D1523559

The Nineteen Forty
MENTAL
MEASUREMENTS
YEARBOOK

The Nineteen Forty

MENTAL
MEASUREMENTS
YEARBOOK

Edited by

OSCAR KRISEN BUROS

Director, The Institute of Mental Measurements

THE GRYPHON PRESS

HIGHLAND PARK · NEW JERSEY

1972

Designed by Luella Buros

Originally published in 1941 by the Mental Measurements Yearbook. Reissued in 1972 by the Gryphon Press, 220 Montgomery Street, Highland Park, New Jersey 08904

ISBN 910674-13-2

Printed in the United States of America

To Luella
and
Allan T. Buros

Cooperating Test Reviewers

* * * * *

Norma A. Albright, *Assistant Professor of Home Economics Education, The Ohio State University, Columbus, Ohio*

John C. Almack, *Professor of Education, Stanford University, Stanford University, California*

Anne Anastasi, *Assistant Professor of Psychology and Chairman of the Department of Psychology, Queens College, Flushing, New York*

Howard R. Anderson, *Associate Professor of Education, Cornell University, Ithaca, New York*

Lawrence Andrus, *Examiner, Board of Examinations, The University of Chicago, Chicago, Illinois*

Christian O. Arndt, *Assistant Professor of Education, Northwestern University, Chicago, Illinois*

S. D. Atkins, *Department of Classics, Princeton University, Princeton, New Jersey*

James C. Babcock, *Assistant Professor of Romance Languages, The University of Chicago, Chicago, Illinois*

Rachel Stutsman Ball, *Psychologist, The Merrill-Palmer School, Detroit, Michigan*

Nancy Bayley, *Research Associate, Institute of Child Welfare, University of California, Berkeley, California.*

Roland L. Beck, *Professor of Education and Director of the Demonstration School, Central State College, Edmond, Oklahoma*

S. J. Beck, *Head Psychologist, Michael Reese Hospital, Chicago, Illinois*

Albert A. Bennett, *Professor of Mathematics, Brown University, Providence, Rhode Island*

H. E. Benz, *Professor of Education, Ohio University, Athens, Ohio*

Robert G. Bernreuter, *Director of the Psycho-Educational Clinic and Associate Professor of Psychology, The Pennsylvania State College, State College, Pennsylvania*

Charles L. Bickel, *Science Department, The Phillips Exeter Academy, Exeter, New Hampshire*

J. M. Blackburn, *Lecturer in Social Psychology, London School of Economics, London, England*

Guy L. Bond, *Associate Professor of Education, The University of Minnesota, Minneapolis, Minnesota*

Ivan A. Booker, *Assistant Director of the Research Division, National Education Association, Washington, D. C.*

Nelson Brooks, *Instructor in French, Westover School, Middlebury, Connecticut*

M. E. Broom, *Assistant Superintendent of Schools, El Paso, Texas*

Andrew W. Brown, *Chief Psychologist, Institute for Juvenile Research, Chicago, Illinois; and Associate Professor of Psychology, University of Illinois, Urbana, Illinois*

vii

CLARA M. BROWN, *Professor and Director of Graduate Studies and Research in Home Economics Education, The University of Minnesota, Minneapolis, Minnesota*

WILLIAM A. BROWNELL, *Professor of Educational Psychology, Duke University, Durham, North Carolina*

LEO J. BRUECKNER, *Professor of Education, The University of Minnesota, Minneapolis, Minnesota*

G. T. BUSWELL, *Professor of Educational Psychology, The University of Chicago, Chicago, Illinois*

W. L. CARR, *Professor of Latin, Columbia University, New York, New York*

HAROLD D. CARTER, *Research Associate, Institute of Child Welfare, The University of California, Berkeley, California*

B. M. CASTNER, *Clinic of Child Development, Yale University, New Haven, Connecticut*

RAYMOND B. CATTELL, *G. Stanley Hall Professor of Genetic Psychology, Clark University, Worcester, Massachusetts*

HESTER CHADDERDON, *Associate Professor of Home Economics Education, Iowa State College, Ames, Iowa*

JOHN R. CLARK, *Principal of the High School, Lincoln School, and Associate Professor of Education, Columbia University, New York, New York*

W. D. COMMINS, *Assistant Professor of Psychology, The Catholic University of America, Washington, D. C.*

CLINTON C. CONRAD, *Lecturer in Education and Associate Director of Practice Teaching, The University of California, Berkeley, California; and Vice-Principal of the University High School, Oakland, California*

HERBERT S. CONRAD, *Associate Professor of Psychology and Research Associate in the Institute of Child Welfare, The University of California, Berkeley, California*

WALTER W. COOK, *Associate Professor of Education, The University of Minnesota, Minneapolis, Minnesota*

STEPHEN M. COREY, *Professor of Educational Psychology and Superintendent of the Laboratory Schools, The University of Chicago, Chicago, Illinois*

A. B. CRAWFORD, *Director of the Department of Personnel Study and Bureau of Appoint-ments and Professor of Psychology, Yale University, New Haven, Connecticut*

R. LENOX CRISWELL, *Teacher of Health and Physical Education, Arts High School, Newark, New Jersey*

EDWARD E. CURETON, *Professor of Education, Alabama Polytechnic Institute, Auburn, Alabama*

FRANCIS D. CURTIS, *Professor of Secondary Education and of the Teaching of Science, The University of Michigan, Ann Arbor, Michigan*

JOHN G. DARLEY, *Director of the University Testing Bureau and Assistant Professor of Psychology, The University of Minnesota, Minneapolis, Minnesota*

FREDERICK B. DAVIS, *Reading and Professional Education Editor, Cooperative Test Service, New York, New York; and Educational Psychologist and Head of the Remedial Department, Avon Old Farms, Avon, Connecticut*

FRANK P. DE LAY, *Department of English, New Trier Township High School, Winnetka, Illinois*

HARRY R. DESILVA, *Director of the Driver Research Center and Research Associate in Psychology, Institute of Human Relations, Yale University, New Haven, Connecticut*

JOSEPH C. DEWEY, *Head of the Department of Education and Psychology, Westminster College, New Wilmington, Pennsylvania*

PAUL B. DIEDERICH, *Assistant Professor of Education, The University of Chicago, Chicago, Illinois*

HARL R. DOUGLASS, *Director of the College of Education, University of Colorado, Boulder, Colorado*

RALEIGH M. DRAKE, *Associate Professor of Psychology, Wesleyan College, Macon, Georgia*

RICHARD M. DRAKE, *Assistant Professor of Education, The University of Buffalo, Buffalo, New York*

JAMES DREVER, *Professor of Psychology, University of Edinburgh, Edinburgh, Scotland*

STANLEY G. DULSKY, *Chief Psychologist, Rochester Guidance Center, Rochester, New York*

HAROLD B. DUNKEL, *Examiner, Board of Examinations, The University of Chicago, Chicago, Illinois*

JACK W. DUNLAP, *Associate Professor of Educational Psychology, The University of Rochester, Rochester, New York*

AUGUST DVORAK, *Professor of Education, University of Washington, Seattle, Washington*

HOWARD EASLEY, *Assistant Professor of Educational Psychology, Duke University, Durham, North Carolina*

BATEMAN EDWARDS, *Head of the Department of Romance Languages, Washington University, St. Louis, Missouri*

MAX D. ENGELHART, *Director of the Department of Examinations, The Chicago City Junior Colleges, Chicago, Illinois.*

EMANUEL E. ERICSON, *Director of the Division of Industrial Education, Santa Barbara State College, Santa Barbara, California*

ALVIN C. EURICH, *Professor of Education, Stanford University, Stanford University, California*

PAUL R. FARNSWORTH, *Acting Professor of Social Psychology, The University of Wisconsin, Madison, Wisconsin*

RAY FAULKNER, *Head of the Department of Fine and Industrial Arts, Teachers College, Columbia University, New York, New York*

HAROLD FAWCETT, *Associate Director of the University School and Associate Professor of Mathematics-Education, The Ohio State University, Columbus, Ohio*

C. E. FICKEN, *Dean of the College and Professor of French, Macalester College, St. Paul, Minnesota*

WARREN G. FINDLEY, *Assistant Director, Division of Examinations and Testing, State Education Department, Albany, New York*

TOMLINSON FORT, *Dean of the Graduate School and Professor of Mathematics, Lehigh University, Bethlehem, Pennsylvania*

JUDSON W. FOUST, *Assistant Professor of Mathematics, Central State Teachers College, Mount Pleasant, Michigan*

CHARLES FOX, *formerly Director of Training, University of Cambridge; 61 Barton Road, Cambridge, England*

VERNE C. FRYKLUND, *Associate Professor of Vocational Education, Wayne University; and Supervisor in the City Schools, Detroit, Michigan*

BESSIE LEE GAMBRILL, *Associate Professor of Elementary Education, Yale University, New Haven, Connecticut*

HENRY E. GARRETT, *Associate Professor of Psychology, Columbia University, New York, New York*

ANN L. GEBHARDT, *Teacher of English, East High School, Madison, Wisconsin*

KARL W. GEHRKENS, *Professor of School Music, Oberlin College, Oberlin, Ohio*

KENNETH E. GELL, *Head of the Department of Social Studies, Washington High School, Rochester, New York; and Special Lecturer in Education, The University of Rochester, Rochester, New York*

J. R. GERBERICH, *Director of the Bureau of Educational Research and Statistical Service and Associate Professor of Education, University of Connecticut, Storrs, Connecticut*

H. H. GILES, *Assistant Professor of Education and Research Associate in the Bureau of Educational Research, The Ohio State University, Columbus, Ohio*

KEITH GOLTRY, *Head of the Department of Education, Parsons College, Fairfield, Iowa*

FLORENCE L. GOODENOUGH, *Research Professor, Institute of Child Welfare, The University of Minnesota, Minneapolis, Minnesota*

HANS C. GORDON, *Division of Educational Research, Public Schools, Philadelphia, Pennsylvania*

GRACE GRAHAM, *Department of History, Columbia High School, Columbia, South Carolina*

HARRY A. GREENE, *Director of the Bureau of Educational Research and Service and Professor of Education, The State University of Iowa, Iowa City, Iowa*

FOSTER E. GROSSNICKLE, *Professor of Mathematics, New Jersey State Teachers College, Jersey City, New Jersey*

J. P. GUILFORD, *Professor of Psychology, The University of Southern California, Los Angeles, California*

HAROLD GULLIKSEN, *Assistant Professor of Psychology and Examiner in the Social Sciences, The University of Chicago, Chicago, Illinois*

JOHN FLAGG GUMMERE, *Chairman of the Latin Department, William Penn Charter School, Philadelphia, Pennsylvania*

LAURA B. HADLEY, *Associate Professor of Home Economics Education, Alabama College, Montevallo, Alabama*

C. H. HANDSCHIN, *Professor of German and Executive Officer of Graduate Work, Miami University, Oxford, Ohio*

LAVONE A. HANNA, *Research Associate, School of Education, Stanford University, Stanford University, California*

J. O. HASSLER, *Professor of Mathematics and Astronomy, The University of Oklahoma, Norman, Oklahoma*

G. E. HAWKINS, *Instructor in Mathematics, University High School, The University of Chicago, Chicago, Illinois*

EARLE R. HEDRICK, *Vice-President and Provost of the University, The University of California, Los Angeles, California*

LOUIS M. HEIL, *Associate Professor of Education, The University of Chicago, and Research Associate in Science, Cooperative Study in General Education, American Council on Education, Chicago, Illinois*

HARRY HELLER, *Head of the French Department, Fieldston School, New York, New York*

JEAN HOARD, *Teacher of English in the University High School, The University of Wisconsin, Madison, Wisconsin*

JAMES R. HOBSON, *Director of Child Placement, Public Schools, Brookline, Massachusetts*

WARREN S. HOLMES, *Department of French, The Gunnery School, Washington, Connecticut*

CHARLES HOLZWARTH, *Principal of the West High School, Rochester, New York*

CLARK W. HORTON, *Department of Educational Research, Dartmouth College, Hanover, New Hampshire*

ROBERT W. HOWARD, *Department of Examinations, The Chicago City Junior Colleges, Chicago, Illinois*

VIOLET HUGHES, *Department of English, East High School, Madison, Wisconsin*

DONCASTER G. HUMM, *Wadsworth-Humm Personnel Service, Los Angeles, California*

E. PATRICIA HUNT, *Vocational Psychologist, Education Office, Birmingham, England*

G. W. HUNTER, *Lecturer in Science Education, Claremont Colleges, Claremont, California*

JOSEPH F. JACKSON, *Professor of French, University of Illinois, Urbana, Illinois*

LAURA B. JOHNSON, *Assistant Professor in the Teaching of French, The University of Wisconsin, Madison, Wisconsin*

PALMER O. JOHNSON *Professor of Education, The University of Minnesota, Minneapolis, Minnesota*

CARLETON C. JONES, *Department of English, State Teachers College, Indiana, Pennsylvania*

EDWARD S. JONES, *Professor of Psychology and Director of Personnel Research, The University of Buffalo, Buffalo, New York*

HAROLD E. JONES, *Director of the Institute of Child Welfare and Professor of Psychology, The University of California, Berkeley, California*

A. M. JORDAN, *Professor of Educational Psychology, The University of North Carolina, Chapel Hill, North Carolina*

WALTER V. KAULFERS, *Associate Professor of Education in Foreign Languages, Stanford University, Stanford University, California*

T. J. KEATING, *Research Fellow, The Training School at Vineland, New Jersey*

TRUMAN L. KELLEY, *Professor of Education, Harvard University, Cambridge, Massachusetts*

GRACE H. KENT, *Psychologist, Danvers State Hospital, Hathorne, Massachusetts*

ROBERT E. KEOHANE, *Instructor in Social Studies, The College, The University of Chicago, Chicago, Illinois*

FORREST A. KINGSBURY, *Associate Professor of Psychology, The University of Chicago, Chicago, Illinois*

L. B. KINNEY, *Associate Professor of Education, Stanford University, Stanford University, California*

DAVID KOPEL, *Department of Education, Chicago Teachers College, Chicago, Illinois*

G. FREDERIC KUDER, *Examiner, Board of Examinations, The University of Chicago, Chicago, Illinois*

F. KUHLMANN, *Director of the Division of Examinations and Classification, State Department of Public Institutions, St. Paul, Minnesota*

Lou LaBrant, *Professor of English-Education, The Ohio State University, Columbus, Ohio*

W. Elmer Lancaster, *Teacher of Mathematics, Cleveland Junior High School, Newark, New Jersey*

Herbert A. Landry, *Research Assistant, Bureau of Reference, Research, and Statistics, Public Schools, New York, New York*

William S. Larson, *Chairman of the Music Education Department and Psychologist in Music, Eastman School of Music, Rochester, New York*

D. Welty Lefever, *Associate Professor of Education, The University of Southern California, Los Angeles, California*

J. Paul Leonard, *Associate Professor of Education, Stanford University, Stanford University, California*

W. Line, *Associate Professor of Psychology, University of Toronto, Toronto, Canada*

Alice K. Liveright, *Principal of the Logan Demonstration School, Public Schools, Philadelphia, Pennsylvania*

Andrew Longacre, *Science Department, The Phillips Exeter Academy, Exeter, New Hampshire*

Irving Lorge, *Executive Officer of the Division of Psychology, Institute of Educational Research and Associate Professor of Education, Columbia University, New York, New York*

C. M. Louttit, *Director of the Psychological Clinics and Associate Professor of Clinical Psychology, Indiana University, Bloomington, Indiana*

W. C. McCall, *Director of the Personnel Bureau and Associate Professor of Education, University of South Carolina, Columbia, South Carolina*

William A. McCall, *Professor of Education, Columbia University, New York, New York*

Robert L. McCaul, *Instructor of Remedial Reading in the Laboratory Schools and the College, The University of Chicago, Chicago, Illinois*

Clara J. McCauley, *Supervisor of Music, Public Schools, Knoxville, Tennessee*

Constance M. McCullough, *Assistant Professor of Education, Western Reserve University, Cleveland, Ohio*

S. P. McCutchen, *Assistant Professor of Education and Research Associate, Bureau of Educational Research, The Ohio State University, Columbus, Ohio*

Jeanette McPherrin, *Director of Admissions, Scripps College, Claremont, California*

J. B. Maller, *Lecturer in Education, New York University, New York, New York*

Berenice Mallory, *Assistant Professor of Home Economics, The University of Texas, Austin, Texas*

Herschel T. Manuel, *Professor of Educational Psychology, The University of Texas; and Director of Research, Texas Commission on Coordination in Education, Austin, Texas*

Francis N. Maxfield, *Professor of Psychology, Psychological Clinic, The Ohio State University, Columbus, Ohio*

Arthur B. Mays, *Professor of Industrial Education, University of Illinois, Urbana, Illinois*

Norman C. Meier, *Associate Professor of Psychology, The State University of Iowa, Iowa City, Iowa*

J. B. Miner, *Professor of Psychology and Director of the Personnel Bureau, University of Kentucky, Lexington, Kentucky*

J. H. Minnick, *Dean of the School of Education, The University of Pennsylvania, Philadelphia, Pennsylvania*

Joseph E. Moore, *Professor of Psychology, George Peabody College for Teachers, Nashville, Tennessee*

Harriet Barthelmess Morrison, *Research Assistant, Bureau of Reference, Research, and Statistics, Public Schools, New York, New York*

Thomas F. Morrison, *Head of the Science Department, Milton Academy, Milton, Massachusetts*

N. W. Morton, *Assistant Professor of Psychology, McGill University, Montreal, Canada*

R. L. Morton, *Professor of Education, Ohio University, Athens, Ohio*

CHARLES I. MOSIER, *Assistant Professor of Psychology and Assistant University Examiner, University of Florida, Gainesville, Florida*

WILBUR F. MURRA, *Executive Secretary, The National Council for the Social Studies, Washington, D. C.*

JAMES L. MURSELL, *Professor of Education, Columbia University, New York, New York*

THEODORE NEWCOMB, *Psychology Department, Bennington College, Bennington, Vermont*

VICTOR H. NOLL, *Head of the Department of Education and Professor of Education, Michigan State College, East Lansing, Michigan*

PAUL A. NORTHROP, *Professor of Physics, Vassar College, Poughkeepsie, New York*

EDWARD S. NOYES, *Chairman, Board of Admissions, and Associate Professor of English, Yale University, New Haven, Connecticut*

C. A. OAKLEY, *Scottish Area Officer of the British Air Ministry; in civil life, Scottish Divisional Director of the National Institute of Industrial Psychology, Glasgow, Scotland*

C. W. ODELL, *Associate Professor of Education, University of Illinois, Urbana, Illinois*

PEDRO T. ORATA, *Special Consultant, Occupational Information and Guidance Service, United States Office of Education, Washington, D. C.*

JACOB S. ORLEANS, *Associate Professor of Education, The College of the City of New York, New York, New York*

W. J. OSBURN, *Professor of Education, The University of Washington, Seattle, Washington*

ALTON O'STEEN, *Research Associate, Bureau of Educational Research, The Ohio State University, Columbus, Ohio*

ANNA PARSEK, *Teacher in the Sixth Grade, Public School No. 6, West New York, New Jersey*

DONALD G. PATERSON, *Professor of Psychology, The University of Minnesota, Minneapolis, Minnesota*

JOHN GRAY PEATMAN, *Assistant Professor of Psychology, The College of the City of New York, New York, New York*

MYRTLE LUNEAU PIGNATELLI, *Clinical Psychologist, Bellevue Psychiatric Hospital, New York, New York*

ROBERT C. POOLEY, *Associate Professor in the Teaching of English, The University of Wisconsin, Madison, Wisconsin*

S. D. PORTEUS, *Director of the Psychological Clinic and Professor of Clinical Psychology, University of Hawaii, Honolulu, Hawaii*

NORMAN T. PRATT, JR., *Department of Classics, Princeton University, Princeton, New Jersey*

ROY A. PRICE, *Dual Professor of Social Science and Education, Syracuse University, Syracuse, New York*

E. V. PULLIAS, *Professor of Educational Psychology, George Pepperdine College, Los Angeles, California*

M. W. RICHARDSON, *United States Civil Service Commission, Washington, D. C.*

PAUL R. RIDER, *Professor of Mathematics, Washington University, St. Louis, Missouri*

HENRY D. RINSLAND, *Director of the Bureau of Educational Research and Professor of School Measurements, The University of Oklahoma, Norman, Oklahoma*

HOLLAND D. ROBERTS, *Associate Professor of Education, Stanford University, Stanford University, California*

ALEC RODGER, *Head of the Vocational Guidance Department, National Institute of Industrial Psychology, London, England*

CARL R. ROGERS, *Professor of Psychology, The Ohio State University, Columbus, Ohio*

FREDERICK RAND ROGERS, *Professor of Education and Director of Physical Education, Boston University, Boston, Massachusetts*

C. C. ROSS, *Professor of Educational Psychology, University of Kentucky, Lexington, Kentucky*

G. M. RUCH, *Chief, Research and Statistical Service, United States Office of Education, Washington, D. C.*

DAVID H. RUSSELL, *Assistant Professor of Education, The University of Saskatchewan, Saskatoon, Canada*

HARRY J. RUSSELL, *Associate Professor of Romantic Languages, Miami University, Oxford, Ohio*

RACHEL SALISBURY, *Director of the Junior High School Department, State Teachers College, Platteville, Wisconsin*

AULUS WARD SAUNDERS, *Head of the Department of Art, State Normal School, Oswego, New York*

ALVIN W. SCHINDLER, *Associate Professor of Education, University of Denver, Denver, Colorado*

LEROY H. SCHNELL, *Department of Mathematics, State Teachers College, Indiana, Pennsylvania*

FRED J. SCHONELL, *Lecturer in Education, Goldsmiths' College, University of London, London, England*

DEAN M. SCHWEICKHARD, *Assistant Superintendent of Schools, Minneapolis, Minnesota*

CARL E. SEASHORE, *Professor of Psychology, The State University of Iowa, Iowa City, Iowa*

ESTHER F. SEGNER, *Assistant Professor of Home Economics Education and Assistant State Supervisor and Teacher-Trainer, University of Idaho, Moscow, Idaho*

L. K. SHUMAKER, *Director of the Education Clinic, University of Oregon, Eugene, Oregon*

C. EBBLEWHITE SMITH, *Lecturer in the Department of Higher Degrees and Research, Institute of Education, University of London, London, England*

PERCIVAL SMITH, *Principal Assistant Organiser, Education Department, Birmingham, England*

C. SPEARMAN, *Professor of Psychology, The University of London, London, England*

ROBERT K. SPEER, *Professor of Education, New York University, New York, New York*

DOUGLAS SPENCER, *Assistant Professor of Psychology, Queens College, Flushing, Long Island, New York*

PETER L. SPENCER, *Professor of Education, Claremont Colleges, Claremont, California*

JOHN M. STALNAKER, *Consultant Examiner, College Entrance Examination Board and Associate Professor of Psychology, Princeton University, Princeton, New Jersey*

CLARENCE R. STONE, *2140 Los Angeles Avenue, Berkeley, California*

RUTH STRANG, *Professor of Education, Columbia University, New York, New York*

PERCIVAL M. SYMONDS, *Professor of Education, Columbia University, New York, New York*

HILDA TABA, *Assistant Professor of Education and Research Associate, The University of Chicago, Chicago, Illinois*

WALLACE TAYLOR, *Assistant Professor of Education and Supervisor in Social Studies, Milne High School, State College for Teachers, Albany, New York*

FLORENCE M. TEAGARDEN, *Professor of Psychology, The University of Pittsburgh, Pittsburgh, Pennsylvania*

LORENE TEEGARDEN, *Psychological Examiner, Public Schools, Cincinnati, Ohio*

EDWARD A. TENNEY, *Associate Professor of English, Cornell University, Ithaca, New York*

JAMES B. THARP, *Associate Professor of Education, The Ohio State University, Columbus, Ohio*

C. L. THIELE, *Director of Exact Sciences, Public Schools, Detroit, Michigan*

CHARLES SWAIN THOMAS, *Associate Professor of Education, Emeritus, Harvard University, Cambridge, Massachusetts*

ALBERT S. THOMPSON, *Instructor of Psychology, The University of Pennsylvania, Philadelphia, Pennsylvania*

GODFREY H. THOMSON, *Professor of Education and Director of the Training Centre for Teachers, University of Edinburgh, Edinburgh, Scotland*

ROBERT L. THORNDIKE, *Associate Professor of Education, Columbia University, New York, New York*

ERNEST W. TIEGS, *Dean of University College and Professor of Education, The University of Southern California, Los Angeles, California*

MILES A. TINKER, *Associate Professor of Psychology, The University of Minnesota, Minneapolis, Minnesota*

M. R. TRABUE, *Dean of the School of Education, The Pennsylvania State College, State College, Pennsylvania*

ARTHUR E. TRAXLER, *Assistant Director, Educational Records Bureau, New York, New York*

MARIE E. TROST, *Teacher of Geography and Science in Grades 7 and 8, School No. 7, Belleville, New Jersey*

ROBERT C. TRYON, *Associate Professor of Psychology, The University of California, Berkeley, California*

R. M. TRYON, *Professor of the Teaching of the Social Sciences, The University of Chicago, Chicago, Illinois*

SIMON H. TULCHIN, *Consulting Psychologist, 136 East 57th St., New York, New York*

CLARENCE E. TURNER, *Assistant Professor of the Romance Languages, Rutgers University, New Brunswick, New Jersey*

A. H. TURNEY, *Professor of Education, The University of Kansas, Lawrence, Kansas*

RALPH W. TYLER, *Chairman of the Department of Education; Professor of Education; and Chief Examiner, Board of Examinations, The University of Chicago, Chicago, Illinois*

P. E. VERNON, *Lecturer in Psychology, University of Glasgow, Glasgow, Scotland*

MORRIS S. VITELES, *Associate Professor of Psychology, The University of Pennsylvania, Philadelphia, Pennsylvania*

ALAN T. WATERMAN, *Associate Professor of Physics, Yale University, New Haven, Connecticut*

EUGENE A. WATERS, *Associate Professor of Education, The University of Tennessee*

RALPH K. WATKINS, *Professor of Education, The University of Missouri, Columbia, Missouri*

GOODWIN WATSON, *Professor of Education, Columbia University, New York, New York*

DAVID WECHSLER, *Chief Psychologist, Psychiatric Division, Bellevue Hospital, New York, New York*

CHARLES C. WEIDEMANN, *Associate Professor of Mathematics and Education, The Ohio State University, Columbus, Ohio*

F. L. WELLS, *Psychologist, Department of Hygiene, Harvard University, Cambridge, Massachusetts*

EDGAR B. WESLEY, *Professor of Education,* *The University of Minnesota, Minneapolis, Minnesota*

HARRY GROVE WHEAT, *Professor of Education, West Virginia University, Morgantown, West Virginia*

CARROLL A. WHITMER, *Assistant Professor of Psychology, The University of Pittsburgh, Pittsburgh, Pennsylvania*

S. S. WILKS, *Associate Professor of Mathematics, Princeton University and Research Associate, College Entrance Examination Board, Princeton, New Jersey*

E. G. WILLIAMSON, *Coordinator of Student Personnel Services and Associate Professor of Psychology, The University of Minnesota, Minneapolis, Minnesota*

MARGARET WILLIS, *Assistant Professor of Social Science Education, University School, The Ohio State University, Columbus, Ohio*

G. M. WILSON, *Professor of Education, Boston University, Boston, Massachusetts*

ERNEST C. WITHAM, *Associate Professor of Education, Rutgers University, New Brunswick, New Jersey*

DAEL L. WOLFLE, *Assistant Professor of Psychology, The University of Chicago, Chicago, Illinois*

HUGH B. WOOD, *Professor of Education, University of Oregon, Eugene, Oregon*

D. A. WORCESTER, *Chairman of the Department of Educational Psychology and Measurements, The University of Nebraska, Lincoln, Nebraska*

C. GILBERT WRENN, *Professor of Educational Psychology, The University of Minnesota, Minneapolis, Minnesota*

J. WAYNE WRIGHTSTONE, *Assistant Director, Bureau of Reference, Research, and Statistics, Public Schools, New York, New York*

LL. WYNN JONES, *Senior Lecturer in Experimental Psychology, University of Leeds, Leeds, England*

LOUIS C. ZAHNER, *Head of the Department of English, Groton School, Groton, Massachusetts*

EDWIN ZIEGFELD, *Instructor in Fine Arts, Columbia University, New York, New York*

Acknowledgment

THE EDITOR WISHES TO EXPRESS HIS INDEBTED-
NESS FOR THE VALUABLE SECRETARIAL ASSIST-
ANCE FURNISHED IN PART BY THE PERSONNEL OF
THE WORKS PROGRESS ADMINISTRATION OFFICIAL
PROJECT NO. 65-1-22-477, SUBPROJECT A-6
SPONSORED BY THE SCHOOL OF EDUCATION,
RUTGERS UNIVERSITY

Preface

* * * * *

TWO hundred and fifty psychologists, subject-matter specialists, teachers, and test technicians have cooperated in making this volume available to test users by contributing frankly critical reviews of standard tests. We who are test users are deeply indebted to these cooperating reviewers for their much-needed criticisms of tests. Their frank, penetrating reviews will help all of us to make more discriminating selections from among the hundreds of tests which are flooding the market. The active participation of such a large number of competent reviewers in this new test-appraisal service marks the end of the days when authors and publishers could successfully market ill-conceived, poorly constructed, and inadequately validated tests with impunity.

The growth of this service from a 44-page noncritical bibliography published in the summer of 1935 to this 700-page yearbook of critical reviews is described in the Introduction. Here I wish only to point out some of the major changes introduced in this volume, to state briefly the objectives of the yearbook series, to point out plans for the improvement and extension of this test appraisal service, and to acknowledge assistance received.

As compared with the corresponding section in *The 1938 Mental Measurements Yearbook*, the following improvements have been made in the section "Tests and Reviews" in this volume: The number of cooperating reviewers has been increased from one hundred and thirty-three to two hundred and fifty. The number of original test reviews has been increased from two hundred and thirty-one to five hundred and three. More space has been allowed to reviewers; the unsatisfactory plan of 40- to 100-word appraisals used in part in *The 1938 Yearbook* has been abandoned for longer test reviews. The various viewpoints held by users and potential users of tests are better represented among the cooperating reviewers. The representation given to other English-speaking countries has been increased from one to sixteen reviewers—this number would have been much larger were it not for the war. The grouping of tests under broader classifications and the expanded Table of Contents make it considerably easier to locate tests and reviews of interest. The presentation of titles of reviewers allows readers to understand better the viewpoints represented. Old as well as new tests are reviewed in this yearbook; for example, the oldest test reviewed was published in 1915 and has not been revised since. This yearbook also contains numerous reviews of non-pencil-and-paper tests and several other classes of tests which were poorly represented in *The 1938 Yearbook*. Finally, the lists of references dealing with the construction, validation, use, and limitations of specific tests have been compiled in a more thorough and comprehensive manner.

The objectives of the section "Tests and Reviews" in this and other yearbooks in the series are as follows: (*a*) to make readily available comprehensive and up-to-date bibliographies of recent tests published in all English-speaking countries; (*b*) to make readily available hundreds of frankly critical test reviews, written by persons of outstanding ability representing various viewpoints, which will assist test users to make more discriminating selections of the standard tests which will best meet their needs; (*c*) to make readily available comprehensive and accurate bibliographies of references on the construction, validation, use, and limitations of specific tests; (*d*) to impel authors and publishers to place fewer but better tests on the market and to provide test users with detailed and accurate information on the construction, validation, uses, and limitations of their tests at the time that they are first placed on the market; (*e*) to suggest to test users better methods of arriving at their own appraisals of both standard and non-standard tests in light of their particular values and needs; (*f*) to stimulate co-operating reviewers—and others to a less extent—to reconsider and think through more carefully their beliefs and values relevant to testing; (*g*) to inculcate upon test users a keener awareness of both the values and dangers which may accompany the use of standard tests; and (*h*) to impress test users with the desirability of suspecting all standard tests—even though prepared by well-known authorities—unaccompanied by detailed data on their construction, validation, use, and limitations.

Readers of *The 1938 Yearbook* will recall that it contains the following three sections devoted to books and review excerpts: "Mental Measurements Books," "Research and Statistical Methodology Books," and "Regional Testing Program Reports." The section on research and statistical books has been omitted from this yearbook in order to make more space for the test reviews. This omitted section will be published as a separate volume early in the spring of 1941. The other two book sections in *The 1938 Yearbook* have been combined in this yearbook to make the section "Books and Reviews."

As compared with the corresponding section in the previous yearbook, the following improvements have been made in the section "Books and Reviews" in this volume: More than a hundred new journals—fifty of which are in medicine

—were searched for reviews of books in testing and closely related fields. Because of this more comprehensive coverage, *The 1940 Yearbook* contains excerpts from reviews which appeared in one hundred and seventy-eight journals as compared to the one hundred and forty-six journals represented in the measurements book section of the preceding yearbook. The scope of the book section has been expanded to include a larger number of books in fields closely bordering mental measurements. Finally, the addition of catchwords to the running heads on the right-hand pages will facilitate the use of the section "Books and Reviews."

The objectives of the section "Books and Reviews" in this and other yearbooks in the series are as follows: (*a*) to make readily available comprehensive and up-to-date bibliographies of recent books published in all English-speaking countries in measurements and closely associated fields; (*b*) to make readily available evaluative excerpts from hundreds of book reviews appearing in a great variety of journals in this country and abroad in order to assist test users to make more discriminating selections of books for study and purchase; (*c*) to stimulate readers to develop more critical attitudes toward what they read; (*d*) to make readily available important and provocative statements which, though appearing in book reviews, have considerable value entirely apart from a consideration of the book under review; (*e*) to point out books which are not being reviewed but which probably merit review; (*f*) to improve the quality of book reviews by stimulating review editors to make greater efforts to choose competent reviewers who will contribute frankly critical reviews; and finally, (*g*) to improve the quality of book reviews by stimulating reviewers "to take their responsibilities more seriously" by refusing to review books which they cannot appraise competently and honestly.

Mention may also be made of three additional improvements which characterize the entire volume. First, several improvements have been made in the format and design of the yearbook. Among these improvements, readers will especially notice the larger type size which makes the book much easier to read. Second, despite the increased size, this yearbook is more up-to-date than any of its predecessors. The lag between the publication date of this volume and the publication date of the latest books, references, reviews, and tests listed has been reduced to a period varying between three and four months. The yearbook may be considered reasonably up-to-date as of October 1, 1940. Third, with the exception of the authors of a few books which were not available locally or in New York City libraries, the names of all authors of books, references, reviews, and tests are listed exactly as they appear in the original source. This practice has also been adopted in the Index of Names.

As rapidly as time and funds will permit, this cooperative service to test users will be improved and expanded. However, changes will have to be made slowly, for the time being, because of my failure to secure financial assistance for the continuation and expansion of this work. Since neither a foundation nor the Works Progress Administration is willing to assist in the preparation of future yearbooks, several changes will have to be made in order to minimize the time and money necessary to continue this service. The first change will be to publish yearbooks every two years instead of annually as originally planned. Despite this shift to a biennial basis, the volumes will continue to be entitled "yearbooks"— for example, the next work will be *The 1942 Mental Measurements Yearbook.* A second change, the establishment of a nonprofit organization to publish this and future yearbooks, has already been made. This organization will publish under the imprint "The Mental Measurements Yearbook" with the subtitle "A Cooperative Nonprofit Service for Test Users." By setting up this publishing organization, the overhead costs of manufacturing and distributing the yearbooks will be decreased considerably without injuring the quality of the publications or the service to yearbook readers. The other changes which must be made to achieve greater economy are not of sufficient interest to be mentioned here.

In order to make the material in the yearbooks more easily accessible to individuals who are interested in only a small part of each volume, a new series of monographs is being planned. If the first two or three monographs prove successful, others will eventually be prepared to cover tests in each of the following fields: business education, character and personality, elementary education, English and reading, fine arts, foreign languages, health and physical education, home economics, industrial arts, intelligence, mathematics, sciences, social studies, and vocational aptitudes. The first publication in each field will include: a comprehensive bibliography of all standard tests in print in that area; a reprinting, in part or in full, of all reviews of these tests which have appeared in previous yearbooks or in the journal literature; new reviews written especially for the monograph (to be, in turn, reprinted, in part or in full, in the following yearbook); and an extensive list of references on the construction, validation, use, and limitations of the tests. Separates in each field will be issued every four, six, or eight years depending upon the frequency of test publication. These monographs will range in size from fifty to two hundred pages. This new series will make it possible for an individual to purchase at a nominal cost every four, six, or eight years a monograph devoted solely to the tests and reviews of most interest to him. These separates will greatly extend the range of service of the yearbooks. The first monograph will be devoted to tests in English and reading and will be published in late 1941 or early 1942. Other titles will be planned for publication at the rate of two monographs each year.

It is with a great deal of pleasure that I express my indebtedness and gratitude to the many persons who have assisted me in the preparation and publication of this volume. I am especially appreciative of the invaluable assistance received from cooperating reviewers. I wish to express my gratitude to the editors who graciously gave me permission to print excerpts from the book reviews appearing in their journals; to the test publishers who cooperated by supplying information and specimen sets of their tests for review; to the American Council on Education for a small grant for extra clerical assistance; and to Librarian George A.

Osborn, Miss Edith Deerr, and other members of the Rutgers University Library staff for facilitating my search for published materials. I am extremely thankful for the valuable assistance—checking of references, copyreading, indexing, proofreading, and typing—provided in part by the personnel of the Works Progress Administration Official Project No. 65-1-22-477, Subproject A-6. I am also grateful to the School of Education of Rutgers University for officially sponsoring the assisting WPA project. It is with pleasure that I express my thanks and appreciation to Rae S. Feinsod, Ruth M. Field, Mary T. Mooney, Serene B. Rabke, Ethel Shine, and Marion S. Traiman for the efficiency, loyalty, and patience with which they have assisted me in the preparation of the manuscript and in seeing the book through the press. Finally, I wish to make a special acknowledgment of my indebtedness and gratitude to my wife, Luella Buros, and to my brother, Allan T. Buros, who together are making it possible for me to publish *The 1940 Yearbook* and to continue this service to test users despite my failure to secure outside financial assistance—to them, this yearbook is affectionately dedicated.

Readers are urged to bring to my attention errors of omission and commission in this yearbook and the earlier publications in the series. Unfavorable as well as favorable criticisms will be gratefully received. Suggestions for the improvement and expansion of this cooperative test-appraisal service will be gladly welcomed. The task of initiating, editing, and publishing a yearbook which aims to be comprehensive in scope, unbiased in treatment, and frankly critical in attitude is not easy. Your candid criticisms and suggestions will help me to approach this goal more closely.

OSCAR KRISEN BUROS

Highland Park, New Jersey
  November 23, 1940

Table of Contents

* * * * *

The Nineteen Forty
MENTAL
MEASUREMENTS
YEARBOOK

Introduction

* * * * *

IN 1934, the Editor of the *Mental Measurements Yearbooks* accepted an invitation to prepare for a well-known journal an annual review of the standardized tests published during the previous year. The review was to be a frankly critical appraisal which would point out both deficiencies and merits of the new tests in all fields. Before the tests could be appraised, they had to be located. This preliminary task promised to be easy, for the Editor prided himself upon his up-to-date—so he thought—knowledge of the tests being currently published; but to make sure, a careful search was initiated. Since the usual bibliographic tools are of little value in locating standard tests, the checking was difficult and time consuming. The little-used monthly record of copyrighted material, the *Catalog of Copyright Entries*, Part 1, Group 2, of the Library of Congress, proved valuable though tedious to use. Several hundred thousand titles of advertisements, directories, leaflets, newpaper and magazine articles, pamphlets, sales letters, and the like were skimmed in search of test titles. The unexpected discovery of many test titles intensified the search. Hundreds of letters were written to possible authors and publishers. A preliminary bibliography of one hundred and nineteen tests was mimeographed and sent to more than fifty test technicians with the request that they look for omissions. Although fewer than ten tests were called to the Editor's attention by the test technicians, eventually, from various sources, the number of tests found to have been published in 1933 and 1934 reached a total of approximately two hundred and fifty—more than twice the number in the preliminary draft!

After having found such an unexpectedly large number of tests of every description, the Editor became convinced that it would be presumptuous for him to go ahead with his original plan to write annually a frankly critical review of all tests published in the previous year. No single person is sufficiently competent to do the task in a thorough manner, even though he were to spend the year round doing this and nothing else. To write a critical evaluation of all standard tests published in a given year would require the combined efforts of a staff of competent psychologists, subject-matter specialists, teachers, and test technicians —with various viewpoints within each group represented. The answer appeared to be the establishment of a test users' research institute with the aid of a substantial grant from one of the large philanthropic foundations interested in serving education. Unfortunately, it is easier to interest such foundations in test-construction and test-promotional activities than in a program which would serve test users by making available frankly critical appraisals of standard tests. Regretfully, plans for a test-the-tests organization had to be abandoned, for the time being, because of lack of financial support.

Instead of a critical review, the Editor prepared the first of a series of unannotated bibliographies of standardized tests. This noncritical listing of tests, *Educational, Psychological, and Personality Tests of 1933 and 1934,** was published in the summer of 1935. The two-year period was chosen in order to supplement Hildreth's bibliography † which covered tests published through 1932. Only five hundred copies of this 44-page bibliography were published. Numerous review copies were sent to the editors of professional journals, but the pamphlet was not reviewed.

Since this small printing of the first test bibliography was soon exhausted— due in large part to gift copies—the next annual bibliography was cumulated so as to include tests published in 1933 and 1934, in addition to the tests of 1935. *Educational, Psychological, and Personality Tests of 1933, 1934, and 1935,*‡ like the first publication in the series, is a carefully prepared but unannotated bibliography of standardized tests. This 83-page list of five hundred and three tests received favorable reviews in fourteen journals.§ Notwithstanding the appreciative book reviews, the second bibliography sold very poorly. It was obvious that the use being made of the first two bibliographies was far too little to justify the expenditure of the time and money necessary to continue the series.

In an effort to make the series sufficiently valuable to justify its continuance, a new feature was planned for the third annual issue. A bibliography was prepared of all books and monographs published in English-speaking countries in the years 1933 through 1936 in the field of measurements and closely related fields.

* Buros, Oscar K. *Educational, Psychological, and Personality Tests of 1933 and 1934.* Rutgers University Bulletin, Vol. 11; Studies in Education, No. 7. New Brunswick, N. J.: School of Education, Rutgers University, May 1935. Pp. 44. Paper. Out of print.

† Hildreth, Gertrude H. *A Bibliography of Mental Tests and Rating Scales.* New York: Psychological Corporation, 1933. Pp. 242. Superseded by a revised edition (*see* B937).

‡ Buros, Oscar K. *Educational, Psychological, and Personality Tests of 1933, 1934, and 1935.* Rutgers University Bulletin, Vol. 13, No. 1; Studies in Education, No. 9. New Brunswick, N. J.: School of Education, Rutgers University, July 1936. Pp. 83. $0.50. Paper.

§ For both the favorable and unfavorable comments of the reviewers, *see* B46 in *Educational, Psychological, and Personality Tests of 1936,* B325 in *The 1938 Mental Measurements Yearbook,* and B856 in this volume.

Considerable pains were taken to prepare accurate and full bibliographic entries for the two hundred and ninety-one books listed. Practically all entries were prepared from an actual examination of the books; very few secondary sources were used. In order to increase the publication's usefulness in all English-speaking countries, both American and foreign publishers and prices were reported.

Approximately one hundred and twenty professional journals in education, psychology, and allied fields were searched for reviews of the two hundred and ninety-one books. More than six hundred book reviews were located in eighty-two journals. Permission was then secured from the editors to reprint the critical portions of the reviews. Every precaution was taken to choose excerpts which would fairly represent the over-all evaluation of each reviewer. The quotations represent the critical portions of all reviews which could be located, even though some of these reviews seemed to have been written by persons who were either incompetent to appraise the book under review or unwilling to speak frankly. These review excerpts were collated with the bibliography of books to make the new book section which was introduced in the third test bibliography.* The sharp increase in size from a 44- to a 141-page bulletin (95 pages of which are in 6-point type set solid) was due to the addition of the section on books and reviews.

The usual review copies were sent to the editors of the leading professional journals in education and psychology. Complimentary copies were also sent to all journals from which reviews had been excerpted. The reception given to this third bibliography by the editors and reviewers was most gratifying. *Educational, Psychological, and Personality Tests of 1936* was favorably reviewed † in twenty-eight journals in this country and abroad—but again, sales were disappointingly low. Had sales been accepted as the criterion of the usefulness of the series, the third annual issue would have been the last.

The first part of the story of the fourth publication ‡ in this series is probably best told by quoting from its Introduction:

> Letters were sent to likely reviewers to determine their willingness to write one or more "frankly critical reviews" if the School of Education of Rutgers University should find it possible to finance their publication. An effort was made to select a representative sampling of able test technicians, subject matter specialists, and psychologists. For example, invitations to review tests were sent to conservatives and progressives, to users and nonusers of the tests to be reviewed, and to friends and opponents of objective-type tests. The response was most encouraging. Approximately eighty per cent of the persons invited indicated a willingness to write one or more critical reviews. The others, with two or three exceptions, expressed a strong interest in the proposal for having tests critically reviewed. Encouraged

---

* Buros, Oscar K. *Educational, Psychological, and Personality Tests of 1936.* Rutgers University Bulletin, Vol. 14, No. 2A; Studies in Education, No. 11. New Brunswick, N. J.: School of Education, Rutgers University, August 1937. Pp. 141. $0.75. Paper.

† For both the favorable and unfavorable comments of the reviewers, *see* B326 in *The 1938 Mental Measurements Yearbook,* and B857 in this volume.

‡ Buros, Oscar Krisen, editor. *The 1938 Mental Measurements Yearbook.* New Brunswick, N. J.: Rutgers University Press, 1938. Pp. xv, 415. $3.00.

by these promises of cooperative support, the School of Education of Rutgers University finally decided to finance the *1938 Yearbook*.

Because of space limitations, reviewers were limited to either 300- to 600-word reviews or 40- to 100-word appraisals. In addition, reviewers were asked to give only as much non-evaluative description as was necessary to serve as a background for their evaluative comments. Other than the request that the review be frankly evaluative, no effort was made to stipulate the kind of review wanted. On the contrary, reviewers were urged to evaluate tests in whatever ways seemed most important to them regardless of any instructions which might be found in textbooks on tests and measurements.

An attempt was made to have each test reviewed by two or more persons in order to obtain a better representation of the various viewpoints in American education. *The Mental Measurements Yearbooks* are to represent all test users, both potential and actual. Unfortunately, space limitations, last-minute refusals, and failures to send in promised reviews are responsible for the fact that many tests have been reviewed by one person only. In future years, the Editor hopes to be able to have all tests reviewed two or more times. Where competent reviewers were not known in a given field, the Editor made a careful search of the literature of that field to locate the most able students. The test users who are most inadequately represented among the reviewers in this *Yearbook* are the classroom teachers at the elementary and secondary school levels. The *1939 Yearbook* will endeavor to correct this underrepresentation of able classroom teachers.

For the most part, tests selected for review were limited to tests published within the past two or three years. Since funds were not available to print reviews of all recent tests, an arbitrary selection had to be made. Hereafter, widely used tests will be reviewed regardless of the number of years since their publication. The objective will be to furnish prospective test purchasers with critical reviews of all tests, both new and old. Most of the tests reviewed in this *Yearbook* will again be evaluated in the *1939 Yearbook*.

Typescripts of reviews as received in the Editor's office were re-typed, collated, and attached to the bibliographic entry of the test reviewed. Carbon copies of the reviews, with the names of reviewers deleted, were then sent to the test publishers with the request that they carefully search the reviews for errors of fact. Originally, the Editor planned to forward to reviewers only those comments which, in his opinion, pointed to errors of fact. However, a negligible percentage of the publishers' and test authors' comments pointed to factual errors. Decision was then made to forward to test reviewers complete copies of the publishers' comments even though the letters were confined to a consideration of questions of value and controversial opinion rather than to questions of fact. Reviewers were asked to study carefully the comments received from the publishers and test authors. If such comments caused the reviewer to appraise the test somewhat differently, he was urged to rewrite his review. However, if the reviewer continued to evaluate the test in the same way, the Editor emphasized that the review should not be changed because of the protests raised by a test publisher or author. Only one reviewer withdrew his review as a result of the protests from a test author. Very few reviewers found it necessary to change their reviews as a result of the comments of the test publishers and authors. Hereafter, the practice of sending typescripts of reviews to publishers in advance of publication probably will be discontinued because of the negligible results obtained. Such a practice entails a tremendous amount of work and would delay publication of future yearbooks by two to three months.

Requests of test authors for the privilege of having their replies published in the *Yearbook* alongside of the reviews were refused because of the expense and delay which such a practice would involve. If adequate financial support is obtained in future years, the Editor hopes to be able to allow test authors the privilege of replying at length in the following yearbook. However, such replies must not consist of matter which should have been published in the manual accompanying the test. The most frequent objection raised by publishers and authors against the reviews submitted to them was that the reviewers were ignorant of unpublished research data in the possession of the test authors and publishers. The Editor has little sympathy for this type of objection. *It is the responsibility of test authors and publishers to furnish in the test manual whatever data they wish to have considered by reviewers and test purchasers.* Test authors and publishers should devote less time and money to constructing new tests and more time to furnishing prospective test consumers with detailed information concerning the construction, validation, and use of the tests which they do publish. Because of the test reviews, three publishers have already informed the Editor that they plan to be more careful in the future about publishing data concerning the construction and validation of their tests. Another publisher admitted that they probably had erred in publishing a test a year or so in advance of the publication of the monograph reporting in detail the supporting research.

When test publishers were told about the plans to review tests in *The 1938 Yearbook*, they appeared to be not only willing but glad to have their tests reviewed. Although it was expected that test publishers would be displeased with any unfavorable reviews which their tests might receive, at no time was the strong emotional reactions of several of the largest publishers anticipated. The Editor had supposed that publishers would recognize the need and inevitability of such a test-appraisal service and would appreciate any reviewing service which attempted to be fair to all concerned—test users, reviewers, authors, and publishers. This supposition was true for the majority of the test publishers, more so for those publishing only a few tests. However, a few of the largest publishers objected strenuously to the unfavorable reviews. So that test users may have a glimpse of some of the problems encountered in the initiation of this cooperative test-appraisal service, the following excerpts from letters received from a few test publishers and authors are presented. Readers will note that the excerpts include favorable as well as unfavorable reactions. The letters of each author and publisher are arranged in chronological order as received in order to show changes in attitudes.

* I am writing to you in a somewhat vigorous protest at the type of language and the tone of the review given by reviewer "A," particularly the last paragraph. * In my opinion, if you publish many reviews in such a condemning manner you certainly will not do your review of psychological tests very much good to the educational public at large, if I may be allowed to offer a hint along the lines of practical psychology. Resort to the use of such characterizations and

general implications, in my opinion, is quite beyond the realm of professional ethics regardless of the merits of the material in question. *   —*Test Author A*

* It makes little difference to me how or what you publish about this test. My only comment is that a certain book on "How to Win Friends and Influence People" is undoubtedly less popular with you than its companion volume of more recent appearance on "How to Lose Friends and Alienate People." It is really too bad that some one has "burned your toast" too often, why try to take the hide off any publisher, author, or group of publications, where does it get you? [Sic] My curiosity is a bit aroused, I may even inquire from some of my good friends on the Rutgers faculty what this is all about, but probably I will not take the trouble.   —*Test Author A*

* I have no corrections or criticisms to make. * We probably should publish a number of the research studies that were done in the standardization of the tests as well as several studies resulting from their use. * I shall try to see that these [studies] get in shape by the end of the summer and get them in the journals next year. *   —*Test Author B*

* Unfortunately, we have been so busy with revisions, factor analyses, and answering the questions of those who use our tests that we have given practically no attention to reporting them in professional magazines . . . [the publishers have] decided that, if possible, there will be plenty of such material available for the next issue of your publication.   —*Test Author C*

Your Reviewer A makes a number of unwarranted assumptions * Therefore, we are certain that you will wish to check further, and carefully, the report of your Reviewer A before considering it for publication in your yearbook. * Reviewer A . . . makes what I understand the Rutgers sophomore would characterize as "a nasty crack"—and a needlessly unfair nasty crack at that. * Professor Buros, we are deeply thankful for the spirit of justice and fairness you show in your letter. * We are certain that in the interest of test users, authors, Reviewer A, the publishers, and your forthcoming yearbook, it would be far better to say nothing whatever about [Test X] . . . in your forthcoming yearbook than to publish A's review, which we regard as definitely misleading and incorrect.
                         —*Test Publisher A*

* Ever since I received your letter . . . with its accompanying "reviews," I have been attempting to understand the viewpoint, the educational and socio-economic backgrounds, the technical training and experience, and the ethical standards of Reviewers A and B. * As a possible explanation of your mailing such literature as you sent with your letter . . . it occurs to me that your other duties were so many and so arduous that you didn't have opportunity to evaluate the "reviews" that A and B submitted. In the event that you believe that . . . [Test Author A] is a reputable and trustworthy student of educational research—without any regard to whatever opinion, if any, you have concerning the publishers of his work —I appeal to you in the name of common decency to withhold from publication in your yearbook or anywhere else the "reviews" submitted by Reviewers A and B. On the other hand, in the event that you concur thoroughly in the beliefs of Reviewers A and B that . . . [here the writer presents a long list of unfavorable comments made by the reviewers]—I assume that you will publish the "reviews" in your yearbook. In this latter event I must comfort myself with the thought

that we are not the first people who have been maligned and grossly misrepresented in a most unfair and scurrilous manner. Undoubtedly we can stand dirty treatment—although, of course, I don't enjoy it. At any rate, I am happy in the knowledge that I am spared the personal acquaintance of those two brave lads, A and B.

—*Test Publisher A*

Now, Oscar! Is this sporting? * Of course I realize that, as a philosopher, you search for the true, the beautiful, and the good and I wish you success in your search. At the same time I am grieved, I am distressed, Oscar, to learn that, in your judgment, the tests of our publication you have examined thus far are not true or beautiful or good. * I confess that . . . during my four years of service . . . in the Army with the A. E. F., it never occurred to me that I would ever be called upon to die for dear old Rutgers—but after all Rutgers is a great school and, since I escaped making the supreme sacrifice in my previous service and as long as I must die some time, why not die for dear old Rutgers? So, Oscar, today three specimen sets of the tests that you mention in your letter of April 21st are starting to you with our compliments. One last thought—wouldn't it be in keeping with modern humanitarian standards to knock them on the head with a mallet before you burn them at the stake? But then, you ruthless seekers after truth are not concerned with observing humanitarian standards, I fear, as long as the chips fall where they may! Anyway, as I go down for the third time, I'll gurgle, "Farewell!"

—*Test Publisher A*

* Your eagerness to have the publishers or authors of the tests . . . check the accuracy of the entries is indeed gratifying, and we hope to co-operate with you to the fullest extent to attain your purpose. * It may be . . . that the authors will not feel quite so alarmed as we have in our guise of publishers. We are asking the authors to let us have word from them immediately. May we repeat that we are eager to aid you to obtain well-rounded reviews (not necessarily favorable) which are accurate and which will make it possible for your publication to represent clearly your purpose?

—*Test Publisher B*

We are sure that by this time you have received the air mail letter from . . . [the authors] in which they set forth their reasons for asking that the review by "A" be withheld, at least until they have had an opportunity to publish the volume in which the data will be given * Many of these points [criticised by Reviewer A] have already been taken up . . . and others will be presented in the second volume, which is to be published as soon as possible. * it is unfortunate that the second volume has not yet appeared * We know that psychologists and educators have in the past found your volumes on tests to be very valuable, and we are eager to cooperate with you in every possible way in producing the 1937 volume satisfactorily.

—*Test Publisher B*

* This reviewer either does not know his stuff or else had a bad night. * I fear that this reviewer has been critical in the sense of fault-finding. At that, he is wrong most of the time. We do not feel that this is the kind of report you desire. If it were printed we feel the reviewer would harm your volume as well as us. In fact, we should protest such a statement as at all representative of this test.

—*Test Publisher C*

* the authors of the tests and the [publisher] . . . believe that the reviews are proper and reasonable with one exception * The entire review is written in an emotional tone, and on the basis of assumptions or major premises which are

not acceptable to us or in harmony with best practices * we seriously object to a report of this kind being reported in a Yearbook which purports to provide the type of evaluation which we know that you desire to present. We see no solution to a situation such as this unless the authors are permitted to prepare a reply to be printed in the next edition. —*Test Publisher C*

We are returning herewith these forthcoming reviews. We should like to compliment you on the thoroughness of your procedure. There's fairness, scholarship and everything good about your procedure in handling reviews. Possibly, however, we may add a comment in regard to the value of reviews. Several years ago we were enthusiastically *for* them. As our experience with them multiplies we are "cooling off" more and more. We have now arrived at the point where we care very little, if at all, whether a "review" of any of our publications is favorable or unfavorable. "Reviews" have no bearing on the run of orders, either to increase or decrease them. As time has gone along it becomes apparent that many of the "reviewers" only half read the item which they "review." It is apparent that most "reviewers" approach their task with no idea of an attitude of surveying but merely to "show off" their brilliance in attempting to pick fault with the publication which is to be their victim. Of course, "reviews" are useful to that extent that they furnish opportunities for the sparkling of doctorial brilliance. We need the entertainment of brilliance. As an illustration of that need "Dopey" is sufficient. "Dopey's in the White House" even, they say. Then there's another trouble with the "reviewers." Many of them are incapable of comprehending advanced concepts by educational leaders, and so proceed majestically to evaluate the work of a real master in terms of thumb-worn creeds. School executives are much more open minded and capable of evaluating in most cases. In the enclosed we took the trouble to try to bring out a little more of the truth in connection with . . . [Test X], but stopped there, not caring to bother further. The "reviewer" "A" who writes on . . . [Test Y] evidently just doesn't see what . . . [the author] is trying to do. Dr. Buros, since you, evidently, have scholarship structure in your mental machinery, why wouldn't it be doing more for education to drop these reviewing gymnastics and help Miss Goodykoontz in what she has started to do in assembling and putting out in mimeograph form "Studies in Progress?" Wouldn't it be service to education to publish in brief form the usable conclusions and recommendations of these studies? Is that what the Phi Delta Kappa people are now undertaking, perhaps? We are hoping that some one will do it. —*Test Publisher D*

* We have watched your work with growing interest. * [The head of the company] has gone through an evolution of first wondering if your project was worthwhile; his reaction of a year ago was that your talents were worthy of a higher cause and he wondered if you were going astray from the main avenues of constructive research; but recent developments and initiative and the constructive thinking you have placed in your work and the growth of its contribution convinces us all that, to use a technical expression, "you've got something there." *
—*Test Publisher D*

* I infer that you have been kind enough to send us these proposed criticisms in order that we might comment upon them in advance of their publication. I want to compliment you on the use of this very fair procedure. * I trust that you will understand that as publishers . . . [our company] welcomes any and all

criticism * I have read the criticisms with entirely an open mind and believe that they are much too harsh. * I believe that impartial and carefully considered reviews, especially when two or more can be presented, are helpful to accompany the announcement of tests. As I read the reviews of books in your bibliography and see how a condemnation by one reviewer is often followed by praise by the next, I am impressed by the fallibility of one person's judgment. I trust your reviewer is aware of this also and that he would grant that it might be better to temper one's own feelings in a review rather than run the risk of doing a publication injustice especially when the author of the test has no recourse. You will understand, of course, that . . . [our] Company is not looking for leniency—merely complete fairness of criticism. I feel sure your reviewer will be willing in the light of these suggestions to reconsider his condemnation of these tests and perhaps send you a revised review. *   —*Test Publisher E*

* The nature of some of the recent reviews has . . . been somewhat disturbing to authors of some of our tests, as well as to the test editors on our staff *
          —*Test Publisher E*

* The following tests . . . are not new publications and we doubt very much that any value is to be derived from publication of reviews at this time. The tests are pretty widely known and a number of them have been exceedingly widely used. *
          —*Test Publisher E*

* In view of the nature of the reviews which some of your reviewers have written in the past it seems to us highly advisable that information on construction and standardization be available to them.   —*Test Publisher E*

* The majority of the reviews appear to have been written by individuals who are unfamiliar with the use of tests. *   —*Test Publisher F*

* Frankly speaking I do not see that your yearbook measures up to the standards of the current professional journals since it is merely a compilation of tests and not as I see it a discriminating reviewing journal *   —*Test Publisher G*

Within a month after publication of *The 1938 Yearbook*, the Editor received from educators and psychologists more than a hundred letters in praise of this new cooperative test-appraisal service. Excerpts from a few of these letters follow:

* I am confident that the tremendous amount of labor which you put upon this volume will be rather generally appreciated. If it is not, my faith in the judgment of educationalists will be rudely shaken. Indeed, I hope that its reception will be accompanied by vigorous demands that the series you have started be continued in its present form.   —*Writer A*

I was quite delighted to find so much useful information in *The 1938 Yearbook*. You are to be congratulated on the work that you have done in bringing together in an orderly fashion what has always seemed to me to be a perfect chaos of materials. I hope that your reviewers in the future will be even more critical because it is only through honest, frank, and friendly criticism that we can hope to advance the scientific standards of work in this field. In the past there has been entirely too much back-slapping and bouquet-throwing to stimulate high standards of work and the exercise of critical judgments. Indeed, it is surprising that psychologists and educationalists have not applied the simple rules of learning to their own business of educational research. If there were some device by means of which good work could be heavily rewarded and poor work heavily punished, the standard would go up pretty fast. I should therefore like to see you use the Yearbook as a kind of a device for doing this very thing. It means that you run the risk of being unpopular with those whose work the Yearbook disapproves, but you will win no end of friends among those who feel that the standards of research in this field must be rapidly improved. —*Writer B*

* You will doubtless get the highest praise from the general run of educators and book reviewers and some from those who really count, as well as a lot of execration from those who got what they deserved. Don't let the latter get your goat. The continued execution of your self-initiated task will, in my judgment, involve almost unsurmountable difficulties unless you give practically all your time to the work. —*Writer C*

* this volume is an indispensible contribution to the working library of every person in the country dealing with the increasingly complex problems of mental measurement. The tremendous number of new tests appearing on the market makes it impossible for the individual worker to keep abreast of what is available to say nothing of being able to separate the wheat from the chaff. Your volume does this to the Queen's taste. I do hope that the tremendous labor involved in putting out such an annual volume will be supported by a foundation so that a real test-users' and test-evaluation research center can be set up. In this connection may I suggest that subsequent volumes contain a section on new evaluation data for tests issued in previous years. All of us in the field owe you our thanks for developing a workable plan and a most usable volume. —*Writer D*

* This marks an important step forward in the appraising and, I hope, the use of various tests and measures. The critical reviews should be invaluable to teachers, supervisors, and others who construct or use tests. * I sincerely hope that you may secure the support of one of the Foundations so that you may expand your services and ultimately set up a test users research organization. * —*Writer E*

I am simply amazed at the amount of material you have been able to include in *The 1938 Mental Measurements Yearbook.* * When we consider all the sums of money that foundations have poured into the production of tests, it seems unbelievable that a few thousand dollars a year could not be set aside for the continuation of this task you have undertaken. * The very fact that your yearbook contains so much highly critical material, will, in itself, tend to produce a recognition and the need for evaluating agencies. Words fail me to express my opinion of this volume, unless I choose from the Hollywood vocabulary, "colossal" etc. * —*Writer F*

* All in all, you have done an excellent piece of work. To me the book suggests the great needs in the field of testing. The task of publishing a book which is relatively unbiased in treatment and frankly critical in attitude is, as you point out, a difficult one. I hope that the inevitable discouragements, the personal abuse, and the financial difficulties which you may encounter will not keep you from reaching your goal of an effective "Test-users Institute." The foundations *should* support such a venture for it is of appreciable educational significance. * —*Writer G*

The 1938 Mental Measurements Yearbook was widely reviewed in this country and abroad. The reviews appeared in professional journals representing a wide range of fields—biology, education, industrial personnel, library administration, mathematics, medicine, psychology, psychiatry, science, and social service. All but two or three of the reviewers were warm in their praise. The critical portions of all known reviews of *The 1938 Yearbook* are reprinted herein. This yearbook series is probably unique in its practice of making readily available to its readers all the favorable and unfavorable criticisms made by reviewers. In a few instances, reviewers of *The 1938 Yearbook* made statements which are definitely in error. However, since other authors have had no opportunity to point out similar errors in reviews of their books, the errors made by reviewers of the yearbook have been reproduced as found. Readers are urged to consider, at this point, the pros and cons presented by the reviewers who represent a great variety of fields and viewpoints.

Following publication of *The 1938 Yearbook*, several foundations were approached without success in an effort to enlist their support in financing the continuance and expansion of this cooperative service to test users. Notwithstanding this failure to secure a subsidy, work was started on the next yearbook.

The first step was the selection of tests to be reviewed. Instead of limiting the volume to reviews of new and recent tests as in *The 1938 Yearbook*, the decision was made to include old as well as new tests. Reviews of old tests may prove effective in eliminating from use many tests which were among the best in their day but are now outmoded and inferior to recently constructed tests. On the other hand, such reviews may result in increasing the use of old tests and testing techniques which compare very favorably with tests being currently published. The sale of outmoded and ever-decreasingly valid tests persists far beyond the sale of textbooks published in the same years. Despite the fact that tests have been on the market for five to fifteen years, there exists, for probably ninety per cent of the tests, a dearth of critical information concerning their reliability and validity. Appraisals and reappraisals of old tests are needed almost as badly as evaluations of new tests. Consequently, the policy of this and of future yearbooks will be to review both old and new tests. It will probably take four to six yearbooks before each of the old but still currently used tests can be reviewed two or more times.

An effort was made to secure reviews of most of the tests published in 1938 and 1939, excluding those specifically constructed for use in state-wide testing programs. In addition, many of the tests which were reviewed in *The 1938 Yearbook* by only one or two reviewers were again chosen for review. This selection of some tests for review in two consecutive yearbooks is in keeping with the editorial policy to have each test reviewed by three to six persons in order to give representation to various viewpoints among test users. Finally, a representative selection of the older tests being currently sold was chosen for review. Because of difficulties in locating competent reviewers, difficulties in obtaining specimen sets for reviewers, last-minute refusals, and failures to send in promised reviews, the list of tests actually reviewed in this volume is less well rounded out than the originally selected list. However, test users are likely to find all classes of tests fairly well represented in this volume with the exception of tests in commercial education and the non-pencil-and-paper tests in physical education. Future yearbooks will cover tests in both of these areas.

The second step in the preparation of *The 1940 Yearbook* was the selection of competent reviewers. Each of the one hundred and thirty-three specialists who contributed test reviews to *The 1938 Yearbook* was asked to recommend persons representing different viewpoints whom he considered especially competent to appraise tests in his field. Numerous other leaders in each field were asked to make similar recommendations. As a final source, hundreds of articles, books, and theses were examined in search of promising reviewers. From these and other sources, a list of approximately six hundred names of potential reviewers was obtained. For each of these, an attempt was made to gather the following information in order to increase the likelihood of securing reviewers who are especially competent to review a particular test: (*a*) bibliography of recent writings; (*b*) courses taught; (*c*) colleges or universities attended; and (*d*) positions held. The high quality of test reviews in *The 1940 Yearbook* is due, in no small part, to the painstaking care with which this list of potential reviewers and accompanying information was gathered.

In selecting reviewers an effort was made to choose persons representing a wide variety of positions and viewpoints among both actual and potential test users. As a result, a very heterogeneous group of reviewers have cooperated in the preparation of this volume—classroom teachers, city school research workers, clinical psychologists, curriculum specialists, guidance specialists, personnel workers, psychologists, subject-matter specialists, and test technicians. Various groups and schools of thought within each of these classes of reviewers have cooperated by appraising tests. For example, the reviewers include Americans and Britishers, authors and nonauthors of standard tests, conservatives and progressives, persons with and persons without experience in administering the tests reviewed, proponents and opponents of essay-type tests, proponents and opponents of objective-type tests, users and nonusers of standard tests, and well-known and little-known persons. It can be truly said that the reviewers represent no one group or school of thought, unless the reviewers are described as representing all test users—actual and potential—who are considered especially competent in their fields and who have the courage to speak frankly and honestly in appraising a standard test. This representation of various viewpoints can only be achieved by having each test reviewed three to six times and, in the case of a few tests, even more. Since the objective is to give different viewpoints representation, test users must not consider two reviews as necessarily incompatible simply because one review praises and another review condemns the same test. Both reviewers may be entirely correct in their appraisals, i.e., correct in light of their respective values.

Ideally, a reviewer of a standard test, such as a high school Latin test, ought to possess the qualifications of a curriculum and teaching specialist, a subject-matter specialist, and a test technician. Unfortunately, all of these qualifications are rarely to be found in any one person. Consequently, the necessity of having each test reviewed by several persons is evident if the test is to receive a well-rounded appraisal. Some test technicians have suggested that each reviewer be supplied with a list of the points which should be covered in a good review. The suggestion was not adopted for fear that reviewers would attempt to cover points about which they may be poorly qualified to judge. For example, the average subject-matter specialist is likely to weaken his review if he tries to review as though he were a test technician. Likewise, the average test technician is on shaky ground when he discusses the validities of tests in subject-matter fields other than the few with which he is best acquainted. The average quality of the reviews is likely to be highest when the reviewers discuss only those points which they feel most competent to appraise even though this practice frequently results in reviews which are not comprehensive. By having three to six persons review each test, the probability of securing a comprehensive appraisal of a test is greatly increased. Unfortunately, this goal has been only partly achieved in the first two yearbooks. For example, some of the subject-matter tests reviewed in this volume were appraised only by subject-matter specialists. It would have been better to have had each of these tests also reviewed by one or two test technicians. Likewise, tests which were reviewed only by test technicians should also have been criticized by subject-matter specialists. Future yearbooks will endeavor to correct most of these underrepresentations.

Special precautions were taken to minimize the effect of possible bias. With a few exceptions, reviewers were not asked to appraise tests prepared by their colleagues or their former teachers. An effort was made to avoid asking a reviewer to appraise a test prepared by a person who is also a coauthor with the reviewer of some other publication. Knowledge of personal animosity or strong personal friendship between a reviewer and a particular test author or publisher was considered sufficient reason for not asking the reviewer to appraise the tests of that particular author or publisher. Authorship of a competing test was not, however, considered a bar to reviewing. In a few cases, reviewers were of the opinion that they should not evaluate tests which are actively in competition with their own. Although authorship of a competing test may introduce into a review an element of bias, the exclusion of authors of competing tests would have ruled out many of the most competent psychologists, subject-matter specialists, and test technicians. It seemed, therefore, wise to urge such reviewers to proceed.

Invitations to write frankly critical reviews of one or more specified tests were finally sent to nearly four hundred psychologists, subject-matter specialists, teachers, and test technicians in this country and abroad. Practically all of the persons invited—including those who were unable or unwilling to accept the invitation—declared a strong belief in the need and importance of providing test users with critical reviews of standard tests. Acceptances were received from approximately seventy per cent of the persons invited. Most of the others indicated a willingness to cooperate by reviewing tests for later yearbooks.

Test publishers were asked to contribute specimen sets of the pencil-and-paper tests which reviewers had agreed to review for this volume. The responses of the publishers varied greatly. Many of them gave their fullest cooperation by promptly supplying reviewers with specimen sets. In general, the smaller, the nonprofit, and the newer test publishers appeared to be most willing to have their tests reviewed. A few publishers refused to send review tests. Whenever possible, specimen sets were purchased from the publishers who refused to supply tests for reviewers. The tests of one of the largest publishers of psychological tests are poorly represented because of the difficulty of securing specimen sets of their tests by gift, purchase or loan. Several publishers not only refused to supply specimen sets of their paper-and-pencil tests for review, but also refused to answer inquiries concerning their tests. In fact, one of the largest publishers not only refused—and still does refuse—to answer or acknowledge letters sent to them by the Editor, but also stopped sending advertising announcements of their new tests to the Editor in his capacity as an instructor of courses in mental measurements.

The following instructions—presented on a mimeographed sheet entitled "Suggestions to Cooperating Test Reviewers"—were sent to each reviewer.

1. *Reviews should be frankly critical.* Noncritical, descriptive matter should be kept to the minimum necessary to support or make meaningful the evaluative portions of the review. The editor will make changes in the assignment of tests if, after examination, the reviewer feels that he prefers not to review the test originally assigned.

2. *Reviews should be concise.* Reviews should average 400 to 500 words in length, and, except in an unusual case, should not exceed 700 words.

3. *The bibliographic entry preceding each review or set of reviews will be prepared by the editor.* These entries will list the following data in the order named: title; subtitle; description of the group for which the test was constructed; copyright date; individual or group test; number of forms; cost; time to administer; author; publisher; references on the construction, validation, and use of the test; and the titles of parts or subtests printed as separate booklets.

4. *The final date on which all reviews should reach the editor's office has been extended to October 1, 1939.* It is hoped that most of the reviews will be in the hands of the editor by September 1.

5. *Test appraisals should be based upon the reviewer's own criteria as to what constitutes a good test.* Do not try to follow the criteria set up in a book on tests and measurements. Reviews should reflect special fields of competence. Remember that we want the reviewer's candid opinion of a test's merits and limitations.

6. *Each test will be reviewed by two or more persons.* In order to more adequately represent the various viewpoints among test users, each test will be evaluated by two to five reviewers. *The Mental Measurements Yearbook* series aims to represent all viewpoints among test users.

7. *The reviewer's name (as he wishes it printed), title, and institution will precede each review.* Titles will be given in order to let test users know whether the reviewer is a test technician, subject-matter specialist, psychologist, or classroom teacher.

8. *Attention should be called to a lack, if any, of accompanying data concerning the test.* Frequently it will be found that a test manual fails to give certain information needed to evaluate the test adequately. Reviews should call attention to these omissions if it is thought test authors and publishers should provide such information. It is the opinion of the editor that the yearbooks can and will render test users a great service by persuading test publishers to present full particulars concerning the construction, validation, and use of their tests. The reviewer can help both test publishers and test users by specifically pointing out the lack of such data in the test manual.

9. *Reviews will be edited only for consistency in style.* All reviews received will be published as written except for minor corrections in style which will be made only with the approval of the reviewer.

10. *Reviewers should include in the test review any comparisons with tests of a similar nature which appear to him to be either better or poorer than the test he is considering.*

11. *Reviewers are urged to skim over the Foreword, Preface, and pages 1-8 of The 1938 Mental Measurements Yearbook.* Persons who did not review tests for *The 1938 Yearbook* are being sent these pages.

All reviews were carefully studied by the Editor in an effort to improve the manuscripts without changing in any way the reviewer's message. Changes of a minor character were made in order to secure greater consistency and uniformity of style. Grammatical errors were corrected, redundancies reduced, and obscure expressions rewritten. References to other tests were checked to make sure that correct titles were being used. References to books and articles were verified and rewritten to conform to the yearbook style. All but a few quotations were checked for accuracy against the original source. This checking involved a tremendous amount of work. Many days were spent trying to find the statements and test items quoted by the reviewers. Although no quotations were seriously in error, many quotations contained minor errors of transcription. Factual errors which appeared to have been made inadvertently by reviewers were corrected. Other factual errors—that is, factual errors in the Editor's opinion—were not arbitrarily corrected but were called to the attention of the reviewers. In most cases reviewers accepted the suggestions and made changes in their reviews. In a few cases reviewers disagreed with the Editor and consequently the suggested changes were not accepted. After the reviews were edited, they were re-typed and copyread. Carbon copies of the reviews were then sent to the reviewers with the request that they copyread the reviews and approve or disapprove the changes made by the Editor. It was strongly emphasized that reviewers should not accept changes which did not meet their full approval. Minor improvements were made by many of the reviewers and several errors missed by the Editor were caught.

A painstaking search was made by the Editor to locate as many references as possible dealing with the construction, validation, and use of the tests listed in this yearbook. All secondary sources which were likely to be of any value were examined. For example: the Editor skimmed over all the abstracts published in *Psychological Abstracts* since it was founded in 1927; numerous measurement textbooks and bibliographies were searched; and bibliographic tools such as *Education Abstracts, Education Index, Psychological Abstracts, Psychological Index, Quarterly Cumulative Index Medicus, Review of Educational Research* and special subject-matter bibliographies were used to locate references on the construction, validation, and use of specific tests. In addition to the references located from these secondary sources, numerous references were located by leafing through back volumes of journals and by direct correspondence with authors. No effort was made to indicate the relative importance of the references. Abstracts and unpublished theses are, as a rule, not included among the references. References written in foreign languages were excluded from consideration because of limitations in time and ability to do the task well. An attempt was made to check all references against the actual article or book. Despite the use of numerous libraries in the New York area, it was found impossible to verify all the references. The percentage of unchecked references is, however, very small —less than five per cent. The names of authors of the references are presented exactly as written in the original source. Both main and secondary titles are presented. Publishers were written, or their catalogs consulted, to make sure that out-of-print books are so marked and that correct prices—both American and English—are given for the others. References are arranged chronologically by years and alphabetically by authors within each year. Literature cited by reviewers is listed among the references in order to avoid the use of footnotes which would frequently duplicate the references. Whether the amount of work which has gone into the preparation of these lists of references is worthwhile or not remains to be seen. If test users find the references on the construction, validation, and use of specific tests of value, the work will be continued in future yearbooks. Unfortunately, these reference lists were not prepared in time to allow the reviewers to get any benefit from them. Yearbook readers are urged to cooperate in making these bibliographies on specific test titles more valuable by calling the Editor's attention to errors and omissions and by sending to him reprints of articles relevant to testing.

Standardized tests are rarely appraised in the book review sections of professional journals in education and psychology. Nevertheless, more than two hundred journals were searched for test reviews. Excerpts consisting of the critical portions of these reviews are listed herein following the reviews written for *The 1940 Yearbook*. In a few cases, excerpts have been taken from books and articles as well as from test reviews. Book-size manuals—e.g., *Tests of Mental Development* *—are frequently reviewed as books. Excerpts from some of these reviews are presented in the test section of this yearbook and other excerpts are presented in the book section. In all cases, however, cross references are given.

The 1938 Yearbook listed practically all tests published up to eight months prior to the yearbook's publication on December 21, 1938. This lag has been cut from eight to between three and four months in *The 1940 Yearbook*. This was accomplished by sending new copy to the printer along with the return of galley proofs. Although costly and time consuming, this procedure has made it possible to include books, references, and tests published through September 1940.

The classification plan used in *The 1938 Yearbook* has been improved upon by grouping similar subjects together. For example, in the first yearbook, tests in algebra, arithmetic, geometry, and general mathematics were scattered throughout the test section. In this yearbook, these same subject headings are used but they are placed together under the more general head, mathematics. The use of general heads such as foreign languages, sciences, and social sciences should greatly facilitate the use of the yearbook. The key to the classification of tests presented in *The 1938 Yearbook* has been omitted from this volume. Its inclusion has been made unnecessary by the more general classification and the improved table of contents.

In order to facilitate cross referencing, the entry numbers follow in consecutive order the numbers used in the three preceding publications † in this series. It is important that test users do not make the mistake of thinking that *The 1940 Yearbook* supersedes the earlier publications in the series. Succeeding yearbooks supplement rather than supplant the earlier volumes.

For each test, an attempt has been made to present the following information in the order given:

1. *Title*. The main titles are presented in boldface type. Secondary and series titles are set in lightface type and are separated from the main title by a colon. Subtest titles are set in small capital letters. When the titles on the test booklet and the test manual differ, the former is used unless the test is much better known by the latter title.

2. *Description of the group for which the test was constructed*. Usually the grade, chronological age, or semester range is given. The designation "Grades 1B, 1A, 2, 3-6, 7-12, 13-17" indicates that there are six test booklets: a booklet for

---

*Kuhlmann, F. *Tests of Mental Development:* A Complete Scale for Individual Examination. Minneapolis, Minn.: Educational Test Bureau, Inc., 1939. Pp. xi, 314. $2.00.

†Buros, Oscar K. *Educational, Psychological, and Personality Tests of 1933, 1934, and 1935.* Rutgers University Bulletin, Vol. 13, No. 1; Studies in Education, No. 9. New Brunswick, N. J.: School of Education, Rutgers University, July 1936. Pp. 83. $0.50. Paper.

Buros, Oscar K. *Educational, Psychological and Personality Tests of 1936.* Rutgers University Bulletin, Vol. 14, No. 2A; Studies in Education, No. 11. New Brunswick, N. J.: School of Education, Rutgers University, August 1937. Pp. 141. $0.75. Paper.

Buros, Oscar Krisen, editor. *The 1938 Mental Measurements Yearbook.* New Brunswick, N. J.: Rutgers University Press, 1938. Pp. xv, 415. $3.00.

each half of grade one; a booklet for grade two; a booklet for grades three to six inclusive; a booklet for grades seven to twelve inclusive; and a booklet for undergraduate and graduate students in colleges and universities. "First, second semesters" indicate that there are two test booklets, one covering the work of the first semester, the other, the work of the second semester.

3. *Date of copyright or publication.* Whenever known copyright dates are reported; otherwise publication dates are given.

4. *Individual or group tests.* All tests are group tests unless otherwise designated.

5. *Number of forms, parts, and levels.*

6. *Cost.* The scale of prices of most publishers varies with the number of tests ordered. In such cases, the yearbook reports only the price per single test or, when the average cost is less, the price per twenty-five tests. Whenever specimen sets are available, their prices are given. Specimen sets and sample tests are usually sold postpaid; other tests are usually sold postage extra. Most prices are net, although a few publishers give discounts similar to those given to book purchasers. For full information on test prices, the catalogs of the publishers should always be consulted. Although every precaution has been taken to insure accuracy of prices, The Mental Measurements Yearbook can assume no responsibility for errors which may have been made. English prices are especially likely to be in error because of the war.

7. *Time.* The number of minutes of actual working time for testees and the approximate length of period necessary for administering the test are reported whenever obtainable. The latter figure is always enclosed in parentheses.

8. *Author.* For most tests, all authors and editorial assistants are reported. Names are written exactly as reported on the test booklets. In the case of tests issued in new form each year, only authors of the most recent forms are listed. Editors are not reported in the case of tests edited by committees of two or more members.

9. *Publisher.* The city in which the main office of the publisher is located and the publisher's full name are reported for each test. Both domestic and foreign publishers are given. For the street address of a given publisher see the index of publishers in this volume.

10. *References.* When known, references on the construction, validation, and use of each test are reported. These referencs are arranged in chronological order by years and alphabetically by authors within years. References cited in the test reviews are also listed among the references.

Tests and Reviews

* * * * *

ACHIEVEMENT BATTERIES

Reviews by William A. Brownell, Herbert S. Conrad, Harl R. Douglass, August Dvorak, Harold Gulliksen, Lavone A. Hanna, Edward S. Jones, A. M. Jordan, D. Welty Lefever, Herschel T. Manuel, Joseph E. Moore, C. W. Odell, E. V. Pullias, C. C. Ross, Robert K. Speer, John M. Stalnaker, Hilda Taba, Ernest W. Tiegs, R. M. Tryon, Ralph W. Tyler, and Hugh B. Wood.

[1182*]

Cooperative Contemporary Affairs Test for College Students. Grades 13-16; 1938-40; Forms 1938, 1939, and 1940; 7¢ per test, 10 to 99 copies; 2¢ per machine-scorable answer sheet; 25¢ per specimen set; 100(110) minutes; Forms 1939 and 1940: Alvin C. Eurich, Elmo C. Wilson, and Edward A. Krug with the editorial collaboration of Robert N. Bush, Easton Rothwell (Form 1939), and Max R. Menschel (Form 1940); New York: Cooperative Test Service.

REFERENCES

1 PATERSON, DONALD G.; SCHNEIDLER, GWENDOLEN G.; AND WILLIAMSON, EDMUND G. *Student Guidance Techniques*, pp. 150-3. New York: McGraw-Hill Book Co., Inc., 1938. Pp. xviii, 316, $3.00. (London: McGraw-Hill Publishing Co., 18s.)
2 AMSTUTZ, WADE S. "A Study of Characteristics of Education Freshmen Who Entered Ohio State University in 1938." *J Exp Ed* 8 : 289-92 Mr '40.
3 CAROW, ARTHUR C. "Relationships of Test Scores of Education College Freshmen to Grades in Selected Courses." *J Exp Ed* 8 : 284-9 Mr '40.
4 ROYER, O. O. "College Students and Contemporary Affairs." *J Exp Ed* 8 : 256-9 Mr '40.
5 FLANAGAN, JOHN C. *Measuring Interests*. Cooperative Test Service of the American Council on Education, Advisory Service Bulletin No. 4. New York: Cooperative Test Service, May 1940. Pp. 4. Gratis. Paper.

* Entries 1-503 will be found in *Educational, Psychological, and Personality Tests of 1933, 1934, and 1935*. By Oscar K. Buros. Rutgers University Bulletin, Vol. 13, No. 1; Studies in Education, No. 9. New Brunswick, N. J.: School of Education, Rutgers University, July 1936. Pp. 83. $0.50. Paper.
Entries 504-868 will be found in *Educational, Psychological, and Personality Tests of 1936*. By Oscar K. Buros. Rutgers University Bulletin, Vol. 14, No. 2A; Studies in Education, No. 11. New Brunswick, N. J.: School of Education, Rutgers University, August 1937. Pp. 141. $0.75. Paper.
Entries 869-1181 will be found in *The 1938 Mental Measurements Yearbook*. Edited by Oscar Krisen Buros. New Brunswick, N. J.: Rutgers University Press, 1938. Pp. xv, 415. $3.00.

Ralph W. Tyler, Chairman of the Department of Education; Professor of Education; and Chief Examiner, Board of Examinations, The University of Chicago.
[Review of Form 1939.] The 1939 form of the *Contemporary Affairs Test for College Students* continued the plan developed by the authors several years ago for the construction of items based upon contemporary topics most frequently mentioned in magazines and periodicals. This test provides the most comprehensive sample of topics to be found in any current events test and includes items classified under national and international politics, social and economic affairs, science and medicine, contemporary literature, arts, music, drama, movies, radio, and sports. From the standpoint of the breadth of content included it is an excellent test.

An achievement test should not only be considered in terms of the breadth of content but it should also be judged by the kind of reaction which the student must make in answering the test questions. Considered from this point of view the *Cooperative Contemporary Affairs Test* requires of the student only a somewhat superficial understanding and recall of current events. In a few cases the items are unnecessarily superficial as in the case of Item 10, Part I, which reads, "The cabinet member most outspoken in his criticism of Nazi activities is Secretary of the Interior (1) Daniel Roper, (2) Henry Morgenthau, (3) Benjamin Cohen, (4) Harold Ickes, (5) Harry Hopkins." Any student who knows the name of the Secretary of the Interior can answer this item correctly without having known that Mr. Ickes has been outspoken in his criticism of Nazi activities. In general, most of the items of this test can be answered by the student who reads the daily press, listens to news broadcasts, or follows the news reels in the movies, and who has a fairly good memory whether or not he has much understanding of the items he has been reading.

The educational significance of contemporary affairs lies not merely in developing the habit of reading and remembering major items in the press but primarily in sensing the implications of these items and thus building a better understanding of contemporary problems, a realization of the probable consequences of proposed courses of action, and developing a more realistic point of view regarding one's own social role. The 1939 form gives a measure of range of contact with contemporary events plus memory. It does not provide a measure of that aspect of contemporary affairs which would be considered very significant by most social studies teachers, namely, the use of this information in explaining important social phenomena and the relating of items of information so as to derive important generalizations about contemporary society.

As a measure of breadth rather than depth the 1939 form of the *Cooperative Contemporary Affairs Test for College Students* is sufficiently reliable for individual use and is easily administered and scored. For use within the limitations set by the qualities it measures, the test can be very helpful to social science teachers.

For a review by Paul M. Limbert, see 948.

[1183]

Cooperative Contemporary Affairs Test for High School Classes. Grades 9-12; 1939-40; Forms 1939 and 1940; 6¢ per test, 10 to 99 copies; 1½¢ per machine-scorable answer sheet; 25¢ per specimen set; 40(45) minutes; Alvin C. Eurich, Elmo C. Wilson, and Edward A. Krug with the editorial collaboration of Robert N. Bush, Easton Rothwell (Form 1939),

and Max R. Menschel (Form 1940); New York: Cooperative Test Service.

John M. Stalnaker, Consultant Examiner, College Entrance Examination Board, Princeton, New Jersey; and Associate Professor of Psychology, Princeton University. [Review of Form 1939.] This is a test of acquaintance with matters discussed in newspapers, magazines, and on the radio. It is divided into several sections. A total of 40 minutes is allowed for the 120 items, divided as follows: 10 minutes for 30 items in each of the fields of "political events" and "social and economic events"; 5 minutes for 15 items in each of the fields, "science and medicine," "literature," "fine arts," "amusements." All items are of the best-answer type (select the best of five given answers). Many of the items deal with names, titles, places, and few of them seem to go deeper than the "who-said-what" sort of thing. Answer sheets for machine scoring are available, or the answers may be written in the test booklet in the usual way.

It is an ambitious undertaking to attempt to secure scores of significance for individual interpretation, based on five minutes of testing time, particularly when the fields being covered are both extensive and heterogeneous. In fact, the significance of scores based on such brief tests is open to severe question.

It would be valuable to know how the content of this test has been selected, and on what basis the classifications have been made. Probably some survey has been made of the amount of space devoted to certain news items in various newspapers and magazines. Has any attention been given, however, to the significance of the information? Some of the items—indeed, many of them—are devoted to trivia which will and should be soon forgotten, whereas other items concern events of more lasting significance. Was each of the fields studied to see that it was thoroughly covered? Do the fields represent relatively homogeneous universes? What is the relationship of scores on this test to scores of general intelligence? Answers to these and many more questions concerning the basis on which the test has been developed and the manner in which it functions should be available for test users.

It is suggested that the test be used to provide a profile of functioning interests. This idea, at first quite appealing, assumes that the sections are long enough to yield dependable scores for individual interpretation, that the classifications or fields are valid, and that interest and not intelligence or some other ability is a principal determiner of the score. A highly intelligent person who skims the newspapers or news magazines will be able to score high on all sections. A less able person, even if his interest is great in one special field, may not score so high.

Should one be classed low in interest in "amusements," for example, because one does not know a few facts about the current movies? The great American sport of baseball is allowed one item. Golf is given one item. Tennis is not represented at all. One's interest in "fine arts" will be counted less if one does not know Hitler's favorite composer, the current slang for a popular swing trombonist, or the artist who wrecked a window display. Surely more significant happenings occurred and even if the tabloids devoted less space to them, is it not of more importance in the functioning of interests to find out if one knows of these significant things?

R. M. Tryon, Professor of the Teaching of the Social Sciences, The University of Chicago. A multitude of present-day teachers of the social sciences on the senior high school level attempt to keep their pupils abreast of contemporary affairs in the realms of politics, science, literature, the fine arts, amusements, and events of a social and economic vintage. To help these teachers evaluate their efforts the Cooperative Test Service has been for the past few years issuing, about May the first, a comprehensive test of current affairs. The test under review here (Form 1939) is the most recent of the Cooperative tests devoted to contemporary happenings.

In taking this test the pupil is confronted with 120 five-response multiple-choice items divided as follows: political events, 30 items; social and economic events, 30 items; science and medicine, literature, fine arts, and amusements, 15 items each. On an average, the testee is allowed twenty seconds for each item in the test. This six-fold division of the test items is in the opinion of the reviewer a decided improvement over the two-fold division utilized in Form 1937 of this test. However, should one desire that pupils meet the events in the list as they are met in the contemporary world, there would be no occasion for even the

six-fold division found in Form 1939. Except for mere administrative purposes, it is difficult to justify any division at all of the items in the test. Probably no high school pupil keeps his knowledge of contemporary affairs pigeonholed to the degree that the tests take for granted.

The content of the test is varied, extensive, and somewhat multifarious. In order to make a high score on it the testee would need to know at least something about nearly two hundred persons, almost forty countries, nearly three dozen books, and stray items concerned with dance steps, vitamins, specific words, aviation, kilovolt-ampere generators, nylon, the Houdry process of refining oil, "mystery control," trade treaties, labor organizations, pension plans, rationing of food, and sit-down strikes. Should the testee make a high score, one would be justified in placing him among the well informed on contemporary political, social, economic, scientific, literary, artistic, and recreational events. While the reviewer has no objective standards for evaluating the validity of the test in question, he cannot escape the impression that it certainly rates high on this characteristic.

If tests in the realm of contemporary affairs ever accomplish anything other than the discovery of the information that pupils possess at a specific time on a multitude of items, they will have to be considerably extended in scope and purpose. Merely to furnish tests that teachers could themselves construct with considerable success does not seem to be enough to demand of experts. Such individuals are expected to do what ordinary folks are incompetent to do. There is urgent need at the present time for a contemporary affairs test that goes beyond rate memory into the realms of attitudes, opinions, beliefs, the interpretation of facts, the sensing of motives, and the pointing out of relations between events.

For reviews by Howard R. Anderson, Walter Barnes, H. H. Giles, and J. Wayne Wrightstone of earlier forms of this test, see 949 and 950.

[1184]
Cooperative General Culture Test. Grades 12-16; 1933-40; Forms 1934, 1935, 1936, 1937, 1938, 1939, and 1940; Form 1933 is out of print; 10¢ per test, 10 to 99 copies; 4¢ per set of machine-scorable answer sheets (Forms 1937, O, P, and Q); 25¢ per specimen set; Form P: H. R. Anderson, L. P. Siceloff, E. F. Lindquist, A. C. Eurich, Rosa Lee Walston,

Margaret W. Moore, and C. P. Swinnerton with the editorial assistance of John Storck, J. H. Randall, R. L. Carey, Duane Roller, F. L. Fitzpatrick, and Alexander Calandra; Form Q: Mary Willis, Richard E. Watson, and Leone E. Chesire with the editorial assistance of Alexander Calandra, F. L. Fitzpatrick, Samuel McKee, Jr., Carl Marcy, Douglas Moore, Lloyd Motz, Martin Y. Munson, L. P. Siceloff, E. W. Sinnott, H. T. Westbrook, Everard M. Upjohn, and members of the faculties of Bethany College, the University of Minnesota, the University of North Carolina, the University of Rochester, and Stanford University; New York: Cooperative Test Service.

REFERENCES

1 LEARNED, WILLIAM S., AND WOOD, BEN D. *The Student and His Knowledge*: A Report to the Carnegie Foundation on the Results of the High School and College Examinations of 1928, 1930, and 1932. Study of the Relations of Secondary and Higher Education in Pennsylvania. With a foreword by Walter A. Jessup. The Carnegie Foundation for the Advancement of Teaching, Bulletin No. 29. New York: the Foundation, 1938. Pp. xx, 406. Gratis. Paper.
2 PATERSON, DONALD G.; SCHNEIDLER, GWENDOLEN G.; AND WILLIAMSON, EDMUND G. *Student Guidance Techniques*, pp. 153-6. New York: McGraw-Hill Book Co., Inc., 1938. Pp. xviii, 316. $3.00. (London: McGraw-Hill Publishing Co., Ltd. 18s.)

Lavone A. Hanna, Research Associate, School of Education, Stanford University. [Review of Form P.] As stated in the publisher's catalog, the purpose of this test is "to provide an indication of the general cultural background of students" and consequently it does not follow any course boundaries. By culture, the authors evidently mean the ability to recall facts, to associate a literary, art, or musical composition with its creator, to identify persons, and to recognize famous quotations. The test makes no attempt to evaluate as part of the student's "general cultural background" his appreciation of the art, literature, or music he is asked to identify; to evaluate the social attitudes which he is developing; to appraise his social sensitivity to persistent social problems or his ability to think scientifically about them. The value of a test of this kind depends upon the acceptance of the assumption that one's "cultural background" rests entirely upon his ability to recall facts.

The authors have attempted to correct the criticism leveled against the earlier general culture tests by adding sections on science and mathematics and more items dealing with current economic, political, and social problems. While some of these items do go beyond mere memorization of fact and call for an understanding of the issues involved in the problem, there is no attempt to appraise this behavior apart from memorization and the number of items calling for such interpretation is too small to be significant in the total score. The mathematics items deal more with the ability to handle symbols used in higher mathematics than to appraise abilities involved in quantitative relationships, while the science section tests the ability of the student to recall specific scientific facts at the expense of appraising his recognition or appreciation of the part science plays in our evolving culture. The emphasis upon current problems and modern art and literature is an encouraging factor in the test although placing these items first gives them an apparent emphasis not warranted when one realizes that only one-third of the social science items deal with present-day problems.

The test items were selected on the consensus of opinion of scholars in the various fields and as such probably adequately sample the facts which a well-informed person should possess. Data on the reliability of this particular form of the test was not included in the available booklet of norms or in the handbook on interpretation.

Since the test is set up for machine scoring the authors have felt themselves limited to two techniques. Two hundred and thirteen of the 600 items are of the single choice or best-answer type with each statement involving four or five possible responses. The other 387 items are of the matching type arranged in two columns and divided so that each of the three items grouped together in the right-hand column is matched with three of the five items making a corresponding group in the left-hand column. The test can, of course, be hand scored by those who do not have machine-scoring facilities.

Although the test does not follow any course boundaries it fails to meet general education or core curricula needs, for it tests factual and not functional information and if used to appraise such courses would tend to determine their content and check the development of curricula based upon pupil needs. The publisher's claim that the test "offers a promising means of exploring the cultural patterns of individual students" is based upon the assumption that appreciation, interest, attitudes, and understandings are closely related to the ability to recall information about a subject or thing.

Edward S. Jones, Professor of Psychology and Director of Personnel Research, The University of Buffalo. [Review of Form P.] This is a three-hour examination composed of over five hundred objective test items, designed for the end of the high school period or the first two years of college. It is the most inclusive of all of the cooperative tests, covering the arts, literature, sciences, mathematics, and the social sciences. The norms are extensive, having been based on the experience of a large number of colleges. This test is designed to be an indicator of the general cultural level of the person, and has shown quite high correspondence with grades and other indicators of success. It can be easily scored and every score compared on a "national" basis.

This reviewer sees a decided value in a test program which includes such a general culture examination—which appears to be a great improvement over the former general culture tests—except for the fact that misleading generalizations can be very easily reached in connection with it. In their book, *The Student and His Knowledge*,[1] William S. Learned and Ben Wood postulate that the answering of a host of multiple-choice items is the best indicator of knowledge that we have. On the other hand, there are many who feel that there is far too much emphasis on very specific memorizations connected between proper names of people or places and specific productions. They disparage the emphasis on recognition items. They do not like the neglect of essays and the recall of ideas. When the general cultural test is compared with college grades there is found to be far more association with freshman English grades than with the grades given the same people when they are juniors or seniors. One may doubt whether it gets at the type of ability that is considered most essential in connection with tutorial work and final comprehensive examinations. It is a comprehensive examination in the sense of being a good survey of the quantity of items known to the student. It may be a poor measure of some phases of insight and expression which are hard to measure objectively.

This test, among others, is used as a basis of analyzing progress in many small colleges throughout the country. Hence, the norms may not be satisfactory for the larger institutions or places with high entrance standards. If it is merely used as a test of specific details which the student has learned, it no doubt fulfills a valuable function; but if, perchance, it is used as a goal or as the main index of education, those applying the test may easily overstep the mark. In spite of the warning issued in their handbook of instructions that "these tests should always be looked upon as *measuring* instruments, not as teaching instruments," there are already indications that some college teaching has been modified in the direction of cramming by such items. The examination would be improved by the reduction of the vast number of proper name items and the inclusion of more inference and definition items, both of which correlate more closely with college grades.

Nearly every specialist in a college field might raise objection to the relative importance or weight given to some sections of the test. To the reviewer the test seems to be unusually well balanced, with a more satisfactory and complete distribution of items than any he has seen. There is very high reliability on such a test, because of the large number of items—over five hundred.

Hilda Taba, Assistant Professor of Education and Research Associate, The University of Chicago. [Review of Form P.] The purpose of this test is stated to be to provide an index of the general cultural level which the individual has attained, disregarding the course limitations. Yet, its five parts correspond to the general areas of social studies, literature, fine arts, science, and mathematics, for each of which part scores are given.

Each of the sections provides a fairly comprehensive sampling of information. Thus, the section on social studies contains items on political, economic, and social problems, history, and current events. The section on literature includes American as well as world literature, covering the classics as well as contemporary literature.

The nature of items is somewhat limited. Most of them are of straight information multiple-choice type, ranging from specific details, such as "The great Protestant leader of the Thirty Years' War was (1) Wallenstein (2) Christian IV of Denmark (3) Gustavus Adolphus and (4) Charles XII of Sweden," to ideas of more general type, such as "The *basic* cause for the decline in the volume of foreign trade in recent years has been the (1) differences in the monetary systems of the various countries (2) tendency for certain backward nations to become more self-sufficient (3) wider application of the principle of territorial division of labor (4) growing feeling of nationalism." There is a good deal of matching of names with events and characteristics or achievements. The section on literature is composed almost wholly of matching authors with titles of books and biographical data, naming and describing characters in works of literature, and matching quotations with books.

On the whole, this test can be grouped with the rather common variety of information tests. For this reason, it is difficult to decide how this test differs from the battery of survey achievement tests appearing in the same series. The one visible difference is that this test takes 180 minutes to give, whereas a battery of achievement tests in the same five areas would take about 225 minutes.

In view of this, the title of the test is somewhat puzzling. By what criterion does a diluted battery of achievement tests become a test on general culture? And what definition of culture do those who make and use these tests have? As a matter of fact, the 1939 form of the *Survey Test in the Social Studies* seems to come closer to deserving the title of "General Culture Test." It calls more for an intelligent and reasoned understanding of social problems and events than does the social studies section of this test.

Because of these characteristics of the test, it is difficult to see how this test would serve any of the purposes stated for the Cooperative test series. It is claimed that these tests provide information about students which is helpful in advising about election of subjects, in discovering causes of failures, in appraising relative achievement in different fields, and in advising about future academic activities. To what degree any test of information will adequately serve these purposes can be questioned. The function of a superficial survey of information in a variety of fields is still more questionable. In schools where achievement tests are used, there seems little need for giving a diluted survey of the same thing. The functions claimed for this test seem to be better covered by other more specific tests. Yet the different parts of this test taken separately do not seem to be representative enough to warrant using it in place of the battery of achievement tests in corresponding fields.

For a review by F. S. Beers, see 871.

[1185]

Entrance and Classification Examination for Teachers Colleges: Elementary Test, 1939 edition. 1933-39; 2 forms; 8¢ per test; 3¢ per machine-scor-able answer sheet; 60¢ per specimen set; 140(150) minutes; Personnel Department of the Colorado State College of Education; Normal, Ill.: Teachers College Personnel Association, c/o C. F. Malmberg.

REFERENCES

Same as for 1280.

[1186]

Glick-Germany Scholastic Aptitude Test. Grades 7-12; 1939; 1 form; $1.50 per 25; 15¢ per specimen set; 53½(60) minutes; Harry N. Glick and Claude B. Germany; Cincinnati, Ohio: C. A. Gregory Co.

[1187]

Gray-Votaw General Achievement Tests. Grades 1-3, 4-8; 1939-40; a revision of the *New-South Achievement Tests* (see 508); 3 forms, 2 levels; Hob Gray and David F. Votaw; Austin, Tex.: Steck Co.
a) PRIMARY TEST. Grades 1-3; $1.25 per 30; 25¢ per specimen set; 52(60) minutes.
b) ADVANCED TEST. *Standard edition*: $2 per 30; 25¢ per specimen set; 149(170) minutes; *Abbreviated edition*: $1.75 per 25; $2 per machine-scorable answer sheets; 25¢ per specimen set; 73(85) minutes.

REFERENCES
1 VOTAW, DAVID F. "Effect of Do-Not-Guess Directions Upon the Validity of True-False or Multiple-Choice Tests." *J Ed Psychol* 27 : 698-703 D '36.

Joseph E. Moore, Professor of Psychology, George Peabody College for Teachers. [Review of the Advanced Test, Standard Edition.] The *Gray-Votaw General Achievement Tests* are recent (1939) revisions of the *New-South Achievement Tests* developed by the same authors. The present Standard Edition of the *Gray-Votaw General Achievement Tests* "includes the original nine divisions, corrected and improved, and includes also a new tenth division, Elementary Science. This addition was made to keep abreast of the curriculum. The added division is applicable to a school regardless of whether the school has formal courses in Elementary Science." The revised test was made to apply to grades four through eight inclusive.

The foregoing quotation by the authors raises several questions concerning the validity of the revised test. The original instrument, the *New-South Achievement Test,* was developed to cover grades four through seven. The questions which went into the achievement test were gathered after a "careful examination of the textbooks, workbooks, courses of study, and reading lists used in southern schools" was made. A comparison of Form A of the *New-South Achievement Test* with the contents of Form A of the Standard Edition of the *Gray-Votaw General Achievement Test* indicates that no questions have been added to this instrument since 1936. The statistical information in the Gray-Votaw Standard Edition manual on the means and standard deviation of each of the average scores remains the same as that found in the New-South test except for alterations made in the total averages for grades 4-8 and in the total number of pupils when the data on grade eight were included. These data obviously seem to indicate that the New-South test, developed for a four grade range (4-7) on the basis of curricular analysis, now becomes a test for grades four through eight, a range of five grades, with the mere process of adding 62 elementary science items and giving the old test plus the new section to 624 eighth-grade pupils.

The test user is entitled to know how the authors can justify the questions selected four years ago (1935), as valid measures of achievement for grades four through seven when those same questions are now given to grades four through eight. The authors appear to have made no fundamental change except in the numbering on the front to include one more grade—a change of the number seven to an eight.

The reliability data have been worked out by the authors but such data are highly questionable when the basic methods of selecting valid questions for the eighth grade have not been made clear. It is entirely possible that if adequate samplings of the curriculum applicable to the eighth grade had been made a number of the basic measures of reliability would have remained the same. A casual inspection of the means and standard deviation would lead one to wonder if the degree of overlapping was not serious between the sixth and seventh and between the seventh and eighth grades.

The second section of the test, dealing with "*a choice of words*" seems to be the weakest of the ten parts of the test, judging from the reliability coefficients stated by the authors in the manual. The "choice" open to a pupil merely means the crossing out of one of two words given. The highest reliability coefficient given by the authors for Test 2 was .66. Tests 1, 3, 5, 9, and 10 appear to lack reliability at the fourth and fifth grades particularly. The probable error of estimate confirms the inconsistency of the measures on separate sections of the test.

The scoring of the Standard Edition of the *Gray-Votaw General Achievement Test* is both difficult and time consuming due to the irregular arrangement of items. The scoring key is printed on a type of paper which wrinkles easily and would show the effects of usage in a very short time. The scoring formula may be unnecessarily involved for general use in the elementary school.

The profile chart is unduly small and contains such fine print that it would be a strain on any teacher's eyes to use it, not to mention the serious possibility of increasing errors in plotting scores. The profile chart cannot be separated from the test without mutilating part of section one.

The quality of paper and the size and legibility of type used in the test are to be commended. The samples, while brief, seem to be adequate enough to get across the method of answering the questions.

It is to be regretted that the authors did not indicate the separate southern states surveyed for the original items of the *New-South Achievement Test*. The test will not be equally valid in all southern states due to differences in textbooks and courses of study. The test is a general achievement test but one based on the curriculum in one or more states in a particular region. A casual survey of the test contents seems to indicate that facts related to Texas dominate all the others.

Joseph E. Moore, Professor of Psychology, George Peabody College for Teachers. [Review of the Advanced Test, Abbreviated Edition.] The abbreviated edition of the *Gray-Votaw General Achievement Tests* was made by selecting three hundred of the six hundred thirty-five items represented in the Standard Edition.

The general criticisms directed at the Standard Edition apply even more directly to the abbreviated edition. The separate parts of the short tests do not correlate very well with the standard-length test. This raises a serious question as to the validity of both the longer and shorter tests. The highest correlation between any part of the abbreviated and the standard editions of the test was .87. The correlations were obtained by giving one test one day and the other the following day and then correlating the partial scores.

The authors of the test point out that "The abbreviated form has less reliability than the standard edition." This statement is not entirely supported by the coefficients given in the manual. The abbreviated form produced a coefficient of .91 on fewer than half the items in reading as against a coefficient of .85 for the whole test. On arithmetic the coefficient of reliability was higher for the abbreviated edition of the test by .02. The reliability of the total average for grades four through eight on the standard edition was .976 in contrast to a reliability coefficient of .968 for the abbreviated test. It would appear that in terms of reliability the abbreviated test would be as consistent as the longer test.

The improved perforated scoring device for hand scoring and the space for machine scoring make the abbreviated form the more desirable instrument. There is little to choose between the abbreviated edition and the standard edition as far as validity and reliability are concerned.

The profile chart in the abbreviated test is markedly improved over that found in the standard edition. The chart covers almost a full page and can be separated from the test without mutilating any of the pupil's responses. The printing, both numbers and letters, is still unnecessarily small for careful plotting without undue eye fatigue to the teacher. The printing throughout the test is excellent and the paper of good quality. The scoring sheet is durable and greatly facilitates rapid grading and probably improves the accuracy of grading. It is possible that the holes in the scoring sheet are too small to detect those answers which have not been placed exactly in the right place.

C. C. Ross, Professor of Educational Psychology, University of Kentucky. [Review of the Advanced Test, Abbreviated Edition.] The abbreviated edition differs from the standard edition mainly in two respects: (*a*) It is reduced in length from 635 items to 300; (*b*) all items are of the multiple-response type with two to five options, and arranged with separate answer sheets for either machine- or hand-scoring.

VALIDITY. The evidence of statistical validity is extremely limited. A correlation of .939 between the abbreviated and standard edition is reported for 302 cases, grades four to eight, inclusive. The item validation of the original test was apparently limited to the selection of items which "show proper 'climb' through the successive grades," a procedure which is less

important than the ability of the items to discriminate between weak and strong students within the same age or grade group.

The authors make a commendable effort to secure curriculum validity. To accomplish this they adopted two somewhat unique procedures: In the first place, the content of the test is based upon a "careful examination of all the instructional materials commonly used in southern schools," such as textbooks, courses of study, teachers' outlines and test questions, and the judgment of expert supervisors. These appear to be located mainly in one state, Texas. The standardization of tests for regional use seems a procedure that should be encouraged. An examination of the test items indicates, however, that this procedure results in very little content that is distinctly local or regional. Even in the language test (choice of words), one looks in vain for such southern expressions as "John *carried* his girl to the show," rather than *escorted* her. All in all, the content is that of the traditional American curriculum which emphasizes isolated knowledges and skills.

In the second place, with the exception of the arithmetic test, the directions to the pupil contain this statement: "Go as far as you can but do not skip any questions." Research by Votaw [1] indicated that was necessary to prevent the tests from reflecting unduly the personality type of the pupil. This is an important hypothesis, but probably needs further verification by other investigators, especially as to why the phenomenon should operate in all other subjects and skip arithmetic. Further study should also be given to the possible effect of such "do-not-skip" instructions upon the conscientious student who gets "stuck" on an item rather early in the test.

RELIABILITY. The reliability coefficient for the abbreviated test, grades four to eight, is .968 as compared with .976 for the longer test. The coefficients for the separate grades are not given. The reliability for the six divisions of the short test is usually only .02 less than for the long test. Although it is doubtless true that test-makers in the past have over-emphasized reliability as an attribute of tests, the present authors have tended toward the other extreme and have given too little information on this point.

USEABILITY. The useability of a test depends mainly upon the ease of the administering and the scoring of the test and upon the ease of interpreting and applying the results. The manual gives brief but adequate directions both for administering and scoring the tests. The keys for hand scoring are the convenient window type. The directions should probably tell the pupil *where* to do his figuring on the arithmetic test, even if he is provided with scratch paper.

Age and grade norms, apparently based upon Texas schools, are conveniently arranged. It is to be hoped that these norms will be further extended to provide separate norms for both seven- and eight-year elementary schools, rural and urban schools, schools with short and long terms, as well as for pupils of various intellectual levels. Up to the present time no publisher has provided a really adequate set of norms. A profile chart greatly facilitates the interpretation of the tests. These charts should be available separately, if it is not feasible to make them a part of the answer sheet.

Suggestions for applying the results are brief but helpful. Many users would probably prefer a change in emphasis: (*a*) less upon *group* analysis and more upon *individual* analysis; and (*b*) less treatment of statistical *methods* easily available elsewhere and more upon the statistical *results* of the test available nowhere else. Unfortunately the usefulness of the abbreviated edition is restricted somewhat by its excessive price, $1.75 for 30, as compared with the much more comprehensive standard edition at $2.00 for 30.

[1188]

Iowa Every-Pupil Tests of Basic Skills. Grades 3-5, 6-8; 1940; Form L, 2 levels; $3.75 per 25 sets of the elementary battery; $1.15 per 25 of any one test in the elementary battery; $4 per 25 sets of the advanced battery; $1.25 per 25 of any one test in the advanced battery; 30¢ per manual; 12¢ per booklet of norms; 40¢ per 25 record cards; single specimen set free; 193(225) minutes for the elementary battery; 266(325) minutes for the advanced battery; H. F. Spitzer in collaboration with Ernest Horn, Maude McBroom, H. A. Greene, and E. F. Lindquist with the assistance of the faculty of the University Experimental Schools, State University of Iowa; Boston, Mass.: Houghton Mifflin Co.
a) TEST A: SILENT READING COMPREHENSION. *Elementary Battery*: grades 3-5; 44(50) minutes; *Advanced Battery*: grades 6-8; 67(85) minutes.
b) TEST B: WORK-STUDY SKILLS. *Elementary Battery*: grades 3-5; 44(55) minutes; *Advanced Battery*: grades 6-8; 78(90) minutes.
c) TEST C: BASIC LANGUAGE SKILLS. *Elementary Battery*: grades 3-5; 51(60) minutes; *Advanced Battery*: grades 6-8; 58(70) minutes.
d) TEST D: BASIC ARITHMETIC SKILLS. *Elementary Battery*: grades 3-5; 54(60) minutes; *Advanced Battery*: grades 6-8; 63(80) minutes.

[1189]

Metropolitan Achievement Tests: Revised Edition. Grades 1, 2-3, 4-6, 7-8; 1931-37; the tests in arithmetic, reading, English, and handwriting are available as separates; the Supervisor's Manual must be purchased separately at 25¢ per copy; the *Primary Handwriting Scale* may be purchased separately at 10¢ a copy; edited by J. S. Orleans; Yonkers, N. Y.: World Book Co.
a) PRIMARY I BATTERY. Grade 1; 1931-35; 3 forms; $1.15 per 25; 20¢ per specimen set; 40(60) minutes; Gertrude H. Hildreth.
b) PRIMARY II BATTERY. Grades 2-3; 1932-35; 3 forms; $1.25 per 25; 20¢ per specimen set; 75(90) minutes; Gertrude H. Hildreth.
c) INTERMEDIATE BATTERY. Grades 4-6; 1932-37; 5 forms. *Complete*: $2 per 25 tests; 25¢ per specimen set; 200(220) minutes; *Partial*: $1.50 per 25; 25¢ per specimen set; 147(165) minutes; Richard D. Allen, Harold H. Bixler, William L. Connor, Frederick B. Graham, and J. S. Orleans.
d) ADVANCED BATTERY. Grades 7-8; 1932-37; 5 forms. *Complete*: $2 per 25; 25¢ per specimen set; 227(245) minutes; *Partial*: $1.50 per 25; 25¢ per specimen set; 162(180) minutes; Richard D. Allen, Harold H. Bixler, William L. Connor, Frederick B. Graham, and J. S. Orleans.

REFERENCES

1 EDUCATIONAL RECORDS BUREAU. *1934 Achievement Tests Program in Independent Schools:* A Summary of the Results of Achievement Tests Given in Elementary and Secondary Independent Schools in April, 1934, pp. 40-53. Educational Records Bulletin No. 13. New York: the Bureau, 1934. Pp. iii, 64, 9. $1.50. Paper, lithotyped.
2 PULLIAS, EARL V. "Commercial Standardized Tests," pp. 65-80. In *Variability in Results from New-Type Achievement Tests.* Duke University Studies in Education, No. 2. Durham, N. C.: Duke University Press, 1937. Pp. 100. $1.00. Paper. (London: Cambridge University Press, 4s. 6d.)
3 PATERSON, DONALD G.; SCHNEIDLER, GWENDOLEN G.; AND WILLIAMSON, EDMUND G. *Student Guidance Techniques,* pp. 101-5. New York: McGraw-Hill Book Co., Inc., 1938. Pp. xviii, 316. $3.00. (London: McGraw-Hill Publishing Co., Ltd. 18s.)

E. V. Pullias, Professor of Educational Psychology, George Pepperdine College. Those aspects of the Metropolitan batteries which one can evaluate on the basis of mere examination are very desirable. This is especially true of the primary batteries. The pictures, maps, and typing are all clear and attractive. Nowhere is there evidence of the crowding that frequently makes a test confusing, particularly at the lower levels. Arrangement throughout is such as to facilitate administration and recording.

Of the 76 pages in the manual only ten pages (pp. 63-73) have any direct bearing upon the technical features of the Metropolitan tests. The first 63 pages of the manual contain essentially the same material as appears in the usual textbook discussion of testing, but its position in the manual and the frequent complimentary reference to the Metropolitan tests make these first 63 pages primarily a piece of advertising. Such advertising is effective and expected in a manual accompanying commercial tests, but the uncritical reader should be reminded that an ideal testing program such as this manual describes is in no sense guaranteed by the use of any particular tests.

The following facts are supplied in the description of the tests: (a) the contents of the tests are "drawn almost entirely from courses of study in large cities and have been checked against the contents of other such courses of study and widely used textbooks in the several subjects"; (b) the tests were standardized according to generally accepted statistical procedures; (c) facts concerning reliability of the tests are given in terms of the commonly used coefficients of correlation between forms of the tests, and in terms of probable errors of a pupil's score; (d) the tests are objective in respect to scoring, provided, of course, the directions and keys are followed scrupulously.

It would have been helpful if the actual courses of study on which the tests were based had been listed. Without this information no very meaningful facts concerning the validity of the tests even within the frame of reference of these courses of study can be adduced. The important question about any achievement test is: Does it measure effectively the achievement of pupils in respect to the aims and contents of the course or courses of study on which the test is based? Obviously this question is difficult to answer in the case of the Metropolitan tests because of the absence of information. As is usually true of standardized tests, the evidence given does not support the claims made in respect to validity.

The facts concerning reliability of the tests are complete and indicate a high degree of excellence at this point.

The available facts seem to indicate that the *Metropolitan Achievement Tests* are among the better of similar tests now on the market; they should be examined carefully by any person interested in such tests. The Metropolitan batteries properly administered and interpreted will uncover valuable data concerning the acquisition of the skills and information covered by the tests. At the same time it is well to remember that there is no convincing evidence that these or any other available tests are sufficiently valid, reliable, and objective to warrant their being used uncritically as a basis for pupil promotion or for instructional evaluation in a particular school system.

Hugh B. Wood, Professor of Education, University of Oregon. The tests were constructed in the twenties and revised in their present form nearly a decade ago. Unfortunately they reflect the philosophy of the conventional school of that date—a philosophy probably not in articulation with general trends in the elementary school today and certainly not with progressive experimental practices. To illustrate: (a) recommended administrative and supervisory uses include, "To rate teacher effectiveness," "Comparison of achievement of school with school," to obtain "accurate estimate of the relative efficiency of schools . . . and of the administrators" (i.e., principals); (b) no test is included on experiences in the realms of science or social living; (c) history, civics, and geography are tested as separate subjects in spite of universal trend in the elementary school towards social studies fusion; and (d) a "promotion age" is computed mathematically from mental ability and achievement test scores.

Validity of tests was established by selecting items from courses of study of large cities, and textbooks. Inasmuch as both sources usually lag behind best practice and not infrequently ignore the teacher's immediate and broader-than-subject-matter objectives, and in the light of the date of the sources, the validity of the tests in general may well be questioned by all save the Essentialists.

Reliability of tests, determined by correlation of two forms, ranges from .758 (single test) to .974 (complete battery) with a median of about .86. No test has a probable error of measurement higher than 4.1 months and the average is about 2.5. Number of cases varied from 142 to 213.

Strong points of the test include: (a) provision of comparable scores between grades and subjects over an 8-grade range; (b) graphical interpretation and effective handling of results; (c) administrative directions are clear, thus contributing to ease and simplicity of administration; (d) scoring is fairly objective and, though long because of the length of test, is made easier by a good format; (e) size of booklet (6 × 10") convenient for students; and (f) the profile sheet may be torn off for filing.

Minor criticisms include: (a) failure to alphabetize items in matching tests; (b) the size of class record sheet (10 × 12") is inconvenient for filing; (c) the spelling sheet is not attached to directions for administering; (d) all possible answers are not given on the key; (e) the punctuation test is difficult to score; (f) like all battery tests, the subtests are too short for real diagnostic value; and (g) the Supervisor's Manual is too academic.

Because changes in the philosophy of teaching skills have been fewer than in the other areas represented, the partial batteries and the primary batteries are (to the reviewer) more valid than the complete batteries. In the typically conventional school or one not too far beyond the average, the former may serve quite well to give group or subject ratings.

For additional reviews by Jack W. Dunlap, Charles W. Odell, and Richard Ledgerwood, see 874. For reviews by Foster E. Grossnickle, Guy M. Wilson, Peter L. Spencer, and Harry Grove Wheat of the arithmetic test, see 892 and 1458. For reviews by Ivan A. Booker, Joseph C. Dewey, and D. A. Worcester of the reading test, see 1105 and 1551.

[1190]

Modern School Achievement Tests. Grades 3-8; 1931; 2 forms, 2 editions; COMPLETE BATTERY: $7.55 per 100; 15¢ per specimen set; (190-200) minutes; SHORT FORM—SKILLED SUBJECTS: $5.25 per 100; 15¢ per specimen set; (120-130) minutes; Arthur I. Gates, Paul R. Mort, Percival M. Symonds, Ralph B. Spence, Gerald S. Craig, DeForest Stull, Roy Hatch, Amy I. Shaw, and Laura B. Krieger; New York: Bureau of Publications, Teachers College, Columbia University.

REFERENCES

1 MORT, PAUL R., AND GATES, ARTHUR I. *The Acceptable Uses of Achievement Tests: A Manual for Test Users.* New York: Bureau of Publications, Teachers College, Columbia University, 1932. Pp. ix, 85. $1.05.
2 FORAN, T. G., AND LOYES, M. EDMUND. "The Relative Difficulty of Three Achievement Examinations." *J Ed Psychol* 26:218-22 Mr '35.
3 WOOLF, HENRIETTE, AND LIND, CHRISTINE. "A Study of Some Practical Considerations Involved in the Use of Two Educational Test Batteries." *J Ed Psychol* 26:629-34 N '35.

William A. Brownell, Professor of Educational Psychology, Duke University. This test battery, the product of several members of the staff of Teachers College, Columbia University, seems to possess no unique feature to distinguish it from the several similar test batteries now on the market.

The opening paragraph of the Short Form manual advises that the "reliability of the individual tests for a single grade ranges from .78 to .96, with a majority of the reliabilities above .87. The reliability of the entire battery for a single grade ranges from .92 to .96." These coefficients indicate satisfactory reliability as reliability is usually measured. With regard to validity, test elements were first selected from "superior" courses of study, as rated by the Bureau of Curriculum Research of Teachers College, and were then checked by "master teachers" of different subjects. Preliminary tests were then tried out, and, it is assumed, needed changes were made. According to the manual, these steps guarantee a high degree of validity for the battery.

Of course, the degree of validity will vary with the purpose for which the tests are used. If used in an ordinary way to make crude comparisons of a given system with a "national" average (the survey function), the tests rate high in validity. If used, however, for diagnostic purposes, obviously the tests possess little validity. Moreover, if used for the purpose implied in the name of the battery —*The Modern School Achievement Tests*— the tests are almost certainly of questionable validity. One does not, of course, measure achievement unless one measures what has been offered for learning in a particular situation, in a given grade, with a particular course of study which has been taught in a certain way. The school administrator or teacher should satisfy himself that this battery, or the separate tests, actually represents what has been taught in his school before adopting these tests to measure the achievement of individual pupils. There seems to have been no justification for these authors to call their battery "achievement tests," except the unfortunate precedent established by the *Stanford Achievemen Tests.*

The battery comes in two forms. The short form, for "skill subjects," contains six tests: Reading: Level of Comprehension, a scaled test of 34 items; Reading: Speed and Accuracy, 50 items; Arithmetic Computation, 35 items; Arithmetic Reasoning (problem solving), 35 items; Diagnostic Test (why diagnostic?), 76 items; and Language Usage, 60 items. The longer form contains these six tests, plus tests on Health Knowledge, 56 items; Social Studies: History and Civics, 60 items; Social Studies: Geography, 60 items; and Elementary Science, 50 items. The items in all tests are of the conventional kind, being factual in character in the "content subjects," and more or less mechanical in the "skill subjects."

Age and grade norms, derived from an adequate population, are printed on the test blanks, each set of norms following immediately the corresponding test.

Herbert S. Conrad, Associate Professor of Psychology and Research Associate in the Institute of Child Welfare, The University of California. GENERAL COMMENTS. The writer is inclined to doubt that any single test battery can adequately cover so wide a span as grades 2-8. There is difficulty in including an adequately large sample of items appropriate for each grade; the test, either as a whole or in some of its subtests, tends to be too hard for the lower and too easy for the higher grades; the directions for some subtests are likely to prove rather difficult for a portion of the cases in the lower grades; the form of response (such as encircling the correct choice), while easy to understand and execute, entails additional time and expense in scoring; etc. The tendency in recent years has been definitely toward using more than one battery (e.g., primary, intermediate, and advanced) to cover the full span of the elementary grades.

THE MANUAL. Information on the construction and validation of this test battery has been condensed to a mere dozen lines in the first paragraph of the manual. Needless to say, so brief a treatment is inevitably inadequate. Not one shred of a posteriori evidence is offered concerning validity, except the vague and casual statement that preliminary forms were "tried out" in practical school situations. After all, there are various degrees of thoroughness of "trying out," ranging from a detailed analysis of each item against multiple criteria (including other items), to a mere inspection of the form of the distribution of total scores. The same casual and unsatisfactory brevity characterizes the description of the derivation of norms (nine lines, page 6 of the manual). Unfortunately, the present manual is by no means a glaring exception in its lack of explicit information. Have achievement tests really reached the stage of development where readers and users may be asked to accept them on faith?

NORMS. As usual among tests for the elementary grades, both grade and age norms are provided. Such norms necessarily fail to supply scores adequately quantitative either for the duller half of the children in the lower grades for which the test is standardized, or for the brighter half in the upper grades for

which the test is standardized. Examination of the norms for the individual subtests indicates definite lack of "bottom" in the tests on arithmetic computation and arithmetic reasoning; and definite lack of "top" at the end of grade 8 in arithmetic computation, arithmetic reasoning, spelling, and (most conspicuously) accuracy of reading. For several of the subtests, the rise in score for grades beyond the sixth appears too small to stimulate much confidence in validity; e.g., there is only a three-point rise in language usage from grade 6.0 to 7.0, the same small rise from grade 7.0 to 8.0 and again the same small rise from grade 8.0 to the end of this grade. An unexplained feature of the norms is the fact that, for example, the CA equivalent of a grade score of 8.0 in arithmetic computation is 13 years 7 months; while the CA equivalent of the same grade score in the history-civics test is 13 years, 11 months. These discrepancies, incidentally, are ignored in the uniform profile chart on which it is recommended that all scores of an individual be plotted.

RELIABILITY. According to the manual, "the reliability of the individual tests for a single grade ranges from .67 to .96, with the majority of the reliabilities over .85." With so wide a range as .67 to .96, it is clearly desirable to present the specific reliability for each test at each grade. Had this been done, we wonder if an occasional coefficient below .67 might not appear—say, for arithmetic reasoning at the end of grade 2 (where half the group make a raw score from 0 to 2, i.e., half the group is virtually undistributed); or for accuracy in reading in grade 8.5 (where 40 per cent make an absolutely perfect score in the test, and another 40 per cent make scores which are between 95 and 99 per cent perfect). In both the instances mentioned, moreover, the arrays of the correlation chart must (through the extreme skewness of the distributions and the concentration of either zero or perfect scores) be extremely heteroscedastic; in this event, no single figure for the reliability coefficient (whether .67 or otherwise) could be adequate. It is interesting to note, by way of comparison, that the three lowest reliability coefficients for subtests in the *New Stanford Achievement Test:* Advanced Examination in grade 4, have been reported in the manual for that test as .31, .34, and .51.

DIRECTIONS. Although each subtest of the

battery is scored simply for the number of items correctly answered, the directions do not include directions to guess when in doubt. This imposes a penalty on those who habitually omit rather than guess.

INDIVIDUAL SUBTESTS. (*a*) *Reading: Level of Comprehension.* A closer approximation to a "life situation" would require the use of at least a few longer paragraphs, and a test of delayed memory. The reading material does not include any tables, graphs, or charts, nor is any measure provided of ability to read an index or a dictionary. Some other standardized tests have, in about the same time as required by this and the following test, achieved a more analytic or diagnostic measure of reading abilities. (*b*) *Reading: Speed and Accuracy.* This test consists of 50 very short paragraphs (2-3 lines), each ending with a question. In several instances, the question can be answered without reading the preceding lines of the paragraphs (e.g., such a question as "How do you think water flows? downhill, uphill, backward, in a circle"). The absence of a separate vocabulary test, as part of the reading examination, is a noteworthy (and undefended) departure from custom. (*c*) *Arithmetic Computation* and *Arithmetic Reasoning.* These appear fairly satisfactory; but as in most computation tests, the printed figures are smaller than those usually written by children in the lower grades; this is an unnecessary and undesirable inconvenience to younger children. No graphs nor diagrams are included in the arithmetic items. The work in computation could have been made the basis for measurement of legibility of number-writing, but this opportunity has here (as in all other achievement tests known to the reviewer) been overlooked. (*d*) *Diagnostic Test in Spelling.* This test, yielding a single total spelling score, is not more "diagnostic" than any other of the subtests. (*e*) *Health Knowledge.* This subtest, like all but the arithmetic and spelling tests, makes use of multiple-choice items. Perhaps health knowledge is of such a nature that nothing but knowledge to the level of *recall* (rather than recognition) should be given credit. (*f*) *Language Usage.* Each item has three choices; occasionally, one of the choices appears rather strained; e.g., "(Bring, take, bear) this book from here to the library"— how many children ever say "bear"? Probably language usage is better tested not by the multiple-choice method (which presents the right as well as the wrong forms), but by a completion (or modified completion) technique. Several aspects of written language usage (punctuation, capitalization, and sentence structure) are untested in the present battery. (*g*) *History and Civics.* This test appears marred to the present reviewer by a few items suggestive of poor teaching practices (e.g., oversimplification and questionable platitudes) ; see the discussion of individual items below. (*h*) *Geography.* The complete absence of maps in a test on geography is rather disturbing. (*i*) *Elementary Science.* See comments under Individual Items, below.

INDIVIDUAL ITEMS. Although the manual claims that the test items were selected "after careful consideration" and "were then checked by master teachers," the items do not seem to the present reviewer either superior or inferior to the usual offering. Careless or inaccurate phrasing occasionally occurs; e.g., "The diameter (a line drawn through the center) of the sun is about . . . 100 times larger than the earth" (meaning 100 times *longer* than the *diameter* of the earth); or, "When a light strikes a mirror, it no longer travels in a straight line" (meaning that when light strikes a mirror obliquely, it no longer travels in the *same* straight line) ; etc. Occasionally, none of the choices offered is correct; thus, according to the key, "Oxygen is . . . needed by almost all plants and animals" (the authors mean that *free* oxygen is needed by almost all plants and animals). Occasionally the supposedly correct answer is questionable; thus, according to the key, "One reason why people should not smoke is that it . . . often harms the lining of the nose and throat" (this hardly seems likely in the case of ordinary indulgence). Occasionally, two choices for an item are both correct; thus, "One reason why the circulation of the blood is important is that it helps . . . to carry air to the heart, to keep the temperature the same all over the body, etc." Occasionally the test item offers multiple cues; e.g., "Two [*sic*] Puritans driven from Massachusetts Bay Colony for religious reasons were . . . Roger Williams and Anne Hutchinson." Some of the items seem excessively easy; e.g., "The United States is a land of many climates because . . . it is so small, it is so far north, it is so large, it is so far south." Occasionally one finds an item that seems misplaced; thus, the item "You are (too, two, to) slow" would appear better placed as part of Spelling than Language Usage. Misleading or undesirable content in items is not difficult to find. Thus, we are told in the body of a paragraph of the reading examination that "A mule . . . likes to kick people" (!). Animism raises its head in (of all places) the science examination; here we find that air, when heated, "needs" more space, and gravity "pulls" things down. Oversimplification and questionable platitude mar the history and civics test. Are not students forced to a grossly oversimplified view when they have to say that "All federal judges obtain their positions through . . . appointment by the President," or that "The object [purpose?] of the Crusades was . . . to regain the Holy Land from the Turks"? The distinction between fiat and fact is certainly not emphasized by such an item as "The Emancipation Proclamation . . . freed all the slaves in the United States"—not even the surrender of Lee quite accomplished that! A very superficial and debatable understanding is betrayed by the item, "Home industries are encouraged by . . . a protective tariff"—*which* home industries? Are not the original, native industries likely to suffer from increased drain of customers' resources to the protected industries? Other faults and faulty items could be catalogued, but space is lacking. Those above should suffice to warn the reader of the danger of unlimited faith either in the self-confessed "careful consideration" of test authors, or a "check" by accommodating "master teachers."

USE OF RESULTS. It is recommended that "profiles" be drawn of grade- or age-equivalents of each individual's raw scores on the various subtests. The drawing of profiles is a time-consuming procedure, and probably not justified except for highly reliable subtests. Exact consideration of inter-test differences is, of course, impossible, without a specific knowledge of the reliability of each of the various subtests at each of the various grades.

The authors recommend, presumably as a measure useful for purposes of guidance and sectioning, the averaging of IQ and EQ. This procedure doubtless has some merit. In any such simple averaging of two scores, however, the weight of each component varies as the standard deviation of its distribution. A *controlled* weighting of IQ and EQ would appear

preferable. Thus, for sectioning, more weight might be given to EQ than IQ; for vocational guidance, more weight to IQ than EQ; etc.

GENERAL SUMMARY. The present reviewer judges this test to be about as reliable and valid as several other batteries of about the same date; it probably is not, however, as reliable and valid as some longer and more recent batteries designed for a narrower grade-span. The critical comments in which we have indulged are designed to indicate possible points of improvement. The test is a good test, even if, in our judgment, it fails fully to reflect the undoubted distinction of its several authors.

Herschel T. Manuel, Professor of Educational Psychology, The University of Texas; and Director of Research, Texas Commission on Coordination in Education. This is a test battery of the type of which the *Stanford Achievement Test* (later the *New Stanford Achievement Test*) is probably the best known example. The test is organized by subjects, including reading (comprehension and speed), arithmetic (computation and reasoning), spelling, language usage, health knowledge, history and civics, geography, and elementary science. Literature, a subject often included in such batteries, is omitted.

The format of the test booklet is in general pleasing, and in six of the tests the blanks for pupil responses are aligned conveniently for the use of a strip key in hand scoring. Three of the tests are of the "recall" type. No test items have fewer than three alternatives. The short form provides a less extensive booklet for those who are interested in the skill subjects alone.

The manual of directions includes few details on the process of constructing the test. Reliability is expressed in the manual for the Complete Battery in two sentences: "The reliability of the individual tests for a single grade ranges from .67 to .96, with a majority of the reliabilities over .85. The reliability of the entire battery for a single grade ranges from .94 to .97." Validity is based upon a "careful selection of materials." The selection was made "after careful consideration of superior courses of study as rated by the Bureau of Curriculum Research, Teachers College, Columbia University," and the selections were "checked by master teachers of the different subjects." Grade and age norms are based upon median scores of 6,710 children in 37 different cities.

On the whole, the battery of tests is probably a good one of its type. The authors (including among others, Gates, Mort, Symonds, and Spence) would themselves constitute a considerable board of "experts" to guarantee its quality if an estimate were to be based upon opinion.

In the use of this test, as in the use of similar tests, one should keep in mind its limitations with respect to the objectives which it samples. It is obviously limited to certain of the language and numerical skills and to information in some of the content subjects. Tests of all of these are important when they are properly interpreted and properly used.

It is not difficult to find points for adverse comment. In the first place, the reading paragraphs are not all constructed in a way that makes necessary the reading of the entire paragraph. This, however, is a rather common fault of reading tests of the completion form. Again, although parts of the test may be used as low as the third grade, the entire manuscript is a rather expensive investment for the little which will be useful for pupils having abilities below the average expected in the latter part of the third grade. One wishes, too, that the test might now be adapted to machine scoring.

Page 2 represents both strength and weakness. It provides space for the recording of supplementary information and for recommendations on adjustments in a pupil's program. The emphasis upon using the test is commendable as is also the suggestion that other information is needed. It is doubtful, however, whether the supplementary information and the recommendations sought should be recorded on the test booklet. There is a danger that the test results will not be seen in perspective and that the recommendations may be too mechanical. The recommendations suggested in the booklet are limited to changes in grade status, changes in grade section, remedial work, omission of activities, and enrichment.

Three comments may be made relative to the norms. First, in spite of the evident care in constructing the norms, this test, like others of its kind, gives no scores that are strictly comparable outside of the series itself. The fact that age and grade norms are based upon

scores of 6,710 children in 37 cities does not mean, of course, that a grade score of 6.0 on this test is the same as a grade score of 6.0 on some other test. The non-comparability of test scores may be illustrated again by listing educational age equivalents of grade 6.0 in this and three other similar batteries: 11-10, 11-6, 11-7, and 11-10, respectively. Second, the emphasis upon grade norms as the basic unit into which raw scores are translated is itself unfortunate in view of the trend away from the concept of grade levels in elementary education. Finally, the use of L, H, and V for scores below and above certain grade scores lessens the discrimination between pupils scoring in these ranges.

[1191]
Municipal Battery: National Achievement Tests. Grades 3-6, 6-8; 1938-39; 2 forms, 2 levels, 2 editions; 25¢ per specimen set; Robert K. Speer and Samuel Smith; Rockville Centre, N. Y.: Acorn Publishing Co.
a) GRADES 3-6. *Complete battery:* $2.85 per 25; 203(225) minutes; *Partial battery:* $2.25 per 25; 138(155) minutes.
b) GRADES 6-8. *Complete battery:* $2.85 per 25; 202(225) minutes; *Partial battery:* $2.25 per 25; 137(155) minutes.

A. M. Jordan, Professor of Educational Psychology, The University of North Carolina. [Review of the complete battery for grades 6-8.] The National Achievement Tests are probably the most complete measures of the outcomes of elementary instruction which have appeared. The construction procedures used in these tests are to be commended. The test items were verified by more than one hundred and fifty experienced superintendents, supervisors, and principals. They were selected in the first place from widely used courses of study, textbooks, etc. The emphasis all through the test is upon the pupil's ability to use the knowledge he has acquired. An attempt is made to sample more of the outcomes recommended by modern trends in curricular construction. The test has been standardized on more than thirty-five thousand pupils and has satisfactory reliability both for the individual tests and for the battery as a whole.

There are several desirable features of the test. (*a*) The scores can be entered directly upon the profile or upon the first sheet of the booklet. No translation of scores is necessary. This advantage has most probably been obtained by a reduction in accuracy. This whole procedure makes for simplicity. (*b*) A code system is used in scoring some of the tests. In five parts of the test the code word is "begin." If any letter occurring in "begin" is underlined the answer is correct. In three of the tests the code word is "forget." The scorer can thus keep in mind without effort the correct answers. (c) Some of the tests are divided into subtests. The reading comprehension test, for example, is divided into following directions, sentence meaning, and paragraph meaning; the arithmetic reasoning test is divided into comparisons, problem analysis, and problems to be solved.

There are some undesirable features, too. So intent are the authors on testing meaning that many of their questions are more suitable for intelligence tests than for achievement tests. For example, the first test depends on arranging names alphabetically for a correct solution; the second, on keeping directions straight. The second test on sentence meaning sounds much like matching proverbs. The paragraphs to be read are short difficult ones about such generalized topics as the laws of nature and commerce which demand accurate deductions. It is no wonder that after using the test for a while the authors felt constrained to give different standards for low, medium, and high IQ's. Curious, too, is it that when speed of reading was tested the material used consisted of very short sentences and very simple constructions. Then, too, arithmetic problems are mixed in with the computation. For example, "800 is ⅔ of ———" occurs among examples of computation. Moreover, some of the number comparisons are too tricky. Two of the tests, "sentence meaning" and "expressing ideas," are quite alike in nature and could have been combined. Finally, many of the questions asked about literature are quite superficial.

As a whole this test is the most thoroughgoing yet to appear. It lends itself to analysis and diagnosis, but to give 30 pages of test material to children in grades 6-8 borders almost on the ridiculous.

Hugh B. Wood, Professor of Education, University of Oregon. [Review of the batteries for grades 6-8.] The Complete Battery includes tests in reading comprehension, reading speed, spelling, arithmetic fundamentals, arithmetic reasoning, English, literature, geography, history and civics, and health. The Partial

Battery omits the last four tests. A four-page manual accompanies each battery.

The authors claim that the tests, which bear a 1938 copyright, are based on "years" of research. Items were checked against "numerous city and state courses of study, widely used textbooks and the judgment of more than one hundred fifty experienced administrators" and criticized by "many classroom teachers." This limited information from the publisher's advertising literature, combined with a study of the tests, leave one in a quandary about the recency of the curricula to which they were adapted. In many respects they may be compared with the *Metropolitan Achievement Tests,* but the authors emphasize that they have been designed to measure "not only the mastery of subject matter but especially the pupil's ability to use knowledge" and "power to apply knowledge." The reviewer's estimate of the tests' validity is "about average."

Reliability varies from .81 to .95, based on the alternate-question method. Norms are based on 35,000 cases.

A unique simplified scoring method on certain tests, which makes the letters of the answers all fall within a code word, makes the format unusual by using such letters as *w, o, b, e,* for answers rather than *a, b, c, d.* The size of the tests is 9 by 12 inches. The format is good. Directions for administering, while adequate, could be improved if parts to be read to pupils were in larger and boldface type. A graphical method of summarizing the results is used.

The reviewer's evaluation (based on analysis only, and limited by lack of familiarity with the tests or any users of them) would place the *Municipal Battery* as equal to *Metropolitan Achievement Tests* but inferior to *Progressive Achievement Tests.*

[1192]

Myers-Ruch High School Progress Test. Grades 9-13; 1936-38; 2 forms; $1.30 per 25; 20¢ per specimen set; 2¢ per machine-scorable answer sheet; 60(65) minutes; Charles Everett Myers, Giles M. Ruch, and Graham C. Loofbourow; Yonkers, N. Y.: World Book Co.

Harl R. Douglass, Director of the College of Education, University of Colorado. This test battery is composed of four subtests of 30 items each and requiring for administration 15 minutes each. The four tests cover the following four fields: English, social studies, mathematics, and science. The test battery is intended for a variety of uses, principally (*a*) to evaluate the work of a pupil or of a school by measurement of the senior class, (*b*) to measure progress of a pupil or class or other group of pupils year by year or semester by semester, (*c*) to furnish a basis for guidance of individual pupils in the early semesters of their high school careers. The authors also suggest its use for the purpose of electing college entrants.

Each item in the test is a five-choice recognition exercise and each test is scored by the appropriate formula Score = $R - 1/4W$. In the English test, Form A, 14 of the 30 items are relative to historical, biographical, or other factual information concerning literature commonly taught in high school; 7, to meanings of words; 5, to matters of grammar; and 4, to spelling. Naturally such outcomes as oral expression, written composition, appreciations, effects upon emotions, ideals, etc. are not measured, except incidently and very crudely.

In the social studies test, Form A, 13 of the 30 items are on American history, 6 on world history, 5 on government, 3 on social problems, and 3 on economics. They are all of the factual information type and measure only indirectly other types of outcomes of teaching the social studies. Taken as a whole the test seems to furnish a fair measure of the informational aspects of high school social studies.

Eighteen of the 30 items of the mathematics test, Form A, relate to algebra, 11 to geometry, and 1 to trigonometry usually taught as algebra. Six of them consist in equation forming from verbal problems. The items in geometry are chiefly definitions and no means of measurement of ability to prove theorems are provided.

Of the 30 items in science, 9 relate to physics, 7 to chemistry and the others to biological science. About half of them cover material commonly taught in general science.

In all four tests the items are rather well chosen, so as to be representative of material taught at the high school level.

The reliabilities of the tests are certain to be reasonably high for measurement of individuals when given to senior classes perhaps also to juniors, but probably only fairly high for first-year students. For comparisons of classes or schools the test is sufficiently reliable for reasonably accurate comparisons even for first-

or second-year student groups. Probably no one of the four subtests which comprise the battery is sufficiently reliable even if valid to be used for accurate measurement of individuals, though for comparison of classes, certainly for comparison of large groups, each of the subtests is sufficiently reliable for rough comparisons in the lower years and for more accurate ones in the upper years of the high school.

The test is of inconvenient length for use in all but a few high schools. Requiring at least 70 minutes to administer it needs more than a single class period.

Each subtest is theoretically equivalent in difficulty to each of the other three and scores on the subtests can be compared directly. The standardization being based on 200 pupils to a form and all 800 pupils being located in one state, Virginia, the comparability may be only approximate in some schools.

An excellent feature of the test is that it has four forms [only two of which have been released] of approximately equal difficulty as judged by the reactions of four sets of 200 Virginian high school pupils.

The directions for giving and scoring and for interpreting scores are very clear and of a superior quality in general.

Percentile norms are available as based on the performances of 9,000 pupils in six states in various sections of the country.

The manual of directions outlines a reasonably useful procedure in judging whether a pupil is working up to his capacity. In comparing scores on the *Myers-Ruch High School Progress Test* and the *Otis Quick-Scoring Mental Ability Tests,* one runs into serious difficulties resulting from the fact that the tables furnished by the authors are based upon 3,000 seniors all in one state, North Carolina, and for the very large part in 11-year schools. Only large differences between relative achievement and intelligence should be regarded as significant. A statistical device for interpreting differences is given by the authors in the manual.

In interpreting the scores of the Myers-Ruch, the Sones-Harry or any other general high school achievement test of individual pupils, or of classes of pupils or of schools, one should not lose sight of two important facts: (*a*) the tests do not measure all aspects of academic achievement in high school, much less all types of growth during attendance at high school, and (*b*) some pupils or even classes or schools may have had much more formal opportunity to learn science (or any of the fields measured) than others. For example, some of the pupils taking the science test may be taking their fourth year of science, and others their first, or again some pupils may have taken 14 or 15, or even all of their 16 units of work in these four fields while others choosing vocational curricula may have taken as little as 8 year-units.

All in all, the Myers-Ruch tests are probably about as good as any available test or test battery for measuring general high school achievement, but that does not mean that much better means of measuring growth in high school should not be expected within the next few years.

August Dvorak, Professor of Education, University of Washington. This achievement test is intended primarily to yield a general measure of mastery of the basic content of the high school course of study. Four subjects are tested; namely, English, social studies, mathematics, and science. There are 30 items in each section of the test, making a total of 120 items in all. The score for any single subject-matter section is not intended to be considered a reliable measure of mastery of that subject for any individual.

An answer sheet, which is printed on the inside of the title page of the test, is used. This answer sheet is so arranged that it can be easily and accurately articulated with each successive page of the test booklet. The use of the separate answer sheet makes it possible to score the test by means of a perforated stencil scoring key. This stencil contains holes so spaced that when the key is placed on the answer sheet only those answer spaces which are correctly marked will show through the perforations. When pupils' responses are recorded on the answer sheet in the booklet the test booklets are expended with each administration.

This test can also be scored on the *International Test Scoring Machine,* but the separate machine-scorable answer sheets must be purchased additionally. These separate machine-scorable answer sheets are similar in type and arrangement to the answer sheet contained in the test booklet, but they are printed on special paper and under the special conditions which the International Business Machines Corporation considers necessary to insure the proper operation of the test scoring machine. If the separate answer sheet designed for machine scoring is used, the test books may be used repeatedly.

The score on the Myers-Ruch test is the number right minus one-fourth of the wrong number. An exact equivalent of this is five-fourths of the number right plus one-fourth of the number omitted minus one-fourth of the total number of items. A perforated stencil scoring key is provided for counting the number right, which makes it unnecessary to mark the papers. For this reason the second formula is preferable for this test, because it does not involve knowing the number of wrong items. While the score can be obtained arithmetically, to facilitate further its computation a double nomograph has been provided.

Two of the authors, Ruch and Loofbourow, are primarily responsible for the construction of the items in this test. Their original items were edited by Myers and submitted by him to *four* experienced secondary school supervisors who were asked to rule on their suitability for this test. From the items found to be satisfactory by these judges, four preliminary forms, each containing 143 questions, were assembled and mimeographed. These preliminary forms were administered to 800 pupils in Virginia, each random fourth of the group taking a different form. On the basis of data obtained in this way a difficulty rating was computed for each item and those items found to be unsatisfactory were discarded. The remaining questions were reassembled into four forms, each form containing 120 questions which were balanced both as to content and as to difficulty.

The probable errors of the scores computed separately for each grade level from the stepped-up values of the split-half reliability coefficients are approximately 4 score points. Consequently, from the author's table of percentile norms it is apparent that if a ninth grade pupil achieves a score of 29 (median for his grade) the chances are 50-50 that his true ability as measured by this test is below the 39th or above the 60th percentile of his grade, and the chances are about 1 in 100 that his true ability is below the 9th or above the 83rd percentile of his group. The differences between grade medians are 5 or 6 points since the norms for grades 9, 10, 11, and 12 are 29, 34, 40, and 46, respectively. The chances are about 1 to 2 that the true measure of a pupil achieving the median score for his grade is actually at the median of the grade above or below.

It is apparent that this test using a sampling of only 30 questions for each of such broad fields as English, social studies, mathematics, and science would be a better measure for comparing groups than individual pupils.

John M. Stalnaker, Consultant Examiner, College Entrance Examination Board and Associate Professor of Psychology, Princeton University. This test is "an achievement test intended primarily to yield a general measure of mastery of the basic content of the high school course of study." Four subjects, English, social studies, mathematics, and science are said to be tested. Each of the four sections contains 30 items of the best-answer form (select the one best of five given responses). The items are mainly of the simple factual type. Each section, of course, must attempt to cover an extensive range of content. The English section, for example, attempts in 30 items to sample from the heterogeneous universe which includes orthography, grammar, vocabulary, and factual knowledge of literature. The sample, of course, cannot be adequate. This test is not in any real sense a measure of the mastery of the *basic* content of the high school course of study—either for individuals or for groups.

Although the authors state in the manual, quite correctly, that "the score for any single subject-matter section is not intended to be considered a reliable measure of mastery of that subject for any individual," they also state, with some inconsistency, that the results may be useful for "administrative and guidance purposes in planning the senior high school program for *individual pupils* [reviewer's italics]." There can be little justification for the use of the results for such purposes.

The one feature of the test worthy of note is the generous time allowance—perhaps more generous than the content deserves—15 minutes for each 30 items, and the pupil has the privilege of going ahead or going back at any time.

The percentile tables supplied are based on 9,000 cases.

Ernest W. Tiegs, Dean of University College and Professor of Education, The University of Southern California. This test, covering the basic content of high school work, has been developed to determine the success with which the major objectives of the high school curriculum are being attained. The authors suggest three specific uses: for survey purposes; for administrative and guidance purposes in planning the senior high school program for individual pupils; and as a college entrance test.

Data reported indicate that all test forms possess sufficient reliability for survey purposes in each of the four grades for which the test is intended. In addition, the separate subject-matter sections are sufficiently reliable to establish group trends in achievement.

Users of the test will find the table for interpreting the significance of differences of special value; too many times raw scores are taken at their face value and chance differences are interpreted to the disadvantage of certain teachers or schools.

Among the special features of the test are a separate answer sheet which can be used easily with each successive page of the test, a separate perforated stencil scoring sheet to use with this answer sheet, and a nomograph which makes it possible to obtain a corrected score from the numbers of items right and omitted. The test is so constructed that scoring machine answer sheets can be used also and the scores obtained on the *International Test Scoring Machine.*

The test provides percentile norms for each grade from nine to twelve. This makes it possible to discover how a class or school ranks in comparison with other classes or schools on the basis of the test scores.

Finally, the results of the test may be used to estimate the quality of achievement in terms of apparent capacity to achieve. Scores of the *Myers-Ruch High School Progress Test* and the *Otis Quick-Scoring Mental Ability Tests: Gamma Test* may be compared directly in terms of standard scores.

In the opinion of the writer, the usefulness of this test will more than justify the modest claims of its authors.

[1193]

Progressive Achievement Tests. Grades 1-3, 4-6, 7-9, 9-13; 1933-38; 4 levels; the tests in reading, arithmetic, mathematics, and language are available as separates; 25¢ per specimen set of any one level; Ernest W. Tiegs and Willis W. Clark; Los Angeles, Calif.: California Test Bureau.
a) PRIMARY BATTERY. Grades 1-3; 1933-38; 3 forms; $1 per 25; 100(115) minutes.
b) ELEMENTARY BATTERY. Grades 4-6; 1933-37; 3 forms; $1.25 per 25 120(135) minutes.
c) INTERMEDIATE BATTERY. Grades 7-9; 1933-37; 3 forms; $1.25 per 25; 150(165) minutes.
d) ADVANCED BATTERY. Grades 9-13; 1934; 2 forms; $1.50 per 25; 150(165) minutes.

REFERENCES

1 PATERSON, DONALD G.; SCHNEIDLER, GWENDOLEN G.; AND WILLIAMSON, EDMUND G. *Student Guidance Technique,* pp. 111-3. New York: McGraw-Hill Book Co., Inc., 1938. Pp. xviii, 316. $3.00. (London: McGraw-Hill Publishing Co., Ltd. 18s.)

C. W. Odell, Associate Professor of Education, The University of Illinois. Although these tests are entitled to rank among the best of their type now on the market, they scarcely fulfill all the claims made for them. They do, as stated, cover many of the important elements in a modern curriculum, but inasmuch as the number of elements devoted to each phase of content is often quite small, even reaching only one, they can hardly deserve the term "diagnostic" so fully as the publisher's statements appear to imply. Perhaps "analytic" would more appropriately designate them. Moreover the directions for administering them are such that power, to the virtual exclusion of speed, is measured. It may be defended as more significant, but scarcely as all important.

The information as to selection of content and general validity is so brief and noninformative as to be practically valueless. Coefficients of reliability are given, but neither more meaningful measures such as errors of measurement and their ratios to means and standard deviations nor the data from which they may be calculated are supplied. The norms were rather indirectly determined, but except for those at the secondary school level are probably as satisfactory as those for most standard tests. Those for the advanced test are based on only fifteen hundred cases from seven high schools.

Although this series is better than several others which the reviewer has examined recently in the quality of English employed, it is not free from some slips therein. Such expressions as "Revision of Norms have," "above

story," and the incorrect placement of interrogatives (this quite frequently) are to be found.

In a large portion of the test for primary grades the designated placement of answers is such as to be unnecessarily difficult to score. Presumably this has been allowed in the interest of rendering pupil responses easier and less confusing, but it has been amply demonstrated that the additional difficulty introduced by placement in more convenient scoring form is so slight as to bother very few children. The same test likewise has much waste space. The chart for the pupil profile on the first page has the lines poorly placed, so that they do not correspond with the names of the sections to which they apply. The correct answers are upon such light stock that it will hardly survive, at least in easily usable form, very much use. In some multiple-answer sections of the tests there is, within a single section, variation in the number of suggested answers, a feature which does not represent the best practice. Elsewhere pupils are directed to underline correct answers as well as copy their numbers or letters in the proper blanks, a practice not necessary above the lower grades and probably not even there. In the vocabulary section, where words are grouped according to their subject-matter fields, it is difficult to see why certain words are classed as they are rather than otherwise. For example, "cause" and "convict" are listed under literature, whereas they appear to belong at least as much under social science.

Despite the various points criticized, the reviewer believes that these tests have real value and rank high in the assistance which they offer teachers in diagnosing the achievements of their pupils, both in the amount thereof and in the ease with which they make it available.

Hugh B. Wood, Professor of Education, University of Oregon. The *Progressive Achievement Tests* are designed to measure comprehension and ability in the basic skills, and comprise five tests: reading vocabulary, reading comprehension, mathematical reasoning, mathematic fundamentals, and language, each with appropriate subtests. In addition to general survey results, the tests provide diagnostic scores for individual pupils, classes, and subjects.

Major advantage of tests over most achievement batteries is high validity and fidelity to objectives of progressive education. The manual is vague on validity beyond reference to "progressive courses of study" but examination and comparison of items with observed progressive practice support commendation on validity. Experimental forms and norms were developed for the most part in progressive schools.

A second advantage of tests is their diagnostic value. Profile chart and diagnostic analysis sheet attached to each test permit general diagnosis for all pupils and specific diagnosis for those needing it. Many teachers will object to the amount of time required for complete diagnosis (including scoring, about 30 minutes), but this is no longer than usually required. The diagnostic value of tests is limited, however, by inadequate sampling in many of the subtests (as few as 5 items in some), but this represents a shortage rather difficult to overcome in a battery test. Subtests include: reading vocabulary in mathematics, science, social science, and literature; reading comprehension in following directions, organization, and interpretations; mathematical reasoning in number concepts, symbols and rules, numbers and equations, and problems; mathematic fundamentals in addition, subtraction, multiplication, and division; and language capitalization, punctuation, complete sentences, grammar, spelling, and handwriting.

Reliability, based on odds-even and two-form techniques, runs from .84 to .98. Revised norms, comparable from grade to grade and subject to subject, are based on one hundred thousand cases.

Major weaknesses of tests lie in the limited sampling and in the exceptional difficulty of the primary battery which many teachers report leads to discouragement on part of pupils. First and second grades should probably have separate booklets. Other weaknesses include: lack of objectivity of scoring handwriting leading to questionable validity and influencing language score too much; scoring directions not entirely clear on some parts and all possible answers not always given; punctuation test difficult to score; text of tests continue into answer columns, making scoring more difficult; paper on which key is printed not sufficiently durable.

The manual of directions and class record sheet provide adequately for administration and interpretation.

Because they avoid the difficulties encountered in battery testing in the content areas, the *Progressive Achievement Tests* are (in the opinion of the reviewer) the best battery tests (of skills) available today.

For a review by D. Welty Lefever, see 876. For reviews by Harry A. Greene and J. Paul Leonard of the language test, see 1292. For reviews by William A. Brownell, C. L. Thiele, and Harry Grove Wheat of the arithmetic test, see 1459. For reviews by Frederic B. Davis, Ivan A. Booker, and Joseph C. Dewey of the reading test, see 1110 and 1563.

[1194]
Public School Achievement Tests. Grades 3-8, 4-8, 6-8; 1928-31; 4 forms, 3 parts; all subtests are available as separates; Jacob S. Orleans, T. L. Torgerson, and Glenn A. Sealy; Bloomington, Ill.: Public School Publishing Co.
a) BATTERY A. Grades 3-8; $5 per 100; 185 (215) minutes for Forms 1 and 2; 170 (200) minutes for Forms 3 and 4.
b) BATTERY B. Grades 6-8; $3 per 100; 105 (120) minutes.
c) BATTERY C. Grades 4-8; $1.75 per 100; (50) 60 minutes.

REFERENCES

1 WILSON, GUY M., AND PARSONS, A. REBECCA. "Critical Examination of a Standardized Spelling Test." *Ed Adm and Sup* 15:494-8 O '29.
2 PULLIAS, EARL V. "Commercial Standardized Tests," pp. 65-80. In *Variability in Results from New-Type Achievement Tests.* Duke University Studies in Education, No. 2. Durham, N. C.: Duke University Press, 1937. Pp. 100. $1.00. Paper. (London: Cambridge University Press. 4s. 6d.)

Herbert S. Conrad, Associate Professor of Psychology, and Research Associate in the Institute of Child Welfare, The University of California. FORMAT. The tests are issued in booklets 6 by 9 inches. This size probably has the advantage of rendering copying somewhat more difficult. On the other hand, the lack of more generous dimensions is likely to lead (as in the present tests) to a print-size somewhat smaller than desirable for the elementary grades, to margins occasionally less ample than convenient for scoring, to space-allowances occasionally less than comfortable for recording an answer or working a problem, etc. Small booklets may also prove less convenient than those of letter-size (8½ by 11 inches) for storage in typical filing equipment.

MANUAL. The practice of issuing unsigned, anonymous test manuals should be stopped. The test manual is part of the test; as such, the author of the test-manual should be known, and held to responsibility for his product. The teacher's handbooks for the present tests (one handbook for Forms 1 and 2, and another for Forms 3 and 4) are rather typical in their failure to present adequate information concerning the construction, preliminary tryout, and results of application of the tests. As opposed to real evidence, we have merely the publisher's statements that "a detailed analysis" was carried out, that "all of these criteria [of reliability and validity] are met," etc. It would be better to present the facts (either in the manual or a separate monograph), and let the facts speak for themselves.

DIRECTIONS FOR ADMINISTRATION. The directions for this battery of tests call for the collection of test booklets and a recess (or change of task) after each subtest. Since five of the ten subtests in Forms 1 and 2 require only 20 minutes, and eight of the ten subtests in Forms 3 and 4 require only from 15 to 30 minutes, this precaution against fatigue or loss of interest seems overelaborate, especially for the upper grades.

Slow pupils in a bright class are likely to be handicapped by a certain elasticity of time limits in the tests for Forms 1 and 2: "If the teacher notices that all but the slowest two or three pupils have finished the test or have worked up to the limit of their abilities, she may stop the test before the expiration of the time limit specified." This direction does not appear in the handbook for Forms 3 and 4.

Although the multiple-choice items in the battery are scored number right (i.e., without penalty for guessing), the directions fail to advise pupils to guess when in doubt; this imposes a penalty on those who (for whatever reason) tend to omit rather than guess.

In the arithmetic reasoning test the directions fail to instruct the pupil to work from left to right (rather than down the columns): this omission may lead to spuriously low scores for pupils in the lower grades. In Part IV of the test on nature study (Forms 1 and 2), the directions are undoubtedly difficult for children in the lower grades; this part could be improved by omission of item-numbers in Column I, and by the occasional use of italics in the directions preceding the part.

Except for the particulars cited above, the directions for subtests in the present battery appear clear and simple and adequate.

SCORING. Forms 1 and 2 of the present battery, since they contain some completion items, cannot be scored perfectly objectively; Forms 3 and 4 are entirely objective. The directions for scoring given in the teacher's handbooks are commendably full and explicit. In the test booklets, however, one misses little refinements for the facilitation of scoring and the prevention of error. Thus, most subtests have no designated place to record total scores.

In some subtests scored right minus wrong, the number wrong is written to the side of (instead of underneath) the number right: this undoubtedly leads to an increase in subtraction errors. Preferable to the formula $R-W$, moreover, is the formula $T-O-2W$ (total items minus omissions minus twice the number wrong): this formula yields exactly the same answer as $R-W$, and in practice improves both speed and accuracy of scoring.

TEST DIFFICULTY. Battery A of the present set of tests is recommended for grades 3-8, Battery B, for grades 6-8, and Battery C, for grades 4-8: the midpoint of the recommended grade-span is, then, for Battery A, grade 6.0, for Battery B, grade 7.5, and for Battery C, grade 6.5. At these "mid-recommended grades," the norms should equal 50 per cent of the maximum possible score (since a test is most efficient when it is composed of "50 per cent items," i.e., items passed by 50 per cent of the group, or about 50 per cent). Examination of the norms for Forms 1 and 2 shows that the norms for the various subtests at the "mid-recommended grades" range from 32 per cent to 62 per cent of the maximum possible scores; for Forms 3 and 4, the range is from 39 per cent to 69 per cent of the maximum. Such a range in percentage-difficulty throws grave question on the competence or care of preliminary standardization of the test. For grades above or below the "mid-recommended," the departure from 50 per cent is, in general, considerably greater. It is of course inevitable, in any achievement tests designed for a wide range of grades, that the tests will be too hard for the lower grades and too easy for the upper.

A few of the subtests appear insufficiently difficult to measure adequately at the end of the eighth grade (i.e., appear lacking in "top"). This is especially true in the spelling test (Form 4), where the norm (103) is 90 per cent of the maximum possible score (114).

RELIABILITY. Practically no statistical data

are provided. The handbook for Forms 3 and 4 gives the reliability coefficients "for Form 3": but only for Battery A, and only for grade 7. The restriction to grade 7 is of special interest, since the reliabilities are almost certainly lower for (say) grade 3 than grade 7. It would appear that the reliability "for Form 3" was obtained by the Spearman-Brown technique; a more usual and probably preferable procedure for achievement tests is the correlation between different forms of the test, administered at different times (in the present case, the correlation between tests in Form 3 and Form 4). Although it is disappointing to notice the absence of proper or complete statistical data, it is necessary to add that, so far as may be judged without actual computation, the present tests appear to be about as reliable as typical tests of their kind.

SUBTEST WEIGHTS. The raw scores of the subtests are combined, without explicit weighting, into a total score. The effective weight of a given test in such a combination depends (*a*) upon its variability (quartile deviation, or standard deviation), and (*b*) upon its correlation with the other tests of the combination. No data are given in the teacher's handbooks or elsewhere on the second of these factors; but following are, roughly, the quartile deviations for the ten tests of the present battery in grade 7 (Form 3): Reading, 11; Arithmetic Computation, 13; Arithmetic Reasoning, 9; Language Usage, 18; Spelling, 19; Grammar, 14; History, 11; Geography, 9; Nature Study, 19; Health, 12. Evidently, the combined weight of Language Usage, Spelling, and Grammar far exceeds that for Reading: Is this desirable? Similarly, the combined weight of Arithmetic Computation and Arithmetic Reasoning also greatly exceeds that of Reading. Other probable disproportions of weighting can be discerned from the figures given above. The figures above pertain strictly to Form 3, but entirely similar conclusions are derived from data for the other forms of the battery.

NORMS. Grade norms are provided for all forms of the test; in addition, quartile norms are provided for Forms 1 and 2, and decile norms (from 10th to 90th percentile) for Forms 3 and 4. It is interesting (though not unusual) that the grade norms for the subtests extend both below and above the grades for which the tests are recommended; thus, the ᵕing test is recommended for grades 3-8,

but grade-equivalents are included as low as grade 2.0 and as high as grade 9.7. Such norms, beyond the range of recommended application of the test, must be obtained either by extrapolation, or by application of the test below or above the recommended grade-limits—a rather undesirable situation, in either event.

The quartile and percentile norms constitute a desirable supplement to the grade norms. It is clear, however, that quartile norms are too coarse to serve adequately; and that decile norms which stop at the 10th and 90th percentiles leave both the lower and upper ten-per-cent groups entirely undifferentiated. The normal range of ability is customarily considered to extend from -3σ to $+3\sigma$, or from -4 *PE* to $+4$ *PE;* the 10-90 percentile range in a normal curve, however, corresponds to the limits -1.3σ to $+1.3\sigma$, or -1.9 *PE* to $+1.9$ *PE*—a distance of *less than half* the customary ability-range, as ordinarily defined. The inadequacy of the decile norms at the "extremes" (i.e., at the upper and lower *half* of the normal ability-range) appears especially regrettable, since it is precisely among cases in these "extremes" that the need for measurement is most urgent. The standardization sample for the present battery was fully large enough to permit reasonably accurate determination of the needed norms.

ALTERNATE FORMS. Forms 1 and 2 are of parallel structure with regard to number of items, types of item, etc.; and Form 3 is similar to Form 4; but Forms 1 and 2 are not entirely similar to Forms 3 and 4. The chief differences lie in the inclusion of completion items in Forms 1 and 2, and some changes in the number of items and timing of certain subtests of Forms 3 and 4. Quite surprisingly, some of the items in Form 3 appear (with little or no change) also in Form 1 or 2; and some of the items in Form 4 appear also in Form 1, 2, or 3. This duplication of items occurs, specifically, in the subtests for history, nature study, and health: 8, 11, and 14 of the items in these subtests, respectively, were recognized by the reviewer as duplicates in Form 3; and 6, 2, and 13, respectively, in Form 4. This duplication, while not crucial, is certainly not desirable: imagine the situation if a so-called "alternate form" consisted *entirely* of duplicates!

It is rather easy, on the basis of a preliminary tryout, to prepare two equally difficult forms of a given subtest; failure to achieve such equality in a standardized test is perhaps legitimately taken as evidence of carelessness or incompetence in test construction. Examining the norms for the subtests of Forms 1 and 2 at the "mid-recommended" (or presumably optimal) grade for each subtest, we find that the ratio of the *norm* to the *maximum possible* score in language usage is 62 per cent in Form 1, but 52 per cent in Form 2; the raw scores are 37 and 31, respectively (the 6-point difference in raw scores equals the median difference between grades 5 and 6, or between grades 6 and 7.5). Similarly, the ratio of norm to maximum in the test on health is 65 per cent for Form 3, but 53 per cent for Form 4; the raw scores are 54 and 44, respectively (the 10-point difference in raw scores equals the median difference between grades 5 and 7, or between grades 6 and 8).

If we extend the foregoing type of comparison to Forms 1 and 2 vs. Forms 3 and 4, the discrepancies are more numerous. Thus, between the average norm-to-maximum ratio for Forms 1 and 2 and the average norm-to-maximum ratio for Forms 3 and 4, there is a 12 per cent discrepancy in reading, a 13 per cent discrepancy in spelling, a 9 per cent discrepancy in grammar, and a 15 per cent discrepancy in nature study. Taken as a whole, Forms 3 and 4 are somewhat easier than Forms 1 and 2. With regard to difficulty, at least, Forms 3 and 4 cannot be said to be adequately comparable with Forms 1 and 2. A brief examination indicates that the same verdict of unsatisfactory comparability also applies with respect to the variability (quartile deviations) of the subtests in Forms 3 and 4 vs. Forms 1 and 2.

TYPES OF ITEMS. Except for the tests in spelling and arithmetic, all the items in Forms 3 and 4 of the present battery measure recognition rather than recall. Since much of the knowledge of the elementary grades should be learned to the level of permanent recall, the exclusive dependence on recognition items appears, if not unusual in an achievement test, at least unfortunate. This applies especially to tests for such subjects as language usage and health: language usage should be tested by recall techniques for the same reason that spelling and computation are so tested; health knowledge should be tested by recall techniques, because the information is of such great importance both to society and the individual.

Matching exercises are used in all four forms of the present battery. Few matching exercises, in the reviewer's judgment, offer as satisfactory alternatives (or "confusions") as reasonably good multiple-choice items.

COMMENTS ON SPECIFIC TESTS. Criticism of the individual subtests should perhaps be reserved to curriculum experts in the various fields; our comments here may well be quite brief. The test in reading fails to realize the possibilities of analysis or diagnosis achieved by other reading tests of no greater length; for example, the present examination does not provide separate vocabulary nor speed-of-reading scores. The test in arithmetic computation is probably somewhat out of date; thus, problems in addition of fractions are written in equation form, and decimals without a common denominator are presented for addition. No problems involving graphs are included. In some problems, it would be well if the printed figures were larger and more widely spaced, and if a more generous space-allotment were provided for the steps in the solution. The test in arithmetic reasoning impresses the present reviewer as interesting and practical. The language usage test appears satisfactory as to content, except that the distinctions between such words as "its" vs. "it's," and "there" vs. "their" seem to belong under spelling rather than usage. The scoring of the language usage test would be greatly facilitated if the choices were numbered, and the pupil directed to write the numbers of his choices in a single column (which could then be scored with the aid of a strip stencil). No tests to measure such features of written language usage as punctuation or capitalization are included in the present battery. The test in grammar is perhaps too long, in view of the generally declining emphasis on formal grammar in the elementary grades. So-called "progressive" educators will probably be especially annoyed by Part V of this test (in Forms 3 and 4); this is a matching exercise based on outright definitions (rather than applications of definitions) of such terms as "clause," "tense," "phrase," etc. The test in history probably corresponds fairly well to current teaching practice; regardless of practice, however, any test in history could well afford to include at least *some* items to measure "time sense," and the recognition of similarit differences between current and historical events. The test in geography is to be commended for its inclusion of questions on a map; but neither the tests in nature study nor health include any diagrams or plates.

INDIVIDUAL ITEMS. Since neither the teacher's handbooks nor any monograph present evidence concerning the validity of specific items of the present battery, it seems proper and necessary to subject the individual items to close scrutiny. We may notice, first, certain items which are questionable as to fact. Is it, for example, true that "The North became more prosperous and powerful than the South because it had a free labor system instead of slaves"; certainly the South does not appear to have prospered mightily since the slave system was abolished. Equally questionable is the item, "A clean, healthy skin is nature's sign of a healthy body"; surely health is not skin-deep, even if beauty is! (The authors thought well enough of a "clean, healthy skin" to include this item in three of the four forms of the test!) Some items appear definitely too easy; e.g., the true-false item, "A clean school room will help prevent the spread of disease." Occasionally one runs across a true-false item which is partly true and partly false; e.g., "Cold, wet weather increases the yield of cherries and apples because it gives the trees much moisture." So-called "specific determiners" in true-false items may occasionally be observed, as in the item, "Bacteria are *always very* harmful" (italics ours). Unnecessary and undesirable multiplication of cues occasionally occurs, as in the true-false item, "You should sit erect and have your book about twelve or fifteen inches from your eyes when reading": this item probably intended to measure the knowledge contained in its second clause, but an answer based on the first clause will receive full credit. Similarly objectionable is such a true-false item as, "Madrid is the capital and largest city in Spain." Cues arising from contiguity of related items are not avoided in the following two completion items, occurring next to each other in the health test: "When a person faints there is very little . . . . in the head and the . . . . should be lowered." "When a person is suffering from sunstroke, there is too much . . . . in the head and the . . . . should be . . . ." Occasionally, an alternative of a multiple-choice item seems too far-fetched to be func-

tional. Sometimes an item supposedly based on paragraph-reading can be answered without reading the paragraph; and in at least one instance the opposite fault occurs (Form 1, Battery A, Item 13). The completion items in Forms 1 and 2 are not as free from technical imperfections as such items should and can be; for example, does the item, "The shape of the earth is . . . . like an orange," measure the pupil's knowledge of the earth or of an orange? Space is unfortunately lacking for the cataloging of further errors or crudities. It would perhaps be too harsh to say that the present tests are worse than others in the respects illustrated above, but it can hardly be claimed that they are much better.

INDIVIDUAL SURVEY CHART. The Individual Survey Chart is a form for the graphical recording of the grade-equivalents of an individual's scores in the various subtests of the battery. The use of such a chart, based on grade norms, involves at least two assumptions; viz., (*a*) that a deviation of one grade above or below the norm for (say) Grammar is equal to a deviation of one grade above or below the norm for (say) Reading; and (*b*) that a deviation of one grade *above* the norm for (say) Arithmetic Computation is equal to a deviation of one grade *below* the norm for Arithmetic Computation. Accepting the customary view that the distance between the 50th and 75th percentiles equals that between the 50th and 25th percentiles, it can be shown that the two assumptions just mentioned are definitely unfulfilled. For example, a deviation of one quartile deviation *below* the norm for grade 7B in Arithmetic Computation (Form 1) represents a deviation of 1.3 grades, while a deviation of one quartile *above* the norm represents a deviation of 2.0 grades. Equally wide discrepancies are observable when the comparison involves not the same, but different, subtests. We may question, further, whether the individual subtests of this (or any other typical) test battery are sufficiently reliable to support the inter-test comparisons which the Individual Survey Chart is designed to promote. It will be recognized that the limitations noted in the present section are not peculiar to the test under review, but apply also to other tests making use of the same techniques.

GENERAL COMMENTS. Despite the critical comments above, we do not consider the present battery inferior to others of about the same date and length. More recent batteries designed for a narrower grade-span are, however, probably more valid.

The four forms of the present battery are "growing old." Instead of preparing simultaneously all the alternate forms of a test, might it not be advantageous to publish only one form the first year, issuing a revised and up-to-date alternate form every year (or every two years)? In this way, the number of alternate forms would not (after the first few years) be reduced; yet the tests could on the whole be kept more nearly abreast of current techniques and developments.

E. V. Pullias, Professor of Educational Psychology, George Pepperdine College. An accurate evaluation of a test can be made only if its authors or publishers furnish sufficient facts concerning the construction, standardization, and use of the test. Except for coefficients of reliability for Battery A (five of the ten subtests that compose one complete form) of Form 3 (one of four forms) such facts are not presented in the manual or other literature describing the *Public School Achievement Tests.* Even the reliability coefficients given are not very meaningful, for no relevant details are provided to show how the coefficients were secured nor the number or kind of cases used.

Excessive claims as to the reliability and the curricular validity of these tests are made in the manual and in the accompanying advertising matter. Not only are these claims unsupported by evidence, but there is little indication that an attempt has been made to secure the data to support them.

It should be said, however, that these tests have been widely used as is stated in the advertising material. The scoring is objective in the usual sense that new-type tests are objective. Norms based upon a very large number of cases are given. So far as one can judge from examining the tests (and from experience in giving some hundreds of them) the Public School achievement batteries are not very different in character of content and in administrative features from similar tests on the market. The *Public School Achievement Tests* may be good tests or they may be poor tests: one simply cannot judge from the facts made available to the public.

However, there is one point about which any person interested in such tests may be

reasonably certain, namely, testing techniques have not advanced to the point where it can be accurately said of any set of achievement tests, as is said of these, "You can use these tests with confidence." Such an unqualified claim is conducive to uncritical and unjustified use, such, for example, as making the test results the sole basis for pupil promotion. There is no adequate evidence to indicate that these or any other available tests measure pupil achievement with sufficient accuracy to warrant their being used with confidence as a basis for pupil promotion or for instructional evaluation in a particular school system.

[1195]

Public School Attainment Tests for High School Entrance: Examinations of Abilities in Reading, English, and Mathematics. Grades 8-10; 1935; a battery assembled from previously published standardized tests; 1 form; $4 per 100; 25¢ per specimen set; 90(100) minutes; Arthur E. Traxler, J. C. Tressler, Henry D. Rinsland, Roland L. Beck, and J. Murray Lee; Bloomington, Ill.: Public School Publishing Co.

REFERENCES

1 LEE, J. MURRAY. *Manual of Directions for the Lee Test of Algebraic Ability,* p. 4. Bloomington, Ill.: Public School Publishing Co., 1930. Pp. 12. $0.15. Paper.

Harold Gulliksen, Assistant Professor of Psychology and Examiner in the Social Sciences, The University of Chicago. This test is a composite consisting of parts of four other tests issued by the Public School Publishing Company. These are the *Traxler Silent Reading Test,* the *Tressler English Minimum Essentials Test,* the *Rinsland-Beck Natural Tests of English Usage,* and the *Lee Test of Algebraic Ability.*

No information is given as to how the items from the previous tests were selected for inclusion in this test, beyond the statement that "an experimental edition of the test was tried out with over two thousand students" and that "After this trial use some slight changes and reorganizations were made and the tests printed in their present form."

To all appearances, however, the test is well-constructed except for the fact that if one follows the scoring key and directions, the student receives credit in Test 8 for one item, the answer to which is printed in the test booklet, and that the form in which the test is set up and the key printed makes scoring needlessly slow.

The scoring directions are adequate, the directions to student and examiner are clear. But one wonders about comparability of performance from school to school when the examiner is told to "Have the pupils stop when all but the slowest two or three have finished" Test 1, Paragraph Comprehension.

The only information on validity and reliability given with the test is that "the enthusiasm of teachers in many schools which have cooperated to perfect this arrangement of the tests and also the appreciation shown by students, indicate the possibilities of the tests for determining quite definitely the student's ability to do high school work." A request by this reviewer to the Public School Publishing Company for such information brought, in reply, a two-page letter dealing with various uses for and merits of the test, but containing no information on validity or reliability.

The only norms given are the quartile points based on 548 cases for grades 8, 9, and 10 for the test as a whole. Apparently more adequate norms are being prepared since there is a form provided for the frequency distribution of scores and a request that it be filled out and mailed to the publishers.

In this reviewer's opinion it would be much better practice to secure adequate norms, and information on validity, reliability, and error of measurement before offering a test for sale, and then to furnish such information, together with an exact description of the population on which these statistics were computed, so that persons using the test could know how to interpret the results.

C. C. Ross, Professor of Educational Psychology, University of Kentucky. The purpose of this test battery is the "discovering, with a minimum of time and expense, students who have the general abilities necessary for success in the regular program of studies and those who are not capable of doing the usual high school work." It has been compiled by the editorial department of the Public School Publishing Company from parts of four well-known tests issued by that organization. There are minor changes in the arrangement of some of the items and sections, but the form of the items and the directions remain essentially the same as for the original tests.

Evidence to support the claim that the battery affords "an accurate check of the individual abilities of each student" is wholly inadequate. It is to be hoped that the day is passed when test users will accept such general statements as that "the battery has demonstrated its worth by successful use throughout the country," no matter how distinguished the authors, in lieu of objective experimental evidence. However, because of the reduced length of the tests in their present form, it is reasonable to assume that when teachers' marks are used as the criterion the validity coefficients will probably fall somewhat below the .56 to .67 reported for the original tests separately. Evidently the editorial department of the company does not take seriously the warning of one of the authors that altering the content or time limits of his test "changes the results so that it is impossible to tell how effective any of the material would be." [1]

Data on the reliability of the tests, either separately or in combination, is altogether lacking. The compilers of the battery should assume neither that the reader will know that the tests from which the material is selected are among the most reliable available in their respective fields, nor that he will be able to make a reasonable inference as to how the reliability will suffer from reducing the length of the tests. This information should appear in the manual.

The usability of the battery is seriously reduced by the meagerness of the norms. At present only the 25th, 50th, and 75th percentiles for the end of grades 8, 9, and 10, based on 548 cases in three schools, are available. Even these tentative norms are for the total battery, rather than for the separate tests. The diagnostic value of a test in guidance depends much less upon the total score than upon the counselor's ability to size up the student's strong and weak points as revealed by his scores on the separate parts of the test.

[1196]

Public School Correlated Attainment Scales: 1938 Revision. Grades 7-8; 1936-39; 3 forms; a battery assembled from previously published standardized tests; $5 per 100; (90-120) minutes. Allan J. Williams, Charles E. Holley, Arthur E. Traxler, W. T. Markham, Paul V. Sangren, Ann Reidy, B. R. Buckingham, L. C. Pressey, S. L. Pressey, and George A. Brown; Bloomington, Ill.: Public School Publishing Co.

REFERENCES

1 LANDRY, HERBERT. "The Disparity of Test Norms," pp. 208-17. In *Yearbook of the New York Society for the Experimental Study of Education, 1938.* New York: the Society (c/o C. Frederick Pertach, Sec.-Treas., 500 Park Ave.) Pp. vii, 228. $1.00. Paper.

C. W. Odell, Associate Professor of Education, University of Illinois. A review of this series of scales involves consideration not only of the scales themselves, but also of the uses suggested for the results. The latter is the point of especial emphasis by the publishers and authors, hence will be dealt with first. The fundamental purpose, to provide means of direct comparison of attainment with aptitude, by subjects, within a class, is sound. The method of doing so, however, is subject to improvement. As has already been amply demonstrated for somewhat similar techniques, such as those of the achievement quotient and accomplishment ratio, the unreliability of measures secured by dividing one fallible score by another is greater than that of either of those involved and rarely so small as to justify placing much confidence in individual measures, and this appears to be no exception to the rule. Indeed, the shortness of the aptitude or intelligence test here included probably makes it even less reliable than similar measures based upon longer tests. No reliability data are given, hence this point cannot be checked. The tenor of the discussion, however, implies that the derived scores suggested may be employed with considerable confidence. Moreover, the discussion of them is far from being as simple and clear as it might be. "Correlation quotient" is employed with different meanings on pages 5 and 6 of the Teacher's Handbook and "efficiency quotient" is used as synonymous with one of them. The graph on Plate II, when interpreted in accordance with the scale thereon, is misleading and requires that a portion of the text be read to correct the false impression.

The scales themselves seem to have been carefully constructed, but the account thereof is too indefinite and lacking in actual details and data to afford the amount of evidence desirable. Their content, however, appears to be suitable for their announced purpose, that is, to represent a good sampling of the subject-matter abilities, skills, and information in the four fields included—reading, vocabulary, spelling, and arithmetic. Incidentally one wonders why language and other subjects were omitted.

The form of the scales, the directions, and the scoring methods are weak in numerous details. The quality of English is not high, including the misplacement of interrogatives, the omission of capitals, reference to questions as statements, and other poor usages.

Directions do not, as they should, inform pupils when to fold back a sheet and when to keep the test booklet open so that two pages show. In some cases they are on the same page as the test to which they apply and are long enough that some pupils will probably "jump the gun" and begin before the signal is given. Pupils are not instructed what to do if they finish before time is called. In Part I, Section D the tester should be told the approximate rate at which to read the material to the class. In Section B of the same part, the word "Mark" is scarcely sufficient in insure the desired response. In the same section each column of a matching exercise contains only four items, too few. Pupils should be directed to reduce the answers to the arithmetic elements to lowest terms, if that is desired, as apparently it is.

Scoring is made unnecessarily difficult by the irregular placement of answers in Part I, Sections A and B. The answers listed as correct for Part II, arithmetic, are not so completely stated as to make evident how to score certain responses almost sure to occur. The placement of answers in columns on sheets which need to be folded is less convenient and durable than their location on strips of cardboard. They cannot be cut and pasted thereon unless two sets are obtained, as they are given on both sides of the sheet. Finally the age score, 17-0, given as equivalent to the highest possible point score is not high enough to measure adequately the attainment or aptitude of the best pupils in the seventh and eighth grades, those for which the scales are intended.

Robert K. Speer, Professor of Education, New York University. [Review of the revised Form A.] Here we have a battery of short tests of achievement, and also three tests of learning aptitude. The achievement tests cover reading, sentence vocabulary, arithmetic, and English. The aptitude tests are in arithmetic problems, selection of synonyms and antonyms, and the detection of number relationships.

An especially valuable contribution of this series is the inclusion of a new type of chart. This chart presents both the aptitude ages and the achievement ages of pupils. An ingenious scale has been constructed that makes it possible to compare a pupil's achievement with his aptitude. This new system of interpretation is in agreement with present disposition to evaluate school attainments on the basis of the learning abilities of the pupils.

The chief defect of both the achievement and the aptitude scales is the unfortunate failure to include enough judgment elements, life situations, or practical applications of skills and knowledge. For the most part, each test continues the old emphasis on facts and isolated skill items, rather than judgments, appreciations, and the power to use knowledge.

Ed Res B 18:145-6 My 3 '39. J. Wayne Wrightstone. * no evidence in the Manual about the reliability or validity of the subtests * The correlation implied in the title of these tests is based on questionable assumption; namely, that by comparing the aptitude age with the attainment age in each or all of the subtests, the teacher or school officer can determine whether John Jones or Mary Smith is mastering in accordance with his or her academic aptitude "the entire elementary course of study as it is now presented" (*see* page 4 of the Manual). The assumption is questionable for three reasons: First, the attainment scales measure only a fraction of the aims of elementary education in the modern school, and they disregard such aims of education as powers of critical thinking, interests, attitudes, and work-study skills. Second, for the narrow skills and informations that the tests do measure the scores on a subtest for a pupil cannot presumably be reliable enough for individual prediction or comparison. Third, the relationship between academic aptitude, especially that obtained by the exercises in this test, and the comparison of separate subtests is too low to do other than mislead a well-meaning, but not statistically trained, teacher. Used as survey tests of the three R's in a school with a traditional curriculum where major emphasis is upon a mastery of narrow academic skills and informations, these tests may well provide for class groups measures of attainment of limited skill objectives. For reasons already stated the writer recommends that the so-called correlation of attainment age in subtests with aptitude age be studiously avoided.

Teach Col J 10:72 Ja '39. E. L. Abell. * The test items seem to be well chosen, but no information is given concerning the statistical valuation of the single items or the test as a whole. No validities or reliabilities are given. *

There are two weaknesses apparent in these tests. One is the use of an aptitude test which has only arithmetic and English items for comparison with the attainment tests which are all arithmetic or English. The other weakness is the use of the per cent score instead of a point score with its relative score equivalent.

For reviews by Herbert S. Conrad and H. E. Schrammel, see 877.

[1197]

Unit Scales of Attainment. Grades 1B, 1A, 2B, 2A, 3, 3-4, 5-6, 7-8; 1932-37; 8 levels, 2 editions; 25¢ per specimen set; nontimed; M. E. Branon, L. J. Brueckner, A. M. Jordan, Prudence Cutright, W. A. Anderson, August Dvorak, and M. J. Van Wagenen; Minneapolis, Minn.: Educational Test Bureau, Inc.
a) PRIMARY DIVISION, GRADE I (FIRST HALF). 1934-36; 2 forms; (40-60) minutes; 75¢ per 25.
b) PRIMARY DIVISION, GRADE I (LAST HALF). 1934-36; 2 forms; (40-60) minutes; 75¢ per 25.
c) PRIMARY DIVISION, GRADE II (FIRST HALF). 1934; 2 forms; (40-60) minutes; 75¢ per 25.
d) PRIMARY DIVISION, GRADE II (LAST HALF). 1934-36; 2 forms; (40-60) minutes; 75¢ per 25.
e) PRIMARY DIVISION, GRADE III. 1934-36; 3 forms; (120) minutes; 75¢ per 25.
f) DIVISION 1. Grades 3-4; 3 forms; 1932-33; *Complete Battery*: $1.50 per 25; (180) minutes; *Minimum Essentials Battery*: $1.10 per 25; (135) minutes.
g) DIVISION 2. Grades 5-6; 1933; 3 forms; *Complete Battery*: $1.50 per 25; (180) minutes; *Minimum Essentials Battery*: $1.10 per 25; (135) minutes.
h) DIVISION 3. *Grades 7-8*; 1933; 3 forms; *Complete Battery*: $1.50 per 25; (180) minutes; *Minimum Essentials Battery*: $1.10 per 25; (135) minutes.

REFERENCES

1 FORAN, T. G., AND LOYES, M. EDMUND. "The Relative Difficulty of Three Achievement Examinations." *J Ed Psychol* 26:218-22 Mr '35.
2 PATERSON, DONALD G.; SCHNEIDLER, GWENDOLEN G.; AND WILLIAMSON, EDMUND G. *Student Guidance Technique*, pp. 88-9, 105-7. New York: McGraw-Hill Book Co., Inc., 1938. Pp. xviii, 316. $3.00. (London: McGraw-Hill Publishing Co., Ltd. 18s.)

D. Welty Lefever, Associate Professor of Education, The University of Southern California. No doubt the most apparent feature of the *Unit Scales of Attainment* is the technical skill with which they were constructed. The individual test items in all parts and divisions of the battery constitute a ladder of difficulty on which the steps are approximately an equal distance apart. This equality of scalar values makes possible a direct comparison of score differences or gains at different C-score levels and for the several forms and divisions comprising the system of scales. It is also possible to study the individual tasks with which each pupil has coped successfully in terms of their relative difficulty.

Unfortunately many teachers will not find it easy to manipulate such technical material nor will they be able to make as ready an interpretation of C-score values as they would a grade placement scale. It may well be argued that the gain of a certain degree of increased precision may be more than offset by a loss in teacher understanding. One example of a possible source of confusion to the teacher is the fact that in the table of norms dated 1937 the C-score values are by no means the same for any educational age or grade level.

The reliability of the several tests is indicated by a probable error of measurement roughly equal to a half year's advance for the average pupil. All achievement batteries should furnish the one using the test with similar measures of errors as they are the least subject to arbitrary definitions of range. However, since reliability coefficients are ordinarily available for grade ranges of one year, it would be helpful if these coefficients were reported in the manual.

Care must be observed in applying the probable error of measurement to the scores of pupils who have done well or poorly for their age or grade level. Pupils with high scores relative to expectancy are much more likely to do less well on a second form of the test than they are to make better scores. Those with relatively poor scores will tend to do better. This, of course, is the familiar phenomenon of regression.

A similar caution must be kept in mind when comparing the outcomes of the primary reading tests with Van Wagenen's *Reading Readiness Test* (not a part of the *Unit Scales of Attainment*). Pupils with high measures of reading readiness will tend to do definitely less well on the reading test and vice versa. It would not be fair to blame (or credit) the child for a tendency resulting from the manner in which the errors of measurement distribute themselves.

Several points of advantage to be mentioned for these scales are: (*a*) The directions for the pupil as read by the teacher are exceptionally clear, simple, and complete. (*b*) Multiple-choice items are well chosen from the standpoint of plausibility so that too much help will not come through the elimination of impossible items. (*c*) The C-score scale values have already been subjected to corrections for guessing. (*d*) Each section of the reading test contains at least one item which emphasizes the paragraph's chief meaning. (*e*) The content of the reading paragraphs and the questions ac-

companying each are closely knit so that clues gained from quick or careless reading are of little help. (*f*) The reading test contains a rather wide variety of materials representing different fields of study, but always in paragraph form. (*g*) In the English usage test the element of guessing has been reduced by requiring the correct form to be written above the erroneous one. (*h*) The spacing of items in the primary scale is excellent from the standpoint of pupil vision. (*i*) A short battery of minimum essentials for the upper grades makes possible the measurement of reading, arithmetic, spelling, and English usage without including the "content scales" on geography, literature, elementary science, and American history.

A number of criticisms appear to be appropriate. (*a*) The art work in the primary tests is poor. (*b*) The arithmetic sections of the third grade test are much too difficult. This is evidenced by the fact that four problems correct is the average for the first half of the third grade while six problems is the norm for the second semester. It is not enough to answer that this difficulty is cared for adequately in the table of norms. We must consider the mental hygiene of the child, particularly the primary child, when confronted with a test on which he can do very little successfully. One problem from this third-grade test will illustrate: "It took a railroad train 12 hours to make a trip of 372 miles. What was the *average* speed of the train an hour?" [Reviewer's italics.] (*c*) The test for capitalization used in Division 1 (grades 3-4) contains many words and phrases strange to pupils of much higher grade level. A few samples follow: "revolutionary," "George Peabody Teachers College," "succeeded by," "democratic party," "elegy," "Breton." Would it not be possible to create sufficient situations requiring the use of capital letters without too many difficult words and phrases? (*d*) It is very difficult in the "content" sections (geography, literature, elementary science, and American history) to present a sampling of items equally acceptable to all sections of the country and to all types of curriculum policy. An added point is that these tests are entirely factual. This emphasis will be criticized by many. Of this group of tests the one on elementary science seems to possess the most universal applicability in terms of content sampling. (*e*) A number of important reading skills are not measured such as the reading of tables of contents, science problems, graphs and charts, book indexes, arithmetic problems, directions for construction, and the like. (*f*) A separation of the elements of reading, reasoning, and computation would add to the diagnostic value of the arithmetic problems test.

By way of summary it may be said that the *Unit Scales of Attainment* are closely knit, well constructed, and quite thoroughly standardized. They could be improved by simplify-ing the machinery for interpretation as used by the classroom teacher and by placing more items on each level of difficulty thus relieving the steepness of the gradient of difficulty. Space for this expansion might be provided by eliminating the "content" sections and their dubious sampling.

For reviews by Herbert S. Conrad and Ethel L. Cornell, see 878. For a review by Joseph C. Dewey of the reading test, see 1115.

CHARACTER AND PERSONALITY

Reviews by S. J. Beck, Robert G. Bernreuter, J. M. Blackburn, Raymond B. Cattell, W. D. Commins, Stephen M. Corey, John G. Darley, Stanley G. Dulsky, Alvin C. Eurich, Warren G. Findley, Bessie Lee Gambrill, J. P. Guilford, Harold Gulliksen, Doncaster G. Humm, Harold E. Jones, Forrest A. Kingsbury, C. M. Louttit, J. B. Maller, Charles I. Mosier, Theodore Newcomb, Pedro T. Orata, Carl R. Rogers, Douglas Spencer, Percival M. Symonds, Robert L. Thorndike, Simon H. Tulchin, P. E. Vernon, Goodwin Watson, Ralph K. Watkins, E. G. Williamson, and Ll. Wynn Jones.

[1198]

A-S Reaction Study: A Scale for Measuring Ascendance-Submission in Personality. College; 1928-39; 1 form, 2 editions; $1.80 per 25; single specimen set free; nontimed (20) minutes; Gordon W. Allport and Floyd H. Allport; Boston, Mass.: Houghton Mifflin Co.
a) FORM FOR MEN. 1928.
b) FORM FOR WOMEN, REVISED. 1928-39.

REFERENCES

1 ALLPORT, FLOYD H., AND ALLPORT, GORDON W. "Personality Traits: Their Classification and Measurement." *J Abn and Social Psychol* 16:6-40 Ap '21.
2 ALLPORT, GORDON W. "A Test for Ascendance-Submission." *J Abn and Social Psychol* 23:118-36 Jl-S '28.
3 BENDER, IRVING EDISON. "Ascendance-Submission in Relation to Certain Other Factors in Personality." *J Abn and Social Psychol* 23:137-43 Jl-S '28.
4 ALLPORT, GORDON W. "The Neurotic Personality and Traits of Self-Expression." *J Social Psychol* 1:524-7 N '30.
5 BECKMAN, R. O., AND LEVINE, MICHAEL. "Selecting Executives: An Evaluation of Three Tests." *Personnel J* 8:415-20 Ap '30.
6 BROOM, M. E. "A Study of a Test of Ascendance-Submission." *J Appl Psychol* 14:405-13 O '30.
7 JERSILD, ARTHUR. "A Study of Personality." *J Abn and Social Psychol* 25:115-20 Jl-S '30.
8 HANNA, JOSEPH V. "Reliability of Two Personality Questionnaires." *Psychol B* 28:621-2 O '31.
9 WANG, CHAS. K. A. "The Internal Consistency of the Allports' Ascendence-Submission Test (Form for Men)." *J Abn and Social Psychol* 26:154-61 Jl-S '31.
10 HOLCOMB, G. W., AND LASLETT, H. R. "A Prognostic Study of Engineering Aptitude." *J Appl Psychol* 16:107-15 Ap '32.
11 MANZER, CHARLES W. "The Effect of Self-Interest on Scores Made on the Allport Test for Measuring Ascendance-Submission." *Psychol Clinic* 21:268-70 D '32.
12 STAGNER, Ross. "The Intercorrelation of Some Standardized Personality Tests." *J Appl Psychol* 16:453-64 O '32.
13 MOORE, HERBERT, AND STEELE, ISABEL. "Personality Tests." *J Abn and Social Psychol* 29:45-52 Ap-Je '34.
14 PERRY, RAYMOND CARVER. *A Group Factor Analysis of the Adjustment Questionnaire.* University of Southern California, Southern California Educational Monographs, 1933-34 Series, No. 5. Los Angeles, Calif.: University of Southern California Press, 1934. Pp. xi, 93. $1.50.
15 STEVENS, SAMUEL N., AND WONDERLIC, ELDON F. "The A-S Reaction Test. A Study of Beckman's Revision." *Personnel J* 13:222-4 D '34.
16 FARRAM, FREDA. "The Relation of Ascendance-Submission Tendencies to Neurosis." *Austral J Psychol and Philos* 13:228-32 S '35.
17 WILLIAMS, GRIFFITH W., AND CHAMBERLAIN, FLORENCE. "An Evaluation of the Use of the Allport Ascendance-Submission Test with High School Girls." *J Genetic Psychol* 49:363-75 D '36.
18 RUGGLES, RICHARD, AND ALLPORT, GORDON W. "Recent Applications of the A-S Reaction Study." *J Abn and Social Psychol* 34:518-28 O '39.
19 WASSON, MARGARET M. "The Agreements among Certain Types of Personality Schedules." *J Psychol* 9:351-63 Ap '40.

Doncaster G. Humm, Wadsworth-Humm Personnel Service, Los Angeles, California. [A review of the 1928 edition.] This behavior-study, according to the authors, aims to discover the disposition of an individual to dominate his fellows.

Its approximate reliability is reported as .74 for men and .78 for women. These figures represent respectively 33 and 37 per cent better than chance. In other words the chances are approximately 1.97 to 1 that a second test will return essentially the same results as the first in the case of men, and 2.20 to 1 in the case of women.

The validity obtained from ratings—the unreliability of which is mentioned by the authors —is reported as from .29 to .79, 4 and 29 per cent better than chance respectively. The chances accordingly are from 1.09 to 1 to 2.26 to 1 that the results will agree with ratings.

Statistical "certainty" is generally accepted as being 369 to 1.

In the light of these reported facts, it is very doubtful that the scale may be employed to advantage in obtaining self-knowledge, choosing a vocation, or in vocational selection and placement without considerable verification and supplementary information.

The authors are to be commended for their statement that the study "be used primarily as a basis of future research in the measurement of personality, rather than as a hard and fast criterion for social guidance."

Users of the *A-S Reaction Study* should interpret the results obtained in the light of a very high probable error, and should certainly not make recommendations without mentioning that probable error.

is led to wonder if success as a manager is an adequate criterion for the tendency to be ascendant or vice versa.

There seems to be no direct measurement of reliability and validity for this scale. Until such is made the following recommendation of the author should be followed: "It is strongly urged that the scores obtained be regarded as suggestive rather than conclusive."

It does not seem established that there is justification for the author's statement: "That the present test may serve as a criterion for the selection of candidates for promotion or of applicants for executive and supervisory positions."

The test does appear to show differences in averages; but differences in individuals' scores is another matter.

[1199]

A-S Reaction Study: Revision for Business Use. Adult men; 1928-32; 1 form; $5 per 100; 25¢ per specimen set; nontimed (20) minutes; the original form of the *A-S Reaction Study* was prepared by Gordon W. Allport and Floyd H. Allport; revision by R. O. Beckman; New York: Psychological Corporation.

REFERENCES

1 BECKMAN, R. O. "Ascendance-Submission Test—Revised." *Personnel J* 11:387-92 Ap '33.
2 ACHILLES, P. S., AND SCHULTZ, R. S. "Characteristics of Life Insurance Salesmen." *Personnel J* 12:260-3 F '34.
3 STEVENS, SAMUEL N., AND WONDERLIC, ELDON F. "The A-S Reaction Test: A Study of Beckman's Revision." *Personnel J* 13:222-4 D '34.
4 SCHULTZ, RICHARD S., AND ROSLOW, SYDNEY. "Restandardization of the A-S Reaction Study as a Personnel Form." *J Appl Psychol* 22:554-7 D '38.

Doncaster G. Humm, Wadsworth-Humm Personnel Service, Los Angeles, California. This is a revision for business use of the Allport *A-S Reaction Study*. The author has shortened the original questionnaire, has changed the language to that which would be more suitable to business, and has endeavored to provide more internal consistency for the test.

He has reported a distribution of scores by occupations which seems to establish that the test affords averages for various occupations which distinguish between the amount of ascendancy required for those occupations. There appears, however, to be large overlapping of ranges.

The correlation between the test and the success on the job of 35 store managers is reported as .27, or 3.7 per cent better than chance. In other words there is 52 per cent agreement and 48 per cent disagreement. One

[1200]

Adjustment Inventory. Grades 9-16 and adults; 1934-38; 1 form, 2 levels; $1.75 per 25; $1.75 per 100 machine-scorable answer sheets; nontimed (25) minutes; Hugh M. Bell; Stanford University, Calif.: Stanford University Press.
a) STUDENT FORM. Grades 9-16; 1934; 15¢ per specimen set.
b) ADULT FORM. Adults; 1938; 25¢ per specimen set.

REFERENCES

1 BELL, HUGH M. *The Theory and Practice of Student Counseling:* With Special Reference to the Adjustment Inventory. Stanford University, Calif.: Stanford University Press, 1935. Pp. 138. $1.00. Paper, lithotyped. (London: Oxford University Press. 4s. 6d.)
2 TURNEY, AUSTIN H., AND FEE, MARY. "An Attempt to Use the Bell Adjustment Inventory for High School Guidance." *Sch R* 44:193-8 Mr '36.
3 TYLER, HENRY T. "Evaluating the Bell Adjustment Inventory." *Jun Col J* 6:353-7 Ap '36.
4 DARLEY, JOHN G. "Tested Maladjustment Related to Clinically Diagnosed Maladjustment." *J Appl Psychol* 21:632-42 D '37.
5 FEDER, DANIEL D., AND MALLETT, DONALD R. "Validity of Certain Measures of Personality Adjustment." *J Am Assn Col Reg* 13:5-15 O '37.
6 KEYS, NOEL, AND GUILFORD, MARGARET S. "The Validity of Certain Adjustment Inventories in Predicting Problem Behavior." *J Ed Psychol* 28:641-55 D '37.
7 DARLEY, JOHN G. "Changes in Measured Attitudes and Adjustments." *J Social Psychol* 9:189-99 My '38.
8 DARLEY, JOHN G. "A Preliminary Study of Relations between Attitude, Adjustment, and Vocational Interest Tests." *J Ed Psychol* 29:467-73 S '38.
9 DROUGHT, NEAL E. "An Analysis of Eight Measures of Personality and Adjustment in Relation to Relative Scholastic Achievement." *J Appl Psychol* 22:597-606 D '38.
10 McNAMARA, WALTER J., AND DARLEY, JOHN G. "A Factor Analysis of Test-Retest Performance on Attitude and Adjustment Tests." *J Ed Psychol* 29:652-64 D '38.
11 PATERSON, DONALD G.; SCHNEIDLER, GWENDOLEN G.; AND WILLIAMSON, EDMUND G. *Student Guidance Techniques,* pp. 185-9. New York: McGraw-Hill Book Co., Inc., 1938. Pp. xviii, 316. $3.00. (London: McGraw-Hill Publishing Co., Ltd., 18s.)
12 BELL, HUGH M. *The Theory and Practice of Personal Counseling:* With Special Reference to the Adjustment Inventory. A revision of *The Theory and Practice of Student Counseling.* Stanford University, Calif.: Stanford University Press, 1939. Pp. v, 167. $1.25. Paper, lithotyped. (London: Oxford University Press. 6s.)
13 GREENE, J. E., AND STATON, THOMAS F. "Predictive Value of Various Tests of Emotionality and Adjustment in a Guidance Program for Prospective Teachers." *J Ed Res* 32:653-9 My '39.
14 PALLISTER, HELEN, AND PIERCE, W. O'D. "A Comparison of Bell Adjustment Scores for American and Scottish Groups." *Sociometry* 2:54-72 Jl '39.
15 PEDERSEN, RUTH A. "Validity of the Bell Adjustment Inventory When Applied to College Women." *J Psychol* 9:227-36 Ap '40.

Raymond B. Cattell, G. Stanley Hall Professor of Genetic Psychology, Clark University. [Review of the Student Form.] To the writing of inventories there is no end, and one would think that today a very potent excuse would be necessary for putting a new one on the market. One looks in vain through this inventory and its equipment for any new research, improvement of technique or even some mere innovation which would justify its existence.

Most of the objections raised ten or fifteen years ago against the self-inventory as an objective measure of adjustment or personality apply to this example, as they have to most of the questionnaire approaches published in the interim, indeed the inventories tend if anything, to be less successful than the original and outstanding personal data sheets of Bernreuter, Woodworth, and Thurstone. What promised to be a passing phase in psychology, a temporary scaffolding to the structure of psychological research and the building of objective tests, threatens, through repeated publication such as this to become accepted as a permanent part of the landscape in applied psychology. One wonders what sort of a personnel is applying psychology.

The questionnaire abounds with questions requiring not only perfect self-knowledge and ruthless honesty but also a wide knowledge of humanity and its standards. Such are: "Are you troubled with shyness?" yes or no; "Are your feelings easily hurt?" yes or no; "Are you often sorry for the things you do?" yes or no; "Do you day-dream frequently?" yes or no (what is frequently?).

The inventory, we are told, has been "validated" in four ways. First, by item validation through internal consistency. Secondly, by being "checked during interviews with four hundred college students"; by what means checked, we are not told. Thirdly, by comparison with judgments of school administrators as to which students are well adjusted. Between groups of such students selected for good and bad adjustment it yields averages differing significantly. But there is no expression showing how effective the test is in differentiating individuals.

Lastly, the test is validated by comparison with a variety of other questionnaire totals. On a population of 39 the "Social Adjustment" pool of the inventory reached a correlation (corrected) of .90 with the B4-D scale [measure of dominance-submission] of Bernreuter's *Personality Inventory*. But it also correlated positively with the Allports' *A-S Reaction Study* (.72, corrected), a test of assertiveness of disposition. What is this inventory aiming at measuring?

Every care appears to have been taken to give the intending user of the test whatever data he might require. He is supplied with "validities" and consistencies, means and standard deviations for high school and college groups, and with an attractive scoring key in a special folder. Everything is given except that which justifies the test's existence—namely, its true validity. As to what the test measures there remains the completest confusion. It is divided into four distinct parts, one measuring home adjustment, one health adjustment (?), one social adjustment, and one emotional adjustment (general emotionality?). But these intercorrelate, so that it looks as if home and social adjustment are the only two measures that are in fact independent. And "emotional adjustment"—unfortunate term since all adjustment is emotional—correlates so much more with the other items than they do with one another that one suspects it is a better measure on its own of whatever tendency is being measured than the whole pool is.

If psychology is to improve in objectivity on psychoanalytic conceptions of adjustment and maladjustment it must find a more objective basis than this. Personal insight can only be abandoned for statistical treatment and measurement if measurement is based on adequate statistical research conceptions.

John G. Darley, Director of the University Testing Bureau and Assistant Professor of Psychology, The University of Minnesota. [Review of the Student Form.] The first two reviews of the *Adjustment Inventory* in *The 1938 Yearbook* were actually reviews of Bell's *School Inventory* [Editor's mistake]; the third review questioned the *Adjustment Inventory* on theoretical grounds. The present review stresses the clinical utility of the test. There are three general methods of validating instruments of this kind: correlation with already established personality tests; group difference techniques; methods based on internal consistency or homogeneity of content. Bell has used all three methods in his work. Data published independently elsewhere include extremely high test-retest correlations over intervals of six to nine months in high school and college age ranges. Such consistency is consonant with a "continuum of stability" concept in personality measurement wherein the more deep-seated personality characteristics presumably tapped by this test are relatively more stable aspects of personality.

In the systematic case study of an individual, personality characteristics are analyzed in four ways: anecdotal reports, rating scales, pencil-and-paper tests, and varying forms of interviewing. Where pencil-and-paper tests are used they are most wisely viewed as clues to identify deviations for more intensive analysis. Pragmatically a good personality test is one which identifies, in its additive score or in its individual items, areas of actual or potential maladjustment for further diagnosis and treatment. If a test picks out a high proportion of adjustment difficulties which a good clinician finds actually existed in the case, and if it misses a small proportion of such difficulties, it is useful in a personnel program. The *Adjustment Inventory* meets this criterion.

Factor analysis of this test as one of a battery of 13 attitude and adjustment test scores indicates that the health and emotional scales in combination may tap anxieties, neuroticism or hypochondriasis as personality characteristics.

The test seems most useful when used as part of a larger battery of personality measurements, thus permitting a cross-check in several areas of adjustment. Its published odd-even correlations have been reproduced in different samples, and these data, together with high test-retest correlations, may be taken as evidence of consistency of measurement.

The inventory yields four adjustment scores: home, health, social, and emotional. A fifth total score, summing all four, is not useful in interviewing or counseling since it lacks the specificity and meaning of the other four. Separate sex norms are provided for both high school and college populations. If the counselor uses these norms in conjunction with the published table of probable errors of measurement, interpretations of borderline cases will be more effective. Bell's selection of clinically well-defined extreme groups for purposes of determining critical ratios on each scale is an important

part of the supporting evidence for the utility of the test.

C. M. Louttit, Director of the Psychological Clinics and Associate Professor of Clinical Psychology, Indiana University. [Review of the Student Form.] This familiar schedule is arranged so that independent scores for home, health, social, and emotional adjustments may be secured, while the total score indicates general adjustment status. The possibility of breaking the scores down into four specific areas increases the usefulness of the scale for the purposes of guidance surveys, as well as for clinical study.

Norms are presented separately for high school and college men and women in terms of a five-point scale. The user is cautioned against overemphasis of the differences between adjacent groups. Reliabilities are high, and the validations are varied and consistent so that use of the schedule for individual analysis and prognosis is warranted.

As is so frequently true of personality schedules, the manual for this instrument is too incomplete. Except for a very brief statement of the meaning of high and low scores, the author fails to give the test user any help in interpreting either group or individual results. In fact there are not even references which might be helpful to the user. Perhaps this lack would be justified by saying that trained psychologists should be able to use the scale without special help. No matter how true this may be, an instrument such as this is freely available to anyone and therefore is open to serious misuse, or at least unintelligent use.

Percival M. Symonds, Professor of Education, Columbia University. [Review of the Student Form.] Bell's *Adjustment Inventory* consists of one hundred and forty simple incidents to be answered by encircling "Yes," "No," or "?." Four scores to serve as measures of home, health, social, and emotional adjustment can be secured as well as a total score. The questions belonging to each of these four special phases of adjustment are spaced at random through the test so that a special key is needed in order to select and score the items belonging to each of the four sections. The questionnaire has the merit of being very compact and simple for the student to answer.

One may question the reliability of the separate sections containing as they do thirty-five items. The manual which accompanies the test states that the coefficient of reliability of the separate sections ranges from .80 to .89. These reliability coefficients would seem to be higher than one would ordinarily expect with these few items.

Even if these scores were reliable enough for individual diagnosis, some skepticism should be exercised in taking the scores at face value as representing the names given to the various sections.

Norms are given in the manual for high school and college students. However, these norms instead of being percentile scores for various groups tested, describe levels on the test by such description as excellent, good, average, unsatisfactory, and very unsatisfactory. This would seem to be an unfortunate practice as it tends to place value judgment on the results of the test that certainly must be a matter for individual interpretation. The writer would prefer to leave to the counselor who is to use the test the privilege of deciding what range of scores he is to consider good and unsatisfactory.

The advantages of Bell's *Adjustment Inventory* are its compactness, simplicity, and the apparent careful selection of questions.

S. J. Beck, Head Psychologist, Michael Reese Hospital, Chicago, Illinois. [Review of the Adult Form.] This reviewer has not used the *Adjustment Inventory*. Critical comments that follow are, therefore, a reaction entirely to a study of the blank and the accompanying directions—reactions based on the reviewer's clinical experience.

This instrument consists of 160 items. The adjustment categories within which they are classified are home, health, social, emotional, and occupational. The directions allow for considerable flexibility, i.e., they make for an adaptability in application. Thus "questions about the meaning of words may be answered by the examiner." Again when subjects inquire concerning the purpose of the test "they should be answered frankly and honestly." This is a flexibility somewhat rare in studies statistically based and certainly commendable. The scoring requires stencils which come with the instructions. It is easy and quick. Norms were obtained from what looks like a good representation of individuals. They ranged in age from 20 to 50 with the majority between 25 and 40. They were taken from adult extension classes in California and in New Jersey, Counseling Service of the Seattle Y.M.C.A., a practice school of the Chicago Y.W.C.A., and adult classes in industrial psychology in Boston.

In fact one lays down this questionnaire with much more satisfaction than with most personality inventory efforts. The first reason is the evidence of much clinical sense in the questions themselves. The author, in other words, appears to have an interest in the entire personality. Confirmation of this is found in the method of validation. Counselors, each of whom had had five or more years of experience in working with maladjusted individuals were put on the alert for "individuals who evidenced during interviews, very good or very poor adjustment in any of the areas covered by the *Inventory*." To these extremes of adjustment the inventory was administered. A check, individual for individual was thus had on the instrument by a totally outside source. Validation, even if not as intensive as one is accustomed to in clinical experience, was real. The result is reflected both in the questions used and also in the subgroupings of adjustment areas. These, even if not elemental in personality or mutually exclusive, still give us a valid picture of the personality. This is not to say a dynamic picture. The questionnaire cannot do that. It can place the individual in a given position relative to the entire group in respect to certain personality tendencies. In turn this can be the starting point for more effective probing.

Some of the intercorrelations found by the author attract attention and certainly arouse interest. The highest positive correlations of reports are those between health and emotional adjustment; social and emotional; emotional and occupational; and home and emotional.

The inventory can be recommended to the clinician when, as, and if he finds himself in need of this type of instrument.

J. P. Guilford, Professor of Psychology, The University of Southern California. [Review of the Adult Form.] This is the familiar type of personality questionnaire, composed of 160 items to be answered by "Yes," "?," or "No." It is similar to the same author's inventory previously designed for students. The responses are scored for adjustment in five respects:

(a) Home Adjustment.—Whether the individual is satisfied with his home life, his living conditions, and his home associates. (b) Health Adjustment.—Whether he has been ill a great deal, having had operations or diseases, and minor ailments. (c) Social Adjustment.—Whether he is shy, retiring, and submissive in social contacts. (d) Emotional Adjustment.—Whether he is subject to emotional upsets of one kind or another; is nervous, or depressed. (e) Occupational Adjustment.— Whether he is satisfied with his job; the kind of work, his associates, his working conditions, and whether he is recognized for what he does.

Only 32 items are scored, with unweighted scoring, for each area of adjustment, no item being scored for more than one category of adjustment. This has the virtue of keeping the correlations among scores as low as possible (the intercorrelations range from −.06 to +.51) at the same time it places a heavy burden of discrimination upon a relatively small number of items. The reliability coefficients, as supplied by the author of the test for the five parts, range from .81 (Health Adjustment) to .91 (Home Adjustment and Emotional Adjustment) with probable errors of measurement between 1.74 (Occupational Adjustment) and 1.10 (Emotional Adjustment). The test items were selected on the basis of their power to discriminate between the upper and lower 15 per cent of an adult population who were selected on the basis of a preliminary scoring. The inventory scores have been found very discriminating between extreme groups that were selected by experienced counselors. A total score is used and though this is probably not as valuable as the part scores, it has a split-half reliability of .94 and a probable error of measurement of 3.14 for men and 3.42 for women.

The test will find its greatest value for the clinician who wishes in a systematic manner to locate the points at which the patient is at odds with the world. Three of the five areas explored—home, health, and occupation—are common places to look for sources of trouble. Incidentally, it will probably have to be determined whether a person with a significant "poor health" score needs medical attention or is merely a hypochondriac. Other areas of adjustment could have been added to make the survey more complete.

Norms are given for both men and women, though the sexes differ very little, as based upon a population ranging in age from 20 to 50, with the majority between 25 and 40. The occupational adjustment score can be obtained only for those who are employed or have recently been employed. Items indicating each type of adjustment in the inventory are labeled by letter so that the clinician may make further analysis within each category. The inventory is said to require not more than 25 minutes to fill out. A translucent scoring key permits complete scoring in about 4 minutes.

Doncaster G. Humm, Wadsworth-Humm Personnel Service, Los Angeles, California. [Review of the Adult Form.] The use of this inventory, as recommended by the author, is as an aid in counseling adults, with the total score indicative of general adjustment status.

The reliability of the inventory as reported is, for the total score, .94. This is 66 per cent better than chance, and indicates a chance of 4.86 to 1 that approximately the same score will be obtained when the test is repeated.

The validity of the inventory is reported in terms of how well it differentiates between a "Very well" adjusted group and a "Very poorly" adjusted group. These groups were selected by experienced counselors. The results clearly indicate that the inventory validly makes such distinction. The inventory seems to have the capability of distinguishing differences between well adjusted individuals and poorly adjusted individuals to the extent of a chance of from 19 to 1 in home adjustment to 499 to 1 in social adjustment. This indicates a high degree of certainty when inventory scores are either very high or very low, diminishing to a lesser degree, of course, in the intermediate classification of average adjustment. These data were collected in counseling situations. We do not know if the same figures hold in other situations, but it seems entirely safe to conclude that this is a valuable measuring instrument for counselors.

Contradictory standards seem to be presented in the suggested "Tentative Norms" presented in the manual and the means of the "Validating Groups Selected by Counselors." The latter would appear to be better standards of evaluation, especially for the counselor.

J Psychol 9:227-36 Ap '40. Ruth A. Pedersen. "Validity of the Bell Adjustment Inventory When Applied to College Women." *

this study was undertaken to determine the validity of the Bell *Adjustment Inventory* when applied to college women * The inventory was administered to . . . 380 freshman women * these individuals were rated by the writer with regard to home, health, social, and emotional adjustment, the categories of the Bell *Adjustment Inventory*. The bases of these ratings were: (*a*) the autobiography written before entrance to college, and (*b*) the Dean's files of the personal records of the students during their freshman year. In addition to these, the Social Advisor rated each subject as to social adjustment during her freshman year, and the Women's Director of Physical Education rated the subjects as to health adjustment. * due to the fact that, in general, both the Dean's files and the autobiographies gave evidence only of maladjustments . . . individuals were rated only "maladjusted" or "no information" * Obviously, many individuals among the "no information" group must have been maladjusted, but for one reason or another, their condition had not received official recognition. To this extent, then, any differences found between the "maladjusted" and the "no information" groups on the Bell will be too small. * By way of summary, it may be said: (*a*) The Bell *Adjustment Inventory* is valid in measuring home adjustment as indicated in the applicant's autobiography, but it does not predict home disturbances which are of sufficient importance to be called to the attention of the Freshman Dean and recorded in the personal records for the freshman year. (*b*) A high score on the health section of the *Inventory* is indicative of poor health as indicated by the autobiography, the personal records, and by the ratings of the Director of Physical Education. Further, individuals rated maladjusted to health tend to have significantly higher scores on the emotional section of the *Inventory* than do other individuals. (*c*) Individuals rated socially maladjusted by the Social Advisor tend to have higher scores on the social section of the Bell than do other individuals. Subjects rated maladjusted socially by other criteria did not, on the whole, have higher scores than the remaining individuals, but the numbers were so small that the results are inconclusive. (*d*) There is no real difference between the emotional scores of individuals rated emotionally maladjusted and other individuals. (*e*) In interpreting and using these results, it should be kept in mind that any differences reported between the "maladjusted" and the "no information" groups have been attenuated due to the fact that there almost certainly are maladjusted individuals in the "no information" group.

For a review by Austin H. Turney, see 912. Although three reviews are listed under 912, only the review by Austin H. Turney is a review of Bell's Adjustment Inventory; *the other two are reviews of Bell's* School Inventory. *See also B30, B309, and B842.*

[1201]

Aspects of Personality. Grades 4-9; 1937-38; 1 form; $1.20 per 25; 15¢ per specimen set; nontimed (30-35) minutes; Rudolf Pintner, John J. Loftus, George Forlano, and Benjamin Alster; Yonkers, N. Y.: World Book Co.

REFERENCES

1 PINTNER, RUDOLF, AND FORLANO, GEORGE. "A Comparison of Methods of Item Selection for a Personality Test." *J Appl Psychol* 21:643-52 D '37.
2 PINTNER, RUDOLF, AND FORLANO, GEORGE. "Four Retests of a Personality Inventory." *J Ed Psychol* 29:93-100 F '33.
3 PINTNER, R., AND FORLANO, G. "Validation of Personality Tests by Outstanding Characteristics of Pupils." *J Ed Psychol* 30:25-32 Ja '39.
4 BROOKS, JAMES J. "A Technique for Determining the Degree of Behavior Maladjustment of Prison Inmates." *J Criminal Psychopathology* 1:339-53 Ap '40.

C. M. Louttit, Director of the Psychological Clinics and Associate Professor of Clinical Psychology, Indiana University. This personality schedule is one of the usual inventory type with the items adapted to the experiences of the school child and the vocabulary reduced to fourth grade level. The three sections of 35 items each refer to ascendance-submission, extroversion-introversion, and emotionality. This instrument is intended for group use by the classroom teacher. The authors suggest that the teacher give the test at the beginning of the school year "in order to acquaint the teacher as soon as possible with the personality make-up of her children." To the clinician this is unwise advice because it assumes that the inventory gives an accurate picture of the child's personality. This is a questionable assumption for any personality inventory, and in the present instance the manual gives no support for it. The validity depends entirely on factors intrinsic to the tests, e.g., selection of items from other instruments, the authors' judgment, an internal consistency of item correlations. Furthermore, the percentile norms given separately for grades 4-6 and for grades 7-9 are based upon an unrevealed number of cases.

Reliabilities by the split-half method for the subsections and for the whole scale by the retest method range from .52 to .92 with a median of about .75. Consideration of reliability, validity, and the norms gives no reason for believing that teachers can safely depend upon an individual's score to reveal his personality.

It must not be understood from what has been written that this scale has no value. Used as a clinical tool we have found it very satisfactory because we can interpret the score in the light of a case history more extensive than anything the teacher usually has at the beginning of a term. We have also found that the individual responses are frequently valuable clues, and an interview with the child based on his responses is often most revealing.

P. E. Vernon, Lecturer in Psychology, University of Glasgow. The construction of the test and establishment of norms appear to have been competently carried out, though the numbers and types of children upon whom the norms were based are not stated. The average reliability coefficient (split-half and retest) for any one part of the test is close to .72. Though this figure is lower than those claimed for many personality inventories, it is, in the reviewer's opinion, adequate. Very high reliability usually means an over-long test. Scoring of the test blanks by means of a stencil should be both convenient and accurate.

The instructions appear very suitable for grades 4-5, but perhaps rather babyish for grades 8-9. The sample items, which are to be read and explained by the teacher, are not very happily chosen. They seem likely to suggest to the children that they should answer according to social respectability, or to what they think the teacher wants. No precautions for reducing this only too common attitude are mentioned.

A commendable feature of the test is that many of the items were worded by children themselves during preliminary trials. Another good point is the inclusion of many "positive" or socially desirable statements in the first two parts. It is a pity that almost all the third part (apart from a few "jokers") consists of "negative" or unattractive statements, which tend to arouse unfavourable attitudes in the subjects. The test shows another advantage over multiple tests like Bernreuter's *Personality Inventory*, namely that one of the criteria for the inclusion of an item in any one part was that the item should not correlate highly with the other two parts. No data are given as to the intercorrelations of total scores on the three parts. They are likely to be substantial, although lower than in the Bernreuter inventory owing to the application of this criterion.

In most respects the test seems to be a distinct advance on other personality inventories for children. Nevertheless the reviewer feels that the directions to teachers, and other users of the test, should have been more cautiously worded, in view of the well-known lack of validity of such inventories. A recent article[3] provided a certain amount of evidence of validity, but the correspondence with the criterion (ratings) was far from high. From the directions teachers are likely to suppose that they can apply the test and measure children's introversion, etc. as easily as their arithmetical disability. They are not even advised to supplement the test findings by careful observations of behaviour. Some useful advice is given on treatment of extremely ascendant, submissive, introverted or unstable children. In view of the assumption that those who fall into these categories require guidance, it is interesting to note small but significant correlations between introversion, emotional instability, and intelligence. The manual does not make clear the direction of these correlations, but apparently the better pupils tend to have more "undesirable" personalities.

See also 913.

[1202]

[**Attitude Scales.**] Grades 7-16; 1934-36; each scale has space for indicating attitude toward five attitude variables; 2 forms; mimeographed; 1½¢ per test; 15¢ per specimen set of any one scale; 3(5) minutes per attitude variable; directed and edited by H. H. Remmers; Lafayette, Ind.: Division of Educational Reference, Purdue University.
a) SCALE FOR MEASURING ATTITUDE TOWARD ANY DISCIPLINARY PROCEDURE. 1936; V. R. Clouse.
b) SCALE FOR MEASURING ATTITUDE TOWARD ANY HOMEMAKING PROJECT. 1934; B. K. Vogel.
c) SCALE FOR MEASURING ATTITUDE TOWARD ANY INSTITUTION. 1934; T. B. Kelly.
d) SCALE FOR MEASURING ATTITUDE TOWARD ANY NATIONAL OR RACIAL GROUP. 1934; H. H. Grice.
e) SCALE FOR MEASURING ATTITUDE TOWARD ANY PRACTICE. 1934; H. W. Bues.
f) SCALE FOR MEASURING ATTITUDE TOWARD ANY SCHOOL SUBJECT. 1934; E. B. Silance.
g) SCALE FOR MEASURING ATTITUDE TOWARD ANY TEACHER. 1935; L. D. Hoshaw.
h) SCALE FOR MEASURING ATTITUDE TOWARD ANY VOCATION. 1934; H. E. Miller.
i) SCALE FOR MEASURING ATTITUDES TOWARD ANY PLAY. 1935; M. Dimmitt.

j) SCALE FOR MEASURING ATTITUDES TOWARD ANY PROPOSED SOCIAL ACTION. 1935; D. M. Thomas.
k) SCALE FOR MEASURING ATTITUDES TOWARD ANY SELECTION OF POETRY. 1935; J. E. Hadley.
l) SCALE FOR MEASURING INDIVIDUAL AND GROUP "MORALE." 1936; L. Whisler.

REFERENCES

1 LIKERT, RENSIS. *A Technique for the Measurement of Attitudes.* Columbia University, Archives of Psychology, No. 140. New York: the University, 1932. Pp. 55. Paper. Out of print.
2 REMMERS, H. H., EDITOR. *Studies in Attitudes:* A Contribution to Social-Psychological Research Methods. Bulletin of Purdue University, Vol. 53, No. 4; Studies in Higher Education, No. 26. Lafayette, Ind.: the University, 1934. $1.25. Paper.
3 REMMERS, H. H., AND SILANCE, ELLA BELLE. "Generalized Attitude Scales." *J Social Psychol* 5:298-312 Ag '34.
4 REMMERS, H. H. "Measuring Attitude toward the Job." *Occupations* 14:945-8 Je '36.
5 REMMERS, H. H., EDITOR. *Further Studies in Attitudes, Series II.* Bulletin of Purdue University, Vol. 37, No. 4; Studies in Higher Education, No. 31. Lafayette, Ind.: the University, December, 1936. $2.25. Paper.
6 WHISLER, LAURENCE AND REMMERS, H. H. "A Scale for Measuring Individual and Group Morale." *J Psychol* 4:161-5 Jl '37.
7 PATERSON, DONALD G.; SCHNEIDLER, GWENDOLEN G.; AND WILLIAMSON, EDMUND G. *Student Guidance Techniques,* pp. 202-4. New York: McGraw-Hill Book Co., Inc., 1938. Pp. xviii, 316. $3.00. (London: McGraw-Hill Publishing Co. Ltd., 18s.)
8 REMMERS, H. H., EDITOR. *Further Studies in Attitudes, Series III.* Purdue University, Division of Educational Reference, Studies in Higher Education, No. 34. Lafayette, Ind.: the University, September, 1938. Pp. 151. $1.50. Paper.
9 DUNLAP, JACK W., AND KROLL, ABRAHAM. "Observations on the Methodology in Attitude Scales." *J Social Psychol* 10:475-87 N '39.

W. D. Commins, Assistant Professor of Psychology, The Catholic University of America. Generalized attitude scales represent an attempt to reduce the amount of preliminary labor and the technical difficulties involved in measuring attitudes. There is perhaps no question about the desirability of this. In using a generalized attitude scale (as in the case of one of the present scales which measures attitude toward any school subject), we are supplied a list of general statements of an evaluative nature both "pro" and "con," and these may be checked off against Latin, English, algebra, etc., in turn. We are able to employ the same list of statements in relation to each subject, the scale value of which has been determined for us in advance. This would mark an immense saving of time over having to devise a special list applicable to only one attitude object at a time. The authors are fully alive to the difficulties involved in this approach and present, in the relevant literature (there is no summary manual however), a comprehensive attempt to answer most of the questions that might be raised. They have, in certain instances, correlated the results of their generalized attitude scales with some of the Thurstone specific scales and have found the correlation to be high. This is offered in evidence of validity, and may be accepted in partial evidence of such, because the present question has to do with the justification of generalized scales and not with all attitude scales as such. Another interesting approach to validity is offered in the comparison of a number of different social groups, the results of which are favorable to the generalized scales. Reliability as determined by correlating equivalent forms is in general high, with some coefficients around .90.

The generalized attitude scales are as a rule longer than special scales, containing forty items or more. This should make for greater reliability if the statements represent variations along the same continuum. One, however, receives the impression that this increase in the number of items introduces a greater variety of "axes," thus compounding the result instead of necessarily making it more differential. For example, such an abstractive intellectual opinion as "Some people like to do this, but more of them dislike it" may not be tapping the same mental source as the personal preference item, "I don't care much about doing this," both items contained in the same scale. In order to make a generalized scale broad enough, moreover, we are likely to include items not universally applicable to all objects supposedly coming under the same general category. Thus, if we were to apply the scale "for any social activity" to dancing or playing baseball, we should be faced with such statements as, "is a destroyer of liberty," "destroys legitimate competition," "is out of focus with the times." This is an extreme instance but it represents one of the difficulties to be surmounted in devising generalized scales, which may reduce the number of effective items and perhaps their scale value.

The statements are arranged in a regular descending order of scale values, a departure from the random order of most special scales. This, according to the authors, results in an immense saving in the time required for scoring. More evidence however should be obtained on whether this innovation effects any change in the reliability and validity of the scale. The present scales are certainly worth a trial in a practical way. One might predict general satisfaction from the use of the less ambiguous ones, such as the scales for measuring attitude toward any school subject or toward any vocation. Many of the others need to be intelligently evaluated, and perhaps also independently checked as to relevance of statement and scale value, at the time of use. As a research technique they offer definite promise of eventually extending the field of attitude measurement.

Theodore Newcomb, Psychology Department, Bennington College. Remmers' generalized attitudes scales, being a modification of the Thurstone technique of equal-appearing intervals in scale construction, must first be examined in the light of Thurstone's general method, and then in the light of Remmers' specific modifications. As to the former, both criticisms of a theoretical nature and empirical evidence are now available in sufficient quantities so that a brief summary may be made with reasonable assurance.

The split-half reliabilities of Thurstone scales have repeatedly been shown to be less than when the same items (or even part of them) have been scored by the Likert method.[1] (It may be objected that the Likert method involves the measurement of strength as well as direction of attitude. This is true, but in every investigation known to the reviewer, correlations of scores obtained by the two methods have reached or exceeded the split-half reliabilities of either measure.) The Thurstone scales are based upon an assumption never realized in practice, namely, that an acceptance of a given scale position involves acceptance of all scale positions less extreme and in the same direction from the neutral position. Their validity is open to doubt except when they are given to the academically sophisticated, by whom the initial judgments (i.e., during the construction of the scales) must almost necessarily be made. Finally, the Thurstone method of scale construction is extremely laborious. In short, briefer scales of greater reliability and probably of greater validity can be constructed by simpler methods.

Remmers has extended Thurstone's work in the direction of mass production, an attempt begun largely because of the laboriousness of applying the Thurstone method anew to every conceivable attitude continuum. Remmers and his collaborators prepared master scales by the same methods. The statements were so worded that they could be applied to any institution, any defined group, any practice, any occupation, etc.—specific groups, occupations, etc., being filled in as the experimenter desires.

Their split-half reliability coefficients, when filled out for various specific attitudes, were almost or quite as satisfactory as those for comparable Thurstone scales; their reliability was somewhat increased, however, by the advantage of being somewhat longer than the Thurstone scales. Scores on those generalized scales, moreover, correlate highly in general with those for Thurstone scales on similar attitudes. The advantages are obvious: time-saving in construction, and ready applicability for a new purpose at a moment's notice. Remmers has also succeeded in using clear and simple language in his scaled statements—though this is not an advantage inherent in the method.

The generalized scales are subject to one disadvantage, however, which is inherent in the method. This is the danger of obtaining responses, not to the actual content of the issue in question, but to the symbol filled in at the top of the page. It has been experimentally demonstrated by others that many individuals whose reaction to such terms as "socialism" and "fascism" is consistently negative, actually accept a large part of what is commonly understood by those terms. The point is not simply that the generalized scales measure stereotyped attitudes evoked by symbols rather than the "true" issues involved, but rather that scores on the generalized scales are not truly comparable—each score represents the subject's reactions to whatever content the symbol evokes for him, whereas a scale specifically designed to measure a given set of issues can (though still dependent, of course, on meanings individually assigned to words) at least avoid the constant error which runs through all the items of the generalized scale.

If the Thurstone technique were clearly the best method of attitude measurement, the advantages of the generalized scale would, under some circumstances, outweigh the disadvantages. But the contrary seems pretty clearly demonstrated, and thus, in this reviewer's opinion, the disadvantages far outweigh the advantages. In view of the simplicity, reliability, and validity of attitude scales constructed by other methods, and in view of the fact that attitudes toward Japanese as a group (for example), or the medical profession as an occupation, do involve specific as well as general considerations, there seems to be no good reason why a scale should not be specifically constructed for any attitude continuum which it seems worth while to measure, rather than resorting to generalized scales.

For a review by Stephen M. Corey, see 897. See also B215, B216, and B1050.

[1203]

[Attitude Scales for Measuring the Influence of the Work Relief Program.] College students and adults; 1940; 1 form, 3 scales; 50¢ per 25; 10¢ per specimen set; nontimed (10-15) minutes; E. D. Hinckley; Gainsville, Fla.: University of Florida Press.
a) SCALE 1, ATTITUDE TOWARD WORK RELIEF AS A SOLUTION TO THE FINANCIAL DEPRESSION.
b) SCALE 2, ATTITUDE TOWARD EARNING A LIVING.
c) SCALE 3, ATTITUDE TOWARD RECEIVING RELIEF.

REFERENCES

1 HINCKLEY, ELMER DUMOND, AND HINCKLEY, MARTHA BROWN. "Attitude Scales for Measuring the Influence of the Work Relief Program." *J Psychol* 8:115-24 Jl '39.

[1204]

Attitudes Toward Child Behavior. Parents and others; 1936; 1 form; $1 per 100; 10¢ per specimen set; nontimed (15) minutes; Ralph M. Stogdill and Henry H. Goddard; Columbus, Ohio: Ralph M. Stogdill, 2280 W. Broad St.

REFERENCES

1 STOGDILL, RALPH M. *The Measurement of Attitudes toward Children.* Unpublished doctor's thesis, Ohio State University, 1934. Pp. 150
2 STOGDILL, RALPH M. "The Measurement of Attitudes toward Parental Control and the Social Adjustments of Children." *J Appl Psychol* 20:359-67 Je '36.

[1205]

Attitudes Toward Parental Control of Children. Parents and others; 1936; 1 form; $1 per 100; 10¢ per specimen set; nontimed (15) minutes; Ralph M. Stogdill and Henry H. Goddard; Columbus, Ohio: Ralph M. Stogdill, 2280 W. Broad St.

REFERENCES

1 STOGDILL, RALPH M. *The Measurement of Attitudes toward Children.* Unpublished doctor's thesis, Ohio State University, 1934. Pp. 150.
2 STOGDILL, RALPH M. "The Measurement of Attitudes toward Parental Control and the Social Adjustments of Children." *J Appl Psychol* 20:359-67 Je '36.

[1206]

Baxter Group Test of Child Personality. Ages 4 through grade 8; 1935; 1 form; 4¢ per test; 25¢ per manual; nontimed (30-40) minutes; Edna Dorothy Baxter; Englewood, Colo.: the Author, Englewood Public Schools.

REFERENCES

1 BAXTER, EDNA DOROTHY. "The Baxter Child Personality Test." *J Appl Psychol* 21:410-30 Ag '37.

[1207]

Baxter Individual Tests of Child Personality. Children ages 4-13 and their mothers; 1935; 1 form; individual; 7¢ per test; 25¢ per manual; nontimed (40-70) minutes; Edna Dorothy Baxter; Englewood, Colo.: the Author, Englewood Public Schools.

REFERENCES

1 BAXTER, EDNA DOROTHY. "The Baxter Child Personality Test." *J Appl Psychol* 21:410-30 Ag '37.

[1208]

Behavior Cards: A Test-Interview for Delinquent Children. Delinquents having a reading grade score of 4.5 or higher; 1940; individual; 1 form; $2.25 per testing outfit; nontimed (20-40) minutes; Ralph M. Stogdill; Columbus, Ohio: the Author, 2280 W. Broad St.

REFERENCES

1 PUSKIN, RUTH. *The Validation of a Test-Interview for Delinquent Boys.* Unpublished master's thesis, Ohio State University, 1938.
2 STOGDILL, RALPH M. "A Test-Interview for Delinquent Children." *J Appl Psychol* 24:325-33 Je '40.

[1209]

Behavior Maturity Blank. Grades 7-16 and adults; 1939; 1 form; $6 per 100; 10¢ per specimen set; nontimed (30) minutes; Walther Joël; Los Angeles, Calif.: Gutenberg Press.

REFERENCES

1 JOËL, WALTHER. " 'Behavior Maturity' of Children of Nursery School Age." *Child Development* 7:189-99 S '36.
2 RICHARDS, T. W. "Note on the Joël Scale of 'Behavior Maturity.' " *J Genetic Psychol* 56:215-8 Mr '40.

[1210]

Behavior Maturity Rating Scale for Nursery School Children. Ages 1½ to 6; 1935; 1 form; $6 per 100; 10¢ per specimen set; (20-30) minutes; Walther Joël and Janet Joël; Los Angeles, Calif.: Walther Joël, Los Angeles City College.

[1211]

Beliefs About School Life: Test 4.6. Grades 7-12; 1940; 1 form; 5¢ per test; 1¢ per machine-scorable answer sheet; 5¢ per interpretation guide; $1 per set of stencils for machine scoring; nontimed (40) minutes; Chicago, Ill.: Evaluation in the Eight Year Study, Progressive Education Association.

[1212]

C-R Opinionaire. Grades 11-16 and adults; 1935; 2 forms; $1.25 per 25 double-form booklets; 75¢ per single-form booklets; 25¢ per specimen set; (20) minutes; Theodore F. Lentz and colleagues; St. Louis, Mo.: Character Research Institute, Washington University.

REFERENCES

1 LENTZ, THEODORE F., JR. "Utilizing Opinion for Character Measurement." *J Social Psychol* 1:536-42 N '30.
2 HANDY, UVAN, AND LENTZ, THEODORE F. "Item Value and Test Reliability." *J Ed Psychol* 25:703-8 D '34.
3 LENTZ, THEODORE F., JR. "Reliability of Opinionaire Technique Studied Intensively by the Retest Method." *J Social Psychol* 5:338-64 Ag '34.
4 LENTZ, THEODORE F. "Generality and Specificity of Conservatism-Radicalism." *J Ed Psychol* 29:540-6 O '38.
5 LENTZ, THEODORE F. "Personage Admiration and Other Correlates of Conservatism-Radicalism." *J Social Psychol* 10:81-93 F '39.

Goodwin Watson, Professor of Education, Columbia University. This questionnaire is a new arrangement of Lentz's items, most of which were previously used in Forms H and I, and all of which were included in Forms E and F. The characteristic measured is called "conservatism-radicalism" and means, in this instance, general tendency to oppose or to welcome cultural change. The items cover a wide range including possibility of cat meat diet, calendar reform, compulsory cremation, new inventions, and new religions. The trait is thus not identical with the contemporary political parties and doctrines commonly called "conservative" or "radical."

In his article on "generality and specificity of conservatism-radicalism" Lentz[4] reported a classification of items under headings of education, religion, government, sex, non-social, and general. Inter-correlations averaged .45 and the self-correlation within any one section .59, indicating almost as much variation in answers within any such classification, as from one to another. No factor analysis was made. On the basis of previous use of the items Lentz predicts a correlation of about .84 between Form J and Form K. Students who rated themselves as conservatives or median, who preferred Hoover to Smith, who had not changed their church affiliation and who were enrolled in small denominational colleges made relatively high scores.

A later study[5] shows "conservatives" favorable toward conventions, the church, moral prudishness, and the status quo. The test thus brings out agreement with the culture syndrome of what Mencken used to call the "Bible belt." The test does not distinguish between persons who accept these ideas because they have had no contact with any others, and those who have some bias toward the traditional.

There are test items (e.g., one concerning the work of Billy Sunday) which seem considerably outdated.

Lentz wisely suggests that the best use of the instrument is tentative experimentation by research experts, or as a springboard for group discussion.

For a review by H. H. Remmers, see 899.

[1213]

California Test of Personality: A Profile of Personal and Social Adjustment. Grades 4-9, 9-14; 1939; 1 form, 2 levels; $1 per 25; 1½¢ per machine-scorable answer sheet; 25¢ per specimen set of any one level; nontimed (45) minutes; Ernest W. Tiegs, Willis W. Clark, and Louis P. Thorpe; Los Angeles, Calif.: California Test Bureau.
a) ELEMENTARY SERIES. Grades 4-9.
b) SECONDARY SERIES. Grades 9-14.

Raymond B. Cattell, G. Stanley Hall Professor of Genetic Psychology, Clark University. These tests are in questionnaire form requiring "yes" or "no" answers. As far as the mechanics of test design are concerned these tests are admirably worked out. The psychometrist is supplied with efficient scoring keys, with will-spaced percentile norms, with probable errors and standard deviations, and with consistency coefficients corrected by the Spearman-Brown prophecy formula.

About validity, however, the handbook becomes persuasively vague. The detailed intention of the authors is, again, good. It is high time that other questionnaire designers should adopt, for example, their plan of disguising the real point of each question item. But it is with regard to the whole plan that one looks in vain for some substantiating research.

The total score is divided into two main parts, Self Adjustment and Social Adjustment. The first part, Self Adjustment, is divided into the following subdivisions: (a) Self-reliance, (b) Sense of Personal Worth, (c) Sense of Personal Freedom, (d) Feeling of Belonging, (e) Withdrawal Tendencies, and (f) Nervous Symptoms. The second part, Social Adjustment, is subdivided as follows: (a) Social Standards, (b) Social Skills, (c) Anti-social Tendencies, (d) Family Relations, (e) School Relations, and (f) Community Relations.

The broad bipartite division has some justification in the well-known clinical classification into personality and behavior disorders, but otherwise it is merely logical. A vein of maladjustment will cut right across these strata, manifesting itself now in personality disorders, now in antisocial behavior.

Moreover, what is this "Self Adjustment"? The notion of adjustment between an individual and his environment is a standard reference frame for analysis of personality; but is it possible to speak of an adjustment of the self to the self? It is possible to speak of adjustment between the ego and the id or the super-ego, or of conflict between some drive and the self-regarding sentiment. If "Self Adjustment" refers to this important internal aspect of adjustment, why then these particular six categories rather than many others which on clinical grounds might be considered equally important? And why is "Withdrawal Tendency" not among the "Social Adjustments"?

Seeking a research basis for such an ambitious application as a "Test of Personality" and especially for the reasoning behind the seemingly arbitrary and incomplete subdivisions, one encounters a small paragraph saying that factor analysis studies "have been in progress for some months." This sounds very promising, but "some months" are scarcely adequate for the whole factor analysis of personality, especially when they do not precede the publication of the test. Finally, we are told that the factor groupings which are emerging do not correspond with "the concepts which abound in the literature on personality and with which teachers are familiar," so that it is undesirable to regroup the items. Is it more important that psychology should be true or that it should avoid transcending the ideas of school teachers? This statement illuminates what is perhaps the real cause of applied psychology remaining at such a low technical level of efficiency.

With sublime indifference to consistency, the handbook follows this statement that the teacher is not trained to understand the complexities of scientific psychology, with some detailed "Suggestions for Treatment" on the basis of the personality analysis. Psychotherapy and remedial treatment are explained to the novice in five pages. To ponder on what may happen to children "treated" by a teacher with the aid of the handbook and the test profile is something of a nightmare. True, the writers remind the reader of the "wholeness" of the adjusting organism; but this is more in the mystical sense of gestalt and in defiance of their own principles of analysis into independent measurements, than with respect to the relativity of symptoms to a purposive whole, as understood by the clinician. If one were making an analysis into syndromes and symptom complexes with a view to remedial treatment it is very doubtful if one would adopt the subdivisions made here, in preference to the main neurotic and problem behavior patterns.

In so far as the questionnaire system can be used with children, and to the extent that a merely logically compartmentalised set of measurements can be useful in making decisions about personality maladjustment, this "test" has some value in routine work. In research, where group average differences in specific traits or social adjustments are being investigated, its value is more definite. After a factor analysis, and the treatment of children's responses not as answers to the questions but as symptomatic responses the meaning of which is to be determined, the test would have great value.

Incidentally, for any purpose, the value of the test is at present impaired by printing on the booklet, in full view of the child filling in the title page, a description of the adjustments in which he is being tested and an indication as to which set of questions determines the score on each.

Percival M. Symonds, Professor of Education, Columbia University. [Review of the Secondary Series.] The *California Test of Personality* appears to be a carefully worked out set of questions designed to reveal the quality of the individual's adjustments. Questions are divided into groups, one dealing with personal adjustment, the other with social adjustment, and each group is divided into six subsections of fifteen questions each. According to the manual of directions, the questions have been very carefully selected by reference to preceding studies and by actual item analysis with the present material. The scoring is objective and a helpful manual of directions accompanies the test.

A questionnaire of this kind furnishes teachers with worthy goals for personality development.

One question which occurs to the reviewer is whether the separate sections of which there are twelve in all can be considered sufficiently reliable to warrant their being scored separately. In the manual, reliability of the separate subsections is reported to range between .60 and .87 and these reliabilities are said to be "sufficiently high to locate more restricted areas of personality difficulty." The question is whether these reliabilities are high enough to do so for individuals.

Still more fundamental query concerns the significance of this questionnaire as a measure of adjustment. It is well known that adjustment is a term which has a variety of meanings. By asking pupils to answer questions about themselves one is securing evidence of only one kind of adjustment, namely the pupil's own attitudes. Adjustment may also mean the reputation that a person has with others, etc. Anyone using this questionnaire should recognize that it is perhaps more limited in its implications than its name, *Test of Personality*, would indicate.

The reviewer would question Part IX (pp. 6-12) in the manual which gives directions for interpreting profiles and guiding adjustment activities. It is his belief that it would be extremely dangerous to believe that simple questions of this kind would constitute a single diagnosis of a pupil's difficulties to serve as a basis for remedial treatment. One might ask whether questions which are asked and answered as part of a school requirement can be expected to reveal underlying trends which may be apparently unconscious in the personality. It is also open to question whether one should attempt to plan a program of treatment without knowing something about the developmental history and the family background of the pupil. This manual would imply that one deals in a rather uniform and stereotyped way with each problem without making inquiry as to the specific background factors which may have induced a given child to select this particular form of behavior or attitude as a way of meeting his frustration. These criticisms would apply with equal force to all personality inventories of this general type.

The *California Test of Personality* would appear to be one of the most carefully prepared questionnaires of this type.

P. E. Vernon, Lecturer in Psychology, University of Glasgow. Great masses of rather woolly verbiage are being published nowadays under the name of mental hygiene, and it seems unfortunate that many professional psychologists encourage and contribute to it. Certainly the ideal of helping teachers to understand their pupils' personalities, which presumably inspired this test, is a very worthy one, but equally certainly personality inventories have not yet been proved to give trustworthy information even to trained psychologists and psychiatrists, much less to untrained amateurs.

The manuals of these tests provide plenty of advice about treatment of pupils whose abnormalities the tests are said to diagnose, but contain a minimum of information about the technique of construction and standardization. In the Elementary Form the reliabilities of the total self- and social-adjustment scores, and the numbers of cases from whom the norms were derived, seem quite adequate. In the Secondary Form the reliabilities are even higher, but the numbers which provided the norms are not stated. Only one set of norms is given for each form, though it seems hardly credible that there should be no significant changes in average scores between 10 and 15, and between 15 and 20 years. One would also like to know the reliabilities of the twelve component parts and their intercorrelations before one can be sure that these components are rea-

sonably self-consistent and distinct from one another. Instead one is told that: "Some of the items of this profile touch relatively sensitive personal and social areas, and such student attitudes may change in a relatively short time," and that: "The obtained correlations among the components emphasize the unity or 'wholeness' of normal individuals." Such statements are not reassuring to psychologists, though they may impress teachers and other amateur testers. If the intercorrelations are high (relative to the reliabilities) this may be due more to halo effect than to "wholeness" of personality.

Wording and instructions appear satisfactory in the Elementary Form, and are suitable for younger pupils, but obviously most unsuitable for college students and adults, in the Secondary Form (e.g., "Are you allowed enough time to play and have a good time?"). It would have been better if, in certain sections, some of the items had been stated in the opposite direction, i.e., so as to suggest socially desirable rather than uniformly undesirable qualities. However, a good attempt has been made to disguise many of the items, so as to reduce their unattractiveness. The scoring will be somewhat lengthy (unless machine-scoring answer sheets are used), and will require careful checking. Since there are only twelve items for measuring each of the separate components—fifteen in the Secondary Form—the ranges of scores are small. The average interquartile range for any one component is only about 4. No evidence whatsoever is given of any correspondence between a pupil's scores and his actual behavior, or other people's impressions of his behavior.

Bus Ed World 20:826 My '40. Marion M. Lamb. It is a satisfaction to find in the California Test of Personality suggestions for curing personality ills as well as for identifying them. * The esoteric terms used by experts in tests and measurements are present for those who want them, but even to the nonexpert the California Test of Personality offers hope for improvement of the maladjusted. *

[1214]

Case Inventory, Third Edition. Grades 5-12; 1935-36; 2 forms; $2.65 per 25; 30¢ per specimen set; nontimed (25-35) minutes; J. B. Maller; New York: Bureau of Publications, Teachers College, Columbia University.

REFERENCES

1 HARRIS, D. B., AND DABELSTEIN, D. H. "A Study of the Maller and Boynton Personality Inventories." *J Ed Psychol* 29:279-86 Ap '38.

Harold E. Jones, Director of the Institute of Child Welfare and Professor of Psychology, The University of California. This personality schedule yields four subscores which are described as measuring (*a*) emotionalized response patterns, (*b*) adjustment, (*c*) honesty, and (*d*) ethical judgment and integration.

Test 1 consists of 50 key words with a choice of associations which are scored as either "rational" or "irrational." Test 2 consists of 50 self-description inventory items selected from Maller's *Character Sketches,* and referring to specific aspects of personal and social adjustment. Test 3 is an overstatement test disguised under the heading "What do you know about sports and hobbies?" Test 4 consists of 9 dual choice discrimination items, regarded as involving ethical judgment, and providing also a measure of integration between the subject's ethical judgment and his own code of behavior.

Two similar forms are available. The individual tests are reported as having a reliability of .90 or above, when odd-even items are correlated for both forms; no statement is made in the manual as to the sample used in the reliability study.

Validity was examined for each test (with the exception of Test 3) by the method of extreme groups, comparing "normals" with children on probation and delinquents. Although there is no statement as to the minimal degree of discrimination which was regarded as acceptable, all of the items included were said to be "valid." It is, of course, possible that items selected to differentiate normals and delinquents may be of restricted value for individual guidance within a relatively normal sample. In a Minnesota testing program a considerable overlapping was found between a normal and a "problem" group, the difference between the averages being in the expected direction but amounting to only about one-half the standard deviation of the normal group. At each age girls appear to be better adjusted than boys, the sex difference being about half as great as the difference between normal and "problem" boys. There is also an apparent age difference, with an improvement in the scores from age 10 to 16.

No attempt has been made to analyze validity in correlational terms, nor to allow for possible group differentials in intelligence, social status, etc. It would also be desirable to present validity data for the subscores as well as for the total scores, particularly in view of the fact that the author considers the individual tests to have greater meaning than the composite.

MERITS OF THE INVENTORY. It is conveniently organized, easy to administer, and in a form which is acceptable to subjects over a wide age range (from grade 4 or 5 to adults). In addition to the four tests, space is provided on the schedule for the recording of data concerning socio-economic background, recreational interests, wishes, fears, and worries.

PRINCIPAL DEFECT. Teachers or guidance workers who are unfamiliar with the sources of error in inventory techniques may attempt to use a schedule such as this for a direct and authoritative diagnosis of personality characteristics. To guard against unwise applications of the test, the manual of directions should include a specific discussion of its limitations.

E. G. Williamson, Coordinator of Student Personnel Services and Associate Professor of Psychology, The University of Minnesota. This inventory consists of four parts: (*a*) Controlled association test, two possible word associations (rational and irrational) with 50 stimulus words. Stereotypy of response is avoided by alternating the positions of the rational and irrational words. The rationality-irrationality score is the number of rational responses. (*b*) Adjustment test, 50 self-description questions involving personal and social adjustments. The adjustment score is the number of normal responses. (*c*) Self-scoring test, 15 questions providing a measure of honesty in classroom situations. The individual's trustworthiness is tested by his willingness to take credit for knowledge which he does not possess. The number of such items for which he has admitted ignorance multiplied by two is his score. (*d*) Ethical judgment test, 9 questions providing for a self-evaluation response in terms of knowledge of ethical standards. This part really yields two scores: *E*, the number of "correct" ethical discriminations; and *I*, the number of times the individual has indicated that he would act according to the ethical pattern. To get the total score for this part, the sum of E and I is multiplied by 2.

The third edition of the inventory includes a section on the student's socio-economic background, interests, preferences, forms of recreation, type of preferred radio and moving picture programs, minor physical complaints and occupational and educational plans.

The inventory is virtually self-administering, especially on the higher levels. In view of the fact that no validity coefficients are presented for the gross total score, the doubling of the part S and E scores seems unnecessary. Otherwise, the method of scoring is extremely simple.

The odd-even reliabilities for the four parts and the total score are: .9203, .9618, .9506, .9909, and .9365, respectively. But the age level of the group upon which these reliabilities were determined is not indicated.

Each question has been selected from the author's earlier forms and has been experimentally validated in several investigations. Items for the association test were selected from a list of 200 used to differentiate 108 patients in psychiatric clinics, an equated group of normal adults, 200 pupils in the New York Probationary Schools and an equated group of normal children.

Items for the adjustment test were selected from a list used to differentiate "well adjusted" children and adults from those exhibiting serious abnormalities. The author states that the "undesirable responses involve extreme introversion, lack of self-control, feeling of inadequacy and inferiority, and symptoms of psycho-neurotic tendencies."

The honesty test was constructed from an earlier test of sports and hobbies and supposedly measures "trustworthiness." The student's "acceptance of credit for these difficult items is evidence of over-statement. The validity of the measure may be considered as self-evident."

The ethical judgment test of 9 items was validated in terms of the extent to which each of a larger number of questions differentiated between delinquents, pupils in probation schools, and normal groups.

Incomplete norms, based upon the second edition, are presented with a table of revised norms and percentiles being promised for the future. The norms presented are based upon a study of 5214 pupils in Minnesota schools. These norms are very inadequate for interpretation of the test. For example, the means of total scores are presented for boys and girls at various age levels, but when deciles are presented, it is for all age groups combined. Since it is the part scores for which the validity is claimed, norms for them would be more useful.

The author does not refer in his manual to research studies reporting in detail his validating experiments. Stott reports an extensive investigation of 695 farm youth, 520 city youth, and 640 town youth in which the *Case Inventory* was used, with other tests, to determine what differences, if any, were, to be found among these three groups. On the adjustment test the urban group ranked, in average score, significantly above the town and farm groups. On the association test, the urban group was, on the average, significantly above the other two groups, the latter two having approximately equal mean scores. On the ethical judgment test, the town youth approximated the city youth in mean score and both groups exceeded the mean score of the farm group. The mean scores of the three groups were approximately the same on the honesty test.

The inventory has merit in that it is not completely dependent upon the subject's frank self-analysis. But the total score cannot be given serious consideration until more evidence is provided for its validity. The nature of the items is such as to raise some question as to its applicability for mature students. This is particularly true of the trustworthiness test. It is possible that more sophisticated subjects will "see through" the device. Studies using college freshmen and adults of various ages are mentioned, but neither data nor references to the literature are cited.

The inventory should be valuable for research studies of groups of cases and should provide valuable, though tentative, leads in the counseling of individuals.

For a review by Richard Ledgerwood, see 916.

[1215]

Character and Personality Rating Scale. 1934; 1 form, separate scales for boys and girls; $2.10 per 100 blanks; 25¢ per specimen set; J. B. Maller; New York: Bureau of Publications, Teachers College, Columbia University.

Bessie Lee Gambrill, Associate Professor of Elementary Education, Yale University. The scale includes fifty items, twenty-five under each of two general categories: I, Aspects of Character; II, Aspects of Personality. The first group includes attitudes, social adjustments and "fundamental habits of character," the summation of whose ratings the author believes will approximate an index of the totality of character. Under the second category, are items of emotional adjustment, "fundamental aspects of personality," and dominant forms of interest. Record blanks for the rating of twenty-five individuals are provided, with different colored cards for boys and girls.

Careful examination of the two divisions of the scale fails to reveal a consistent theory of character and personality underlying the selection of many of the items and their classification under the two major categories. For example, on what basis is a student's liking for school and his regard for teachers the first two items under character? Information as to these attitudes is desirable as a point of departure for further study—of pupil and school situation—but is it valid for rating character? Might a high rating in some situations merely indicate docility, or an uncritical mind? Again, a question arises as to why foresight, sense of humor, and responsiveness are classified under character, while intellectual interest, neatness, and social mindedness are grouped under personality. Since the sums of the ratings on each of the two parts of the scale are to be recorded as character rating and personality rating, such questions as these seriously affect the validity of the scale. The purpose of the scale is not defined further than the statement "intended primarily for classroom use, but may be found of value in work with young people's clubs or groups of employees." Obviously, a low rating on character or personality for any of these purposes, without interpretation of total scores in terms of the items of the scale itself, and without great care in safeguarding such criteria of validity as common understanding of separate scale items by all judges, opportunity and ability to secure reliable evidence on each item by the judges, etc., may lead to grave injustice.

The reliability of the scale was determined by the re-rating of 381 pupils in grades 7 and 8 by their respective teachers after an interval of six weeks, the correlation between the two sets of total scores being .90. There is no information on the more important question of consistency of judgment on the individual items of the scale. Without this knowledge it is possible that the high correlation results from many shifts on single items which tend to balance each other. No evidence is offered on agreement of different judges. To guard against unreliability resulting from lack of opportunity to observe certain characteristics, raters are properly advised to omit these items. In the following paragraph, however, it is recommended that when comparison with norms is desired such items be given the intermediate rating of 2. This seems to recommend provision for statistical facilitation at the expense of reliability of judgment.

Norms for the test in terms of distribution of total scores of 1,219 junior high school pupils of New York City are given. In view of the facts: that this is a three-step scale; that the rating instructions recommend that in a normal group about one-fourth of the group be rated respectively 1 and 3 and the remaining fifty per cent be marked 2; that a "normal group" for the qualities included in this scale has not been defined; that no information is given about the social-intellectual status of the group on which the standardization is based, use of the norms would be misleading. While the author states that the main value of the scale is for inter-group comparison, he is not emphatic in discouraging its use for group comparisons.

[1216]

Concept Formation Test. Normal and schizophrenic adults; 1940; 1 form; $15.50 per testing outfit (No. 36118); Jacob Kasanin and Eugenia Hanfmann; Chicago, Ill.: C. H. Stoelting Co.

REFERENCES

1 KASANIN, JACOB, AND HANFMANN, EUGENIA. "An Experimental Study of Concept Formation in Schizophrenia: I. Quantitative Analysis of Results." *Am J Psychiatry* 95:35-52 Jl '38.

[1217]

Cowan Adolescent Personality Schedule: Revision No. 2. Ages 12-18; 1935-37; 1 form; $2 per 25; 50¢ per specimen set; nontimed (10-30) minutes; Edwina A. Cowan; Wichita, Kan.: Wichita Child Research Laboratory.

REFERENCES

1 COWAN, EDWINA ABBOTT; McCLELLAN, MERNERVA CHURCH; PRATT, BERTHA M.; AND SKAER, MAE. "An Adolescent Personality Schedule." *Child Development* 6:77-87 Mr '35.
2 BRIGDEN, ROBERT L. "A Diagnostic Adolescent Personality Schedule," pp. 38-9. In *Proceedings, Second Biennial Meeting*. Society for Research and Child Development. Washington, D. C.: National Research Council, 1936.
3 BRIGDEN, R. L. "The Cowan Adolescent Personality Schedule: Its Function in Psychological Diagnosis." *Am J Med Jurisprud* 2:97-9 F '39.

Goodwin Watson, Professor of Education, Columbia University. This questionnaire on symptoms of maladjustment, to be answered by pupils in junior or senior high school, has developed refinements and improvements at every point except the fundamental ones. "Holy Gee!" said one thirteen-year-old boy, "I'm going to be careful how I answer this test!" It remains true of the Cowan schedule, as of its predecessors (Woodworth, Woodworth-Matthews, Thurstone, Colgate, Bernreuter, Bell, Symonds, Pinter, *et al.*), that a subject can answer it to give any impression that he may deem it advantageous to present. The directions take no account whatever of this basic limitation. Despite criticisms on this point in the literature for a decade or more, the authors fail to suggest that the validity of the test is a function of the rapport between examiner and adolescent. The "Instructions to be read or recited to the subject" seem to be based on the false assumption that no genuine relationship is necessary to persuade an adolescent to bare his soul with check marks.

Even granted the best will in the world, youngsters do not always mean what the author meant by his question. One boy read "People have told me 'scary' things," and checked "Yes" which is interpreted as a fear, but the boy hadn't been in the least disturbed by horror-tales which, as a matter of fact, he enjoys. Another answered "Yes" to "Have you ever been told that you were stupid?" because he and the other fellows often said such things in fun. This went mechanically into the profile as an inferiority score, although the boy usually rated tops in intellectual matters, and was well enough aware of it. One girl answered "Yes" to a feeling of smothering; what she meant was that sometimes it was hard to breathe when her nose was stopped up by a cold.

There are questions in the schedule which seem unnecessarily stupid. To answer a question mark to "I have a lot of friends" is supposed to show "childish immaturity." To answer a question mark to "I believe that most people are real good," gets one into the column "neurotic, keyed up emotionally, and frustrated." To answer that saying your prayers make you feel better is scored good adjustment—to answer "No" is interpreted as "avoids

people and problems." A little hard on children not reared to orthodoxy!

One of the most untenable assumptions is that questions have the same value for boys and girls, in every culture group, and over the age range from 12 to 20. The statement "I like to fight" for example, is scored alike for both sexes, all ages, and every type of community atmosphere. Not having definite plans about what to do after finishing school is rated "irresponsibility" for the twelve-year-old in the same degree as for the boy of nineteen or twenty.

The instrument has the advantage of yielding nine scores (fear, family emotion, family authority, inferiority, nonfamily authority, responsibility, escapes, neurotic, and compensation) along lines that facilitate diagnosis. An ingenious scoring method, with a wire gadget, enables one quickly to strike an average and to observe "peaks" and "valleys." An "interpretation" of various combinations of peaks and valleys is furnished—complete almost to the point of being ridiculous. For example, "hypothyroid?" is suggested for an individual who has shown considerable "irresponsibility" by answering with a question mark such ambiguous queries as "Are you usually to blame for your mistakes?" and "Can you persuade other boys and girls to do things for you that you dislike to do yourself?"

The Cowan schedule is one more example of the delight of some psychologists in any kind of probe which purports to give insight into others by merely mechanical means, obviating the necessity for personal rapport, keen observation, broad experience, and common sense.

For a review by Harold E. Jones, see 918.

[1218]
Environment Inventory for College and University Students. 1938; 1 form; 5¢ per copy; sample copy free; Robert H. Morrison and M. Ernest Townsend; St. Louis, Mo.: Webster Publishing Co.

REFERENCES

1 TOWNSEND, M. E. "Environment Inventory in College Personnel Work," pp. 111-4. In *Research on the Foundations of American Education.* National Education Association, American Education Research Association, Official Report of the 1939 Meeting, Cleveland, Ohio, February 25-March 1, 1939. Washington, D. C.: the Association, 1939. Pp. 215. $1.50. Paper.

E. G. Williamson, Coordinator of Student Personnel Services and Associate Professor of Psychology, The University of Minnesota. This 15-page inventory is a special case-history form consisting of questions organized in the form of a questionnaire. On the basis of their counseling experiences, the authors selected items of information which they judged necessary for the work of the counselor. The inventory is to be filled out by the student before he is interviewed or during his interview with the counselor. It provides a convenient summary of important case data as reported by the student.

In addition to the usual identifying items (name, age, sex, etc.) the inventory includes questions on the following topics: usual ways of traveling to and from college; regular place of eating (e.g., home, campus, cafeteria, etc.); extent and ways of self-support and part-time employment; conditions and place of studying for each day of the week; name and extent of participation in extracurricular activities; educational and occupational plans; living, financial, and study conditions in the home; cultural aspects of the home and kind of furnishings of the home; education and occupation of parents; and 21 questions sampling the student's attitudes toward a number of socio-economic-political issues and problems.

A number of such inventories or case-history forms are now available and widely used. They are convenient methods of collecting directly from the student certain information necessary to effective counseling. To a certain extent the use of such an instrument makes unnecessary the long and tedious interview method of case history taking used by the doctor and the social worker. But there are some serious limitations in the use of such an inventory. The many unique and highly individual phases of each student's experiences and problems may be masked by the form of the general questions and statements. Such detailed and supplementary information must be collected in the personal interview. Secondly, it must be remembered by the counselor that such an inventory properly filled out constitutes but one part of a total and comprehensive case history. Many other sources of data must be tapped to round out the case history. Thirdly, the student's answers to questions in such an inventory as this one must be checked or verified. The student's reports cannot be accepted at face value unless they have been substantiated. This may be done incompletely in the personal interview but in many cases the counselor should seek verification from other counselors, parents, teachers and other individuals. When used with these limitations in mind, such an inventory can prove to be invaluable in providing the counselor with important information in advance of the interview, thereby making easier the task of establishing rapport and understanding and may also reduce to a minimum the routine collecting of information by the question and answer technique.

This particular inventory includes very important questions, well-phrased to elicit proper answers. It has the virtue of not requiring that the student attempt, through the dubious process of self-analysis, to diagnose his own capabilities and problems. Rather the student is asked to summarize for the counselor some of the important data by means of which the counselor and the student together may arrive at such an understanding of the latter's problems.

[1219]

Experience Variables Record: A Clinical Revision. College and adults; 1928-38; 1 form; individual; reprinted from the February 1938 issue of *Psychiatry*; 10¢ per copy; Joseph Chassell; Towson, Md.: Sheppard and Enoch Pratt Hospital.

REFERENCES

1 CHASSELL, J. O. *The Experience Variables*: A Study of the Variable Factors in Experience Contributing to the Formation of Personality. Bennington, Vt.: the Author, Bennington College, 1928. Pp. 42. $0.75. Paper.
2 CHASSELL, JOSEPH. "A Clinical Revision of the Experience Variables Record." *Psychiatry* 1:67-77 F '38.

[1220]

"F" Test. Ages 9 and over; 1938; 1 form; an individual test for ages 9-10 and group or individual for ages 11 and over; 5s. 6d. per 12; 15(20) minutes; Raymond B. Cattell with the assistance of L. G. Studman and C. A. Simmins; London: University of London Press, Ltd.

REFERENCES

1 BERNSTEIN, E. *Quickness and Intelligence*: An Enquiry Concerning the Existence of a General Speed Factor. British Journal of Psychology Monograph Supplements, Vol. 3, No. 7. London: Cambridge University Press, 1924. Pp. viii, 55. 7s. Paper.
2 HARGREAVES, H. L. *The "Faculty" of Imagination*: An Enquiry Concerning the Existence of a General "Faculty," or Group Factor, of Imagination. British Journal of Psychology Monograph Supplements, Vol. 3, No. 10. London: Cambridge University Press, 1927. Pp. viii, 55. 7s. Paper.
3 WYNN JONES, LL. "An Investigation into the Significance of Perseveration." *J Mental Sci* 74:653-9 '28.
4 KARVE, B. D. *An Experimental Investigation of 'Fluency' in School Children*. Unpublished master's thesis, University of Leeds, 1929.
5 STUDMAN, L. G. "Measurement of the Speed and Flow of Mental Activity." *Brit J Med Psychol* 14:124-31 '34.
6 WYNN JONES, LL. Chapter 10, "Fluency of Association and Imagination," pp. 112-7. In *An Introduction to Theory and Practice of Psychology*. London: Macmillan and Co., Ltd., 1934. Pp. x, 308. 12s. 6d.
7 STUDMAN, L. G. "The Factor Theory in the Field of Personality." *Char and Pers* 4:34-43 S '35.
8 STUDMAN, L. G. "Studies in Experimental Psychiatry: 'V', 'W' and 'F' Factors in Relation to Traits of Personality." *J Mental Sci* 81:107-37 '35.
9 CATTELL, RAYMOND B. *A Guide to Mental Testing*: For Psychological Clinics, Schools, and Industrial Psychologists, pp. 148-63. London: University of London Press, Ltd., 1936. Pp. xvi, 312. 10s. 6d.
10 CATTELL, RAYMOND B. "Temperament Tests in Clinical Practice." *Brit J Med Psychol* 16:43-61 pt 1 '36.

J. M. Blackburn, Lecturer in Social Psychology, London School of Economics. Is it overcompensation for an inferiority complex in relation to other sciences that has made so many—too many—psychologists the servants of statistics instead of remaining their masters? Do they think that the application of precise quantitative methods will endow indefinite data with a measure of exactitude, and thus allow them to hold up their heads again in the presence of workers from other sciences? Or can it be they sometimes feel that the presentation of complicated mathematical formulae will persuade many persons, who might otherwise be critically disposed, into a more ready acceptance of their views? Whatever the cause the principal result is a grotesque overemphasis on objectivity that ruins many tests for most clinical purposes. Subjects are hammered into the same objective situation regardless of their relative malleability; the responses of one subject are considered to be equivalent to the same responses of another in the same situation, although the attitudes of the two may be entirely different; and great emphasis is laid on arithmetical scores irrespective of how they are obtained. This great defect is to be found in most of the factorial tests, most acutely, perhaps, in those which are supposed to investigate *p* (so-called "perseveration"), because these are difficult to interpret other than quantitatively. Cattell's *"F" Test* has at least the advantage that one *can* ignore his method of scoring and interpret the results in a qualitative manner. Such interpretation is what the clinical worker finds most useful in filling in the picture of a subject's case history. Even from the most accurately standardised tests of intelligence it is the subject's grade of intelligence together with a knowledge of how the test was tackled that is of far greater importance to the clinical worker than a quantitative measure expressed in a single figure, the IQ. People are not condemned to permanent treatment in institutions for the mentally defective on the basis of one point of IQ alone, and it is to be hoped they never will be.

Cattell's test is useful to the clinician who ignores Cattell's instructions. In the Subtest 4, Topics, for example, the Cattell score is the number of significant words given in 30 seconds, omitting *a, the, and,* but counting the topic (man going up a ladder, dog barking, etc.) where repeated. This method of scoring is clearly somewhat arbitrary and it may, amongst other things, prejudice the results against a verbose though imaginative subject. It is certainly ridiculous to believe that an arithmetical score obtained in this way will represent with any fine degree of accuracy a subject's temperamental type. Thus, instead of counting the number of words, things, or drawings in estimating a subject's score and then solemnly looking in the appropriate table for an arithmetical figure to express his temperament—more valuable clinical material may be obtained by noting the kind of topics, drawings, etc., that the subject offers, paying not too strict attention to the timing of the test, and finally interpreting the results in terms of the kinds of topics, drawings, etc. mentioned, the relationship between them, and—most important—the way in which the subject gave them.

Cattell himself admits that the consistency of the *"F" Test* varies according to the subject's state of health, mood, fatigue, etc., and this provides all the stronger argument against an uncritical acceptance of the arithmetical scores. Instead, therefore, of concentrating his attention on the correlation coefficient between letters of the alphabet (*f, c, g,* etc.) he might have been better advised to have developed his test as a useful clinical tool.

P. E. Vernon, Lecturer in Psychology, University of Glasgow. Fluency of association or "*f*-factor" is one of the group factors in mental operations which, with *p* and *o,* are stressed by Spearman and his followers. Cattell's battery of five tests depends on the speed of naming objects which might appear in certain pictures, the speed of associations with ink-blots, speed of writing things which are "round," "eatable," "begin with S," and so on. The author discovered that such tests gave moderately high correlations with ratings of traits such as cheerfulness, sociability, humorousness, adaptability, quickness of apprehension, etc., i.e., traits which belong to the conventional extravert pattern. He gives this group of traits the name "surgency." Correlations of .60 to .65 between *f* tests and ratings on "surgent" traits have been obtained in three small groups of subjects. This leads the author to claim that the test is "of higher validity than any other yet discovered in the realm of temperament testing."

Though these results are as yet unconfirmed there is actually a good deal of evidence suggesting that such tests do correlate more highly with extraversion than do most objective personality tests (e.g., the June Downey or p tests) with the traits they are supposed to measure. They seem to be especially useful with mental hospital patients. Certainly f tests are worth more thorough study, and this battery should provide a good starting point, although its construction and norms are by no means satisfactory as yet.

The battery correlates about .30 with intelligence, and the author recommends a rough correction for high and low IQ. This needs to be worked out more accurately. The reliability is stated to be .78 with 14-year-olds; apparently the figure is based only on about 15 cases. The norms for 14 years are derived from 450 children, but for other ages the numbers are quite insufficient. Sex differences are not mentioned.

Ll. Wynn Jones, Senior Lecturer in Experimental Psychology, University of Leeds. The "F" Test is a temperament test of fluency of association and imagination and consists of five subtests: (1) Unfinished Pictures—Score: one point for each idea. (2) Word Series (things round, things to eat, words beginning with S)—Score: number of things or words. (3) Completing Forms—Score: number of drawings completed multiplied by three. (4) Topics—Score: number of significant words divided by two. (5) Ink Blots—Score: double the number of items conceived. Three periods of one minute are needed for each subtest, except Subtest 4 which needs six periods of half a minute. Fluency is a factor which has been extensively studied by the Spearman School.

The instructions for administering the "F" Test are given in Chapter 5 of Cattell's *Guide to Mental Testing.*[9] The f score was found to correlate about 0.3 with g (intelligence). Because of this, a correction for IQ has been empirically obtained for ages between 10 and 14 years. The results can then be converted to decile scores from the table given on page 162. Cattell found a correlation of 0.65 ± 0.07 between fluency and surgency and in his studies of temperament traits he prefers the terms surgent and desurgent to extravert and introvert. Cattell further claims that the "F"

Test remains the best objective test of a definite temperament so far discovered. Although the reviewer has not had experience in applying the above correction for IQ yet it appears to be a procedure which can be confidently recommended. The reviewer can also testify to the satisfactory reliabilities of such subtests.[4, 6] The reviewer's experience when similar tests were applied to manic and melancholic patients was also favourable to the view that such tests are objective tests of a definite temperament type.[3] It is, of course, essential to distinguish between fluency in the education of relations and correlates, that is, fluency in its noetic aspect and fluency in its reproductive aspect. The former figures in tests of g, the latter in tests of f. Thus the fluency of finding the fourth term of "soot : black :: snow : ———" is noetic, but the fluency in finding a large number of correlatives like salt, snow, note-paper, etc. which would form a fourth term of "black : soot :: white : ———" is reproductive.

Brit J Med Psychol 17:394 pts 3-4 '38. *J. C. Raven.* Cattell has . . . prepared in leaflet form his material for testing fluency or 'surgency' of ideas. The usual series of suggestive pictures, forms, ink blots, and stimulating phrases are employed. The only difference is that the subject is asked to write a list of his associations at the side of the test material. The psychological value of the material is naturally reduced. The leaflets are useful for experimental work but anyone who wishes to use them for practical purposes must bear in mind that they give low consistency coefficients.

[1221]
Fels Parent-Behavior Rating Scales. "For the use of the trained home visitor in appraising certain aspects of parent-child relationships"; 1939; 1 form, 30 parts; $1.50 per 30 sets; 25¢ per specimen set; Horace Champney; Yellow Springs, Ohio: Antioch Press.

REFERENCES
1 CHAMPNEY, HORACE. *Measurement of Parent Behavior as a Part of the Child's Environment.* Unpublished doctor's thesis, Ohio State University, 1939.
2 CHAMPNEY, HORACE, AND MARSHALL, HELEN. "Optimal Refinement of the Rating Scale." *J Appl Psychol* 23:323-31 Je '39.

[1222]
Haggerty-Olson-Wickman Behavior Rating Schedules. Kindergarten through grade 12; 1930; $1 per 25; 10¢ per specimen set; M. E. Haggerty, W. C. Olson, and E. K. Wickman; Yonkers, N. Y.: World Book Co.

REFERENCES
1 HAGGERTY, M. E. "The Incidence of Undesirable Behavior in Public School Children." *J Ed Res* 12:102-22 S '25.
2 WICKMAN, E. K. *Children's Behavior and Teachers' Attitudes.* New York: Commonwealth Fund, 1928. pp. ix, 247. $2.00. (London: George Allen & Unwin, Ltd. 9s.)

3 OLSON, WILLARD C. *Problem Tendencies in Children*: A Method for Their Measurement and Description. Minneapolis, Minn.: University of Minnesota Press, 1930. Pp. xi, 92. $2.00.

4 OLSON, WILLARD C. "The Clinical Use of Behavior Rating Schedules." *J Juvenile Res* 15:237-45 O '31.

5 OLSON, WILLARD C. "Utilization of the Haggerty-Olson-Wickman Behavior Rating Schedules." *Childh Ed* 9:350-9 Ap '33.

6 ELLIS, D. B., AND MILLER, L. W. "Teachers' Attitudes and Child Behavior Problems." *J Ed Psychol* 27:501-11 O '36.

6.1 KIRK, SAMUEL A. "Behavior Problem Tendencies in Deaf and Hard-of-Hearing Children." *Am Ann Deaf* 83:131-7 Mr '38.

7 DUREA, M. A. "Introversion-Extroversion and Problem Tendencies in Children." *Ed Res B* 18:103-6+ Ap '39.

8 BROOKS, JAMES J. "A Technique for Determining the Degree of Behavior Maladjustment of Prison Inmates." *J Criminal Psychopathology* 1:339-53 Ap '40.

Harold E. Jones, Director of the Institute of Child Welfare and Professor of Psychology, University of California. Schedule A, a behavior problem record, presents a list of 15 problems (such as defiance to discipline, speech difficulties etc.) to be checked in one of four columns according to frequency of occurrence in an individual. In summating for a total score, weights are assigned in terms of the frequency and seriousness of a given problem. It may be noted that these are standardized weightings and are not adjustable for variations in the significance of a problem for an individual.

Schedule B consists of a graphic 5-point rating scale for 35 traits classified in four groups—intellectual, physical, social, and emotional. For a given trait, each position on the scale is weighted in terms of its predictive relation to the problem tendency score on Schedule A. In general, extremes of a trait (such as quiet-talkative) receive higher problem-weightings than intermediate positions.

A re-rating correlation of .86 and a split-half correlation (raised) of .92 are reported for elementary school children on Schedule B. No reliability data are given in the manual for Schedule A.

A composite score on A and B has shown a correlation of .76 with frequency of referral for discipline or other action by the school principal. A comparison of normals with clinic cases has shown that only about ten per cent of the former equal or exceed the median of the latter.

The two schedules are printed conveniently in a single folder; a class record form and tally chart are provided on a separate sheet. Included in the manual of directions are tables for converting raw scores into percentile ranks; these apply to Schedules A and B, to the four divisions of Schedule B, and also to an abbreviated form of Schedule B recommended for

use with preschool children. It is pointed out, however, that the percentile tables may not be equally applicable for all groups, and that scores should be taken as relative to the mean scores of the group which is being studied.

A sound understanding of the limitations of rating scales is shown in a cautioning statement which indicates the importance of using ratings, together with supplementary data, in a program of further study and guidance, rather than as a final classification.

[1223]

Humm-Wadsworth Temperament Scale, 1940 Edition. Adults; 1934-39; 1 form; sold only to qualified testers; $2.50 per 25; 50¢ per specimen set; nontimed (30-90) minutes; Doncaster G. Humm and Guy W. Wadsworth, Jr.; Los Angeles, Calif.: Wadsworth-Humm Personnel Service, 245½ South Western Ave.

REFERENCES

1 HUMM, DONCASTER G., AND WADSWORTH, GUY W., JR. "The Humm-Wadsworth Temperament Scale: Preliminary Report." *Personnel J* 12:314-23 Ap '34.

2 HUMM, DONCASTER G., AND WADSWORTH, GUY W., JR. "The Humm-Wadsworth Temperament Scale." *Am J. Psychiatry* 92:163-200 Jl '35.

3 WADSWORTH, GUY W., JR. "Temperament Tests as Personnel Aids." *Personnel J* 15:341-6 Mr '37.

4 HUMM, DONCASTER G. *The Analysis of Disposition or Temperament.* Los Angeles, Calif.: the Author, 416 West Eighth St., 1938. Pp. 20. $0.50. Paper.

5 KRUGER, BARBARA L. "A Statistical Analysis of the Humm-Wadsworth Temperament Scale." *J Appl Psychol* 22:641-52 D '38.

6 MOSIER, CHARLES I. "On the Validity of Neurotic Questionnaires." *J Social Psychol* 9:3-16 F '38.

7 PATERSON, DONALD G.; SCHNEIDLER, GWENDOLEN G.; AND WILLIAMSON, EDMUND G. *Student Guidance Techniques*, pp. 197-201. New York: McGraw-Hill Book Co., Inc., 1938. Pp. xviii, 316. $3.00. (London: McGraw-Hill Publishing Co., Ltd. 18s.)

8 DYSINGER, DON W. "A Critique of the *Humm-Wadsworth Temperament Scale.*" *J. Abn and Social Psychol* 34:73-83 Ja '39.

9 HEMSATH, MARY ELIZABETH. "Theory and Practice of Temperament Testing." *Personnel J* 18:3-12 My '39.

10 HUMM, DONCASTER G. "Discussion of 'A Statistical Analysis of the Humm-Wadsworth Temperament Scale.'" *J Appl Psychol* 23:525-6 Ag '39.

11 HUMM, DONCASTER G. "Dysinger's Critique of the Humm-Wadsworth Temperament Scale." *J Abn and Social Psychol* 34:402-3 Jl '39.

12 HUMM, DONCASTER G.; STORMENT, ROBERT C.; AND IORNS, MARTIN E. "Combination Scores for the Humm-Wadsworth Temperament Scale." *J Psychol* 7:227-54 Ap '39.

13 WASSON, MARGARET M. "The Agreements among Certain Types of Personality Schedules." *J Psychol* 9:351-63 Ap '40.

Forrest A. Kingsbury, Associate Professor of Psychology, The University of Chicago. [Review of the Second Edition.] This is a profile scale, yielding scores on seven traits or "components of temperament." In general makeup it resembles neurotic questionnaires of the yes-no type, except for its greater length, 318 items, of which only 164 yield scores, the remaining 154 being padding. The authors, however, believe that these 154 help create "test atmosphere" and influence responses to the 164 valid questions, so they have declined thus far to publish a shortened form and thus risk invalidating the present norms.

In scoring and interpretation, however, the scale is distinctive in several ways. The seven components, taken from Rosanoff's theory of personality, are summarized in a recent article [12] as follows:

COMPONENT	SYMBOL	CONSTITUTED OF TRAITS ASSOCIATED WITH:
"Normal"	N	Self-control, self-improvement, inhibition, etc.
Hysteroid	H	Self-preservation, selfishness, crime, etc.
Manic Cycloid	M	Elation, excitement, sociability, etc.
Depressive Cycloid	D	Sadness, retardation, caution, worry, etc.
Autistic Schizoid	A	Daydreams, shyness, sensitiveness, etc.
Paranoid Schizoid	P	Fixed-ideas, restiveness, conceit, etc.
Epileptoid	E	Ecstasy, meticulousness, inspiration, etc.

Each significant yes- or no-response is assigned weighted log-scores of from 1 to 5 points on one or more components. These are totaled to make the 7 raw scores, which in turn are rated from "Very Strong" ($+3$) to "Very Weak" (-3), each rating being further divisible into upper, middle, and lower ranges.

Due to the tendency of many subjects to answer *No* too often while others mark too many items *Yes,* a validation device is provided by which questionnaires showing too many or too few no-responses can be identified and either rejected or accepted provisionally as doubtful. The 1939 article cited describes a new procedure for broadening this range of valid and semi-valid scores by taking into account "combination scores"; i.e., correcting each log-score in terms of scores on the other components.

Reliability coefficients (split-half, corrected) for the seven components range from .70 to .88. Validity, as determined by comparison of scores with case studies and clinical records of the original standardization group, is stated to be very high, "only .355 per cent of the cases showed discrepancy." This, of course, means merely that the weighting of this group's responses was done so carefully that their numerical scores describe them accurately. More impressive are the findings (1939 article) from 705 public service employees, college students, abnormals, and criminals. In one corporation, out of 185 engineering employees selected on the basis of temperament score, only 2 (of whom 1 had originally been rated doubtful) had been discharged for reasons arising out of temperamental maladjustment; 1500 other shop employees similarly selected lost only 18 (1.2 per cent) for like reasons. If these results are typical of what others can

do with this instrument, there can be no question of its high potential value; for the 7 characteristics measured are prima facie of great practical and theoretical importance.

A more explicit account might well have been given of the methods and criteria employed in obtaining the original standardization groups, beyond the bare statement that they were "selected" from state prison, state hospitals, homes for indigents, and private patients.

Scoring the Humm-Wadsworth—also taking it—is a time-consuming enterprise. This, of course, is a minor criticism, but it does affect the chances of error. More hazardous, perhaps, is the practice of employing distinctly pathological categories (even when valid), such as "Hysteroid," "Paranoid," "Manic," "Epileptoid," etc., in characterizing "normal" subjects. Even the qualifying "Border-line" or "Moderately Weak" does not altogether eliminate the stigma. The authors are justified in forbidding mention of these terms or giving out scores; but under pressure from advisees (curious, perhaps, about the large *H, P, M, E,* etc., on their blanks), or employers or others with a legitimate interest in the diagnoses, there is always the risk of unintentionally using aloud the terms in which one is thinking. Whether the answer lies in substituting more innocuous component-names, the reviewer does not know; but he feels the need of reassurance.

P. E. Vernon, Lecturer in Psychology, University of Glasgow. [Review of the Second Edition.] This test is, in the reviewer's opinion, much the best of the many questionnaires which are supposed to measure several different traits simultaneously. First, it is based on a logically worked out classification of normal and abnormal personalities, instead of being aimed at some ill-defined hotch-potch like introversion or psychoneurotic tendency. Rosanoff's seven-fold classification may or may not be widely accepted, but his components are clear-cut and should be fairly distinctive. These components are the normal or rational inhibition tendency, the hysteroid or antisocial tendency, the manic, depressive, autistic, paranoid, and epileptoid tendencies. One defect in the authors' presentation is that they do not tell us the actual amount of correlation between the scores of a normal group on these various components. However there should be far less overlapping than between introversion, emotionality, and submissiveness.

Secondly, the items of the questionnaire have been empirically validated. Each scorable response has been proved to differentiate persons who are high in one of the components from other persons, and the criterion for selecting the persons high in each component consisted of psychiatric case-studies. A complaint must, however, be raised here about the authors' data on validity. They fail to state the numbers of persons representing each component, with whom this validation was carried out. Almost certainly the numbers were too small, since the total for all seven components was only 436. Again we are told that the scale as a whole was validated by comparing its diagnoses with psychiatric case-studies of additional subjects, yielding a "coefficient of validity of $+.98 \pm .01$." But the numbers of subjects and the extent of agreement with the case studies are not given. If the validity is as good as it is claimed, then to withhold such important details is stupid.

A third point is the admission that some 25 per cent of presumably normal persons and 45 per cent of abnormal patients produce invalid blanks, usually through being too negativistic or too suggestible. Checks are provided for determining when the blanks have been filled in sufficiently conscientiously to be accepted as valid. A recent article provides a new scoring method, again based on empirical investigations, which allows many of the previously unacceptable blanks to be scored. The scoring is, unfortunately, very elaborate; but this is justified by the usefulness of the results.

Another apparently unique feature is the retention in the scale of items which were proved invalid during the final standardization, on the grounds that the response to an item is not determined by that item alone, but also by the context in which it occurs. This means that half the items are not scored at all, and that the scale takes a very long time to answer. Again the trouble seems to be worth while.

Finally, we are particularly pleased to see restrictions imposed on the sale of the test. In the future it will only be supplied to members and associates of the American Psychological Association or the American Psychiatric Association, to qualified employment managers, and the like. There is far too much commercial-ism about present-day mental testing. It would be one of the greatest advances in the history of testing if psychologists would forego some of their royalties, and only sell intelligence, educational, and personality tests to persons competent to use them wisely.

For a review by Daniel A. Prescott, see 920.

[1224]

Information Blank EA: A Questionnaire on Emotional Adjustment, Provisional Form. Grades 10-16; 1938; 1 form; $1.00 per 50 machine-scorable test-answer sheets; 10¢ per specimen set; nontimed (10-20) minutes; H. T. Manuel, F. J. Adams, and Paul White; Austin, Tex.: Steck Co.

Stanley G. Dulsky, Chief Psychologist, Rochester Guidance Center, Rochester, New York. The *Information Blank EA* is "a questionnaire on emotional adjustment" designed for use with senior high school and college students and may be scored either by hand or by machine. It consists of thirty questions "of the type commonly used in inventories of emotional adjustment and of the type which psychiatric and clinical experience have found useful in dealing with personality difficulties." The questions are directed toward the individual's internal (as opposed to external) adjustment and are concerned mainly with feelings of anxiety, guilt, tension, and fantasy. Such questions are more difficult to answer than those applying to a person's overt behavior. "Its purpose is to direct attention to the emotional difficulties of students in school and college and to furnish a little of the personal information needed in student counseling."

It must be clearly understood that this blank is now only in provisional form. Correspondence with Mr. Manuel, one of the authors, revealed the following data: (*a*) Reliability of the test as determined by repetition of it to 98 college freshman after an interval of one to nine days is $r = .89$. (*b*) "The total score did *not* select freshmen who later became patients of the university psychiatrist." (*c*) "A psychiatric study . . . of a group of 14 students in a class in mental hygiene showed only moderate agreement with test scores."

It is obvious from the above that although the reliability is satisfactory the validity is not. To this reviewer the *raison d'être* of such a blank is its potentiality for selecting from a large group of students those who need psychiatric assistance. Did those students who made low scores (indicating emotional difficulty) need psychiatric help? This is another method of evaluating the efficacy of the blank. On this point we have no information.

Manuel stated that much of the information needed to evaluate the blank is still lacking. Further work is planned and is being done by the authors. It is too early to make a final judgment about the value of this blank and, therefore, it cannot now be recommended for use.

[1225]

Interests and Activities: Tests 8.2b and 8.2c. Grades 7-12; 1939; 2 forms (both of which must be given); an experimental edition; 3¢ per test; 1¢ per machine-scorable answer sheet; 15¢ per key to classification of items; nontimed (40) minutes; Chicago, Ill.: Evaluation in the Eight Year Study, Progressive Education Association.

REFERENCES

1 RATHS, LOUIS. "Evaluating the Program of Lakeshore School." *Ed Res B* 17:57-84 Mr 16 '38.
2 SHEVIAKOV, G. V., AND FRIEDBERG, JEAN. *Evaluation of Personal and Social Adjustment:* Report of Progress of the Study. Chicago, Ill.: Evaluation in the Eight Year Study, Progressive Education Association, 1939. Pp. iii, 65. $0.75. Paper, mimeographed.
3 AMSTUTZ, WADE S. "A Study of Characteristics of Education Freshmen Who Entered Ohio State University in 1938." *J Exp Ed* 8:289-92 Mr '40.
4 BITTNER, REIGN H., AND BORDIN, EDWARD. "The Study of an Interest Questionnaire." *J Exp Ed* 8:270-7 Mr '40.
5 CAHOW, ARTHUR C. "Relationships of Test Scores of Education College Freshmen to Grades in Selected Courses." *J Exp Ed* 8: 284-9 Mr '40.
6 SHEVIAKOV, G. V., AND FRIEDBERG, JEAN. "Use of Interest Inventories for Personality Study." *J Ed Res* 33:692-7 My '40.
7 SHEVIAKOV, G. V., AND FRIEDBERG, JEAN. "Use of Interest Inventories for Personality Study," pp. 87-90. In *Official Report of 1940 Meeting:* American Educational Research Association, A Department of the National Education Association, St. Louis, Missouri, February 24-27, 1940. Washington, D. C.: American Educational Research Association, May 1940. Pp. 192. $1.50. Paper.

[1226]

Interest Index: Test 8.2a. Grades 7-12; 1939; 1 form; revision of Test 8.2; 3¢ per test; 1¢ per machine-scorable answer sheet; 10¢ per key to classification of items; 5¢ per explanation sheet and interpretation guide; $2 per set of stencils for machine scoring; nontimed (40) minutes; Chicago, Ill.: Evaluation in the Eight Year Study, Progressive Education Association.

REFERENCES

1 RATHS, LOUIS. "Evaluating the Program of Lakeshore School." *Ed Res B* 17:57-84 Mr 16 '38.
2 SHEVIAKOV, G. V., AND FRIEDBERG, JEAN. *Evaluation of Personal and Social Adjustment:* Report of Progress of the Study. Chicago, Ill.: Evaluation in the Eight Year Study, Progressive Education Association, 1939. Pp. iii, 65. $0.75. Paper, mimeographed.
3 SHEVIAKOV, G. V., AND FRIEDBERG, JEAN. "Use of Interest Inventories for Personality Study." *J Ed Res* 33:692-7 My '40.
4 SHEVIAKOV, G. V., AND FRIEDBERG, JEAN. "Use of Interest Inventories for Personality Study," pp. 87-90. In *Official Report of 1940 Meeting:* American Educational Research Association, A Department of the National Education Association, St. Louis, Missouri, February 24-27, 1940. Washington, D. C.: American Educational Research Association, May 1940. Pp. 192. $1.50. Paper.

[1227]

Interest Questionnaire: Games and Sports: Test 8.3. Grades 9-12; 1939; an experimental form; 5¢ per test; 1¢ per machine-scorable answer sheet; $1.50 per set of stencils for machine scoring; [W. H. Lauritsen]; Chicago, Ill.: Evaluation in the Eight Year Study, Progressive Education Association.

[1228]

Interest-Values Inventory. Grades 9-16 and adults; 1939; 1 form; $7.20 per 100; 35¢ per record sheet; 20¢ per specimen set; nontimed (30) minutes; J. B. Maller and Edward M. Glaser; New York: Bureau of Publications, Teachers College, Columbia University.

REFERENCES

1 GLASER, E. M. *A Determination of Personality Patterns through Measurements of the Relative Dominance of Certain Basic Personality Interests.* Unpublished master's thesis, University of Kansas, 1936. Pp. 82.
2 GLASER, EDWARD M., AND MALLER, JULIUS B. "The Measurement of Interest Values." *Char and Pers* 9:67-81 S '40.

Loyola Ed Digest 15:9 N '39. *Austin G. Schmidt.* This inventory is designed to measure the relative dominance of four major types of interest or basic values within the individual: theoretic, esthetic, social, and economic. *

[1229]

Inventory of Factors STDCR. College; 1940; 1 form; $2.25 per 50; $1 per scoring key; 15¢ per specimen set; nontimed (30) minutes; J. P. Guilford; Beverly Hills, Calif.: Sheridan Supply Co.

REFERENCES

1 GUILFORD, J. P., AND GUILFORD, RUTH B. "Personality Factors D, R, T, and A." *J Abn and Social Psychol* 34:21-36 Ja '39.

[1230]

Jones Personality Rating Scale. High school; 1939; 1½¢ per scale; Harold J. Jones; New York: Gregg Publishing Co.

[1231]

Minnesota Rating Scale for Personal Qualities and Abilities, Fourth Revision. College students and adults; 1925-38; reprinted from the *Minnesota Rating Scale for Home Economics Teachers* (out of print); $1 per 100; 10¢ per specimen set; Clara M. Brown; Minneapolis, Minn.: University of Minnesota Press.

REFERENCES

1 BROWN, CLARA M. *An Evaluation of the Minnesota Rating Scale for Home Economics Teachers.* Minneapolis, Minn.: University of Minnesota Press, 1931. Pp. 29. $0.50. Paper.

[1232]

Occupational Personality Inventory. Applicants for sales positions in department stores; 1939; 1 form; $3 per 100; 15¢ per specimen set; nontimed (10) minutes; Arthur F. Dodge; New York: Psychological Corporation.

REFERENCES

1 DODGE, ARTHUR F. "Social Dominance and Sales Personality." *J Appl Psychol* 22:132-9 Ap '38.
2 DODGE, ARTHUR F. "What Are the Personality Traits of the Successful Sales-Person?" *J Appl Psychol* 22:229-38 Je '38.
3 DODGE, ARTHUR F. "Personality Measuring Stick." *Retailing* (Executive Edition) F 13 '39.

[1233]

P. Q. or Personality Quotient Test, 1938 Revision. Grades 7-13; 1936-38; 2 editions; the title on the test booklet is *Inventory of Activities and Interests;* $5.00 per 100; 25¢ per specimen set; $2 per 100 machine-scorable answer sheets; nontimed (30-40) minutes; Henry C. Link with the assistance of G. K. Bennett, Rose G. Anderson, Sydney Roslow, and P. G. Corby; New York: Psychological Corporation.
a) FOR BOYS AND YOUNG MEN.
b) FOR GIRLS AND YOUNG WOMEN.

REFERENCES

1 LINK, HENRY C. "A Test of Four Personality Traits of Adolescents." *J Appl Psychol* 20:527-34 O '36.

1.1 LINK, HENRY C. "Personality Can Be Acquired." *Readers Digest* 29:1-4 D '36.
2 GIBBONS, CHARLES C. "A Short Scoring Method for the Link P.Q. Test." *J Appl Psychol* 22:653-6 D '38.
3 LINK, HENRY C. *The Rediscovery of Man*, pp. 55-90. New York: Macmillan Co., 1938. Pp. xi, 257. $1.75. (London: Macmillan & Co., Ltd., 1939. 7s. 6d.)
4 THOMSON, WILLIAM A. "An Evaluation of the P.Q. (Personality Quotient) Test." *Char and Pers* 6:274-92 Je '38.
5 DRAKE, MARGARET J.; ROSLOW, SYDNEY; AND BENNETT, GEORGE K. "The Relationship of Self-Rating and Classmate Rating on Personality Traits." *J Exp Ed* 7:210-3 Mr '39.

Douglas Spencer, Assistant Professor of Psychology, Queens College. The difficulties of personality measurement are so numerous and baffling that they invite a tolerant and respectful consideration for new attempts to overcome them when claims are limited by scientific caution and supporting data are made available.

The so-called "PQ Test," however, has little claim to such consideration. Probably no other test has been introduced to such a vast popular audience with such confident claims, before its promise could be verified. Witness: "The well-known 'IQ' or intelligence quotient is a measure of the kind of intelligence required in school—a test in terms of what a person *knows* about things and people. The 'PQ' or personality quotient is a new measure of what a person *does* about things and people. It is a yardstick of the traits required to get along in the world." [1.1]

If the popular reader were astonished at this great accomplishment, or a bit skeptical as to some of the confident directions for developing personality revealed as "findings," he was reassured by a note that "the scientific details of the construction of the test are described in the October (1936) Journal of Applied Psychology."

This citation is disappointing. Anticipating, on the basis of the claims, evidence of validity and trait isolation if not age-level norms comparable to the MA, one finds little more than a report of progress and promise. There is an interesting armchair discussion of the author's theory that personality is measured by "the extent to which the individual has learned to convert his energy into habits and skills which influence and serve other people." The test held to incorporate the assumptions underlying this theory is another self-report inventory. There are the usual stepped-up, odd-even reliability coefficients for the preliminary form. An item analysis is described. But the crucial question of validation is treated as follows: "If the general assumptions made in this study are correct then the validity of the scale in terms of the conventional measures of validity is of secondary importance. The primary problem is a scale which reasonably exemplifies these fiats, both logically and statistically." [1]

Confident claims have been repeated in other popular articles and also in the publisher's catalogue (Catalogue of Test Division of the Psychological Corporation, 1939 Edition): "By means of concrete questions five personality traits are measured: extroversion, social aggressiveness, self-determination, economic self-determination, adjustment to the opposite sex." If the test measures these or any other traits significant to personality functioning, this reviewer has been unable to find the evidence.

Nor can the manual of the 1938 revision be accused of understatement: "This test . . . is unique in that its validity has been demonstrated in a nation-wide study of 74 schools, as detailed on pages 11 and 12." Page 11 reports a classification of 1138 students from different high schools into four groupings of boys and girls based on teachers' ratings as to scholarship and leadership. Means and standard deviation of Scale X scores are given for these groupings and indicate that the groups rated high as leaders scored higher on Scale X on the average than those rated low in leadership. This rough comparison of an unvalidated instrument with a criterion as inadequate as teachers' ratings does not achieve validation. Since page 12 yields only a listing of schools "participating in the standardization," the evidence for the claim of nation-wide demonstration of validity is, after ten years, still unreported.

As to reliabilities, those reported are based on a tryout of an earlier form (1936) on 421 boys. The five scales yielded odd-even, corrected coefficients ranging from .73 to .87, according to the manual. These are too low for individual prediction. No evidence is found in the manual as to the reliability of the 1938 revision, which offers separate forms for boys and girls.

Of course the instrument is not a "test" in the strict sense of the term, and certainly does not "measure what a person does about things and people." It is a self-report blank inviting the subject, under his signature, to respond to highly vague and subjective questions many of which he may not be able or willing to answer. The first page offers an easy opportunity for the kind of deception revealed on other blanks of this kind. Here each subject can make a good impression by checking lists of group activities in which he has taken "an active part," hobbies at which he "spends a great deal of effort," games (athletics) in which he "practices hard and regularly," etc. The 150 items which follow are little different from those found in older self-report inventories. The manual describes them as "questions regarding habits and activities, rather than feelings and emotions." Nevertheless, there are many questions like the following: Does your temper occasionally explode? Do you cry when you are angry? Are you usually in a cheerful or happy frame of mind? Do you often get discouraged? Do your classmates often make remarks that hurt your feelings? Are you a rather nervous person? Are you planning to get married before you are 25?

The chief difference from other attempts of its kind is the introduction of the PQ score. PQ is derived from the scoring of only Scale X which the author assumes to be a measure of extroversion $[PQ = \frac{17}{\sigma}(X - M) + 100$, the mean PQ value for each sex and for each grade grouping being 100]. The promise of comparability with the IQ falls far short. Lacking evidence of validity, it is not easy to justify such a promising label as "Personality Quotient" except on the basis of market appeal.

Simon H. Tulchin, Consulting Psychologist, 136 East 57th St., New York, New York. This is a revision of an earlier test and consists of 150 questions which are intended to measure the personality of normal students in grades 7 to 13—ages 12 to 20. Separate inventories have been provided for boys and girls. These inventories are designed to measure five traits: personality, which includes nearly all the items; social initiative, which includes items concerned with "habits" of taking initiative in dealing with people; self-determination, or items representing "habits" of doing things considered desirable even if unpleasant; economic self-determination, or those items which consist of "habits" of earning money; and adjustment to the opposite sex, which includes "habits" of action toward members of the opposite sex.

Percentile norms based on 3,131 tests given to students in 74 schools throughout the country are recorded separately for each subtest for boys and for girls in grades 6, 7-8, 9-10,

11-12, and 13. Reliability has been determined from the 1936 edition administered to 421 boys. The reliability for each of the five scales was computed on the basis of the correlation between the odd and even scores, and the coefficients of reliability range between .73 and .88.

The definition of personality is a narrow and limited definition which considers personality in terms of "the possession of habits which interest and serve other people." "Personality is measured by the extent to which the individual has learned to convert his energies into habits and skills which *interest* and *serve* other people." "Our theory of personality assumes that it is the result of habits which can be developed just as education now develops the habits measured by scholastic tests." Having determined the weak points by means of the test, a personality building program can be developed for individuals and groups. The test "also lifts the subject of personality to the wholesome level of normal psychology and the practical problems of habit formation." The authors assert that habits and activities are stressed in the test questions rather than feelings and emotions, yet we find such questions as: "Do you frequently lose your temper?" "Do your classmates often make remarks which hurt your feelings?" "Do you often brood over your mistakes or hard luck?" A number of questions which seem significant carry no scoring value, as for example, "Do you often just sit and think or imagine things?" A number of questions which deal with adjustment to the opposite sex, such as, for example, "Have you had a steady girl friend for three months or more?" or, "Are you indifferent to girls?", certainly must have different meaning to a ten-year-old than to a twenty-year-old, but no attempt is made to consider this problem.

A table is presented for the purpose of converting the total score obtained on the personality test into a P.Q., or Personality Quotient, interpreted in the same way as the familiar intelligence quotient, with a P.Q. of 100 as average. Without presenting any evidence, it is claimed that the P.Q. indicates "the development or growth of the individual's personality," and is taken to be "valuable in giving a measure of effective personality."

Link evidently accepts replies to a questionnaire as factual data and seems satisfied in as-

signing Personality Quotients on admittedly
partial sampling of personality traits. He attacks critics who demand that personality tests
demonstrate their validity and suggests that
"some of the criticism of the validity of personality scales should be directed rather at the
situation which makes validation difficult." [1]
On page one of the manual we find the statement that the test "is unique in that its validity
has been demonstrated in a nationwide study
of 74 schools, as detailed on pages 11 and 12."
When we turn to these pages we find that
only one attempt to validate the test is recorded
by comparing scores made by 1,138 students
who were classified by their teachers into four
categories of leadership and scholarship. There
follows merely a list of representative schools
which participated in the standardization.

Determining the validity of a personality test
is unquestionably difficult but it must remain
its most essential requisite. It seems naive to
assume that personality is but an aggregate of
"habits" and activities which can be developed
and modified by the simple process of habit
training. It is equally dangerous to disregard
the possibility that psychopathologic processes
can be easily concealed by giving "proper"
answers to test questions.

*For reviews by C. M. Louttit and Edmund
G. Williamson, see 921.*

[1234]
P-S Experience Blank: Psycho-Somatic Inventory.
Late adolescents and adults; 1938; 1 form; $1.25 per
25; 25¢ per specimen set; nontimed (20-60) minutes;
Ross A. McFarland and Clifford P. Seitz; New York:
Psychological Corp.

REFERENCES

1 McFarland, Ross A., and Seitz, Clifford P. "A Psycho-
Somatic Inventory." *J Appl Psychol* 22:327-39 Ag '38.
2 Mosier, Charles I. "On the Validity of Neurotic Questionnaires." *J Social Psychol* 9:3-16 F '38.

*Doncaster G. Humm, Wadsworth-Humm
Personnel Service, Los Angeles, California.*
The authors state that the purpose of this
inventory is to help physicians, clinicians, social
workers, and school psychologists ascertain
neurotic tendencies in late adolescents and
adults.

Some objection may be had to the term
"neurotic." This seems to be a euphemism
which has gained currency as a substitute for
"psychopathic." If psychoneuroses or neuroses
are connoted by this term and findings are
confined to hysteria, psychasthenia, neuras-
thenia, and the anxiety neuroses, this connota-

tion should be made plain. In such a case some
distinction should be provided to differentiate
between these four subclasses.

Reliability for the inventory was determined
by the split-half method and found to be .87,
or 51 per cent better than chance. This is
about a 3 to 1 chance that retesting will give
about the same result as the original testing.
From retesting 52 males a reliability of .75
or 34 per cent better than chance was secured.
This offers a retest chance of 2.02 to 1.

The inventory indicates trustworthy differences between the "normal group" and the
"psychoneurotic group" in both males and
females. For males the average chance seems
to be 1.83 to 1 that it will differentiate between
individuals; for females, 1.48 to 1. The high
probable error for individual scores seems to
be due to the selection of "normal" and
"neurotic" subjects. There is considerable overlapping between these two control groups.

This inventory represents an excellent attack on the problem of determining individuals
incapacitated by reason of personality. The
methods used are sound. Probably the only
weakness is in the selection of subjects, a
weakness against which it is exceedingly difficult to guard.

*Charles I. Mosier, Assistant Professor of
Psychology and Assistant University Examiner, University of Florida.* This inventory
consists of two scales of forty-six questions
each, to be answered "often," "at times,"
"seldom," or "never," designed to measure
physiological dysfunction and psychological
maladjustment, and to select those individuals
in a normal group who exhibit excessive
psychoneurotic tendency. The manual gives
no description of construction, but does refer
to such a description. It provides directions
for administration and scoring, and percentile
norms for each sex separately for normal and
for psychoneurotic groups, based, except for
the normal men, on less than two hundred subjects. The manual also reports reliability coefficients and validating evidence. Particularly
noteworthy is the modesty of the manual's
claim: "No questionnaire can be a final basis
for classification, although it should direct attention to those cases which require further
investigation."

The items composing the inventory were
selected on the basis of their power to dif-

ferentiate a group of psychoneurotics from a group of normal subjects. This mode of validation, granting the assumption that there is some single trait in which psychoneurotics differ from normal subjects, is superior to that used for many personality schedules. However, the work of Landis and his co-workers renders the validity of that assumption at least doubtful. The reported reliability coefficients by the Spearman-Brown method, based on only 100 normal subjects, were .86 and .80 respectively for Parts I and II, and .87 for the entire test. Test-retest coefficients based on only 52 subjects were .75. These reliabilities are not low by comparison with those of other similar tests, but are too low to justify much faith in the meaning of an individual score.

The validity of the scale is reported in terms of the differences between mean scores for normal and psychoneurotic groups. These differences were from thirteen to nineteen times their standard errors, and indicate, on the surface, unusually high validity, since workers with other inventories usually fail to find any difference of statistical significance. The fact that the validating groups were the same ones as those used in the selection of the items tends to produce, of course, a spuriously high validity, but this effect is mitigated by the fact that the scoring weights were computed on the basis of only a small part of the total number of subjects, and high critical ratios were also found for groups containing none of the individuals used to establish those scoring weights. In connection with validity, the authors' statement: "tubercular or cardiac patients might make equally low scores on the psycho-somatic inventory as the neurotics," [1] should be noted.

The correlation coefficient between the two parts of the scale as reported (but not in the manual) is of the order of the magnitude of .70, which, when corrected for the unreliability of the scales, is seen to approach unity. The scales do not measure two distinct traits, but only one, and that one, if the evidence of other workers with highly similar material is valid, a composite of a number of traits. (Seventeen of the items on the second scale were among the forty shown by Mosier [2] to be measuring six distinct traits. What combination of these traits is represented in any individual score on the *P-S Experience Blank* cannot be determined.) The distinction which the authors

claim between physiological dysfunction and psychological maladjustment is not maintained by their own reported results. Their suggestion, however, that "Experienced clinicians should find the separate items a good basis for further questioning," should be commended.

In general, the authors' modest claim (not repeated in the manual) that: "In a certain percentage of the cases, depending on the degree of cooperation of the subjects, such an inventory will detect the subject in the normal group who might profit by psychiatric guidance and treatment," [1] is probably justified. However, the words, "a certain percentage of cases," should be underscored, and the qualifying phrase, "depending on the degree of cooperation," should be extended to cover a number of other possible distorting factors.

[1235]
Parents Rating Scale. Self and mutual rating of parents; 1935; 1 form; $15 per 100; 25¢ per specimen set; nontimed (60) minutes; Walther Joël and Janet Joël, Los Angeles, Calif.: Walther Joël, Los Angeles City College.

[1236]
Personal History Record, 1937 Revision. Grades 9-16 and adults; 1928-37; a test of emotional stability; 1 form; $2.50 per 25 (No. 24524); 25¢ per manual (No. 24524A); nontimed (30) minutes; Lorin A. Thompson, Jr.; Chicago, Ill.: C. H. Stoelting Co.

REFERENCES

1 THOMPSON, LORIN A., JR. "Personal History, Intelligence, and Academic Achievement." *J Social Psychol* 5:500-7 N '34.

[1237]
Personal Index. Boys in grades 7-9; 1933; 1 form; 75¢ per 25; 25¢ per specimen set; nontimed, (30-40) minutes; Graham C. Loofbourow and Noel Keys; Minneapolis, Minn.: Educational Test Bureau, Inc.

REFERENCES

1 LOOFBOUROW, GRAHAM C. *Test Materials for Problem Behavior Tendencies in Junior High School Boys.* University of California Publications in Education, Vol. 7, No. 1. Berkeley, Calif.: the University, 1932. Pp. 62. $1.25. Paper.
2 LOOFBOUROW, GRAHAM C., AND KEYS, NOEL. "A Group Test of Problem Behavior Tendencies in Junior High School Boys." *J Ed Psychol* 24:641-53 D '33.
3 KEYS, NOEL, AND GUILFORD, MARGARET S. "The Validity of Certain Adjustment Inventories in Predicting Problem Behavior." *J Ed Psychol* 28:641-55 D '37.
4 RIGGS, WINIFRED C. *A Validation of the Loofbourow-Keys Personal Index.* Unpublished master's thesis, University of Denver, 1937. Pp. 47.
5 RIGGS, WINIFRED C., AND JOYAL, ARNOLD E. "A Validation of the Loofbourow-Keys Personal Index of Problem Behavior in Junior High Schools." *J Ed Psychol* 29:194-201 Mr '38.

J. B. Maller, Lecturer in Education, New York University. The test consists of four subtests: False Vocabulary—a test of overstatement; Social Attitudes—each key word or phrase is followed by one socially desirable and three undesirable alternatives (adapted from Raubenheimer); Virtues—(adapted from the moral knowledge tests of Hartshorne and May); Adjustment Questionnaire—(adapted from the psychoneurotic inventories of Wood-worth, Mathews, Cady and Symonds).

The discrimination between the problem cases and normal groups on each of the four tests as reported by the authors is surprisingly high. Of particular interest is the evidence presented in the manual that the test results show a higher correlation with behavior ratings obtained after a lag of three years than with similar ratings of behavior obtained at the time the test was given. If this finding were substantiated by repeated studies and based on larger numbers of cases it would be considerable significance.

Numerous recent studies of problem cases reveal consistently that such behavior disorders are as a rule the result of environmental factors, teacher-pupil conflicts, and the like, rather than some inherent difficulty in the child himself. This finding would hardly lead one to expect that maladjustment could be predicted several years in advance on the basis of a series of highly specific pencil-and-paper responses such as those evoked by this test.

The authors indicate that its value might be "destroyed if the test were given in a way to arouse self-consciousness, suspicion, or open resentment." Therein lies the most serious weakness of tests of this type for the results will depend unduly upon the conditions under which the test is given and even upon the personality of the examiner. In spite of the authors' suggestion that the test results must be "interpreted with due scientific caution" it is likely that once such a test is placed in the open market it will be used under conditions quite different from those which prevailed in the process of validation. Diagnosis based on such indiscriminate usage and comparison with the "norms" will result in dubious value to the person using such tests as well as to the science of psychometrics.

A few words should be added about the subtests. Aside from the ethical problem involved in the inclusion of fictitious words there is of course a likelihood that many children will mistake these for similar words which they do know—for example: rettle for rattle, faline for feline, tromer for tremor, etc. It would be more desirable to include real but extremely difficult words. Of course, that involves the probability of an occasional child who may actually know the meaning of a difficult word but that, in the opinion of the re-

viewer, would be less hazardous than the presentation of fictitious words which differ from real and relatively easy words by a slight variation in spelling. In fact, children who are poor in spelling and who have a fairly good comprehension vocabulary are likely to appear very dishonest on this test.

Even more puzzling is the validity of the Virtues Test. Self-descriptions of a high degree of rectitude have been found in other studies to be indicative of untruthfulness, rather than of high moral standard. But this test is scored in such a way that in many items highly favorable self-descriptions are given positive weights.

Perhaps further research with the test on different groups will throw light on the surprisingly high degree of discrimination which this test yielded in the population upon which it was standardized.

Carl R. Rogers, Professor of Psychology, The Ohio State University. This test was designed primarily for boys, but is applicable both to boys and girls of junior high school age. It is intended to identify the individual who is or may become a serious disciplinary problem.

The test shows evidence of much careful preliminary work. Ten different types of paper-and-pencil tests were tried out on problem and control groups of boys and the degree to which they discriminated was determined. On the basis of this study all but four were discarded, and later one of these was discarded. The remaining tests have been evaluated item by item and only those showing a significant critical ratio have been retained. As revised, the test as a whole shows a critical ratio (difference divided by the standard error of the difference) of 16.8 between a group of 100 San Francisco disciplinary problems and a matched group of unselected high school boys. Between two groups chosen by the principal as the "best" and the "worst" boys in school the test gave a critical ratio of 25, with very little overlapping of score between the two groups. In another study institutionalized delinquent boys were compared with 500 nonproblem boys. Seventy-three per cent of the delinquent boys made scores over 35, while only 21 per cent of the nonproblem boys scored in this group.

An interesting further check on validity was

made by a follow-up study of 130 boys, three years after test scores and behavior ratings had first been obtained. It was discovered that the later behavior status of these boys was slightly more accurately predicted by the original scores on the *Personal Index* than by the original ratings of high school counselors and principals.

In its present form the test consists of three parts. First is a "vocabulary" test, essentially a test of falsification or tendency to make extravagant statements. The second portion is a measure of antisocial attitudes toward school, minor delinquencies, the law, and society. The third portion is a combination of a neurotic inventory (largely from the *Woodworth-Matthews Personal Data Sheet*) and a test of school adjustment. In general the questions are interestingly worded. The use of "yes-no" responses rather than multiple choice in Test 3 seems unfortunate. The manual gives adequate though not complete information regarding the construction and validation of the test.

The most serious drawback to the use of the test is that for the most part it would reveal only the obvious. The alert principal or counselor will know the problem individuals in his school. This test is sufficiently valid to confirm this knowledge, but it goes little further. It would discover a few problem individuals not recognized as such by the school counselor. It does not however, add very significantly to our knowledge of the causes of these tendencies. Even an inspection of the individual responses would give few clues to such causes, except for the twenty-one items on school adjustment in Test 3. The greatest possibility for usefulness would seem to lie in quickly identifying problems in a new group. Thus, given at the outset in a junior or senior high school, the test would select with considerable accuracy those individuals upon whom the personnel workers should concentrate their efforts.

[1238]

Personality and Interest Inventory. Grades 4-9, 9-12; 1935-36; 1 form, 2 levels; Gertrude Hildreth; New York: Bureau of Publications, Teachers College, Columbia University.
a) ELEMENTARY FORM. Grades 4-9; 1935; nontimed (45) minutes; $2.10 per 100; 10¢ per specimen set.
b) HIGH SCHOOL FORM. Grades 9-12; 1936; nontimed (45) minutes; $4.20 per 100; 15¢ per specimen set.

REFERENCES
1 HILDRETH, GERTRUDE. "Adolescent Interests and Abilities." *J Genetic Psychol* 43:65-93 S '33.
2 HILDRETH, GERTRUDE. "An Interest Inventory for High School Personnel Work." *J Ed Res* 27:11-9 S '33.

3 HILDRETH, GERTRUDE, AND KELLER, VICTORIA M. "Results of an Experience Inventory in the High School." *Teach Col Rec* 38:581-92 Ap '37.

Stephen M. Corey, Professor of Educational Psychology and Superintendent of the Laboratory Schools, The University of Chicago. In 1933 the author of the *Personality and Interest Inventory* wrote:

The objection to the questionnaire method when the record is made by the child and unchecked by other methods is that the child may be unable to give an accurate picture of himself with respect to the traits in question or he may intentionally falsify his record to make it fit the picture he wants his teachers and advisors to have of him.[2]

This is a profound criticism of inventories and led the reviewer to expect some research data that would indicate the extent to which the present questionnaires were free from such weakness. No such data were presented however. In a second article the author wrote:

Results from the present questionnaire indicate in the main a serious attitude on the part of the pupils responding, and little attempt to give an imaginary picture in place of the real one. The questionnaire results tally well with known facts about individual pupils.[1]

So far as the reviewer can judge, these were merely the author's casual impressions. No quantitative evidence was presented. As a matter of fact, the reviewer was unable to locate any data that would enable him to judge the value of the *Personality and Interest Inventory*. Inspection of the forms indicates that information of interest is called for and that the format of the sheets as well as the administrative procedures are satisfactory.

The manual of directions to accompany the *Personality and Interest Inventory* includes no data on reliability or validity. The author suggests that the "reliability of the inventory can be determined in three ways: by examining the inner consistency of the record, by comparing the written record with the student's observed conduct, and by studying the change in trend of interest and activity in groups of different age and maturity." No statement appears as to whether this had or had not been done for the inventory under consideration. No norms of any sort appear. No description is given of the source of the items which appear under headings such as: I, Activities; II, Games-Sports; III, School Subjects; IV, Types of Books, etc.

For a review by Jack W. Dunlap, see 924.

[1239]

Personality Inventory. Grades 9-16 and adults; 1931-38; 1 form, 6 scoring scales; $1.75 per 25; 25¢ per 25 individual report blanks; 25¢ per specimen set; nontimed (25) minutes; Robert G. Bernreuter (Scales F1-C and F2-S were prepared by John C. Flanagan); Stanford, Calif.: Stanford University Press.

REFERENCES

1 BERNREUTER, ROBERT G. *The Valuation of a Proposed New Method for Constructing Personality Trait Tests.* Unpublished doctor's thesis, Stanford University, 1931.
2 FINCH, F. H., AND NEMZEK, C. L. "The Relationship of the Bernreuter Personality Inventory to Scholastic Achievement and Intelligence." *Sch and Soc* 36:594-6 N 5 '32.
3 WELLES, HENRY HUNTER, 3RD. *The Measurement of Certain Aspects of Personality among Hard of Hearing Adults.* Columbia University, Teachers College, Contributions to Education, No. 545. Rudolf Pintner, faculty sponsor. New York: Bureau of Publications, the College, 1932. Pp. viii, 77.
4 BENNETT, WILHELMINA. *A Study of Several Well Known Personality Tests.* [New York: Psychological Corporation], October 1933. Pp. ii, 25. Paper, mimeographed. Out of print.
5 BERNREUTER, ROBERT G. "The Measurement of Self-Sufficiency." *J Abn and Social Psychol* 28:291-300 O-D '33.
6 BERNREUTER, ROBERT G. "The Theory and Construction of the Personality Inventory." *J Social Psychol* 4:387-405 N '33.
7 BERNREUTER, ROBERT G. "Validity of the Personality Inventory." *Personnel J* 11:383-6 Ap '33.
8 BROTEMARKLE, R. A., "What the Bernreuter Personality Inventory Does Not Measure." *J Appl Psychol* 17:559-63 O '33.
9 CAHOON, G. P. "The Use of the Bernreuter Personality Inventory in the Selection of Student Teachers." *Univ H Sch J* 13:91-103 D '33.
10 HARGAN, JAMES. "The Reaction of Native White Convicts to the Bernreuter Personality Inventory." *Psychol Clinic* 22:138-40 Je-Ag '33.
11 MARSHALL, HELEN. "Clinical Applications of the Bernreuter Personality Inventory." *Psychol B* 30:601-2 O '33.
12 BERNREUTER, ROBERT G. "The Imbrication of Tests of Introversion-Extroversion and Neurotic Tendency." *J Social Psychol* 5:184-201 My '34.
13 DARLEY, JOHN G., AND INGLE, DWIGHT J. "An Analysis of the Bernreuter Personality Inventory in Occupational Guidance," pp. 32-41. In *Research Studies in Individual Diagnosis.* Edited by D. G. Paterson. University of Minnesota, Bulletin of the Employment Stabilization Research Institute, Vol. 3, No. 4. Minneapolis, Minn.: University of Minnesota Press, August 1934. Pp. 55. Paper. Out of print.
14 GILLILAND, A. R. "What Do Introversion-Extroversion Tests Measure?" *J Abn and Social Psychol* 28:407-11 Ja-Mr '34.
15 JOHNSON, WINIFRED B. "The Effect of Mood on Personality Traits as Measured by Bernreuter." *J Social Psychol* 5:515-22 N '34.
16 KUZNETS, G. "Analysis of Bernreuter's Personality Inventory." (Abstract.) *Psychol B* 31:585 '34.
17 LANDIS, CARNEY, AND KATZ, S. E. "The Validity of Certain Questions Which Purport to Measure Neurotic Tendencies." *J Appl Psychol* 18:343-56 Je '34.
18 LASLETT, H. R., AND BENNETT, ELIZABETH. "A Comparison of Scores of Two Measures of Personality." *J Abn and Social Psychol* 28:459-61 Ja-Mr '34.
19 LAYCOCK, SAM R. "The Bernreuter Personality Inventory in the Selection of Teachers." *Ed Adm and Sup* 20:59-63 Ja '34.
20 LENTZ, THEODORE F., JR. "Reliability of Opinionaire Technique Studied Intensively by the Retest Method." *J Social Psychol* 5:338-64 Ag '34.
21 PERRY, RAYMOND CARVER. *A Group Factor Analysis of the Adjustment Questionnaire.* University of Southern California, Southern California Educational Monographs, 1933-34 Series, No. 5. Los Angeles, Calif.: University of Southern California Press, 1934. Pp. xi, 93. $1.50.
22 STAGNER, ROSS. "Validity and Reliability of the Bernreuter Personality Inventory." *J Abn and Social Psychol* 28:413-8 Ja-Mr '34.
23 BERGEN, GARRET L. *Use of Tests in the Adjustment Service*, pp. 51-2. Adjustment Service Series Report [No.] 4. New York: American Association for Adult Education, 1935. Pp. 70. Paper. Out of print.
24 BERNREUTER, ROBERT G. "Chance and Personality Inventory Scores." *J Ed Psychol* 26:279-83 Ap '35.
25 BLOOM, BENJAMIN S. *Further Validation of the Bernreuter Personality Inventory.* Unpublished master's thesis, Pennsylvania State College, 1935. Pp. 48.
26 BURNHAM, PAUL S., AND CRAWFORD, ALBERT B. "The Vocational Interests and Personality Test Scores of a Pair of Dice." *J Ed Psychol* 26:508-12 O '35.
27 DODGE, ARTHUR F. *Occupational Ability Patterns.* Columbia University, Teachers College, Contributions to Education, No. 658. Harry Dexter Kitson, faculty sponsor. New York: Bureau of Publications, the College, 1935. Pp. v, 97. $1.60.
28 FLANAGAN, JOHN C. *Factor Analysis in the Study of Personality.* Stanford University, Calif.: Stanford University

Press, 1935. Pp. x, 103. $1.25. Paper, lithotyped. (London: Oxford University Press. 6s.)
29 FLANAGAN, JOHN C. "Technical Aspects of Multi-Trait Tests: A Reply to Dr. Lorge." *J Ed Psychol* 26:641-51 D '35.
30 FRANK, BENJAMIN. "Stability of Questionnaire Response." *J Abn and Social Psychol* 30:320-4 O-D '35.
31 LANDIS, CARNEY; ZUBIN, JOSEPH; AND KATZ, SIEGFRIED E. "Empirical Evaluation of Three Personality Adjustment Inventories." *J Ed Psychol* 26:321-30 My '35.
32 LINE, W., AND GRIFFIN, J. D. M. "The Objective Determination of Factors Underlying Mental Health." *Am J Psychiatry* 91:833-42 Ja '35.
33 LINE, W.; GRIFFIN, J. D. M.; AND ANDERSON, G. W. "The Objective Measurement of Mental Stability." *J Mental Sci* 81:61-106 Ja '35.
34 LORGE, IRVING. "Personality Traits by Fiat: [Part] I, The Analysis of the Total Trait Scores and Keys of the Bernreuter Personality Inventory." *J Ed Psychol* 26:273-8 Ap '35.
35 LORGE, IRVING. "Personality Traits by Fiat: [Part] II, A Correction." *J Ed Psychol* 26:652-4 D '35.
36 LORGE, IRVING; BERNHOLZ, ELNA; AND SELLS, SAUL B. "Personality Traits by Fiat: [Part] II, The Consistency of the Bernreuter Personality Inventory by the Bernreuter and by the Flanagan Keys." *J Ed Psychol* 26:427-34. S '35.
37 ZERILLI, VIRGINIA I. "Note on Scoring Tests of Multiple Weighted Items." *J Ed Psychol* 26:395-7 My '35.
38 BILLS, MARION A., AND WARD, L. W. "Testing Salesmen of Casualty Insurance." *Personnel* J 15:55-8 Je '36.
38.1 GUILFORD, J. P., AND GUILFORD, R. B. "Personality Factors S, E, and M and their Measurement." *J Psychol* 2:109-27 '36.
39 CONWAY, CLIFFORD B. "A New Scoring Apparatus for the Bernreuter Personality Inventory." *J Appl Psychol* 20:264-5 Ap '36.
40 JOHNSON, ELEANOR HOPE. "Objective Tests, Including the Bernreuter Personality Inventory, as Constructive Elements in a Counseling Technique." *Am J Orthopsychiatry* 6:431-6 Jl '36.
41 SHLAUDEMAN, KARL W. "A New Scale for Scoring the Bernreuter Personality Inventory." *J Social Psychol* 7:483-6 N '36.
42 SPEER, G. S. "The Use of the Bernreuter Personality Inventory as an Aid in the Prediction of Behavior Problems." *J Juvenile Res* 20:65-9 Ap '36.
43 DODGE, ARTHUR F. "Relation of 'Social Dominance' to General Intelligence." *J Ed Psychol* 28:387-90 My '37.
44 DODGE, ARTHUR F. "Social Dominance of Clerical Workers and Sales-Persons as Measured by the Bernreuter Personality Inventory." *J Ed Psychol* 28:71-3 Ja '37.
45 HOLLINGWORTH, LETA S., AND RUST, METTA MAUND. "Application of the Bernreuter Inventory of Personality to Highly Intelligent Adolescents." *J Psychol* 4:287-93 O '37.
46 KEYS, NOEL, AND GUILFORD, MARGARET S. "The Validity of Certain Adjustment Inventories in Predicting Problem Behavior." *J Ed Psychol* 28:641-55 D '37.
47 PINTNER, RUDOLF; FUSFELD, IRVING S.; AND BRUNSCHWIG, LILY. "Personality Tests of Deaf Adults." *J Genetic Psychol* 51:305-27 D '37.
48 ST. CLAIR, WALTER F., AND SEEGERS, J. CONRAD. "Certain Aspects of the Validity of the Bernreuter Personality Inventory." *J Ed Psychol* 28:530-40 O '37.
49 ANDERSON, ROSE G. "Some Technological Aspects of Counseling Adult Women." *J Appl Psychol* 22:455-69 O '38.
50 BAER, LENONA OPAL. *A Comparison of Ratings on the Bernreuter Personality Inventory with Case History Records.* Unpublished master's thesis, State University of Iowa, 1938.
51 BENNETT, GEORGE K. "A Simplified Scoring Method for the Bernreuter Personality Inventory." *J Appl Psychol* 22:390-4 Ag '38.
52 BILLS, MARION A., AND DAVIDSON, CHARLES M. "Study of Inter-relation of Items on Bernreuter Personality Inventory and Strong's Interest Analysis Test, Part VIII, and Their Relation to Success and Failure in Selling Casualty Insurance." *Psychol B* 35:677 N '38.
53 DODGE, ARTHUR F. "Social Dominance and Sales Personality." *J Appl Psychol* 22:132-9 Ap '38.
54 DODGE, ARTHUR F. "What Are the Personality Traits of the Successful Sales-Person?" *J Appl Psychol* 22:229-38 Je '38.
55 FARNSWORTH, PAUL R. "A Genetic Study of the Bernreuter Personality Inventory." *J Genetic Psychol* 52:3-13 Mr '38.
56 FARNSWORTH, PAUL R., AND FERGUSON, LEONARD W. "The Growth of a Suicidal Tendency as Indicated by Score Changes in Bernreuter's Personality Inventory." *Sociometry* 1:339-41 Ja-Ap '38.
57 HORSCH, ALFRED C., AND DAVIS, ROBERT A. "Personality Traits of Juvenile Delinquents and Adult Criminals." *J Social Psychol* 9:57-65 F '38.
58 JARVIE, L. L., AND JOHNS, A. A. "Does the Bernreuter Personality Inventory Contribute to Counseling?" *Ed Res B* 17:7-9+ Ja '38.
59 McQUITTY, LOUIS L. "An Approach to the Measurement of Individual Differences in Personality." *Char and Pers* 7:81-95 S '38.
60 MOSIER, CHARLES I. "On the Validity of Neurotic Questionnaires." *J Social Psychol* 9:3-16 F '38.
61 NEMZEK, CLAUDE L. "The Value of the Bernreuter Personality Inventory for Direct and Differential Prediction of Academic Success as Measured by Teachers' Marks." *J Appl Psychol* 22:576-86 D '38.

62 St. Clair, Walter F., and Seegers, J. Conrad. "Certain Aspects of the Validity of the F Scores of the Bernreuter Personality Inventory." *J Ed Psychol* 29:301-11 Ap '38.

63 Stogdill, Emily L., and Thomas, Minnie E. "The Bernreuter Personality Inventory as a Measure of Student Adjustment." *J Social Psychol* 9:299-315 Ag '38.

64 Traxler, Arthur. *The Use of Tests and Rating Devices in the Appraisal of Personality*, pp. 15-7, 40-2. Educational Records Bulletin No. 23. New York: Educational Records Bureau, March 1938. Pp. vii, 80. $1.50. Paper, lithotyped.

65 Cook, P. H. "The Clinical Testing of Personality." *Austral J Psychol and Philos* 17:151-7 '39.

66 Greene, J. E., and Staton, Thomas F. "Predictive Value of Various Tests of Emotionality and Adjustment in a Guidance Program for Prospective Teachers." *J Ed Res* 32:653-9 My '39.

67 Hathaway, S. R. "The Personality Inventory as an Aid in the Diagnosis of Psychopathic Inferiors." *J Consulting Psychol* 3:112-7 Jl-Ag '39.

68 Kirkpatrick, Forrest H. *The Measurement of Personality*. Psychological Record, Vol. 3, No. 17. Bloomington, Ind.: Prinicipia Press, Inc., October 1939. Pp. 211-24. $0.30. Paper.

69 Laycock, S. R., and Hutcheon, N. B. "A Preliminary Investigation into the Problem of Measuring Engineering Aptitude." *J Ed Psychol* 30:280-8 Ap '39.

70 St. Clair, Walter F. "The Relation of Scholastic Aptitude to 'Withdrawal' Personality." *J Ed Psychol* 30:295-302 Ap '39.

71 Babcock, Harriet. "Personality and Efficiency of Mental Functioning." *Am J Orthopsychiatry* 10:527-31 Jl '40.

Charles I. Mosier, Assistant Professor of Psychology and Assistant University Examiner, University of Florida. The *Personality Inventory* is a multitrait test of the questionnaire type, designed to yield measures on six traits of personality adjustment, viz., neurotic tendency (B1-N), self-sufficiency (B2-S), introversion-extroversion (B3-I), dominance-submission (B4-D), self-confidence (F1-C), and sociability (F2-S). The manual provides a description of the construction and validation of the scales, and reports validity and reliability coefficients. Percentile norms are supplied for each sex at high school, college, and adult levels. The manual reports corrected split-halves reliabilities on college students for the B scales ranging from .85 to .91, and for the F scales of .86 and .78. Reliabilities obtained by other workers have been slightly lower. These reliabilities are rather low to warrant use in work with individuals. Validation was originally against other tests—Thurstone's *Personality Schedule,* Bernreuter's *Self-sufficiency Scale,* Laird's *C2 Introversion Test,* and the Allport's *A-S Reaction Study.* Since the items comprising the *Personality Inventory* were taken from or adapted from these tests originally,[16] it is not surprising that the author can report that "the four traits measured by the *Personality Inventory* are identical with four traits which have been measured by previously validated tests."[6] The validity of the Bernreuter test is thus seen to depend on the validity of these four scales.[60] Of the six personality traits measured, B3-I is identical with B1-N, and only one of the two scales need be used. The F scales were derived from the B scales by factorial analysis of the intercorrelations of total scores,[28] and reduces the four B scales to the two F scales. If the test is used, all of the information contained in the first four B scales, is obtained by use of the F scales only.

Other work by factor analysis of individual responses [38a, 60] indicates that the B1-N scale measures a composite of at least six identifiable traits, which may combine in any unknown proportions to yield a particular score. Attempts to validate the test clinically have, in general, been unsuccessful, due to the heterogeneity of the traits combined in a single total score. While Stagner[22] reports a subjectively observed agreement between scores and interview impressions (the interviews were made with knowledge of the scores) for selected cases, the general conclusion from clinical use is that while an extremely high score probably indicates maladjustment, a low score does not indicate adjustment. Landis and co-workers[17, 31] found that none of the Bernreuter scales would differentiate groups of normal college students from groups of hospitalized psychotic and psychoneurotic patients. Their conclusion concerning the validity of the test is probably the best guide to its use.

This analysis, together with the previous studies . . . indicates clearly the unsatisfactory nature of the personality inventories at present available. Until we have personality inventories which measure or at least indicate those factors in the life of the individual which the inventory purports to measure, psychologists can do no other than regard these questionnaires as instruments of research not yet ready for general application.[6] Even if the test does select the individual in need of psychiatric advice, the test user should remember that the assignment of the test title as a trait does not constitute a diagnosis of any value.

The *Personality Inventory* does, however, present an extremely useful checklist of symptoms, and without regard for the scales or scores from them, a study of the responses to individual questions should be far more revealing in the individual case than the total scores on all six scales.

The usefulness of the test as a group test to select those individuals most in need of mental hygiene is definitely limited. For this purpose the best single scale is probably F1-C. Even so, it must be remembered that while those individuals scoring extremely high are probably in need of assistance, those scoring low cannot be assumed to be adjusted, and some with low scores may be in as great or greater need of assistance as the individual with the highest score.

In the hands of the trained clinical psychologist, the *Personality Inventory* may be an extremely useful instrument, but for other users, even those with a course in "Tests and Measurements," the uncertainties in the field of personality measurement, particularly with the questionnaire type of test, make such tests, in the reviewer's opinion, of little value, and of some potential harm.

Theodore Newcomb, Psychology Department, Bennington College. Certain obvious disadvantages inhere in the method of asking direct yes-or-no questions of subjects who are bound to impute some personal significance to their replies, and who vary in the degree of their willingness to reveal whatever they imagine that significance to be. It is not difficult to prepare such schedules in such a manner that their split-half reliability can be demonstrated to be very satisfactory. But responses are determined by so many factors other than those necessarily involved in the trait ostensibly being measured that the validity of scores yielded by such methods is exceedingly doubtful. The rank order of scores obtained by a given population on a schedule of this type is thus of questionable significance. When given under favorable conditions, however, it is often true that either the high-scoring or the low-scoring individuals—rarely both, for one extreme of most scales is commonly considered more desirable than the other—will be found, following more exact study, actually to be characterized by a considerable degree of the trait in question.

Bernreuter's *Personality Inventory* must be evaluated in terms of this basic methodology, but it is in certain ways unique. As originally published, each reply (yes-no-?) to each of its 125 brief questions received a given score-value for each of four traits. These are neurotic tendency, self-sufficiency, introversion-extroversion, and dominance-submission, respectively labeled as B1-N, B2-S, B3-I, and B4-D. Each of the 125 items was initially selected as having high differentiating power, for one of the four traits, between high and low criterion groups as determined by previously existing measures of those traits. Each item-response was then weighted for the other three traits, on the basis of empirical differentiating power for those traits.

The split-half reliabilities, as reported both by the author and by other investigators, are satisfactory by common standards, most of them ranging between .85 and .90 when corrected by the Spearman-Brown prophecy formula. But the validity of the several traits can scarcely be regarded as satisfactory, in view of their high intercorrelations. The correlation between B1-N and B3-I is actually higher (.95) than the reliability coefficient of either, and that between B1-N and B4-D (r's of $-.80$ and $-.83$ are reported by the author) is nearly as high as the reliability coefficient of either ($-.80$ and $-.83$). For all practical purposes it must be concluded that B1-N, B3-I, and B4-D are alternative measures of the same thing, whatever it be called. The author himself has proposed that either B1-N or B3-I be discarded.

It may be, of course, that neurotic tendency and introversion are actually indistinguishable, and that submissiveness (or nondominance) is almost equivalent to either of them. But few psychologists are prepared to concede this, and none have obtained such high intercorrelations by other measures. It is probable, therefore, that the method of differential weighting of the same responses is responsible for the apparent equivalence of these traits. For such reasons Flanagan,[28] using Hotelling's method of principal components, has more recently shown from an analysis of responses to the Bernreuter items, that by a revised weighting of item responses two unrelated scores can be obtained. These are tentatively labeled self-confidence and sociability. Self-confidence is by no means the same as Bernreuter's self-sufficiency, nor is sociability closely related to the constellation B1-N, B3-I, B4-D, judging from correlations presented.

If one starts with the assumption that the psychologist's task is to find important human traits which are not correlated, even though it is not quite clear what they represent, the Flanagan scores are certainly among the best personality measures available to date. It should not be forgotten, however, that his results depend upon the particular loading of items which Bernreuter happened to offer him. The only genuine validation of the measure is the empirical demonstration that they correspond to some significant human behavior, and this demonstration may yet be made. If one assumes that traits which it is important to measure may or may not be correlated, measures like the Bernreuter Schedule, which result in intercorrelations as a result of methodological artifacts, will be avoided. If one assumes, with this reviewer, that the results of yes-no-? questionnaires are valuable not for their rank-ordering of individuals but for their isolating of individuals for more intensive clinical or experimental study, one will wonder whether such crude means of obtaining data merit so much statistical refinement, and for one's own purposes (if one is to use such methods at all) will have recourse to briefer schedules which are equally reliable and perhaps more valid.

See also B108 and B358.

[1240]

Personality Inventory for Children. Ages 9-14; 1935; 1 form; $2.00 per 100; 15¢ per specimen set; nontimed (15) minutes; Fred Brown; New York: Psychological Corporation.

REFERENCES

1 BROWN, FRED. *An Experimental Study of the Psychoneurotic Syndrome in Childhood.* Unpublished doctor's thesis, Ohio State University, 1933. Pp. 175.
2 BROWN, FRED. "A Psychoneurotic Inventory for Children between Nine and Fourteen Years of Age." *J Appl Psychol* 18:566-77 Ag '34.
3 BROWN, FRED. "The School as a Subsidiary of the Psychological Clinic in the Prevention of Neuroticism in Childhood." *Ed Method* 13:254-8 F '34.
4 BROWN, FRED. "The Problem of Nervousness and Its Objective Verification in Children." *J Abn and Social Psychol* 31:194-207 Jl-S '36.
5 BROWN, FRED. "Neuroticism of Institution versus Non-Institution Children." *J Appl Psychol* 21:379-83 Ag '37.
6 BROWN, FRED. "Social Maturity and Stability of Non-Delinquents, Photo-Delinquents, and Delinquents." *Am J. Orthopsychiatry* 8:214-9 Ap '38.
7 SPRINGER, N. NORTON. "A Comparative Study of the Psychoneurotic Responses of Deaf and Hearing Children." *J Ed Psychol* 29:459-66 S '38.
8 SPRINGER, N. NORTON, AND ROSLOW, SYDNEY. "A Further Study of the Psychoneurotic Responses of Deaf and Hearing Children." *J Ed Psychol* 29:590-6 N '38.

S. J. Beck, Head Psychologist, Michael Reese Hospital, Chicago, Illinois. This reviewer has not used the inventory. The comments that follow are therefore a reaction entirely to a study of the blank and the accompanying directions.

This inventory consists of eighty items. In the directions accompanying the material the author classifies the items within five categories of personality area—home, school, physical symptoms, insecurity, and irritability. The questionnaire was standardized on "2,748 unselected cases between nine and fourteen years of age from the fourth to the ninth grade inclusive, and including equal distribu-

tion of both sexes." The scoring method has the advantage that it is simplified in the extreme, not even requiring the use of a key.

Examination of the eighty questions in the inventory reveals the difficulty so common in questionnaires. What does the question really mean? For example: "Are you very particular about the things you eat?" "Do your parents get angry with you often?" "Is your mother too strict with you?" The common experience when two or more persons get together to iron out the meanings of the questions in a questionnaire has been much time in mulling over the words and usually disagreement in the end. We are faced here with the old difficulty that the same experience cannot have the same meaning to two individuals. In this connection the author's dependence on unselected children deserves some comment. Unselected material is the lodestone of statistical studies. With intelligent adults having the difficulty they do in pinning down the content of the inventory items how intelligible could these questions have been to children at the average and lower end of the intelligence scale in the ninth, to say nothing of the fourth grades?

A second difficulty with inventories is the problem of how much faith can we put in the answers as speaking truth? This criticism must be asserted in spite of the effort at reassurance in the directions: "These questions have nothing to do with your regular school work. There are no right or wrong answers in this list. No one except the person giving this test will know how you answered the question. You will not be asked to explain your answers." The fact is that children are cagey and the number of untrue answers is pretty certain to vary with the amount of suspiciousness in the child. In other words, the one from whom we most need the truth is by the very fact of his emotional maladjustment, likely to cover it up. Anonymity is the one antidote; but that defeats, of course, the purpose of the questionnaire since it covers up the identity of the individual to be treated. The author's assurance to himself of "a tendency in children to regard the inventory as a sympathetic and unemotional recipient of confidences, which leads us to believe that questions are sometimes answered more truthfully in questionnaires than in person-to-person interviews," sounds a bit naive and inconsistent with clinical experience. The claim for the inventory's usefulness in treatment must again be challenged. The information obtained is at the best descriptive and static; not a presentation of the dynamics producing the overt behavior, i.e., not explanatory. And how can treatment be directed except by knowing the causative sequences? Does, for example, the fact that a child considers his work too hard (Item 66) or that he stutters (Item 7) have the same symptomatic value irrespective of the personality which produces this behavior? Then, too, why the five particular categories? Are they independent variables? The clinician must ask, for example, when is irritability (Category 5) an expression of insecurity (Category 1) or a physical symptom (Category 3)? Will the inventory answer these questions? Or again, when are the physical symptoms emotional reactions and when are they products of actual tissue pathology?

The big difficulty this reviewer senses throughout this questionnaire is the lack of clinical sense. This brings us to our chief criticism, namely the validation on which the author depends. This was based on the literature concerning the neurotic child and statistical technics for final selection of the items. There is no report of validation of findings in individuals' inventories with study of the same individual by other methods. The defect is one which the author, no doubt, shares with much present day study of personality. The fallacy it seems should be simple in its recognition, namely, statistics is a tool of science, an aid to it, but it is not a method of science. It cannot substitute for actual investigation. There is no more royal road to science than there is to any other learning.

A bibliography appended to the directions includes nine titles by the author and three other papers. The clinical literature is represented by its absence.

Carl R. Rogers, Professor of Psychology, The Ohio State University. It is difficult to know the purpose of this carelessly devised instrument. In the original published reference it is discussed as a measure of neurotic tendency, and this would seem to be its most accurate description. In the brief manual there seems to be complete confusion as to whether it is a measure of neuroticism or a measure of behavior maladjustment, and the norms are phrased to indicate the latter view. The fact

that symptoms of nervousness, fear, guilt, hypochondria, and worry are not identical with behavior problems in children, is not even considered. Not every problem child is neurotic, nor does every neurotic exhibit behavior problems, but the author of the test seems unaware of this.

The questions are exceedingly direct and obvious, making evasion likely. Few children would give truthful answers to such a question as "Do you usually get headaches when you are told to do something which is disagreeable to you?" Likewise the "yes-no" technique, with no possibility of shaded or neutral responses, seems inexcusable. The questions are concerned primarily with neurotic physical symptoms, worries, fears, and irritability. There are a few questions regarding home and school adjustment.

There is little that can be commended in the construction of the test. The items were chosen from a review of the literature, and the scoring of the items is also based entirely on the literature. With this a priori choice of items, and an a priori method of scoring, the author proceeds to "validate" the test by comparing the group making high scores with those making low scores. This is lifting oneself by the bootstraps with a vengeance! Even this dubious type of validation is only mentioned, and not presented, in the manual.

This reviewer can see little usefulness in such an inventory. It is too blunt in its questions to be of very much help as a preliminary to interviewing. It is certainly not a valid measure of a child's maladjustment. It may be a measure of a child's neurotic tendencies, but no real study has been carried out to indicate whether it does discriminate between stable and neurotic children. The most that can be said for it is that it measures the degree to which children admit the existence of symptoms which are classed in the literature as neurotic.

[1241]
Personality Rating Chart for Preschool Children. Nursery school; 1938; 5¢ per chart; Rachel Stutsman; Detroit, Mich.: Merrill-Palmer School, 71 East Ferry Ave.

REFERENCES
1 WILSON, CHARLES A.; SWEENY, MARY E.; STUTSMAN, RACHEL; CHESIRE, LEONE E.; AND HATT, ELISE. *The Merrill-Palmer Standards of Physical and Mental Growth.* Detroit, Mich.: Merrill-Palmer School, 1930. Pp. ix, 121. $0.50. Paper.

[1242]
Personality Rating Scale for Preschool Children. Nursery school; 1938; 9 schedules; 20¢ per set of 9 schedules; 50¢ per reprint of article in the *Journal*

of *Genetic Psychology*; Katherine Elliott Roberts and Rachel Stutsman Ball; Detroit, Mich.: Merrill-Palmer School, 70 East Ferry Ave.

a) SCHEDULE 1, ASCENDANCE—SUBMISSION.
b) SCHEDULE 2, ATTRACTIVENESS OF PERSONALITY.
c) SCHEDULE 3, COMPLIANCE WITH ROUTINE.
d) SCHEDULE 4, INDEPENDENCE OF ADULT AFFECTION OR ATTENTION.
e) SCHEDULE 5, PHYSICAL ATTRACTIVENESS.
f) SCHEDULE 6, RESPECT FOR PROPERTY RIGHTS.
g) SCHEDULE 7, RESPONSE TO AUTHORITY.
h) SCHEDULE 8, SOCIABILITY WITH OTHER CHILDREN.
i) SCHEDULE 9, TENDENCY TO FACE REALITY.

REFERENCES

1 ROBERTS, KATHERINE ELLIOTT, AND BALL, RACHEL STUTSMAN. "A Study of Personality in Young Children by Means of a Series of Rating Scales." *J Genetic Psychol* 52:79-149 Mr '38.

[1243]

Personality Schedule, 1929 Edition. College and adults; 1928-30; 1 form; $1.25 per 25; 15¢ per specimen set; nontimed (30-40) minutes; L. L. Thurstone and Thelma Gwinn Thurstone; Chicago, Ill.: University of Chicago Press.

REFERENCES

1 ALLPORT, GORDON W. "The Neurotic Personality and Traits of Self-Expression." *J Social Psychol* 1:524-7 N '30.
2 THURSTONE, L. L., AND THURSTONE, THELMA GWINN. "A Neurotic Inventory." *J Social Psychol* 1:3-30 F '30.
3 HARVEY, O. L. "Concerning the Thurstone 'Personality Schedule.'" *J Social Psychol* 3:240-51 My '32.
4 STAGNER, ROSS. "The Intercorrelation of Some Standardized Personality Tests." *J Appl Psychol* 16:453-64 O '32.
5 WILLOUGHBY, RAYMOND ROYCE. "Some Properties of the Thurstone Personality Schedule and a Suggested Revision." *J Social Psychol* 3:401-24 N '32.
6 HERTZBERG, OSCAR E. "Emotional Stability as a Factor in a Teachers College Administration and Training Program." *Ed Adm and Sup* 19:141-8 F '33.
7 HABBE, STEPHEN. "The Selection of Student Nurses." *J Appl Psychol* 17:564-80 O '33.
8 SMITH, HATTIE NESBIT. "A Study of the Neurotic Tendencies Shown in Dementia Praecox and Manic Depressive Insanity." *J Social Psychol* 4:116-28 F '33.
9 STAGNER, ROSS. "Improved Norms for Four Personality Tests." *Am J Psychol* 45:303-7 Ap '33.
10 HANNA, JOSEPH V. "Clinical Procedure as a Method of Validating a Measure of Psychoneurotic Tendency." *J Abn and Social Psychol* 28:435-45 Ja-Mr '34.
11 LANDIS, CARNEY, AND KATZ, S. E. "The Validity of Certain Questions Which Purport to Measure Neurotic Tendencies." *J Appl Psychol* 18:343-56 Je '34.
12 MOORE, HERBERT, AND STEELE, ISABEL. "Personality Tests." *J Abn and Social Psychol* 29:45-52 Ap-Je '34.
13 FARRAM, FREDA. "The Relation of Ascendance-Submission Tendencies to Neurosis." *Austral J Psychol and Philos* 13:228-32 S '35.
14 MORAN, THOMAS F. "A Brief Study of the Validity of a Neurotic Inventory." *J Appl Psychol* 19:180-8 Ap '35.
15 NEPRASH, J. A. "The Reliability of Questions in the Thurstone Personality Schedule." *J Social Psychol* 7:239-44 My '36.
16 CONKLIN, EDMUND S. *Three Diagnostic Scorings for the Thurstone Personality Schedule.* Indiana University Publications, Science Series, No. 6, Bloomington, Ind.: Indiana University Bookstore, 1937. Pp. 25. $0.50. Paper.
17 FEDER, DANIEL D., AND MALLETT, DONALD R. "Validity of Certain Measures of Personality Adjustment." *J Am Assn Col Reg* 13:5-15 O '37.
18 KIRKPATRICK, FORREST H. "The Validity of the Thurstone Personality Schedule." *Proc W Va Acad Sci* 10:204-9 S '37.
19 MOSIER, CHARLES I. "A Factor Analysis of Certain Neurotic Symptoms." *Psychometrika* 2:263-86 D '37.
20 PAI, T.; SUNG, S. M.; AND HSÜ, E. H. "The Application of Thurstone's Personality Schedule to Chinese Subjects." *J Social Psychol* 8:47-72 F '37.
21 SCHOTT, EMMETT, L. "Personality Tests in Clinical Practice." *J Abn and Social Psychol* 32:236-9 Jl-S '37.
22 HALL, MARGARET E. "Mental and Physical Efficiency of Women Drug Addicts." *J Abn and Social Psychol* 33:332-45 Jl '38.
23 KUZNETS, GEORGE M. "An Analysis of a Group of Most Differentiating Items of the Thurstone Personality Schedule. *Psychol B* 35:525 O '38.
24 MOSIER, CHARLES I. "On the Validity of Neurotic Questionnaires." *J Social Psychol* 9:3-16 F '38.
25 REMMERS, H. H.; WHISLER, LAURENCE; AND DUWALD, VICTOR F. "'Neurotic' Indicators at the Adolescent Level." *J Social Psychol* 9:17-24 F '38.
26 MCCANN, WILLIS H. "Responses of Psychotic Patients to the Thurstone Personality Schedule before and after Metrazol Treatment," pp. 187-9. In *Proceedings of the Indiana Academy of Science [for 1938]*, Vol. 48. Edited by Paul Weatherwax. Indianapolis, Ind.: the Academy, State Library, 1939. Pp. xxx, 253. $3.00. Paper.
27 MCKINNEY, FRED. "Personality Adjustment of College Students as Related to Factors in Personal History." *J Appl Psychol* 23:660-8 D '39.
28 PINTNER, RUDOLF, AND FORLANO, GEORGE. "A Note on the Relation between Divergent Interests and Emotional Stability." *J Abn and Social Psychol* 34:539-41 O '39.

J. P. Guilford, Professor of Psychology, The University of Southern California. This extensive inventory of 223 questions was prepared in 1928 for the general purpose of singling out those college freshmen who were in need of special attention from psychologist or psychiatrist. Presumably, it is still of greatest value for that and similar purposes, although the variety of duties it has been asked to perform has been larger than that. Beginning with questions, gathered from all sources, that describe symptoms and causes of neurotic disorders of various kinds, the authors selected the final list on the basis of internal consistency, assuming that since the preliminary scoring was based upon every available common description of neurotic conditions, there was no better criterion than the test itself. The 50 highest and 50 lowest students in a population of nearly 700 were criterion groups, a latitude of difference that would result in few, if any, rejections if items are diagnostic at all.

The manual of instructions states that "thirty minutes is ample time for answering the questions" but in the reviewer's experience more time is required by many students. A single score is conveniently obtained in five to six minutes by means of a translucent stencil. No weights are used, which suggests that the schedule would be easily adaptable to machine scoring.

The reliability (split-half) for the total score is given as .95; and for one-half of the inventory as .90. The validity is more or less taken for granted, in view of the accepted symptomatic nature of the questions, assuming, of course, as the authors frankly do, that the student takes the test seriously and does his best to respond truthfully. They point out that only the very rare student would artificially raise his score toward the high (unfavorable) end, and that while an occasional neurotic is overlooked because of falsification, in this case we err on the side of safety.

In the light of factor-analysis studies of such test items since the time this inventory was published, and in view of the more analytical approaches of Bernreuter and Bell, it would seem that the Thurstone schedule would by now have some partial scorings. So extensive a list of questions should have the same analytical possibilities as are exploited in similar inventories. Perhaps such scorings have been developed; to the knowledge of the reviewer they have not yet been published.

The authors warn testers against comparing scores from different groups of individuals, lest the same diagnostic value of the items not obtain. Studies have shown that the same inventory that is validated on one population may not give the expected results when applied to another of different background and mental set. For example, lists of items validated with psychotic and psychopathic individuals may not give the expected differentation when applied to normals, and vice versa. The Thurstone schedule, and others like it, will fail to distinguish the mental patient from the normal in many cases. Furthermore, a high "neurotic tendency" score, no matter from what inventory it is obtained, may mean merely that the individual has indeed had numerous incidental factors that frequently "cause" neurotic breakdowns, but that because of a strong mental constitution he has not broken under them. Another individual with few such indicators has one of them to a severe degree and cracks under it. All we can say is that for a person with a high score the probability of a neurotic difficulty is greater than for a person with a low score. It is these probabilities that lead us to explore certain individuals further for expected trouble. A small amount of advance information that may serve as a warning is better than none at all.

The correlation of the schedule scores with college aptitude tests like the *American Council on Education Psychological Examination* is given as approximately zero. On the other hand, the correlation of the schedule scores with scholarship is positive, though low. This situation would make the inventory score an ally in the better prediction of scholarship. But it probably contributes much less to a multiple prediction than do other scores and so will rarely be included in a regression equation.

[1243.1]

Pressey Interest-Attitude Tests. Grades 6 to adults; 1933; 1 form; 75¢ per 25; 15¢ per specimen set; nontimed (30) minutes; S. L. Pressey and L. C. Pressey; New York: Psychological Corporation.

REFERENCES

1 PRESSEY, SIDNEY L., AND PRESSEY, LUELLA C. "Development of the Interest-Attitude Tests." *J Appl Psychol* 17:1-16 F '33.
2 HARRIS, A. J. "A Note on Three Recent Personality Tests." *J Social Psychol* 7:474-9 '36.
3 PRESSEY, SIDNEY L. "A Note on the Critical Note." *J Appl Psychol* 22:659-61 D '38.
4 THORNDIKE, ROBERT L. "Critical Note on the Pressey Interest-Attitudes Test." *J Appl Psychol* 22:657-8 D '38.
5 THORNDIKE, ROBERT L. "Responses of a Group of Gifted Children to the Pressey Interest-Attitude Test." *J Ed Psychol* 30:587-93 N '39.

Douglas Spencer, Assistant Professor of Psychology, Queens College. This reconstruction of the Pressey's *X-O Test* makes available in greatly improved form an instrument that has long proved an interesting addition to the clinician's battery. As heretofore, it has the advantage of being non-threatening to the subject because its purpose is disguised. Although many of the *X-O Test* items are retained, the mechanics of the old blank have been altered to simplify the administration and the scoring, and careful work has been done to reduce vocabulary difficulties and to eliminate insignificant items.

The new test, for use from the sixth grade to the adult level, "furnishes a simple and expedient way of investigating the maturity of the interests and attitudes of a group with respect to a large number of items," according to the authors.

Four subtests of 90 items each concern the following: (1) Things the subject considers wrong; (2) Things which interest him; (3) Things he worries about; and (4) Characteristics of persons he admires. He responds to each section by putting an X in front of words arranged in columns, and to register very strong feelings he can put two X's in front of any item. The 360 items were selected through a painstaking item analysis of 950 words, each item being retained on the basis of its power to differentiate between younger and older subjects. Separate norms are available for boys (2099 cases) and for girls (2088). The test is easy to give and to score.

Reliability by the split-half method for the entire test was found to vary for single grades from .94 to .96, and for the subtests varied from .85 to .96.

As to validity, while the authors stress the need for more research, the efforts thus far reported are encouraging. These findings include confirmation of expected differences between groups contrasting as to the apparent sophistication of their community, and also between groups of assumed contrast in racial maturity.

Correlation of scores with estimates of emotional maturity by various guidance workers are promising, varying from .66 to .72. Further research on clinically contrasting groups to reveal more clearly what the test measures, should prove worth the effort. More light needs to be thrown on the meaning of extreme high and low scores, especially when these occur in marked discrepancy with MA or CA. This would require a careful case study approach.

As on the older *X-O* blanks, the strong feeling responses often yield valuable clues for investigation through interviews. These may make the test well worth giving even when the numerical scoring is not taken seriously.

[1244]

Pupil Portraits. Grades 4-8; 1934; 2 forms; $2.10 per 100; 25¢ per specimen set; nontimed (25-40) minutes; R. Pintner, J. B. Maller, G. Forlano, and H. C. Axelrod; New York: Bureau of Publications, Teachers College, Columbia University.

REFERENCES

1 PINTNER, RUDOLF; MALLER, J. B.; FORLANO, G.; AND AXELROD, H. "The Measurement of Pupil Adjustment." *J Ed Res* 28:334-48 Ja '35.
2 PINTNER, RUDOLF. "An Adjustment Test with Normal and Hard of Hearing Children." *J Genetic Psychol* 56:367-81 Je '40.

Simon H. Tulchin, Consulting Psychologist, 136 East 57th St., New York, New York. The test consists of 100 items and is available in two forms. The items are phrased in language readily comprehended by pupils in grades 4 to 8 and include both positive and negative statements dealing with specific habits and attitudes presented in the form of impersonal descriptions of other children. For example, such statements as "This child thinks school helps children," "This child thinks everybody copies, so why shouldn't he," and "This child thinks his friends do not care much for him," etc., are made and the child is to draw a circle around the letter *S* if he thinks the same and around the letter *D* if he thinks he is different. The items are grouped into five subtests dealing with the relationship of the pupil to his school environment, to his teacher, to his classmates, to himself, and to his home and family. The score is the number of statements answered in agreement with the key. The scores show no definite relation to age. The correlations between total score and age are —.17 for 270 boys, and —.03 for 289 girls in grades 6 and 7. A wider age scatter would have been more desirable.

This test has been standardized on 1,720 boys and 1,434 girls in grades 4 to 8. Because the girls made significantly higher scores than the boys separate norms are given for the two sexes. No separate norms are given for the several subtests. However, norms are given for the first four subtests which are grouped under the heading of school adjustment and the last subtest under the heading of home adjustment as well as for total score on all items. Percentile equivalents have been calculated.

The reliability coefficient based on the correlation between the two forms administered to 600 pupils in grades 4 to 8 is .935 ± .004.

The authors employed several procedures [1] to determine the validity of the test. The test was given to a group of "problem" children in a probation school. The mean score of the normal group was 20 points higher than the mean score of the "problem" children and the difference was found to be statistically significant. However, this difference of 20 points was found during the preliminary study when 287 statements were used. Only items which differentiated between the two groups were included in the final form. In the article a table shows the correlation of each item with total test score, percentages of pupils who failed each item and the difference between percentages of failures in the normal and "problem" groups. The authors also had 36 matched pupils in each of two groups. In the one group were pupils who received C or D in conduct and in the other group those with the grade A. The difference in score was 9.25 in favor of the A group and this difference was more than 3 times its standard deviation. The correlation between the school adjustment items and Maller's *Character Sketches* is .46 ± .03. The correlation with intelligence quotients for 180 pupils is .13 ± .05 and with mental age on McCall's *Multi-Mental Scale* the correlations are .13 for 270 boys and .23 for 289 girls. The test also offers a series of 30 questions under the general heading of Background. Here questions dealing with the father's occupation, the home, and several miscellaneous items are scored and the result is considered a measure of socio-economic status. The correlation between this total score and score on the *Sims Score Card for Socio-Economic Status* is .86. A number of other items included in the background series are in the nature of an association test and the authors offer no discussion as to their relative significance. Some of these items are "I wish ....," "I like ....," "I feel sad when ....," etc.

The authors of *Pupil Portraits* are fully aware of the need for determining the validity of their test. It is to be regretted that only 54 "problem" children and 36 matched conduct grade children were studied. One would like to see the use of more clinical material and more investigations dealing with a great many children whose adjustment in school and in the home is known. Until the results of such studies become available the test should be considered in an experimental stage.

[1245]

Radio Checklist. Grades 9-12; 1939; 4¢ per copy; nontimed (30) minutes; Chicago, Ill.: Evaluation in the Eight Year Study, Progressive Education Association.

[1246]

Record Blank for the Rorschach Method of Personality Diagnosis, Revised. Ages 3 and over; 1939-40; individual; $1.75 per 25; 5¢ per blank, 100 or more; 10¢ per sample blank; Bruno Klopfer and Helen H. Davidson; New York: Rorschach Institute, Inc., c/o Helen H. Davidson, Secretary of the Folder Committee, 601 West 115th St.

REFERENCES

1 RORSCHACH, H., AND OBERHOLZER, E. "The Application of the Interpretation of Form to Psychoanalysis." *J Nerv and Mental Dis* 60:225-48, 359-79 '24.
2 BECK, SAMUEL J. "Personality Diagnosis by Means of the Rorschach Test." *Am J Orthopsychiatry* 1:81-8 O '30.
3 BECK, S. J. "The Rorschach Test and Personality Diagnosis: I, The Feeble-Minded." *Am J Psychiatry* 10:19-52 Jl '30.
4 BECK, SAMUEL J. "The Rorschach Test and Personality Diagnosis: The Feeble-minded," pp. 221-61. In *Institute for Child Guidance Studies:* Selected Reprints. Edited by Lawson G. Lowrey. New York: Commonwealth Fund, 1931. Pp. viii, 290. Out of print.
5 BECK, SAMUEL J. "The Rorschach Test in Problem Children." *Am J Orthopsychiatry* 1:501-11 O '31.
6 LEVY, D. M., AND BECK, S. J. "The Rorschach Test in Manic Depressive Psychosis," pp. 167-81. In *Manic Depressive Psychosis.* Proceedings of the Eleventh Annual Meeting of the Association for Research in Nervous and Mental Disease held in New York, December 29 and 30, 1930. Edited by W. A. White, T. K. Davis, and A. M. Frantz. Baltimore, Md.: Williams & Wilkins Co., 1931. Pp. xxix, 851. $10.00.
7 BECK, S. J. *The Rorschach Test as Applied to a Feeble-Minded Group.* Columbia University, Archives of Psychology, No. 136. New York: the University, 1932. Pp. 84. $1.00. Paper.
8 OESER, O. A. "Some Experiments on the Abstraction of Form and Color: Rorschach Tests, Part II." *Brit J Psychol* 22:287-323 Ap '32.
9 WERTHAM, F., AND BLEULER, M. "Inconstancy of the Formal Structure of the Personality: Experimental Study of the Influence of Mescaline on the Rorschach Test." *Arch Neurology and Psychiatry* 28:52-70 Jl '32.
10 BECK, SAMUEL J. "The Rorschach Method and Personality Organization: II, Balance in Personality." *Am J. Psychiatry* 13:519-32 N '33.
11 BECK, SAMUEL J. "Configurational Tendencies in Rorschach Responses." *Am J Psychol* 45:433-43 Jl '33.
12 BECK, SAMUEL J. "The Rorschach Method and Personality Organization of Personality: I. Basic Processes." *Am J Orthopsychiatry* 3:361-75 O '33.
13 BENNETT, WILHELMINA. *A Study of Several Well Known Personality Tests.* [New York: Psychological Corporation], October 1933. Pp. ii, 25. Paper, mimeographed. Out of print.
14 MACCALMAN, DOUGLAS R. "The Rorschach Test and Its Clinical Application." *J Mental Sci* 79:419-24 Ap '33.
15 SHUEY, HERBERT. "A New Interpretation of the Rorschach Test." *Psychol R* 40:213-5 Mr '33.
16 VERNON, PHILIP E. "The Rorschach Ink-Blot Test: I." *Brit J Med Psychol* 13:89-118 pt 2 '33.
17 VERNON, PHILIP E. "The Rorschach Ink-Blot Test: II." *Brit J Med Psychol* 13:179-200 pt 3 '33.
18 VERNON, PHILIP E. "The Rorschach Ink-Blot Test: III." *Brit J Med Psychol* 13:271-295 pt 4 '33.
19 BECK, SAMUEL J. "The Rorschach Method and Person-

ality Organization: III, The Psychological and the Social Personality." *Am J Orthopsychiatry* 4:290-7 Ap '34.
20 DIETHELM, O. "The Personality Concept in Relation to Graphology and the Rorschach Test." *Proc Assn Res Nerv Mental Dis* 14:278-86 '34.
21 HERTZ, MARGUERITE R. "The Reliability of the Rorschach Ink-Blot Test." *J Appl Psychol* 18:461-77 Je '34.
22 KERR, MADELINE. "The Rorschach Test Applied to Children." *Brit J Psychol* 25:170-85 O '34.
23 LEVY, DAVID M., AND BECK, S. J. "The Rorschach Test in Manic-Depressive Psychosis." *Am J Orthopsychiatry* 4:262-82 Ap '34.
24 MELTZER, H. "Personality Differences among Stutterers as Indicated by the Rorschach Test." *Am J Orthopsychiatry* 4:262-82 Ap '34.
25 BECK, SAMUEL J. "Problems of Further Research in the Rorschach Test." *Am J Orthopsychiatry* 5:100-15 Ap '35.
26 BLEULER, M., AND BLEULER, R. "Rorschach's Ink-Blot Test and Racial Psychology: Mental Peculiarities of Moroccans." *Char and Pers* 4:97-114 D '35.
27 DIMMICK, GRAHAM B. "An Application of the Rorschach Ink-Blot Test to Three Clinical Types of Dementia Praecox." *J Psychol* 1:61-74 Ja '35.
28 GUIRDHAM, ARTHUR. "On the Value of the Rorschach Test." *J Mental Sci* 81:848-869 O '35.
29 GUIRDHAM, ARTHUR. "The Rorschach Test in Epileptics." *J Mental Sci* 81:870-93 O '35.
30 HACKFIELD, A. W. "An Objective Interpretation by Means of the Rorschach Test of the Psychobiological Structure Underlying Schizophrenia, Essential Hypertension, Graves' Syndrome, etc." *Am J Psychiatry* 92:575-88 '35.
31 HARRIMAN, PHILIP LAWRENCE. "The Rorschach Test Applied to a Group of College Students." *Am J Orthopsychiatry* 5:116-20 Ap '35.
32 HERTZ, MARGUERITE R. "The Rorschach Ink-Blot Test: Historical Summary." *Psychol B* 32:33-66 Ja '35.
33 HERTZ, MARGUERITE R. "Rorschach Norms for an Adolescent Age-Group." *Child Development* 6:69-76 Mr '35.
34 LINE, W., AND GRIFFIN, J. D. M. "The Objective Determination of Factors Underlying Mental Health." *Am J Psychiatry* 91:833-42 Ja '35.
35 LINE, W., AND GRIFFIN, J. D. M. "Some Results Obtained with the Rorschach Test, Objectively Scored." *Am J Psychiatry* 92:109-14 '35.
36 LINE, W.; GRIFFIN, J. D. M.; AND ANDERSON, G. W. "The Objective Measurement of Mental Stability." *J Mental Sci* 81:61-106 Ja '35.
37 MELTZER, H. "Talkativeness in Stuttering and Non-Stuttering Children." *J Genetic Psychol* 46:371-90 Je '35.
38 POWELL, MARJORIE. "Relation of Scholastic Discrepancy to Free Associations on the Rorschach Tests." *Ky Personnel B* 14:3-4 My '35.
39 ROSENZWEIG, SAUL. "Outline of a Cooperative Project for Validating the Rorschach Test." *Am J Orthopsychiatry* 5:121-3 Ap '35.
40 VERNON, P. E. "Recent Work on the Rorschach Test." *J Mental Sci* 81:894-920 O '35.
41 VERNON, P. E. "The Significance of the Rorschach Test." *Brit J Med Psychol* 15:199-217 '35.
42 WELLS, F. L. "Rorschach and the Free Association Test." *J Gen Psychol* 13:413-33 O '35.
43 BECK, S. J. "Autism in Rorschach Scoring: A Feeling Comment." *Char and Pers* 5:83-5 S '36.
44 BOOTH, GOTTHARD C., AND KLOPFER, BRUNO. "Personality Studies in Chronic Arthritis." *Rorschach Res Exch* 1:40-8 N '36.
45 BOOTH, GOTTHARD C.; KLOPFER, BRUNO; AND STEIN-LEWINSON, THEA. "Material for a Comparative Case Study of a Chronic Arthritis Personality." *Rorschach Res Exch* 1:49-54 N '36.
46 BRYN, DAG. "The Problem of Human Types: Comments and an Experiment." *Char and Pers* 5:48-60 S '36.
47 GARDNER, G. E. "Rorschach Test Replies and Results in 100 Normal Adults of Avearge IQ." *Am J Orthopsychiatry* 6:32-60 Ja '36.
48 GUIRDHAM, ARTHUR. "The Diagnosis of Depression by the Rorschach Test." *Brit J Med Psychol* 16:130-45 '36.
49 GUIRDHAM, ARTHUR. "Simple Psychological Data in Melancholia." *J Mental Sci* 82:649-53 S '36.
50 HERTZ, MARGUERITE R. *Frequency Tables to be Used in Scoring the Rorschach Ink-Blot Test.* Cleveland, Ohio: the Author, Brush Foundation, Western Reserve University, 1936. Pp. v, 283. $3.50. Paper, mimeographed.
51 HERTZ, MARGUERITE R. "The Method of Administration of the Rorschach Ink-Blot Test." *Child Development* 7:237-54 D '36.
52 KERR, MADELINE. "Temperamental Difference in Twins." *Brit J Psychol* 27:51-9 Jl '36.
53 KLOPFER, BRUNO, AND SENDER, SADIE. "A System of Refined Scoring Symbols." *Rorschach Res Exch* 1:19-22 N '36.
54 PIOTROWSKI, ZYGMUNT. "On the Rorschach Method and its Application in Organic Disturbances of the Central Nervous System." *Rorschach Res Exch* 1:23-39 N '36.
55 SENDER, SADIE, AND KLOPFER, BRUNO. "Application of the Rorschach Test to Child Behavior Problems as Facilitated by a Refinement of the Scoring Method." *Rorschach Res Exch* 1:5-17 S '36.
56 SUNNE, DAGNY. "Rorschach Test Norms of Young Children." *Child Development* 7:304-13 D '36.

57 THORNTON, GEORGE R. "A Note on the Scoring of Movement in the Rorschach Test." *Am J Psychol* 48:524-5 Jl '36.

58 THORNTON, GEORGE R., AND GUILFORD, J. P. "The Reliability and Meaning of Erlebnistypus Scores in the Rorschach Test." *J Abn and Social Psychol* 31:324-30 O-D '36.

59 VERNON, P. E. "Rorschach Bibliography No. III." *Rorschach Res Exch* 1:89-93 S '36.

60 BARRY, HERBERT, JR., EDITOR. "The Significance of the Rorschach Method for Consulting Psychology: Author's Abstracts of the Contributions to the Round-Table Conference at the Eighth Annual Meeting of the Association of Consulting Psychologists, May 7-8, 1937, at the New York State College for Teachers, Albany, New York." *Rorschach Res Exch* 1:157-66 Jl '37.

61 BECK, S. J. "Some Present Rorschach Problems." *Rorschach Res Exch* 2:15-22 S '37.

62 BECK, SAMUEL J. *Introduction to the Rorschach Method: A Manual of Personality Study.* Preface by F. L. Wells. Monograph No. 1 of the American Orthopsychiatric Association. New York: the Association, 1937. Pp. xi, 278. $4.00.

63 BECK, SAMUEL J. "Psychological Processes in Rorschach Findings." *J Abn and Social Psychol* 31:482-8 Ja-Mr '37.

64 BINDER, HANS. "The 'Light-Dark' Interpretations in Rorschach's Experiment." Translated by J. Jervis Carlson. *Rorschach Res Exch* 2:37-42 D '37.

65 BINDER, HANS; BLEULER, MANFRED; BENJAMIN, JOHN D.; BOOTH, GOTTHARD; HERTZ, MARGUERITE R.; KLOPFER, BRUNO; PIOTROWSKI, ZYGMUNT; AND SCHACHTEL, ERNST. "Discussion on 'Some Recent Rorschach Problems.'" *Rorschach Res Exch* 2:43-72 D '37.

66 BOOTH, GOTTHARD COHEN. "Personality and Chronic Arthritis." *J Nervous and Mental Dis* 85:637-62 Je '37.

67 GOLDSTEIN, KURT. "Personality Studies of Cases with Lesions of the Frontal Lobes: I, The Psychopathology of Pick's Disease." *Rorschach Res Exch* 1:57-64 Ja '37.

68 HERTZ, MARGUERITE R. "The Normal Details in the Rorschach Ink-Blot Test." Discussions by Sadie Sender and Bruno Klopfer. *Rorschach Res Exch* 1:104-20 Ap '37.

69 HUNTER, MARY. "Responses of Comparable White and Negro Adults to the Rorschach Test." *J Psychol* 3:173-82 Ja '37.

70 JACOBSEN, WILHELMINA E. "A Study of Personality Development in a High School Girl." *Rorschach Res Exch* 2:23-35 S '37.

71 KLOPFER, BRUNO. "The Present Status of the Theoretical Development of the Rorschach Method." *Rorschach Res Exch* 1:142-7 Jl '37.

72 KLOPFER, BRUNO. "The Technique of the Rorschach Performance." *Rorschach Res Exch* 2:1-14 S '37.

73 PIOTROWSKI, ZYGMUNT. "A Comparison of Congenitally Defective Children with Schizophrenic Children in Regard to Personality Structure and Intelligence Type." *Proc Am Assn Mental Def* 61:78-90 '37.

74 PIOTROWSKI, ZYGMUNT. "The M, FM, and m Responses as Indicators of Changes in Personality." *Rorschach Res Exch* 1:148-56 Jl '37.

75 PIOTROWSKI, ZYGMUNT. "Personality Studies of Cases with Lesions of the Frontal Lobes: II, Rorschach Study of a Pick's Disease Case." *Rorschach Res Exch* 1:65-76 Ja '37.

76 PIOTROWSKI, ZYGMUNT. "The Reliability of Rorschach's Erlebnistypus." *J Abn and Social Psychol* 32:439-45 O-D '37.

77 PIOTROWSKI, ZYGMUNT. "The Rorschach Inkblot Method in Organic Disturbances of the Central Nervous System." *J Nerv Mental Dis* 86:525-37 N '37.

78 PIOTROWSKI, ZYGMUNT. "Rorschach Studies of Cases with Lesions of the Frontal Lobes." *Brit J Med Psychol* 17:105-18 pt 1 '37.

79 "A Review of Rorschach Scoring Samples." *Rorschach Res Exch* 1:94-101 Ja '37.

80 SCHACHTEL, ERNST, AND HARTOCH, ANNA. "The Curve of Reactions in the Rorschach Test: A Contribution to the Theory and Practice of Rorschach's Psychodiagnostic Ink Blot Test." *Am J Orthopsychiatry* 7:320-48 Jl '37.

81 TALLMAN, GLADYS, AND KLOPFER, BRUNO. "Personality Studies of Cases with Lesions of the Frontal Lobes: III, Rorschach Study of Bilateral Lobectomy Case." *Rorschach Res Exch* 1:77-88 Ja '37.

82 TROUP, EVELYN, AND KLOPFER, BRUNO. "Sample Case Studies: from A Comparative Study of the Personality Development of Twenty Pairs of Monozygotic Twins by Means of the Rorschach Test." Summary and Records by Evelyn Troup; Scoring and Interpretations by Bruno Klopfer. *Rorschach Res Exch* 1:121-39 Ap '37.

83 VARVEL, W. A. "Suggestions toward the Experimental Validation of the Rorschach Test." *B Menninger Clinic* 1:220-26 '37.

84 BECK, SAMUEL J. *Personality Structure in Schizophrenia: A Rorschach Investigation in 81 Patients and 64 Controls.* Preface by C. MacFie Campbell. Nervous and Mental Disease Monograph No. 63. New York: Nervous and Mental Disease Publishing Co., 1938. Pp. 88. $2.00.

85 BENJAMIN, JOHN D., AND EBAUGH, FRANKLIN G. "The Diagnostic Validity of the Rorschach Test." *Am J Psychiatry* 94:1163-78 Mr '38.

86 CLAPP, HAZEL S.; MIALE, FLORENCE ROSENBLATT; AND KAPLAN, A. H. "Clinical Validation of a Rorschach Interpretation: The Case of Lillian K." *Rorschach Res Exch* 2:153-62 Je '38.

87 DAVIDSON, HELEN H., AND KLOPFER, BRUNO. "Rorschach Statistics: Part I, Mentally Retarded, Normal, and Superior Adults." *Rorschach Res Exch* 2:164-169 Je '38.

88 DAVIDSON, HELEN H., AND KLOPFER, BRUNO. "Rorschach Statistics: Part II, Normal Children." *Rorschach Res Exch* 3:37-43 O '38.

89 FOSBERG, IRVING ARTHUR. "Rorschach Reactions under Varied Instructions: On the Use of Chi-Squares as a Measure of the Reliability of the Rorschach Psychodiagnostic Technique." *Rorschach Res Exch* 3:12-30 O '38.

90 HERTZ, HELEN, compiler. "Binder's Shading Responses." Translated by Mary Hunter Sicha. *Rorschach Res Exch* 2:79-88 Mr '38.

91 HERTZ, MARGUERITE R. "The 'Popular' Response Factor in the Rorschach Scoring." *J Psychol* 6:3-31 Jl '38.

92 HERTZ, MARGUERITE R. "Scoring the Rorschach Ink-Blot Test." *J Genetic Psychol* 52:15-64 Mr '38.

93 HERTZ, MARGUERITE R. "Scoring the Rorschach Test with Specific Reference to 'Normal Detail' Category." *Am J Orthopsychiatry* 8:100-121 Ja '38.

94 KLOPFER, BRUNO. "A Further Rorschach Study of Mr. A." *Rorschach Res Exch* 3:31-35 O '38.

95 KLOPFER, BRUNO. "The Shading Responses." *Rorschach Res Exch* 2:76-79 Mr '38.

96 KLOPFER, BRUNO, AND MIALE, FLORENCE ROSENBLATT. "An Illustration of the Technique of the Rorschach Interpretation: The Case of Anne T." *Rorschach Res Exch* 2:126-52 Je '38.

97 PATTERSON, M., AND MAGAW, DAVID C. "An Investigation of the Validity of the Rorschach Technique as Applied to Mentally Defective Problem Children." *Proc Am Assn Mental Def* 62:179-85 '38.

98 PESCOR, M. J. "Age of Delinquents in Relationship to Rorschach Test Scores." *Pub Health Reports* 53:852-64 My '38.

99 PIOTROWSKI, Z. "Recent Rorschach Literature: Rorschach Bibliography No. IV." *Rorschach Res Exch* 2:172-5 Je '38.

100 PIOTROWSKI, ZYGMUNT. "Blind Analysis of a Case of Compulsion Neurosis." *Rorschach Res Exch* 2:89-111 Mr '38.

101 PIOTROWSKI, ZYGMUNT. "The Prognostic Possibilities of the Rorschach Method in Insulin Treatment." *Psychiatric Q* 12:679-89 O '38.

102 RICKERS-OVSIANKINA, MARIA. *Rorschach Scoring Samples.* Worcester, Mass.: Worcester State Hospital, 1938. Pp. [v, 166]. $3.00. Paper, mimeographed.

103 RICKERS-OVSIANKINA, MARIA. "The Rorschach Test as Applied to Normal and Schizophrenic Subjects." *Brit J Med Psychol* 17:227-57 pt 2 '38.

104 SHUEY, HERBERT. "Further Discussion on Some Recent Rorschach Problems." *Rorschach Res Exch* 2:170-1 Je '38.

105 SILL, JANE B. "A Case Study Comparing the Performance on the Binet and on the Rorschach." *Rorschach Res Exch* 2:112-124 Mr '38.

106 SUARES, NADINE. "Personality Development in Adolescence." *Rorschach Res Exch* 3:2-11 O '38.

107 TALLMAN, GLADYS. "Further Results of Retesting Mr. A." *Rorschach Res Exch* 3:35-6 O '38.

108 TROUP, EVELYN. "A Comparative Study by Means of the Rorschach Method of Personality Development in Twenty Pairs of Identical Twins." *Genetic Psychol Monogr* 20:461-556 N '38.

109 VAUGHN, JAMES, AND KRUG, OTHILDA. "The Analytic Character of the Rorschach Ink Blot Test." *Am J Orthopsychiatry* 8:220-9 Ap '38.

110 BECK, SAMUEL J. "Thoughts on an Impending Anniversary." *Am J Orthopsychiatry* 9:865-8 O '39.

111 BOOTH, G. C. "Objective Technics in Personality Testing." *Arch Neurology and Psychiatry* 42:514-30 S '39.

112 FRANK, LAWRENCE K. "Comments on the Proposed Standardization of the Rorschach Method." *Rorschach Res Exch* 3:101-5 My '39.

113 HERTZ, HELENE. "A Rorschach Comparison Between Best and Least Adjusted Girls in a Training School." *Rorschach Res Exch* 3:134-9 My '39.

114 HERTZ, MARGUERITE R. "On the Standardization of the Rorschach Method." *Rorschach Res Exch* 3:120-33 My '39.

115 HERTZ, MARGUERITE R., AND RUBENSTEIN, BORIS B. "A Comparison of Three 'Blind' Rorschach Analyses." *Am J Orthopsychiatry* 9:295-314 Ap '39.

116 HIRNING, L. C. "Case Studies in Schizophrenia." *Rorschach Res Exch* 3:66-90 F '39.

117 HUNTER, MARY. "The Practical Value of the Rorschach Test in a Psychological Clinic." *Am J Orthopsychiatry* 9:287-94 Ap '39.

118 KELLEY, DOUGLAS M. "Announcement of the Rorschach Institute." *Rorschach Res Exch* 3:92-100 My '39.

119 KELLEY, DOUGLAS M., AND KLOPFER, BRUNO. "Application of the Rorschach Method to Research in Schizophrenia." *Rorschach Res Exch* 3:55-66 F '39.

120 KELLEY, DOUGLAS M., AND RIETI, ETTORE. "The Geneva Approach to the Rorschach Method." *Rorschach Res Exch* 3:195-201 Ag '39.

121 KLOPFER, BRUNO. "Should the Rorschach Method Be Standardized?" *Rorschach Res Exch* 3:45-54 F '39.

122 KLOPFER, BRUNO; KRUGMAN, MORRIS; KELLEY, DOUGLAS M.; MURPHY, LOIS BARCLAY; AND SHAKOW, DAVID. "Shall the Rorschach Method Be Standardized? Round Table, 1939 Session [Rorschach Institute]." *Am J Orthopsychiatry* 9:514-28 Jl '39.

123 KLOPFER, BRUNO, IN COLLABORATION WITH EDWARD M. L.

BURCHARD, DOUGLAS M. KELLEY, AND FLORENCE R. MIALE. "Theory and Technique of Rorschach Interpretation." *Rorschach Res Exch* 3:152-94 Ag '39.
124 MIALE, FLORENCE R. "The Rorschach Forum at the Sixteenth Annual Meeting of the American Orthopsychiatric Association, February 23, 1939, in New York City." *Rorschach Res Exch* 3:106-19 My '39.
125 PESCOR, M. J. *Marital Status of Delinquents in Relationship to Rorschach Test Scores.* United States Public Health Service, Supplement No. 153 to the Public Health Reports. Washington, D. C.: Government Printing Office, 1939. Pp. 6. $0.05. Paper.
126 PIOTROWSKI, ZYGMUNT. "Rorschach Manifestations of Improvement in Insulin Treated Schizophrenics." *Psychosom Med* 1:508-26 O '39.
127 SARBIN, THEODORE R. "Rorschach Patterns under Hypnosis." *Am J Orthopsychiatry* 9:315-8 Ap '39.
128 WOLFSON, RUTH. "Scoring, Tabulation and Interpretation of the Two Sample Cases." *Rorschach Res Exch* 3:140-50 My '39.
129 BROSIN, H. W., AND FROMM, ERIKA OPPENHEIMER. "Rorschach and Color Blindness." *Rorschach Res Exch* 4:39-70 Ap '40.
130 HALLOWELL, A. IRVING. "Rorschach as an Aid in the Study of Personalities in Primitive Societies." Author's abstract. *Rorschach Res Exch* 4:106 Jl '40.
131 HARROWER-ERICKSON, M. R. "The Contribution of the Rorschach Method to Wartime Psychological Problems." *J Mental Sci* 86:366-77 My '40.
132 HARROWER-ERICKSON, M. R. "Personality Changes Accompanying Cerebral Lesions: I, Rorschach Studies of Patients with Cerebral Tumors." *Arch Neurology and Psychiatry* 43:859-90 My '40.
133 HARROWER-ERICKSON, M. R. "Personality Changes Accompanying Cerebral Lesions: II, Rorschach Studies of Patients with Focal Epilepsy." *Arch Neurology and Psychiatry* 43:1081-1107 Je '40.
134 HARROWER-ERICKSON, M. R., AND MIALE, F. R. "Personality Changes Accompanying Organic Brain Lesions: Pre- and Post-Operative Study of Two Pre-Adolescent Children." *Rorschach Res Exch* 4:8-25 Ja '40.
135 HERTZ, MARGUERITE R. "Problems on the Validity of the Rorschach Method." Author's abstract. *Rorschach Res Exch* 4:104-5 Jl '40.
136 HERTZ, MARGUERITE R. "The Shading Response in the Rorschach Ink-Blot Test: A Review of Its Scoring and Interpretation." *J Gen Psychol* 23:123-67 Jl '40.
137 HERTZ, M. R., AND KENNEDY, STEPHANIE. "The M Factor in Estimating Intelligence." Author's abstract. *Rorschach Res Exch* 4:105-6 Jl '40.
138 KELLEY, DOUGLAS M. "Survey of the Training Facilities for the Rorschach Method in the U. S. A." *Rorschach Res Exch* 4:84-7 Ap '40.
139 KELLEY, D. M., AND BARRERA, S. E. "The Present State of the Rorschach Method as a Psychiatric Adjunct." *Rorschach Res Exch* 4:30-6 Ja '40.
140 KLOPFER, BRUNO. "Personality Aspects Revealed by the Rorschach Method." *Rorschach Res Exch* 4:26-9 Ja '40.
141 KLOPFER, BRUNO, in collaboration with Helen Davidson, Evelyn Holzman, Douglas M. Kelley, Helen Margulies, Florence R. Miale, and Ruth Wolfson. "The Technique of Rorschach Scoring and Tabulation." *Rorschach Res Exch* 4:75-83 Ap '40.
142 KOGAN, WILLIAM. "Shifts in Rorschach Patterns During a Critical Period in the Institutional Experience of a Group of Delinquent Boys." *Rorschach Res Exch* 4:131-3 Jl '40.
143 KRUGMAN, MORRIS. "Out of the Ink Well: The Rorschach Method." *Rorschach Res Exch* 4:91-101 Jl '40.
144 MIALE, F. R. "Personality Structure in the Psychoneuroses." *Rorschach Res Exch* 4:71-4 Ap '40.
145 MUNROE, RUTH. "The Use of the Rorschach in College Guidance." *Rorschach Res Exch* 4:107-30 Jl '40.
146 ROSS, W. D. "The 'Anxiety Neurosis' Rorschach Record Compared with the Typical Basically Neurotic Record." *Rorschach Res Exch* 4:134-7 Jl '40.
147 TULCHIN, SIMON H. "The Pre-Rorschach Use of Ink-Blot Tests." *Rorschach Res Exch* 4:1-7 Ja '40.

[1247]

Report Form on Temperament and Social Behaviour. For recording observations of children ages 2-7; 1940; 4s. 6d. per 12; C. W. Valentine; Birmingham, England: Birmingham Printers, Ltd.

REFERENCES

1 VALENTINE, C. W. "The Specific Nature of Temperament Traits and a Suggested Report Form." *Brit J Ed Psychol* 10:25-48 F '40.

[1248]

Revision of the Babcock Examination for Measuring Efficiency of Mental Functioning. Ages 7 and over; 1940; a revision of *Babcock's Mental Deterioration Scale* (No. 37058); 1 form; $10 per test booklet and manual (No. 37058A); $2 per 25 record

blanks (No. 37058R); 10¢ per *Color Naming Test*: Woodworth-Wells (No. 12309); $1.25 per *Cube Imitation Test*: Pintner (No. 33304); $1 per *Memory for Designs Test*: Army Performance Scale (No. 32317); nontimed (70+) minutes; Harriet Babcock and Lydia Levy; Chicago, Ill.: C. H. Stoelting Co.

REFERENCES

1 BABCOCK, HARRIET. *An Experiment in the Measurement of Mental Deterioration.* Columbia University, Archives of Psychology, No. 117. New York: the University, 1930. Pp. 105. $1.25. Paper.
2 BABCOCK, HARRIET. "Psychological Testing in Psychopathology." *J Appl Psychol* 15:584-9 D '31.
3 SCHWARZ, RUDOLPH. "Measurement of Mental Deterioration in Dementia Praecox." *Am J Psychiatry* 89:555-60 N '32.
4 BABCOCK, HARRIET. *Dementia Praecox: A Psychological Study.* Lancaster, Pa.: Science Press Printing Co., 1933. Pp. 167. $2.50.
5 WITTMAN, PHYLLIS. "The Babcock Deterioration Tests in State Hospital Practice." *J Abn and Social Psychol* 28:70-83 Ap-Je '33.
6 GILBERT, JEANNE G. *Mental Efficiency in Senescence.* Columbia University, Archives of Psychology, No. 188. New York: the University, July 1935. Pp. 60. $1.00. Paper.
7 SIMMONS, C. "Mental Incapacity: The Intelligence of Patients in Mental Hospitals." *Char and Pers* 4:25-33 S '35.
8 HARBINSON, M. R. "An Investigation of Deterioration of 'General Intelligence' or 'G' in Psychotic Patients." *Brit J Med Psychol* 16:146-8 '36.
9 ALTMAN, CHARLOTTE HALL, AND SHAKOW, DAVID. "A Comparison of the Performance of Matched Groups of Schizophrenic Patients, Normal Subjects, and Delinquents on Some Aspects of the Stanford-Binet." *J Ed Psychol* 28:519-29 O '37.
9.1 BOOKHAMMER, R. S., AND RUBIN, BEATRICE. "Babcock Test for Mental Deterioration." Discussion by Arthur P. Noyes, Frederick H. Allen, and J. C. Yaskin. *Arch Neurology and Psychiatry* 37:1204-6 My '37.
10 JASTAK, JOSEPH. "Psychometric Patterns of State Hospital Patients." *Del State Med J* 9:87-91 Ap '37.
11 BARNES, MARGARET R., AND FETTERMAN, JOSEPH L. "Mentality of Dispensary Epileptic Patients." *Arch Neurology and Psychiatry* 40:903-10 N '38.
12 HALL, MARGARET E. "Mental and Physical Efficiency of Women Drug Addicts." *J Abn and Social Psychol* 33:332-45 Jl '38.
12.1 CAPPS, HARRY MARCELLUS. *Vocabulary Changes in Mental Deterioration:* The Relationship of Vocabulary Functioning as Measured by a Variety of Word Meaning and Usage Tests to Clinically Estimated Degrees of Mental Deterioration in 'Idiopathic' Epilepsy. Columbia University, Archives of Psychology, No. 242. New York: the University, September 1939. Pp. 81. $1.25. Paper.
13 KENDIG, ISABELLE, AND RICHMOND, WINIFRED V. *Psychological Studies in Dementia Praecox,* pp. 14-22, and passim. Ann Arbor, Mich.: Edwards Brothers, Inc., 1940. Pp. x, 211. $0.50. Paper, lithotyped.
14 BABCOCK, HARRIET. "Personality and Efficiency of Mental Functioning." *Am J Orthopsychiatry* 10:527-31 Jl '40.

[1249]

Roback Sense of Humor Test. Adolescents and adults; 1939; 1 form; $1.25 per 25 (No. 24412); nontimed (15) minutes; A. A. Roback; Chicago, Ill.: C. H. Stoelting Co.

[1250]

Scale of Beliefs: Tests 4.21 and 4.31. Grades 9-12; 1939; 1 form, 2 parts (both of which must be given); revision of Tests 4.2 and 4.3; 5¢ per set of both parts; 1¢ per machine-scorable answer sheet; 5¢ per explanation sheet and interpretation guide; $2 per set of stencils for machine scoring; nontimed (40) minutes; Chicago, Ill.: Evaluation in the Eight Year Study, Progressive Education Association.

REFERENCES

1 GRIM, PAUL R. "A Technique for the Measurement of Attitudes in the Social Studies." *Ed Res B* 15:95-104 Ap '36.
2 RATHS, LOUIS. "Evaluating the Program of Lakeshore School." *Ed Res B* 17:57-84 Mr 16 '38.
3 *Social Sensitivity:* An Approach to Evaluation in Social Studies. Chicago, Ill.: Evaluation in the Eight Year Study, Progressive Education Association, March 1939. Pp. [34]. Paper, mimeographed. Out of print.
4 AMSTUTZ, WADE S. "A Study of Characteristics of Education Freshmen Who Entered Ohio State University in 1938." *J Exp Ed* 8:289-92 Mr '40.
5 CAHOW, ARTHUR C. "Relationships of Test Scores of Education College Freshmen to Grades in Selected Courses." *J Exp Ed* 8:284-9 Mr '40.
6 GIBBONS, C. C., AND SCHRADER, W. A. B. "Liberalism

and Consistency: A Study of Social Attitudes." *J Exp Ed*
8:259-67 Mr '40.
    7 SCHRADER, W. A. B. "Analysis of Variance Applied to
Liberalism Scores." *J Exp Ed* 8:267-70 Mr '40.

[1251]

Scale of Beliefs for Junior High School: Tests
4.4 and 4.5. Grades 7-9; 1940; an adaptation of *Scale
of Beliefs*: Tests 4.21 and 4.31; 1 form, 2 parts (both
of which must be given); 5¢ per set of both parts;
1¢ per machine-scorable answer sheet; 5¢ per explanation sheet and interpretation guide; $2 per set
of stencils for machine scoring; nontimed (30) minutes; Chicago, Ill.: Evaluation in the Eight Year
Study, Progressive Education Association.

REFERENCES

    1 *Social Sensitivity*: An Approach to Evaluation in Social
Studies. Chicago, Ill.: Evaluation in the Eight Year Study,
Progressive Education Association, March 1939. Pp. [34].
Paper, mimeographed. Out of print.

[1252]

School Inventory. Grades 10-12; 1937; 1 form; $1.00
per 25; 15¢ per specimen set; nontimed (10-15) minutes; Hugh M. Bell; Stanford University, Calif.:
Stanford University Press.

REFERENCES

    1 BELL, HUGH M. *The Theory and Practice of Student
Counseling*: With Special Reference to the Adjustment Inventory. Stanford, Calif.: Stanford University Press, 1935. Pp.
138. $1.00. Paper, lithotyped. (London: Oxford University
Press. 4s. 6d.)
    2 TYLER, HENRY T. "Evaluating the Bell Adjustment In-
ventory." *Jun Col J* 6:353-7 Ap '36.
    3 BELL, HUGH M. *The Theory and Practice of Personal
Counseling*: With Special Reference to the Adjustment Inventory. A revision of *The Theory and Practice of Student Counseling*. Stanford University, Calif.: Stanford University Press,
1939. Pp. v, 167. $1.25. Paper, lithotyped. (London: Ox-
ford University Press. 6s.)
    4 RYANS, DAVID G., AND PETERS, EDWIN F. "An Analysis
and Adaptation of the Bell *School Inventory* with Respect to
Student Adjustment in a Women's College." *J Appl Psychol*
24:455-62 Ag '40.

    EDITOR'S NOTE: In *The 1938 Yearbook*,
    two reviews of Bell's *School Inventory*
    were incorrectly listed as reviews of
    Bell's *Adjustment Inventory*. These two
    reviews are herein reprinted under the
    correct test title.

*Robert G. Bernreuter, Director of the Psy-
cho-Educational Clinic and Associate Professor of Psychology, The Pennsylvania State
College.* The *Bell School Inventory* is intended
to determine the attitude of pupils toward their
school. According to the results obtained by
the author, the inventory is sufficiently reliable
to be used to determine the attitudes of individual students. Also, according to the data
obtained by the author, the scores agree reasonably well with the ratings given pupils by
their teachers.

An analysis of the items indicates that they
fall into two major categories. One includes
items expressing general attitude toward the
school. The other includes attitudes toward
such specific things as teachers, classmates, the
curriculum, and extracurricular activities.

The only method of scoring developed by
the author consists of finding the total number

of items on which the student has expressed
dissatisfaction regardless of whether the items
are general or specific in nature. The inventory
would be a more useful instrument if it could
be scored to serve two purposes: first, to disclose dissatisfied pupils, and second, to disclose
causes of dissatisfaction. The first is reasonably well done by the present scoring method
but the second is not. The second purpose
would be accomplished if the items were classified into subcategories on the basis of the types
of specific items they involve and scored accordingly.

The inventory will need to be used with
considerable caution and only after a good
rapport has been established because it is particularly susceptible to invalidation through a
desire on the part of the pupils to make a good
showing before their teacher.

*J. B. Maller, Lecturer in Education, New
York University.* This inventory directs the
student to answer "honestly and thoughtfully"
a number of questions about his school. He is
asked to state whether some of his teachers are
"bossy," narrow-minded, lazy, lack a sense of
humor, lack enthusiasm for their work, nervous
and easily excited, etc. Some of the questions
are even more forceful. "Do you think that
this school is run as if it were a prison? Do
you dislike intensely certain teachers in this
school?"

It is questionable whether high school students would have the courage and the desire
to answer such questions honestly in a test
which is given in school and which requires
them to write their names on it. Furthermore,
in schools which are poorly adapted to the
needs and interests of their pupils would it be
fair to label the outspoken students as "poorly
adapted to the school"?

The inventory could hardly be used as a
group test, if one is to follow the author's
admonition that "the inventory should not be
administered until the examiner has developed
a feeling of cooperation among the students
being tested."

The evidence of validity and the "norms"
are based on the responses of 391 pupils in
California high schools located at Chico, Yreka,
Oroville, and Durham.

In view of the enormous differences between
schools the norms are not only meaningless but
also misleading. Even within one school the

responses will probably vary from class to class, and from examiner to examiner. The statement in the directions that "your answers will be treated with the strictest confidence" will probably be of little reassurance for the directions also state that "the school will endeavor to improve the conditions which your answers indicate need improvement."

See also B842.

[1253]

Social Intelligence Test. High school, college, and adults; 1930; 1 form; $12.00 per 100; 20¢ per specimen set; 45(50) minutes; F. A. Moss, T. Hunt, and K. T. Omwake; Washington, D. C.: Center for Psychological Service, George Washington University.

REFERENCES

1 GROSVENOR, EDITH LOUISE. "A Study of the Social Intelligence of High School Pupils." *Am Physical Ed R* 32:649-57 N '27.
2 HUNT, THELMA. "What Social Intelligence Is and Where to Find It." *Industrial Psychol* 2:605-12 D '27.
3 MOSS, F. A., AND HUNT, T. "Are You Socially Intelligent? An Analysis of the Scores of 7,000 Persons on the George Washington University Social Intelligence Test." *Scientific Am* 137:108-10 Ag '27.
4 PINTNER, R., AND UPSHALL, C. C. "Some Results of Social Intelligence Tests." *Sch and Soc* 27:369-70 Mr 24 '27.
5 BROOM, M. EUSTACE. "A Note on the Validity of a Test of Social Intelligence." *J Appl Psychol* 12:426-8 Ag '28.
6 HUNT, THELMA. "The Measurement of Social Intelligence." *J Appl Psychol* 12:317-34 Je '28.
7 MCCLATCHY, VIVIENNE ROBISON. "A Theoretical and Statistical Critique of the Concept of Social Intelligence and of Attempts to Measure Such a Process." *J Abn and Social Psychol* 24:217-20 Jl-S '29.
8 BROOM, M. E. "A Further Study of the Validity of a Test of Social Intelligence." *J Ed Res* 22:403-5 D '30.
9 STRANG, RUTH. "Measures of Social Intelligence." *Am J Sociol* 36:263-9 S '30.
10 STRANG, RUTH. "Relation of Social Intelligence to Certain Other Factors." *Sch and Soc* 32:268-72 Ag 23 '30.
11 STAGNER, ROSS. "The Intercorrelation of Some Standardized Personality Tests." *J Appl Psychol* 16:453-64 O '32.
12 STRANG, RUTH. "An Analysis of Errors Made in a Test of Social Intelligence." *J Ed Sociol* 5:291-9 Ja '32.
13 RHINEHART, JESSE BATLEY. "An Attempt to Predict the Success of Student Nurses by the Use of a Battery of Tests." *J Appl Psychol* 17:277-93 Ap '33.
14 STAGNER, ROSS. "Improved Norms for Four Personality Tests." *Am J Psychol* 45:303-7 Ap '33.
15 Human Engineering Laboratory. *Revision of Form A of Worksample 169, Judgment in Social Situations.* Human Engineering Laboratory, Technical Report No. 6. Boston, Mass.: the Laboratory, 1936. Pp. xii, 56. $1.00. Paper, mimeographed.
16 HUNT, THELMA. *Measurement in Psychology*, pp. 335-51. New York: Prentice-Hall, Inc., 1936. Pp. xx, 471. $3.00.
17 THORNDIKE, ROBERT L. "Factor Analysis of Social and Abstract Intelligence." *J Ed Psychol* 27:231-3 Mr '36.
18 BURKS, FRANCES W. "The Relation of Social Intelligence Test Scores to Ratings of Social Traits." *J Social Psychol* 8:146-53 F '37.
19 THORNDIKE, ROBERT L., AND STEIN, SAUL. "An Evaluation of the Attempts to Measure Social Intelligence." *Psychol B* 34:275-85 My '37.
20 Human Engineering Laboratory. *Statistical and Graphic Analysis of Three Forms of Worksample 169, Judgment in Social Situations.* Human Engineering Laboratory, Technical Report No. 15. Boston, Mass.: the Laboratory, 1938. Pp. viii, 140. $1.00. Paper, mimeographed.

Robert L. Thorndike, Associate Professor of Education, Columbia University. Following up the suggestion made by E. L. Thorndike in 1920 that it might be profitable to make a tripartite division of intelligence into abstract, mechanical, and social intelligences, the authors of this test have endeavored to develop a paper-and-pencil technique of assaying differences in ability to respond to social situations.

The subtests require the individual to (a) select the best course of action in a briefly outlined social situation, (b) attach the appropriate emotional term to a brief quotation, (c) judge the truth or falsity of a number of statements about human behavior, (d) memorize names and faces and subsequently attach the right name to the right face, (e) choose the best completion of a series of jokes. All of these tests are in some degree verbal, and some of them seem to call for a high level of verbal comprehension. This being the case, it is not surprising to find that the test as a whole shows substantial correlation with tests of abstract intelligence. To what extent it measures abilities other than verbal abilities is not so easy to determine.

Hunt presents evidence for the validity of the test consisting of (a) the fact of marked occupational differences—executives, teachers, and salesmen scoring much higher than clerks and unskilled laborers, (b) the fact that students engaging in several extracurricular activities have a higher median score on the test than those engaging in few or none, (c) the fact that score on the test correlated rather well with rating by a superior executive in a large sales company. In none of these cases, however, was the effect of abstract intelligence partialled out. Whether these discriminations would hold up in groups equated in abstract verbal ability seems questionable to this reviewer. Other investigators have found very low correlations between test score and frequency of activity or rating for social adjustment.

In a factor analysis of the subtests of the *Social Intelligence Test* and the subtests of a general intelligence test, the writer was unable to find evidence of any clear-cut unity within the social intelligence test or differentiation between it and the general intelligence test.[17]

All in all, it seems to the reviewer that no satisfactory validation of this test has been presented. Until this has been done, he views it with suspicion, and doubts whether a test which is so predominantly verbal and abstract will give information about the individual's ability to actively handle social situations, except insofar as abstract comprehension is involved therein.

[1254]
Social Problems: Test 1.42. Grades 9-12; 1938-40;
1 form; revision of Tests 1.4 and 1.41; 5¢ per test;
1¢ per machine-scorable answer sheet; 5¢ per explanation sheet and guide; $1.50 per set of stencils
for machine scoring; nontimed (90) minutes; Chicago, Ill.: Evaluation in the Eight Year Study, Progressive Education Association.

REFERENCES

1 *Social Sensitivity*: An Approach to Evaluation in Social
Studies. Chicago, Ill.: Evaluation in the Eight Year Study,
Progressive Education Association, March 1939. Pp. [34].
Paper, mimeographed. Out of print.

[1255]
**Study of Attitudes toward the Administration of
Justice.** College and adults; 1938; 1 form; $1 per 25;
20¢ per specimen set; nontimed (60) minutes; [F. C.
Sumner]; Washington, D. C.: the author, Howard
University.

REFERENCES

1 SUMNER, F. C., AND CAMPBELL, ASTREA S. "Attitudes
toward the Administration of Justice." *J Psychol* 8:23-52 Jl
'39.

[1256]
Teacher's Rating Scales for Pupil Adjustment.
Kindergarten through grade 14; 1937; 1 form; 25¢
per rating scale (only one copy is needed for a class
of 40 students); 25¢ per 25 individual record blanks;
25¢ per specimen set; Frank N. Freeman and Ethel
Kawin; Chicago, Ill.: University of Chicago Press.

*Bessie Lee Gambrill, Associate Professor of
Elementary Education, Yale University.* Developed in the Laboratory Schools of the University of Chicago and in the public schools
of Glencoe, Illinois, these rating scales are designed as a service instrument to help teachers
in understanding and managing pupils rather
than for research purposes. There are five
scales, one for each of the following general
categories: intellectual characteristics, work
and study habits, emotional adjustment, social
adjustment, scholastic achievement. While dis-
claiming any assumption that these are mutually exclusive categories and voicing the belief that a child's behavior is an expression of
his total personality, the authors state that
their experimentation indicates that teachers
can discriminate among the categories and that
pupils may show considerable variability on the
five scales. To help the teacher define these
five concepts a list of traits or characteristics
is provided opposite each scale: three taken
at random for illustration from the twelve
which define *Intellectual Characteristics* are,
"possession of average intelligence," "discrimination in selecting tasks," and "imagination."
The ratings, from 1 to 5 in each scale division,
are to be given, not in these defining terms,
but in terms of the composite categories. A
rough approximation to the normal curve of
distribution in terms of percentages is sug-

gested as proper distribution of ratings for a
large number of pupils. Provision is made on
a separate sheet for a summary of individual
ratings and a pupil graph, and for an anecdotal
report on pupils who have been given a rating
of 5 (lowest) on any scale. The purpose of
this report is to serve as a background for
study and understanding of the pupil. The
individual sheets become a part of the student's
cumulative record.

No attempt at establishing the reliability of
the scales is attempted beyond the statement
that in actual experimental use teachers do
succeed in discriminating among the areas represented by the five scales. This seems sufficient
in view of the stated purpose of the scales.
The defining terms under each scale division
should improve its validity in use. The authors'
explanation of the effect of a teacher's own
attitudes upon personality responses and personality ratings should operate in the same
direction. Caution against halo effect and suggestions on how to reduce it are given.

Such an instrument as this has its greatest
value as a supervisory device for helping
teachers to form the habit of studying their
children continuously and for developing skill
in such study. The reviewer questions the
value of emphasizing the general concept rating. Since the purpose is to improve the guidance given children, defining characteristics as
given under each scale category would seem
to be the focal points for teachers' attention.
For this purpose, as well as for giving greater
validity to any ratings undertaken, it is important that teachers should note and record
adequate behavioral evidence for such defining
categories as "Intellectual curiosity," "Being
independent in one's work," "Has emotional
reactions well controlled." The authors do not
suggest this practice.

[1257]
**Tentative Check List for Determining Attitudes
on Fifty Crucial Social, Economic, and Political
Problems.** Grades 9-16 and adults; 1935-39; a revision of *A Tentative Check List for Determining
the Positions Held by Students in Forty Crucial
World Problems (see 72)*; 1 form; 35¢ per check list;
35¢ per specimen set; nontimed (120) minutes; Herbert B. Bruner, Arthur V. Linden, and Hugh B.
Wood; New York: Bureau of Publications, Teachers
College, Columbia University.

[1258]
Test of Personality Adjustment. Ages 9-13; 1931;
1 form, separate editions for boys and girls; $1.75
per 20; 40¢ per specimen set; Carl R. Rogers; New
York: Association Press.

REFERENCES

1 ROGERS, CARL R. *Measuring Personality Adjustment in Children Nine to Thirteen Years of Age.* Columbia University, Teachers College, Contributions to Education, No. 458. New York: Bureau of Publications, the College, 1931. Pp. v, 107. $1.50.
2 BABCOCK, MARJORIE E. *A Comparison of Delinquent and Non-Delinquent Boys by Objective Measures of Personality.* Ralph B. Spence, faculty sponsor. Honolulu, H. I.: the Author, 1932. Pp. 74. Paper.

C. M. Louttit, Director of the Psychological Clinics and Associate Professor of Clinical Psychology, Indiana University. Although this instrument for personality investigation of children is entirely different from the usual schedules, it is sufficiently familiar that a detailed description is unnecessary. It covers areas of personal inferiority, social maladjustment, family maladjustment, and daydreaming, by setting six tasks none of which are of the yes-or-no answer type. Our experience with the scale shows that children find it more interesting and game-like than schedules of the inventory type.

The statistician would frown upon this test because norms are based upon only 167 children, and the scoring is rather complicated. However Rogers carefully warns that, while the tests may be given to small groups, it is intended as a clinical tool. A section on interpretation of results in the manual is especially complete in that it suggests the many clues obtainable from a study of individual responses. In fact, the author does not seem to be particularly concerned about the numerical scores. This is a very refreshing attitude in a world filled with statistically minded psychometricians. Further help is given the test user in four case studies in which the significance of responses is related to items of the case history.

We have used this test in our clinics, and with the exception of the time-consuming method of scoring, have found it the most satisfactory instrument of personality measurement.

[1259]

Tests of the Socially Competent Person. Grades 7-12; 1936-37; 1 form; $6.30 per 25; 15¢ per specimen set; 75(80) minutes; Paul R. Mort, Ralph B. Spence, V. C. Arnspiger, and Laura K. Eads; New York, N. Y.: Bureau of Publications, Teachers College, Columbia University.

REFERENCES

1 SPENCE, RALPH B. "One Approach to the Appraisal of the Competence of High School Pupils." *Teach Col Rec* 40:507-20 Mr '39.

Alvin C. Eurich, Professor of Education, Stanford University. This test of the socially competent person is designed to measure reactions to situations in four areas of living: Health (Test I); Personal Economics (Test II); Family Community Relations (Test III); and Social-Civic Relations (Test IV). The items in Tests I and II call for reactions to generalizations on situations which a pupil can do something about as an individual; in Test III, to situations which a pupil can do something about with the cooperation of other members of his family or community; in Test IV, to situations which a pupil can do something about only as a member of a large group. Within each test the items are arranged in groups, each of which is preceded by a description of a situation. If the pupil agrees with an item he encircles an *A*; if he disagrees, he encircles a *D*.

Reliability coefficients for the total test, based on a single grade of about 300 cases, range from .83 to .94. Grade norms are provided for "typical schools" and for "superior curriculum schools." Validity is inferred from the value of the items and from the fact that children in superior curriculum schools make higher scores than pupils in typical schools.

The authors suggest that the test has three outstanding uses: (*a*) a broad check on the effectiveness of the school curriculum; (*b*) motivation of instruction through the presentation of practical problems to the pupils; and (*c*) individual diagnosis and guidance. They suggest also that individual problems might be prepared, although they fail to give the reliability of each part, so that the test user will know how much reliance he can place on the part scores.

A more accurate label for this test would be: A Test of Beliefs and Knowledge Concerning Four Areas of Living. The following is an example of a belief item: High school boys and girls should "have outdoor recreation or sports every day." The knowledge items may be illustrated by the following: "The differences in insurance rates for standard types of insurance from one company to another are small." If one agrees that beliefs and knowledge in the four areas of living determine whether or not a person is soundly competent, the test is a good one. If, however, one believes with the reviewer that social competence involves more than beliefs and knowledge—that it includes methods and habits of approaching and communicating with people, as well as other characteristics—the test is wholly inadequate as a measure of social competency, and a score is likely to be misleading.

Within the limited scope established by the nature of the items, the test is carefully prepared and should be useful for the purpose designated by the authors if the major limitation is kept in mind.

Warren G. Findley, Assistant Director, Division of Examinations and Testing, State Education Department, Albany, New York. The four parts of this test are designed to measure competence in four areas: health, personal economics, family and community relationships, and social-civic problems. The areas thus are arranged in ascending order of size of group through which the individual operates and by the same token in descending order of immediate personal control and responsibility.

The test is to be commended as an instrument which presents real situations for consideration. The claim that it may be used for "motivating instruction through the presentation of practical problems" seems wholly reasonable. It should be useful not only to the teacher who wishes to motivate pupils, but also to the supervisor who wishes to motivate teachers to relate their work to pupil problems.

Some credence may also be given to the claim that the test may be used to pick out for special attention pupils notably incompetent in the areas covered by the test.

On the other hand, the test cannot be recommended as a *measuring* instrument even for surveys. And the construction of individual pupil profiles from the scores on the various parts would be extremely dubious. In many places in the first three scales the correct answering of a single true-false item makes a difference of half a grade in the individual's rating. No matter how carefully these scales have been standardized, they are too coarse and unreliable for individual diagnosis.

Two factors combine to make the test a poor measuring instrument. First, the fact that it is a simple pencil-and-paper questionnaire of opinion makes its validity very doubtful. While the test exercises present real situations, the expression of agreement or disagreement with statements does not mean the making of real choices. Even though the situations are real and related especially to adolescents and though the answers allowed are as free from criticism as one can expect in such controversial areas,

the validity of a direct questionnaire for measuring social competence must be questioned.

The second source of weakness is the type of item that has been used. The agree-disagree or true-false item is the least reliable item in the test constructor's repertory. When one adds to this the fact that instructions about guessing and corrections for guessing are omitted, a greater degree of unreliability is certain. Moreover, the examination of individual questions leads to the conclusion that the negative answers do not reflect a clear position. In many comparative statements, of which there are 66 in the test, to disagree may mean that one believes the two items compared are equal or that the opposite comparison is true or that one does not know whether the two items compared are equal, or unequal in the opposite sense. Multiple-choice items would be better in most of these cases and, indeed, are generally better adapted to reflect the balanced "judgments characteristic of the socially competent person." One should also mention that of 33 statements which contain as *critical* words "all," "always," "every," "never," 29 are false. The effect of these and other items is to cause a preponderance of "disagree" answers on the scoring key for each part. If one were to mark all statements in the test "disagree," he would obtain a measurable score on the test.

In summary, then, the test should serve a very useful purpose in a "test-teach" plan but should not be considered adequate for objective appraisal of social competence or of effects of instruction on competence.

Pedro T. Orata, Special Consultant, Occupational Information and Guidance Service, United States Office of Education, Washington, D. C. The French naturalist, Cuvier, was once asked to pass judgment on the following definition: "A crab is a small red fish that walks backward." Cuvier replied: "The definition is entirely correct except at three points; the crab is not a fish, it is not red, and it does not walk backward." *Tests of the Socially Competent Person* is a perfect instrument except at three points: first, it is not a test, if by the term *test* is meant a valid measure of competent social behavior; second, it does not provide situations to which a person may act in a social way; and, third, it is entirely possible for a person to score perfectly in the test and still be a social misfit. As someone has so aptly put it, "Saying is not believing and believing is not behaving." A competent person is to be judged not by what he says or believes, but by what he does.

This weakness of the test is evidently recognized by the authors, because in the first paragraph of the manual of directions they state definitely that "The ultimate test of education is found in the behavior patterns produced in the pupils." Nevertheless, since to secure evidence for "behavior patterns" requires trained observers and the methods are very expensive of time, "A more practical method is to give pupils an opportunity to react to descriptions of situations similar to those which they face in everyday life."

The catch is in the meaning of the word *practical.* A test can be practical in the sense implied by the term *attainable* without being in the least useful. We have thousands of tests now that are practical in this sense whose validity, however, has been demonstrated to be very low indeed. The need is not more of the same kind. This world would be greatly benefited if we valued practicability less and usefulness more, especially in the field of tests and measurements, in which he who runs may make a test—and usually does.

Apart from the theoretical unsoundness of the test, it has manifest shortcomings in other respects. A careful reading of the items should enable one to classify an undue proportion of them under the following categories:

1) *Too Obviously Absurd or Wrong.* Test III, Problem I: "A group of high school boys and girls agreed that the people in the community should be actively interested in community problems." One of their reasons is: *"In order to reduce the free services for the poor."* Test II, Problem IV: "Harry's mother has always wanted him to be a lawyer. She worked hard sewing for a living, in order to send him to law school. Whenever he failed in an examination she provided private tutors for him. He tried the bar examination three times and finally passed them. He is now working as a clerk in a large law office. In general, persons like Harry probably: *Will be able to give better legal advice than most lawyers."*

2) *Too Obviously Right or May be Readily Granted.* Test II, Problem: "Jim is especially interested in bookkeeping and has decided that he would like to study to be an accountant.

To be well suited for this work he should rate high on . . .: *General intelligence."* Test I, Problem II: "High school boys and girls should plan their after-school hours wisely." One of the "sensible things that they might do" is: *"Carefully plan their recreation as well as their study."*

3) *Highly Ambiguous or Controversial, or Question-Begging.* Test IV, Problem XIII: "Following are some statements concerning present-day economic problems which are of particular importance to high school pupils today. Indicate those with which you agree and those with which you disagree: *If all people were consistently more thrifty there would be no poverty."* Test III, Problem III: "A group of high school boys and girls, disturbed by conflicting ideas concerning the value and importance of the home in American life today, decided to study this problem. As a result of their study they came to the conclusion that some of the following ideas were true and some were false. Indicate those with which you agree and those with which you disagree: *If all parents were well-educated, schools would be unnecessary."*

4) *Requiring Expert Information or Specific Knowledge.* Test IV, Problem IX: "Below are a few things, some of which have changed considerably within the last one thousand years and some of which have not. Indicate those you think have not: *Man's physical strength."* Test IV, Problem XII: "Because business depressions affect them and their futures so seriously high school pupils should understand the causes of such depressions. Among the factors contributing markedly to the occurrence of the depression in the United States during the years from 1929 on, were: *Unsound expansion of credit; increased government control of production; Lack of balance between production and distribution."*

In brief, it seems to the present reviewer that *Tests of the Socially Competent Person* lacks validity both in what it should measure according to the title and in what it is intended to measure according to the introductory statement of its makers. It may be highly practical from the point of view of the mechanical phases of execution and administration, but it may be practically useless from the point of view of the end to be served.

In spite of the shortcomings indicated the test has outstanding contributions to make toward the improvement of evaluation, among which may be mentioned the following: (*a*) seriously attempting to obtain evidence for one of the "intangibles" in education; (*b*) focusing attention upon the areas in life at the present time in which there exists the greatest need for emphasis—health, personal economics, family and community relationships, and social-civic problems; (*c*) suggesting a way of integrating school experiences in the various subjects around problems of personal and social concern; and (*d*) going one step forward in emphasizing "behavior patterns produced in the pupils" as "the ultimate test of education."

For reviews by Douglas E. Scates and Hilda Taba, see 1154.

[1260]
Test of Social Attitudes. Grades 13-17; 1939; 1 form; $1.25 per 25; 25¢ per specimen set; nontimed (25) minutes; E. C. Hunter; New York: Psychological Corporation.

[1261]
Walther Social Attitudes Test. Grades 12-16; 1937; 2 forms; 50¢ per 25; 15¢ per specimen set; nontimed (25-40) minutes; E. Curt Walther; Towson, Md.: the Author, State Teachers College.

[1262]
Washburne Social-Adjustment Inventory: Thaspic Edition. Age 12 and over; 1936-40; 1 form; $1.30 per 25; 20¢ per manual; 15¢ per specimen set (without manual); nontimed (45) minutes; John N. Washburne; Yonkers, N. Y.: World Book Co.

REFERENCES

1 WASHBURNE, JOHN N. "An Experiment in Character Measurement." *J Juvenile Res* 13:1-18 Ja '29.
2 WASHBURNE, JOHN N. "The Impulsions of Adolescents as Revealed by Their Written Wishes." *J Juvenile Res* 16:193-212 Jl '32.
3 WASHBURNE, JOHN N. "A Test of Social Adjustment." *J Appl Psychol* 19:125-44 Ap '35.
4 WASHBURNE, JOHN N. "The Social Adjustment of Adolescents," pp. 288-92. In *Reconstructing Education Thru Research.* Official Report, American Educational Research Association, A Department of the National Education Association, St. Louis, Missouri, February 22-26, 1936. Washington, D. C.: the Association, May 1936. Pp. 301. $1.50. Paper.

For a review by Daniel A. Prescott of an earlier edition, see 928.

[1263]
What Do You Think? Grades 7-12; 1934-35; 2 forms; $3.15 per 100; 35¢ per manual; 40¢ per specimen set; nontimed (35-45) minutes; Victor H. Noll; New York: Bureau of Publications, Teachers College, Columbia University.

REFERENCES

1 NOLL, VICTOR H. "Measuring Scientific Thinking." *Teach Col Rec* 35:685-93 My '34.
2 NOLL, VICTOR H. "Measuring the Scientific Attitude." *J Abn and Social Psychol* 30:145-54 Jl-S '35.
3 BLAIR, GLENN M. "The Validity of the Noll Test of Scientific Thinking." *J Ed Psychol* 31:53-9 Ja '40.

Ralph K. Watkins, Professor of Education, The University of Missouri. This is an attempt to measure scientific attitude and habits of thinking. The tests are intended for school pupils in grades 7-12.

Each form includes 75 true-false items, 15 added true-false items based upon the analysis of a diagram, and a final exercise requiring the numbering of 22 terms in alphabetical order.

The front page asks for certain personnel data concerning the pupil. There are some peculiar discriminations and lacks of discrimination in this. For example, there is a space for marking the number of years' experience in physical geography or general science as if these two courses were considered as of equivalent value in training in scientific attitudes. The space for recording training in history is marked "yrs. History (not U.S.)" as if training in United States history has not assumed training value for scientific attitudes and other history has.

One-half page at the front is devoted to questions concerning the likes and dislikes of pupils for various types of leisure activities. There is no apparent relationship between this material and the traits which the test purports to measure.

Of the first 75 true-false items in Form 1, 59 are keyed as false, 13 as questionable, and only 3 as true.

The tests may be considered useful as experimental tools for teachers interested in trying to train pupils in scientific attitudes. Teachers using the tests need to be cautious in forming conclusions concerning the exact status of the attitudes of their pupils as a result of scores on such tests.

Workers in education and in educational psychology are by no means in agreement upon the definition of scientific attitudes, nor of scientific habits of thinking. There is serious question on whether the "habit of accuracy of observation" can be attained as such, or whether accuracy of observation is always an attribute of definite situations or things. Is an individual accurate, or must he be accurate in *something*? This same type of question arises concerning all the other five "habits of thinking" which these tests purport to measure.

At least one other of the basic assumptions underlying the validity of the tests may be seriously questioned. In the handbook accompanying the tests the author says, "First, if the tests really measure habits of thinking, scores on them should be little dependent upon native mental capacity or intelligence." This, in effect, says that intelligence is little related to the formation of desirable habits of thinking or the formation of scientific attitudes. The writer of this review seriously questions the validity of this assumption.

Finally, the most important question concerning these tests is that of just what do they measure. Teachers may well restrict the use of these tests to experimental and tentative trials until this fundamental question can be more definitely answered.

J Ed Psychol 31:53-9 Ja '40. Glenn M. Blair. "The Validity of the Noll Test of Scientific Thinking." * The Noll test of scientific thinking has been devised to measure the extent to which school children can take an objective, scientific viewpoint toward a variety of problems. In brief, it purports to measure the scientific attitude. In order to check its validity, this test was given to sixteen top ranking scientists on the faculty of the University of Illinois. Each of these men holds the Ph.D. degree, and has a rank of associate professor or higher in the University. The branches of science represented by these scientists are: Bacteriology, botany, chemistry, entomology, physics, psychology, and zoology. The results of the investigation show that for many items of both forms of the test, the answers given by the scientists disagree with those given in the published scoring key. Several questions are found for which none of the sixteen scientists give acceptable answers according to the Noll key. There are twenty-six invalid items in Form 1 and twenty-five invalid items in Form 2, if it be held that for an item to be considered valid it must be answered according to the scoring key by three-fourths of the scientists. These facts cause one to question the validity of this test as a measure of scientific thinking. It is suggested, however, that the validity could be improved considerably by revising the scoring key so that it would fall in line with the answers of the group of scientists who took the tests. In a number of questions there is almost complete disagreement among the scientists as to what are the correct answers. It is suggested that these questions be eliminated from the tests altogether.

For a review by Francis D. Curtis, see 1139.

[1264]
What Should Our Schools Do? A Poll of Public Opinion on the School Program. Adults; 1938; 1 form; $2.10 per 100; 10¢ per specimen set; Paul R. Mort, F. G. Cornell, and Norman H. Hinton; New York: Bureau of Publications, Teachers College, Columbia University.

Loyola Ed Digest 14:12 Ap '39. Austin G. Schmidt. This is a questionnaire containing one hundred items, and is intended as a measure of the extent to which school authorities and the public are prepared to accept newer practices. One scores high if he says that children who do not know their subject matter should not be required to repeat the matter, if he denies that children have as much need for practicing restraint as they have for practicing freedom, and so forth. In justice to the authors it should be noted that they do not defend in the accompanying set of instructions these new and progressive ideas. Users of the questionnaire are at liberty to condemn as an undesirable citizen one who scores high in it. Not all the practices, of course, are equally extreme or radical.

[1265]
What Would You Do? A Survey of Student Opinion. Grades 7-12; 1939; 1 form, 2 parts; 75¢ per 25; 10¢ per specimen set; nontimed (15-20) minutes per part; Ruth E. Eckert and Howard E. Wilson; Cambridge, Mass.: Committee on Publications, Harvard Graduate School of Education.
a) PART I, SCHOOL AFFAIRS.
b) PART II, COMMUNITY AFFAIRS.

REFERENCES

1 WILSON, HOWARD E. *Education for Citizenship,* pp. 66-79. New York: McGraw-Hill Book Co., 1938. Pp. xii, 272. $2.75. (London: McGraw-Hill Publishing Co., Ltd., 1939. 15s.)

[1266]
Wrightstone Scale of Civic Beliefs. Grades 9-12; 1938; 2 forms; $1.00 per 25; 15¢ per specimen set; 15(20) minutes; J. Wayne Wrightstone; Yonkers, N. Y.: World Book Co.

REFERENCES

1 WRIGHTSTONE, J. WAYNE. "Appraising Newer Practices in Teaching Social Studies." *Sch R* 42:688-93 N '34.
2 WRIGHTSTONE, J. WAYNE. "Civic Beliefs and Correlated Intellectual and Social Factors." *Sch R* 42:53-58 Ja '34.
3 WRIGHTSTONE, J. WAYNE. "Measuring Some Major Objectives of the Social Studies." *Sch R* 43:771-9 D '35.

Stephen M. Corey, Professor of Educational Psychology and Superintendent of the Laboratory Schools, The University of Chicago. The most important single question that anyone can ask about a scale purporting to provide "a valid and reliable measure of civic attitudes" is: What hint do the scores give us as to the way the subjects will behave? This to the reviewer is the real test of the validity of attitude questionnaires. Some scale makers identify an attitude with a verbal statement checked on an inventory. Such an "attitude" has little significance psychologically or sociologically. The pragmatic justification of attitude questionnaires is the accuracy with which they make possible the prognostication of overt behavior. Especially is this true of scales such as Wrightstone's which are developed to measure attitudes because of "their importance as dynamic factors which exert a powerful influence on behavior." This concept of the validity of attitude scales is not emphasized in either the manual of directions or the three articles [1,2,3] the reviewer read which dealt with the scale. Wrightstone apparently believes that the validity of his scale was established by demonstrating that: (a) the items differentiated between liberals and conservatives, and (b) expert judges agreed that the items scored "liberal" and "conservative" were really so. No data were presented to indicate the degree to which the scale discriminated between the two groups (liberal and conservative) nor was there any description of the method employed to select the groups originally. The reliability coefficient between Forms A and B for 252 pupils in grades 10-12 inclusive was .90.

In the *Catalog of Standard Tests* (Spring 1940, p. 59) published by the World Book Company appears the statement: "This test [Wrightstone's] provides a measure of an individual's liberalism or conservatism with respect to social, economic, and political issues. It meets the need for a reliable index of the extent to which certain attitudinal or non-intellectual objectives of educational procedure are being attained." The reviewer doubts the accuracy of the second sentence. He has found no convincing evidence that scores on the *Wrightstone Scale of Civic Beliefs* are in any way related to the liberal or conservative *behavior* of children. It is the latter with which educators are primarily concerned. The scales are attractively put up, easy to administer, and economical of scoring time. The reviewer has found them interesting to children and provocative of much valuable classroom discussion.

Harold Gulliksen, Assistant Professor of Psychology and Examiner in the Social Sciences, The University of Chicago. From the viewpoint of the mechanics of administering and scoring, the test is well-constructed. The directions to the student and examiner are clear. The test is completely objective, and a convenient scoring stencil is provided. Percentile norms are provided for a single form and for the combined score using both forms of the test. These norms are given separately for grades 9, 10, 11, and 12.

The reliability of the test is high, .90 for a single form and .94 for the combined score on both forms. However, we are told that the reliability was computed from a sample including pupils from grades 10 to 12 inclusive while norms are given for each grade separately. Since the "liberalism" score increases steadily from the ninth to the twelfth grade, the reliability for a single grade would certainly be less than .90, although in this case probably not much less. The best practice would be to give reliability figures for the same groups as those on which the norms are calculated. In addition to information on reliability, it should be common practice to give the standard error of measurement since this statistic probably is not as sensitive to changes in variability of the total population as is the reliability coefficient.

It is gratifying to note that when the author suggests the use of part scores on the test, he also points out that the reliability of these scores is low, that they are "not sufficiently reliable for accurate individual diagnosis."

The techniques used in selecting the test items and in validating the scale are described. These techniques, while indicating careful work, are not scaling techniques such as are now available. The need for scaling techniques can be illustrated. For example, agreement with either of the following statements adds the same amount to the "liberalism" score: "United States citizens have been jailed because of their political beliefs"; and "Business and industry increasingly need some government regulation"; whereas they should probably be weighted differently. Attitude measurement is a field in which factor analysis techniques could be used with considerable profit. There is no indication that they have been used or that the test items form a one-dimensional system. It would be desirable to take the precaution of determining this before constructing attitude scales, or to use a scaling technique which includes a test of linearity.

Some of the statements in the test seem to this reviewer to be so largely factual in nature that—barring considerable evidence to the contrary—they hardly constitute appropriate material for a scale of "liberalism." The following three statements will illustrate this point: "Democracy, unlike dictatorship, has certain limitations for dealing quickly with emergencies"; "Other nations approved our getting Panama from Colombia"; and "The United States is now entangled in European affairs." Also in view of our present knowledge of the precariousness of generalizations concerning nations, it seems somewhat unjustified to include the statement "German people are on the whole industrious and thrifty," and to score a person who agrees with this statement as more "liberal" than one who does not.

ENGLISH

Reviews by John C. Almack, Roland L. Beck, M. E. Broom, Walter W. Cook, Frank P. De Lay, Joseph C. Dewey, Paul B. Diederich, Charles Fox, Ann L. Gebhardt, H. H. Giles, Keith Goltry, Harry A. Greene, Jean Hoard, Robert W. Howard, Violet Hughes, Carleton C. Jones, G. Frederic Kuder, Lou LaBrant, Herbert A. Landry, J. Paul Leonard, Constance M. McCullough, Jeanette McPherrin, Edward S. Noyes, Jacob S. Orleans, Robert C. Pooley, Henry D. Rinsland, David H. Russell, Rachel Salisbury, L. K. Shumaker, C. Ebblewhite Smith, Robert K. Speer, John M. Stalnaker, Edward A. Tenney, Charles Swain Thomas, Arthur E. Traxler, G. M. Wilson, J. Wayne Wrightstone, and Louis C. Zahner.

GRAMMAR AND USAGE

[1267]

Barrett-Ryan-Schrammel English Test. Grades 9-16; 1938; 2 forms; $1.10 per 25; 15¢ per specimen set; 2¢ per machine-scorable answer sheet; 40(50) minutes; E. R. Barrett, Teresa M. Ryan, and H. E. Schrammel; Yonkers, N. Y.: World Book Co., (London: George G. Harrap & Co., Ltd.)

G. Frederic Kuder, Examiner, Board of Examinations, The University of Chicago. Part I contains 30 points on sentence structure and diction, the student being required to judge whether each selected word or phrase in the passage presented is correctly used. The same technique is used in Part II for 35 words selected from a continuous passage, the errors being grammatical in this case. In addition to judging whether an item is right or wrong the student is required to indicate what the correct construction would be for the wrong items. Part III calls for judgments as to the correctness of 50 instances of punctuation selected from a continuous passage.

Requiring the student to identify errors in context is a highly commendable characteristic of the test. Whether it is justifiable to allot one-third of the points to punctuation in a test of this sort is doubtful. No reasons are given for the distribution of points used. It may be that the authors have found that the particular weighting used is most effective for predicting freshman composition grades. Certainly the validities obtained sound like the answer to a test builder's dream. Correlations of .73, .74, .73, and .75 were obtained for three groups of first-semester college freshmen and one group of first-semester college sophomores numbering respectively 88, 76, 93, and 51, between test scores obtained at the beginning of a semester and marks in English composition obtained at the end of the semester. To what extent similar correlations will be found in other institutions will depend largely, probably, upon the nature of the measure of achievement used.

The reliabilities reported appear to be satisfactory although final judgment on this point must be suspended since no data concerning the nature of the groups from which the reliabilities were obtained are given except for the number of subjects used. Correlations of .88 and .89 between different forms, and Spearman-Brown reliabilities of .94, .91, and .91 for Forms A, B, and C, respectively, were obtained.

Although the authors state that the test may be used for diagnostic purposes, to what extent the scores on the separate parts may be so used is open to question since reliabilities for the parts are not reported. Norms are not given for the parts.

The authors appear to have been successful

in avoiding trivialities which tend to creep into English tests. The material used apparently covers a wide range both as to types of errors represented and difficulties of specific questions.

Robert C. Pooley, Associate Professor in the Teaching of English, The University of Wisconsin. A test of English grammar and usage in three forms, prepared with a detachable answer sheet which is quickly scored by means of a perforated key. The test is reported to have coefficients of reliability between odd and even items of single forms from .91 to .94; the probable error of a score ranges from 3.1 to 3.3. Exact directions for administering and scoring are furnished and norms based on the scores of 31,937 high school students and 7472 college freshmen are supplied. The test is well constructed, easily administered and scored, and its results are capable of useful interpretation.

Each form contains three parts. Part I is a test of sentence structure and diction, formed by underlining words in a running narrative. The student is required to indicate whether the underlined word is right or wrong in its setting. It is a test, of course, of skill in proofreading, but proofreading under extraordinary conditions where each error is heavily underscored. What relationship this skill in proofreading bears to the ability to correct one's own manuscript is not revealed by the authors of the test. Recent studies seem to agree that the relationship is slight. Nevertheless, until better devices are discovered, this one will have to serve if pupils must be tested.

Part II is a combined test of correctness and grammatical knowledge. Each sentence in a running narrative contains one underlined word which must be marked right or wrong. At the same time, one of three grammatical explanations for the form of the word must be selected to explain the reason for marking it right or wrong. Part III is a long and dull exercise on punctuation.

This test should delight a great number of teachers. It tests what they know and what they teach. It belongs to a world in which a comma is of greater importance than a child, and where a grammatical form, duly labeled with a reason, is venerated. Undoubtedly it tests grammar as it is taught in the schools, and to some extent reveals weaknesses in the

student's command of cultivated usage. But it is not, and should not be called a test of English. We may rejoice that English cannot be enmeshed in a test of three parts, scored with a perforated card.

Charles Swain Thomas, Associate Professor of Education, Emeritus, Harvard University. The *Barrett-Ryan-Schrammel English Test* is a simple, practical test that makes a direct appeal to all English teachers—those who have had special training in statistical methods and those who have **not**.

The test is designed to give an objective measure of a student's degree of mastery of the mechanics of English.

Part I, Sentence Structure and Diction, is provided with these specific directions:

In the following paragraphs some expressions are underlined. (The expression may be a word or a group of words.) If the expression is rightly used and rightly placed, make a heavy mark like this in the space between the dots under R on the Answer Sheet. If the expression is either wrongly used or wrongly placed, make a heavy mark in the space under W on the Answer Sheet, as shown in the sample. (See the sample answer on the Answer Sheet.)

Sample. Even though you don't succeed at first,
                  a
     you had ought to try again. ....
              b

This is followed by a page of composition sprinkled with errors commonly made by high-school and college students. Here are the opening sentences:

In the senior class were six of us boys who ranked high in scholarship and who ......
                                                    1
wanted to go to college. Five of us could not of gone even for one year without we ......
          2   3
worked not only for our living expenses but ......
                                          4
also for our tuition and books. Wishing to ......
  4   5
get work, it was our plan to write to several colleges and asking what our chances were ......
                    6
for employment. Having received encourag- ......
                        7
ing letters from one of the colleges, three of us decided to attend that college. The other ......
                      8
two preferred to remain at home rather than working to pay their way.   ......
9

In Part II—Grammatical Forms, we have this set of directions.

In each numbered portion of the story below there is an underlined word. Some of these underlined words are right and some are wrong. If the word is right, make a mark under R on the Answer Sheet. If the word is wrong, as shown in the sample below, make a mark under W. (See the mark under W on the Answer Sheet.) Then look at the three items numbered 1, 2, and 3, one of which names the correct form to be used. Only one of these items is the right explanation. Choose the right one, and make a mark on the Answer Sheet under the number of that item.

There follows a composition, freely interlarded with mistakes such as these which are underlined—and which the students are asked to correct.

1. Before school closed in June us girls were making plans to spend part of our vacation camping out.
2.
   1. possessive case, to modify *girls*
   2. nominative case, subject of *were making*
   3. objective case, in apposition with *girls*

3. It was left to Jane and I to get a chaperon, for we must have one. After much
4.
   1. nominative case, subject of *get*
   2. objective case, object of *was left*
   3. objective case, object of *to*

5. deliberation as to whom of our teachers would like to spend two weeks in camp, Jane suggested
6.
   1. objective case, to agree *teachers*
   2. nominative case, subject of *would like*
   3. objective case, object of *to*

7. that we have Miss Lee, who we agreed was our favorite teacher. The group was satisfied with
8.
   1. objective case, object of *agreed*
   2. nominative case, subject of *was*
   3. objective case, to agree with *Miss Lee*

9. our choice. It was either Jane or I who was to ask her whether she would consent to go. Then
10.
    1. objective case, object of *was*
    2. objective case, to agree with *Jane*
    3. nominative case, in the predicate with *was*

11. we decided both would ask her. Jane and myself went to her classroom. We found her still busy.
12.
    1. objective case, after *and*
    2. nominative case (I), subject of *went*
    3. pronoun ending in *self*, after *and*

To facilitate the scoring, the publishers provide a stencil. The whole procedure is simple and practical.

Indeed, the whole test is extremely sensible. The items chosen are carefully selected—selected largely because the errors made are of frequent occurrence and can be corrected only by drills. The test itself is one of these drills.

[1268]

Basic Language Skills: Iowa Every-Pupil Tests of Basic Skills, Test C. Grades 3-5, 6-8; 1940; Form L, 2 levels; 30¢ per manual; 12¢ per booklet of norms; 40¢ per 25 record cards; single specimen set free; H. F. Spitzer in collaboration with Ernest Horn, Maude McBroom, H. A. Greene, and E. F. Lindquist with the assistance of the faculty of the University Experimental Schools, State University of Iowa; Boston, Mass.: Houghton Mifflin Co.
a) ELEMENTARY BATTERY. Grades 3-5. $1.15 per 25; 51(60) minutes.
b) ADVANCED BATTERY. Grades 6-8. $1.25 per 25; 58(70) minutes.

For reviews by William A. Brownell, J. Murray Lee, and Charles W. Odell of an earlier form of the complete battery, see 872.

[1269]

Cleveland English Composition and Grammar Test. Grades 7-12; 1931-32; 2 forms; 50¢ per 25; single specimen set free; Clarence Stratton, William L. Connor, and Frank A. Redmond; Boston, Mass.: Houghton Mifflin Co.

Frank P. De Lay, Department of English, New Trier Township High School, Winnetka, Illinois. It is not only the lazy teacher who appreciates a test so mechanically constructed that it is quickly and easily corrected. The time of the good teacher is greatly over-filled with work, and an efficiently constructed test such as the Cleveland is a boon. The thing that impresses me most about this test, in addition to its mechanical makeup, is the fact that so much of its space is given to functional grammar. The grammar of recognition, in which the student merely identifies numerous grammatical forms, is largely wasted on the high school student; but he certainly can use that grammar which points out ways of varying his sentence structure, or of being correct by showing the logic of correctness. My only criticism of the test is that Part I merely tests the ability of the student to name a grammatical form, and that Part II does not contain the serious errors most often found in student compositions, but rather deals with finer points in usage the seriousness of which may be debatable in the light of recent studies. The other parts, especially Part VII, really test the student's ability *to use language.*

[1269.1]

College English Test: National Achievement Test. Grades 12-13; 1937; 1 form; $2.50 per 25; 5¢ per specimen set; nontimed (45-60) minutes; A. C. Jordan; Rockville Centre, N. Y.: Acorn Publishing Co.

REFERENCES

1 MARCKWARDT, ALBERT H., AND WALCOTT, FRED G. *Facts about Current English Usage*: Including a Discussion of Current Usage in Grammar from "Current English Usage" by Sterling A. Leonard. National Council of Teachers of English, English Monograph No. 7. New York and London: D. Appleton-Century Co., Inc., 1938. Pp. ix, 144. $0.90; 4s. 6d. Paper.

Constance M. McCullough, Assistant Professor of Education, Western Reserve University. This 120-item test, one of the comprehensive battery entitled National Achievement Tests, is evidently designed for college English placement programs or for prospective college entrants. The advertisement reads, "Every high school student who expects to enter college should take this test." Not a timed test, it is advertised as requiring from 45 to 60 minutes.

Part I, Punctuation, consists of 40 items which the student is to punctuate by inserting the necessary marks and enclosing each of them in parentheses. In the 22 items of Part II, Capitalization, the student is to indicate the need for capitalization by underlining the words which should begin with capital letters. Part III, Language Usage, contains 20 items of 4 sentences each. For each item, the student is to write in the margin the letter preceding the sentence which he thinks is best written. Each item deals with a single type of language error. Part IV, Sentence Structure, offers 20 items of 4 sentences each, to which the student is to make similar responses in the margin. With few exceptions, each item exemplifies one type of error. The types concern pronoun reference, verbosity, tense sequence, placement of modifiers and clauses, subordination and coordination of ideas, and the case of the relative pronoun. Part V, Modifiers, comprises 8 sets of 4 sentences which illustrate the proper and improper placement of modifiers. The student is to respond to this section as he did to the preceding two. Part VI, Miscellaneous Principles, is a matching section of 10 items, which requires the identification of structural and grammatical errors and the recognition of the technical terms appropriate to them. The student is to write after each sentence the letter referring to the principle which applies to the error. The only norm reported for the *College English Test*—which is apparently still in the process of standardization—is an undefined median score. The reliability coefficient, estimated from the correlation between scores on the odd- and even-numbered items and based upon an unidentified population, is .88. The validity of the test proceeds from consultation of "numerous city and state courses of study, widely used textbooks and the judgment of more than one hundred fifty experienced administrators. The tests were further evaluated and criticized by many classroom teachers."

The teacher's directions, class record, scoring key, and "norms" appear with convenient compactness on the two sides of a single sheet.

It is curious, in view of all the available studies of frequency of use and frequency of error, that the author should have chosen textbooks, courses of study, and the judgment of school administrators for the validation of his test items. This type of validation is probably responsible for many of the unusual emphases observable in the test. Perhaps there are those who would agree that three of six parts of an English test should be devoted to matters of sentence structure, that there should be half as many items on grammatical usage as on punctuation, that about one-third of all the items on structural errors should involve the placement of modifiers. But surely few would advocate having three items on the case of the relative pronoun, with only one on the use of the adjective for the adverb; none of the twenty-eight items of sentence structure, exclusive of the technical section, concern parallel construction or the use of the adverbial for the noun clause.

There are peculiar inconsistencies throughout the test. Item 9 in the punctuation section demands a correction in capitalization. The divorce, by the way, of punctuation and capitalization makes it possible for the student to derive clues to the correction of items in the one from items in the other. The principle tested in Item 14 of the language usage section is violated in the very next item and, according to the Marckwardt-Walcott report [1] on current usage, is no longer an issue. Another item in the language usage section appears to be a matter of verbosity better placed in the sentence structure section. An item on the case of the relative pronoun and another involving the use of *says* for *said*, both of which have sister items in the language usage section, appear in the sentence structure section. Three items in this section deal with the placement of modifiers, although the next section is devoted to similar items. It is not clear on what basis the author selected the items on verb form, subject and verb agreement, and sentence structure for the section on miscellaneous principles, which requires a knowledge of technical terms for correct response. While the directions for this section state that the ten sentences are incorrect, one of the optional "principles" listed in the section is, "Sentence is correct as it stands." Marginal spaces for responses are provided for all parts of the test even though the student uses them in only four of the parts. Some students may find this situation confusing.

A high reliability coefficient may be achieved on an English test if niceties and uncommon usages are included. The score on such a test, however, makes a rather doubtful index of a student's actual language ability and encourages teachers to emphasize in their teaching the niceties at the expense of the fundamentals. It is a plausible conjecture that most people have lived entire lifetimes without being called upon to punctuate "LLD" and "I Sam IX 13."

Although there are several items in Parts I and II to which more than one response could be correct, the key provides only one answer for each item. In the capitalization section some responses are highly disputable. Many teachers will consider certain answers in the key utterly wrong. I refer especially to Items 7, 21, and 22.

For both survey and diagnostic purposes, test users will find a number of carefully validated and well constructed tests in this field.

Robert W. Howard, Department of Examinations, The Chicago City Junior Colleges, Chicago, Illinois. This test is a short, easily administered test designed for entering freshmen. Its six parts measure skills in punctuation, capitalization, language usage, sentence structure, modifiers, and miscellaneous principles. The first two parts seem difficult to score since they require corrections within the text. The remaining four parts, however, are easily scored by the strip method. With a little revision, the entire test could be adapted to machine scoring.

The parts devoted to language usage, sentence structure, and modifiers require the student to choose the best sentence from groups of four. The student who selects the correct

sentence from each ingeniously arranged group undoubtedly has a feeling for what is right in English prose. Whether he carries out this feeling in his own writing remains to be proved. The last section, requiring the matching of principles with sentences illustrative of common errors, raises the question of whether the student may not know right from wrong in matters of grammar without possessing the ability to identify the rule governing his performance.

[1270]
Columbia Research Bureau English Test. Grades 11-16; 1925-26; 2 forms; $1.50 per 25; 20¢ per specimen set; 105 (120) minutes; Harrison R. Steeves, Allan Abbott, and Ben D. Wood; Yonkers, N. Y.: World Book Co.

L. K. Shumaker, Director of the Education Clinic, University of Oregon. This test is compact and easy to handle not only by the pupil who has limited desk space at which to work, but also for the teacher whose files must be kept restricted. Part I, Spelling, does not appeal to me because the pupil is asked to choose a correct spelling from a noncontextual setting; the number of words appears to be too small; the incorrect spellings tend to confuse even rather good spellers. Part II, Mechanical Accuracy in Composition, does not make use of contextual setting and the device of copy-editing has not been employed to get the best results possible. The test seems to be too short. It is probably rather hard to score. Part III, Vocabulary, fails to use contextual settings which would tend to sharpen the pupil's power to discriminate, in my opinion. Part IV, Literary Knowledge, ought to be particularly useful to teachers who are attempting to estimate the preparation of pupils in the field of literature. It is long enough and sufficiently diversified to give a fair cross section of ready knowledge of a purely factual nature. It does not seem to me to indicate much about literary discrimination, unless this trait is concomitant with factual knowledge about literature.

The time limit feature is both an asset and a liability. As an asset, the time limit makes it possible to plan carefully for the use of the test in a busy program; as a liability, it tends to restrict the sampling of the work of those unable to finish the test and therefore handicaps the teacher who wishes to use the test papers themselves for diagnostic purposes. The chief value I see in the *Columbia Research Bureau English Test* is that it is a useful kind of achievement test in terms of facts retained, for students who have completed some study of literature at the secondary level; and perhaps even at the end of a course in the history of English literature at the college level. Whether or not I should use this test would depend entirely upon the purpose to which I wished to put it. I should never select it as a "language aptitude test"; only as a special type of achievement test.

Louis C. Zahner, Head of the Department of English, Groton School, Groton, Massachusetts. This test is a measure of achievement in a small, limited, elementary area of English studies. It is confined entirely to the more mechanical aspects of English. Familiar testing techniques are used, and the test is thus laid open to criticisms that also are familiar. Composition receives attention only in proofreading tests for recognition of errors in such mechanical elements as spelling, punctuation, reference, grammatical form, and elementary sentence-structure. Vocabulary is given only a test in synonym-matching. Literary knowledge is tested only by multiple-choice items based entirely on factual detail.

Even within this limited area of mechanical matters, serious questions are raised as to just exactly what is being tested. Operationally described, the spelling test is a measure of the pupil's ability to recognize the one correct spelling out of four given versions of the word. Whether performance in this is a measure of his ability to spell the word correctly in his own composition is uncertain. Similarly, even in its limited area of testing mechanical accuracy, the composition test, demanding as it does merely proofreading, is not necessarily even a measure of the pupil's ability to write mechanically accurate composition. It is certainly not a test of his ability to select and to arrange materials gathered from his reading and from his firsthand experience; to develop his ideas in a clear, logically planned essay. The vocabulary test, similarly, measures the pupil's reading-recognition of a word, and his ability to recognize one of its synonyms when it is given to him. It is not a measure of the pupil's ability to select and to use the word in his own writing and speech in a situation in which the use of that word and not another would not only be correct but would also exactly convey the meanings and effects

he wishes to convey. Nor is it a test of the ability of the student fully to comprehend the meanings and effects of the word when he reads it in a context. The literary knowledge section, likewise, tests the pupil's familiarity with some of the factual content of traditional works and his ability to remember a book he has read well enough to identify a fact connected with it. It does not test his assimilation of what he has read; nor does it test his ability to interpret and to criticize literature; nor does it test his ability to see relationships that hold between different books he has read and between literature and his experience with life.

Within these limits, the test is adequate. It might, for instance, be a reasonably accurate instrument for detecting pupils who are close to illiteracy; a pupil making an extremely low score on this test would probably be a poor risk for specialization in the field of English in school or college. A low-scoring pupil would very likely be deficient in his use of English. But it by no means follows that a high-scoring pupil would have special aptitude in English, or would of necessity be a better risk for specialization in the field. Successful work in English demands many things that are not covered by this test.

In the manual of directions, however, the publishers make almost unlimited claims. Among those implicitly or explicitly made are these: that the test measures the entire field of requisites in English studies, and that it will, by itself, furnish a measure of achievement in this entire field; that it will be found useful by supervisors in standardizing the English work in their schools; that college administrators can safely use it in selecting students for admission without any other tests or examinations in English, and in placement and guidance of their students; that its results should be used by teachers in adjusting their teaching and in establishing standards for the teaching of English.

To make such claims for a test limited to the mechanics of composition and the recall of factual details of books is completely to disregard the most important aims and objectives of English studies. That these objectives do not yield results amenable to present techniques of objective testing is not evidence of the unimportance of the objectives, nor is it evidence of the unreality of the results they can yield and are in fact yielding. It is rather an indication of the handicaps under which objective tests labor in this field. These handicaps can possibly be overcome. Already much progress has been made here and there. Extravagant claims made for objective tests in their present stage of development, however, will not only do harm to the teaching of English, but will also retard the development of adequate tests. To make such claims is completely to misunderstand and to underestimate the growing demands put upon English studies today, and the progress being made in meeting these demands. A test of a limited part of the field of English studies is not a test of the whole field, and no talk about reliability and validity, no figures of correlations and norms, will make it so.

[1271]

Cooperative English Test: Usage, Spelling, and Vocabulary. Grades 9-16; 1932-39; 4 editions; 25¢ per specimen set of any one edition; Form P: Sterling A. Leonard, M. H. Willing, V. A. C. Henmon, M. F. Carpenter, E. F. Lindquist, W. W. Cook, D. G. Paterson, F. S. Beers, Charles Swain Thomas, and Geraldine Spaulding with the assistance of Henry S. Dyer and Robert L. McCaul; Form PM: M. F. Carpenter, E. F. Lindquist, W. W. Cook, D. G. Paterson, F. S. Beers, Geraldine Spaulding with the editorial assistance of H. A. Domincovich, Constance M. McCullough, and Natalie D. Starr; New York: Cooperative Test Service.
a) SERIES 1, FORMS 1932 AND 1936. Forms 1933, 1934, and 1935 are out of print; 6¢ per test, 10 to 99 copies; 95(105) minutes.
b) SERIES 2, FORMS 1932 AND 1936. Forms 1933, 1934, and 1935 are out of print; 6¢ per test, 10 to 99 copies; 75(80) minutes.
c) FORMS 1937, O, AND P. 1937-39; 6¢ per test, 10 to 99 copies; 80(85) minutes.
d) FORMS OM AND PM. 1938-39; 8¢ per test, 10 to 99 copies; 1½¢ per machine-scorable answer sheet; 70(75) minutes.

REFERENCES

1 THORNDIKE, E. L. *A Teacher's Word Book*. New York: Bureau of Publications, Teachers College, Columbia University, 1921. Pp. 134. $0.80.
2 HORN, ERNEST. *A Basic Writing Vocabulary*: 10,000 Words Most Commonly Used in Writing. State University of Iowa, Monographs in Education, Series 1, No. 4. Iowa City, Iowa: the University, 1926. Pp. 225. Cloth, $2.25; paper, $1.75.
3 HORN, ERNEST, AND ASHBAUGH, ERNEST J. *Fundamentals of Spelling*: For Grades 1-8, Incorporating the Findings of a Tabular Analysis of 5,100,000 Words of Ordinary Writing. Philadelphia, Pa.: J. B. Lippincott Co., 1928. Pp. xxvii, 148. $0.60.
4 BECK, R. L. *The Reliability and Validity of a National Test of English Composition for High School Seniors and College Freshmen*. Unpublished doctor's thesis, University of Oklahoma, 1932. Pp. 173.
5 BECK, ROLAND L. "A Natural Test of English Usage." *J Exp Ed* 1:280-6 Mr '33.
6 GLADFELTER, M. E. "The Value of the Cooperative English Test in Prediction for Success in College." *Sch and Soc* 44:383-4 S 19 '36.
7 DRAKE, LEWIS E., AND HENMON, V. A. C. "The Prediction of Scholarship in the College of Letters and Science at the University of Wisconsin." *Sch and Soc* 45:191-4 F 6 '37.
8 STUIT, DEWEY B., AND JURGENSEN, CLIFFORD E. "The Effect of Method of Presentation on Spelling Scores." *J Exp Ed* 5:271-3 Mr '37.
9 PATERSON, DONALD G.; SCHNEIDLER, GWENDOLEN G.; AND WILLIAMSON, EDMUND G. *Student Guidance Techniques*, pp. 116-20. New York: McGraw-Hill Book Co., Inc., 1938. Pp.
xviii, 316. $3.00. (London: McGraw-Hill Publishing Co., Ltd., 18s.)
10 HANNA, JOSEPH V. "A Comparison of Cooperative Test Scores and High School Grades as Measures for Predicting Achievement in College." *J Appl Psychol* 23:289-97 Ap '39.
11 MCCULLOUGH, CONSTANCE M., AND FLANAGAN, JOHN C. "The Validity of the Machine-Scorable Cooperative English Test." *J Exp Ed* 7:229-234 Mr '39.

Carleton C. Jones, Department of English, State Teachers College, Indiana, Pennsylvania. [Review of Forms P and PM.] In setting out critically to review an educational test labeled "English," the reviewer has really to answer just one question—a question which the test publishers themselves should already have answered—namely: *Does the instrument yield a valid measure of a student's ability to speak or write the English language?* If a test does not yield such a measure, it merits no consideration whatsoever; for, in the final analysis, the sole defensible objective of English instruction is the development of the student's powers of linguistic expression. We teach spelling, grammar, punctuation, capitalization, and all the rest, not because they are important in themselves, but because they are integral to the total process of composition. Any evaluation instrument, therefore, which undertakes to investigate student achievement in these matters must do so in such a way that the test results will bear a known relationship to functional usage. And this relationship should always be clearly indicated by experimental data published in conjunction with the test itself. In other words, every test issued in the English field should be accompanied by correlation tables indicating the exact relationship existing between test scores and the actual performance of students in practical composition situations.

In theory, at least, the original authors of the *Cooperative English Test* were in agreement with this reviewer that their test, as a test of usage, should yield evidence of a student's ability actually to express himself in the medium of language. They wrote, when the series was first inaugurated, that the purpose of the test was "to measure ability in English composition"; but they immediately made the unwarranted assumption that such ability could be measured by probing a student's ability "to detect or correct errors and difficulties in expression in composition by others"—an assumption which this reviewer, for one, feels has never been adequately established. But it is on this assumption, nevertheless, that the *Cooperative English Test* is still predicated, despite the fact that the authors apparently have made no effort to establish the validity of their procedure since 1928, when they reported "a substantial correlation with final marks in Freshman English at the University of Wisconsin and elsewhere." Today, of course, there is a general and justifiable skepticism concerning anything, the validity of which has been established on the basis of a correlation with teachers' marks!

An analysis of the *Cooperative English Test*, therefore, leaves this reviewer with one fundamental doubt concerning each of the several parts of the instrument: We doubt, first, that ability to detect and correct errors in English usage in someone else's writing, or ability to select the most appropriate of several alternative constructions for any given sentence can be taken as very conclusive evidence of a student's ability to write grammatically in his own compositional enterprises. We doubt, also, that ability to select the best of four sentences, each expressing the same general idea in a different way, or ability to recast sentences according to a prescribed pattern constitutes too sound an index of a student's ability, on his own part, to compose acceptable sentences. We doubt, furthermore, that the discovery of 30 or 40 misspelled words in a list of 250 can be taken as much of an indication of what a student would normally do in avoiding spelling defections in his own writing. And finally, we doubt that a student's score on the kind of vocabulary test used in this instrument would indicate anything concerning the vocabulary which that student himself would employ in connection with his own efforts at composition; really, the test would seem to give evidence of a student's *reading* vocabulary, rather than of his *compositional* vocabulary.

However, if the test user is willing to accept the basic assumption on which the instrument has been constructed, the *Cooperative English Test* is perhaps as good a test of its sort as is commercially available. The format is good. The items appear to have been carefully constructed. The content has been arrived at on the basis of a careful scientific study. A satisfactory degree of objectivity has been maintained throughout. Reliability of component parts is unusually high. Detailed national norms are available each year as new forms are issued. But the test user needs to be aware that whatever "ability" the test actually measures, it probably is not—certainly is not of necessity—the ability which the English specialist means when he refers to "ability in English."

Jeanette McPherrin, Director of Admissions, Scripps College. This test is divided into subtests of usage, spelling, and vocabulary. The part of the test devoted to usage is really a test of punctuation, points of grammar, and the ability to recognize a simple, direct style in writing. The punctuation items are too simple and too often repeated for students of high school and college level—for example, the numerous uses of contractions. The grammar items are very restricted in number and certain simple points are tested again and again —for example, the difference between the words *their* and *there*. The third section of the usage subtest is composed entirely of multiple-choice items requiring the examinee to discriminate between good and bad sentence structure. None of the items in this section tests the examinee's ability to use concise, grammatical English in writing.

In Part II, devoted to spelling, the words are well chosen for the most part, but a multiple-choice arrangement makes this a test of the ability to recognize misspelled words, rather than a test of the ability to spell. The test manual fails to indicate the correlation between scores on this part of the test and scores made by groups spelling the same words from dictation.

Part III, devoted to vocabulary, would seem to be the best part of the test, although a few of the words have little importance in lifelike situations and would have been learned only by chance—for example, *neap, pomaceous, tarantella.* Parts II and III of the test cannot be described as functional, since the words do not appear in sentences.

The distribution of emphasis among the various parts of the test constitutes one of its greatest weaknesses. Of the possible 267 raw-score points, 117 are given to the usage section of the test (in my opinion the poorest section), and of these 117, almost two-thirds are directly or indirectly concerned with punctuation.

In the first two sections of Part I, the examinee is not penalized for adding irrelevant or even incorrect punctuation. In the third section of Part I, no correction is made for guessing. The same correction is made for guessing in Parts II and III, although the examinee may guess with more chance of success in Part II than in Part III.

The statement in the manual that the choice of test items was based on curriculum surveys, textbook analyses, and consultation with specialists does not constitute a proof of acceptable selection, since no specific titles of surveys and texts or names of specialists are given. The manual offers no evidence of validity beyond a statement that the test has been "tried out on large groups" to choose for retention items that discriminate between good and bad students. The desirability of this type of discrimination is in itself questionable.

The booklet of norms gives reliability coefficients for the total test and for the separate parts of the test, but it does not give coefficients for single grades nor describe the groups of students tested to provide data for the building of coefficients. In giving percentile norms for three types of high schools, the test authors are making a move in the right direction, but still the numbers upon which the norms are based are too large and the various types of schools are not described in sufficient detail to make the norms valuable for comparison with individuals or small groups.

The scoring of the test is complicated by the fact that the raw scores must be converted first into "scaled scores" and then into percentile ranks. The authors claim that scaled scores make possible the comparison of different types of tests without conversion of raw scores into percentiles or "other cumbersome measures." Why the scaled scores are considered less cumbersome than percentile ranks is not clear. Scaled scores are based on the accomplishment of an "average child" who has attended an "average school" and taken the "usual amount" of a subject. These hypothetical averages are meaningless because incapable of definition.

Louis C. Zahner, Head of the Department of English, Groton School, Groton, Massachusetts. [Review of Form P.] This test undertakes, according to its subtitle, to test "Usage, Spelling, and Vocabulary." The word "usage" has a wide and ill-defined range of meanings. Exactly what is meant here by "usage" is not entirely clear. A teacher looking for a test of usage in the sense in which Leonard used the word in his study of modern usage will not find it in this test, which is perhaps more accurately described as a test in the mechanics of composition. This comment upon the title of the test does not imply that the test is intended to cover more ground than it does cover. The authors make no extravagant claims for it. In the admirable handbook describing the purpose, content, and interpretation of the Co-operative Test Service Tests, there is a clear and fair statement of what this test can be expected to show, how results can safely be interpreted, and what action can safely be taken upon the basis of these results. The claims are modest, and teachers and principals are warned against reading into tests results interpretations they will not fully bear. Any teacher who uses this test with an understanding of its limitations as described by its authors and publishers is on firm ground. This test, furthermore, bears sure marks of forward-looking experiment in the field of the construction of objective tests in English.

The mechanics of composition are tested in Part I, Sections 1 and 2, and in Part II (Spelling). The first and last of these are tests of the proofreading type, raising the old question as to how well proofreading tests measure the ability to write correctly. There is no conclusive evidence either way. Probably such a test would be a good measure of this ability for some pupils and not for others. Here a teacher is driven back to examination of a pupil's original work. An objective proofreading test might be useful as a check upon the teacher's more subjective judgment. This question is fully understood by the authors of this test, who claim only that these items are "probably of value in getting a picture of what a class will do in actual composition." Part I, Section 2, is an ingenious departure from the straight proofreading type of test that deserves further exploration and development. This form of item, however, is limited in the number of elements it can test, and will therefore not be likely to take much of the load now carried by the proofreading type.

Part I, Section 3, calls for the choice of one "best" sentence out of four given sentences. This section could have been more carefully and consistently constructed. The "best" sentence in some of the groups is demonstrably the best by virtue of being the only one free from grammatical blunders. In other groups, however, the "best" sentences would be best only for certain rhetorical effects, while one or another of the discarded sentences might be better for other rhetorical effects. An intelligent choice would require an interpretation of a full context in which the sentence is to be placed. In still other groups the "best" sentence and the discarded sentences simply make different statements. The "best" sentence would be best only if it made the statement the writer wished to make. Here again full context would be necessary for intelligent choice. The danger of this section as it stands is that it may lead some teachers and pupils to believe that sentence-making is simply a matter of applying a priori rules without any necessity of giving attention to the precise meanings and effects the sentence is intended to convey, and without any realization of the importance of the context in determining these meanings and effects. It is dangerous to imply that any sentence is good, let alone "best," apart from the total situation in which it is being used.

The same criticism can be brought against Part III, a vocabulary test of the synonym-matching type that deals with single words out of context. The effective use of language in straight thinking, in reading for full comprehension of meanings, in clear and logical writing and speaking, requires so much more that a bowing acquaintance with a list of synonyms that the claims made for vocabulary tests as measures of general power over language are subject to grave question. In this field the type of item being developed in the verbal section of the *Scholastic Aptitude Test* of the College Entrance Examination Board is unquestionably better.

It is unfortunate that in this particular section the authors themselves have used language so loosely. Most of their supposed synonyms are indeed synonyms. But there are too many items in which the right response is not a synonym at all, but something entirely different. *Drug*, for example, is not a synonym for *insulin*, but a class that includes *insulin*. *Three dramas* is not a synonym for *trilogy*, but a member of the class *trilogy*. The distinction between synonyms and class-words is one of the fundamentals in the study of words and language, involving as it does both the theory of symbols and the principles of classification. Is it too much to ask that authors of tests in English should set themselves rigorous standards in their use of words? "If gold ruste, what shal iren do?" If the teaching and testing of language is to prosper, test-makers must work from sound principles of language, their subject matter, as well as from sound principles of testing and measuring.

Henry D. Rinsland, Director of the Bureau of Educational Research and Professor of School Measurements, The University of Oklahoma. [Review of Form PM.] The English test is in 3 parts: (*a*) English usage, including grammar and diction of 75 items, punctuation of 60 items, capitalization of 30 items, and sentence structure of 15 items; (*b*) spelling, consists of 45 items; (*c*) vocabulary of 100 words.

The objective test labeled *usage* departs far from securing a natural or normal response which any one gives when he uses English in a written form. The sample illustrates what the student is to do; it also illustrates the psychological validity of the test, that is, the performance measured. The sample given is:

$$\text{That} \begin{Bmatrix} 1 \text{ aren't} \\ 2 \text{ ain't} \\ 3 \text{ isn't} \end{Bmatrix} \text{right.}$$

The student is required to choose the correct form. Now this is just what no one does when he writes; it isn't exactly what any one does when he edits; it is just what some one does when he takes an artificial, unnatural English usage test of this type. It is true that occasionally when one thinks of right and wrong forms, such as the nominative or the objective case of six personal pronouns, that he does do a sort of choosing. It is obvious from the research of Roland L. Beck [4,5] on the validity of the *Rinsland-Beck Natural Test of English Usage* that the present *Cooperative English Test* has sacrificed validity for an objective and machine scoring device. Perhaps this is one reason why the *Cooperative English Test*, administered during the school year 1934-35, correlated only .50 with school marks when the scores of the psychological examinations were rendered constant. Further, the titles and the subtitles of the usage test are misleading, as there is no grammatical term mentioned in the 75 items, but merely usage. One could make perfect on this test without any knowledge of grammar if he only recognized correct usage of words and phrases. This reviewer cannot understand why the Cooperative group have omitted the measurement of grammar, that is, grammatical terminology and rules of grammar, nor why they have not chosen a more valid measure of English usage, even though it does not lend itself to rapidity of scoring—desirable as the latter is. Certainly in the writings of the authors whose names appear on the title page, none have suggested that validity be sacrificed for objectivity and speed of scoring.

The second part is spelling. This test consists of a presentation of four different words. The student is to find the misspelled word and mark it, or if none are misspelled, to check the phrase *none*. Forty-five sets of four words each are given. From the published studies of the validity of different objective forms, the right or wrong spelling form is about as good as any, except dictation. Dictating 45 words to be spelled may take more time than reading 180 words. Since no description of the sources of these words is furnished with the 1939 edition, one finds a reference to validity on page 17 of *Cooperative Achievement Tests:* A Handbook Describing Their Purpose, Content and Interpretation. The spelling words were chosen from the first five thousand most frequently used words in the Ernest Horn list, *A Basic Writing Vocabulary*.[2] The question arises whether or not the first five thousand most frequently used words represent the proper group for sampling the spelling of students in grades 7-12. Almost all elementary textbooks in spelling in grades 2-8 have approximately four thousand words. Horn's textbook[3] has approximately this number.

The vocabulary test is in the form of multiple choice; a word being given with five choices, only one of which corresponds in meaning as,

1 resistant

    1–1 confusing
    1–2 conjunctive
    1–3 systematical
    1–4 assisting
    1–5 opposing

No statement of the validity of the 1939 vocabulary test is found, however in the 1936 handbook (p. 16) is the information that the words of the vocabulary series are chosen from the E. L. Thorndike, *Teacher's Word Book*.[1] The words chosen come from the first

ten thousand most frequently used words. The reviewer agrees with the authors of the test that the synonym form of five choices presents a broader understanding for the meaning of words than any other objective form. A test of 100 words seems to be a very meager sampling of a reading vocabulary of somewhere around twenty or thirty thousand words, although with the synonym form the complete knowledge runs somewhere from 100 words to 500. However, at least 16 additional groups of words could be added to the last page of the test, as page 15 has available space.

The test can be scored by hand, using perforated sheets, or by the *International Test Scoring Machine*. This is probably the most efficient scoring device available. Norms are in terms of percentages of students (percentiles) attaining and exceeding scaled scores. Scaled scores seem to offer a linear scale which will increase in usefulness as teachers and administrative officers understand it. The reliability of the 1938 test shows the coefficient of reliability of the total English test to be above .98, and the standard errors of measurement of the revised series is approximately six points in terms of raw score. This fluctuation out of a possible 260 points indicates an exceedingly stable score for each individual student. Because this English test is in a series of other subjects with comparable norms, the use and value of such a test is superior in many respects to an independent test of higher validity not in such a series with comparable norms.

L. K. Shumaker, Director of the Education Clinic, University of Oregon. [Review of Form P.] There are certain elements which commend this test at once upon first inspection. It has been prepared under reliable auspices. Without this guarantee, anyone using the test would have to do over again all the laborious work of inquiring into the why's and wherefore's of the original test construction. Then the presentation of test material in contextual form is good. The cross-out-and-write-in feature of Section 2 is good because this form of copy-editing is one way to get discriminative judgment without the use of grammatical terminology. Section 3 does not appeal to me so much because of the limited context and the possibility of debate concerning separate items in the key. Part II should be a fair test of spelling; although I have found that very frequently individuals of a good deal of ability do not give a very sound indication of their capacity to spell if they are asked to recognize correctly spelled words in settings of. misspelled words. Part III would be stronger in my opinion, if the choices were presented in contextual settings. I can foresee quite a bit of hand labor in scoring the test; and this is always a drawback. I should expect this test to be quite effective in separating low from high ability pupils. The norms furnished ought to make the test very useful to teachers who have limited numbers of pupils at different school levels.

The time limit feature of the Cooperative test would enable a busy teacher to estimate how best to fit the test into a full program. On the other hand, time limits in tests of this type deprive them to some extent of their "power testing" quality. A poor student, unable to finish the test, would not give as good a basis for the teacher to make a fair diagnosis of the kind of difficulties which should be removed (if they can be!) to enable this weak student better to meet the competition of stronger ones.

For reviews by John M. Stalnaker, Charles Swain Thomas, and John H. Thompson, see 961.

[1272]

Cross English Test. Grades 9-13; 1923-26; 3 forms; $1.20 per 25; 20¢ per specimen set; 45(50) minutes; E. A. Cross; Yonkers, N. Y.: World Book Co.

REFERENCES

1 HARVEY, NATHAN A. "The Cross English Test." *Am Schoolmaster.* 18:85-6 F '25.
2 FOLEY, LOUIS. "A Test Case." *Engl J* 17:387-94 My '28.
3 EDDS, JESS H., AND MCCALL, W. MORRISON "Predicting the Scholastic Success of College Freshmen." *J Ed Res* 27:127-30 O '33.

Roland L. Beck, Professor of Education and Director of the Demonstration School, Central State College, Edmond, Oklahoma. The *Cross English Test* is composed of eight parts: spelling, pronunciation, recognizing a sentence, punctuation, verb forms, pronoun forms, idiomatic expressions, and miscellaneous faulty expressions.

Part I, Spelling, is an alternative form of spelling test with one of the two words misspelled. The validity and psychology of such a test of spelling is, at least, questionable. There is not sufficient evidence to show that such a form does not help to form incorrect spelling habits to recommend its use. Further-

more, the ability to spell a word correctly is not the same as the ability to select the word which is spelled correctly.

Part II, Pronunciation, is also an alternative form of objective test. This part is subject to, at least, part of the criticism mentioned for Part I. The guessing element is also maximum in both parts—that is, there are fifty chances in one hundred that a student may guess the answer without knowing it.

Part III, Recognizing a Sentence, also involves two choices. Certainly, the student needs to be able to know how to write in terms of sentences which are not faulty. Here, again, the ability to use complete and correct sentences is highly desirable. The guessing element is present, as well as the assumption that a student's ability to recognize complete, faulty, or correct sentences in a printed test is the same as the ability to write complete and correct sentences in his own composition.

Part IV, Punctuation, is proofreading which does not measure a student's ability to punctuate his own writing.

Part V, Verb Forms; Part VI, Pronoun Forms; Part VII, Idiomatic Expressions; and Part VIII, Miscellaneous Faulty Expressions —all use the alternate-response or multiple-choice form of recognition. Except for Items 4 and 7 of Part V, guessing is at its maximum; the psychology of this is questionable. For example, in Sentence 4 of Part V, Verb Forms, a boy might say, "I have never 'et' such good pears before." Every student has his own vocabulary of errors. For this reason, if a student is not allowed to supply the missing word in a sentence completion form, one would not be able to know for sure what he would use in his own writing.

The test as a whole is objective, but one should not wonder why many teachers of English prefer to grade subjective tests rather than to place faith in tests of an objective nature, merely because they are objective.

The content of the test is good—that is, if the test really measured a student's ability to use the English forms in his own writing which the test evidently intends to measure, it would be an excellent test.

Edward S. Noyes, Chairman, Board of Admissions and Associate Professor of English, Yale University. Each form of this test deals with composition in the fields of spelling, grammar, pronunciation, etc. Each is divided as follows, the number of items being given in parentheses: Part I, Spelling (32); II, Pronunciation (32); III, Recognizing a Sentence (in five groups totalling 40 items); IV, Punctuation (15); V, Verb Forms (16); VI, Pronoun Forms (12); VII, Idiomatic Expressions (10); VIII, Miscellaneous Faulty Expressions (15). Collation indicates accurate pairing of Forms A and C, in number, kind, and difficulty of items.

Tests of this kind cannot reproduce the conditions under which a student normally exercises the skill being tested. The section devoted to spelling, for instance, has 32 items, each consisting of a word spelled once wrongly and once correctly. The examinee's task is to check the correct spelling. A pupil may be able to recognize the correct spelling of a word on the printed page, by contrast with the incorrect spelling, without being able, in free composition, to spell that same word correctly. Similarly, a student's score on the section on pronunciation might indicate his degree of familiarity with diacritical marks rather than his ability to pronounce the test words correctly in ordinary speech.

These tests assume the inviolable authority of dictionary and grammar-book. They assume that a sentence must be either correct or faulty by itself, as judged by rigid grammatical rules, without consideration of its possible context. Such assumptions are now under fire by a growing number of teachers of English who prefer what might be called a functional approach to grammar and who do not believe that a living and growing language can be treated in a stereotyped fashion. A good deal of water has flowed over the dam since 1923, when these tests were apparently constructed.

On the other hand, even the modern functionalist would scarcely find fault with most of the items in the *Cross English Test* on the ground that they deal with dubious questions of grammatical rules. The errors which they require students to correct are generally so gross as to be unmistakable. According to the manual, these tests were "designed primarily for high school seniors and college freshmen." The present reviewer has been a reader of college entrance examinations for over twenty years, but has only infrequently met on such examinations errors as palpable as "might of" for "might have," "suspicion" as a verb, for

"suspect," or "leave me" for "allow me"—to mention three which are stressed in Forms A and C of the Cross tests. Either he has been dealing with a select group of students, or there has been a general improvement of students at this level. Unless scoring is to be done by the pupils themselves, a key seems hardly necessary.

Occasionally, it is true, there is a question whether an "error" actually exists. The directions in Group B of Part III state: "Place a figure 1 in the parentheses before each expression which should be written as one sentence and a figure 2 before each which should be written as two sentences." Among the items, however, there is at least one expression which, according to the key, should be written as two sentences, but which, according to acceptable modern usage, could be kept as a single sentence if a comma were changed to a colon. In Group D, again, one "faulty" sentence could as easily be corrected by the insertion of a semicolon as by making it into two separate sentences. Such cases are, however, rare.

The time allowance for the test is forty-five minutes, which seems ample. Whether or not the number of items in each part is large enough to measure accurately a student's skill in the field tested is a matter which cannot be decided a priori; it must be left to the judgment and the statistics of those who have administered the tests.

[1273]
Davis-Schrammel Elementary English Test. Grades 4-8; 1934; 2 forms; 50¢ per 25; 15¢ per specimen set; 20(25) minutes; Vera Davis and H. E. Schrammel; Emporia, Kan.: Bureau of Educational Measurements, Kansas State Teachers College.

Keith Goltry, Head of the Department of Education, Parsons College. This test is available in two forms, with percentile norms for both midyear and end-of-year testing in grades 4-8 inclusive. Each form consists of the following parts: punctuation, 20 items; capitalization, 10 items; sentence recognition, 10 items; and language usage (words and forms of words), 50 items. Norms are not available for the separate parts. The test has been developed in connection with the Nation-wide Every Pupil Scholarship Testing Program and is intended solely for survey purposes.

The items of the test are a good representative sample of the items stressed in elementary school textbooks of English. As such, of course, it is a test of the pupil's ability to use textbook English, not acceptable colloquial English. The proofreading test on punctuation, capitalization, and sentence recognition is an acceptable measure of pupils' abilities and much less open to the charge of invalidity than is the multiple-response test of language usage.

The norms, based as they are on large numbers of pupils in a nation-wide survey, possess the so-called characteristic of universality as well as one could ask for. But despite the fact that the test has 90 items, the range of scores is not great and improvement from grade to grade of median scores is only 3 to 7 points, while the semi-interquartile range of scores within each grade varies from 5.5 to 7.5. The reliability of the test is only .87 for all five grades combined, and the average reliability for a single grade is only .77.

Rachel Salisbury, Director of the Junior High School Department, State Teachers College, Platteville, Wisconsin. Each form contains 90 items, printed in two parts on two sides of a single sheet, so that manipulatory problems are reduced to a minimum. The type is large and readable. Part I contains items regarding punctuation, capitalization, and sentence recognition (40 items). Part II is devoted to language usage (50 items).

Part I is true-false, the child being asked to judge whether a sentence is correctly printed or not. Apostrophes are included among the punctuation items. Some of the items seem debatable. Children may well disagree about the comma after an introductory adverbial clause; and "July 1933 was a long, hot month" is accepted by many publishers while it is condemned by many teachers. Probably the example of single quotation marks within doubles should not be included in an elementary test at all. Under Sentence Recognition there are no examples of the run-together sentence; one appears under Punctuation.

Part II is multiple-choice, and includes principal parts of verbs, agreement of subject and verb, homonymns, contractions, double negatives, reflexives, agreement and case of pronouns, split infinitives, comparatives, potential mode, and faulty use of connectives, prepositions, adjectives, and adverbs. Some of the examples seem to labor the point. For example, "For captain they elected me, who (is, are, am) the largest." No grade school child would say

such a sentence; he would use *because*. In "(Who, Whom) shall we ask?" the first form is quite regularly accepted in conversation. Such an item as "All of the boys brought (their, his) skates" is pure test waste; no child would use the singular, for all oral pressure is toward the plural pronoun.

It is easy, of course, to criticize the selection of items in a list of 40. But this reviewer wonders why split infinitives are included when the principal parts of *do* and *go* are omitted; and why the test omits the double subject, such as "(He, Him) and (I, me) never stay for the game," while it includes the less resented "They sang (like, as though) they enjoyed it," and the regularly accepted "You (have, have got) a good bicycle." Most of the "really trulies" are included, however; and the test should discriminate effectively among students who have studied the textbooks.

The test has a reliability coefficient of .87 for a five-grade range (grades 4-8) and an average of .77 for the separate grades. As for validity, "the items were carefully selected from a number of leading elementary school textbooks of English," and the selected items were checked by the subjective judgments of competent teachers and supervisors of English. No statistical evaluation is presented. The use of textbooks as criteria naturally accounts for the inclusion of the debatable or recently accepted items cited above; for it is well known that textbooks continue to present puristic forms long after the dictionaries have acknowledged changes in language. A good language test should be as free as possible of debatable items.

Grade norms, based upon over 16,000 cases in 21 states, give a reliable scale for grade placement, by midyear and end-of-year scores. The raw scores are translated into percentiles, the 50th percentile being the norm for a given grade. There is a useful table for translating percentile ranks into school marks. A class record sheet and a strip key accompany the test.

The Davis-Schrammel test should be an inexpensive and effective instrument for diagnostic use, for ability grouping, and for measuring progress in classes that base their work upon standard textbooks in language.

[1274]

Diagnostic Tests in English Composition. Grades 7-12; 1923; 4 forms, 4 parts; 15¢ per specimen set; S. L. Pressey, L. C. Pressey, F. R. Conkling, E. V.

Bowers, Helen Ruhlen, and Blythe Pearce; Bloomington, Ill.: Public School Publishing Co.
a) CAPITALIZATION. 75¢ per 100; nontimed, (10) minutes.
b) PUNCTUATION. 75¢ per 100; nontimed, (15) minutes.
c) GRAMMAR. $1.50 per 100; nontimed, (20) minutes.
d) SENTENCE STRUCTURE. $1.50 per 100; nontimed, (17) minutes.

Harry A. Greene, Director of the Bureau of Educational Research and Service and Professor of Education, The State University of Iowa. Four general areas of language skill are sampled by brief four-page tests: Test A, Capitalization; Test B, Punctuation; Test C, Grammar; Test D, Sentence Structure. Each test is available in four practically equal forms.

Test A comprises 28 proofreading exercises sampling a number of important capitalization skills. The spread of items fails to cover a number of variants of socially useful skills emphasized today in the upper grades and high school. Reliability seems to be secured by multiplying the responses to certain types of skills many times within each item.

Test B is made up of 30 proofreading items on punctuation. Here again the sampling is limited in the range of skills and usages tested.

Test C is composed of 30 four-response multiple-choice exercises described as measuring grammar, but much more probably measuring simple usage. Each exercise is made up of four statements, three of which contain correct usages and one of which is incorrect. The usages presented as correct are usually but not always related to the usage error in the incorrect statement. The exercises are grouped to conform to certain grammatical rules governing the usages, but no measure of the knowledge of the rule is involved.

Test D is designed to measure sentence structure. The 24 items comprising this test are four-response multiple-choice exercises similar to those used in Test C. The test is partly a measure of sentence sense, that is, the ability to discriminate fragments from sentences, and partly a measure of the ability to discriminate between sentences of differing levels of quality of structure.

Recent evidence on the best testing techniques for measuring the mechanical aspects of language indicates that the forms used in these tests are not the most effective. Certainly they are far from economical in terms of scoring time when compared with modern quick-scoring techniques. Little or no evidence on

the actual validation process is given by the authors although the items are selected on the basis of data showing the socially useful skills as identified by the authors prior to making the tests. Reliability indices are also not given for the tests. Only grade medians are presented as norms. Grade distributions and percentile tables are not given. The very slight grade growths in the skills measured by these tests as shown by the tables of grade norms are further limitations on the interpretation of the tests. The practical possibilities of the tests are increased somewhat through the use of analytical tabulation sheets which aid in identifying for each pupil the items and skills in which weakness is revealed.

The use of the word *diagnostic* in the title of any language test is doubtless just as optimistic today as it was at the time these tests were made. Language expression is complicated by so many interrelated factors that diagnosis in the strict sense is very difficult if not impossible to secure. At best, these tests, sampling briefly into only four areas of expressional skills, provide an extremely sketchy and vague diagnostic picture of language ability. There are many other tests which are markedly superior for this purpose.

Jean Hoard, Teacher of English in the University High School, The University of Wisconsin. This is a series of tests of English grammar and usage in four forms. The tests provide a teacher of English with the information necessary to evaluate the ability of her students to use correctly the fundamentals of English composition.

Directions for administering the tests are clear; the record sheet accompanying each test enables the teacher to have an individual picture of the strength and weakness of each of her students. Most of the tests are well constructed, and their results should provide useful measurements of student knowledge and ability.

Test A is arranged to give the teacher and the students analytic information about the knowledge of good usage in capitalization. All sentences in the test are correct except that they lack all capitalization. The problem set before the student is to underline each letter that should be a capital. This test demands skill in proofreading, and requires a knowledge of the correct use of capital letters. The sentences used for testing this knowledge cover a wide area of usage and are well balanced.

Test B is a test of correctness in punctuation. It should contain actual errors from student themes, topics, and informal letters in addition to those gathered from magazines, periodicals, and business letters. For the most part, this test is a dull exercise; some of the errors listed are too far-fetched. Sentences 15, 28, 29, and 30 illustrate this point; they do not represent the typical errors made by the average student.

There is no relationship between this test and the ability of students to punctuate their own sentences accurately.

Test C is a better test because it presents errors made in the written work of students. It tests a student's ability to recognize common mistakes in grammar and contains twenty problems of four sentences each. Only one out of the four is wrong and the student must place a check before that one. This test would be more valid if provision were made to underline the error and to insert the correct usage. As it stands the test does not check student knowledge and it does encourage guesswork. To illustrate: a student may place his check correctly because the sentence doesn't sound or look right; he doesn't know the reason for doing it, nor does he possess the grammatical knowledge necessary to effect the change. Therefore, there is no tie-up between this test and the ability to avoid making similar errors the next time a student writes a theme.

Test D seeks to have students recognize common errors in sentence structure. It contains actual sentences from the written work of students. Only one sentence in each group is not well expressed, and a check is to be placed before the poor sentence. Provision should be made to show why the sentence is poor, and to test the student's ability to correct it. Without such provision, the test loses its effectiveness and evidences no valid proof of knowledge.

All four tests in this series are to be used in testing the composition skill of students from the seventh through the twelfth grades. I would like to have a division made in the tests, so that the materials pertaining to the junior high school could be given separately. The first part of each test is too easy for the upper level students and causes carelessness in their proofreading. By the time the upper level

is challenged, the lower level is entirely out of its depth; they either give up trying to solve the problem or else they resort to guessing. Either case destroys the validity of the test's purpose; it encourages bad habits and it definitely fails to present a true picture of student knowledge.

[1275]

"Dingwall" Test in English Usage. Ages 9-10; 10-12; 1937; 1 form, 2 levels, 2 booklets at each level; 25(30) minutes per booklet; 1s. 3d. per specimen set; Educational Institute of Scotland; London: University of London Press, Ltd.
a) PUPILS AGES 9-10, PUPIL'S BOOKLET I: CONTAINING PARTS 1-4. 3d. per test, 2s. per 12; 3s. 6d. per 25.
b) PUPILS AGES 9-10, PUPIL'S BOOKLET II: CONTAINING PARTS 5-9. 3d. per test; 2s. 6d. per 12; 4s. 6d. per 25.
c) PUPILS AGES 10-12, PUPIL'S BOOKLET I: CONTAINING PARTS 1-4. 3d. per test; 2s. per 12; 3s. 6d. per 25.
d) PUPILS AGES 10-12, PUPIL'S BOOKLET II: CONTAINING PARTS 5-9. 3d. per test; 2s. per 12; 3s. 6d. per 25.

Charles Fox, formerly Director of Training, University of Cambridge. This test is issued by the Educational Institute of Scotland and is intended for pupils from 9 to 12 years of age. There are 2 forms of the test; one for pupils 9-10 years in which the instructions are read by the examiner, and the other for those from 10-12 in which the instructions are printed in the test booklets. A table of *tentative* norms for each age group is given.

The present reviewer tried the tests on a group of 70 boys aged 10-11 years and obtained the same total mark as that given in the manual, but with considerable variations in the different subtests; so that it would be unwise to draw any conclusions from the separate parts of the test.

There are a few expressions which are not in accordance with English usage, though they are familiar to Scottish pupils, e.g., "message boy" and "score out" instead of "messenger boy" and "cross out." And, if "I take my breakfast" means "I eat it," very few English boys would use the expression, nor do they use the word "forenoon." Though these locutions make little difference to the results, they are unfortunate in a test intended for general use.

The various parts of the test are concerned with those elementary parts of grammar which every pupil of the ages tested should be familiar with; and many teachers would prefer to construct their own examples instead of the trivial ones given. If they wish to compare their pupils with others they would desire definitive norms instead of tentative ones. In a test of English usage it is desirable to select some, at least, of the examples from acknowledged literary sources instead of inventing them *ad hoc* as the latter tend to have an air of artificiality. There is no lack of English classical or modern writers from which to make a suitable choice for the ages concerned, and these are more appropriate than the stilted sentences given in the test.

[1276]

Effectiveness of Expression Test: Cooperative English Test, Tests B1 and B2. Grades 7-12, 11-16; 1940; 2 levels, Form Q; 5¢ per test, 10 to 99 copies; 1½¢ per machine-scorable answer sheet; 25¢ per specimen set; 40(45) minutes; Geraldine Spaulding with the editorial assistance of Dudley H. Cloud, H. A. Domincovich, E. F. Lindquist, Robert C. Pooley, Marion C. Sheridan, and George Summey, Jr.; New York: Cooperative Test Service.
a) TEST B1, LOWER LEVEL. Grades 7-12.
b) TEST B2, UPPER LEVEL. Grades 11-16.

REFERENCES

1 Cooperative Test Service. *The Cooperative English Expression Tests:* Information Concerning Their Construction, Interpretation, and Use. New York: Cooperative Test Service, 1940. Pp. 4. Gratis. Paper.
2 TRAXLER, ARTHUR. "The Cooperative English Test, Form Q: Correlations with School Marks and Intercorrelations," pp. 42-50. In *1940 Achievement Testing Program in Independent Schools and Supplementary Studies.* Educational Records Bureau Staff. Educational Records Bulletin, No. 30. New York: the Bureau. June 1940. Pp. xii, 76. $1.50. Paper, lithotyped.

[1277]

English Classification Test for High Schools and Colleges: Form X. 1940; 1 form; $1.25 per 25; 10¢ per specimen set; nontimed (90-120) minutes; R. D. Scott, A. A. Reed, and Ruth E. Pike; Lincoln, Neb.: University Extension Division, University of Nebraska.

[1278]

English Placement Test: Form F. Entering college freshmen; 1935-39; 1 form; 5¢ per test; 15¢ per key; nontimed (90) minutes; L. K. Shumaker; Eugene, Ore.: the Author, Friendly Hall, University of Oregon.

REFERENCES

1 SHUMAKER, L. KENNETH. "The Prediction of Success in English Composition," pp. 72-9. In *Research in Higher Education.* United States Department of Interior, Office of Education, Bulletin 1931, No. 12. Washington, D. C.: Government Printing Office, 1932. Pp. vi, 133. $0.15. Paper.
2 SHUMAKER, LAWRENCE K. *A Predictive Measure for Estimating Success in English Composition at the College Level.* Unpublished master's thesis, University of Oregon, 1932. Pp. 65.

Roland L. Beck, Professor of Education and Director of the Demonstration School, Central State College, Edmond, Oklahoma. [Review of Form D.] The *English Placement Test* is divided into four parts—namely, Part I, Words; Part II, Grammar; Part III, Punctuation; and Part IV, Usage.

Part I, Words, is a good objective test in spelling and vocabulary. The device used in this part is much better than selecting the misspelled word in a series of five, or the selection of the correctly spelled word in a series of five.

The use of either method mentioned would permit machine scoring. Teachers and college professors need to realize that ease in scoring tests is not the only important criteria in measurement. Measurement and grading, especially in English, probably never will be validly done if only a machine is used. This part serves very satisfactorily the measurement of spelling and vocabulary.

Part II, Grammar, is a proofreading test of the knowledge of grammar. The numbering of the italicized words is an improved device in proofreading. If the purpose of this part is to measure the ability of a student to do proofreading, then the only question that remains is "Should ability to do proofreading be a part of an English placement test?" Certainly, this part does not measure a student's habitual grammatical usage, but his ability to recognize grammatical errors in someone else's composition.

Part III, Punctuation, is an improved form of proofreading. Attention of the student is called to the necessity for punctuation at specific places in or between the sentences. The form might be improved some by eliminating words, to be supplied by the student, which are associated with, or make necessary, the punctuation. Although, one might question that the test measures a student's ability to punctuate his own composition; nevertheless, a student who would make a good score on this part would have considerable knowledge of punctuation.

Part IV, Usage, is more a form of recognition than of completion. Credit is given if a student can recognize errors in a printed test. This is not proof that a student would or would not use the correct form.

The test as a whole does measure abilities which college freshmen will need in their English classes. However, a student might have the ability to use very good English and still not make a high score on this test. The principal criteria which the test fails to meet is that it measures a student's ability to compose. The test does measure very satisfactorily ability in spelling and vocabulary and the recognition of correct usage in someone else's writing.

Robert W. Howard, Department of Examinations, The Chicago City Junior Colleges, Chicago, Illinois. [Review of Form D.] This test is divided into four parts: words, grammar, punctuation, and usage. The one hundred items in each part make percentages easy for the classroom teacher, and one man's guess is as good as another's in the matter of proportions.

Part I requires the student to recall the correct word to complete a sentence. The clues are the initial letter of the word and parenthetical italicized synonyms or definitive words and phrases. Three pages of the test and 23 minutes of time are required for the testing of 100 words. Since the student must write the recalled word in the indicated space and spell it correctly, he is tested not only in vocabulary but also in spelling. After the guessing game, comes a spelling contest! What are we testing?

In the grammar test, the student is asked to indicate whether certain italicized words are used correctly in a contextual background. An effort has been made, first, to show words as they appear in natural reading conditions, and, second, to present the student with interesting material. Although the aim is admirable, the effect is often the opposite, since the attention of the student is centered only on the italicized and numbered words or phrases, and he will not be interested in any case.

Similarly, in Part III the student is asked to punctuate two pages of material reprinted from a popular magazine, with the author's own punctuation the criterion for the correct marks, while in Part IV he is asked to exercise judgment in usage. In each case he is told to consider certain numbered spaces or italicized words. The usage test includes items which might easily be reclassified as spelling or grammar.

The manual of instructions accompanying the test indicate that in 1937-1938 it was used successfully for placement and diagnosis in thirty northwestern colleges and normal schools. Any English test containing 400 items should serve to distribute students satisfactorily enough for purposes of placement. There are tests of linguistic abilities, however, investigating a wider variety of field, which should provide a more satisfactory basis for diagnosis and remedial instruction.

[1279]

English: Thanet Mental Tests. Age 11; 1937; 1 form; 3s. 6d per 25; 1s. per handbook; 1s. 6d. per specimen set, including the arithmetic and school aptitude tests in the same series; 45(50) minutes; W. P. Alexander; London: University of London Press, Ltd.

C. Ebblewhite Smith, Lecturer in the Department of Higher Degrees and Research, Institute of Education, University of London. This test is to be used in conjunction with the *School Aptitude Test* and the *Arithmetic Test* in the series Thanet Mental Tests. It is designed to test the minumum essentials of English expected of a child about to enter an English secondary school. The test is in three parts.

(1) Reading Comprehension. This part, though short, is well designed involving a minimum of intelligence and a maximum of reading ability.

(2) Test of Punctuation and Use of Capitals. The form of this test is satisfactory but here again the test is too short. It is always a dangerous policy when scoring to subtract marks for errors. For example, it is questionable whether a child who inserts the question mark after the quotation marks should lose a mark when the child who omits it altogether is not similarly penalized.

(3) Spelling. I thought the type of spelling test which gave the correctly spelled word among four misspelled alternatives was universally condemned but here it appears again. Educationally the method is not sound. On what basis were the words chosen?

Children are allowed to hand in their papers when they have finished. This always creates some measure of confusion in the class and anxious souls are worried when others are obviously ahead of them.

The norm for 10-year-old boys is 37 marks; for 11-year-old boys, 40 marks; and for 12-year-old boys, 43 marks. These differences are so small as to be comparable with the standard error of the test. Admittedly it is difficult to prepare a minimum essentials test in English but surely a test could be prepared that would have more than three marks between those who pass the test and those who are one whole year behind standard!

[1280]

Entrance and Classification Examination for Teachers Colleges: English Test, 1939 Edition. 1933-39; 2 forms; 8¢ per test; 3¢ per machine-scorable answer sheet; 30¢ per specimen set; 100(110) minutes; Normal, Ill.: Teachers College Personnel Association (c/o C. F. Malmberg).

REFERENCES

1 HEILMAN, J. D. *Report of the Cooperative Testing Program of the Teachers College Personnel Association.* Greeley, Colo.: Colorado State Teachers College, February 1932. Pp. 65. $0.50. Paper, mimeographed.

2 HEILMAN, J. D. *Report on the 1932–33 Testing Program of the Teachers College Personnel Association.* Greeley, Colo.: Colorado State Teachers College, February 1933. Pp. 71. $0.50. Paper, mimeographed.

3 HEILMAN, J. D. *Report on the 1933-34 Testing Program of the Teachers College Personnel Association.* Greeley, Colo.: Colorado State Teachers College, February 1934. Pp. ii, 83. $0.50. Paper, mimeographed.

4 HEILMAN, J. D. *Report on the 1934–35 Testing Program of the Teachers College Personnel Association.* Greeley, Colo.: Colorado State Teachers College, February 1935. Pp. iii, 74. $0.50. Paper, mimeographed.

5 HEILMAN, J. D. *The 1936 Report on the Cooperative Testing Program of the Teachers College Personnel Association.* Greeley, Colo.: Colorado State College of Education, February 1936. Pp. iii, 87. $0.50. Paper, mimeographed.

6 HEILMAN, J. D. *The 1937 Report on the Cooperative Testing Program of the Teachers College Personnel Association.* Greeley, Colo.: Colorado State College of Education, February 1937. Pp. ii, 102. $0.50. Paper, mimeographed.

7 HEILMAN, J. D. *The 1938 Report on the Cooperative Testing Program of the Teachers College Personnel Association.* Greeley, Colo.: Colorado State College of Education, February 1938. Pp. iii, 71. $0.50. Paper, mimeographed.

8 HEILMAN, J. D. *The 1939 Report on the Cooperative Testing Program of the Teachers College Personnel Association.* Greeley, Colo.: Colorado State College of Education, February 1939. Pp. iii, 44. $0.50. Paper, mimeographed.

9 CONGDON, NORA A. *The 1940 Report on the Cooperative Testing Program of the Teachers College Personnel Association.* Greeley, Colo.: Colorado State College of Education, February 1940. Pp. 32. $0.25. Paper, lithotyped.

[1281]

Essentials of English Tests. Grades 7-13; 1939; 1 form; $1 per 25; 25¢ per specimen set; 45(50) minutes; Dora V. Smith and Constance M. McCullough; Minneapolis, Minn.: Educational Test Bureau, Inc.

[1282]

Gregory Diagnostic Tests in Language. Grades 4-9; 1935; 2 forms; $2.50 per 100; 10¢ per specimen set; nontimed (20-40) minutes; Helen Gregory and C. A. Gregory; Cincinnati, Ohio: C. A. Gregory Co.

Keith Goltry, Head of the Department of Education, Parsons College. This test consists of two forms of 156 two-response items. It is designed to measure the pupil's ability to recognize correct forms in common every-day language expressions. Each item consists of a sentence involving the use of some word or phrase which is not correct according to some standard of usage. In each case the questionable word or words and the so-called correct form are given, and the task of the pupil is to choose the one he believes to be correct. The scoring key is convenient and interpretation of results easy. For convenience in diagnosis the items are divided into 20 groups, each group including expressions involving similar grammatical constructions.

No evidence is presented in the manual as to the validity of the test. No doubt it is, as are most such tests, rather a poor measure of actual ability to speak in accordance with commonly accepted standards of usage. The items involve the most common of questioned usages, but recognition of acceptable forms is no guarantee that such forms are used in speech. In a number of items the form which is marked incorrect by the key is quite ac-

ceptable, at least in colloquial usage, though the test leans less toward the purist view of language than do many courses of study, textbooks, and teachers of English. Such items can of course be ignored in diagnosing pupil difficulties, and interpretation of total scores is probably not seriously altered unless the course of study is unusually generous in recognizing colloquial usage.

No evidence is presented as to what is sometimes termed universality of the norms. It even seems a bit strange that crude scores, sigma scores, and months of chronological age all should happen to increase from one level to another by such regular increments as are shown in the manual. Throughout the range of scores for third- to eleventh-grade pupils, with few exceptions, an increase of one in total score equals an increase of one in sigma score and the equivalent age increment is three months.

J. Paul Leonard, Associate Professor of Education, Stanford University. The authors of the Gregory test recommend it for either diagnostic or survey purposes in everyday language expressions, stressing the fact that the test is comprehensive and able to show language deficiencies which need remedial work. To do this they have prepared two forms, A and B, each form consisting of 156 common language expressions divided into the following 20 groups under three major headings: Pronouns—55 sentences divided into 9 groups of items running from 4 to 9 sentences in each group; Verbs—60 sentences divided into 6 groups of items running from 7 to 16 sentences in each group; Miscellaneous constructions—41 sentences divided into 5 groups of items running from 6 to 12 sentences in each group.

The sections in the pronoun group deal with: compound subjects in the nominative case, the pronoun subject of a comparative clause in the nominative case, the complement of a copulative verb in the nominative case, use of objective case when pronoun is object of a preposition; correct use of compound personal pronouns; objective form with infinitive; possessive form with gerund; use of direct and indirect object, and correct form following indefinites.

The sections in the verb groups deal with tense forms of present, past, and past participial forms, verbs with contractions and with indefinite pronouns, and other common miscellaneous verb usages.

The miscellaneous constructions deal with the use of adverbs; plural, singular, and possessive nouns; prepositions, conjunctions, and adjectives.

All the items in the tests are in complete sentences and for each sentence two possible forms are given. The pupil is to check the one he considers correct, the score being the total of all correct items, or the total for each group may be used as a separate score.

The user of the test is given no indication of the validity or reliability of the test. He is to be content with the statement that "Great care has been taken to select sentences which are in common use and which will illustrate frequently misused constructions." There is no good reason for the number of items in each group and in some of the most difficult usages only four sentences are used whereas in the easier usages eight sentences are used. The sentences are all short and do not give a fair picture of average composition. The material is the same for grades 4-9, but by no means should considerable of the material be taught in these lower grades. A test measuring language proficiency over a range of these six years of study is ill adjusted to the lower grades. The test manual describes each section in terms of a grammatical principle rather than in terms of usage.

The test scores may be converted into "raw scores," "crude scores," "equivalent sigma scores," "age norms," and "grade norms." For these numerous statistical devices not one bit of data are given. The user has to take everything on faith, even the authors' statement that "language achievement, as measured by this test, increases approximately four points per year, or one point for each additional three months of age."

The test deals with common daily usages, is clear and simple for pupils in the upper grades to understand, and for the upper elementary or junior high school years the test could be used as a substitute for exercises which the teacher might make herself. Any good teacher with a few hours of careful study can prepare a test as good as this one and probably better suited to her immediate teaching. The statistical impedimenta of the test are misleading to a teacher who takes them seri-

ously as a measure of growth in language power.

[1283]

Judging the Effectiveness of Written Composition: Test 3.8. Grades 9-12; 1938; and experimental form; 5¢ per test; 1¢ per machine-scorable answer sheet; $1.50 per set of stencils for machine scoring; nontimed (40) minutes; Chicago, Ill.: Evaluation in the Eight Year Study, Progressive Education Association.

REFERENCES

A Descriptive Summary of Evaluation Instruments in the Field of English. Chicago, Ill.: Evaluation in the Eight Year Study, Progressive Education Association, March 1939. Pp. 10. Paper, mimeographed. Out of print.

[1284]

Kentucky English Test: A General Achievement Test for High School Students and College Freshmen [1939 Revision]. Grades 9-13; 1937-39; 2 forms; $3.50 per 100; 10¢ per specimen set; nontimed (25-85) minutes; E. J. Asher and T. E. McMullen; Lexington, Ky.: Kentucky Cooperative Testing Service, University of Kentucky.

REFERENCES

1 ASHER, ESTON J. "The Reliability and Validity of the Kentucky General Scholastic and Kentucky English Tests." *Ky Personnel B* 21:1-2 S '38.

For a review by Henry D. Rinsland of an earlier form, see 966.

[1285]

Leonard Diagnostic Test in Punctuation and Capitalization. Grades 5-12; 1930-31; 2 forms; 90¢ per 25; 20¢ per specimen set; nontimed (20-40) minutes; J. Paul Leonard; Yonkers, N. Y.: World Book Co.

REFERENCES

1 LEONARD, J. PAUL. "The Use of Practice Exercises in Teaching Punctuation and Capitalization." *J Ed Res* 21:186-90 Mr '30.
2 LEONARD, JOHN PAUL. *The Use of Practice Exercises in the Teaching of Capitalization and Punctuation.* Columbia University, Teachers College, Contributions to Education, No. 372. New York: Bureau of Publications, the College, 1930. Pp. vii, 78. $1.50.

Jean Hoard, Teacher of English in the University High School, The University of Wisconsin. There are two forms to this test which covers a wide area of punctuation and capitalization difficulties. The test is well constructed, and shows a careful study of the needs of students in this field of writing fundamentals. The sentence problems are chosen well and are challenging as they increase in problem difficulty. The instructions for giving the test are clear, and the directions are easy to follow. It is one of the most satisfactory tests that has come to my attention.

Form A contains 52 sentences, all of which are correct, except that they lack some of the necessary punctuation marks and capital letters; these are to be supplied by the student. Not only is this a test of skill in proofreading, but also an exercise for testing a student's ability to correct errors similar to his own.

The test reveals to a student how much, or how little he knows, and likewise informs the teacher about the remedial work to be done. The test is of value, because the types of errors contained in it are common to all students.

Form B is like Form A and contains the same number of problems; they are more difficult, and accurate knowledge is necessary to solve them. The sentences are challenging and should produce interesting results.

Both of these tests present sentence problems that demand knowledge and judgment from the student; they are valuable as a check-up on classroom teaching and student learning.

[1286]

Mechanics of Expression: Cooperative English Test, Test A. Grades 7-16; 1940; Form Q; 5¢ per test, 10 to 99 copies; 1½¢ per machine-scorable answer sheet; 25¢ per specimen set; 40(45) minutes; Geraldine Spaulding and W. W. Cook with the editorial assistance of Dudley H. Cloud, H. A. Domincovich, E. F. Lindquist, Robert C. Pooley, Marion C. Sheridan, and George Summey, Jr.; New York: Cooperative Test Service.

REFERENCES

1 Cooperative Test Service. *The Cooperative English Expression Tests*: Information Concerning Their Construction, Interpretation, and Use. New York: Cooperative Test Service, 1940. Pp. 4. Gratis. Paper.
2 TRAXLER, ARTHUR. "The Cooperative English Test, Form Q: Correlations with School Marks and Intercorrelations," pp. 42-50. In *1940 Achievement Testing Program in Independent Schools and Supplementary Studies*. Educational Records Bureau Staff. Educational Records Bulletin, No. 30. New York: the Bureau, June 1940. Pp. xii, 76. $1.50. Paper, lithotyped.

[1287]

Linguistic Awareness Test. High school; 1938; 1 form; $1.25 per 25; sample copy free; 45(50) minutes; Elmer R. Smith; Atlanta, Ga.: Turner E. Smith & Co.

[1288]

Literary Information Test: American Literature: Test 3.5. Grades 9-12; 1937; 1 form; 5¢ per test; 1¢ per mimeographed key; nontimed (90) minutes; Chicago, Ill.: Evaluation in the Eight Year Study, Progressive Education Association.

REFERENCES

1 *A Descriptive Summary of Evaluation Instruments in the Field of English*. Chicago, Ill.: Evaluation in the Eight Year Study, Progressive Education Association, March 1939. Pp. 10. Paper, mimeographed. Out of print.

[1289]

Literary Information Test: English Literature: Test 3.4. Grades 9-12; 1939; 1 form; 5¢ per test; 2½¢ per set of machine-scorable answer sheets; 1¢ per mimeographed key; $1.50 per set of stencils for machine scoring; nontimed (90) minutes; Chicago, Ill.: Evaluation in the Eight Year Study, Progressive Education Association.

REFERENCES

1 *A Descriptive Summary of Evaluation Instruments in the Field of English*. Chicago, Ill.: Evaluation in the Eight Year Study, Progressive Education Association, March 1939. Pp. 10. Paper, mimeographed. Out of print.

[1290]

Nelson's High School English Test. Grades 7-12; 1931-32; 2 forms; $1.65 per 25, including 25 answer booklets; 75¢ per 25 answer booklets; single speci-

men set free; 40(50) minutes; M. J. Nelson; Boston, Mass.: Houghton Mifflin Co.

Frank P. De Lay, Department of English, New Trier Township High School, Winnetka, Illinois. The self-correcting nature of this test will make it most desirable to the busy teacher, if the student is made to understand clearly what he is to do. Students, through inattention to instructions, often do work incorrectly; and this test requires most careful explanation, especially in Part IV. However, training in the accurate following of directions is a thing greatly needed in our work, and a test such as this may afford as a by-product an example of the importance of such accuracy.

The fact that the Nelson test contains a large number of questions in each section makes it a more accurate test. The sections on word usage, sentence structure, and punctuation are functional, and can be used to the end of improving the ability of the student in writing accurate and effective sentences. The section on grammar does not meet with my personal favor because it is for the purpose of testing the student's ability to *name* the various grammatical elements in a sentence; but it does not deal in involved grammatical constructions, and all of the elements it seeks to identify should be included in the student's information for all are needed in the most simple explanation of sentence construction.

The *Cleveland English Composition and Grammar Test* and *Nelson's High School English Test* make a good pair, both for diagnostic and remedial work; however, if one of the two must be selected, I prefer the Nelson test.

Jacob S. Orleans, Associate Professor of Education, The College of the City of New York. This test is offered to serve four purposes, two administrative (grouping and prediction), and two instructional. In view of the fact that the test is entirely of the recognition type it is questionable that the analysis of the results can be accepted at their face value for teaching or remedial purposes as far as the student's *use* of language and of the mechanics of language are concerned. The test covers four phases of the mechanics of English (language usage, sentence structure, grammar, and punctuation) with 196 items in all. The information provided by the authors indicates a sound basis for content validity. The statements made concerning statistical validity may be questioned in view of the fact that, apart from grades eight and nine, a point of test score represents about a month and one-half of achievement for the test as a whole. In the case of the individual parts a single point represents on the average from two and one-half months to seven months of achievement.

The reliability coefficients are high, approximately .90 for the entire test. However, the coefficients were computed for populations covering a range of four years. No data are given on the reliability of scores on the entire test for a single-year group. It is doubtful that the separate divisions are, for most grades and for most parts of the test, reliable enough even for group measurement. No reliability data are available for the separate parts.

The test has the very marked advantage of saving much time and effort in the scoring of the papers, since it uses the Clapp-Young self-marking technique. However, in the case of part four in particular the method of indicating the answers is rather complicated. It may lead to errors on the part of the examinee in indicating the answer when he does mean to note the correct answer. The type size is rather small, especially for the junior high school grades.

Norms are provided for apparently representative groups for the end of the school year in the form of percentile ranks of scores for each of grades seven to twelve for each part of the test as well as the total scores. Comparisons in terms of grade levels are hardly feasible except for total score because of the very small differences in norms between grades.

The tenth percentile score for the seventh grade is 85 points. As is to be expected many of the items (approximately a third) are answered correctly by almost all of even the poorest pupils. This condition is bound to hold true for a test in language usage and the mechanics of English if it is to be valid, from the standpoint of content, for learning purposes. If the test is to be used only for administrative purposes, content validity is of significance only in so far as it produces accuracy in the interpretation of scores for administrative purposes. The effect of trying to cover both learning and administrative purposes is a much longer test (at the easier levels) than is needed for administrative purposes, and a consequent reduction of the dis-

criminative power of the test. That is, despite the length of the test (the total score is 226 points) only 12 points represent the two years from the end of grade 10 to the end of grade 12. The entire range of five years of achievement (grades 7 to 12) is represented by 45 points or only one-fifth of the entire range of possible scores.

This test would hardly seem to serve better the need for an analytical achievement test in English than is already provided for by other available tests.

[1291]
Pressey English Tests for Grades 5 to 8. 1923-38; an abbreviated adaptation of *Diagnostic Tests in English Composition*; 3 forms; $2 per 100; 15¢ per specimen set; 30(40) minutes; S. L. Pressey and others; Bloomington, Ill.: Public School Publishing Co.

Ed Res B 19:60 Ja 17 '40. J. Wayne Wrightstone. * The tests probably measure capitalization, good usage, punctuation, and sentence structure as validly as such factors can be measured in a test of recognition of language errors. Many questions have been raised about the validity of testing such language skills in a so-called new type objective test. The assumption that the proficiency in skills which pupils use in oral and written language may not correlate highly with recognition of errors in the test situations, is unquestioned by the authors. For those who are willing to make a similar assumption these tests do provide one index of the ability of pupils to recognize errors in selected language skills.

Teach Col J 10:72 Ja '39. Mary Reid McBeth. The new adaptation of the Pressey tests is well planned to give definite and detailed information concerning each pupil's knowledge of the essentials of capitalization, punctuation, word usage, and sentence structure. * All of the material is practical, and a maximum of diagnosis is done in a minimum of time and space. Directions for administering and for taking the test are simple and concise, and the scoring key is efficiently arranged. A particularly excellent and useful feature of the Pressey tests is the accompanying *Diagnostic Record Chart* with correlated scale and concise summary of the rules covered by the test *

[1292]
Progressive Language Tests. Grades 1-3, 4-6, 7-9, 9-13; 1933-39; 4 levels; identical to the language tests in the battery *Progressive Achievement Tests*; 2¢ per machine-scorable answer sheet; 15¢ per speci-

men set of any one level; Ernest W. Tiegs and Willis W. Clark; Los Angeles, Calif.: California Test Bureau.

a) PRIMARY. Grades 1-3; 1933-38; 3 forms; 50¢ per 25.
b) ELEMENTARY. Grades 4-6; 1933-37; 3 forms; 50¢ per 25; *Machine Scoring Edition*: 1933-39; 2 forms; 5¢ per test.
c) INTERMEDIATE. Grades 7-9; 1933-37; 3 forms; 50¢ per 25; *Machine Scoring Edition*: 1933-39; 2 forms; 5¢ per test.
d) ADVANCED. Grades 9-13; 1933-37; 3 forms; 75¢ per 25; *Machine Scoring Edition*: 1933-37; 2 forms; 5¢ per test.

Harry A. Greene, Director of the Bureau of Educational Research and Service and Professor of Education, The State University of Iowa. These tests are identical in content with the language sections of the battery *Progressive Achievement Tests.* Capitalization, punctuation, usage and sentence sense, spelling, and handwriting are measured at different levels of difficulty in the three tests comprising the series. The test content itself is compressed on the two inside pages of a four page folder for the elementary and intermediate tests. The advanced test requires three pages. A diagnostic profile chart and an analysis of learning difficulties represented by the items in the test occupy the first page of the folder. It is apparent that the analysis of skills is more valuable as a teaching aid than the profile chart due to the obviously inadequate sampling provided in each of the parts of the test. The spelling tests and the grammar test (in the advanced examination) are the only subtests composed of as many as thirty items.

The tests are described by the authors as "diagnostic tests keyed to the curriculum." The entire series of tests comprising the Progressive achievement battery is not extensive enough to function as a reliable diagnostic instrument, so it is apparent that the brevity of these language tests and the inadequate sampling of language skills they afford could not furnish a reliable diagnostic measure in written expression. While it is true that the capitalization and punctuation skills sampled may be those of high social significance, it is doubtful if ten or fifteen reactions in these fields constitute a sufficiently reliable sampling to provide meaningful results.

The evidence presented on the validity of the tests is not particularly conclusive. The use of the term *diagnostic* in connection with any brief four-page (or even longer) test is optimistic. The complexity of language expression is so great that brief cross-sections of isolated areas of skill can scarcely be taken as diagnostic evidence. The sampling of items covered in these tests would indicate a very narrow and limited curriculum.

The reliability coefficients reported for the elementary or intermediate tests are adequate, but they are based upon talent ranging over two or three school grades. Thus, a reliability coefficient of .92 for the elementary examination based on a three-grade range is not too convincing. Furthermore, the reliabilities reported are based on odd-even correlations stepped up by formula rather than the intercorrelation of the two forms of the test. No data of the extent of the population involved in the reliability computations are given.

Convincing norms based upon more than one hundred thousand cases are provided for both the elementary and intermediate tests. Grade and percentile norms based upon fifteen hundred cases are given for the advanced tests. Grades and percentile norms, taking into account differences in mental level, accompany the elementary and the intermediate tests.

Machine-scored editions of the intermediate and the advanced tests are available. The importance of this procedure in the case of such brief tests is not apparent. Furthermore, the numerous changes in the administration of the tests, and the somewhat unusual procedures in recording the answers on the separate answer sheets introduce factors which should necessitate separate norms for the machine-scored and the hand-scored tests.

J. Paul Leonard, Associate Professor of Education, Stanford University. All three batteries of the *Progressive Language Tests* are designed to diagnose for individual pupils their language proficiency. The items which the tests measure are the "skills and abilities which are included in the objectives of education" and are "based upon the results of scientific studies," selected from skills "which represent the essential elements of the basic skills now being taught . . . in recent courses of study." Just what courses or objectives or studies were used is not told the reader.

The test makers claim further that the tests will produce "a diagnostic profile which reveals graphically the pupil's actual achievement in relation to normal achievement for his particular grade placement" and reveal "which pupils are achieving satisfactorily," thus enabling the teacher to determine "the particular type of remedial work necessary for those who are experiencing one or more of the different types of learning difficulty." In these claims the makers place themselves in a position of criticism by modern students of language growth who believe the determination of general minimum language essentials to be a myth and the determination of satisfactory language growth by resort to norms based upon average achievement to be a fallacious method of diagnosis.

All three batteries of the test deal with capitalization, punctuation, words and sentences, spelling and handwriting. The authors claim that "while the basic elements of these skills are the same on all levels, the increasing difficulty and complexity of the materials of instruction require a corresponding increase in tool mastery." They claim, therefore, to have increased the difficulty of these items in the three batteries and "selected test situations which reveal the extent to which tool mastery is adequate to the demands put upon it." If any language test could do these things adequately, curriculum workers would flock to it. The intermediate battery adds a section on parts of speech, while the advanced battery adds a section on grammar, to the basic four sections in all three batteries. Norms for the elementary and intermediate batteries are based upon 100,000 cases and for the advanced battery upon 1500 cases.

These tests offer a meagre survey of a few language uses and in the manual tend to overemphasize by far the validity and diagnostic value of the tests. The number of items to cover the different usages are entirely too small. For instance, in the elementary battery 33 sentences are used to cover 17 different groups of language usage (counting such things as tense, good usage, case, and commas as one group); the intermediate battery used 36 sentences to cover 26 different groups and the advanced battery 80 sentences to cover 28 different groups. The advanced battery is the only one having enough items to warrant any reasonable claim to having diagnostic values. The tests may be fairly useful for general survey purposes but seem to be of very little value for individual diagnostic purposes. They are not nearly so diagnostic as the *Gregory Diagnostic Tests in Language* in the items covered by both tests.

For reviews by D. Welty Lefever, C. W. Odell, and Hugh B. Wood of the complete battery, see 876 and 1193.

[1293]

Rinsland-Beck Natural Test of English Usage. Grades 9-13; 1934-39; 2 forms; $1.50 per 25; 10¢ per teacher's handbook; 50¢ per specimen set; Henry D. Rinsland and Roland L. Beck; Bloomington, Ill.: Public School Publishing Co.
a) TEST I [MECHANICS]. 45(50) minutes.
b) TEST II [GRAMMAR]. 30(35) minutes.
c) TEST III [RHETORIC]. 45(50) minutes.

REFERENCES

1 BECK, R. L. *The Reliability and Validity of a Natural Test of English Composition for High School Seniors and College Freshmen.* Unpublished doctor's thesis, University of Oklahoma, 1932. Pp. 173.
2 BECK, ROLAND L. "A Natural Test of English Usage." *J Exp Ed* 1:280-6 Mr '33.
3 BECK, ROLAND L. "Predicting Success in College English." *Col Engl* 1:541-2 Mr '40.

John M. Stalnaker, Consultant Examiner, College Entrance Examination Board and Associate Professor of Psychology, Princeton University. These tests are designed to measure the ability to use language needed by high school seniors and college students. Three tests are offered: one in mechanics, one in grammar, and one in rhetoric. The tests are timed so that almost all pupils complete them.

The tests are of the recall rather than the more popular recognition type: the pupil does not check one of several given answers but must supply the correct answer himself. Test III, in particular, requires the actual writing of complete sentences by the pupil. It is a hopeful sign to find on the market a test labeled "English" which requires some actual writing. Such tests, of course, are not easily scored when compared with the modern machine-scoring procedures. Because numerous judgments must be made, the authors advise that persons scoring the tests should have a knowledge of English. It is claimed, however, that the entire test can be scored with a high degree of objectivity. If the test does provide a dependable measure of the ability to use language, the increased time required and the increased cost of scoring will be justified. Certain important skills and abilities may never lend themselves to measurement in a short time or to techniques which permit rapid and cheap scoring. It is to be hoped that they will not be sacrificed in favor of less important abilities measured more cheaply.

In general the three tests are too easy and do not give as wide a range of scores as is desirable. A perfect score on the combined three tests is 223 points. The lower quartile for high-school seniors is 143 points and the upper quartile is 175.

The manual describes how the tests have been developed, and discusses the reliability and validity of the tests. Percentile norms are given. A diagnostic record chart is available for each test. The items of the test are classified according to the item of English which is being tested.

Charles Swain Thomas, Associate Professor of Education, Emeritus, Harvard University. The first query that confronts a critic of the *Rinsland-Beck Natural Test of English Usage* is the authors' very peculiar use and position of the word *natural*. No objective test of elaborate design can be a *natural* test; it is, in fact, highly artificial. But the critic soon discovers that *natural* does not in actual meaning here modify *test;* it modifies *English Usage.* That fact immediately suggests another question. What is *natural usage*? The authors give an alternative adjective—*habitual.* Here is their own explanation: "The words supplied by the student probably represent his natural or habitual language usage . . ." Could there not be a revision of the title—a revision that would accurately express the fundamental concept of the test, and at the same time carry out in the placement of adjectives one of the grammatical principles that the authors evidently wish to enforce?

The exercises which the forms provide are, for the most part, excellent. They were constructed for the purpose of correcting the types of errors that by objective experiments have been found to be most common among high-school pupils.

A few items of the test arouse specific queries. In Item 4 of Test II, Division 2, Section a, we have this interrogative sentence: "How many boys (———4———) there at your birthday party yesterday?" The key prints *were* as the correct response. When you read the completed sentence you discover that the deletion of *there* would improve the sentence.

In Test II, Division 2, Section b, we have this sentence: "I will never be able to (——2——) you geometry." When the able students fill in the proper word *teach,* may they not wonder why the authors did not use *I shall* rather than *I will*?

The items which deal with sentence structure have been carefully prepared and should in

practice prove helpful in developing greater care and greater skill in placing words and phrases and clauses in positions that will make the meaning unmistakable.

The technical material in the Diagnostic Record Chart is sufficiently involved to suggest this somewhat skeptical query: How many classroom teachers will care to compute the "Cumulative Frequency" and then convert each frequency into a percentile? To "get the reciprocal of the number of cases ($1/N = 1/24 = .0417$) and multiply by each cumulative frequency" seems a bit menacing to those who still uneasily loiter around the corridors that lead to the secret statistical chambers.

Ed Res B 19:117-8 F 14 '40. J. Wayne Wrightstone. * In techniques these tests are constructed so that the methods or items used are completion questions and controlled essay questions. The completion questions offer the usual difficulties of scoring which include, among other things, variable standards of scoring among teachers and variable interpretations of students' responses. To measure certain aspects of English usage controlled essay questions are used. If essay questions are included in the test, it would seem wise to summarize the guiding principles and findings of Stalnaker and others on how to achieve more reliable reading and grading of responses to such essay questions. The authors of this test do not provide such information or guidance in the manual for test scorers and, in the opinion of the reviewer, have weakened thereby the reliability and validity of certain parts of their test. The publishers claim that the tests are diagnostic, and the authors report that these tests can be used for diagnostic purposes because the total test score has a high coefficient of reliability. An essential condition for reliable diagnosis, however, is that the parts of the test used for diagnosis should meet reliability standards which cannot be inferred or borrowed from the reliability of a total test score. The authors of this test seem to have hold of a valuable idea which needs to be refined and improved, if the tests are to be made sufficiently practical and economical in scoring so that they will be used widely among high schools and colleges.

[1293.1]

Schonell Diagnostic English Tests. Ages 8-14; 1940; 1 form; 6d. per test; 5d. per test, 25 to 49 copies; 53(60) minutes; F. Eleanor Schonell; Edinburgh, Scotland: Oliver & Boyd, Ltd.

REFERENCES

1 SCHONELL, FRED J., AND SCHONELL, F. ELEANOR. *Diagnosis and Remedial Teaching in English.* Edinburgh, Scotland: Oliver & Boyd, Ltd. In press.

LITERATURE

[1294]

Alphabetical List of 1000 Fiction Authors Classified by Subject and Maturity Level. Grades 9-12; 1939; a revision and expansion of Jeanette Howard Foster's basic list of some 250 authors; 10¢ per copy; Irvin C. Poley and B. J. R. Stolper, assisted by Jeanette Foster and Douglas Waples; Chicago, Ill.: Evaluation in the Eight Year Study, Progressive Education Association.

REFERENCES

1 EBERHART, WILFRED. "Evaluating the Leisure Reading of High-School Pupils." *Sch R* 47:257-69 Ap '39.

[1295]

Analytical Scales of Attainment in Literature. Grades 7-8, 9-12; 1933; 1 form, 2 levels; 75¢ per 25; 15¢ per specimen set; nontimed (45) minutes; A. M. Jordan and M. J. Van Wagenen; Minneapolis, Minn.: Educational Test Bureau, Inc.
a) DIVISION 3. Grades 7-8.
b) DIVISION 4. Grades 9-12.

Carleton C. Jones, Department of English, State Teachers College, Indiana, Pa. According to the authors, *Analytical Scales of Attainment in Literature* are "designed to measure the abilities and ranges of information of the pupils." For all practical purposes, however, the scales are merely information tests; and any insinuation that other "abilities" incident to literary attainment are also measured is simply a misrepresentation of the facts. Two separate forms of the tests are available. Division 3 is designed for grades 7 and 8, and Division 4 for grades 9 to 12 inclusive; but the two forms are so nearly alike in content that there seems to be little purpose in their separate publication.

Each form of the scales is composed of four parts of forty items each. The first probes a student's "information about literature"; the second, his "information about authors"; the third, his knowledge of the "content of literature," especially in the matter of "outcomes"; and the fourth, his "general impressions" concerning particular pieces of literature, together with his knowledge of "characters." The analytical or diagnostic intent of these subtests is, of course, highly commendable. But the test items comprising each part are so little differentiated in character from the items comprising all the other parts that the diagnostic purpose of the sectioning is largely negated.

The actual content of the scales is, for the most part, exceedingly conventional; that is, the literary information which the instruments seek to explore is limited almost exclusively to the standard materials of traditional courses in school literature. The 160 items of each form are divided about equally between English and American literature, with a very few devoted to Greek and Roman mythology, to the Bible, and to three or four continental writers long popular with children. The richness of the dozen or more foreign literatures now generally included (in excellent English translations) in the curricula of progressive schools is almost entirely neglected.

Another limitation in sampling is evidenced in the scales' failure adequately to explore the various literary types. Poetry is made to assume an inordinately important place by virtue of the fact that approximately one-half of all the test items are devoted to that one literary type alone. The novel, certainly more important than poetry in present-day living, has items comprising only about one-fourth of the total. The short story, almost equally important with the novel, has items comprising only about one-eighth of the total. The rich fields of biography and the essay have been virtually disregarded, and the drama is represented by only five items, all of which pertain to Shakespeare.

Further weaknesses in sampling are evident also in the number of authors, selections, and literary periods represented. Roughly, only 50 different authors are referred to in the scales—25 English and 25 American. Of these, at least ten are mentioned five times or more; and Longfellow—to point out the most glaring violation of the principle of sampling—alone claims nearly one-eighth of the total items of each form! Moreover, a number of pieces of literature, which at best are of only minor literary significance, are given unusual prominence. For example, in one form alone four items pertain to Pyle's *Men of Iron* and three to Wiggin's *Rebecca of Sunnybrook Farm.* But probably the most damaging fault in sampling is evidenced in the tests' failure to explore modern literature. Only about one-eighth of the items pertain to the modern period (1900 on), and hardly a single item can be said to deal with truly contemporary materials. More than two-thirds of the items are devoted to authors and works dating from 1800 to 1900—which fact, of course, completely obviates the adequate sampling of other important literary periods.

Finally, the scales must be criticized on the grounds that individual test items are frequently in violation, not only of the most elementary principles of item construction, but also of the most obvious facts of literary history. For example, one item reads: "Life on the ocean was written about by (1) Irving, (2) Cooper, (3) Dana, (4) Scott, (5) Dickens"; to which the student is expected to answer "Dana", although both "Cooper" and "Scott" would be equally appropriate answers. Another item reads: "Bret Harte was (1) a short story writer, (2) an English poet, (3) an American poet, (4) an English novelist, (5) a New England novelist." For this item, Response 1 is designated as the only correct response, yet no student of American literature would be satisfied if Response 3 were not also mentioned.

Robert K. Speer, Professor of Education, New York University. These tests comprise one scale of 160 questions for grades 7-8, inclusive, and another similar scale for grades 9-12, inclusive. The scales purport to measure powers related to the following aspects of literature, each aspect being given forty questions: (*a*) information about literature; (*b*) information about authors; (*c*) outcomes; (*d*) general impressions and characters.

Despite the titles of (*c*) and (*d*) above, most of the questions are of an informational character. On the whole, these scales measure power to recall names, titles, and plot-events, with a few questions included on recall of the moods of literary classics.

There is some doubt as to the allotment of items. Thus, in the second part of the scale for grades 7-8, Information About Authors, 15 out of a total of 40 questions deal with only 4 authors: Stevenson, Scott, Poe, and Dickens. The remaining 25 questions are about 22 different authors. No mention is made of some popular classics more often found in the respective grades than certain other classics about which many questions are included.

The scales do cover a wide range of readings, however, and should prove useful for testing the memoriter aspects of learning. It is unfortunate that the authors stopped here and did not develop more questions in the field of appreciations of literary moods, effects, and interpretations.

[1296]

Awareness Test of 20th Century Literature. Grades 9-16; 1937; 1 form; $1.50 per 25; sample copies free; 45(50) minutes; edited by Harold H. Bixler; Elmer R. Smith; Atlanta, Ga.: Turner E. Smith & Co.

H. H. Giles, Assistant Professor of Education and Research Associate in the Bureau of Educational Research, The Ohio State University. This test is valuable if only to prove that some educators are interested in contemporary writing and the use made of it by students. It is of the "Ask Me Another" type and fun to take. On the whole the authors have avoided obvious and narrow commitments to a particular line of clichés or a lofty ignorance of popular and not quite respectable literature. For example, they list Zane Grey and Harold Bell Wright as well as Mark Twain and Thomas Wolf. Section III, dealing with characters and backgrounds, exemplifies the fault of any such test made without reference to a particular situation in that it presupposes that all readers will or should, remember the same things as significant in particular books.

The test is designed to take 45 minutes and can be finished easily in 25. It takes 5 to 8 minutes to correct and record one student's work. It does not take into account sufficiently, perhaps, the immense importance of biographical and historical writing in our time. The assumptions back of the test are that the student will be compared to others in his group, and that the norm is not necessarily an acceptable standard of achievement since many factors other than class work enter in. Its chief value is to provide an objective basis for planning future reading in contemporary literature. These assumptions are valid for this test. Better still, one of a comparable nature made by students could be stimulating and useful.

Ann L. Gebhardt, Teacher of English, East High School, Madison, Wisconsin. This test is most comprehensive and approaches the subject of modern literature from several interesting angles. It is the kind of test which a teacher of English in a secondary school hesitates to criticise, because of its very nature and the nature of the ever shifting requirements of high school courses in literature. In order to check the most precocious pupils, the test would have to be revised almost annually, so that it would include current prize books and best sellers. Its apparent usefulness is limited because no three schools could agree upon what to include in their curricula, and only those few juniors and seniors who read everything because that is what they see their parents do could pass it satisfactorily. And even these students who belong definitely to a small cultured group do not often have the incentive to busy themselves with such literature.

All high schools include twentieth century literature in their courses in English, but there is a great variety in the books selected. This is partly due to the fact that tradition still clings to the "classics," which means that more recent books are on free reading lists or are projects for advanced or independent work. New books which have been made into movies would be familiar to a larger number of high school students, but even these would necessarily include only those who live in larger towns where such pictures are shown soon after their release.

There are also a few specific objections to the style of the test. In Part V several statements are misleading. For example: Item 16 states: "Bret Harte suggests that even the dissolute may be unselfish and heroic in . . ." and then lists stories by other writers as well as by Bret Harte. Item 18 states: "Sympathy for the downtrodden appears in Edwin Markham's . . ." and includes also poems of other poets. Item 37 states: "Truer happiness within her own Vermont family circle than what she might find abroad comes to the heroine of Dorothy Canfield Fisher's . . ." and includes books of other writers also.

The technique is confused. The statements are partly true-false, attributing to an author his works and those of other writers; and partly multiple choice, in that one of the quoted books is both by the specified author and characterized by the specific quality named. That might be acceptable, but it is not the technique used throughout, and the inconsistency thus created is necessarily confusing to both teacher and pupil. At least each section should conform to the same scheme if the test is to be of any real value.

In Part VI, Trends, some of the terminology would be confusing to even exceptionally "aware" students; namely, "psychographs" and "Freudian interpretation." Of course some students would understand these terms, but only a very few, and a usable test would scarcely be published for such a limited group.

It would be interesting to see a comprehensive tabulation of the results of these tests. One must not lose sight of the fact, however, that regional requirements must necessarily influence the rankings, and that the average high school English course will not quite fit any general scheme of testing, except one that is too general to be very valuable.

[1297]

Checklist of One Hundred Magazines. Grades 9-12; 1939; 5¢ per copy; Chicago, Ill.: Evaluation in the Eight Year Study, Progressive Education Association.

[1298]

Cooperative Literary Acquaintance Test. Grades 9-16; 1933-40; 40- and 45-minute editions; 25¢ per specimen set; 5¢ per test, 10 to 99 copies; Forms P and Q: Rosa Lee Walston and Edward E. Cureton with the editorial assistance of Henry W. Adams (Form P), Telfair B. Peet (Form P), Constance Churchyard, H. A. Domincovich (Form P), Constance M. McCullough (Form P), Leonard A. Rice, Arthur S. Roberts, Natalie D. Starr (Form P), Russell D. Trebilcox (Form P), Catherine L. Walston (Form P), and K. W. Wright (Form Q); New York: Cooperative Test Service.
a) FORMS 1934, 1935, AND 1936. Form 1933 is out of print; 45(50) minutes.
b) FORMS 1937, O, P, AND Q. 1937-40; 1½¢ per machine-scorable answer sheet; 40(45) minutes.

Lou LaBrant, Professor of English-Education, The Ohio State University. [Review of Form P.] The *Cooperative Literary Acquaintance Test* designed "to fill the need for a comprehensive measure of an individual's acquaintance with the field of literature" expresses all too well our present confusion in teaching literature to secondary school and college students. One hundred and fifty multiple choice questions are offered.

Just what is meant by "acquaintance" is not clear. Frequently (in over 40 of the 150 questions), correct answers could be given without the reading of a word written by the authors in question. Certainly a person may know that Moses was called "The Great Law Giver," and that Scarlett O'Hara is the heroine of *Gone With the Wind* without having read either *Old Testament* or modern novel. These and a few questions dealing with form suggest that "literary acquaintance" may mean acquisition of facts or opinions about literature.

Other questions, however, suggest that the makers of the test may have had in mind pieces chosen because they appeal to adolescent interests, or because they may be matter for close reading by students. As a means for introducing the essay, a number of anthologies have included White's article on the death of his daughter. *Ethan Frome* is a usable novel in high school. Only a few of the questions, however, appear to be offered because they sample material simple enough for independent reading by high school students. On what basis these few could be found reliable samples of the enormous amount of simple, well-written essays and novels, is not clear to this reviewer. Several questions deal with recognition of quotations from pieces presumably studied or memorized. Another considerable group calls for generalizations not warranted by the actual reading of adolescents: that Eugene O'Neill is influenced by psychoanalysis; that Chekhov expresses the tragedy among middle class people of failure to act; that Anatole France "usually" shows gentle irony. The apparent basis for selection here is that the questions deal with writers and selections frequently included in current school anthologies, and with statements made in histories of literature.

With the literature of the world from which to make selection, any sampling must be open to question. The field of this test is so extensive as to include David, Homer, Greek dramatists, Virgil, Boccaccio, Norse mythology, Shakespeare, Tolstoy, Chaucer, Cervantes, and Rousseau, along with such minor moderns as William Allen White, Hugh Walpole, and the creator of Scarlett O'Hara. When this enormous range in time, nationality, type, subject, style, and importance are to be covered by 150 questions, it is difficult to explain the inclusion of more than thirty on English poets (not including Shakespeare), with three for Browning alone. Kipling rates two! A whole precious question is used to ask the meaning of "passing fair."

Lovers of Browning might resent characterizing "Dare, never grudge the throe" as a "typical line," whatever that means, and Maxwell Anderson has himself not emphasized his writing of historical plays. These are minor matters, perhaps.

Taken as a whole the 150 questions illustrate a series of approaches: facts about the great, mere knowledge of names; recognition of popularly taught quotations from English and American verse; superficial facts about the events of certain novels or stories; generalizations about the themes or style of writers, perhaps assumed after reading one piece, perhaps read in a text on literature. That the test is a hodgepodge is no fault of its makers. It probably measures (as indeed its validation

shows) the superficiality and almost total lack of direction in our teaching.

Edward S. Noyes, Chairman, Board of Admissions and Associate Professor of English, Yale University. [Review of Form P.] ITS APPARATUS. Materials received for review include: (*a*) a handbook describing the purpose, content, and interpretation of Cooperative achievement tests (1936); (*b*) a booklet of norms (1938); (*c*) a booklet of directions for using the Cooperative tests (1939); (*d*) a single sheet showing scaled score percentiles in each of the four college years of three types of colleges, for all forms 1932-37 of the *Cooperative Literary Acquaintance Test;* (*e*) a similar sheet (revised to May 1937) for three types of secondary schools; (*f*) a key for scoring this test (Form P, but undated); (*g*) a catalog describing Cooperative tests (Nov. 1938); and (*h*) the test itself (Form P, 1939).

There is, in all this apparatus, no indication of the student group for which the test is particularly designed, except a statement on page 14 of the catalog, that it is suitable for both school and college classes. This raises the question: What is the nature of literary acquaintance which can be measured equally well in high school freshmen and college seniors by the same test?

ITS SCOPE. The test consists of 150 items of the "controlled response" variety. Twenty-eight of these items deal with foreign literature, which might be classified as follows: Greek and Roman, 11 items; French, 4; the Bible, 4; Old English, 3 (classified here because probably read in translation); German, 2; Italian, 1; Russian, 1; Scandinavian, 1; Spanish, 1. One hundred and ten items deal with American and English literature classified as shown in Table 1.

TABLE 1

Classification of Test Items Dealing with American and English Literature in the Cooperative Literary Acquaintance Test, Form P

Period	Prose			Drama	Poetry		Total
	Fiction	Essay	Other Prose		Lyric	Other Poetry	
Before Elizabeth..	..	..	..	1	..	2	3
Shakespeare......	..	..	..	8	1	..	9
Other Elizabethans	..	1	..	2	1	1	5
17th Century.....	1	1	1	..	..	3	6
18th Century.....	2	1	1	1	2	2	9
19th Century.....	19	7	1	4	20	13	64
20th Century.....	7	..	2	2	2	1	14
Totals........	29	10	5	18	26	22	110

Twelve items defy classification by either of the two categories used above: e.g., "Albion is the poetic name for 1 Sussex," etc. The classification is based on the correct answers to items, and while probably not exactly accurate, suffices to show the scope of the test. Since 78 items deal with English and American literature since 1800, it is clearly this period with which students are supposed to be acquainted; for other periods and nationalities the items are so few and scattering as to warrant slight confidence in the breadth of literary acquaintance of even a student who scored well in all these items.

The thinness of the test, as regards any real knowledge of any single author, is revealed by an author-analysis of items dealing with English and American writers, disregarding chronology: Addison, 1 item; Maxwell Anderson, 1; Bacon, 1; Bennett, 1; Browning, 3; Bryant, 1; Bunyan, 1; Burns, 1; Byron, 2; Cather, 2; Chaucer, 2; J. F. Cooper, 1; Coleridge, 2; Dunsany, 1; G. Eliot, 1; Emerson, 1; Frost, 1; Goldsmith, 1; Hardy, 1; O. Henry, 1; Housman, 1; Howells, 1; Irving, 1; S. Johnson, 1; Jonson, 1; Keats, 2; Kipling, 2; Lamb, 1; Lanier, 1; S. Lewis, 1; Longfellow, 2; J. R. Lowell, 1; C. Morley, 1; E. Markham, 1; Marlowe, 1; Masefield, 1; Millay, 1; Milton, 3; O'Neill, 1; Poe, 1; Pope, 1; Richardson, 1; E. A. Robinson, 1; Sandburg, 1; Scott, 2; Shaw, 1; Shelley, 2; Sheridan, 1; Spenser, 1; Shakespeare, 9; Tennyson, 3; Twain, 2; H. Walpole, 1; Wells, 1; Wharton, 1; Whitman, 1; Whittier, 1; Wordsworth, 3.

Obviously, some great names, such as Swift, are absent. Equally obvious is the scanty space allotted to all but Shakespeare. The test, therefore, can scarcely give a valuable answer to the question "What does this student know about this author?" just as it cannot, in its present form, completely test the student's acquaintance with any period prior to the nineteenth century. It would probably be unfair to argue, from this analysis, that the test-makers consider it as important that a student be acquainted with Bennett as with Bacon, with Cather as with Chaucer, with O. Henry as with Johnson, or with Kipling as with Keats. They would rightly object that this test is not a measure of *knowledge*, but of "acquaintance." We return, then, to the question raised in the first paragraph. What does "acquaintance" mean?

Analysis of the content of the items would seem to show that it means strictly a "bowing acquaintance"—except, perhaps, for the dozen or so items which are of the "spot passage variety." Several items (10, 18, 25, etc.) could be answered correctly by a student who had looked through digests or tables of contents without reading the actual works. Others (2, 36, 102, 106, 148) could be answered from information obtained through the movies or movie magazines. Still others depend upon information of a fairly trivial kind. Item 88 asks the student which of five American authors listed is frequently called "The Laureate of the Common Heart." Who cares?

Another type of item, while requiring some information about the author or book mentioned, is more dangerous than those just mentioned because it implies that only one of several answers can be "correct." Consider Item 62. "Samuel Johnson's popular reputation rests largely on his 1 dictionary 2 club 3 literary dictatorship 4 eccentricities 5 kindness to young authors." The key gives 4 as the correct answer; an extremely good defense could be made for any one of the other four possibilities. A still better answer would be: 6 Boswell. Response 4 cannot be the *only* "correct" answer unless the test-makers have conducted a poll of all the people in the world who have any knowledge of Samuel Johnson. Among other items presenting roughly similar difficulties are 9, 17, 23, 59, 63, 82, 96, 100, 140.

CONCLUSIONS. If the test is taken for what it is—an index of ingenuity as much as of an acquaintance, generally superficial, with some authors and books—it should provide interesting though hardly significant information about a student or a class. If it begins to influence what literature is taught and how it is taught, the test is a potential menace. It will tend to inculcate such notions as: (*a*) that there is one and only one correct answer to any question about literature; (*b*) that the trivial and the essential are of equal importance; (*c*) that the whole work of an author can be summed up in a neat little phrase (of dubious correctness sometimes, as when Item 100 declares that "A British poet whose cynicism and pessimism are expressed in exquisite, haunting verse is A. E. Housman . . ."); (*d*) that it is much simpler and more profitable to read digests than to wade through original works of art. Since tests, once widely used, almost inevitably influence teaching, one hopes that English teachers will use this one with circumspection. Such a caution, indeed, is given by the authors of the handbook (page 7), who urge that "no test . . . can be taken as a safe guide to what specific materials should be taught in the subject tested." In spite of such warnings, the history of tests and teaching shows a constant influence of one on the other, as Louis C. Zahner clearly emphasized in his address on "The Testing and Teaching of Meaning" at the Eighth Educational Conference in New York, October 26th. The test will influence, if not the materials, at least the way in which they are presented. The able group of editorial assistants listed on the cover of Form P should consider this problem with care before a new form is issued. There are many skillfully constructed items in the present form. Item 81, for instance, requires a fairly sound knowledge of *Julius Caesar*; Item 73, again, hits at the core of the story of the "Purloined Letter"; Item 99 has four red herrings most ingeniously but not unfairly dragged across the trail. With a scope frankly limited to a given period of literature, and with a larger number of items, answers to which can be given correctly only after a reading of the books involved, the test could be made to show something more significant about a student's acquaintance with literature than it seems to show at present.

For reviews by Carleton C. Jones and John H. Thompson, see 970.

[1299]

Cooperative Literary Comprehension Test. Grades 9-16; 1935-40; 40- and 45-minute editions; 25¢ per specimen set; 5¢ per test, 10 to 99 copies; Form Q: M. F. Carpenter and E. F. Lindquist; New York: Cooperative Test Service.
a) FORM 1936. Forms 1935 and 1937 are out of print; 45(50) minutes.
b) FORMS O, P, AND Q. 1½¢ per machine-scorable answer sheet; 40(45) minutes.

REFERENCES

1 FLANAGAN, JOHN C. "A New Type of Reading Test for Secondary-School and College Students Which Provides Separate Scores for Speed of Comprehension and Level of Comprehension," pp. 195-9. In *Practical Values of Educational Research*. National Education Association, American Educational Research Association, Official Report of 1938 Meeting, Atlantic City, N. J., February 26–March 2, 1938. Washington, D. C.: the Association, May 1938. Pp. 216. $1.50. Paper.
2 TRAXLER, ARTHUR E. "The Relation between Speed and Level of Literary Comprehension," pp. 51-56. In *1938 Achievement Testing Program in Independent Schools*. Educational Records Bureau, Educational Records Bulletin No. 24. New York: the Bureau, June 1938. Pp. xi, 59, 14. $1.50. Paper, lithotyped.
3 FLANAGAN, J. C. "A Study of the Effect on Comprehension of Varying Speeds of Reading," pp. 47-50. In *Research on the Foundations of American Education*. National Education Association, American Educational Research Association, Official Report of the 1939 Meeting, Cleveland, Ohio, February 25–March 1, 1939. Washington, D. C.: the Association, 1939. Pp. 215. $1.50. Paper.

Lou LaBrant, Professor of English-Education, The Ohio State University. [Review of Form P.] This test is designed to go beyond the usual rate-comprehension test and examine the student's ability to recognize and understand literary devices and patterns. The writers have considerable success in presenting questions which discover whether the reader comprehends the figures of speech, tone, implied relations, and similar characteristics of the piece. There is some doubt, however, as to whether the seventy-one questions on twelve brief quotations meet the rather large ends stated in the Handbook.

The selections are brief and not especially subtle: they are simple and somewhat factual in style. No opportunity is given for testing whether the reader notes contradictions or basic assumptions. Indeed, the test itself seems to imply that literary comprehension involves merely discovering what the writer wants the reader to discover. This is undoubtedly one essential in comprehension. The test should be used, however, with full knowledge of its limitation. Limited also to excerpts of a single paragraph each, it is open to the criticism common to most reading tests, that interest in isolated bits is so slight as to weaken the performance of many students.

For the most part the test assumes that the whole is equal to the sum of the detailed parts of a paragraph, an assumption scarcely acceptable for a well-organized unit of writing. As a measure, however, of the student's ability to comprehend literary details the test is helpful for both examining and teaching.

Edward A. Tenney, Associate Professor of English, Cornell University. [Review of Form P.] This test should go far toward setting a standard of literacy for students of literature. The disrepute into which the teaching of English has fallen may be removed if tests like this one are used to judge the quality of both the teacher and the student. For if the student has not been taught to read closely and to interpret precisely, he will fare ill on this examination. The break-up of the old course of reading has often left the teacher with nothing solid to tie to and has often opened the way to vague, desultory, general classroom discussions of "social" questions wherein the mind is more likely to be titillated than trained. This test shows up both the dull student and the glib but untrained student, and it is therefore to be commended.

Its most important aspect is that it is designed to measure both "speed" of comprehension and "level" of comprehension. A study of the test reveals that there is scant relation between these two aspects of reading.[1] In other words, this means that in testing what is sometimes called "reading ability" or "power to interpret the written word" the timed test is not especially useful or especially important. Since the power to understand literature and to interpret it is what we teachers of English strive to develop and since the speed at which a student understands is of secondary or tertiary importance, this test is to be welcomed; for it enables the teacher of English to escape from the whole system of timed tests, and it also enables the slow but clear-thinking and well-trained student to meet his more agile fellow student in a situation where mere speed is of no particular advantage.

For reviews by Charles Swain Thomas and John H. Thompson, see 971.

[1300]

Davis-Roahen-Schrammel American Literature Test. High school and college; 1938; 2 forms; 50¢ per 25; 15¢ per specimen set; 60(65) minutes; V. A. Davis, R. L. Roahen, and H. E. Schrammel; Emporia, Kan.: Bureau of Educational Measurements, Kansas State Teachers College.

Paul B. Diederich, Assistant Professor of Education, The University of Chicago. The test consists of 20 titles to match with authors, 16 multiple-choice questions revealing acquaintance with 14 titles, 24 multiple-choice questions most of which reveal acquaintance with authors, 25 quotations to match with authors and titles, 20 brief statements of the central thought of literary works to match with titles, and 20 characters to match with titles. The test requires 60 minutes, is appropriate for grades nine through college, presumably after at least a year's study of American literature, and yields only a single score. Each item in the test is given one point credit. Norms are based on 641 scores reported by cooperating schools in the Every Pupil Testing Program for April, 1938. There are two comparable forms of the test.

To set such a test loose upon a state, and to set teachers to work preparing for it, would be the equivalent of a Kansas dust storm to literary appreciation. I grew up in Kansas, where this test hails from, and I still visit there occasionally. It seems to me to be as far from civilization as the North Pole. Maybe these famous Emporia tests have something to do with it, either as cause or effect. The authors are probably not to blame, for they have done a competent job with their unsavory assignment, but this test and all that it stands for does not represent, in my opinion, a promising direction of the human spirit.

Violet Hughes, Department of English, East High School, Madison, Wisconsin. As a comprehensive "achievement test for high school and college classes in the general field of American Literature," this test falls short of its purpose.

The range of selections and authors upon whom the test is based is too limited. While Captain John Smith, Governor Bradford, Jonathan Edwards, Increase Mather, Joel Barlow, Charles B. Brown, Anne Bradstreet, Michael Wigglesworth, "Boy Psalm Book," "New England Primer," Margaret Fuller, George Ripley are all included, many important authors and selections of the later nineteenth and of the twentieth century are not included. Such writers as Sinclair Lewis, Pearl Buck, Willa Cather, Ole Rolvaag, Edna Ferber, Edna St. Vincent Millay, Sara Teasdale, Helen Keller, Jane Addams are among those omitted. Missing also are questions on orators from Patrick Henry down to the present time, on many of our important patriotic songs and poems, and on drama except for *Emperor Jones* and *Clarence*.

On the other hand, undue emphasis has been placed upon the history of American literature during the Colonial and the early National periods, upon the beginnings of American literature, upon selections of junior high level, and often upon selections of relatively little importance, as *Elsie Venner* and *Blithedale Romance.* Moreover, such selections as "Barbara Frietchie," "Skipper Ireson's Ride," "Rip Van Winkle," "Legend of Sleepy Hollow," "Paul Revere's Ride," "Courtship of Miles Standish" are considered so important that two and often three or more questions are based upon them.

In some instances in Part IV, the statement of the "central thought" of a literary selection is misleading since it is the central thought of an excerpt rather than of the entire selection, as in Item 114: "Imitating the style of a good writer is a great aid to learning good English."—*Autobiography*.

The 150 questions of each form of the test are of the following types: Part I, 20 questions matching a selection with its author; Part II, 40 completion questions with multiple choice; Part III, 50 questions matching quotations with source and author; Part IV, 20 questions matching central theme with selection; Part V, 20 questions matching characters with selections in which they appear.

A more helpful test for use in high schools today would include more contemporary material and questions checking the student's progress in appreciation rather than just his memory.

[1301]

English Tests for Outside Reading. Grades 9-10, 11-12; 1939; 1 form, 100 tests; $2.50 per 100; 15¢ per key for any one set; $1 per specimen set of any one set; $3.75 per complete specimen set; nontimed; Henrietta Silliman; Toulon, Ill.: the Author.

a) SET NO. 1. Grades 9-10.

Bob, Son of Battle.
Call of the Wild.
Captains Courageous.
The Casting Away of Mrs. Lechs and Mrs. Aleshine.
Daddy Long-Legs.
Florence Nightingale.
Huckleberry Finn.
Lad: A Dog.
The Lance of Kanana.
Last of the Mohicans.
The Little Shepherd of Kingdom Come.
Little Women.
Man Without a Country.
Oliver Twist.
Penrod.
Rebecca of Sunnybrook Farm.
The Secret Garden.
Seventeen.
The Three Musketeers.
Tom Brown's School Days.
Tom Sawyer.
Treasure Island.
Two Years Before the Mast.
Understood Betsy.
Wild Animals I Have Known.

b) SET NO. 2. Grades 9-10.

Adventures of Sherlock Holmes.
Aeneid.
The Amateur Gentleman.
Anne of Green Gables.
Arabian Nights.
Ben Hur.
Gulliver's Travels.
High Benton.
Hoosier School Boy.
In Brightest Africa.
Ivanhoe.
Martin Hyde, The Duke's Messenger.
Master Skylark.
Miss Lulu Bett.

The Promised Land.
Robin Hood.
Rudder Grange.
The Story of My Boyhood and Youth.
The Story of My Life—Helen Keller.
Tanglewood Tales.
Under the Big Top.
Up From Slavery.
The Virginian.
White Fang.
Wild Life in the Rockies.

c) SET NO. 3. Grades 11-12.

Abraham Lincoln.
The Alhambra.
Alice Freemen Palmer.
The Americanization of Edward W. Bok.
The Beloved Vagabond.
The Crises.
David Copperfield.
Franklin's Autobiography.
Giants of the Earth.
The Harbor.
House of Seven Gables.
Jane Eyre.
The Light That Failed.
The Little Minister.
Lorna Doone.
Man Who Married a Dumb Wife.
Maria Chapdelaine.
Mill on the Floss.
Monsieur Beaucaire.
My Antonia.
Ramona.
Representative Plays.
So Big.
The Soul of Ann Rutledge.
We—Charles Lindbergh.

d) SET NO. 4. Grades 11-12.

Adam Bede.
Adventures in Friendship.
Alice Adams.
The Bent Twig.
Covered Wagon.
David Harum.
Drums.
Gray Dawn.
The Greene Murder Case.
The Green Mirror.
Kidnapped.
Kim.
Main Street.
A Man for the Ages.
Moby Dick.
My Home in the Field of Honor.
Oregon Trail.
Pride and Prejudice.
Royal Road to Romance.
Scaramouche.
Show Boat.
Tess of D'Urbervilles.
Twelve Tests of Character.
Twenty Years at Hull House.
Woman in White.

[1302]

Literature Questionnaire: The Drama: Test 3.21. Grades 9-12; 1937; an experimental form; 5¢ per copy; 1¢ per machine-scorable answer sheet; Chicago, Ill.: Evaluation in the Eight Year Study, Progressive Education Association.

REFERENCES

1 *A Descriptive Summary of Evaluation Instruments in the Field of English.* Chicago, Ill.: Evaluation in the Eight Year Study, Progressive Education Association, March 1939. Pp. 10. Paper, mimeographed. Out of print.

[1303]

Literature Questionnaire: The Novel: Test 3.2a.
Grades 9-12; 1937; an experimental form; 5¢ per
copy; 1¢ per machine-scorable answer sheet; Chicago, Ill.: Evaluation in the Eight Year Study, Progressive Education Association.

REFERENCES

1 *A Descriptive Summary of Evaluation Instruments in the
Field of English.* Chicago, Ill.: Evaluation in the Eight Year
Study, Progressive Education Association, March 1939. Pp. 10.
Paper, mimeographed. Out of print.

[1304]

Literature Test: National Achievement Test. Grades
7-12; 1937; 2 forms; $2.00 per 25; 5¢ per specimen
set; nontimed (40-60) minutes; Robert K. Speer and
Samuel Smith; Rockville Centre, N. Y.: Acorn Publishing Co.

*H. H. Giles, Assistant Professor of Educa-
tion and Research Associate in the Bureau of
Educational Research, The Ohio State University.* The authors state that this test is relevant to the appreciation of literary effects,
qualities, moods, and the knowledge of facts.
It is extremely difficult to attempt any such
testing because in the first place there are so
many kinds of literary effects, qualities, moods,
and facts, and in the second place, a standard
test implies that the selection that must be
made is valid for all kinds of students and
teachers in all kinds of situations. To put it
bluntly, no standard test can possibly take into
account purposes and values determined by a
particular teacher and a particular group of
pupils, this with the single exception of such
tests as have no "right answers" and depend
on interpretation and further use by those who
take them rather than on scoring by any absolute method.

There is some value, which varies according to the situation, in learning how to read
and interpret the meaning and intention of an
author. Part I of the test presumes to prove
this ability. It does not raise the question of
the value of the selections given for pupil purposes. Part II deals with such qualities as
choice of words, convincingness, exaggeration,
authorship, and force. Again it is difficult to
see how any of these qualities matter except
in relationship to a purpose, more important
than the general purpose of getting a good
mark on a test. It is not at all sure that correct
answers in any of these cases would be a real
measure of the ability of students to analyze
effects and qualities in general. The selections
in Part III on moods, like those in the foregoing, are not chosen from literature written
in the last ten years. Part IV is certainly mis-

cellaneous and the variety is good, but it might
strike the high school student as incomplete and
irrelevant even though he might know all the
scattered facts asked for.

Such a test as this is difficult to make and
the criticisms given above are all related to one
major criticism, the omission of pupil purpose
from the assumptions back of the test. If this
omission is not important, the test is excellent
of its kind. It does require careful comparative
thinking.

*Robert C. Pooley, Associate Professor in
the Teaching of English, The University of
Wisconsin.* Any test which ventures to measure the results of literature instruction in terms
of aptitudes and appreciations rather than in
terms of facts is worthy of respectful notice.
This test consists of four parts, three of which
are nonspecific, testing the recognition of "Effects," "Qualities," and "Moods." Part IV is
called Miscellaneous Facts, and can be dismissed briefly. This part contains 30 items,
drawn from the whole range of English and
American literature, with side references to
French and Russian literatures. That Amy
Lowell wrote free verse, and that Jane Eyre
married Mr. Rochester are, in the eyes of the
authors, two of the 30 most important facts in
the literature of the world. Others might disagree. Had the section been labeled *Miscellaneous and Irrelevant Facts*, it would be more
accurate.

Parts I, II, and III are interesting and ingenious. They endeavor, through the comparison of short paragraphs or stanzas from
poetry, to test the pupils' sensitivity to various
aspects of mood, suggestiveness of words, degrees of humor and pathos, and consistency of
style. But while the authors must be commended for an original approach, the test is a
long cry from being a valid instrument in the
appreciation of literature. For one thing, it
touches lightly only a few of the hundred or
more recognitions and sensitivities which make
up that complex thing called appreciation. In
the second place, the exercises on the few
recognitions offered are too scanty to be really
valid. No one attempts to measure skill in
arithmetic by means of two or three problems.
Finally, the exercises are spotty in quality,
ranging from excellent to mildly absurd. For
example, the child is asked to state the effect
of the words "shall not perish from the earth"

by selecting one of these three choices; (*a*) "a dramatic tragedy," (*b*) "a defense of demo-cratic ideals," and (*c*) "the need of a new government." The words as given suggest only one thing—*perpetuity,* which is not given in the answers. In Part II, Recognizing Qualities, the issue is confused by including some factual information worded, "paragraph IV might have been written by Daniel Defoe," etc., which is not pertinent to the test.

On the whole, this test can be given only a limited recommendation. It is definitely better than the pure fact test, and it will measure vaguely some of the elements of appreciation. But hopeful teachers will have to look further for the test of genuine, nonspecific literary appreciation.

[1305]

Questionnaire on Voluntary Reading: Test 3.31. Grades 10-12; 1939; 1 form; revision of Test 3.3; 5¢ per questionnaire; 1¢ per machine-scorable answer sheet; $1.50 per set of stencils for machine scoring; nontimed (40) minutes; Chicago, Ill.: Evaluation in the Eight Year Study, Progressive Education Association.

REFERENCES

A Descriptive Summary of Evaluation Instruments in the Field of English. Chicago, Ill.: Evaluation in the Eight Year Study, Progressive Education Association, March 1939. Pp. 10. Paper, mimeographed. Out of print.

[1306]

Stanford Test of Comprehension of Literature. Grades 7-12; 1929; 2 forms, 3 parts; 75¢ per 25 parts; 20(25) minutes per part; Mary C. Burch; Stanford University, Calif.: Stanford University Press.
a) TEST I, NARRATION AND DESCRIPTION.
b) TEST II, CHARACTER AND EMOTION.
c) TEST III, EXPOSITION.

REFERENCES

1 BURCH, M. C. *Determination of a Content of the Course in Literature of a Suitable Difficulty for Junior and Senior High School Students.* Genetic Psychology Monographs, Vol. 4, Nos. 2-3. Worcester, Mass.: Clark University Press, 1928. Pp. 163-332. $3.00. Paper.

J. Wayne Wrightstone, Assistant Director, Bureau of Reference, Research, and Statistics, Public Schools, New York, New York. The *Stanford Tests of Comprehension of Literature* are made up of ten to twelve short samples for each form. These samples are taken from books frequently recommended for use in secondary schools. According to the author, each test is designed to measure the accuracy with which certain types of literature are read. Test I contains samples from types of literature whose main interest is action and event: the adventure story, the novel of incident, the epic, and narrative and descriptive prose and poetry. Test II contains samples from types whose main interest is character portrayal and emotional appeal such as the character sketch, the novel of emotion, lyric poetry, and the drama. Test III contains samples from types whose main appeal is to the intellect such as the essay and the oration. The functions of the tests, says the author, are to classify students of each grade into ability groups for purposes of instructions in literature, to measure growth in reading ability of an individual or group over a period of time, and to indicate what books are suitable reading materials (so far as difficulty is concerned) for a particular individual or group.

The reviewer has five criticisms of these tests as they relate to the functions claimed by the author and publisher. In the first place, the test does not measure reading comprehension of literature, but only two or three aspects of such reading comprehension. Reading comprehension is not a simple unitary process but rather a complex psychological process, involving multiple abilities of pupils. It is the opinion of the reviewer that the only kinds of reading comprehension ability measured by these tests are the ability to locate specific facts and the ability to identify general ideas in the paragraphs. Moreover, the items for such abilities are not arranged in the tests so that they can be scored and used for diagnostic purposes.

The second criticism is that the test exercises, which are paragraphs followed by questions, are not necessarily representative of the books. A primary assumption of the author is that the ability to identify the ideas in one paragraph represents the ability to comprehend the ideas and relationships of a book. This is not necessarily true and the author presents no evidence to support the assumption.

A third criticism is that the three different tests do not measure intrinsically different kinds of comprehension. The author has divided the literary selections into three arbitrary categories and has assumed that the series' three tests measure three different phases of literature comprehension. She presents no evidence to support this assumption.

The fourth criticism is that the information as to norms, validity, and reliability is entirely inadequate.

The fifth criticism is that the scores on these tests do not necessarily indicate what books children should read—a function claimed for the tests. The problem of choosing books that are suitable and interesting to boys and girls is far more complex than interpreting a score on a comprehension of literature test.

As survey tests on comprehension of paragraphs from such "classic" literature as Scott's novels, Burns' lyrics, and Emerson's essays, this series of three tests has limited values. For the modern high school curriculum and objectives of instruction in literature, this series of tests needs far-reaching reconstruction.

[1307]

Tests for the Appreciation of Literature. Grades 9-16; 1926; 1 form, 6 parts; 10¢ per set of six parts; 15¢ per specimen set; nontimed (60-100) minutes; Hannah Logasa and Martha McCoy Wright; Bloomington, Ill.: Public School Publishing Co.

a) TEST 1, DISCOVERY OF THEME.
b) TEST 2, READER PARTICIPATION.
c) TEST 3, REACTION TO SENSORY IMAGES.
d) TEST 4, COMPARISONS.
e) TEST 5, TRITE AND FRESH EXPRESSIONS.
f) TEST 6, RHYTHM.

Ann L. Gebhardt, Teacher of English, East High School, Madison, Wisconsin. One of the outstanding features of this test is its definiteness and objectivity. The average high school student has not been very enthusiastic about reading poetry, because he feels that 'here is something vague about it, so that he never knows whether he understands what it is attempting. When he takes this test he probably is not even aware of the logical, thorough way in which he is being examined, but he cannot help realizing that he is being checked on his comprehension of specific things. The test items progress from an apparently simple one, from which the teacher can at once determine whether the student can understand only an idea that is baldly stated, or whether he can grasp an idea that is imaginatively stated, through a series of increasingly difficult problems that determine where his appreciation of poetry ends.

Test 2 is perhaps a better index of the kind of teaching that preceded it than of the student's actual comprehension. Not all students can grasp the differences between the emotions the poet is attempting to arouse in the reader himself and those of the person he is writing about.

The sensory images, which are examined in Test 3, are a little harder to recognize than the simpler emotions tested in Test 2, but the transition is made logically. The references to *muscle* in Items 4 and 6 are confusing; they employ a mixed technique, demanding first recognition of personification, a figure of speech, for which there has been no adequate preparation or warning, and then discrimination between the sensory appeals of the thing personified.

Perhaps this criticism of Test 4 is a little severe, but one feels that it demands a niceness in distinction that is rather mature and sophisticated, and is often quite lost to the imaginative student who is swept away by the sensory or emotional appeal of the verse picture and forgets to be critical of it. Physical enjoyment that is so vivid, although it may never lead to keen critical perception, is nevertheless a definite achievement too seldom realized in the teaching of poetry. Too many high school students lack the capability for much more than that. Perhaps it is mere chance, but the least obvious examples of far fetched or mixed comparison are those set to the more vigorous rhythms in this group.

Although Test 5 demands those critical qualities which are not difficult to develop in a student whose standards of effectiveness are predetermined by what he hears most frequently, the problems are so definite and obvious that even the least "aware" student can pick out some examples of the things no true poet would say. Composition training and radio work should make this test easier to do than Test 4.

Test 6 is the one that unquestionably would be too difficult for the pupil who has had no training in choral reading or music. And even some of the most sensitively "aware" would have trouble in matching the patterns depicted here. In spite of this the test is a great improvement upon most tests of this nature.

Definite and objective as this set of six tests is, it would almost appear that the value of the entire group could not be defined until results from a great many student papers could be tabulated and interpreted. It is to the great credit of the compilers that its terminology and range are not confined to the classical tradition which has frightened off so many adventurers in the realm of poetry.

SPEECH

[1308]

Bryan-Wilke Scale for Rating Public Speeches. Speech audiences; 1939; 40¢ per 25; 10¢ per specimen set; nontimed (5-10) minutes; Alice I. Bryan and Walter H. Wilke; New York: Psychological Corporation.

SPELLING

[1309]
Australian Council for Educational Research Spelling Test. Ages 8-14; 1936; 6 forms; 9d. per booklet of tests; Victoria, Australia: Australian Council for Educational Research.

REFERENCES

1 QUANCE, F. M. *The Canadian Spellers.* Toronto, Canada: W. J. Gage and Co., 1936.

David H. Russell, Assistant Professor of Education, The University of Saskatchewan. The words of these tests are in six lists, said to be of equal difficulty for Australian children. The fifty words of increasing difficulty in each list are accompanied by illustrative sentences which contain the individual words to be written by the pupils. This is a usual form of spelling test and should be suitable for "primary school" children of from eight to fourteen years. The lists, with their accompanying sentences, are contained in a 35-page manual whose content varies from very elementary directions to teachers (such as not using the lists for teaching lists) to instructions for elaborate statistical manipulation difficult for the average teacher to perform. The manual, however, seems to accomplish its purpose of providing "reliable norms of attainment in spelling for Australian children."

The manual states clearly the methods used to obtain lists of typical useful words. It is an interesting question whether or not the system of borrowing from several United States lists and submitting these to the subjective criticism of a number of headmasters will ensure a completely valid test for Australia. It would seem that the Australian Council might undertake a word frequency count for their own country. When this was done by Quance [1] in Canada, for example, a few interesting differences were found in Canadian and American usage and such differences might also occur in Australia.

The reliability of the tests was determined by having children work two lists on successive mornings. It is expressed in terms of the probable error of a score on one list, or on the average of two lists, and not in terms of the more usual reliability coefficients.

The directions for the administration of the tests and the norms both allow the giving of "bands" or partial lists at different times of year. The norms have been worked out elaborately as age norms, percentiles, "age-in-grade"

norms, and grade norms for February, May, August, and November, and are given separately for each state. All this, with norms given for "bands" at the beginning and end of the year, provides a system which seems needlessly complex for the ordinary teacher. In addition, the manual suggests corrections for the ages and also the sex of pupils for any class unusual in these respects. These may be of limited value in comparing whole classes but would seem to be of little use in understanding the difficulties of individual pupils. While the stated purpose of the manual is to "provide reliable norms of attainment in spelling" the manual seems to contain an undue emphasis on general results and an unjustified worship of norms. When this manual is placed in the hands of a teacher, it should be accompanied by one discussing the diagnosis and treatment of individual difficulties in spelling. The system of taking seven tenths of a word from a girl's score or adding seven tenths of a word to a boy's score when comparing them with the percentile tables, as suggested in the manual, or the use of norms for comparing classes, is hardly the crux of the spelling problem in elementary schools.

[1310]
Buffalo Spelling Scale. Grades 2-8; 1938; 2 forms; 15¢ per specimen set; no materials needed for pupils; (15) minutes; Allan J. Williams; Bloomington, Ill.: Public School Publishing Co.

John C. Almack, Professor of Education, Stanford University. The words in this scaled test were taken from the *Buckingham Extension of the Ayres Spelling Scale.* The grade norms are based upon results from five thousand pupils to the grade. There is no fixed time limit.

The words are presented in sentences. Since one aim is to include several test words in each sentence so as to reduce the time required for the test, a difficult problem arises. Some of the sentences do not make clear the meaning of the words, and may indeed border on the absurd, as

Come sit back here.
Mother, send that cold child home.
However, tonight father will *change* his *store.*
Endeavor to *eliminate judgment* in marking examinations.

Some half of the hundred words in each form are comprised in the interval which is expected to be covered by the second grade.

Thereafter, the word list in each grade interval is very brief: about ten words. This is a close sampling, and a longer step would give greater accuracy and refinement in the test.

The reviewer agrees that there are advantages in presenting the test words in sentences. To serve their purposes, they must be good sentences. Usually these sentences may be improved by using only one test word to each. If one does this, he then increases the amount of time the test demands for giving. It may be that some other answer can be found to this problem; it may be best to use one word to a sentence, read the whole sentence, and require the pupil to write the test word only. Or perhaps, the entire sentence may be printed, with a blank left for the test word, which is pronounced and written in the blank or in a column with other words at one side of the paper.

This test compares favorably with others of its kind. It is convenient to give and score. Its norms seem well founded.

M. E. Broom, Assistant Superintendent of Schools, El Paso, Texas. Each of the two forms includes 100 words selected from the *Buckingham Extension of the Ayres Spelling Scale.* The 100 words are included in 24 sentences in Form A and in 21 sentences in Form B. These sentences are to be read in their entirety, and then by parts thereafter, while the pupils write the sentences. The test is not timed, but the examiner is instructed to urge slow pupils to write more quickly, if they are holding back the rest of the class.

Research has shown the sentence dictation form of spelling test to be almost as valid as the dictated list of spelling words. This test has the advantage of having very few words which are not scored for correctness, with the majority of such words very easily spelled, as *on, with,* and *will.* Form B has more difficult unscored words than Form A.

Evidence is lacking in the manual as to the equivalence of the two forms, and as to the validity and reliability of the instrument. Grade placement norms are available, but the number of cases on which they were established is not stated. The test author merely says concerning these matters: "Care was taken to have the two forms of the scale balanced by an equal number of words from each column of the Buckingham-Ayres Scale. The scale was standardized by giving it to approximately five thousand pupils in each grade."

For a review by Henry D. Rinsland, see 1158.

[1311]

Davis-Schrammel Spelling Test. Grades 1-9; 1935-36; 4 forms; 15¢ per specimen set; no materials needed for pupils; (15) minutes; Vera Davis and H. E. Schrammel; Emporia, Kan.: Bureau of Educational Measurements, Kansas State Teachers College.

REFERENCES

1 HORN, ERNEST. *A Basic Writing Vocabulary*: 10,000 Words Most Commonly Used in Writing. State University of Iowa, Monographs in Education, Series 1, No. 4. Iowa City, Iowa: the University, 1926. Pp. 225. Cloth, $2.25; paper, $1.75.

Walter W. Cook, Associate Professor of Education, The University of Minnesota. The words of this survey test of general spelling ability were selected from the *Buckingham Extension of the Ayres Spelling Scale.* Each of the four forms contains 96 words arranged in grade tests with enough overlapping to provide 20 words appropriate for each grade. The mean accuracy of each grade list on the original scale is 72 per cent. Percentile norms for midyear and end-of-year testing are furnished for each grade. Reliability coefficients reported for each grade list range from .84 to .93 with a mean of .87. The average probable error of measurement is reported as 1.1 words.

There is no excuse for building a spelling test in 1935 based on a pioneer scale developed in 1918. The list might at least have been checked against the most commonly used words in writing as determined by Ernest Horn in the Commonwealth Investigation.[1]

The difficulty of the words used in the test is also questionable. Although Ayres recommended that words with an average of 84 per cent correct spellings be used, and in the Springfield, and Cleveland Surveys used words of 70, and 73 per cent accuracy respectively, recent investigations are unanimous in recommending words of 50 per cent accuracy for classification purposes.

In schools using modern spelling lists and modern methods of teaching, it is difficult to conceive of any vital purpose being served by this test.

Joseph C. Dewey, Head of the Department of Education and Psychology, Westminster College. This series of spelling tests, with its four forms and its simple, easy-to-understand manual, appears to be a rather useful instrument for use in testing spelling achievement in grades one to nine. The authors state in the manual that there are four equivalent forms but submit no evidence that the four forms are actually equivalent. This leads one to the suspicion that either the forms are not actually equivalent or that the authors have been negligent in submitting evidence to support their claim.

The reliability coefficients, as given by the authors in the manual, ranging from .84 to .93 with an average of .87 seem reasonably high although the number of cases used in determining reliabilities was only 1506 with little geographical distribution, all the cases being in Kansas.

The manual is well written, easy to understand and to use. Percentile norms are provided for midyear testing as well as for end-of-year testing which is an excellent feature and enables one to use the tests at the middle of the year as well as at the end. This feature together with the four forms provided makes these tests a rather flexible and useful instrument in a variety of circumstances.

These tests provide administrators and teachers with an instrument that is easy to administer, easy to score, and to interpret. However, before choosing this test for use in any school system one must be sure that the tests are valid in terms of the word list taught by the particular school system concerned. If this is not done it may be that the tests will give a very distorted view of the effectiveness of spelling instruction in the school system.

[1312]

High School Spelling Test. Grades 7-12; 1929; 4 forms; 25¢ per specimen set; no materials needed for pupils; Harold H. Bixler; Atlanta, Ga.: Turner E. Smith & Company.

REFERENCES

1 HORN, ERNEST. *A Basic Writing Vocabulary:* 10,000 Words Most Commonly Used in Writing. State University of Iowa, Monographs in Education, Series 1, No. 4. Iowa City, Iowa: the University, 1926. Pp. 225. Cloth, $2.25; paper, $1.75.
2 SIMMONS, ERNEST P., AND BIXLER, HAROLD HENCH. *The Standard High School Spelling Scale,* Revised edition. Atlanta, Ga.: Turner E. Smith & Co., 1935. Pp. 63. $0.48. Paper.

Walter W. Cook, Associate Professor of Education, The University of Minnesota. This test is designed to measure general spelling ability at the junior and senior high school levels in order to determine which pupils may be excused from spelling classes. January norms (medians only) are furnished for grades 7, 8, 9, and 12. An exemption score of 80 is recommended.

Each of the four equivalent forms consists of 100 words selected from the *Standard High School Spelling Scale.*[2] This scale consists of the 2560 words most frequently misspelled by high school pupils selected from the 5000 most commonly used words as determined by the Commonwealth Investigation.[1]

A reliability coefficient of .93 was secured by administering Forms I and II to 132 eighth-grade pupils on successive days.

The word-used-in-sentence list dictation is employed. This technique requires that the administrator pronounce a word, read a sentence containing the word, and pronounce the word again. One test form in the hands of the administrator is required.

The test could probably be improved by selecting those words from the *Standard High School Spelling Scale,*[2] the spelling of which correlates highest with general spelling ability.

[1313]

Spelling Test: National Achievement Tests. Grades 3-4, 5-8, 7-9, 10-12; 1936-39; 2 forms; 50¢ per 25; Robert K. Speer and Samuel Smith; Rockville Centre, N. Y.: Acorn Publishing Co.
a) GRADES 3- 4. (20) minutes.
b) GRADES 5- 8. (25) minutes.
c) GRADES 7- 9. (25) minutes.
d) GRADES 10-12. (25) minutes.

For a review by W. J. Osburn, see 1161.

[1313.1]

Standard Elementary Spelling Scale. Grades 2-8; 1940; a 115-page book consisting of 3,679 words alphabetically arranged with difficulty percentages for each grade; Harold Hench Bixler; Atlanta, Ga.: Turner E. Smith & Co.

[1314]

Standard High School Spelling Scale, Revised Edition. Grades 7-12; 1925-35; a 63-page book containing 64 40-word lists to be used for either testing or teaching; 48¢ per copy; Ernest P. Simmons and Harold Hench Bixler; Atlanta, Ga.: Turner E. Smith & Co.

[1315]

Unit Scales of Attainment in Spelling. Grades 3-4, 5-6, 7-8; 1932-33; 3 forms, 3 levels; identical to the spelling tests in the battery *Unit Scales of Attainment*; 10¢ per single form; 25¢ per 25 answer blanks; 15¢ per specimen set; (15) minutes; W. A. Anderson; Minneapolis, Minn.: Educational Test Bureau, Inc.

REFERENCES

1 THORNDIKE, EDWARD L. *A Teacher's Word Book:* The Twenty Thousand Words Found Most Frequently and Widely in General Reading for Children and Young People. New York: Bureau of Publications, Teachers College, Columbia University, 1931. Pp. vii, 182. $1.60.

John C. Almack, Professor of Education, Stanford University. These spelling scales are part of an achievement battery "for measuring abilities and ranges of information." The norms for the battery were standardized on 60,000 cases in 1937.

There are three divisions, for grades 3-4, 5-6, and 7-8. A list of forty words is found in each division. The examiner is directed to "pronounce each word distinctly but not in a 'giveaway' manner." A second pronunciation is allowed if it is needed, and "a short sentence or phrase may be given to convey the meaning of any word." There is no fixed time limit, but some fifteen minutes is made available. This is adequate.

Some of the words found in Division 1 for the third and fourth grades are *many, written, independent, secretary,* and *valuable*. Fifth- and sixth-grade words are *increasing, securing, height, noticeable,* and *recommendation*. Seventh- and eighth-grade words are *several, accommodate,* and *privilege*.

Key words are repeated in each division, scaled about ten steps apart, and lower in each succeeding list. The word *being* which is No. 11 in Division 1 is No. 1 in Division 2. The word *local* is No. 28 in Division 1, No. 18 in Division 2, and No. 8 in Division 3.

These scales furnish a satisfactory method for comparing spelling attainment among those pupils who have been taught these words in the grades to which they have been assigned in this test. There is such variation in the grade placement of words in different series of spelling books that the probability of identical grade placement of these words in any two spelling series or courses of study is very remote. The reviewer estimates that any two of the most used texts in spelling *for any grade* will have from twenty-five to forty per cent of their words in common; in a list of the ten most used texts, he anticipates ninety per cent will be common to all. The two or three books for consecutive grades will ordinarily have sixty per cent of their words in common.

The test also measures only a part of what is properly comprised in spelling; namely, the writing of the letters of these words in their correct order, from the pronunciation as given. Certainly, this is an important part of the results desired, but not as important as to be able to use the words in their proper meaning; to use the words in oral speech in their proper meaning, and to use them in the right form and in correct relation to each other.

To contend that any spelling test given in this fashion measures spelling attainment in general demands two big jumps between the data at hand and the generalizations: (*a*) that the sampling is adequate and significant; and (*b*) that other elements in the spelling process correlate to a significant degree with what is measured.

The statement on page 7 of the publisher's catalog (No. 24) to the effect that the profile charts are "an index of where remedial work is needed," needs considerable qualification. The diagnosis of spelling and the prescribing of remedies for deficiencies is not as simple as this suggests. Deficiencies may exist for several reasons: (*a*) because we have not made use of the forces which produce learning of spelling; (*b*) because obstacles exist to the operation of these forces; (*c*) because of lack of media or deficiencies in the media of learning; and (*d*) because of combinations of the foregoing as well as other reasons. This test is not adapted to revealing any of the major causes of spelling deficiency, though it may reveal the symptoms.

There remains also the problem of conveying to the children by some standard and uniform method the "name" of the word, the idea to be symbolized, and the meaning of the word to be spelled. Pictures may be used to do this, records on which the words have been inscribed, and by putting meaningful context which calls for the word into the hands of the subjects. This test contributes nothing new to the problem here described.

So far as statistical treatment is concerned, and so far as test mechanics are of service, this seems to be an excellent test.

G. M. Wilson, Professor of Education, Boston University. The spelling words in this scale consist of forty words in each of three divisions, namely: Division 1, grades 3-4; Division 2, grades 5-6; and Division 3, grades 7-8. It is not possible for anyone to evaluate spelling words on the basis of general impressions. It is, however, possible to apply such an instrument as Thorndike's *Teacher's Word Book* [1] and in such manner as to give at least a rough evaluation of the words.

Table 1 shows an analysis of the three divisions of words as compared with the *Teacher's Word Book*. Division 1 is designed for third and fourth grade pupils. The words in this division run up into the sixth thousand. Words in Division 2, grades 5-6, run up to the seventh, the eighth, and even the fifteenth thousand. The words in Division 3, grades 7-8, go beyond that.

TABLE 1

Frequency of Occurrence of the Words in the *Unit Scales of Attainment in Spelling*, Form B, According to Thorndike's *A Teacher's Word List*

Thorndike's Placement	Number of Words		
	Division 1 Grades 3–4	Division 2 Grades 5–6	Division 3 Grades 7–8
1a	13	4	1
1b	7	5	2
2a	6	5	9
2b	7	9	4
3a	2	5	4
3b	1	2	2
4a	1	2	2
4b	0	0	0
5a	1	1	1
5b	1	2	2
6	1	0	1
7	0	1	3
8	0	3	2
9	0	0	1
10	0	0	1
11	0	0	1
12	0	0	1
13	0	0	1
14	0	0	1
15	0	1	0
16	0	0	0
17	0	0	1
18	0	0	0
19	0	0	0
20	0	0	0
Total	40	40	40

Read table thus: Of the 40 words in Division 1, 13 are listed by Thorndike as being among the first 500 words found in "the general reading for children and young people"; 7 are in the second 500; 6, in the third 500; 1, in the sixth 1,000; etc. Read likewise for Divisions 2 and 3.

The questions involved in word selection for spelling lists are primarily curriculum questions. One of these questions is: How many words should children undertake in their spelling lists? A second question is: How far up the scale of difficulty or unfamiliarity should the words run? Just a very few years ago such questions could not be answered with any degree of certainty. Today, however, we know that few eighth grade pupils have a writing vocabulary that exceeds 3,000 words. Furthermore, we know that if pupils undertake too many words, they are going to fail; that is, the primary requirement of drill is that the load shall be sizable.

The above questions indicate that the word lists in the *Unit Scales of Attainment in Spelling* are extended unreasonably. Doubtless, no words for the third and fourth grade should go above the second thousand. Many would insist that no sixth grade words should go

above the second thousand. Few who have studied the matter would extend the eighth grade list above the third thousand; certainly the fourth thousand would be the limit. In other words, this test has sadly neglected to observe the most fundamental principles relating to the curriculum and good teaching.

The test is in convenient form. It has been fully standardized. If the fundamental objections were not so weighty, the test might be looked upon with favor.

VOCABULARY

[1316]

Clinton General Vocabulary Test. High school and college; 1936; 2 forms; $1.15 per 25; 10¢ per specimen set; nontimed (30) minutes; R. J. Clinton; Corvallis, Ore.: O. S. C. Cooperative Association.

[1317]

Columbia Vocabulary Test. Grades 3-12; 1939; 1 form; $1 per 25 machine-scorable test-answer sheets; 25¢ per specimen set; nontimed (15-20) minutes; Irene Gansl and H. E. Garrett; New York: Psychological Corporation.

REFERENCES

1 GANSL, IRENE. *Vocabulary: Its Measurement and Growth.* Columbia University, Archives of Psychology, No. 236. New York: the University, March 1939. Pp. 52. $1.00. Paper.

[1318]

Cooperative Vocabulary Test. Grades 7-16; 1940; Form Q; 5¢ per test, 10 to 99 copies; 25¢ per specimen set; nontimed (10-30) minutes; Frederick B. Davis, F. S. Beers, D. G. Paterson, and Mary Willis; New York: Cooperative Test Service.

REFERENCES

Cooperative Test Service. *The Cooperative Vocabulary Test: Information Concerning Its Construction, Interpretation, and Use.* New York: Cooperative Test Service, 1940. Pp. 2. Gratis. Paper.

[1319]

English Recognition Vocabulary Test. Grades 1-16 and adults; 1937-38; 1 form; $3.50 per 100; 15¢ per specimen set; Robert H. Seashore and Lois D. Eckerson; Evanston, Ill.: Robert H. Seashore, Northwestern University.

REFERENCES

1 ECKERSON, L. E. *The Estimation of Individual Differences in the Total Size of English Recognition Vocabulary.* Unpublished master's thesis, University of Southern California, 1938.
2 SEASHORE, ROBERT H., AND ECKERSON, LOIS D. "The Measurement of Individual Differences in General English Vocabularies." *J Ed Psychol* 31:14-38 Ja '40.
3 SMITH, MARY KATHERINE. *Measurement of the Size of General English Vocabulary through the Elementary Grades and High School.* Unpublished doctor's thesis, Northwestern University, 1940. Pp. 62.

[1320]

Michigan Vocabulary Profile Test. Grades 9-16; 1937-39; a revision of the *Michigan Vocabulary Profile (see 1171c)*; 2 forms; $1.50 per 25; 3¢ per machine-scorable answer sheet; 25¢ per specimen set; nontimed (40-60+) minutes; Edward B. Greene; Yonkers, N. Y.: World Book Co.

REFERENCES

1 GREENE, EDWARD B. "Michigan Vocabulary Profile: A Sampling of Vocabularies of Superior Adults." *J Higher Ed* 9:383-9 O '38.
2 GREENE, EDWARD B. "Vocabulary Profiles of Groups in Training." *J Ed Res* 33:569-75 Ap '40.

Herbert A. Landry, Research Assistant, Bureau of Reference, Research, and Statistics, Public Schools, New York, New York. The author states in the manual that "this test is designed to give a profile of an individual's vocabulary in eight fields of information which are considered to be important and independent to a marked degree." This profile is presumed to be "more valuable than a single general vocabulary score because it shows the extent of the individual's knowledge in particular fields."

It would appear then that the chief contribution to be made by the test is in the additional information it can provide in studying the individual. One would agree that for this purpose a knowledge of the differential quality of an individual's vocabulary would be very useful in many specific situations. Value of this profile however depends upon such limiting conditions as are imposed by the extent of the validity and reliability of the instrument.

Concerning the former, it can be said that the test appears to be a valid measure of the specialized vocabulary of each of the eight different fields selected. Painstaking refinement procedures have resulted in the selection of what seems to be a graded representative sampling of the technical vocabularies involved.

Concerning the reliability of the test, the author states that the correlation between equivalent forms provides reliability coefficients for the separate subdivisions which range from .87 to .94, median .91. While they are relatively high on most of the divisions, they do not meet the minimum standard of .94 suggested by Kelley as the lowest reliability a test should have if it is to be used for individual diagnosis. The reliabilities when expressed in terms of the probable error of individual scores, which do not appear in the manual but were obtained on request from the publisher, range from .47 to .94 score points, the median is .91. There is, therefore, a one-to-one chance that an obtained score on four of the eight divisions will not vary more than approximately one score point from the true score. However, it must also be remembered that there is the same chance that the variation from the true score may be more than one score point. Now a one score point difference may seem insignificant until one inspects the table of norms. From this table, it is seen

that on the lower levels, grades 9-12, the mean increase in the median scores for the eight divisions for the four year span is only 4.5 score points. Thus a one point deviation is equivalent to a one year difference in the grade norms. Within a single grade level the difference between the 31st and 69th percentile ranks seldom vary by more than two score points. Thus the possible extent of the error of measurement and its effect upon the pupil's percentile rank are apparent.

It is obvious that the scores obtained on the divisions of the test have little value unless properly interpreted. A high score on a particular division for a given grade level may be the result of several factors such as (a) a special interest (b) a formal course (c) the wide collateral reading common to bright pupils (d) certain environmental factors which result in bringing an individual into more extensive contact with a given area than is usually the case. These and other factors may operate to varying degrees in different situations. Because of this, scores become meaningful only to the extent that they have been carefully analyzed in the light of the factors that may give rise to them. This would seem to necessitate extensive use of cumulative records and interviews.

The hazards involved in an uncritical use of the test are apparent. However, since it represents the only available measure of differential vocabulary ability it can provide useful information if used with full knowledge of its limitations. Results must be carefully interpreted by persons who have both the time and the facilities to follow through each case in order to determine the real significance of an individual's scores. Further experimentation will undoubtedly lead to the overcoming of some of its present limitations for individual analysis.

The test may also be used as a general vocabulary test by combining the scores on all divisions. Percentile norms are provided for interpretation of the total scores. Used as a 240-item general vocabulary test it should provide highly reliable measures of breadth of vocabulary.

The physical aspects of the test are very satisfactory. The arrangement for machine or hand stencil scoring simplifies scoring procedure greatly. The answer sheet provides for the profile and other data and may be easily filed with a student's record for future use. The modest claims of the author together with his cautioning statements concerning its use which are included in the manual are to be commended.

Ed Res B 19:117 F 14 '40. * designed to test the vocabulary of high-school and college students in eight fields of information * The authors expect the test to provide evidence about: how growth and retention of specific information is connected with training and interest, what vocabularies are essential to certain vocations, what is the importance of vocabulary in reading, what is the importance of vocabulary in educational and vocational planning, and which terms are important tools for thinking. It would seem to the reviewer that such comprehensive and diverse purposes cannot adequately be served by this single test. The authors present little or no evidence to show that it has been used or is valid for serving any of these purposes. Further experimentation and application are needed to provide answers for these questions. The test does provide some new and challenging possibilities in vocabulary analysis, but the users of this test must finally determine for what purposes it is valuable and practical.

For reviews by Richard Ledgerwood, M. R. Trabue, John G. Darley, John M. Stalnaker, and Arthur E. Traxler of an earlier edition, see 1171.

[1321]
Schrammel-Wharton Vocabulary Test. Grades 7-12; 1938; 2 forms; 50¢ per 25; 15¢ per specimen set; 40(45) minutes; H. E. Schrammel and LaVerna P. Wharton; Emporia, Kan.: Bureau of Educational Measurements, Kansas State Teachers College.

Arthur E. Traxler, Assistant Director, Educational Records Bureau, New York, N. Y. The widespread awareness of the importance of knowledge of word meaning in school success is shown by the fact that there are now about fifty published vocabulary tests, aside from many such tests that exist as parts of other tests. These tests cover all levels from preschool through college.

The *Schrammel-Wharton Vocabulary Test,* which was used in the 1938 Nation-wide Every Pupil Testing Program, is similar in nearly every way to some of the earlier vocabulary tests. Each of the two forms contains 140 items, each consisting of a test word followed by four words from which the subject must choose the one which defines the test word. The test is designed for use throughout the junior and senior high school and in college. It yields only a total score and has no diagnostic features. According to the manual of directions, the words were selected from the Pressey list and other supplementary lists and "all words were checked against the Thorndike word lists in order to insure an equitable distribution according to difficulty and frequency of use."

The test is long enough to be highly reliable. It is somewhat surprising, therefore, to note that a reliability coefficient of only .85 is reported in the manual of directions. This is fairly high reliability for tests in general, but it is lower than the reliability of most vocabulary tests that contain a hundred or more items. For example, the reliability of the *Inglis Test of English Vocabulary,* containing 150 items, is above .90 and that of the vocabulary part of the *Cooperative English Test,* containing 100 items, is about .95. It should be observed, however, that the reliability coefficient given for the Schrammel-Wharton test is based on the scores of only seventy-two college juniors and seniors. It is possible that further study with a more adequate sampling will show higher reliability.

The time limit for the test is forty minutes, which is long enough for most persons to complete a vocabulary test containing 140 items. This is a desirable feature. In a vocabulary test, one is interested in measuring the subject's knowledge of word meaning and not his rate of work. If the time limit is so brief that few if any pupils can cover the test in the time allowed, the scores will be determined partly by speed of reading and will not show vocabulary alone. It is noteworthy that this test avoids that pitfall.

Certain aspects of the format of the test probably involve limitations. One of these is that each test word is presented alone rather than in a sentence or phrase. A disadvantage of not presenting the words in context is that the exact meaning of each word may not be clear to the subject. For example, *draft,* word number ninety-nine in Form A, has twenty-six meanings when used as a noun, eight meanings when used as a verb, and three meanings when used as an adjective. The only clue that the person taking the test has concerning which of these thirty-seven meanings is to be applied to the word is the series of choices following it.

Another apparent limitation is that in some instances the word which the subject is expected to select as a definition of the test word is not very well suited to this purpose. For instance, in the eightieth item of Form A, the test word is *metabolism* and the expected response is *growth,* and in the second item of Form B, the test word is *possessive* and the response that is presumed to be correct is *designating.* A number of the other items could be criticized in the same way.

Fairly adequate midyear and end-of-year percentile norms for grades 7-12 are given in the manual of directions. The number of cases included in the distributions on which the midyear norms are based ranges from 327 for grade 7 to 1,311 for grade 9. The groups contributing to the end-of-year norms are smaller. As yet, the only norms for the college level are tentative norms for the beginning of the freshman year.

In all probability, the *Schrammel-Wharton Vocabulary Test* has served a useful purpose in the Nation-wide Every Pupil Testing Program, but in view of the availability of several vocabulary tests that are apparently more thoroughly validated and more adequately standardized, the recommendation of this test for use in other testing programs would hardly be warranted at its present stage of development.

[1321.1]

Vocabulary: Parr Skill-Ability Tests. Grades 9-16; 1938; 2 forms; 10¢ per test, 50 or more; 28(35) minutes; Frank W. Parr; Corvallis, Ore.: O. S. C. Cooperative Association.

[1322]

Vocabulary Power Tests. Grades 4-8, 7-9; 1938; 2 levels; 25¢ per 30; specimen set free; nontimed (15-20) minutes; Norman K. Frick; Chicago, Ill.: Scott, Foresman and Co.
a) INTRODUCTORY FORM A. Grades 4-8.
b) JUNIOR FORM A. Grades 7-9.

FINE ARTS

Reviews by Raleigh M. Drake, Paul R. Farnsworth, Ray Faulkner, Karl W. Gehrkens, William S. Larson, Clara J. McCauley, Norman C. Meier, Joseph E. Moore, James L. Mursell, Aulus Ward Saunders, Alton O'Steen, Carl E. Seashore, and Edwin Ziegfeld.

ART

[1323]

Knauber Art Ability Test. Grades 7-16 and adults; 1932-35; 1 form; 10¢ per test; $1.00 per manual; 15¢ per sample test; $1.10 per specimen set; nontimed (180) minutes; Alma Jordan Knauber; Cincinnati, Ohio: the author, 3331 Arrow Ave.

REFERENCES

1 KNAUBER, ALMA JORDAN. *Testing for Art Ability.* Unpublished master's thesis, Ohio State University, 1928.
2 BIRD, MILTON H. Chapter 6. "Tests," pp. 37-48. In *A Study in Aesthetics.* Harvard University, Harvard Monographs in Education, No. 11; Studies in Educational Psychology and Educational Measurement. Cambridge, Mass.: Harvard University Press, 1932. Pp. x, 117. $1.00. Paper. (London: Oxford University Press. 4s. 6d.)
3 KNAUBER, ALMA JORDAN. "Testing for Art Ability." *Ed* 55:219-23 D '34.
4 KNAUBER, ALMA JORDAN. "The Construction and Standardization of the Knauber Art Tests." *Ed* 56:165-70 N '35.

Norman C. Meier, Associate Professor of Psychology, The State University of Iowa. The main test is classified as a production test, thereby requiring a semi-subjective scoring and also verging toward the testing of skills and knowledge acquired in the classroom as contrasted with a functional use of some psychological process such as aesthetic judgment. Exercises required of the subject in the ability test include drawing a design from memory; drawing figures within space limitations from memory or of a stereotyped character such as Santa Claus; arranging within a given space a specified composition and creating and completing designs from supplied elements. Additional exercises require the spotting of errors in drawn compositions, these being errors in ordinary drawing practice, such as incorrect perspective, misplaced or incorrectly proportioned details, and inconsistent or incongruous elements. A final type of material is the requirement of producing some compositions which are intended to bring out the subject's creative imagination, ingenuity, ability to represent an idea symbolically or to plan and express a universal idea. This latter problem has for its instruction, "Draw a composition using your own symbol for labor."

The reviewer believes that complex functions

such as these—likewise creative imagination—could hardly be tested adequately by a single exercise. In some of the exercises success may be dependent largely upon how well the subject has mastered stereotypes and the traditional problems of art instruction. The primary function of the test would appear to be that of measuring school progress with some indication of the degree to which habits of observation and aspects of imagination are now serviceable. Hence, it would be expected that she would find in giving the test to a group of college art majors a median score of 95 whereas a group of non-art majors yielded 52, but it is not clear to the reviewer why this outcome should be taken as a measure of *native* ability, since it could just as well indicate the measure of learned increment and skills derived through longer practice. Possibly it measures both, but in what proportions it would be difficult to discover. Likewise, the median of 123 for art teachers contrasted with a median of 61 for non-art teachers could be explained as a measure of familiarity with the type of teaching problems making up much of the test content.

The measurement of reliability offered, indicated by a correlation of .95 by the split-half technique using 83 students, is open to question if it is true that these 83 students were within the influence of her own or similar teaching rather than being widely distributed geographically. The factor of community of ideas possibly explains the high reliability co-efficient and the results on retakes (.96—nine students). Undoubtedly the restricted limit within which scoring may spread through the use of scoring keys contributes also to this end. But the data offered on validity and reliability would be more convincing had individuals with different training and different ideas of what constitutes success in art been included.

The test should find good use in indicating progress in art classes and offer some indications of unusual ability from study of the individual products obtained.

[1324]

Knauber Art Vocabulary Test. Grades 7-16 and adults; 1932-35; 1 form; 7¢ per test; 25¢ per manual; 35¢ per specimen set; nontimed (40) minutes; Alma Jordan Knauber; Cincinnati, Ohio: the author, 3331 Arrow Ave.

REFERENCES

1 KNAUBER, ALMA JORDAN. *Testing for Art Ability.* Unpublished master's thesis, Ohio State University, 1928.
2 KNAUBER, ALMA JORDAN. "Testing for Art Ability." *Ed* 55:219-23 D '34.
3 KNAUBER, ALMA JORDAN. "The Construction and Standardization of the Knauber Art Tests." *Ed* 56:165-70 N '35.
4 MOORE, JOSEPH E. "A Note on the Reliability of the Knauber Art Vocabulary Test." *J Ed Psychol* 29:631-5 N '38.

Ray Faulkner, Head of the Department of Fine and Industrial Arts, Teachers College, Columbia University. The purpose of this test is to measure knowledge of art vocabulary from the seventh grade through high school. Inasmuch as this is a pioneer attempt to produce a separate test of art vocabulary, it deserves attention.

However, there are several technical faults, both in test construction and presentation of data, which minimize its value. First, the basis of selection of terms is not stated, and the selection of terms in a vocabulary test is of utmost importance. Second, it appears that no work has been done on the discriminating power of the items, and it is reasonable to suppose that a more efficient instrument could be developed from selected, discriminating terms. Third, the validity of the test has been established only by a comparison of median scores of art and non-art groups, but the significance of these differences has not been computed. Thus, there is no proof that these differences are real. Fourth, the reliability of the test is too low for general use. Two coefficients of reliability are reported by the author: .67 and .78. These coefficients were computed on groups varying markedly in ability and age level, and indicate that the test is not sufficiently reliable for general use. Thus, although the basic idea is good, the test should have been studied more carefully before being published.

Joseph E. Moore, Professor of Psychology, George Peabody College for Teachers, Nashville, Tennessee. This test consists of one hundred multiple-choice art terms which are arranged in order of difficulty. The subject answers each question by underlining the one of the responses which he thinks makes the most meaningful statement. The form is attractive and the type clear and easy to read.

The manual fails to give any information concerning the sources consulted for purposes of getting the original words and fails to tell how the various sources were sampled. The mere term *art knowledge* is far too broad to convey any specific meaning adequately. The test user is not told whether the words were selected principally for college students majoring in art or for art school students. It is highly improbable that any list of one hundred words would present a well-rounded picture of art knowledge and yet no mention is made of the special phase of art covered by the instrument.

The manual gives no information concerning the group on which the test was standardized. The user of these tests would not have any idea whether those taking the test were all art majors, or non-art students. The author of this test should certainly state specifically the number of subjects used in each grade and the *amount* and *kind* of art training possessed. The test norms include groups ranging from the seventh grade through the senior year in college. It is to be regretted that the exact method of selecting the subjects used at each grade level was not included along with measures of central tendency and variability. The mid-score given by the author for each grade is almost without meaning unless the number of individuals participating is given. At no place does the author state whether the subjects were all boys or all girls or how many of each were included.

The table of norms published by the author does indicate a rise in score from grade to grade but *not* a consistent rise. In four of the nine comparisons between grades the difference between the mid-scores was not greater than *two* points. This lack of discrimination between the scores of the eighth and ninth grades, the tenth and eleventh, the eleventh and twelfth, and at the college level between the juniors and seniors would seem to indicate that the test is not equally well standardized at each grade level. No statistical treatment of the differences was made; hence, it is not known if the obtained differences between grades were significant.

In support of the above criticism Moore [4] compared the achievement of 21 art teachers with that of 23 art majors and found no statistically reliable difference in performance. Between art majors and art minors and between art teachers and art minors no statistically reliable difference was found. The vocabulary test does seem to be making a differentiation between the vocabulary knowledge of art teachers and art majors when compared to those who have not had art training. There is no statistically significant difference between the vocabulary possessed by art minors and non-art students.

The percentage of overlapping scores in Moore's data should probably make one cautious in concluding that art training per se is responsible for vocabulary knowledge as measured by this test. In the non-art group twenty per cent of the 98 non-art students scored higher on the vocabulary test than did the median student minoring in art. Three per cent of the non-art group made better scores than that score represented by the median of the art majors. Slightly more than three per cent of the non-art group scored above the median of the art teachers. The validity of the *Knauber Art Vocabulary Test* should probably be questioned when it claims to be a measure of art knowledge and yet can only reveal statistically reliable differences between extremes—such as art teachers and non-art students. It appears that the crucial test of validity for the Knauber test will come when some investigator applies the test and arranges the subjects on the basis of art training by type and extent, then checks to see if there is a consistent and statistically reliable difference between the various gradations of training.

The scoring of the *Knauber Art Vocabulary Test* is very time consuming. A marked copy of the test is generally used for scoring.

The reliability of the *Knauber Art Vocabulary Test,* as reported by the author, was based on 100 students. The training or special qualifications of these subjects was not mentioned but it was indicated that they were from various grades. The scores of these 100 subjects were divided into odd and even items and then correlated. The coefficient of correlation was found to be .78 but no mention was made as to whether this coefficient was corrected by the Spearman-Brown Prophecy formula. Moore attempted to verify the reliability of the vocabulary test by applying it to 158 subjects divided as follows: 23 art majors, 21 art teachers, 7 art minors, and 98 educational psychology students. The coefficient resulting from correlating the odd-even items was .81 which becomes .90 when corrected by the Spearman-Brown Prophecy formula. The scaling of the instrument seems to be satisfactory judging from the foregoing data.

[1325]

McAdory Art Test. All grades, colleges, and art schools; 1929; $15.75 per folio of 72 plates; 40¢ per 25 record sheets; nontimed (90) minutes; Margaret

McAdory; New York: Bureau of Publications, Teachers College, Columbia University.

REFERENCES

1 McAdory, Margaret. *The Construction and Validation of an Art Test.* Columbia University, Teachers College, Contributions to Education, No. 383. New York: Bureau of Publications, the College, 1929. Pp. 35. $1.50.
2 Bird, Milton H. Chapter 6, "Tests," pp. 37-48. In *A Study in Aesthetics.* Harvard University, Harvard Monographs in Education, No. 11; Studies in Educational Psychology and Educational Measurement. Cambridge, Mass.: Harvard University Press, 1932. Pp. ix, 117. $1.00. Paper. (London: Oxford University Press. 4s. 6d.)
3 Carroll, Herbert A., and Eurich, Alvin C. "Abstract Intelligence and Art Appreciation." *J Ed Psychol* 23:214-20 Mr '32.
4 Carroll, Herbert A. "What Do the Meier-Seashore and the McAdory Art Tests Measure?" *J Ed Res* 26:661-5 My '33.
5 Kintner, Madaline, under the supervision of Paul S. Achilles. *The Measurement of Artistic Abilities:* A Survey of Scientific Studies in the Field of Graphic Arts, pp. 8-10, 18-20. Prepared for the Carnegie Foundation. New York: Psychological Corporation, 1933. Pp. 90. $0.10. Paper.
6 Siceloff, Margaret McAdory, and Woodyard, Ella. *Validation and Standardization of the McAdory Art Test.* New York: Bureau of Publications, Teachers College, Columbia University, 1933. Pp. 33. $0.75. Paper.
7 Steggerda, Morris. "The McAdory Art Test Applied to Navaho Indian Children." *J Comp Psychol* 22:283-5 O '36.
8 Voss, Mildred Dow. "The Validity and Reliability of a Modified Form of the McAdory Art Test for Use at Lower Grade Levels," pp. 68-84. In *Studies in the Psychology of Art, Vol. II.* Edited by Norman C. Meier. Psychological Monographs, Vol. 48, No. 1, Whole No. 213; University of Iowa Studies in Psychology, No. 19. Columbus, Ohio: American Psychological Association, Ohio State University, 1936. Pp. xi, 172. $2.50. Paper.
9 Bingham, Walter V. *Aptitudes and Aptitude Testing,* pp. 352-3. New York and London: Harper & Bros., 1937. Pp. ix, 390. $3.00; 10s. 6d.
10 Dewar, Heather. "A Comparison of Tests of Artistic Appreciation." *Brit J Ed Psychol* 8:29-49 F '38.
11 Paterson, Donald G.; Schneidler, Gwendolen G.; and Williamson, Edmund G. *Student Guidance Techniques,* pp. 213-6. New York: McGraw-Hill Book Co., Inc., 1938. Pp. xviii, 316. $3.00. (London: McGraw-Hill Publishing Co., Ltd., 18s.)
12 Steggerda, Morris, and Macomber, Eileen. "A Revision of the McAdory Art Test Applied to American Indians, Dutch Whites and College Graduates." *J Comp Psychol* 26:349-353 O '38.
13 Horton, Samuel P. *A Study of Factors in the Art Appreciation Test, Worksample 172.* Human Engineering Laboratory, Technical Report No. 23. Boston, Mass.: the Laboratory, 1939. Pp. vii, 42. $1.00. Paper, mimeographed.

Norman C. Meier, Associate Professor of Psychology, The State University of Iowa. The test follows a multiple-choice plan, each plate having four variations of the same theme, each to be ranked in order of merit. Scoring is on a basis of one point for each placement corresponding to the key. The scoring norms were first derived by obtaining a consensus of rankings by 100 competent judges. This was later revised by the Division of Psychology, Institute of Educational Research at Teachers College, Columbia University, with the result that several of the 72 plates are now not scored and in several other instances the rankings of two places of equal correctness.

The test is usually given individually but may be given to a group by having the plates displayed along a rack or from a cord. Grade and age norms are now available and the test theory is presented in the bulletin, *The Construction and Validation of an Art Test.*[1]

The test materials form six groups—furniture and utensils, texture and clothing, architecture, shape and line arrangements, dark and light masses, and color. The selection, therefore, has the advantage of including practical material along with the disadvantage of basing a test on material which is subject to changes in taste or prevailing interests and vagaries of design. Automobiles, furniture and clothing particularly are cases in point, and to a lesser extent architecture. In the reviewer's opinion, this is a basic weakness which can not be wholly overcome by the thoroughgoing and wholly admirable statistical derivation of scoring procedure and norms.

The test classifies as a functional test of aesthetic judgment and is designed to meet the needs of a general test of art appreciation in educational, vocational, and consumer fields. Because of the variety and prevailing utilitarian character of the materials, it has high interest value to the subject which compensates for the rather long period required for its administration. The preparation of the test materials represents an effort, extending over a period of six years followed by considerable labor (6,000 subjects) on the part of the Institute of Educational Research to secure a commendable degree of standardization which, however, is limited to the New York City area. Save for the possibility that time may outmode some of the prevailing standards on which both the scoring norms and the consensuses were based, the test represents a definite achievement in providing a test of general art appreciation.

Edwin Ziegfeld, Instructor in Fine Arts, Columbia Univerity. The *McAdory Art Test* is based on the assumption that a measure of an individual's judgment in art can be secured by the degree to which his ranking of art objects agrees with that of art experts. The test consists of 72 plates each containing four items which the subject is required to rank in order of merit. Plates include examples of a wide variety of objects such as furniture, utensils, clothing, architecture, painting, and other plastic and graphic art objects. Some of the plates are in color—a commendable feature, since most published art tests are in black and white only.

The *McAdory Art Test* was carefully constructed, validated, and standardized. The test reliability varies with different groups, Mc-

Adory herself reporting coefficients from .79 to .93, the highest for an unselected group of adults. As with all available art tests, the correlation with intelligence is low, and girls score significantly higher than boys. The test measures either innate talent or traits not generally subject to improvement in art classes, as training does not appear to alter scores significantly. Nothing is known of its correlation with creative ability.

Although from all external appearances the test is an excellent instrument for educational purposes, the results obtained with it are on the whole disappointing and must be used with discretion. In particular, those using the test should remember that there is no evidence that this test measures creative art ability. A high score on the test does not necessarily indicate pronounced creative art ability and a relatively low score does not prove that the person has little creative art ability. Creative art ability is evidently a distinct trait. Furthermore, the correlation of the *McAdory Art Test* with other measures of art judgment is generally low. An exception is the *Christensen Test of Appreciation of Art,* containing items of the same type, and with which there is a correlation coefficient as high as the reliability of the Christensen test. Experimental evidence has indicated that art judgment is very specific, and there is little relation between judgments in different fields. The *McAdory Art Test* measures well what it measures, but it is not certain what this trait is. Until better art aptitude tests are available, a subjective opinion on a student's work is a more valid index of his ability than a score on any art test.

The *Meier-Seashore Art Judgment Test* seems to be slightly superior to the *McAdory Art Test* for the following reasons: it requires less time and is easier to administer; it correlates more highly with college teachers' ratings of art students (no studies have been done at lower levels); it correlates more highly with scores of other art and intelligence tests; and it differentiates art majors from non-art majors more sharply.

[1326]

Meier-Seashore Art Judgment Test. Grades 7-12; 1929-30; 1 form; 75¢ per book of test pictures; 10¢ per manual; $2.00 per 100 record sheets; 90¢ per specimen set; nontimed (45-50) minutes; Norman Charles Meier and Carl Emil Seashore; Iowa City, Iowa: Bureau of Educational Research and Service, State University of Iowa.

REFERENCES

1 MEIER, NORMAN CHARLES. *Aesthetic Judgment as a Measure of Art Talent.* University of Iowa Studies, Vol. 1, No. 19; Series on Aims and Progress of Research. Iowa City, Iowa: the University, August 1926. Pp. 30.
2 MEIER, NORMAN C. "Special Artistic Talent." *Psychol B* 25:265-71 My '28.
3 SEASHORE, CARL E. "Meier-Seashore Art Judgment Test." *Sci* 69:380 Ap 5 '29.
4 MURRAY, ELSIE. "Some Uses and Misuses of the Term Aesthetic." *Am J Psychol* 42:640-4 O '30.
5 EURICH, ALVIN C., AND CARROLL, HERBERT A. "Group Differences in Art Judgment." *Sch and Soc* 34:204-6 Ag 8 '31.
6 FARNSWORTH, PAUL R., AND MISUMI, ISSEI. "Notes on the Meier-Seashore Art Judgment Test." *J Appl Psychol* 15:418-20 Ag '31.
7 BIRD, MILTON H. Chapter 6, "Tests," pp. 37-48. In *A Study in Aesthetics.* Harvard University, Harvard Monographs in Education, No. 11; Studies in Educational Psychology and Educational Measurement. Cambridge, Mass.: Harvard University Press, 1932. Pp. ix, 117. $1.00. Paper. (London: Oxford University Press. 4s. 6d.)
8 CARROLL, HERBERT A., AND EURICH, ALVIN C. "Abstract Intelligence and Art Appreciation." *J Ed Psychol* 23:214-20 Mr '32.
9 CARROLL, HERBERT A. "What Do the Meier-Seashore and the McAdory Art Tests Measure?" *J Ed Res* 26:661-5 My '33.
10 KINTNER, MADALINE, under the supervision of Paul S. Achilles. *The Measurement of Artistic Abilities*: A Survey of Scientific Studies in the Field of Graphic Arts, pp. 8-10, 14-7. Prepared for the Carnegie Foundation. New York: Psychological Corporation, 1933. Pp. 90. $0.10. Paper.
11 BERGEN, GARRET L. *Use of Tests in the Adjustment Service,* pp. 58-9. Adjustment Service Series Report [No.] 4. New York: American Adult Association for Adult Education, 1935. Pp. 70. Paper. Out of print.
12 BINGHAM, WALTER V. *Aptitudes and Aptitude Testing,* pp. 350-2. New York and London: Harper & Bros., 1937. Pp. ix, 390. $3.00; 10s. 6d.
13 DEWAR, HEATHER. "A Comparison of Tests of Artistic Appreciation." *Brit J Ed Psychol* 8:29-49 F '38.
14 PATERSON, DONALD G.; SCHNEIDLER, GWENDOLEN G.; AND WILLIAMSON, EDMUND G. *Student Guidance Techniques,* pp. 210-3. New York: McGraw-Hill Book Co., Inc., 1938. Pp. xviii, 316. $3.00. (London: McGraw-Hill Publishing Co., Ltd., 18s.)
15 SISSON, E. DONALD. "Suggestion in Art Judgment." *J Gen Psychol* 18:433-5 Ap '38.

Paul R. Farnsworth, Acting Professor of Social Psychology, The University of Wisconsin. Before evaluating the *Meier-Seashore Art Judgment Test,* the critic would do well to read Appendix A of the manual which accompanies the tests. In this the authors offer a rather unusual definition of natural capacity as it refers to art talent. "It does not necessarily involve inborn or inherited facility," they say. Rather, capacity implies "an untaught facility in perceiving aesthetic quality." If such a definition is accepted, the critics can pick no quarrel with the authors' claims that their test detects capacity. One of their proofs lies in the fact that many people without formal art training score well on the test. This finding must not be taken to mean that art training can never improve test scores; even a relatively small amount of pertinent training can raise certain subjects' scores.

When compared with its most potent rival in the art judgment field, the *McAdory Art Test,* the Meier-Seashore wins on at least two counts. (*a*) The majority of the "correct" items (plates) are more valid in the sense that they have withstood the test of time, i.e., they have been created by so-called great masters.

(*b*) The items are less affected by fashion changes. Already many of the McAdory items are hopelessly out of date. The McAdory wins in being a trifle more reliable. However, the Meier-Seashore has sufficient reliability for most purposes.

To be found in the Meier-Seashore test manual are references to the publications which contain the substantiating data. As all too often tests are put on the market without such corroborating data, the Meier-Seashore policy deserves much praise.

The only question this reviewer wishes to raise anent the claims made by Meier and Seashore refers to the idea that the test "measures the key-capacity, . . . the most trustworthy and significant *index* to talent and to probable success in an art career." This statement seems rather a bold one to make while the philosophy of the arts is in its present confused state. One might imagine that an executant rather than a judgment capacity would furnish a more significant index to talent. However, time will judge the correctness of the authors' assertion.

Aulus Ward Saunders, Head of the Department of Art, State Normal School, Oswego, New York. The test is in the form of a booklet of 125 pairs of pictures. Each pair is presented as a separate situation in which the subject makes a choice of preference between the two pictures, identical except for one unlike portion. The unlike portion is arranged with the intention of making one of the pictures inferior aesthetically to its near-duplicate. The subject selects from each pair of pictures the one which is more artistic, more pleasing, more satisfying to him. The test is an individual capacity measure, requiring something less than an hour to take.

Not attempting to cover a wide range of reactions that might possibly determine art ability the test singles out aesthetic judgment as being a crucial factor and centers all its attention on that quality. This basis is definitely acceptable since taste or judgment is vital in the art situation, and is a variable that should permit of reliable measurement.

In carrying out the mechanics of the test the authors were evidently intent upon designing a measure that would be clear-cut and decisive. Therefore they chose to measure perception of quality rather than the production of it. The test recognizes only some component sensitivities in the total scheme of recognition of quality in art, namely rhythm, proportion of space, balance of mass, unity and harmony of treatment, and ignores other factors that are perhaps less easily isolated and measured. Consequently the caliber of art represented is determined by the presence, largely, of these several qualities. However, the result is acceptable in that a definite difference in art quality is represented in the two pictures making up each test situation. The test would have been improved by an increase in the size of the pictures, and by the use of color. It would be more valuable if two forms were available, rather than only one. As it stands, it is valid in its material and treatment and represents a useful measure of individual sensitivity to aesthetic organization of graphic form.

[1327]

Selective Art Aptitude Test. Grades 7 and over; ages 14 and over; 1939-40; 1 form; $1.34 per permanent test section, including a student's test section; 28¢ per student's test section; 68¢ per examiner's manual and keys; 76¢ per scoring and interpretation manual; $1.34 per validation, reliability, and rating manual; (45) minutes; William H. Varnum; Scranton, Pa.: International Textbook Co.

[1328]

Seven Modern Paintings: Test 3.9. Grades 9-12; 1939; 1 form; "based on 7 large, framed reproductions of the following modern paintings, which can be sent only to schools in the Eight Year Study": Alexander Brook's *Portrait of My Wife*, Paul Cezanne's *House on a Hill in Provence*, George Grosz's *Central Park*, Pablo Picasso's *Figure*, Eugene Speicher's *Semi-Nude*, Maurice Sterne's *Plum Girl*, and Vincent Van Gogh's *Vegetable Garden;* 5¢ per test; 1¢ per machine-scorable answer sheet; nontimed (45) minutes; Chicago, Ill.: Evaluation in the Eight Year Study, Progressive Education Association.

[1329]

Tests in Fundamental Abilities of Visual Arts. Grades 3-12; 1927; 1 form, 3 parts; 35¢ per manual; $5.00 per color chart; 50¢ per specimen set, without color chart; 30(35) minutes per part; Alfred S. Lewerenz; Los Angeles, Calif.: California Test Bureau.
a) PART I. $2.00 per 100.
b) PART II. $2.00 per 100.
c) PART III. $3.50 per 100.

REFERENCES

1 LEWERENZ, ALFRED S. "Scientific Measurement in the Realm of Art," pp. 43-8. *1927 Yearbook of the Southwestern Educational Research and Guidance Association.* Los Angeles, Calif.: [California Test Bureau], 1927. Gratis.
2 LEWERENZ, ALFRED S. "I.Q. and Ability in Art." *Sch and Soc* 27:489-90 Ap 21 '28.
3 LEWERENZ, ALFRED S. "Sex Differences on Ability Tests in Art." *J Ed Psychol* 19:629-35 D '28.
4 LEWERENZ, ALFRED S. "Predicting Ability in Art." *J Ed Psychol* 20:702-4 D '29.
5 BIRD, MILTON H. Chapter 6, "Tests," pp. 37-48. In *A Study in Aesthetics.* Harvard University, Harvard Monographs in Education, No. 11; Studies in Educational Psychology and Educational Measurement. Cambridge, Mass.: Harvard University Press, 1932. Pp. ix, 117. $1.00. Paper. (London: Oxford University Press. 4s. 6d.)

6 KINTNER, MADELINE, under the supervision of Paul S. Achilles. *The Measurement of Artistic Abilities*: A Survey of Scientific Studies in the Field of Graphic Arts, pp. 8-10, 24-7. Prepared for the Carnegie Foundation. New York: Psychological Corporation, 1933. Pp. 90. $0.10. Paper.

Ray Faulkner, Head of the Department of Fine and Industrial Arts, Teachers College, Columbia University. The purpose of this test is to provide an instrument which will measure scientifically the art abilities developed in the public schools, and with this test as a basis to conduct studies which will improve our meager knowledge of these art activities. There is striking need for such an instrument. To date there have been few art tests, partly because of the difficulty of the problem, and partly because of the resistance of art teachers to any intrusion on their sacred domain. This is an attempt well worth attention as one way of attacking a difficult problem.

Nine separate tests are based on an analysis of art abilities into such categories as recognition of proportion, originality of line drawing, and observation of light and shade, these abilities being regarded as essential to "an appreciation of what constitutes pattern in form and color." Naturally the interpretations of this test will depend on the extent to which the user agrees with this approach to art. It is of little value to those who believe that art is an integrated activity rather than a series of separate skills, nor is it of great value to those who believe that an approach to art through such general and abstract art elements as light and shade, color, and proportion is less desirable than through such specific fields as architecture, industrial art, and the like. Thus its value is highly dependent on one's philosophy and psychology of art.

Technically, the test is well constructed. Its validity rests primarily on the fact that it is based on classroom practices of the Los Angeles schools at the time it was constructed. A correlation of .40 with marks in art classes is given as further evidence that the instrument is valid. A reliability coefficient of .87 computed on 100 pupils in grades 3 to 9 suggests that the test is sufficiently reliable for group use, but that individual scores should be treated with discretion.

Aulus Ward Saunders, Head of the Department of Art, State Normal School, Oswego, New York. Lewerenz' tests are a battery of nine arranged in three parts, as follows: Part I, (1) Recognition of Proportion, (2) Originality of Line Drawing; Part II, (3) Observation of Light and Shade, (4) Knowledge of Subject Matter Vocabulary, (5) Visual Memory of Proportion; Part III, (6) Analysis of Problems in Cylindrical Perspective, (7) Analysis of Problems in Parallel Perspective, (8) Analysis of Problems in Angular Perspective, (9) Recognition of Color.

They are meant to measure basic powers in visual art and are consequently built on an assumption that the powers listed in the test titles are basic. There is considerable doubt that such an assumption has foundation.

To being with, a number of the tests measure general intelligence rather than specific art ability, insofar as they measure anything. Tests 3, 6, 7, and 8 are of this nature—tapping the ability of the subject to perceive variations in the accepted natural pattern in outline drawings of buildings, cubes and other such objects. The fact of perspective cannot be considered coexistent with the fact of art, perspective being merely a tool serving the artist or draftsman in the production of a three-dimensional image.

Since art may be considered the production of form rather than the reproduction of it, Test 5 may be censured on this score. The test presents the shape of a vase to be studied for a period of two minutes by the subject, who then reproduces from memory the outlines of the shape. The "photographic eye" may be helpful to the artist in the same manner as a steady hand may be helpful. The expected superior ability of the artist in visual perception may very well be due to his necessity of seeing when he looks. How he gets this ability does not matter. The fact that the vase's shape is to be reproduced rather than judged places this reaction outside the field of art.

Test 9 is another psycho-physical capacity test that indicates the ability of the subject to distinguish specific color. There is no basis in the assumption that the ability to classify a color as red constitutes any part of art ability.

Tests 1 and 2 strike in the right direction. The first deals with taste, or judgment, in 15 multiple-choice situations in which the subject selects one from a group of four items in each situation. The procedure is satisfactory, but the subject matter of the test unfortunately repeats the accepted symbols, conventional forms that have been for years the stock in trade of the drawing teacher of the last generation. This same criticism is due other tests in the battery. A fairly close similarity between a knowledge of these forms as measured by the tests and grades or marks in high school art classes of this regime is to be expected. The second test is superior to the others: it is concerned with aesthetic excellence of original drawing. Ten separate areas are to receive drawings, each area being equipped with a number of dots that are to be incorporated with the drawing made in that area. Reliability is lowered by the necessity of using a 5-value scale in the scoring process.

MUSIC

[1330]

Drake Musical Memory Test: A Test of Musical Talent. Ages 8 and over; 1934; 2 forms; 25¢ per musical-score booklet of either form; 25¢ per manual; 2¢ per score sheet; 75¢ per specimen set; (25) minutes; Raleigh M. Drake; Bloomington, Ill.: Public School Publishing Co.

REFERENCES

1 DRAKE, RALEIGH M. "Four New Tests of Musical Talent." J Appl Psychol 17:136-47 Ap '33.
2 DRAKE, RALEIGH M. "The Validity and Reliability of Tests of Musical Talent." J Appl Psychol 17:447-58 Ag '33.

Paul R. Farnsworth, Acting Professor of Social Psychology, The University of Wisconsin. Research some years ago on the Seashore's *Measures of Musical Talent* made it clear that, of the capacities this battery was attempting to measure, musical memory seemed to be yielding the best results, both in the matter of validity and in reliability. It was thus quite natural that Drake should select the field of musical memory for further explorations.

The Drake test can probably be regarded as coming closer in two respects to ordinary musical experience than can the Seashore measure of tonal memory. The Drake test employs piano rather than flute tones. And it brings in the phenomena of key and time as well as note changes. Its method of presentation, however, is far less accurate. Testers, it would be imagined, vary widely in their ability to play the melodies precisely as the directions demand. Moreover, no directions are given for the metronome time. This ambiguity must contribute to further inaccuracies.

However, the reviewer's major quarrel is not with Drake's measure itself but rather with his test philosophy. Time and again he has maintained that through his musical memory test one can discover innate talent. Now a review of this sort is not the place in which to marshal the arguments against the idea that innate capacity can be tested. As a matter of fact, the very problem itself is in large part a pseudo problem. It would appear to the reviewer that about all one can reasonably say is that Drake has a fairly reliable test in the field of musical memory. His test will probably aid considerably in culling out those who will not profit in great degree by further instruction in music. But whether or not these cullings are inherently unmusical cannot be decided by an inspection of the scores on the Drake test.

James L. Mursell, Professor of Education, Columbia University. The assumption on which this test is made is that immediate recognition memory for melodic material is an important and valid sign of musical ability. The test comes in two forms; each consists of twelve melodies, and each melody is followed by a number of variants in which changes are made in key, time, and notes. These are interspersed with repetitions of the original melody. The task of the subject is to indicate with regard to each item whether it is the same or different from the original, and whether it differs in key, time, or note content. The melodies are given on the piano. It is not a speed test, but each form requires about twenty-five minutes to administer. Age norms, based on 1,979 cases, are worked out for ages 8 to 22. The split-half reliability on both forms combined is .93 for musical subjects, and .85 for nonmusical subjects. The test has been validated against estimated musicality and against a musical examination, and the coefficients are reported of .49 to .67. Just how significant this validation may be, it is difficult to say. The claim is that the test is relatively independent of musical training, a point which does not appear adequately substantiated. It is said to measure "musicality." That is the factor in common as between conductors, performers, and composers. The general notion that musical memory is a significant factor seems interesting and defensible. The test should probably be regarded as a stage in the development of a more complete battery. Its interest lies in its use of musically significant materials and situations.

[1331]
Hillbrand Sight-Singing Test. Grades 4-6; 1923; individual; 1 form; 90¢ per 25; 10¢ per specimen set; (10) minutes; E. K. Hillbrand; Yonkers, N. Y.: World Book Co.

REFERENCES

1 HILLBRAND, EARL K. *Measuring Ability in Sight-Singing.* Ann Arbor, Mich.: Edwards Bros., 1924. Pp. 41. Paper. Out of print.

Alton O'Steen, Research Associate, Bureau of Educational Research, The Ohio State University. This is a test to measure the mechanics of oral sight reading in vocal music by individuals. This rather narrow purpose is met by the test to some degree. However, the range of difficulty of the items of the test is far too small. There are no test items using sixteenth notes or dotted notes and there is only one chromatic in the entire test. No six-eight meter is included.

The chief value I see in the test is the suggestion of a useful way to record errors in sight reading as they occur. The music reading ability measured by such a test as this is not the kind we see people use when they actually undertake to sing new music. Tests of individual sight-singing ability should, in my opinion, have a relatively small place in the program of music education in our schools.

[1332]
Knuth Achievement Tests in Music: For Recognition of Certain Rhythmic and Melodic Aspects. Grades 3-4, 5-6, 7-12; 1936; 2 forms, 3 levels; $1.35 per 25; 35¢ per 25 answer sheets; 60¢ per manual; 75¢ per specimen set; nontimed (40-45) minutes; William E. Knuth; Minneapolis, Minn.: Educational Test Bureau, Inc.
a) DIVISION 1. Grades 3-4.
b) DIVISION 2. Grades 5-6.
c) DIVISION 3. Grades 7-12.

REFERENCES

1 KNUTH, WILLIAM E. *The Construction and Validation of Music Tests Designed to Measure Certain Aspects of Sight-reading.* Unpublished doctor's thesis, University of California, 1932. Pp. 390.

Carl E. Seashore, Professor of Psychology, The State University of Iowa. This test is accompanied by a complete manual containing sections on purpose, validity, reliability, procedure, administration, scoring keys, percentile norms, and use of the test results, together with the complete musical scores.

The test materials needed for each student consist of a test booklet containing the test material in the form of musical scores, a device for making a complete record on one sheet without writing on the test material, and the record sheet. These materials are all published in excellent type and format; the directions are clear and explicit; and the use of material is economical in that the same test material can be used an indefinite number of times—the only thing consumed being the single record blank.

The test provides "a valid and reliable measure of the pupil's ability to recognize and comprehend music from its notation." This is accomplished through the measuring of complete musical phrases composed of melodies containing certain specific idioms which are presented to the pupil through the medium of the piano, each in a single playing. The general scheme of procedure is on the principle of the four-response multiple-choice type of exercise. The instructor first strikes a full chord which sounds the key and then, after a pause, plays four measures which represent one of the four musical scores in the hands of the student. The pupil is directed to recognize the last two measures after hearing a single playing and place a cross in the square which represents the melody played. In general, the trials proceed in the order of difficulty. There are forty trials for each division.

The whole procedure is well conceived in terms of scientific measurement in that it becomes a distinctive measure of achievement in a single specific issue and the conclusions drawn therefrom are limited to the factors measured. The validity of the test is self-evident in that it deals with actual musical situations and the statistical treatment seems satisfactory. Specific elements may be isolated statistically. The test sets up one of the distinctive goals toward which sight reading is directed. It also motivates achievement in that there is a well defined goal. This test may well be regarded as setting a pattern for coming tests in musical achievement.

For reviews by Jay W. Fay and James L. Mursell, see 1085.

[1333]
Kwalwasser-Ruch Test of Musical Accomplishment. Grades 4-12; 1924-27; 1 form; 6¢ per test; 15¢ per specimen set; 40(50) minutes; Jacob Kwalwasser and G. M. Ruch; Iowa City, Iowa: Bureau of Educational Research and Service, State University of Iowa.

REFERENCES

1 KWALWASSER, JACOB. *Tests and Measurements in Music,* pp. 65-73, 107-37. Boston, Mass.: C. C. Birchard and Co., 1927. Pp. xiii, 146. $2.00.

William S. Larson, Chairman of the Music Education Department and Psychologist in Music, Eastman School of Music, The Uni-

versity of Rochester. This test is in ten parts: Test 1, Knowledge of Musical Symbols and Terms; 2, Recognition of Syllable Names; 3, Detection of Pitch Errors in a Familiar Melody; 4, Detection of Time Errors in a Familiar Melody; 5, Recognition of Pitch Names; 6, Knowledge of Time Signatures; 7, Knowledge of Key Signatures; 8, Knowledge of Note Values; 9, Knowledge of Rest Values; and 10, Recognition of Familiar Melodies from Notation. Each part has a definite time limit of from three to eight minutes; the total working time is forty minutes. It is designed for use in grades four to twelve, and the manual of directions gives norms in deciles for each grade from four through eight and a composite norm for grades nine through twelve.

In the manual the authors give the reliability of the test as .97. They state that the validity of the test rests primarily upon the specifications adopted by the Music Supervisors' National Conference in 1921. However, reference to the seven recommended standards of attainment of this conference indicates that this test could apply only to a limited part of these recommended standards of accomplishment. It is in this respect that even the title of this test might be considered a misnomer to a considerable extent, for the term, musical accomplishment, usually infers musical progress based on actual musical performance, be it vocal or instrumental. And it is evident from a glance at the names of the various parts of the test that probably with the exception of parts three and ten, which make demands on musical imagery and related musical aptitudes, the test as a whole is built upon the factual or mechanical elements of musical notation, an aspect of musical learning that, incidentally, is relatively easy to measure objectively. As it is generally conceded that there is little correlation between musical talent and intelligence, the brighter but unmusical child would have a decided advantage over a more musically talented but less intelligent student in a test largely factual in construction; it would not necessarily mean that the student who makes a high score in this test would have the necessary sensory and motor capacities basic for musical accomplishment. Therefore it is advisable in its use to weigh the importance of the factual part of musical accomplishment with which this test is largely concerned, and

consider its validity as a measure of musical accomplishment in this light. Flagrant errors have been made in the interpretation of data of studies having to do with the relationship of talent to accomplishment, etc., because the factual elements in tests of this kind have been accepted as complete and valid criteria of musical accomplishment.

This test is well constructed and can be used profitably by those who will weigh the relative importance of the aspects of musical accomplishment found therein.

James L. Mursell, Professor of Education, Columbia University. The Kwalwasser-Ruch test is based upon the recommendations of the Music Supervisors' National Conference, as published in 1921, and proposes to establish the items regarded as important by that body. These included such matters as knowledge of musical symbols, recognition of syllable names, detection of errors in a melody, knowledge of time and key signatures, and the like. That is to say, it is in the main a test of musical knowledge and of an area of knowledge defined as stated above. It has a reported reliability of .97. Grade norms from the fourth to the twelfth grade inclusive are worked out for 5,415 pupils. In format and physical makeup the test meets practical standards quite adequately. It has, like most other standard achievement tests, a definite usefulness in situations where the outcomes to be measured are of considerable importance, but comparatively little beyond its field.

[1334]
Kwalwasser Test of Musical Information and Appreciation. Grades 9-16; 1927; 1 form; 5¢ per test; 10¢ per specimen set; 40(45) minutes; Jacob Kwalwasser; Iowa City, Iowa: Bureau of Educational Research and Service, State University of Iowa.

REFERENCES
1 SEMEONOFF, BORIS. "A New Approach to the Testing of Musical Ability." *Brit J Psychol* 30:326-40 Ap '40.

Raleigh M. Drake, Associate Professor of Psychology, Wesleyan College, Macon, Georgia. Although a test of this type is necessarily limited largely to use with special classes who have taken a special course in music information (one is hardly justified in calling it appreciation), this test covers a wide range and, because of this wide sampling, should have a satisfactory validity.

The test could be improved in a few details which would facilitate scoring. Some of the subtests, those having true-false, or alternative answers, require the right-minus-wrong correction which increases the scoring time considerably. This correction is not necessary where percentile norms are used as is the case with this test. There is no reason why the entire test cannot be scored as a point scale, or further effort saved by keeping the score in the number of mistakes rather than the number correct. Further consideration could be shown the scorer by making all of the answer-key sections align with the corresponding sections in the test. A description of the number and selection of cases for the construction of the norms is much in order, although they appear on the surface to be adequate, judging by the tremendous range of scores.

Karl W. Gehrkens, Professor of School Music, Oberlin College. The purpose of this test is to determine whether or not high school and college students (who may or may not have taken a course in music appreciation) have acquired a mass of information which, presumably, constitutes at least a part of what is termed "music appreciation." The material upon which the student is tested is in the first place selected from the bias of the instrumentalist who has but little sympathy with vocal music; and is in the second place not too wisely chosen at best. Finally, the test was published in 1927 so that some of the material included is entirely out of date, as for example, its reference to artists like Galli Curci, Mary Garden, and DeGogorza.

But an even more serious criticism is the fact that, basically, the test attempts to measure music appreciation and it is a grave question whether such factual material as this has much to do with the individual's reaction to music. Certainly the pupil's ability to recognize the violin as a bowed string instrument and the oboe as a wind instrument is worth something and such knowledge concerning the music itself will undoubtedly increase his appreciation. But whether the statement "Clara Wieck became the wife of Schumann" has any similar effect is open to grave doubt.

Our chief criticism of the test, then, is that it is not valid. It tests the pupils for certain items of information about music under the assumption that these constitute an important ingredient in music appreciation. But it would be possible to know all the items and yet not appreciate music at all. And even at that the items are not well chosen and the test would have to be drastically revised to have any value at all at this time.

So far as mechanics is concerned the test is easy to administer, entirely objective, and it is accompanied by a table of norms making it possible for the administrator of the test to ascertain at least in a general way how his pupils stand in comparison with students in other schools.

[1335]

McCauley Examination in Public School Music.
Grades 4-9; 1933; 1 form; $1.50 per 25; 20¢ per specimen set; (100) minutes; Clara J. McCauley; Knoxville, Tenn.: Jos. E. Avent.

Alton O'Steen, Research Associate, Bureau of Educational Research, The Ohio State University. According to the manual of directions this test is "to ascertain the degree to which pupils are actually learning what is supposedly being taught." This is far too expansive a claim. The test actually measures sight and oral identification of melodies; certain information about types of compositions, musical instruments, famous names in music, and musical terms; the ability to identify syllable and letter names of notes and a paper-and-pencil knowledge of note and rest values, meter and key signatures, and chromatics. What is "supposedly being taught" in music is far more than this. The test does not include the use in musical situations of any of the skills and facts it purports to measure. Natural, lifelike situations are, of course, difficult to achieve in a test.

The test is considerably more comprehensive than the Gildersleeve test which is constructed along similar lines. This comprehensiveness has made the test too long for a single administration and anyone using the test would do well to plan for at least an hour and a half.

The manual leaves much to be desired. Only meager information is given about the methods used in determining items to be included, in defining the terms used, and in computing reliability. One wonders, for example, how "requiem" got into the test and why a cantata is defined so academically, as a "setting for sustained thought, by means of solos and choruses." There is even a rather serious typographical error, the word "renumber" being printed as "remember."

Perhaps before long we will concern ourselves with the measurement of such important objectives of music education such as voluntary singing outside of school, choosing a variety of music on the radio, and participation in church and community music groups. In the meantime, if it seems desirable to measure knowledge of syllable names and the like, it is probably better to construct your own test on the basis of your own teaching.

[1336]
Musical Achievement Test. Grades 4-8; 1933; 1 form; $3.15 per 100; 10¢ per specimen set; 22(30) minutes; Glenn Gildersleeve and Wayne Soper; New York: Bureau of Publications, Teachers College, Columbia University.

Raleigh M. Drake, Associate Professor of Psychology, Wesleyan College, Macon, Georgia. As an achievement test designed to measure certain elementary knowledge of musical notation, use of symbols, recognition of familiar melodies, types of compositions, authors and their works, and definitions of musical terms, this test fills a restricted need. Most any music teacher could construct one as good in a few minutes and it would probably fit the individual teaching situation even better. As a standard of comparison from school to school, or section to section, however, it will be found serviceable. If it is to find any considerable use it would gain much from a revision. Percentile norms for each grade from 4 through 8 would give a much more adequate basis for interpreting test scores. Only "tentative medians" are given for each class at present, although all data must be available for percentile scores since the "tentative medians" are based on 3,000 cases. Much improvement is possible in the method of scoring. The four subtests are scored separately, with two of them receiving special weightings of 3 and 2 respectively. No basis for this weighting is stated. Such a procedure is to be avoided unless based on some very definite principle indicated as a result of statistical analysis, or if each subtest is to have a separate norm so that the total test performance can be diagnosed. Such weighting, if desirable, could much better have been accomplished by incorporating it in the construction of the test by lengthening such subtests. This procedure also has the advantage of increasing the reliability of the test.

[1337]
Providence Inventory Test in Music. Grades 4-9; 1932; 1 form; $1.10 per 25; 15¢ per specimen set; 28(45) minutes; Richard D. Allen, Walter H. Butter-

field, and Marguerite Tully; Yonkers, N. Y.: World Book Co.

William S. Larson, Chairman of the Music Education Department and Psychologist in Music, Eastman School of Music, The University of Rochester. This test contains ten sections: 1, Naming Notes; 2, Placing "Do"; 3, Naming Note Values; 4, Naming Key Signatures; 5, Naming Measure Signatures; 6, Naming Rest Values; 7, Naming Syllables; 8, Naming Melodies; 9, Naming Syllables (Bass Staff); and 10, Naming Symbols. It is intended for grades four through nine. Each part has a definite time limit of from one to six minutes; the total working time is twenty-eight minutes.

The manual contains a table of norms in deciles for each of grades 4-9, and an associated letter rating scale of A, B+, B, B−, C+, C, C−, D+, D, D−, and E.

The authors state that they designed this test to be an improved measure, especially in its use in the junior high school grades, for they believe that some of the tests on the market contain too many elements that are not covered in the regular public school music course. They explain that its purpose is the measurement of the ability to read and understand music, and they claim that it has helped teachers and supervisors to know and understand the reading difficulties of children in the field of music, thus allowing remedial instruction to be made more specific. They further claim that the test is most useful in measuring the ability to read music when the student enters junior high school and in evaluating growth in the same ability as a result of three years of junior high school music instruction.

An examination of the various parts of the test shows that, with the exception of Part 8, the items are almost entirely drawn from the rudiments of music which are factual in nature, and—a matter of importance to test-builders—they constitute a part of musical achievement which is readily adaptable to objective measurement. In this test, as with most tests of this kind, it is questionable that an indication of proficiency in this type of factual learning necessarily means that the student will have the ability to read music, for capacities of musical talent, to which the more mechanical aspects of music reading do not directly relate, are undoubtedly of prime importance and basic for musical response. The use of a test of this kind for comparative purposes before and after a period of training such as indicated above may have the effect of directing the attention of the teacher toward the more mechanical aspects of music reading at the expense of the more musical values, thus emphasizing a procedure which is now entirely too prevalent in school music teaching in the opinion of many prominent music educators. This issue is of paramount importance in the use of this kind of test from the point of view of considering its validity as a measure of musical achievement.

Clara J. McCauley, Supervisor of Music, Public Schools, Knoxville, Tennessee. This test in the field of public school music rightly does not attempt to measure musical aptitude. It covers the following phases of music: naming notes; placing "do"; naming note values; naming key signatures; naming measure signatures; naming rest values; naming syllables; naming melodies (at sight); naming syllables (bass staff); and naming symbols.

This test squares with the criteria of objectivity, ease of administering and scoring, the availability of grade norms, and alternative forms. It also has a useful and well-prepared manual of directions.

This test measures up to the criterion of validity less adequately than it measures up to the other criteria. Validity is the degree to which a test adequately samples, or parallels, that which is usually taught in the subject and grades concerned. For example, the *Providence Inventory Test in Music* does not measure the following outcomes of music education: knowledge of musical terms employed in grades 4 to 9; recognition knowledge of the composers of familiar melodies; aural recognition of familiar melodies; knowledge of composition types; and recognition knowledge of musical instruments. These latter phases of music are usually found in elementary courses of study in public school music, especially incidentally.

[1338]

Seashore Measures of Music Talent, Revised edition. Grades 5-16 and adults; 1919-39; 2 series of 3 records each; $9 per album of 6 records including manual and 200 test blanks; $1.50 per record; 50¢ per manual; 40¢ per 200 test blanks; (60-80) minutes; Carl E. Seashore, Don Lewis, and Joseph G. Saetveit; Camden, N. J.: RCA Manufacturing Co., Inc.

a) SERIES A. For the testing of unselected groups in general surveys.

b) SERIES B. For the testing of musicians and prospective or actual students of music.

REFERENCES

1 SEASHORE, CARL E. "Measurement of Musical Talent." *Music Q* 1:129-48 Ja '15.
2 SEASHORE, CARL EMIL. *The Psychology of Musical Talent.* New York: Silver, Burdett and Co., 1919. Pp. xvi, 288. $3.00.
2.1 GILLILAND, A. R., AND JENSEN, C. R. "The Reliability of the Seashore Phonograph Record for the Measurement of Pitch Discrimination." *J Exp Psychol* 5:214-22 Je '22.
2.2 HEINLEIN, CHRISTIAN PAUL. "An Experimental Study of the Seashore Consonance Test." *J Exp Psychol* 8:408-33 D '25.
2.3 MOSHER, RAYMOND M. *A Study of the Group Method of Measurement of Sight-Singing.* Columbia University, Teachers College, Contributions to Education, No. 194. New York: Bureau of Publications, the College, 1925. Pp. vi, 75. Out of print.
3 HOLLINGWORTH, LETA S. "Musical Sensitivity of Children Who Test Above 135 IQ (Stanford-Binet)." *J Ed Psychol* 17:95-109 F '26.
3.1 LANIER, LYLE H. "Prediction of the Reliability of Mental Tests and Tests of Special Abilities." *J Exp Psychol* 10:69-113 Ap '27.
4 BROWN, ANDREW W. "The Reliability and Validity of the Seashore Tests of Musical Talent." *J Appl Psychol* 12:468-76 O '28.
5 FARNSWORTH, PAUL R. "The Spearman-Brown Prophecy Formula and the Seashore Tests." *J Ed Psychol* 19:586-8 N '28.
5.1 HEINLEIN, CHRISTIAN PAUL. "A Brief Discussion of the Nature and Function of Melodic Configuration in Tonal Memory, with Critical Reference to the Seashore Tonal Memory Test." *J Genetic Psychol* 35:45-61 Mr '28.
6 McGINNIS, ESTHER. "Seashore's Measures of Musical Ability Applied to Children of the Pre-School Age." *Am J Psychol* 40:620-3 O '28.
7 SCHOEN, M. "Musical Talent and its Measurement." *Music Q* 14:255-82 '28.
8 STANTON, HAZEL M. "Measuring Musical Talent: Seashore Tests as Administrative Aids." *Personnel J* 7:286-92 D '28.
9 VITELES, MORRIS S. "The Mental Status of the Negro." *Ann Am Acad Pol and Social Sci* 140:166-77 N '28.
10 WRIGHT, FRANCIS A. "The Correlation between Achievement and Capacity in Music." *J Ed Res* 17:50-6 Ja '28.
11 BROOM, M. E. "A Note Concerning the Seashore Measures of Musical Talent." *Sch and Soc* 30:274-5 Ag 24 '29.
12 FARNSWORTH, PAUL R. "Reply to Dr. Lanier's Note on the Seashore Tests." *J Ed Psychol* 20:693-4 D '29.
13 HEINLEIN, CHRISTIAN PAUL. "Critique of the Seashore Consonance Test: A Reply to Dr. Larson." *Psychol R* 36:524-42 N '29.
14 HIGHSMITH, J. A. "Selecting Musical Talent." *J Appl Psychol* 13:486-93 O '29.
15 LANIER, LYLE H. "Note on Reliability Predictions for the Seashore Music Tests." *J Ed Psychol* 20:691-2 D '29.
16 SALISBURY, FRANK S., AND SMITH, HAROLD B. "Prognosis of Sight Singing Ability of Normal School Students." *J Appl Psychol* 13:425-39 O '29.
17 STANTON, HAZEL M. *Prognosis of Musical Achievement*: Study of the Predictive Value of Tests in the Selection of Degree and Certificate Students for the Eastman School of Music. University of Rochester, Eastman School of Music, Studies in Psychology, Vol. 1, No. 4. Rochester, N. Y.: Eastman School of Music, 1929. Pp. 89. $1.00. Paper.
18 STANTON, HAZEL M. "Psychological Tests—A Factor in Admission to the Eastman School of Music." *Sch and Soc* 30:889-91 D 28 '29.
19 WILLIAMS, C. O. "A Critique of Measures of Musical Talent." *Music Sup J* 16:67-81 O '29.
20 LARSON, RUTH CREWDSON. *Studies on Seashore's "Measures of Musical Talent."* University of Iowa Studies, First Series, No. 174; Series on Aims and Progress of Research, Vol. 2, No. 6. Iowa City, Iowa: the University, March 1930. Pp. 83. $0.75. Paper.
21 LARSON, WILLIAM SEVERT. "Measurement of Musical Talent for the Prediction of Success in Instrumental Music," pp. 33-73. In *University of Iowa Studies in Psychology, No. XIII.* Edited by Christian A. Ruckmick. Psychological Monographs, Vol. 40, No. 1, Whole No. 181. Columbus, Ohio: American Psychological Association, Ohio State University, 1930. Pp. v, 214. $3.25. Paper.
22 McCARTHY, DOROTHEA. "A Study of the Seashore Measures of Musical Talent." *J Appl Psychol* 14:437-55 O '30.
23 MOOS, J. C. "Yardstick Applied to Musical Talent." *Mus Q* 16:238-62 Ap '30.
24 SEASHORE, C. E. "Measures of Musical Talent: A Reply to Dr. C. P. Heinlein." *Psychol R* 37:178-83 Mr '30.
25 WILSON, M. E. "The Prognostic Value for Music Success of Several Types of Tests." *Music Supervisors J* 16:83 '30.
26 FARNSWORTH, PAUL R. "An Historical, Critical, and Experimental Study of the Seashore-Kwalwasser Test Battery." *Genetic Psychol Monog* 9:291-393 My '31.
27 JOHNSON, GUY B. "A Summary of Negro Scores on the Seashore Musical Talent Tests." *J Comp Psychol* 11:383-93 Ap '31.
28 MERRY, RALPH V. "Adapting the Seashore Musical Talent Tests for Use with Blind Pupils." *Teach Forum* 3:15-9 Mr '31.
29 MURSELL, J. L. "Evaluation of the Seashore Tests." *Mus Superv J* 17:62+ My '31.

30 TILSON, LOWELL M. "A Study of the Predictive Value of Music Talent Tests for Teacher Training Purposes," pp. 5-20. In *Eighteenth Annual Conference on Educational Measurements*: Held at Indiana University, April 24 and 25, 1931. Bulletin of the School of Education, Indiana University, Vol. 7, No. 5. Bloomington, Ind.: Indiana University Bookstore, 1931. Pp. 80. $0.50. Paper.

31 TILSON, LOWELL MASON. "A Study of the Predictive Value of Musical Talent Tests for Teacher-Training Purposes." *Teach Col J* 3:101-29 N '31.

32 FARNSWORTH, PAUL R. "Psychology and Music: A Discussion of Certain Points of Contact." *Sch Music* 32:3-4 N-D '32.

33 MORE, GRACE VAN DYKE. "Prognostic Testing in Music on the College Level: An Investigation Carried on at the North Carolina College for Women." *J Ed Res* 26:199-212 N '32.

34 MURSELL, JAMES L. "Measuring Musical Ability and Achievement: A Study of the Correlations of Seashore Test Scores and Other Variables." *J Ed Res* 25:116-26 F '32.

35 TILSON, L. M. "Music Talent Tests for Teacher-Training Purposes." *Music Superv J* 18:26 '32.

36 WHITLEY, MARY T. "A Comparison of the Seashore and the Kwalwasser-Dykema Music Tests." *Teach Col Rec* 33:731-51 My '32.

37 CHADWICK, J. ELBERT. "Predicting Success in Sight-Singing." *J Appl Psychol* 17:671-4 D '33.

38 DRAKE, RALEIGH M. "The Validity and Reliability of Tests of Musical Talent." *J Appl Psychol* 17:447-58 Ag '33.

39 STANTON, HAZEL M. "Quantitative Yard-Stick for the Measurement of Musical Capacities." *Eug News* 18:78-81 Jl-Ag '33.

40 STANTON, HAZEL M. "Testing the Cumulative Key for Prognosis of Musical Achievement." *J Ed Psychol* 25:45-53 Ja '34.

41 BERGEN, GARRET L. *Use of Tests in the Adjustment Service*, p. 59. Adjustment Service Series Report [No.] 4. New York: American Association for Adult Education, 1935. Pp. 70. Paper. Out of print.

42 FARNSWORTH, PAUL R. "Are 'Music Capacity' Tests More Important than 'Intelligence' Tests in the Prediction of the Several Types of Music Grades?" *J Appl Psychol* 19:347-50 Je '35.

43 SEASHORE, CARL E. Chapter 21, "The Discovery and Guidance of Musical Talent," pp. 447-61. In *Educational Diagnosis*: The Twenty-Fourth Yearbook of the National Society for the Study of Education. Bloomington, Ill.: Public School Publishing Co., 1935. Pp. x, 559. Cloth, $4.25; paper, $3.00.

44 STANTON, HAZEL MARTHA. *Measurement of Musical Talent*: The Eastman Experiment. Foreword by Carl E. Seashore. University of Iowa Studies, Studies in the Psychology of Music, Vol. 2. Iowa City, Iowa: the University, 1935. Pp. 140. Cloth, $1.50; paper, $1.00.

45 SEASHORE, CARL E. "The Psychology of Music: V, Measurement of Musical Talent." *Music Ed J* 23:24-5 D '36.

46 DEAN, CHARLES D. "Predicting Sight-Singing Ability in Teacher-Education." *J Ed Psychol* 28:601-8 N '37.

47 MURSELL, JAMES LOCKHART. "What About Music Tests?" *Music Ed J* 24:16-8 O '37.

48 FARNSWORTH, PAUL R. "Further Notes on the Seashore Music Tests." *J Gen Psychol* 18:429-31 Ap '38.

49 Human Engineering Laboratory. *Steps Toward the Isolation of Tonal Memory as a Mental Element*. Human Engineering Laboratory, Technical Report No. 21. Boston, Mass.: the Laboratory, 1938. Pp. vii, 49. $1.00. Paper, mimeographed.

50 SEASHORE, CARL E. *Psychology of Music*, pp. 302-45, 383-6. New York: McGraw-Hill Book Co., Inc., 1938. Pp. xxi, 408. $4.00. (London: McGraw-Hill Publishing Co., Ltd. 24s.)

51 BURNS, SAMUEL T. "Measurement in Music," pp. 3-9. In *Twenty-Sixth Annual Conference on Educational Measurements*: Held at Indiana University, April 11, 1939. Bulletin of the School of Education, Indiana University, Vol. 15, No. 4. Bloomington, Ind.: Indiana University Bookstore, September 1939. Pp. 50. $0.50. Paper.

52 FRIEND, RUBY S. "Influences of Heredity and Musical Environment on the Scores of Kindergarten Children on the Seashore Measures of Musical Ability." *J Appl Psychol* 23:347-57 Je '39.

53 MURSELL, JAMES L. "Intelligence and Musicality." *Ed* 59:559-62 My '39.

54 SEASHORE, C. E. "Revision of the Seashore Measures of Musical Talent: Psychology of Music, XXI," *Music Educators J* 26:31-3 '39.

55 WYATT, RUTH. "A Note on the Use of 'Omnibus' Training to Validate Seashore's 'Capacity' Hypothesis." *Am J Psychol* 52:638-40 O '39.

[1339]

Strouse Music Test. Grades 4-16; 1937; 3 forms; 90¢ per 25; 20¢ per specimen set; (60) minutes; edited by H. E. Schrammel; Catherine E. Strouse; Emporia, Kan.: Bureau of Educational Measurements, Kansas State Teachers College.

REFERENCES

1 STROUSE, CATHERINE E. *The Construction of a Test in General Musical Knowledge for the Intermediate Grades*. Unpublished master's thesis, Northwestern University, 1933.

Clara J. McCauley, Supervisor of Music, Public Schools, Knoxville, Tennessee. This is a test designed to measure certain phases of musical ability enumerated and discussed below.

The phases of musical aptitude to be measured may be thought of as: aural recognition of the relative pitch of tones; aural recognition of the relative length of tones; aural recognition of whether a measure may be a two-part, three-part, or four-part measure. The phases of musical ability to be measured are: ability to write on the staff four notes heard twice; ability to distinguish between major and minor melodies heard; ability to recognize a tone *heard* which is different from one *seen* in a melody; ability to perceive likenesses and differences in pairs of melodies; ability to perceive difference in a measure heard from one seen and read; ability to place measure bars, after hearing the melody; knowledge of meaning of terms and symbols, composition types, and composers (true-false, 48 items); ability to place "do" and write name of key; ability to write the letter names of notes seen and read; ability to write syllables for notes, including chromatics; ability to determine measure signatures; ability to place bars, the measure sign being given; ability to determine minor scales; knowledge of musical signs, and instruments (a quadruple-choice test).

The organization of the test material would be improved by a thoroughly homogeneous grouping of items in Division Two, Parts I and VIII. The validity of the test would be increased by dissociating the aptitude phases from the achievement phases. It is possible that the importance of aptitude testing justified its entire separation from an achievement test. The brevity of the aptitude features of this test does not give sufficient data concerning the musical aptitude of the student. The achievement phases of the test, while each includes a few items from each type of material usually taught through the grades 4 to 9, the number of items in each class of items is too small to square adequately with the criterion of validity. True validity calls for a much more extensive and comprehensive sampling of the subject matter of music in grades 4 to 9. There are no data available by which to judge the test from standpoint of the criterion of reliability.

This test squares with the criteria of objectivity, alternative forms, and ease of administering and scoring. There are no norms available. The manual of directions could·be improved by including data on the validity and reliability of the test and on how to interpret and apply the results.

Carl E. Seashore, Professor of Psychology, State University of Iowa. This is primarily a test of information as an element of achievement. It purports to cover musical aptitude, knowledge, attainment, skill, and appreciation, and involves both auditory and visual reactions. It uses primarily the method of multiple-choice, true-false, and identification. Items seem to be well chosen for the purpose of covering features taught in public school music classes.

For a review by Paul R. Farnsworth, see 1087.

FOREIGN LANGUAGES

Reviews by Lawrence Andrus, Christian O. Arndt, S. D. Atkins, James C. Babcock, Nelson Brooks, W. L. Carr, Paul B. Diederich, Harold B. Dunkel, Bateman Edwards, C. E. Ficken, John Flagg Gummere, C. H. Handschin, Harry Heller, Warren S. Holmes, Charles Holzwarth, Joseph F. Jackson, Laura B. Johnson, Walter V. Kaulfers, Norman T. Pratt, Jr., Harry J. Russell, James B. Tharp, and Clarence E. Turner.

[1340]

Foreign Language Prognosis Test. Grades 8-9; 1930; 2 forms; $7.35 per 100; 25¢ per specimen set; 44(60-65) minutes; Percival M. Symonds; New York: Bureau of Publications, Teachers College, Columbia University.

REFERENCES

1 SYMONDS, PERCIVAL M. Chapter 6, "A Modern Foreign Language Prognosis Test," pp. 91-126. In *Prognosis Tests in the Modern Foreign Languages*: Reports Prepared for the Modern Foreign Language Study and the Canadian Committee on Modern Languages. By V. A. C. Henmon and others. Publications of the American and Canadian Committees on Modern Languages, Vol. 14. New York: Macmillan Co., 1929. Pp. xviii, 182. Paper. Out of print.
2 SYMONDS, PERCIVAL M. "A Foreign Language Prognosis Test." *Teach Col Rec* 31:540-56 Mr '30.
3 LAU, LOUISE MARGARET. *The Use of the Symond's Foreign Language Tests in Beginning French.* Unpublished master's thesis, University of Chicago, 1933. Pp. 41.
4 RICHARDSON, H. D. "Discovering Aptitude for the Modern Languages." *Mod Lang J* 18:160-70 D '33.
5 VIRGIL, SISTER. "Prognosis in German." *Mod Lang J* 20:275-87 F '36.
6 MARONPOT, RAYMOND P. "Discovering and Salvaging Modern Language Risks." *Mod Lang J* 23:595-8 My '39.

Walter V. Kaulfers, Associate Professor of Education in Foreign Language, Stanford University. Prepared some ten years ago, this test is apparently designed to forecast achievement in foreign language classes taught by the formal grammar-translation method. An eighth or ninth grader who can pass this examination should be able to qualify in almost any subject, for the test is hardly more than a linguistically weighted intelligence test. At that, its correlation with foreign language achievement (when both forms are combined into one test) averages only .71. Since no probable errors are given, nor statements made concerning the number of cases upon which the coefficient is based, it is difficult to judge the true significance of this measure. It is certain, however, that the correlations of .60 and .61 between prognosis test scores and achievement test scores when only one form of the test is used, are not sufficiently high to warrant the rejection of any particular student on the basis of his test score alone. For purposes of homogeneous grouping, in the relatively few schools having large enough enrollments in any one language to make such grouping possible, the IQ alone would be just about as satisfactory.

From the standpoint of testing time (44 minutes per form) and ease of administration and scoring, the test ranks high among such foreign language prognosis tests as are available to date.

The validity of almost any prognosis test in foreign languages, however, varies with the type of course offered. Almost every foreign language prognosis test published to date has for certain groups yielded correlations as high as the test under discussion. The correlation is often high when the types of abilities involved (grammar-translation, in this case) are identical in the test and course work. The correlation tends to be low when different abilities are utilized in the course from those measured in the test. The user of this test should, therefore, make certain that the course in which the success of any student is to be predicted follows more or less closely the traditional grammar-translation method. Otherwise, the test is not likely to be any more valid in predicting ability to learn a foreign language than an ordinary intelligence test. This fact is emphasized because most schools are now breaking away from the traditional approach to foreign languages.

Moreover, the relative difficulty of many of the items makes the use of the test below the eighth grade undesirable. Whether or not the test predicts achievements equally well in German, French, Spanish, or Latin, as claimed, is debatable in view of the absence of separate data for the several languages. Since no norms are available, the interpretation of pupils' scores is still to some extent a matter of personal discretion. On the basis of a tryout of the test with prospective pupils of Spanish, the author advises that "pupils scoring under 50 on Form B and under 25 on Form A should have considerable difficulty in learning a foreign language."

Foreign language prognosis tests of the Symonds and Luria-Orleans type are usually excellent means for reducing foreign language enrollments in nonfunctional courses taught by teachers incapable of adjusting either method or content to the needs, interests, and abilities of children.

[1341]
Luria-Orleans Modern Language Prognosis Test. Grades 7-13; 1928-30; 1 form; $1.30 per 25; 15¢ per specimen set; 76(85) minutes; Max A. Luria and Jacob S. Orleans; Yonkers, N. Y.: World Book Co.

REFERENCES

1 KAULFERS, WALTER VINCENT. *The Forecasting Efficiency of Current Bases for Prognosis in Junior High School Beginning Spanish.* Unpublished doctor's thesis, Stanford University, 1933. Pp. 381.
2 YOUNG, JOSEPHINE A. *Derived Practical Instruments for Predicting Success in High School French.* Unpublished master's thesis, University of Pittsburgh, 1933. Pp. 46.
3 SEAGOE, MAY V. "Prediction of Achievement in Foreign Languages." *J Appl Psychol* 22:632-40 D '38.

Walter V. Kaulfers, Associate Professor of Education in Foreign Languages, Stanford University. The theory underlying the construction and organization of this test is that "to determine how well one can do a job, it is best to let him try it." Consequently, the examination consists of vocabulary exercises (recognition of cognates, memorization, etc.) and some eight grammar-translation lessons in Spanish and French. The test, therefore, is seemingly designed to predict achievement in the traditional grammar-translation type of course of a

decade or more ago. The correlation between the prognosis test scores and achievement test scores was .68 before the test was revised. In its present form the validity is estimated at .75.

Since this type of test cannot be standardized, no norms or standards are available. This makes the interpretation of scores rather difficult. According to the authors, "the usual per cent failing in the school should be the main basis of determining how many and which pupils should be eliminated."

Although fairly easy to score, the test is by virtue of its length and numerous subtests, by no means economical in administration or scoring.

In 1930 the reviewer administered the prognosis test to 461 pupils beginning Spanish in the eighth grade, and to 209 pupils beginning Spanish in the ninth grade. The correlation between prognosis test scores and achievement test scores at the end of the first semester was .35 for the eighth grade group, and .51 for the ninth grade group. For teachers' marks in Spanish, the correlations with prognosis test scores were .43 and .52 respectively. In this study the test did not prove itself sufficiently superior to ordinary intelligence tests to warrant use. In general, the test seems to be too difficult to provide a fair measure of pupil ability below the ninth grade. Above the eighth grade, the test may have some validity for predicting achievement in traditional grammar-translation types of work—at least for purposes of homogeneous grouping, but for this purpose it has not demonstrated itself sufficiently superior to IQ's, English test scores, or even to a simple twelve-minute test of English vocabulary, to claim any significant practical advantage.

Reliability is difficult to compute for a test of this type. It can be assumed, however, to be at least as high as the validity coefficient for the test.

FRENCH
[1342]
American Council Alpha French Test. Grades 9-16; 1926-27; 2 parts, 2 forms; 35¢ per specimen set; 40(50) minutes per part; V. A. C. Henmon, Algernon Coleman, and Marion R. Trabue; Yonkers, N. Y.: World Book Co.
a) PART I, [VOCABULARY AND GRAMMAR]. $1.25 per 25.
b) PART II, [SILENT READING AND COMPOSITION]. $1.25 per 25.

REFERENCES

1 HENMON, V. A. C. *French Word Book*: Based on a Count of 400,000 Running Words. University of Wisconsin,

Bureau of Educational Research, Bulletin No. 3. Madison, Wis.: the University, 1924. Pp. 84. Paper. Out of print.

2 SYMONDS, PERCIVAL M. *Ability Standards for Standardized Achievement Tests in the High School.* New York: Bureau of Publications, Teachers College, Columbia University, 1927. Pp. x, 91. $1.05.

3 BEATLEY, BANCROFT. Appendix 2, "A Comparative Study of Two Tests of French Vocabulary: The American Council Test and the Twigg French Vocabulary Test," pp. 346-53. In *Achievement Tests in the Modern Foreign Languages*: Prepared for the Modern Foreign Language Study and the Committee on Modern Languages. By V. A. C. Henmon. Publications of the American and Canadian Committees on Modern Languages, Vol. 5. New York: Macmillan Co., 1929. Pp. xxvii, 363. $1.00. Paper. (London: Macmillan & Co., Ltd. 4s. 6d.)

4 HENMON, V. A. C. *Achievement Tests in Modern Foreign Languages*: Prepared for the Modern Language Study and the Canadian Committee on Modern Languages, pp. 1-266. Publications of the American and Canadian Committees on Modern Languages, Vol. 5. New York: Macmillan Co., 1929. Pp. xxvii, 363. $1.00. Paper. (London: Macmillan & Co., Ltd. 4s. 6d.)

5 VANDER BEKE, GEORGE E. *French Word Book.* Publications of the American and Canadian Committees on Modern Languages, Vol. 15. New York: Macmillan Co., 1929. Pp. xiii, 188. $1.10. Paper. (London: Macmillan & Co., Ltd. 5s. 6d.)

6 BREED, FREDERICK S. Chapter 4, "The Reliability of the Trabue French Composition Scale," pp. 187-98. In *Studies in Modern Language Teaching*: Reports Prepared for the Modern Foreign Language Study and the Canadian Committee on Modern Languages. By E. W. Bagster-Collins and others. Publications of the American and Canadian Committees on Modern Languages, Vol. 17. New York: Macmillan Co., 1930. Pp. xxxi, 491. $1.75. Paper. (London: Macmillan & Co., Ltd. 9s.)

7 FORD, H. E. Chapter 5, "The Reliability of the Trabue French Composition Scale for Scoring Ten-Minute Compositions," pp. 201-10. In *Studies in Modern Language Teaching*: Reports Prepared for the Modern Foreign Language Study and the Canadian Committee on Modern Languages. By E. W. Bagster-Collins and others. Publications of the American and Canadian Committees on Modern Languages, Vol. 17. New York: Macmillan Co., 1930. Pp. xxxi, 491. $1.75. Paper. (London: Macmillan & Co., Ltd. 9s.)

8 SEIBERT, LOUISE C., AND GODDARD, EUNICE R. "The Use of Achievement Tests in Sectioning Students." *Mod Lang J* 18: 289-98 F '34.

9 STEVENSON, MARY LOU. "The Use of Modern Language Placement Tests at the University of Pittsburgh." *Mod Lang J* 18:433-50 Ap '34.

C. E. Ficken, Dean of the College and Professor of French, Macalester College. This test, first copyrighted in 1926, has the distinction of having pioneered in its field and yet remains one of the best tests on the market for the objective measurement of silent reading, recognition vocabulary, and English-French grammar. The publishers are to be commended for reporting that "reliability for different parts for single years is from .84 to .95," while "probable error of a score is about two points." Validity coefficients are not given but have undoubtedly become available since the first printing and should therefore be added.

Part I, i.e., booklet one, contains a fifteen minute vocabulary test of seventy-five words and a twenty-five minute English-French grammar test of fifty items. Part II devotes thirty-two minutes to a silent reading test of twenty-eight responses, and eight minutes to a free composition based upon a picture to be scored on the basis of a composition scale.

Words for the vocabulary test were "chosen at regular intervals from each successive fifty words in a word count of 400,000 running words" and therefore measure in accurate progression of difficulty the recognition power of students into fairly advanced levels. The five-responses answer-words are in English, thereby avoiding the ambiguities which the French synonym technique involves for the English speaking student.

The grammar test likewise contains items chosen according to frequency in textbooks and presented in the order of progressive decrease in difficulty from semester to semester. "The testing technique varies throughout the test in accordance with what seems best for each grammatical point," being of the recall type in twenty-seven cases. Sixteen items require mutation of forms and hence involve the disturbing factor of nomenclature. Only the remaining seven items use the now prevalent multiple-choice technique.

The silent reading test "consists of seven paragraphs of increasing difficulty, with questions on the text in French, the answers to be given in English." Again the gradation is admirable to test the power of the advanced student as well as the student of limited training.

To the authors and publishers this reviewer urges revised editions and ventures several suggestions. For convenience of scoring, the answer-words of the vocabulary test should be numbered for response in blanks on the margin. The grammar test as well as the reading test should use the multiple-choice technique throughout. This would not only facilitate scoring but permit either economizing of time or the lengthening of the content with a consequent improvement of reliability. Furthermore, the procrustean pairing of subtests into two booklets, each to fit a forty-minute period is too arbitrary. If, as seems probable, the composition part is rarely used anyway, a single booklet built on lines of maximum efficiency and greatly reduced cost should bring this test back to the wider use which it merits.

Warren S. Holmes, Department of French, The Gunnery School, Washington, Connecticut. Each of the two forty-minute tests consists of two sections: Part I, Vocabulary and Grammar; and Part II, Silent Reading and Written Composition. Together they form a good test, as would be expected from the distinguished names of their authors. However, there are a few points that should be brought out in examining this instrument.

First, it is a comparatively old test (1926). This fact necessarily affects the vocabulary section, as it is based on the Henmon [1] count rather than on the considerably more extensive and scientific work of Vander Beke,[5] which was not to appear until eight years later. Although the statement in the manual dealing with this section is not wholly clear, it would appear that the words were selected from the first 4,000 in the Henmon count. Yet, there are several words that do not appear at all in the Vander Beke list (over 6,000 words), and others that are in very low frequency ranges. Does this react on the value of the test as an implement of measurement? Probably not seriously.

In the grammar section, I do not like the use, in the directions, of such expressions as partitive, possessive adjective, demonstrative pronoun, etc., although in fairness it should be added that illustrations of these somewhat formidable labels make clear what is desired.

My principal objections to Part II are in the matter of time required for scoring. The comprehension section, while raising no great difficulties of scoring, would demand more time on the part of the reader than, for example, multiple-choice items, and the reader would have to be thoroughly familiar with the language. The written composition test offers undeniable problems, both in the amount of material to be read and in the scoring. The difficulty of scoring is somewhat alleviated, but certainly not removed, by the careful scale prepared by M. R. Trabue. As the reader must familiarize himself with seventeen sample compositions in order to use this scale, the question as to whether the result obtained justifies the effort expended arises of itself. My inclination would be to answer in the negative. The Cooperative tests of the American Council on Education, which may be machine-scored throughout, if desired, would surely provide nearly, if not quite, as accurate a measurement, and the time saved in dealing with a large number of papers would be very considerable. And the Cooperative tests, at least the recent ones, require only 40 minutes to administer as against 80 minutes for the test under consideration.

[1343]

American Council Alpha French Test: Aural Comprehension. 1 to 6 semesters, high school; 1933; 2 forms; $4.20 per 100; 25¢ per specimen set; (35)

minutes; Agnes L. Rogers and Frances M. Clarke; prepared for the Committee on Modern Language Teaching under the auspices of the American Council on Education; New York: Bureau of Publications, Teachers College, Columbia University.

REFERENCES

1 HENMON, V. A. C. *Achievement Tests in Modern Foreign Languages*: Prepared for the Modern Language Study and the Canadian Committee on Modern Languages, pp. 311-21. Publications of the American and Canadian Committees on Modern Languages, Vol. 5. New York: Macmillan Co., 1929. Pp. xxvii, 363. $1.00. Paper. (London: Macmillan & Co., Ltd. 4s. 6d.)
2 CLARKE, FRANCES MARGUERITE. "Results of the Bryn Mawr Test in French Administered in New York City High Schools." *B High Points* 13:4-13 F '31.
3 ROGERS, AGNES L., AND CLARKE, FRANCES M. "Report on the Bryn Mawr Test of Ability to Understand Spoken French." *Mod Lang J* 17:241-8 Ja '33.

Nelson Brooks, Instructor in French, Westover School, Middlebury, Connecticut. The authors of this test have made a serious effort to isolate and measure a single ability, the ability to comprehend spoken French. Such information, if it can be obtained, is valuable indeed, and there is much of value in this test. Yet many users will have occasion to question some points of the theory on which it is constructed and certain details of its printed form.

The test is composed of eighty questions in French, each with five possible answers in English. The questions are short and simple and, to quote the authors, of "such a selection of content that the maximum degree of intelligence and of information required is below that possessed by the poorest student to be examined." To test comprehension in a language by giving questions in that language and answers in another raises immediate and serious objection, for there is no assurance that the student does not merely translate a few isolated words from the foreign tongue into his own, in which he then comprehends them as a sentence and makes an answer. As every language teacher knows, this is a process to be avoided at all costs, and the form of this test seems not only to provide the student with a crutch but also to insist that he use it. All classroom methods of teaching a foreign language, while not necessarily actual verbal processes in that language, should at least be projected against the natural use of the language as a background. The thought process required in answering a question on this test is something which simply never happens in a French person's mind.

To reduce the intelligence level of the questions to a point far below that of most of the students to be tested is a dubious procedure also, for the student remains a human being even while he is being analyzed by devices such as this, and the test may turn into a measure of his resentment at being asked questions that seem to him stupid.

The questions are of different types, and differ considerably in their value for a test of this kind. In one type, the answer is implicit in the question itself, such as Item 76 of Form B: "Qui appelle-t-on en cas de maladie?" In another type, no answer can be given until further information is supplied, as, for example, Item 47 of Form A: "Quel est le plus fier de ces animaux?" A third type is a question so wide in scope that one is, to say the least, bewildered until some limits are given, as in Item 61 of Form B: "Qu'est-ce qui ne dure qu'un instant?" Only questions of the first type can fairly be included in a test of ability to understand spoken French; the others obviously test something quite different, that is, the ability to understand a language pattern composed of a sentence spoken in French and five words written in English.

The test would be more satisfactory to both student and teacher if the questions were arranged in order of difficulty, and the student's mind would be clearer for the main business of the test if the perplexing chart for indicating his previous experience in French were at the end rather than at the beginning.

The dullness of many of the questions and the generally stuffy atmosphere of this test suggest that perhaps the advice of Otto Jespersen to makers of language textbooks, "It seems never to have occurred to the authors of some (schoolbooks) that there might be a limit to the amount of rubbish that can be offered children under the pretext of teaching them grammar," should be taken to heart by the makers of language tests as well.

[1344]

American Council Beta French Test. Grades 7-11; 1926-27; 2 forms; $1.30 per 25; 20¢ per specimen set; 90(100) minutes; prepared for the Modern Language Study under the auspices of the American Council on Education and the Conference of Canadian Universities; Jacob Greenberg and Ben D. Wood; Yonkers, N. Y.: World Book Co.

REFERENCES

1 Wood, Ben D. *New York Experiments with New-Type Modern Language Tests*: Including a Survey of Modern Language Achievement in the Junior High Schools of New York City, June, 1925; the Regents Experiment of June, 1925, with New-Type Tests in French, German, Spanish, and Physics; and a Second Survey of Modern Language Achievement in the Junior High Schools of New York City, June, 1926, pp. 3-103, 323-39. Publications of the American and Canadian Committees on Modern Languages, Vol. 1. New York: Macmillan Co., 1928. Pp. xxii, 339. Paper. Out of print.

2 Giduz, Hugo. "The 1935 French Placement Tests at The University." *H Sch J* 18:227-8 N '35.

Bateman Edwards, Head of the Department of Romance Languages, Washington University. This test is published in two forms which the makers claim to be equivalent. In the year which elapsed between the copyrighting of Form A and Form B certain improvements were introduced, such as the provision of a place for recording the score at the end of each part, and the instruction at the bottom of the odd-numbered pages for the student to go right on to the next page. With these exceptions, the material form of the two tests is identical. Since the key for Form A alone was included with the tests, all references, unless indicated, are to that form.

Part I, a vocabulary test of 100 items, presents four or five English words as possible translations of a given French word. It would be difficult to invent a method better designed to elicit misinformation from the student. Series of words, lacking their context, soon lose all power to provoke response, and the confusion is not reduced by the occasional inclusion, among the correct equivalents, of words possessing several meanings, such as: "grave," "to oblige," "nail," or by the inconsistent use of "to" as the sign of the infinitive. To avoid bewilderment, the student would be wise to translate in his mind each French word, before referring to the suggested possibilities. And even then his problem may be complicated by one of the following: (*a*) the required translation is not the best or the most usual (*ménager* "to manage," *vœu* "vow"); (*b*) the translation required by the key is not the only acceptable one among the given possibilities (*fin* "end" also "fine," *souris* "mouse" also "smile," and in Form B *que* "that" also "why"); (*c*) the key is in error (*border* is translated as "to bare").

Part II is a comprehension test, offering 60 French sentences to be completed, at the end, by the addition of one out of five suggested words or phrases. Here the objections to Part I do not apply, since the words are presented in their context. However, the extreme platitude of these synthetic sentences is not conducive to inspiring the student with any enthusiasm for the French language. Since only the ability to understand French is here in question, an English answer to a question based on a passage of real French prose, of the type adopted by the College Entrance Examination Board, presents a far more interesting and trustworthy means of evaluation. The only objection to such a test could be that it is not susceptible of mechanical marking. Part II presents one typographical error in the omission of the question mark in Item 14. In Item 41 the use of *sept jours*, even in quotation marks, as synonymous with *une semaine* is of dubious correctness.

Part III, a grammar test, requires the insertion of one to four French words to complete the meaning in 60 French sentences of which the English translation is given. In five cases the omitted words comprise the entire sentence. This is the only part of the examination in which the scoring can not "be done mechanically by clerks who know nothing of French." The intention of the makers of the key has been "to include all satisfactory forms of possible answers," but in a good number of cases this has not been done. The long form of the interrogation may be used in Items 15, 29, and 42; the feminine pronoun is as correct as the masculine in Items 32, 53, and 60; the second person singular may be used in Item 30; the past definite is correct for Item 40. It is possible to accept *quelques pommes* instead of *des pommes* for "some apples" (Item 5), *fort* instead of *très* for "very" (Item 47), and *il doit travailler* instead of *il lui faut travailler* for "he must work" (Item 58), not to mention the less obvious possibility of circumlocutions in several of the other sentences. In addition, the key is in error for Item 48 in omitting the definite article which is not translated in the test. No uses of the conditional or subjunctive are included.

In the Manual of Directions the authors point to the difficulties inherent in an objective test of this sort in order to explain the lack of measurement of any cultural or oral-aural elements. A still greater lack is, I fear, that of material capable of giving the student any confidence whatsoever that he can handle the French language as a living means of communication. A French sentence for complete translation, where the student will have to conquer problems not only of vocabulary but also of syntax, is far more valuable than the recognition of any number of isolated words. When reading for comprehension the student should feel that the information imparted is mature enough not to insult his intelligence. In translating into French, the value of expressing a complete thought with all its elements is far superior to that of spotting a series of unrelated grammatical points in sentences artificially designed for the purpose. Perhaps the fault lies in the very conception of the wholly objective examination. An examination which subordinates the encouragement of independent thought to speed and objectivity in marking, and which does not require, on the part of the marker, intelligence and a knowledge of the subject superior to that of the examinee, may very likely prove not worth administering.

[1345]

American Council French Grammar Test. Grades 9-16; 1927; 2 forms; $1.25 per 25; 20c per specimen set; 22(27) minutes; prepared for the Modern Foreign Language Study under the auspices of the American Council on Education and the Conference of Canadian Universities; Frederic D. Cheydleur; Yonkers, N. Y.: World Book Co.

REFERENCES

1 CHEYDLEUR, F. D. *The American Council French Grammar Test (Selection Type)*: A Preliminary Experiment at the University of Wisconsin. University of Wisconsin, Bureau of Educational Research, Bulletin No. 8. Madison, Wis.: the University, 1927. Pp. 35. Out of print.
2 CHEYDLEUR, F. D. "The Construction and Validation of a French Grammar Test of the Selection or Multiple-Choice Type." *J Ed Res* 17:184-96 Mr '28.
3 CHEYDLEUR, FREDERIC D. "Results and Significance of the New Type of Modern Language Tests." *Mod Lang J* 12:513-31 Ap '28.
4 HENMON, V. A. C. *Achievement Tests in Modern Foreign Languages*: Prepared for the Modern Language Study and the Canadian Committee on Modern Languages, pp. 1-8, 10-11, 18-19, 295-300. Publications of the American and Canadian Committees on Modern Languages, Vol. 5. New York: Macmillan Co., 1929. Pp. xxvii, 363. $1.00. Paper. (London: Macmillan & Co., Ltd. 4s. 6d.)
5 CHEYDLEUR, FREDERIC D. "The Relationship between Functional and Theoretical Grammar: An Experiment Carried on with the American Council French Grammar Test, Selection Type, in Seven State Institutions." *Mod Lang J* 16:310-33 Ja '32.

Harry Heller, Head of the French Department, Fieldston School, New York, New York. This is an old and well-known test, prepared originally for the Modern Foreign Language Study. Much that this reviewer has said elsewhere in these pages concerning the *Cooperative French Test* in general, and its grammar section in particular, applies here too. Further comparison reveals that the publishers of the Cheydleur test have been much less generous with research data on the test's construction, etc. The reliability coefficient for 9,664 cases, given in the accompanying manual, is .87, but for some single years and semesters is too low for accurate measurement of individual students, ranging from .72 to .92. Correlation coefficients with other tests appear for the most part adequate although based on relatively few cases. Tables of percentile norms are given but it is not indicated how recently they were compiled.

Both alternate forms of this test are composed of 50 items of the selection type. An English sentence is followed by four alternative French translations among which the student chooses the correct one. As stated elsewhere, the device of confronting the student with incorrect alternatives is suspect to this reviewer who holds it to be educationally unsound, especially in the language arts where no governing "logic" can be posed in the early stages of study but is acquired only with a long mastery that few students achieve. Experimental evidence on this point would be valuable. However, in most of the items the alternative French translations are arranged around a common correct portion, thus throwing into better relief the grammatical usage being tested —an improvement over the grammar section of the *Cooperative French Test*.

A record of student achievement in French based on this one objective test alone would be a barren thing. Unless a grammar test is needed for some special reason the teacher would do well at least to combine this measure with a comprehension test or use the three-part *Cooperative French Test*.

Charles Holzwarth, Principal of the West High School, Rochester, New York. Since this test is also of the recognition type, the objections which I voiced in my review of the *American Council on Education French Reading Test* are applicable here, although to a somewhat lesser degree since the responses offered for the choice of the pupil are not so tricky and there seems to be only one possible choice. Personally I much prefer to test pupils by the actual translation into French of sentences based on a known vocabulary and with a controlled grammatical range of difficulty, something which is impractical in a standard test.

If one has to use a standard test, I see considerable merit in this one, but I believe it should be revamped. Of course, the minute even minor changes are made, goodbye standards and comparisons!

As to the range of grammar topics, I find it touches on most of the points covered in our school grammars. There are, however, a few rough spots, e.g.,

1. *There is little testing of verb forms.* (*a*) In the classroom we spend a great deal of time on tense formation, conjugation of verbs, principal parts of irregular verbs, etc. Yet this test which purports to evaluate our work fails to take them into account. (*b*) Tense usage is tested in Items 38, 39, 42, of Form A and in Items 1, 3, 6, 27 and 32 of Form B. (*c*) Verbs conjugated with *être*, which we classroom teachers consider rather important, appear only in B17 (i.e., Item 17 in Form B) and in A43, which latter case tests not only this principle but also the use of the subjunctive. (*d*) The agreement of the past participle with *avoir* appears only in B24. Surely this is cavalier treatment for such an important topic—or do we classroom teachers merely think it important? (*e*) The agreement of the past participle in reflexive verbs appears in A2 and B5, B43, while we find the perplexing agreement with *entendre parler* in A29 and *voir se battre* in B31.

2. *Pronouns.* (*a*) Personal pronouns, which we teachers believe relatively important, are tested only in A7 and A37, B7, B22, and B46. The position of pronouns (word order) is stressed apparently only in A7. The emphatic forms occur in A22 and B20. (*b*) Relative and interrogative pronouns seem more adequately handled. (*c*) Possessive pronouns occur only in A19.

3. *Prepositions are neglected.* They occur only in A4, B11 (à + place name), A26, B48 (*dans* + country), and A25 (*avant de*).

4. *Idiomatic and tricky usages are tested* (whether adequately enough, who shall say?) e.g., (*a*) se fait faire, A36; faire couper, B43; (*b*) venir de, B14; (*c*) plus de, A46, B35; (*d*) first (last) two, A40, B45; (*e*) enseigner à Louise à chanter, A30; (*f*) penser à (de), B39; and (*g*) gender of gens, B40.

Naturally some of the examples are hard to classify or present double difficulties, e.g., B1 (verb form and position of adjective), B22 (use of conjunction or preposition and indicative or subjunctive), B28 (use of *dont* and confusing word order), A25 (pronouns and preposition), etc.

If one of the strong points of the recognitional type of test is to concentrate attention on a single point, this has been overlooked in a number of cases.

To sum up, the test gives me the impression of a cross section of grammar cut on somewhat of a bias—but I don't say I could do better, for I appreciate the difficulties which faced the author. I merely affirm that some review and reconstruction would seem to be in order.

[1346]

American Council on Education French Reading Test. 2 semesters or more of college French; 1937-39; Forms A, B, and C; 5¢ per test, 10 to 99 copies; 25¢ per specimen set; 50(55) minutes; prepared for the Committee on Modern Languages; F. D. Cheydleur, V. A. C. Henmon, and M. J. Walker; New York: Cooperative Test Service.

REFERENCES

1 VANDER BEKE, GEORGE E. *French Word Book.* Publications of the American and Canadian Committees on the Modern Languages, Vol. 15. New York: Macmillan Co., 1929. Pp. xiii, 188. $1.10. Paper. (London: Macmillan & Co., Ltd. 5s. 6d.)

Charles Holzwarth, Principal of the West High School, Rochester, New York. This test is what is known as an objective, standardized test. Is there, however, such a thing as a purely objective test? Possibly so far as scoring is concerned but certainly not so far as the subject matter of the test is concerned for this, despite the best efforts of the editor or editors, is bound to be subjective in choice of materials, manner of presentation, etc. Any competent classroom teacher can make up a test better suited to test the progress and the knowledge of his own particular classes but, of course, it will not be standardized. Score one, therefore, for the standardized test.

This test is of the recognition type. Whatever advantages may inhere in this type of test, there are certainly just as inherent disadvantages, one of the most important of which, to my mind, is the fact that only passive knowledge is tested. This observation will stamp me at once as being a conservative of the old school who actually believes that pupils should achieve a certain oral-aural mastery of the language which the "new type" or "standardized" tests do not attempt to measure or even more or less highhandedly consider a mere ancillary of the power to read for comprehension. I grant, of course, that oral-aural ability is very difficult to measure except aurally, but I do not grant the premise that because a pupil does well on a reading test, he will necessarily do well in oral-aural work.

My chief additional objection to the recognition type test is that its very form makes it a guessing game or sets up an additional hazard which tests not one's comprehension of the written word in the basic paragraph but rather one's ability to choose carefully among the solutions offered, making the test one of

logical ability and clear thinking. This is particularly true of the first test of this kind undertaken by a given pupil. He has to learn the technique before he can show his real ability, i.e., before the test becomes really a fair and accurate test of his comprehension of the paragraph set for comprehension. Let me illustrate.

Let us consider Item 111, Form B. The question is: "Que ferait-elle quand elle serait riche?" Response 1 states: "She would have a beautiful house and magnificent dresses" (cf. "J'aurais une belle maison et des robes magnifiques" of the text) but that is not the correct answer, for Response 3 says: "She would marry the richest farmer in the country" ("J'épouserais le plus riche fermier du pays"). Both answers agree with the text but, of course, the question asks: Que *ferait*-elle? Here it hinges on the ability of the pupil to comprehend the question, not on his ability to comprehend the reading selection. My point is merely this, is the test supposed to test the pupil's ability to comprehend the passage set or his ability to comprehend questions based on the passage?

Consider also Item 112, Responses 2 and 3— here is a logical distinction rather than a factual distinction. Consider also Item 126, Responses 2 and 3. Here the pupil has to have not casual comprehension but mastery of *raille*.

In Item 108 the test tempts the pupil with Response 1 to see if he will fall for village. But the question itself says to *a* nearby city rather than *the* nearby city as in the text. Why be more critical of the pupil than the test?

Sometimes the questions are harder than the text, e.g., "châteaux en Espagne" of Item 113 or cf. Item 129 or Item 143. Here again the test is rather of the pupil's ability to understand the question rather than to comprehend the text.

Do you now see why I prefer to ask a pupil to translate into English rather than read a French question and pick an English answer which may trip him?

Or consider Item 149 (where I assume that Response 1 is the correct answer). Yet the passage doesn't really say so, it leaves the pupil to make the connection between "remplissait son assiette à fleurs" and "Oh! la bonne odeur de soupe au fromage!" And the author tries to trip the pupil with Response 2.

Consider Item 147 (where I assume Response 3 is the acceptable answer) and yet the text says "il va trouver *sa chambre* encore chaude . . . et tout *son petit chez lui* bien rangé," i.e., the pupil must be logical. Heaven forfend that I should object to setting up training in logical thinking as one of the by-products of language well taught; I merely question the validity of such procedure in a test which aims to discover whether the pupil can read and comprehend. Do we arrive at the goal via a double aim?

I object also to Item 107. Here the author is testing the pupil's concept of morality rather than his understanding of the story.

Have I illustrated what I consider to be some of the inherent faults of recognitional testing? For the classroom I believe translation is the most reliable form of testing comprehension. For purposes of comparison I grant the value of the standard test, but, oh, how careful must the author be!

I now come to a different type of objection to this particular test (Form B), namely extent of vocabulary. The description of the reading test given by the publishers says that the passages of Form A contain no words of a frequency above 2,000 except "22 words, such as proper names, cognates, and a few others whose meanings can be inferred from the text or whose English meanings are given." I have before me only Form B, but since A and B are held to be interchangeable, I assume that the above should apply to the passages of Form B also.

Is *confiseur* one of the 22? It is a vital word in the first selection but it is not translated in the text nor would I classify it as one of the cognates whose meaning an average pupil could guess. On the other hand it is not in the Vander Beke word list [1] and hence cannot be a particularly common word. Hence the pupil is entirely out of luck on Item 101.

Laitière of the second selection is also foreign to the Vander Beke list and yet is important to the understanding of the text. Do we infer that this is one of the 22 easy-to-guess words? Try it on a high school pupil!

The verb *quereller* of the third selection does not appear in Vander Beke. Another to be guessed at? And yet Item 116 depends upon it. I believe also that the wording of Item 117 is likely to stump the average high school pupil, i.e., this use of *offrir* is not commonly met in high school reading.

Again *conseillères* of the fourth selection is

not in Vander Beke. Hence I object to Item 123 which might well tempt the pupil to guess at *consolation*. The verb *railler* seems to rank 5,115 in Vander Beke. Although, to be sure, I have Form B before me rather than Form A for which the claim is made not to go above 2,000 (i.e., only 3 words between 1,500-2,000 and none between 2,001 and 2,500).

In the fifth selection *blanchâtre* is not in Vander Beke. *S'assombrir* ranks 5,057 in Vander Beke, while *terne* is 4,399, *étain* is 5,459, *réseau* is 5,236, and *s'enlacer* and *déformer* are not in Vander Beke.

In the sixth selection *culbuter* is not in Vander Beke, *assaillir* ranks 4,556, *égorger* 5,172, *narine* 5,988, and *désordonné* and *marmite* are not in Vander Beke.

Part I, the vocabulary test, is open to the same general objection that I have offered against Part II, i.e., that it is a guessing game where technique must be mastered before it is fair to gauge the pupil by what he accomplishes. My objection here is, however, much less strong for there is not the ambiguity of question to lead the pupil astray.

Inasmuch as the words which make up the vocabulary test are carefully chosen from the Vander Beke list, I believe it has decided value once the pupil knows the technique.

For a review by Nelson Brooks, see 984.

[1347]

Columbia Research Bureau Aural French Test. Grades 9-16; 1930; 2 forms; $1.25 per 25, 20¢ per specimen set; (45-60) minutes; Louise C. Seibert and Ben D. Wood; Yonkers, N. Y.: World Book Co.

REFERENCES

1 VANDER BEKE, GEORGE E. *French Word Book.* Publications of the American and Canadian Committees on Modern Languages, Vol. 15. New York: Macmillan Co., 1929. Pp. xxvii, 363. $1.10. Paper. (London: Macmillan & Co., Ltd. 5s. 6d.)

Clarence E. Turner, Assistant Professor of the Romance Languages, Rutgers University. This test is designed to measure the extent to which students, when listening to spoken French, can (*a*) understand a question, (*b*) understand the relation of facts, (*c*) understand a continuous paragraph, and (*d*) understand dictated sentences and copy them. In Part I the examiner reads a series of statements concerning each of three pictures which are before the student, who then indicates whether each statement is true or false. In Part II the examiner reads a series of questions which the student answers by indicating "yes" or "no." In Part III the examiner reads a paragraph, then identifies it by a letter. The student turns to that letter in his booklet, where he finds in English three statements concerning the paragraph, each statement to be completed by indicating the best of four possible answers. Part IV consists of a dictation exercise of fifteen sentences. The material in the test booklet is well arranged, without crowding or ambiguity.

The accompanying manual discusses the construction and validity of the test. Validity is claimed because of the wide sampling of items, the selection of content, the number of distinct functions measured, and the extent of differentiation among students who have had the same number of years of the subject, and between the averages of students who have had different amounts of training. Statistical support is offered for the claim of differentiation. The authors explain how they have sought to control the extent to which the test becomes a measure of vocabulary: 827 of its words are found in the Vander Beke list,[1] 47 per cent in the first thousand, 67 per cent in the first two thousand, 85 per cent in the first four thousand, and 92 per cent in the first six thousand. They state further that the selection of content was made with a view to avoiding as far as possible the measurement of general intelligence, information, or memory. Nevertheless, particularly in Part III, general intelligence and recall seem clearly to be measured. The authors' assertion that, "In Part III, for instance, all the paragraphs were first tested in English as to length, grasp of general meaning, perception of details and so on," does not prove, or mean, anything as it stands. The authors have sought to meet the objection that Part IV measures factors other than comprehension (e.g., grammar, spelling) by a method of scoring which minimizes errors not primarily of comprehension.

The reviewer believes this to be on the whole a sound and well-constructed test, capable of furnishing a usable measure of aural comprehension. Its usefulness and validity are somewhat reduced, perhaps unavoidably, by certain factors relating to the examiner, and to the means used for securing discrimination among students of superior ability.

The examiner is intended to be the teacher of the students tested. He must be able to pronounce French, which the authors optimistically take for granted, and he must furthermore train himself to read at three different speeds and to time pauses accurately. The speeds are those at which a sentence like *L'ouragan déracine les arbres les plus vigoureux* would be read in 30 (normal), 50 (slow), and 80 (very slow) seconds respectively. While an intelligent person can with reasonable practice arrive at an accurate performance, one can not help wondering whether some verification of the examiner's skill should not be requisite to the inclusion of scores in the norm-tables. The latter would have their maximum utility if based on scores obtained when the test is administered by *any* person of proven ability to pronounce French and to follow the authors' directions. Comparable scores could then be obtained for large groups of students from different schools, like college freshmen whom it might be wished to place according to their aural comprehension.

An examination of the more difficult items reveals a paradox underlying the test's construction. Fundamentally, the test, like the Vander Beke list with which it has been checked, is based on written French. It measures the ability to understand written French read aloud. This is a useful measure, but it must not be mistaken for a measure of the ability to understand spoken French. The simpler items when read aloud are like sentences which may be heard spoken, but the more difficult ones owe their difficulty in considerable part to the introduction of processes characteristic of literary French—longer sentences, more difficult syntax, less familiar words. Now spoken French becomes harder to understand as the speakers change, as the speed increases, as the vocabulary is extended, and as the style grows colloquial. In this test the speaker does not change. The vocabulary is carefully controlled, and though it increases, does not increase colloquially. The speed increases only to that rate called "normal," and which is definitely slower than that of rapid colloquial French. The style never grows colloquial either. Hence, the only devices left to secure discrimination among the better students are essentially those of literary French.

[1348]

Columbia Research Bureau French Test. Grades 9-15; 1926; 2 forms; $1.30 per 25; 20¢ per specimen set; 90(100) minutes; A. A. Méras, Suzanne Roth, and Ben D. Wood; Yonkers, N. Y.: World Book Co.
REFERENCES
1 MÉRAS, A. A.; ROTH, SUZANNE; AND WOOD, BEN D. Chapter 25, "A Placement Test in French," pp. 247-63. In *Contri-*

butions to Education, Vol. 1. Edited by J. Carleton Bell. New York Society for the Experimental Study of Education. Yonkers, N. Y.: World Book Co., 1924. Pp. ix, 364. Out of print.
2 WOOD, BEN D. *New York Experiments with New-Type Modern Language Tests*: Including a Survey of Modern Language Achievement in the Junior High Schools of New York City, June, 1925; The Regents Experiment of June, 1925, with New-Type Tests in French, German, Spanish, and Physics; and A Second Survey of Modern Language Achievement in the Junior High Schools of New York City, June, 1926, pp. 105-319. Publications of the American and Canadian Committees on Modern Languages, Vol. 1. New York: Macmillan Co., 1927. Pp. xxii, 339. Paper. Out of print.
3 CHEYDLEUR, FREDERIC D. "The Relative Reliability of the Old and New Type Modern Language Examinations." *French R* 2:530-50 My '29.

Joseph F. Jackson, Professor of French, University of Illinois. Forms A and B are equivalent and are similarly constructed. Part I, Vocabulary, consists of 100 French words for each of which the student is to choose the nearest English equivalent from 4 or 5 alternates; Part II, Comprehension, 75 true-false statements in French; and Part III, Grammar, 100 English sentences, each followed by an incomplete translation to be completed by the student.

In Form A the items of Part I are well chosen, excepting two cognates (Items 29 and 90) and several alternates which could serve as well in certain contexts as the expression desired (Items 16, 48, 62, and 100). For an objective test the items of Part II are less generally satisfactory, as the answers in some cases depend at least as much on the student's judgment, opinion, or experience as on his knowledge of French (e.g., Items 40, 45, 55, 61, 67, 72, and 73). Granted that any test of intellectual ability involves the use of intelligence and memory, it is possible to devise a sounder gauge of a student's language skill than is provided by the type of sentences indicated. The grammar-completion elements of Part III are quite satisfactory, but the scoring of them is less objective than the manual of directions indicates. All the possible alternate answers are not given in the key. In the directions for using the key, it is stated that "the student's answer should receive credit even if it is not in the key, provided there is no doubt that it is correct." One naturally wonders whether a scorer's doubt necessarily invalidates a student's answer.

Form B is less acceptable than Form A. There are more debatable points in Part I (Items 4, 13, 37, 58, 68, and 100) and in Part II (Items 17, 18, 22, 23, 29, 30, 39, 41, 43, 45, 51, 53, 55, 61, 65, and 72). In connection with Part II of both forms, it is interesting and perhaps significant to note that the reliability

coefficient for Part II is .84, while those of Part I and Part III are respectively .93 and .94. Similarly the correlation of Part II with each of the other parts is .71, while the correlation between Parts I and III is .74.

The manual of directions treats in detail validity, derivation, construction, application, administration, establishment of norms, scoring and interpretation of scores. The vocabulary of the test was drawn from words common to at least four of sixteen recognized textbooks. Items were pretested for validity and practicability; those retained were then arranged according to order of difficulty. It is affirmed that this test "affords a measure two or three times as reliable as those of old-type examinations of three hours' duration," but the basis of this affirmation is not indicated. In a discussion of possible limitations of the test, there is no mention of lack of measurement of the student's ability to translate connected passages thoroughly and accurately from and into French, yet this is an ability which is considered of primary importance in instruction. There seems to be some confusion about the character of Part II (Comprehension) which, according to the manual, was intended to afford a wide sampling of French grammar. It is difficult to see what grammatical points are included in Part II. Norms were established from the results obtained in giving the test to high school students of New York State. These norms should be too high for some sections of the country. The key is somewhat awkward to operate. One of the alternate answers given for Item 77 of Part III, Form A, is incorrect.

In summary, the material and makeup of this test are interesting and significant within the indicated limits, but in execution it falls short of its potentialities.

Laura B. Johnson, Assistant Professor in the Teaching of French, The University of Wisconsin. These tests are among the most satisfactory standardized French tests for high-school students. Divided into three parts they test quite adequately recognition of vocabulary, reading ability, and grammar knowledge. The 75 items in the vocabulary test are well chosen. The multiple-choice technique is used, five English words being given as possible translations of each French word. Cognates are avoided and misleading similar words are suggested. One may question the validity of *instance* as a translation of *cas,* or *carry out* as a translation of *accomplir,* but, on the whole, it seems as good a way to measure recognition of isolated words as has yet been devised.

The comprehension part of the test is based on 75 disconnected statements to be identified as true or false. The statements are based on a reasonable vocabulary and increase gradually enough in difficulty to permit of clear differentiation in each year of language study. In at least two instances there is sufficient ambiguity to permit of two possible interpretations which make them invalid as testing instruments. One wonders, however, if accurate interpretation of isolated sentences is as good a test of reading power as comprehension of a connected passage with opportunity for cumulative inference, correlation of ideas, understanding of implication, emphasis, idiomatic phrasing, etc.

The 100 items which make up the grammar test are fairly representative of the grammatical points stressed in high-school classes. However, in some cases, there seems to be rather too much emphasis on unimportant idiomatic usage rather than on significant constructions as such. Because the French words to be inserted into the French context in translating a given English sentence are to be written in the margin apart from the sentence, students often omit a vital word and hence are penalized for an omission rather than a commission.

The chief advantage of this examination is that it includes a sufficient number of relatively easy items to measure adequately achievement in the first- and second-year work and has sufficient range to challenge the most advanced students in fourth-year work. Forms A and B are considered equivalent and duplicable forms.

[1349]

Cooperative French Test [Advanced Form]. 4 semesters or more: high school, or 2 semesters or more: college; 1933-40; 40- and 90-minute editions; 25¢ per specimen set of either edition; Advanced Form P: Geraldine Spaulding and Paule Vaillant; Advanced Form Q: Geraldine Spaulding and Paule Vaillant with the editorial assistance of Algernon Coleman, E. B. DeSauzé, Henry M. Fiske, Stephen L. Pitcher, and Lenore Thomas; New York: Cooperative Test Service.
a) FORMS 1934, 1936, AND 1937. Forms 1933 and 1935 are out of print; 6¢ per test, 10 to 99 copies; 90(95) minutes.
b) REVISED SERIES, ADVANCED FORMS N, O, P, AND Q. 1937-40; 5¢ per test, 10 to 99 copies; 40(45) minutes.

REFERENCES

1 VANDER BEKE, GEORGE E. *French Word Book.* Publications of the American and Canadian Committees on the Modern Languages, Vol. 15. New York: Macmillan Co., 1929. Pp. xiii, 188. $1.10. Paper. (London: Macmillan & Co., Ltd. 5s. 6d.)
2 FICKEN, CLARENCE ELWOOD. *Intercorrelations of Part Scores in Foreign Language Tests.* Unpublished doctor's thesis, University of Wisconsin, 1937. Pp. 120.
3 HANNA, JOSEPH V. "A Comparison of Cooperative Test Scores and High School Grades as Measures for Predicting Achievement in College." *J Appl Psychol* 23:289-97 Ap '39.
4 GIDUZ, HUGO. "The 1939 French Placement Tests at the University of North Carolina." *H Sch J* 23:28-31 Ja '40.

C. E. Ficken, Dean of the College and Professor of French, Macalester College. [Review of Advanced Form P.] This test "is recommended for those students who have had four or more semesters of study in high school French, or at least a year in college, and has the same scope and objectives as indicated . . . for the 90-minute edition." It, therefore, purports to measure throughout this range in forty minutes the nonliterary elements of linguistic achievement other than free composition, pronunciation, and aural skill. The pattern of the longer test is followed in designating the three parts as Reading, Vocabulary, and Grammar but the time proportions of 25, 25, and 40 minutes are revised to 15, 10, and 15 minutes respectively. Test item totals of 80, 100, and 100 are consequently reduced to 45, 40, and 40.

Without a test supply for obtaining empirical data the reviewer undertakes merely an armchair appraisal. The authors give but small consolation when they admit that the shorter tests "are slightly less reliable than the longer tests but are adequate for most purposes," while the manual of directions does not give a reliability coefficient for either. A nonprofit organization of first-rate prestige thereby misses a valuable opportunity to discipline the more mercenary test makers. Meanwhile the cautious examiner can scarcely be blamed for questioning the reliability of a ten or fifteen minute test.

It is encouraging to find that "all test material was given to large numbers of students in order to obtain data from which indices of difficulty and validity could be secured." But again there are no coefficients to demonstrate the statistical validity of the test or any of its three parts. We are merely assured that the successive forms are comparable and equivalent measures of whatever they measure. In short, evaluation of the test is reduced to an analysis of its probable curricular validity.

Part I, Reading, contains twenty-nine items involving word and sentence meaning, while the remaining sixteen items require a multiple-choice interpretation of four brief paragraphs. The proportion suggests that we are measuring vocabulary rather than reading. Ninety-five per cent of the vocabulary used is from Vander Beke's *French Word Book* [1] and hence within the six thousand commonest reading words. This evidence of scientific care is commendable but also points to the absence of sufficiently difficult passages to test the recognition power of a fourth-semester college student. In spite of these limitations, the test probably measures reading ability as well as it can be done in fifteen minutes.

Part II, Vocabulary, adds little of value and should either have been pooled with Part I or omitted. Out of forty words, no fewer than ten are English cognates, whose response word (in French) is likewise a cognate. "Gigantesque" for example, is rendered by "énorme," which would be evident without the slightest knowledge of French. Of the remaining thirty words four or five have answer-synonyms of lower frequency than the test word. In four other cases the answer word merely categorizes the test word and hence credits a most hazy response, as for example, "cigale" is rendered by "insecte." In short, the "direct" method may be good technique for *teaching* vocabulary but becomes a very "indirect," if not abortive, method of *measuring* vocabulary. Furthermore, this reviewer fails to detect any "decoy" elements among the incorrect answer-words. And finally, there is no perceptible progression from easy to difficult question-words.

Part III, Grammar, consists of forty English sentences, each with five French translations. It, therefore, directly measures composition grammar rather than a recognition knowledge of reading essentials. As such it appears to be entirely successful.

To examiners, this reviewer suggests the reduction of the test to thirty minutes by omitting Part II, thus measuring comprehension in a broad sense with Part I and composition grammar with Part III. The results should then be treated as approximations to be interpreted in the light of past or future performance or additional testing. With all its limitations we must recognize that this test is a far better measuring instrument than the traditional examination of yesterday.

Harry Heller, Head of the French Department, Fieldston School, New York, New York. [Review of Advanced Form P.] A survey of our achievements to date in the field of objec-

tive modern foreign language testing is, in general, discouraging. Test makers continue to address themselves, with varying degrees of moderate success, to those aspects of language learning that are most obviously measurable. Nowhere would our survey yield evidence of any concerted pioneering effort to measure the outcomes sought by the best practices of progressive language teaching. A lag between good teaching practice and the production of corresponding instruments of measurement may well be inevitable but, far from assuming any large responsibility for progress, test makers continue to produce instruments—in some cases, as in the one under review, ably constructed and validated on the basis of what it is proposed to measure—that sanction the outworn materials, if not methods, of the days before the Modern Foreign Language Study. These assertions are difficult to support fully within the scope of this review although general and specific considerations bearing upon them will be noted.

In the light of our poor achievements in this field and measured merely against its own claims, this latest form of the *Cooperative French Test* stands favorable comparison with other tests on the market. A teacher or supervisor content to understand the skills of reading, vocabulary, and grammar as presented by the authors, implicit in their test, will find that this instrument attains its stated goal with better than average success. Descriptive and explanatory material concerning the test's construction, validation, norms, etc., is available in rather extensive accompanying booklets, some at a small extra cost. This material appears to be the fruit of considerable research and is marked throughout by sincerity. Useful tables for the conversion of raw scores into special scaled scores for greater comparability are supplied. Tables of percentile norms of recent compilation and for different types of secondary schools and colleges represent another real advantage. The test is adapted to hand or machine scoring.

The three divisions of the test have already been indicated. Part I is made up of short passages of French. The student is invited to select from five choices the word, or small group of words, which completes the prefaced statement. These passages are for the most part too meager to be considered real reading situations. The power to comprehend the unfamiliar when it is in context with the known is barely called into play. In many cases only one of the five choices has any relevance or plausibility. In fact, many items reduce themselves to questions of vocabulary, *acheter* suggesting *argent* and *livre* eliciting *bibliothèque*. The authors will claim that "easy" items must be inserted to provide measurement of individual differences in the lower percentiles. This may not be the place to point out that our tests so far do not reveal important individual *human* differences but only differences from an artificial norm, although it may fairly be asked whether the range of difficulty is wide enough on the upper level to measure individual differences in the higher percentiles. What is involved here, however, is not the difficulty of the reading items but the very definition of the reading skill.

Part II is a vocabulary test of the multiple-choice type. It is difficult to justify, or even discover, any unifying basis on which the words given may have been chosen. Some are common or useful only in specific forms or connections, like *agréer*. Here, too, as in the reading section, many items offer only one alternative, out of five, that is in any way related to the given word. Here even to a lesser extent than on the reading portion will "careful judgment" and "shrewd guessing based on intelligent inference," both invited by the authors' directions to the student, enter into performance. But, above all, this reviewer wishes to question whether vocabulary can usefully be tested by giving words *out of context.*

The grammar section, Part III, contains forty items. In Items 1 to 8 the student chooses the correct form among five to complete the French translation of an English sentence. In Items 9 to 40 he selects the correct French translation among five of an English sentence. It would be difficult to formulate a definition of functional grammar to which competent teachers could subscribe that is met by this test. The most inept French student with the greatest gift for whimsy should feel most at home among these wrong alternative translations! The multiple-choice question admittedly lends itself to objective measurement but is this use of it a good educational procedure? Is it psychologically sound? Many of the items on this part of the test cover fundamental forms, verb tenses, etc., that good teaching and testing alike must treat as simple habit

responses not to be dislocated by offering confusing choices that cannot be distinguished from one another by any process of reasoning or even useful rules. And as for the properly functional aspects of grammar, why not build a multiple-choice test where four out of five alternatives are *correct* or *approximately correct* and only one wrong for some *important reason*? The student could be asked to indicate the best answer as well as the wrong one. The choices he made among items placed in such a juxtaposition would reflect his acquisition of functional grammar concepts in an interesting way.

It should be repeated in all fairness that the *Cooperative French Test* is a relatively good contribution to the measurement of the reading, vocabulary, and grammar skills, although important *redefinitions* of these skills have been suggested. Yet the skills measured, while fundamental in any language teacher's hierarchy of values, received but a few scant lines, and with different emphasis, in the list of desirable outcomes promulgated recently by a "records" committee of language teachers on which this reviewer sat. A director of languages in a large school system has declared publicly that his teachers are not primarily teachers of French, German, or Spanish, but of the social studies! In the second place, said he, they were teachers of language in general. Only lastly, and almost incidentally, were they concerned with the French subjunctive or German word order. This reviewer has little sympathy for this viewpoint. It is like looking through the wrong end of a telescope! It is cited, however, as a symptom of real and growing concerns among language teachers. The test makers are challenged to redefine their old goals and to essay new roads—a difficult task, indeed. They must look to the best, as well as to the most usual, educational procedures for material that is socially significant and interesting to maturing minds and developing personalities. They are challenged to devise tests that are significant educational experiences, the standard by which the teaching art measures itself.

Joseph F. Jackson, Professor of French, The University of Illinois. 〔Review of Advanced Form P.〕 According to a descriptive pamphlet, this form is designed for students who have studied French for four or more semesters in high school or at least one year in college. It consists of three parts. Part I, Reading, 15 minutes, 29 sentences or brief passages, each to be completed by a choice of one of five words or phrases, and 4 longer passages with 16 questions based on them, each to be answered by a choice of one of five words or phrases. This part is entirely in French. Part II, Vocabulary, 10 minutes, 40 French words, each with a series of five French words from which the one most nearly corresponding in meaning to the original is to be selected. Part III, Grammar, 15 minutes, 8 English sentences, each with an incomplete translation to be completed by a choice of one of five expressions, and 32 English sentences, the correct translation of each to be indicated by a choice of one of five options.

The material, which is based almost entirely on the Vander Beke and Cheydleur lists, is well chosen and carefully prepared. The items were pretested for validity and for order of difficulty. The student indicates throughout by number his choice of answers. The test can thus be scored purely objectively, as there is no question of interpretation or of alternate answers.

From the standpoint of rigid measurement a test which lends itself completely to objective scoring is most satisfactory, but the teacher may well find this type of test highly mechanical and narrowly limited. The student is not called upon to write any French, he is asked only to identify correct answers. Nowhere is he required to dip into his own fund of knowledge. The authors of the test recognize as the most generally accepted objectives of modern foreign language study "the acquisition of skill in reading, writing, speaking, and understanding the language." Yet they admit that, since ability to compose in writing and speaking, as well as general oral and aural skill, do not readily lend themselves to objective techniques of testing, there is no attempt made to measure them. This raises a broad, fundamental question which is applicable to all tests of this type. If there are important aspects of language study which can not be scientifically tested and objectively measured, does the objective test furnish an adequate description of the student's general ability?

With reference to the test under consideration, the second section of Part III, which offers for each of 32 English sentences five

French versions, four-fifths of which are barbarisms, represents a device which is antagonistic to sound teaching. Students learn largely by example. Eighty per cent of bad examples in an important section of a formal test can not have a good effect, particularly in the case of a student who chooses and retains a number of improper constructions.

The explanatory and descriptive material dealing with derivation, validity, applicability, establishment of different norms, scoring and interpretation of the scores from various points of view is instructive and interesting. The key is ingeniously constructed and easy to use.

For a review by Nelson Brooks, see 985.

[1350]
Cooperative French Test [Elementary Form]. First 3 semesters: high school, or first semester: college; 1933-40; 40- and 90-minute editions; 25¢ per specimen set of either edition; Elementary Form P: Jacob Greenberg and Geraldine Spaulding; Elementary Form Q: Jacob Greenberg and Geraldine Spaulding with the editorial assistance of Algernon Coleman, E. B. De Sauzé, Henry M. Fiske, Stephen L. Pitcher, and Lenore Thomas; New York: Cooperative Test Service.
a) JUNIOR FORMS 1936 AND 1937. Forms 1933, 1934, and 1935 are out of print; 6¢ per test, 10 to 99 copies; 90(95) minutes.
b) REVISED SERIES, ELEMENTARY FORMS O, P, Q. 1937-40; Form N is out of print; 5¢ per test, 10 to 99 copies; 1½¢ per machine-scorable answer sheet; 40(45) minutes.

REFERENCES

1 VANDER BEKE, GEORGE E. *French Word Book.* Publications of the American and Canadian Committees on Modern Languages, Vol. 15. New York: Macmillan Co., 1929. Pp. xiii, 188. $1.10. Paper. (London: Macmillan & Co., Ltd. 5s. 6d.)
2 EMERY, M. A. *The Composition and Amount of a Minimum Vocabulary for Reading Ungraded French Texts.* Unpublished master's thesis, University of Chicago, 1931. Pp. 39.
3 PURIN, C. M. *A Standard German Vocabulary of 2000 Words and Idioms.* Chicago, Ill.: University of Chicago Press, 1931. Pp. xvi, 195. Out of print.
4 HAYGOOD, J. D. *A Minimum Essential French Reading Vocabulary.* Unpublished master's thesis, University of Chicago, 1932. Pp. 51.
5 THARP, JAMES B. *A Basic French Vocabulary,* Revised edition. New York: Henry Holt and Co., Inc., 1934. Pp. 222. $0.72.
6 GREENBERG, JACOB. *Le Français et la France:* Premier Cours. New York: Charles E. Merrill Co., 1939. Pp. xiii, 433. $1.48.

Warren S. Holmes, Department of French, The Gunnery School, Washington, Connecticut. [Review of Elementary Form P.] This is an excellent test. It is divided into three parts: reading, vocabulary, and grammar. The multiple-choice technique has been used throughout, making the following of directions extremely simple and allowing very rapid and accurate scoring. In fact the test may be machine scored if desired. The accompanying material is abundant, and includes all that could be desired in the matter of use, validation, administration, scoring, and tabulation.

Prospective buyers of this test should realize, however, that it attempts to measure only those skills which "lend themselves readily to objective techniques of testing." It is not a test of the ability to translate a connected passage of French into English or to write connected French prose, either free or from an English model. Yet these are still important objectives, if one is to judge by the emphasis placed upon them in class and preparation time, as well as in examinations set for entrance to many of our universities. Would it not be possible to show a correlation between an objective test of this sort and ability to translate from English to French and vice versa? Such a correlation, if obtainable and made readily accessible in the manual, would be sure of a welcome from practical teachers.

James B. Tharp, Associate Professor of Education, The Ohio State University. [Review of Elementary Form P.] When one considers the careful research and attention to detail based on an expert knowledge of testing techniques and sensitivity to educational purposes that have characterized the construction, validation, and interpretation of the Cooperative tests, one must, generally speaking, accord them first place among educational measurements today. The tests have employed the most objective techniques and have been organized to avoid misunderstanding of directions and to facilitate rapid scoring. Besides a carefully annotated catalogue of test forms, there have been prepared booklets of directions, of norms, and of "purpose, content, and interpretation."

That the French tests have profited from these professional contributions goes without saying. From the thousands of administrations of the 90-minute regular and junior forms from 1933 ending with 1937 among all types of high schools and colleges there have accumulated enough cases to permit establishing norms for three categories of secondary schools and three types of colleges. In each of these six groups hundreds if not thousands of students were tested—sufficient to level off the variation in types of instruction, methods, and content. Reliability coefficients and intercorrelations with other types of measurements are so high that few other tests may rival them. The system of scaled scores and the elaborate tables of percentile ranks make possible many

kinds of educational uses with reasonable confidence in the accuracy of interpretation.

With the highest possible statements of confidence and praise in the mechanical and statistical features, the same cannot be said for the range and selection of content. While some users may quarrel with the lack of variety in the technique of response, this reviewer recognizes the accuracy in objective scoring and accepts the principles of selection. With respect to measurement of grammar, the selection response comes the nearest to testing that type of grammar needed for comprehension, rather than that usually stressed in testing—the grammar needed for expression and creative composition. I say "nearest" because even yet the system of completion of partial translations of English sentences is mainly a measurement of powers of composition rather than of comprehension. When we shall invent nearly pure measurements of the latter, the writer just now cannot predict.

Of 35 items in the grammar portion, 27 are these completions and the remaining 8 are best-answer (5-item choice) exercises, testing the correct rendering in French of an idea expressed in English. It is only by having this second type that word position and order can be measured. This type is also the best device to measure comprehension as well as expression of idioms. The items are well chosen in range of coverage and reflect well the estimated frequency of grammatical phenomena in French discourse. (Only in Spanish has a frequency count in syntax been completed.) Other than to say that there seem to be too many items based on inflections in proportion to the total number of items, the reviewer has only praise for the grammar test.

Part I, Reading, and Part II, Vocabulary, cannot have the same bill of health from this reviewer. In the booklet on purposes, the test authors subscribe to current objectives of reading skill, and while making no promise to use only vocabulary items from the frequency lists for fear that "rigid exclusion . . . would seriously restrict the range of subject matter," state that at least the vocabulary portions "are based directly on the Modern Foreign Language word lists for the respective languages." These statements are made for all the languages, but on the junior forms there is a variation: "The vocabulary part of the Spanish test is derived from the first half of the word book, only. In the German test, the vocabulary items are taken from Purin's *Standard German Vocabulary*.[3] In the French test, it was decided not to limit the choice of words to those of higher frequency in the word book, partly because of the considerable number of 'environmental' words which are widely taught in the first years of French study, but which do not rank high in the frequency list."

It is apparent that these differences represent the different opinions of the authors working in the three languages, for it is especially in French and Spanish that surveys by Haygood,[4] Emery,[2] and others have shown that 80 per cent to 93 per cent of ordinary discourse stays within the first 2,000 words in the word lists. If there still remains a considerable number of low frequency words "widely taught" in French, the reviewer submits that the proportion of environmental words runs quite similar with respect to frequency in each of the languages measured. If the authors of this test accept the word counts as quoted above, it must be that teachers and school syllabi continue to use books written before the word counts or that they do not put first the reading objective. That it is the present trend for authors of new books to use the frequency lists and even restricted selection therefrom is generally accepted. Greenberg, in the preface of his beginners' text *Le Français et la France* [6] says: "The total basic vocabulary of the book is limited to a minimum number of useful words and phrases that are generally chosen on the basis of their range as rated by the Vander Beke *French Word Book*." [1]

Recent published vocabulary syllabi in French (The New York State List, the Secondary Education Board List, the *Basic French Vocabulary*,[5] etc.) all contain at least the first 2,000 words, and idioms proportionately, and add a scattering of words of lower frequency —less than a fifth of the total—somewhat as indicated by the Haygood, Emery, and similar studies.

Finally, there is another reason to question the quoted reasons for validity of a higher proportion of low-frequency words in French than in Spanish or German. While the 90-minute Junior Form may have been devised for and widely used "within the narrow range of junior high school work," this new 40-minute Elementary Form is "especially adapted to beginning classes" (according to the cata-

logue) both in junior and senior high schools and in colleges. The vocabulary problem of beginners at various levels varies only by quantity and speed of assimilation, not by range of selection.

Of the 50 items of the vocabulary test, 30 are from the first thousand, 9 more from the second thousand, the remaining 11 of still lower frequency, the whole having an Index of Frequency of 2.74. Form N (1937) of this series has an index of 2.80 in the Elementary Form as against an index of 6.01 in the Advanced Form. (In this Advanced Form, 27 out of 50 items are beyond the 2,000 range and 26 of these are not found in the *Basic French Vocabulary*. The 50 odd-numbered items in the vocabulary portion of the 1934 "regular" test have an index of 6.6; and 30 of the 50 do not appear in the *Basic French Vocabulary*.) Noting that the Miller-Davis second-year test has an index of 2.37, it is the opinion of the reviewer that on a frequency basis the vocabulary portion of the *Cooperative French Test* seems placed somewhat too high for an elementary test.

The same criticism is advanced on the reading portion. Many of the key words of the sentences set for comprehension, are not among the 3,340 words in *Basic French Vocabulary;* two, *ragoût* and *réveille-matin,* are not among Vander Beke's 6,136 words. A large proportion of words in the 5-item selection responses are not in the *Basic French Vocabulary;* words like *muguets, boucher, épicier,* are not in Vander Beke.

The reading portion of the regular 90-minute forms and of the advanced 40-minute forms begin with short sentences describing an idea or establishing a situation which only one of the selection choices will complete, but the items grow longer and become short paragraphs. The Elementary Form uses exclusively the incomplete sentence, a device that requires the authors to assemble "universally known facts" to which responses are not ambiguous. Of 40 of such sentences, the reviewer judges only 10 to be plain facts; the other 30 are intelligence-test type, of which several are arithmetic problems.

Some of the factual items are ambiguous: e.g., Item 3, Part I, "La fête nationale des États-Unis a lieu (1) très souvent (2) très rarement (3) au mois de juillet (4) en hiver (5) à Paris seulement." May a reader not reason that one day a year is "très rarement"? And suppose the test is measuring reading achievement in Canada and some luckless boy doesn't know the United States' national holiday (do we know that of Canada?)! Another example is Item 38, Part I: "On dit que les chiens qui aboient (1) sont très grands (2) mangent beaucoup de viande (3) aiment à jouer (4) courent dans les rues (5) ne mordent pas." If a reader perchance had never met this famous proverb, must his comprehension of French suffer? He reasons that dogs do two or three things and that the "barking" is merely a confusion item, so he does *not* mark the last choice. It must be admitted that this technique runs the risk of other factors affecting a pure measurement of comprehension of written French. Moreover, the series of disconnected sentences puts too strong a stress on mere vocabulary memory, a factor being measured in a separate part. There is lacking the successive build-up of connected ideas in longer passages and the operation of syntax and idiom as affecting comprehension.

Unfortunately, the tables of norms in terms of scaled scores merge the raw scores of all four types of test, so there is no evidence given of successive achievement levels on this test. It would be interesting to see intercorrelations of the reading and vocabulary measurements— of the relations of the reading and vocabulary measurements, of the regular with the revised series. The high coefficients of reliability (lowest in the vocabulary portion) do not give evidence of validity.

The reviewer would recommend a selection of vocabulary test items (some of them idioms which should not be tested as grammar) more in harmony with research on frequency burden in typical French prose rather than that in widely used beginners' textbooks, until the gap between these two bases becomes narrowed by more genuine adoption of the frequency criterion. For the reading test the reviewer would suggest a series of short paragraphs, each long enough to establish a central idea on which the language, which has been used to express the idea, may be tested on broader factors of comprehension. If a series of sentences is used, why cannot they be connected in thought, perhaps in groups of five or six, based on story pictures so that the hazard of "universally known fact" need not be present to inject a variable error? There are several other types

of reading that we must find ways of measuring before we can consider the field covered.

Although the reviewer sees the difficulty of change of style in maintaining norms on earlier forms, it is probable that the system of scaled scores would safeguard a revision of the reading and vocabulary portions of this test. There is no shadow of doubt that the Cooperative tests, as a general battery of measurements, offer the best instruments available at this date. They have taken testing many strong strides forward.

For a review by Walter V. Kaulfers, see 986.

[1351]
French Life and Culture. High School and College; 1935; 1 form; 50¢ per 25; 15¢ per specimen set; 40(45) minutes; Minnie M. Miller; Emporia, Kan.: Bureau of Educational Measurements, Kansas State Teachers College.

REFERENCES

MILLER, MINNIE. "A Test on French Life and Culture." *Mod Lang J* 20:158-62 D '35.

Bateman Edwards, Head of the Department of Romance Languages, Washington University. This test raises the problem of the possibility of imparting to students in elementary French courses a grasp of the essentials of French life and culture. The objective is admirable, but, if this knowledge were to be gained in the French course alone, it is difficult to see how teachers could maintain normal progress in the acquisition of the language and at the same time furnish the necessary "information on French geography, history, government, art, literature, science, and customs." Even if some one of the manuals of French civilization which are now on the market were to be included in the student's reading, their necessarily summary treatment of a large number of subjects would not be sufficient to impress detailed points on the student's mind. Consequently, the test becomes, in some measure, one of general information gleaned from a variety of sources, requiring no knowledge of French as a language.

Leaving aside the question of how cultural information is to be obtained, the value of such information is obvious. The test under discussion organizes its material of 100 questions into three parts, which represent differing techniques of examination. Part I is the most valuable, since it tests the student's own factual information by means of 40 questions with no prompting lists of answers. Part II consists of 30 questions grouped into two equal sections, the first covering geography, history, and government, the second covering art, literature, and science. Corresponding to each section is an alphabetical list of 20 possible answers. Part III contains 30 statements to be completed by one of three possibilities.

The need for inclusion of some of the items represented may be questioned. For example: questions based on the comparison of French and American systems of measure lack value if there has been no practical experience with both; a knowledge of the present-day population of France and of Paris is significant only when related to that of other countries and cities, or of other centuries; the ability to choose between the Place de la Concorde and the Place de la République as the largest public square in Paris does not necessarily imply any worth-while grasp of French life and culture.

A graver criticism results from the fact that a test of cultural values is, of all tests, the least suited to the present fashion for examinations which can be marked by clerks who need have no knowledge of the subject. Of what value is it to be able to state that the French Renaissance took place in the sixteenth century, unless one can also state what the qualities and influence of that Renaissance are? Is the student who, from a list of twenty names, can pick out that of André Maurois as "a well-known writer of present-day France" to be compared to one who could state some significant fact about the writings of Maurois or of any one of a number of authors of greater merit? The ultimate test of our knowledge of a civilization is not the ability to fit a word into its proper place, to recall or select the isolated fact, but to understand the meaning and importance of the fact, to put in order a number of facts so that their relations and the implications of those relations are apparent. Insistence on the single unrelated and undefined fact, such as demanding the word "gothic" to characterize the style of architecture used in the French medieval cathedrals, leads to partial and ill-digested knowledge. Certainly, a factual examination has its place in any study of a civilization, and the present examination is well-balanced and comprehensive in the facts it demands, but it would be ridiculous to claim that its results could point to more than a superficial knowledge of the subject.

In at least three cases in Part III (Items 86, 88, and 89), the words offered to complete the sense suffer from a lack or a superfluity of definite articles. It is impossible to speak of "the Notre-Dame de Paris" or of "Jardin du Luxembourg," and to call the wood or park in the west part of Paris "Boulogne" is distressingly ambiguous. A more careful wording of the sentences might remove such faults.

Clarence E. Turner, Assistant Professor of the Romance Languages, Rutgers University. This test purports to measure "such information on French geography, history, government, art, literature, science, and customs as students may reasonably be expected to acquire in two years of high school, or one year of college French." All the questions are in English. Part I calls for one- to three-word answers in English to forty factual questions. Part II calls for the matching of fifteen questions on geography and history with twenty possible answers, and of fifteen questions on literature and the fine arts with twenty other answers. Part III offers a choice of best answer from among three to each of thirty questions representing all of the fields mentioned. The material is somewhat crowded on the page, especially in Parts II and III.

The accompanying manual gives no account of the test's construction and validity beyond the following assertion: "The items were selected from valid sources. The items themselves, as well as their proportional distribution among the various fields of subject matter, were carefully checked by teachers of French in high schools and colleges." The omission of some further demonstration of the test's validity is particularly regrettable for two reasons. First, because it purports to measure achievement in a field where there is no readily accepted valid criterion of achievement. Second, because many of the items appear to have little or no discriminatory power with reference to the achievement under test.

Actually, the test measures factual information. Much of this information is often, and some of it is almost always, acquired by students prior to the study of French: "Name one Frenchman who aided the thirteen colonies during the American Revolution." "Who was commander-in-chief of the allied armies at the close of the World War?" Other questions may be answered by a significant number of students on the basis of information acquired elsewhere in the curriculum: "Is the kilogram more or less than the pound?" "What duke of Normandy conquered England?" Some are both extraneous and trivial: "What colors are used in the French flag?"

About seventy of the items call for information which would normally be encountered only in the French classroom, and then only if emphasis were there placed upon one or more of the manuals which convey that thin mixture of geography, history, sociology, and literature which is sometimes called Civilization. Information gained from one of these books is necessarily superficial and unrelated to that which gives it significance. Consequently, some items of the test under review remind one, by their stressing of the small fact for its own sake, of a well-known radio program: "What is the largest public square in Paris?" "The approximate population of Paris is: (1) 3,000,000 (2) 5,000,000 (3) 1,500,000."

There are a few inaccuracies. The key wrongly insists on "No" as the answer to Item 21, "Are the church and state separated in France?" Dumas *père* and not just Dumas ought perhaps to be exacted as the answer to Item 39. Item 46 may be missed by the student with the best information, who knows that the chateau of Versailles was begun under Louis XIII. Item 86 offers a choice of three impossible answers, since the wood or park in the west part of Paris is not called *Boulogne,* any more than it is called *Tuileries* or *Luxembourg.*

One's total judgment of the test is bound up with that of the curriculum which it reflects, since it has been noted that only for a certain type of curriculum could the test claim validity. It will seem to many teachers that there is no possibility on this earth of building a significant knowledge of any national life and culture without founding it upon a fluent command of the language of that culture. Imparting such command of the printed and spoken language is surely the legitimate business of the modern language teacher, and no other comparable contribution to the student's ultimate knowledge and understanding of a national culture lies within his power. The time spent in preparing students to produce odd bits of information about kilograms, bridges, and authors one-to-a-century, is time spent at the expense of the student in his progress toward meaningful knowledge.

[1352]

French Reading: Dominion Tests. Grade 10; 1940; 2 forms; 2¢ per test in quantity; 15¢ per preliminary manual; 5¢ per sample test; 30(40) minutes; Toronto, Canada: Department of Educational Research, University of Toronto.

[1353]

French Vocabulary Test: Dominion Tests. Grades 9-10; 1940; 2 forms; 2¢ per test in quantity; 15¢ per preliminary manual; 5¢ per sample test; 30(40) minutes; Toronto, Canada: Department of Educational Research, University of Toronto.

[1354]

Lundeberg-Tharp Audition Test in French. High school and college; 1934; 2 forms; $2 per 100; 75¢ per 25; percentile rank norms furnished on request; 10¢ per specimen set; James B. Tharp and Olav K. Lundeberg; Columbus, Ohio: James B. Tharp, Ohio State University.

REFERENCES

1 THARP, JAMES B. "Effect of Oral-Aural Ability on Scholastic Achievement in Modern Foreign Languages." *Mod Lang J* 15:10-26 O '30.
2 THARP, JAMES B. "Lundeberg-Tharp Audition-Pronunciation Test in French." *Mod Lang Forum* 16:4-7 Ja '31.
3 THARP, JAMES B. "A Modern Language Test." *J Higher Ed* 6:103-4 F '35.

Nelson Brooks, Instructor in French, Westover School, Middlebury, Connecticut. The first question that arises when one is confronted with a highly objective test is this: what is the relation between the score one makes on this test and one's actual success in applying in real life the ability being measured? The maker of a test in oral comprehension of a foreign language has an unusual opportunity, for he can make his test of problems that are almost identical with those of normal social contact. The makers of this test have profited well by this opportunity, and have devised problems that are as natural as that of understanding a name over the telephone.

The test contains three groups of questions. In the first, the student sees before him four words or word groups that are similar but not identical in sound, and upon hearing one of them pronounced, indicates which one he has heard. In the second, the student listens while the examiner reads aloud in French a sentence that is complete except for the final word. The student then writes, in either French or English, the word that rightly completes the thought of the sentence. In the third type, the examiner reads aloud a definition of an object or an idea and the student then writes in a single word what it is that has been described. In these last two groups, the answer is to be found in the question itself, and a well-trained student can do all parts of the test without any reference to English.

Part III, the definition series, is the least satisfactory section, for definitions are devious at best, and such a one as Item 20 (Form B, Part III) "action de se mettre la nourriture dans la bouche, la mâcher avec les dents, l'infiltrer de salive and ensuite de l'avaler" seems to go a very long way around. But such heaviness and artificiality occur only rarely, and a much more typical item is Item 24 of the same section: "plante dont on fume les feuilles desséchées."

The authors provide one or two reassuring bits of information that may forestall criticism on certain points. In the first part, the test of "phonetic accuracy," two methods of administration were employed, one in which the student heard four words or word groups and saw one, the other in which he saw four groups and heard one. As there was no appreciable difference in the results of these two methods, the second and obviously shorter method was retained. Also, the scores on this part of the test were compared with ratings based on phonograph recordings of individual pronunciation by several classes of high school and college students, with correlations as high as .84 on the two types of test. The writers feel, therefore, that they have devised what is a reasonably reliable index of a student's pronunciation.

The test contains many useful reminders such as "account for every test sheet; avoid pantomime; do not finish the incompleted sentence inadvertently" and to the students "avoid coughing and shuffling of feet." The presence of such practical details gives the user confidence that the authors have done a thorough job in perfecting this test in the only way such a test can be perfected, that is, in collaboration with the student.

[1355]

Miller-Davis French Test. First, second years; 1935; 1 form, 2 levels; 50¢ per 25; 15¢ per specimen set; 40(45) minutes; Minnie Miller and Vera Davis; Emporia, Kan.: Bureau of Educational Measurements, Kansas State Teachers College.
a) TEST I. First year.
b) TEST II. Second year.

REFERENCES

1 VANDER BEKE, GEORGE E. *French Work Book.* Publications of the American and Canadian Committees on Modern Languages, Vol. 15. New York: Macmillan Co., 1929. Pp. xiii, 188. $1.10. Paper. (London: Macmillan & Co., Ltd. 5s. 6d.)

Walter V. Kaulfers, Associate Professor of Education in Foreign Languages, Stanford University. Tests I and II are about as reliable and valid as any short 40-minute omnibus tests of general achievement in a foreign language can be. Whether or not the tests serve adequately to measure all the things claimed—vocabulary, pronunciation, grammar, translation, reading for thought content, and information on French life and culture, is questionable. No effort has seemingly been made to compute the reliability and validity of the individual parts devoted to vocabulary, grammar, pronunciation, etc. Consequently, the test cannot be considered diagnostic except in the sense of indicating general areas of weakness. Even for this purpose, however, the items on French culture are too few (only 8 in Test II, and only 5 in Test I) to be indicative of anything at all. In Test II these few items are included among purely vocabulary items with the result that the validity of the section is jeopardized.

Nevertheless, this innovation, feeble as it is, represents a significant beginning in achievement testing in the foreign languages. It represents the probable trend of the future. Indeed, many frontier workers in the foreign languages are ready even now to evaluate their offerings primarily in terms of functional reading ability and functional cultural acquirements in the way of useful information and desirable attitudes, interests, and appreciations acquired in and through the foreign language conceived as a means of communication. Apparently the cultural objective is taking root sufficiently to be given incidental consideration in testing programs. However, if the *Miller-Davis French Tests* truly represent answers to the prayers of high-school teachers for tests that will do justice to what they teach, then it is evident that most French teachers are still spending most of their time drilling students on nonfunctional grammar-translation or proofreading exercises. In reality, Parts III and IV in both tests might well be omitted as failing to measure anything worth measuring as an indication of the student's ability to use French correctly in his *own* original oral or written speech. The transfer value of proofreading or translation exercises in formal grammar to actual extemporaneous or impromptu speech has yet to be demonstrated in any language. The evidence to date tends overwhelmingly to indicate that there is little or no transfer value at all. Despite this fact Tests I and II devote more items to grammar than to any other phase of French. The number of items devoted to grammar even exceeds the number assigned to reading. The reading sections are, in fact, the least objective of the six parts of the tests. It is unfortunate that multiple-choice or true-false correction-type items could not have been used here.

By and large the tests are about as satisfactory and inexpensive as any brief omnibus measures of general achievement in conservative French courses. The tests have the advantage of brevity and simplicity in giving and scoring (except Part VI in both tests which involves handwriting). One disadvantage is the small type in which the tests are printed. Moreover, the norms must be used with some caution since they are based on only 469 cases for Test I and 500 cases for Test II. Fortunately these norms represent the achievement of students in several different schools and localities.

James B. Tharp, Associate Professor of Education, The Ohio State University. Of the 100 points to be scored, 5 points each are given to pronunciation and to cultural information in Test I, and similarly, 10 and 8 points respectively in Test II. While highly desirable from the point of view of coverage, the smallness of the sampling renders this use of the time consumed rather dubious. These areas merit measurement each by a separate test. Unless the samplings can be increased to a point more safely valid, these sections had better be omitted.

Part I of each test lists 30 vocabulary items (of which the last 5 are high-frequency idioms). The items have been well chosen and the selection responses thoughtfully arranged. There are 19, 8, and 3 items respectively from the first three 500-word groups of the *French Word Book*[1] in Test I; and 12, 4, 8, 3, and 3 items from respective groups in Test II. On a point-ratio basis, calling the first 500 groups worth 1, the second, 2, etc., the Index of Frequency of Test I is 1.13; of Test II, 2.37. Again the only danger is the small size of the sampling; the range is excellent. Of the various techniques employed to measure grammar, the most nearly valid is that of Part III of Test I, a completion exercise with 4-item selection responses. The partial-translation completions of Part IV, as usual, permit only the testing of forms and agreements. The translation to

French of English verb forms of Part III, Test II, is valid for composition aims, but the arrangement of the partial-translation completions of Part IV leaves much to be desired. It causes such a hybrid as *"nous* of it *avons besoin,"* a child that neither a French nor an English mother would recognize. Had the English phrase been placed in front of the incomplete French sentence with no blank indicated, both form and position could have been measured by requiring the complete sentence to be written with the missing item in its proper place. Preferably, with a preceding sentence to set the problem, a mutation exercise could have measured this phenomenon much more effectively.

In Part VI, paragraph comprehension is tested by two and three paragraphs of 100 to 200 running words, very well chosen as to advance of vocabulary burden between the two levels. Unfortunately, there are too many questions on each paragraph, and of the 25 in Test I, 12 are of yes-no type, good only for vocabulary testing through the requirement to respond only in English. Fewer items, factual and thought questions, weighted if it is desired to give more value to reading, would probably give a more valid measurement of comprehension.

One serious defect of all the multiple-choice sections of the test is the failure to provide for the correction formula [Score $= R - W/(N - 1)$]. For example, when a four-choice response is used, one may score 25 per cent by a random guess. The writer tried this out in the 30-item vocabulary tests, marking the third response down the list. There were 7 and 9 items on Tests I and II, respectively, correct by this guess. The test author virtually spotted the candidate fourteen points on each test, as proved when the reviewer guessed at all the other selection type exercises in the same way. With correction formulas provided for, a stiffening of the questions on paragraph comprehension, a refinement of technique in measuring grammar, and omission of pronunciation and culture tests in favor of more extensive testing of these areas by other instruments (in particular the *Miller Test on French Life and Culture* and one of several aural tests), the excellent range and choice of content of these tests could be reworked into highly desirable measurements of general achievement in French.

[1356]
Standard French Test: Vocabulary, Grammar, and Comprehension. Semesters 1-5: high school; 1929; 1 form; $1.50 per 25; 15¢ per specimen set; Peter Sammartino and Carl A. Krause; Bloomington, Ill.: Public School Publishing Co.
a) PART I. 28(35) minutes.
b) PART II. 32(40) minutes.

REFERENCES

1 SAMMARTINO, PETER. "An Experiment in Modern Languages." *B High Points* 10:15-21 N '28.
2 SAMMARTINO, PETER. "A Standardized Test in Modern Languages." *J Ed Res* 20:231-3 O '29.

Laura B. Johnson, Assistant Professor in the Teaching of French, The University of Wisconsin. This test covers vocabulary, grammar, and comprehension in each of its two parts. The reviewer's opinion that Part II is definitely more difficult than Part I is corroborated by the higher score made throughout Part I by first, second, third, and fourth semester students in all but two instances. It leads one to wonder why first or even second semester students should spend time taking the second part on which they can hope to recognize relatively few items. If one considers both parts as a whole, the test includes 100 words to be identified in five-response multiple-choice exercises, 50 grammatical items to be filled in with the correct French words, and five brief reading passages on each of which five English questions are to be answered. The words in the vocabulary test are wisely chosen, with few exceptions, and the grammatical items are based on constructions most frequently drilled in class. The test on comprehension seems quite inadequate because of the extreme brevity of the passages chosen and the nature of the questions which seem to reduce interpretation of the reading passage to almost verbatim translation. The test can be easily and quickly administered, graded, and scored.

GERMAN

[1357]
American Council Alpha German Test. Grades 9-16; 1926-27; 2 forms, 2 parts; 35¢ per specimen set; 40(45) minutes per part; V. A. C. Henmon, B. Q. Morgan, Stella M. Hinz, C. M. Purin, and Elizabeth Rossberg; prepared for the Modern Language Study under the auspices of the American Council on Education and the Conference of Canadian Universities; Yonkers, N. Y.: World Book Co.
a) PART I [VOCABULARY AND GRAMMAR]. $1.30 per 25.
b) PART II [SILENT READING AND COMPOSITION]. $1.25 per 25.

REFERENCES

1 MORGAN, B. Q., EDITOR. *German Frequency Word Book*: based on Kaeding's Häufigkeitswörterbuch der deutschen Sprache. Publications of the American and Canadian Committees on Modern Languages, Vol. 9. New York: Macmillan Co.,
1928. Pp. xv, 87. $0.75. Paper. (London: Macmillan & Co., Ltd. 2*s.* 6*d.*)
2 HENMON, V. A. C. *Achievement Tests in Modern Foreign Languages*: Prepared for the Modern Language Study and the Canadian Committee on Modern Languages, pp. 1-266. Publications of the American and Canadian Committees on Modern Languages, Vol. 5. New York: Macmillan Co., 1929. Pp. xxvii, 363. $1.00. Paper. (London: Macmillan & Co., Ltd. 4*s.* 6*d.*)
3 American Association of Teachers of German, Committee on the Word List. "Minimum Standard Vocabulary for German." *German Q* 7:87-119 My '34.

C. H. Handschin, Professor of German and Executive Officer of Graduate Work, Miami University. REVIEW OF PART I. This is an effective test, as far as the general technique goes. An adequate manual of directions and key are supplied. The first item is a multiple-choice vocabulary test, and consists of 100 German words, each followed by five English words, one of which is the equivalent of the German word. The task is to select this equivalent from among the five English words.

This multiple-response exercise is well known. However, it is not suited in this form to modern language testing because the one being tested must spend his time studying English words, instead of German words; i.e., he must compare the English words, one after another, with his idea of what the German word means. His attention is therefore predominantly on the English words.

It would be far better in these multiple-choice responses as used in foreign language tests, if there were one English word and five German words, one of which were the equivalent of the German word. It would be presumed that he knew the English word and his time would be spent on trying to recall the meaning of the five German words, all of which would redound to his knowledge of German.

Another weakness of this vocabulary test is the fact that the words were taken from Morgan's adaptation [1] of Kaeding's frequency list. It should instead be based on the "Minimum Standard Vocabulary for German," [3] the official list of the American Association of Teachers of German. This list was not available when this test was written.

This official list is far superior to Kaeding's list. (*See* Morgan's *German Frequency Word Book*, which is based on Kaeding's list.) In the first place, about 400 words were eliminated as belonging to realms not needed by our American students, and then quite a number of use-words eminently useful for our students were added. Future tests should be based only on this list.

The second item in the test is made up of multiple-choice exercises on grammatical forms in sentences. There are fifty English sentences. Each one is followed by four German sentences, one of which is correct. This is the proper technique, as the time and effort of the one being tested is spent in studying the four German sentences.

The grammatical knowledge necessary to do these exercises is what is known as recognitional (not functional) knowledge of grammar. Since the recognitional grammar is now in many schools the sole grammatical objective, this sort of test may be welcomed.

The test shows another weakness in that it is nowhere stated what stage of ability (how many semesters of work) the test proposes to test. It is assumed that it is meant to test two years of college, or four years of high school work.

REVIEW OF PART II. Item 1 of this test is writing a composition in eight minutes about the picture reproduced on the first inside cover page. This is a difficult task and should be demanded only of classes that have had considerable work in writing German. Writing is a perfectly legitimate objective, if time is ample. In most schools the first, sometimes the only objective, is a reading knowledge. In such classes as this the exercise might be omitted.

The scoring is not as simple as on the other parts of the test. It is done by the aid of the scale supplied and can be done only by the teacher, or other competent person.

Item 2 is a test of silent reading, and consists of seven paragraphs of increasing difficulty, chosen on the basis of preliminary testing. Whether the gradation of difficulty is absolutely correct or not makes no great difference.

The technique employed is to base a number of German questions on each paragraph. These are to be answered in English. This is a proper gauge of comprehension, as the precise thought must be reproduced.

The weakness of the test is that it does not state what portion of the frequency word list it tests, whether the first 1,000, 1,500 or 2,000 words, or what.

It is necessary that the test be based on a certain portion or on the entire frequency word list, and that this be then stated in the description of the test. For no teacher can guarantee that his pupils know any portion of the frequency word list—no matter how many ordinary reading texts his class has read, unless he teaches the words of the word list somehow in addition. If, therefore, his class is to take a test successfully he should know what portion of the frequency word list it tests.

[1358]
American Council on Education German Reading Test. 2 semesters or more of college German; 1937-38; Forms A and B; 5¢ per test, 10 to 99 copies; 25¢ per specimen set; 50(55) minutes; prepared for the Committee on Modern Languages; E. P. Appelt and V. A. C. Henmon; New York: Cooperative Test Service.

For a review by Curtis C. D. Vail, see 999.

[1359]
Columbia Research Bureau German Test. Grades 9-15; 1926-27; 2 forms; $1.30 per 25; 20¢ per specimen set; 90(95) minutes; C. M. Purin and Ben D. Wood; Yonkers, N. Y.: World Book Co.

REFERENCES

1 WOOD, BEN D. *New York Experiments with New-Type Modern Language Tests*: Including a Survey of Modern Language Achievement in the Junior High Schools of New York City, June, 1925; The Regents Experiment of June, 1925, with New-Type Tests in French, German, Spanish, and Physics; and A Second Survey of Modern Language Achievement in the Junior High Schools of New York City, June, 1926, pp. 105-319. Publications of the American and Canadian Committees on Modern Languages, Vol. 1. New York: Macmillan Co., 1927. Pp. xxii, 339. Paper. Out of print.

Harold B. Dunkel, Examiner, Board of Examinations, The University of Chicago. These tests consist of three parts: I, Vocabulary, 25 minutes; II, Comprehension, 20 minutes; and III, Grammar, 45 minutes. The norms are derived from the New York Regents examination of 1925.

Part I presents 100 isolated German words with the answers in multiple-choice form. That the words are not given in context is certainly a serious objection. Whatever the instructional method followed, reading is always an important, and usually the primary, objective; and vocabulary is usually taught and learned with reading in view. Hence it seems logical that vocabulary should be tested in some manner which approximates the reading situation. But even granting the present technique, we find flaws in its execution. In a good many cases, the student selects his answer, not from all four or five possibilities offered (unfortunately only four possibilities are printed for some items), but from fewer. For example, although the capitalization plainly indicates which German words are nouns—English verbs, adverbs, and adjectives are offered as possible distractors for them. These possibilities the student immediately rules out. Or, frequently the correct answer and its opposite (e.g., wet, dry) are both included. The experienced test-taker guesses that the correct answer is one of these, and his chances become one out of two, not one out of five.

Part II contains 75 statements of the true-false type and shows all the faults of this form. The familiar determiners (manchmal, alle, nie, immer, oft selten, and the like) frequently betray the answer. Even worse are some statements of doubtful validity in a German examination. That "Ein Pfund Eisen wiegt mehr als ein Pfund Wolle" is obviously a false statement, but one can catch too many people on this item in English for it to be a valid item in a German test. Similarly, to decide the truth or falsity of "Damit der Luftballon in die Höhe steige, muss er mit einem Gase gefüllt werden, das schwerer ist als die atmosphärische Luft" demands some knowledge of physics as well as of German. Even worse are statements of the proverbial sort like: "Oft sprechen die Leute am meisten, welche nichts zu sagen haben," or "Jede Dummheit findet einen, der sie macht." Before I can pass judgment on "Nach einem heissen Tage folgt manchmal eine kühle Nacht," I must have some idea of what the author means by "manchmal" and some reports from the weather bureau. With items like these, it is nothing short of miraculous that this section ever attained its published reliability of .80. In any event, I doubt whether the ability here tested is ability to read with some comprehension continuous passages of German.

Part III, though called grammar, really tests, through sentence completion, active ability to use the language in writing and speaking rather than ability to read. Aside from such help as this power may give in reading, writing and speaking have a legitimate place in modern foreign language instruction. I wonder, however, whether this place is sufficiently great to merit one-half the testing time. If we dismiss this objection, this section of the test, as might be expected from the time devoted to it, does seem an adequate sampling of the actual knowledge required for writing and speaking on an elementary level, and appears to merit its reliability of .95.

The norms are based on examinations of 1925. Considering the changes in language instruction which have taken place since that date, I am extremely dubious of the value of these norms. The fact that they are based on pupils from New York state alone also makes them of questionable national value. Furthermore, they are entirely in terms of high school years; consequently, for high school no semester norms are available, and the college instructor must content himself with his best guess as to how his semesters or quarters correspond with high-school years in New York during the year 1925.

In the past thirteen years more progress has been made in testing than in automobile construction. To say that this test and a 1926 Ford appear odd to us is no reflection on the authors or Mr. Ford. Both the test and the car were good in their day; but that day has passed.

[1360]

Cooperative German Test [Advanced Form]. 4 semesters or more: high school; or 1 year or more: college; 1933-40; 40- and 90-minute editions; 25¢ per specimen set of either edition; Advanced Form P: Miriam Van Dyck Hespelt, E. Herman Hespelt, and Geraldine Spaulding; Advanced Form Q: Miriam Van Dyck Hespelt, E. Herman Hespelt, and Geraldine Spaulding with the editorial assistance of E. W. Bagster-Collins, E. E. Cochran, Warner F. Gookin, C. M. Purin, and E. H. Zeydel; New York: Cooperative Test Service.

a) FORMS 1935, 1936, AND 1937. Forms 1933 and 1934 are out of print; 6¢ per test, 10 to 99 copies; 90(95) minutes.

b) REVISED SERIES ADVANCED FORMS N, O, P, AND Q. 1937-40; 5¢ per test, 10 to 99 copies; 1½¢ per machine-scorable answer sheet; 40(45) minutes.

REFERENCES

1 MORGAN, B. Q. *A German Frequency Word Book*: Based on Kaeding's Häufigkeitswörterbuch der deutschen Sprache. Publications of the American and Canadian Committees on Modern Languages, Vol. 9. New York: Macmillan Co., 1928. Pp. xiii, 87. $0.75. Paper. (London: Macmillan & Co., Ltd. 2s. 6d.)
2 HAUCH, EDWARD F. *A German Idiom List*: Selected on the Basis of Frequency and Range of Occurrence. Publications of the American and Canadian Committees on Modern Languages, Vol. 8. New York: Macmillan Co., 1929. Pp. xi, 98. $0.80. Paper. (London: Macmillan & Co., Ltd. 2s. 6d.)
3 PATERSON, DONALD G.; SCHNEIDLER, GWENDOLEN G.; AND WILLIAMSON, EDMUND G. *Student Guidance Techniques*, pp. 143-5. New York: McGraw-Hill Book Co., Inc., 1938. Pp. xviii, 316. $3.00. (London: McGraw-Hill Publishing Co., Ltd. 18s.)
4 HANNA, JOSEPH V. "A Comparison of Cooperative Test Scores and High School Grades as Measures for Predicting Achievement in College." *J Appl Psychol* 23:289-97 Ap '39.

C. H. Handschin, Professor of German and Executive Officer of Graduate Work, Miami University. [Review of Advanced Form P.] This test is designed for groups having had four semesters or more of high school work, or at least one year of college work. The test is divided into three parts. Part I, Reading, consists of 45 sentence-completion exercises. An incomplete German sentence is given, followed by five German words or phrases, only one of which makes sense. Beginning with Item 32, several exercises are based on a single

portion of text. There are 45 exercises all told in this part.

Part II is a multiple-choice vocabulary test. A German word is followed by five other German words, only one of which is an equivalent of the first word given. The task is to select the equivalent word.

This also is a proper technique; i.e., giving one German word or phrase, followed by a number of German words or phrases. This technique can be employed whether the test attempts to test single words, phrases, sentences, or syntactical expressions.

Part III contains 40 multiple-choice completion exercises, the part to be supplied consisting in this case of grammatical forms. An English sentence is given, followed by a correct German translation except that one word is omitted. There follow five forms, only one of which is correct in the sentence as given. The task is to choose and insert this correct form.

The knowledge called for includes articles, interrogative pronouns, verb forms, personal pronouns, adjectives, possessives, relative pronouns, case and inflections of nouns and pronouns, auxiliary verbs, and cases after (prepositions, word position, etc.).

The knowledge called for is of functional grammar, since the examinee must not only recognize the form in question but must choose a form to fit into the sentence.

This is an effective test. Here again, however, there is no proper account of the derivation of the test given. There is merely a footnote on page eighteen of the Handbook implying that the source of the material used is Morgan's *German Frequency Word Book*,[1] and Hauch's *German Idiom List*.[2] As in the case of the other texts discussed above, there is no statement as to what portions of the word or idiom list the test is based on. To be sure there is no frequency list of syntactical expressions for German yet.

For a review by Curtis C. D. Vail, see 1000.

[1361]

Cooperative German Test [Elementary Form]. 1-6 semesters: grades 6-9; 1937-39; 25¢ per specimen set of either edition; Elementary Form P: Emma Popper, Alice Miller, and Lucy M. Will; New York: Cooperative Test Service.
a) JUNIOR FORMS 1933 AND 1934. Form 1935 is out of print; 6¢ per test, 10 to 99 copies; 90(95) minutes.
b) ELEMENTARY FORMS N, O, AND P. 1937-39; 5¢ per test, 10 to 99 copies; 1½¢ per machine-scorable answer sheet; 40(45) minutes.

For a review by Curtis C. D. Vail, see 1001.

ITALIAN

[1362]

Cooperative Italian Test. 2 semesters or more: high school or college; 1940; Experimental Form Q; 6¢ per test, 10 to 99 copies; 25¢ per specimen set; 70(75) minutes; Peter Riccio and Anthony Cuffari; New York: Cooperative Test Service.

LATIN

[1363]

Cicero Test. High school and college; 1937; 1 form; 50¢ per 25; 10¢ per specimen set; 40(45) minutes; Mary Alice Seller and H. E. Schrammel; Emporia, Kan.: Bureau of Educational Measurements, Kansas State Teachers College.

S. D. Atkins, Department of Classics, Princeton University. Part I contains a long passage taken from Cicero's second speech against Verres and twenty appended true-false statements. Its aim is to test the student's ability to read and comprehend Ciceronian Latin. That aim has been admirably achieved by a careful choice of the reading passage and a skillful construction of the true-false statements. This is the most important and valuable section of a test that has many good features, but is very badly proportioned. This first portion is almost a complete test of 40 minutes in itself and yet that is the time allowance for the whole test. The reading selection consists of 1½ Teubner pages or, more exactly, 54 lines. Even the most brilliant student at the Cicero level cannot read and really comprehend 54 lines of a Verrine oration which he has not previously seen, and adequately handle the appended statements in less than 20 or 25 minutes. That leaves 15 or 20 minutes to answer the 56 other items on the test. All items weigh equally in the determination of the final score. It is my opinion that the time limit for this test should be extended 20 minutes at least and Part I should count much more heavily than the other two parts or the whole test should be drastically pruned. In either case the time allotments *for each part* ought to be clearly indicated.

Part II (14 items) examines a knowledge of syntax through the medium of the continuous narrative. Certain words and phrases are printed in bold face in the narrative and then are printed again below followed by technical terms descriptive of various grammatical constructions. The student is required to make a correct choice from the several possibilities. For example: "( ) 22. *nullīs.* 1. dative, ind. obj. 2. dat. of possession. 3. dat. of person judging." The Latin passage consists of 36 Teubner lines taken from the third speech *In Catilinam.* The employment of the continuous narrative as an instrument for testing syntax is praiseworthy. The attachment thereto of questions that emphasize correct "pigeonholing" rather than correct perception of relations is deplorable, particularly when it necessitates a familiarity with such absurd artificial refinements as a "dative of person judging" which, according to the key, is the correct answer in the example cited above.

Part III, comprising 42 true-false statements, is divided into two sections. Section A continues the examination of an ability to remember technical labels and formal rules of grammar. The statements are of this kind: "( ) 41. There are at least seven ways of expressing purpose in Latin." For some reason not apparent to me there are two statements in this group totally unrelated to the rest, one concerning consuls and the other the praetorship. It is my belief that this section might be deleted with little loss. Section B tests a factual knowledge of social life, political events and figures, and governmental organization in the Ciceronian period. In general, the statements are well-formulated, of a sufficiently wide range, and as thought-provoking as any of a true-false type can be.

The following corrections are suggested: *causa* for *causā* in line 45, Part I; "Sicily" for "Italy" in Item 5 of Part I (or − for + on the answer key); *ac* for *as* in line 4, Part II, Section A; *restitisse* for *resistisse* in line 4, Part II, Section B; and "causal" for "casual" in Item 28 of Part II. It is also suggested that the words translated or explained in the footnotes to the comprehension selection in Part I receive some sort of identification mark in the text itself.

With some revision this could be made an acceptable test of the objective type.

[1364]

Cooperative Latin Test [Advanced Form]. 2 years or more of Latin; 1933-40; 40- and 90-minute editions; 25¢ per specimen set of either edition; Advanced Form P: John C. Kirtland assisted by Ruth B. McJimsey and Bernard M. Allen; Advanced Form Q: George A. Land; New York: Cooperative Test Service.
a) FORMS 1933, 1936, AND 1937. Forms 1934 and 1935 are out of print; 6¢ per test, 10 to 99 copies; 1½¢ per

machine-scorable answer sheet for Form 1937; 90(95) minutes.
b) REVISED SERIES, ADVANCED FORMS N, O, P, AND Q. 1937-40; 5¢ per test, 10 to 99 copies; 1½¢ per machine-scorable answer sheets; 40(45) minutes.

For a review by Norman T. Pratt, Jr., see 1064.

[1365]

Cooperative Latin Test [Elementary Form]. 1-3 semesters: high school; 1933-40; 40- and 90-minute editions; 25¢ per specimen set of either edition; Elementary Form P: John C. Kirtland assisted by Ruth B. McJimsey and Geraldine Spaulding; Elementary Form Q: George A. Land; New York: Cooperative Test Service.
a) JUNIOR FORMS 1934, 1936, AND 1937. Forms 1933 and 1935 are out of print; 6¢ per test, 10 to 99 copies; 1½¢ per machine-scorable answer sheet for Form 1937; 90(95) minutes.
b) REVISED SERIES, ELEMENTARY FORMS O, P, AND Q. 1937-40; Form N is out of print; 5¢ per test, 10 to 99 copies; 1½¢ per machine-scorable answer sheet.

Harold B. Dunkel, Examiner, Board of Examinations, The University of Chicago. [Review of Form P.] This test consists of the three sections common to the Cooperative foreign language tests: Part I, Reading, is tested by the paragraph-question method; Part II, Vocabulary, is represented by 100 isolated words; Part III, Grammar, is tested by the correct completion of Latin sentences. All sections are in multiple-choice form.

If we are sincere in our claims that the student's ability to read Latin understandingly is the primary aim in elementary instruction, Part I is the most important part of the test. Yet I doubt whether Part I is an instrument able to bear the responsibility of measuring the primary objective. The difficulties of producing adequate passages with words drawn from a frequency list, of framing searching yet unambiguous questions on them, and of cramming all this material into one testing period are familiar to anyone who has attempted the task himself. Yet even to a kindly judge, this section appears to have serious shortcomings. The passages themselves are not bad; but the thought moves very jerkily with little by way of transition. Hence, the stories rather fly along, and I was tempted to mark the first passage as "absurd" though the key indicates "sorrowful." The chief fault lies in the questions which are too few in number to test adequately the student's comprehension. Very few of the questions are searching. Some of them are slightly ambiguous; some of them even answer preceding questions. These shortcomings are surprising since many of the items are good. My main criticism is, however, that there are too few penetrating questions for even the necessarily elementary subject matter. In its present form this section gives unnecessary aid and comfort to those who believe that translation is the only valid test of reading ability.

Part II would be much more valuable if the words were presented in context. Depending upon the context, a rare word may be easily understandable or a common word puzzling. Vocabulary in itself is nothing; it is only an aid to reading, and we test it only because of its relation to reading. Hence, the student's vocabulary is important only in context and should be tested there.

The desirability of Part III is even more questionable. In the case of the modern foreign languages which the student may sometimes write or speak, the ability tested by this section (which might better be labeled composition rather than grammar) may be important. But in Latin, the student needs only enough grammatical knowledge to be able to read intelligently. Certainly that is not the ability tested here. The active knowledge demanded by this section may well contribute to reading ability, but I should consider it questionable whether its contribution entitles it to fifteen minutes of a forty-minute test.

In general, I feel that Part I should have better questions and more of them so that it is, in itself, a valid test of reading comprehension. This change would involve lengthening this section. Why not take time for an adequate measurement of our prime objective? Measurement of vocabulary is important only in diagnosis of reading progress. It should, then, probably be measured on the reading passages. Then we shall know that Johnny can't read because he doesn't know the words. If he doesn't know the words and yet can read, knowing the words is not important. The same statement is true of grammar. In short, if—and it is no easy task—Part I could be expanded to form the entire test with certain items included which would yield part-scores on functional vocabulary and grammar, we should have a much better instrument than the present one whose value in testing attainment of the reading objective seems very limited.

John Flagg Gummere, Chairman of the Latin Department, William Penn Charter School, *Philadelphia, Pennsylvania.* [Review of Form P.] Part I consists of reading for comprehension. There are four passages of made Latin of approximately the same length, but graded in difficulty. Each passage is followed by five incomplete statements. With each incomplete statement there are given five words or phrases, and the pupil is to select the word or phrase in each instance which "most correctly" (sic!) completes the statement. It is difficult to say much in a short Latin passage with the limited vocabulary permitted in an elementary test; as a result, little could be said for the literary quality or narrative attainment of the four selections. Yet this should not be considered as preventing pupils from revealing their ability to comprehend Latin. Moreover, the type of question is necessitated by the fact that the tests are to be marked objectively. Translation is a better guide to an evaluation of a pupil's knowledge of Latin, but this test does not pretend to furnish that kind of evaluation.

Part II is a multiple-choice vocabulary test. With each Latin word are given five words or phrases, and the pupil is to select the word or phrase "which most nearly corresponds in meaning." It is true that such a test tends to equate the meaning of a Latin word with a definite English word; such practice is a direct violation of the principles of real semantic study. On the other hand, we are dealing with a test that is supposed to reveal a pupil's knowledge, and this type of multiple-choice exercise will be done well by a pupil who has a good Latin vocabulary, and poorly by one who has not. It is my opinion that no real harm is done by equating Latin *socius* and English *ally*, for instance. If the classroom work emphasizes the fact that *sequor* and *socius* are from variant forms of the same root, the semantic development of the word *socius* will be clear; if not, the situation will be made no worse by the equation of meaning. It is evident that a better test could be made by asking the meaning of words in a context, but that procedure is prevented by practical considerations of testing. Some multiple-choice tests of this type include nonsense words among the possibilities offered to the pupil. In this test objection could be made to the giving of such words as *pulley* and *comport*. An intelligent student knows quite well that he has not met the word for *pulley*; a great many students, regardless of intelligence would, at this age, be entirely ignorant of the meaning of the verb *comport*.

Part III contains thirty-five incomplete sentences each to be completed by selecting one of a group of five words or phrases. I object to giving, among the possible answers, forms that do not actually exist in Latin (e.g., viren, hominos, mitteberis), since it is not good practice to permit pupils to see such pseudo forms at any time, least of all in print.

The time and percentage of questions are divided thus: Part I—15 minutes, 19 per cent; Part II—10 minutes, 48 per cent; Part III—15 minutes, 33 per cent. I think that the time and the value given to Part I is proportionately too small, and should prefer that it be given half the time and half the questions.

The examiner is furnished with every possible assistance: a scoring key, complete tables of norms, and a 16-page booklet giving directions for administering the tests and interpreting the results. Percentile scores have been compiled from a satisfactorily large number of student scores; the tables are divided according to the location and type of schools so that public-school records are separated from independent-school records.

The test has been so carefully proofread that nowhere is there an error; in fact, misprints are limited to exactly one piece of type, from a wrong font, in Part III, Item 17-2. This bespeaks the great care that has been exercised in its preparation.

For a review by S. D. Atkins, see 1065.

[1366]

Holtz Vergil Test. High school and college; 1937; 1 form; 60¢ per 25; 10¢ per specimen set; 40(45) minutes; W. L. Holtz and H. E. Schrammel; Emporia, Kan.: Bureau of Educational Measurements, Kansas State Teachers College.

W. L. Carr, Professor of Latin, Columbia University. This test, which is offered in only one form, is described as including "translation, thought content, syntax, scansion, and mythology based on selected passages from the Aeneid I-IV." This description is inaccurate in four particulars. No "translation" is called for; Part V, ostensibly on scansion and requiring a choice of one of five words which "correctly completes" each of five incomplete "hexameter verses," is really a test in recalling the verse as Vergil wrote it; the 18 items in Part III and the 22 items in Part V call for a knowledge of the content and back-

ground of Aeneid I-VI and not of Aeneid I-IV alone; and Parts I and II are based on a single passage, not on "passages."

Part I consists of 23 true-false statements based on a thirty-line passage taken from the beginning of the second book of the Aeneid and is obviously intended to test the "thought content" (i.e., the pupil's comprehension) of the passage. This passage is almost sure to have been read by the pupils taking the test, and one or more passages which the pupil had presumably *not* seen would provide a better test of his ability to comprehend Latin. The 18 items in Part III also test comprehension, for they consist of questions in Latin with multiple-choice answers in Latin, although these questions would seem to be intended primarily as a test of the pupil's ability to identify certain persons, places, and events mentioned in Aeneid I-VI. Part VI also calls for some comprehension, but it is obviously primarily intended to test the pupil's knowledge of the identity of the twelve persons and places listed.

The test consists of a total of 96 items arranged in six parts, but except for Part II (on forms and syntax) it would be hard to say just what each part really tests. Furthermore, the 96 items are lumped together in the scoring, a procedure which would be justifiable only if all the items were of equal weight and if a wrong response in the true-or-false portions of the test were no more serious than a wrong response in the multiple-choice portions. This lump score would have some value as a measure of general proficiency in Latin and of a general knowledge of the content of Aeneid I-VI, but its diagnostic value would seem to this reviewer to be very low.

Careless proofreading in the matter of macrons seriously lessens the value of the test, e.g., *Troia eversa* is used as an ablative absolute phrase in a Latin question in which all the other long vowels are indicated. Some of these Latin questions are pretty bad in other ways; e.g., "Qui cognatus Ascanio erat Hector"?

Norman T. Pratt, Jr., Department of Classics, Princeton University. This test, including "items concerned with translation, thought content, syntax, scansion, and mythology based on selected passages from the *Aeneid*, Books I-IV," "was constructed for use as an achievement test for classes pursuing work in this field in high school or college." It is crowded in format and appears to contain more material than can properly be tested in the forty minutes allotted. Of its six parts two are, laudably, based directly upon the first thirty lines of the fourth book of the *Aeneid*. Part I consists of twenty-three questions on thought content, some of which seemingly could easily be guessed by anyone familiar with the general context and none of which touch the pathos of the passage very deeply; indeed, it is doubtful that the significance of such a passage *can* really be penetrated by any such technique as the true and false questions here employed. Also appended to the passage are sixteen Latin words selected therefrom; beside each is a designation of form and construction to be marked true or false. Knowledge of forms and syntax is thus well tested in context. There are a few minor imperfections: the case of Item 27 might as well be dative as ablative; in Item 31 *vellum* is misprinted for *vellem*; and the grammatical terminology of Item 35, "substantive volitive clause," is unnecessarily obscure. Parts III and IV may be considered together. The former contains eighteen questions in Latin concerning the story and background of the *Aeneid*, each with five brief Latin answers of which the correct one is to be indicated; their function is to test knowledge of factual details. In the latter there are twenty-two incomplete statements in English concerning the story, meter, mythology, and literary matters, each to be completed by the selection of one of five possibilities also given in English. Most of these questions, too, are of a mechanical nature, and it is noteworthy that the attempt to introduce more weighty matters results in a question of the following type: "From the Roman standpoint the strongest element in the character of Aeneas was: 1. courage in battle; 2. consideration for his companions in distress; 3. obedience and submission to the will of Fate; 4. devotion to his father; 5. affection for his son." Number three is the correct answer, but it is at least very presumptuous to rule out numbers one, four, and five. Herein lies an indication of the most serious deficiency in the objective Latin test in general. Even if the faults of inanity, transparency, and over-subtlety are avoided in the construction of the questions, there still remains

the unavoidable shortcoming that the examinee can not be asked to give a synthesis of his own knowledge. The fundamental capacities to apprehend meaning and to organize material are thus left unexamined and unstimulated. Implicit in any good test should be the examiner's conception of what is significant in his subject matter, and one may be so bold as to say that the objective Latin test never will succeed in representing satisfactorily what is valuable in the study of Latin.

In the fifth part are five incomplete hexameters which the student is to complete by selecting one of five Latin words. This is a good functional test of memory and of skill in meter; it should be made clear in the directions, however, that both the meter and the original reading of each line are to be restored. Finally, Part VI consists of twelve proper names to be identified from a list of seventeen possibilities given in Latin. Here again, whereas it is necessary and desirable that the student of Latin have a knowledge of ancient folklore and geographical terminology, the objection is not so much to this test as to any objective Latin test, namely, that there is much too much emphasis upon mechanical knowledge rather than real comprehension and the use of knowledge.

[1367]

Hutchinson Latin Grammar Scale. High school; 1928; 2 forms; 50¢ per 25; 10¢ per specimen set; 25(30) minutes; Mark E. Hutchinson; Bloomington, Ill.: Public School Publishing Co.

REFERENCES

1 HUTCHINSON, MARK E. "A Standard Latin Grammar Test." *Sch and Soc* 27:47-8 Ja 14 '28.

2 AMERICAN CLASSICAL LEAGUE, ADVISORY COMMITTEE. *The Classical Investigation*: Part One, General Report: A Summary of Results with Recommendations for the Organization of the Course in Secondary Latin and for Improvement in Methods of Teaching. Princeton, N. J.: Princeton University Press, 1924. Pp. vi, 305. Out of print. (An abridged edition, consisting of a reprint of pp. 29-235, may be obtained from the American Classical League, New York University, New York, N. Y. at fifty cents a copy. The abridged edition was published in 1928 and has paper covers.)

S. D. Atkins, Department of Classics, Princeton University. This test involves no knowledge of technical terms usually employed to describe features of syntax but only requires from the student an ability to select from four choices offered the Latin sentence which correctly renders the syntactical principle presented in a complete English sentence. Measured by the recommendations made in *The Classical Investigation* [2] with respect to the principles to be incorporated in the normal four-year course and the distribution of these by semesters, the test, both Scales A and B, covers the first six semesters. Approximately 34 per cent of the items of Scale A belong to the first-semester level, 14 per cent to the second, 23 per cent to the third, 12 per cent to the fourth, and 17 per cent to the fifth and sixth. The corresponding percentages of Scale B are 34 per cent, 17 per cent, 25 per cent, 12 per cent, and 12 per cent. (These figures are only roughly approximate.) As far as constructions tested are concerned Scales A and B are exactly identical in some 25 or 26 items out of 35. The testing sentences and their order, of course, are different. The difficulty value assigned to these sentences by the test author is, in the majority of cases, greater for Scale B. The prospective consumer might like to know how the author can arrive at an assessment of 90 for Item 13, let us say, in Scale A and 96 for Item 17 in Scale B, both of which test the use of the ablative of description in sentences that are quite similar. Such information regarding value-criteria might well be included in the direction folder or references, at least, to sources where that information may be obtained, should be made therein.

The coverage of both scales is satisfactorily comprehensive, save that the pronoun and the uses of the dative should, perhaps, have greater representation, and more time, certainly, should be devoted to the verb, even to the point of lengthening the test. None of the tasks on either scale appears to be excessively difficult. The average time of 42 seconds per item is a generous allowance. The ocular energy required of the student could be reduced considerably and much time, space, and expense saved by changing the format. For example, Item 1 (Scale A), instead of being set up in five separate sentences, could be presented as follows: 1. ( ) The consul, a friend of the soldiers, has set out. *Cōnsul* (a. *amīcus*, b. *amīcī*, c. *amīcō*, d. *amīcum*) *militum profectus est.* All items on both scales, without exception, are adaptable to such revision.

The reviewer must raise the question as to whether a test of this type has justification for existence. The primary immediate objective of an elementary Latin course is to develop an ability to read and understand Latin. For the attainment of that objective educators in recent years have insisted upon a very early introduction of connected reading into the initial stages of Latin study and have emphasized the use of this continuous narrative as a more effec-

tive instrument for developing principles of syntax than detached, isolated sentences. It is my opinion that the continuous narrative and questions built thereupon make a far better testing agent than the collection of colorless insipid drill-sentences found in this test.

[1368]

Kansas First Year Latin. First, second semesters: high school; 1936; 2 forms, 2 levels; 50¢ per 25; 15¢ per specimen set; 40(45) minutes; Mary Alice Seller, H. E. Schrammel, and Lois Bellinger; Emporia, Kan.: Bureau of Educational Measurements, Kansas State Teachers College.

a) TEST I, FORMS A AND B. First semester.
b) TEST I, FORMS C AND D. Second semester.

REFERENCES

1 College Entrance Examination Board. *A Latin Word List*: Prepared in Accordance with the Recommendation of the Commission Which Revised the Definition of the Requirement in Latin. New York: the Board, 1927. Pp. 31. $0.25. Paper.

John Flagg Gummere, Chairman of the Latin Department, William Penn Charter School, Philadelphia, Pennsylvania. It is difficult to believe that these tests are actually in use. In spite of an evidently sincere effort to provide valid testing material, the authors have signally failed to provide the thoroughly accurate and well-edited material which the users of tests have a right to demand. The very title omits a hyphen that belongs in the compound modifier "first-year." The directions for securing the raw score state that from the "possible score" should be subtracted the "number wrong and omitted" instead of the number wrong *or* omitted. These are small points, but typical of the tests as a whole. It is quite proper to mark vowel length, but there are almost twenty errors in the markings in each form. There are downright blunders such as *"lex Romanus,"* "King Philippi" (both in Form C), "they are lead" (Form B). Further examples are:

FORM A. The word *cicada*, marked feminine in the vocabulary, is referred to seven times in the questions by a masculine pronoun. Misprints are *prevēnit* and *thonsand*. Two verbs in the Latin reading, supposedly referring to the same time, are in different tenses (*rogāvit* and *respondet*). *Comparābās* is wrongly divided into syllables. *Impecunious* is supposed to mean *lack of money; amiable* to mean *affectionate.* The use of *inquit* outside the quotation which it accompanies is questionable.

FORM C. *Dicione* is written three times with long *e*, suggesting that it is not a mere misprint. The word *imperātor,* used to refer to Flamininus we find translated as *emperor* though the event described took place in 195 B.C. The Latin reading deals with events in Greece after the war between the Romans under Flamininus and King Philip. The following statement appears in the true-false questions: " 'S. P. Q. R.' meant that it was the will of the emperor alone." Observe that the sentence is not English; it is precisely this kind of inexactness that a study of foreign language, particularly of Latin, should eliminate. The question is the more objectionable because S. P. Q. R. is given in its full form in a footnote. Misprints are *adīvisse* and *fratem*.

FORM D. Certain rules of grammar, to be used in answering questions in Part III, are said to be "at the right"; as a matter of fact, they are on the next page (not good) and below the questions that run over onto the next page. *Amābant* is to be translated as *did love*. Misprints are *appelāvit* and *mūtibus*.

The Latin text is set in small type and in Forms A, C, and D the lines are very close together. We are told that "the content of these tests is based on . . . recommendations of the national committee on Latin teaching." What national committee?

The proportion of questions in the two types of test is as follows: Forms A and B, about 43 per cent on comprehension of Latin and Latin grammar, 23 per cent on word study, and 33 per cent on "background" material; Forms C and D, 57, 17, and 26 per cent respectively. The ratio of questions on Latin itself to other questions is, therefore, in Forms A and B, about 2 to 3; in Forms C and D, about 3 to 2. The ratio should be higher in both types.

With the tests are furnished: a mimeographed sheet of directions (erroneously called a "manual"), a scoring key, and a class record sheet.

The direction sheet gives directions and tables of percentile scores with suggestions for translating such scores into school marks. The percentile scores have been based, for Forms A and B, on 4,035 student scores; for Forms C and D, on 4,354 scores. All these scores were sent in by "410 cooperating schools in four nation-wide testing programs."

If thoroughly edited and revised, the tests would be useful to some schools.

[1369]

Kansas Second Year Latin Test. First, second semesters: high school; 1935; 2 forms, 2 levels; 50¢ per 25; 15¢ per specimen set; 40(45) minutes; W. L. Holtz and H. E. Schrammel; Emporia, Kan.: Bureau of Educational Measurements, Kansas State Teachers College.

a) TEST II, FORMS A AND B. First semester.
b) TEST II, FORMS C AND D. Second semester.

REFERENCES

1 College Entrance Examination Board. *A Latin Word List*: Prepared in Accordance with the Recommendation of the Commission Which Revised the Definition of the Requirement in Latin. New York: the Board, 1927. Pp. 31. $0.25. Paper.

W. L. Carr, Professor of Latin, Columbia University. This test appears in four forms. Forms A and B, outwardly comparable, are intended for use at the end of the first semester of second-year Latin and Forms C and D, also outwardly comparable, are intended for usc at the end of the second semester. The manual of directions gives percentile norms computed from 4,217 student scores.

FORM A. Form A consists of four parts. Part I is intended to test comprehension. It consists of a single 184-word Latin passage taken from Ritchie's "Fabulae Faciles," followed by 25 true-or-false statements. This story about Hercules and the Amazons is found in several second-year textbooks and is, furthermore, fairly familiar to a good many pupils from sources other than Latin. The pupil's responses, therefore, might be based in part on something other than comprehension of the Latin passage. The use of several sight passages dealing with less familiar themes would provide a better test of comprehension. Furthermore, Item 5 calls for the identification of Mars as the Roman god of war, a response not to be secured from the passage alone. Two minor faults are noted in the true-or-false statements: first, the tricky linking of Items 2 and 3 by the word "however" and, second, the use of a negative in Item 8. Part II consists of a multiple-choice test of 20 points of syntax in the Latin passage set for comprehension in Part I. Devoting 20 out of 65 items to formal syntax and only 25 to comprehension does not seem to this reviewer justifiable, especially when Parts III and IV are also mainly concerned with forms and syntax, Part III consisting of 16 completion exercises and Part IV calling for the choice of the Latin sentence which best translates each of 5 English sentences.

The "final score," and the only score apparently used in the validation of the test, is found by subtracting the "wrong and omitted" items from the total number of items, a procedure which would be acceptable only if all the items were of equal weight, if a wrong response were no more serious than an omitted response, and if a wrong response in the true-or-false portions of the test were no more serious than a wrong response in the multiple-choice portions of the test. This criticism of the scoring technique applies also to Forms B, C, and D.

FORM B. Form B is constructed on the same pattern as Form A and the same general criticisms are applicable. The single Latin passage set for comprehension in Part I consists of 193 words and is a continuation of the Hercules-Amazon episode begun in Form A. A minor fault is the use of the tie-up words "nevertheless" and "however" to introduce three of the true-or-false statements. A much more serious fault, as this reviewer sees it, is the overemphasis given to syntax in Parts II, III, and IV, which have a total of 40 items while Part I on comprehension contains only 25 items.

FORM C. Form C follows in general the pattern of Forms A and B, but consists of a total of 70 items, only 20 of which are concerned primarily with testing the pupil's ability to comprehend Latin. This lack of emphasis upon comprehension seems even less justifiable in Forms C and D than in Forms A and B. Part I consists of a single Latin passage of 143 words, adapted from Caesar's *Gallic War*, Book I, Chapter 36, followed by 20 true-or-false statements. Pupils taking this test may or may not have previously read this particular passage. It is found in several second-year Latin textbooks.

Part II consists of 18 true-or-false statements about syntax in the Latin passage set for comprehension in Part I. Part III calls for the completion of 14 Latin sentences to test the pupil's functional knowledge of forms and syntax. Part IV employs the multiple-choice technique for testing the pupil's recognition knowledge of 18 Latin words or phrases mostly of technical nature. Examples are: lorica, vexillum, vinea, aquilifer, sarcina, speculator, and testudo. Only ten of the 18 words in Part IV are included in the College Entrance Examination Board's *Latin Word List* [1] for the first two years. The "final score" is found by subtracting the number of "wrong and omitted" items from the "possible score" of 70 unweighted items.

FORM D. Form D follows the pattern of Form C in its distribution of items by parts and in the testing techniques used. The single 123-word passage set for comprehension in Part I is taken without adaptation from Caesar's *Gallic War*, Book I, Chapter 52. Item 2 requires more than ability to comprehend the Latin, namely, the background knowledge that a Roman *quaestor* was a "quartermaster" and that probably there was only one such officer assigned to Caesar's army. Item 20 likewise demands the background knowledge that *tertiam aciem* here means the "reserve line." Minor criticisms are the use of the tricky tie-up word "nevertheless" in Item 9 and of a negative in Item 14. Part II employs a true-or-false technique for testing knowledge of formal syntax and Part III consists of completion exercises to test a functional knowledge of forms and syntax. Item 44 practically repeats Item 45 in Form C and Item 51 is ambiguous. Part IV tests the pupil's understanding of certain technical terms, proper names, and background material in connection with the Gallic War. Unfortunately, Items 54, 61, 63, 64, and 65 exactly repeat items in Form C.

In the opinion of this reviewer any of these four tests would serve as rough measure of the knowledge and abilities which the authors claim that the tests measure, with the single exception of "derivatives," for which there is no provision whatsoever. Furthermore, their diagnostic value would seem to be very low, because of the failure to distinguish clearly among the objectives the attainment of which each part is supposed to measure.

[1370]

Powers Diagnostic Latin Test. First year; 1930; 2 forms; $1.25 per 25; 15¢ per specimen set; non-timed (90) minutes; Francis F. Power; Bloomington, Ill.: Public School Publishing Co.

Paul B. Diederich, Assistant Professor of Education, The University of Chicago. The test consists of fifteen parts of English sentences to be translated into Latin, 21 noun forms to be diagnosed and then written in some other form, 21 verb forms ditto, 60 Latin words to match with English equivalents, 2 Latin stories of 44 words each about which 10 comprehension questions are asked, and from which ten words are selected to match with their construction, and 25 English derivatives for which the student finds Latin roots. It is appropriate for first year Latin, requires two 45-minute periods, and yields part scores of high statistical reliability. Norms for each part are based upon 571 scores from 33 schools after 7 months of instruction in Latin. Two comparable forms of the test are available.

It is a perfectly conventional objective test of the usual elements of a first-year Latin course. The words and constructions used give evidence of a careful study of their frequency of occurrence in first-year Latin texts. The only grave objection a conservative teacher might have would be that the ability to read Latin receives scant attention. Eighty-eight words of very simple Latin prose, followed by comprehension questions which can be figured out one at a time are hardly an adequate sample of the ability to read Latin.

A more progressive teacher would be likely to complain that no one needs a standardized test to find out how well students have learned these simple mechanical elements of Latin grammar. The ultimate objectives of the study of Latin are represented only by the 25 very easy derivatives, with no attempt to determine what increment of meaning is added by knowing the Latin root. The effect of Latin on English, the study of classical civilization, a beginning acquaintance with the great stories of the classics, and the discipline of thinking which this study can give are all ignored. It is true that these outcomes are more difficult to test, but these are the points at which the Latin teacher really needs the help of the test technician.

Norman T. Pratt, Jr., Department of Classics, Princeton University. These tests are designed "to measure the extent to which pupils in first-year Latin have mastered the vocabulary, word forms, and translating skills necessary for a good foundation in the subject" and may be used also "in canvassing the basal preparation of a second, third, or fourth year class at the beginning of a term." The two forms are planned exactly alike, and their "high reliability (.80 to .90 by parts)" renders them valuable for determining the results of remedial instruction. The time required is estimated at "two forty-five-minute periods." Except for one misprint in the key for Form 2, English-Latin Translation, Item 4 (*magnam* for *magnum*), the accompanying literature is clear and useful.

There are seven parts. The first consists of twelve sentences in English followed by partial Latin versions thereof to be completed by the insertion of one Latin word in each of the total of fifteen blank spaces; this constitutes an adequate functional test of memory for the rules governing such constructions as object, complementary infinitive, ablative of cause, etc., as well as vocabulary.

Parts 2 and 3 are constructed alike. The former contains a column of 21 Latin nouns and adjectives, each followed by five spaces in which the student enters the number, gender, case, nominative singular, and another designated form from the declension of the word. The third section serves the same purpose for verb forms, calling for the identification of voice, tense, person, and number (all 21 forms are in the indicative) and for the construction of another form; the items herein are apparently of graded difficulty. Both parts seem well constructed, even to the nicety that for the purpose of initiation the first item is much like the model given at the beginning of each section. In Part 4 there are three columns of twenty Latin words each. Below each column is a list of twenty English words arranged alphabetically from which the student is to select the one which translates the meaning of each Latin word. In addition to the objection which may be made to all such techniques, namely, that the testing of the mental process involved in finding the correct answer amid a group of possibilities is less rigid and fundamental than the testing of independent and original knowledge, a more serious charge must be brought against the whole group of Parts 2-4: they test aspects of the knowledge of Latin through media completely detached from any context. This is especially serious in the province of vocabulary wherein context is so important, and could have been avoided by attaching the analysis of forms and meanings to real passages of Latin, perhaps in conjunction with the two following sections.

There follow two brief passages of inferior quality to each of which are attached ten English questions concerning the contents to be answered briefly in English. It is praiseworthy that the factor of ease of correction has not eliminated this section as it has in some marketed tests. The questions should, however, include some of a more inferential variety; all of them as now constituted can be answered by the bald translation of one, two, or at the most three words. Also appended to each passage are ten Latin words from the passage and ten constructions to be matched with the words by which they are illustrated. The test is concluded with a column of twenty-five English words; the student is to give the Latin word from which the English is derived.

These tests are in the reviewer's opinion essentially good and could easily be improved, chiefly by basing Parts 2-6 upon more, continuous Latin of better calibre and by so designing the comprehension-questions as to test and develop the students' imagination and insight which are not merely valuable translating skills but indispensable ends in themselves.

SPANISH

[1371]

American Council Alpha Spanish Test. Grades 9-16; 1926-28; 2 forms, 2 parts; $1.25 per 25; 35¢ per specimen set; 45(50) minutes; prepared for the Modern Language Study under the auspices of the American Council on Education and the Conference of Canadian Universities; Milton A. Buchanan, J. P. W. Crawford, Hayward Keniston, and V. A. C. Henmon; Yonkers, N. Y.: World Book Co.
a) PART I [VOCABULARY AND GRAMMAR].
b) PART II [SILENT READING AND COMPOSITION].

REFERENCES

1 HEMMERLING, WALTER. "A Study of Four Standardized Achievement Tests in Spanish." *Mod Lang Forum* 14:10-4 O '29.
2 HENMON, V. A. C. *Achievement Tests in Modern Foreign Languages*: Prepared for the Modern Language Study and the Canadian Committee on Modern Languages, pp. 1-266. Publications of the American and Canadian Committees on Modern Languages, Vol. 5. New York: Macmillan Co., 1929. Pp. xxvii, 363. $1.00. Paper. (London: Macmillan & Co., Ltd. 4s. 6d.)
3 BUCHANAN, MILTON A. *A Graded Spanish Word Book*, Fourth edition. Publications of the American and Canadian Committees on Modern Languages, Vol. 3. Toronto, Canada: University of Toronto Press, 1933. Pp. 195. $1.25. Paper.
4 KENISTON, HAYWARD. *Spanish Syntax List*: A Statistical Study of Grammatical Usage in Contemporary Spanish Prose on the Basis of Range and Frequency. Publications of the Committee on Modern Languages, American Council on Education. New York: Henry Holt and Co., 1937. Pp. xi, 278. $1.75. Paper.

Lawrence Andrus, Examiner, Board of Examinations, The University of Chicago. The vocabulary section contains 100 items, using the 5-response multiple-choice technique, with responses in English. A check of the Spanish words in the Buchanan *Graded Spanish Word Book* [3] shows the following percentages (for Forms A and B respectively) in the 500-word groups in Buchanan's word book (arranged in descending order of range and frequency)—first 500: 23, 23; second 500: 10, 10; third 500: 11, 11; fourth 500: 9, 9; fifth 500: 8, 9; sixth 500: 9, 8; seventh 500: 10, 10; eighth 500: 10, 10; ninth 500: 8, 8; tenth 500: 2, 2. The validity of vocabulary

selection and the equivalence of Forms A and B in vocabulary are obvious. For lower and intermediate levels of instruction, this section should still give excellent results.

In the grammar section there are 50 items, using multiple-choice and completion techniques. Eight items in each form demand merely the recall of verb forms, by no means the most significant type of item. One item in Form A and two in Form B involve very common idioms. The remaining items are syntactical in nature. Following are the percentages (for Forms A and B respectively) of these syntactical items found in the different ranges of the Keniston *Spanish Syntax List*, [4] the range figures representing the number of 10,000-word units (out of a total of 60 such units counted) in which a given construction occurs—range 60: 29.27 and 35; range 55-59: 7.32 and 5; range 50-54: 14.64 and 17.5; range 45-49: 2.44 and 0; range 40-44: 14.64 and 12.5; range 35-39: 0 and 2.5; range 30-34: 2.44 and 5; range 25-29: 0 and 0; range 20-24: 4.88 and 5; range 15-19: 9.76 and 7.5; range 10-14: 4.88 and 2.5; range 5-9: 7.32 and 7.5; and range 0-4: 2.44 and 0.

The foregoing data show remarkably good validity and fair equivalence of Forms A and B in a test published eleven years before the *Spanish Syntax List.* Unquestionably better could now be done in both respects. The adoption of a uniform technique throughout the grammar section would enable more items to be tested in the same allotted time.

The silent reading section has eight Spanish paragraphs accompanied by 50 questions in Spanish to be answered in English. The paragraphs are well graded in difficulty and varied in content. The questions are generally well phrased and well chosen, with the exception of two in Form A and one in Form B where the student has merely to choose between two possibilities.

The composition section is undoubtedly the weak point of the test. The student is confronted with an "action picture" of a rather emotional type and told to write in Spanish the best composition he can in eight minutes about the picture. Compositions are to be graded by means of a Spanish Composition Scale. While such a scale is admittedly an attempt to remedy the evils of purely subjective grading, the difficulties arising in its use are so great that it is probably better to omit altogether free composition as such from achievement tests.

Reliability coefficients based on apparently adequate samplings of high school pupils are reported as follows: Vocabulary, .92; Grammar, .84 to .91; Silent Reading, .86. We are not told by what procedure these coefficients were obtained. The probable error of measurement for each of these three parts is given as approximately two score points.

Distribution of scores, percentile ranks, and norms are given in the manual of directions for eight semesters of high school in all four sections and for six semesters of college in vocabulary and grammar, five in silent reading, and four in composition. Some of the norms for vocabulary, grammar, and silent reading in both high school and college are based on a rather small number of cases. Adequate directions for administration and scoring are furnished in the manual.

Christian O. Arndt, Assistant Professor of Education, Northwestern University. Although this test suffers from certain weaknesses it nevertheless possesses considerable value as a measuring device for evaluating the progress of students.

The test is divided into four sections which deal with vocabulary, grammar, silent reading, and composition. Two class periods are required for administration. In reference to the vocabulary section it should be said that words are generally well chosen, although the reviewer questions the functional value of the inclusion of such words as *ajo, aguantar, pereza, tez, bóreda,* and *desollar.* It is doubtful whether the vocabulary test measures ability other than general intelligence, and whether word tests without context should therefore be given if one would test vocabulary in a foreign language.

The section dealing with grammar gives the student a good opportunity to make direct application to his knowledge of Spanish. By way of criticism of this part in Form B, the examiner would point out the disproportionate emphasis of questions on the irregular verb at the expense of the regular verb (*see* Item 11). Again in Item 13, could the number of examples not be increased above one!

Some teachers may raise the criticism that the sections devoted to silent reading and composition involve a certain amount of sub-jective evaluation in scoring. Though this be true, however, these sections nevertheless afford a valuable instrument for determining the actual ability of the examinee to comprehend written Spanish.

The reliability of the separate parts of this test vary from .84 to .92. Scores are presented in terms of percentile ranks.

Unfortunately, no data are available in the manual of directions concerning the validity of this test. Until more information is at hand to show that such language tests are actually measuring what they purport to measure the results can only be accepted with considerable reservation.

Several other Spanish tests are available which offer advantages beyond those afforded by this test.

[1372]

Columbia Research Bureau Spanish Test. Grades 9-15; 1926-27; 2 forms; $1.30 per 25; 20¢ per specimen set; 90(100) minutes; Frank Callcott and Ben D. Wood; Yonkers, N. Y.: World Book Co.

REFERENCES

1 KENISTON, HAYWARD. "Common Words in Spanish." *Hispania* 3:85-96 My '20.
2 CARTWRIGHT, C. W. "A Study of the Vocabularies of Eleven Spanish Grammars and Fifteen Spanish Reading Tests." *Mod Lang J* 10:1-14 O '25.
3 WOOD, BEN D. *New York Experiments with New-Type Modern Language Tests:* Including a Survey of Modern Language Achievement in the Junior High Schools of New York City, June, 1925; The Regents Experiment of June, 1925, with New-Type Tests in French, German, Spanish, and Physics; and A Second Survey of Modern Language Achievement in the Junior High Schools of New York City, June, 1926, pp. 105-319. Publications of the American and Canadian Committees on Modern Languages, Vol. 1. New York: Macmillan Co., 1927. Pp. xxii, 339. Paper. Out of print.
4 HEMMERLING, WALTER. "A Study of Four Standardized Achievement Tests in Spanish." *Mod Lang Forum* 14:10-4 O '29.
5 KENISTON, HAYWARD. *A Spanish Idiom List:* Selected on Basis of Range and Frequency of Occurrence. Publications of the American and Canadian Committees on Modern Languages, Vol. 11. New York: Macmillan Co., 1929. Pp. xiii, 108. $0.60. Paper. (London: Macmillan & Co., Ltd. 2s. 6d.)
6 BUCHANAN, MILTON A. *A Graded Spanish Word Book,* Fourth edition. Publications of the American and Canadian Committees on Modern Languages, Vol. 3. Toronto, Canada: University of Toronto Press, 1933. Pp. 195. $1.25.
7 KENISTON, HAYWARD. *Spanish Syntax List:* A Statistical Study of Grammatical Usage in Contemporary Spanish Prose on the Basis of Range and Frequency. Publications of the Committee on Modern Languages, American Council on Education. New York: Henry Holt and Co., 1937. Pp. xi, 278. $1.75. Paper.

James C. Babcock, Assistant Professor of Romance Languages, The University of Chicago. It is not easy to find exact information on the derivation of the present test. In the manual of directions it is stated that "the derivation of the test is exactly like that of the *Columbia Research Bureau French Test* as described in the manual of directions for that test." If the user or potential user of the Spanish test happens to have the French manual at hand, which can by no means be assumed, he will find that the derivation of the French test "is described in detail in *Yearbook of the New York Society for the Experimental Study of Education*, Volume I." Without continuing his search beyond the French manual, however, he will learn that the criterion governing the construction of the French test was the degree of community shown in sixteen well-known French texts (twelve grammars and four composition books). From this he may deduce that the Spanish test is based on the common content of a number of Spanish texts, all published, necessarily, before the date of the test (1926). It seems scarcely necessary to point out at the present time the serious limitation of a criterion involving the assumption that the subject matter found in texts (especially those written at least fourteen years ago) is what should appear there. The test, then, is out of date. If it is to be of use, it must be revised in the light of the frequency counts of vocabulary, syntax, and idiom, and other information made available since its publication. In Part I (vocabulary), of Form A, for example, a check of the words tested with the Buchanan *Graded Spanish Word Book* [6] would seem to indicate the presence in the test of a number of unprofitable items. Approximately one-third of the items are either among the starred words or the first 500, while about 13 per cent are above 3,000. Regardless of the teaching method employed and the degree of advancement of the students, it is obvious that in classes taught with recently published texts, a number of these items would be either too easy or entirely beyond the range of the student's vocabulary experience. Similar criticisms could be made of the content of Part II (comprehension) and Part III (grammar).

The alternative-response recognition technique employed in Part I is satisfactory, the four or five English words which follow each Spanish word being, on the whole, well chosen. The Spanish words, however, are not arranged in order of difficulty. The comprehension section is much less satisfactory. It is composed entirely of true-false sentences, no attempt being made to test the comprehension of paragraphs. In Part III, grammar is tested by use of the completion type in which the student writes out the Spanish word or words necessary to complete correctly the Spanish translation of 100 rather short English sentences. The manual's claim that this section is

"equally objective" is debatable, especially since the key is not entirely adequate. A few of the items in Part III test vocabulary rather than usage.

The manual states that the reliability coefficient for the test as a whole is .97; for Parts I, II, and III separately the figures are .92, .68, and .95 respectively.

Harry J. Russell, Associate Professor of Romanic Languages, Miami University. Two forms of this test are available, Forms A and B. They are supposed to be comparable, and the results, if administered simultaneously, should be the same.

The format is all that could be desired, the type is clear, and the items are arranged in a comprehensible manner.

The reliability coefficient, arrived at by finding the correlation between random halves of the same form of the test, is given as .97. The validity coefficient, found by correlating the test scores with college grades in Spanish courses, and the Regents examinations for 1925, is given at .70 in the college group, and for second-, third-, and fourth-year high school students as, .55, .65, and .71.

Each test consists of three parts, vocabulary, comprehension, and grammar, to be completed in 20, 25, and 45 minutes respectively. The 100 vocabulary items are tested by giving a Spanish word followed by 5 English words, one of which is right. Comprehension is tested with 75 Spanish sentences, some of which are true and others false. The division on grammar consists of 100 English sentences, each one followed by an incomplete Spanish translation, to be completed by supplying the untranslated word or words.

At the time these tests were formulated there were no scientific studies on vocabulary and syntax. The authors did have access, however, to the Keniston [1] and Cartwright [2] word lists.

A brief analysis of the vocabulary content of Part I reveals many low frequency words such as *almohada, legumbre, panadería, oveja, sugerir*, etc., however, there are a surprising number of words belonging to the first 1,500 in the *Graded Spanish Word Book*, [6] (75 per cent of the first 50 words falling in that category).

The items found in the grammar test are principles of common occurrence in Spanish texts of the time. Many of these syntax items have been proven relatively unimportant by the recent *Spanish Syntax List*,[7] but, of course, that was not available to the authors at the time the test was constructed.

The device of testing the foreign word by means of a native one has been improved upon by recent test technicians. True-false tests are not very reliable. Some of the statements made in Part II of this test might be either true or false; e.g., Items 1, 12, 17, 23, 35, etc. A more satisfactory measure of comprehension could be devised.

There should be some sort of reading test that would measure reading ability in a natural reading situation. This division of the test should carry the bulk of the weight, being given the major role in the test rather than the minor one that it occupies in this test. The test on grammar should be changed from the present active type to some sort of passive, recognition exercise. It should be given the least weight in the total test. As the tests now stand, fifty per cent of the time is devoted to Part III, Grammar.

The tests need re-editing in the light of the above criticisms, making full use of available scientific studies, and the more advanced techniques developed within the past few years.

[1373]

Cooperative Spanish Test [Advanced Form]. 4 semesters or more: high school; or 1 year or more: college; 1933-40; 25¢ per specimen set of either edition; 40- and 80-minute editions; Advanced Form P: E. Herman Hespelt, Robert H. Williams, and Geraldine Spaulding; Advanced Form Q: same authors with the editorial assistance of Helen B. Collins, Mary B. MacDonald, Nell Morris, Trudie Wilson, and G. W. Umphrey; New York: Cooperative Test Service.

a) FORMS 1934, 1936, AND 1937. Forms 1933 and 1935 are out of print; 6¢ per test, 10 to 99 copies; 90(95) minutes.

b) REVISED SERIES, ADVANCED FORMS N, O, P, AND Q. 1937-40; 5¢ per test, 10 to 99 copies; 1½¢ per machine-scorable answer sheet; 40(45) minutes.

REFERENCES

1 BUCHANAN, MILTON A. *A Graded Spanish Word Book*, Fourth Edition. Publications of the American and Canadian Committees on Modern Languages, Vol. 3. Toronto, Canada: University of Toronto Press, 1933. Pp. 195. $1.25. Paper.
2 KENISTON, HAYWARD. *Spanish Syntax List*: A Statistical Study of Grammatical Usage in Contemporary Spanish Prose on the Basis of Range and Frequency. Publications of the Committee on Modern Languages, American Council on Education. New York: Henry Holt and Co., 1937. Pp. xi, 278. $1.75. Paper.
3 HANNA, JOSEPH V. "A Comparison of Cooperative Test Scores and High School Grades as Measures for Predicting Achievement in College." J Appl Psychol 23:289-97 Ap '39.

Lawrence Andrus, Examiner, Board of Examinations, The University of Chicago. [Review of Advanced Form P.] This test has three parts: I, Reading (45 items, 15 minutes); II, Vocabulary (40 items, 10 minutes); III, Grammar (40 items, 15 minutes). The multiple-choice technique, with five suggested responses for each item, is used. Timing for each part is reasonable.

The reading section is too easy throughout to provide sharp discrimination at the third and fourth year levels in high school or the second and third year levels in college. Possibly the time limit may help overcome this deficiency.

The vocabulary section contains no English, for which it is to be commended. Each of the forty lead words is followed by five words from which the student must select the one closest in meaning to the lead word. A check of the lead words and the responses in the Buchanan *Graded Spanish Word Book* [1] shows the following percentages of lead and response words respectively in the 500-word groups in Buchanan's word book (arranged in descending order of range and frequency)—first 500: 25, 16; second 500: 25, 19.5; third 500: 15, 14.5; fourth 500: 0, 7; fifth 500: 2.5, 9.5; sixth 500: 7.5, 7.5; seventh 500: 5, 5.5; eighth 500: 0, 4.5; ninth 500: 2.5, 2; tenth 500: 5, 3.5; eleventh 500: 7.5, 4; twelfth 500: 5, 2.5; thirteenth 500: 0, .5; fourteenth 500: 0, 0; not in the *Graded Spanish Word Book*: 0, 3.5.

While individual users may not approve the exact percentage chosen from each 500-word group, it is evident that an attempt has been made to use the most valid criterion available in choice of vocabulary, i.e., the word count. It may be noted that the words used are practically all content words. It would be advisable to include more form words among those chosen from the commonest two thousand. This test is inferior in distribution of vocabulary difficulty to the *American Council Alpha Spanish Test*, but does include more difficult words, which should make it more discriminating than the Alpha Spanish test at higher levels of instruction.

Of the forty items in the grammar section, three are idiomatic in nature. The remaining thirty-seven items are definitely syntactical. The following table shows the percentage of these syntactical items found in the different ranges of the Keniston *Spanish Syntax List*,[2] the range figures representing the number of 10,000-word units (out of a total of sixty such units counted) in which a given construction occurs—range 60: 43.24; range 55-59: 5.45; range 50-54: 8.11; range 45-49: 8.11; range 40-44: 10.81; range 35-39: 8.11; range 30-34: 8.11; range 25-29: 0; range 20-24: 0; range 15-19: 2.70; range 10-14: 2.70; range 5-9: 2.70; range 0-4: 0. This distribution of construction difficulty is satisfactory, although it could be made more even.

No reliability coefficients for Form P have yet been reported. Percentile norms for both secondary schools and colleges are differentiated, for secondary schools according to geographical location and type of institution, for colleges on the basis of the performance of entering college freshmen on the *American Council on Education Psychological Examination.* College norms are given for entering freshmen and for college students who have had no instruction in Spanish in secondary school. These types of differentiation show a wholly laudable effort to make the norms mean more for individual students than published norms often do mean. Although we are told in the booklet of norms that "these norms represent carefully smoothed and weighted values so that the numbers of cases do not provide a proper basis for judging their accuracy of sampling," this reviewer would feel safer in using norms based on at least one hundred cases—which is not true for certain norms given—particularly in the absence of details about the smoothing and weighting. Furthermore, all these norms are presented in terms of the scaled scores, the critical worth of which must be evaluated in the light of the information finally available in a bulletin devoted especially to them.

A complete and very satisfactory manual of instructions for administration and scoring accompanies the test.

Harry J. Russell, Associate Professor of Romanic Languages, Miami University. [Review of Advanced Form P.] The users of this test would undoubtedly like to know (*a*) exactly who could be tested by it, (*b*) precisely what they were being tested in, or for, (*c*) what the test means in terms of achievement and, (*d*) what learning possibilities it has. Questions one and three are answered adequately by the handbook, the booklet of norms, and other data supplied to prospective users. The information contained in the handbook answering questions *b* and *d* are definitely in-

adequate. The rather vague statements made about the vocabulary range of the reading and vocabulary divisions, and the grammar content of the test leave much to be desired from the point of view of the teacher who wishes to administer it, or the examiner who would like to critically evaluate it.

Part I, the reading section of this test consists of 45 items, and is to be completed in fifteen minutes. Items 1 to 26 are, for the most part, single sentences of the completion type, five choices being given after each incomplete statement, one of which is correct. The remaining nineteen items are based upon five separate short paragraphs and one letter. There are from two to four incomplete sentences, similar to those found in the first twenty-six items, based on each paragraph or letter.

The vocabulary basis of this test is nowhere stated other than the rather vague statement made in the handbook. A brief analysis of various items reveals the fact that many words, such as *neumáticos, perforado, melocotones, tenis,* do not occur in the *Graded Spanish Word Book.*[1] Of course, some of these words are partially cognate, and might be understood in spite of their unusualness, but why include such problematical items when legitimate ones could just as easily be found?

Items 27 to 45 are more nearly true reading situations than the others. It is the author's opinion that reading ability can best be tested by items more nearly comparable to the normal reading activities engaged in by Spanish students than those found in Items 1 to 26 inclusive.

Part II, the vocabulary division of this test, is composed of forty words, each one followed by five choices, one of which is an exact, or near synonym of the item being tested. The test is to be completed in ten minutes.

The vocabulary chosen for the test consists of 19 words (47.5%) taken from the first 1,000 words in the *Graded Spanish Word Book;* 7 words (17.5%) from the second 1,000; 5 words (12.5%) from the third 1,000; 4 words (10%) from the fifth 1,000; and 5 words (12.5%) from the sixth 1,000.

The answer words, contrary to the statement made in the handbook, are not usually of a higher frequency than the words being tested. As proof of this statement see Items 1, 3, 4, 5, 6, 9, 10, 11, 12, 13, 14, etc. The answer word, being more difficult than the test word, makes the test somewhat unfair.

The items that go into the test might have been selected more scientifically to give a more adequate cross section of the specific vocabulary being tested. If the test, for instance, is to examine the student on his knowledge of the 3,000 most common Spanish words the tester might pick every seventy-fifth word, thus eliminating the element of chance selection that seems to have been employed in choosing the words used in this test.

Part III, the grammar division, is made up of forty items. The first 21 items consist of English sentences partially translated into Spanish, the student to supply the one missing word or part of word from the five Spanish choices that are given after each item. The remainder of the test consists of 19 English sentences, each of which is followed by five possible Spanish translations one of which is correct.

We are not told whether the recent study [2] on Spanish syntax was used in selecting the grammatical items to be tested. A hurried comparison, however, of the most common grammatical phenomena as revealed in Keniston's *Spanish Syntax List* with those contained in this test proves that some of the items tested are relatively unimportant.

The validity of the techniques employed in this test, the translation of English to Spanish, might well be questioned.

[1374]

Cooperative Spanish Test [Elementary Form]. 1-6 semesters: grades 6-9; 1933-39; 40- and 90-minute editions; 25¢ per specimen set of either edition; Elementary Form P: Jacob Greenberg, Robert H. Williams, and Geraldine Spaulding; New York: Cooperative Test Service.
a) JUNIOR FORM 1934. Forms 1933 and 1935 are out of print; 6¢ per test, 10 to 99 copies; 90(95) minutes.
b) REVISED SERIES, ELEMENTARY FORMS N, O, AND P. 1937-39; 5¢ per test, 10 to 99 copies; 1½¢ per machine-scorable answer sheet; 40(45) minutes.

Christian O. Arndt, Assistant Professor of Education, Northwestern University. [Review of Elementary Form P.] This test should meet the practical needs of all teachers who desire an accurate measuring device for the evaluation of progress in Spanish in secondary schools. The test is divided into three parts covering reading, vocabulary, and grammar. The multiple-choice method whereby words are selected for completing sentences is used in the section devoted to reading. This method

has been widely used by psychologists for many years and is set up to good advantage in this test. There may be some legitimate questioning of the value of Part II devoted to vocabulary since the meaning of words is contingent upon their context. Results of vocabulary tests have long been known to correlate highly with the intelligence of those tested and do not necessarily indicate proficiency in language. The section dealing with grammar should test for grammar and not be concerned with idioms as well. Idioms might better be tested under the section on vocabulary.

Some of the examples employed in Part III are open to criticism because of the choice of alternative words; for instance, Item 8: "The maid will serve us right away." Instead of the pronouns *yo, me, mi,* it would appear better to use *nuestros, usos,* and *os.* In Item 3, two things are tested, the object pronoun and the idiom. This is obviously undesirable. Giving the first few letters of the verb rather than the infinitive in the case of Items 23, 26, 27, 28, and 33 is confusing to the examinee. In general more aspects of grammar should be treated in this section.

The short time (40 minutes) required for administering the test will be appreciated by all busy teachers. Scores are presented in terms of percentiles which makes for ready understanding.

Norms are based upon adequate sampling from widely separated geographical areas. This enables one to compare the relative standing of students in various parts of the country. Furthermore, interesting comparisons may be drawn between the work done in public and independent secondary schools.

The test has a reliability coefficient of .93 which indicates that it possesses value as a reliable diagnostic device. It is regretted by the examinee that no information is at hand concerning the validity of the test.

The three authors of this test are to be commended for the objective approach and meticulous care with which the test has been constructed and standardized. It should find wide acceptance by teachers of Spanish in secondary schools throughout the country.

For a review by Walter V. Kaulfers, see 1156.

[1375]

Spanish Life and Culture. Two years: high school, or 1 year: college; 1937; 1 form; 50¢ per 25; 15¢ per specimen set; Minnie M. Miller; Emporia, Kan.: Bureau of Educational Measurements, Kansas State Teachers College.

James C. Babcock, Assistant Professor of Romance Languages, The University of Chicago. The construction of useful tests of students' knowledge of foreign "life and culture" is perhaps one of the most difficult tasks confronting those who are trying to improve the standard tests for use in foreign language courses. The difficulty arises from the lack of uniformity in cultural background instruction in our elementary courses, both with regard to the relative importance of this part of the course and, in the case of Spanish, the question of emphasis on Spain or Spanish America. It arises also from the fact that the significant objective of an understanding and appreciation of the peculiar genius of a people and the role of that people's civilization in world culture is much less easily tested than the less meaningful aim of memorizing dates and names.

The author of the present test does not attempt to test understanding and appreciation. The test "covers such information on geography, history, government, art, literature, science, and customs of Spain and Spanish America as students may reasonably be expected to acquire in two years of high school, or one year of college Spanish." The word "information" should be taken to mean primarily a knowledge of the subjects listed sufficient to identify, recognize or (in Part I) produce the names of people and places. No explanation of the choice of materials is given in the manual of directions other than the assertion that "the items were selected from valid sources" and "the items themselves, as well as their proportional distribution among the various fields of subject matter, were carefully checked by teachers of Spanish in high schools and colleges." In the opinion of the reviewer, some six or eight at least out of the total of 100 items are of too little significance to merit inclusion in the test. It is likely that many teachers would have preferred more than five items dealing with art. This number could easily be increased without adding to the length of the test by omitting a few very easy and probably unprofitable items such as: "There are many Spanish names for towns in: I. Virginia, 2. California, 3. Wisconsin." Approximately forty per cent of the items have to do primarily with Spanish America or the activities of Spaniards in Spanish America.

Three types of responses are called for in the three parts of the test. In Part I, the student is to write out the answers to short questions. Since these questions call for nothing other than the names of people, cities, mountains and the like, a more objective type of response might be preferred. The matching type in Part II and the multiple-choice type in Part III are more satisfactory, although it would probably have been well to include more detractors in the answer columns of Part II and use four rather than three possible responses in Part III. The items are not arranged in order of difficulty.

It should be noted that the table of percentile norms was computed from the scores of only 343 students. The test showed a reliability coefficient of .73.

For a review by Walter V. Kaulfers, see 1157

INTELLIGENCE

Reviews by Anne Anastasi, Rachel Stutsman Ball, Nancy Bayley, Robert G. Bernreuter, J. M. Blackburn, Andrew W. Brown, B. M. Castner, Raymond B. Cattell, James Drever, Jack W. Dunlap, August Dvorak, Howard Easley, Charles Fox, Henry E. Garrett, Florence L. Goodenough, J. P. Guilford, E. Patricia Hunt, A. M. Jordan, T. J. Keating, Truman L. Kelley, Grace H. Kent, F. Kuhlmann, W. Line, Herschel T. Manuel, Francis N. Maxfield, Myrtle Luneau Pignatelli, S. D. Porteus, C. Ebblewhite Smith, Percival Smith, C. Spearman, Florence M. Teagarden, Lorene Teegarden, Godfrey H. Thomson, Robert L. Thorndike, Robert C. Tryon, A. H. Turney, David Wechsler, F. L. Wells, Carroll A. Whitmer, D. A. Worcester, and Ll. Wynn Jones.

[1376]

Alexander Performance Scale. Ages 9 and over; 1935; individual; 1 form, 3 subtests; 12s. 6d. or $3.15 per manual; [2] (40-60) minutes; W. P. Alexander.
a) PASSALONG TEST. 1932-37; 21s. per box of blocks, cards, and manual; London: University of London Press, Ltd.
b) BLOCK DESIGN TEST. 1919-36; Drever and Collins' modification of Kohs' *Block Design Test* (using only Designs 1-3, 5, 7-9, and 14-16); 12s. 8d. per set of 16 color cubes; 6s. per 10 design cards; Edinburgh, Scotland: Andrew H. Baird, Scientific Instrument Maker.
c) CUBE CONSTRUCTION TEST. 1918-25; Gaw's modification of Doll's *Cube Construction Test*; 8s. 6d. per 26 cubes and 3 blocks; London: National Institute of Industrial Psychology.

REFERENCES

1 ALEXANDER, W. P. "A New Performance Test of Intelligence." *Brit J Psychol* 23:52-63 Jl '32.
2 ALEXANDER, WILLIAM PICKEN. *Intelligence, Concrete and Abstract:* A Study of Differential Traits. British Journal of Psychology Monograph Supplements, Vol. 6, No. 19. London: Cambridge University Press, 1935. Pp. x, 177. 12s. 6d. Paper.
3 ALEXANDER, W. P. "Intelligence, Concrete and Abstract." *Brit J Psychol* 29:74 Jl '38.

J. M. Blackburn, Lecturer in Social Psychology, London School of Economics. In the pilot survey on 71 adults made before he finally chose the three tests to form his performance scale, Alexander found that the frequency distribution of scores on Kohs' *Block Design Test* was skewed at the bottom, indicating that the test was rather difficult for some of the subjects; that the distribution for the *Cube Construction Test* was skewed at the top, showing that it was on the easy side; and that the distribution for the *Passalong Test* approached the normal curve of error.

Alexander therefore came to the conclusion that a combination of the three tests met the principal requirements for a performance scale suitable for vocational and educational guidance between the ages of 14 and 18 years. The weakest subjects score positively on the scale while the strongest subjects are still well within the maximum score. He subsequently standardised this scale on four groups of subjects,

totaling 374 cases, employing an alteration—and, in my opinion, a definite improvement on the methods of scoring Kohs' *Block Design Test* and the *Cube Construction Test*.

From my own experience I would say without hesitation that Kohs' *Block Design Test* is far more diagnostic for clinical purposes than either of the other two. The *Passalong Test* I have found to be scored on the lenient side. If this were its only defect it could be easily remedied, but in addition to this it depends too much on the chance factor. If a subject in one of the early subtests properly assimilates the significance of breaking down a rectangular vertical block composed of two square blocks into a rectangular horizontal block, he will gain an advantage, which is out of all proportion to the importance of this piece of "insight," over another subject who fails to see it until later, or who fails to see it at all. It is true that after the time limit for each subtest has expired, the experimenter demonstrates the solution to the subject, but this hardly affects the point at issue. Though I readily agree that the more intelligent subject will be likely to acquire the piece of knowledge more readily than the less intelligent, my argument is that it is unfortunate that so much may depend on the fact of its acquisition.

The *Cube Construction Test*, even with Alexander's improved method of scoring, I have never found to be satisfactory, except as a shock absorber. The careful, plodding subject is, in my experience, unduly penalised and the impulsively quick subject gains many more chance successes than he deserves. As a shock absorber, however, the test has its place, and its next most useful purpose is in helping the experimenter to make some qualitative observations on a subject's temperamental qualities.

But neither of these tests approaches the importance of Kohs' *Block Design Test*. Alexander's method of scoring is a definite improvement on that of Drever and Collins and on that of Kohs, because it presents a *graduated* score for the designs on the basis of the time taken. It was a defect of the other methods—particularly of that suggested by Kohs—that so many points in a subject's score might turn on a second or two, the subject getting no points if he exceeded the time limit for the design, but—in one case—as many as 9 points if he took a few seconds less. For this reason, and because of the important observations about a subject's temperamental characteristics that may be made by a skilled clinician who watches the subject as he performs the test, I regard it as unfortunate that Alexander chose to use the Drever and Collins reduction in the number of designs from 16 to 10. Much more can be learnt about a subject who is given the full 16 designs, for there are more designs of the same type for the subject to become familiar with before he is suddenly shifted to a new type of design, and it is at this point that emotional stability or instability often betrays itself. In the 10-card test he is more directly oriented towards a sudden change of design, he does not lose his balance so readily when the type of design is altered, and so this information is frequently submerged. Consequently I would like to see the full Kohs' test of 16 designs, scored on Alexander's principles, employed as the *Alexander Performance Scale*.

[1377]

American Council on Education Psychological Examination for College Freshmen, Form 1939. Grade 13; 1939; a new form has been issued annually since 1924; 3 editions; 7¢ per test; 15¢ per specimen set; L. L. Thurstone and Thelma Thurstone; Washington, D. C.: American Council on Education.
a) HAND-SCORING EDITION. 37 (55-60) minutes.
b) PERFORATED MACHINE-SCORED EDITION. 33 (55-60) minutes.
c) SEPARATE ANSWER SHEET MACHINE-SCORED EDITION. 2¢ per machine-scorable answer sheet; 33 (55-60) minutes.

REFERENCES

1 THURSTONE, L. L. "Psychological Tests for College Freshmen." *Ed Rec* 6:69-83, 282-94 Ap, O '25.
2 NELSON, M. J., AND DENNY, E. C. "The Terman and Thurstone Group Tests as Criteria for Predicting College Success." *Sch and Soc* 26:501-2 O 15 '27.
3 OWENS, WILLIAM A. "On a Certain Value of the Thurstone (American Council on Education) Tests in Predicting Scholarship." *Ed Adm and Sup* 13:495-9 O '27.
4 THURSTONE, L. L. "Psychological Examinations for College Freshmen." *Ed Rec* 8:156-82 Ap '27.
5 KENT, R. A., AND SCHREURS, ESTHER. "Predictive Value of Four Specified Factors for Freshman English and Mathematics." *Sch and Soc* 27:242-6 F 25 '28.
6 STALNAKER, JOHN M. "American Council Psychological Examination for 1926 at Purdue University." *Sch and Soc* 27:86-8 Ja 21 '28.
7 THURSTONE, L. L. "Norms for the 1927 Psychological Examination." *Ed Rec* 9:102-7 Ap '28.
8 CONDIT, PHILIP M. "The Prediction of Scholastic Success by Means of Classification Examinations." *J Ed Res* 19:331-5 My '29.
9 KELLOGG, CHESTER E. "Relative Values of Intelligence Tests and Matriculation Examinations as Means of Estimating Probable Success in College." *Sch and Soc* 30:893-6 D 28 '29.
10 THURSTONE, L. L., AND THURSTONE, THELMA GWINN. "The 1929 Psychological Examination." *Ed Rec* 11:101-28 Ap '30.
11 FREEMAN, FRANK S. "Predicting Academic Survival." *J Ed Res* 23:113-23 F '31.
12 THURSTONE, L. L., AND THURSTONE, THELMA GWINN. "The 1930 Psychological Examination." *Ed Rec* 12:160-78 Ap '31.
13 THURSTONE, L. L., AND THURSTONE, THELMA GWINN. "The 1931 Psychological Examination." *Ed Rec* 13:121-36 Ap '32.
14 HUNSICKER, LILIAN. "A Comparison of Scores on Two College Freshman Intelligence Tests." *J Ed Res* 26:666-7 My '33.
15 RHINEHART, JESSE BATLEY. "An Attempt to Predict the Success of Student Nurses by the Use of a Battery of Tests." *J Appl Psychol* 17:277-93 Ap '33.
16 SEGEL, DAVID, AND GERBERICH, J. R. "Differential College Achievement Predicted by the American Council Psychological Examination." *J Appl Psychol* 17:637-45 D '33.
17 THURSTONE, L. L., AND THURSTONE, THELMA GWINN. "The 1932 Psychological Examination." *Ed Rec* 14:183-97 Ap '33.
18 WAITS, J. VIRGIL. "The Differential Predictive Value of the Psychological Examination of the American Council on Education." *J Exp Ed* 1:264-71 Mr '33.
19 JORGENSEN, C. "Analysis of Some Psychological Tests by the Spearman Factor Method." *Brit J Ed Psychol* 4:96-109 F '34.
20 McCONNELL, T. R. "Change in Scores on the Psychological Examination of the American Council on Education from Freshman to Senior Year." *J Ed Psychol* 25:66-9 Ja '34.
21 THURSTONE, L. L., AND THURSTONE, THELMA GWINN. "The 1933 Psychological Examination." *Ed Rec* 15:161-75 Ap '34.
22 JONES, GEORGE A. A., AND LASLETT, H. R. "The Prediction of Scholastic Success in College." *J Ed Res* 29:266-71 D '35.
23 MOSIER, CHARLES I. "Group Factors in College Curricula." *J Ed Psychol* 26:513-22 O '35.
24 THURSTONE, L. L., AND THURSTONE, THELMA GWINN. "The 1934 Psychological Examination." *Ed Rec* 16:226-40 Ap '35.
25 DAVIES, J. EARL. "The Relative Effects of Two Kinds of Provision for Response upon the Validity of an Artificial Language Test." *J Ed Res* 29:593-5 Ap '36.
26 LIVESAY, T. M. "Racial Comparisons in Performance on the American Council Psychological Examination." *J Ed Psychol* 27:631-4 N '36.
27 THURSTONE, L. L., AND THURSTONE, THELMA GWINN. "The 1935 Psychological Examination." *Ed Rec* 17:296-317 Ap '36.
28 DRAKE, LEWIS E., AND HENMON, V. A. C. "The Prediction of Scholarship in the College of Letters and Science at the University of Wisconsin." *Sch and Soc* 45:191-4 F 6 '37.
29 LIVESAY, T. M. "Sex Differences in Performance on the American Council Psychological Examination." *J Ed Psychol* 28:694-702 D '37.
30 SCHMITZ, SYLVESTER B. "Predicting Success in College: A Study of Various Criteria." *J Ed Psychol* 28:465-73 S '37.
31 THURSTONE, L. L., AND THURSTONE, THELMA GWINN. "The 1936 Psychological Examination for College Freshmen." *Ed Rec* 18:252-73 Ap '37.
32 UPSHALL, C. C. "Contrast of the Upper and Lower 16 Percent on the American Council Psychological Examination (Abstract)," pp. 45-6. In *The Role of Research in Educational Progress*: Official Report, American Educational Research Association, A Department of the National Education Association, New Orleans, Louisiana, February 20-24, 1937. Washington, D. C.: the Association, May 1937. Pp. 255. $1.50. Paper.
33 Educational Records Bureau. *1937 Fall Testing Program in Independent Schools*: Including a Study of the California Test of Mental Maturity, pp. 1-16. Educational Records Bulletin No. 22. New York: the Bureau, January 1938. Pp. x, 60. $1.50. Paper, lithotyped.
34 KOHN, HAROLD A. "Achievement and Intelligence Examinations Correlated with Each Other and with Teacher's Rankings." *J Genetic Psychol* 52:433-7 Je '38.
35 McGEHEE, WILLIAM. "Freshman Grades and the American Council Psychological Examinations." *Sch and Soc* 47:222-4 F 12 '38.
36 THURSTONE, L. L., AND THURSTONE, THELMA GWINN. "The 1937 Psychological Examination for College Freshmen." *Ed Rec* 19:209-34 Ap '38.
37 BUTSCH, R. L. C. "Improving the Prediction of Academic Success through Differential Weighting." *J Ed Psychol* 30:401-20 S '39.

38 CURETON, EDWARD E. "Note on the Validity of the American Council on Education Psychological Examination." *J Appl Psychol* 23:306-7 Ap '39.

39 LIVESAY, T. M. "Does Test Intelligence Increase at the College Level?" *J Ed Psychol* 30:63-8 Ja '39.

40 SEDER, MARGARET. "The Reliability and Validity of the American Council Psychological Examination, 1938 Edition," pp. 51-8. In *1938 Fall Testing Program in Independent Schools and Supplementary Studies.* Educational Records Bulletin No. 26. New York: Educational Records Bureau, January 1939. Pp. x, 69. $1.00. Paper, lithotyped.

41 THURSTONE, L. L.; THURSTONE, THELMA GWINN; AND ADKINS, DOROTHY C. "The 1938 Psychological Examination." *Ed Rec* 20:263-300 Ap '39.

42 TRAXLER, ARTHUR. "Summary of Test Results, Fall 1938," pp. 1-21. In *1938 Fall Testing Program in Independent Schools and Supplementary Studies.* Educational Records Bulletin No. 26. New York: Educational Records Bureau, January 1939. Pp. x, 69. $1.00. Paper, lithotyped.

43 BARNETTE, W. LESLIE. "Norms of Business College Students on Standardized Tests: Intelligence, Clerical Ability, English." *J Appl Psychol* 24:237-44 Ap '40.

44 FLORY, CHARLES D. "The Intellectual Growth of College Students." *J Ed Res* 33:433-51 F '40.

45 SEDER, MARGARET. "The Reliability of the American Council on Education Psychological Examination, 1939 Edition," pp. 34-8. In *1939 Fall Testing Program in Independent Schools and Supplementary Studies.* Educational Records Bulletin No. 29. New York: Educational Records Bureau, January 1940. Pp. x, 50. $1.00. Paper, lithotyped.

46 SUPER, DONALD E. "The *A.C.E.* Psychological Examination and Special Abilities." *J Psychol* 9:221-6 Ap '40.

47 THOMSON, WILLIAM A. "Note on Retest Results on the ACE Psychological Examination for College Students." *J Ed Psychol* 31:229-33 Mr '40.

48 THURSTONE, L. L., AND THURSTONE, THELMA GWINN. "The American Council on Education Psychological Examinations, 1939 Editions," pp. 3-38. In *Psychological Examinations, 1939.* American Council on Education Studies, Series 5, Vol. 4, No. 2. Washington, D. C.: the Council, May 1940. Pp. v, 53. $0.25. Paper.

Jack W. Dunlap, Associate Professor of Educational Psychology, The University of Rochester. This examination is designed for use primarily in colleges. It provides two scores—a linguistic value based on the composite of the scores on the same-opposite test, the completion test, and the verbal analogies test; and a quantitative score based on the results on the arithmetic test, the number series test, and the tables or figure analogies test. Considerably more weight is attached to the linguistic score than to the quantitative score—roughly in the ratio two to one. This is not chance as is attested by the authors' statement, "In general, a scholastic aptitude test should be rather heavily saturated with language factors, since these represent scholarship." There is, therefore, some question as to the suitability of such an instrument for use in technical schools, such as the scientific and engineering schools. No evidence is offered as to the validity of the Q and L scores. Such evidence should be available to test users.

This test is put out in two forms, one for hand-scoring and one for machine-scoring. The forms are identical, with two exceptions: (*a*) the order for presentation of the tests; and (*b*) the substitution in the hand-scoring form of a "tables" test for the figure analogy test in the machine-scored edition. The shift from the figure analogies test to the "tables" test in the hand-scored edition will affect the comparability of the two tests, but this effect should be slight. The new test is ingenious and requires the subject to examine a series of simple facts and to deduce from them certain relationships. In its simplest form it consists of giving the total number and the number in class A, and requiring the subject to determine the number in class B.

The total time for administration of the test is fifty-two minutes for each form. On the machine-scored form, this is distributed as nineteen minutes for practice tests and thirty-three minutes for the testing, and on the hand-scored edition as fifteen minutes for practice tests and thirty-seven minutes for testing. The use of practice exercises is commendable, but personal experience indicates that the time devoted to these might be reduced to about two minutes, thus saving about seven minutes, which would allow the test proper to be lengthened. The amount of test time allowed seems inadequate to the reviewer, in view of the importance attached to the results by administrative officers and personnel workers. No evidence is submitted as to the reliability of the instrument. Some data are presented as to the validity of the 1938 forms, where it is shown that the examination correlates approximately .50 with the results of each of four six-hour examinations in introductory courses in biology, the humanities, physical sciences, and the social sciences.

Robert L. Thorndike, Associate Professor of Education, Columbia University. These new forms continue the series of annual tests for college freshmen prepared by the Thurstones since 1924. Like the earlier forms of the test, these forms are characterized by: (*a*) a variety of subtests, both verbal and quantitative in character; (*b*) norms from a large college population, reported fully and with various breakdowns; and (*c*) data on the comparability of successive forms.

The new forms show a number of changes. These include: (*a*) Preparation of a machine-scored form of the test, and rearrangement of the hand-scored form so that its format resembles that of the machine-scored form. (*b*) The introduction of practice exercises, upon which a substantial part of the total testing time is to be spent. (*c*) Certain changes in the subtests, as follows: the addition of a number series subtest to all the forms; the replacing of the artificial languages test in both 1939 forms by a verbal analogies test; and the replacing of the figure-analogies test in the hand-scored 1939 form by a tables test. (*d*) The provision, in all forms, for a *quantitative* and a verbal subscore.

The advantages of the machine-scored test from the point of view of efficiency of scoring can hardly be questioned. That it calls for more complicated instructions is suggested both in the volume of instructional material and by the provision of practice exercises. Some question might be raised as to the "efficiency" of a test which devotes 19 minutes to practice and 33 minutes to testing. Does the preliminary practice permit the actual test time to be used enough more effectively to give a more reliable and valid result for the total time expenditure?

The several changes in subtests cannot be judged in terms of information made available at this time.

The provision of separate quantitative and verbal scores is a first step in the direction of differential diagnosis with this test. Now that separate scores are available, research will be possible to determine the value of these subscores for differentiating between aptitude for literary and scientific curricula.

These tests represent, then, the continuation of a well-planned hour test for college students with certain new variations, the value of which remains to be determined by further research.

For reviews by Anne Anastasi and David Segel, see 1037.

[1378]

American Council on Education Psychological Examination for High School Students, Form 1939. Grades 9-12; 1939; a new form has been issued annually since 1933; 2 editions; 5¢ per test; 10¢ per specimen set; 33(60) minutes; L. L. Thurstone and Thelma Gwinn Thurstone; Washington, D. C.: American Council on Education.
a) HAND-SCORING EDITION.
b) MACHINE-SCORING EDITION. 2¢ per machine-scorable answer sheet.

REFERENCES

1 THURSTONE, L. L.; THURSTONE, THELMA GWINN; AND ADKINS, DOROTHY C. "The 1938 Psychological Examination." *Ed Rec* 20:263-300 Ap '39.
2 THURSTONE, L. L., AND THURSTONE, THELMA GWINN. "The American Council on Education Psychological Examinations, 1939 Editions," pp. 3-38. In *Psychological Examinations, 1939.* American Council on Education Studies, Series 5, Vol. 4, No. 2. Washington, D. C.: the Council, May 1940. Pp. v, 53. $0.25. Paper.
See also references for 1377.

A. H. Turney, Professor of Education, The University of Kansas. The use of the *American Council on Education Psychological Examination for College Students* is so widespread that a description of these tests would be superfluous. The figures [1] in the *Educational Record* for April, 1939, would seem to indicate that the *American Council on Education Psychological Examination for High School Students* is not so widely known. The high school tests are the same in form and content (not identical items, of course) and the manuals are in the same form. Both hand- and machine-scorable forms are available. There seems to be no reason why the high school forms are not as serviceable and valuable as the college forms.

The reviewer has used the latter for seven years, testing new students to the number of about ten thousand, and has been well satisfied with the results.

These two editions have separated the test into a language and a quantitative section, giving respectively an *L* and *Q* score and also a gross score. These may appeal to many users. The manual and scoring devices are simple yet entirely adequate. It seems only just to say that a very valuable service is being rendered by the makers and publishers of these tests.

For a review by V. A. C. Henmon, see 1038.

[1379]

Arthur Point Scale of Performance Tests. Ages 6 and over; 1925-30; 2 forms; $62.50 per complete testing outfit for Form I (No. 37047); $29.75 per set of four additional tests necessary for Form II; $1 per 25 record blanks for Form I (No. 44003); (35-90) minutes; Grace Arthur; Chicago, Ill.: C. H. Stoelting Co.

REFERENCES

1 ARTHUR, GRACE, AND WOODROW, HERBERT. "An Absolute Intelligence Scale: A Study in Method." *J Appl Psychol* 3:118-37 Je '19.
2 ARTHUR, GRACE. "A Standardization of Certain Opposites for Children of Grade School Age." *J Ed Psychol* 14:483-95 N '23.
3 ARTHUR, GRACE. "A New Point Performance Scale." *J Appl Psychol* 9:390-416 D '25.
4 ARTHUR, GRACE. "A Group Point Scale for the Measurement of Intelligence." *J Appl Psychol* 10:228-44 Je '26.
5 ARTHUR, GRACE. "An Attempt to Sort Children with Specific Reading Disability from Other Non-Readers." *J Appl Psychol* 11:251-63 Ag '27.
6 ARTHUR, GRACE. "The Re-Standardization of a Point Performance Scale." *J Appl Psychol* 12:278-303 Je '28.
7 RILEY, G. "Stanford Binet 'Indicators' of Mechanical Ability." *Psychol Clinic* 18:128-32 My-Je '29.
8 ARTHUR, GRACE. *A Point Scale of Performance Tests:* Vol. I, Clinical Manual. New York: Commonwealth Fund, 1930. Pp. ix, 82. $1.50. (London: Oxford University Press. 6s. 6d.)
9 BROWN, ANDREW W. "The Correlations of Non-Language Tests with Each Other, with School Achievement, and with Teachers' Judgments of the Intelligence of Children in a School for the Deaf." *J Appl Psychol* 14:371-5 Ag '30.
10 ARTHUR, GRACE. *A Point Scale of Performance Tests:* Volume II, The Process of Standardization. New York: Commonwealth Fund, 1933. Pp. xi, 106. $1.50. (London: Oxford University Press, 6s. 6d.)
10.1 MACKANE, KEITH. *A Comparison of the Intelligence of Deaf and Hearing Children: A Study of the Reactions of Comparable Groups of Deaf and Hearing Children to Three Performance Scales and a Non-Language Test.* Columbia University, Teachers College, Contributions to Education, No. 585.

Rudolf Pintner, faculty sponsor. New York: Bureau of Publications, the College, 1933. Pp. ix, 47. Out of print.

11 KNIGHT, MAXINE WISLER. "A Comparative Study of the Performance of Feeble-Minded and Juvenile Delinquents on the Arthur Performance Scale and the Stanford-Binet Test of Intelligence." *J Juvenile Res* 18:5-12 Ja '34.

12 MAHAN, HARRY C. "A Battery of Performance Tests: The Arthur Scale Revised." *J Appl Psychol* 18:645-55, 859, O, D '34.

13 HILDEN, ARNOLD H., AND SKEELS, HAROLD M. "A Comparison of the Stanford-Binet Scale, the Kuhlmann-Anderson Group Test, the Arthur Point Scale of Performance Tests, and the Unit Scales of Attainment." *J Exp Ed* 4:214-30 D '35.

14 HUMM, KATHRYN A. "The Applicability of the Grace Arthur Performance Scale to an Adolescent Group." *Psychol B* 32:538 O '35.

15 BISHOP, HELEN M. "Performance Scale Tests Applied to Deaf and Hard of Hearing Children." *Volta R* 38:447 Ag '36.

16 ARTHUR, GRACE. "The Predictive Value of the Kuhlmann-Binet Scale for a Partially Americanized School Population." *J Appl Psychol* 21:359-64 Ag '37.

Andrew W. Brown, Chief Psychologist, Institute for Juvenile Research, Chicago, Illinois; and Associate Professor of Psychology, University of Illinois. The *Arthur Point Scale of Performance Tests* is a restandardization of twelve of the formboards of the *Pintner-Paterson Performance Scale* and in addition the *Porteus Maze Test* and the *Block Design Test.* These fourteen tests are divided into two forms. The *Knox Cube Test,* the *Seguin Formboard,* the *Porteus Maze Test,* and the *Block Design Test*—the most discriminative tests—are included in both forms, but presented in a different way in each form. Two of the tests, the *Two-Figure Formboard* and the *Gwyn Triangle Test,* are given as practice tests and are not scored. The material and methods used in the construction of the test are clearly and systematically presented in Volume II.[10] Volume I is the clinical manual.[8]

Theoretically the scale has two distinct advantages over some of the other performance tests. First, it is a point scale and second, the various tests are weighted according to their "discriminative value." The tests which most sharply discriminate one age group from the other receive the greatest weight in the total score. The age norms for Form I are based upon the scores of 1,100 public school children of a good middle class "American" district. The norms for Form II are based upon scores of 535 of the same children who had already been tested on Form I.

The probable error of measurement between the IQ's on the two forms ranges from 4.52 at age six to 8.45 at age fourteen. There are norms for ages six to fifteen. In contrast to some of the verbal tests the material seems interesting and attractive to most children.

The scale in its present form is intended as a clinical instrument to be used by adequately trained clinicians in psychological and psy-chiatric clinics. As such it has fulfilled its purpose well, especially between the ages seven or eight and twelve or thirteen. It does not appear to work as well above this level as does the *Cornell-Coxe Performance Ability Scale.*

The primary value of the Arthur scale is its use with foreign children or those who come from homes where a foreign language is spoken or those with educationally impoverished environment or those with reading difficulties.

With one or two exceptions the tests can be given by pantomime directions, and although verbal directions were used in the standardization, the test results by pantomime would probably deviate little if any from those obtained by verbal directions. It can therefore be used effectively in the examination of deaf children.

The scale is a valuable clinical instrument. One is often surprised, after having inspected the growth curves in Pintner and Paterson's *A Scale of Performance Test,* that it works as well as it does. Frequently the results correspond more closely with clinical impressions and the child's history, than the results of verbal tests. Correlations ranging between .50 and .75 have been reported between this and the Stanford-Binet. Because of these relatively low correlations and because of its fairly high reliability the scale serves as a good supplement to verbal tests of the Binet type. The scale also gives the examiner an opportunity to observe the child under different conditions than those during a verbal test. The child's method of approach in a concrete situation, his insight, his motor coordination and his persistence in a task can be noted.

On the other hand the clinician must not take the results too seriously especially for older dull children. Tests such as the *Seguin Formboard,* the *Casuist Formboard,* and the *Mare and Foal Test* are for children at this level more tests of speed-of-motor-performance than tests of "intelligence." Frequently older dull children of juvenile court age make relatively high scores on the performance tests which are entirely discrepant with performance in school, in shop, in the community or with clinical impressions.

Carroll A. Whitmer, Assistant Professor of Psychology, The University of Pittsburgh. The *Arthur Scale of Performance Tests* is composed of the following individual tests:

Knox Cube Test, Seguin Formboard, Two-Figure Formboard (used only as a transition between the solid block board and the divided block board and not scored), *Casuist Formboard, Manikin and Feature Profile* (scored in series), *Mare and Foal Test, Pictorial Completion Test I, Porteus Maze Test* and the *Block Design Test.* Form II consists of the *Knox Cube Test, Seguin Formboard, Gwyn Triangle Test, Five-Figure Formboard, Glueck's Ship Test, Pictorial Completion Test II, Porteus Maze Test,* and *Block Design Test.*

The subjects used in standardizing Form I, after a preliminary period of experimentation, numbered 1,125 and ranged in age from five to fifteen. These subjects were chosen from a public school in a middle class "American" district. Out of this standardization group, 574 children with Kuhlmann or Stanford-Binet IQ's in an approximate range of 57-125 were used for the mental age norms.

The process involved in fitting each test into the scale and in standardizing the scale as a whole is described in detail in Volume II [10] accompanying the manual [8] for the tests. It is sufficient to say in review that each test takes its point score value from its capacity to discriminate between successive age levels and is used in the manner which yielded the highest discriminative value according to the formula employed. It is obvious that the experience reported in the standardization volume would be of definite value to any other worker who considers using any of these tests in a new scale. The author reports a probable error between the Kuhlmann-Binet IQ's and Form I of the Arthur scale of 4.97. The corresponding probable error between Form I and Stanford-Binet IQ's was 4.92.

Form II of the scale is less well standardized and according to the author would require more work before it could equal Form I in reliability. It is obvious to any one experienced in formboard use that retesting with any formboard or scale of formboards presents an almost insurmountable problem of dealing with practice effects. For that reason and after having observed some retest cases with Form II, the writer feels that the primary serviceability of the Arthur scale is in Form I.

A method of extrapolation of scores is presented for use in the case of the subject whose score falls outside the norms for the chronological ages 6.5 to 16.5 years inclusive. The author admits the relative inaccuracies of such procedures particularly in respect to the lower extension. In view of the fact that the subject who scores less than the points required for the 5½-year rating must certainly score below the norm on some tests, it would seem that that subject is relatively unmeasured. In practice we have found the scale less suitable than the *Merrill Palmer Scale of Mental Tests* for measuring the child of preschool age or the dull child who scores below the 7-year level.

Although the inaccuracies of the extrapolation for the brighter or older subject are admitted, we have found the method of extrapolation useful because of its possibility for use with the foreign speaking or deaf subject who under normal conditions would not be a logical subject for formboards.

The Arthur scale provides a means of interpreting the total point value obtained when one test is omitted from the scale. We have found this treatment of the score useful when the subject has had some specific experience with one of the tests.

As compared with the *Pintner-Paterson Performance Scale* we feel that the Arthur scale is better suited to the examination of school children because of its method of standardization. In comparison to other formboard scales it is relatively easy to administer and score. The directions for presenting the tests are simple and the scoring does not require the counting of moves or errors. All tests are scored on time or success in parts or as a whole. The author has used what seems to us a very awkward means of handling the child in the test situation in requiring him to turn his head or hide his eyes while the material of the test is being arranged. It would seem much more reasonable to arrange the material on the back of the boards before the subject appears, then the parts could be quickly slid onto the table and the board placed at the time the directions are being given, thus facilitating the administration process.

We have found the Arthur scale a very valuable supplement to the Binet type of test. In cases of deaf, foreign language speaking, or emotionally blocked subjects, the test provides a substitute which with qualitative observation plus the score gives a fair index of general mental level. We feel that the Arthur should be used as a *substitute* only when the Binet cannot be accurately done, but it certainly should be a part of the equipment of any well-equipped clinic for mental examinations of children.

J Ed Psychol 21:716-7 D '30. *Donald Snedden.* * The chief disadvantage of the scale as a whole is its inelasticity. Good age norms are available for the total point score, but not for the separate tests. This means that in case a test is "spoiled" an adjustment (that is not simple) has to be made to the incomplete total score. It seems to the reviewer that the advantages far outweigh the disadvantages and that the scale should have and will have a very wide clinical usefulness.

[1380]

Australian Council for Educational Research Non-Verbal Tests. Ages 9-14; 1936; 1s. per 25; 5d. per manual; 24 (40-45) minutes; Melbourne, Australia: Australian Council for Educational Research.

REFERENCES

1 McIntyre, G. A. *The Standardization of Intelligence Tests in Australia.* Australian Council for Educational Research, Educational Research Series, No. 54. Melbourne, Australia: Melbourne University Press, 1938. Pp. 82. 4s. Paper. (London: Oxford University Press, 1939. 4s.) (New York: G. E. Stechert & Co. $1.00.)

[1381]

Bristol Group Reasoning Tests. Ages 10½-14; 1926; 3 forms; 1s. 8d. per 25; 8d. per 25 practice sheets; 6d. per manual; 9d. per specimen set; nontimed (90) minutes; A. Barbara Dale; London: University of London Press, Ltd.

REFERENCES

1 Dale, A. Barbara. "Group Tests in Reasoning Ability." *Brit J Psychol* 16:314-38 Ap '26.

Charles Fox, formerly Director of Training, University of Cambridge. This admirable test is based on Burt's individual test of reasoning, amplified and recast so as to be suitable for group testing. There are three equivalent forms of the test, each containing 15 items, and a practice test to act as a shock absorber. There is no time limit as speed is not of importance in testing reasoning; but one hour is sufficient to enable each testee to do all he is capable of doing. It is essential for reliability to emphasize the fact that there is no need to hurry, and to make arrangements accordingly in the testing room. The table of norms given in the manual of directions covers the age-range 10½ to 14 years for primary school children; but the tests can be applied up to 16 years at least. The construction and validation of the tests have been described by the author in the *British Journal of Psychology.*[1] There appears to be no difference in the standardization for English or American children; nor any appreciable sex differences. Objectivity of marking, which is a

great difficulty in reasoning tests, is secured by allowing the testee to select by underlining among a number of alternatives. Much ingenuity has been displayed in the alternatives given, so that guessing is precluded.

Many individual or group tests include tests of reasoning as subtests, but there are few tests of reasoning alone, and the Bristol test is the best of them. The present reviewer has given a selection from these tests to brighter and duller classes of 12 years of age in a central school, and found a marked difference in average scores. He was able also to confirm the finding of the author of the tests that there is a correlation between the total class position of the testees and excellence in the tests. The tests are, therefore, useful for diagnostic purposes to get an estimate of general suitability for school work. The three alternative forms of equal difficulty provide a ready means of estimating the growth of ability over a prolonged period of time.

Percival Smith, Principal Assistant Organiser, Education Department, Birmingham, England. These tests have been very carefully constructed. The fact that they are based on an early test-scale prepared by Cyril Burt who has written an introductory note to the instructions is evidence that the tests may be accepted, within certain limits, as scientific and reliable. Dale, however, in overlooking Burt's statement that "the power to reason is *one of the most important* mental capacities," puts her claim too high when she asserts that one of her chief aims has been to "use as a measure of mental ability the fundamental process of reasoning." The tests are reasoning tests and the results should and no doubt do give a valuable and reliable assessment of one facet of mental ability.

The instructions are clear and thorough although minor criticisms might be made. For instance, it seems unwise to "provide each child with pen or pencil." It is preferable and usual for pencils only to be allowed in such tests.

Two tables of norms are supplied and two methods have been followed in their preparation. The first table gives the average score obtained by children from 10½ to 14 years of age at intervals of six months.

The second table gives the average score obtained by children in Standards IV, V, VI, and VII respectively. This second table at once dates the test as it is no longer the practice to grade children in English elementary schools in such a simple manner. As a rule children are graded according to their age in "year groups" and secondarily in streams according to their capacity. Although exact details are not supplied it would appear that the norms were prepared some 13 years ago. It is suggested that a useful purpose would be served by calculating up-to-date norms. These useful tests would then be of even greater value.

[1382]

California First-Year Mental Scale. Ages 1-18 months; 1933; individual; 1 form; $73.82 per complete testing outfit (No. 37018); $36.07 per testing outfit not including the crib, table, high chair, and mirror; 55¢ per manual; $1.12 per 25 record blanks; Nancy Bayley; Chicago, Ill.: C. H. Stoelting Co.

REFERENCES

1 BAYLEY, NANCY. *The California First-Year Mental Scale.* University of California, Syllabus Series No. 243; Institute of Child Welfare. Berkeley, Calif.: University of California Press, May 1933. Pp. 24. $0.50. Paper.

Florence L. Goodenough, Research Professor, Institute of Child Welfare, The University of Minnesota. The standardization of the *California First-Year Mental Scale* is unique in that it was based upon repeated examinations of the same group of infants who were tested at monthly intervals from 1 through 15 months and were again tested at 18 and at 21 months. The total number of cases was 61; the average number tested at each of the specified ages was 54, and the smallest number tested at any age was 46. Although this seems like a small group for normative purposes, the developmental changes in performance are probably more reliably established than they could have been by the use of much larger numbers selected by the usual cross-sectional method. Inasmuch as all the children came from the city of Berkeley, where, owing to the large proportion of families connected with the University of California the average intellectual level of the population has been shown to be above that of the country as a whole, it is probable that the standards given are somewhat above those for the infant population in general, particularly since the author states that the socio-economic status of the families was slightly higher, on the average, than even the Berkeley standards. However, it is obvious that such an error, if it exists, would operate equally at all ages at which the test was given. The test should therefore be relatively free from the irregularities not uncommonly met with in tests standardized on a cross-sectional basis in which it may chance that the children tested at one age are on the average truly inferior to those tested at another age.

The instructions for giving and scoring the test are clear and concise. Results may be expressed in terms of an absolute scale value derived by the Thurstone method, the sigma deviation from the mean of the age-group, or in mental age units. The use of the IQ or Developmental Quotient is not recommended since the standard deviations do not increase in proportion to age beyond the first few months.

Although the scale appears to provide a fairly accurate appraisal of the child's developmental status at time of testing, it does not afford a basis for predicting mental status after the period of infancy has passed. As a matter of fact, the author has shown that the correlations between individual test performance during the first year of life and standing on other recognized tests of intelligence after the age of three years show a low but consistently negative trend. This is in accordance with the findings of other investigators with tests designed for infants. A number of interesting theoretical questions are thereby raised, but a probable explanation appears to be that the content of the tests included in the infant scales may be psychologically so dissimilar from that of the tests used with older children that no clear-cut relationship could be expected. It should be noted that the tests used for infants are largely concerned with relatively simple motor and perceptual items of a kind that have never been found to correlate highly with intelligence at any age.

Perhaps at some time a future student of child development will be able to single out other aspects of infantile behavior that will provide more stable indications of his mental potentialities. On the other hand, it may be that the overt manifestations of that which we later call "intelligence" do not reach the threshold of perceptibility until after the period of infancy is past. In attempting to predict the later mental status of a child on the basis of his behavioral capacity during infancy, we may be in much the same case as if we were to attempt to predict the later growth of the beard of a male child at the same age. Except by inference from other known facts, no character can be predicted until its emergence has at least begun.

Although the writer has not lost hope that the first possibility may in time be realized, there is no use in blinding ourselves to the fact that the time is not yet come. In the meantime, it should be noted that the so-called mental tests for infants have done much to acquaint the scientific world with the normal course of certain aspects of behavioral growth during its early stages, but that thus far these tests have not proved to be useful instruments for the clinical prediction of later mental capacity.

[1383]

California Preschool Mental Scale. Ages 1½-6 years; 1934; individual; 1 form; $27.95 per testing outfit without manual, carrying case, or record blanks; $10 per carrying case; 75¢ per manual; 5¢ per record blank, 50 or more (the manual and record blanks must be ordered from the University of California Press, Berkeley, California); Adele S. Jaffa; Berkeley, Calif.: Joseph Dominion, 2734 Milvia St.

REFERENCES

1 JAFFA, ADELE S. *The California Preschool Mental Scale*: Form A. Foreword by Herbert R. Stolz. University of California, Syllabus Series, No. 251; Institute of Child Welfare. Berkeley, Calif.: University of California Press, November 1934. Pp. v, 66. $0.75. Paper.

B. M. Castner, Clinic of Child Development, Yale University. We have here a group of test situations, mostly borrowed from previously published scales, and arranged in developmental sequences under ten headings, some of which refer to important basic fields of behavior, such as "Language" and "Manual Facility," while others are simply descriptive categories, such as "Block-Building" and "Completion." The selection of tests is good, on the whole, and the normative placement of the individual items does not vary significantly from their original placement in the scales from which they were taken. The amount of testing material called for seems unnecessarily great, with many small items, difficult to keep in order.

Details of the standardization procedures are not given, nor is there any detailed presentation of results. The number of cases—there were about 2,000 tests on approximately 800 children—is relatively large as preschool standardization groups go. Since large groups representative of the general population are not available within this age range, as they are in the case of school children, it is particularly necessary to present details as to selection of subjects, conditions of testing, variability of response, and the like, in order that the results may be properly evaluated. It is conceded

that a major group, which has furnished the basis for one method of scoring, is definitely superior.

Three methods of scoring are provided: (a) an "approximate" mental age and IQ score; (b) a sigma score; and (c) a profile score, in which the maturity levels indicated in the respective test categories are considered individually and collectively. The MA-IQ type of scoring for preschool children will not appeal to those who have sufficient experience, based upon follow-up study of many children over a period of several years, to know in how large a number of cases such measures can be seriously misleading. Unfortunately, it will appeal, because of its simplicity, to those who attempt to use the tests without a background of training and experience, and are likely to put precisely similar interpretations upon MA and IQ that they are accustomed to make in the case of school children. The sigma score would be expected to have more value, but is here based upon the results obtained in a superior group. The "profile" score has definite advantages over the other two types in that it encourages an analytic interpretation of the total performance, and emphasizes acceleration or retardation in specific fields of behavior, so commonly met with in preschool children, and so important for the proper understanding of the test results, particularly from the point of view of prognosis. The value of this method of scoring would be increased if the test-categories were better defined in terms of significant basic fields of behavior. It is unfortunate, too, that the profile scores have not been thoroughly studied, and are "offered principally as an interesting departure from traditional method." They are, even so, if applied with clinical judgment based upon adequate experience, better than either of the two other methods.

But the gravest defect in the scale, from the social as well as the clinical point of view, lies in the extremely brief and quite inadequate description of what are to be scored as "successes" in response to the individual items, and the omission of any discussion of the significance of qualitative variations from the prescribed responses. Much less than older persons do normal preschool children respond in the cut-and-dried way which might be expected from reading the brief statements given here; and interpretation of failures is often extremely difficult, even for the experienced examiner. There is little in this presentation to discourage the inexperienced tester from attempting developmental diagnosis on the basis of tests given according to formula and woodenly scored by a plus-and-minus rating, as has been done to the point of scandal in the case of older children. Within the preschool age range, the serious injustice that often results from such methods is certain to be even more frequent.

In summary, it may be said that this scale contains a good group of individual tests, probably well placed from the normative point of view, but inadequately standardized as a scale. Since none of the scoring methods are completely satisfactory, and since the discussion of the significance of test-responses is too brief to be clinically useful, most examiners will prefer to use one of the other available preschool scales in which the requirements are more adequately met. Further research, however, might convert this into a useful method for preschool study.

Florence L. Goodenough, Research Professor, Institute of Child Welfare, The University of Minnesota. The *California Preschool Mental Scale* was prepared especially for use in certain research projects at the University of California Institute of Child Welfare and has been little used elsewhere. The items were selected from a number of other published scales with some additions by the author. A distinctive feature of the test is the attempt to maintain psychological uniformity of content from age to age by dividing the items into ten categories, roughly described as (*a*) manual facility, (*b*) block-building, (*c*) drawing, (*d*) form discrimination, (*e*) spatial relations discrimination, (*f*) size and number discrimination, (*g*) language comprehension, (*h*) language facility, (*i*) immediate recall, (*j*) completions, with one or more tests in each category (with a few exceptions) included at each age level. The record booklet is prepared in the form of a profile chart by which the child's standing on each of the ten categories is shown separately. However, inasmuch as this standing is based upon so few tests that lie near the developmental level of any individual child, it is questionable whether the individual profiles can be said to have much clinical significance since the reliability of the separate point-determinations cannot be high. The

author gives no data on this head. Undoubtedly, however, uniformity of test-meaning from age to age has been increased by this arrangement.

The instructions for scoring are needlessly complicated but the method itself is not difficult, once it has been worked through. A technique is devised whereby the child is not penalized for the accidental omission of items or for items that he refuses to attempt. Results may be expressed in the usual terms of mental age and intelligence quotient, in sigma units, or in a point score scaled according to the Thurstone technique.

The test items seem to have been very well selected both from the standpoint of children's interests and variety of content. The scale merits a wider use than it has received.

[1384]

California Test of Mental Maturity. Grades Kgn.-1, 1-3, 4-8, 7-10, 9-adults; 1936-39; 1 form, 3 editions; $1.25 per 25 copies of the regular edition; 75¢ per 25 copies of the short-form edition; 25¢ per specimen set of any one edition at any one level; 2¢ per machine-scorable answer sheet; (90) minutes for the regular edition; (45) minutes for the short-form editions; Elizabeth T. Sullivan, Willis W. Clark, and Ernest W. Tiegs; Los Angeles, Calif.: California Test Bureau.
a) PRE-PRIMARY BATTERY. Grades Kgn.-1; [*Regular Edition*]; *Pre-Primary S-Form.*
b) PRIMARY BATTERY. Grades 1-3; [*Regular Edition*]; *Primary S-Form.*
c) ELEMENTARY BATTERY. Grades 4-8; [*Regular Edition*]; *Elementary S-Form; Elementary S-Form: Machine Scoring Edition.*
d) INTERMEDIATE BATTERY. Grades 7-10; [*Regular Edition*]; *Intermediate S-Form; Intermediate S-Form: Machine Scoring Edition.*
e) ADVANCED BATTERY. Grades 9-adults; [*Regular Edition*]; *Advanced S-Form; Advanced S-Form: Machine Scoring Edition.*

REFERENCES

1 TIEGS, ERNEST W. "Breaking Down the I.Q." *Prog Ed* 13:603-5 D '36.
2 MAXFIELD, FRANCIS N. "California Test of Mental Maturity." *Ed Res B* 16:188-9+ O '37.
3 TRAXLER, ARTHUR E. "A Study of the California Test of Mental Maturity," pp. 49-60. In *1937 Fall Testing Program in Independent Schools:* Including a Study of the California Test of Mental Maturity. Educational Records Bulletin No. 22. New York: Educational Records Bureau, January 1938. Pp. x, 60. $1.50. Paper, lithotyped.
4 TRAXLER, ARTHUR E. "Some Correlation Data for the California Test of Mental Maturity," pp. 63-9. In *1938 Fall Testing Program in Independent Schools and Supplementary Studies.* Educational Records Bulletin No. 26. New York: Educational Records Bureau, January 1939. Pp. x, 69. $1.00. Paper, lithotyped.
5 TRAXLER, ARTHUR E. "Study of the California Test of Mental Maturity, Advanced Battery." *J Ed Res* 32:329-35 Ja '39.

Raymond B. Cattell, G. Stanley Hall Professor of Genetic Psychology, Clark University. This test has a regular and a short form and is available in hand-scored or machine-scored printings. However, since the same principles of construction are well observed throughout, it is possible to consider the merits of the test as a whole.

A plan of which most psychologists will approve is the breaking-up of the range of mental improvement into several ranges, each of two or three years' span. In this way the measurement is made finer by more items and the type of test is better adapted to the child's mental age. On the other hand, the tester needs to know beforehand, by some preliminary omnibus test, in what range of mental age any given child is likely to fall.

These tests are exceedingly well designed from the point of view of adaptation to school needs and the convenience of the teacher. All the data regarding consistencies, standardization, correlation with school progress, etc., that one could reasonably demand, are clearly presented in the handbook of instructions. In only one case is there some danger of misunderstanding, and then only by the test user not familiar with the statistical and psychological notions of the professional psychologist. This occurs in the table on "IQ's and Related Data as Shown by School Surveys" in which one finds opposite IQ 114, 99th percentile; and opposite IQ 85, 5th percentile. Many teachers will probably need to be emphatically warned that this is not the percentile distribution of individual IQ's, but of group medians (and how big are these groups?). In the same table, years of retardation in reading are set against IQ levels. That this relation depends on the absolute age of the pupil is not conspicuously suggested by the table.

An admirable feature of this test is the courageous manner in which the authors come out into the open regarding the purpose, principles, and theory of test design. They point to factor analysis as their foundation, but reject the two-factor theory of a general intellective power g in favor of a multiple-factor supposition. They are, of course, quite entitled to do this, since either of these theories fits the correlations, but it seems a little wayward deliberately to adopt the more complex rather than the more simple explanation, with special cause for doing so.

A possible reason for this behavior becomes evident when we come to the application of results. People having little acquaintance with intelligence test research, as is well known, like to pass beyond the mere IQ, possibly because they feel that a single index is a small return for so much labor of testing. They wish to elaborate their analysis of the child and will generalize, from particular test items, or even from the child's manner of answering or his handwriting, in a far-reaching way about temperament or special abilities. Every psychologist is familiar with the tendency in teachers or parents, but not all are willing to cater to it.

The authors evidently feel that this desire to find out more than about intelligence from an intelligence test alone is to be encouraged, for they write, "dealing only with mental ages and intelligence quotients obscures and ignores the separate important factors." They add, rightly, that independent special factors have been found in verbal and arithmetical fields and (incorrectly) in spatial performance but then proceed to speak as if the separate subtests in their test measure these factors and are independent. They offer a profile which "analyzes and summarizes the various factors which are measured by the test situations," and claim that this "reduces the 'mystery' which has surrounded the meaning of mental age and intelligence quotient." This attempt to produce for special consumption a "psychology without mystery" ends by appearing to the psychologist to be "mystery without psychology." No proof is offered that these subtests do, in fact, test independent factors or that one is justified in generalizing from them to performances in everyday life which happen to have the same verbal label.

A useful application of ingenuity in these tests is the introduction of tests of visual acuity and hearing at the beginning of the test. Most psychologists have known "mental defectives" who turn out only to be somewhat deaf.

Ingenuity is less happy in the use of terms; indeed, originality here seems to have become perverse. Why, for example, "Foresight in Spatial Situations," or why call the familiar and correctly described "Classifications" test a "Similarities" test? Why bring confusion and mystery into a very good intelligence test by departing from custom so far as to call it a "Mental Maturity" test? The term "maturity" in personality measurement has become increasingly associated with the notion of emotional maturity. Intelligence is not "maturity," otherwise we should count a child's teeth in assessing it, and it would continue in growth far beyond adolescence. It is to be hoped, both in the interests of their test and of avoiding disruption of clear discussion in psychology, that the authors will indicate by a better label that their test belongs to the category of intelligence tests.

F. Kuhlmann, Director of the Division of Examinations and Classification, State Department of Public Institutions, St. Paul, Minnesota. These tests include five batteries to cover the range from kindergarten to grade 14, inclusive. There is a long and short form, the long form requiring two sessions of about forty-five minutes each to give. In each battery there is a test on visual acuity, auditory acuity, and motor co-ordination. Following this the tests are grouped as tests of Memory, Spatial Relationships, Reasoning, and Vocabulary. The tests in these four groups are also classed as "Language Factors" tests, and "Nonlanguage Factor" tests. Age norms are given for each of these and for the total number of right responses on the whole battery, making it possible to compute seven sets of mental ages and corresponding IQ's. Profile scoring is provided for and recommended.

The outstanding features of these batteries are : first, the inclusion of tests on vision, hearing, and motor co-ordination, which, if defective, would invalidate the results on the other tests ; second, the wealth of material included in each battery ; third, the underlying theory on which the selection of the tests and construction of the batteries are based.

We do not believe there is much merit in labeling tests as regards functions measured, as the authors have done ; first, because it cannot be done correctly by inspection ; and second, because these labels are not of much value until we know also how these functions enter into school achievement in different school subjects. Also, when a battery is divided into several different measures the tests assigned to measure any particular function tend to become inadequate in number and range to do so reliably. It would be hazardous, indeed, to conclude from the score on two brief tests that a child has a poor memory, for example. It seems to be implied also that the child mind is simply the adult mind in miniature, so that tests should measure the same function at all ages. We believe the empirical and more usual procedure is better. This starts out experimentally to find tests of maximum discriminative capacity at each age, and regards the question of what

functions are measured at any age by such tests as of minor importance. The authors' distinction between language factor and nonlanguage factor tests is also somewhat misleading. Language enters both, the real distinction being that in the former the child has to read test material, while in the latter he is told what to do with picture material and, with a few exceptions, no reading is involved.

The authors have probably built much better than they planned. The different tests in each battery probably measure a much greater variety of functions than they are intended to measure. They should have given more evidence that the tests are arranged in order of difficulty in each battery and that they are more or less equally spaced on the basis of difficulty. The increase in total raw score with increase in age does this only rather roughly. Outside of this, we believe the *unabbreviated* batteries are to be classed among the very best on the market for determining general levels of mental maturity. It is gratifying to see authors with the courage to offer tests that take more than a single class period to give and who do not attempt to get the maximum economy in time and dollars, by sacrificing everything necessary to attain this end.

Chicago Sch J 21:304 My-Je '40. D(avid) K(opel). [Review of the Short Form.] * Each test contains six sub-tests, of which three are designated as "non-language" and three as "language." It is claimed, quite reasonably, that this feature is particularly valuable in cases where reading or language difficulties may invalidate the results obtained from use of the ordinary group verbal test of intelligence. An unusual feature is the inclusion of a pretest of visual acuity. Since many items in each test consist of pictures and other symbols containing fine details, it is thought necessary to identify individuals suffering from gross visual defect for whom the test is therefore inappropriate.

For reviews by W. D. Commins, Rudolf Pintner, and Arthur E. Traxler see 1042.

[1385]

Carl Hollow Square Scale. Ages 10 and over ; 1939 ; 1 form ; $36.00 per testing outfit ; (25-60) minutes ; George P. Carl ; Philadelphia, Pa.: Psychological Service, Institute of the Pennsylvania Hospital.

REFERENCES

1 CARL, GEORGE P. *Manual of Directions for the Carl Hollow Square Scale.* Philadelphia, Pa.: Psychological Service, Insti-

tute of the Pennsylvania Hospital, 1939. Pp. 30. Sold only with testing outfit. Mimeographed.
2 CARL, GEORGE P. "A New Performance Test for Adults and Older Children: The Carl Hollow Square Scale." *J Psychol* 7:179-99 Ja '39.

T. J. Keating, Research Fellow, The Training School at Vineland, New Jersey. The *Carl Hollow Square Scale* meets the need for a formboard test which has enough top to be useful for superior adults. The materials used —a frame and blocks—are well made and conveniently arranged in a portable wooden box. The blocks are so labeled that those used in a particular subtest—the scale is composed of twenty—may be easily identified.

Contrary to one's initial impression, administration is relatively easy. The time consumed is fairly long, twenty-five minutes or more. Scoring, which is based on time, moves, and a correction, is somewhat cumbersome. The effect of readministration is not indicated in the author's manual. The subtests do not appear to become increasingly difficult in a regular progression. The length of the scale acts as a corrective to this irregular progression; results may therefore be accepted with some assurance.

[1386]

Cattell Intelligence Tests, Revised Edition. Mental ages 4-8, 8-11, 11-15, 15 and over; 1930-35; 2s. for manual for Scales I-III; 6s. per specimen set; R. B. Cattell; London: George G. Harrap & Co., Ltd.
a) SCALE O (DARTINGTON SCALE). Mental ages 4-8; 1933; individual; 1 form; 6s. per 25; 6s. per set of cards; 2s. per manual; (45) minutes.
b) SCALE I (NON-VERBAL) REVISED. Mental ages 8-11; 1930-35; 2 forms; 6s. per 25; (45-50) minutes.
c) SCALE II, REVISED. Mental ages 11-15; 1930-35; 5s. per 25; 6s. per set of cards; 2 forms; 66(75) minutes.
d) SCALE III, REVISED. Mental ages 15 and over; 1930-35; 2 forms; 5s. per 25;.66(75) minutes.

REFERENCES

1 CATTELL, RAYMOND B., AND BRISTOL, HILDA. "Intelligence Tests for Mental Ages of Four to Eight Years." *Brit J Ed Psychol* 3:142-69 Je '33.
2 CATTELL, RAYMOND B. "Occupational Norms of Intelligence, and the Standardization of an Adult Intelligence Test." *Brit J Psychol* 25:1-28 Jl '34.
3 CATTELL, RAYMOND B. "Standardization of Two Intelligence Tests for Children." *Brit J Psychol* 26:263-72 Ja '36.

Godfrey H. Thomson, Professor of Education and Director of the Training Centre for Teachers, University of Edinburgh. These tests are in many ways excellent. The handbooks give full and clear directions, and give references to the articles in easily accessible journals where the ingenious standardisation of the tests is described. I do not think, however, that any reliabilities are given either in the handbooks or in the articles referred to. If there are any they are at least not given a prominent place. And there is one statement

(that "Scale III is at the moment the most widely standardised of adult tests") which appears to be entirely unsupported. As I have no experience of Cattell's Scale 0 (for mental ages of 4-8 years) I shall in the remarks which follow speak only of his Scales I, II, and III.

The chief criticism I have to make of the handbook to these scales is that it does not warn the purchaser sufficiently that these tests have the peculiarity that they give a much wider scatter of intelligence quotients than is usual. My criticism, as I wish to make very clear, is not against this feature of Cattell's tests in itself, but against inadequate warning of the peculiarity. The only sentence in the handbook concerning this point is that "the scatter of IQ's is decidedly greater than on the Binet Test and in accordance with recent research," with a reference to an article [2] by Cattell. Even in that article, however, the purchaser, if he refers to it, will not easily find a quantitative statement of how much greater the Cattell scatter is than the Binet scatter. The standard deviation of Binet IQ's is about 15 or 16 points. In the article referred to, I find by calculations on Figures 7 and 8 a standard deviation of 27 points of Cattell IQ and on Figure 3 about 20 points. A calculation on Figure 5 in another article [3] of Cattell's, which refers to Scale IIA, gives a standard deviation of 21 points of Cattell IQ. Our experience at Moray House in giving tests to university graduates of about 22 years of age is that the excess of IQ over 100 needs to be reduced about two-thirds in order to be comparable with other tests.

In the diagram showing intelligence levels in various occupations, reproduced in the handbook, there is indirect evidence, for those familiar with vocational IQ's, of the wide scatter of Cattell IQ's. The average IQ of 90 elementary schoolteachers for example is given as 137, which is much higher than their average Binet IQ.

It is of course possible that Cattell is right in finding this scatter. In his 1934 article he quotes my own experience in finding higher standard deviations with group tests than with the Binet test. I did not, however, conclude that the Binet scatter was wrong, though I anticipated the rise from Terman's Californian 13 points to the Scottish Survey's 16 or 17 points. I have reread Cattell's articles on standardising his tests and find much to praise and nothing to criticise except the small number of cases on which some points depend, and the very daring way in which he multiplies up his actual 1,039 men on page 8 of his 1934 article to obtain a balanced population of 227,081. But I do not think his wide scatter of IQ's is explicable by these features. There should be, I think, further research on the lines he has indicated. Meanwhile, however, the handbook to his tests should more emphatically, and *quantitatively*, warn the purchaser that Cattell IQ's, if they are high, are too high, and if they are low, are too low, compared with most other measures of IQ.

[1387]

Chicago Non-Verbal Examination. Ages 7-adults; 1936-40; 1 form; individual; may be administered using either verbal or nonverbal directions; $1.50 per 25 tests; 60¢ per manual and keys; 10¢ per sample test; (40) minutes; A. W. Brown with the assistance of S. P. Stein and P. L. Rohrer; New York: Psychological Corporation.

REFERENCES

1 BROWN, ANDREW W. "The Development and Standardization of the Chicago Non-Verbal Examination." *J Appl Psychol* 24:36-47, 122-9 F, Ap '40.

Robert G. Bernreuter, Director of the Psycho-Educational Clinic and Associate Professor of Psychology, The Pennsylvania State College. The *Chicago Non-Verbal Examination* is intended to measure the nonverbal aspects of intelligence. It is a group test, composed of ten subtests, which may be administered either orally or by pantomime. It requires 25 minutes of actual working time, plus the time necessary for making the task clear in each of the subtests.

Reliability coefficients varying from .80 to .93 are reported by the author. They were obtained by both the split-half and the retest techniques, on groups with ranges of two and three years in chronological age, and two to six grades in school placement. As a consequence, the test is probably not reliable enough to use in comparing a child with his classmates within a single grade, but probably is reliable enough to compare him with the children in a wider range of grades.

Four criteria were used to determine the validity of the test: correlation with chronological age, comparison of normal and feebleminded children, the normality of the distribution of scores, and the correlation with other tests. So far as can be told by these criteria, the test seems to be reasonably valid. Furthermore, the types of items of which the ten sub-

tests are composed are all well known and have been shown by previous investigators to be useful. However, the author has not made a multiple factor analysis of the intercorrelations of his subtests. Had he done so, the validity of the test as measures of Thurstone's primary abilities might have been disclosed. Lacking this information, it is impossible to say more than that the test measures the "nonverbal aspects of intelligence." Considered in the light of Thurstone's work, this is very nearly a meaningless phrase.

A total of over 6,000 cases, from age six to adulthood were tested during the process of standardization. Mental ages, percentile scores and so-called "modified standard scores" have been prepared for the test administered orally. The latter serve as a substitute for IQ's above 14 years and are reasonably similar, numerically, to IQ's obtained on the Revised Stanford-Binet. However, a comparison of the table for obtaining mental ages from raw scores with the one for obtaining percentile scores, discloses some discrepancies in the derived scores. If, for example, a child has a constant IQ at each age from 6 to 14, his percentile scores will vary unsystematically, sometimes as much as 20 points. If he has a constant percentile score, his IQ will vary unsystematically. Because of these characteristics, the norms must be treated as tentative.

Myrtle Luneau Pignatelli, Clinical Psychologist, Bellevue Psychiatric Hospital, New York, New York. The *Chicago Non-Verbal Examination* is a test purporting to measure general intelligence without the use of verbal symbols. It is especially suitable for those children who are deaf or are hard of hearing, who have reading difficulties, who come from environments where there is limited use of the English language, and in general those who have difficulty in manipulating verbal concepts. It will especially be useful in urban centers which have large foreign populations.

The author has selected for the battery, tests which can be administered by both verbal and pantomime directions. Using the verbal directions, the test can be applied to children from age 6 through the adult level, and with the nonverbal directions, to children of age 7 through the adult level. The tests include the following performances: (*a*) common digit-symbols test; (*b*) marking out what does not belong in a series of pictures or designs; (c) counting number of blocks in a pile; (d) selecting from a series of geometrical forms, two of which can be put together to make a given form; (e) selecting from a series of designs one of which is just like a given design; (f) arranging the parts of a picture to make a complete picture; (g) numbering pictures according to a certain sequence; (h) marking the thing that is wrong in each of a number of pictures; (i) selecting from a series of pictures, the one that goes with or is a part of a given picture; and (j) learning, of a more difficult type than that in a.

The norms for the tests were established on 1844 normal hearing children from the middle-economic class in Chicago. The sampling is held to be respresentative of children of elementary school age up to year 14. Norms are given for mental ages, percentile ranks, and modified standard scores for each age up to 14 years. For groups above 14 years, only percentile ranks and standard scores are available. Reliability obtained for both verbal and pantomime directions is between .80 and .90. Clinical use of the tests by the authors has shown its value for the child with language difficulty, and ratings are reported to compare favorably with Stanford-Binet rating in the middle IQ range.

The examination compares favorably with the *Pinter Non-Language Mental Test* and the *Revised Beta Examination* as an instrument for the measurement of general intelligence, although it covers a wider range of mental functions. The tests make demands on the powers of association, visualization, depth imagery, integrative perceptual capacity, momentary perceptive retentiveness for purposes of gestalt organization, social apperception, and judgment. The instrument shows how difficult it is to devise tests which do not make use of verbal concepts in some forms. Of the ten tests in the battery, only four appear entirely free of such concepts, while the remaining tests make wide demands on general information and knowledge of things associated with everyday life.

The directions are clear, but for some types of individuals, may not be readily grasped. The scoring is objective, and facilitated by the use of stencils. The pictures in some of the tests could be clearer and less detailed, though the printing is fairly distinct.

The examination will not be a good measure of general intelligence for persons with uncorrected visual difficulties or slow psycho-motor reactions, but clinically it may prove to be a very good indicator of the efficiency of mental functioning in certain types of mental cases. It has possibilities for use as a research instrument, and from a practical standpoint, if used with individuals who are functioning up to capacity, it will tap, somewhat more thoroughly than other instruments of its type, the essential aspects of intelligence.

S. D. Porteus, Director of the Psychological Clinic and Professor of Clinical Psychology, University of Hawaii. This scale consists of ten subtests. Tests 1 and 10 are digit substitution tests, the former being much simpler than the latter. In Test 10 there are no less than twelve drawings which look like Chinese characters to be paired with digits. If the person is test-wise he can make a good score without much mental exercise by taking one form at a time throughout the series and putting the digit underneath it wherever it occurs. If he is not test-wise it is a rather difficult exercise in associating symbols arbitrarily. This, of course, is not the common use of symbols. Ordinarily symbols are used to shortcut reasoning processes as in algebra, but there is no exercise of memory required in remembering what the symbol stands for. Symbol substitution of the kind examined in the test is of little or no importance in our thinking. To weight it by including two tests of this nature in the series is unwise.

Test 2 is a test of the ability to see quickly the incongruous item in a pictured series. Unfortunately, some of the objects are so badly drawn that precious time is consumed by the effort to see what the drawing represents. The writer could not tell whether one item was a woman's hat or a handbag, and in another was confused in determining whether the picture represented a telegraph key or a patent can opener.

Test 3 is a cube counting test in which the cubes are drawn in most unnatural perspective. In my opinion, it should be declared unconstitutional as involving cruel and inhuman punishment of the subject. Anyone who can count those cubes without eyestrain has exceptional vision. Is the test one of cube counting or is it intended to examine persistence in the face of ocular distress?

Test 4 presents a task in recognizing space relationships, the task being to duplicate a given shape by selecting from a number the appropriate segments. This kind of visual ability is, of course, very useful in working out jigsaw puzzles, but the ordinarily intelligent person can get along with a very moderate degree of ability in this direction. The writer is aware of this fact because he usually does very poorly in this kind of exercise. Test 6 provides another trial of capacity to mentally manipulate pictured forms, while Test 5, like Test 3, sets a problem in matching complicated forms that is certainly hard on the eyes.

Test 7, arrangement of pictured events in proper time sequence, is one of the most interesting, but unfortunately as the test becomes more difficult the artist (*sic*) becomes more careless. This criticism applies chiefly to the last three sequences, which are annoyingly unintelligible. Among three psychologists who attempted the final sequence, there were four opinions as to the correct solution. It showed (*a*) a boy riding on a bicycle, (*b*) a man sitting on his hunkers looking at two roadside lunch wagons (or alternatively—by stretching your imagination and the man's legs—a person running towards a train), (*c*) a man receiving a telegram, (*d*) a man blowing his nose at what might be a death bed scene. All this is interesting but it could be anybody's guess whether the person died first or last in the sequence. Relatives must sometimes be sent for *after* a person's demise, especially if that person has been inconsiderate enough to die without warning.

Unfortunately, the artistry of Tests 8 and 9 is equally atrocious. In the latter the subject is shown an object and then he is supposed to select one of four others with which the first picture naturally belongs. For example, Item 5 shows a little boat with two seats (presumably to carry five persons) suspended from davits (with no mechanism for lowering the boat so that the only way to launch it would be to cut the ropes and let it fall into the sea). The unhappy testee is required to say whether this boat belongs with an ill-drawn yacht, a pleasure cruiser, a liner, or another steamship—all equally ill drawn. The right answer is, of course, that it goes with none of them—least

of all the liner, which is scored correct. These may seem like picayune criticisms of trifles, but it is attention to details that the test is supposed to examine. One wonders whether the artist ever saw a ship.

Undoubtedly a great deal of ingenuity has gone into the making of this test, and one can assume that a psychologist of Andrew Brown's status will have done all the work necessary on validation and standardization. The test needs redrawing, for in its present form it offends again two prime requisites of a good test—namely, intelligibility and nonambiguity of the problem. If by increasing the size of the pictures and improving the drawings these objections can be obviated, then the scale may have a useful function.

[1388]

Cornell-Coxe Performance Ability Scale. Ages 4½-16; 1934; 1 form; individual; $26.95 per complete testing outfit (the testing outfit should be ordered from Ellen Wilson, 1013 N. Madison St., Rome, N. Y.); $1.50 per examination manual;[1] 90¢ per 25 individual record blanks; Ethel L. Cornell and Warren W. Coxe; Yonkers, N. Y.: World Book Co.

REFERENCES

1 CORNELL, ETHEL L., AND COXE, WARREN W. *A Performance Ability Scale*: Examination Manual. Yonkers, N. Y.: World Book Co., 1934. Pp. iv, 88. $1.50.
2 BRILL, MOSHE. "Performance Tests as Aids in the Diagnosis of Maladjustment." *J Genetic Psychol* 49:199-214 S '36.
3 LINCOLN, HAZEL. "A Study of the Cornell-Coxe Performance Ability Scale with Superior Children." *J Genetic Psychol* 50:283-92 Je '37.

Francis N. Maxfield, Professor of Psychology, Psychological Clinic, The Ohio State University. This scale consists of a series of six nonverbal tests, with a seventh test which may be used as an alternate for Test 3. Test 2 is a modification of Kohs' *Block Design Test.* The other six were used in the *Army Performance Scale.* The material is less expensive than that required for the Pintner-Paterson or Arthur scales and less cumbersome. The directions for giving and scoring the tests (Chap. 5) are very clear and unequivocal. Coloring the sample block designs on page 71 will facilitate scoring. Speed as well as accuracy is scored in four tests. Raw scores on each test are translated into weighted scores, which are added to derive a point score for the scale. This is translated in turn into a mental age score.

As Thurstone pointed out years ago the concept of "mental age" is ambiguous. One may use, as most authors have done, the respective mean or median scores of successive age groups to determine his mental age score, or he may use the respective mean or median chronological ages of those making a series of scores. The authors of this scale profess (p. 33) a preference for the latter determination, but go on (p. 34) to use a compromise method for their own table of norms, so that the mental ages derived from the scale do not conform to either definition of mental age. The IQ, or "PIQ," is derived in the usual way, though directions are not given as to what one should use for a divisor in the case of a feebleminded adult with a mental age score of six years.

Scores in terms of mental age or IQ are often misleading or ambiguous because they do not indicate the degree of deviation of the score in question below or above the norm for the pupil's age group. If a boy of seven makes a mental age score of 7 years, 7 months on Form L of the *Revised Stanford-Binet Scale,* his IQ being 108, one can give this rating a standard score of 0.5, or a centile rank of 69. Unfortunately the authors of the Cornell-Coxe scale give no tables from which deviation within the pupil's age group may be determined.

The scale will be found most useful in testing children of elementary school age. Its use in differentiating different types among overage children who test low on the Stanford-Binet is well illustrated in Chapters 3 and 4. With slight modification, the scale can be given to children who are deaf or who understand little English. For children over thirteen, it is not as satisfactory as the Arthur scale.

Chapter I, *Functions of a Performance Scale,* is a clear statement of the practical method of the clinical psychologist in his use of tests in general and of nonverbal or "performance" tests in particular. Psychologists and psychoclinicians of limited experience should reread this chapter every three months, and those of longer experience occasionally check their practice by it. Think how much unnecessary misunderstanding might have been avoided in some recent discussions of changes in intelligence if everyone had noted this sentence carefully. "We," the authors state, meaning not themselves but authors of tests in general, "have constructed tests on the theory that we could measure differences in intelligence by measuring differences in performance when experience and opportunity were the same, and then we have often proceeded to ignore the differences in experience and opportunity and

considered that we had *bona fide* differences in intelligence." (p. 4)

Correlations: between original and retest scores made by 125 pupils on this scale, $r = .93$; between mental ages on the Stanford-Binet and on this scale (306 pupils from kindergarten through the eighth grade), $r = .79$; between CA and MA on this scale, $r = .78$.

Carroll A. Whitmer, Assistant Professor of Psychology, The University of Pittsburgh. The *Cornell-Coxe Performance Ability Scale* is composed of the following tests: Test 1, Manikin-Profile; Test 2, Block-Designs; Test 3, Picture-Arrangement; Test 4, Digit-Symbol; Test 5, Memory-for-Designs; Test 6, Cube Construction; and Test 7, Picture-Completion. Only six of the tests are used, Test 7 being a substitute for Test 3.

Detailed description of the tests and the procedure involved in the standardization of the tests is presented in the examination manual. The manual also includes a very good discussion of the functions of the performance scale as well as a discussion of interpretations illustrated by case studies.

The raw scores on the separate tests are computed on a combined time and accuracy basis and stated in points. The standardization process involved weighting the raw scores so that each test would contribute equally to the total raw score. The method used to achieve this end was to distribute the scores for each test on a 10 sigma base line. According to the authors: "In order to find a score on the Block-Designs Test equivalent to any sigma value, say 3.0, we determined from a statistical table the per cent of cases which should fall below this sigma value (2.28 per cent), then found this same per cent of our 306 cases (i.e., 7 cases), and calculated the score below which this number of cases fell (score 3.7). In a similar way we located every sigma value in terms of the test score." (p. 30) Arbitrary weights from 1 up were then assigned to the sigma values of the scores. The computed test score equivalent and the corresponding weights assigned for each test score were then plotted and a line of best fit adjusted to these data. The final weighted test scores were taken from the line of best fit.

The total battery score is the sum of the weighted score values for the six tests of the battery. Age norms for the total scores were read from a line drawn midway between the regression lines plotted first, upon the best fit for the means of chronological ages corresponding to each score, and, second, for the means of the scores corresponding to each chronological age.

According to the authors the validity of the battery is substantiated by its relationship to other test results (correlation with *National Intelligence Test*, .74 and with Binet, .79) and in the fact that the correlation with chronological age is .78. An indirect indication of validity is claimed in results shown by individual case analysis. The reliability of the battery is indicated by a correlation of .93 between the two performances of 125 children reexamined after an interval of 11 months.

In summarizing the standardization data the reviewer feels that 306 cases ranging in grade placement from kindergarten through eighth grade is a very questionable sampling. The manual does not include an adequate description of the standardization group with respect to age other than grade placement. Consequently, adequate age norms for performance on the separate tests are lacking.

For practical clinic purposes the Cornell-Coxe scale offers a variety of tests not found in the other performance scales. It is unfortunate that adequate age norms are not presented for the performance on the separate tests in order to allow the examiner some standard reference point for the child's performance.

The administration and scoring of the battery is somewhat more complicated than that of either the Arthur or the Pintner-Paterson scales. A special record blank which includes the Digit-Symbol Test and the tables for scoring conversions and norms as well as a record of performance on the other tests is provided for using the test. The need for the special blank increases the cost of using the test. The record blank would be improved if the locations for drawing the designs were not outlined. The subject frequently attempts to use the lines bounding the space provided and when not actually permitted to make them part of his drawing still uses them as guides.

In our experience we find that the scale fails to measure the average or superior child above 10 or 12 years of age because of its inadequacy in the upper range. We find also that the directions for the Pintner-Paterson and the Arthur scales are easier to explain to the deaf or non-English-speaking child.

For the experienced examiner the Cornell-Coxe scale provides a variety of material of interest to the child and a means of observing the qualitative aspects of his performance. We could recommend the battery with its present standardization as a supplement to rather than in place of either the Binet type of test or the other formboard batteries mentioned above.

See also B77 and B335.

[1389]

Dawson Mental Test. Ages 11-12; 1936; 2 forms; 3*s.* 6*d.* per 25; 6*d.* per test; 1*s.* per manual; 40(45) minutes; Shepherd Dawson; London: George G. Harrap and Co., Ltd.

Raymond B. Cattell, G. Stanley Hall Professor of Genetic Psychology, Clark University. The design of this test shows the throughness, common sense perspective and care over detail which characterised all the research enterprises of the late Shepherd Dawson.

The test is in omnibus form with a reasonably adequate number (80) of pass or fail items, and a working time (40 minutes) which is not too brief. The A and B forms are well designed in parallel, almost item for item, but it seems a mistake to supply only one norm table for both, on the assumption that they will coincide in difficulty over all ranges of performance.

There is no indication in the booklet as to the number or quality of the child populations used in standardization, nor is there any reference to articles in which these particulars might be found. That validity and consistency coefficients are overlooked is not so important; for consistency is meaningless without particulars of the dispersion of the population concerned, while validity as measured against a Binet test might in this case be an attempt to assess a good test against a less *g* saturated medley.

For the subtest forms mixed in this omnibus —opposites, classification, analogies, etc.—are all such as have been shown by many previous researches and factor analyses to have high *g* saturation for children of this age range (9 years and upwards). There has also been much care to avoid unusual words or words likely to belong only to a bigger vocabulary. Increasing difficulty has not been produced by the fallacious procedure of demanding more verbal education but by requiring nicer judgment among words and ideas known presumably to all children.

Nevertheless there is no research proof that every word is within the vocabulary of the youngest children taking the test. The reviewer's opinion is that the test attempts to measure too wide a range of mental age with one test form. It is probable too that the omnibus design, involving special instruction on each item or group of items is wasteful of testing time in comparison with the test constituted by half a dozen subtests, each having items graded in difficulty.

Percival Smith, Principal Assistant Organiser, Education Department, Birmingham, England. This mental test is prepared in the cycle omnibus style but not with the cycle omnibus system. Each alternative test consists of 80 questions of very varied types, including reasoning, analogies and numbers. The alternative tests appear very similar but it would be interesting to know whether the two have been correlated and if so what coefficient was obtained.

The test can apparently be applied to children between the ages of 9 and 18 years; at any rate the published table of norms gives scores for all ages between these limits. The reviewer finds it difficult to believe that the test can be reliable for such a wide age range. It is always wise when placing a mental test on the market to publish data in regard to its standardization. No doubt this test was given to a considerable number of children during its preparation and particulars are known as to its correlation with other mental measures. Such information would be helpful to teachers and others who desire to make use of the test.

The instructions allow 40 minutes for giving the test. The reviewer found that at the end of 25 minutes a girl of 17 had completed the test and had been through the answers a second time. The table of norms gives a mental age of 18 to a child getting a perfect score of 80. It is not usual for a group intelligence test to be constructed in such a way that a perfect score can be obtained.

For additional reviews, see 1043.

[1390]

Dearborn-Anderson Formboards 2 and 2b. Ages 5-10, 10 and over; 1916; 2 levels; also called *Formboard 2, Dearborn Formboard 2, or Reconstruction Puzzle*; Walter F. Dearborn and John E. Anderson. *a)* FORMBOARD 2. Ages 10 and over; 8-depression board; $8.00; (8-20) minutes for first trial; Cambridge, Mass.: Psycho-Educational Clinic, Palfrey House, Harvard University. *b)* FORMBOARD 2b. Ages 5-10; 4-depression board; $5; (5-10) minutes for first trial; Cambridge, Mass.: Psycho-Educational Clinic, Palfrey House, Harvard University. ($6.50 (No. 27165); Chicago, Ill.: C. H. Stoelting Co.)

REFERENCES

1 DEARBORN, W. F.; ANDERSON, J. E.; AND CHRISTIANSEN, A. O. "Form Board and Construction Tests of Mental Ability." *J Ed Psychol* 7:445-58 O '16.
2 DEARBORN, WALTER F.; SHAW, EDWIN A.; AND LINCOLN, EDWARD A. *A Series of Form Board and Performance Tests of Intelligence.* Harvard University, Harvard Monographs in Education, Series 1; Studies in Educational Psychology and Educational Measurement, No. 4. Cambridge, Mass.: Graduate School of Education, Harvard University, September 1923. Pp. 64. $1.00. Paper.
3 BRONNER, AUGUSTA F.; HEALY, WILLIAM; LOWE, GLADYS M.; AND SHIMBERG, MYRA E. *A Manual of Individual Mental Tests and Testing*, pp. 155, 229. Judge Baker Foundation Publication No. 4. Boston, Mass.: Little, Brown and Co., 1927. Pp. x, 287. $3.50.
4 SCHIEFFELIN, BARBARA, AND SCHWESINGER, GLADYS C. *Mental Tests and Heredity*: Including a Survey of Non-Verbal Tests, pp. 169-70. New York: Galton Publishing Co., Inc. 1930. Pp. ix, 298. Out of print.

Grace H. Kent, Psychologist, Danvers State Hospital, Hathorne, Massachusetts. Two formboards, published as Formboards 2 and 2b, are built to carry the same insets. These three insets are irregular quadrilateral blocks, markedly unlike in size and form but having certain dimensions in common. Each block can be matched against either of the others in any of five ways. There are many different ways of assembling these three blocks in a group; and thus it is possible to obtain the outlines for many irregular figures which are equal in area while differing widely in form. Board 2 has eight recesses thus outlined, and Board 2b has four.

The four-hole board, which is the more convenient both in size and in degree of difficulty, is used at Danvers State Hospital for a practice series of at least three trials. The board is presented as shown in the publisher's catalog illustration, with its three blocks in the upper left corner from the subject's point of view. The subject is informed that all three blocks can be fitted into each of the holes; and is instructed (in language appropriate to his mental level) to insert them in each recess, in a clockwise circle, without stopping until the blocks are back in the starting place. It is made clear that he is being timed for the whole circle, not for individual figures; and if he pauses after filling one recess he is hurried along to the completion of the circle. After the time is recorded for the first trial he is requested to try again and see if he can do it more quickly.

The number of trials need not be kept constant for different examiners nor for different subjects, but the third trial is perhaps the most significant one for the average subject. It may be expected that the first performance will be by trial and error. The mathematical nicety of construction—at all times a delight to the examiner—is usually lost on the subject at first; but his appreciation of it is frequently apparent in the later trials. Occasionally he carefully seeks the middle block for first placement in each recess, thus marking off clearly the exact positions for the other two blocks.

The reviewer would not wish to see this board standardized, because standardization would of necessity destroy its adaptability to the individual subject. The discriminative capacity of a single formboard is rarely wide enough to justify the effort and cost of standardization, and it is doubtful if norms would add anything important to the usefulness of this test.

The board is inexpensive, easily portable, and so simple that it can be made by hand from several layers of cardboard. (Not, however, from any published drawings seen recently by the reviewer.) Requiring very little time for presentation and very little space in the briefcase, it can be recommended as a convenient addition to the equipment of the traveling clinic.

[1391]

Dearborn Formboard 3. Ages 6 and over; 1916; also called *Construction Puzzle, Block Test,* or *Formboard 3*; individual; $10 (No. 27179); worklimit (10-20) minutes; Walter F. Dearborn; Chicago, Ill.: C. H. Stoelting Co. ($10; Cambridge, Mass.: Psycho-Eduational Clinic, Palfrey House, Harvard University.)

REFERENCES

1 DEARBORN, W. F.; ANDERSON, J. E.; AND CHRISTIANSEN, A. O. "Form Board and Construction Tests of Mental Ability." *J Ed Psychol* 7:445-58 O '16.
2 DEARBORN, WALTER F.; SHAW, EDWIN A.; AND LINCOLN, EDWARD A. *A Series of Form Board and Performance Tests of Intelligence.* Harvard University, Harvard Monographs in Education, Series 1; Studies in Educational Psychology and Educational Measurement, No. 4. Cambridge, Mass.: Graduate School of Education, Harvard University, September 1923. Pp. 64. $1.00. Paper.
3 YOAKUM, CLARENCE S., AND YERKES, ROBERT M., EDITORS. *Army Mental Tests,* pp. 107-9, 122. Published with the authorization of the War Department. New York: Henry Holt and Co., 1920. Pp. xiii, 303. Out of print.
4 YERKES, ROBERT M., EDITOR. *Psychological Examining in the United States Army,* pp. 132-3, 152-3, 184-5, 191, 307, 400, and passim. Memoirs of the National Academy of Sciences, Vol. 15. Washington, D. C.: Government Printing Office, 1921. Pp. vi, 890. Out of print.
5 GAW, FRANCES. *Performance Tests of Intelligence,* pp. 24-7. Medical Research Council, Industrial Research Board, Report No. 31. London: H. M. Stationery Office, 1925. Pp. iv, 45. 2s. 6d. Paper.
6 BRONNER, AUGUSTA F.; HEALY, WILLIAM; LOWE, GLADYS M.; AND SHIMBERG, MYRA E. *A Manual of Individual Mental Tests and Testing,* pp. 123-4, 219-20. Judge Baker Foundation Publication No. 4. Boston, Mass.: Little, Brown, and Co., 1927. Pp. x, 287. $3.50.

7 WELLS, F. L. *Mental Tests in Clinical Practice,* pp. 129-31. Yonkers, N. Y.: World Book Co., 1927. Pp. x, 315. $2.16.
8 SCHIEFFELIN, BARBARA, AND SCHWESINGER, GLADYS C. *Mental Tests and Heredity:* Including a Survey of Non-Verbal Tests, pp. 170. New York: Galton Publishing Co., Inc. 1930. Pp. ix, 298. Out of print.

Grace H. Kent, Psychologist, Danvers State Hospital, Hathorne, Massachusetts. Of all the performance tests used in Danvers State Hospital, this formboard is the favorite. There are no norms that can be recommended, nor is there any published series of tasks in which full utilization of the test-possibilities of the board is even approached; but the construction of the board itself—so far as this reviewer is concerned—is absolutely beyond criticism.

The board contains nine recesses, one being a 2-inch square and another, a circle of 2-inch diameter. The other seven recesses are multiples either of these figures or of their component parts, in various combinations. The most distinctive inset is made by taking a semicircle of 1-inch radius out of one side of a 2-inch square. (The remaining portion of the square is referred to here as a "concave," for lack of a better name.) For the nine recesses there are twenty-one insets, as follows: five whole figures, including three squares, one circle and one double-concave; sixteen half-figures, consisting of six triangles, six semicircles and four concaves.

The smallest recess can be filled only by a single block of its own form; whereas the largest one can be filled by any one of at least eleven different combinations. The possibilities of setup for the entire board are practically innumerable, and the number of tasks to be included in a series is entirely optional. (The reviewer uses eight tasks of increasing difficulty, plus a demonstration task.)

The unit task, which serves as the basis for more complicated tasks, may be described as follows: The board is presented with one whole square on the outside, and with no vacant places in the board except a semicircle in one figure and its complementary "concave" in another figure. The subject is instructed to make a place for the square in the frame without making any more moves than are necessary. If he can spot a square filled with the blocks needed for these two openings, he can in three moves transfer these blocks to the appropriate vacant places and then insert the square in the place thus left vacant.

The distinctive feature of the test is that it permits an accurate move-count, thus making possible a scoring system which is not dependent upon speed. It is permissible, if desired, to record the time of performance as well as the number of moves; and to evaluate the achievement by two independent variables. But the reviewer prefers to measure the subject's speed of performance by some test which does not admit of being scored except by speed, and to assure the subject in advance that his performance on this test will not be timed. In the great majority of performance tests the slow worker is very heavily discriminated against. This test owes its unique value to the fact that it gives the slow worker a fair opportunity to show what he can do. As an untimed test, it is applicable even to the pathologically retarded patient.

Another very strong feature of the test is that a failure from the examiner's point of view is not usually apparent to the subject as a failure. The young child, interested primarily in filling the board, easily forgets that his moves are being counted. The subject who empties the board and replaces the blocks by trial and error is as a rule well satisfied with his performance. For him, it is a real achievement to complete the task of filling the board.

Although not quite essential, it is highly desirable to have a board for each task and to prepare the setup in advance of the examination. It is worth-while also to have a specially-built cabinet with a shelf for each board.

[1392]
Detroit Advanced First-Grade Intelligence Test. Grades 1-2; 1925-28; 1 form; $1.10 per 25; 10¢ per specimen set; (30-35) minutes; Harry J. Baker; Yonkers, N. Y.: World Book Co.

A. M. Jordan, Professor of Educational Psychology, The University of North Carolina. The purpose of this test is to furnish an instrument for measuring the unclassified pupils of the first grade and those of the low second. Seven tests constitute the whole. In none of these tests is reading required. The recognition of printed numbers is demanded in all to designate position and in one to designate the number of items to be counted. The tests are the usual ones: marking drawings or objects from their names and from a description of them; discovering similarities; drawing in missing parts; recognizing one object among five others, recognizing parts of objects from their description, recognizing printed numerals up to 18 and then counting the designated

number of objects. The test has developed through preliminary editions in mimeographed form. It uses the old Stanford-Binet technique of measuring tests against a high group, middle group, and low group which to say the least is open to question since the very division into higher, middle and lower was determined by a preliminary use of these very tests. The items are roughly scaled in each part of the test. The scoring is simple and quickly done. There are tables for transmuting these scores into letter grades for each six months from 5½ to 11 years. This is a distinct advantage. The letter ratings are based on 2,975 cases tested, curiously enough, in the year 1926. Approximate MA equivalents are also available. The reliability of the test with repeated measures of the same test is given as .94. The reviewer believes that the probable error of measurement should also be furnished with each test. This measure does not appear. The second testing produced a gain of 9 points. The correlation with Stanford-Binet MA's in the case of 46 unselected pupils was .85; but in the case of 227 mentally backward, .57.

The drawings except in two or three cases are easily recognizable. In one case the reviewer could not tell whether the picture was a ball, an orange, or some other unrecognizable object. Then, too, some of the directions seem at least a little fuzzy. For example, "Mark the part of the pail to carry it . . . and the part of the tea kettle where the water [*sic!*] comes out," or again, mark "the part of the face that talks" and "the part of the bee that helps him fly." These statements which seem confusing to an adult might not be so to a six-year old.

As a whole the test will fill a useful niche in the testing of young children.

[1393]
[**Detroit Intelligence Tests.**] Grades 2-4, 5-9, 9-16; 1924-34; 2 forms, 3 levels; $3.00 per 100; 15¢ per specimen set of any one level; Harry J. Baker; Bloomington, Ill.: Public School Publishing Co.
a) DETROIT PRIMARY INTELLIGENCE TEST. Grades 2-4; 1924-34; (30-35) minutes.
b) DETROIT ALPHA INTELLIGENCE TEST. Grades 5-9; 1924; (45-50) minutes.
c. DETROIT ADVANCED INTELLIGENCE TEST. Grades 9-16; 1924; 29(40) minutes.

REFERENCES
1 KUHLMANN, F. "The Kuhlmann-Anderson Intelligence Tests Compared with Seven Others." J Appl Psychol 12:545-94 D '28.
2 SEAGOE, M. V. "An Evaluation of Certain Intelligence Tests." J Appl Psychol 18:432-6 Je '34.

W. Line, Associate Professor of Psychology, University of Toronto. The series is of a fairly traditional type. In form the tests are satisfactory, and the instructions appear to be adequate and clear. The standardization is based on a population sufficiently large to warrant confidence in their usefulness for general school purposes. The manual presents some evidence suggesting that the various sections of the test are less homogeneous than might be desired if the instrument is to be used beyond the local setting in which it was constructed. For that reason, local norms and reliabilities differ from those based on nationwide data. Perhaps tests of the information type are partly responsible for this. Justification for the plan of interpreting results by subsections (e.g., under such captions as Memory, Reasoning, etc.) is not given, since detailed analysis of the results of the standardization is not given.

[1394]

Ferguson Formboards. Ages 4 and over; 1920; individual; $58.50 per set of 6 formboards (No. 37007); (10-40) minutes; George Oscar Ferguson, Jr.; Chicago, Ill.: C. H. Stoelting Co.

REFERENCES

1 FERGUSON, GEORGE OSCAR, JR. "A Series of Form Boards." *J Exp Psychol* 3:47-58 F '20.
2 MCFARLANE, MARGARET. *A Study of Practical Ability,* pp. 68-9. British Journal of Psychology Monograph Supplements. Vol. 3, No. 8. London: Cambridge University Press, 1925. Pp. viii, 75. 7s. Paper.
3 BRONNER, AUGUSTA F.; HEALY, WILLIAM; LOWE, GLADYS M.; AND SHIMBERG, MYRA E. *A Manual of Individual Mental Tests and Testing,* pp. 126-7, 220. Judge Baker Foundation Publication No. 4. Boston, Mass.: Little, Brown, and Co., 1927. Pp. x, 287. $3.50.
4 MACPHEE, E. D., AND BROWN, A. J. "An Inquiry into the Standardization of the Ferguson Form Boards." *J Ed Psychol* 21:24-36 Ja '30.
5 SCHIEFFELIN, BARBARA, AND SCHWESINGER, GLADYS C. *Mental Tests and Heredity:* Including a Survey of Non-Verbal Tests, pp. 166-7. New York: Galton Publishing Co., Inc. 1930. Pp. ix, 298. Out of print.
6 GARRETT, HENRY E., AND SCHNECK, MATTHEW R. *Psychological Tests, Methods, and Results,* Part 2, pp. 85-6. New York and London: Harper and Bros., 1933. Pp. x, 137, 235. $2.75; 10s. 6d.
7 PESCOR, M. J. "A Further Study of the Ferguson Form Board Test." *Pub Health Rep* 51:1195-1201 Ag 28 '36.
8 WILLIAMS, GRIFFITH W., AND LINES, JANET. "An Evaluation of the Ferguson Form Boards and the Derivation of New Age and Grade Norms: Part I, Procedure and Derivation of Norms." *J Appl Psychol* 21:556-71 O '37.
9 WILLIAMS, GRIFFITH W., AND LINES, JANET. "An Evaluation of the Ferguson Form Boards and the Derivation of New Age and Grade Norms: Part II, Presentation of Norms and Discussion." *J Appl Psychol* 21:673-87 D '37.
10 WOOD, LOUISE, AND KUMIN, EDYTHE. "A New Standardization of the Ferguson Form Boards." *J Genetic Psychol* 54:265-84 Je '39.
11 WERNER, HENRY. "A Comparative Study of a Small Group of Clinical Tests." *J Appl Psychol* 24:231-6 Ap '40.
12 FOWLER, H. L. "Report on Psychological Tests on Natives in the North-West of Western Australia." *Australian J Sci* 2:124-7 Ap '40.

Grace H. Kent, Psychologist, Danvers State Hospital, Hathorne, Massachusetts. This is a series of six tasks of increasing difficulty, each board having six somewhat irregular recesses fitted with insets. The first board has one block for each recess, and all the others have two for each. In Boards 3, 5, and 6 the two

blocks for each recess are fitted together by matched beveled edges; and in Board 4 one block of each pair has a double bevel which fits into a groove in the other block. The tasks are essentially self-corrective, and can be presented without use of language.

The test was used by the reviewer in 1923, as an instrument for observation rather than for numerical results. The series marked an important advance over the detached form boards of the Pintner-Paterson scale; establishing beyond question the advantage of a graded series starting at the six-year level and leading up to a task discriminative at the adult level. The Ferguson series furnished the stimulus for the development of other performance test series having tasks graded in difficulty but similar in kind.

It is not, however, a strictly continuous series. The six tasks are quite varied in kind; (unavoidably so, inasmuch as it is almost impossible to increase the difficulty of a formboard series without introducing new principles of construction); and the six problems of a given task are also somewhat varied in nature. For example: one of the figures in Board 2 is an all-but-regular octagon having its diagonal dimensions slightly greater than the vertical and horizontal dimensions, divided diagonally into halves. No other figure of the board is divided diagonally into halves, and therefore there is nothing to suggest a diagonal placement for these two blocks. Almost any subject for whom the task is discriminative will try to insert the blocks in a vertical position, a placement which just barely misses being possible. Frequently the subject will make repeated attempts to insert the blocks either vertically or horizontally, apparently quite unable to accept the evidence that such placement is impossible. He may spend more time on this one figure than on the other five figures; may remove blocks correctly placed in other recesses, in his efforts to find a place for these blocks; may lose credit for the entire task because of his failure to solve this one problem; and occasionally may become so irritated by his failure as to react unfavorably to the rest of the examination. It seemed to the reviewer, when using the test, that this board offered material which might better have been used in two independent tasks.

What is measured by a test depending largely upon form perception is not easy to state, but there is no reasonable doubt concerning the value of the test. The lower end of the series appears to the observer to have some significance as a measure of mental capacity, but the upper end appears rather to be a test of mechanical aptitude. The form perception required for the performance of the first task is of so elementary a nature that it must almost of necessity be possessed by any person who has learned to dress himself; whereas the principles underlying the tasks at the upper end are rarely used except by engineers, skilled tradesmen and other technically trained persons. Experience in handling concrete materials is a strong factor in a subject's achievement. A dressmaker may achieve a high score, although women are generally weak in the test as compared with men. A cabinet maker of low achievement in language tests may spot the place for each block with almost unerring accuracy; while a university professor who has had comparatively little occasion to use his hands may startle the observer by the utter stupidity with which he attempts impossible placements.

The norms developed by the Judge Baker Foundation staff are much more adequate than those originally offered by Ferguson; but the value of the test is by no means dependent upon norms.

[1394.1]
Essential Intelligence Test. Ages 7-12; 1940; 1 form; 4d. per test; 3d. per test, 25 to 49 copies; 45(50) minutes; Fred J. Schonell and R. H. Adams; Edinburgh, Scotland: Oliver & Boyd, Ltd.

[1395]
Fiji Test of General Ability. Ages 9 and over; 1935; 1 form; 6d. per test; 1s. 6d. per manual; 27(60) minutes; Cecil W. Mann; Suva, Fiji: Government Printer.

REFERENCES

1 MANN, CECIL W. *Objective Tests in Fiji.* Suva, Fiji: Government Printer, 1937. Pp. i, 39. 1s. 6d. Paper.
2 MANN, CECIL W. "A Test of General Ability in Fiji." *J Genetic Psychol* 54:435-54 Je '39.

[1396]
General Intelligence Test for Africans. "African youths and adults who have received a certain amount of schooling"; 1932-37; 1 form; 25½(90) minutes; R. A. C. Oliver; Nairobi, Kenya Colony, East Africa: Government Printer.

REFERENCES

1 OLIVER, R. A. C. "The Adaptation of Intelligence Tests to Tropical Africa." *Oversea Ed* 4:186-91 '33
2 OLIVER, R. A. C. "The Adaptation of Intelligence Tests to Tropical Africa II." *Oversea Ed* 5:8-13 '33.
3 OLIVER, RICHARD A. C. "Mental Tests in the Study of the African." *Africa* 7:40-6 Ja '34.
4 OLIVER, R. A. C. Chapter 15, "Mental Tests for Primitive Races," pp. 165-75. In *The Testing of Intelligence.* Edited by H. R. Hamley. London: Evans Brothers, Ltd., 1937. Pp. 175. 2s. 6d. Paper.

[1397]
Group Test of Intelligence, Advanced: Dominion Tests. High School and college; 1940; 2 forms; 2¢ per test in quantity; 15¢ per manual; 5¢ per sample test; 30(40-45) minutes; Toronto, Canada: Department of Educational Research, University of Toronto.

[1398]
Henmon-Nelson Test of Mental Ability. Grades 3-8, 7-12, 13-16; 1932-35; 2 forms, 3 levels; 75¢ per 25; single speciment set free; 30(35) minutes; V. A. C. Henmon and M. J. Nelson; Boston, Mass.: Houghton Mifflin Co.
a) ELEMENTARY SCHOOL EXAMINATION. Grades 3-8.
b) HIGH SCHOOL EXAMINATION. Grades 7-12.
c) INTELLIGENCE TEST FOR COLLEGE STUDENTS.

REFERENCES

1 DRAKE, LEWIS E., AND HENMON, V. A. C. "The Prediction of Scholarship in the College of Letters and Science at the University of Wisconsin." *Sch and Soc* 45:191-4 F 6 '37.
2 HENMON, V. A. C., AND NELSON, M. J. *The Measurement of Intelligence.* Educational Progress Bulletin, Vol. 13, No. 2. Boston, Mass.: Houghton Mifflin Co., September 1937. Pp. 21. Gratis. Paper.

Anne Anastasi, Assistant Professor of Psychology and Chairman of the Department of Psychology, Queens College. The three levels of this test, for elementary school, high school, and college, are closely similar in construction and administration. Each of the equivalent forms at each level consists of 90 items arranged in order of increasing difficulty. A wide variety of items is included, such as vocabulary, sentence completion, disarranged sentences, classification, logical selection, series completion, directions, analogies, anagrams, proverb interpretation, and arithmetic problems. Spatial, as well as verbal and numerical materials, are employed. The different types of items are not segregated but are arranged in a "scrambled" sequence. Administration is very simple, the examiner reading with the subjects the directions and sample exercises printed on each test. Scoring is by the Clapp-Young self-marking device and requires no key.

The validity of the tests was checked against scholastic achievement as well as against scores on other common intelligence tests. The authors report that for each of their tests the original selection of items was made by the method of contrasted groups, i.e., "only such items as proved to differentiate between pupils of known superior and known inferior mental ability were retained." We are not told in what way the subject's superior or inferior ability was "known," but presumably the criterion was scholastic success. In some of the college groups, correlations are also reported between test scores and grades in various courses, as well as composite first term grades. The latter correlation was .60, the others ranging from

.46 to .60. These correlations compare fairly well with those obtained between most scholastic aptitude tests and college grades. Correlations between the Henmon-Nelson scores and scores on other well-known and widely-used group intelligence scales are also fairly high. Among the college groups, they range from .68 to .79. In the high school groups, they range from .77 to .88, and in the elementary school from .54 to .90. The number of subjects in each of the groups upon which these correlations were based was usually over 100, ranging from 57 to 554.

Reliability of the college form was determined by correlating the scores of 171 freshmen on Forms A and B. The correlation proved to be .89. For the other levels, reliability was found by the odd-even technique and the Spearman-Brown formula, but we are not told which of the three parallel forms of the test was employed in finding these correlations. Separate reliability coefficients are reported for each age and each grade. In the high school group, 100 cases were employed in finding each correlation, but no number is reported for the elementary school data. The reliabilities thus found are all high, being consistently in the upper .80's or in the .90's.

Percentile norms are reported for each grade in elementary and high school and for each of the four college classes. In the elementary and high school forms, tables of mental age equivalents are also included. Each of the three sets of norms was obtained on approximately 5,000 cases. In addition, the mental age equivalents for elementary and high school groups were subsequently checked on much larger samplings covering a wide geographical area. Further details regarding the selection of subjects are not given, except for the statement that the college students were drawn from colleges of different sizes and in different parts of the country. It would seem, in general, that the representativeness of the norms compares quite favorably with that found in the general run of intelligence tests.

The use of the mental age equivalent for point scores, as well as the use of percentile scores, are, of course, open to criticism. For a crude evaluation of the individual's relative standing in the group, however, such devices serve adequately. Similarly, the use of a single score based upon a hodgepodge of different types of items could be questioned, if one wanted a particularly fine or discriminative measure. But like other tests of its kind, this scale serves the practical purposes of (*a*) preliminary rapid exploration, and (*b*) rough classification of broad groups. It is interesting to note, in conclusion, that at the college level, the tests are described as a measure of "the aptitude of college students for academic work, or what has ordinarily been termed 'mental ability' or 'intelligence'." At the elementary and high school level, on the other hand, the prospective tester is told flatly and with no qualification that the tests measure mental ability. It is to be hoped that the distinction made by the authors in their manual is not a reflection on the relative psychological perspicacity of testers at the respective levels.

August Dvorak, Professor of Education, The University of Washington. These tests are designed to measure the mental ability of students in junior and senior high schools or in grades seven to twelve inclusive. Three forms of the test, which are identical in difficulty and construction, are available. Each form consists of ninety items arranged in order of increasing difficulty. Scoring is done in a remarkably short time, since the Clapp-Young self-marking device is employed. No scoring keys are necessary.

Two hundred fifty items were originally prepared and submitted to *experienced teachers* for their criticisms. The number was thus reduced to 202 items. These were divided into two forms and administered to about 500 students. The two forms of 90 items each were made from the items having the best predictive value. The tests were then printed in their present form and it is on the basis of the administration of this printed edition that the statistical data herein presented were derived.

In determining the validity of these intelligence tests, the authors secured correlation coefficients between IQ's of $r = .72$ to $r = .88$ for groups varying from 57 to 554 pupils to whom these tests and one of five other tests (Otis, Terman, American Council, Kuhlmann-Anderson, and Illinois) had been administered. It should be remembered that these coefficients were inflated by the common factor, chronological age, in both IQ's (spurious index correlation). Correlations between MA's and/or scores were $r = .78$ to .81. The validity of these tests may better be estimated when it is remembered that the alienation coefficient for $r = .80$ is $.60\sigma$.

The chief advantages of these tests lie in their ease of administration and scoring and that the relatively small number (90) of items require only 30 minutes of pupils' time. They may be an adequate measuring instrument for measuring intelligence if a low-cost (3¢ per pupil), 30-minute, quick-scoring test is desired.

Howard Easley, Assistant Professor of Educational Psychology, Duke University. These three tests are of the omnibus type. The materials of each test are very similar, consisting of, with minor variations, information, sentence completion, logical selection, classification, verbal analogies, number relations, anagrams, disarranged sentences, geometrical analogies, proverbs, word meaning, identifying family relationships, and arithmetic problems. Each test consists of 90 items, arranged in order of increasing difficulty. The validity of the individual items was determined by administering a much larger number of items to approximately 500 students and selecting the items which had the best predictive value.

The validity of the tests was determined by correlating these with a number of well-known tests. The correlations for the elementary test ranged from .54 to .92. Nine of the 19 correlations reported were above .80. The correlations for the high school test ranged from .72 to .88.

The reliability of the test for grades 3-8, determined by correlating odd-even halves, ranged from .89 to .94 for the separate age groups 8 to 14, and from .86 to .90 for the separate age groups 3 to 8. Similar reliability coefficients for the high school examination range from .91 to .94 for ages 12 to 17, and from .88 to .90 for grades 7 to 12.

For each of the lower grade tests mental age equivalents and the more important percentile points for the appropriate ages and grades are given; also tables for reading IQ directly from age and score. These tables are merely the result of computations of the MA divided by CA, and are unaffected by the varying significance of a given score made by children of different ages. It is not clear from the description in the manual whether the mental age equivalents represent the average scores made by children of certain ages, or the average ages of children who make certain scores.

The reliability of the college examination, determined by correlating the Form A scores with the Form B scores of 171 college freshmen, is reported as .89. The validity was determined by correlating the test with the *Psychological Examination for High School Graduates and College Freshmen* and the *Otis Self-Administering Test of Mental Ability.* In four studies in different institutions these correlations ranged from .68 to .79. The correlations between the test and grades earned in six subjects at Iowa State Teachers College ranged from .46 to .60. Thirteen important percentile points for each of the four college classes are given.

The content and standardization of these three tests seem as satisfactory as those of the better group tests of intelligence, but not strikingly more so. In two respects they have definite advantages—viz., price and mechanical features. They are almost completely self-administering and self-scoring. The scoring device (a carbon record) is simple and fool-proof, and has about the highest degree of convenience and perfection short of machine scoring.

J. P. Guilford, Professor of Psychology, The University of Southern California. An examination of these group tests and the manuals and scoring keys that accompany them impresses one immediately with the kind of care and expertness with which one wishes all tests were constructed.

The tests are appropriately entitled "Tests of Mental Ability" rather than "Tests of Intelligence" though the authors imply very clearly that "intelligence" is the important unity which they are measuring. This being the emphasis, it is fortunate that they include a variety of items which demand a variety of mental operations, thus touching many areas of mental ability sampled in so-called tests of intelligence. The kinds of items include: following directions; arithmetical problems; common sense (as in Army Alpha); word meaning; word opposites; and geometric analogies. These varieties are scrambled and rotated so that when taken in order an equal number of each kind will be attempted. It is fortunate that the attempt was made to keep the composition of the tests constant from lowest to highest ages, though in the elementary test the authors were less successful in this. To the extent that the content is uniform, the scores and IQ's will consequently have an unusual constancy of meaning at all ages.

As a preliminary to the preparation of every test form, many experimental items were tried out and an item analysis made, usually two times. As a consequence the highest validity and reliability that is now attainable was probably assured. At any rate, the reliability coefficients are typically up in the low .90's, even within the narrow ranges of ability provided by single age or grade groups. Validity coefficients, as indicated by correlations with the Stanford Revision, Otis, Terman, and Kuhlmann tests, are between the limits of .75 and .90 and are usually in the .80's. The various forms at the same level are equated for difficulty so that scores are directly comparable. Mental-age evaluations and IQ's can be computed even with the high school forms by those testers who prefer these measurements. Convenient tables are given for computing IQ's from mental ages in terms of months. The validity of the college form as an indicator of scholastic aptitude is as high as can now be obtained from so short a test, with coefficients ranging between .45 and .65 for both specific courses and general scholastic averages.

Every form makes use of the Clapp-Young self-marking system, with its carbon impressions, which makes the counting of correct responses a quick and easy mode of scoring. The print is quite legible except at the college level in which forms it is unduly crowded. Short practice exercises are provided for the testee before he begins the test proper. Norms are based upon 5,000 or more scores in every case, including in the standardizing population testees from various parts of the country.

Ed Res B 17:143-4 My '38. Francis N. Maxfield. * Standardization on five thousand pupils and checking on over two hundred thousand gives a basis for superior statistical treatment and data on which interpretation of test scores may be based. * The authors provide tables for translation of raw scores into mental-age scores and *I.Q.*'s, but commendably urge those who use these tests to substitute centile ranks for these measures, against which so many objections may be raised, particularly at the high-school level. *

[1399]

Herring Revision of the Binet-Simon Tests. Grades 1-12; 1922; individual; 1 form; $1.50 (5s.) per 25 indi-vidual record cards; $1.50 (4s. 6d.) per examination manual; [1] John P. Herring; Yonkers, N. Y.: World Book Co. (London: George G. Harrap & Co., Ltd.)

REFERENCES

1 HERRING, JOHN P. *Herring Revision of the Binet-Simon Tests*: Examination Manual, Form A. Yonkers, N. Y.: World Book Co., 1922. Pp. 56. $1.50. (London: George G. Harrap & Co., Ltd. 4s. 6d.)
2 WILNER, CHARLES F. "Mental Age Equivalents for a Group of Non-Reading Tests of the Herring Revision of the Binet-Simon Tests." *J Ed Psychol* 14:296-9 My '23.
3 AVERY, GEORGE T. "Comparison of Stanford and Herring Binet Revisions Given to First Grade Children." *J Ed Psychol* 15:224-8 Ap '24.
4 HERRING, JOHN P. "Avery's Comparison of the Stanford and Herring Revisions." *J Ed Psychol* 15:383-8 S '24.
5 HERRING, JOHN P. "Herring Revision of the Binet-Simon Tests." *J Ed Psychol* 15:172-9 N '24.
6 HERRING, JOHN P. *Herring Revision of the Binet-Simon Tests and Verbal and Abstract Elements in Intelligence Examinations.* Yonkers, N. Y.: World Book Co., 1924. Pp. 71. $0.60. Paper.
7 HERRING, JOHN P. "Reliability of the Stanford and the Herring Revision of the Binet-Simon Tests." *J Ed Psychol* 15:217-23 Ap '24.
8 WILNER, CHARLES F. "A Comparative Study of the Stanford and Herring Revisions of the Binet-Simon Tests." *J Ed Psychol* 15:520-9 N '24.
9 REMMERS, H. H. "Systematic Differences in the Various Parts of the Herring Revision of the Binet-Simon Test When Applied to Normal Dull Adults." *J Ed Psychol* 20:622-7 N '29.
10 CARROLL, HERBERT A., AND HOLLINGWORTH, LETA S. "The Systematic Error of the Herring Binet in Rating Gifted Children." *J Ed Psychol* 21:1-11 Ja '30.
11 NEMZEK, CLAUDE L. "Is the IQ Constant?" *Peabody J Ed* 9:123-4 S '31.
12 GARRETT, HENRY E., AND SCHNECK, MATTHEW R. *Psychological Tests, Methods, and Results*, Part 2, pp. 11-2. New York and London: Harper and Bros., 1933. Pp. x, 137, 235. $2.75; 10s. 6d.
13 NEMZEK, CLAUDE L. "The Comparative Constancy of Stanford-Binet and Herring-Binet IQ's." *J Appl Psychol* 17:475-7 O '33.

Andrew W. Brown, Chief Psychologist, Institute for Juvenile Research, Chicago, Illinois; Associate Professor of Psychology, University of Illinois. The *Herring Revision of the Binet-Simon Tests* was constructed as an alternative form for the 1916 *Stanford Revision.* The contents of the two tests are therefore very similar. Their structure, however, is quite different. First, the Herring is a point scale rather than a mental age scale which according to most test theorists is an advantage. Second, it is divided into five groups of tests. These groups are accumulative, i.e., each group consists of each preceding group and eight or nine additional tests. At the end of each group are directions for the omission of certain tests in the next group. These omissions are determined by the score in Group A (the first group) and include those tests in which the examinee is certain to make either a perfect score or a zero score. The examinee is given full credit for the former and no credit for the latter. Mental age norms are available for each group of tests. The author, however, because of the small number of items advises against the use of these norms for the first two groups except as rough approximations.

The test is unusually easy to administer and to score. The examination manual is arranged so that the instruction for giving a test and the test itself are on the same page, e.g., in Test 3, Reproduction of Thought, the passage to be read by the subject and the instructions for giving and scoring are on the same page; the former facing the child, the latter, the examiner.

Although the test has a number of unique features it also has a number of limitations. First it is extremely verbal in nature. Eighteen of the thirty-eight are regarded by the reviewer as distinctly verbal. Four of these tests yielding a total of 55 points are "Reproduction of Thought" tests, which depend upon ability to read and comprehend the English language. This distinctly verbal aspect of the test, although in accord with Herring's general theory that intelligence is the ability to carry on abstract thinking, makes it of limited use in a clinic or school situation where there are a large number of children with reading difficulty or language handicaps.

A second limitation is that the test is poorly standardized in comparison with other individual tests. One hundred fifty four cases were used and the norms for the various age levels derived by statistical manipulation.[5] As a consequence the test results often do not give true mental ratings. Carroll and Hollingworth [10] have shown that the test rates gifted children about 17 points lower in terms of IQ than does the Stanford. They state further that "Invalidity rests with Herring-Binet, since when the criterion of subsequent scholastic success under conditions of full opportunity is applied, Herring-Binet makes, on the average, a minus error of prediction amounting to about eighteen points of discrepancy between IQ and EQ." Whether the same degree of invalidity exists at other levels of intelligence has not been determined. There is no evidence, however, to indicate that it does not. The very high correlations (.98 and .99) between the Herring and the Stanford reported by Herring and Wilner [8] (which, incidentally, have not been confirmed by other studies) do not necessarily indicate a close correspondence in individual scores.

The test has many original features which should be further developed, but until it is better standardized it has very limited use.

[1400]
Junior School Grading Test. Age 7 or entrants to the junior school; 1937; 1 form; 6s. 6d. per 25; 9d.

per manual; 1s. per specimen set; 12(30) minutes; W. P. Alexander; London: University of London Press, Ltd.

E. Patricia Hunt, Vocational Psychologist, Education Office, Birmingham, England. This intelligence test for classifying seven-year-old pupils when they enter Junior Schools supplies a great need and should prove very valuable. It has been constructed by an expert of considerable experience and can be used without hesitation by those wanting a reliable test for seven-year olds. The general notes and instructions for giving and scoring are admirable, and due warning is given concerning any points on which the giver of the test might come to grief. The reviewer is strongly opposed to psychological tests being given by persons untrained in the technique of psychological testing, but, as yet, in many instances this cannot be avoided. Alexander has produced a test which can be given even by untrained persons with the expectation of achieving reliable results.

One criticism does arise in the reviewer's mind regarding the table of norms. A mental age of 57 months is assigned to children obtaining a score of 1. Surely anyone would hesitate to assign any value to a score of 1 on any test! At the other end of the scale a mental age of 150 months is assigned to the score of 90. This is the maximum total score, and in a sound intelligence test, as the reviewer judges this to be, no candidate should be able to achieve the maximum total score. Hence it seems redundant to assign a mental age to this score. It would appear that in this table of norms the author has allowed theoretical enthusiasm to override practical common sense. This criticism, however, must not be regarded as throwing any doubt on the reliability of the norms which, having been constructed by Alexander, can be accepted with full confidence.

[1401]
Kent-Shakow Formboard. Ages 6 to adult; 1928; 1 form, 2 models; revision of the *Worcester Formboard*; Grace H. Kent and David Shakow; Chicago, Ill.: C. H. Stoelting Co.; Worcester, Mass.: Sven G. Nilsson, 16 Maverick Road.
a) INDUSTRIAL MODEL. (20-40) minutes; Stoelting: $120; Nilsson: $45 including container and instructions.
b) CLINICAL MODEL. (15-30) minutes; Stoelting: $120; Nilsson: $40 including container and instructions.

REFERENCES

1 SHAKOW, DAVID, AND KENT, GRACE H. "The Worcester Formboard Series." *J Genetic Psychol* 32:599-611 D '25.
2 BRONNER, AUGUSTA F.; HEALY, WILLIAM; LOWE, GLADYS M.; AND SHIMBERG, MYRA E. *A Manual of Individual Mental*

Tests and Testing. pp. 174-5, 233-4. Judge Baker Foundation Publication, No. 4. Boston, Mass.: Little, Brown and Co., 1927. Pp. x, 287. $3.50.
3 KENT, GRACE H., AND SHAKOW, DAVID. "Graded Series of Form Boards." *Personnel J* 7:115-20 Ag '28.
4 SCHIEFFELIN, BARBARA, AND SCHWESINGER, GLADYS C. *Mental Tests and Heredity*: Including a Survey of Non-Verbal Tests, pp. 171-2. New York: Galton Publishing Co., Inc. 1930. Pp. ix, 298. Out of print.
5 GROVE, WILLIAM R. "An Experimental Study of the Kent-Shakow Industrial Formboard Series." *J Appl Psychol* 19:467-73 Ag '35.
6 BRILL, MOSHE. "Performance Tests as Aids in the Diagnosis of Maladjustment." *J Genetic Psychol* 49:199-214 S '36.
7 EARL, C. J. C. "The Performance Test Behaviour of Adult Morons." *Brit J Med Psychol* 17:78-92 pt 1 '37.
8 PATERSON, DONALD G.; SCHNEIDLER, GWENDOLEN, G.; AND WILLIAMSON, EDMUND G. *Student Guidance Techniques*, pp. 229-33. New York: McGraw-Hill Book Co., Inc., 1938. Pp. xviii, 316. $3.00. (London: McGraw-Hill Publishing Co., Ltd., 18s.)
9 SHAKOW, DAVID, AND PAZEIAN, BESSIE. "Adult Norms for the K-S Clinical Formboards." *J Appl Psychol* 23:495-502 Ag '39.

Lorene Teegarden, Psychological Examiner, Public Schools, Cincinnati, Ohio. This formboard is made in a small size called the clinical board, and a larger size called the industrial formboard. The reviewer has used the industrial board only, in work with adults over sixteen years of age.

The board contains five holes or recesses into which are to be fitted eight sets of blocks presenting a graded series of tasks or problems. In each task the blocks for the five holes are cut by the same pattern, so that the pattern is presented five times in the five holes. This feature minimizes chance in solution, for although the blocks may be correctly placed by chance in one or two of the holes, this cannot happen for all the holes in any task.

The test possesses intrinsic interest for a wide range of age and ability. The blocks are sufficiently large to fit the adult hand, and while the simplest tasks can be completed by young children, the more difficult tasks offer a challenge to even the superior adult. Because of this interest, the test is valuable for establishing rapport with the adult applicant who may be a bit scornful or fearful of manipulative tests. The first five tasks can be completed by all adults except a few of very poor ability. The last three are too difficult for those who exceed certain time limits on the simpler tasks. The time required for the test is from 20 to 40 minutes, depending upon the ease and rapidity with which the subject works. Though the test has been used in several studies which have been reported, norms for general use have not yet been published.

Each task except the first is timed and scored by percentile rating or other method. The reviewer uses percentile ratings (unpublished) developed at the Cincinnati Employment Cen-

ter, which are combined into two mean ratings, one for the simple tasks, and one for the complicated tasks of the series. These ratings may differ widely for a given individual. In addition to numerical ratings, the test yields information as to the subject's manner of work which should be recorded in the examiner's notes. Such qualitative data may relate to poise under difficulties, insight into the problem, adaptability and resourcefulness in varying the method and trying new methods, or rapidity of movement in handling objects.

Industrially the *Kent-Shakow Formboard* is useful for selecting workers for jobs involving complicated situations, especially those of a mechanical nature. Perhaps the most useful standards for industrial use will prove to be those developed by each industry in relation to its specific jobs. The test is valuable also for aid in guidance. It has a wider usefulness than the *Minnesota Spatial Relations Test* since it includes problems of a wide range of difficulty. In certain situations it should be supplemented by tests measuring manual or finger dexterity and eye-hand co-ordination.

[1402]
Kentucky General Scholastic Ability Test [1939 Revision]. Grades 10-13; 1937-39; a revision of the *Kentucky Classification Test (see* 338); 1 form; $3.50 per 100; 10¢ per specimen set; nontimed (30-80) minutes; E. J. Asher; Lexington, Ky.: Kentucky Cooperative Testing Service, University of Kentucky.

REFERENCES

1 McQUITTY, JOHN V. "Student Mortality in Relation to Scores on the Kentucky Classification Test." *Ky Personnel B* 19:1-2 My '37.
2 ASHER, ESTON J. "The Reliability and Validity of the Kentucky General Scholastic and Kentucky English Tests." *Ky Personnel B* 21:1-2 S '38.
3 BISHOP, HELEN. "A Study in Prediction and Mortality." *J Am Assn Col Registrars* 14:62-3 O '39.

For a review by Richard Ledgerwood of an earlier form, see 1048.

[1403]
Kingsway Intelligence Tests. 1939; a 29-page booklet of 15 practice tests; 7d. per pupils' edition; 10d. per teachers' edition with answers; London: Evans Brothers Ltd.

Scottish Ed J 23:273 Ap '40. The object of these Tests is to familiarise children, especially pupils sitting for special places in English secondary schools, with the usual type of Group Intelligence Tests, so that they may be able to show their full capacity when called upon to work them under examination conditions. Fifteen different sets of tests, containing twenty items each of different types, are given in the booklet. Much less practice than this is now believed to produce the maximum effect, and teachers coaching pupils through the whole fifteen sets may be wasting valuable time. The collection itself is quite satisfactory, although the correction might have been simplified.

[1404]
Kuhlmann-Anderson Intelligence Tests, Fourth Edition. Grades 1B, 1A, 2, 3, 4, 5, 6, 7-8, 9-12; 1927-39; 1 form, 9 levels; $1.25 per 25; 40¢ per manual; 25¢ per 100 individual record cards; 40¢ per specimen set; 15¢ per 25 copies of any single page for individual testing; (40-60) minutes; F. Kuhlmann and Rose G. Anderson; Minneapolis, Minn.: Educational Test Bureau, Inc.

REFERENCES

1 KUHLMANN, F. "A Median Mental Age Method of Weighting and Scaling Mental Tests." *J Appl Psychol* 11:181-98 Je '27.

2 KUHLMANN, F. "The Kuhlmann-Anderson Intelligence Tests Compared with Seven Others." *J Appl Psychol* 12:545-94 D '28.

3 KUHLMANN, F. "The Pearson Formula, and a Further Note on the Kuhlmann-Anderson Tests." *J Appl Psychol* 13:32-45 F '29.

4 KUHLMANN, F. "Effect of Degree of Difficulty on Operation of Intelligence Tests." *J Juvenile Res* 14:8-21 Ja '30.

5 STECKEL, MINNIE L. "The Restandardization of IQ's of Different Tests." *J Ed Psychol* 21:278-83 Ap '30.

6 CATTELL, PSYCHE. "The Heinis Personal Constant as a Substitute for the IQ." *J Ed Psychol* 24:221-8 Mr '33.

7 CHARLES, C. M. "A Comparison of the Intelligence Quotients of Three Different Mental Tests Applied to a Group of Incarcerated Delinquent Boys." *J Appl Psychol* 17:581-4 O '33.

8 KUHLMANN, F. "What the IQ Means Today." *Nation's Sch* 11:33-8 F '33.

9 BOYNTON, PAUL L. "A Reply to Professor Nemzek." *Peabody J Ed* 12:239-41 Mr '35.

10 HILDEN, ARNOLD H., AND SKEELS, HAROLD M. "A Comparison of the Stanford-Binet Scale, the Kuhlmann-Anderson Group Test, the Arthur Point Scale of Performance Tests, and the Unit Scales of Attainment." *J Exp Ed* 4:214-30 D '35.

11 NEMZEK, CLAUDE L. "A Note Concerning the Kuhlmann-Anderson Tests." *Peabody J Ed* 12:238-9 Mr '35.

12 BRADWAY, KATHERINE PRESTON, AND HOFFEDITZ, E. LOUISE. "The Basis for the Personal Constant." *J Ed Psychol* 28:501-13 O '37.

13 HALES, W. M. "Results of a Group Intelligence Re-test with a Reformatory Group." *J Juvenile Res* 21:181-7 Jl '37.

14 SPACHE, GEORGE. "The Use of the Kuhlmann-Anderson Intelligence Tests in Private Schools." *J Ed Psychol* 30:618-23 N '39.

15 ANDERSON, ROSE G. "Fifth Revision of Kuhlmann-Anderson Tests." *J Appl Psychol* 24:198-206 Ap '40.

Henry E. Garrett, Associate Professor of Psychology, Columbia University. This well-known test series was first published in 1927, and in its present revised form in 1933. The battery consists of 39 separate tests which contain from 5 to 28 items each. These tests have been assembled into 9 booklets and cover the ability-range from the first to the twelfth grades. The average chronological age of those children in the standardization group who passed 1, 2, 3, or more of the items of each test has been calculated; and the "median mental age" of a given child is the median of the "ages" which he earns on the tests. Since abilities of school children are relatively undifferentiated as compared to the abilities of adults, this is probably as satisfactory a method as any for obtaining the typical level at which a child functions.

The instruction manual which accompanies the tests contains explicit directions for giving and scoring the tests, as well as a 20-page description of the theory and methods employed in the construction of the scale. The directions are detailed and clear; but the theoretical introduction is badly written—it reads like a poor translation—and contains some astonishingly naive and inaccurate statements. In discussing validity criteria, for instance, the authors discard the usual methods. Instead, they propose to use the "discriminative capacity" of the tests—by which is meant the ability of a test to show—or not to show—steady and significant increases in score with age. Although much is made of the superiority of this technique over other methods in the advertising which describes the scale, the notion itself is not new and has nothing essentially to do with test validity. It is necessary, of course, that we compute the discriminative capacity of a test if we wish to know its difficulty and the age range over which the test is most effective. But since physical strength, motor agility, and emotional control (to mention a few), all increase with age, mere increase in score with age is no guarantee that a test is an adequate measure of intellect. The authors really admit this when they say (p. 9): "we have depended on common sense analysis in the selection of tests." As practical people who know and have had wide experience with both children and tests the authors' scale is very probably a valid measure of intelligence—but not for the reasons which they and their publishers give.

Several curious statements regarding test validity appear on page 7 of the manual. In arguing against the need for obtaining validity correlations with such criteria as school marks, our authors say: "But it is conceded by psychologists that test scores themselves are a better criterion of intelligence than anything else available." It would be enlightening to know how "test scores" become criteria of intelligence in the first place; and what "psychologists" are willing to make so broad a concession. Again, with reference to validity, our authors write: "Too close an agreement between test scores and school marks is evidence that the tests are not entirely valid tests of intelligence, because school marks are not determined entirely by intelligence. From this example (*sic*), it is clear that a knowledge of the amount of correlation between test scores and any other criteria may mislead instead of inform about the value of the tests." It is difficult to guess just what the authors are trying to say here. Should criterion correlations with school marks be low because school marks are not simon-pure measures of intelligence? If so, how low? And how high must test correlations with "any other criteria" be before they "mislead" instead of "inform"? Though admittedly fallible—if they were not we should not need intelligence tests—school marks constitute our best single criterion of that kind of intellectual activity which intelligence testers, since Binet, have attempted to measure. If our tests measure something radically different from that ability measured by school marks, then they are not useful estimates of the intellectual ability of school children, no matter what their discriminative capacity.

In introducing the topic of reliability, Kuhlmann and Anderson remark that: "The literature on this subject is in a badly muddled condition" (p. 10). Their subsequent discussion is the best exhibit they could offer of the truth of this statement. Apparently our authors have completely confused "goodness" of a test (validity) with consistency of test scores (reliability). They write: "If either circumstances or the children are different the second time they (*sic*) are given the same tests, the tests would be poor instead of good if they gave the same results. . . . In other words, close agreement between the first and second set of scores, and as expressed by the coefficient of correlation, may be evidence that the tests are poor instead of good." What our authors intend to say, apparently, is that high self-correlation is no guarantee of high reliability—*if* circumstances and children have changed between testings. What they really say is that high reliability does not necessarily imply high validity ("goodness"). The latter statement is, of course, true. But the former statement is true only if one can conceive of a test which would give more consistent retest results when circumstances are altered and children different (practised, coached, emotionally upset, etc.) than the same test would give when these factors have been rigidly controlled. A test may be highly reliable and not be a valid measure of intellect (e.g., the tapping test) ; and by the same token, a test may be a "good" measure of intellect (e.g., syllogisms) and still not show

"close agreement" on two successive occasions. Sameness of score is no measure of "goodness" or "poorness"; and goodness in a test does not necessarily lead to highly stable scores.

An interesting conception of the reliability coefficient is given by our authors on page 11. In contending that high reliability coefficients are evidence of a "good" test only when difficulty of items has been cared for, they write: "But high correlations also result when the tests are either too easy or too difficult, because all scores then tend to be the same. Perfect reliability would result if the tests were so easy that all children could easily get a maximum score on them any time, no matter what the circumstances, or if they were so difficult that no children could get above a zero score on them at any time." In the highly improbable (not to say absurd) situation in which children's scores are either all zero or all maximum on both test and retest, there is, of course, perfect agreement between test and retest scores. But a reliability coefficient in such a situation has no meaning—and would never be calculated outside of an insane asylum. In the more likely situation in which all scores—test and retest—show little spread and cluster around some common point, say the mean, the self-correlation approaches zero, not 1.00.

A final word may be said of our authors' use of the "Heinis growth units"—of which much is made. Heinis units are derived values obtained by fitting an arbitrarily selected exponential equation to certain poorly described data, gathered by Heinis from various sources. Our authors' data are so much superior to and more extensive than those used by Heinis that it is surprising that they did not derive "growth units" from their own test scores.

For reviews by Psyche Cattell, S. A. Courtis, and Austin H. Turney, see 1049.

[1405]

Leiter International Performance Scale. Ages 4 and over; 1936-40; 1 form; 68 nonlanguage tests which can be given without language or pantomime; $68 per testing outfit, including manual and 100 record blanks; $2 per manual; $2 per 100 record booklets; (30) minutes at the 6-year-old level and (90) minutes at the high school level; Russell Graydon Leiter; Santa Barbara, Calif.: the Author, 601 East Valerio St.

REFERENCES

1 LEITER, RUSSELL G. *The Leiter International Performance Scale.* University of Hawaii Bulletin, Vol. 15, No. 7; Research Publications, No. 13. Appendix by Stanley D. Porteus. Honolulu, Hawaii: the University, May 1936. Pp. 42. $0.30. Paper.
2 LEITER, RUSSELL GRAYDON. *The Leiter International Performance Scale*: Vol. 1, Directions for the Application and

Scoring of Individual Tests. Santa Barbara, Calif.: Santa Barbara State College Press, 1940. Pp. ix, 95. $2.00.

[1406]
Merrill-Palmer Scale of Mental Tests. Ages 24-63 months; 1926-31; individual; 1 form; $46.60 per testing outfit (No. 37061); $1.50 per 25 record blanks (No. 44088); $2.45 per manual [5] (No. 46621) (the manual may be purchased directly from the publisher for $2.20); test purchasers having the following tests may save approximately $9.15: *Mare and Foal Test*: Pintner-Paterson, *Manikin Test*: Pintner, and the *Block Design Test*: Kohs; Rachel Stutsman; Chicago, Ill.: C. H. Stoelting Co.

REFERENCES

1 STUTSMAN, RACHEL. *Performance Tests for Children of Pre-School Age.* Genetic Psychology Monographs Vol. 1, No. 1. Worcester, Mass.: Clark University Press, January 1926. Pp. 67. $2.00. Paper.
2 STUTSMAN, RACHEL. *A Scale of Mental Tests for Pre-school Children.* Unpublished Doctor's thesis, University of Chicago, 1928. Pp. 350.
3 WILSON, CHARLES A.; SWEENY, MARY E.; STUTSMAN, RACHEL; CHESIRE, LEONE E.; AND HATT, ELISE. *The Merrill-Palmer Standards of Physical and Mental Growth.* Detroit, Mich.: Merrill-Palmer School, 1930. Pp. ix, 121. $0.50. Paper.
4 KAWIN, ETHEL, AND HOEFER, CAROLYN, assisted by Edna Mohr, Maria G. Linder, and Marian W. Taylor. *A Comparative Study of a Nursery-School versus a Non-Nursery-School Group.* Chicago, Ill.: University of Chicago Press, 1931. Pp. 52. $0.75. Paper.
5 STUTSMAN, RACHEL. *Mental Measurement of Preschool Children*: With a Guide for the Administration of the Merrill-Palmer Scale of Mental Tests. Yonkers, N. Y.: World Book Co., 1931. Pp. xi, 368. $2.20.
6 DRISCOLL, GERTRUDE PORTER. *The Development Status of the Preschool Child as a Prognosis of Future Development.* Columbia University, Teachers College, Child Development Monographs, No. 13. New York: Bureau of Publications, the College, 1933. Pp. xiv, 111. $1.50.
7 GORDON, R. G. "The Merrill-Palmer Scale of Intelligence Tests for Pre-School Children Applied to Low-Grade Mental Defectives." *Brit J Psychol* 24:178-86 O '33.
8 MOWRER, WILLIE MAE C. "Performance of Children in Stutsman Tests." *Child Development* 5:93-6 Je '34.
9 STUTSMAN, RACHEL. "Factors to be Considered in Measuring the Reliability of a Mental Test, with Special Reference to the Merrill-Palmer Scale." *J Ed Psychol* 25:630-3 N '34.
10 BRISTOL, HILDA. "An English Norm for the Merrill-Palmer Performance Tests: Based on a Study of 530 Children between the Ages of Two and Six Years." *Brit J of Ed Psychol* 6:250-66 N '36.
11 OBERLIN, DIANA S. "Verbal and Manual Functions at the Preschool Level." *Del State Med J* 9:95-8 Ap '37.
12 WELLMAN, BETH L. *The Intelligence of Preschool Children as Measured by the Merrill-Palmer Scale of Performance Tests.* University of Iowa Studies, New Series No. 361; Studies in Child Welfare, Vol. 15, No. 3. Iowa City, Iowa: the University, October 1938. Pp. 150. Cloth, $1.35; paper, $1.00.
13 DEFORREST, RUTH. *A Study of the Prognostic Value of the Merrill-Palmer Scale of Mental Tests and the Minnesota Preschool Scale.* Unpublished master's thesis, University of Pittsburgh, 1939. Pp. 21.

Nancy Bayley, Research Associate, Institute of Child Welfare, University of California. The Merrill-Palmer scale has the handicap of all preschool scales which have been so far standardized: that is, its predictive value is very limited. Its merits must lie in any ability it may have to measure children's present intellectual capacities. It is one of the earlier tests for preschool children for which norms are based on an adequate sample of cases. (The scale was first published in 1926.) The norms are based on 631 cases ranging in age from 18 to 77 months, and secured from a variety of sources. These included kindergarten and first grade children from the public schools, children from child care agencies and health clinics,

and children on the Merrill-Palmer nursery school waiting list. The test items are to a large extent nonlanguage, and they have been selected for their intrinsic interest to young children. Their outstanding merit is in the children's interest in performing most of the tasks set to them. On the other hand, a fault of the scale lies in its generous use of time-scores. The abilities of young children can not be adequately measured by speed of performance, because speed has not yet become a goal for them, and their shifting attention often alters the score in a way which obscures skill of manipulation and insight into the solution of a problem.

Although Stutsman claims *r*'s of .79 between scores on her scale and the Stanford-Binet, she obtained these *r*'s without partialling out chronological age, in an age range where her own data show a marked correlation between test performance and chronological age. Actually, the tests have been found by other investigators to have rather low relationship to Stanford-Binet IQ's. From these later investigations it is evident that the two tests do not measure the same array of abilities. A number of the items in the Merrill-Palmer scale test motor skills and co-ordinations rather than learning or insightful behavior. For these reasons, the scale should not be used as a substitute for the Binet type of tests, but it should rather be considered a supplementary measure.

Stutsman describes the processes of standardization in some detail, and in addition gives other material of value to the person who wishes information about preschool tests generally. This information includes a historical summary of preschool testing, short descriptions of other preschool scales, and a discussion of technics and problems of preschool testing. This latter discussion includes a section on the tendency of preschool children to refuse tests, with suggested ways of surmounting this difficulty. Stutsman also takes account of this tendency in her scoring, so that a child is not penalized for resistive behavior. Other sections deal with the effects of environment on test scores, sex differences, a guide for observing personality, and case studies which illustrate various factors which are relevant in judging a child's mental level.

B. M. Castner, Clinic of Child Development, Yale University. This is one of the better-constructed preschool scales, its defects lying rather in the scope of its sampling of abilities, and in the limited age-range covered, than in details of the scale itself. The ages covered are from 18 to 77 months, with 6-month intervals; but Stutsman does not recommend use of the scale above 63 months or below 24 months. This seriously limits its clinical usefulness, particularly at the lower end. The age of referral of children is steadily dropping, and the examiner whose practice includes the ages below 2 years will by preference make use of a scale which is continuous from infancy upward, permitting the study of growth sequences through follow-up examinations in terms of a unitary group of tests.

No attempt has been made to group tests on the basis of specific fields of behavior. Such a grouping aids materially in the analytic interpretation of test results, and can be more definitely made in the preschool years than in the case of older children, whose behavior is more complexly integrated. It is particularly useful in bringing into relief, fields showing specific retardation or acceleration which may be overlooked in a more heterogeneous grouping of tests. This lack is partially, but not wholly, compensated for by a far better discussion of qualitative individual differences in response and their interpretation, than is sometimes found in manuals for preschool testing.

The range of abilities tested seems inadequate for a thorough clinico-developmental study of a child, although it will usually be roughly satisfactory when only an approximate general rating is desired. The important fields of postural, locomotor, and gross motor behavior, deviations which may greatly influence the total clinical picture, are untapped. Drawing, which has a high diagnostic value aside from its purely normative significance, could to advantage be extended beyond the three tests included. Items based upon personal-social behavior are omitted, although there is an excellent chapter on the significance of personality observations as made in the examination. Language—important not only in itself, but by reason of the vital part it plays in the gradual integration of the individual's total behavior—should be more extensively represented. The principal language test—the Action-Agent—is perhaps the best single test in the scale. The "Simple Questions," however, designed for the ages below 3 years, have not proved very satisfactory in clinical practice; they are often annoying to give, and the wide individual differences in response make the interpretation of failure difficult.

Details as to standardization methods and selection of subjects—problems offering peculiar difficulty in the case of preschool children—are fully and clearly presented. There is adequate tabular presentation of results, and the statistical treatment is satisfactory without going beyond limits justified by the nature of the material.

Scoring is provided for by any of three methods—standard deviation in terms of either MA or IQ, or on a percentile basis. Stutsman does not recommend the IQ method, because of the undetermined relationship of such a measure at this age to the IQ obtained on higher-age scales. The same objection applies in part to the use of MA; some such rating in terms of behavior maturity age is useful, but it would be desirable to use a term which does not carry with it so many connotations, some helpful but many misleading, acquired through its use in the case of school children and adults. It is, in fact, doubtful whether any strict numerical method of scoring a complete examination is justified at present below the age of 5 or 6 years, especially since there are no correction formulae for such factors as inattentiveness, temporary retardation in specific fields, lack of normal environmental experience, deviations caused by illness, personality complications, and others, which are more frequent and more pronounced in their effects during the preschool years, when development is more rapid and more easily disturbed in its manifestations, and when a difference of a few months or even weeks in the developmental rating looms much larger than in later years.

Florence L. Goodenough, Research Professor, Institute of Child Welfare, The University of Minnesota. The Merrill-Palmer tests for preschool children have been widely used in nursery schools and preschool behavior clinics throughout the country. Undoubtedly, their popularity with children has had a good deal to do with their popularity among clinicians since in many other respects they fall short of modern technical requirements in the field of mental measurement. The method of scoring with its emphasis upon speed of performance is hardly in accordance with present-day knowledge of the psychology of early childhood which has shown the very rudimentary concepts of time usually found among children of preschool age. On the other hand, the scale has so many excellent features that one can only hope that its author will at some future time see fit to prepare a revision which will preserve its good points while correcting those details that at present interfere with its usefulness.

In any test designed for young children, the intrinsic interest of the tasks and the materials is of first-rank importance. In this respect the Merrill-Palmer scale easily takes the lead. The tests have been selected on the basis of an intimate understanding of child psychology and are put up in gay-colored boxes which, piled where the child can see them, keep him in a state of happy anticipation as to what is coming next. The order of administration may be varied in whatever way seems best suited to the child's interests, thus permitting the examiner to seize upon a favorable moment for interjecting the more difficult or the less attractive items.

The tests are largely of the "performance" type but there are a small number of language tests, including a modification of the Woodworth and Wells Action-Agent test. Other tests include formboards, block building, peg boards, picture puzzles, copying simple designs, following directions, buttoning, etc. Since instructions are given verbally, some degree of language comprehension on the part of the child is presupposed; yet these instructions are so simple and obvious that a rough appraisal of the abilities of young deaf children can be had by giving certain parts of the test in pantomime. The use of the test with handicapped children or those unusually difficult to manage is greatly facilitated by an ingenious method of making allowance for omitted items or those which the child refuses to try so that the total score is not affected.

The most serious difficulty in the practical use of the test has been pointed out by its author. This is the fact that the standard deviations of scores do not increase in proportion to age throughout the age range for which the test is designed (18 to 66 months) but reach their maximum at three and one-half years and decrease thereafter. The result is that the test results are likely to be misleading when used by persons with little statistical sophisti-cation. The use of intelligence quotients as a means of indicating the degree of brightness is ruled out for the reason just given; for example, an IQ of 166 at 45 months has the same meaning as one of 122 at 27 months. For this reason, norms are also given in terms of standard deviation units and percentiles but in such broad steps that interpolation must be made if fine units are desired. Such interpolation is, however, hardly warranted at the ages beyond four, since the decreasing variability of the scores at the later ages makes the significance of small differences decidedly questionable, especially when, as in this case, those differences depend largely upon speed of performance. A fundamental defect in the construction of a test cannot be wholly overcome by any statistical devices.

For children between the ages of 18 and 42 months the test is a valuable one. Thereafter its usefulness steadily decreases until, except for those intellectually backward, it becomes of little service for children who have passed the age of 54 months. In the hands of a skillful clinician it affords an excellent opportunity for observing personality characteristics. A useful guide for such observations together with a series of case studies is provided in the manual.

Florence M. Teagarden, Professor of Psychology, The University of Pittsburgh. After several years in which it has been used and compared with other preschool tests, this test must still be considered one of the best available. The careful standardization of the scale largely accounts for this fact. From 49 to 81 children at each six-month interval from 18 months through 77 months of chronological age constituted the standardization group, 300 girls and 331 boys in all. (It is to be noted, however, that Stutsman recommends the use of the scale for only those children 24 to 63 months of age.) The standardization group was selected from 20 widely different sources. Stutsman's evidence as to reliability and validity of the test is certainly as convincing as that given for most scales.

The entire scale includes 38 different tests. Sixteen of these score at only one point and are, therefore, called "all-or-none" tests. The remaining 22 tests have variable score values and score at 77 different points on the scale. In all there are thus 93 different items arranged in six-month intervals beginning at 18 to 23 months and running through 66 to 72 months. The tests require manipulation of body (opposition of thumb and fingers, standing on one foot and the like), language, and the use of such objects as ball, mirror, blocks, peg boards, scissors, paper and pencil, form boards, jigsaw puzzles, buttons, colors, manikin, etc. The commercialized material for the test is needlessly expensive and this prevents its being standard equipment in many testing centers where it should be found.

Ratings are secured by use of *score, mental age, standard deviation,* and *percentile rank.* In actual practice it sometimes happens that there is a slight discrepancy in the rating of a child by the use of one of these methods as compared with another. Stutsman does not recommend the use of the IQ technique for this test. There is also a "personality blank" which although almost entirely subjective in nature is suggestive as to items of behavior for which one should look in evaluating the reactions of preschool children. The provisions for scoring "omitted" and "refused" test items are exceedingly helpful even though one is sometimes in doubt as to whether a test item should be scored "refused" or "failed." Some of the items are "timed" tests. However one might wish that preschool children's responses need not be scored by the use of a stop watch, nevertheless there is probably no satisfactory substitute in making certain differentiations.

Mastery of the testing technique requires more time perhaps than is true of certain other tests but this may after all be a merit rather than otherwise. One has a feeling that Stutsman has been perfectly straightforward in her directions for administering and scoring. In her book there is none of the "esoteric" that one so often finds in manuals for testing infants and young children.

Several years use of the scale has demonstrated to the writer that children *like* the test and, as a rule, a skilled examiner has no difficulty in getting cooperative response from children to the test. In the hands of an expert the test has great value also in attempts to evaluate the intelligence of older children who for undetermined reasons are not talking.

An unpublished master's thesis by Ruth De-Forrest [13] gives data on 170 children who were given Merrill-Palmer ratings while in nursery school and who were subsequently given the *Revised Stanford-Binet Scale.* Prediction of

subsequent Binet IQ became less and less accurate the older the child at the time his Merrill-Palmer was secured. For the age range 24 to 63 months Revised Binet IQ could be predicted from Merrill-Palmer ratings 16 per cent better than by chance. For children 24 to 42 months of age when given the Merrill-Palmer, prediction of Binet IQ was 30 per cent better than by chance while it was only two per cent better than by chance for the 51 to 63 months age group. DeForrest also found that IQ's obtained by Merrill-Palmer were as reliable as the standard deviation which Stutsman very greatly prefers.

[1407]

Minnesota Preschool Scale. Ages 1½ to 6 years; 1932; 2 forms; individual; nontimed; $9.50 per testing outfit for a single form; 75¢ per 25 individual record blanks; Florence L. Goodenough, Josephine C. Foster, and M. J. Van Wagenen; Minneapolis, Minn.: Educational Test Bureau, Inc.

REFERENCES

1 MOWRER, WILLIE MAE C. "Intelligence Scales for Preschool Children." *Child Development* 4:318-22 D '33.
2 CURTI, MARGARET WOOSTER, AND STEGGERDA, MORRIS. "A Preliminary Report on the Testing of Young Maya Children in Yucatan." *J Comp Psychol* 28:207-24 O '39.
3 DEFORREST, RUTH. *A Study of the Prognostic Value of the Merrill-Palmer Scale of Mental Tests and the Minnesota Preschool Scale.* Unpublished master's thesis, University of Pittsburgh, 1939. Pp. 21.

Rachel Stutsman Ball, Psychologist, The Merrill-Palmer School, Detroit, Michigan. The *Minnesota Preschool Scale* is a well-organized, easily administered test for preschool children, consisting of 26 separate test items. The test is largely an adaptation of items chosen from earlier Binet materials, but includes some other original and perhaps more interesting additions. In producing a test scale which is compact and relatively inexpensive in price, the authors have profited wisely and well from earlier and cruder Binet test scales. The test has the advantage of giving language and nonlanguage scores, thus eliminating the necessity when time is limited for more complex double testing procedures. The test blank is carefully and conveniently set up. It contains a section for recording test reactions that is a decided contribution to test record forms. There are two test forms, A and B, so set up as to have equivalent value for testing. This should have the advantage of decreasing the practice effect upon retesting if a different form is used.

The test is not sufficiently interesting or varied to be very satisfactory with many children under three years of age, particularly in clinic situations. The authors suggest that the scores for children under three should not be separated into verbal and nonverbal. There is no device for scoring omitted or refused tests and this lack makes for inaccuracy of scoring the responses of young children. Deaf children or those with other language problems such as foreign language handicaps and aphasia cannot be tested by the test. There is no plan for omitting easy test items, thus shortening testing time for older children. However, the test may be shortened for the younger ages by omitting similar more difficult items when others have been failed. The test is most suited for children from 3 to 5 years of middle ability ranges. It is inferior to the Stanford-Binet for older bright children because it does not offer sufficient range of difficulty to establish the upper limit of his ability.

The test was standardized on 900 children representing a cross section of different socio-economic levels in the city of Minneapolis. Each test form was given to 75 children. The raw point scores are converted into C-scores which in turn can be interpreted in terms of IQ equivalents, percentile scores, or standard deviation scores. For half-year age ranges the product moment correlation between the C-scores on the two forms with a 1- to 7-day interval varies at the different ages from .68 to .94 for the verbal scales, .67 to .92 for the nonverbal scales, and from .80 to .94 when verbal and nonverbal scales are combined.

The brief statement about the standardization in the test manual is hardly satisfying to those who wish to be thoroughly familiar with the test. The statistical competence of the authors of this test cannot be questioned, but one cannot help wishing that the long promised monograph giving details of the standardization procedures might soon be available.

Nancy Bayley, Research Associate, Institute of Child Welfare, University of California. Intelligence tests for preschool children must be used with precautions and reservations. Their value is exceptionally dependent on the skill of the examiner in getting the child willingly to put forth efforts in the desired directions. For this reason careful training and experience in dealing with young children are necessary before adequate test scores can be secured. Furthermore, even when the scores are reliable, it is problematic whether intelligence in such young children develops at predictable rates. The predictive value of preschool test scores

has been found to be very uncertain, and hence emphasis should be placed, instead, on their evaluation of the child's present status.

The manual of directions for the Minnesota scale gives a summary of the procedures of standardization. The scale has been carefully standardized on 900 children, 100 at each of 9 half-year intervals. These cases were selected, on the basis of parents' occupation, to form a representative socio-economic cross section of the population. Two forms were administered on alternate days with careful procedures for determining practice effects. The reliability coefficient for a single scale is .89. The tests are arranged so that scores can be computed separately for verbal, nonverbal, and total items. The tests are scored in C-score absolute units, and tables are given for converting these into percentile ranks, standard deviation placements, and IQ equivalents. Although the method of obtaining a child's score of relative ability is somewhat more abstruse than is the computation of the IQ, it is statistically preferable, and IQ equivalents are available for those who wish them.

The test items used are in their general nature similar to the Binet tests, a number of them having been adapted from the Kuhlmann-Binet. The scale has been carefully assembled and, if one wishes to test at preschool levels the same functions as are measured in the Binet type of school-age test, it is one of the best of the preschool scales. It is sufficiently verbal in character to have some similarity to the tests more generally employed with older children. On the other hand, most of the items have intrinsic interest for young children. Another factor in favor of this scale is the omission of time-scores. At these early ages speed of performance is a very inaccurate measure of a child's ability because his attention often shifts, he has no notion of "working fast" as a goal, or if he does the very effort for speed often disturbs his co-ordinations and lowers his scores. The provision for the separate scoring of verbal and nonverbal items, in addition to giving information on relative abilities in different fields, takes care, in part, of the difficulty of obtaining scores for children who refuse some of the tests. Most refusals are among the verbal items, which tend to make the child self-conscious and more aware of the examiner's presence in the situation. For children who refuse to respond under these conditions the nonverbal score will often give a more adequate measure of mental status.

Florence M. Teagarden, Professor of Psychology, The University of Pittsburgh. The test was standardized on 100 children at each half-year age level from 18 months to 6 years, making 900 children in all. There are two alternate forms of the test, which permits of periodic examination if first one form and then the other is used. Each form contains items which together make up a "verbal" section and other items which constitute a "nonverbal" section. Reliability coefficients approximating .90 are quoted for the scale as a whole. No measures of validity are given in the manual which accompanies the test.

The test material, which is reasonable in price, comes in a box which is easy to carry. Much of the equipment is contained in a series of envelopes which are bound together and which carry abbreviated directions for administering the test. The child's folder, however, when ready to file is likely to be somewhat disorderly with its assortment of separate pieces of paper that have been used for "tracing," "folding," and the like.

There are 26 separate items in the scale and with few exceptions all must be given to each child. The result is that the test requires rather too much time for younger children, and even older preschool children tend to tire before the test is completed. There is no provision in the scoring for "omissions" or "refusals."

The statistical work of standardization and derivation of scoring units of equal difficulty at all points along the scale are merits not found in most preschool tests. For children over three years of age the verbal and nonverbal parts are scored separately. One finds for each child a verbal C-score, IQ equivalent, percentile, standard deviation, and mental age. Similar measures for the nonverbal section and for the total examination are also found. Obviously, the scoring becomes somewhat tedious. The scoring of separate test items is very difficult at places also. This is particularly true of the picture test where varying credit is given for nouns, verbs, and prepositions in the child's responses to pictures. The child's usage of the word is the basis of scoring, however, rather than grammatical classification. A page and a half of the manual is required for explaining these scoring directions, and experience shows

that even then many questions arise on the scoring of this part of the test. Again in the scoring of a test requiring that the child trace a form with a pencil, difficulties arise. If the child's pencil *touches* the boundary, there is no penalty; if it crosses the boundary the distance between where his pencil leaves the line and where it returns to the line is measured and all such measurements are added. This procedure implies a statistical accuracy that the circumstances do not seem to warrant.

A commendable feature of the test is that it provides fore-exercises which are very fine for young children. In some instances, however, the amount of time spent on the fore-exercises is out of proportion to the value of the test item which they are meant to illustrate. Perhaps the greatest weakness of the test is that many preschool children do not care for it and become bored by the monotonous repetition and similarity of test items. The record blank provides space for entering sociological data about the parents, and personality and behavior data about the child.

Ruth DeForrest [3] found on 44 cases that the Minnesota total IQ and the Minnesota verbal IQ predicted Revised Stanford-Binet IQ with approximately the same degree of success as the Merrill-Palmer IQ.

[1408]

Modification of the Kent-Shakow Formboard. Adult males; 1937; 1 form; $25 per set of unpainted formboards made of masonite; 50¢ per blue print for those wishing to construct their own formboards; (15-30) minutes; William R. Grove; Pittsburgh, Pa.: William R. Grove, Behavior Clinic of the Criminal Court, County of Allegheny.

REFERENCES

1 GROVE, WILLIAM R. *Modification of Kent-Shakow Formboard Series.* Unpublished doctor's thesis, University of Pittsburgh, 1937. Pp. iv, 70.
2 GROVE, WILLIAM R. "An Experimental Study of the Kent-Shakow Industrial Formboard Series." *J Appl Psychol* 19:467-73 Ag '35.
3 GROVE, WILLIAM R. "Modification of the Kent-Shakow Formboard Series." *J Psychol* 7:385-97 Ap '39.

[1409]

Moray House Test 10. Ages 10-12½; 1934; 2s. 9d. per 12; 17s. 6d. per 100; 1s. per 12 practice tests; 7s. per 100 practice tests; 6d. per manual; 9d. per specimen set; 45(60) minutes; Godfrey H. Thomson and colleagues; London: University of London Press, Ltd.

REFERENCES

1 THOMSON, GODFREY, H. "The Standardization of Group Tests and the Scatter of Intelligence Quotients: A Contribution to the Theory of Examining." *Brit J Ed Psychol* 2:92-112, 125-38 F, Je '32.

C. Ebblewhite Smith, Lecturer in the Department of Higher Degrees and Research, Institute of Education, University of London.

English test users have learned to place great value on the Moray House Tests. The *Moray House Test 10* is well up to the standard that Moray House has set itself and is perhaps the best English intelligence test for children of 11+. The idea of preceding the test proper by a ten-minute practice test is to be commended. The test is of satisfactory length and of suitably graded difficulty giving a very good spread of marks with 11-year-olds. Instructions to supervisors are practical and adequate.

Norms have been obtained with over 5,000 children from various English Counties, County Boroughs or Boroughs, the entire age group 10-6 to 11-6 being taken in each case. Scores have been adjusted for age and expressed as "standard scores" having a mean of 100 and a standard deviation of 15. This method constitutes a good compromise for obtaining IQ's when complete figures for norms cannot be obtained. This is an excellent test for its purpose.

[1410]
Northox Group Intelligence Test. Ages 11-12; 1933; 1 form; *3s. 6d.* per 25; *3d.* per test; *1s.* per key; *2d.* per manual; 30(35) minutes; G. Perrie Williams; London: George G. Harrap & Co., Ltd.

E. Patricia Hunt, Vocational Psychologist, Education Office, Birmingham, England. Each of the five subtests in this booklet is of a type recognised as suitable for testing general intelligence, viz: (*a*) pictorial observation, (*b*) pictorial classification, (*c*) pattern-completion, (*d*) substitution, and (*e*) arithmetic: missing digits. It is a pity, however, that some form of analogies test is not included as this is recognised as a most valuable test of *g*.

The subtests are well constructed. They are clearly set out, and each subtest contains one type of question only. The time limits, however, appear overgenerous and the reviewer doubts whether there are a sufficient number of items in each subtest to occupy the time allowed. This would need trying out, but if it is the case, it is a bad fault. Any test should be of such a length that the brightest candidate cannot succeed in completing it in the given time. Only in this way can a true estimate of the ability tested be obtained.

The absence of "practice" tests is a weak point. "Practice" tests should always be included to help the candidates to overcome initial nervousness and also to diminish any disparity among the candidates due to previous experience of, or coaching in intelligence tests. The whole test is entirely nonverbal and the reviewer thinks that it is more suitable for a younger age-group than 11-12 years.

The instructions are carefully worded and well set out. It would, however, be advisable to add to the "general instructions" a regulation that the printed instructions must be adhered to. No warning of this kind is included and the reviewer's personal experience provides many examples of untrained persons using tests and deviating considerably from the printed instructions.

It is unfortunate that the whole value of this test is vitiated by the absence of any norms. When the test has been given and scored the examiner is no wiser as to the intelligence rating of the candidates; all that has been obtained is a ranking within a particular group. The test, as an intelligence test, is therefore valueless. The author should have procured norms before publication; having failed in this, norms should have been procured as soon as possible after publication. The test was published in 1933. It is now 1939 and apparently published norms are still non-existent.

For an additional review, see 1050.

[1411]
Ontario School Ability Examination. Ages 3-15; 1936; "a performance test prepared more especially for use among children who are deaf, whose native tongue is other than English or who for any reason are lacking in language facility"; authorized by the Minister of Education for use in the schools of Ontario, Canada; 1 form; individual; $1.75 per box of testing materials; 90¢ per manual;[1] 75¢ per 50 test blanks; (20-40) minutes; H. Amoss; Toronto, Canada: Ryerson Press.

REFERENCES

1 AMOSS, HARRY. *Ontario School Ability Examinations*: A Performance Test Prepared More Especially for Use among Children Who Are Deaf, Whose Native Tongue Is Other than English or Who for Any Reason Are Lacking in Language Facility. Toronto, Canada: Ryerson Press, 1936. Pp. ii, 54. $0.90.
2 MORRISON, W. J. "The Ontario School Ability Examination." *Am Ann Deaf* 85:184-9 Mr '40.

W. Line, Professor of Psychology, University of Toronto. In the manual,[1] Amoss presents his point of view regarding intelligence and its measurement, an account of the experimental work in establishing the scale, a description of the materials used, and detailed instructions for administering and scoring the tests.

The statement of point of view is of interest mainly as describing the general nature of the examination itself—which seeks to observe the three principles: (*a*) limitation of trial and error procedure; (*b*) progressions of increasingly complex situations, rather than scattered samplings; and (*c*) elimination of all special skills.

The experimental work involved preliminary tryouts with 31 backward and 8 average pupils of the Ontario School for the Deaf, 30 deaf pupils in the Day Classes of Toronto, and some 50 hearing children. Scaling of the selected test items was based on results obtained with an unspecified number of hearing pupils who had previously been examined by means of the Stanford Revision, and with deaf students who had taken the original form of the test. When administered to 288 deaf students (age range, 5 to 22), the examination gave a fairly normal distribution of intelligence quotients about the median 94. The 6-point shifting to the left agrees with results obtained when the IQ's of deaf and of hearing children were compared. The author has used the scale extensively in connection with the work of his staff in selecting candidates for special education in the Ontario schools.

The materials include adaptations of performance tests from Gesell, the Stanford Revision, Drever and Collins, Kohs, Knox, and Pintner, and some which the author his devised.

The instructions are clear. A few minor misprints (e.g., Series G-Weight Arrangement) are not likely to lead to confusion, since the corrections are fairly obvious.

The scale as a whole is easy to administer, although the more complex items in the tapping series will make demands on the examiner's skill.

The author, his staff, and other examiners have found the scale of great value in the Provincial Elementary Schools, in determining the school ability of "deaf children, retarded children, and children whose home language is other than English." As with all empirical instruments of this kind, adequate evaluation can be made only after extensive use.

[1412]

Otis Self-Administering Test: Adapted by Australian Council for Educational Research. Ages 9-15, 13-17; 4 forms, 2 levels; 6*d.* per 12; 5*d.* per manual; 30 (35-40) minutes; Melbourne, Australia: Australian Council for Educational Research.

[1413]

Otis Quick-Scoring Mental Ability Tests. Grades 1A-4, 4-9, 9-16; 1936-39; 3 levels; 2¢ per machine-scorable answer sheet; Arthur S. Otis; Yonkers,

N. Y.: World Book Co. (London: George G. Harrap & Co., Ltd.)
a) ALPHA TEST. Grades 1A-4; 1936-38; 2 forms; may be given as a verbal or nonverbal test or both; 20(25) minutes for either verbal or nonverbal administration; $1.15 per 25; 25¢ per specimen set.
b) BETA TEST. Grades 4-9; 1937-39; 4 forms; 85¢ per 25 (Forms A and B); 90¢ per 25 machine-scorable tests (Forms CM and DM); 20¢ per specimen set; 30(35) minutes.
c) GAMMA TEST. Grades 9-16; 1937-39; 4 forms; 85¢ per 25 (Forms C and D); 90¢ per 25 machine-scorable tests (Forms AM and BM); 15¢ per specimen set; 30(35) minutes.

F. Kuhlmann, Director of the Division of Examinations and Classification, State Department of Public Institutions, St. Paul, Minnesota. The chief objective of these three batteries of tests seems to be economy in administration. This has been achieved to a considerable degree, except for Alpha which when given as a "verbal" is not self-administering. Quick scoring concerns the rapidity with which the number of right responses may be counted with the aid of a single cut-out stencil placed over the single test-sheet, except with Alpha in which the test material consists of a booklet of ten pages which must be scored two pages at a time. Deriving mental ages and intelligence quotients from the number of right responses is, on the whole, more involved than with most other tests.

Judged from inspection only, one would say that the choice of the different test items is ingenious and exceptionally well done, though lacking in variety, resulting in the reduction of the number of abilities measured by the battery. Where Otis uses a total of 80 or 90 trials in a battery some other tests use two or three times that number to cover the same range of mental levels.

In the reviewer's experience self-administering tests have not compared favorably with others, possibly largely because they do not keep the child motivated as well as tests do in which he is motivated anew with each successive test in the battery. A given type of question, such as opposites, recurs a number of times without others intervening. This removes some of the novelty which other tests continue to present throughout. Conceivably this may further reduce interest and motivation. When many children work with poor effort resulting age norms will be too low which in turn gives too high mental ages thereafter for those who work with good effort. This could account for the abnormally high variability in IQ's that he finds when they are computed in the usual way.

One is somewhat surprised at Alpha, which, though offered as a measure of general mental ability, consists, as a "nonverbal" test, entirely of recognition of similarities. Given as a "verbal" test it is almost equally limited in this respect.

The ages for which norms are given include a much larger range than the ages that are normal for the grades to which the tests were given to get norms. This makes the accuracy of these norms somewhat doubtful at both the lower and upper ends for each battery. All norm data were apparently obtained from volunteer contributions from schools using the tests, and are to be verified in the same manner. Nothing is said about the mental testers who gave the tests.

The need of arbitrarily allowing two months in mental age for every one point in raw score after age thirteen in Beta—instead of using the age norms unchanged—in order to keep the variability in IQ's down to what was found on a Binet scale suggests error elsewhere in the scale. Further, when raw scores exceed 70 they are increased by one to ten points to make the "IQ's more constant for a given individual than ordinary IQ's." For all three batteries the "IQ's" are not quotients, but are obtained by subtracting a child's raw score deviation from the age norm from 100, if the score is below the age norm, and adding this deviation to 100, if the raw score is above the age norm. The resulting measure may be as useful as true IQ's but it is unfortunate that the author suggests applying the term "IQ" to it. There is much arbitrary procedure in computing it. The difference is often considerable.

An attempt was apparently made to arrange the test questions in each battery in order of difficulty. This is a vital matter for any battery or scale, and some statistical evidence that this has been achieved should have been given. Without it one is not assured that the battery does not give results similar to what a Binet scale would give if it had a dozen or more tests for one age group, and only one or two for some other age group.

The reviewer has long contended that the range of abilities found in school children from grades 1 to 12 cannot be adequately measured by as few as three or four batteries that are brief enough for practical administrative purposes. When attempted, either the range of difficulty of test items is smaller than the existing range of abilities to be measured, or the number of test items is so small as to give a poor sampling of abilities at different levels, or there may be a compromise between these two faults. The Otis batteries represent such a compromise, but on the whole with more leaning toward small number of items than toward restricted range in difficulty of items.

Occupational Psychol 13:159 Ap '39. The intelligence tests of Dr. Otis are undoubtedly popular. * Scoring is an easy matter and can be accomplished with astonishing rapidity. We feel, however, that ease and rapidity are to some extent gained at the expense of the testee, who is, at any rate in the Beta and Gamma tests, asked to record his replies and manipulate his booklet in a rather involved fashion. Further, we are not convinced that all the items included in the tests are reasonable ones for intelligence, or "mental ability," tests. The norms quoted in the manuals of directions are for American children.

For reviews by Psyche Cattell and Rudolf Pintner, see 1053.

[1414]

Passalong Test: A Performance Test of Intelligence. Ages 8 and over; 1932-37; individual; 1 form; suitable for hearing and deaf cases; 21s. per box of blocks, cards, and manual; 1s. 6d. per set of cards; 1s. per manual; (10-15) minutes; W. P. Alexander; London: University of London Press, Ltd.

REFERENCES

1 ALEXANDER, W. P. "A New Performance Test of Intelligence." *Brit J Psychol* 23:52-63 Jl '32.
2 ALEXANDER, WILLIAM PICKEN. *Intelligence, Concrete and Abstract*: A Study of Differential Traits. British Journal of Psychology Monograph Supplements, Vol. 6, No. 19. London: Cambridge University Press, 1935. Pp. x, 177. 12s. 6d. Paper.
3 EARL, C. J. C. "The Performance Test Behaviour of Adult Morons." *Brit J Med Psychol* 17:78-92 pt 1 '37.
4 VERNON, P. E. "A Study of the Norms and the Validity of Certain Mental Tests at a Child Guidance Clinic." *Brit J Ed Psychol* 7:115-37 Je '37.
5 FOWLER, H. L. "Report on Psychological Tests on Natives in the North-West of Western Australia." *Australian J Sc* 2:124-7 Ap '40.

James Drever, Professor of Psychology University of Edinburgh. This is a very interesting test, and, for general purposes, probably one of the best of the available performance tests. Its chief defect arises from the fact that the grading of difficulty is by no means uniform. The step between Test 3 and Test 4 is a very considerable one as compared with the step from 1 to 2 or from 2 to 3. The step between Tests 4 and 5 is approximately of the same difficulty as is the step from 5 to 6 and possibly that from 6 to 7. Again, however, we come to a more difficult step still between 7 and 8, a step which, if intelligently taken, makes that from 8 to 9 too easy. At the same time it must be freely admitted that Alexander deserves the greatest credit for his attempt at grading a test of this kind.

Like most performance tests trial and error with chance success may obtain an unmerited high score, but the *Passalong Test* is superior to most performance tests in this regard. As one of a battery of performance tests, with, say Kohs' *Block-Design Test*, Healy's *Pictorial Completion Test II*, and the *Cube Construction Test*—the *Passalong Test* merits further attention.

T. J. Keating, Research Fellow, The Training School at Vineland, New Jersey. This test consumes little time but appears to give fairly satisfactory results. It is quickly set up and quickly scored, the scoring being based on timing. A reasonable time is allowed the examiner for making qualitative observations. In this respect the test is superior to many others in the performance category, especially those requiring counting of moves.

The test is so designed that the goal set is easily comprehended by the subject, which makes it useful, for example, for testing the deaf. It has intrinsic appeal to subjects and is thus practically self-motivating. It could readily be adapted for blind subjects.

The scoring might be too liberal. A study of the results with 16 to 34 mentally deficient subjects showed that, in these cases at least, the median test age of the group on the *Passalong Test* was at least a year above the median test ages obtained on the 1916 *Stanford-Binet*, the *Vineland Social Maturity Scale* and the *Porteus Maze Test*. Further work with the test may explain this discrepancy, which is superficially explained by the known relative superiority of mentally deficient subjects on performance tests. The inclusion in the test manual of the scores obtained by the standardization group, arranged by age levels, would make possible comparative studies. The test seems too useful to be discarded without further study because of the supposed weakness of unduly generous norms. There are no data available on the practice effect of the test but it is felt on the basis of inspection of a few cases that this is not great.

Preliminary indications from a small number (16 to 34) of mentally deficient subjects

suggests that the *Passalong Test* correlates low with the *Stanford-Binet* ($r = .21$), a point perhaps in its favor as a nonverbal test; moderately well with the nonverbal *Porteus Maze Test* ($r = .61$), and intermediately ($r = .47$) with the *Vineland Social Maturity Scale*.

Grace H. Kent, Psychologist, Danvers State Hospital, Hathorne, Massachusetts. This test is based upon a mechanical puzzle commonly known as a toy, developed here into a nine-task graded series. For each task a small tray holds several rectangular blocks of the sizes: 1×1 inch, 1×2 inches, or 2×2 inches; with an area of at least one square inch left open to permit the blocks to be moved in the tray without being lifted from it. Two opposite edges of the tray are painted red and blue, respectively; and the tray is invariably presented with blue blocks at the red edge and red blocks at the blue edge. The task is to slide each block to the edge of its own color, arranging the blocks according to a painted pattern which is kept before the subject.

Four trays of different sizes serve for the nine tasks, and the setup for each task can be prepared in a few seconds during the examination. The entire outfit is sufficiently compact to be carried in a briefcase and taken to the traveling clinic.

The test is one of absorbing interest, one which usually commands the spontaneous cooperation of the subject. For this reason it affords the examiner an unusual opportunity for observation. The task holds the subject's attention so completely that he is hardly aware of being observed.

The presentation is needlessly time-consuming, because the performance is to be continued until there have been two consecutive failures. Two nonconsecutive failures might safely be accepted as evidence that the subject has reached his limit, and a first failure on Task 8 might be accepted as final. A little time might be saved also by using Task 1 for demonstration only instead of for credit, the subject being permitted to perform it for practice.

The reviewer has not seen anyone solve Task 9 within the time limit. The interval between 8 and 9 is wider than between any other adjacent tasks, and yet these two tasks differ only in the arrangement of certain blocks. The first step in the solution of 9 is to change its setup to that of 8; but it more often happens that the subject changes the setup of 8 to that of 9, thereby destroying all likelihood of success. These two tasks are more tricky than is desirable in a test intended to measure "intelligence"; but the test could hardly have been made discriminative at the upper levels without involving some play of chance. The actual interference is slight, because failure by chance is more common than success by chance. Accidental failure is an accident which cannot easily happen to a subject who has grasped the principles of the test.

Evaluation is wholly in terms of speed, and some important factors are left unrecorded. The test could not be scored accurately by move-count, but it is worth while at least to record a subject's tendency to keep repeating a course of procedure which has already been proven fruitless.

The scoring system is notably weak as compared with the test itself. The weighting at the upper end is entirely inadequate, while at the lower end full credit is allowed for a one-minute performance of tasks requiring only a few seconds. The subject who scores one point on Task 8 is usually credited with five points each on the Tasks 3 to 7; but the single point which he achieves on the difficult task is more significant than the 25 points he has earned by rapid performance of the five easy tasks.

One who is dissatisfied with the scoring system is of course dissatisfied also with the norms; but even if there were no norms at all, the reviewer would eagerly adopt this test as an attractive and very valuable unit of a performance test battery.

For a review by J. M. Blackburn of the Alexander Performance Scale *which includes the* Passalong Test, *see 1376.*

[1415]

Personnel Test. Adults in business and industrial situations; 1939; an adaptation of the *Otis Self-Administering Tests of Mental Ability*: Higher Form by Arthur S. Otis; 3 forms; $5 per 100; 75¢ per specimen set; sale is restricted to technically qualified personnel workers in business and industry; 12(20) minutes; E. F. Wonderlic; Chicago, Ill.: the Author, 919 North Michigan Avenue.

REFERENCES

1 HOVLAND, CARL IVER, AND WONDERLIC, E. F. "A Critical Analysis of the Otis Self-Administering Test of Mental Ability —Higher Form." *J Appl Psychol* 23:367-87 Je '39.
2 WONDERLIC, E. F., AND HOVLAND, CARL IVER. "The Personnel Test: A Restandardized Abridgment of the Otis S-A Test for Business and Industrial Use." *J Appl Psychol* 23:685-702 D '39.

[1416]

Pintner General Ability Tests: Verbal Series. Grades kdgt.-2, 5-8, 9-12; 1923-39; 2 forms, 3 levels;

$1.25 per 25; Yonkers, N. Y.: World Book Co. (London: George G. Harrap & Co., Ltd.)
a) PINTNER-CUNNINGHAM PRIMARY TEST. Grades kdgt.-2; 1923-39; 15¢ per specimen set; (25) minutes; Rudolf Pintner, Bess V. Cunningham, and Walter N. Durost.
b) PINTNER INTERMEDIATE TEST. Grades 5-8; 1931-39; a revision of the *Pintner Intelligence Test* published in 1931 by the Bureau of Publications, Teachers College, Columbia University; 20¢ per manual; 20¢ per specimen set; 45(55) minutes; Rudolf Pintner.
c) PINTNER ADVANCED TEST. Grades 9-12; 1938-39; 20¢ per manual; 20¢ per specimen set; 55(65) minutes; Rudolf Pintner.

REFERENCES

1 KIRKPATRICK, FORREST H., AND RUPP, ROBERT A. "The Pintner Test at the College Level." *J Ed Res* 33:357-9 Ja '40.

Am J Psychol 53:477-8 Jl '40. Roger M. Bellows. * Form A of the Primary Test is like the original Pintner-Cunningham Primary Mental Test except that the pictures have been redrawn and new items have been substituted for dated ones. * A well prepared manual of 16 pages for the Intermediate and Advanced Tests gives a description of the series, a brief but unusually adequate statement of the requirements of a good test, characteristics of statistical data and standardization of the series, and suggestions for interpretation and use of the tests. * Directions for administering and scoring which have been carefully edited are given in a separate manual. Sampling procedures as well as number of cases used in establishing the norms (the total is above 100,000 Ss) would seem to be satisfactory. Every child in the public schools in the appropriate grades of the coöperating communities took the test, and the authors believe they have eliminated Sampling errors which might arise from intracommunity selection. Communities were chosen which were widely different in size, socio-economic status, and geographic location. * Reliabilities for the total tests are high enough for group comparison but test performance must of course be interpreted with great caution when the purpose is individual diagnosis or orientation. * Reported statistical validity of the tests is very high. The Intermediate Test correlates 0.84 with total scores on the Metropolitan Achievement Tests for 168 cases in grade 5, and 0.79 for 209 cases in grade 7. Coefficients between the Pintner General Ability Tests and seven other psychological tests range from 0.71 for the Revised Stanford Binet to 0.87 for the Otis Group Intelligence Scale. The reviewer was favorably impressed, not only by the care used in the development of the tests, their elaborate standardization, and their detailed evaluation *before* publication, but also by the clear and conservative presentation of interpretative material in the manual. Repetition of such statements as the following quotation from the manual will do much to aid test users in general to appreciate limitations of adequate instruments of measurement—"success or failure must be interpreted in terms of variety of additional facts concerning the child."

Ed Res B 18:117-8 Ap '39. J. Wayne Wrightstone. * These tests follow the generally accepted ideas of exercises which should constitute a test of academic aptitude. Apparently no factor analysis of the components of academic aptitude, such as that proposed by Thurstone, has been applied to these tests. No correlations of these tests with other tests of academic aptitude or tests of academic achievement are supplied. * Inadequate data are provided in the Manual about the reliability and the validity of these tests, but it may be presumed that in both of these aspects, the tests are as good as most currently available tests of "verbal intelligence." Another inadequacy is the lack of explanation of the derivation and meaning of the so-called "standard scores" which are provided. Until psychological research has revealed more convincing evidence about the components of academic aptitude, the *Pintner General Ability Tests* may be recommended for use in schools. The apparent care in construction is noteworthy.

Ed Res B 19:60 Ja 17 '40. J. Wayne Wrightstone. [Review of the *Pintner-Cunningham Primary Test.*] The revision . . . has not included any radical departures from its previous edition. * The reliability coefficients of this test are high, approximating .88 in each grade for which it is designed to be used. An innovation in terms of scores is a standard-score scale which has been established for the series of batteries of the Pintner General Ability Test. This test in its previous form has been widely used in the primary grades to provide an index of academic aptitude and probably will continue to be used widely until other and better tests are constructed to replace it. Its main value is that it does provide an index of a primary-grade child's ability to deal with abstract symbols which correlate with ability to do verbal and number work efficiently in the early school grades.

[1417]

Progressive Matrices: A Perceptual Test of Intelligence. Mental ages 3 and over; 1938; individual; 1 form, 3 editions (this entry refers only to the published booklet edition; for information about the Board Form and the Portfolio Form *see* the article "Matrix Tests" [8]); 10s. 6d. per testing outfit; 3s. per 100 record forms; nontimed (20-60) minutes; prepared for the Research Department, Royal Eastern Counties' Institution, Colchester, England; J. C. Raven; London: H. K. Lewis & Co., Ltd.

REFERENCES

1 PENROSE, L. S., AND RAVEN, J. C. "A New Series of Perceptual Tests: Preliminary Communication." *Brit J Med Psychol* 16:97-104 pt 2 '36.
2 SPEARMAN, CH. E. "Measurement of Intelligence." *Scientia* 64:75-82 Ag '38.
3 DAVIDSON, MARSH. "Studies in the Application of Mental Tests to Psychotic Patients." *Brit J Med Psychol* 18:44-52 pt 1 '39.
4 MILLER, F. M., AND RAVEN, J. C. "The Influence of Positional Factors on the Choice of Answers to Perceptual Intelligence Tests." *Brit J Med Psychol* 18:35-9 pt 1 '39.
5 RAVEN, J. C. "The R.E.C.I. Series of Perceptual Tests: An Experimental Survey." *Brit J Med Psychol* 18:16-34 pt 1 '39.
6 RAVEN, J. C., AND WAITE, A. "Experiments on Physically and Mentally Defective Children with Perceptual Tests." *Brit J Med Psychol* 18:40-3 pt 1 '39.
7 SPEARMAN, C. " 'Intelligence' Tests." *Eug R* 30:249-54 Ja '39.
8 RAVEN, JOHN C. "Matrix Tests." *Mental Health* 1:10-8 Ja '40.

T. J. Keating, Research Fellow, The Training School at Vineland, New Jersey. The *Progressive Matrices*, a series of perceptual tests, qualifies as a desirable instrument in these practical respects: equipment is simple—only the booklet of matrices and a scoring sheet are needed; administration and scoring are easy; self-administration is possible; applicability is extended to deaf, aphasic, and foreign subjects; and readministration affects results but slightly.

Its useful range is limited to years nine to thirteen inclusive. (A formboard variation of the test is available for younger subjects.) The norms at year fourteen are less reliable than others, according to the authors. As an individual test it is time-consuming, especially with brighter subjects. If, however, an examiner's time needs to be spared, the subject may work alone. For subjects who appear to be perturbed by the presence of an examiner, working alone may be advantageous. No item analysis has been attempted, but it is apparent that Item E-8 is unsatisfactory.

[1418]

Psychological Examination, Form D—1939 Edition. Grades 12-13; 1935-39; 1 form (Form D replaces the five earlier editions); machine scorable; 50(60) minutes; Intelligence Test Committee of the Teachers College Personnel Association; Normal, Ill.: the Association, c/o C. F. Malmberg.

REFERENCES

Same as for 1280.

Howard Easley, Assistant Professor of Educational Psychology, Duke University. [Review of Form D.] Form D of this examination is the 1939 edition, Forms A, B, and C having appeared in 1934, 1935, and 1938. The major changes in the 1939 edition are the omission of the completion test, the addition of some number-series items, changing the form of the examination from the subtest type to the omnibus type, and, new since 1937, provision for machine scoring.

This test is prepared especially for use in teachers colleges, but, according to the manual "may be used alone for all purposes common to intelligence tests." The test material reveals, as one might expect, no selection with the view to its peculiar usefulness to teachers colleges. The norms (percentile ranks on Forms B and C) are based entirely on scores from teachers college freshmen. We may expect this test to do a better job of ranking students according to the abilities of teachers college students in general, no better job of ranking them among students of a given institution, and a poorer job of ranking them among college students in general, than is done by other college entrance psychological examinations with norms based on a wider selection of college students.

D. A. Worcester, Chairman of the Department of Educational Psychology and Measurements, The University of Nebraska. This is a fourth form of a psychological examination which has been prepared by a committee of the Teachers College Personnel Association.

The committee explains in detail the statistical procedures by which the items have been validated and presents reliable coefficients (which run from .720 to .920 for the various tests) for previous forms of the test. The committee presents evidence of the discriminative value of the test, and it can undoubtedly be used with confidence.

The content of the test is from six conventional fields, namely: vocabulary, number series, same-opposite, arithmetic reasoning, completion, and analogies. In justification of these fields the somewhat naive statement is made: "We recognize the fact that in recent studies arithmetic reasoning and number completion tests have not been found particularly valuable for predicting academic success. Language and number, however, are the two fundamental social arts that all must acquire. It

was felt, therefore, that an intelligence test should include both these elements."

There are some who might argue that tests used more generally would offer a desirable possibility of comparison of students in teacher-training institutions with those in other colleges and universities. Whereas the content of this test does not show any observable internal evidence of being peculiar to the experience of those who are preparing to teach, it would perhaps be better to secure norms from non-teacher-training students and to use it more generally.

The reviewer has one serious question concerning the test. The instructions, including the sample exercises, are somewhat long and complicated, occupying about one and one-third pages. The time spent in familiarizing oneself with these instructions and practice exercises is included in the fifty-five minutes of working time allowed for the test. This would appear to be a significant advantage to the student who has had earlier experience with tests of this kind. There are two blank pages in the booklet, and it would seem desirable to have the instructions and sample exercises presented separately and then to have a uniform working time on the test proper.

Instead of giving zero scores to tests apparently marked according to some different plan, as is recommended, the booklet should be thrown out and the student treated as "not tested." The manual of instructions and the instructions in the test booklet need more careful editing.

For a review by John C. Flanagan, see 1054.

[1419]

Revised Beta Examination. Grades 3 and over; 1931-35; 1 form; $7 per 100; 25¢ per specimen set; (40-75) minutes; C. E. Kellogg assisted by N. W. Morton; New York: Psychological Corporation.

REFERENCES

1 YOAKUM, CLARENCE S., AND YERKES, ROBERT M., EDITORS. *Army Mental Tests,* pp. 79-92, 276-84, and passim. New York: Henry Holt and Co., 1920. Pp. xiii, 303. Out of print.
2 YERKES, ROBERT M., EDITOR. *Psychological Examining in the United States Army,* pp. 162-7, 235-58, 368-95, 466-8, and passim. Memoirs of the National Academy of Sciences, Vol. 15. Washington, D. C.: Government Printing Office, 1921. Pp. vi, 890. Out of print.
3 KELLOGG, C. E., AND MORTON, N. W. "Revised Beta Examination." *Personnel J* 13:94-100 Ag '34.
4 HORTON, SAMUEL P. *Relationships Among Nineteen Group Tests and Their Validity for Freshman Engineering Marks.* Human Engineering Laboratory, Technical Report, No. 46. Boston, Mass.: the Laboratory, 1939. Pp. viii, 141. $1.00. Paper, mimeographed.

S. D. Porteus, Director of the Psychological Clinic and Professor of Clinical Psychology, University of Hawaii. Of the tests that were either devised or assembled by the committee that worked on the Army examinations, the most unsatisfactory effort was, in the writer's opinion, the *Beta Performance Scale*. There was a hopeful assumption that it could serve as a substitute for *Army Alpha*, but this, in a clinical sense, it was not. I doubt very much if we can ever substitute a nonverbal for a verbal test, any more than we can substitute a musical test for one in mathematics. For the illiterate, the *Army Beta* provided a most inadequate appraisal of abilities.

One of the chief reasons for this lay in the choice of tests which put a premium on memory of one kind or another. In the revised Beta this choice of tests has been improved so that there is not the same emphasis on immediate memory for unrelated material. The scale, however, still suffers because some of its individual tests are limited to material that can be readily applied to groups.

Test 1, a form of maze test, was copied from the writer's earlier individual maze test, but the imitation was no flattery. The Beta form is scored on accuracy—with a time limit—which damns it completely as a measure of planning capacity, the only feature which, in my opinion, makes a maze test worth using. Obviously, speed can only be attained by sacrificing the time that should be taken for planning and preconsideration. In the second place, using the test as a group test robs the examiner of any opportunity to watch the subject at work and thus observe the characteristics that make for nonsuccess.

Test 2 is a substitution test which examines the subject's ability to make purely arbitrary associations between two sets of symbols such as digits and letter-like forms. The capacity tested would be valuable in code-writing or possibly to a mild degree in learning the vocabulary of a foreign language. I cannot see, however, that it has any particular function in our everyday thinking or behavior. In other words, it is a good test of an unimportant ability.

The third test is one in which the subject marks the faulty item in pictures arranged in series of fours. It was this test which, it must be confessed, roused the ire of the reviewer. The pictures are so small and ill-drawn as to be almost unintelligible, and in some cases the scoring is ambiguous. The first picture in Item 9 could be anything from a baby in a bath to a castle on a sea of vegetation. A picture in Item 11 shows a man using an axe to split wood, with his foot in such a position that there is grave danger that it will be badly cut—yet that is not, according to the key, the faulty item. The next picture shows a man pulling on a rope over a pulley that hangs unattached in the air—yet that, too, in the artist's conception, is correct! Item 13 has nothing wrong with it, although it shows a balance held down with a smaller weight—which, of course, often happens when heavy material is balanced against lighter. Items 18 and 19 are so unintelligible that they might qualify as tests of imagination, but of nothing else. Anything, apparently, will do for a mental test!

Test 4 is one of the well-known mental formboards—ingenious enough, but like Test 2, examining a capacity that seems of little importance. The next test is a rather simple missing-feature test, which seems to be overweighted in the scoring. Test 6 resolves itself into a visual rote memory test.

The best feature of the *Revised Beta Examination* is the opportunity that is given for fore-exercise. On the whole, the reviewer doubts the value of an attempt, no matter how painstaking, to revive a justly discarded performance scale such as the Beta.

David Wechsler, Chief Psychologist, Psychiatric Division, Bellevue Hospital, New York, New York. The test offered by the authors may be best described as a modification rather than a revision of the *Army Beta*. Of the seven tests originally constituting the *Army Beta* only Test 1 (Maze) is retained unaltered. Test 2 (Cube Analysis) and Test 3 (X-O Series) have been entirely omitted. Test 4 (Digit-Symbol) has been altered so that the subject writes the numbers instead of symbols. Test 5 (Number Checking) has been expanded to include pictures and symbols as well as numbers. Test 6 (Pictorial Completion) and 7 (Geometrical Construction) are kept in substantially the original form but have been lengthened. For the two tests omitted, the authors have substituted a new one (Picture Discrimination Test), so that the entire examination consists of six instead of seven tests. On the whole the modification of the examination seems to be an improvement on the old Beta. The Cube Counting and X-O series were the poorest of the original Beta examination.

The added new test, however, does not seem to be a very happy choice. The pictures are too miniscule and decidedly hard on the eyes. It also appears to be one of the tests that is still hard to get across in spite of the preliminary practice exercises.

The chief feature and most noteworthy contribution of the Kellogg-Morton revision is the elimination of the pantomime method of presentation and its replacement by the practice exercise. The pantomime method of presentation was laborious and costly, requiring an elaborate and expensive blackboard setup. It had the advantage of enabling the examiner to test the totally deaf as well as individuals who did not understand English at all. This advantage is largely lost by the revision, but is more than made up by the test's new features.

The revised Beta was standardized on Canadian children, ages 7 to 18 and grades 3 through 11. Mental age score equivalents and grade norms are available. Although standardized on Canadian children the norms appear applicable to corresponding American age groups. Thus, Morris Krugman of the Bureau of Child Guidance of the Board of Education of the City of New York informed the reviewer that data obtained from New York City school children furnished norms which do not deviate markedly from those furnished by the author. The test shows good reliability (.987) as measured by inter-test correlations (odd versus even items). The retest *r*, however, is relatively low showing only an *r* of .77 between first and second administrations of the test. The main shortcoming of the revision is its continued omission of any attempt to weight the different tests. Thus Test 1 (Maze) which is one of the best, contributes a possible maximum score of only 10 as against the possible maximum of 25 on the number-checking test which, in the reviewer's opinion, is one of the poorest tests of general intelligence. There is also the fact that while the author furnishes mental age equivalents for test scores, no distribution of MA's at different age levels is given. The result is that one is again confronted with a problem as to how to interpret IQ's obtained by dividing an MA by a CA for classification purposes. In this respect, however, the revised Beta sins no more than most other tests on the market.

In spite of certain merits the revised Beta lends itself to only limited application. Unlike the original Beta it does not seem to have been devised merely for the speedy testing of large groups of illiterates. Knowing the avidity of many clinicians for new instruments, one suspects that it may be used as a paper-and-pencil performance type of test as a substitute and shortcut for the Pintner-Paterson, the Grace Arthur, or similar scales. It is important therefore to point out that it cannot be so used. Except for Test 1, the revised Beta contains no test which can be classified as performance. Most of the remaining tests involve functions which measure very much the same things that verbal tests do except that the raw data furnished the subject is given in pictures and symbols and not in words. That this is so, is attested, for example, by the fact that the highest correlation furnished by the revised Beta was that obtained between it and the time and error scores of the Thurstone's *Examination in Clerical Work* (.81).

[1420]

Revised Stanford-Binet Scale. Ages 2 and over; 1937; a revision of the Stanford-Binet Scale published in 1916; 2 forms (Forms L and M) ; $2 (7s. 6d.) per 25 record booklets ; 60¢ (3s. 6d.) per record form; $1.75 (4s. 6d.) per set of printed card material for each form; $8 (45s.) per testing outfit for each form; $2.25 (10s. 6d.) per copy of the manual ; [99] $1.35 per abbreviated directions for administering ; [98] Lewis M. Terman and Maud A. Merrill; Boston, Mass.: Houghton Mifflin Co. (London: George G. Harrap & Co., Ltd.)

REFERENCES

[1] TERMAN, LEWIS M., AND CHILDS, H. G. "A Tentative Revision and Extension of the Binet-Simon Measuring Scale of Intelligence." *J Ed Psychol* 3:61-74, 133-43, 198-208, 277-89 F, Mr, Ap, My, '12.
[2] TERMAN, LEWIS M. "Suggestions for Revising, Extending and Supplementing the Binet Intelligence Tests." *J Psycho-Asthenics* 18:20-33 S '13.
[3] TERMAN, LEWIS M. *The Measurement of Intelligence*: An Explanation of and a Complete Guide for the Use of the Stanford Revision and Extension of *The Binet-Simon Intelligence Scale*. Boston, Mass.: Houghton Mifflin Co., 1916. Pp. xix, 362. $2.00. (London: George G. Harrap & Co., Ltd. 8s. 6d.)
[4] TERMAN, LEWIS M.; LYMAN, GRACE; ORDAHL, GEORGE; ORDAHL, LOUISE ELLISON; GALBREATH, NEVA; AND TALBERT, WILFORD; ASSISTED BY HERBERT E. KNOLLIN, J. H. WILLIAMS, H. G. CHILDS, HELEN TROST, RICHARD ZEIDLER, CHARLES WADDLE, AND IRENE CUNEO. *The Stanford Revision and Extension of the Binet-Simon Scale for Measuring Intelligence*. Educational Psychology Monographs, No. 18. Baltimore, Md.: Warwick & York, Inc., 1917. Pp. v, 179. $2.58.
[5] CUNEO, IRENE, AND TERMAN, LEWIS M. "Stanford-Binet Tests of 112 Kindergarten Children and 77 Repeated Tests." *J Genetic Psychol* 25:414-28 D '18.
[6] TERMAN, LEWIS M. "The Vocabulary Test as a Measure of Intelligence." *J Ed Psychol* 9:452-66 O '18.
[7] SKAGGS, E. B. "A Comparison of Results Obtained by the Terman Binet Tests and the Healy Picture Completion Test." *J Ed Psychol* 11:418-20a O '20.
[8] TERMAN, L. M. *Condensed Guide for the Stanford Revision of the Binet-Simon Intelligence Test*. Boston, Mass.: Houghton Mifflin Co., 1920. Pp. 32. $1.00. (London: George G. Harrap & Co., Ltd. 4s. 6d.)
[9] BURT, CYRIL. *Mental and Scholastic Tests*, pp. 68-72. London: P. S. King and Son, Ltd., 1921. Pp. xv, 432. 18s.
[10] ODELL, C. W. "A Few Data on the Use of the Stanford Revision of the Binet-Simon Tests by Halves." *J Ed Res* 4:437-8 D '21.
[11] RUGG, HAROLD, AND COLLOTON, CECILE. "Constancy of the Stanford-Binet I.Q. as Shown by Retests." *J Ed Psychol* 12:315-22 S '21.

12 YERKES, ROBERT M. EDITOR. *Psychological Examining in the United States Army*, pp. 172-82, 271-4, 397-9, 407-11, and passim. Memoirs of the National Academy of Sciences, Vol. 15. Washington, D. C.: Government Printing Office, 1921. Pp. vi, 890. Out of print.

13 BALDWIN, BIRD T., AND STECHER, LORLE I. "Additional Data from Consecutive Stanford-Binet Tests." *J Ed Psychol* 13:556-60 D '22.

14 GARRISON, S. C. "Additional Retests by Means of the Stanford Revision of the Binet-Simon Tests." *J Ed Psychol* 13:307-12 My '22.

15 GORDON, KATE. "Some Retests with the Stanford-Binet Scale." *J Ed Psychol* 13:363-5 S '22.

16 JEWETT, STEPHEN PERHAM, AND BLANCHARD, PHYLLIS. "Influence of Affective Disturbances on Responses to the Stanford Binet Test." *Mental Hyg* 6:39-56 Ja '22.

17 MORGENTHAU, DOROTHY RUTH. *Some Well-Known Mental Tests Evaluated and Compared.* Columbia University, Archives of Psychology, No. 52. New York: the University, 1922. Pp. 54. Paper. Out of print.

18 RICHARDSON, C. A. "Note on a Method of Estimating the True Stanford-Binet Intelligence Quotients of Adults." *Brit J Psychol* 12:383-4 Ap '22.

19 STENQUIST, JOHN L. "Constancy of the Stanford Binet-IQ as Shown by Retests." *J Ed Psychol* 13:54-6 Ja '22.

20 CORNELL, ETHEL L., AND LOWDEN, GLADYS L. "A Comparison of the Stanford and Porteus Tests in Several Types of Social Inadequacy." *J Abn and Social Psychol* 18:33-42 Ap-Je '23.

21 KENT, GRACE H. "A Combination Mental Test for Clinical Use." *J Appl Psychol* 7:246-57 S '23.

22 SYMONDS, PERCIVAL M. "A Second Approximation to the Curve of the Distribution of Intelligence of the Population of the United States, with a Note on the Standardization of the Stanford Revision of the Binet-Simon Scale." *J Ed Psychol* 14:65-81 F '23.

23 AVERY, GEORGE T. "Comparison of Stanford and Herring Binet Revisions Given to First Grade Children." *J Ed Psychol* 15:224-8 Ap '24.

24 HERRING, JOHN P. "Avery's Comparison of the Stanford and Herring Revisions." *J Ed Psychol* 15:383-8 S '24.

25 HERRING, JOHN P. "Reliability of the Stanford and the Herring Revision of the Binet-Simon Tests." *J Ed Psychol* 15:217-23 Ap '24.

26 MADSEN, I. N. "Some Results with the Stanford Revision of the Binet-Simon Tests." *Sch and Soc* 19:559-62 My 10 '24.

27 WALTERS, FRED C. "Language Handicap and the Stanford Revision of the Binet-Simon Tests." *J Ed Psychol* 15:276-84 My '24.

28 WILNER, CHARLES F. "A Comparative Study of the Stanford and the Herring Revisions of the Binet-Simon Tests." *J Ed Psychol* 15:520-9 N '24.

29 PAL, SATYAJIVAN. *The Tests of the Stanford Revision of the Binet-Simon Intelligence Scale*: Adapted for Use with Bengali Boys and Translated into the Bengali Language, with Notes on the Procedure. Foreword by M. West. Dacca University Bulletins, No. 5. Published for Dacca University. Bombay, India: Oxford University Press, 1925. Pp. iv, 55. Rs. 1-8.

30 HILDRETH, GERTRUDE. "Stanford-Binet Retests of 441 School Children." *J Genetic Psychol* 33:365-86 S '26.

31 MAITY, H. "A Report on the Application of the Stanford Adult Tests to a Group of College Students." *Indian J Psychol* 1:214-22 '26.

32 LINCOLN, EDWARD A. "The Reliability of the Stanford-Binet Scale and the Constancy of Intelligence Quotients." *J Ed Psychol* 18:621-6 D '27.

33 RANDALL, FLORENCE B. "A Study on the Constancy of the IQ." *Sch and Soc* 26:311-2 S 3 '27.

34 WALLIN, J. E. W. "A Further Note on Scattering in the Binet Scale." *J Appl Psychol* 11:143-54 Ap '27.

35 WELLS, F. L. *Mental Tests in Clinical Practice*, pp. 32-53. Yonkers, N. Y.: World Book Co., 1927. Pp. x, 315. $2.16.

36 GREENE, EDWARD B. "A Graphic Summary of the Stanford-Binet Test." *J Appl Psychol* 12:343-7 Je '28.

37 THOMPSON, E. M. "The Stanford Revision Vocabulary Test." *South African J Sci* 25:461-3 '28.

38 TOWNSEND, REBECCA R. "Tests of the Stanford Revision of the Binet-Simon Scale Most Frequently Failed by Children in Orthogenic Backward Classes." *Psychol Clinic* 17:200-3 N-D '28.

39 BROOKS, FOWLER D. "The Accuracy of the Abbreviated Stanford-Binet Scale." *Psychol Clinic* 18:17-20 Mr-Ap '29.

40 HAYES, SAMUEL P. "The New Revision of the Binet Intelligence Tests for the Blind." *Teach Forum* 2:2-4 N '29.

41 MARINE, EDITH LUCILE. *The Effect of Familiarity with the Examiner upon Stanford-Binet Performance.* Columbia University, Teachers College, Contributions to Education, No. 381. New York: Bureau of Publications, the College, 1929. Pp. v, 42. $1.50.

42 RILEY, G. "Stanford Binet 'Indicators' of Mechanical Ability." *Psychol Clinic* 18:128-32 My-Je '29.

43 THURSTONE, L. L., AND ACKERSON, LUTON. "The Mental Growth Curve for the Binet Tests." *J Ed Psychol* 20:569-83 N '29.

44 WALLIN, J. E. WALLACE. *A Statistical Study of the Individual Tests in Ages VIII and IX in the Stanford-Binet Scale.* Mental Measurements Monographs, No. 6. Baltimore,

Md.: Williams & Wilkins Co., June 1929. Pp. vii, 58. $1.00. Paper.

45 SCHOTT, EMMETT L. "Variability of Mental Ratings in Retests of Neuropsychiatric Cases." *Am J Psychiatry* 87:213-27 S '30.

46 SULLIVAN, ELIZABETH T. "The Mental Development of Thirty-Three Ten Year Old Children." *J Juvenile Res* 14:27-33 Ja '30.

47 WILSON, CHARLES A.; SWEENY, MARY E.; STUTSMAN, RACHEL; CHESIRE, LEONE E.; AND HATT, ELISE. *The Merrill-Palmer Standards of Physical and Mental Growth.* Detroit, Mich.: Merrill-Palmer School, 1930. Pp. ix, 121. $0.50. Paper.

48 CATTELL, PSYCHE. "Constant Changes in the Stanford-Binet IQ." *J Ed Psychol* 22:544-50 O '31.

49 GREEN, HELEN J. *Qualitative Method for Scoring the Vocabulary Test of the New Revision of the Stanford-Binet.* Unpublished master's thesis, Stanford University, 1931.

50 JONES, HAROLD ELLIS. *The Pattern of Abilities among Adult and Juvenile Defectives.* University of California Publications in Psychology, Vol. 5, No. 2. Berkeley, Calif.: University of California Press, May 1931. Pp. 47-61. $0.25. Paper.

51 McFADDEN, JOHN HOLMAN. *Differential Responses of Normal and Feebleminded Subjects of Equal Mental Age, on the Kent-Rosanoff Free Association Test and the Stanford Revision of the Binet-Simon Intelligence Test.* Mental Measurement Monographs, No. 7. Baltimore, Md.: Williams & Wilkins Co., February 1931. Pp. 85. $1.50. Paper.

52 DURLING, DOROTHY. "Note on the Comparative Reliability of the Stanford-Binet below the Age of Six." *J Appl Psychol* 16:331-33 Je '32.

53 FEINBERG, HENRY. "The Stanford Revision of the Binet-Simon Tests Compared with the Pintner-Paterson Short Performance Scale." *J Genetic Psychol* 40:486-99 Je '32.

54 JONES, H. E.; CONRAD, H. S.; AND BLANCHARD, M. B. *Environmental Handicap in Mental Test Performance.* University of California Publications in Psychology, Vol. 5, No. 3. Berkeley, Calif.: University of California Press, January 1932. Pp. 63-99. $0.40. Paper.

55 JORDAN, JOHN S. "Reliability of Stanford-Binet Intelligence Quotients Derived by Student Examiners." *J Ed Res* 26:295-301 D '32.

56 MADDEN, RICHARD. "A Note on the Eight and Nine Year Levels of Stanford-Binet." *Sch and Soc* 36:576 O 29 '32.

57 PERKINS, RUTH E. "A Study of the Relation of Brightness to Stanford-Binet Test Performance." *J Appl Psychol* 16:205-16 Ap '32.

58 PHILLIPS, ARTHUR. "An Analytical and Comparative Study of the Binet-Simon Test Responses of 1,306 Philadelphia School Children with an Attempt to Evaluate and Grade the Separate Tests." *Psychol Clinic* 21:1-38 Mr-My '32.

59 SKALET, MAGDA. "A Statistical Study of the Responses of a Group of Normal Children to the Individual Tests in the Stanford-Revision of the Binet-Simon Scale." *Psychol Clinic* 21:183-95 S-N '32.

60 CATTELL, PSYCHE. "Do the Stanford-Binet IQ's of Superior Boys and Girls Tend to Decrease or Increase with Age?" *J Ed Res* 26:668-73. My '33.

61 CHARLES, C. M. "A Comparison of the Intelligence Quotients of Three Different Mental Tests Applied to a Group of Incarcerated Delinquent Boys." *J Appl Psychol* 17:581-4 O '33.

62 LINCOLN, E. A. "Preliminary Report on the Stanford Binet IQ Changes of Superior Children." *J Exp Ed* 1:287-92 Mr '33.

63 LOUDEN, MARY V. "Relative Difficulty of Stanford-Binet Vocabulary for Bright and Dull Subjects of the Same Mental Level." *J Ed Res* 27:179-86 N '33.

64 LOUDEN, MARY V. "Relative Difficulty of Vocabulary Lists in the Stanford-Binet Scale." *J Ed Res* 26:601-7 Ap '33.

65 MOWRER, WILLIE MAE C. "Intelligence Scales for Preschool Children." *Child Development* 4:318-22 D '33.

66 NEMZEK, CLAUDE L. "The Comparative Constancy of Stanford-Binet and Herring-Binet IQ's." *J Appl Psychol* 17:475-7 Ag '33.

67 NEMZEK, CLAUDE L. "The Constancy of the IQ." *Psychol B* 30:143-68 F '33.

68 RHINEHART, JESSE BATLEY. "An Attempt to Predict the Success of Student Nurses by the Use of a Battery of Tests." *J Appl Psychol* 17:277-93 Ap '33.

69 STOKE, STUART M. "The Eight and Nine Year Levels of the Stanford-Binet Scale." *Sch and Soc* 37:459-61 Ap 8 '33.

70 WALLIN, J. E. WALLACE. "Further Data on Stanford-Binet VIII- and IX-Year Tests." *Psychol Clinic* 22:94-100 Je-Ag '33.

71 BURNSIDE, LENOIR H. "A Comparison of the Abbreviated and the Complete Stanford Revision of the Binet-Simon Scale." *Child Development* 5:361-7 D '34.

72 KNIGHT, MAXINE WISLER. "A Comparative Study of the Performance of Feeble-Minded and Juvenile Delinquents on the Arthur Performance Scale and the Stanford-Binet Test of Intelligence." *J Juvenile Res* 18:5-12 Ja '34.

73 MADSEN, I. N. "The Reliability and Validity of the Stanford-Binet Tests when Administered by Student Examiners." *J Ed Res* 28:265-70 D '34.

74 PARKER, H. T. "Fluctuations in the Intelligence Quotients of Subnormal Children." *J Juvenile Res* 16:163-8 Jl '34.

75 SÁNCHEZ, GEORGE I. "The Implications of a Basal Vocabulary to the Measurement of the Abilities of Bilingual Children." *J Social Psychol* 5:395-402 Ag '34.

76 ELWOOD, M. I. "A Statistical Study of Results of the Stanford Revision of the Binet-Simon Scale with a Selected Group of Pittsburgh School Children." *Pittsburgh Sch* 9:116-140 Mr '35.

77 FEINBERG, HENRY. "The Examinee Defines 'Shrewd,' " pp. 549-57. In *Papers of the Michigan Academy of Science, Arts and Letters,* Vol. 20: Containing Papers Submitted at the Annual Meeting in 1934. Edited by Eugene S. McCartney and Alfred H. Stockard. Ann Arbor, Mich.: University of Michigan Press, 1935. Pp. xv, 755. Cloth, $4.00; paper, $2.25.

78 HILDEN, ARNOLD H., AND SKEELS, HAROLD M. "A Comparison of the Stanford-Binet Scale, the Kuhlmann-Anderson Group Test, the Arthur Point Scale of Performance Tests, and the Unit Scales of Attainment." *J Exp Ed* 4:214-30 D '35.

79 LINCOLN, EDWARD A. "The Stanford Binet IQ Changes of Superior Children." *Sch and Soc* 41:519-20 Ap 13 '35.

80 MAYER, BARBARA A. "Negativistic Reactions of Preschool Children on the New Revision of the Stanford-Binet." *J Genetic Psychol* 46:311-34 Je '35.

81 ODEN, MELITA H., AND MAYER, BARBARA A. "A Study of the Effect of Varying the Procedure in the Ball and Field Test." *J Genetic Psychol* 46:335-48 Je '35.

82 ROACH, CORNELIA BELL. "A Discussion of the Six, Seven and Eight Year Levels of the Stanford-Binet Scale." *J Ed Res* 29:216-8 N '35.

83 BRILL, MOSHE. "A Comparison of the Abbreviated and the Complete Stanford Binet Scales." *Sch and Soc* 43:102-4 Ja 18 '36.

84 FEINBERG, HENRY. "The Examinee Defines 'Mellow.' " *J Ed Psychol* 27:179-92 Mr '36.

85 LINCOLN, EDWARD A. "Stanford-Binet IQ Changes in the Harvard Growth Study." *J Appl Psychol* 20:236-42 Ap '36.

86 LOUTTIT, C. M., AND STACKMAN, HARVEY. "The Relationship between Porteus Maze and Binet Test Performance." *J Ed Psychol* 27:18-25 Ja '36.

87 MAHAN, HARRY C., AND WITMER, LOUISE. "A Note on the Stanford-Binet Vocabulary Test." *J Appl Psychol* 20:258-63 Ap '36.

88 PEATMAN, LILLIE BURLING, AND PEATMAN, JOHN GRAY. "The Adequacy of the Shortened, Single-List Vocabulary Test of the Binet-Simon Tests (Terman Revision)." *J Ed Psychol* 27:161-72 Mr '36.

89 ALTMAN, CHARLOTTE HALL, AND SHAKOW, DAVID. "A Comparison of the Performance of Matched Groups of Schizophrenic Patients, Normal Subjects, and Delinquent Subjects on Some Aspects of the Stanford-Binet." *J Ed Psychol* 28:519-29 O '37.

90 CATTELL, PSYCHE. "Stanford-Binet IQ Variations." *Sch and Soc* 45:615-8 My 1 '37.

91 CATTELL, RAYMOND B. "Measurement versus Intuition in Applied Psychology." *Char and Pers* 6:114-31 D '37.

92 DAVIDSON, MARSH. "A Study of Schizophrenic Performance on the Stanford-Binet Scale." *Brit J Med Psychol* 17:93-7 pt 1 '37.

93 HARRIS, ALBERT J., AND SHAKOW, DAVID. "The Clinical Significance of Numerical Measures of Scatter on the Stanford-Binet." *Psychol B* 34:134-50 Mr '37.

94 MACMURRAY, DONALD. "A Comparison of the Intelligence of Gifted Children and of Dull-Normal Children Measured by the Pintner-Paterson Scale, as Against the Stanford-Binet Scale." *J Psychol* 4:273-80 O '37.

95 PIOTROWSKI, ZYGMUNT A. "Objective Signs of Invalidity of Stanford-Binet Tests." *Psychiatric Q* 11:623-36 O '37.

96 ROBERTS, J. A. F., AND GRIFFITHS, R. "Studies on a Child Population: II, Retests on the Advanced Otis and Stanford-Binet Scales, with Notes on the Use of a Shortened Binet Scale." *Ann Eng* 8:15-45 '37.

97 ROTHNEY, J. W. M. "The New Binet—A Caution." *Sch and Soc* 45:855-6 Je 19 '37.

98 TERMAN, LEWIS M., AND MERRILL, MAUD A. *Directions for Administering Forms L and M: Revision of the Stanford-Binet Tests of Intelligence.* Boston, Mass.: Houghton-Mifflin Co., 1937. Pp. v, 116. $1.35. Spiral binding.

99 TERMAN, LEWIS M., AND MERRILL, MAUD A. *Measuring Intelligence: A Guide to the Administration of the New Revised Stanford-Binet Tests of Intelligence.* Boston, Mass.: Houghton Mifflin Co., 1937. Pp. xiv, 461. $2.25. (London: George G. Harrap and Co., Ltd., 1939. 10s. 6d.)

100 VERNON, P. E. "The Stanford-Binet Test as a Psychometric Method." *Char and Pers* 6:99-113 D '37.

101 VERNON, P. E. "A Study of the Norms and the Validity of Certain Mental Tests at a Child Guidance Clinic." *Brit J Ed Psychol* 7:72-88 F '37.

102 BENTON, ARTHUR L. "Performances of School Children on the Revised Stanford-Binet and the Kent E-G-Y-Test." *J Genetic Psychol* 52:395-400 Je '38.

103 BERNREUTER, ROBERT G., AND CARR, EDWARD J. "The Interpretation of IQ's on the *L-M* Stanford-Binet." *J Ed Psychol* 29:312-4 Ap '38.

104 BOND, ELDEN A. "Some Verbal Aspects of the 1937 Revision of the Stanford-Binet Intelligence Test, Form L." *J Exp Ed* 6:340-2 Mr '38.

105 BUHLER, CHARLOTTE. "The Ball and Field Test as a Help in the Diagnosis of Emotional Difficulties." *Char and Pers* 6:257-73 Je '38.

106 HARRIS, ALBERT J., AND SHAKOW, DAVID. "Scatter on the Stanford-Binet in Schizophrenic, Normal, and Delinquent Adults." *J Abn and Social Psychol* 33:100-11 Ja '38.

107 HILDEN, A. H. "Training Kindergarten Teachers to Test

108 LODGE, TOWNSEND. "Variation in Stanford-Binet IQ's of Pre-school Children According to the Months in Which Examinations Were Given." *J Psychol* 6:385-95 O '38.

109 MERRILL, MAUD A. "The Significance of IQ's on the Revised Stanford-Binet Scales." *J Ed Psychol* 29:641-51 D '38.

110 ROBERTS, J. A. F.; NORMAN, R. M.; AND GRIFFITHS, R. "Studies on a Child Population: IV, The Form of the Lower End of the Frequency Distribution of Stanford-Binet Intelligence Quotients and the Fall of Low Intelligence Quotients with Advancing Age." *Ann Eug* 8:319-36 '38.

111 SHAKOW, DAVID, AND GOLDMAN, ROSALINE. "The Effect of Age on the Stanford-Binet Vocabulary Score of Adults." *J Ed Psychol* 29:241-56 Ap '38.

112 ARTHUR, GRACE. "The Agreement of Kuhlmann-Binet and Stanford-Binet Ratings for 200 Cases." *J Appl Psychol* 23:521-4 Ag '39.

113 ATWELL, C. R. "Comparison of Vocabulary Scores on the Stanford-Binet and the Revised Stanford-Binet." *J Ed Psychol* 30:467-9 S '39.

114 BALINSKY, B., ISRAEL, H., AND WECHSLER, D. "The Relative Effectiveness of the Stanford-Binet and the Bellevue Intelligence Scale in Diagnosing Mental Deficiency." *Am J Orthopsychiatry* 9:798-801 O '39.

115 BLACK, IRMA SIMONTON. "The Use of the Stanford-Binet (1937 Revision) in a Group of Nursery School Children." *Child Development* 10:157-71 S '39.

116 BURT, CYRIL. "The Latest Revision of the Binet Intelligence Tests." *Eug R* 30:255-60 Ja '39.

117 DAVIS, FREDERICK B. *Table of Equivalence Values for Intelligence Quotients Derived from the 1916 and 1937 Revisions of the Stanford-Binet Scales.* Avon, Conn.: Avon Old Farms, 1939. Pp. 4. Privately distributed. Paper.

118 ELWOOD, MARY ISABEL. "A Preliminary Note on the Vocabulary Test in the Revised Stanford-Binet Scale, Form L." *J Ed Psychol* 30:632-4 N '39.

119 HARRIMAN, PHILIP LAWRENCE. "Irregularity of Successes on the 1937 Stanford Revision." *J Consulting Psychol* 3:83-85 My-Je '39.

120 HILDRETH, G. "Retests with the New Stanford-Binet Scale." *J Consulting Psychol* 3:49-53 Mr-Ap '39.

121 HILDRETH, GERTRUDE. "Comparison of Early Binet Records with College Aptitude Test Scores." *J Ed Psychol* 30:365-71 My '39.

122 KRUGMAN, MORRIS. "Some Impressions of the Revised Stanford-Binet Scale." *J Ed Psychol* 30:594-603 N '39.

123 MACMEEKEN, A. M. *The Intelligence of a Representative Group of Scottish Children.* Publications of the Scottish Council for Research in Education, [No.] 15. International Examinations Inquiry. London: University of London Press, Ltd., 1939. Pp. xvi, 144. 5s.

124 MANN, CECIL W., AND MANN, HELENE POWNER. "An Analysis of the Results Obtained by Retesting Juvenile Delinquents." *J Psychol* 8:133-41 Jl '39.

125 Scottish Council for Research in Education, Terman Revision Committee, D. KENNEDY-FRASER, CONVENER. *Modifications Proposed for British Use of the Revised Stanford-Binet Tests of Intelligence in Measuring Intelligence* by LEWIS M. TERMAN AND MAUD A. MERRILL published by George G. Harrap & Company, Ltd., 1937. Edinburgh, Scotland: the Council, January 1939. Pp. iv, 16, i, 11. Paper, mimeographed.

126 WRIGHT, RUTH E. "A Factor Analysis of the Original Stanford-Binet Scale." *Psychometrika* 4:209-20 S '39.

127 BERGER, ARTHUR, AND SPEEVACK, MORRIS. "An Analysis of the Range of Testing and Scattering among Retarded Children on Form L of the Revised Stanford Binet." *J Ed Psychol* 31:39-44 Ja '40.

128 BRODY, M. B. "A Note of the Use of the 1937 Revision of the Stanford Binet Vocabulary List in Mental Hospital Patients." *J Mental Sci* 86:532-3 My '40.

129 CARLTON, THEODORE. "Performances of Mental Defectives on the Revised Stanford-Binet, Form L." *J Consulting Psychol* 4:61-5 Mr-Ap '40.

130 HOAKLEY, Z. PAULINE. "A Comparison of the Results of the Stanford and Terman-Merrill Revisions of the Binet." *J Appl Psychol* 24:75-81 F '40.

131 KENDIG, ISABELLE, AND RICHMOND, WINIFRED V. *Psychological Studies in Dementia Praecox,* pp. 10-18, 49-85, and passim. Ann Arbor, Mich.: Edwards Brothers, Inc., 1940. Pp. x, 211. $0.50. Paper, lithotyped.

132 STOTT, M. BOOLE. "The Relation between Intelligence and Proficiency in Binet-Simon Testing." *Brit J Ed Psychol* 10:135-42 Je '40.

133 WALLIN, J. E. WALLACE. "The Results of Multiple Binet Re-Testings of the Same Subjects." *J Exceptional Children* 6:211-22 Mr '40.

134 WERNER, HENRY. "A Comparative Study of a Small Group of Clinical Tests." *J Appl Psychol* 24:231-6 Ap '40.

Their Pupils on the Stanford-Binet Scale." *Sch and Soc* 48:123-4 Jl 23 '38.

Eug R 30:255-60 Ja '39. Cyril Burt. Nearly twenty-five years ago, when the Binet-Simon tests were first coming into vogue, I endeavoured to examine, in two articles in this *Review,* their merits and limitations as a means of measuring innate intelligence. * Terman's new revision is now at length available; and those whose work entails the assessment of intelligence are inquiring whether the new version is, as it claims to be, genuinely superior to the older versions, and whether it has successfully eliminated the defects that had become obvious in the first scale without destroying any of the merits. A large committee, comprising all the leading educational psychologists in Great Britain, together with representatives or members of every body or institution engaged in mental tests, has been set up to work through the wording of the new revision, test by test, and to check the age standardizations on the basis of extensive experiments all over the country. A provisional "translation" (if I may so call it) is now available, and may be obtained from the Psychological Department, University College, London, for private experimental use. Thanks to the prompt co-operation of teachers, psychologists and medical officers, a large mass of data has already come to hand; and it may be of interest to summarize briefly the chief conclusions that emerge from a first preliminary survey of the results. * As regards the chief practical purpose of the scale—the diagnosis of dull and defective children—there seems little question that the new revision is decidedly more efficient than the old. As regards the wording and the age-assignments of the numerous tests that have been retained, the new revision frequently accepts the modifications proposed in the former London version. The principle of "internal grading," too, which was advocated in this Review, has been far more freely used—notably, in the vocabulary test. Many of the problems, however, are entirely new; and here the American age-assignments and even the American wording seem often far from appropriate to English children. * In the revised scale, most of the poorer tests that figured in the original scale (e.g., "Suggestion," "Months," "Age," "Sex," "Surname") have silently been dropped. The newer tests inserted in their place are based on accepted psychological principles; nevertheless those principles have really been derived more from group testing than from individual examinations. An intensive item analysis for each test separately is thus an urgent requisite. Such an investigation, however, will call for a long and patient research. * As I pointed out in my original examination of the scale, its difficulties and defects arise largely from the adoption of the plan of "external" instead of "internal grading." This plan proves convenient for the practical examiner; but makes it far from easy to test the tests themselves. With "internally graded" tests we can arrange the persons tested in order according to their ability in each test, and so correlate the tests with each other or with an independent criterion in the ordinary way. With "externally graded" tests, we can only say whether each person passes or fails, and so at best estimate the correlation between test and intelligence from fourfold tables by a "coefficient of colligation" or the like—never a very satisfactory procedure. * With an externally graded scale, like the Binet-Simon series, everything turns upon the relative difficulty of the test-problems. The standardization of each problem in terms of a mental age assumes that the order of difficulty is constant for the two sexes, for different social classes, for different ages, for different types of child, and above all for different localities. Thus, if a child repeats four numbers backwards, Terman would give him a mental age of 9; if he repeats six numbers forwards, i.e., in the order in which they have been recited to him, he would get a mental age of 10. Now with London children it is found that the latter test is actually easier than the former. And so with many other tests: the order of difficulty is often reversed. Worse still, when we experiment with the scale as a whole, there seems to be no fixed order at all: what is easier for one child may be harder for another. Indeed, the early critics of the scale were constantly pointing out how no two editors of Binet's scale ever agreed over the relative difficulty of the several tests. The orders of difficulty seem to vary with different examiners as well as with different examinees. At the very outset, therefore, in examining the validity of the whole proposal, the task of the psychologist must be to compare these different orders, and see whether they vary so widely as to invalidate the very foundations of the scale. * Now the original Binet scale had a heavy verbal bias; and such a bias is particularly hard upon the mentally defective child, who, as every teacher knows, is better at practical things than he is at reading, writing, spelling, and rational conversation. This defect in Binet's own series has, of course, not escaped

Professor Terman: and, indeed, the chief difference between the former Terman series and the new is that, whereas the former was still overweighted with verbal tests, the new is, if anything, overweighted with practical or manual tests. * the question is this: how much of the total "variance" (i.e., of the variations in performance due to any and every type of cause) is attributable to a single general factor common to all children, and how much is due to specific and irrelevant factors—sex, social opportunity, school teaching, and above all perhaps qualitative difference in mental type? The data that have already been received enable us to give some first provisional answer to this question. * The figures . . . are so far based on but comparatively few cases: but, so far as they go, they indicate that the new scale is appreciably more reliable than the old. But far more numerous data are needed. * the whole diagnostic value of the scale turns on the way we shall ultimately answer this preliminary question: how far is our order of difficulty trustworthy and how far is that order —and consequently our whole scheme of age-assignments—liable to be disturbed by wholly irrelevant conditions? With a little ingenuity we may perhaps turn the defect into a merit, and even ultimately make the scale to do two things at once: measure the child's general intelligence with a rough but reasonable degree of accuracy and at the same time throw side-lights on the kind as well as on the nature and extent of the special abilities or the special defects that he displays.

Psychol Rec 1:409-32 N '37. Grace H. Kent. "Suggestions for the Next Revision of the Binet-Simon Scale." * The new Stanford-Binet scale is of course a much stronger test than the 1916 edition, especially quantitatively. On the qualitative side it should be mentioned with approval that the blood-curdling absurdities of the older edition have given place to statements which are emotionally neutral and yet interesting; also that the memory test has been greatly improved by substituting a single sentence of suitable length for two sentences combined in one task. It is especially with reference to the set-up of the scale that the authors have failed to take advantage of the contributions published since 1916. * The basic construction of the Binet-Simon scales— the age-grade or year-scale method used by Binet and followed by Terman—is needlessly cumbersome and uneconomical as compared with a scoring system in which the responses are evaluated by points. Unconditional acceptance or rejection of a response is unfair to the subject whose response just barely misses being acceptable. * Within the year-scale system, the subject matter of the Stanford-Binet scale is used with unnecessary wastefulness. When a child responds correctly to only three of the five absurdity questions, he of course fails to achieve ten-year credit on that item [referring to the 1916 edition]; but might he not be given nine-year credit for three acceptable responses, and possibly eight-year credit for two responses? * The year-scale method is essentially an uneconomical scoring system for a subject of whatever age, because each examination includes so many items which add nothing to its adequacy. It is strictly required that the examination be carried low enough in the scale to yield six correct responses at a given age-level; and that it be carried high enough to elicit six consecutive failures. Thus there are at least twelve items (some of them multiple items requiring considerable time for presentation) which are frankly non-discriminative for the particular subject examined * It is not for the purpose of shortening the examination that the non-discriminative material should be reduced to the minimum, but rather to gain time for the use of additional tests not included in the scale. * Furthermore, the time thus wasted in a psychometric examination is much worse than wasted. The typical clinical subject over ten years of age is usually sensitive about being brought to a clinic at all. The items which are most annoying to a self-conscious child or adolescent are these questions at the upper and lower ends of his natural range. * it is nothing less than inhuman to use a larger amount of inappropriate material than is necessary to the adequacy of the examination. * A thoroughgoing revision of the Binet-Simon scale is too costly a project to be undertaken more than once or twice in a generation; also, the standardization requires so many years that there is time for items to lose something of their significance before the test is ready to be used. We cannot depend upon such a scale as Stanford-Binet without being forced to make considerable use of outdated material. * The great need of the clinic is a test system that can be adapted to the individual subject. * It is impossible that the Stanford-Binet scale or any other inflexible system should be suitable for cases of unusual types. * The climax of complexity is reached in the new Stanford-Binet, with all the rigidity of the earlier form still retained. If each item . . . which admits of being graded in difficulty had been made up in the form of an independent graded series, discriminative for the range of mental levels for which it is appropriate, the resulting collection of tests would offer a wealth of material sufficiently varied to contain something suitable for almost any subject who can be tested at all. This scale contains the raw material for a remarkably adequate system, but it is given us in a form which renders it inconvenient in all cases, wasteful of time in all cases, and invalid—in varying degrees—in a very large proportion of clinical cases. It is in the clinic that we are especially in need of a flexible test that can be adapted to the individual subject; but the test which has been individually standardized for clinical use has been made so inflexible that it is almost exceptional to have a subject for whom it can be used with satisfactory validity. * * * Of all the items included in the Stanford-Binet scale, the one which seems to the writer most strikingly to fall short of its possibilities is the vocabulary test. In the first place, 100 words (or 50 words) selected by rule from a dictionary of 18,000 words do not afford a large enough sampling to justify a conjectural estimate of the subject's total vocabulary, nor is such estimate of any use in determining the subject's "mental age." * If we require the subject to give an oral definition . . . there would be many advantages in using words which admit of being defined by the person who recognizes them—words which would elicit more uniform responses and which would permit more uniform evaluation. In the second place, the plan of having the words orally defined by the subject at all is open to serious objections: 1. It involves the personal equation of the examiner both in presenting the words and in scoring the results. 2. The request to define a word is unduly annoying to a large proportion of subjects; and the succession of failures with which the series is usually brought to a close makes it an instrument of torture to the extremely sensitive subject. 3. It measures the subject's willingness

to attempt a definition, not invariably his actual ability to offer an acceptable response. Subjects differ widely in respect to the standards of certainty which seem to them to justify a response. It is sometimes the highly intelligent person who is most reluctant to offer anything short of a definition worthy of the dictionary, and who will decline to answer at all rather than attempt a crude explanation which does not satisfy his own standard of definition. * 4. For the typical clinical subject (as opposed to the school children upon whom tests are standardized) the request to define a word seems unnatural and wholly remote from everyday experience. We use words at all times, but only rarely have occasion to define them. * * * It is recommended that language test material be developed according to the method used by Pintner and Paterson for a group of performance tests. Any item which can be graded in difficulty may be developed into a graded series and standardized as an independent unit. Each unit should be so graded as to cover the entire range of mental levels for which it can appropriately be used; but for economy of presentation, the standardization should be for overlapping sections rather than for the series as a whole * If independent norms be published for each section, the non-discriminative material to be used in a given examination may be reduced to a negligible quantity. When sufficient test-units have been thus developed and standardized, an examiner may make up a battery by selecting for each case such units as are individually suited to the subject. The examination will be custom-made to fit each subject, instead of the subject being held responsible for fitting the test. The battery of tests used in a given examination will yield a series of independent ratings, the median of which may be placed on record for reference. When a one-figure numerical rating is required, this median rating is the figure to be reported. *

J Ed Psychol 30:594-603 N '39. M. Krugman. "Some Impressions of the Revised Stanford-Binet Scale." * For this paper, the writer approached the evaluation of Form L of the new scale by four different methods: (1) Impressions of ten psychologists of the Bureau of Child Guidance on eight specific questions were obtained. (2) An examination of one thousand two hundred cases was made for the complaint that frequently we cannot be certain, after obtaining a basal and a final year, that the child has been adequately measured. (3) A study of ninety clinic cases, in which both the old and the new scales were administered to the same children, was made. (4) A study was made of surveys conducted in four schools in widely separated areas of the city, surveys in which individual examinations were administered to entire grades. In these schools the old and the revised scales were administered at different times and random samplings of their populations were obtained by examining one or all of the first three grades. There were one thousand three hundred sixty-one children to whom the old Stanford-Binet scale had been administered, and four hundred three who were given Form L. * In conclusion, the experience at the Bureau of Child Guidance with Form L of the Revised Stanford-Binet scale would indicate that it is much superior to the old scale statistically; that it is better standardized and better validated, as a whole; that it eliminates successfully many of the objections to the old by including new lower levels, extending the upper, and filling in the gaps; that the lower levels no longer give results that seem too high, and the upper levels, results that seem too low; that the dispute over using thirteen, fourteen, fifteen or sixteen for maximum CA for adults has finally been settled; that, on the one hand, preschool and very dull kindergarten and first-grade children can now be examined without the use of an additional preschool battery, and, on the other hand, the superior adolescents can be reached; that directions have, in general, been simplified; that, in the main, it is a much more refined psychological scale, but, apparently, so much attention has been paid to these refinements in the process of revision, that some of the old weaknesses in content were not eliminated, and others have crept in. These are some of the weaknesses: (1) Longer time required for administration—twenty-five to thirty per cent more time, on the average. (2) Emphasis on verbal material still present, possibly to a greater extent, especially in middle and upper levels. (Admitted by Terman.) (3) Years VIII and XI seem especially poor in this respect. (4) Rote memory still seems emphasized too much at the upper levels. (5) Possibly because of refinements, there is considerably more scatter on the new scale.

(6) A single basal or final year is not as conclusive as it was on the old scale. (7) In attempting to simplify directions, confusion to the child has resulted on some tests. (8) Scoring directions and criteria are sometimes not clear. (9) Many tests seem misplaced for New York City children. (10) Many situations and many words seem unfair to New York City children. (11) Much of the content is unsuited to clinic children who show emotional disturbances. (12) For clinic work, more flexibility in administration would be desirable. Since in the year-by-year testing, the easy material is presented all at one time, and the difficult material at another, consecutive failure introduces an additional emotional stress. All in all, then, Form L of the new scale seems to be a better constructed instrument, much superior to the old for survey purposes, and possibly even for clinical purposes, but with many shortcomings which, if corrected, would make it much more satisfactory for clinic use.

For reviews by Francis N. Maxfield, J. W. M. Rothney, and F. L. Wells, see 1062. Also see B497.

[1421]
Ryburn Group Intelligence Tests for Senior Children. Ages 10-14; 1940; 1 form; 3s. per 20; 5s. per 50; 60(65) minutes; H. V. Clark; Glasgow, Scotland: Robert Gibson & Sons, Ltd.

[1422]
School Aptitude Test: Thanet Mental Tests. Age 11; 1 form; 5s. per 25; 1s. per handbook; 1s. 6d. per specimen set, including the arithmetic and the English tests in the same series; 30(40) minutes; W. P. Alexander; London: University of London Press, Ltd.

C. Ebblewhite Smith, Lecturer in the Department of Higher Degrees and Research, Institute of Education, University of London. For many English children, the Entrance Scholarship Examination taken at the age of 11 plus, constitutes a hurdle which must be successfully negotiated if they wish to proceed to higher education. Competition is keen, and with the whole future career of the child depending upon the result of this one examination it behooves examiners to make it as reliable and as valid an instrument as present day knowledge of examining and testing will allow. The three Thanet Mental Tests are together designed to perform the function of the Entrance Scholarship Examination. The *School Aptitude Test* is an intelligence test; the other two tests are minimum essential tests of English and of the fundamentals of arithmetic.

Most weight in the examination is placed on the results of the *School Aptitude Test* which is largely a verbal intelligence test, of the self-administering type, comprising 75 items, and taking 30 minutes working time.

What is it that causes the author to believe that on the basis of this 30-minute group test fine distinctions having far-reaching importance can be drawn between individuals? Is the test more than usually reliable? We are given no clue in the handbook. Is the test very valid? We are not told in the handbook of any measures taken to compare test scores with an outside criterion or of any measures taken to ensure item validity. Indeed, one has reason to believe that the item validity of some of the types of item used will not be high. Perhaps the special merit of the test in the author's eyes is that it measures *g* and *v* in equal proportions (*sic*). One would wish to see some reference to the experimental work by means of which such a result was obtained. There is some evidence that *g* and *v* have in the past been measured in about equal proportions in English Secondary School Examinations but is there any reason for perpetuating this? How does Alexander propose to distinguish the child with low *g* and high *v* from the child with high *g* and low *v*? It is always difficult to interpret the results of a test designed to measure several mental factors at the same time. A test which measures *g* and *v* in equal proportions for 11-year-olds of average mental age will measure *g* and *v* in different proportions for 11-year-olds of superior intelligence. The effect of familiarity with intelligence test material will be to change the relative proportion of *g* and *v* measured by the test. In the test here reviewed, insufficient preliminary practice material is given.

Surely the payment of one shilling for the test handbook should entitle the purchaser to learn something of the standardization of a test. Beyond a somewhat casual reference to the fact that norms have been obtained on five thousand cases no other mention is made of standardization. One would like to know how the cases were chosen, apart from this information the graphs given on pages 8 and 9 are meaningless.

The test is simple to administer and the instructions are good. The scoring is simple and speedy.

This test will be useful as a survey test for obtaining a distribution of mental ages over a wide range, but in the absence of further information from the author one would hesitate to use it as a major factor in making individual selection for competitive scholarships.

[1423]

Southend Group Test of Intelligence. Ages 10½-13; 1939; 1 form; 6s. per 25; 9d. per handbook; non-timed (40-60) minutes; selected from tests originated by William Stephenson; London: George G. Harrap & Co., Ltd.

Scottish Ed J 23:273 Ap 19 '40. The characteristic feature of this Group Test is that whereas half the sections are of the verbal type, the other half consists exclusively of comparisons of shapes. * No information is given as to the population on whom the Test was standardised. What validity the Test has, if any, is likewise not disclosed.

[1424]

Terman Group Test of Mental Ability. Grades 7-12; 1920; 2 forms; $1.20 (6s.) per 25; 20¢ (2s.) per specimen set; 27(40) minutes; Lewis M. Terman; Yonkers, N. Y.: World Book Co. (London: George G. Harrap & Co., Ltd.)

REFERENCES

1 BRIGHT, IRA J. "The Intelligence Examination For High-School Freshmen." *J Ed Res* 4:44-55 Je '21.
2 FRANZEN, RAYMOND. "Attempts at Test Validation." *J Ed Res* 6:145-58 S '22.
3 AVERY, GEORGE T. "A Study of the Binet and Terman Intelligence Tests, with Eleven-Year-Old Children." *J Ed Res* 7:429-33 My '23.
4 HINES, HARLAN C. *A Guide to Educational Measures,* pp. 96-104. Boston, Mass.: Houghton Mifflin Co., 1923. Pp. xxiii, 270. $1.90.
5 JORDAN, A. M. "The Validation of Intelligence Tests." *J Ed Psychol* 14:348-66, 414-28 S, O '23.
6 MILLER, W. S. "The Variation and Significance of Intelligence Quotients Obtained from Group Tests." *J Ed Psychol* 15:359-66 S '24.
7 WILSON, J. H. "Comparison of Certain Intelligence Scales." *Brit J Psychol* 15:44-63 Jl '24.
8 BROOKS, FOWLER D. "The Accuracy of Intelligence Quotients from Pairs of Group Tests in the Junior High School." *J Ed Psychol* 18:173-86 Mr '27.
9 GUILER, W. S. "The Predictive Value of Group Intelligence Tests." *J Ed Res* 16:365-74 D '27.
10 NELSON, M. J., AND DENNY, E. C. "The Terman and Thurstone Group Tests as Criteria for Predicting College Success." *Sch and Soc* 26:501-2 O 15 '27.
11 SYMONDS, PERCIVAL M. *Ability Standard for Standardized Achievement Tests in the High School.* New York: Bureau of Publications, Teachers College, Columbia University, 1927. Pp. x, 91. $1.05.
12 KUHLMANN, F. "The Kuhlmann-Anderson Intelligence Tests Compared with Seven Others." *J Appl Psychol* 12:545-94 D '28.
13 COLE, ROBERT D. "A Conversion Scale for Comparing Scores on Three Secondary School Intelligence Tests." *J Ed Res* 20:190-8 O '29.
14 KEFAUVER, GRAYSON N. "Need of Equating Intelligence Quotients Obtained from Group Tests." *J Ed Res* 19:92-101 F '29.
15 MILLER, W. S. "Variation of IQ's Obtained from Group Tests." *J Ed Psychol* 24:468-74 S '33.
16 TURNEY, AUSTIN H., AND FEE, MARY. "The Comparative Value for Junior High School Use of Five Group Mental Tests." *J Ed Psychol* 24:371-9 My '33.
17 MOORE, HERBERT, AND TRAFTON, HELEN. "Equating Test Scores." *J Ed Psychol* 25:216-9 Mr '34.
18 SEAGOE, M. V. "An Evaluation of Certain Intelligence Tests." *J Appl Psychol* 18:432-6 Je '34.
19 FINCH, F. H. "Equating Intelligence Quotients from Group Tests." *J Ed Res* 28:589-92 Ap '35.
20 MITCHELL, CLAUDE. "Prognostic Value of Intelligence Tests." *J Ed Res* 28:577-81 Ap '35.
21 WILSON, J. H. "The Exactness of '*g*' as Determined by Certain Intelligence Tests." *Brit J Psychol* 26:93-8 Jl '35.

22 FINCH, F. H., AND ODOROFF, M. E. "The Reliability of Certain Group Intelligence Tests." *J Appl Psychol* 21:102-6 F '37.
23 PATERSON, DONALD G.; SCHNEIDLER, GWENDOLEN G.; AND WILLIAMSON, EDMUND G. *Student Guidance Techniques*, pp. 56-8. New York: McGraw-Hill Book Co., Inc., 1938. Pp. xviii, 316. $3.00. (London: McGraw-Hill Publishing Co., Ltd. 18*s*.)
24 BISHOP, HELEN. "A Study in Prediction and Mortality." *J Am Assn Col Registrars* 14:62-3 O '39.
25 KEYS, NOEL. "The Value of Group Test IQ's for Prediction of Progress beyond High School." *J Ed Psychol* 31:81-93 F '40.

Anne Anastasi, Assistant Professor of Psychology and Chairman of the Department of Psychology, Queens College. Both forms of this test consist of ten subtests: (*a*) information; (*b*) best answer, including interpretation of proverbs and questions of fact; (*c*) word meaning, and opposites test; (*d*) logical selection; (*e*) arithmetic reasoning; (*f*) sentence meaning, each sentence containing a single term or concept whose understanding determines the response; (*g*) analogies; (*h*) mixed sentences; (*i*) classifications; and (*j*) number series completion. Administration and scoring are very simple. Directions are printed at the top of each subtest and the examiner reads these with the subjects. Sample items are also included in all the tests except arithmetic reasoning, a fact which insures much better understanding of procedure. The omission of samples in the arithmetic reasoning test is understandable in view of the familiarity of this task to the subjects.

Percentile norms are reported for each grade from 7 to 12 inclusive. These norms are based upon a total of 41,241 white children, the number varying from approximately four to ten thousand for each grade level. The subjects were drawn chiefly from city schools, about two-thirds of them being from California and the remainder being chiefly from the Middle West. These restrictions should, of course, be borne in mind in any attempt to use the test with other groups. A table is also provided for transmuting the raw scores into mental age equivalents. No further data regarding the construction or standardization of the test are furnished in the manual.

One could, of course, take issue with the use of percentile scores which do not represent a scale of equal units. Similarly, the practice of estimating mental ages from scores on a test which is not standardized in terms of age levels is open to question. The content of the test, furthermore, is highly overweighted with verbal material for a test which purports to measure "mental ability." These are criticisms, however, which could be leveled against the large majority of intelligence tests. As traditional "intelligence tests" go, this scale has much to commend it. It will serve more or less adequately for purposes of rough classification and especially in the classification of school children, to which its author specifically refers in the manual. Since this function seems to have been uppermost in the author's mind, it would perhaps have been more accurate to have labeled the test a measure of scholastic aptitude rather than general mental ability.

For any problem requiring very accurate measurement or fine discrimination, such a test would be unsuited, as would any test which attempts to measure in a single score such a composite and ill-defined characteristic as "general intelligence." Undoubtedly, tests of separate aptitudes will gradually replace the general intelligence tests for this purpose. It should be noted in this connection that the author himself is quite cautious and explicit in describing the use of his test. Thus, for example, he calls attention in the manual to the fact that a score on such a test should serve chiefly as a "point of departure for further study" of the individual, and he emphasizes the need of supplementing such a score with other data.

Howard Easley, Assistant Professor of Educational Psychology, Duke University. This test consists of ten subtests, with separate directions for each, namely: Information, Best Answer, Word Meaning, Logical Selection, Arithmetic, Sentence Meaning, Analogies, Mixed Sentences, Classification, and Number Series. Such an arrangement hardly seems justified, because (*a*) the part scores are of little use. No norms for them are given, and no indication of their significance. (*b*) Even if they measure different aspects of mental ability they can hardly do it well with so small numbers of items, 11 to 20, in the various subtests. The 370 items in the two forms were selected from an original list of 886. Each item was required to distinguish between children of known brightness and children of known dullness. The total working time is twenty-seven minutes, and the whole test is supposed to be administered "easily within a school period of thirty-five minutes." Experience indicates, however, that this time is about the absolute minimum, and that forty minutes is practically required.

The scoring is objective and simple, but time

consuming compared to the more recent economical devices. Each test is on a separate page, and five different answer strips are required.

Percentile grade scores, based on 41,241 cases, and mental age equivalents, based on 1,422 cases, are given. The mental age equivalents involve an error common to many such norms, due to failure to take account of the regression of mental age on scores. "If a pupil obtains a score of 49, his mental age is 138 months, since 49 is the average of the scores obtained by pupils who are 138 months old" (Manual, p. 11). It would be more nearly correct to give as the mental age equivalent for a score of 49 the average age of pupils who made scores of 49.

This was a good test when it was first published in 1920, both in terms of its intrinsic and relative values. There were no other group tests which were unmistakably better. It is not certain that other more recent tests do a better job of measuring mental ability, but many of them do it more economically and conveniently. Many improvements have been made, especially in the mechanics of testing, since 1920; but this test remains in its original form.

[1425]

Test of General Knowledge. Ages 14 and over; 1938; a disguised intelligence test; 1 form; $3 per 20; specimen sets obtainable on approval; 23½(30) minutes; Eugene J. Benge; Philadelphia, Pa.: Management Service Co.

REFERENCES

1 BENGE, EUGENE J. "Tests in Selecting Employes." *Soc Adv Mgmt J* 3:72-5 Mr '38.

[1426]

Tests of Mental Development. Ages 3 months and over; 1939; 1 form; individual; $6.80 per testing outfit including the necessary materials for 25 examinations; $1.60 per manual; $2.75 per carrying case; F. Kuhlmann; Minneapolis, Minn.: Educational Test Bureau, Inc.

REFERENCES

1 PORTER, E. H., JR. "A Method of Organizing Test Materials of the Kuhlmann Tests of Mental Development." *J Appl Psychol* 24:92-5 F '40.

Grace H. Kent, Psychologist, Danvers State Hospital, Hathorne, Massachusetts. The raw material for this scale is taken from many sources, especially the Binet and Stanford-Binet scales, the Kuhlmann-Anderson tests, the Gesell tests, and the Buehler tests.

The children employed as subjects for standardization were from the public schools of certain carefully-selected Minnesota towns. Preschool children were selected from the birth registries as being exactly of the ages desired

and were examined in their homes by appointment. Less than one per cent of the parents refused to permit the examination. In each case the child's feeding time and sleeping time were ascertained in advance, in order to avoid all danger of finding a child hungry or sleepy. The discriminative capacity of the scale starts at four to six months. The standardization for children of school age includes 140 cases for each year, and for preschool children about 106 for each year.

The tests form a continuous series of increasing difficulty and are not grouped according to age levels; but the presentation is similar to that of the Binet scale, in that the examination is to be carried far enough upward to exclude any chance of further success and far enough downward to exclude possibility of failure.

The scale is constructed on the Heinis mental growth curve. Passing scores for tests are located at every third point in the growth curve, and each test is placed at the level at which it is passed by fifty per cent. The tests are scored in terms of mental growth values, and the Percent of Average (P.A.) is recommended as a substitute for the IQ.

The reviewer believes the lower end to be the most valuable part of the scale, because of the scarcity of properly standardized test material for infants. The toys included in the outfit are exceptionally attractive as compared with the materials of most preschool tests. Some of the pictures for preschool levels are excellent, but it is to be regretted that others are too small and very poorly proportioned. In one series of pictures intended for the six-year level, the potato and pumpkin and radish are so nearly equal in size as to be confusing to the mature subject. One member of our psychological department mistook the radish for a beet, and another thought it was a turnip.

The scoring system, based largely upon speed, is too complicated to be described in the space allowed here. The author states that the scale is not more difficult of presentation than its predecessors and that the scoring is "easier because more objective." It may be easy to one who has mastered it, but to the beginner it seems very much like trying to read a strange language without having a dictionary at hand. There ought to be a one-page index to the abbreviations used in the manual, many of which are far from being self-explanatory;

and there is serious need also of a general index.

The inherent weakness of the composite scale, which can be used only as a whole, is indicated by the author's instructions for evaluating the achievement of the child who suffers from some special handicap. Each test apparently affected by the handicap is to be scored *minus* with an interrogation point, and the child is to be given credit for half the tests thus scored. But if the various tests had been evaluated independently, as in the Kuhlmann-Anderson series, there would be no need of taking liberties with the results in order to be fair to the child, inasmuch as any particular test affected by the handicap could be omitted. It is highly disappointing to find the author of a flexible school test reverting to the composite scale when developing a new test for individual examination.

The manual of instructions is for the most part rather heavy reading matter, but there is one chapter which can be recommended for careful study on the part of every clinical examiner who uses mental tests—the fifth chapter, on the conduct of a clinical examination.

Francis N. Maxfield, Professor of Psychology, Psychological Clinic, The Ohio State University. One would hardly expect a snapshot photograph of the Norris dam, even if the man behind the camera had some knowledge of engineering and economics, to be a very significant item in a discussion of power control or of hydraulic engineering. This scale of Kuhlmann's rests on such a broad basis of author-experience and both theoretical and practical research that anything more than a snapshot would be presumptious within the limits of this review and in light of the recency of publication.

In that many of the test items in the scale are not found in the Binet-Simon scale of 1911 or in early revisions and translations, including Kuhlmann's own, some will hesitate to call this scale the "Kuhlmann-Binet," yet it is clearly in the Binet tradition in many of its theoretical and practical aspects. Yet the author himself frequently speaks of the "Binet method" in contrast with his own. A preliminary list of one hundred twenty-one tests prepared in 1933 was given to some 15,000 persons ranging in age from three months to sixty years. Thirteen test items discarded and

nineteen retained as "supplementary tests" left eighty-nine for the final scale.

The directions for administering the scale are an improvement on those in Kuhlmann's 1922 manual. Test materials are packed in a carrying case, but are still cumbersome and inconvenient. E. H. Porter,[1] an assistant at Ohio State University, has devised a convenient arrangement of the many-sized cards and the directions for the tests in which they are used which should be put out by the publishers as a "condensed guide." For the time-limit tests taken over from the Kuhlmann-Anderson series, critical scores for scoring when the full time is taken should be written in a third line, as below.

For example, Test 73 (p. 167):

Scoring

M.U. —	312 —	330 —	375 —	399
R/T —	.039 —	.054 —	.088 —	.105

Critical score
when T = 120″ 5   7   11   13

The most common source of error in psychometric work done by assistants lies in arithmetical calculation. The author endeavors to eliminate these errors by including in the appendix one hundred twenty pages of tables from which most results may be read.

Kuhlmann abandons age grouping of tests, assumes the validity of Heinis's mental growth curve, and has at least one test scoring at every third point on this curve from 21 to 528. The scale is scored in points on this curve. The score may be translated into a mental age score or an IQ. Heinis's P.C. (personal constant) is rechristened "P.A.," or "percent of average," and is recommended for prediction. Scores for speed, accuracy, and variability for test items No. 71 and following add to the list, so that each full use of the scale yields seven scores. The author raises statistical objections to the use of standard scores or centile ranks. He rejects the assumption of a normal surface of distribution for measures of intelligence. Yet his own distributions of P.A. values for five different age groups in Table 30 do not indicate marked skewness. The probable errors of these "percents" of average, taken as half the interquartile distance, are small (about .07) for psychometric values and relatively uniform for age groups six to fourteen. The clinician dealing with an individual case is interested in degree of deviation from average as well as status

(M.U.) and prediction (P.A.). Forgetting nice points as to skewness and the doubtful validity of extreme values, the clinician should set up tables from which deviations may be read more readily than from Tables 28 and 30.

The use of the 1916 Stanford-Binet became so nearly universal in this country that the revised Stanford-Binet will go ahead with some of that momentum, as well as on its own merits. Nine out of ten of those that use it give little thought to the theoretical questions discussed so ably by Kuhlmann. Even if they give his scale a trial, they will be prejudiced from the start, not only by their previous experience, but by the uniform cards, the convenient Directions for Administering, and the dual forms of the Terman-Merrill revision. Kuhlmann's scale will not find extensive use unless his publishers make it easier for the clinician to discover its merits.

Myrtle Luneau Pignatelli, Clinical Psychologist, Bellevue Psychiatric Hospital, New York, New York. The scale, *Tests of Mental Development*, recently standardized by Kuhlmann, differs essentially from the older type of Binet scale. The author feels that in using experience gained with thousands of problem cases as well as normal individuals, a more solid foundation was established for the scale as a whole. Only those tests were chosen which had: (*a*) discriminative capacity with age, (*b*) variety in make-up, (*c*) freedom from practice effect and coaching, (*d*) freedom from variable training, (*e*) objectivity in scoring, (*f*) and the right degree of difficulty of separate items or trials.

The scale has 89 tests and 19 supplementary ones. The levels extend from 3 months of age through the superior adult. Final norms were obtained in Minnesota on 3,000 white nonselected public school and preschool children down to the age of three months. Instead of age-level scoring, the test items are placed at equally spaced distances on the Heinis mental growth curve. The norms for each test represent 50 percentile scores, and are expressed in terms of scale or mental units. The 89 tests of the scale represent Heinis scale numerical values ranging from 21 to 528 mental units. Mental growth values after the age of 16 are assumed values, and have been extended to a level equivalent to a mental age of 45 years.

Outstanding features of the scale, are: (*a*) the ingenuity of its author in devising the tests, (*b*) the demands that the instrument makes on the "power" of mentality under examination, (*c*) the technique of administering the scale seems more detailed and it makes more demands on the testing judgment of the examiner, than other similar scales, (*d*) the scoring of the tests at many levels permits the measurement of mental traits by degrees, (*e*) the inclusion of paper and pencil tests which can be given to subjects in small groups, (*f*) the stress on the time factor throughout the scale, with time as well as accuracy entering into the scoring of all tests at the upper levels, (*g*) the use of P.A. (percent of average) instead of the IQ, and in addition, scoring for mental age, mental level (M.U.), speed, accuracy and variability, (*h*) the use of many tables for computations and for the converting of scores.

On first acquaintance, the scale seems very difficult. Experienced examiners, however, will find it interesting and easy to master. A thorough understanding of the theoretical basis of the scale and the concepts introduced therein, as well as a mastery of technique are essential. Inexperienced examiners and students will need special training in order to use the instrument intelligently, as it makes greater demands on psychological background and clinical technique, than other instruments of its kind. Time for giving the test runs from 30 minutes to over an hour, depending on the age of the subject. The examiner must use his judgment as to what constitutes adequate testing, as there are no established critical points, such as basal age and upper limit.

There is only one form of the scale, but practise effect is not great after a lapse of several months. Kuhlmann's idea to add supplementary tests to the scale to be used with individuals who have special handicaps, would add to its usefulness. The test manual is unusually good, though it is unfortunate that an index was omitted, and that data were not given on problem cases. Information for scoring is adequate, with the exception of a few tests which need additional scoring data.

Characteristics of the scale which will limit its use are the following: (*a*) the extensive material which must be handled during the process of a single examination; (*b*) the complicated procedure associated with scoring and obtaining final ratings; (*c*) the demand which the tests make on perception and reading will make it unfeasible for reading disability cases, illiterate adults and persons who have visual defects.

The test content is not as familiar as that of the *Revised Stanford-Binet Scale,* and the test is not so generally applicable to adults who come to clinics, as the *Wechsler-Bellevue Intelligence Scale,* but it offers new avenues of approach to the measurement of mentality, which will be challenging to those psychologists who can appreciate its possibilities as a clinical instrument.

F. L. Wells, Psychologist, Department of Hygiene, Harvard University. This work is based in large part on the Kuhlmann-Binet series, but the metamorphosis is too great to be classed as a "revision." The number of separate tests, 89 plus 19 alternates, is comparable to the Binet systems, but the year level division is done away with, and a scale in units of mental growth is substituted. It can of course be transmuted into the more familiar terms of mental age and IQ.

The feature of essential distinction in this scale is actually its foundation on the Heinis "Personal Constant," here known as "percent of average," P.A. This is offered as a measure of considerably greater reliability than the conventional IQ, and the data on pp. 85-92 would seem to justify this. The IQ has long been under fire from various quarters, and probably survives for reasons other than scientific. The superiority claimed for the new measure raises serious question as to the advisability of reworking other psychometric procedures in its terms.

The standpoint from which the writer desires to discuss the work especially is its internal methodology. Here, as in other ways, it occupies a position between the Binet systems and the *Wechsler-Bellevue Intelligence Scale* and *Detroit Tests of Learning Aptitude;* on the whole nearer the Binet. The main issue is between a large number of disparate procedures, each aimed at a single or narrow range of developmental levels, and a much smaller number, each covering a considerable range of developmental levels. Kuhlmann is clearly a partisan of variety, in the Binet tradition. The background of the present writer definitely favors the other policy, as embodied originally in the performance scales, and now

very effectively in the Bellevue. It is probably a matter of differential interests; Kuhlmann's being primarily in the juvenile and defective areas, the present writer's in the adult of normal or superior intellectual functions (cf. the earlier and later portions of the present scale). Here one lays stress on the better understanding that accrues to each procedure, in respect to both administration and evaluation. One acquires a feel for a wide range of response adequacies, both quantitative and qualitative, that is not approached with numerous discrete items of the Binet type.

Naturally there are limits to which this can be carried. Procedure for infant and preschool ages cannot be adapted to the superior adult, as Kuhlmann points out very forcibly. But this only brings into question the wisdom of organizing test series to cover so wide a range. It has official advantages, where one is administratively concerned with large numbers, as Kuhlmann presumably is. Whether the skilled examiner gets as good an understanding through such means, is another matter.

Though it is many years since Gesell set an example of differential categories for the early ages, development in this direction has been relatively slow. The *Minnesota Preschool Scale* and the *Wechsler-Bellevue Intelligence Scale* make specific distinctions of verbal and nonverbal accomplishments. Many users should find it convenient similarly to reorganize the upper levels of the present scale, for which its resources are ample. In series like the Bellevue and Detroit, individual test procedures may be strong enough to acquire notable intrinsic significance, as is also incidentally the case here. But the technology continues largely under the spell of a global figure of some sort, which heavily masks the status in such disparate functions as e.g., vocabulary range, abstracting power, and imaginative richness.

On the other hand, a real advance is made in the special consideration given to speed and error, apart from age level scores. The discussion of this point is very pertinent, though one may find it difficult to go along with all the reasoning. The Kuhlmann-Binet test gave more than usual recognition to these factors, but made too much attempt to get them into a single score. Here they are treated more analytically, as they should be.

Kuhlmann apparently feels that the existing

variety of test devices is reasonably satisfactory, at any rate it has not appeared necessary to strive for novelty in this respect. Borrowings from other systems are freely acknowledged. The underlying viewpoint requires somewhat more rigidity in response patterns than is usual in most clinical methods; in the name of objectivity, as little as possible is left to "qualitation." This may account for the absence of problems in the "absurd sentence" or "comprehension" class. Such restrictions might be a liability in work with problem cases, unless qualitation is supplied from elsewhere, as, of course, it can be. To purposes essentially educational the new scale is well adapted, either as a basic procedure, or as an alternate to whatever already has the prestige of use.

Aside from the necessary juvenile content at times, the material includes effective elements for aphasia examination; the writer has elsewhere commented on the usefulness from this standpoint of certain Kuhlmann-Anderson procedures. Items of the present scale especially suggesting themselves are the tests numbered 23, 26, 28, 32 (in principle), 33, 35, 39, 40, 42, 45, 55, 67, 73, 74, and 19s.

Range for range the new scale seems easier to learn than the Stanford-Binet, less easy than the Detroit, more foolproof than either, so far as scoring goes. Administrative convenience is impertinent to judge without experience in giving, but here it probably does not differ greatly in the early ages from the revised Stanford-Binet; at the later ages it looks more cumbrous. This is owing to considerations of material; its recording system is distinctly preferable. In respect to convenience it cannot properly be compared with Bellevue or Detroit, because of their smaller age ranges; the Detroit, however, seems the only procedure that has really exerted itself in this direction. Two suggestions may be offered on this point, towards facilitating the diffusion of the present device. (*a*) Make the record blank available in sheet rather than card form. (*b*) Put Chapter VI of the manual, together with such portions of the Appendix as are not functions of simple arithmetic, in a separate spiral binder, possibly somewhat condensed.

All in all, the present offering probably represents the best instrument available over a fairly wide area, denoted as follows: (*a*) where it is desired to represent the intelligence function by a single figure; (*b*) for healthy individuals up to say fourteen years of age; and (*c*) for individuals with intelligence defect.

J Consulting Psychol 3:128-30 Jl-Ag '39. Gertrude Hildreth. * departs radically in scoring and item selection from the classic Binet type test. From our first preliminary experience with the scale it appears to constitute a marked step in advance over the 1922 Kuhlmann revision. Any attempt to make a complete appraisal at this time would be premature. The scale needs an extensive tryout in order to determine its advantages and possible limitations. * For the most part the materials are simple in character and at the younger age levels capitalize the child's interest in natural play materials. The first tests requiring response to printed verbal symbols come at age eight years, six months. This may work a hardship on the very gifted child of six who has not yet learned to read, but there is no actual reading test in the sense of deriving thought from consecutive content until near the end of the scale. Objectivity in scoring is increased by the inclusion of multiple choice items throughout the scale. * [the] scaling scheme makes the whole scale more flexible than the traditional Binet scale, for any separate test, such as a form board, that is standardized and scaled in the same way may be admitted into the scale at any point. Furthermore, there is the practical advantage that the examiner need not go through any set number of tests before he concludes that no more items would be passed or failed. * We find that Item 53, memory for pictured objects, has diagnostic value in beginning stages of reading, but this capacity in no way invalidates the test. Our preliminary experience with the scale indicates that the child has somewhat less opportunity for verbal response than on other Binet revisions. On the other hand, a premium is placed on the subject's ability and tendency to listen to verbal instructions, and to give sustained mental effort while doing so. * We have found that for the young, bright child some of the items that must be used are not intrinsically very interesting. Certain items are rather tedious and require close attention to directions that must be read verbatim from the manual. Young gifted children may also be at some disadvantage in responding to tests that are closely timed. Handling the large quantity of paper and card material will require considerable practice to insure efficiency. We use a large notebook with manila pockets to hold the materials, numbered according to the test items, and arranged in proper sequence. The toys and materials for the infant and nursery levels are conveniently handled in a small container. One must learn from experience where to begin the test and how far up or down in the scale to go in order to complete the test. It is important to score the test as much as possible while it is being given so that two testing sessions need not be necessary. * The new scale contains considerable material that entails response to spatial relations, geometrical in character. This material is advantageous because it requires no verbal response, but it seems to narrow somewhat the subject's repertory of responses. It is impossible to give the test properly unless one is completely free of all distractions. The timing must be done precisely with a stop watch. All computations should be checked twice for accuracy. Carelessness will vitiate the ultimate rating obtained. On the whole, the separate items can be scored with a minimum of deliberation. The examiner will, however, puzzle over how to score some items; he will be uncertain at some points what to consider a "pass" or "fail." Each examiner will need to develop his own scoring standards for doubtful items through practice with the test. Fortunately the items in which this need arises are comparatively few in number. There appear to be some slight irregularities in the placement of subitems within tests, and even of total test items. The blank could be improved upon, for school testing purposes at least, by omitting some of the squares now provided for scoring and leaving space at the top for note-taking. Although at first glance the scale appears to be rather formidable and intricate, there are no intrinsic difficulties that do not yield to faithful study and practice. One advantage of the scale is that it will not be readily coached. Furthermore, few but serious clinical workers will be apt to develop expertness with the scale, and the casual testing done by untrained persons that has so frequently brought testing into disrepute will be eliminated. In the hands of qualified workers it will prove to be a highly reliable, stable, and accurate mental measurement scale.

Loyola Ed Digest 15:11-2 O '39. Austin G. Schmidt. * Particularly gratifying to the reviewer is the author's forthright rejection of the coefficient of reliability, which he brands as useless and even misleading. It is indeed true that the importance of the coefficient of reliability has been grossly overemphasized. Virtue has been attached to high reliability, as if the fact that a test consistently did the same thing was proof of its validity. Dr. Kuhlmann's wide experience and scientific background are a sufficient guarantee of the merit of these tests. * an important contribution in the field of mental measurement.

[1427]
Tests for Primary Mental Abilities, Experimental Edition, 1938. High school and college; 1938; 1 form, 3 parts; 40¢ per set of 3 parts, 5 to 39 sets; 25¢ per set, 40 or more; $1 per specimen set; 153(270) minutes; L. L. Thurstone; Washington, D. C.: American Council on Education.

REFERENCES

1 THURSTONE, L. L. "The Factorial Isolation of Primary Abilities." *Psychometrika* 1:175-82 S '36.
2 THURSTONE, L. L. "A New Conception of Intelligence." *Ed Rec* 17:441-50 Jl '36.
3 THURSTONE, L. L. "A New Concept of Intelligence and a New Method of Measuring Primary Abilities." *Ed Rec* 17: Sup 10:124-38 O '36.
4 THURSTONE, L. L. *Primary Mental Abilities.* Psychometric Society, Psychometric Monograph No. 1. Chicago, Ill.: University of Chicago Press, 1938. Pp. ix, 121. $2.00. Paper. (London: Cambridge University Press. 9s.)
5 THURSTONE, L. L. *Primary Mental Abilities*: This Supplement Contains the Experimental Psychological Tests that Were Used in the Factorial Analysis Described in the Monograph. Supplement to Psychometric Monograph No. 1. Published for the Psychometric Society. Chicago, Ill.: University of Chicago Press, 1938. Pp. 274. Paper, lithotyped. Out of print.
6 SHANNER, WILLIAM M. "A Report on the Thurstone Tests of Primary Mental Abilities," pp. 54-60. In *1939 Achievement Testing Program in Independent Schools and Supplementary Studies.* Educational Records Bulletin No. 27. New York: Educational Records Bureau, June 1939. Pp. xiii, 76, 11. $1.50. Paper, lithotyped.
7 STALNAKER, JOHN M. "Primary Mental Abilities." *Sch and Soc* 50:868-72 D 30 '39.
7.1 WRIGHT, RUTH E. "A Factor Analysis of the Original Stanford-Binet Scale." *Psychometrika* 4:209-20 S '39.
8 CRAWFORD, A. B. "Some Observations on the Primary Mental Abilities Battery in Action." *Sch and Soc* 51:585-92 My 4 '40.
9 STALNAKER, JOHN M. "Results from Factor Analysis: With Special Reference to 'Primary Mental Abilities.'" *J Ed Res* 33:698-704 My '40.
10 ADKINS, DOROTHY C. "The Relation of Primary Mental Abilities to Vocational Choice," pp. 39-53. In *Psychological Examinations, 1939.* American Council on Education Studies, Series 5, Vol. 4, No. 2. Washington, D. C.: the Council, May 1940. Pp. v, 53. $0.25.

Henry E. Garrett, Associate Professor of Psychology, Columbia University. This unique examination has as its purpose the measurement of seven primary mental abilities or "factors." These seven factors are designated by capital letters and may be described as follows: *P*, perceptual ability; *N*, numerical ability; *V*, verbal ability; *S*, spatial-visualizing ability; *M*, memory; *I*, induction or generalizing ability; and *D*, deductive or reasoning ability. The test battery consists of three booklets which comprise a total of 16 separate tests. Many of these tests cover familiar ground (same-opposite, arithmetic, completion, number series) but many are original in content or in form (marks, cards, number patterns, figures). Fore-exercises are provided; and the tests are timed individually, the whole examination requiring about four hours. An examinee's standing in each of the seven abilities is summarized graphically by an individual profile.

The seven primary abilities measured by the test battery were identified by Thurstone through the application of his centroid method of factor analysis to the intercorrelations of 56 tests administered to 240 college freshmen. A "primary mental ability" may be defined as a function which cuts across many mental operations, and is involved to a greater or lesser degree in various tasks, much as physical strength or visual acuity is involved in many different activities. In the present study, the seven primary abilities are assumed to be independent. It is theoretically possible to think of the fundamental mental traits as being unique; and practically it is much easier to calculate factors which are statistically uncorrelated. But it may be remarked that the assumption of independence of factors is not necessary to factor theory. Comments upon the test may be grouped conveniently under several heads.

IDENTIFICATION OF FACTORS. Derivation of factors by any method of analysis from a table of correlations involving 56 tests and more than 1,500 coefficients is a huge task. Cut-and-fit and approximation methods as well as arbitrary decisions as to what factor weights should be considered significant are, therefore, a practical necessity; but as a result the identity of several of the postulated factors becomes doubtful. The two factors I and D may be artifacts and are certainly not definitely established; while factor P is probably what other investigators have called "mental speed." The four factors, V, N, M, and S have been so consistently found by other workers in a variety of experimental setups that their identity seems reasonably sure. The present study of Thurstone verifies and extends earlier work.

INDEPENDENCE OF FACTORS. While it was undoubtedly convenient for Thurstone to assume orthogonality (statistical independence) among factors in the present study in order to analyze mathematically a correlational matrix involv-

ing so many coefficients, from the psychological point of view the assumption of unique factors has its drawbacks. Words, numbers, and geometrical figures are all symbols; and it is hard to conceive of independent brain and neural structures underlying V, N, and S. It is easier, perhaps, to think of speed (synaptic resistance) or of memory (cortical retentiveness) as being independent functions; though even here strict independence seems far fetched. Considerable experimental work with factors indicates that, if not zero, the intercorrelations of V, N, S, and M are not high—probably from .20 to .30. Hence, it is not likely that the assumption of independence among mental factors in the present study introduces any great error.

TEST. In administering the *Tests for Primary Mental Abilities* to graduate and professional students, the reviewer noted several minor criticisms of the test as a practical instrument. The fore-exercises are nearly all too long; many of the tests are interesting and challenging, but several are so obviously of the puzzle type that students are either amused or bored —a bad test attitude in either case; the memory tests are too short, too superficial, and rely too much upon the factor of confusion; and the battery as a whole is too long.

These shortcomings in the test as well as other criticisms are to be expected in a new instrument. The test is certainly a step in the right direction—that is, toward the differentiation and measurement of certain essential mental traits. From both the theoretical and practical points of view such an approach is vastly superior to that taken by makers of omnibus tests who hope by averaging scores on a hodgepodge of functions to obtain, finally, a measure of some worth-while ability.

Truman L. Kelley, Professor of Education, Harvard University. The experimental and statistical analysis of mental life into a number of independent factors is the modern equivalent of the philosophical endeavors of earlier times to typify men and to assign different activities to fundamentally different psychological categories. It is the reviewer's belief that these typological psychologies are discredited because, like phrenology, palmistry, and astrology, they were built upon hypotheses pure and undefiled and not upon demonstrable and proven individual differences.

This modern attempt by Thurstone differs

from the just mentioned earlier attempts in that he gets mental factors from the findings of contemporary experimental and mental factor psychologists, verifying and supplementing these by his own experimental investigations. In short, his mental factors are not purely hypothetical, but are demonstrable and capable of measurement by means of objective measuring devices.

Though this is altogether an improvement in methodology over that of the armchair analysts, it still seems to the reviewer to be essentially weak in that the mental factors thus enumerated may be trivial. That there are demonstrable individual differences of a certain sort is no guarantee that they are important. The reviewer agrees with the viewpoints of Thorndike, Tryon, and Thomson that, due to the infinite variety of genetic structure and of psychological associative process, real and provable individual differences of infinite multiplicity are to be expected. If this is so it is not sufficient that Thurstone have evidence that his mental traits exist in demonstrably different amounts from subject to subject. He certainly should be called upon to show that they differentiate individuals in respects that are important in academic, vocational, and avocational living if he proposes them as essential rubrics, which he does in using the title "Primary Mental Abilities."

There seems to be a serious hiatus in his argument for he calls them "primary" and then admits that he does not know whether they serve any function. He writes: "It is too early in these investigations to make any definite statements about the particular combinations of abilities that are called for by each vocation . . . Before attempting to give individual vocational advice, it is well to recall that a man might be a success in accounting without being quick in adding a column of figures, that he might be a success in some phase of engineering or architecture without being superior in the factor S [space] which may be involved in design, and that he might be a success in law without being superior in the verbal factors." That Thurstone makes these hedging statements is highly commendable in view of the known facts about his measures, but that he needs to make them signifies that the issuance of the tests for public consumption is premature. As it is, the public is overwhelmed with tests. The crucial weakness of the test movement today is not primarily paucity of good tests, but lack of widely-known, sound, and helpful interpretative techniques. The *Tests for Primary Mental Abilities* not only cannot be interpreted in a sound and helpful manner by lay users, they cannot be so interpreted by experts. They would seem to but further confuse a market already surfeited with meaningless or bewildering measures.

Though the reviewer believes this to be the case with the battery entire he would, nevertheless, readily grant that certain of the seven measures are more important and more interpretable than certain others. Without documenting the accumulated evidence it seems believable that four of the seven abilities—number, verbal, space, and memory—are serviceably independent and it seems certain that two of these are widely important in forecasting academic and vocational differences. If these four stood alone and if the measures did not have grievous technical shortcomings the battery would be highly promising.

The shortcomings are, first: The use of speeded tests for functions never before ascertained to be speed functions—perception, number, verbal, space, memory, induction, and reasoning. The tests are so timed that no subjects are expected to finish them within the time limits set, thereby making speed a function of each and every one. This raises the reliability coefficients, which are high as reported, but it lowers the purity of the measures. It introduces a correlation between the tests, which the author acknowledges, but does not use, nor does he note that it is largely due to a common speed factor. The most obvious measure to be gotten from these seven is one of "mental speed," but no scoring for such is provided.

The second serious technical shortcoming is that an inadequate scoring formula is employed throughout—the score being the number of "rights." The correct formula for multiple-choice tests is $R - W/(n-1)$, where R is the number of rights; W, the number of wrongs; and n, the number of options. It is particularly important that this formula be used if many subjects do not attempt all the items, otherwise a mere marking at random will increase a person's score.

A third serious shortcoming lies, not in the tests, but in the record sheet provided, which omits any place for recording "sex"—a trait far more important than any of the seven constituting the battery.

The reviewer is aware of the severity of his criticisms, but is constrained not to temper them because of his knowledge of the history of the general-intelligence-test movement. The analytical outlook and the temperate claims of Binet quickly gave way in his followers to the general-intelligence fetish, which has blighted the study of individual mental differences for nearly a generation and is still the source of befuddlement of sincere but nonanalytical teachers and counselors. If the use of analytical mental measures is not to follow a similar course it is necessary that pragmatic values and not wishful thinking—even though introduced in so inconspicuous a manner as in the selection of the original tests to be subjected to factor analysis—be the basis of trait analysis.

If this battery of "Primary Mental Abilities" is recognized as an initial attempt to accomplish a very difficult task, for which we can be very grateful to the author, and if it leads to an investigative attitude rather than to one of trust and confidence in this as yet uncharted realm it will prove an important stepping stone in the transition from reliance upon "general intelligence" to knowledge and use of "analytical and independent mental measures."

C. Spearman, Professor of Psychology, The University of London. [Joint review of the *Tests for Primary Mental Abilities* and the English version of the *Otis Quick-Scoring Mental Tests (see* 1413).] Here are two recent works of the highest interest, partly by the renown of their authors, partly by their intrinsic merits, and again by the extraordinary contrast between them.

To begin with, the test of Otis is above all things practical. At the start, indeed, and particularly in the development of group testing, this author displayed remarkable originality. But afterwards, he seems to have settled down to groping after improvement of detail; he has sought above all to supply the needs of ordinary teachers. Thurstone, at the other extreme, has from first to last been theoretical and original. His present work is the crown of a long series of fundamental and inspiring researches.

This contrast between them comes strikingly to expression in the fact that, whereas the test of Otis can be completed in twenty minutes, that of Thurstone requires the intolerable

amount of twelve hours. Again, the Otis test is drawn up in three separate versions, each carefully adapted for a different age group—7-10, 10-15, and 15-18. With Thurstone, on the other hand, the point seems to find little if any consideration. He takes into account exclusively the application of the tests to university students. The opposite occurs in respect to the nature of the ability tested. For here it is Otis who is content with one single value; he simply follows the old and still almost universal custom of throwing all the test scores into one indiscriminating pool and so measure one single "general ability." Thurstone, instead, reintroduces the venerable doctrine that the mind is made up of several "primary mental abilities," each of them is determined by two or three different tests taken to be "fairly heavily saturated" with it. These abilities are: Perception, Number, Verbal, Space, Memory, Induction, and Reasoning. As for the elsewhere almost universally admitted "general" ability, this now completely vanishes.

Of these two new tests, undoubtedly that of Thurstone is the more open to criticism. For he is the daring pioneer, a role full of honour, but also of danger. One objection that might be raised is that we have to await indications of his faculties being really serviceable to practical teachers, psychiatrists, and industrialists. More dubious still is the question as to whether such workers in the field of applied psychology will ever be able to dispense with the said "general ability" or at least something akin. But I must venture to suggest something yet worse. In general, I myself yield to nobody with respect to Thurstone's admirable contributions to statistical psychology. But I have been forced to the conclusion that in his present study he has at last gone quite astray. The paradoxical absence of any general factor in this analysis I have been obliged to attribute to a grave fault of method. (*See* my article, "Thurstone's Work Re-worked," *J Ed Psychol* 30:1-16 Ja '39.) And this conclusion has been immediately confirmed by the reappearance of the general factor in another study [7.1] made by the same School.

On the whole, then, the chief value of Thurstone's tests would seem to lie, not so much in application as rather in stimulation.

Godfrey H. Thomson, Professor of Education and Director of the Training Centre for

Teachers, University of Edinburgh. It is seldom that tests can be published with so thorough and complete a scientific backing as these. The manual of instructions [4] is clear and almost beyond criticism and the references to articles and books justifying the standardisation and significance of the tests are complete, except that the study at the Hyde Park School, Chicago, has not yet been published, though it is promised "in the near future." The estimated reliabilities of the tests are given, and their estimated "validity," defined as the estimated correlation between the score and a pure test of the relative primary factor. But since it is the function of a critic to be critical, let me see what minor faults I can descry.

There is nowhere an explicit statement that the tests are intended for young adults. That has either to be known by the reader from his previous acquaintance with Thurstone's articles, or deduced from the reference to high schools and from the use of the word "students" for those taking the test.

The whole interpretation of the tests depends, of course, on the user's acceptance of Thurstone's theory of simple structure and primary factors. It is perhaps too much to expect the manual to explain that other systems exist and to give references to adverse articles by workers who disagree.

As a "test technician" I am myself most troubled by two things. The first is the absence of any information by which I can check the estimated reliabilities and validities. I am not even quite sure what the estimated validity exactly is.

The second point is concerned with the "compromise which was made in adapting the tests for practical use." The manual is to be commended for making quite clear what that compromise is, and what the ideal but very laborious method would be. My first reaction, however, was one of great disappointment that Thurstone, after all the spade-work he has done towards measuring these primary abilities as accurately as possible, should have descended to the crude plan of offering the sum of the raw scores in a couple of tests as the measure of each factor.

And this brings me back to the first point. For to know how much has been lost by this compromise I would need to be sure of what the "estimated validity" means. In his *Primary Mental Abilities* [4] one can calculate (though he does not give them explicitly) the determinable part of each factor as estimated from the whole battery of 57 tests, by post-multiplying Table 7 (p. 98) by Table 3 (p. 96). Thus, for example, one finds the determinate part of the P factor there to be .616, and of the N factor to be .825. If the squares of the "estimated validities" in the present tests are to be compared with these quantities, they are .65 squared and .63 squared, or .423 and .397, indicating a very considerable loss of "validity" by the compromise of simplicity. And if this comparison is not the proper one to make, then I criticise the manual for not making perfectly clear what is meant by "estimated validity." Possibly, however, these criticisms might have been unnecessary had the Hyde Park School article appeared. Yet I do not really think so. These tests of primary mental abilities are a new departure along a pioneer track. The manual accompanying them ought to have been, in part, a summary of their theoretical justification, to be read, of course, with the assumption that the relevant articles in the journals were known.

But having now done my duty as a critic I would like to conclude by saying, without any implication that I am subscribing to Thurstone's theories, that I should be very proud to have produced these tests and this manual.

Robert C. Tryon, Associate Professor of Psychology, The University of California. The reviewer is frankly defeatist regarding the theory that there exist a few important functional, primary unities in human behavior and that factor analysis provides the means of discovering them. This test which purports to measure seven such primary traits as isolated by Thurstone's factor method requires, in the reviewer's mind, restricted use. The troubling thought is that the test—developed by such an eminent and brilliant authority and bolstered by an awe-inspiring mathematics—may set a new tradition of a few faculties of the mind, just at the time psychologists are showing some signs of recovering from the pall of the IQ doctrine.

In his manual of instructions, the author does indeed urge caution, recommending the use of the test only in schools employing a competent psychologist. But competence in evaluating these "primary traits" requires a grounding in factor theory; one should, for example, be conversant with Thomson's *Fac-*

rial Analysis of Human Ability, in which Thurstone's arbitrary assumptions are set off against a variety of others which could equally well be made. Probably not a handful of school psychologists have such a training.

The intent of the test is to measure several important *functions*, but the author admits uncertainty regarding the psychological nature of these. Factor P "*seems* to be a perceptual ability," "those who excel in [factor V] . . . are *probably* verbally-minded in their thinking," "it *seems reasonable* to expect" that ability S refers to visualization; "factor M can be *tentatively* named the ability to memorize," "the hypothesis that the factor I is associated with inductive thinking] . . . *seems plausible*," "factor D *seems* to represent facility in formal reasoning." [Words italicized by the reviewer.]

What is clearly wanted is convincing evidence of the psychological validity of these abilities. The manual presents the "estimated validity" of each type of ability score, which is a composite of two or more subtests. But validity is defined as "the estimated correlation between the composite score and a pure test of the primary factor." One not familiar with factor logic might suppose that this means a correlation between the test score and a superlatively constructed experimental or empirical criterion. But its real meaning is geometric, to wit: the projection of the test on a primary trait vector which, as such, is not experimentally determined. The primary trait vectors are *theoretical* abilities inferred from the intercorrelations between the tests and governed by the assumptions of Thurstone's factor methods.

Taken at face value, furthermore, all of the validities of the seven measures are discouragingly low, being of the order .6. As an illustration of the inadequacy of this value, the variance of the measure of Reasoning (D) as scored in the experimental sample of subjects is only about 36 per cent determined by the pure reasoning factor and 64 per cent by factors having nothing to do with reasoning. These other nonreasoning factors would correlate as high as .8 with the D scores. Individual diagnosis of a trait is precarious where the diagnostic score is only about a third determined by a pure measure of the trait and where the pure measure itself is a theoretical and undefined continuum.

The test is an interesting and ingenious research instrument to be used by factor-trained psychologists. The reviewer believes that years of research will be necessary before the test can be shown to possess practical value in vocational counseling.

J Ed Res 33:698-704 My '40. John M. Stalnaker. "Results from Factor Analysis." * The most striking characteristic of the tests, obvious from inspection, is that they are all short speed tests. Manual dexterity in operating a pencil and speed of reaction are of unquestioned importance in almost all the tests. Speed is so important, and the tests are so brief, that slight errors in timing must assume major importance. The test results would differ greatly for various age groups. Adults, on the average, cannot work at the speed demanded—such as in the "same-opposites" test in which twenty items per minute are offered and then the response word may be the same or the opposite of the stimulus word. In using machine-scorable sheets some subjects, it has been found, blacken the space between the lines very carefully. Such a person will be found deficient in all primary mental abilities. There is evidence that a very different factor pattern would emerge if these tests were given without time limits. Although speed is certainly of primary significance in these tests, no factor or primary mental ability of speed has been found. That it has not may be a reflection on or limitation of the method of analysis used. Does it make psychological sense to ignore speed? * To summarize: the mathematical theory underlying factor analysis techniques will doubtless be perfected in time so that factor analysis will be recognized as a powerful mathematical tool. Its application to the results of valid tests given to various but known types of populations may yield data of value for a better understanding of the functioning of the mind and for purposes of practical educational guidance. At the moment, however, the greatest need seems to be for vastly improved basic tests, tests developed with but one object in view—a thorough and dependable measure of certain types of ability. Such tests will require more time from the candidates; some of the tests may be more difficult to score; all of them will require great care in construction. Until such tests are used as a source for the primary data, positive conclusions from any system of factor analysis must be viewed as conjecture. To Mr. Thurstone we are all indebted for stimulating interest in this problem by offering the experimental edition of his tests, tests which he personally advocates be restricted at this time to experimental purposes and to group not to individual interpretation. One can but hope that a like amount of intelligence, energy, and industry will be devoted, by him and by others, to producing tests of the high quality necessary to make the results from mathematical analyses of test data of practical significance, not alone for basic theoretical studies, but also for the use of those who are merely "faithful workers in the vineyards."

Sch and Soc 50:868-72 D 30 '39. John M. Stalnaker. "Primary Mental Abilities." * Of practical importance is the question of the value of this particular set of tests for individual diagnosis and guidance. Even if the theory on which the tests are based were beyond question, there is still the problem of how thoroughly it has been applied and how well prepared the present series is. The analysis here reported throws some light on the question. In spite of the enormous amount of research which directly or indirectly has gone into the preparation of the present set of tests and the careful editing to which they have been subjected, the results obtained with one group of candidates do not support in full the theory of the seven primary abilities. Speed, although not recognized as a "factor," appears to be of utmost importance. The time allowed for each test is brief, and the resulting individual scores, therefore, are not as dependable as if longer tests had been used. The tests could be materially improved by the elimination of items of low validity, by arranging the items in order of difficulty and by adjusting the time limits. It will be interesting to observe the relationship found for university freshmen between the test scores of a perfected set of tests, tests given without time limits, and also to note the factors which may be postulated to account for the correlations thus obtained. Although tests given by the amount-limit method usually require more careful preparation than those given under very short time limits, such care and attention may be justified if a theory of primary mental abilities is to be established. A definite arrangement of the items according to difficulty may be desirable if time limits, even generous ones, are to be used. Longer tests may yield scores sufficiently dependable for indi-

vidual diagnosis. The present experimental edition is an interesting and stimulating initial attempt. The psychologists, the personnel and guidance groups, will all undoubtedly eagerly await a revision and improvement of these tests. The present tests are more useful in suggesting new lines of experimentation, needed developments and points of weakness, than they are in yielding data useful for individual diagnosis or guidance.

Sch and Soc 51:585-92 My 4 '40. A. B. Crawford. "Some Observations on the Primary Mental Abilities Battery in Action." Now that the Thurstone Primary Mental Abilities battery has been made generally available in readily scorable form, many personnel officers and educational authorities in schools and colleges alike are eager to learn how it can be utilized to serve practical problems of student orientation and guidance. A recently published analysis [6] . . . of current experience with this battery at one of the larger independent secondary schools in the East is . . . of timely interest. * With due appreciation of the care and completeness with which Mr. Shanner has marshalled and presented his data, I venture to question certain of the associated comments and conclusions. * The concluding paragraph of Mr. Shanner's report is as follows:

A comparison of the three different types of profiles suggests that groups selected upon the basis of academic achievement may differ significantly with respect to their mental abilities. In so far as the Thurstone *Tests for Primary Mental Abilities* are capable of accurately defining these abilities, we may use the tests for guidance purposes and for predicting performance on various achievement tests. The battery of tests is satisfactorily reliable and the intercorrelations for the ability scores are sufficiently low to indicate considerable independence of mental factors measured, even though they are not so low as one should desire. Although there should be additional refinement and improvement of the tests and further research concerning the interpretation of the results, the available evidence indicates that the tests in their present form unquestionably constitute a valuable addition to the field of aptitude testing.

Though Mr. Shanner has put us in his debt by the careful analysis and complete presentation of his data, I cannot find justification therein for these conclusions. He is, of course, entitled with all proper respect, to his own opinions. Those of a different nature here presented are doubtless open to considerable criticism in turn. Yet, with no intention to be arrogant, I submit (*a*) that, to quote Mr. Shanner again, i groups selected upon the basis of academic chievement" do really "differ significantly vith respect to their mental abilities" (as is ltogether likely), such difference is *not* re-ealed by this particular trial of the tests in uestion; and (*b*) that intercorrelations as re-orted in the study are *not* "sufficiently low to ndicate considerable independence of mental actors measured," although they certainly *are* not so low as one should desire." That "the ests in their present form unquestionably con-titute a valuable addition to the field of apti-ude testing" I sincerely hope and believe; but nis demonstration of their diagnostic powers s unconvincing. The results thus reported ap-ear, at least to the present writer, distinctly ess encouraging than had been hoped for, vhen the long-awaited primary ability mea-ures became generally available. Having of-ered some suggestions as to why they may not ave operated, in the situation so carefully nalyzed by Mr. Shanner, as their author had eason to expect, I still maintain faith in their ltimate importance as significant contributions ot only to psychological theory, but to prac-cal guidance needs as well. That the desired bjectives were not satisfactorily realized in nis early trial should but serve as a challenge o further experiment. * Thurstone . . . has een under continued pressure to make at least ome preliminary form of the P. M. A. bat-ery available for field experimentation and nmediate use. That he has consented to do so, ven though the present composite instruments dmittedly do not satisfy his standards of purity," represents, under the circumstances, generous concession which should be duly ap-reciated. Yet the current battery bears the rimary Mental Abilities label and generally regarded as measuring the traits so desig-ated. Its imperfections in this respect are less idely recognized than its objectives. * Obvi-usly, however, this one administration and e resultant analyses herein discussed neither rove nor disprove the value of Professor hurstone's battery. They do distinctly indi-ate the need for further investigation of how ese measures, conceived in scientific purity, n meet realistic educational and human emands. *

See also B503 and B1099.

[1428]

nit Scales of Aptitude. Grades 4-5, 6-7, 8-9, 10-12; 34-38; 2 forms; $1.00 per 25; 25¢ per specimen set;

(50-60) minutes; M. J. Van Wagenen; Minneapolis, Minn.: Educational Test Bureau, Inc.

Herschel T. Manuel, Professor of Educational Psychology, The University of Texas, and Director of Research, Texas Commission on Coordination in Education. This test is designed to yield measures of five "significant mental functions"—rate of comprehension of simple paragraphs, perception of relations (verbal analogies), reading vocabulary, composition vocabulary, and range of general information. The five together provide an "index of verbal competence," which is roughly comparable to the intelligence quotient. The difference between the reading vocabulary and the composition vocabulary test is illustrated by the following examples, respectively: (*a*) *commence* begin keep on stop rest delay; (*b*) He put up a *brave* fight prudent discreet uncouth inglorious valiant. In the first the stimulus word is supposed to be more difficult than the responses; in the second this is reversed.

The test bears evidence of careful work. The mechanical arrangement of the test booklet is satisfactory for hand scoring. With the exception of the first test (rate of comprehension), in which a cross-out technique is used, pupil responses are indicated by writing numbers in conveniently aligned blanks. The publication of the test in four divisions, each for a group of grades, avoids the bulkiness sometimes found in tests covering a wide range.

Although the manual of directions is fairly extensive and detailed, it seems to offer unnecessary difficulty to the reader. Perhaps the C-score is itself a difficult concept, but one feels that the explanation is not as clear as it might be. The use of terms with meanings that are unexpected (at least to the reviewer) is a possible source of difficulty. Verbal analogies, for example, bear the name "*perception* of relations." "Percent placement" turns out to be based, not upon the frequency of the score as one might expect, but upon the scale itself. It is simply a score for an age group scaled in terms of P.E. with a median of fifty. Thus a "percent placement" of 10 is a score of -4 P.E. This is 10 per cent "of the way between the lowest and highest cases among a representative thousand." Another possible criticism is that the number of different numerical measures used in interpreting scores seems rather formidable.

The test as a whole is probably a fairly satisfactory basis for an index of general ability such as is obtained from a short verbal group test of intelligence. Reading, vocabulary, analogies, and general information are acceptable components of such a test. The total score could be made more useful, however, by including in the individual profile an index of the level of total ability as well as an index of relative standing.

The most serious questions to be raised by this reviewer center around the five analytic measures, the "significant mental functions," which the test is said to measure. Perhaps the question of reliability—measuring five functions in 45 minutes—may be passed with the observation that a second form of the test might be administered to make the measures more stable if one had use for this particular analysis. Too, one should not lightly discourage any analysis that may prove to be useful. Factor analysis is too young for anyone to know just what analyses will be most useful. It is safe, however, to observe that nothing which the reviewer has found in the test material or elsewhere makes clear the specific use which a teacher may make of the separate measures. "Just how difficult content he knows and understands in each of the functions measured can be readily seen"—but what then? In verbal analogies, for example, what useful information would a high score give the teacher which would not be given much more reliably by the test as a whole?

[1429]

Wechsler-Bellevue Intelligence Scale. Age 10 and over; 1939; individual; $12.50 per outfit of testing material (not including the manual) ; $3.50 per manual; 75¢ per 25 record blanks ; David Wechsler; New York: Psychological Corporation.

REFERENCES

1 BALINSKY, B.; ISRAEL, H.; AND WECHSLER, D. "The Relative Effectiveness of the Stanford-Binet and the Bellevue Intelligence Scale in Diagnosing Mental Deficiency." *Am J Orthopsychiatry* 9:798-801 O '39.
2 WECHSLER, DAVID. *The Measurement of Adult Intelligence.* Baltimore, Md.: Williams & Wilkins Co., 1939. Pp. ix, 229. $3.50. (London: Baillière, Tindall, and Cox. 16s.)

F. L. Wells, Psychologist, Department of Hygiene, Harvard University. This series is by a considerable margin the best available procedure for adults, in a clinical setting. The writer will here discuss it from the standpoint not of general organization, which may be left to reviews of Wechsler's book, but of technical matters having special concern for a workaday user, as the writer has for some time had the good fortune to be. Naturally this involves

mention, if not enumeration, of real or fancied flaws in detail. In important features, the scale' status is as above set forth ; as it deserves grea use, it can also bear minute scrutiny withou captiousness.

To begin with, the question of the preceding president will obviously vary in difficulty according to the length of the current incumbency. The "pints" question is an interesting one suggesting that its relative value may have something to do with the misleading association furnished by "quart" (quarter, fourth) The writer does not like the use of the word "obtain" ; too high-brow for a question so early in the series. The standard answer to the thermometer question is also of a high level for so early a position, and since the test may be often given in general hospital surroundings, attention should be paid to response in terms of clinical thermometers. "Average height" again seems rather complicated from a vocabulary standpoint for its position in the series. The writer has always favored formulating an information question in the simplest possible terms (e.g., What does rubber come from? About how tall are American women mostly?) even if it involves a recasting of norms. Few things are so disturbing to an examinee's attitude as a question with an unintelligible or even very unfamiliar expression in it. The airplane, North Pole, and United States population questions are specially interesting for their distribution of erroneous answers. The instructions for certain items should make clearer what is the limit of tolerance in the responses as in, e.g., apocrypha, habeas corpus.

In the comprehension subtest the first question would probably benefit by specifying a "new" (uncancelled) stamp. The scoring of the leather question seems needlessly cumbrous. The second alternate involves rather too many variables to be satisfactory from the standpoint of intelligence, whatever might be its significance for an evaluation of personality Comprehension questions in general give good insights into the examinee's intellectual processes, but it is hard to set up satisfactory scoring criteria for them. The present questions illustrate dependence on attitude and background ; cf., urban and rural background to the "forest" question.

Digit span hardly calls for comment. The most meaningful of the verbal subtests is surely Similarities. The directions are particularly well found. But it is impossible to avoid repeating the criticism that more levels of credit should be recognized, and especially given a wide spread. As to specific items, wood and alcohol make trouble on account of the "wood alcohol" association, and Wechsler must have somehow escaped wrestling with dialect pronunciations of "poem."

Among the arithmetical questions the sugar problem has seemed placed a little late in the series. It is embarrassing to raise invidious questions of commercial ethics, but so much complication has arisen over the prescribed wording of the making change problems, that the word "should" appears preferable to "will." As on other grounds, "get back" is preferable to "receive." (Also in Item 8 of the same, "how much did it cost new" rather than ". . . was it worth new.")

The organization of performance tests always presents greater difficulty than obtains with language content. A more distinctive name than "picture completion" might have been found for the first listed. It is not clear whether there has been a studied inclusion of misleads in such items as the hinge on the door (knobs are hardly more "important" than hinges), the discontinuous cane in the sunset, and the missing antennae of the ship.

Picture arrangement is an excellent testing device, limited by its cumbrousness. (The Bellevue series could have spared itself much of this by printing, as it could easily have done, each one of its pictures on a separate 3 × 5 card.) Cultural difficulties enter, e.g., the taxi outside an urban environment. It has been objected that in the holdup situation the A, B, D, C order is too reasonable to be scored zero, especially since the outmoding of prison "stripes."

The block design series is probably the strongest of the performance subtests. One could wish that more use had been made of the principle, which could well include three-dimensional models. The object-assembly test is cumbrous for what it distinctively contributes, and pencil-and-paper tests, even though nonverbal, seem out of place in a strictly "performance" scale. Fortunately the scale is not a tightly closed system and it is perhaps not too much to hope that the performance scale may be amplified into a manipulative (e.g., block design) and non-manipulative (e.g., digit-symbol) series.

An alternate subtest has been added, a vocabulary test of the Terman type (other words) being taken for the purpose; probably as wise a choice as available. Notation would be easier with double and single credits, as elsewhere, rather than single and half.

That very important and often neglected feature of a test series, the record form, is only moderately well designed. In addition to some rearrangement of material, the writer would prefer to have most of the rulings omitted; they cramp eye movements as well as size of writing, and disregard the consideration that little or nothing may need recording on one item, with a long note on the next.

Special mention should also be made of age norms, tracing the gradual decline of performance after early adult years. In terms of mental age this is some 20 per cent between ages 20 and 60 (pp. 56, 196).[2] Although little cited here, perhaps the strongest feature of the scale is its structure, which can serve as a model, in its facility of comparison between records of different well-constructed subtests. For the author of a treatment of Army Alpha from this standpoint, Wechsler lays less stress on this feature than might be anticipated. The chief use of global scores is administrative.

Arch Neurology and Psychiatry 43:614 Mr '40. * a clear presentation * provides a scale which is simple to give and is reliable. *

Psychol B 37:251-4 Ap '40. Grace H. Kent. * The book opens with a ten-page chapter on the nature of intelligence, which is defined as "the aggregate or global capacity of the individual to act purposefully, to think rationally and to deal effectively with his environment." No question is raised by the author concerning the measurability of intelligence as thus defined. The need for a test system intended specifically for study of adult intelligence as opposed to juvenile intelligence is stated in a way which must strike a responsive chord in every clinical examiner who has had occasion to present the Binet scale to a mature subject of average or superior achievement. * In spite of his opposition to the IQ as we know it, the author considers "Intelligence Quotient" too happy a term to be discarded. In his standardization of the Bellevue tests he presents the norms, as determined by standard deviation procedure, in tables by means of which the weighted scores can be converted directly into what he calls the "IQ." This use of the term, as applied to something entirely different from what we understand by it, is likely to be misleading. The strongest feature of the system is the selection of cases for standardization. The norms are based upon scores obtained from 1750 subjects ranging in age from seven to seventy, selected out of 3500 subjects to whom the tests had been presented, the selection being a sampling based upon the occupational distribution of the country's adult white population, as indicated by the 1930 census. The adult subjects were divided into age groups by five-year intervals, the number of cases in a group ranging from 50 subjects in the later fifties to 195 subjects in the later twenties. The collection of such a mass of data is a marvelous achievement. The scale consists of ten test units (plus one alternate), each unit having a wide range of discriminative capacity. Correlations and intercorrelations have been calculated for all possible combinations, and the units are ranked in value according to their correlation with the scale as a whole. The scores have been so weighted as to make the numerical values approximately uniform for the eleven units. Three tables of norms are based upon these weighted scores: one for ten tests, one for five language tests, and one for five performance tests. The student who is not too scrupulous about manipulations of results will be able to obtain approximate ratings from other combinations. Most of the tests are modified forms of tests already in use. The strongest unit of the scale is "Similarities," a series of 12 pairs beginning with *orange—banana* and ending with *fly—tree*. Following Binet, Dr. Wechsler has apparently given more careful attention to criteria for standardization than to criteria for selection of test items. He includes Memory Span for Digits, although acknowledging it to be a weak test as a measure of intelligence. Furthermore, he combines digits forwards and digits backwards under one score, allowing the same credit for five digits forwards as for five digits backwards. He uses also the Symbol-Digit test, observing that the scores show a marked decline with advancing age, but making no mention of visual strain as a possible explanation of this decline. In the tests called "Picture Arrangement" and "Picture Completion," he has used pictures which are too small and too sketchy to be easily understood. It appears that the value of a test, for him, is statistical rather than psychological. The text

is carelessly written. "Like" is used as a conjunction, and "where" as a relative pronoun. Throughout the book the author refers to himself as "we," as if the work were a joint product. His irregular use of the "editorial we" is at times misleading, especially when he uses "we" as including (apparently) the small group of students who assisted in making the examinations or the larger group of psychologists who may be expected to use the test in the future. Some of the test materials are contained in six pasteboard boxes, each of which has the name *Bellevue Intelligence Test* blazoned on the cover. Before placing these boxes on the table in full view of the subject, the examiner would do well to cover the offensive labels with something in code. Clinical examiners who are relatively satisfied with some form of the Binet-Simon scale for examination of children will welcome a test which is intrinsically better adapted to adult interests and which is adequately standardized for adults. To this extent, the Bellevue scale will meet a need that has been keenly felt for more than twenty years. It does not, however, show any such advance over the Binet scale as might be expected as a result of our collective experience in the use of tests for a full generation. Students engaged in the development of tests for individual study can learn much from Dr. Wechsler's plan of standardization. The table by means of which a score can be converted directly into the IQ (or its equivalent, preferably under some other name) marks a very important advance over the current method of deriving the IQ. If all tests were thus standardized, the public demand for a one-figure rating could be satisfied honestly and without distortion of results. But the "mental age," although it lends itself to gross abuse, need not be wholly discarded. Many students, with full appreciation of Dr. Wechsler's contribution to higher standards of accuracy in evaluation of test results, will be disappointed because he has made it difficult to derive a satisfactory "mental age" from the scores of his tests. So long as this way of expressing results is so nearly universal, the "mental age" is indispensable as a common denominator. It is a mistake for any author of tests to assume that others will wish to adopt his system as a whole and use it exactly as he himself uses it. Some of us prefer a flexible system to any composite scale. If Dr. Wechsler had included a table of true mental age" norms for the ages seven to seventeen, not for this three scales, but for each individual unit, the Bellevue tests would be incomparably more useful and would presumably see much wider service. A full-size textbook is too large to be used conveniently as a manual of instructions for test presentation. The third part of this book, containing the instructions and norms, might better have been separated from the reference material in the first two parts. For the convenience of the examiner it is to be hoped that the author will publish additionally a compact booklet or pamphlet containing only what is needed for the daily use of the tests. It is strongly urged that he offer norms (for each unit individually) in the form of simple decile scores for each age group, unweighted and wholly free from mathematical manipulation. He has in his possession much material which would be invaluable to clinical examiners.

See also B1121.

[1430]

"West Riding" Tests of Mental Ability. Ages 9-14; 1925; 2 parts; 6s. 6d. per 25 test booklets; 1s. 9d. per 25 answer sheets; 6d. per manual; 1s. per specimen set; 55(65) minutes; T. P. Tomlinson; London: University of London Press, Ltd.
a) SET Y.
b) SET Z. For use only with examinees who have taken Set Y on the day previous to taking Set Z.

Ll. Wynn Jones, Senior Lecturer in Experimental Psychology, University of Leeds. Each set consists of eight subtests: Test A, Instructions; Test B, Word Meaning; Test C, Arithmetic; Test D, Analogies; Test E, Incongruities; Test F, Logical Selection; Test G, Jumbled Sentences; and Test H, Classification. These tests were standardised by Tomlinson in preparation for an M.Ed. thesis entitled *A Group Scale of Mental Ability* which was approved by the University of Leeds in June, 1923.

In the main Tomlinson based his statistical evaluation of the tests on the Spearman technique. For each subtest the reliability and the correlation with the central intellective factor or *g* are high, whether for city, rural, or small town children. The reliability of the scale as a whole is as high as .95. Some of the subtests, however, cannot be marked as quickly as the more modern forms. Thus in the analogies test Tomlinson decided that the form which requires the testee to find the correct answer was

more valid than the more modern form of underlining one of five given words and therefore adopted it. This also applies to the incongruities test where the testee has to express his answer in words. The word meaning test, the logical selection test, and the classification test were new, at least in the form in which Tomlinson used them.

In the Examiners' Manual there is a table giving the mental age equivalents, so that an approximate value for the IQ of each testee may be obtained. In one rural school Tomlinson found the average IQ of the native children to be 82.5, a standard deviation of 15.3, and a range of 58 to 110. These figures may be compared with the corresponding figures given by Burt for a Warwickshire Village, viz., 81.6, 15.7, and 38 to 112. The distribution of IQ's in an average city school was found to agree very closely with the normal distribution given by Terman. Tomlinson himself points out in his thesis that the word meaning test, the incongruities test, and the classification test have little distributing value for the lower 25 per cent of the 9-year-old children tested. This means that the tests are not effective for mental ages below 7. This, of course, is partly due to the fact that any group test of a literary nature would tend to correlate highly at low mental ages with scholastic attainments in reading and writing. Coefficients of correlation were obtained with teacher's estimates of .84 at age 12 and of .71 at age 13. There was a greater range of *g* in the rural schools where there was a high percentage of low as well as of high IQ's. Godfrey Thomson refers to the migration of the more intellectual elements of rural districts to the city. Tomlinson mentions the migration of the lesser intellectual elements from the villages to a neighbouring township which offers abundance of employment of an unskilled nature. In some cases there has been immigration of higher intellectual elements into villages on the outskirts of big towns and is probably one of the factors operating to provide Thomson with his highest IQ's in such localities.

[1430.1]

Word-Number Test of Scholastic Aptitude. Grades 4-8, 9-16; 1939-40; 1 form, 2 levels; $1.75 per 30; $1.50 per 100 machine-scorable answer sheets; 10¢ per specimen set; 30(35-40) minutes; H. T. Manuel, James Knight, J. A. Floyd, and R. C. Jordon; Austin, Texas: Steck Co.
a) FORM X. Grades 4-8.
b) FORM A. Grades 9-16.

MATHEMATICS

Reviews by Albert A. Bennett, H. E. Benz, William A. Brownell, Leo J. Brueckner, John R. Clark, Edward E. Cureton, Harl R. Douglass, Richard M. Drake, Harold Fawcett, Tomlinson Fort, Judson W. Foust, Foster E. Grossnickle, J. O. Hassler, G. E. Hawkins, Earle R. Hedrick, L. B. Kinney, W. Elmer Lancaster, J. H. Minnick, R. L. Morton, W. J. Osburn, M. W. Richardson, Paul R. Rider, G. M. Ruch, Leroy H. Schnell, Fred J. Schonell, C. Ebblewhite Smith, Peter L. Spencer, C. L. Thiele, Charles C. Weidemann, Harry Grove Wheat, S. S. Wilks, and G. M. Wilson.

[1431]

Cooperative General Mathematics Test for College Students. 1933-37; a duplicate of the *Cooperative General Mathematics Test for High School Classes* with the addition of a fourth section made up of more advanced material; Forms 1934, 1935, 1936, and 1937; Form 1933 is out of print; 6¢ per test, 10 to 99 copies; 25¢ per specimen set; 120(130) minutes; H. T. Lundholm and L. P. Siceloff; New York: Cooperative Test Service.

Tomlinson Fort, Dean of the Graduate School and Professor of Mathematics, Lehigh University. [Review of Form 1937.] This is a good examination as "new-type" tests go. There are in all 164 questions. Of these, 95 can be described as of the short problem and 69 of the multiple-choice type. According to the authors, in that portion of the examination suitable for high school students such topics are covered as the interpretation of graphs, the use of algebraic symbols, functional relations, geometrical relations in two-dimensional and three-dimensional space, and trigonometric relations. The complete examination adds a section of 44 questions of a more advanced nature including a little calculus.

It is assumed that this complete test is intended for students who have completed one year of work in college. However, if this is so, the college teacher is apt to feel that as an achievement test there is too much emphasis on precollege mathematics and not enough on the work that he himself has taught. Particularly will this be the case if the student has not had as much as one semester of calculus. Many students complete their freshman year with no calculus and for this group the introduction of calculus at all may prove confusing. As a matter of fact, in the opinion of the reviewer, any examination on general mathematics is subject to the following criticism. If throughout the examination there occur questions on which the student is entirely uninformed, an element

of confusion is introduced which may vary as greatly as between individuals. If the material is strictly segregated by topics the examination ceases to be an examination in general mathematics.

In that portion of the examination of secondary grade the great emphasis on short problem questions (95 as against 25 multiple-choice questions) attaches great importance to facility in arithmetic computation, probably more than is deserved when judged by the importance of arithmetic computation in mathematics. Moreover, the structure of the examination necessarily reduces the emphasis on geometry except in so far as mensuration is concerned. As a matter of fact, any new-type examination seems certain to slight formal geometry and it is only in his geometry that the average student ever learns what proof consists in. And so to the mathematician who realizes the predominant position of proof in more advanced mathematics, any slighting of formal geometry is to be deplored. The ability to solve more serious problems than can appear in an examination like this one is most important. Many college teachers believe that the new-type examination is not adequate to test this ability, nor to test the ability to carry out formal proof. This is one reason that this kind of examination is not more widely used in colleges. However, in his own work the reviewer has succeeded very well, it seems to him, in obtaining the advantages of the new-type as well as the problem-proof examination by dividing examinations into two distinct parts, one a new-type and the other a problem-proof examination. It is surprising that this procedure is not more generally followed.

Finally, the present examination seems a good one within the limitations of the new-type test. It is to be recommended. The dominance of the short problem as against the multiple-choice question strengthens it.

For a review by M. W. Richardson, see 1071.

[1432]

Cooperative General Mathematics Test for High School Classes. 2-4 years of mathematics; 1933-38; 40- and 90-minute editions; 5¢ per test, 10 to 99 copies; 25¢ per specimen set of either edition; H. T. Lundholm and L. P. Siceloff; New York: Cooperative Test Service.
a) FORMS 1934 AND 1935. Forms 1933, 1936, and 1937 are out of print; 90(95) minutes.
b) REVISED SERIES FORMS N AND O. 1937-38; 1½¢ per machine-scorable answer sheet; 40(45) minutes.

REFERENCES

1 HANNA, JOSEPH V. "A Comparison of Cooperative Test Scores and High School Grades as Measures for Predicting Achievement in College." *J Appl Psychol* 23:289-97 Ap '39.

L. B. Kinney, Associate Professor of Education, Stanford University. [Review of Form O.] This test is intended as a comprehensive achievement test to classify individual students in mathematics even though they may have very different backgrounds. It is also intended as an instrument for measuring increments in the field.

The objectives upon which the selection of items is based are primarily those concerned with a development of understanding and skill relative to the processes, principles, relationships, and concepts that constitute specific content of the field. The items represent a wide sampling of materials covered in the secondary school courses in mathematics, as revealed by analyses of textbooks and courses of study. They include multiplication of decimal and common fractions, percentage, interpretation of graphs, algebraic computations, logarithms, trigonometric functions, and a variety of problems.

Administratively, the test is very well planned. The directions are clear and concise. The time limit, forty minutes, is convenient for most schools. The scoring is very simple, since the questions are all of the multiple-choice type. The reliability of .91 indicates a high degree of consistency of performance.

The multiple-choice form of question raises an interesting point as regards the ability measured by the test. Logically, it would seem that performance on such a test would require an ability to arrive at an approximate solution or check a solution obtained by someone else, rather than the ability to present an independent solution. It may be that these abilities are identical, but no evidence to this effect is of-

fered in the literature descriptive of the test. In the field of vocabulary, it has been found that the functions measured by multiple-choice tests have some degree of independence from those measured by completion tests. Reasoning by analogy, in the absence of better evidence, one may question whether the convenience of the multiple-choice question is not obtained at too great a sacrifice in a mathematics test.

The material presented for the purpose of facilitating the interpretation of scores is probably more complete and useful than for any other test in the field. Percentiles are given for various groups of high school students, based not only on mathematics courses completed, but also on geographic location. The literature accompanying the test describes the derivation and use of the norms and test results.

For a review by Maurice Hartung, see 1072.

[1433]

Cooperative Mathematics Test for Grades 7, 8, and 9. 1938-39; Forms O, P, and Q; 5¢ per test, 10 to 99 copies; 1½¢ per machine-scorable answer sheet; 25¢ per specimen set; 40(45) minutes; Forms P and Q: Alice H. Darnell, John C. Flanagan, Stevenson W. Fletcher, and Rose E. Lutz with the editorial assistance of Ralph Beatley, Ruth Sayward (Form P), Dorothy S. Wheeler (Form P), W. D. Reeve (Form Q), C. L. Thiele (Form Q), and C. C. Weidemann (Form Q); New York: Cooperative Test Service.

REFERENCES

1 SEDER, MARGARET. "A Correlational Study of the Cooperative Mathematics Test for Grades 7, 8, and 9," pp. 49-53. In *1939 Achievement Testing Program in Independent Schools and Supplementary Studies.* Educational Records Bulletin No. 27. New York: Educational Records Bureau, June 1939. Pp. xiii, 76, 11. $1.50. Paper, lithotyped.
2 SEDER, MARGARET. "An Experimental Study of a New Mathematics Test for Grades 7, 8, and 9." *Math Teach* 32:259-64 O '39.

Richard M. Drake, Assistant Professor of Education, The University of Buffalo. [Review of Form P.] The directions for administering this test are very explicit. The directions for scoring should be read and studied by all teachers whether they make use of the test or not. The authors of this test have provided answer sheets, which reduces the cost considerably. The test is well organized and in good form. Since the test is quite recent, no scaled scores are available nor is the reliability indicated. Publication of a test before such data has been compiled is a questionable procedure.

The content of this test is such that it would not be valid for use in schools where formal algebra is stressed in the ninth grade. The authors claim that it is appropriate for use in schools employing the integrated approach.

Since the content of such courses is ordinarily in a constant state of revision, it is doubtful if a test could be set up which would be valid for all such revisions.

In Part II an attempt is made to test vocabulary and concepts. The items included in this part are excellent but there should be more stress on this part of the test.

For each item in the test five possible responses are set up. The pupil is to choose the correct response and record its number as his answer. This procedure simplifies the scoring by eliminating partial credit and the possibility of having answers in several different forms. However, it is not a typical problem-solving situation. When one is confronted with a problem in life, one does not often know in advance the possible solutions. Furthermore, this multiple-choice procedure limits to four the possible number of incorrect procedures in solving the problem. Diagnosis of difficulties in solving problems often shows more than four typical errors.

Within the reviewer's experience this test is the best of its kind. However, it is doubtful if one should attempt to test so much material by means of a single test requiring eighty minutes of working time.

Judson W. Foust, Assistant Professor of Mathematics, Central State Teachers College, Mt. Pleasant, Michigan. [Review of Form P.] The test consists of four parts with questions presented in multiple-choice form. Each part is concerned with one of the following four types of material on mathematics and allotted the respective time intervals stated below. Part I, Skills—30 minutes; Part II, Facts, Terms, and Concepts—10 minutes; Part III, Applications—30 minutes; Part IV, Appreciation—10 minutes.

These divisions outlined seem reasonable and adequate. The amount of material given in each part, as suggested by specific time allotments, places emphasis on skills and applications rather than on memorized facts, terms, and concepts except as these are *used* in connection with exercises. This is fully justified.

It is heartening to see a test, such as this, requiring 80 minutes testing time and hence providing space for a wide sampling. The test allows the better student to stretch out since the amount of material presented is such that it is not expected that a student answer all the questions in any part within the time limit. The test is capable of being given in two 40-minute periods so as to fit into the school program.

From every indication the test should prove satisfactory. However since Form P appeared as late as May 1, 1939 there are presented no reliability coefficients to statistically justify the above inference. Lack of norms, at this time, will also retard its use.

Perhaps the most doubtful part is the section on appreciation. Some of this material seems to call for skills. Since appreciations are admittedly hardest to test and this is an initial attempt to provide some material along that line, one is tempted to compliment the material given and ask that this section be expanded somewhat in future revisions.

G. M. Ruch, Chief, Research and Statistical Service, United States Office of Education, Washington, D. C. [Review of Form P.] This test is a 16-page booklet in four parts: (*a*) Skills, (*b*) Facts, Terms, and Concepts, (*c*) Applications, and (*d*) Appreciation. The numbers of items, by parts, respectively, are 45, 30, 30, and 25, or a total of 130. It is suitable for grades 7, 8, and 9 in schools teaching general mathematics, as contrasted with arithmetic in grades 7 and 8 and algebra in grade 9. Its content is similar to that of recent courses of study and textbooks based upon a true junior high school organization. The easiest items begin at about the third grade level, and move rapidly to the higher grade levels. There is a considerable number of elements of algebra and geometry. These are selected, however, with a view to life situations. The relative proportions of elements drawn from the fields of arithmetic, algebra, geometry, etc., are judged to be reasonable ones; no fixed criteria are possible in a field in which there is considerable flux at present. In the opinion of the reviewer, the sampling is about as adequate as any one group of competent authors would be likely to arrive at. There is little or no trace of the domination of secondary and collegiate subject matter traditions.

Few verbal problems, in the typical sense, are provided; this statement is not to be taken as implying that reasoning and judgment (mental processes by which problems are justified) are not measured.

All items are of the 5-choice variety, adapted to rapid hand scoring by strip stencils or by response on separate answer sheets to be scored by the International scoring machine. Compact (perhaps too compact for easiest use) tables for correcting for chance eliminate much calculation and reduce resulting errors.

The fourth section of the test (Appreciation) is probably the most novel, and probably the most "spotted." Generally excellent, it suddenly presents several items that call for little more than inspectional placement of decimal points in multiplication and division. This admittedly useful and greatly neglected skill probably fits better in Parts I and II.

Taken in its entirety, this is one of the promising tests in mathematics. As to its technical excellence in a statistical sense, the reviewer can make no comment because he was not furnished with the necessary data; possibly because the test itself was published in advance of a full treatment of its validation and standardization. It is apparently geared to all other tests in the Cooperative series so far as common norms, profile graphs, methods of interpretation, and the like, are concerned.

The obvious defects of the test are chiefly those of printing. Typesetting by a linotype machine is limited in a field involving symbols and mathematical algorisms. Modern textbooks are almost invariably monotype-set with the result that linotype-set tests present somewhat strange visual patterns, especially below the secondary school level. Examples are: .12½ instead of .12$\frac{1}{2}$ (because linotype fonts do not carry "piece" fractions), mixed type faces such as 1⁹⁄₁₆, and the use of bold-face type for literal expressions such as **3a(a + 2a)** instead of the conventional roman and italic style $3a(a + 2a)$. Another marring typographical feature is the varying use of the hyphen and dash for the minus sign. The use of caps in such formulas as **I = PRT** is hardly conventional in the right member of the equation. The make-ready for the press shows signs of haste. There are one or two questionable mathematical usages, but none that could be held to be definitely at variance with common practices.

[1434]

Survey Test in Mathematics: Cooperative General Achievement Test, Part III. High school and college placement; 1937-39; Forms N, O, and P; 6¢ per test, 10 to 99 copies; 1½¢ per machine-scorable answer sheet; 25¢ per specimen set; 40(45) minutes; Form O: John A. Long and L. P. Siceloff; Form P: Constance M. McCullough, Emma Spaney, and L. P. Siceloff with the editorial assistance of Ruth Lane, Rose Roll, M. F. Rosskopf, and C. N. Stokes; New York: Cooperative Test Service.

Paul R. Rider, Professor of Mathematics, Washington University. [Review of Form O.] My first impression of this test is that it is too long. There are 75 questions to be answered in 40 minutes. This gives only 32 seconds per question and many of the questions require a certain amount of computation.

The questions, on the whole, are good, but in some instances could be improved. For example, one of the possible answers or distractors for Item 8, "$\frac{3}{10} + \frac{1}{2}$ is equal to," should be $\frac{4}{12}$, as a student who does not really know how to add fractions is very likely to guess that they can be added by adding their numerators and adding their denominators. Similarly, for Item 62, "If $x^2 = \frac{A + B}{C^2}$, then x equals," one choice should be $\frac{\sqrt{A} + \sqrt{B}}{C}$. Seeing the excerpt from a table of tangents in Item 73, the student might naturally suppose that he is expected to interpolate. If he does so, the answer is not given among the possible choices.

Two of the five questions devoted to solid geometry have the words parabola, ellipse, hyperbola (or the corresponding adjectives) among the answers to be chosen from. This seems inexcusable, particularly since most courses in high school solid geometry do not even mention the conic sections. This part of the test is not well balanced; it contains a disproportionate amount of material concerning cones and cylinders. It should include some questions about the relations between lines and planes, e.g., The number of lines which can be drawn parallel to a plane through a point exterior to the plane is: (*a*) none (*b*) 1 (*c*) 2 (*d*) any number.

For reviews by Arnold Dresden, Palmer O. Johnson, M. W. Richardson, and S. S. Wilks, see 870.

[1434.1]

Test of General Proficiency in the Field of Mathematics: Cooperative General Achievement Tests, Revised Series, Part II. High school and college; Form QR; 6¢ per test, 10 to 99 copies; 1½¢ per machine-scorable answer sheet; 25¢ per specimen set; 40(45) minutes; Emma Spaney with the editorial assistance of Alice H. Darnell, Rose E. Lutz, Hiram E. Pratt, and Robert Widdop; New York: Cooperative Test Service.

REFERENCES

1 Cooperative Test Service. *The Cooperative General Achievement Tests (Revised Series)*: Information Concerning their Construction, Interpretation, and Use. New York: Cooperative Test Service, 1940. Pp. 4. Gratis. Paper.

ALGEBRA

[1435]

Breslich Algebra Survey Test. First, second semesters: high school; 1930-31; 2 forms, 2 levels; 75¢ per 25; 10¢ per specimen set of either level; E. R. Breslich; Bloomington, Ill.: Public School Publishing Co.
a) FIRST SEMESTER. 41(50) minutes.
b) SECOND SEMESTER. 52(60) minutes.

John R. Clark, Principal of the High School, Lincoln School, and Associate Professor of Education, Columbia University. The first-semester booklet includes the following sub-tests: Part I, recognition of algebraic concepts, a matching test in which the pupil is to associate algebraic symbolism with its appropriate conceptual name (3 minutes); Part II, changing algebraic expressions to simpler forms (3 minutes); Part III, solving equations both integral and fractional involving one unknown (8 minutes); Part IV, deriving equations from verbally stated problems (5 minutes); Part V, finding the value of a formula (6 minutes), a test in the evaluation of algebraic expressions, translating verbal statements into formulas (3 minutes) and the translation and construction of graphs (3 minutes); Part VI, factoring (6 minutes).

The author conceives some of the major powers to be developed by the study of algebra to be: (*a*) to understand the terminology of the algebra taught during the semester; (*b*) to perform the fundamental operations that have been taught; (*c*) to combine and decompose simple algebraic expressions; (*d*) to derive equations from problems; (*e*) to solve equations; (*f*) to understand formulas; (*g*) to evaluate formulas; (*h*) to solve formulas for a given letter; (*i*) to translate verbal statements into formulas; (*j*) to understand graphical representation; (*k*) to use graphical representation.

Assuming the validity of the author's major purposes to be achieved by the study of algebra, we must conclude that the content of the test is justified. We wish to give special approval to the items in Part IV. For the most part these may be called genuine problems in the solution of which algebra is truly instrumental or functional. We should also commend

Breslich for his emphasis upon the construction of formulas as given in Part V.

In the manual of directions for the use of the test there appear standards for each part of the test. These include the lower quartile, the median and the upper quartile on each of the test's six parts based upon the scores of 5,963 pupils.

The second-semester test, similar in construction to the test for the first semester, is divided into the following parts; Part I, algebraic concepts (3 minutes); Part II, algebraic processes (8 minutes); Part III, solving equations with numerical coefficients (5 minutes) and with literal coefficients (5 minutes); Part IV, deriving equations from problems (8 minutes) and solving problems (5 minutes); Part V, fractions (8 minutes); Part VI, evaluating algebraic expressions (3 minutes), telling how changes in the value of one variable change the value of another (2 minutes), interpreting graphs (2 minutes), and graphical solutions of a system of equations (2 minutes).

Standards similar to those supplied for the first-semester test are included, together with percentile norms. Breslich argues that the test is valid because its items were common to five widely used textbooks in algebra.

A careful study of the *Iowa Every-Pupil Test in Ninth Grade Algebra* and the *Breslich Algebra Survey Tests* raises certain larger problems. These tests give little weight to certain important objectives such as generalizations, drawing inferences from data, and recognizing basic algebraic meanings of axiom, definition, and deduction.

[1436]

Columbia Research Bureau Algebra Test. Grades 9 or 13, 9-14; 1927-33; 2 forms, 2 levels; 30¢ per specimen set; Yonkers, N. Y.: World Book Co.
a) TEST 1. First semester; Grade 9 or 13; 1929; $1.20 per 25; 80(90) minutes; Joseph B. Orleans, Jacob S. Orleans, and Ben D. Wood.
b) TEST 2, REVISED. First year: grades 9-14; 1927-33; $1.30 per 25; 100(110) minutes; Arthur S. Otis and Ben D. Wood.

REFERENCES

1 ORLEANS, JOSEPH B., AND SYMONDS, PERCIVAL M. "The Comparative Reliabilities of Standardized and Teacher-Made Achievement Tests When Given in the Middle of the Year." *J Ed Res* 25:127-8 F '32.

L. B. Kinney, Associate Professor of Education, Stanford University. This is a series of two tests designed to measure achievement in the traditional types of college preparatory algebra. They undoubtedly present a well-planned and comprehensive instrument for this purpose.

Test 1 of this series is intended to provide a final examination for the end of the first semester of the customary high school algebra course. The test is in two parts, each requiring a forty-five minute period to administer. Part I consists of thirty-six examples in the mechanics of algebra. It includes items in algebraic operations, including factoring and equations; use and evaluation of formulas; and construction and interpretation of graphs. Part II is designed to measure ability to express relationships algebraically, to set up equations, and to solve problems. There are two forms of Test 1, the correlation between the forms being from .89 to .94 on various groups.

Test 2 is designed to serve as a final examination at the end of the year's instruction in algebra, or to serve as a college entrance test in that subject. Like Test 1, Test 2 also consists of two parts, each requiring fifty minutes. Part I consists of twenty equations each requiring special manipulation for solution, such as clearing of fractions, factoring, or graphing. Part II consists of twenty-five verbal problems for which the student is required to set up the equation and provide the solution. There are two forms of Test 2, the correlation between the two forms being .917.

The data for interpretation of scores is adequate and clearly explained. The norms for Test 1 are based on 598 students who had just completed a semester of algebra. The percentile rank for each score is given, as obtained from these groups.

The mechanical set-up of the tests is very satisfactory. The directions are clear, and the pages are arranged to obtain rapidity and ease of scoring.

S. S. Wilks, Associate Professor of Mathmatics, Princeton University; and Research Associate, College Entrance Examination Board, Princeton, New Jersey. Test 1, in two forms, is designed as an achievement test to be given at the end of the first semester of the average high school algebra course. It is constructed in two parts. The first part consists of thirty-six short-answer examples most of which involve formal algebraic manipulations, and the second part consists of a list of twelve short word problems in which the

student is asked to set up expressions algebraically and six longer word problems calling for solution by algebra, in which the student is asked to give the equation involved and also its solution.

The coefficient of reliability as found by correlating the two forms of the test is given as .94 for a group of 115 students and .89 for a second group of 147 students. Correlations of .68 and .72 between the test and teachers' marks are claimed.

This test has the commendable property, which is lacking in many of the current objective algebra tests, that the short and purely manipulative items in Part I are supplemented by the longer items in Part II which require deeper algebraic insight. Although it is known that there is rather high correlation between performance on "sufficiently clever" short-answer items and that on longer "multiple-step" problems, there are many who are dubious of the extent to which power at formal demonstration can be gauged by responses on short-answer items, particularly if the short items are essentially manipulative in character. Such individuals are probably strongly influenced by what they have actually seen in objective tests and not by any a priori argument that it would be impossible to devise short items so that performance on these items would be highly related to performance on the more elaborate mathematical problems.

Test 2 is similar to Test 1 in every respect except that it is designed as a final achievement test for first-year algebra to be given at the end of one year of algebra. It has been standardized on many more students than Test 1.

[1437]

Colvin-Schrammel Algebra Test. First, second semesters: high school; 1937-38; 2 forms, 2 levels; 50¢ per 25; 15¢ per specimen set; 40(45) minutes; Edgar S. Colvin and H. E. Schrammel; Emporia, Kan.: Bureau of Educational Measurements, Kansas State Teachers College.
a) TEST I. First semester.
b) TEST II. Second semester.

J. H. Minnick, Dean of the School of Education, The University of Pennsylvania. In this review of the *Colvin-Schrammel Algebra Test* the questions of scientific construction, validity, and reliability of the test are passed over, and discussion is devoted to that which seems to the writer to be far more important.

The authors define the purpose of the test as the measurement of achievement in first year algebra. Since the term "achievement" is not limited by the authors, it is naturally supposed that the purpose is to measure the ultimate outcome resulting from the study of first year algebra. It is the writer's opinion that if the study of first year algebra does not result in outcomes beyond that measured by this test, the subject has no rightful place in the school curriculum. The essence of a first year algebra course should be the equation, the formula, and the graph as tools for solving problems. Through the mastery of these phases of algebra, the child should learn not only their practical uses, but come to appreciate the place and value of algebra in civilization. For the most part, the test deals with the mechanics of algebra. It includes no graph materials; there is slight reference to the formula, but no attempt to test the child's ability to use it. While Part IV involves the use of equations for the solution of problems, the value of the type of problem selected is seriously questioned.

There is no question that the materials included in this test are *generally* useful for realizing the final purpose of the study of algebra. However, the teacher should be aware that the test measures the degree of mastery of certain algebraic materials which are valuable only as a means of arriving at the ultimate purpose of the study of algebra. Unless this is clearly understood the use of the test will tend to cause the study of algebra to degenerate into an attempt on the part of the child to master abstract facts which have no useful relationships and, therefore, have little or no educational value.

Attention is called to three doubtful minor features of the test. First, the language in Part I may be questioned. The child is asked to indicate whether "$x^2 + 2x = 0$ is a quadratic equation" is a true equality. Although the statement is true, it is not an equality. In like manner, the child is asked to indicate whether "The difference between any two numbers is represented by x/y" is a true equality. Of course, the statement is false; but if it were true, it would not be an equality.

Second, Part II is a multiple-choice test. The writer cannot see any advantage in the use of this form of test. For example, if in the formula $S = 2\pi hr$, $h = 10$, and $r = 14$, the child is to select the correct value of S from 880, 440, 220, 22, why not ask him to find the value of S when $h = 10$ and $r = 14$? This would eliminate the possibility of guessing, and it would test his ability to answer the question in the form in which it occurs in practical situations.

Third, Part IV, which attempts to measure the child's ability to solve problems by means of the equation, is crowded into a small space through the use of fine type. Have the authors of the test determined the psychological effect of this variation in print? Does this treatment of perhaps the most important part of the test render it insignificant in the mind of the child?

For a review by Maurice Hartung, see 879.

[1438]
Cooperative Algebra Test: Elementary Algebra Through Quadratics. High school; 1933-40; 40- and 90-minute editions; 5¢ per test, 10 to 99 copies; 25¢ per specimen set of either edition; Form P: John A. Long and L. P. Siceloff; Form Q: John A. Long and L. P. Siceloff with the editorial assistance of A. A. Bennett, Rose E. Lutz, Mary A. Potter, and W. D. Reeve; New York: Cooperative Test Service.
a) FORMS 1934 AND 1937. Forms 1935 and 1936 are out of print; 90(95) minutes.
b) REVISED SERIES FORMS N, O, P, AND Q. 1937-40; 1½¢ per machine-scorable answer sheet; 40(45) minutes.

Harl R. Douglass, Director of the College of Education, University of Colorado. [Review of Form P.] This test consists of 63 five-choice items. Part I is composed of 20 items testing accuracy in fundamental operations with monomials and polynomials including exponential axioms, removal of parenthesis, simplifying fractional terms, simultaneous equations, and handling of radicals.

The 15 items of Part II are verbal problems emphasizing thinking involved in this type of problem solving, as applied to percentage, ratio, equation construction, and graph reading.

Part III, composed of 28 items, measures very much the same skill in algebraic manipulation but includes more difficult exercises and includes some verbal problems.

As compared with other tests for measuring abilities developed in first year algebra this test is probably as good as is available, particularly if employed to measure mastery of the conventional first year course in algebra. It is relatively free from the more complicated and seldom employed manipulative puzzlers. As judged by the claims made for first year algebra, like all other algebra tests, it overemphasizes manipulative skills.

The multiple-choice feature possesses some

advantages and some disadvantages. It facilitates speedy scoring. It avoids the difficulties involved in deciding whether an answer equal but not in the same form as the answer given in the key is correct or not. In some exercises, however, the correct answer may be located at least in part by the process of elimination even though the student's answer is not accurate. Repeating the number of the problem before each of the five alternative answers printed beneath the exercises is confusing and not really necessary.

The correct answers to several of the 15 items in Part II may be identified accurately by authoritative reasoning without use of algebra, though they do measure roughly problem solving abilities developed in the study of algebra. The tests avoid use of sequences of exercises in which some items are certain to be incorrectly answered if earlier items are not correctly answered. For the very large part, the incorrect alternatives given among the five choices are sufficiently good decoys and are not obviously impossible answers.

Like all algebra tests commonly used for measuring progress in the first year of algebra, it should never be used in any way which would furnish an incentive to teachers to teach for the test. It gives heavy weight to the fundamental manipulative skills in algebra; it does not measure abilities to use statistical methods; because of time limitations it does not measure the ability involved in the construction of graphs; it does not place much emphasis upon measurement of the ability to apply algebra to situations likely to be within the past or near future experience of most high school pupils. Because these things are so, to use such tests in ways likely to influence teachers to neglect the objectives of algebra growth toward which the test does not measure or emphasize, and to include and concentrate upon those which are included and emphasized in the test, would be unfortunate.

The test is much better suited for use at the end of or during the second semester than at the end of or during the first semester, since many of the items involving abilities are not commonly taught in the first semester. The portion of the test useful for measuring mastery of first year algebra would not require more than 20 or 25 minutes and the reliability would very likely be too low for useful individual measurement.

By use of tables furnished by the publishers it is possible to convert any pupils' scores into "scaled scores" permitting comparisons with similarly scaled scores when available for tests in other subjects. The norms supplied by the publishers are usually based upon comparatively large numbers. Separate norms are available for 12-year public high schools, for 12-year independent secondary schools, and for 11-year schools.

The test possesses little diagnostic value and can not be used satisfactorily for that purpose. It seems to possess relatively high reliability. The publishers report of a coefficient of .924 based upon 260 cases which is higher than that usually obtained for a 40-minute algebra test. They also report a coefficient of correlation of .73 with school marks, a good indication of reasonable validity. It is reasonably priced.

Harold Fawcett, Associate Director of the University School and Associate Professor of Mathematics-Education, The Ohio State University. [Review of Form P.] Since one of the most powerful forces giving direction to the mathematics program in any school is found in the tests by which the effectiveness of that program is measured, the significance of any test is largely determined by the desirability of the objectives it appears to emphasize. To what extent then does this particular test promote the development of important educational values such as relational thinking, conceptual training, and the like, and to what extent does it encourage manipulation and the mechanical aspects of the subject?

If a pupil scores high on this test it probably indicates that he has, at least, temporary control of the following abilities: (*a*) He can recall certain facts from elementary mathematics. (*b*) He understands the language and symbolism of elementary algebra. (*c*) He can perform the fundamental operations with simple algebraic expressions. (*d*) He can interpret circle, straight line, and very simple bar graphs.

It is not possible, however, to say with any degree of certainty that the student is able to solve equations or simple verbal problems even though the test includes a number of such items. Since five responses are suggested for each of the sixty-three exercises in the test, it is quite possible to find through substitution that response which satisfies the equation

$x/2 - 4 = 5$ without solving it, and the same thing is true of the other problems which call for the solution of an equation. Some of the verbal problems can be similarly handled. Thus, when one of the given conditions is that "the denominator of a given fraction is 10 greater than the numerator" and among the five results suggested there is only one in which this condition is met, it seems quite probable that the student might select the correct response, 7/17, without actually solving the problem. Furthermore, a student who is skilful at multiplication might well select the correct factors of $b^2 - 14b + 24$ from among those suggested without knowing how to factor an expression of this sort.

The general format of the test is inviting. The spacing is good, the drawings are well made, and the print used is attractive. In Item 10, Part III, perhaps the question, "Which one of the following is true?" should be changed to "Which one of the following statements is an identity?" since $a(ax) = a^2x^2$ is "true" for both $x = 0$ and $x = 1$ whereas it is quite obviously not the response which the authors desire. Similarly, in Item 20, Part III, the idea which the authors wished to express by "the sum of the weight (B) of the deflated balloon plus the weight (G) of the gas with which it is filled" would be more accurately stated if the "plus" were changed to "and." With these possible exceptions, however, the directions are easily understood and the problems are clearly stated.

While this test does recognize to some extent the importance of the language and symbolism of algebra it places a heavy premium on the manipulative and mechanical aspects of the subject and the effect of the test will be to perpetuate the conventional type of algebra teaching. The pupils' growth in ability to do relational thinking, the building of sound concepts, appreciations and attitudes are involved only indirectly if at all and wherever the test is used teachers will be encouraged to ignore the ever increasing demands for more dynamic and functional teaching in algebra.

For reviews by William Betz, Helen M. Walker, and S. S. Wilks, see 880.

[1439]

Cooperative Intermediate Algebra Test: Quadratics and Beyond. High school; 1933-40; 40- and 90-minute editions; 5¢ per test, 10 to 99 copies; 25¢ per specimen set of either edition; Form P: John A.

Long and L. P. Siceloff; Form Q: John A. Long and L. P. Siceloff with the editorial assistance of G. E. Hawkins, Harvey O. Jackson, Joseph A. Nyberg, and Jack Wolfe; New York: Cooperative Test Service.
a) FORMS 1934, 1935, 1936, AND 1937. Form 1933 is out of print; 90(95) minutes.
b) REVISED SERIES FORMS N, P, AND Q. 1937-40; Form O is out of print; 1½¢ per machine-scorable answer sheet; 40(45) minutes.

Albert A. Bennett, Professor of Mathematics, Brown University. [Review of Form P.] Despite the adventurous subtitle "Quadratics and Beyond," the field covered is well understood by preparatory school teachers and is quite prosaic. Topics touched upon include the quadratic equation and prior material, arithmetic and geometric progressions, variation, permutations and combinations, probability, and even very simple graphs of conic sections in standard form. To cover the twenty-two questions in forty minutes demands short problems. These are very short indeed, and naturally fail to test any powers of analysis requiring more than one step. Five more or less plausible alternative answers of which exactly one is correct, are given in each case for the contestant to select among. Blundering and confused thinking or ignorance cannot yield a good score.

The authors succeed admirably in the accomplishment of their aim. The questions are clearly put, cover many standard topics, and one correct answer is included each time. The "rights" of the individual to secure credit for any item of knowledge he may have in any of the many little topics covered by the course are scrupulously respected. In short, this test should be thoroughly acceptable to a teacher absorbed in the systematic drill of docile (and perhaps stupid) pupils in rudiments of formal algebra. Scaled norms are provided.

One might perhaps question whether the aim is justified. Only the most direct applications of the simplest formal rules are being tested. No ingenuity is called for, nor judgment, nor continuity of effort, nor computational accuracy, no selection of data, formulation of problems, recognition of logical principles, and so on, through almost any list of the ostensible reasons for teaching algebra. To one so bold as to ask why should the future citizen study algebra, an examination of this test would seem to suggest as the only intended answer,—to obtain familiarity with the abstractness and symbolism of algebraic notation. In testing for information which students are likely soon to forget, tests of this sort can only help to bolster any prejudice of intelligent and responsible leaders of public thought against specific mathematical study.

Earle R. Hedrick, Vice-President and Provost of the University, The University of California. [Review of Form P.] This test appears to be a thorough test of some aspects of algebra in the portion called "Quadratics and Beyond." The organization is definitely affected by the arbitrary choice of a grading scheme which definitely limits the questions that may be asked.

In the very nature of the examination, only formalized questions seem to be possible. Hence, the examination leans very heavily on the side of formalized algebra, to the exclusion of anything that might be called a "thought-process."

Only one question is set which has to do with the solution of a problem stated in English, and that problem is almost necessarily a highly artificial type of problem. In its solution, no "thinking-through" is required, for the steps are taken by the examiners, with no alternative for the student except to choose falsely or correctly from among stated possibilities. Synthesis and coordinated thought are wholly eliminated. This does not appear to be the fault of the examiners but rather of the method prescribed for setting up the examination and for grading it.

Similarly, there is a complete absence of anything that touches upon the *function concept,* which has been emphasized by every thoughtful discussion of the teaching of algebra for a generation. It seems impossible to set any questions that touch this concept under the method employed.

Although the test is called "Quadratics and Beyond," there is only one question out of fifty-three which requires in any way a knowledge of the solution of quadratic equations by any other than trial processes, for all of the other quadratics given have rational roots and can be solved by the most elementary factoring, except that one so-called "pure" quadratic is given.

By contrast, there are seven of the fifty-three questions that ask for the solution of first degree equation, and in five of these there is only one unknown.

The fact that the test is heavily formalized is evidenced by the fact that ten of the fifty-three questions deal with formal operations on radicals or exponents, without any pretense of other than formal meanings. This count does not include several formal questions on logarithms, which may be said to be in this same general category.

While the test may, therefore, be a true indication of ability in formalized processes, it omits large portions of what should be the more thought-provoking side of the subject, and it very nearly omits even the solution of problems set in English and the solution of serious types of ordinary quadratic equations in one unknown.

For reviews by J. O. Hassler and S. S. Wilks, see 881.

[1440]

Cooperative Mathematics Test for College Students: Comprehensive Examination in College Algebra. 1937; Experimental Form A; 5¢ per test, 10 to 99 copies; 25¢ per specimen set; 240(250) minutes; prepared by the Committee on Tests of the Mathematical Association of America; Ralph Beatley, E. W. Chittenden, A. R. Crathorne, L. L. Dines, and Marie M. Johnson; New York: Cooperative Test Service.

REFERENCES

1 Mathematical Association of America, Committee on Tests, E. W. Chittenden, Chairman. "Report of the Committee on Tests." *Am Math Mo* 47:290-301 My '40.

Albert A. Bennett, Professor of Mathematics, Brown University. [Review of Form A.] The test has 90 short questions, some of the multiple-choice type. The material touched upon includes elementary algebra in general, evaluation of simple determinants, logarithms, complex numbers, theory of equations, permutations and combinations, probability, partial fractions, convergence of series, and statistics. Although algebra is basic to all college mathematics, this examination in college algebra covers many items with which a student, pushed early into the calculus, may remain unfamiliar.

Many of the questions are particularly brief for any one who understands the principal idea, and is reasonably ingenious. A few test accuracy in computation. The scope of the paper is much wider than formerly traditional in algebra, and considerable skill has been exercised in securing a variety of searching questions with a minimum of manipulative detail.

The general tone is formal and conservative. For example, no questions are asked which might test the student's ability to select appropriate data, to name applications, to recognize historical aspects, to acknowledge hypotheses, or criticise faulty definitions (save possibly in the case of convergence), to reduce verbal statements to formulas, to supply a step in a proof, to name a property, or to apply mathematical induction. The tank-filling problem is here despite its dubious applicative value and the oft-noted fact that turning on the cold water may affect the rate of flow from the hot-water faucet. Logarithms to unknown bases still flourish.

The student is called upon to remain docile and naive in attempting what the expert might hesitate to undertake: he is asked to name the equation of a familiar but poorly-drawn graph; to guess the n'th term of a series of which three or four terms only are given; to assume in connection with complex numbers that the letters used indicate real numbers although not so stated; to guess that a smooth curve is called for when he is asked to plot all integral values of x from $x = -1$ to $x = 3$; and to infer from an undescribed diagram certain exact relations intended.

Minor criticisms include the following: while certain areas are given as numbers, the approved answers using them appear in cubic inches. The student is supposed to know what a "defective" equation is. In the offset printing, the distinction between the numeral "one" and the letter "l," is unrecognizable, although the student needs to know always which is intended. The omnibus term "simplify" is still used to designate a variety of operations.

Paul R. Rider, Professor of Mathematics, Washington University. [Review of Form A.] "The test is designed to give a very comprehensive and thorough measure of a student's mastery of algebraic processes and concepts developed in a college course in this field." It seems to have been carefully worked out with regard to content, degree of difficulty of questions, and time allotted for completion.

Some criticism might be offered of the inclusion of questions on least squares, standard deviation, and correlation coefficient, on the ground that few textbooks on college algebra treat these topics. Although they are admittedly important, the inclusion of questions on them might discriminate against a good student simply because his instructor has confined the attention of the class to the subject matter found in a standard text. Certainly students who are to be subjected to the test should be apprised of the fact that questions on elementary statistics, including least squares, may be expected to occur. If this is done, there would be no objection to such questions; in fact they add to the test instead of detracting from it.

On the whole, this is recommended as an excellent test.

For reviews by Arnold Dresden, Marion W. Richardson, and Henry L. Rietz, see 882.

[1441]

Iowa Algebra Aptitude Test. Grade 9; 1931; 1 form; 85¢ per 25; 10¢ per manual; 15¢ per specimen set; 35(45) minutes; Harry A. Greene and Alva H. Piper; Iowa City, Iowa: Bureau of Educational Research and Service, State University of Iowa.

REFERENCES

1 PIPER, A. H. *The Validity of Certain General and Special Tests for Prognosis in First Year Algebra.* Unpublished master's thesis, State University of Iowa, 1929. Pp. 49.

Richard M. Drake, Assistant Professor of Education, The University of Buffalo. The validity of this type of test is a very important consideration. The results of this test were correlated with the results of a single standardized achievement test given at the end of the semester. Only 105 cases were used and the correlation was found to be .66. It would seem desirable and necessary to use more than one test as a measure of final achievement and to use more cases. Furthermore, a correlation of .66 is not high enough to justify the claims made for the test.

The directions for giving the test are well worked out and explicit. The answer key is clear and concise. The norms were established on 223 pupils and are expressed in terms of percentiles for each part. This latter aids in diagnosis from the test results. The number of cases used for establishing the norms is too small.

The reaction of some who have used this test is that there is too much emphasis on arithmetic and that the test might well be shortened by the elimination of some of this material. The section on abstract computation is important. Perhaps this part should receive more emphasis in the way of a better arrangement according to difficulty of items, and the inclusion of additional simpler examples.

No attempt has been made to test the vocabulary of arithmetic. The reviewer has found by extensive experimentation that this is a very important factor of success in algebraic achievement. Since many of the words and expressions of arithmetic are common to algebra, it would seem that this is a serious omission.

Much of the test implies some previous knowledge of algebra. Pupils who have attended a school where algebra is introduced in the seventh and eighth grades would have a considerable advantage.

The reviewer feels that this type of test could play a very important part in our guidance system. However, it is doubtful if we can ever devise a test which by itself will be valid enough to warrant prediction in individual cases.

M. W. Richardson, United States Civil Service Commission, Washington, D. C. This test is designed to predict achievement in first-year algebra. The four subtests were selected, empirically, from a larger number of preliminary subtests, and further checked for validity by estimating the correlation of the total score with teachers' grades and with the *Columbia Research Bureau Algebra Test.*

The reported validity coefficient ($r = .76$) is rather higher than might be expected from a test requiring only 35 minutes of working time. It is regrettable that although the test was published in 1931, the norms are based on only 223 cases, and the validity measures upon only 105. Surely this test has been given to many more pupils since 1931, and the manual should have been periodically revised to include results up to the end of the last preceding school year.

The manual is intended to serve as a guide to interpretation of scores. Its value is vitiated somewhat by an unfortunate statement (p. 10) relative to the interpretation of the probable error of a score, and by inexact use of technical terms generally. Incidentally, the probable errors of scores given on page 9 of the manual are calculated by the wrong formula; the true values are fortunately lower than those given. Such errors are based on misunderstanding, or, at best, careless use of the theory of testing.

The test is well conceived and well constructed, and probably deserves further use when supplemented with further results presented in a revised manual, which should be freed from errors and unnecessary crudities. Until these steps are taken, this reviewer feels

constrained in all honesty to suggest that the test is not yet ready for general use, although published eight years ago.

[1442]

1939 Iowa Every-Pupil Test in Ninth Year Algebra: Eleventh Annual Iowa Every-Pupil High School Testing Program. High school; 1939; a new form is scheduled for publication each May; 4¢ per test; 5¢ per key; 10¢ per summary report of norms; 55(60) minutes; H. Vernon Price; Iowa City, Iowa: Bureau of Educational Research and Service, State University of Iowa.

John R. Clark, Associate Professor of Education and Principal of the High School, Lincoln School, Columbia University. Part I, Fundamental Processes (19 minutes), includes seventeen tasks involving removal of parentheses, division, solution of equations, the additions of two literal fractions, the solutions of quadratic equations, literal factoring, the solution of a pair of simultaneous linear equations, simplification of a radical expression, literal equations, and the evaluation of an algebraic expression.

Part II, Algebraic Relations and Representations (18 minutes), includes twenty-three tasks involving the translation of simple verbal statements into algebraic symbolism, the plotting of points, reading of a graph, the solution of problems whose equations are literal, and the analysis of functional relationships as expressed by literal equations.

Part III, Verbal Problems (18 minutes), includes the traditional problems about number relations, motion, areas of geometric figures, age, coins, mixture, rates of work, and altering the terms of a fraction.

Along with the test is a valuable booklet entitled Summary Report of Results which discusses the use and interpretation of test results, the relation of test content to curriculum content, the value of tests in educational guidance, the use of tests in evaluating instruction and the relation of testing to the improvement of teaching. This booklet provides percentile norms for the entire group of some nine thousand pupils who supplied the data for these norms, and the median grades of four classifications of schools according to enrollment.

The author of the test selected the items to be included in the test from the textbooks in use in Iowa and on this basis he argues that the test has validity. I find no data concerning the reliability of this test.

The format of the test is good. It is easy to

read, the test items are well spaced, there is space for the pupil to do his work, and there is a unique plan for the pupil to record his answers in a manner designed to facilitate scoring.

The test appears to be difficult. The median score for all the pupils was 14.1 examples correct. It is discouraging to teachers and to pupils to discover that roughly two-thirds of the content of a test is beyond the attainment of half the pupils. It might be equally correct to conclude that the test is all right but that instruction is poor. If the tasks in the tests are valid for ninth-grade pupils then certainly the instruction is bad.

[1443]

Lee Test of Algebra Ability. Grade 9; 1930; 1 form; $1.00 per 25; 15¢ per manual; 20¢ per specimen set; 25(35) minutes; J. Murray Lee; Bloomington, Ill.: Public School Publishing Co.

REFERENCES

1 TORGERSON, T. L., AND AAMODT, GENEVA P. "The Validity of Certain Prognostic Tests in Predicting Algebraic Ability." *J Exp Ed* 1:277-9 Mr '33.

S. S. Wilks, Associate Professor of Mathematics, Princeton University; and Research Associate, College Entrance Examination Board, Princeton, New Jersey. This test is designed as a prognostic test of algebraic ability for students who have never studied algebra. The test consists of a battery of four subtests: Test 1, Arithmetic Problems; Test 2, Analogies; Test 3, Number Series; and Test 4, Formulas. These four subtests were selected from an original battery of nine tests, which was given for the first time to ninth-grade students in the Horace Mann School for Girls in New York in the spring of 1928. Later in 1928 the tests were revised and given to 800 students in Los Angeles, and the final four subtests were selected from among the nine tests by multiple regression methods, using the results of an algebra achievement test, given a few months later, as the validating criterion. Using the battery of the four selected tests, a somewhat more extensive validity study was made on 318 students in the Harvard High School of Glendale, California. The correlation between the weighted scores of the selected tests and of an algebra achievement test was reported as .71. This validity study was apparently made between 1928 and the time at which the test was copyrighted which was in 1930. There is no evidence that validity of the test has been investigated since that date.

The reliability coefficient of the test, estimated by the "split-halves" method, is reported as .93.

No information is furnished regarding the difficulty of the items on the individual tests. Inspection of the items suggests that there may possibly be a slight graduation of items with respect to difficulty, but it is doubtful that the difficulty ranges very widely. The items themselves do not appear to penetrate very deeply into the extremely narrow regions which are supposed to be sampled by the various subtests. The subtests contain from 15 to 20 items each, or a total of 72 items, and the total working time designated for the test is 35 minutes. With this small amount of time allotted for the 72 items, together with the limited range of difficulty represented by the items, one may well raise the question whether some of the reliability found for the test may not be due to the time element. That is, if the students were allowed more time, how much would the reliability coefficient diminish?

The items within each of the first three subtests, particularly the second and third ones, are extremely homogeneous. Each item in subtest two is one requiring the completion of a proportion: that is, three numbers, let us say *a b*, and *c*, are given, and the student is asked to find a fourth number which bears the same ratio to *c* that *b* bears to *a*. The author of the test unfortunately uses the ambiguous word "relation" in place of "ratio" when he says in the directions for Test 2: "Find a number which has the same relation to the third number as the second number has to the first."

Each item in the number series test consists of a given sequence of six numbers, and the student is asked to continue the sequence through two further numbers.

This test is undoubtedly of some value in detecting ability in algebra, but, in the opinion of the reviewer, it would be a much better instrument if the items within each subtest were not quite so homogeneous, if they had a wider range of difficulty, and if more time were allowed for the test.

[1444]

Orleans Algebra Prognosis Test. Grades 7-9; 1928-32; 1 form; $1.50 per 25; 15¢ per specimen set; 81(90) minutes; Joseph B. Orleans and Jacob S. Orleans; Yonkers, N. Y.: World Book Co.

REFERENCES

1 GROVER, C. C. "Results of an Experiment in Predicting Success in First Year Algebra in Two Oakland Junior High Schools." *J Ed Psychol* 23:309-14 Ap '32.
2 TORGERSON, T. L., AND AAMODT, GENEVA P. "The Validity

of Certain Prognostic Tests in Predicting Algebraic Ability."
J Exp Ed 1:277-9 Mr '33.
3 ORLEANS, JOSEPH B. "A Study of Prognosis of Probable
Success in Algebra and in Geometry." *Math Teach* 27:165-80,
225-46 Ap, My '34.
4 SEAGOE, MAY V. "Prediction of Achievement in Elementary
Algebra." *J Appl Psychol* 22:493-503 O '38.

S. S. Wilks, Associate Professor of Mathematics, Princeton University; and Research Associate, College Entrance Examination Board, Princeton, New Jersey. This test is devised as a prognosis test for algebra to be given before beginning the study of algebra. The test consists of the following twelve parts: (1) Substitution in monomials; (2) Rise of exponents; (3) Meaning of exponents; (4) Substitution in monomials with exponents; (5) Substitution in binomials with exponents; (6) Like and unlike terms; (7) Representation of relations; (8) Representation of expressions; (9) Positive and negative numbers; (10) Problems; (11) Addition of like terms; and (12) Summary test. Of these twelve parts, eleven include both a lesson and a test on the lesson. The test was validated in 1926 on three hundred students in the George Washington High School, New York. The test was revised and again tried out in 1927 in two other New York City high schools. The actual validation procedure consisted in correlating the scores on the prognosis test with those of an objective achievement test in algebra given at the end of the first semester. Correlation of .71 is claimed. No reliability study for the test is reported.

Perhaps the greatest criticism to make of this test is the cramped amount of time allowed for the test. This entire test, including the lessons which are attached to eleven of the parts, is scheduled to require eighty-one minutes. The time allotted to each lesson varies from one to four minutes, and the number of lines (some of which are very short) of reading material to be covered in these time intervals varies from twelve to thirty. The time allotted to the various tests varies from one and one-half to eight and one-half minutes, while the number of items varies from ten to sixteen. From an inspection of the items, there appears to be very little graduation of items with respect to difficulty in most of the parts. This fact, coupled with the fact that small bits of time are allowed for the several parts, immediately raises the question as to whether or not a considerable amount of whatever reliability the test might have is due to sheer differences of students in reaction time. If the items in the parts had been carefully graduated with respect to difficulty, then this particular question would not loom quite so large, but there would still remain the question as to whether any very significant information can be obtained about a student in a test of twelve items to be done in one and one-half minutes!

[1445]
Survey Test in Elementary Algebra, Preliminary Edition. One year: high school; 1939; 1 form; 75¢ per 25; 25¢ per specimen set; 80(85-90) minutes; Harl R. Douglass and Dale O. Patterson; Minneapolis, Minn.: Educational Test Bureau, Inc.

[1446]
Votaw Algebra Test. High school; 1939; 3 forms; $1 per 30 (usable with or without answer sheets); $2 per 100 machine-scorable answer sheets; $2 per 100 answer sheets for hand scoring; 10¢ per specimen set; 50(60) minutes; David F. Votaw, Sr., and David F. Votaw, Jr.; Austin, Texas: Steck Co.

ARITHMETIC

[1447]
Analytical Scales of Attainment in Arithmetic. Grades 3-4, 5-6, 7-8; 1933; 2 forms, 3 levels; 90¢ per 25; 20¢ per specimen set; 80(90) minutes; L. J. Brueckner, Martha Kellogg, and M. J. Van Wagenen; Minneapolis, Minn.: Educational Test Bureau, Inc.
a) DIVISION 1. Grades 3-4.
b) DIVISION 2. Grades 5-6.
c) DIVISION 3. Grades 7-8.

R. L. Morton, Professor of Education, Ohio University. Each of the divisions is composed of four parts: quantitative relationships (multiple-choice items); problems; vocabulary (multiple-choice items); and fundamental operations. There is considerable overlapping of items from division to division. The tests in problems and fundamental operations are identical in contents with the contents of the previously published *Unit Scales of Attainment in Arithmetic.*

Norms are said to be based upon results obtained from 60,000 cases in 1937. Whether or not each item of each test was given to 60,000 persons is not stated.

Validity has been determined (*a*) by checking against textbooks and leading courses of study and (*b*) by noting the extent to which the items discriminated between upper-grade and lower-grade pupils or between those who had studied the topic and those who had not. However, it is suggested that an item may discriminate between the performances of pupils of different levels and yet not discriminate with reference to the trait, capacity, or skill which is being measured. For example, one may question whether an item on the composition of the dime which occurs in the test of Quantitative Relationships really measures the pupil's grasp of quantitative relationships at all.

Reliability is expressed in terms of the probable error of the derived C-score units. No reliability coefficients are given. The reviewer suggests that reliability coefficients should have been supplied in spite of the fact that they depend in part upon the range of the scores. It is very difficult to compare the reliability of this test with the reliability of other tests because of the absence of comparable data.

W. J. Osburn, Professor of Education, The University of Washington. The tests furnish separate measures of quantitative relationships, arithmetic vocabulary, fundamental operations, and ability to solve arithmetic problems. The content of the tests for fundamental operations and problem solving is identical with the corresponding portions of the *Unit Scales of Attainment in Arithmetic.* The technique for scoring and the time limits are also the same for both tests. The purpose of repeating so much of a former test is not apparent.

The new contributions of the tests are in number relations and arithmetic vocabulary. The questions of reliability and validity are met very sketchily by the simple direction "See the Directions for the Unit Scales of Attainment." But a reference to those directions yields no light concerning quantitative relations and vocabulary. Apparently the authors are telling us only that the same technique and care has been used with these tests as was true in the former case. No other information is given concerning how the test items were selected. Furthermore, some of the items look doubtful; quantitative relations are not prominent in such items as "We should loan money only to people whom we . . . trust" (It would be better to say *lend* money.) ; "The figure of a buffalo is on the . . . nickel"; "Which can most conveniently be used for money?" (the answer is silver) and numerous other items. On the other hand the authors seem to have largely avoided such genuine quantitative relations as may be found in ratios, proportions, and series. The test seems to be a measure of

arithmetical information. Its validity for quantitative relationships seems very doubtful.

The vocabulary tests are also open to question. One misses such useful words as sum, remainder, product, dividend, and the like. Instead we find such words as postpone, ancient, plentiful, temporary, and sufficient. Grade placement is badly out of adjustment, for example: vacant, withdraw, postpone, overdue, and ancient—all among the first 20 items for grades 3-4. Moreover in the same list of words it is illogical to encourage children that *double* means the same as *twice*, that *circle* is equivalent to *round*, and that *inch* is the same as *length*, and others of like maladjustment.

The tests of quantitative relations and vocabulary are definitely below the high and scholarly standard set by the *Unit Scales of Attainment.*

G. M. Wilson, Professor of Education, Boston University. The test covers quantitative relationships, problems, vocabulary, and fundamentals. The attempt to measure quantitative relationships and vocabulary is relatively new in the field. There is little basis for judgment as to the merits of the work done. The type of answer called for is the multiple response. The pupil checks one of the suggested answers.

The writer's inclination is to regard these phases of the *Analytical Scale of Attainment in Arithmetic* as good for informal testing but very doubtful as a part of a standardized test. The final judgment, of course, must come after the material has been used and the effects of such usage become evident. The teacher undoubtedly needs more fundamental preparation than is common. It is doubtful if such preparation will be stimulated by the items of this test. In other words, when general concepts, appreciation opportunities, or business terms are placed into a standardized test without regard to the preparation of the teacher or the work of the pupils, it is more likely to be detrimental than otherwise. Items appearing in a standardized test should be in the nature of definite drill material where perfect mastery is a reasonable requirement.

The problem scales of this test are of the usual type. For the most part they are simple and yet they have elements of puzzle in them. It is doubtful if problem work has been improved by the use of the ordinary problem scale. Such scales help to perpetuate a practice that never was profitable and is now obsolete in all progressive schools.

Testing of the drill phases of arithmetic should be (*a*) limited to processes used often enough by adults to justify perfect mastery, and (*b*) should show a coverage sufficient to enable the teacher to diagnose pupil weaknesses.

Giving attention to the first item, we note in the present test that third- and fourth-grade children are expected to have experience in addition, subtraction, multiplication, short division, long division, and multiplication and subtraction of fractions. Undoubtedly this program is too extensive for fourth-grade pupils. Long division should not occur before the fifth grade. Simple fractions will be used from the first grade up but should not be tested upon at this level.

In the second division of the scales, grades 5-6, the coverage in fundamental operations is further extended to include addition of fractions, subtraction of mixed numbers, division of fractions and mixed numbers, addition, subtraction, and multiplication of compound numbers, and percentage. It should be noted that division of fractions and mixed numbers and work in compound numbers find little or no place in ordinary adult usage. Therefore, they should not appear in a standardized test where drill mastery is the reasonable expectation.

In Division 3 of this test the work in fractions, decimals, compound numbers, and percentage is further extended. Of the twenty-five examples appearing in Division 3, at least eight of the examples go beyond reasonable adult usage.

Our second question relates to the coverage of the processes which may properly be noted as drill processes. At least no one would object to calling addition, subtraction, multiplication, and division drill processes. In Division 1 of this test 16 of the 100 primary facts in addition are covered and 3 of the 300 upper decade facts in addition. In other words, 19 of the 400 drill facts for column addition are covered. In Division 2, 32 of the 100 primary facts in addition are covered and 12 of the 300 decade facts. In Division 3, 29 of the 100 primary facts in addition are covered and 24 of the 300 decade facts. In other words, the coverage in such a fundamental process as addition is not adequate.

The coverage for the other processes is very much like that in addition. Division 1 of the test covers 31 of the 100 subtraction facts. Division 2 covers 28 of the 100 subtraction facts. Division 3 covers 29 of the 100 subtraction facts. The 100 multiplication facts are covered as follows: Division 1, 37 facts; Division 2, 34 facts; Division 3, 58 facts.

It is possible to note with equal definiteness the coverage in short division. It is a little less adequate than in the other processes. The coverage in long division cannot be noted except in very general terms.

The general conclusion must be that the coverage of fundamental processes is inadequate for the diagnosis of difficulties and, therefore, as a guide for teaching. The test can only be used for very general classification.

[1448]

Arithmetic: Midland Attainment Tests. Ages 7-13; 1938; 1 form, 2 parts; 2s. 9d. per 25; 6d. per manual; 9d. per specimen set; R. B. Cattell; London: University of London Press, Ltd.
a) ARITHMETIC NO. 1, KNOWLEDGE OF METHODS. 60(65) minutes.
b) ARITHMETIC NO. 2, MECHANICAL SKILL. 8(13) minutes.

Fred J. Schonell, Lecturer in Education, Goldsmiths' College, University of London. ARITHMETIC TEST NO. 1. This test consists of 49 graded questions arranged in order of difficulty and following the order of difficulty in method knowledge commonly found in primary school syllabuses. In the main the computational aspects of each sum are sufficiently simple for the work to be done mentally.

The questions are designed to cover an age range of from 4 to 14 years. In the 4+ to 5-year-old allotment there are 3 questions based on recognition of the concrete and on counting thus, recognition of 3 (fingers), counting to 5, and addition of 2 and 1 (pennies). Then up to the 11-year-old level there are examples in problem form of the four rules and common applications to weights and measures. Between age 11 and 14+ there is the introduction, in graded form, of fractions and decimals.

The number of questions for each age year varies from 4 to 6, so that scoring is done by adding the appropriate fraction for success in each question in an age group. For example, for age group 7 add one fourth of a year per question answered correctly, or for age 11 add one-sixth of a year per question answered correctly.

Norm tables for the tests are also given and are based on the scores of some 800 children in city elementary schools. The norms range from a 6½-year-old level—a score of 3.1—to a 14-year-old score of 46.0. Use of the test reveals somewhat unreliable norms at the lower end of the age scale, perhaps due to the comparatively few cases used in standardization. It is possible that the test would be slightly improved if the small printed instruction to examiners, in the left hand margin, were omitted.

The test is useful for general testing purposes, particularly for a rapid assessment of arithmetical standard in knowledge of method.

ARITHMETIC TEST NO. 2. This is essentially a test of mechanical skill in the four processes—both speed and accuracy are tested. The author says that "to avoid the effects of fatigue and for greater reliability of measurement, each section (addition, subtraction, multiplication, and division) occurs twice." Thus, there are 6 examples in addition, 6 in subtraction, 6 in one-figure multiplication, and 6 in one-figure division; then this plan is repeated giving 8 sections in all with a total of 48 examples.

As an estimate of mechanical skill in the four processes the test is adequate enough for ages of 9 and beyond, but the grading of the examples is too coarse to admit of any really satisfactory assessment of skill for the ages of 6+ to 8+. For example, no young pupil should be expected to show his powers of division in sums with only 5 figure dividends.

Attainment ages for age groups 6½ to 14 are given, based on results from 800 children, a somewhat meagre sample for standardization. There is no evidence given to show what precautions for reliability or validity were taken in the construction of the tests.

[1449]

Arithmetic Test: National Achievement Tests. Grades 3-8; 1936-38; 2 forms; $1.35 per 25; 5¢ per specimen set; Robert K. Speer and Samuel Smith; Rockville Centre, N. Y.: Acorn Publishing Co.
a) FUNDAMENTALS. (55-85) minutes.
b) REASONING. Nontimed (40) minutes.

R. L. Morton, Professor of Education, Ohio University. The test in arithmetic fundamentals is in three parts. The time allowed for Parts I and II is 18 minutes. There is no time limit for Part III. The test in arithmetic reasoning is in four parts. It has no time limits.

Reliability coefficients .93 and .86 are given for the fundamentals and reasoning tests, respectively. Validity was determined by checking against courses of study, textbooks, and the judgments of administrators and classroom teachers. Batteries of tests are said to have been standardized by administration to more than 35,000 pupils. Whether or not this number was used in standardizing the arithmetic tests under review is not stated.

Parts I and III of the test in fundamentals require a variety of straightforward computations for answers. Part II is a test in number comparisons. Some computation is necessary before the pupil can select the correct statement from each set of four statements. The items of the test in fundamentals seem to be well selected and well arranged although one may take exception to such items as

$$\text{ADD } 0 \qquad \qquad$$
$$\qquad 2 \qquad 8\,|\,\overline{106\text{ lbs. } 16\text{ oz.}}$$

and an item requiring the addition of decimal mixed numbers in which the number of decimal places in the various addends is not equal. The first would never occur in isolated form in the world of practical affairs; the dividend of the second would ordinarily be expressed as 107 lbs.; the third implies neglect of the subject of accuracy of measurement and significant figures.

The reasoning test is in four parts. Part I requires comparisons; Part II is called a test in problem analysis; Part III requires the pupil to find the key to a problem; Part IV is a test in problem solving. Considerable ingenuity seems to have been used in selecting and arranging the items of the four parts of this test. It is the reviewer's subjective opinion that the test will be found to measure rather well the desirable outcomes of arithmetic instruction in problem solving.

Leroy H. Schnell, Department of Mathematics, State Teachers College, Indiana, Pennsylvania. The publishers of the National Achievement Tests state that "the questions of each test were checked against numerous city and state courses of study, widely used textbooks and the judgment of more than one hundred fifty experienced administrators. . . . The tests were further evaluated and criticised by many classroom teachers. Every precaution was taken to include important subject matter emphasized in contemporary curricula." In the light of this imposing array of checks on the validity of items in the test, the only possible conclusion is that something went seriously amiss during the construction of the arithmetic test. This reviewer finds nothing to recommend the test as superior to other currently published standardized tests, and feels that it is definitely inferior to most of them.

The test is divided into two sections—Arithmetic Fundamentals and Arithmetic Reasoning. The fundamentals test covers the usual fundamental operations with whole numbers, fractions, and decimals. The reasoning test follows, in general, the usual pattern although there are features which apparently are assumed to make it different from the ordinary reasoning test. Of the two sections, the one on reasoning is the more valid.

Disregarding the fact that the format is unattractive and confusing even to the adult eye, the first obvious weakness in the fundamentals test is that it gives scant attention to some of the important fundamentals. The topic of percentage, for example, is emphasized even in *conservative* "contemporary curricula." In fact this topic may be regarded as one of the most important fundamentals of the seventh and eighth grades. In this section of the test, only three items involve percentages—two classified as Case I percentage situations and one as Case II. On the reasoning test, seven problems involve percentage, all of them Case I situations.

In actual practice, many computations involving percentage are performed by using fractional equivalents. This test does not check on a pupil's knowledge of these fundamental relationships, unless it is in one far-fetched situation where the authors want to know if "40% of $75.82 is less than $\frac{2}{5}$ of 76.00." Percentages less than one (or mixed) and greater than 100 are not used.

The inclusion of a number of antiquated computational forms in the test is entirely inexcusable. Complex fractions in arithmetic have been out of vogue for many generations. However, eight such expressions are employed in this test, the most absurd of which is $\frac{80}{7\frac{5}{6}}$. The item in which this appears requires the child to decide if "$\frac{18}{2}$ is more than $\frac{80}{7\frac{5}{6}}$." Why any defenseless child should be expected to answer this is beyond comprehension, particularly since even the wildest imagination could not concoct a practical illustration on the level of child experience which requires such reasoning. Inclusion of such ridiculous and meaningless busywork is a menace to the all too slow progress we make in arithmetic instruction. Unfortunately we teachers are inclined to assume that standardized tests of recent copyright date, which are allegedly meticulously validated, will include items on material which we should expect pupils to master.

Modern practice requires that even abstract computational exercises shall conform to practical usage. In one item, $\frac{2}{5}$, $\frac{5}{9}$, and $\frac{1}{3}$ are to be added. In what single practical situation are fractions of these denominators added? Certainly not as parts of a dozen, nor as parts of a foot, dollar, pound, hour,—nor, for that matter, as parts of any measurement in the English or French systems. The answer given in the key is $1\frac{13}{45}$, which certainly is not a practical form for interpretation.

In most cases in this test, the denominators used in fractions need no defense, although the authors show an insatiable penchant for fifths far beyond practical requirements (over one-third of the items involving fractions in the fundamental test have at least one denominator of five), while no fraction with a denominator of sixteenths is used.

In one item, 39 is written as 039 in a column of three-digit *whole number* addends. Some of the column additions are too long and some of the "ragged" columns do not conform to usage.

The "number comparisons" idea introduced in the fundamentals test is commendable but the execution of the idea most certainly is not. In fact, this part of the test is the most indefensible and fantastic of the entire test. No single item requires any reasoning or skill beyond the dull level of meaningless computation. Children are asked to decide if "4.5 + 8 + 7 + 3.4 is equal to 9.4" or "more than 24.7," or "less than 23," or "more than $24 \div \frac{1}{2}$." They are asked if "6 bu. + 9 pecks is equal to 7 bu. + 3 pecks + 8 qts.," or if it "is more than 6 bu. $\times$ $1\frac{3}{4}$," or, etc. These are only *moderate* samples of the meaningless tasks required. Number comparisons are a vital part of intelligent social living. It is indeed regrettable that in the construction of this test, so little insight into an important social problem was shown.

The Reasoning Test has some merit and can be used for diagnostic purposes, although there is nothing startling in the techniques employed to rank it as superior. The "number comparisons" on this section of the test are more easily defended as better adjusted to social situations and child comprehension than the comparisons required on the fundamentals test.

Some of the problem material is open to serious criticism. Mentioning pencils, hats, candy, and other merchandise, does not necessarily make a problem real or practical, nor does it bring the problem within the scope of child experience. When, for example, will a child "buy seven books at a price of 2 dollars each"? When will he buy "two pounds of candy that costs 1 dollar for six pounds," and if he does, would he be concerned about *comparing* the cost of the candy with the cost of a "pound of meat [which] costs 40 cents," and with the cost of two pounds of cake which costs 80 cents for four pounds?

Users of this test, who follow a curriculum, or use textbooks, based on the report of the Committee of Seven, cannot expect their pupils to achieve the norms established for this test and it is hoped that such teachers will not be persuaded to revise their curricula to conform to the many patently obsolete items included in the arithmetic tests in the National Achievement Test series.

For reviews by William A. Brownell and W. J. Osburn, see 889.

[1450]
Arithmetic: Thanet Mental Tests. Age 11; 1937; 1 form; 7s. per 25; 1s. per handbook; 1s. 6d. per specimen set, including the English and school aptitude tests in the same series; 34(40) minutes; W. P. Alexander; London: University of London Press, Ltd.

Fred J. Schonell, Lecturer in Education, Goldsmiths' College, University of London. It is intended that this test should be used at the age of 11+, as a basis of selection for secondary schools and for classification of pupils in senior, modern, and central schools.

The test booklet contains five subtests. Test 1 covers simple addition and ranges from examples of two figures in two columns to an example of four figures in eight columns. There is a total of ten examples in this test. Test 2, Subtraction, consists of ten examples, seven of which have millions in the subtrahend and minuend. These seem somewhat artificial ex-

amples for pupils of 11+, and it is possible that the same number combinations could be covered by numerous small sums more closely related to life. Test 3, Multiplication, consists of ten examples ranging from one-figure to three-figure multiplication, while the ten examples of Test 4 give a measure of division with no divisor greater than two figures. The fifth test consists of nine examples in addition and subtraction of money. This test might have included one or two examples in multiplication and division of money, as these processes may be regarded as fundamental for those proceeding to post primary education.

In the manual, averages based on 5,000 cases are given for 10-, 11-, and 12-year-olds. The test is specifically for the narrow age range cited above, and for this particular purpose it functions satisfactorily. Examples involving smaller figures would probably make the test more attractive.

No reliability or validity coefficients are given.

C. Ebblewhite Smith, Lecturer in the Department of Higher Degrees and Research, Institute of Education, University of London. This test is to be used in conjunction with the *School Aptitude Test* and the *English Test* in the series Thanet Mental Tests. It is designed to test the minimum essentials of arithmetic expected of a child about to enter an English secondary school.

A minimum essentials test does not aim at providing a normal distribution of scores; ideally it should be composed of a large number of items of approximately the same difficulty so that it may readily be seen whether candidates do or do not reach the standard set by the test. Candidates who have reached the required standard will answer the majority of the questions correctly, candidates who have not reached the standard will fail in the majority of questions. The test aims at creating as sharp a division as possible between those who reach the standard and those who do not. Such a test is difficult to prepare and requires a vast amount of experimental investigation of difficulty values of questions. The Thanet arithmetic test is not this kind of a test at all. It apparently aims at producing a normally distributed set of scores. The questions are carefully graded for difficulty: the ten addition questions, for example, range from the addition of 46 and 33 for the easiest question to the addition of eight four-figure numbers for question ten. Other tests (subtraction, ten questions; multiplication, ten questions; division, ten questions; money, nine questions) are similarly arranged from very easy to, in most cases, unnaturally long questions. The result is to produce for Entrance Scholarship candidates a distribution of marks with (for boys) the mean at 27 (out of a possible 49) and a very narrow spread. At ten years the mean is 22 and at twelve years, 32. The author does not give any figures for the reliability of the test with the eleven-year-old candidates, but surely the small difference of five marks between the eleven-year norm and the ten-year norm is of the order of the standard error of the test. On a minimum essentials test designed for eleven-year-olds the twelve-year-old norm should be a *very definite* pass and the ten-year-old norm should be a fail.

In each of the five subtests, items have been chosen to cover a wide range of number combinations. It would be of advantage to test users if authors would explain briefly in their test handbooks the process by which the final choice of test items was made.

[1451]

Basic Arithmetic Skills: Iowa Every-Pupil Tests of Basic Skills, Test D. Grades 3-5, 6-8; 1940; Form L, 2 levels; 30¢ per manual; 12¢ per booklet of norms; 40¢ per 25 record cards; single specimen set free; H. F. Spitzer in collaboration with Ernest Horn, Maude McBroom, H. A. Greene, and E. F. Lindquist with the assistance of the faculty of the University Experimental Schools, State University of Iowa; Boston, Mass.: Houghton Mifflin Co.
a) ELEMENTARY BATTERY. Grades 3-5. $1.15 per 25; 54(60) minutes.
b) ADVANCED BATTERY. Grades 6-8. $1.25 per 25; 63(80) minutes.

For reviews by William A. Brownell, J. Murray Lee, and Charles W. Odell of an earlier form of the complete battery, see 872.

[1452]

Chicago Arithmetic Readiness Test. Grades 1A-2A; 1939; 1 form; $1.25 per 25; nontimed (30) minutes; J. T. Johnson; Milwaukee, Wis.: E. M. Hale and Co.
REFERENCES
1 JOHNSON, JOHN T. "The Chicago Arithmetic Readiness Test." *Chicago Sch J* 21:121-3 D '39.

[1453]

Chicago Arithmetic Survey Tests. Grades 3-4, 5-6, 7-8; 1939; 1 form, 3 levels; J. T. Johnson; Milwaukee, Wis.: E. M. Hale and Co.
a) TEST A. Grades 3-4; 60¢ per 25; 3¢ per sample test; 60(70) minutes.
b) TEST B. Grades 5-6; 75¢ per 25; 4¢ per sample test; 80(90) minutes.

c) TEST C. Grades 7-8; 75¢ per 25; 4¢ per sample test; 90(100) minutes.

Ed Res B 18:118 Ap '39. J. Wayne Wright-stone. * No data are presented about the reliability and validity of these tests. Inspection of the exercises leads the writer to the conclusion that they are designed to be used in the conventional-school curriculum. These tests do not represent any advance in testing practices, but merely an adaptation of familiar testing exercises to the measurement of arithmetical computation and reasoning. The tests may serve survey purposes, but they must be supplemented if they are used for diagnosis.

[1454]

Compass Diagnostic Tests in Arithmetic. Grades 2-8; 1925; 1 form, 20 parts; 20¢ per manual; 60¢ per specimen set; G. M. Ruch, F. B. Knight, H. A. Greene, and J. W. Studebaker; Chicago, Ill.: Scott, Foresman and Co.
a) TEST I, ADDITION OF WHOLE NUMBERS. Grades 2-8; 25¢ per 25; 27(35) minutes.
b) TEST II, SUBTRACTION OF WHOLE NUMBERS. Grades 2-8; 25¢ per 25; 18(25) minutes.
c) TEST III, MULTIPLICATION OF WHOLE NUMBERS. Grades 3-8; 50¢ per 25; 31(40) minutes.
d) TEST IV, DIVISION OF WHOLE NUMBERS. Grades 4-8; 50¢ per 25; 60(65) minutes.
e) TEST V, ADDITION OF FRACTIONS AND MIXED NUMBERS. Grades 5-8; 50¢ per 25; 50(55) minutes.
f) TEST VI, SUBTRACTION OF FRACTIONS AND MIXED NUMBERS. Grades 5-8; 25¢ per 25; 40(45) minutes.
g) TEST VII, MULTIPLICATION OF FRACTIONS AND MIXED NUMBERS. Grades 5-8; 25¢ per 25; 30(35) minutes.
h) TEST VIII, DIVISION OF FRACTIONS AND MIXED NUMBERS. Grades 5-8; 50¢ per 25; 40(45) minutes.
i) TEST IX, ADDITION, SUBTRACTION, AND MULTIPLICATION OF DECIMALS. Grades 5-8; 50¢ per 25; 45(50) minutes.
j) TEST X, DIVISION OF DECIMALS. Grades 6-8; 50¢ per 25; 40(45) minutes.
k. TEST XI, ADDITION AND SUBTRACTION OF DENOMINATE NUMBERS. Grades 6-8; 50¢ per 25; 25(30) minutes.
l) TEST XII, MULTIPLICATION AND DIVISION OF DENOMINATE NUMBERS. Grades 6-8; 50¢ per 25; 30(35) minutes.
m) TEST XIII, MENSURATION. Grades 7-8; $1.00 per 25; 54(60) minutes.
n) TEST XIV, BASIC FACTS OF PERCENTAGE. Grades 6-8; $1.00 per 25; 38(45) minutes.
o) TEST XV, INTEREST AND BUSINESS FORMS. Grades 7-8; $1.00 per 25; 44(50) minutes.
p) TEST XVI, DEFINITIONS, RULES, AND VOCABULARY OF ARITHMETIC. Grades 4-8; 50¢ per 25; 25(30) minutes.
q) TEST XVII, PROBLEM ANALYSIS: ELEMENTARY. Grades 5-6; $1.25 per 25; 35(40) minutes.
r) TEST XVIII, PROBLEM ANALYSIS: ADVANCED. Grades 7-8; $1.25 per 25; 35(40) minutes.
s) TEST XIX, GENERAL PROBLEM SCALE: ELEMENTARY. Grades 5-6; 25¢ per 25; 20(25) minutes.
t) TEST XX, GENERAL PROBLEM SCALE: ADVANCED. Grades 7-8; 25¢ per 25; 20(25) minutes.

William A. Brownell, Professor of Educational Psychology, Duke University. This is by all odds the most elaborate and most comprehensive battery of diagnostic tests available in any subject-matter field. Comprising twenty separate tests, each containing an average of five parts, the battery provides material for a total testing time of nearly eleven and a half hours (though it is only fair to say, of course, that no child would conceivably be subjected to the whole battery).

Tests I to IV cover computation with whole numbers, one test for each of the four fundamental processes. Tests V to VIII deal with fractions and mixed numbers in a similar fashion. Tests IX and X are devoted to computation with decimals, and Tests XI and XII, with denominate numbers. Test XIII is on mensuration; Test XIV, the basic facts of percentage; Test XV, interest and business forms; Test XVI, arithmetical definitions, rules, and vocabulary; Tests XVII and XVIII, formal problem analysis; and Tests XIX and XX, problem-solving. Tests XVII and XIX are elementary forms; Tests XVIII and XX, advanced forms.

The general organization can best be explained by illustration. Test I, Addition of Whole Numbers, contains: Part 1, 70 basic addition facts in vertical and horizontal form; Part 2, 66 higher-decade addition facts; Part 3, 13 examples in column addition of three to seven single digits; Part 4, 13 examples in more difficult column addition, ranging from two 2-place numbers to seven 3- and 4-place numbers; Part 5, seven examples similar to those in Part 4, these to be checked. Test XIII, Mensuration, consists of: Part 1, 54 terms to be identified in geometric figures; Part 2, 15 examples dealing with the measurement of plane surfaces; Part 4, 14 examples involving areas and volumes; and Part 5, matching exercises covering 15 formulas used in mensuration.

The average working time per test is slightly more than 30 minutes, with a high of 54 minutes (Test XIII) and a low of 18 minutes (Test II). The tests are, of course, to be given to classes, and must be carefully administered so that precisely the designated amount of time will be allowed for each part.

All the tests are attractively arranged, and plenty of space has been left for work and for answers. The exercises in each part are roughly scaled for difficulty. Both age and grade norms, based upon large samplings of pupils, are furnished for each test as a whole, for each part of a test, and for a number of combinations of various tests.

The battery as a whole gives every indication of careful preparation, though the manual provides no information whatsoever with regard to reliability and validity. However, each test is long enough practically to guarantee a reliable measure, though this may not be true for the separate parts. So far as validity is concerned, this is perhaps best assured by the reputation of authors, who have worked long in the field of arithmetic. Nevertheless, the validity of the tests can be high only for the types of measures which can be obtained therefrom. It should be noted that, except for a few scattering items, the first fifteen tests deal almost exclusively with computation. Arithmetical meanings are pretty generally neglected, except for rather formal testing in Test XVI; and arithmetical or quantitative thinking is evaluated only in Tests XVII to XX by means of traditional verbal problems. Tests XIX and XX are really problem scales, and can be expected to yield few diagnostic data of value. Tests XVII and XVIII are intended through formal analysis to reveal sources of difficulty in children's problem solving.

One may question the value of norms in these tests. A score when translated into its age and grade equivalents can tell only how many correct answers a given child obtained in the allotted time. For purposes of diagnosis this information is not very helpful. Moreover, analysis of the scores secured and of errors made in the examples of the separate parts can reveal only the *location*, but not the *nature* of a given child's difficulty. Information on this latter point, which is crucial for the teacher, is hardly to be had from group tests, and this handicap the *Compass Diagnostic Tests in Arithmetic* share in common with all other so-called group diagnostic tests which have not been so painstakingly constructed as have these.

Foster E. Grossnickle, Professor of Mathematics, New Jersey State Teachers College, Jersey City, New Jersey. There are twenty different tests in the *Compass Diagnostic Tests in Arithmetic*. The number of tests and the topics treated are as follows: 4 tests in whole numbers; 4 tests in common fractions; 2 tests in decimal fractions; 2 tests in denominate numbers; 1 test each in mensuration, percentage, business forms, and vocabulary; 2 tests in problem analysis; and 2 tests in problem scales. The range in grade for each test varies from grades 2 to 8 depending upon the place for teaching a particular topic. The range in time for administering each test varies from 18 minutes to 60 minutes with an average of about 35 minutes.

Each of the tests, except the problem scales and the vocabulary test, is subdivided into levels of difficulty for a given process. Thus, the levels for addition of integers include the following parts: (*a*) basic facts; (*b*) higher decade addition; (*c*) single column addition; (*d*) carrying in column addition; and (*e*) checking answers in addition. Grade norms are provided for each part of a test as well as for the test as a whole. The manual of directions does not indicate whether the median or average scores are to be used for finding the grade norms for a given test or any of its parts.

It is unfortunate that the phrase, "diagnostic test in arithmetic," does not have a fixed meaning. If a diagnostic test should show the particular type of example which is not known, then the Compass tests are diagnostic only in name. No insight into the thought pattern of a pupil can be obtained by the use of these tests. They are diagnostic only in the sense that they show the particular level at which a pupil's work is unsatisfactory.

The Compass tests are essentially speed and power tests. Each part of the test is timed and norms are established in terms of a fixed working time. The incorrect examples are not included in arriving at a pupil's score, hence, the particular kind of example within a given level may be overlooked in the diagnosis because the total score on this level was equal to or above grade norm. As an illustration, consider one example of the type $2\overline{)\,241}$. If a pupil gets this zero type wrong, the chances are about 95 out of 100 that he will get all similar examples incorrect. A truly diagnostic test will make an analysis of each incorrect response or example and not lump scores into group data. Therefore, the results from the Compass test show symptoms but they give a limited amount of information which is fundamental for remedial instruction.

Considering the scope of the tests, the subject matter is well selected. There are certain to be exceptions to this statement. One of these is the perpetuation of short division. One whole section of the division test is devoted to short division. The space provided for the solution is so limited that the long form cannot be used. Some of the work in decimals is very obsolete and should not appear in a standard test. The following two examples are exemplary of obsolete subject matter: $244 + 24.4 + 2.44 + .244 + .0244$; and $36.724 - 36.0724$.

The tests in which an analysis is made of unrelated problems for diagnosis in problem-solving ability are of questionable value. There is a gradual acceptance of a philosophy that unrelated and disintegrated problems are not conducive for quantitative thinking. Such tests as these pertaining to problem analyses and problem scales tend to lend dignity and to perpetuate disassociated problems.

The *Compass Diagnostic Tests in Arithmetic* may well be used for survey purposes for a given process, but their value is very limited for diagnosis for specific remedial instruction.

[1455]

Compass Survey Tests in Arithmetic. Grades 2-4, 4-8; 1927; 2 forms, 2 levels; 50¢ per 25; 15¢ per manual; specimen set free; H. A. Greene, F. B. Knight, G. M. Ruch, and J. W. Studebaker; Chicago, Ill.: Scott, Foresman and Co.
a) ELEMENTARY EXAMINATION. Grades 2-4; 25(30) minutes.
b) ADVANCED EXAMINATION. Grades 4-8; 35(40) minutes.

William A. Brownell, Professor of Educational Psychology, Duke University. The elementary examination, for grades 2-4, deals exclusively with computation with whole numbers and consists of four parts: Part 1 contains 30 examples in addition; Part 2, 25 examples in subtraction; Part 3, 35 examples in multiplication; and Part 4, 25 examples in division. The advanced examination, for grades 4-8, is organized in a similar manner, except in two respects: (*a*) there are six instead of four parts, the new parts being devoted to percentage and to problem-solving; and (*b*) Parts 1-4 call for computation, not only with whole numbers, but also with decimals and common fractions. Each of the six parts contains 10 examples.

The chief virtues of these examinations seem to be the following: (*a*) attractive arrangement of content, with ample working space; (*b*) adequate grade norms (based upon records obtained from over 34,000 pupils) and age norms (based upon records from over 8,500 pupils), these norms being supplied separately for the parts of each examination; (*c*) correct title—it is properly called a survey test; (*d*) careful grading of examples for difficulty and equally careful distribution of use with respect to the basic number facts; (*e*) two "equal and equivalent" forms; (*f*) relative absence of exaggerated claims for the tests; (*g*) simple and helpful suggestions in a convenient manual.

Among the less desirable features of the tests are: (*a*) Only the traditional outcomes of arithmetical instruction are measured, and these imperfectly. That is to say, the emphasis is almost wholly upon computation, there being no verbal problems at all in the elementary examination and only ten in the advanced examination. No attempt has been made to get at arithmetical meanings (except as they are indirectly but inadequately measured through computation) or at the social significance which children attach to the number ideas and skills which they possess. (*b*) No means are provided in the advanced examination for securing accurate and comprehensive knowledge concerning children's ability to use different kinds of numbers in computation. Part 1, devoted to addition, contains 3 examples with whole numbers, 2 examples with decimals, 4 examples with fractions, and 1 example with denominate numbers. Parts 2, 3, and 4 likewise contain small samplings of these different kinds of numbers. (*c*) No data of any kind are presented with regard to the reliability of the tests, nor with regard to the procedures used in validation. (*d*) The keys, printed on single heavy sheets, one for each examination, cannot be used conveniently. Recent developments to improve ease of scoring might well be adopted in a revision which is surely now due, since the test is twelve years old.

In spite of the criticisms offered, the *Compass Survey Tests in Arithmetic* are probably as good as any instrument available at present for securing rough measures of attainment in the computational phases of arithmetic.

[1456]
Diagnostic Test for Fundamental Processes in Arithmetic. Grades 2-8; 1925; an individual test; 2 forms; $2.50 per 50; 25¢ per specimen set; nontimed (20) minutes; G. T. Buswell and Lenore John; Bloomington, Ill.: Public School Publishing Co.

REFERENCES

1 BUSWELL, G. T., with the co-operation of LENORE JOHN. *Diagnostic Studies in Arithmetic.* University of Chicago, Supplementary Educational Monographs, No. 30. Chicago, Ill.: Department of Education, the University, July 1926. Pp. xiii, 212. $1.50. Paper.

H. E. Benz, Professor of Education, Ohio University. Some people will not recognize the diagnostic instrument here under review as being a test at all. It is not timed, has no norms, and does not yield a numerical score. But in spite of the absence of these usual paraphernalia of standard tests, the point of view embodied in this test may, perhaps, be said to represent educational measurement at its best.

There are many kinds and types of diagnosis in arithmetic. Mass methods in education have led us to rely chiefly on diagnostic techniques which involve groups of pupils. In many instances group measurement helps only slightly in efforts to get at the underlying reasons for the bewildering vagaries apparent in the work of pupils. The test here under review is strictly an individual one. It is intended that the teacher shall sit down with an individual pupil and watch him work a carefully arranged set of examples involving the fundamental operations with whole numbers, register her observations regarding his arithmetical behavior, and when advisable obtain from the pupil by means of his explanation an understanding of the reasons for getting a wrong answer.

The authors of this test examined many samples of pupils' work in order to obtain illustrations of the most common wrong habits. They observed and studied pupils actually at work. The difficulties and wrong habits which are common have been listed on the teachers' diagnostic chart which accompanies the test. The examples were so constructed that they would give these bad habits or wrong procedures an opportunity to appear if they happened to be part of the mental equipment of the pupil being tested.

A large amount of experimental work went into the construction of this test. It represents educational diagnosis in this particular subject at its best. Some teachers will be disappointed to discover that the prescription of remedial measures is not reduced to the same simple formula as the discovery of the difficulties. This of course is another problem and has nothing to do with the merits of the test as a diagnostic instrument.

It seems doubtful that under present day conditions many schools will develop educational procedures involving the use of instructional instruments of such precision as the test here under review. But such procedures should be encouraged. Teachers should be familiar with this test and should be urged to make such use of it as available time will permit. It is this reviewer's belief that if they once experience the satisfaction which comes from using such a sharp tool, they will wish to use it more often.

Foster E. Grossnickle, Professor of Mathematics, New Jersey State Teachers College, Jersey City, New Jersey. This chart is to be used to locate difficulties of pupils whose progress is unsatisfactory in any of the four fundamental operations in arithmetic. The pupil is given a work sheet with the examples in each operation graded according to difficulty. The examiner has a chart containing a list of errors and questionable habits of work which a pupil may make in each of the four fundamental operations. Each response by the pupil is given orally. If a response is incorrect, or obtained in an indirect manner, the examiner checks the appropriate item or items on his chart. In this way an inventory is made of the pupil's habits of work so as to determine the reason for poor achievement in a given process. No time limit is set for the test. The condition under which the test is given necessarily makes it an individual and not a group test.

The favorable and unfavorable features of this test will be considered separately. The favorable qualities will be discussed first.

First, the test has two very important qualities of a diagnostic test, namely the absence of a time limit and the individual method of administration.

Second, the test attempts to analyze the thought process of a pupil. This is the only test in the field of arithmetic which the reviewer has seen, that does not deal entirely with the answers to examples. A chart of this kind enables the examiner to gain insight into the pupil's performance.

Third, there are no norms or standards to be met. The results are for diagnostic purposes and not for comparative purposes.

Fourth, on the whole, the examples selected are within the realm of minimum essentials for each operation. There are very few examples which cannot be justified from the standpoint of social utility. One exception to this rule is the following multiplication problem:

$$\frac{68}{9878}$$

There are several unfavorable features to this test which detract from its usefulness. First, the authors made no distinction between errors and what may be considered questionable habits of work. An error results in an incorrect result. If a pupil uses a questionable habit of work, his result may be correct. Thus, such things as crutches are placed in the same category as a faulty procedure or a combination error. Many competent authorities endorse and encourage the use of crutches and other aids. Hence, the chart should differentiate between errors and questionable habits of work. Such things as a differentiation between short and long division should not be perpetuated in a standard test.

Second, the examples should be arranged according to types and not according to difficulty. Since zero was the cause of many errors in each process, the examples on the pupil's work sheet typifying zero difficulties, should have been grouped. A corresponding grouping of the errors resulting from zero should have been made on the diagnostic chart. In this way a particular defect could be seen, hence, the test would be much more diagnostic than it is at present.

Third, the sampling of different skills or elements in a process is not sufficient to use for making a reliable diagnosis. As an illustration, there are six basic facts in addition, four in subtraction, eight in multiplication, and five even and one uneven division facts. Since these few basic facts occur but once, a reliable diagnosis cannot be made from a pupil's response because of the factor of chance error.

Fourth, the check list of errors is far from being complete. This is especially noticeable in multiplication and division. In the latter process, the examples in which the divisor contains a one-figure number should be in one group, and those in which the divisor contains a two-or-more-figures number in another group. One of the very frequent and serious errors in division results from faulty placement of the quotient figure, although this is not mentioned on the chart.

The reader can judge whether or not the favorable features of this test outweigh its shortcomings. The reviewer looks upon this test as the first successful effort in standard test construction in arithmetic to devise an instrument for measuring the thought pattern rather than the finished product. To that extent the authors have made a contribution in the field of testing in arithmetic. The test is in serious need of revision so that some of its most objectionable features may be removed.

[1457]

Kansas Arithmetic Test. Grades 3-5, 6-8; 1934; 2 forms, 2 levels; 50¢ per 25; 10¢ per specimen set; 30(35) minutes; Emporia, Kan.: Bureau of Educational Measurements, Kansas State Teachers College.
a) TEST 1. Grades 3-5. Ruth E. Otterstrom and H. E. Schrammel.
b) TEST 2. Grades 6-8. H. E. Schrammel, Mildred Peak, and Dodds M. Turner.

H. E. Benz, Professor of Education, Ohio University. The *Kansas Arithmetic Test* is a survey test intended to cover all of the material usually taught in grades 3-8. Each test contains two parts, the first made up of "examples" and the second of "problems." Test I comprises 40 and 28 items in the two parts respectively, while Test II comprises 30 and 25 items.

Examination of the first part of each test indicates that the examples are well distributed among the various phases of arithmetic. However, certain questions must be raised about the social utility of some of the examples. An example like "$468 \times 0 =$　" does not seem to this reviewer to help to measure the ability of a pupil to use arithmetic in concrete situations. In fact, he is unable to think of a concrete situation in which this particular ability is used. (The ability to multiply two numbers together, when one of them contains a 0 is something else.) Also, two examples out of thirty in Test II, Part I, seem to represent a disproportionate emphasis on the ability to find square roots.

The problems in Part II were evaluated in terms of criteria usually used for this purpose. Test I, Form A, was found to contain 19 good problems, 5 of doubtful value, and 4 undesirable. For Form B the figures are 23, 4, and 1. For the two forms of Test II the figures are 16, 4, and 5, and 21, 1, and 3, respectively. It should, however, be remembered that these figures represent the reviewer's subjective judgment.

The tests seem to have been carefully prepared. Examples and problems were collected from textbooks, courses of study, and research studies. They were criticised by arithmetic teachers and supervisors. Changes in the preliminary form were made in the light of error studies. The tests as published were used in the 1934 Nation-wide Every Pupil Scholarship Testing Program as administered by the Bureau of Educational Measurements of the Kansas State Teachers College at Emporia. Norms for individual grades and for separate parts of the test are based on varying numbers of pupils, ranging from 573 to 3,239. These pupils were scattered over 20 states. These norms are expressed in the form of percentiles.

Reliability coefficients average .85 when only one grade is considered, and for a range of talent involving three grades the reliability coefficients for the two tests are .91 and .88.

Mechanically the tests are satisfactory. Each one covers both sides of an $8\frac{1}{2} \times 11$ inch sheet. Typography and arrangement are attractive. Pupils will need extra paper for the problem-solving work. The scoring key is convenient. The manual of directions includes the usual material. A class record sheet is included.

By way of summary it may be said that this appears to be a suitable test for the purpose for which it is intended. Any substantial increase in its effectiveness would involve lengthening it. More adequate evaluation of the test would necessarily involve statistical analysis.

W. J. Osburn, Professor of Education, The University of Washington. These tests are an outgrowth of the Nation-wide Every Pupil Scholarship Testing Programs. Reliability coefficients range from .81 to .91. The tests are validated in terms of teacher judgment and contents of textbooks. Standard medians and percentile norms are based on more than 20,000 pupil scores in 20 different states.

Each test contains both fundamentals and problem solving. In the sections on fundamentals the equation form is used thus introducing much unnecessary trouble particularly in the case of common fractions. The addition of decimals without a common denominator is represented and should not be. Extracting the square root is included in spite of a general tendency in textbooks to present square root by table only. The division of decimals is presented together with the difficulties of nonapparent quotients. In Test I, Form B, long division is presented in only one exercise and it is far too difficult for the fourth and fifth grades. Neither the conventional nor the increase-by-one rule yields a correct quotient figure.

The problems are all of a practical nature, but the forms are not accurately parallel in some cases. One problem requires the extraction of the square root without a table. There are no age norms or T-scores.

In spite of these defects the tests are worth what they cost.

[1458]

Kansas Primary Arithmetic Test. Grades 1-3; 2 forms; 50¢ per 25; 15¢ per specimen set; 38(45) minutes; Charlotte Foster, Emma Humble, Gladys Kemp, Mildred Miller, and H. E. Schrammel; Emporia, Kan.: Bureau of Educational Measurements, Kansas State Teachers College.

W. J. Osburn, Professor of Education, The University of Washington. The test has five parts: Part I contains abstract addition and subtraction; Part II, abstract multiplication and division; Part III, a mixture of all four processes, all abstract; Part IV, a combination of number relations, denominate numbers, notation and Roman numerals; and Part V, problem solving. The entire test requires 38 minutes (two sittings of 15 and 23 minutes respectively). The one striking defect of the tests is the abstract character of the first three parts. Apparently the new literature of concrete arithmetic has made no impression upon these authors. There is a large and growing body of evidence to show that the presentation of abstract number exercises to first- and second-grade children is one thing that we should *not* do. The first half of this test, therefore, cannot expect endorsement from those who hold the newer point of view concerning the teaching of primary arithmetic.

In another respect also the test fails to observe the more recent research results in arithmetic in that short division is favored in preference to the long form. This procedure seems as definitely wrong as any procedure could be.

The latter part of the test is much better but it could be improved by the use of number series which involve counting backward as well as forward. It would also be helpful if a few words in Part V such as *costume, refreshments,* and *decided* were changed to bring them well within the vocabulary of the first three grades.

The test is to be commended for its build-up which precedes the mixed fundamentals of Part III, for its use of illustrated solutions in Parts I and II, and for the generally well-selected content of Parts IV and V. The authors claim a high degree of validity. Reliability coefficients of .90 and .89 are reported for grades 2 and 3 respectively. Adequate grade norms and directions are to be found in the manual of directions. There are no age norms.

G. M. Ruch, Chief, Research and Statistical Service, United States Office of Education, Washington, D. C. The *Kansas Primary Arithmetic Test* has 5 parts. Part I covers addition and subtraction of integers (25 and 17 items, respectively); Part II, multiplication and division (17 and 7 items, respectively); Part III, mixed fundamentals of the types included in the first two parts (6, 5, 4, and 1 items, respectively, for addition, subtraction, multiplication, and division); Part IV, 37 items of varying kinds (chiefly counting, choice of larger of two numbers, and knowledge of money and measures); and Part V, 19 problem-solving, or reasoning items. The total number of items in the five sections is 138. The total working time is 38 minutes, but provision is made for two sittings so that two class periods may be employed and fatigue factors minimized.

Considerable diagnostic value is claimed for this test, in addition to its use as a general measure of achievement. It is difficult in the available space to suggest the real situation with reference to diagnosis. Ability to handle the basic facts in addition, subtraction, and multiplication may be differentiated satisfactorily from higher levels of skills (taken more or less as a group) in these three operations. Further diagnosis is possible through tabulation of errors on individual items in the same sense that this may be done for tests making no claim for diagnostic functions. Neither the basic facts nor the higher skills of division are adequately provided for. Part IV, the miscellaneous section, permits of estimates of differentiated skills in the several fields already mentioned; how reliably no one can tell by inspection, and the manual is of no help in this decision. As a diagnostic instrument, the test falls in a position midway between survey, or general achievement tests, with no claim to diagnosis, and several of the more comprehensive group diagnostic tests in arithmetic that do permit of considerable differentiation.

The statistical evidence of validity and reliability supplied by the authors and publisher is totally inadequate; the former is a 3-line statement in the most general terms, and the latter does no more than list three reliability coefficients obtained under undefined conditions that permit of no statistical judgment or interpretation by the reviewer. The norms are medians based upon 7,109 pupils in 159 schools in 19 states. They are given, grade by grade, for midyear and end-year, by parts, and total scores; percentile scores are also provided. The dubious innovation of supplying a basis for turning scores into letter-grades (A, B, C, D, and F) is provided for, and presumably advocated.

It should be noted that the *Kansas Primary Arithmetic Test* bears the copyright date 1935. Since two or more years are ordinarily required to produce a standard test, the thinking back of this test is properly dated as falling between 1930 and 1935. This period is almost exactly that characterized by striking upward shifting of arithmetic topics in courses of study and textbooks under such influences as the Committee of Seven and other experimental work. It is not surprising, therefore, that this test represents elements of both the "old" and "new" orders, with reference to 1940 standards. The authors' evidence is fully acceptable that the test functions at the end of the first grade in the schools employed in the standardization for pupils of average or superior ability, Parts II and III excepted. Inspection of the content is sufficient proof that this test should not be used in first grades having the "new" grade placement; that is, those that attempt only meanings, concepts, and simple counting, etc., in the first grade. (Perhaps a dozen items in Part IV are valid for the "new" grade placement.) On the other hand, if grade three is taken as the point of reference, only the extremists could find large fault with the kind of content included, judged by practices at the date of publication, and the number of items provided should allow most pupils enough opportunity to "make a showing."

The mechanical features of the test are open to many criticisms, such as poor spacing, broken type, etc. The paper is of good quality, but it is too transparent and too white. Directions to pupils are set in type that is at least two points too small for primary pupils. The largely abandoned short division algorism is employed, and the symbols used in subtraction samples violate mathematical principles. Several problems are poorly phrased.

[1458.1]

Metropolitan Achievement Tests in Arithmetic, Revised Edition. Grades 1-3, 4-6, 7-8; 1932-35; identical to the reading tests in the battery *Metropolitan Achievement Tests*; 3 forms, 3 levels; 25¢ per supervisor's manual; edited by J. S. Orleans; Yonkers, N. Y.: World Book Co.

a) PRIMARY ARITHMETIC TEST. Grades 1-3; 1932-35; $1.15 per 25 tests; 20¢ per specimen set; 45(60) minutes; G. H. Hildreth.

b) INTERMEDIATE ARITHMETIC TEST. Grades 4-6; 1932-36; $1 per 25 tests; 10¢ per specimen set; 65(70) minutes; R. D. Allen, H. H. Bixler, W. L. Connor, and F. B. Graham.

c) ADVANCED ARITHMETIC TEST. Grades 7-8; 1932-36; $1 per 25 tests; 10¢ per specimen set; 70(75) minutes; R. D. Allen, H. H. Bixler, W. L. Connor, and F. B. Graham.

Peter L. Spencer, Professor of Education, Claremont Colleges. These tests are issued separately and as parts of a battery of tests which the publishers assert "provide reliable measures of group achievement, of average achievement of individual pupils, and also of individual achievement in each of the school subjects." The particular details as to how the scores are to be interpreted in order to secure these results are set forth in a supervisor's manual which must be ordered separately and in addition to the regular test materials and directions for administering and scoring.

The test sections entitled Arithmetic Fundamentals contain too few examples of any type and the sampling of known types is too limited to provide reliable and reasonably adequate data for individual diagnosis. The sections entitled Arithmetic Problems contain many instances of very poor usage of arithmetic language.

The primary test section entitled Numbers is heavily loaded with potential vocabulary difficulties. It includes in addition to the reading and writing of number symbols and a few instances of discriminations of number sequence, tests of ordinals, distinguishing differences in apparent length and size of geometric figures, the identification of geometric forms by name, reading clock faces, interpretation of simple fraction expressions, and the reading of numerous pictures. These are admittedly parts of arithmetic development, but one wonders what a single score covering such widely divergent discriminations can possibly signify in terms of individual achievement. Age and grade ratings equivalent to test scores are provided for those who wish to use them.

A careful study of these tests does not reveal evidence which indicates that they are either superior or inferior to other instruments of the same type and designed for a similar purpose. The inclusion of both classification and detailed analysis of specific achievement within the functions of a single test instrument is a practice open to criticism.

Harry Grove Wheat, Professor of Education, West Virginia University. The primary test is in three sections. The first section, Numbers, is intended for pupils in grade one, and deals chiefly with the discrimination of numerals and numbers. The second and third sections, Arithmetic Fundamentals and Arithmetic Problems, are intended, either with or without the first section, for pupils in grades two and three. These sections deal predominantly with whole numbers. In the second section six of the eighty-five examples, and in the third section four of the twenty problems, require computation with dollars and cents. The idea of the fraction appears six times in the first section and twice in the third. The intermediate and the advanced tests have two sections each, namely, Arithmetic Fundamentals and Arithmetic Problems. The intermediate test includes exercises with whole numbers, fractions, decimals, percentage, and denominate numbers. The advanced test includes similar exercises on a somewhat more difficult level and, in addition, exercises in interest, square measure, and simple equations.

Explicit directions for administering and scoring accompany the tests. A pupil's score on any given section is either the number of his correct responses, as is the case in the primary test, or an equivalent of the number of his correct responses, as is the case in the other tests, in the time limit of the section. A score is thus one of accuracy and speed. Whether the pupil understands or merely performs as he remembers he should as a result of drill and of rule-of-thumb directions is thus not revealed in his score. A pupil who is inclined to deliberate or who has been trained in deliberation in his work in arithmetic and who has not as yet attained expertness in deliberation is under a handicap in taking the test. His low score which in his case should be an indication of progress is not distinguishable from the corresponding low score of the pupil who relies wholly upon memory or who works by hit-or-miss methods. Moreover, in the sections on Arithmetic Problems no distinction is made in the scoring between the pupil who recognizes and chooses the correct procedure but makes a mistake in computation and the pupil who is wholly unaware of the situation which the wording of the problem seeks to describe. A pupil's score, when compared with the table of norms which is provided, gives him a grade-placement without the revelation of the extent of his preparation for the work of the grade.

The tests are "achievement" tests. They give a measure of achievement in general. They do not show specific weaknesses or successes. They are not adapted to purposes of diagnosis. They are useful in determining quickly, but very roughly indeed, the classification of a large group of pupils. In the case of small groups or of individual pupils, they do not reveal as much as the skillful teacher can discover through careful observation.

For reviews by Foster E. Grossnickle and Guy M. Wilson, see 892. For reviews by Jack W. Dunlap, Richard Ledgerwood, E. V. Pullias, and Hugh B. Wood of the total battery, see 874 and 1189.

[1459]
Progressive Arithmetic Tests. Grades, 2-3, 4-6, 7-9; 1933-39; 2 forms, 3 levels; 75¢ per 25; 2¢ per machine-scorable answer sheet; 15¢ per specimen set of any one battery; Ernest W. Tiegs and Willis W. Clark; Los Angeles, Calif.: California Test Bureau.
a) PRIMARY BATTERY. Grades 2-3; 1933-37; 50(60) minutes.
b) ELEMENTARY BATTERY. Grades 4-6; 1933-37; 60(70) minutes; *Machine Scoring Edition*: 1933-39.
c) INTERMEDIATE BATTERY. Grades 7-9; 1933-37; 75(85) minutes; *Machine Scoring Edition*: 1933-39.

C. L. Thiele, Director of Exact Sciences, Public Schools, Detroit, Michigan. The *Progressive Achievement Tests,* of which the *Progressive Arithmetic Tests* are a part, are divided into three batteries, Primary, Elementary, and Intermediate, and aim to test the essential abilities which constitute the elementary school subjects. In the field of arithmetic, reasoning ability and skill in the fundamental processes are tested. There are two equivalent forms for each battery.

A complete manual accompanies the tests. It contains statements of purpose, data pertaining to the reliability, the validity, and to the norms and standards of the tests. The manual also provides time allotments and suggestions for administering, scoring, and interpreting the test results. Interpretation is facilitated by class data sheets and individual pupil profiles printed on each test form. When the forms have been properly filled out they reveal such things as chronological grade placement, educational quotient, and intelligence grade placement. From these figures, grade acceleration and retardation may be computed. This somewhat full description is offered to indicate the completeness of the test plan from the point of view of test construction.

It is significant to note that the authors suggest that the tests may be used both as group and as individual measures of arithmetical ability. Used as group tests, they are intended to reveal whether or not schools are keeping abreast of the times because it is claimed that the types of abilities measured—"are indicated as desirable educational objectives in recent courses of study and are in accordance with progressive educational practice."

Used as individual measures, the tests indicate not only grade, age, and intelligence placement in general arithmetical ability but also the particular skills in which a given pupil may need strengthening. In the words of the authors, "The test is intended to be primarily of immediate practical value to the teacher in revealing which pupils are achieving satisfactorily, and for determining the particular type of remedial work necessary for those who are experiencing one or more types of learning difficulty." The latter is facilitated by analyses of the larger skills into constituent elements of difficulty.

Whether or not the arithmetic tests will serve the school administrator, supervisor, or teacher, as claimed by the authors, is the question facing the reviewer. More specifically the reviewer may ask: Is the prospective user of the *Progressive Arithmetic Tests*, after reading the manuals and other advertising material, justified in concluding that these tests will give reliable information about such matters as: (a) the standing of the arithmetic program; (b) grade, chronological and educational age; and (c) individual and group weaknesses in the mastery of arithmetic.

In the first place, the criterion upon which arithmetic tests must be evaluated depends upon the purposes accepted for the teaching of the subject. Many leaders in arithmetic teaching believe that the facts of arithmetic, by the very nature of the number system, are related and should be studied from that point of view. There are those, on the other hand, who argue that if the facts of arithmetic are to be of service in everyday life, they must be recognized as unrelated and specific things, and therefore must be singled out and mastered, one more or less independent of the other. If the former outlook is accepted, arithmetic tests will necessarily deal with basic principles and

generalizations of which the particular skills are outgrowths. On the other hand, if the acquisition of each minute skill is considered as the goal of instruction, reliable arithmetic tests should contain a proper sampling of all of the skills to indicate the extent to which the subject has been mastered.

A cursory examination of the *Progressive Arithmetic Tests* is sufficient to indicate that the tests are wholly inadequate as measures of the principles and generalizations of arithmetic. The records obtained from these tests would in no way indicate what concepts and generalizations of arithmetic have not been acquired and hence would be of little service for diagnostic and remedial purposes.

Whether or not the *Progressive Arithmetic Tests* would serve those in sympathy with a mechanistic program of arithmetic teaching depends in a large measure upon the extent to which the tests contain an adequate sampling of both the topics of arithmetic and of the skills and abilities into which they are sometimes analyzed.

In the sections devoted to arithmetic fundamentals, the sampling devices employed by the authors may be questioned. As an illustration, almost one-half of the basic addition, subtraction, and multiplication combinations are included in the primary form to measure mastery of these fundamental facts. This sampling is more than adequate in contrast with that of long division, which is measured in the three forms, primary, elementary, and intermediate by exactly eight problems, one appearing in the primary form, four in the elementary, and three in the intermediate forms. The samplings made of the other fundamental processes are as meager as that of long division. It is on this basis that the authors claim that the tests will reveal "the particular type of remedial work necessary for those who are experiencing one or more types of learning difficulties."

The selection of the items included in the section of the test designed to test reasoning ability may also be questioned. In the primary form number and sequence knowledge of money value, telling time, recognizing signs and symbols, are combined with word problems to test reasoning ability. The word problems are assigned ten points credit and the other items mentioned above thirty.

By most authorities, telling time, knowledge of money values, and the recognition of signs and symbols are considered to be specific skills of arithmetic and hence have no place as such in a reasoning test. Actual problem solving likewise comprises only a small part of the reasoning tests in the elementary and intermediate forms.

In view of the sampling methods alone, it would be difficult to accept the tests as measures which indicate the educational status of a given arithmetic program, or the extent to which both groups and individuals have mastered larger topics and specific skills in arithmetic. The elaborate and imposing sets of norms and standards and record forms in the last analysis have little value unless the contents of the tests are adequate measures of that which they purport to measure.

Harry Grove Wheat, Professor of Education, West Virginia University. Each test has two parts—one on Arithmetic Reasoning, and the other on Arithmetic Fundamentals—each of which is subdivided into three to five sections. The sections of the "reasoning" test deal in each case with the recognition of numerals, symbols, and rules, the written expression of quantities, and problem-solving. The sections of the "fundamentals" test deal in each case with the four operations on progressively higher levels of difficulty. In the primary test the operations are simple ones with whole numbers and in the intermediate test the operations are complex ones with whole numbers, fractions, decimals, and denominate numbers. The tests as a whole are largely informational and computational. The sections of each "reasoning" test other than the one in problem-solving are tests of the pupil's knowledge, not of his ability to reason or to recognize ideas of combination in practical situations. These sections are given values in the pupil's possible score two to three times the values that are given the sections on problem-solving, and the sections on computation are given four to five times the values accorded those on problem-solving. Ability to compute in relation to ability to determine what computation to use in any given case is given a progressively more important place in the objectives of instruction of pupils as they move up through the grades of the school.

The tests are intended to be useful both for survey and diagnostic purposes. The administration of the tests provides opportunity for securing a measure of ability on each item of the content. Timing is such as to require attention to each section. For the purpose of diagnosis, each test may be given individually or as a group test. In either case the scores on the various sections are available for diagnosis. A feature of the tests is the Diagnostic Profile which shows at a glance the pupil's general successes and weaknesses. Another feature is the Analysis of Learning Difficulties. This analysis breaks down the requirements of each section into specifics. For example, the Problems section of the primary test is analyzed into "one step," "two step," "sharing and arranging," and "budgeting" problems; and the Number Concept section of the intermediate test is analyzed into the requirements of "writing numbers," "writing money," "Roman numbers," "concept of whole numbers," "concept of fractions and decimals," and "concept of negative numbers." Thus the teacher can resolve the pupil's total score into its constituents and note at a glance his special points of difficulty. At what points remedial instruction is needed is thus revealed. What the remedial instruction should be is not, of course, indicated, because the causes of disabilities are not revealed by the tests. Like the usual objective test these tests measure accuracy of response, but they give no hint as to how the pupil arrived at his responses.

For a review by William A. Brownell, see 893. For reviews by D. Welty Lefever, C. W. Odell, and Hugh B. Wood of the complete battery, see 876 and 1193.

[1460]

Sangren-Reidy Survey Tests in Arithmetic. Grades 2-3, 4-6, 7-9; 1933; 1 form, 3 levels; $2.00 per 100; 25¢ per specimen set; Paul V. Sangren and Ann Reidy; Bloomington, Ill.: Public School Publishing Co.
a) DIVISION I. Grades 2-3; 27(35) minutes.
b) DIVISION II. Grades 4-6; 44(50) minutes.
c) DIVISION III. Grades 7-9; 34(40) minutes.

Leo J. Brueckner, Professor of Education, The University of Minnesota. Division I consists of tests in each of the four fundamental operations, including whole numbers and addition and subtraction of fractions. Division II contains tests in all processes, and a test in problem solving. Division III contains tests in the division of decimals, problem solving, mensuration, and percentage. Tentative norms based upon results for beginning sections of each grade for October 1 are given in the teacher's manual. No data are given concerning the reliability of the tests. The scale values of the items in the tests have not been determined statistically. The class tabulation sheet accompanying the tests provides a means of making an item by item analysis of the work of the pupils in the class which the authors believe should be helpful in determining the needs of the various pupils. The supplementary use of the *Sangren-Reidy Instructional Tests in Arithmetic* is suggested by the authors when need of more analytical diagnosis is indicated.

In the opinion of the reviewer, Divisions II and III of this series of tests are probably as usable as most of the survey tests that have been published, although exception may be taken to such items as examples in ragged addition or subtraction of decimals, compound denominate numbers of three places, and very difficult percentages. Division I (grades 2-3) should not be used in its present form since it contains many items that are entirely beyond the limits of the contents of practically all courses of study for these grades. For example, the addition test contains the examples, $5\frac{1}{6} + 3\frac{1}{2}$, and $4\frac{1}{3} + 2\frac{1}{4}$; similar examples are found in the subtraction test; the multiplication test contains an example in which the pupil is required to multiply a four-place number by a four-place number; the division test contains the example, $605,420 \div 203$. These examples which appear late in the tests are the culmination of a series of examples of increasing difficulty. Obviously the inclusion of such items in a test that may be widely used may have a very harmful effect on instruction since teachers inevitably tend to teach the items to their classes which are included in tests such as these that are too often used to secure an index of their skill as teachers. This division of the test should be radically revised so that it will more nearly meet the requirements of the first three grades. Tests should also be added to the series which deal with the social and informational functions of arithmetic.

C. L. Thiele, Director of Exact Sciences, Public Schools, Detroit, Michigan. The purposes of *Sangren-Reidy Survey Tests in Arithmetic* according to the authors are: (*a*) "to provide a measure of the general level of ability of pupils in the major processes of arithmetic"; and (*b*) "to determine the phases of arithmetic and to locate the level of difficulty

in which the pupil needs further analytical testing in order to discover his instructional needs."

The usefulness of the tests depends upon the validity of the method by which the test items were selected. This was done by analyzing the treatment of the major topics of arithmetic in eight textbook series published from 1925 to 1929. Obviously, to accept the tests it is incumbent upon the user to concur in the point of view held by those who constructed the texts upon which the tests are based.

In the light of the developments in the field of arithmetic teaching during the last ten years, of certainty is the fact that texts written from 1925 to 1929 contain a mechanistic treatment of the topics of arithmetic. This in itself destroys in almost entirety the diagnostic value of the *Sangren-Reidy Survey Tests in Arithmetic* for the increasingly large number of educators who now look with despair upon a mechanistic treatment of arithmetic. For example, those who now contend that the prime purpose for the teaching of arithmetic is the cultivation of general ideas rather than training in trivial particular skills will find little diagnostic value in an analysis of the subtraction of whole numbers into 32 "essential abilities, judgments and procedures" as outlined in the Sangren-Reidy Teacher's Handbook. Those who believe that the essential subtraction abilities are limited to a working knowledge of place value, inherent in a decimal number system, want subtraction tests which will enable them to determine what basic meanings must be acquired to enable children to subtract whole numbers meaningfully rather than mechanistically. The criticisms which have been made regarding the treatment of the subtraction with whole numbers in the Sangren-Reidy tests may likewise be made about the methods by which the other skills and abilities are tested.

In fairness to the authors, it may be said that the tests should be valuable survey instruments for those who still analyze the major topics of arithmetic into constituent elements of mechanical difficulty. The eight texts upon which the tests are based were without question among the best of the arithmetic texts produced from 1925 to 1930.

The diagnostic value of the Sangren-Reidy tests for those who accept a mechanistic psychology of learning may be questioned on grounds that the samplings of the skills found in the tests are too few in number. The authors suggest that this shortcoming may be overcome provided the teacher will—"locate the level of difficulty in which the pupil needs further analytical testing to discover his individual needs." In other words, the analytical values of the tests depend upon the ability of the teachers to determine the nature of the errors from a very limited number of cues. At best then the *Sangren-Reidy Survey Tests in Arithmetic* will remain survey tests for most teachers.

The reviewer would be remiss in the discharge of his obligations if he did not suggest that the problem confronting arithmetic test makers today seems to him to be that of taking into account the advances that have been made in the teaching of arithmetic since the publication of the Tenth Yearbook of the National Council of Teachers of Mathematics in 1935 and then constructing arithmetic tests in keeping with the point of view expressed in the Tenth Yearbook and in other more recent publications.

[1461]

Schonell Diagnostic Arithmetic Tests, Third Edition. Ages 7-13; 1936-39; 1 form; 6d. per test; 4d. per test, 25 to 49 copies; 2s. 6d. per manual; [1] Fred J. Schonell; Edinburgh, Scotland: Oliver and Boyd Ltd.

REFERENCES

[1] SCHONELL, FRED J. *Diagnosis of Individual Difficulties in Arithmetic.* Edinburgh, Scotland: Oliver and Boyd Ltd., 1937. Pp. xi, 115. 3s. (Toronto, Canada: Clarke, Irwin & Co., Ltd. $0.75.)
[2] VERNON, P. E. "Educational Tests in Scottish Schools." *Scottish Ed'J* 23:80-1 F 9 '40.

C. Ebblewhite Smith, Lecturer in the Department of Higher Degrees and Research, Institute of Education, University of London. These are 12 comprehensive, carefully graded, but not overlong tests. Schonell has tried to ensure that the tests will not occasion fatigue by dividing them up into sections each of which may be suitably completed at a sitting.

The tests are very well arranged. Test 1 comprises the 100 basic addition facts; these are given in approximate order of difficulty in five numbered columns of 20, so that the exact position of a particular item may be readily found when the test is given or corrected orally. Tests 2, 3 and 4 consist of the basic subtraction, multiplication, and division facts respectively. Test 5 is a miscellaneous test consisting of 100 of the most difficult items (as determined by error frequency) from Tests 1, 2, 3 and 4.

Subsequent tests are graded addition, subtraction, multiplication, short division and long division, constructed on the basis of four similar examples to each step of increasing difficulty. Finally there is a test of problems in mental arithmetic.

The items in Tests 6 to 12 have been well chosen to cover all possible sources of error, and enable psychologists and teachers to find out the exact levels and the nature of difficulties of pupils in all the fundamental processes.

Under ordinary circumstances the test is worked without regard to time limit—it is essentially diagnostic—but with older pupils it is sometimes useful to have an estimate of speed plus accuracy, and hence norms are provided for achievement with a time limit for each test. The details of the extensive experimental work by which the norms were obtained are not given in the handbook—we are told that they were obtained from normal samples of children from junior and senior schools.

The tests are clearly printed in good type with adequate spacing between items. They are, in their construction and production, a great advance on anything that has hitherto been produced in this country.

[1462]

Schorling-Clark-Potter Arithmetic Test, Revised Edition. Grades 5-12; 1926-28; 2 forms; 80¢ per 25; 10¢ per specimen set; 40(45) minutes; Raleigh Schorling, John R. Clark, and Mary A. Potter; Yonkers, N. Y.: World Book Co.

W. J. Osburn, Professor of Education, The University of Washington. The test consists of 100 examples divided into six sections: Part I, addition; II, subtraction; III, multiplication; IV, division; V, fractions, decimals, and percentages; and VI, a general list composed of number relations, interest, discount and percentage. The authors claim that this test measures fine gradations in computation because it includes a much wider sampling of phases of computation used in daily life. "It not only measures skills with whole numbers but it also involves the various steps by which skills are built up in the less frequently measured subjects of common fractions, decimals, percentage, and denominate numbers." All of this is a special help in diagnosis. Space is provided in which the pupil may do his computations thus avoiding the damage to diagnosis which follows when side sheets are used for computation. It is encouraging to find authors who have the courage to resist the presentation of the addition and subtraction of decimals without a common denominator. Here is at least one attempt to break the vicious circle which exists when standard tests are validated in terms of textbooks containing useless material which violates social usage. The authors are also to be commended for devoting serious attention to number relations.

The two forms of the test are matched item by item with unusual care. In the first four parts the exercises are arranged according to process in order to facilitate diagnosis. Norms also are given for each division separately. A form is provided which aids in the measurement of progress. Reliability coefficients range from .85 to .91. Provisions for validity are adequate. Useful models are provided for the use of the supervisor.

The chief defect of the test is the failure to provide age norms and some form of the T-score technique. In the addition and subtraction of common fractions it would have been better if the equation form had been avoided. The use of such forms will later present an almost irresistible invitation to the child to use cancellation. Test items relating to long division are inadequate in number. In the multiplication of decimals the notorious type ".2 × .3" should be represented. The same is true also for the type "change ½% to a decimal."

After all, however, the faults of the test are relatively minor in character. The *Schorling-Clark-Potter Arithmetic Test* is undoubtedly worth what it costs. The reviewer recommends its use.

[1462.1]

Southend Attainment Test in Mechanical Arithmetic. 1939; 1 form; 8 sets of test sheets; *2s.* per 50 of any one set; *6d.* per handbook; London: George G. Harrap & Co., Ltd.

[1463]

Unit Scales of Attainment in Arithmetic. Grades 3-4, 5-6, 7-8; 1932-33; 3 forms, 3 levels; 60¢ per 25; 15¢ per specimen set; (45) minutes; L. J. Brueckner and M. J. Van Wagenen; Minneapolis, Minn.: Educational Test Bureau, Inc.
a) DIVISION 1. Grades 3-4.
b) DIVISION 2. Grades 5-6.
c) DIVISION 3. Grades 7-8.

W. J. Osburn, Professor of Education, The University of Washington. The contents of these tests are identical with the contents of corresponding forms in the *Unit Scales of Attainment.* The tests measure ability to do the fundamental operations and to solve prob-

lems. The norms have been determined on 60,000 cases. Special keys are furnished for unfinished tests.

These tests are distinctly in the first class. Laborious and painstaking care has undoubtedly gone into their construction. The validity of the tests is based on careful studies of expert opinion and pupil performance. In reliability we are told that the probable error of the scale is 3—a truly notable achievement. C-scores are similar to the T-scores of other tests. The unit of the C-score is one tenth of the quartile deviation with an arbitrary zero point set at 60 C-score points or 6 quartile deviations below the median ability of normal children having a mental age of ten years. No reason is given for basing C-scores on the quartile deviation instead of the sigma unit. This is a bit odd since the sigma unit is the more reliable of the two.

The three divisions of the test overlap so that the tests represent a truly continuous scale. A pupil achieves the same C-score regardless of the division used in testing. The C-score units are constant throughout the entire scale. The authors claim that they are constituted so as to eliminate guessing on the part of the pupil. It is encouraging to note that the gain in problem solving from the ages of ten to fifteen is 40 C-score points as compared to a gain of 25 points in reading during the same period. Perhaps we are at last learning how to teach problem solving in arithmetic.

The authors present claims to two features that are both unique and highly useful. The C-score is said to be independent of the amount of time spent on the tests. Such a feature enables us to free ourselves from the ever obnoxious rigidity of time limitations. Each pupil may have as much time as he needs.

Even more than this, for schools which have not time to permit such extension of time, the authors have provided a table for unfinished tests in which the examiner may read what the child would do if he had as much time as he needs.

There should be some way to improve the scoring and interpretation of these tests. For a single division of the arithmetic test there are two scoring keys, two tables showing the relation of raw scores and C-scores, two class record sheets, an individual profile chart for each pupil in terms of age and grade, one class record sheet, and one C-score key for unfinished tests—nine in all printed on six separate sheets of different sizes. A person who is concerned with all three divisions of the arithmetic test and all three forms of the arithmetic test thus has 54 separate pieces of paper to look after. When an examiner wants to know, for example, what a given raw score on some division of some form means in terms of grade level, he is faced with a task that is bewildering if not maddening. The authors of the unit scales should abate this nuisance.

In spite of the careful attention given to the matter of validity there are some gaps and inadequacies in the test items. The addition and subtraction of decimals without a common denominator are retained although they appear nowhere in the world outside of school. There is also a complete neglect of ratio and proportion. Complex fractions also might have been included to advantage.

The problem scales seem short in the applications of percentages, commission, simple interest, and taxation. Insurance and bonds would seem to deserve at least some attention. Problems involving number relations also fail to appear.

None of these adverse criticisms are of major importance. The fact remains that the authors have made an earnest and scholarly attempt to produce the "best battery of tests yet constructed." Who can prove that they have failed to do so?

Peter L. Spencer, Professor of Education, Claremont Colleges. These scales are members of a battery of scales covering eight subject fields. The pattern governing the construction of this battery is an important factor in its use. The manual states, "Within each scale the questions or tasks are arranged in the order of their difficulty and spaced approximately even distances apart." This indicates that the choice of items has been governed by a statistical analysis of current accomplishment with the arithmetic tasks included rather than by the potentiality of the use of such material in the determination of the nature of student's learning. The scale is, therefore, most useful for purposes of general classification and least useful for diagnosis of specific characteristics of accomplishment. This point is recognized by the authors who have developed and recommended the use of *Analytical Scales of Attainment in Arithmetic* "Where more accurate

measurements are needed in particular functions." Elaborate statistical techniques have been utilized in the selection of scale items and in the development of the norms. The critical test of usefulness is, however, the way in which the scales fit the measurement demands of the school. The items within each division of the arithmetic scale are divided about equally between verbal problems and computational examples. The verbal problems are traditional in type but somewhat better stated than is common. The computational examples are presented in excellent type and well arranged for convenient work, but the types are too few to supply a satisfactory measure of a pupil's knowledge of computational operations.

For reviews by Herbert S. Conrad, Ethel L. Cornell, and D. Welty Lefever of the complete battery, see 878 and 1197.

[1464]

Wisconsin Inventory Tests in Arithmetic. Grades 2-8; 1924-29; 1 form, 12 parts; 75¢ per 100 of any one test, except Tests XI and XII which each sell at 90¢ per 100; 20¢ per manual; 45¢ per specimen set; non-timed; Worth J. Osburn; Bloomington, Ill.: Public School Publishing Co.

a) TEST I, ADDITION, FIRST DECADE. Grades 2-6.
b) TEST II, 100 COMBINATIONS IN FIRST DECADE SUBTRACTION. Grades 2-6.
c) TEST III, MULTIPLICATION—SIMPLE COMBINATIONS. Grades 2-6.
d) TEST IV, SHORT DIVISION—DIFFICULT COMBINATIONS. Grades 4-8.
e) TEST V, MOST USEFUL COMBINATIONS IN ADDITION—HIGHER DECADES. Grades 4-7.
f) TEST VI, ADDITION COMBINATIONS NEEDED FOR CARRYING IN MULTIPLICATION. Grades 3-8.
g) TEST VII, ALL COMBINATIONS WHICH GIVE ZERO QUOTIENTS. Grades 4-8.
h) TEST VIII, LONG DIVISION. Grades 5-8.
i) TEST IX, BRIDGING IN THE ADDITION OF MIXED NUMBERS. Grades 5-8.
j) TEST X, BRIDGING IN THE SUBTRACTION OF MIXED NUMBERS. Grades 5-8.
k) TEST XI, PROBLEM SOLVING. Grades 3-5.
l) TEST XII, DENOMINATE NUMBERS. Grades 3-5.

Leo J. Brueckner, Professor of Education, The University of Minnesota. The *Wisconsin Inventory Tests in Arithmetic* consists of a series of twelve tests. The first eight tests provide comprehensive inventories of specific phases of processes with whole numbers only, including knowledge of basic combinations in the four processes, of combinations in higher decade addition, of combinations required for carrying in multiplication, and of processes in "short" and "long" division. Two inventory tests are also provided for steps in addition and subtraction of mixed numbers. The last two tests deal with problem solving and denominate numbers. None of the tests are timed. For each test norms for appropriate grades based on October-November testing of large numbers of pupils in the white schools of Maryland are presented in the folder of directions. The medians and the lower and upper quartiles are given. No data are included as to the reliability of the tests. The tabulation sheet that is provided makes it possible to tabulate the particular combinations each pupil had incorrect. This information is helpful in diagnosis, although recent research has indicated that many errors on combinations and examples are not persistent but apparently are accidental. Hence an error on a particular combination or item does not necessarily indicate a weakness on the part of the pupil.

The author states that this series of tests "guarantees an almost perfect measure of specified parts of the subject because all of the essential items are included in each test," but that the series must necessarily be supplemented by inventory tests dealing with phases of arithmetic not included in it. The author also presents data in the Teacher's Handbook showing the improvement that has taken place in schools where these tests have been used. For check-up purposes these inventories have undoubtedly considerable value.

GEOMETRY

[1465]

Becker-Schrammel Plane Geometry. First, second semesters: high school; 1934; 2 forms, 2 levels; 60¢ per 25; 15¢ per specimen set; 40(45) minutes; Ida S. Becker and H. E. Schrammel; Emporia, Kan.: Bureau of Educational Measurements, Kansas State Teachers College.
a) TEST I. First semester.
b) TEST II. Second semester.

REFERENCES

1 BECKER, IDA S. *The Construction and Standardization of a Test in Plane Geometry.* Unpublished master's thesis, Kansas State Teachers College, Emporia, Kansas, 1934. Pp. 84.

Harold Fawcett, Associate Director of the University School and Associate Professor of Mathematics-Education, The Ohio State University. After a careful study of this test one is inclined to agree with the authors' claim that it is "a comprehensive and thoroughly objective test in plane geometry" if "comprehensive" is defined to mean that the factual content usually covered in the conventional course is adequately sampled. There are, in general, four distinct types of exercises in each

of the four tests: (*a*) those involving the completion of statements by recalling the needed geometric facts; (*b*) those calling for numerical answers to be obtained through the recall and application of certain geometric relationships; (*c*) those requiring certain geometric constructions; and (*d*) those calling for the proof of certain suggested conclusions. There is little doubt that the sort of completion exercise found in this test encourages memorization and when the word or words necessary for completing a statement are to be selected from a list supplied for this purpose, one might raise the question as to what is actually tested in all such cases. Perhaps the greatest weakness of this test is found in that part which relates to "proof." Here a figure is drawn accompanied by a statement of what is given and what is to be proved. The student is then asked to "write the steps of the proof on the lines left for this purpose" and he is told that "there should be as many steps in a correct proof as there are lines left for them." Thus, in Exercise 3 of Part IV, Test I, Form B, he must use seven steps and only seven steps in proving that $DF = EF$ for if he uses any more or any less his proof will not be "correct." Surely no such procedure can be defended for it is based on the assumption that in each of the given situations there is only one correct pattern of thinking by which the suggested conclusions can be established and that is an assumption which the reviewer cannot accept. There is wide agreement today among thoughtful teachers of demonstrative geometry that one of the chief contributions of this subject to the general education of the student is to improve the quality of his thinking and to fix the "number of steps" by which he must reach any given conclusion is to stifle this very desirable outcome. Neither children nor adults follow identical patterns of thought and to call a proof "incorrect" because it has eight steps rather than seven is to encourage intellectual dishonesty. In Test II, Form B, the authors do suggest in Part III that "several additional correct steps may be included" even though the preceding statement indicates that the number of steps in a "correct" proof should correspond to the number of lines given. It is then suggested that these "additional correct steps" should be written in the "extra space" although no "extra space" is provided for this purpose. In fact the space given for the entire proof seems altogether too small for the best results. The "list of reasons" from which the student is to select those which support the steps in his proof should, in the judgment of the reviewer, be omitted and the student required to provide his own evidence as he would be called upon to do in any real life situation.

Teachers of demonstrative geometry, whose effectiveness is to be measured by this test, will tend to emphasize the factual side of the subject, memorization will be encouraged, genuine creative thinking will be stifled, and the chief contribution of "demonstration" to the general education of the student will be largely ignored.

Judson W. Foust, Assistant Professor of Mathematics, Central State Teachers College, Mt. Pleasant, Mich. The test material is chosen and arranged so that Test I may be given at the end of four months work and Test II given at the end of eight months work. The material of Test II admittedly overlaps that of Test I. Due to the necessity of having a limited sampling in an achievement test to be given in 40 minutes, it would seem that this overlapping is undesirable. A stronger test set would have been achieved had Test II dealt more specifically with the second four months work so as to give this wider sampling. Test II attempts to sweep over the entire year's work. It is doubtful if a 40-minute test alone can adequately test the work of a year in plane geometry. Time limitations imposed on a testing program may, however, prevent wider sampling.

Each test (Tests I and II) deals with four types of material: completion of definitions and statements of theorems, simple geometric exercises requiring computation, proofs of theorems, and the performing of certain constructions. The selection of these groups as well as the material within each group is quite satisfactory.

It may seem to some, however, that the weight in amount of material and hence in score given to each type of material is unsatisfactory. Too few questions are concerned with reasoning and proof as compared with memorized materials such as definitions and completion of statements of theorems. More work on drawing conclusions from given data and judging the correctness of conclusions

could better replace some of the work on definitions, statement of theorems and constructions. Exercises could be devised so as to require this knowledge of definitions, concepts, and theorems to be used in reasoning and proof rather than merely recalled.

The test may be adequate for the great mass of ordinary geometry students who apply themselves to learn some geometry as it is often taught. The distribution of emphasis in this test will only partially satisfy one who subscribes to present trends stressing the acquaintance with the nature of proof and ability to handle proof as the main objective of geometry.

The correlations between Forms A and B for Parts I and II are .71 and .73 respectively. This is adequate for group testing and comparison but is not outstanding for a test in which interpretation of individual scores is suggested.

[1466]
Columbia Research Bureau Plane Geometry Test. Grades 10-12; 1926; 2 forms; $1.20 per 25; 25¢ per specimen set; 60(65) minutes for Parts I and II; 70(80) minutes for Parts III-VI; Herbert E. Hawkes and Ben D. Wood; Yonkers, N. Y.: World Book Co.

W. Elmer Lancaster, Teacher of Mathematics, Cleveland Junior High School, Newark, New Jersey. Part I consists of 65 true-false items which are, for the most part, well stated and thought-provoking. The items range in difficulty from simple statements of theorems and definitions to relatively difficult items such as Item 58: "If three non-parallel transversals intercept two parallel lines so that the ratio of the two segments of one of the parallel lines is equal to the ratio of the two segments of the other, the transversals are concurrent." The 20-minute time limit does not allow the examinee enough time to exercise the careful, critical thinking which the majority of the items should receive. Furthermore, in view of the direction that "Unless a statement is true, wholly and without exception, it must be marked false," Item 42, "All congruent line segments are equal and all equal line segments are congruent," is incorrectly marked true in the key.

The majority of the 35 problems in Part II require the student to construct his own diagrams. Many of these items are clever adaptations of traditional textbook problems of varying degrees of difficulty. Short numerical answers are required. The time allowed for this part is more liberal, being 40 minutes.

The test is easy to administer and score, although the key must be shifted six times during the scoring of each paper. The scoring of Part I is completely objective. A few of the items in Part II may be answered in several ways—thus requiring, as the authors point out, that the scorer must have a knowledge of algebra.

The manual does not make clear whether the elements common to previously existing plane geometry tests, or the elements common to present day textbooks, or both, have served as the basis for this test. More detailed information about the construction and validation of the test should have been presented in the manual.

The test items cover only the traditional skills and facts of plane geometry. No effort is made to measure the development of *general* reasoning ability, i.e., reasoning ability in other than purely geometric situations. Consequently, teachers interested in the broader objectives of geometry instruction will not find this test a sufficiently comprehensive measure of pupil growth toward their teaching objectives.

Reliability coefficients of .62, .90, and .93 are reported for Parts I, II, and the total test respectively. No probable errors of measurement are reported. Unfortunately, the reliability coefficients are of doubtful value since no information is given concerning the variability of the group upon which they were based or the method used to obtain them.

Test users who know how to read percentile graphs may obtain percentile rank norms based upon the scores of 2049 college freshmen. No norms are presented for grades 10-12—the grades for which the test was constructed.

A supplementary manual presents an augmented test consisting of four parts involving worth-while items on loci, converses, definitions, and demonstrations. The time allowed for the part on converses seems too little. The questions for the supplementary test are to be written on the blackboard or mimeographed; a key and suggested method of scoring these items is included.

In summary, the *Columbia Research Bureau Plane Geometry Test* is a fairly comprehensive achievement test covering the traditional subject matter of plane geometry. Despite the fact that the test was published fourteen years ago,

it compares very favorably with newer tests, such as the *Cooperative Plane Geometry Test*.

J. H. Minnick, Dean of the School of Education, The University of Pennsylvania. The purpose of this test is to measure pupil achievement in plane geometry. The test has been developed scientifically. Directions for administering the test and interpreting the results are clear and exact.

The authors have provided Forms A and B of the test. Each form consists of six parts. Parts I and II constitute the regular test and Parts III-VI constitute an augmented test. The entire test covers a wide range of well-selected materials. In addition to measuring the pupil's mastery of geometrical concepts, it also measures his ability to think within the field of geometry.

The form in which Parts I and II are printed is good. Doubtless, the users of the tests will wish that Parts III-VI were in as usable a form. In using these parts it is necessary for the examiner to furnish the pupil with mimeographed copies or to write the questions on the board.

While this test is usable and covers a wide range of essential geometrical material, it is to be noted that it measures the pupil's achievement in the field of abstract or pure geometry. It is entirely possible for a pupil to make an exceptionally high score on this test, but have no conception of the relation of the subject to the affairs of life. Except for the pupil who will pursue the study of pure mathematics, achievement in geometry as measured by this test is, in itself, of but very little value. It is the writer's opinion that the test does measure achievement that is essential to the accomplishment of the ultimate purpose for which geometry should be studied. If this test is used as a final measure of pupil achievement, the teacher will doubtless lose sight of the higher values which may be obtained from a study of geometry and for a majority of students the subject will have little or no value. They will fail to see how, through the ages, geometry has been a factor in developing civilization and how the social fabric of today is dependent upon it.

The writer would emphasize the fact that in his opinion this is one of the best geometry tests available. It does measure mastery of essential materials, but it does not measure the extent to which the pupil has realized the ultimate purpose for which geometry should be studied.

[1467]

Cooperative Plane Geometry Test. High school; 1933-40; 40- and 90-minute editions; 5¢ per test, 10 to 99 copies; 25¢ per specimen set of either edition; Form P: John A. Long and L. P. Siceloff; Form Q: Emma Spaney and L. P. Siceloff with the editorial assistance of Alice H. Darnell, Ruth Lane, Eloise B. Voorheis, and C. C. Weidemann; New York: Cooperative Test Service.
a) FORMS 1934 AND 1937. Forms 1933, 1935, and 1936 are out of print; 90(95) minutes.
b) REVISED SERIES, FORMS N, O, P, AND Q. 1937-40; 1½¢ per machine-scorable answer sheet; 40(45) minutes.

Leroy H. Schnell, Department of Mathematics, State Teachers College, Indiana, Pennsylvania. [Review of Form P.] In spite of the assertion that the staff of the Cooperative Test Service "are cognizant of trends in secondary . . . education," there is little evidence of such cognizance in their *Cooperative Plane Geometry Test*. The test is distinctly and exclusively subject-matter centered, in the most conservative sense. While it can be argued that a single test of forty minutes' duration (or even the longer form requiring ninety minutes) cannot measure all desirable objectives, it is, nevertheless, true that many teachers will assume that this test measures achievement of the primary objectives of a modern course in geometry, particularly since it is "recent" and apparently has the stamp of approval of a group of eminent educators. The influence of this test, therefore, becomes vicious in so far as teachers are led through the test to believe that subject matter is the chief end of geometry teaching.

Extreme left progressives may not be concerned with the acquisition of subject matter as such, and may even abhor such a conservative notion. Most modern educators of progressive tendencies, however, still insist that their students shall acquire mastery of that subject matter which has meaning and practical application for the learner. It is not because of any leftist view that this reviewer is critical of the subject-matter concentration of the test, but rather because the implication exists that this instrument measures the alpha and omega of objectives and also because the tèst emphasizes considerable abstruse material which is of small consequence to anyone except those who will use their geometry for technical purposes.

Educators interested in mathematics education who are cognizant of the trends at the secondary level know that during the last two or three academic generations the geometry curriculum has undergone considerable change, and furthermore, they recognize that the following attitudes and practices epitomize the modern course of geometry in the secondary school:

1) Much of the conventional subject matter has been deleted. The present tendency is toward still further restriction of the number of theorems in the elementary sequence. Many topics traditionally regarded as essential are now maintained only as optional topics but will unquestionably be eliminated entirely during the present transition period. Many topics are now being treated informally which formerly were given "rigorous" treatment. The present trend is toward greater emphasis than heretofore on induction and is based on the common-sense observation that students generally accept the validity of a theorem before they study or develop the deductive proof.

2) An attempt is made to help the pupil develop his ability to apply techniques of logical thinking to nonmathematical situations as well as to mathematical ones.

3) It is generally believed that one major objective, possibly *the* major objective, is to acquaint pupils with the nature of proof so that they will know what constitutes a good argument, what procedures lead to logical or to faulty reasoning, what the types of reasoning employed in geometry are and how they are to be transferred to nonmathematical reasoning situations; so that pupils will know how to isolate the underlying and unstated assumptions when considering the validity of a conclusion, etc.

4) It is believed that these objectives will not be realized mysteriously and result merely because formal geometry has been studied but that materials and methods must be changed to give them emphasis.

5) It axiomatically follows that if achievement of these objectives is to be measured, they must be given at least as specific attention in testing as they are given in instruction.

It is readily admitted that many of these objectives are not easily measured. Nevertheless, it is imperative that instruments be developed which will explore objectives other than that of subject matter if the needs of the modern classroom are to be met. There is little evidence to date that ability to reason logically in subject matter has any connection with ability to reason logically in typical everyday nongeometric problem situations. Modern practice is based on the psychological principle that methods of instruction, and the selection of subject matter, must force transfer of mathematical techniques to nonmathematical situations and that whatever transfer is desired must be sought for specifically. Thus we have no right to assume that a subject-matter test will yield evidence of a student's general reasoning ability, even though individual items on a factual-computational test "are so constructed as to emphasize logical reasoning and originality in geometry." Hence, the *Cooperative Plane Geometry Test* does not begin to measure what teachers of the subject in the modern secondary school are trying to teach.

Almost one-half of the items in the test can be challenged on the ground that they are abstruse and have no practical meaning or use for students who will not use geometry technically. Some of these items are challenged mainly because they involve relationships of minor significance. While in progressive classrooms a considerable amount of the conventional subject matter of geometry has been deleted or is given scant attention, nevertheless, students in such classes can be expected to "pass" the test. The test items which this reviewer does not challenge—approximately fifty per cent of the test's items—involve concepts and relationships which every person probably should know for adequate social living. Furthermore, the testing techniques employed in the test require that the student must do independent thinking in the geometric situations.

This subject-matter test could be improved by requiring reasons and defenses for geometric conclusions in many of the test items (required now in only two out of fifty items), and by giving attention to indirect reasoning, and possibly to loci. It could then be used as the subject-matter test in a battery, each section of which had been constructed to measure other important objectives of geometry.

For reviews by Charles C. Weidemann and S. S. Wilks, see 993.

[1468]
Cooperative Solid Geometry Test. High school; 1932-38; 40- and 90-minute editions; 5¢ per test, 10 to

99 copies; 25¢ per specimen set of either edition; Form P: H. T. Lundholm, John A. Long, and L. P. Siceloff; New York: Cooperative Test Service.
a) FORM 1932. Forms 1933, 1934, and 1935 are out of print; 90(95) minutes.
b) REVISED SERIES FORMS O AND P. 1938; 1½¢ per machine-scorable answer sheet; 40(45) minutes.

J. O. Hassler, Professor of Mathematics and Astronomy, The University of Oklahoma. [Review of Form P.] The test is in three parts, consists of fifty questions, and is supposed to require forty minutes.

Part I has twenty true-false questions. Six are based on factual knowledge of theorems and five on factual knowledge of definitions or fundamental concepts. The remaining nine require some independent thinking in order to adapt material learned to special cases. The subject matter covered is very good.

Part II consists of fifteen five-choice questions all of which deal with mensuration. Three are based on direct computation by means of formulas as usually stated in the book. Ten require solution of the formula-equation before or after substituting given numerical values. The remaining two require some original thinking. For example, Item 33: "The length of an edge of a cube whose volume in cubic inches is numerically equal to one-sixth its area in square inches is (1) 1 inch; (2) 2 inches; (3) 36 inches; (4) ⅙ inch; (5) 6 inches."

Part III is composed of fifteen questions like Part II except that there are more questions requiring independent thinking, a few locus problems are included, and the problems are harder.

If the true-false type and the multiple-choice type of test is to be used, this test is a very good sample. Because of the nature of such tests, it is of course impossible to test a student on his ability to put several logical steps together to prove an original exercise or theorem. As is usual in such tests, mechanical manipulation, memory, and factual knowledge are unduly emphasized. Because of this, I consider it a poor test.

If Part I is graded according to the scheme suggested in this test of subtracting the number wrong from the number right, it is an injustice to a fairly good student who does not guess, but tries all questions (nearly half of which require independent thinking) and misses, let us say, eight out of twenty. His knowledge is twelve answers out of twenty, but credit given him is four out of twenty. Another student, knowing none of the answers, can get half of them correct by marking all true, which naturally demands that some scheme like subtracting the wrongs from the rights be used. Any method of scoring is faulty and all true-false testing in mathematics should be thrown out on the junk heap.

With regard to the multiple-choice questions one may wonder what is accomplished, for example, in Item 33 quoted above by asking the question as it is and putting down five answers, one of which is correct. Why not state the problem thus: What is the length of an edge of a cube whose volume in cubic inches is numerically equal to ⅙ its area in square inches?

Two other general criticisms should be made. Only ten minutes is allowed for Part I where most of the independent thinking is done. Too great a percentage of the test is on mensuration.

Earle R. Hedrick, Vice-President and Provost of the University, The University of California. [Review of Form P.] I have more than once pointed out that it is impossible to set tests that cover adequately any mathematics beyond the most elementary arithmetic when the examination must conform to the stock "yes or no" types or to the "selection" type of answer.

There is no case in which the difficulty just mentioned becomes as obvious as it does in the case of this examination, which is supposed to cover solid geometry.

Thus it is evident that there can be no question which deals with any shade of ability in sustained reasoning; nor is there any trace of any such thing in this examination. This is not the fault of the men who made the examination; it is predestined from the start after the manner of the examination had been arbitrarily fixed.

Geometry is not per se a question of logical deduction, but it has been and should be associated with the logical processes. There is none of this here, nor can there be in an examination of this sort. The fault is in the prescription of this form of examination by those who are in charge of such prescription, for they are evidently fanatically convinced that an examination in any subject can be conducted by this particular method. What

they do not see is that the limitations of the method then load the examination heavily to one side of a subject, and eliminate or emasculate what may be—and they are in this case—the most vital phases of the subject concerned.

Thus this examination, which is supposed to represent a rational course in solid geometry, actually has become an examination in the formal mensuration formulas. Of fifty questions listed, thirty-six are actually nothing but such mensuration formulas, directly or indirectly. The almost unbelievable emphasis on this very formalized phase, almost to the exclusion of everything else, is at least striking.

Possibly between ten and fourteen of the fifty questions may be said to have some connection with geometric thinking in space other than formalized mensuration. Thus even the idea of space perception and the appreciation of the relationships between space elements is nearly or wholly lost.

This examination would seem to me to serve its highest purpose in demonstrating to any person whose mind is still open to any sort of argument that this type of examination is highly unsuited to such a subject, and that the influence which is exerted upon classroom teaching by the effort to throw examinations into this stereotyped form is to destroy in those classes the most vital and important phases of the subject.

[1469]

Iowa Plane Geometry Aptitude Test. High school students who have studied no geometry; 1935; 1 form; 85¢ per 25; 10¢ per manual; 15¢ per specimen set; 44(50) minutes; Harry A. Greene and Harold W. Bruce; Iowa City, Iowa: Bureau of Educational Research and Service, State University of Iowa.

Edward E. Cureton, Professor of Education, Alabama Polytechnic Institute. This is a 4-page test containing four parts: Part 1, Reading Geometry Content; Part 2, Algebraic Computation; Part 3, Algebraic and Arithmetical Reasoning; and Part 4, Visualization. There are 75 items of the recall type, and the test requires 44 minutes working time.

VALIDITY. The four subtests were selected from a battery of nine administered to a group of 131 students from a number of classes. The criterion was a 90-minute achievement examination of 85 items. In the final test, the items of the original subtests were rearranged in descending order of difficulty and the time limits were shortened considerably. An item analysis appears to have been made, on the basis of 61 cases, but there is no evidence that the individual items of lowest discriminating power were discarded.

For the original validation group, a correlation of .705 was obtained between the total score on the four parts (total time, 68 minutes) and the scores on the 90-minute objective achievement test. Using another group of 146 students, and (apparently) the revised time limit of 44 minutes, the correlation between the geometry aptitude test scores and the average of first and second semester grades was .592.

RELIABILITY. The odd-even reliability coefficient, "raised" by the Spearman-Brown formula, was .901 for the revised test, based on 414 cases. Since the time limits of the subtests have been reduced sharply, this coefficient is spuriously high.

NORMS. Thirteen selected percentiles are presented for each part and for the total score, based on 413 unselected pupils enrolled in plane geometry classes in a number of public school systems. No data are given regarding the selection of the particular schools included.

FORMAT. The materials for this test have been "forced" into a four-page, 8½ by 11 inch booklet. The result is unfortunate. Part of Part 1 is on the front page, so that it will be difficult for the examiner to enforce the instructions not to commence working on the test until the signal is given. To do Part 1 of the test the student must look back and forth from page 1 to page 2 on the opposite side of the same leaf. Part 2 commences in the middle of page 2, and the instruction "Do not work on Part 2 until told to do so," is omitted. This part of the test is arranged very inconveniently in two columns, apparently to save space. A considerable improvement could have been effected merely by interchanging Parts 1 and 2. All of Part 2 would have gone on page 1, underneath the general instructions, and all of Part 1 could have been put on page 2. Parts 3 and 4 are much better arranged, each on a separate page.

MANUAL. This is handsomely printed as a 20-page booklet with an orange-colored cardboard cover, but it is full of misleading information. After presenting the validity coefficient already mentioned, the authors give the same information for the original validation group (where the time limit was 68 minutes) in the form of a quintile table. From this table the authors conclude that there is "convincing evidence of the prognostic power of these tests." According to the authors' own spuriously high reliability coefficient, the probable error of the total raw score, when laid off up and down from the median, would extend approximately from the fortieth to the sixtieth percentile. "In spite of this somewhat wide displacement on the percentile scale the total scores of this test afford reasonably accurate indices to the abilities measured," say the authors. A scoring key is provided, but the arrangement of the answers on this key does not match the spacing of the items in the test booklet. The directions for administering are unusually long, the examiner being required to read aloud the instructions to the students which are printed in the test booklet. These instructions are not reprinted in the manual, so the examiner is required to look back and forth from manual to test booklet to manual again in reading the instructions for each subtest.

GENERAL EVALUATION. The practical validity of this test is likely to be rather low for purposes of individual prognosis. It is probably a little more valid, however, than the 35-minute *Lee Test of Geometric Aptitude* but appreciably less valid than the 70-minute *Orleans Geometry Prognosis Test*.

Charles C. Weidemann, Associate Professor of Mathematics and Education, The Ohio State University. The examiner's manual consists of 20 pages describing in clear language the author's experience in construction, directions for administration, and ways of checking and scoring the test. The validity is reported as .71. The grades-aptitude score validity coefficient is .59. Data are presented on the power of the test to discriminate sharply between superior and inferior pupils. The reliability is .90 based on a 44-minute test. The directions for giving the test are quite specific and clear.

The class record sheet is set up for duplicate copies—one to be mailed to the authors. It provides for entries of names, chronological and mental ages, geometry grades, achievement test scores, and the geometry aptitude scores.

The *Iowa Plane Geometry Aptitude Test* consists of 4 pages in four parts requiring 9 minutes for Part 1 (20 items), 9 minutes for Part 2 (17 items), 13 minutes for Part 3 (18 items), and 13 minutes for Part 4 (20 items)—

a total of 44 minutes with a possible score of 75. The administrative convenience, form of organization, and language in the main, seem satisfactory. Part 1, the reading of geometry content, consists of explanatory materials and 20 test items bearing on parts of angles, naming angles, included side and included angle.

The 20 items are factually clear and probably require little in the way of reasoning ability. Part 2, on algebraic computation, consists of 17 items on solving equations for unknowns: 12 of these are linear; 5 are quadratic equations; 9 are fractional equations; and the use of enclosure signs occurs 3 times. One item is a simple simultaneous linear equation. The 17 equations are a good sampling of such materials for algebraic computation. Part 3, on algebraic and arithmetical reasoning, consists of 18 items as verbal statements and problems. The number of words and number values in these range from 14 to 25. The words are simple, excepting those of a mathematical vocabulary. The sentence structures are not complex, mostly simple statements and questions. This test reads easily and the range of the sample of materials seems good. Part 4, on visualization, consists of 20 items limited mainly to cubes, involving arithmetical answers relative to faces, corners, edges, planes, and colored faces. Use of the imagination seems necessary to arrive at right results. This part of the test is unusual and probably interesting to the person examined. All the items are in question form.

The scoring key seems satisfactory for hand scoring of the test.

In summary, my study of this test causes me to judge it to be of good form. Choice of content would depend upon the viewpoint of the reviewer. The test may predict fairly well the probable academic success of a person in formal geometry. It may be questioned severely, relative to its value to predict the probable success of a person to become able as a critical logical thinker.

[1470]

Lee Test of Geometric Aptitude. High school students who have studied no geometry; 1931; 1 form; 75¢ per 25; 15¢ per specimen set; 31(40) minutes; Doris M. Lee and J. Murray Lee; Los Angeles, Calif.: California Test Bureau.

REFERENCES

1 LEE, J. MURRAY, AND LEE, DORIS MAY. "The Construction and Validation of a Test of Geometric Aptitude." *Math Teach* 25:193-203 Ap '32.

Edward E. Cureton, Professor of Education, Alabama Polytechnic Institute. This test is an 8-page booklet consisting of four parts, in which the student demonstrates his ability to learn and apply some elementary theorems on angles, to work simple arithmetical problems, to find the lengths of lines and the perimeters of subfigures (rectangles, triangles, parallelograms) within a complex figure, and to solve elementary problems in mensuration. There are fifty items, all of the recall type, and the subtests are weighted so that the maximum score is 80. The test requires approximately thirty-five minutes of working time.

VALIDITY. The four subtests were selected by a multiple correlation technique from a battery of eight given to about 600 students in schools in and around Los Angeles. The complete battery was applied at the beginning of the year, and the criterion was a comprehensive geometry achievement examination given at the end of the first semester. The median correlation between the prognosis test scores and the achievement test scores was .765, and the median correlation between the prognosis test scores and geometry marks was .530. There was apparently no item analysis, the four subtests being carried over intact from the preliminary battery into the final test. The validity coefficients reported were obtained from the same data used in selecting the subtests, and the "selection error" will therefore make them a little too high. A "face validity" error occurs at the beginning of the first test, where the conventional symbols for lines and angles are used without specific explanations.

RELIABILITY. A coefficient of .811 is reported, based on the scores of 107 unselected tenth grade pupils. This coefficient was obtained by correlating odds against evens, and "raising" by the Spearman-Brown formula. Since speed is a large factor in such a test as this, the odd-even procedure of computation gives an exaggerated estimate of the reliability.

NORMS. Eleven selected percentiles are presented, based on the 450 cases used in validating the test. A table is also given showing the distribution of scores of those students, among the 450, who failed or received grades of *D*. From a study of this table, the authors derive a "critical score." Students making higher scores than this are presumed to be able to understand elementary geometry, and students making lower scores are considered likely to encounter great difficulty in this field.

MANUAL. This is adequate in most respects, though the data on validity and reliability are presented in a slightly misleading manner. The directions for administering and scoring the tests are brief but quite adequate. A fan-type scoring key is provided, permitting rapid and accurate scoring.

FORMAT. Some of the drawings are rather poor, and many of the equal-signs can hardly be distinguished from minus-signs. In most other respects the arrangement is good.

GENERAL EVALUATION. This test is so short that its practical validity is somewhat doubtful. It appears slightly inferior to the 44-minute *Iowa Plane Geometry Aptitude Test* and appreciably poorer than the 70-minute *Orleans Geometry Prognosis Test.*

Charles C. Weidemann, Associate Professor of Mathematics and Education, The Ohio State University. The materials received for review consisted of a standardized test construction report, a manual of directions, Form A of the test, and the scoring key.

The standardized test construction report consists of 4 pages briefly describing the purpose, validity data in tabled form, reliability data in tabled form, objectivity, administration, norms and standards, equivalent forms (none), preliminary forms used, and cost data.

The manual of directions consists of 8 pages of closely printed materials which further describe the purpose, validity and reliability of the test; details for administering the test to children and suggestions for guidance use of the test results.

The *Lee Test of Geometric Aptitude* aims to predict success in geometry. It consists of eight pages in four tests requiring 31 minutes with a total possible score of 80. The administrative conveniences of the test, form of organization and language statement seem satisfactory. Test 1 consists of 3 explained geometric examples and 12 problems, the answers to which require the use of 3 figures and the explained examples. Items 1, 3, 7, and 10 are so related that a correct answer to one might aid a correct answer to the others; this is also true for incorrect answers in which cases either the advance or the penalty in score would be disproportionate to actual information known by the pupil. Test 2 consists of a

body of given data on prices of 12 different goods, 3 sample items, and 14 problems requiring use of given data. All fractions are to be reduced to lowest terms. These seem good, quite clear and unambiguous. Test 3 consists of explanatory material and 12 problems on length of line segments and perimeters of a series of geometric figures. The explanations are clear as to meaning yet in one or two places technically in need of improvement. Example: a figure has angles and vertices of angles, not corners. One of the sevens in the 17-s looks a little like a 2 and might unintentionally lead a pupil to read the segment CrH as 21 instead of 17. This test seems good. Test 4 consists of 12 algebraic problems based on formulas of perimeter, area, and volume of geometric figures and solids. This test could be improved in many details in practically every problem. Example: Item 1, "What is the area of a board L feet long and W feet wide?" The key says LW. The item would be better as follows: What is the area, A, of a board l feet long and w feet wide? The key would be A = lw. Similarly for every item in this test. Line segments are usually represented by small letters, angles by capital letters and a formula is an algebraic expression of a relationship. The ideas expressed in this test are good. Form A seems short. The claimed 25 validity coefficients range between .47 and .82 and the median is .65. The reliability coefficient is .91. The Form A is limited almost entirely to certain arithmetical computations many of which have a geometric basis.

The scoring key seems satisfactory for ordinary hand methods of scoring. The answers to Test 4 might be somewhat improved.

In summary, my study of this test causes me to judge it to be satisfactory in form, probably too short, and in need of some minor technical improvements. The content will be more or less critically questioned depending upon the viewpoint of a reviewer. Its validity in terms of individual pupil development—namely, its *valuidity*—is not available.

[1471]

Orleans Geometry Prognosis Test. High school students who have studied no geometry; 1929; 1 form; $1.70 per 25; 15¢ per specimen set; 70(80) minutes; Joseph B. Orleans and Jacob S. Orleans; Yonkers, N. Y.: World Book Co.

REFERENCES

1 PERRY, WINONA M. "Prognosis of Abilities to Solve Exercises in Geometry." *J Ed Psychol* 22:604-9 N '31.

2 Cooke, Dennis H., and Pearson, John M. "Predicting Achievement in Plane Geometry." *Sch Sci and Math* 33:872-8 N '33.
3 Orleans, Joseph B. "A Study of Prognosis of Probable Success in Algebra and in Geometry." *Math Teach* 27:165-80, 225-46 Ap, My '34.

Edward E. Cureton, Professor of Education, Alabama Polytechnic Institute. This test is a 20-page booklet consisting of nine short lessons on various types of geometric materials, each followed by a short test, and the whole followed by a summary test. The parts are as follows: (*a*) Axioms; (*b*) Reading Angles; (*c*) Kinds of Angles; (*d*) Complementary and Supplementary Angles; (*e*) Understanding Geometrical Relationships; (*f*) Bisection; (*g*) Geometrical Notation; (*h*) Analyzing Geometrical Statements; (*i*) Geometrical Problems; and (*j*) Summary Test.

The test contains 185 items all together, and requires seventy minutes of working time. This includes the time necessary to study the lessons as well as the time required to take the tests. The items are of the recall, matching, and multiple-choice types.

VALIDITY. Preliminary forms of the tests were given at the beginning of the year to 250 students in (apparently) four New York City high schools, and the results compared with scores on an objective achievement test in geometry given at the end of the first semester. A median multiple correlation of .73 between the achievement test and the several subtests of the prognosis battery is reported. The authors then state that two new parts were added, that the test in its present form is more than twice as long as the original test, that the time allotments have been increased, and that this would undoubtedly raise the validity coefficient to more than .80. No further data are given and apparently no item analysis was made.

RELIABILITY. No reliability coefficients of any sort are reported in the authors' manual.

NORMS. No norms are provided. The manual contains a statement that when more data are available they will be presented, but so far none have been. Two tables are presented for the interpretation of scores, both based, apparently, on the assumption of a correlation of .80 between scores on the test and final grades. The manual contains excellent additional advice regarding the interpretation of scores. It recommends that a test of achievement in algebra, a group intelligence test, and a school habit rating scale be used along with this test for the prognosis of ability in plane geometry.

MANUAL. The manual, as noted, is rather vague regarding the construction and validation of the test. The directions for administering however, are quite clear, brief, and explicit, conforming to the best modern practice. A fan-type scoring key is included, as is also a class record and distribution blank. The back cover of the manual contains the *New York Rating Scale for School Habits*, providing for the estimation of attention, neatness, honesty, interest, initiative, ambition, persistence, reliability, and stability.

GENERAL EVALUATION. In spite of the obvious paucity and vagueness of the data on validity and reliability provided, it is the reviewer's general opinion that this is the best test available at the present time for its intended purpose. It is appreciably superior to both the *Lee Test of Geometric Aptitude* and the *Iowa Plane Geometry Aptitude Test*, particularly if used in conjunction with other prognostic instruments as recommended by the authors.

Charles C. Weidemann, Associate Professor of Mathematics and Education, The Ohio State University. The materials received for review consisted of a manual of directions, Form A of the test, a class record form, and the scoring key.

The manual of directions consists of 12 pages describing the test, validity, directions for giving, scoring and recording scores, norms, applying results, and evaluating the test for a particular school. On page 12 is included a copy of the *New York Rating Scale for School Habits* by Cornell, Coxe, and Orleans. These directions are clear and useful.

The *Orleans Geometry Prognosis Test* consists of 20 pages, in 10 parts, each of which is made up of a lesson and a test based on the lesson.

The title of each part, the number of minutes allowed for each lesson, the number of minutes allowed for each test, and the possible score on each test are as follows: Part 1, Axioms (3, 4, 15); Part 2, Reading Angles (3, 3, 15); Part 3, Kinds of Angles (2, 4, 20); Part 4, Complementary and Supplementary Angles (3, 4, 21); Part 5, Understanding Geometrical Relationships (3, 4, 21); Part 6, Bisection

(2, 3½, 14) ; Part 7, Geometrical Notation (2, 4, 14) ; Part 8, Analyzing Geometrical Statements (1½, 3, 14) ; Part 9, Geometrical Problems (4, 9, 30) ; Part 10, Summary Test (0, 8, 21) ; totals 23½, 46½, 185.

The lesson or instructional material preceding each test is used as a means to answer the items in the test—that is, the content of Lesson 1 is used to answer the items in Test 1 and so on. The lessons are fully explained with plenty of examples and geometric figures. The 170 test items are supplemented by 75 carefully labeled, geometric figures. The test includes responses on information from factual to more general reasoning abilities, including some material on critical logical thinking. It does not test application of the principles of reflective thinking beyond geometric situations. The test allows 70 minutes to read 20 pages of materials involving responses to 170 items in the 10 tests and 27 items in the 10 lessons ; also some consideration must be given geometric figures—34 in the lessons and 75 in the tests. The written material is mostly simple statements with easy general vocabulary and in generally chosen mathematical vocabulary. Since the test is quite long, it seems that a detailed item review is not a part of this review. A few minor technical improvements might be made, but in general the administrative conveniences, form of organization, and language content is satisfactory.

The class record form consists of 2 pages and provides for names, age, score, class percentile ranks, grades, and distribution of scores.

The scoring key seems satisfactory for hand scoring. Details for its use are provided.

In summary, my extended study of this test causes me to judge it to be one of the better tests of its kind. Even though its choice of content may be questioned depending upon the reviewer, nevertheless it is fairly comprehensive in nature and should have some value in many situations. It probably has little value in predicting individual pupil development in logical as well as geometric thinking. It may indicate fairly well the superior or inferior future success of individual pupils in formal geometric situations.

[1472]

Survey Test in Plane Geometry. High school; 1939; 2 forms; 75¢ per 25; 25¢ per specimen set; 50(55) minutes; Harl R. Douglass, Richard M. Drake, and Virgil R. Walker; Minneapolis, Minn.: Educational Test Bureau, Inc.

TRIGONOMETRY

[1473]

American Council Trigonometry Test, Revised. Grades 11-15; 1928-30; 2 forms; $1.25 per 25; 15¢ per specimen set; 80(90) minutes; Joseph B. Orleans, Henry W. Raudenbush, L. Parker Siceloff, and Ben D. Wood; Yonkers, N. Y.: World Book Co.

J. O. Hassler, Professor of Mathematics and Astronomy, The University of Oklahoma. Twelve out of the twenty four-choice questions in Part I merely test ability to remember formulas. The remaining eight require some thinking to apply facts learned.

Among the twenty-nine single-answer questions in Part II are fourteen problems which require in some cases several steps. In at least half of them a student might do several things right and by a slight mistake in arithmetic get the wrong answer. By the method of objective grading he would, of course, get no credit.

In each of Parts III, IV, and V there are six applied problems dealing with methods of solution of both right and oblique triangles. The longer ones (Part V) have several steps. The statement of the problem and the manner of grading are so arranged that the student is given credit for how much he knows and not merely for a final answer which depends on a series of steps. As a matter of fact, methods of solution rather than answers are expected. It is a good attempt to test a student's ability to analyze and set up complicated problems and to grade him objectively. The thing lacking is the measure of his ability to get correct numerical answers to long problems as Part II does in the case of shorter problems. Objective testing as exemplified by current tests never does do this.

Trigonometric equations, inverse functions, and the methods of development of formulas are ignored on the test. Aside from one question relating to the recognition of a graph, there is nothing that would test a student's understanding of the real functional nature of trigonometric functions.

G. E. Hawkins, Instructor in Mathematics, University High School, The University of Chicago. This examination consists of five parts. Parts I and II cover knowledge of the fundamental facts of trigonometry. In Part I, the items are of the multiple-choice type; in Part II, of the short-answer type. Part III contains six problems for which the student is to draw the diagram, label it properly, and name the part whose value is to be found. Part IV contains six problems for which the triangles are drawn and the given parts labeled. The student is to give the formula used in finding certain remaining parts, and then to repeat the formula with the necessary numerical substitutions in it. Part V contains six more complicated problems for which the diagrams are given. The student is to outline the method of solution. A sample outline is shown in the test. The test stresses particularly achievement in the solution of triangles. The manual states that this is the most important part of the course in trigonometry.

The only data available on the validity of the test are the correlations between scores on this test and marks on the New York State Regents Examination in trigonometry for two groups of 129 and 131 cases. The coefficients were .63 and .72 respectively. There is no description of the method used in constructing the test. The large number of items in it and the range of content sampled are indicative of fairly high validity.

The measure of reliability of the test was obtained by correlating the scores made on the two forms of the test. For 126 cases this coefficient was .84. This figure would seem to indicate fairly high reliability, although further information regarding distribution of the scores is desirable if one is to get a very precise idea of the reliability.

The manual states that the scoring of the test is objective throughout. The statement is true for Parts I and II but questionable in others parts, particularly in Part V. There students will present a variety of outlines for the solutions, and it seems highly probable that some degree of subjectivity would enter into the scoring.

Norms for the test are given in the form of percentile scores. These percentiles are based on the scores of 351 students in three public high schools. Due to the fact that these percentiles are based on such a few cases from only three schools, these norms would probably have little value for many users of the test.

In a particular school the usefulness of this test would depend to a large extent on the objectives sought in the course in trigonometry. If the major objective is the development of ability in solving triangles and if reliable norms are not particularly essential, this test should

prove a useful instrument in measuring the achievement of students.

[1474]

Cooperative Trigonometry Test. High school; 1933-39; 40- and 90-minute editions; 5¢ per test, 10 to 99 copies; 25¢ per specimen set of either edition; Form P: John A. Long and L. P. Siceloff; New York: Cooperative Test Service.
a) FORMS 1934, 1935, AND 1937. Forms 1933 and 1936 are out of print; 90(95) minutes.
b) REVISED SERIES FORMS O AND P. 1938-39; 1½¢ per machine-scorable answer sheet; 40(45) minutes.

REFERENCES

1 Educational Records Bureau. *1936 Fall Testing Program in Independent Schools and Supplementary Studies*, p. 87. New York: the Bureau, January 1937. Pp. x, 111. $1.50. Paper, lithotyped.

G. E. Hawkins, Department of Mathematics, University High School, The University of Chicago. [Review of Form P.] The Cooperative Test Service of the American Council on Education was established for the fundamental purpose of making continuously available to schools the best instrument for the measurement of educational achievement that present knowledge and skill in the field of test construction, and cost considerations, will permit. The test under review is the 1939 form of their trigonometry test.

The examination is divided into two parts and requires 40 minutes to administer. It contains 45 questions of the multiple-choice type; five possible answers are given, only one of which is correct. It is adapted to machine scoring, if that feature is desired.

Materials published by the Cooperative Test Service give a rather detailed description of the construction, uses, and characteristics of this test. The purpose is to measure the extent to which students have progressed toward attaining an understanding of, and skill in the use of, those processes, principles, relationships, ideas, etc., that constitute the specific content of the course in trigonometry. The publishers make no claim for its usefulness as an instrument for measuring directly attainments in the less tangible objectives such as the development of general habits, attitudes, powers, appreciations, and ideals. The criteria used for the selection of specific content for the test was the frequency of its occurrence in courses of study and in extensively used textbooks. It includes a wide sampling of the many conventions, facts, and relationships included in the typical course in trigonometry.

The authors of the test have attempted to place emphasis on genuine understanding of principles and relationships and upon generalized ability to apply the associated skills and abilities, rather than upon mechanical manipulation and upon rote memory. The principal technique employed in this attempt is that of phrasing some of the questions in a manner that differs from that frequently employed in textbooks and in the classroom, yet in such a manner that a correct response by a student indicates genuine understanding of the principle. The following question taken from the test illustrates this idea.

If $\log 20 = \log x - \log 5$, then x equals

$$\sqrt[5]{20}, \ 15, \ 100, \ 4, \ 25$$

Extensive statistical data regarding the test scores are available. Most of these were derived from scores made on comparable forms of the test used in past years. As one measure of validity, scores made by boys in private secondary schools on an earlier form of the *Cooperative Trigonometry Test* were correlated with school marks. The coefficient was .73.[1] For the 1938 form, the reliability coefficient obtained by correlating scores on even- with odd-numbered items was .925. Other data seems to indicate that the test has high reliability. The scoring is entirely objective.

Three norms are available; those for public secondary schools of the East, Middle West, and West; those for public secondary schools of the South; and those for independent secondary schools mostly in New England. These norms are expressed in standard scores and also in percentiles. They are based on a large number of cases well distributed geographically.

The test is subject to certain limitations pointed out above. The publishers are aware of these, and the users should be. The content is necessarily that common to many courses offered in the schools. It may or may not parallel closely the course offered in a particular school. It is not intended to be used as a measure of achievement in all of the objectives for which the teacher may be striving. In order to permit machine scoring, it has only the multiple-choice type of question. It is a short test. It has little or no diagnostic value. It is intended to give, in a short time, a fairly reliable measure of the student's mastery of the content of the course. The test is a carefully constructed instrument. Experience with similar forms made in past years have aided the publishers in perfecting it. The various norms for the test are a unique and highly desirable feature of it.

For reviews by J. O. Hassler and S. S. Wilks, see 1074.

MISCELLANEOUS

Reviews by Norma A. Albright, John C. Almack, Clara M. Brown, Hester Chadderdon, R. Lenox Criswell, John G. Darley, Harry R. DeSilva, Emanuel E. Ericson, Verne C. Fryklund, Laura B. Hadley, Berenice Mallory, H. T. Manuel, Arthur B. Mays, Frederick Rand Rogers, Dean M. Schweickhard, Esther F. Segner, and A. H. Turney.

AGRICULTURE

[1475]

Clinton-Walker General Farm Mechanics Test. High school and college; [1936]; 2 forms; $1.75 per 25; 10¢ per specimen set; nontimed (60) minutes; Clyde Walker and R. J. Clinton; Corvallis, Ore.: O. S. C. Cooperative Association.

BUSINESS EDUCATION

[1476]

Bookkeeping Ability Tests: National Clerical Ability Tests, Series 1939. Bookkeepers; 1939; a new form is scheduled for publication each May for use in the annual testing program of the Joint Committee on Tests of the National Office Management Association and the National Council of Business Education; $1.35 per examinee is the fee charged for the administration and scoring of this "vocational ability test" along with the *Fundamentals Test* (*see* 1484) and the *General Information Test* (*see* 1485); 25 or more copies, 20¢ per copy (Series 1939); 50¢ per sample copy (Series 1939); $1.55 per set of sample copies of all National Clerical Ability Tests (Series 1939); 180(190) minutes; Cambridge, Mass.: Joint Committee on Tests, 16 Lawrence Hall, Kirkland St.

REFERENCES

1 Eastern Commercial Teachers' Association. *Measuring for Vocational Ability in the Field of Business Education.* Tenth Yearbook. Edited by Clinton A. Reed. New York: New York University Book Store, 1937. Pp. xx, 442. $2.00.

2 BRIGHAM, LESTER H. "National Clerical Ability Tests." *J Bus Ed* 15:25 O '39.

3 COWAN, HAROLD E. "Popularity of National Clerical Ability Tests." *J Bus Ed* 15:30 S '39.

4 Joint Committee on Tests. *National Clerical Ability Tests:* Sponsored by National Office Management Association and National Council of Business Education As a Service to Trainers and Employers of Office Workers. Bulletin No. 1. Cambridge, Mass.: Joint Committee on Tests, Lawrence Hall, Kirkland St., November 1939. Pp. iv, 40. Gratis. Paper, mimeographed.

5 "National Clerical Ability Tests." *Bus Ed World* 20:117-8 O '39.

6 "National Clerical Ability Tests: Comments and Suggestions for Their Improvement Made by Sponsors of Test Centers and Teachers of Testees with Reactions of Joint Committee on Tests." *J Bus Ed* 15:28-31 D '39.

7 FORD, GERTRUDE C. "Implications of the National Clerical Ability Tests for Teacher-Training Institutions," pp. 3-6. In *Proceedings of the Twelfth Annual Conference of the National Association of Business Teacher-Training Institutions,* Cleveland, February 25, 1939. Edited by A. Brewington. Bulletin 17. Akron, Ohio: the Association (c/o H. M. Doutt, Sec., University of Akron), 1939. Pp. 34.

8 HITTLER, GEORGE M. "Our Experience with the National Clerical Ability Tests." *Bus Ed World* 20:715-7 Ap '40.

9 "List of Schools Giving the Tests in 1939." *J Bus Ed* 15:28 F '40.

[1477]

Breidenbaugh Bookkeeping Tests: Division I, Single Proprietorship. High school; 1936; 1 form, 4 parts; 35¢ per specimen set; V. E. Breidenbaugh; Bloomington, Ill.: Public School Publishing Co.

a) TEST I, FIRST HALF OF COURSE. $1 per 25; 6¢ per key; nontimed (50-60) minutes.

b) TEST 2, FIRST HALF OF COURSE. 50¢ per 25; 4¢ per key; nontimed (50-60) minutes.

c) TEST 3, SECOND HALF OF COURSE. $1 per 25; 6¢ per key; nontimed (50-60) minutes.

d) TEST 4, SECOND HALF OF COURSE. $1.50 per 25; 8¢ per key; nontimed (100) minutes.

Bus Ed World 19:434 Ja '39. Jessie Graham. These tests, designed for the single-proprietorship high school bookkeeping course, may be used with any textbook. The tests cover journalizing, adjustments, balance sheet, statement of profit and loss, closing entries, and work sheet. They are of the completion, true-false, matching, and equation type. They are easily scored with use of the key. Tentative norms are provided. Instructions for calculating medians are printed on the record sheet. Self-check sheets for pupils' remedial work are included. Teachers using these tests will get the benefit of the large amount of preliminary work done by Mr. Breidenbaugh in constructing, trying out, and improving these tests.

[1478]

Business Backgrounds Test. High school; 1939; 1 form; $1 per 25; 10¢ per specimen set; 60(70) minutes; Mathilde Hardaway; El Paso, Tex.: the author, Austin High School.

REFERENCES

1 HARDAWAY, MATHILDE. "A Business Backgrounds Test." *Balance Sheet* 21:244-7, 279, 292-4, 336 F, Mr '40.

Balance Sheet 21:90 O '39. * Designed to cover the type of general business knowledge which an independent consumer should possess. * Teachers interested in evaluating their commercial courses to determine how well they are imparting the consumer type of general business knowledge will find this test a valuable aid.

[1479]

Clinton-LeMaster Commercial and Business Law Test. High school and college; 1936; 2 forms; $2.40 per 25; 15¢ per specimen set; nontimed (60) minutes J. Lloyd LeMaster and R. J. Clinton; Corvallis, Ore.: O. S. C. Cooperative Association.

[1480]

Commercial Education Survey Tests. First-, second-year typewriting; [1931]; 1 form, 2 levels; $1 per 25; 25¢ per manual; 40¢ per specimen set; Jane E. Clem; Bloomington, Ill.: Public School Publishing Co.

a) JUNIOR TYPEWRITING. First-year typewriting; 95(105) minutes.

b) SENIOR TYPEWRITING. Second-year typewriting; 120(130) minutes.

Bus Ed World 19:523 F '39. Jessie Graham. The Horn list of 1,000 commonest words was drawn upon for 73 per cent of the material in these stroking tests (Test 1). Each word is numbered in the key to the end that scoring is very easily done. Test 2 deals with the mechanics of the business letter and the ability to follow instructions. In the Senior Test, the pupil is required to supply capitals and punctuation marks. Test 3 is based on typewriter mechanics and typescript arrangements. Test 4 is on placement and tabulation test. Test 5 deals with centering and rough drafts. Each of these tests is issued in both junior and senior form. Final medians for some tests and tentative medians for others are reported. If you are familiar with Miss Clem's book, "The Technique of Teaching Typewriting" (Gregg), you will know that these are well-constructed tests of typing ability.

[1481]

Diagnostic Test of Letter-Writing Ability. High school students, teachers, and adults; 1939; 7¢ per test; $2 per test including scoring and a personal diagnosis by the test author; nontimed; Ralph R. Rice; Oakland, Calif.: the Author, 291 Lester Ave.

Bus Ed World 19:523-4 F '39. Jessie Graham. Teachers of business correspondence who take this test will reap not only benefits for themselves but, also, many ideas that will help to objectify their teaching. They will also have a good time while they are taking the test. The test is designed to measure letter-writing ability. It is not a check chart for letter copy. Persons who take the test learn why their letters do not function as they should, and are offered ways and means to overcome this ineffectiveness. The test also reveals natural abilities and provides personal information that enables the counselor to make recommendations for developing those abilities to the utmost. There are 17 pages of test material, comprising everything from copy reading to the construction of a technical letter. * The teacher who takes this test and has the results evaluated will gain self-assurance in teaching business correspondence. Mr. Rice is both a teacher and a specialist in the writing of business letters. His diagnoses are, therefore, reliable.

[1482]
Dictating Machine Transcription Test: National Clerical Ability Tests, Series 1939. Stenographers; 1939; a new form is scheduled for publication each May for use in the annual testing program of the Joint Committee on Tests of the National Office Management Association and the National Council of Business Education; $1.35 per examinee is the fee charged for the administration and scoring of this "vocational ability test" along with the *Fundamentals Test* (see 1484) and the *General Information Test* (see 1485); 25 or more copies, 20¢ per copy (Series 1939); 50¢ per sample copy (Series 1939); $1.55 per set of sample copies of all National Clerical Ability Tests (Series 1939); 60(65) minutes; Cambridge, Mass.: Joint Committee on Tests, 16 Lawrence Hall, Kirkland St.

REFERENCES
Same as for 1476.

[1483]
Filing Test: National Clerical Ability Tests, Series 1939. File clerks; 1939; a new form is scheduled for publication each May for use in the annual testing program of the Joint Committee on Tests of the National Office Management Association and the National Council of Business Education; $1.35 per examinee is the fee charged for the administration and scoring of this "vocational ability test" along with the *Fundamentals Test* (see 1484) and the *General Information Test* (see 1485); 25 or more copies, 20¢ per copy (Series 1939); 50¢ per sample copy (Series 1939); $1.55 per set of sample copies of all National Clerical Ability Tests (Series 1939); 120(130) minutes; Cambridge, Mass.: Joint Committee on Tests, 16 Lawrence Hall, Kirkland St.

REFERENCES
Same as for 1476.

[1484]
Fundamentals Test: National Clerical Ability Tests, Series 1939. Applicants for office work; a new form is scheduled for publication each May for use in the annual testing program of the Joint Committee on Tests of the National Office Management Association and the National Council of Business Education; $1.35 per examinee is the fee charged for the administration and scoring of one vocational ability test (see 1476, 1482-3, 1487, and 1490-1), the General Information Test (see 1485), and this test; 25 or more copies, 20¢ per copy (Series 1939); 50¢ per sample copy (Series 1939); $1.55 per set of sample copies of all National Clerical Ability Tests (Series 1939); 120(130) minutes; Cambridge, Mass.: Joint Committee on Tests, 16 Lawrence Hall, Kirkland St.

REFERENCES
Same as for 1476.

[1485]
General Information Test: National Clerical Ability Tests, Series 1939. Applicants for office work; 1939; a new form is scheduled for publication each May

for use in the annual testing program of the Joint Committee on Tests of the National Office Management Association and the National Council of Business Education; $1.35 per examinee is the fee charged for the administration and scoring of one vocational ability test (see 1476, 1482-3, 1487, and 1490-1), the Fundamentals Test (see 1484), and this test; 25 or more copies, 20¢ per copy (Series 1939); 50¢ per sample copy (Series 1939); $1.55 per set of sample copies of all National Clerical Ability Tests (Series 1939); 40(45) minutes; Phillip J. Rulon, Henry S. Dyer, and George B. Simon; Cambridge, Mass.: Joint Committee on Tests, 16 Lawrence Hall, Kirkland St.

REFERENCES
Same as for 1476.

[1486]
Grading Scales for Typewriting Tests. 18 to 72 weeks of instruction; 1939; a 28-page booklet for converting stroke and error scores into words typed per minute and percentage grades; 75¢; Howard Z. Stewart; Champaign, Ill.: Garrard Press.

Bus Ed World 22:165-6 O '39. Marion M. Lamb. The twenty-two grading scales, with directions for use, found in this book have been designed to assist the instructor in objectively grading the timed writings of high school students. The twenty-two scales cover two years of typewriting instruction. The person checking need only follow down the "Strokes" column until he finds the range in which lies the number of strokes written. Upon moving to the right to the proper "Error" column, he finds the net rate per minute and the percentage grade. At the discretion of the teacher, the letter grade equivalent for the percentage grade may be used. Those progressive teachers of typewriting who have adopted the plan of permitting students properly and neatly to erase errors and insert the correct letter or character will find the scales may be used successfully, for as the errors decrease through erasing, the strokes decrease proportionately. Thus, improved erasing efficiency will result in higher percentage grades. Probably the most important among the several values to be found in the use of the scales lies in the opportunity given students to know how they rank in such tests because the scales are objective statements of student achievement in proportion to the weeks spent in study.

[1487]
Key-Driven Calculating Machine Ability Test: National Clerical Ability Tests, Series 1939. Electric- or hand-operated machine calculators; 1939; a new form is scheduled for publication each May for use in the annual testing program of the Joint Committee on Tests of the National Office Management Association and the National Council of Business Education; $1.35 per examinee is the fee charged for the administration and scoring of this "vocational ability test" along with the *Fundamentals Test* (see 1484)

and the *General Information Test* (*see* 1485); 25 or more copies, 20¢ per copy (Series 1939); 50¢ per sample copy (Series 1939); $1.55 per set of sample copies of all National Clerical Ability Tests (Series 1939); 120(130) minutes; Cambridge, Mass.: Joint Committee on Tests, 16 Lawrence Hall, Kirkland St.

REFERENCES
Same as for 1476.

[1488]
Qualifying Test for Ediphone Voice Writing. Typists; 1938; 1 form; 40¢ per 12 tests; to schools, 30¢ per 12 tests; 24(40) minutes; Raymond C. Goodfellow and Ediphone Educational Committee; West Orange, N. J.: Thomas A. Edison, Inc.

[1489]
Scale of Problems in Commercial Arithmetic. High school; [1926]; 3 levels; $1 per 25; 25¢ per specimen set; Lucien B. Kinney; Bloomington, Ill.: Public School Publishing Co.
a) SCALE A, PART 1. First 10 weeks; 20(25) minutes.
b) SCALE A, PART 2. First 10 weeks; 10(15) minutes.
c) SCALE B. First semester; 2 forms; 40(45) minutes.
d) SCALE C. Second semester; 2 forms; 40(45) minutes.

REFERENCES
1 KINNEY, LUCIEN B. "A Program for the Determination of the Mathematical Requirements of Commercial Positions Taken by High School Graduates," pp. 60-75. In *Research Studies in Commercial Education, III.* Edited by E. G. Blackstone. University of Iowa Monographs in Education, No. 9. Iowa City, Iowa: the University, 1928. Pp. 230. $0.75. Paper.
2 KINNEY, LUCIEN B. *The Mathematical Requirements of Commercial Positions Open to High School Commercial Graduates.* Unpublished doctor's thesis, University of Minnesota, 1931.
3 KINNEY, LUCIEN B. "The Relationship of Certain Factors to Success in Clerical Positions." *J Appl Psychol* 17:55-62 F '33.

Bus Ed World 19:434 Ja '39. *Jessie Graham.* Although these tests are designed to be used at various stages of a one-year course in commercial arithmetic, they could be used equally well for diagnosis of pupils' needs in schools in which commercial arithmetic, as such, is not a part of the curriculum. Provision is made for retesting after the remedial drill following the first testing. Directions for giving the tests, answer keys, and record sheets are included. Tentative norms are reported. Space is provided for self-analysis by pupils. Problems range from those in the four fundamental processes to interest and percentage. The problems represent a good sampling of the entire commercial-arithmetic course.

[1490]
Stenographic Ability Tests: National Clerical Ability Tests, Series 1939. Stenographers; 1939; a new form is scheduled for publication each May for use in the annual testing program of the Joint Committee of Tests of the National Council of Business Education; $1.35 per examinee is the fee charged for the administration and scoring of this "vocational ability test" along with the *Fundamentals Test* (*see* 1484) and the *General Information Test* (*see* 1485); 25 or more copies, 20¢ per copy (Series 1939); 50¢ per sample copy (Series 1939); $1.55 per set of sample copies of all National Clerical Ability Tests (Series 1939); 180(190) minutes; Cambridge, Mass.: Joint Committee on Tests, 16 Lawrence Hall, Kirkland St.

REFERENCES
Same as for 1476.

[1490.1]
Turse Shorthand Aptitude Test. 1937-40; 1 form; $1.30 per 25; 10¢ per specimen set; 45(50) minutes; Paul L. Turse; Yonkers, N. Y.: World Book Co.

[1491]
Typing Ability Test: National Clerical Ability Tests, Series 1939. Typists; 1939; a new form is scheduled for publication each May for use in the annual testing program of the Joint Committee of Tests of the National Office Management Association and the National Council of Business Education; $1.35 per examinee is the fee charged for the administration and scoring of this "vocational ability test" along with the *Fundamentals Test* (*see* 1484); and the *General Information Test* (*see* 1485); 25 or more copies, 20¢ per copy (Series 1939); 50¢ per sample copy (Series 1939); $1.55 per set of sample copies of all National Clerical Ability Tests (Series 1939); 120(130) minutes; Cambridge, Mass.: Joint Committee on Tests, 16 Lawrence Hall, Kirkland St.

REFERENCES
Same as for 1476.

COMPUTATIONAL AND SCORING DEVICES

[1492]
International Test Scoring Machine. Rents for $480 per year to all except schools and colleges, to whom the rental is $400 per year; standard answer sheets printed on one side vary in price from 1½¢ per sheet when less than 500 are purchased to ¾¢ per sheet when 5,000 or more are purchased; the corresponding prices for standard answer sheets printed on two sides vary from 2¢ to 1¼¢; mechanical pencils (filled with electrographic lead) vary from 10¢ per pencil when only 12 pencils are purchased to 7¢ per pencil when 144 are purchased; 14¢ per box of 12 electrographic leads; New York: International Business Machines Corporation.

REFERENCES
1 WOOD, BEN D. *Bulletin of Information on the International Test Scoring Machine.* New York: Cooperative Test Service, October 1936. Pp. 12. Gratis. Out of print.
2 SCHROEDEL, E. C. "Potentialities of the New Test Scoring Machine in the Field of Educational and Vocational Guidance." *Am Assn Col Registrars B* 12:318-21 Jl '37.
3 WOOD, BEN D. "Test Scoring by Machine." *Nation's Sch* 20:34-6 Ag '37.
4 International Business Machines Corporation, Test Scoring Machine Department. *Methods of Adjusting Tests for Machine Scoring:* International Test Scoring Machine. New York: the Corporation, [1938]. Pp. 24. Gratis. Paper.
5 KUDER, G. FREDERIC. "Use of the International Scoring Machine for the Rapid Computation of Tables of Inter-Correlations." *J Appl Psychol* 22:587-96 D '38.
6 LANGLIE, T. A. "Objective Tests for Machine Scoring." *J Ed Res* 32:156-7 O '38.
6.1 SCHROEDEL, E. C. "Score Your Tests by Machine." *Personnel Adm* 1:6 O '38.
7 HORCHOW, REUBEN. *Machines in Civil Service Recruitment:* With Special Reference to Experiences in Ohio, pp. 10-16. Introduction by Joseph W. Hawthorne. Civil Service Assembly of the United States and Canada, Pamphlet No. 14. Chicago, Ill.: the Assembly, October 1939. Pp. 43. $0.50. Paper.
8 KORAN, SIDNEY W. "Adapting Tests to Machine Scoring." *J Appl Psychol* 23:709-19 D '39.
9 McCULLOUGH, CONSTANCE M., AND FLANAGAN, JOHN C. "The Validity of the Machine-Scorable Cooperative English Test." *J Exp Ed* 7:229-34 Mr '39.
10 NELSON, ERLAND. "Logic—Machine Scored?" *J Appl Psychol* 23:414-5 Je '39.
11 VOTAW, DAVID F., AND DANFORTH, LILY. "The Effect of Method of Response upon the Validity of Multiple-Choice Tests." *J Ed Psychol* 30:624-7 N '39.
12 WILGUS, GEORGE. "An Analysis of the Test-Scoring Machine." *Personnel Adm* 2:1-5 N '39.

13 DUNLAP, JACK W. "Problems Arising from the Use of a Separate Answer Sheet." *J Psychol* 10:3-48 Jl '40.
14 MARTIN, F. D., AND ALLEN, F. J. "The 'Clerical Facility' Factor for Students Taking Objectively Scored Tests by Direct Answer on the Test Sheet versus Separate Answer Sheets." *J Chem Ed* 17:76-7 F '40.

John G. Darley, Director of the University Testing Bureau and Assistant Professor of Psychology, The University of Minnesota. The second model of this much-needed device has been on the market long enough to have received a thorough try-out. Most of the defects of the experimental model have been eliminated, although improvements might still be made in the visibility of the reading dial by the use of a straight-line scale under a magnifying glass.

The machine rents for $400 a year to schools and colleges with an additional annual rental of $180 for an item analysis unit. An aggregate weighting unit is also available for purposes of establishing weighted averages such as grade point ratio, average of differently weighted ratings, etc. The company's service policy includes the issuance of a periodic news letter citing additional uses of the machine as they are developed. Item analyses, correlation analysis, and analysis of pattern of responses are now possible in addition to straight scoring by most of the standard formulae. Routine class room examinations can be set up in advance and machine scored; item analyses can be made in these situations as well, which should act as an impetus to more effective examination methods.

Procedures for scoring an increasingly large number of tests composed of items with multiple weights, such as vocational interest blanks and personality tests, are gradually being developed. Keys have recently been released for the machine scoring of the Strong's *Vocational Interest Blank for Men,* but there are not yet sufficient cost and time studies to indicate the amount of superiority of this method over the method using Hollerith cards and tabulating machine equipment. It is probable that where fifty or more blanks are to be scored at one time, the test scoring machine will be less expensive although no more rapid than other machine techniques. Specific information on these points can be obtained from J. W. Dunlap, University of Rochester; E. K. Strong, Stanford University; and J. G. Darley, University of Minnesota.

Since cost studies vary so much with individual institutions, and since testing loads are equally variable, no simple formula can be given for prospective users of this equipment. Some of the present charges made for scoring service seem rather high according to our local cost studies. If a great deal of testing is done, savings can be made by the purchase of smaller quantities of test supplies used on a staggered testing schedule. These savings may not be noticeable in the first year because of the necessity of purchasing specially prepared pencils and answer sheets. With the average life of a pencil-and-paper test falling in the range of 6 to 18 testing periods, however, considerable savings in supplies may be possible over a period of time. Decreased costs for labor in scoring are immediately possible since the machine in a normal working day can score between 400 and 500 tests per hour using a scoring formula that yields one score per answer sheet. As subscores for each test and scoring formula increase, this output is correspondingly decreased.

The machine is most economical for large numbers of the same test. If many different tests are being scored, the operator must change scoring keys frequently with consequent decrease in units scored in units of time. A possible defect in design is the location of the scoring key rack and crank which the operator must manipulate in these key-changing operations.

The test scoring machine will undoubtedly become increasingly valuable as time goes on. Its present use in large scale testing programs is definitely less expensive, more rapid, and more accurate than equivalent clerical methods.

H. T. Manuel, Professor of Educational Psychology, The University of Texas, and Director of Research, Texas Commission on Coordination in Education. This "review" is written from the standpoint of a consumer. The Texas Commission on Coordination in Education installed one of the early machines two years ago and shifted to the new desk model last September. Probably the review is not without bias, for the reviewer has earnestly hoped that the machine will be successful and widely useful.

That the machine is a marvelous mechanism no one will deny. If a student taking a test follows directions and if the machine operator does his part well, the machine will give an approximation of a pupil's score which on the whole will probably be more nearly accurate than the score yielded by a single scoring of the paper by hand. Moreover, it works with incredible speed even though it must be hand-fed and the scores must be recorded by hand. Naturally, since it is a mechanical thing, its repertoire of tricks is limited, but undoubtedly its full possibilities have yet to be explored.

Mechanically, it is sensitive and must be handled with intelligence and care. The operator must check at frequent intervals and watch for signs of difficulty. In the earlier machine we were greatly troubled with shorts involving usually a single item, but the new model has so far been almost free of the difficulty. Even though the student's answer sheet may have stray marks or other irregularities, or may be improperly inserted, the machine must react to what it finds—a fact which calls for extra care on the part of the operator or his assistants.

Although a great deal of ingenuity has been shown in producing an answer sheet of great flexibility, it has significant limitations. For example, the 750 sensing areas are arranged in ten fields which must behave as units, alone or in combination. Again, the positions of the sensing areas are definitely fixed, and the test maker has no choice other than to conform to them. Only relatively brief test materials can be printed on one side of the test sheet itself. If longer tests are used, either separate answer sheets are required or so many sheets are needed for the test that the saving in mechanical scoring is greatly reduced or may even disappear. The use of a separate answer sheet introduces factors the full bearing of which are yet to be explored. There is evidence that separate answer sheets can be used at least as low as the fourth grade, and our experience indicates that average six-year-olds can use a sheet adapted to machine scoring if the test material is appropriately printed on the sheet itself.

One of the least favorable factors in considering the machine for general use is its rental cost, the cost of answer sheets, and the cost of the pencils which must be provided. It takes a considerable volume of testing to justify the investment required. If there is the volume of testing suitable for machine scoring, however, it is true here as elsewhere that hand labor cannot compete successfully with machines. Not only this, but its use will free the

teacher for other important activities which only human beings can do.

One is tempted to caution educators against the attempt to over-mechanize testing in the attempt to take advantage of the saving in time and effort which the machine makes possible. There is, of course, no present hope that all needed measures can be cast in form for machine scoring, and it would be extremely unfortunate if the use of the machine were to discourage the use of other forms of measurement.

[1493]
Morgan IQ Calculator. For calculating IQ's between 66 and 125 from MA's and CA's between 8 and 14 years; [1939?]; 4s. per calculator; S. A. Morgan; Glasgow, Scotland: Robert Gibson & Sons, Ltd.

Brit J Ed Psychol 10:176 Je '40. * An ingenious device, very suggestive in its method of the sliding rule. It consists of a bakelite disc, on which mental ages are marked, including divisions for each month. On this revolves a smaller disc on which chronological ages are marked (also with month divisions). One only has to revolve the inner disc until the chronological age (say 9¼) is opposite the mental age (say 10½) to find displayed in a special opening the correct intelligence quotient, viz., between 113 and 114. The age limits are 8 and 14 * should be most serviceable for those who need to calculate quickly a fairly large number of intelligence quotients * The inventor is to be congratulated and so is the publisher on producing it in such a convenient and attractive form.

EDUCATION

[1494]
Brown Rating Profile for Student Teachers and Teachers of Physical Education. 1938; 1 form; 7¢ per scale; Margaret C. Brown; East Orange, N. J.: the author, Panzer College of Physical Education and Hygiene.

[1495]
Clinton-Castle Self-Rating Scale for County School Superintendents. 1936; 1 form; $1 per 25; 10¢ per sample scale; R. J. Clinton and E. H. Castle; Corvallis, Ore.: O. S. C. Cooperative Association.

[1496]
College Efficiency-of-Instruction Index. Student rating of college instructors; 1937; 1 form; $1 per 25; 10¢ per specimen set; R. J. Clinton; Corvallis, Ore.: O. S. C. Cooperative Association.

REFERENCES
1 CLINTON, R. J. "Qualities College Students Desire in College Instructors." *Sch and Soc* 32:702 N 22 '30.

[1496.1]
Educational Aptitude Test. Students wishing to do "advanced work in the professional educational in-

stitution or teachers' college"; 1940; 1 form; $9 per 100; 10¢ per test; 15¢ per specimen set; 55(60) minutes; Thelma Hunt and James Harold Fox; Washington, D. C.: Center for Psychological Service, George Washington University.

[1497]

Rating Instrument for the Evaluation of Student Reactions, Form 2. For student rating of high school teachers and teaching procedures; 1939; 1½¢ per scale; 3¢ per sample scale; nontimed (25-35) minutes; Roy C. Bryan and Otto Yntema; Kalamazoo, Mich.: the authors, Western State Teachers College.

REFERENCES

1 BRYAN, ROY COULTER. *Pupil Rating of Secondary School Teachers.* Columbia University, Teachers College, Contributions to Education No. 708. Percival M. Symonds, faculty sponsor; New York: Bureau of Publications, the College, 1937. Pp. vi, 96. $1.60.
2 BRYAN, ROY C., AND YNTEMA, OTTO. *A Manual on the Evaluation of Student Reactions in Secondary Schools.* Kalamazoo, Mich.: Western State Teachers College, January 1939. Pp. ii, 56. $0.50. Paper, mimeographed.

For reviews, see B323, B854, and B855.

[1498]

Rating Instrument for the Evaluation of the Reactions of College Students. For student rating of college teachers and teaching procedures; 1939; 1½¢ per scale; 3¢ per sample scale; nontimed (25-35) minutes; Roy C. Bryan and Otto Yntema; Kalamazoo, Mich.: the authors, Western State Teachers College.

REFERENCES

1 BRYAN, ROY COULTER. *Pupil Rating of Secondary School Teachers.* Columbia University, Teachers College, Contributions to Education No. 708. Percival M. Symonds, faculty sponsor; New York: Bureau of Publications, the College, 1937. Pp. vi, 96. $1.60.
2 BRYAN, ROY C., AND YNTEMA, OTTO. *A Manual on the Evaluation of Student Reactions in Secondary Schools.* Kalamazoo, Mich.: Western State Teachers College, January 1939. Pp. ii, 56. $0.50. Paper, mimeographed.

For reviews, see B323, B854, and B855.

HEALTH

[1499]

Brewer-Schrammel Health Knowledge and Attitude. Grades 4-8; 1935; 2 forms; 40¢ per 25; 15¢ per specimen set; 30(35) minutes; John W. Brewer and H. E. Schrammel; Emporia, Kan.: Bureau of Educational Measurements, Kansas State Teachers College.

REFERENCES

1 WEIDEMANN, CHARLES CONRAD. *How to Construct the True-False Examination.* Columbia University, Teachers College, Contributions to Education, No. 225. New York: Bureau of Publications, the College, 1926. Pp. ix, 118. Out of print.

John C. Almack, Professor of Education, Stanford University. This is a true-false and multiple-choice type of test of 100 items. According to the publisher's catalog, "A high correlation was obtained between pupils' scores on the test and teachers' estimates of their efficiency in respect to healthful living," but this conclusion is not substantiated by the manual of directions. On the contrary, one reads that a contingency coefficient of .38 was found, based

on only 287 junior high school students. Reliability for the eighth grade on the basis of 204 cases was given as .76.

Under "Use of Test Results," the manual says the "knowledge" items may be separated from the "attitude" items. This separation is not shown in the tests nor in the manual, nor is it an easy matter to make the division. A personal survey of the items indicates that there are many more "knowledge" items than there are "attitude" items. One also concludes that there are two kinds of "knowledge" items: (*a*) those that state facts, and (*b*) those that state generalizations from facts.

Several items are expressed in negative form; for example, "Strenuous exercise *decreases* the need for food. Which one of the following is *not* found in the air? The *lack of food* is the only cause of malnutrition." (Reviewer's italics.)

There are several items which seem to convey the obvious and should, so far as they measure *health*, give one hundred per cent answers. Among these are: "Good teeth are necessary for good health"; "A healthy body is the best defense against disease"; "Unclean food spreads disease"; and "A dirty kitchen sink is unsanitary," which is equivalent to saying a dirty kitchen sink is dirty.

A few items lead to wrong conclusions or may lead the student to believe that it expresses all the truth when in fact it expresses only part of the truth. One example is the item which says, "Antitoxins are used to prevent disease," from which one might conclude that all immunization measures make use of antitoxins. Also the statement that "Oil poured on the surface of stagnant pools makes the pools *unfit* for mosquitoes." (Reviewer's italics.) Speaking literally, in such cases, the mosquito wrigglers die because they cannot get air. Again, the item which says, "Most diseases may be *cured* by vaccination," (reviewer's italics) carries the inference that *some* diseases may be *cured* by vaccination. In Item 67, Form A, there apparently is expressed the theory that dim light *weakens* the eyes; and conversely that light of high intensity will make the eyes strong, neither of which is true. Item 12, Form A says that if the purity of water is doubted, the water should be tested. From the point of view of child education in health, it might be better to say that such water should not be used.

Another item which is marked false says that air whose humidity is 20 to 30 per cent of saturation is about right. People live and flourish in such low humidities; but the important point is that humidity is not the vital health factor; it is temperature, and the relation of humidity to physical condition can only be known when one also knows the temperature. With a humidity of 15 to 25 per cent, the temperature of a room should measure about 75 degrees in order for one to be comfortable. The item which precedes this one marks as true the statement that a temperature of 78 degrees is too warm. This is not the case, if the humidity is very low.

Teachers of health also doubt the advisability of using false statements or items on health that convey false ideas and generalizations. Testing is also teaching, and the presentation of the conclusion, "Tuberculosis patients are always kept inside," may confirm a false view and practice. Doubtless greater certainty is attached to the truth of all statements after one has taken a test than before, and while it is true that children will be exposed outside the school to false ideas and generalizations about health, the school should not multiply these. "I shall put only truth into his head," Rousseau said of Emile, "and then he shall know nothing but the truth."

The conclusion is that this test should be used with caution and only after careful weighing of its merits. On the testimony of published matter concerning it, the rating is low in validity and reliability. Many of the items are not truly objective and in answering the questions, the subject is required to accept untenable inferences. Perhaps the form should be altered, the false items eliminated, and items of fact and principle separated from items of judgment and value. In many other fields of study, sadly enough, such criticisms might be held of little weight; in health, on which happiness, efficiency, even life itself depend, every care should be exercised.

Frederick Rand Rogers, Professor of Education and Director of Physical Education, Boston University. Health knowledge tests are still relatively deficient in number, form, and completeness, but particularly in the subject matter covered. There is still no significant agreement among health teaching specialists as to what should be taught children concerning their own bodies and behavior to conserve vitality. Moreover, it is the exception rather than the rule for educators to secure competent medical advice in the selection of information to pass on to pupils. And finally, health education tests are still largely confined to tests of information rather than behavior. Such a defect is comparatively inescapable in the social science field, but not in health.

The Brewer-Schrammel test is superior to subjective tests of health knowledge prepared by individual teachers chiefly because it is standardized in two forms with a scoring key and percentile norms. It is deficient otherwise, both in construction and in subject matter covered. Of the true-false type, it includes some relatively ambiguous statements, such as "Organs are sometimes called the workmen of the body," and "If the purity of water is doubted, the water should be tested." Concerning the second statement, does the test-creator wish the child to say "no, it should be boiled" or "yes, it should be tested if possible, convenient, and economical"? The use of "all or never" modifiers in many other statements indicates lack of critical judgment in test-construction: such questions may—almost always—be answered in the negative. For there are exceptions to—almost—all rules or conditions. One exception renders an "all or never" statement wrong. When pupils learn this they automatically score such true-false statements "minus." Thus, for instance "*All* bacteria are harmful. . ." "Colds can be prevented *entirely*. . ." "Well-ventilated homes are *always* healthful." "The food one likes best is *always* best for him." (Reviewer's italics.) The use of unfamiliar and unimportant words in test questions for fourth to eighth grade pupils is also of questionable value: *anopheles* is a good example, having value chiefly to sanitarians of tropical countries, and none whatever, perhaps, to children in Kansas or New York.

Such errors in test construction are common in tests in other fields of knowledge. They are called to the reader's attention here for two reasons: to improve tests everywhere, but especially in that field which ought to be best served because it is of paramount importance to life and learning. It would be well for true-false test builders to study Weidemann's *Construction of True-False Tests*.[1]

The reliability coefficients of the Brewer-Schrammel test are low, too; while one looks in vain for proper evidence of their validity in measuring information necessary for health conservation. Even a statement of the method used to select items is missing.

[1499.1]
Byrd Health Attitude Scale. Grades 10-14; 1940; 1 form; $1.75 per 25; nontimed (30) minutes; Oliver E. Byrd; Stanford University, Calif.: Stanford University Press.

[1500]
Gates-Strang Health Knowledge Tests. Grades 3-8, 7-12; 1937; 3 forms, 2 levels; $3.15 per 100; 15¢ per specimen set; Arthur I. Gates and Ruth Strang; New York: Bureau of Publications, Teachers College, Columbia University.
a) ELEMENTARY TESTS. Grades 3-8; 40(45) minutes.
b) ADVANCED TESTS. Grades 7-12; 30(35) minutes.

REFERENCES
1 GATES, ARTHUR I., AND STRANG, RUTH. "A Test in Health Knowledge." *Teach Col Rec* 26:867-80 Je '25.

Frederick Rand Rogers, Professor of Education and Director of Physical Education, Boston University. Among the very few health knowledge tests the Gates-Strang tests are outstanding. These tests are of the multiple-choice or best-answer type in which the pupil selects the most appropriate of five alternatives which range from improper to ideal. Technically, the construction of the Gates-Strang tests is excellent, the printing is attractive, and the questions asked appear to be from selections of relatively important subject matter.

A typical Gates-Strang question is the following: "Bacteria cannot enter the body through a. The mouth. b. The nose. c. A small scratch. d. The unbroken skin. e. A hole in the tooth that has reached the pulp chamber."

The use of the best-answer technique is relatively wasteful of space: a Gates-Strang test of 7 pages includes only 60 items, whereas a Brewer-Schrammel test of 2 pages includes 100 items. The reliability coefficients of the Gates-Strang tests are higher than those of the Brewer-Schrammel, but still relatively low.

No validity coefficients are reported for Gates-Strang tests. Who knows whether the items they test have any significant relation to the maintenance of physical fitness for the average child? Nor is there any information given in the manual concerning methods used to select material, or the body of information from which questions were chosen. Moreover, these tests cover a broad range of topics related to health such as food habits, cleanliness, games and sports, anatomy, safety, first aid, and mental and social hygiene.

A. H. Turney, Professor of Education, The University of Kansas. The field of health education is as inclusive as an old-time garret; and, although the contents of the former are presumably of more value, the total picture is almost as disordered in one as the other. Moreover, much useful material is not found in either. Though we pretend to teach for a changing and complicated order of society, children learn little from the schools to protect them against the vicious barrage of propagandists' salesmanship interested in patent medicines, "food" and "drinks," cosmetics, and what-have-you.

But we do "teach" them to brush the teeth, drink milk (whether allergic to it or not), and a few other simple facts. These are thinly spread over twelve or thirteen years of school experience, taught incidentally sometimes and at other times in classes. Health is a major objective in theory and a minor and neglected one in practice.

The lot of a test maker in this field cannot be enviable if his test reflects the curriculum and the maker of the test is at all self-conscious. Most of the tests do reflect this hodge-podge we call the health curriculum.

The Gates-Strang test is undoubtedly among the best in the field. The division into two levels is fortunate and the three forms highly desirable. The tests are correctly named health *knowledge* tests, which is no discredit to them. One of the authors has for a long time been an authority on the curriculum in health education. This gives the authors some advantage in test construction in this field. The tests are easy to administer and score. On the whole, the reviewer considers them first choice in the field.

Sci Ed 23:112 F '39. L(ois) M. S(hoemaker). * These tests can be used to gain a better understanding of needs of individual pupils, to provide information essential to guidance of pupils, to show progress in health instruction, to indicate areas of instruction needing greater attention, and to measure pupils' knowledges in the health field.

[1501]
Health Awareness Test. Grades 4-8; 1937; 1 form; $3.20 per 100; 15¢ per specimen set; 30(40) minutes; Raymond Franzen, Mayhew Derryberry, and William A. McCall; New York: Bureau of Publications, Teachers College, Columbia University.

REFERENCES
1 FRANZEN, RAYMOND. *Health Education Tests*: A Description of the Tests Used in the School Health Study, with Norms for

Fifth and Sixth Grade Children, and Directions for Giving the Tests. School Health Research Monographs, No. 1. Washington, D. C.: National Education Association, 1929. Pp. xxi, 70. Cloth, $0.90; Paper, $0.60.

R. Lenox Criswell, Teacher of Health and Physical Education, Arts High School, Newark, New Jersey. The publishers describe this test in their catalogue as follows: "A group test of health information, attitudes, and practice applicable in Grades 4 to 8 inclusive; composed of a story test, a matching test, and a true-false test, each constructed from tests developed by the School Health Study of the American Child Health Association. The reliability and validity are high, independent of intelligence. Time required 30 minutes."

The test manual presents a somewhat different story. The grade range for which this test is intended is not directly reported in the manual but grade-score norms for grades 1 to 14 are supplied! No information is given as to how these grade norms were obtained. This is all the more perplexing since the original tests were "prepared specifically for the fifth and sixth grades with ages ranging from nine to thirteen years." [1]

Despite this restriction, the abbreviated test reports age-score norms ranging from 5.5 to 21.8! The authors and publishers should have provided a description of the manner in which these startling norms were secured. Justification should also have been presented for the discrepancy between the grade and age ranges for which the original and abbreviated tests are intended.

Scoring difficulties are needlessly increased by the failure of the publishers to provide ready-to-use answer keys. Examiners are given the correct answers but must prepare their own scoring keys.

The story test consists of four short, simple stories in which the pupil is told to: "Underline everything that is good for the health. Cross out everything that is bad for the health." This test may be of some value as a health information test in grades 4 and 5. However, the repetition of such elementary choices as "eating bread and butter" rather than "candy" before meals seems scarcely challenging enough for upper grade pupils.

The matching test consists of three exercises containing a total of twenty-one statements to be matched with correct answers picked from a list of thirty items in a second column. For example, "Should be very clean" is to be matched with "Bedroom" and "Should not be too warm" with "Babies' milk." These responses could be interchanged and still be correct. By reversing the position of the two columns in this test, *subjects,* on the left could be matched with *predicates,* on the right. That should prove simpler for the younger children.

The 40-item true-false test seems more mature and better suited for upper grade pupils. Directions to guess answers not known seem to be ill advised. Furthermore, the true-false test should have been scored rights minus wrongs. As it is, the rights score makes no distinction between wrong and omitted answers.

The test manual reports no information on the test's reliability. The only information which the manual presents concerning the test's validity is the statement that "The correlation between scores on this test and scores on the larger battery are .95 for the fifth grade and .95 for the sixth grade." Reference to the research monograph, *Health Education Tests,*[1] reveals numerous statistics and tables of dubious value in establishing the reliability and validity of the original 90-minute battery. Perhaps no paper and pencil test can adequately rate pupil growth in a subject that has the diversification and ramifications of health education. Certainly the difficulty of the task is greatly increased when a single test is expected to cover all five of the upper grades of elementary school. Notwithstanding the fine auspices under which the original battery was constructed, this reviewer is unable to recommend either the original or the abbreviated edition.

Hygeia 16:366 Ap '38. W. W. B(auer). * The test should be interesting to teachers of health as a means of measuring the success which they have attained in imparting information. It is, of course, no test of the true criterion of health education; namely, motivation toward healthful conduct.

For a review by Austin H. Turney, see 1006.

[1502]

Health Test: National Achievement Tests. Grades 3-8; 1937-38; 2 forms; $1 35 per 25; 5¢ per specimen set; nontimed (40) minutes; Robert K. Speer and Samuel Smith; Rockville Centre, N. Y.: Acorn Publishing Co.

[1503]

Kilander Health Knowledge Test. Grades 12-13; 1936; 1 form; $1.40 per 25 tests; nontimed (40-50) minutes; H. F. Kilander; East Orange, N. J.: the

Author, Panzer College of Physical Education and Hygiene.

REFERENCES

1 KILANDER, H. F. "Health Knowledge of High School and College Students." *Res Q* 8:3-32 O '37.

J Health and Phys Ed 10:432 S '39. * includes one hundred multiple-choice questions in the several fields of health education. A score sheet and tentative norms are also included.

Sci Ed 22:379 D '38. L(ois) M. S(hoemaker). This test consists of 100 multiple-choice questions dealing with health knowledge in the fields of Nutrition, Communicable Diseases, Sanitation, Safety and First Aid, Social and Mental Health, including common errors and superstitions in these fields. Time required is 40 minutes. Such a test can be used for diagnostic purposes and for student motivation.

[1504]

Physical Examination Record. Grades 1-16; 1938; $1.25 per 25; 20¢ per specimen set; Edward MacDonald; Lancaster, Mass.: College Press.

REFERENCES

1 MACDONALD, EDWARD. *The Interrelations Between Certain Physical and Mental Capacities Together with Social Attitudes as Factors Affecting Educational Growth.* Unpublished doctor's thesis, Boston University, 1940.

HOME ECONOMICS

[1505]

Engle-Stenquist Home Economics Test. Grades 5-10; 1931; 2 forms, 3 parts; $1.00 per 25 parts; 35¢ per specimen set; 60(65) minutes; Edna M. Engle and John L. Stenquist; Yonkers, N. Y.: World Book Co.
a) FOODS AND COOKERY.
b) CLOTHING AND TEXTILES.
c) HOUSEHOLD MANAGEMENT.

Clara M. Brown, Professor and Director of Graduate Studies and Research in Home Economics Education, The University of Minnesota. These tests cover three aspects of subject matter: clothing and textiles, foods and cookery, and household management. They were the first home economics tests to provide equivalent forms, and are without doubt superior to any of the earlier tests in the field. The manual of directions discusses the purpose of the tests, describes how they were constructed and presents statistical evidence of their validity and reliability. It provides clearly stated directions for administering the tests and scoring them. Norms are set up for each form of each test in terms of both grade and age of pupils. Certain suggestions are offered for the interpretation of test results for pur-

poses of measuring achievement, classification of students, for analysis of students' weaknesses and of teachers' instruction, and for educational guidance.

The reliability coefficients found by the authors ranged from .85 to .96, which would indicate that the tests compare favorably with those in other subjects.

The tests were standardized on the basis of results obtained from giving them to from ten to fifteen thousand children in the city of Baltimore, Maryland, in 1929-30. The fact that the tests were standardized on the basis of children in a single city limits the value of the norms.

Each test consists of four parts: including 4-response multiple-choice items, true-false items, matching items, and completion items. Each section of a test is preceded by explicit directions for answering it and a correctly answered example. The tests are planned for grades 5 to 10, which is too great a range and the norms for grades above the ninth are extrapolated values which experience suggests are too low.

The mechanical features of the test are reasonably satisfactory and strip keys are furnished which make it possible to score tests rapidly and accurately. The completion statements are so phrased that the final word is always the one to be supplied; hence answers are recorded in the right-hand margin for these items as well as for the others.

A form for recording the score on each part of the test separately is located on the first page of each test. Unfortunately this score form is too small and does not provide enough space for writing in the scores.

As is true with most other commercial tests, few questions demand more than reproduction of facts and despite the care exercised in the selection of test items one finds many instances where the key may be questioned.

Hester Chadderdon, Associate Professor of Home Economics Education, Iowa State College. This test was designed to measure the acquisition of knowledge in the field of home economics. The authors imply in their manual of directions that it includes the whole field but an examination of the items included reveals many gaps and relatively little attention to some other phases. The items chosen were common to twelve of the "best up-to-date" textbooks and twenty-five "outstanding" courses of study and the questions were submitted to home economists for criticism. Since the test was published in 1931, it seems fair to everyone concerned to suggest that the test be revised in the light of more recent developments in the field.

The section devoted to foods and cookery is largely a test of meal planning and cookery with a few items relating to table service, etiquette, and food purchasing. This is probably the best of the three tests as far as breadth of subject matter is concerned and teachers will find it of value in helping to estimate the extent of learning.

It is unfortunate that the one section is titled Home Management since approximately 84 per cent of the items relate to housing; house planning, house furnishing, and care of the house. No attention is given to the management of time and energy and little to money. Only 15 of the 119 questions are concerned with social relations and these pertain largely to etiquette.

The section relating to textiles and clothing places major emphasis on textiles and construction although selection, care, and repair are not neglected. Some of the subject matter on textiles is relatively unimportant. A revision of the test should contain more questions on the art aspects and the broad social implications of selection.

Norms have been developed based on ten to fifteen thousand cases in one city system. Recent developments in the field imply some need for changes in the key. The parts making use of the matching technique are probably more intelligence than achievement tests; in most cases there is only one answer which makes "sense."

[1506]

Food Score Cards. High school and college; 1940; 25¢ per set of 53 cards; Clara M. Brown with the cooperation of Lillian Butler, Alice M. Child, Grace Kern, Kathryn B. Niles, Isabel Noble, and Rosalind Simon; Minneapolis, Minn.: University of Minnesota Press.

[1507]

Frear-Coxe Clothing Test. One to four semesters of dressmaking in high school; 1928; $1.25 per 25; 15¢ per specimen set; nontimed, (60) minutes; Florence D. Frear and Warren W. Coxe; Bloomington, Ill.: Public School Publishing Co.

Laura B. Hadley, Associate Professor of Home Economics Education, Alabama College. The *Frear-Coxe Clothing Test* is planned to cover knowledge of "fundamental principles and processes of clothing construction" and

"related subject matter" for one to four semesters of work. Norms have been worked out for the end of the first, second, and third semesters. A test is a good test in so far as it reveals pupil progress toward *desired* objectives. Since (at least in home economics) the objectives must be determined for the individuals or groups concerned, and "a semester's work in clothing" may vary greatly from one class to another even in the same school, a commercial semester test has limited usefulness.

The authors make no claim to measuring anything but knowledge; and no attempt is made to evaluate ability to use knowledge in thinking through problems, or even understanding of the facts sampled. None of the important objectives in clothing except *recall of information* is measured. The facts called for in the sections on construction and care of clothing seem to cover essential material. In hygiene of clothing, appropriateness of clothing, and economics of clothing the test calls for recall of rather arbitrary rules or procedures rather than basic principles. For example, "Sensible dressing requires that: (*a*) Woolens should be worn in winter. (*b*) Thin clothing should be worn in summer. (*c*) All clothing should be selected according to the temperature in which one is." Among the true-false items are the following examples: "Cambric is the most satisfactory material for fine underwear," and "Large people should choose light colors rather than dark ones."

No date is given, but the failure to include material on recent developments in textiles (especially rayons) and consumer-buyer knowledge indicates that the test has not been revised recently. Some of the material called for is little used for high school girls today.

In the directions the statement is made that the five parts may be given separately "permitting the test to be used as a diagnostic instrument." This is true only in so far as the desired diagnosis relates to the kinds of facts the pupil knows.

The authors have used an ingenious device making it possible to use the test booklets more than once. The directions are clear. Adequate instructions are given for scoring, tabulating, and interpreting results. The key is convenient.

Only two kinds of items are used, yes-no and multiple-choice. Only three choices are given in the latter. Some items require definite choices where none can be made on basis of data given. For example, "In using a commercial pattern the most important markings to understand are those: (*a*) Relating to grain of material; (*b*) Relating to putting seams together; (*c*) Relating to placing of decorative pieces," and "It is wiser to combine two partly worn garments than to buy part new material." The correct response depends upon the particular situation.

Norms are given, but no information is supplied as to the number, age, or situation of the pupils included in the study.

The test may be useful to teachers who want a test covering information in the whole field of clothing, taking account of the omissions cited above.

Esther F. Segner, Assistant Professor of Home Economics Education and Assistant State Supervisor and Teacher-Trainer, University of Idaho. If this test is to have any present or future value it must be brought up-to-date factually and from the standpoint of emphasis. Most of the points in it represent facts that students need to know, and material that teachers are still presenting in clothing classes. Many questions do not give detailed enough information about a situation to warrant a logical decision; for example, in Part I, Item 17 does not tell where the binding is to be placed, Item 27 does not indicate quality of voile nor use of dress, and Item 33 does not indicate whether it is machine or hand hemstitching.

The test is definitely out-moded as indicated by the facts that rayon and current problems in consumer buying are not mentioned and, the key represents obsolete styles as correct. In Part III the heading makes many of the answers pretty obvious. The answers to many of the questions in Part V represent opinion rather than fact or judgment and involve the old "should" complex that home economics teachers formerly had so frequently.

It is doubtful whether this kind of test administered on a wholesale basis could ever be recommended in accordance with our present philosophy of state teachers guides which are flexible in the extreme.

The evaluation of the *Frear-Coxe Clothing Test* was approached in the manner described below. At the University of Idaho there were fourteen graduate students enrolled in a summer school course called Problems in Teaching

Home Economics; all of these students were teachers with some experience at the high school level.

Each member took the test and marked all of the questions which she felt should be so labeled as: (*a*) controversial, (*b*) obsolete, or (*c*) vaguely stated. These data were tabulated after the papers had been scored.

Nothing was done with the scores except it was noted that, as one would expect, they were well above the norms as set up. The other data were tabulated and interpreted with the results stated in the first three paragraphs.

Each student was asked to give her opinion of the test. Complete agreement was indicated on the fact that it is useless in its present state.

[1508]

Information Test on Foods: Illinois Food Test. High school; 1924; 1 form; 75¢ per 25; 10¢ per specimen set; 35(40) minutes; prepared by the Test Committee of the Illinois Home Economics Association; Adah H. Hess, Georgina Lord, Mabel Trilling, and Anna Belle Robinson; Bloomington, Ill.: Public School Publishing Co.

REFERENCES

1 PERRY, FAY V., AND BROOM, M. E. "A Study of Standard Tests and of Teacher-Made Objective Tests in Foods." *J Ed Res* 26:102-4 O '32.

Norma A. Albright, Assistant Professor of Home Economics Education, The Ohio State University. As the title would indicate, this test claims to test only knowledge on various aspects of foods. The chief criticism is the emphasis on testing pure knowledge. It might be well to restate some questions due to recent practices as Items 34 and 46. The danger I see in using such a test is in having students attach more importance to acquiring knowledge and losing sight of other values which we hold more important in their development, namely, ability to work with others, ability to sense relationships, ability to recognize all the various factors which alter and determine directions in solving problems. If provision is made for measuring these latter values, then such a pencil-and-paper test would find its place in an evaluation program.

There is at present a need for tests which are broader in scope and which would attempt to measure all the various values and purposes in home economics offerings. Since many are of common concern in education, home economics people need to cooperate with other educators in developing tests and methods of measurement.

Clara M. Brown, Professor and Director of Graduate Studies and Research in Home Economics Education, The University of Minnesota. The *Information Test on Foods* was one of the earliest home economics tests published, and it was among the best of the early tests; but it has never been revised and it does not meet the requirements recognized today as desirable for tests. Only one form of test item is utilized, namely, four-response single-choice items—a form which is very space consuming.

Correct answers are staggered throughout the page, making it impossible to use a strip key; and the key is very difficult to use because it is printed in very small type at the end of the class record and direction sheet.

Only one norm is furnished, that of the "Median Score for High School Students—April Testing," and this has no real significance because no information is furnished regarding the size and composition of the group for which the norm was established, or regarding the reliability of the test.

The test items deal largely with isolated factual information about food sources, composition, functions, and methods of preparation; they do not check on many of the objectives of present-day foods courses. Much of the information has little if any value in a foods class, and is more likely to be taught in geography than in home economics, as "Most of our rice comes from the United States Japan Ceylon Great Britain." Students are not asked to indicate *why* certain procedures are good or poor; there is no evaluation of knowledge of meal planning and practically nothing dealing with food costs.

The section labeled "Principles Employed in the Preparation of Different Foods" is misnamed because few of the statements are really principles and some of the key answers in this, as well as in other sections, are incorrect in the light of present knowledge.

Many of the items are ambiguous, frequently because they are not grammatically correct, such as "A good citizen supports pure food legislation because . . . it is more economical" or "When one has no help and has dinner guests, one should . . . spend several days in preparing it." The latter item would probably seem obviously wrong to even the poor students and hence would have no differentiating value.

[1509]

Minnesota Check List for Food Preparation and Serving. Grades 8 and over; 1938; an adaptation of a similar check list [1] prepared by Edna Amidon in 1927; $1 per 100; 10¢ per specimen set; Clara M. Brown; Minneapolis, Minn.: University of Minnesota Press.

REFERENCES

[1] AMIDON, EDNA P. *The Development of a Method of Evaluating Ability in Meal Preparation.* Unpublished master's thesis, University of Minnesota, 1927.

Ed Res B 18:146 My 3 '39. * an adaptation of the one constructed in 1927 by Edna Amidon. The device has been modified and refined as a result of various experimental studies conducted on both the secondary-school and the college levels. The present form describes fourteen characteristics or abilities which experience has shown are assets to those who prepare and serve food and which can be checked by the classroom teacher as she observes students' work as well as by the students in evaluating their own accomplishments. The primary purpose of the check list is to provide a device for rating the ability to perform the laboratory techniques required in food courses, which should show a transfer of learning from the laboratory to normal home situations or to those in which food is prepared in large quantities. An analysis of the characteristics desired by prospective employers indicates that most of the points included in the check list are regarded as highly desirable for home-economics teachers and dietitians, although certain points are of more concern in some fields than in others. *

[1510]

Tests in Comprehension of Patterns. Grades 6-12; [1927]; 1 form; $1.00 per 25; 15¢ per specimen set; nontimed; L. Stevenson and M. Trilling; Bloomington, Ill.: Public School Publishing Co.

Laura B. Hadley, Associate Professor of Home Economics Education, Alabama College. The best features of this test are: (*a*) It measures achievement in a specific unit of experience and may be used whenever it is needed. It does not depend for its usefulness upon a standardized course of study in clothing. (*b*) It is fairly well worked out as a diagnostic instrument. Particular difficulties of students can be located. There is one important omission— it does not attempt to measure the student's *ability to use the pattern guide* which is found in most commercial patterns, although it does test for understanding of notches. This part is inadequate because many patterns use other kinds of symbols. (*c*) It makes use of diagrams which improve the validity of the test. (*d*) It considers most of the problems common to the use of all patterns; but makes use of out-of-date garments (e.g., bloomers, kimono nightgowns, and middy blouse). It has apparently not been revised recently and no date was given. (*e*) An attempt is made to measure ability to use knowledge, or judgment.

Its chief value is in diagnosing pupil difficulties. It would be useful for large classes where this is not easy to do by working directly with pupils in using their own patterns. It might be used as a measure of effectiveness in teaching two paired groups of students by different methods.

Directions are given for scoring and tentative norms are given (although no explanation is provided about how they were arrived at). There is no practical need in real life for knowing a student's position with relation to *norms* in pattern comprehension, so it would seem that the authors were sensible not to bother to work this out beyond the "tentative" stage, even though the test has been out several years. If one needs a pattern test, this is as good as any I know.

Berenice Mallory, Assistant Professor of Home Economics, The University of Texas. This test is made up of five brief tests designed to measure comprehension of patterns. The tests are the identification type and are organized as follows: Test 1, Recognition of Parts of Patterns; Test 2, Comprehension of Pattern Lines; Test 3, Comprehension of Notches; Test 4, Alteration of Patterns; and Test 5, Placing the Pattern on the Material.

Diagrams of various pattern pieces are used in each test. There is some lack of accuracy in the various pattern pieces, and this with the lack of a uniform scale for the pattern pieces would probably tend to confuse students. Teachers will no doubt question the value of this measuring device to secure reliable evidence of the ability of a class or an individual to make profitable use of patterns. They may question if it is possible with a pencil-and-paper test to determine pupils' ability to use patterns.

The briefness of the test tends to reduce its usefulness as does the pattern pieces that are selected for identification and alteration. Neither the middy blouse, bloomers, nor kimona nightgown are patterns with which students are likely to be working, for these garments are not a part of many girls' wardrobes today.

The physical make-up of the test is fair. The directions for giving and scoring are adequate, but in some parts the key is confusing. The key furnishes the correct answers but even with it some of the scoring is subjective. This is particularly true in Test 4 where students are asked to draw lines on diagrams of pattern pieces to indicate where alterations are to be made.

Tentative norms in terms of medians are given for grades 9 and 10 only. The test is designed for grades 6 to 12. The authors suggest that in view of the fact that instruction in the use of patterns differs for each grade in various school systems, it is practically impossible to get reliable norms from grade to grade. The authors suggest that instead of giving too much emphasis to norms the teacher put most emphasis on the individual needs of the pupils as they are revealed by the tests. This seems to be a desirable point of view. No information concerning the reliability or validity of the test is furnished.

[1511]

Unit Scales of Attainment in Foods and Household Management. Grades 7-9; 1933; 2 forms; 90¢ per 25; 20¢ per specimen set; nontimed (50) minutes; Ethel B. Reeve and Clara M. Brown; Minneapolis, Minn.: Educational Test Bureau, Inc.

Norma A. Albright, Assistant Professor of Home Economics Education, The Ohio State University. The title of this test, *Unit Scales of Attainment in Foods and Household Management,* is somewhat misleading. The questions are almost all on attainment in foods and only four or five questions can be considered household management. There should be a better distribution of questions and more emphasis given to management as this would give more opportunity for measuring judgment and ability to do critical thinking. More questions on selection of foods and household equipment would aid in measuring an understanding of consumer problems.

This test may be welcomed by home economics teachers as a way of measuring growth of certain acquired knowledge but does not in any way serve as a means of measuring the more important values and purposes which we hold for home economics offerings in grades seven to nine.

Hester Chadderdon, Associate Professor of Home Economics Education, Iowa State College. This test was "devised for the purpose of enabling teachers of home economics to see how much the pupils in their classes actually know about the facts in this field, how much they gain during the course, and the extent to which they differ in their amounts of information." Each form contains two subtests which are referred to as "scales." Data are given to facilitate the interpretation of the raw scores into C-scores, and the comparison of scores with MA's based on the results of administering the test and the *Kuhlmann-Anderson Intelligence Test* to "several hundred girls." No coefficients of reliability are given but the assumption is made that since the probable error of the C-scores is 2.5 points in each scale, the "Scales are sufficiently reliable to be satisfactory measuring devices and are approximately equal in this respect to scales of the same length in other subject-matter fields." No indication is given of the basis used for the selection of test items.

The directions for administering and scoring the test are clear and, for the most part, the test is well set up mechanically. Some authorities will question the key at a few points.

Approximately 63 per cent of the 70 items in Form A are devoted to cookery and nutrition. Table service, purchase of foods, management of time, money, and equipment, house furnishings, and etiquette each are given a small amount of attention. It seems unfortunate that so short a test includes such a large number of aspects of the field and that such unrelated items as cookery and house furnishings are included in one test.

Teachers will find this test helpful in making a general survey of status and attainment as far as subject matter in cookery and nutrition are concerned. It will need to be supplemented, however, if broad objectives are accepted and if there is a concern for actual changes in practice and attitudes.

INDUSTRIAL ARTS

[1512]

Achievement Test in Mechanical Drawing. High School and College; [1931]; 1 form; $2.00 per 25; 20¢ per specimen set; nontimed (60-65) minutes; Harry M. Wright; Bloomington, Ill.: Public School Publishing Co.

REFERENCES
1 WRIGHT, HARRY MARVIN. *Development of a Test to Measure Achievement in Mechanical Drawing.* Unpublished master's thesis, Purdue University, 1929.

Verne C. Fryklund, Associate Professor of Vocational Education, Wayne University; and Supervisor in the City Schools, Detroit, Michigan. In any creative world activity there are two major considerations of subject matter; one involves the essential elements (as in arithmetic) and the other the problems (as in arithmetic). This is true in any activity whether it is industrial or any other. The essential elements in combination plus reasoning are necessary in the solution of a particular problem. The teacher must teach these elements, somehow, in application in practical problems. The learner must learn them and be able to apply them.

This principle holds true in teaching mechanical drawing. The teacher must teach the drawing essentials in practical application. An achievement test is assumed to measure the results of teaching in terms of ability to apply what has been learned up to the time of the test. The essential elements in mechanical drawing, as in any industrial area, are determined by the analysis technique. One way to determine how thorough a test is, is to check it with an inventory of essential elements made through analysis. An evaluation of the Wright test made by checking it, item for item, with an inventory of essential elements in drafting shows that it is comprehensive in coverage of information of essentials that could be expected in an elementary course. Performance is not covered. The test considers in its measurement only mechanical drawing and none of the various specialties. This would make the test more generally useful than if specialties were included. Most schools over the country cover the elements involved in the Wright test, but only scattered schools cover the various specialties in various courses.

There is much more commendation than criticism, however. The reviewer believes strongly in application-type questions and the true-false section of the test is weak in application value. True-false questions are weak at their best in constancy of reliability and should not be used if the same elements can be measured by application situations. The test of reading ability of working drawings is quite involved for beginners and it is quite suggestive of machine drafting knowledge rather than understanding of elementary mechanical drawing.

[1512.1]

Drawing Aptitude Test. Grades 7-14; 1940; 1 form; 10¢ per test; 20¢ per manual; 60(65) minutes; Weston W. Mitchell; Bloomington, Ill.: McKnight & McKnight.

[1513]

Mechanical Drawing. High school; 1937; 1 form; 50¢ per 25; 10¢ per specimen set; 60(65) minutes; Charles Schoonover, C. L. Jackson and H. E. Schrammel; Emporia, Kan.: Bureau of Educational Measurements, Kansas State Teachers College.

Dean M. Schweickhard, Assistant Superintendent of Schools, Minneapolis, Minnesota. This test is arranged in six parts differing essentially from each other in the method of approach and manner of presentation.

Part I, consisting of sixteen items, utilizes a combination of two methods of approach. The first four items have to do with the recognition of representative symbols which for nation-wide use would present the defect of varying with different authors and localities. The remaining twelve items in Part I have to do with the ability to visualize three-dimension sections from two-dimension representation. The element of difficulty is increased by the diminutive size of the figures and the poor quality of the shading used. A further element of difficulty encountered in Part I arises from the necessity of matching numbered items with numbered responses. The questions requiring responses might more appropriately be given alphabetical designations.

Part II utilizes the test device commonly known as multiple choice, and should be comprehended readily by the person taking the test without essential chance of misunderstanding.

Part III is arranged on the true-false basis and in the extent to which this device is accepted as an authentic means of testing this part is well arranged. Items 32 and 53, however, involve an element in the true-false test which is likely to be misleading, namely, the introduction of a negative in a statement, the response to which should be positive. The person being tested is likely to think in terms of a double negative and give the wrong response.

Part IV, a test of the matching type, consists of items well selected and arranged. There is strong possibility that the same confusion mentioned in Part I may arise in this part because of the use of numbers in both items and responses. In this instance, as in the other, let-

tered designations might well be used for the responses.

Part V involves the ability to interpret a given length of line on paper in terms of various scales of measurement. The device is good and calls for specific knowledge and ability on the part of the one being tested, but the statement of directions is not particularly clear.

Part VI presents a three-view orthographic drawing of an object with all dimensions given on one view or another. The requirement in the test consists in translating measurements from the positions and views where they are given to certain specified locations on other views and recording the quantities in an accompanying table. Again, the device used is good and the knowledge required is very specific. The execution of the drawing, however, is poor, in that the lines used for the outlines of the views are distinguishable from dimension and construction lines with extreme difficulty. Likewise, the figures and letters used to designate dimensions are of a mediocre quality, in some instances even being difficult to read.

The key for scoring the test is much more clearly prepared and printed than is the test itself. By means of the key, scoring should be extremely simple and rapid. A descriptive sheet accompanying the test gives clear information concerning its interpretation and reliability so far as these matters have been established.

The present status of this test should be considered experimental rather than in any way a finished product. If used in that sense, it should serve to give a fair degree of understanding concerning the nature and stage of advancement reached by a given group in the field of mechanical drawing.

[1514]

Mechanical Drawing Performance Test. High School; 1935; 1 form; part individual; 4 of the 24 problems require the use of drawing instruments; 25¢ per student's set; 60¢ per teacher's set; (120-360) minutes; Ernest W. Baxter; Milwaukee, Wis.: Bruce Publishing Co.

REFERENCES

1 BAXTER, ERNEST W. *Determination of Objective Test Content for Mechanical Drawing.* Unpublished master's thesis, Iowa State College, 1931. Pp. 62.

Emanuel E. Ericson, Director of the Division of Industrial Education, Santa Barbara State College. This test consists of twenty-four problems in orthographic projection with dimensions but no lettering. Four problems are arranged upon each of six sheets 8½ by 11 inches in size. The working area for each problem is marked in ⅛-inch squares in order to facilitate the drawing. In the upper right hand quarter of this area is located a dimensioned pictorial drawing of the object to be reproduced with the remaining area available for the three orthographic views required. Transparent check sheets containing the correct drawings desired are available, making it easy for the instructor to evaluate the results by simply placing the check sheets over the drawings produced by students.

Apparently this test does just what it proposes to do namely to offer a performance test to see to what extent the student has acquired skill in making three-view mechanical drawings from sketches. The twenty-four problems are so selected that they present a wide range of practices and situations on the drafting board. The assignments are clear and the pictorial drawings are attractively made. Outside the possible use of some additional dimensions on Problem 17 all data that might be desired by those taking the test seem to be supplied.

The test makes no claim of being standardized and no norm is furnished. Whether used as test materials or simply as drafting room assignments these problems should be valuable in any high school or beginning college drafting class. The test may well be used for entering college students who expect to have their high school drawing recognized.

For an additional review, see 1034.

[1515]

Mechanical Drawing Tests. High schools, trade schools, and entering college students; 1929; 1 form, 2 parts; $1 per 25 sets of two parts; $1 per specimen set; 38(43) minutes per part; Ferdinand A. P. Fischer; Milwaukee, Wis.: Bruce Publishing Co.
a) PART I, TECHNICAL INFORMATION TESTS.
b) PART II, PERFORMANCE TESTS.

Emanuel E. Ericson, Director of the Division of Industrial Education, Santa Barbara State College. There are two tests involved in this series—Part I, a technical information test; and Part II, a performance test. Each part consists of four separate tests. The content of these tests in their final forms is the result of extensive research and experimentations. As a preliminary measure the author graded and tabulated more than 5,000 tests based upon 130 trial problems taken from textbooks and other organized teaching material in mechanical drawing. Then the material was

reorganized and presented to a large number of cooperating teachers in various parts of the United States. More than 2,500 completed tests which were received by this procedure were marked and tabulated. After the rearranging of the problems in order of apparent difficulty the author distributed the tests to sixty high schools for further tryout and checking.

A norm or "Median Score Curve" is furnished indicating average accomplishment for students with a range of from 1,000 to 50,000 minutes of time spent in mechanical drawing.

This series of tests should be of value to mechanical drawing teachers as a check upon the achievement of students. It presents a wide range of subject matter in the field. Since a variety of solutions to some of the problems is acceptable according to the interpretation of the teacher, the tests can probably not be considered truly objective in nature. The statement in the marking key for Part II, Test 2 that "Many different methods may be used by students to solve each problem" and the "Instructor must decide if pupil's method is correct" obviously places the test on the subjective level and places the student at the mercy of a teacher who may not himself know all the different methods permissible.

Better drafting technique in the tests themselves and particularly in the keys for marking while not required for the purpose for which these tests are used, would help to inspire both students and teachers with the need for improved appearance of mechanical drawings in our schools.

[1516]

Newkirk-Stoddard Home Mechanics Test. Grades 7-9; 1928; 2 forms; $4 per 100; 10¢ per manual; 25¢ per specimen set; 40(45) minutes; Louis V. Newkirk and George D. Stoddard; Iowa City, Iowa: Bureau of Educational Research and Service, The State University of Iowa.

REFERENCES

1 NEWKIRK, LOUIS VEST. *Validating and Testing Home Mechanics Content.* University of Iowa Studies, New Series No. 201; Studies in Education, Vol. 6, No. 4. Iowa City, Iowa: the University, 1931. Pp. 39. $0.50. Paper.

Arthur B. Mays, Professor of Industrial Education, The University of Illinois. This test is designed "to measure in an objective and diagnostic manner the essential knowledge that the pupils should acquire from a well-organized course in home mechanics." With the exception of the section dealing with electric wiring, the entire test is concerned with the order of procedure in performing certain jobs. Consequently, the test is based on the assumption that such knowledge is indicative of the possession of the knowledge "that the pupils should acquire from a well-organized course." There is much to be said for this assumption but it is questionable whether a test confined to the pupil's ability to arrange processes in proper sequence will indicate a possession of the knowledge which a pupil should have as a result of a well-organized course in home mechanics. Part 2, dealing with electric wiring, while in a different form from Part 1, really tests the same sort of factor in pupil understanding.

It is not clear as to what the test diagnoses except knowledge of sequence of job processes. If home-mechanics courses have any other objectives than teaching sequence of procedure, the test should take into account some sort of classification of content to be learned. The manual states that "the test is designed to have *diagnostic power*," and that the procedure-type question was found by the authors to permit "diagnosis within the single job." However, it is not evident just what content knowledge "within the single job" other than sequence is revealed by the test. For example, in answering Job 9, the student may recognize the proper sequence of steps to be taken "to grind a chisel," and yet not be able to answer questions like the following: What is the "proper angle" at which the chisel should be held? How does one "remove the wire edge"? How does one "determine the bevel"? This same criticism may be made with reference to nearly all of the jobs. In fact, it would seem to be a more important matter to test these items of knowledge, than merely to test a knowledge of the order of procedure. Obviously, to know the order of procedure does not necessarily imply a knowledge of how to perform the processes.

Although the key is carefully worked out and easy to understand, it would be much easier to use if the answers in the margins were spaced so as to correspond exactly with the spacing of the answers on the test sheet. This could be easily corrected.

There is, of course, also the question with reference to the value of a standard test in a field that is far from standardized and probably never can be standardized. This weakness is recognized by the authors who suggest that the test may contribute to standardizing the courses in home mechanics.

Technically, with the exception of the scoring key, the test is excellently designed and conforms to the best accepted practice of tests of this type. The manual of directions is well worked out and gives the information usually desired concerning such a test. The authors have been careful to point out some of the limitations of the test, and the instructions for giving it are clearly stated and easy to follow.

[1517]

Standard Test in Fundamental Mechanical Drawing. Grades 7-12; [1929]; 1 form, 3 parts; this test is commonly referred to as the *Badger Mechanical Drawing Test*; $2.00 per 25 sets of the 3 parts; 20¢ per specimen set; nontimed; Alex J. Badger; Bloomington, Ill.: Public School Publishing Co.
a) TEST 1, USE OF TOOLS, LINEWORK, DIMENSIONING, AND LETTERING.
b) TEST 2, PROJECTION, INCLUDING SECTIONS AND AUXILIARY VIEWS.
c) TEST 3, PICTORIAL DRAWING (ISOMETRIC, CABINET, OBLIQUE).

Verne C. Fryklund, Associate Professor of Vocational Education, Wayne University; and Supervisor in the City Schools, Detroit, Michigan. The Badger test is much like Wright's *Achievement Test in Mechanical Drawing* in coverage of the essential elements involved in elementary mechanical drawing. Compared with the Wright test, it covers more of the abilities necessary to identify good lettering and fewer of the abilities necessary to read working drawings in their composite. The Badger test likewise does not cover any of the specialties of drafting such as electrical or sheetmetal pattern drafting; therefore it also would have general use throughout the country. This examination is not a test of ability to make drawings according to accepted techniques; rather it is an information test. Each of the three parts is a test in itself and covers a certain group of essentials. This makes for flexibility in use and renders it somewhat diagnostic in value. However there should be a part devoted to reading drawings in their composite inasmuch as ability in reading drawings is assumed to form a part of the pattern of abilities involved in drafting.

The test situations are mostly of multiple-choice nature. This tends to tax more limited human abilities than would a test of more varied test situations. Three choices are offered in each situation. This is just one step from a true-false situation. At least four choices and even five would allow for better testing of discriminative ability.

RECORD AND REPORT FORMS

[1518]

Indiana Psychodiagnostic Blank, Fourth Edition. For history taking in psychological clinics; 1934-39; Publications I. U. Psychological Clinics, Series II, No. 7. 6¢ per blank; 5¢ per blank, 100 or more; 3¢ per psychometric data insert (Section VI of the blank) for recording the results of a second series of phychometric examinations; 2½¢ per insert, 100 or more; 75¢ per manual; [2] C. M. Louttit and Jerry W. Carter, Jr.; Bloomington, Ind.: Principia Press, Inc.

REFERENCES

[1] Louttit, C. M. "A Blank for History Taking in Psychological Clinics." *J Appl Psychol* 18:737-48 D '34.
[1.1] Louttit, C. M. *Clinical Psychology*: A Handbook of Children's Behavior Problems, pp. 33-44. Foreword by L. T. Meiks. New York and London: Harper & Brothers, 1936. Pp. xx, 695. $3.50; 12s. 6d.
[2] Carter, Jerry W., Jr. *Manual for the Psychodiagnostic Blank*. Psychological Record, Vol. 3, No. 20. Bloomington, Ind.: Prinicipia Press, Inc., March 1940. Pp. 251-90. $0.75. Paper.

[1519]

[Pupils' Record Cards.] Cumulative record forms for use in infant, primary, and senior schools; 1937; 1s. per 12; sample cards free; Teachers Advisory Committee of the Wiltshire Education Committee; London: Evans Bros., Ltd.
a) INFANT ADMISSION CARD.
b) INFANT CARD.
c) JUNIOR AND SENIOR CARD.
d) MEASURES TAKEN CARD.

REFERENCES

[1] Hamley, H. R.; Oliver, R. A. C.; Field, H. E.; and Isaacs, Susan. *The Educational Guidance of the School Child*: Suggestions on Child Study and Guidance Embodying a Scheme of Pupil's Records. Foreword by Sir Percy Nunn. Introduction by Keith Struckmeyer. London: Evans Brothers, Ltd., 1937. Pp. 122. 3s. 6d.

RELIGIOUS EDUCATION

[1520]

Test in Religious Instruction. High school; 1938; 1 form; $1 per 25; 50¢ per specimen set; nontimed (40) minutes; Alfred Schnepp; Milwaukee, Wis.: Bruce Publishing Co.

SAFETY EDUCATION

[1521]

Auto and Highway Safety Test. Grades 8-12; 1938; 2 forms; $1.25 per 50 machine-scorable test-answer sheets; 10¢ per specimen set; nontimed (20) minutes; H. T. Manuel; Austin, Tex.: Steck Co.

Harry R. DeSilva, Director of the Driver Research Center and Research Associate in Psychology, Institute of Human Relations, Yale University. Each form of this test contains 48 brief multiple-choice questions. Three choices are given for each item. The test is printed on one sheet and is designed to be scored by the *International Test Scoring Machine*. Scoring by hand, however, is possible with the keys that are supplied, but some users

may find these inconvenient. The test is to be given without a time limit.

About one-sixth of the items are based on diagrams dealing with safe driving practices. An equal number of the items deal with the mechanical features of an automobile, for example: "What does the backfiring or coughing of a motor usually mean? Mixture too rich Mixture too lean Too much oil." There may be some question as to the relevancy of such items. They have been included, according to the author, because "knowledge of the car contributes something to the ability of a driver." The reviewer feels that their use is justified. Too often individuals drive a car without fully appreciating its mechanical operation.

According to the manual of directions "the forms are similar in content and difficulty." An inspection of the two forms indicates that this might be true but the reliability is not indicated. The reliability coefficient, which is given only for Form A, is computed by the method of split halves and is given as .71 for one group of 50 students and as .605 for another group of 83 students. These low reliability coefficients and the fact that no attempt was made to validate the test items may be overlooked if we bear in mind the fact that the purposes of this test are merely to stimulate interest in safety and to test briefly a student's information relating to the operation of an automobile.

[1522]

General First-Aid Test for Senior-High-School Students: National Safety Education Tests. Grades 10-12; 1940; 3¢ per test; 30(35) minutes; New York: Center for Safety Education, New York University.

[1523]

General Safety Education Test for Junior-High-School Pupils: National Safety Education Tests. Grades 7-9; 1940; 3¢ per test; 30(35) minutes; New York: Center for Safety Education, New York University.

[1524]

Home Safety Test for High-School Students and Adults: National Safety Education Tests. Grades 7-12; 1940; 3¢ per test; 30(35) minutes; Leon Brody; New York: Center for Safety Education, New York University.

[1525]

Judgment Test on Safe Driving Practices. Grades 9-16 and adults; 1939; 1 form; $3.50 per 100; 6¢ per test; 5¢ per manual; nontimed (40-60) minutes; Ammon Swope; Bloomington, Ill.: McKnight & McKnight.

Harry R. DeSilva, Director of the Driver Research Center and Research Associate in Psychology, Institute of Human Relations, Yale University. This test is divided into three parts: (*a*) 24 multiple-choice items; (*b*) 59 true-false items; and (*c*) a picture test of 7 parts, illustrating correct and incorrect methods of making turns, parking, etc. A convenient scoring key is supplied.

The author has attempted to limit the scope of this test—as its title indicates—so that it deals "exclusively with judgment factors in driving." The question of whether the author has succeeded is a debatable one. Although judgment factors are emphasized, there are also several items that deal purely with acquired knowledge. There is, for example, the item: "One can first distinguish two headlights on an oncoming automobile at a distance of approximately (1) 1 miles; (2) ½ miles; (3) 2000 feet; (4) 1000 feet; (5) 500 feet; (6) 100 feet." (*Sic.*)

It is questionable whether even the safest and most experienced drivers can answer this item correctly. Its correct solution can probably be found only in a course on safe driving —either in the textbook or the teacher's discussion. Also the fact that the distance between the headlights depends on the age and make of a car would seem to nullify the usefulness of such an item. There are a few other items, particularly those dealing with stopping distances that are not of a purely judgment character. The reviewer feels, therefore, that the test would more accurately be called "A General Test on Safe Driving Practices."

The manual of directions contains the means and standard deviations of 1,151 high school students of both sexes and for the age group 14, 15, 16, 17, and 18 years or over. The number of cases in each group ranges from 61 to 159. In view of the fact that the norms are for students in only one school, there is some doubt as to their suitability. Scores will undoubtedly depend on whether the students have taken a course in safe driving or not and whether they have driven a car on the highway or are nondrivers. The manual does not state to which group the 1,151 students belong. The reviewer feels that in tests of this type it is most desirable to have norms that are based on driving experience.

The items from which this test was compiled were originally based on observations made in actual driving situations and were then submitted to commercial drivers, noncommercial drivers, and university students. After checking the answer to a question, the examinee was asked, "Should this item be included in a safe driving practices test?" The final criterion in the selection of an item was agreement among 75 per cent of the subjects favoring its use. This method of compiling the test has resulted in the inclusion of a number of original and significant items.

Although it is recommended that the test be used for accident analysis, there is no statistical information which would lead one to believe that there would be any significant relationship between automobile accidents and performance on this test.

The correlation between this test and the *Otis Self-Administering Tests of Mental Ability* is given as .70. The result is based on 298 random sample cases.

The items in this test were "selected on the basis of clearness of statement, lack of ambiguity in meaning, absence of any legal phase of automobile driving, and objectivity as measuring instruments." With few exceptions, this characterizes the items in this test. As a general test on safe driving practices, this test contains many well-chosen items that deal with most of the important situations encountered in the operation and care of an automobile. It is a comprehensive test and seems well suited for use among high school and college students. Because of the technical nature of some of the items in this test, it is advisable to use this test in conjunction with a course on safe driving.

Clearing House 14:60-2 S '39. Joseph S. Roucek. * Swope has provided us with a clever test, the items of which are taken from a long list of observations made on highways and city streets. They are the final agreement of groups of commercial and non-commercial drivers on important judgment factors. The responses of eleven hundred high-school boys and girls were used in standardizing the test. School officials may use the test for remedial instruction and for suggestions in driver training courses. The manual contains directions, norms, and further information.

Safety Ed 19:42-3 S '39. This test consists of 93 statements dealing with driving practices. The items are of three types, two of which follow and the third being a series of diagrams: "1. When traveling in traffic of more than one lane in that direction, one should pull from right to left; or left to right (1) hastily;

(2) slowly." "T F 42. The motorist should keep to the right of the center of the traveled part of the road at all times, with the exception of passing another car." A manual and scoring key accompanies the test. The manual discusses selection of items, validity, reliability and scoring. A table of norms for boys, ages 14 through 17, and for girls of the same ages is given. The experimental test was given to three groups: (1) commercial drivers, (2) non-commercial drivers and (3) university students. No data are given to indicate the degree of reliability of the test when given to different groups or to the same pupil at different times. In addition to checking the items, the members of the experimental groups were asked to indicate whether or not the items should be included. "Agreement of the three groups," the manual states, "and a response of 75 per cent favoring the inclusion of an item were the final criteria for making up the test." One wonders what is meant by the phrase "agreement of the three groups." It is assumed that this means agreement as to which was the right answer, but what standard constituted agreement within each group? The reviewer wonders also how the key was prepared. The phrase "agreement of the three groups" leads one to suppose that the key may have been based on the responses from the experimental group. Is this a valid procedure for determining such a key? It seems to the reviewer that in a case such as this expert opinion is needed in key preparation. Some of the difficulties in using the key are seen in the following. Driving practices are often determined by state laws. (Agreement of the experimental group would not change the state law.) In this case the Indiana state laws are reflected so that *if the test is used in another state, the most careful check should be made to see that the answers given are not scored incorrect because they conform to the laws of the state in which the test is given rather than to Indiana laws.* The best example of this is on page 7 under (Three diagrams are given. The correct one is to be selected.) "left turns." Diagram No. 1 shows a left turn which would be correct in Cleveland at signalized intersections. The middle diagram is correct in Indiana and is given as correct in the key. Diagram No. 3 might easily be interpreted as correct by those states which have adopted the Uniform Vehicle Code where the turn about the center of the intersection is not

required. In any case, the diagrams are all somewhat confusing because one of the vehicles is shown straddling the center line, which is frowned upon in all states. In many other cases there are some confusions of statements and over-simplifications of situations. For example, Item 42 . . . is, according to the key, to be marked "true"; and yet, technically speaking, there are situations in which one may drive to the left side of the road (for example on a one-way street, and when directed to do so by a policeman). If these additional exceptions are considered, the statement as it appears would be false. Again, in Item 76, ("If a car stops suddenly in front of you it is well to turn into the opposite lane of traffic in order to avoid hitting it.") The correct answer to the question would depend upon the circumstances. If there is no oncoming traffic, or if the likelihood of oncoming traffic is small and the ditch to the right is bad, one might turn to the left with greater safety; whereas if there is heavy on-coming traffic, and especially if the ditch to the right has smooth shoulders, one might turn to the right. In a few other cases words are used which are not well enough understood by the ordinary driver to make this a good test. For example, in Item 11 the term "odometer"; Item 29, "deceptive"; and Item 78 "intermediate." A few slang expressions are also used which may not be understood by certain groups of the public such as "road-hog," and "back-seat driving." Under such circumstances the tests are for language rather than for judgment in safe driving. In summary it would seem that the test will find more usefulness in the classroom as an instrument to be examined and criticized by the group rather than as an evaluatory instrument.

[1526]

National Bicycle Tests. Ages 10-16; 1940; 1 form; 4¢ per test; Alfred L. Lorenz; New York: Center for Safety Education, New York University.

SENSORY-MOTOR

[1526.1]

Tests for the Hearing of Speech by Deaf People. 1939; 4s. 6d. per set of six cards; directions for administering and scoring test are available only in the *Lancet* article; [1] D. B. Fry and P. M. T. Kerridge; London: H. K. Lewis & Co., Ltd.

REFERENCES

1 FRY, DENNIS BUTLER, AND KERRIDGE, PHYLLIS MARGARET TOOKEY. "Tests for the Hearing of Speech by Deaf People." *Lancet* 6020:106-9 Ja 14 '39.

Birmingham Med R 14:58 Mr '39. This set of six cards supplies a useful series of words and sentences for testing the ability of deaf patients to hear speech. They are most effective if read by a relative or friend of the patient, as this gives approximation to the normal environment of the deaf person, and are especially helpful in testing the efficacy of deaf aids.

Brit J Children's Dis 36:80-1 Ja-Mr '39. M(acleod) Y(earsley). * The method of use

of these cards was detailed in a recent number of the 'Lancet' this year; it would have been of additional advantage had a reprint thereof been attached to the cards. * It will be of much interest if, in the near future, the results of the application of the method by otologists could be seen. Such results alone can show their practical value both for adults and children.

Glasgow Med J 131:192 Ap '39. * The method is particularly useful when a voice test with some measurable result is required *

READING

Reviews by Guy L. Bond, Ivan A. Booker, M. E. Broom, G. T. Buswell, Frederick B. Davis, Joseph C. Dewey, Alvin C. Eurich, J. R. Gerberich, Hans C. Gordon, James R. Hobson, Edward S. Jones, David Kopel, Alice K. Liveright, W. C. McCall, William A. McCall, Robert L. McCaul, Constance M. McCullough, Harriet Barthelmess Morrison, W. J. Osburn, Henry D. Rinsland, Holland D. Roberts, David H. Russell, Rachel Salisbury, Clarence R. Stone, Edward A. Tenney, Miles A. Tinker, D. A. Worcester, C. Gilbert Wrenn, and J. Wayne Wrightstone.

[1527]

Analysis of Controversial Writing: Test 5.31. Grades 10-12; 1939; 1 form; revision of Test 5.3; 15¢ per test; 1½¢ per machine-scorable answer sheet; 5¢ per explanation sheet and interpretation guide; $1.50 per set of stencils for machine scoring; Chicago, Ill.: Evaluation in the Eight Year Study, Progressive Education Association.

[1528]

Application of Certain Principles of Logical Reasoning: Test 5.12. Grades 10-12; 1939-40; 1 form; revision of Tests 5.1 and 5.11; 5¢ per test; 1¢ per machine-scorable answer sheet; 5¢ per explanation sheet and interpretation guide; $1 per set of stencils for machine scoring; Chicago, Ill.: Evaluation in the Eight Year Study, Progressive Education Association.

REFERENCES

1 RATHS, LOUIS E. "Evaluating Some Aspects of Proof." *Ed Res B* 17:108-14 Ap '38.
2 RATHS, LOUIS E. "Evaluating the Program of Lakeshore School." *Ed Res B* 17:57-84 Mr 16 '38.
3 RATHS, LOUIS E. "Measuring the Ability to Apply Scientific Principles." *Ed Res B* 17:86-98 Ap 13 '38.
4 *The Evaluation of Abilities Involved in Dealing with Quantitative Relationships.* Chicago, Ill.: Evaluation in the Eight Year Study, Progressive Education Association, March 1939. Pp. [24]. Paper, mimeographed. Out of print.

[1529]

"Brighton" Reading Tests. Ages 8-14 or 9-14; 1931; 6 forms; 1s. 9d. per 50 test papers (nonconsumable); 1s. 9d. per 50 question papers; 6d. per manual; 1s. 3d. per specimen set; Educational Research Sub-Committee of the Brighton and Hove Teacher's Association; London: University of London Press, Ltd.

a) MACAULAY TEST. Ages 8-14; 40(45) minutes.
b) BEE TEST. Ages 8-14; time limit not reported.
c) STEVENSON TEST. Ages 9-14; 34(40) minutes.
d) STURLUNGA TEST. Ages 9-14; 32½(40) minutes.
e) PEPYS TEST. Ages 9-14; 27½(35) minutes.
f) WALPOLE TEST. Ages 9-14; 30(35) minutes.

Frederick B. Davis, Reading and Professional Education Editor, Cooperative Test Service, New York, New York; and Educational Psychologist and Head of the Remedial Department, Avon Old Farms, Avon, Connecticut. The purposes of these tests, as stated in the accompanying manual of instructions, are as follows: "It is the double purpose of these tests to enable a teacher to compare a child's powers of understanding a passage which he has read silently, with the normal powers of children of his age, and later, after an interval, to ascertain whether the child's powers in that respect are improving or not."

The tests include six forms, for each of which separate question papers and norms are provided. When one of the forms is administered, the pupils are given ten minutes in which to read the passage, after which the papers are collected and the question sheets are distributed. At the expiration of a second time limit, which varies from 22½ to 30 minutes, the question sheets are collected. The directions provided in the manual are sufficiently clear, but the time limit for one of the question sheets has been omitted.

No information is given regarding the construction of the tests; there is no statement concerning the specific reading skills which they are intended to measure. As a matter of fact, it seems questionable to call them "reading" tests because the method of administration introduces a memory factor which must greatly influence the scores and affect their validity as measures of comprehension. A rough classification of the 100 items included in the six question papers reveals the following distribution of items:

Items testing factual content	41
Items requiring inference	41
Items testing vocabulary	12
Items testing background knowledge	5
Unanswerable item	1

The last item in the list occurs in the *Macaulay Test* and reads as follows: "What was the longest day's journey you could make from London in the coach which took the Great North Road? I do not mean the longest day's journey."

Unfortunately, the items in the various categories listed above are not evenly distributed among the six forms; that is, one form consists almost wholly of fact items, another form almost wholly of inference items. In view of the low correlations which have been found experimentally between scores on these two types of items, one must conclude that the several forms of the *"Brighton" Reading Tests* are not comparable since they do not measure the same functions. For this reason, successive testings with the various forms could not properly be used to accomplish the second purpose of the test as stated in the manual; namely, the measurement of growth to discover the effect of practice.

The manual contains no information about the reliability coefficients of the various forms. Age norms ranging from ages eight to fourteen for two tests and from nine to fourteen for four tests are provided, but the variability of the scores at each age level is not mentioned and the number of cases is not stated. The extent to which the test discriminates between the various age levels can, therefore, only be estimated by an inspection of the raw-score differences between the age norms. On the best-discriminating test the average raw-score difference between grades is 1.6 points but between ages thirteen and fourteen the raw-score difference is only .3 of a point. On the least-discriminating test there is an average raw-score difference of .6 of a point between grades. On the *Sturlunga Test,* which includes

fifteen questions, there is no raw-score difference between the norms for ages nine and ten, the total raw-score difference over the entire range of the test from ages nine to fourteen being only 3.3 points. From these data we can conclude with considerable assurance that most of the differences between the age norms are too small to be significant for individual measurement. It is probable that an individual's score could easily vary by pure chance over the entire range of norms provided. Hence, we must conclude that the tests cannot be used singly to accomplish the first purpose stated in the manual, that of comparing a child's power of understanding a passage with the normal powers of children of his age.

SUMMARY. These tests do not seem to be valid reading-comprehension tests. Furthermore, their apparent lack of discriminating power between the ages for which norms are provided and their probable lack of reliability and comparability combine to make them poor tests of the combination of memory ability and reading-comprehension skills which they appear to measure.

[1530]

Critical-Mindedness in the Reading of Fiction: Test 3.7. Grades 9-12; 1938; an experimental form; 5¢ per test; 1¢ per machine-scorable answer sheet; 2¢ per summary sheet; nontimed (40) minutes; Chicago, Ill.: Evaluation in the Eight Year Study, Progressive Education Association.

REFERENCES

A Descriptive Summary of Evaluation Instruments in the Field of English. Chicago, Ill.: Evaluation in the Eight Year Study, Progressive Education Association, March 1939. Pp. 10. Paper, mimeographed. Out of print.

[1531]

Chicago Reading Tests. Grades 2-4, 4-6, 6-8; 1939; 2 forms, 4 levels; $1.00 per 25; 60¢ per specimen set; Max D. Engelhart and Thelma Gwinn Thurstone; Milwaukee, Wis.: E. M. Hale and Co.
a) TEST A. Grades 1-2; 31(40) minutes.
b) TEST B. Grades 2-4; 42(60) minutes.
c) TEST C. Grades 4-6; 45(55) minutes.
d) TEST D. Grades 6-8; 45(55) minutes.

REFERENCES

1 ENGELHART, MAX D., AND THURSTONE, THELMA G. "Chicago Reading Tests." *Chicago Sch J* 20:74-81 N '38.

Robert Lawrence McCaul, Instructor of Remedial Reading in the Laboratory Schools and the College, The University of Chicago. [Review of Tests B, C, and D.] Underlying the construction of the *Chicago Reading Tests* is a philosophy consisting of two main principles: (*a*) reading ability is a composite of many abilities and skills, each of which must be measured by an adequate reading test; and (b) the materials of a reading test should correspond to the materials of those courses of the school curriculum which entail reading. As a theory of the nature of reading, the first principle may easily be carried to extremes. Its proponents often consider reading ability a loose conglomeration of independent abilities and skills and ignore the interdependence of these components and the fused unitary way in which they function in normal reading activity. Tests constructed upon this theory customarily afford measurements of a large number of what the authors subjectively judge to be important component reading abilities and skills, and these tests forthwith are labeled "diagnostic." However the reliability of their subtests is usually such that they cannot be safely employed for individual diagnosis. There also remains a question of whether a total measure secured from relatively unanalytical tests, like the *New Stanford Reading Test* or the *Nelson-Denny Reading Test,* is not more valid than a total measure secured from an analytical test where the measures of many subtests are lumped together. So much in general for the theory.

Their adherence to the first principle has caused the authors to make the Chicago tests very broad in sampling. Test C, for example, assesses vocabulary, sentence comprehension, speed, story comprehension, map reading, skimming, paragraph comprehension, drawing conclusions, discerning central ideas, knowledge of details, and interpretation. To facilitate diagnosis, at the end of each of the three tests is a profile chart for numerical and graphic records of the derived scores earned by the pupils from subtests and the whole test. Unfortunately for the diagnostician no reliabilities of the subtests are reported, nor are there probable or standard errors which would enable him to determine when variations in achievement upon the subtests are of real significance. Owing to their espousal of the second principle, the authors have incorporated within the tests literary, social studies, science, health, and other course materials. This is a distinct advantage, for the pupils' ability to read their curricula books is appraised by material analogous to that in their texts.

Preliminary work upon the tests, including the evaluation and final choice of items, appears to have been carefully done. Especially good are the picture items of Test B. They are not subject to the ambiguity which in the case of some tests, notably *Gates Primary Reading Test,* leads a child now and then to fail certain items because he misinterprets the pictures rather than because he misreads the words to be paired with the pictures. Frequently the word choices of vocabulary items in the Chicago tests may not demand precise discrimination. A bright child with a modicum of phonics might be able to answer the items correctly even though he could recognize in context none of the words.

The *Chicago Reading Tests* were tentatively standardized by administering them to approximately 25,000 pupils of grades two to eight in "a representative sample of thirty Chicago Elementary Schools." Before applying the norms to his own pupils, the non-Chicago schoolman should know more about this population and especially more about what is meant by "representative" than he is told by the authors. Grade norms for the subtests of Test B extend from 2.0 to 4.9, for the subtests of Test C they extend from grades 4.0 to 6.9, and for the subtests of Test D the norms extend from grades 6.0 to 8.9. Certain percentages of children will assuredly earn scores entitling them to reading grade placements below the lowest grade norm or above the highest grade norm of the particular subtest that they take. Consequently, no grade ratings of their reading abilities and skills can be obtained unless another reading test, at a lower or higher level, is administered. It would be both a convenience and an economy for the user of these tests were the norms of the subtests expanded by one or more grades above and below their present extremes. This likewise would serve to extricate the authors from the anomalous position in which they place themselves when they recommend that Test B (published as being for grades 2, 3, and 4) be given ordinarily only in grades 2 and 3 and Test C (published as being for grades 4, 5, and 6) be given ordinarily only in grades 4 and 5.

Two final comments about the tests are warranted. First, the skimming sections could be improved by placing the information asked of the pupil less consistently in the same location within the test paragraphs. Second, for the benefit of pupil and scorer the test items might be numbered.

W. J. Osburn, Professor of Education, The University of Washington. [Review of Tests B, C, and D.] Two sittings are recommended for each test. Each test covers comprehension of words, comprehension of sentences, comprehension of paragraphs, and rate. Story comprehension and following directions are found in Test B. Story comprehension and map comprehension in Test C. Story comprehension, map comprehension, and graph comprehension in Test D. The tests show that they have been constructed with a great amount of care. In general, they are well graded so far as vocabulary is concerned. Vocabulary is directly measured under word comprehension. The tests are unique in that they include the interpretation of maps, graphs, and statistical tables. Tests C and D contain a generous amount of material which involves skimming. The exercises in Test D in which a pupil is required to read a paragraph in order to find (*a*) a statement that is true, and (*b*) a statement that is false, are of particular interest.

The tests are of unusual importance because of their possibility as diagnostic instruments. By using them, it is possible to diagnose vocabulary, skimming, and the ability to locate details, antecedents, and central thoughts. In addition there is extensive material dealing with interpretation and inference. The reviewer knows of no other test which includes so many types of reading. Consequently, these tests are to be recommended as among the best of our diagnostic reading instruments.

Standard scores are supplied which are based upon the test papers of more than eight thousand Chicago school pupils. Answer sheets and class record sheets are furnished.

On the adverse side there are only a few things to say. It would be quite an advantage if the questions were numbered. A few of the test items are questionable. In Test B, page 10, the child is invited to respond that "one time a big dog chased Uncle Toby," but the paragraph hardly warrants this inference. On the same page there are two possible answers to the item "the noise which Tippie heard." On page 4 of the same test, "red" and "color" are presented as synonyms. In Test C, page 4, the pupil is required to identify "doubt" and "question" as synonyms. In the same test, page 10, a neighbor is identified as "one who lives in the next village." Elements of this sort seem to

contribute to fuzzy thinking. They could easily be eliminated.

There are some evidences that more attention should have been given to the matter of scaling in the separate tests. For example, in Test B which applies to grades 2-4, most of the words are on the first-grade level. A few more are on the second-grade level. The test closes with two words on the fifth-grade level, but no words at all are included for the third and fourth grades. Furthermore, the word "rapidly" is one upon which we do not have accurate information as to its grade level. Possibly it should have been omitted.

While the test contains an unusually wide sample of different types of reading, the frequencies are not so well balanced. In Test B there are only two questions each for "detail" and "central thought," while there are twenty which are concerned with interpretation. Special emphasis upon interpretation is found in all the tests, with consequent neglect of other types. Test D has no questions relating to antecedents and only one relating to central thought. The tests overlap with reference to grade levels, but there is no overlapping of content. This would not be a disadvantage, if the overlapping areas were carefully matched, but no evidence is given on that point. No discussion of validity is presented although an inspection of the tests assures one that that quality has not been overlooked. Grade standards are available, but the T-score technique is not used.

In spite of all this, the tests are well worth what they cost. Indeed, with respect to some features such as map interpretation, graph interpretation, and skimming, they stand almost alone in the field.

[1532]

Diagnostic Examination of Silent Reading Abilities. Grades 4-6, 7-9, 10-16; 1939; 1 form, 3 levels; 10¢ per test; 5¢ per machine-scorable answer sheet; 10¢ per manual; $1 per scoring key for any one level; 25¢ per specimen set; part timed, part nontimed (110-140) minutes; M. J. Van Wagenen and August Dvorak; Minneapolis, Minn.: Educational Test Bureau, Inc.

a) INTERMEDIATE DIVISION. Grades 4-6.
b) JUNIOR DIVISION. Grades 7-9.
c) SENIOR DIVISION. Grades 10-16.

Univ Wash Col Ed Rec 6:80 Mr '40. Worth J. Osburn. This is one of the few "diagnostic tests" which really diagnoses. It can be used also for general survey purposes. The diagnostic features apply to "ten silent reading abilities" which is a larger number than any other test presents. The tests for each division are presented in three parts: Part I tests Rate of Comprehension; Part II includes vocabulary of two types, word relations and general information; Part III furnishes a basis for the diagnosis of "ability to group the central thought of the paragraph, ability to note the clearly stated details, ability to interpret the content of the paragraph, ability to grasp an idea when spread through several sentences and the ability to draw inferences from the ideas of a paragraph." * In the opinion of the reviewer, the authors could have improved their excellent test further by informing the teacher what diagnostic value each question in Part III has. They could also have enhanced the attractiveness of their test by explaining and emphasizing the diagnostic value of those tests which relate to vocabulary, word relationships, and general information. Their presentation of these tests is overly modest. If the authors have been a bit reticent and modest, the fact remains that they have given us a test that has high validity as a diagnostic instrument. No one truly interested in the diagnosis of reading ability can afford to be without it.

[1533]

Durrell Analysis of Reading Difficulty. Grades 1-6; 1933-37; 1 form; individual; $1.50 per 25 individual record blanks; 50¢ per booklet of reading paragraphs; 50¢ per tachistoscope; 80¢ per 30 blank tachistoscope cards; 25¢ per manual; $1.65 per examiner's kit, including 5 record blanks; a minimum of (30) minutes; Donald D. Durrell; Yonkers, N. Y.: World Book Co.

Guy L. Bond, Associate Professor of Education, The University of Minnesota. In diagnosing a reading disability case, it is necessary to locate any discrepancy that exists between the various reading attainments as well as to locate the factors associated with the cause of the disability. These discrepancies indicate the nature of the remedial work while the causal factors indicate the adjustments of instruction needed. The worth of a diagnostic battery is determined, in no small degree, by the insight into the disability derived from a comparison of the relative proficiency in the attainments measured. The worth is also determined by the insight it gives as to the causal factors.

The *Durrell Analysis of Reading Difficulty* test makes possible some revealing comparisons between various reading attainments. The specific abilities measured are: oral reading and

recall, silent reading and recall, flash recognition of words, word pronunciation, and difficulties in writing and spelling. Although each of the comparisons that can be made between the parts of this battery of tests give valuable results, the real contribution is in the use of a simple tachistoscopic technique for comparing flash recognition of words with word pronunciation under long time exposure conditions. This latter comparison gives, among other things, an indication of any tendency toward overanalysis.

The areas in which this instrument seems to be weakest are those of isolating differences in the various sensory capacities and of appraising certain personality characteristics and interests which would prove helpful in formulating remedial instruction. The remedial worker may find the results of the appraisals do not give data to indicate the adjustment of instruction that is needed for some of the more stubborn cases. For the vast majority of cases, however, the analysis will give sufficient information to prescribe the remedial instruction.

A comprehensive check list of difficulties has been included in the individual record blank. Observational methods and subjective judgment must be used in making most of the entries. Nevertheless, the list should aid the diagnostician in making a complete analysis of the difficulties.

Miles A. Tinker, Associate Professor of Psychology, The University of Minnesota. This test consists of materials designed to measure comprehension, recall, and speed for oral and silent reading as well as phonetic ability and word analysis. Difficulties in spelling are also checked. It is suggested that these results may well supplement those on reading capacity and achievement tests.

Important criteria for an adequate reading test might well include: (*a*) satisfactory standardization, (*b*) data on consistency of measurement, and (*c*) proven validity.

This test was standardized on approximately one thousand children. Use of the norms is not clear in some instances. For paragraphs designed to measure comprehension in oral reading, only rate of reading norms are presented although errors in reading and comprehension are tabulated. In the manual of instructions, it is stated that inability to answer, or wrong answers to two questions on a given paragraph indicates low comprehension. It is, of course, contrary to good practice to use rate of reading to determine reading grade· when comprehension is being measured. Is grade location determined by noting the place of the rate score for the most difficult paragraph that is read with no more than two comprehension questions missed? Or is it based upon rate for paragraph established as the "upper level"? Similar difficulties are encountered in using norms for oral recall on oral reading. For written recall on silent reading the norms for oral recall are used although the author admits that they may not be equivalent. He suggests, however, that they are adequate for rough analysis. The norms for word recognition, pronunciation, spelling, and handwriting are readily interpreted. Use of the profile chart furnished in the record blank involves the difficulties inherent in interpretation of the norms.

No reliability coefficients are furnished with the test nor are any other indications of consistency of measurement given. Also little concerning validity is cited. It is stated that after standardization, 3,000 tests were given to children with reading difficulties and the norms were found to check satisfactorily against other tests of reading ability. No correlations or other figures are given.

Directions for procedure in giving the test are clearly stated. The author correctly emphasizes the usefulness of the test for standard observation of errors and faulty reading habits and that these are more important than the norms. The check list of difficulties is extensive and well selected with the exception of those items concerning eye movements which are of dubious value.

For a review by Marion Monroe, see 1098.

[1534]

Emporia Silent Reading Test. Grades 3-8; 1933-34; 4 forms; 50¢ per 25; 15¢ per specimen set; 15(20) minutes; H. E. Schrammel and W. H. Gray; Emporia, Kan.: Bureau of Educational Measurements, Kansas State Teachers College.

M. E. Broom, Assistant Superintendent of Schools, El Paso, Texas. Each of the four forms of this test includes fifteen paragraphs and a total of forty-one scorable answers, presented in multiple-response form. The test content is largely taken from literary and social science materials, with some content from sci-

ence. A good reading test should include variety in its content, in the types of reading skills measured, and in the form of the exercises used in measuring the varied reading skills. This test does not do these things sufficiently. Furthermore, no test with only forty-one scorable items can measure adequately over a six-grade range, yielding discriminative scores at all levels. The percentile norms bear this out, since on three of the four forms one per cent of third-grade pupils at midyear earn scores of zero, while one per cent of these pupils earn scores above 33. From one to three per cent of the pupils in grades seven and eight at midyear earn perfect scores.

The tables of percentile norms raise some question as to the equivalence of the forms. For example, tracing the percentile equivalents for scores of 10, 20, and 30 for both midyear and end-of-year testing for the four forms shows marked differences in the percentile equivalents for each of these three score values among the four forms.

Reliability coefficients were obtained in each of the six grades by the Spearman-Brown technique, based on odd versus even scores for Forms A and B separately. The average of the six coefficients for Form A was .88; for Form B, .86. The numbers of cases are not given in the manual. Sufficient evidence as to the reliability of this test is not given.

Validity was determined, using the *Burgess Silent Reading Scale,* the *Los Angeles Reading Test,* and the *Thorndike-McCall Reading Scale* as criteria. The average of the coefficients between the test and the criterion was .86. At least one of the criterion instruments, the Los Angeles test, has not been sufficiently identified; there are several Los Angeles reading tests. Furthermore, a better choice of criterion instruments might have been made, including such tests as the *Sangren-Woody Reading Test,* the *Gates Silent Reading Tests,* the *Ingraham-Clark Diagnostic Reading Tests,* etc.

Norms are based on 25,000 cases. Forms A and C were used for midyear testing, and the end-of-year norms were computed statistically from the midyear scores. Forms B and D were used for end-of-year testing, and the midyear norms were computed statistically from the end-of-year scores.

Distinctly better reading tests than the *Emporia Silent Reading Test* are available for use in grades three to eight.

Harriet Barthelmess Morrison, Research Assistant, Bureau of Reference, Research, and Statistics, Public Schools, New York, New York. Each form consists of fifteen paragraphs arranged according to difficulty and 41 questions based thereon, of the usual multiple-response type. The highly satisfactory two-column arrangement is used, the paragraph on the left, and the questions on the right.

The test is attractive in appearance, well edited, easy to administer, and simple to score, with the answer key arranged to fit the pupil's answers spacially.

The content is varied and interesting. The questions are well chosen, and the multiple answers have been carefully constructed so that usually the pupil cannot—except by chance—choose the correct answer without reading the paragraph. Form A, however, is less satisfactory in this respect than the other forms. The score yielded is an undifferentiated score of general comprehension, no provision being made for specific types of reading skills.

The validity of the test for measuring general reading comprehension appears, from inspection of the test, to be high. This judgment is confirmed by the statistical validity, which is shown by an average correlation of .72 per grade with the *Thorndike McCall Reading Scale,* the *Burgess Silent Reading Scale,* and the *Los Angeles Reading Test.* The number of cases involved in this validating is not stated in the manual nor are the separate correlations given.

The reliability is indicated by an (a) average correlation of .71 per grade (grades 4-6) between Form A and Form B, (b) reliability coefficients ranging between .82 and .93 and averaging at .88 per grade in grades 3 to 8 inclusive, secured by the odd-versus-even method on Form A, (c) results similar to the foregoing, based on Forms B, C, and D. The separate correlations are not stated in the manual. These reliabilities are not high enough to warrant using one form of the test alone for individual diagnosis, but they do not lessen the usefulness of one form as a survey instrument.

Percentile norms for each grade, midyear and end-of-term, are reported for grades 3 to 8 inclusive, for each of the four forms. These are based on "the scores made by 25,000 pupils." Analysis indicates that this means about 900 pupils per grade for each of Forms

A, B, and C, and 1,600 for Form D. Comparison of pupil progress by the use of different forms in successive testings rests on the questionable assumption of the equality of the samplings used for the norms for the various forms and grades.

The test should not be used in grade 3 in a normal situation since approximately half the children at midyear can get a score of 10, which is within the area of chance.

The usefulness of the test is impaired by its inadequate standardization. When the four forms have been equated on identical groups, with the practice factor controlled, the test should provide one of the most useful general reading tests available.

[1535]
Examiner's Reading Diagnostic Record for High School and College Students. 1938-39; 20¢ per record blank, 10 or more; 25¢ per specimen set; Ruth Strang with the assistance of Margaret E. Martin, Margaret G. McKim, and Mary Alice Mitchell; New York: Bureau of Publications, Teachers College, Columbia University.

Henry D. Rinsland, Director of the Bureau of Educational Research, and Professor of School Measurements, The University of Oklahoma. The record is a 20-page booklet for recording the following: (a) identifying data with names of parents, language spoken at home, and so forth; (b) summary of results of standardized tests including intelligence, achievement and reading, with space for observations and analyses; (c) summary of scholastic achievement giving general trends, years covered in each subject, and attitude of student toward each subject; (d) medical examination and reports of physical conditions, which includes a report of oculist, results of Betts' tests, and photographic record of eye movements; (e) development and educational history, most of which concern reading and its influences on activities and interests; (f) present interests in reading, with lists of books recently read, and reading habits as they concern reading newspapers, magazines and books; (g) other interests and activities; (h) present reading status, which includes an analysis of reading ability through interview, oral reading of four paragraphs with analysis of reading errors, speed of reading, likes and dislikes of materials in the paragraphs, and a practical test of looking up words in the dictionary; (i) summary; (j) recommendations; and (k) follow-up.

It is obvious that the record is very thorough. The questions provided under many headings are just the type to bring into consideration factors which indicate reading habits and interests; as, "How does the student spend his week end?" and "What things and activities apparently give the student the keenest pleasure and satisfaction?" One regrets that the oral reading paragraphs are not standardized in a manner similar to the *Standardized Oral Reading Check Tests* by Gray for the elementary school, and that a diagnostic record of the kinds of errors is not provided. More anecdotal records of this nature, combining life history and results of tests and scales, are needed in other high school subjects, especially English.

Ed Res B 19:118 F 14 '40. * The unusual attribute of this diagnostic record is the part played by an oral-reading test. In the reviewer's opinion the quickest and surest way to detect a student's reading difficulties is for a discriminating listener to hear him read aloud.

Loyola Ed Digest 15:7-8 N '39. Austin G. Schmidt. Contains a number of tests, including passages for oral reading, designed to obtain a complete measure of a student's reading ability and interests. The record is diagnostic in the sense that it calls for data on significant factors, but neither the record itself nor the accompanying manual gives the examiner much assistance in interpreting the data obtained.

Q J Speech 25:685-6 D '39. Seth A. Fessenden. * The blank, when scored by one trained in clinical observation and interpreted by one trained in reading diagnosis, should be of very considerable value for diagnostic work. It would have little value, except to point out the complexity of reading diagnosis, in the hands of the untrained teacher or administrator. The form should be of primary value for individual analyses of cases of reading disability in which the cause is in question, and its use should do much to show that remedial reading work is clinical in nature rather than subject to group classification.

[1536]

First Year Reading Test. Grades 1B, 1A; 1938; 2 levels; 75¢ per 25; 10¢ per specimen set; part non-timed (30-35) minutes; Marie Garrison; Cincinnati, Ohio: C. A. Gregory Co.

a) TEST I, MID-YEAR.
b) TEST II, END OF YEAR.

REFERENCES

1 EVANS, MARIE GARRISON. *The Revision and Standardization of a First Grade Reading Test.* Unpublished master's thesis, University of Michigan, 1938.

[1537]

Gates Reading Readiness Tests. Grade 1; 1939; 1 form; $3.75 per 100; 25¢ per specimen set; (50) minutes; Arthur I. Gates; New York: Bureau of Publications, Teachers College, Columbia University.

REFERENCES

1 GATES, ARTHUR I., AND BOND, GUY L. "Reading Readiness: A Study of Factors Determining Success and Failure in Beginning Reading." *Teach Col Rec* 37:679-85 My '36.
2 WILSON, FRANK T.; FLEMMING, CECILE WHITE; BURKE, AGNES; AND GARRISON, CHARLOTTE G. "Reading Progress in Kindergarten and Primary Grades." *El Sch J* 38:442-9 F '38.
3 GATES, ARTHUR I. "Basal Principles in Reading Readiness Testing." *Teach Col Rec* 40:495-506 Mr '39.
4 GATES, ARTHUR I. "An Experimental Evaluation of Reading-Readiness Tests." *El Sch J* 39:497-508 Mr '39.
5 GATES, A. I.; BOND, G. L.; AND RUSSELL, D. H.; ASSISTED BY EVA BOND, ANDREW HALPIN, AND KATHRYN HORAN. *Methods of Determining Reading Readiness.* New York: Bureau of Publications, Teachers College, Columbia University, 1939. Pp. iv, 55. $0.60. Paper.
6 GATES, ARTHUR I. "A Further Evaluation of Reading-Readiness Tests." *El Sch J* 40:577-91 Ap '40.

Loyola Ed Digest 15:8 N '39. Austin G. Schmidt. It is interesting to note how frequently psychology, after losing itself in dark labyrinths, finally works out into clear open spaces. Convinced some years ago that the possession of a mental age of six and a half years was not a sufficient guarantee that a child would succeed in reading, research workers analyzed the physical, mental, emotional, and social factors involved in reading and developed such a multiplicity of tests that teachers were baffled in their search for a simple and scientifically reputable index of reading readiness. Dr. Gates with that simplicity which is one of the secrets of his success, concludes that the only safe index of ability to go forward in reading is previous success in those approaches toward reading to which the natural environment invites every child. His test consists of five parts. In the first part the child is shown pictures and required to make certain marks according to the directions given by the examiner. This requires ability to listen, to understand, and to remember. In the second test the child is required to find among four words two that are identical. In the third he is required to find among four printed words one that is identical with the one printed on a card shown by the examiner. In the fourth he is shown pictures in sets of four and required to find one the name for which sounds almost the same as the first. In the fifth he names as many as he can of the letters of the alphabet and the numbers. The author does not propose any score as an index of reading readiness. The percentile standing shows whether the testee can be expected to experience less or greater difficulty than the average child. The mental age merely accentuates for better or for worse whatever condition is found to exist.

Sight-Saving R 10:165-6 Je '40. * In the first test it is necessary to have many details in the pictures. These may at first prove somewhat confusing to the young child who is not used to close eye work. The examiner will do well to take this into consideration. The printing and the pictures of the other tests are in good size and the type is clear and well chosen. * should be of great value to those interested in beginning reading.

[1538]

Gates Reading Survey for Grades 3 to 10: Vocabulary, Level of Comprehension, Speed, and Accuracy. 1939; 2 forms; $5.25 per 100; 20¢ per specimen set; part timed and part nontimed (60-90) minutes; Arthur I. Gates; New York: Bureau of Publications, Teachers College, Columbia University.

[1539]

Gates Silent Reading Tests. Grades 3-8; 1926-35; 3 forms, 4 parts; $2.10 per 100; 25¢ per specimen set; Arthur I. Gates; New York: Bureau of Publications, Teachers College, Columbia University.
a) TYPE A, READING TO APPRECIATE GENERAL SIGNIFICANCE. 6(12) minutes.
b) TYPE B, READING TO PREDICT THE OUTCOME OF GIVEN EVENTS. 8(15) minutes.
c) TYPE C, READING TO UNDERSTAND PRECISE DIRECTIONS. 8(15) minutes.
d) TYPE D, READING TO NOTE DETAILS. 8(15) minutes.

REFERENCES

1 FORAN, T. G. *The Present Status of Silent Reading Tests:* Part II, The Measurement of Rate of Reading. Catholic University of America, Educational Research Bulletin, Vol. 2, No. 2. Washington, D. C.: Catholic Education Press, February 1927. Pp. 27. $0.50. Paper.
2 GATES, ARTHUR I. "Methods of Constructing and Validating the Gates Reading Tests." *Teach Col Rec* 29:148-59 N'27.
3 FORAN, T. G., AND ROCK, ROBERT T., JR. *The Reliability of Some Silent Reading Tests.* Catholic University of America, Educational Research Bulletin, Vol. 5, No. 6. Washington, D. C.: Catholic Education Press, June 1930. Pp. 23. $0.35. Paper.
4 GATES, ARTHUR I. *The Improvement of Reading,* Revised edition. New York: Macmillan Co., 1935. Pp. xvii, 668. $2.50. (London: Macmillan & Co., Ltd. 8s. 6d.)
5 LANDRY, HERBERT. "The Disparity of Test Norms," pp. 208-17. In *Yearbook of the New York Society for the Experimental Study of Education,* 1938. New York: the Society (c/o C. Frederick Pertach, Sec.-Treas., 500 Park Ave.). Pp. vii, 228. $1.00. Paper.

Joseph C. Dewey, Head of the Department of Education and Psychology, Westminster College. These tests consist of four different types each designed to measure one specific reading skill. Each type test contains three forms called equivalent by the author but no evidence is submitted to show that this is true. An excellent manual provides clear and careful directions for using the tests for individual

and group diagnosis. Regular age and grade norms are provided as well as those for the lower and upper quartiles. The manual provides the answers to the various tests but no actual answer keys seem to be provided.

The manual states that each test measures a type of reading ability that is important. No evidence is submitted to support this contention. Evidently test makers do not agree on what are the important skills.

These tests provide such small bits of reading material in each case that test results may not give a true picture of what children can do reading longer selections.

Little or no provision is made for measuring speed of reading. It is possible to get some measure of speed of reading from the number of attempts made but no norms are provided to show how fast children should read this material.

No statements regarding validity or reliability coefficients are given in the manual although the author does state that the reliability of the tests depend upon how carefully they are given.

The reading material seems better adapted for third-grade pupils than for eighth graders and seems to possess little literary quality and might prove rather uninteresting to upper-grade pupils.

It is doubtful if these tests give an accurate picture of reading ability since they are almost entirely verbal in nature and there is evidence available that pencil-and-paper verbal tests give distorted pictures of children's reading ability when checked against picture and object tests and by individual interviews.

Certainly the ability to read to appreciate the general significance as found in the Type A test is a valuable reading skill. However, one wonders if each of the various paragraphs of reading material is equal in difficulty so as to give equal credit for each correct response. The reading material in this test apparently lacks variety as the pupil is always asked how some one feels about something. Is the general significance of a paragraph only how one feels about something?

The Type B test, Reading to Predict the Outcomes of Given Events, seems to be the only test in the series wherein the pupil is expected to make inferences concerning his reading. This is again a valuable skill in reading and as such this test is valuable. The alternate responses used are often rather obvious and the pupils are presented with an even chance of guessing correctly in some cases.

The Type C test, Reading to Understand Precise Directions, seems a great deal like the type of reading found in the Type D test, Reading to Note Details. Both tests seem to test ability to understand detail in the reading material. This test makes use of pictures many of which are rather poorly drawn or are printed from old plates. Some of the pictures might not convey to children intended meanings.

The Type D test is entitled Reading to Note Details. To be able to read carefully and accurately to get the details is no doubt an important skill in reading. However, in this test the test paragraphs are so short, especially for upper-grade pupils, that there are few details to note. Some of the material is so well known to the children that they might answer questions correctly even though they did not read the material carefully.

It appears that Gates has provided a rather valuable instrument for measuring the specific phases of reading that he thinks are important. However, one must not conclude that these tests will give an accurate and complete measure of reading ability as there is no provision for measuring how difficult reading the pupils can do nor how fast they can read. There is no assurance that if a pupil excels in these reading skills he will excel in general all-around reading ability. We must also recognize that these tests have the weakness inherent in all verbal tests that pupils may answer in words and not actually understand what the responses mean.

James R. Hobson, Director of Child Placement, Public Schools, Brookline, Massachusetts. This series of four separate tests is referred to by the author as a "team of tests" and is designed to serve two purposes—namely, to furnish a "general measure of silent reading ability" and to provide "an intelligible diagnosis of special needs for follow-up work." The four skills measured by this team of tests were selected from the list of silent reading skills generally recognized because, according to the author, each measures a particular kind of reading ability which is important and which can be acquired. Considerable emphasis is

placed upon the differences in difficulty for the average child of these four types of reading as well as the differences in probable and desirable rates of speed in reading for each of the four purposes indicated.

Unlike most tests of reading comprehension the paragraph units in this series apparently do not increase in difficulty from the beginning to the end of each test. Each pupil's proficiency in each of the four abilities tested is not measured in terms of the depth of his power of comprehension but rather on the basis of the number of test units attempted, the number correct, and the percentage of accuracy. Although this team of tests covers a range of six grades, each paragraph in them is within the ability range of the average third-grade pupil.

The manual which accompanies this test series goes into considerable detail in giving directions for the diagnosis of both individual and group difficulties in reading through the use of these tests in conjunction with other measures. Complete norms based upon more than 300,000 cases in all parts of the United States are given in terms of grade level, reading age, and percentiles.

Despite the wide use and evident popularity of this series of tests, there are many questions about their construction and use and several features of their physical make-up upon which more light needs to be thrown. To begin with, no reasons are given in the manual for the selection of the four types of reading skills measured by these tests. No experimental evidence is produced to show that these are the basic silent reading skills in grades 3-8. There seems to have been no attempt made to validate these tests and no reliability coefficients are reported in the manual. If data on these points are available they should be reported in the manual.

Each of the twenty-four questions in Reading to Appreciate General Significance asks the pupil to select one from among five words which best describes the feelings of some person or character mentioned in the paragraph. This appears to the reviewer to be a very narrow delimitation of "reading to appreciate general significance."

A valid criticism of any reading comprehension test, which requires specially written paragraphs or a special physical make-up in order to permit questions of a certain type to be asked about it, is that the kinds of comprehension which a pupil needs in order to gain meaning from textbook material or from general literature are not being measured. When a pupil reads a paragraph in normal reading he is not ordinarily reading it for one narrow specific purpose. Reading of this type is valuable as a practice exercise to develop a somewhat specific ability, but such an ability is genuine only if it can be demonstrated in a normal reading situation.

Finally, it seems to the writer that a series of tests covering a range of six grades in which each paragraph is entirely within the comprehension range of a pupil in the lowest grade cannot measure anything except the speed of comprehension and cannot be classed as "an accurate measure of reading ability in general." Important as speed of reading admittedly is, the increase in reading comprehension from grade to grade cannot be measured without measuring the increase in "depth of power of comprehension." In this series of tests there is nothing to prevent a rapid reader in grade four or five from attaining a higher score than a reader of average speed but great power in grade eight. Yet his true ability in reading comprehension of any one of the types measured would normally be much less.

The greatest usefulness of this group of tests appears to lie in their ability to detect lack of facility in four of the reading comprehension skills and to point the way to needed teaching of these skills, rather than as a measure of general reading ability.

Dolch, Edward William. A Manual for Remedial Reading, pp. 137-8. (Champaign, Ill.: Garrard Press, 1939. Pp. x, 166. $2.00.) * The reading matter in the Gates Silent Reading Tests, though intended for grades 3 to 8, is all at one level of difficulty, about grades 4 or 5. Therefore these tests are excellent for use with children whose actual reading ability ranges from fourth grade to sixth grade. Readers at lower reading levels find too many hard words and therefore do too much guessing. High school teachers who have readers as low as fourth to sixth grades can use these tests to advantage. For first testing of a large group only one type needs to be used as this makes the testing quite inexpensive. It is recommended that type D, "Reading for Details," be chosen because it is perhaps closest to the

kind of thing these children are supposed to be doing with their high school textbooks. If, however, the teacher is concerned with the child's outside reading she would choose type A, "Reading to Predict Coming Events." For a remedial case, the "Reading to Follow Directions" is probably best because one can watch best the child's thought processes. Here is a clear case in which the teacher's purpose influences her choice of tests. For better understanding of the remedial cases, all four of the Gates Tests are helpful. *

[1540]

High School Reading Test: National Achievement Tests. Grades 7-12; 1939; 1 form; $2.50 per 25; 15¢ per specimen set; nontimed (40) minutes; Robert K. Speer and Samuel Smith; Rockville Centre, N. Y.: Acorn Publishing Co.

[1541]

Hildreth Diagnostic Reading Record. Grades 1-16; 1939; $1.25 per 25; 25¢ per specimen set; Gertrude Hildreth; New York: Psychological Corporation.

[1542]

Individual Reading Test. Grades 1-3; [1933?]; 1 form, 3 parts; individual; 2s. 6d. per set of cards for testing; 3d. per manual; L. W. Allen; Melbourne, Australia: Australian Council for Educational Research.
a) WORD READING TEST.
b) READING COMPREHENSION TEST.
c) SPEED OF READING.

[1543]

Instructional Reading Tests for the Intermediate Grades. Grades 4, 5, 6; 1938-39; 3 forms, 3 levels; 50¢ per 25; single specimen set free; 15(20) minutes; M. J. Nelson; Boston, Mass.: Houghton Mifflin Co.

[1544]

Interpretation of Data: Tests 2.51 and 2.52. Grades 9-12; 1939-40; 2 forms (Tests 2.51 and 2.52); revision of Test 2.5; 5¢ per test; 1¢ per machine-scorable answer sheet; 5¢ per explanation sheet and interpretation guide; $1.50 per set of stencils for machine scoring; nontimed (90) minutes; Chicago, Ill.: Evaluation in the Eight Year Study, Progressive Education Association.

REFERENCES

1 HARTUNG, M. L. *Interpretation of Data.* Progressive Education Association, Evaluation in the Eight Year Study, Bulletin No. 3. Chicago, Ill.: the Study, October 1935. Pp. 11. Paper, mimeographed. Out of print.
2 RATHS, LOUIS E. "Evaluating Some Aspects of Proof." *Ed Res B* 17:108-14 Ap 13 '38.
3 RATHS, LOUIS, "Evaluating the Program of Lakeshore School." *Ed Res B* 17:57-84 Mr 16 '38.
4 RATHS, LOUIS E. "Measuring the Interpretation of Data." *Ed Res B* 17:98-107 Ap 13 '38.
5 *Evaluation Materials Developed for Various Aspects of Thinking.* Chicago, Ill.: Evaluation in the Eight Year Study, Progressive Education Association, March 1939. Pp. [22]. Paper, mimeographed. Out of print.
6 *The Evaluation of Abilities Involved in Dealing with Quantitative Relationships.* Chicago, Ill.: Evaluation in the Eight Year Study, Progressive Education Association, March 1939. Pp. [24]. Paper, mimeographed. Out of print.
7 AMSTUTZ, WADE S. "A Study of Characteristics of Education Freshmen Who Entered Ohio State University in 1938." *J Exp Ed* 8:289-92 Mr '40.
8 AMSTUTZ, WADE S., AND KOENINGER, RUPERT C. "A Study of a Test for Measuring Skill in the Interpretation of Data." *J Exp Ed* 8:251-5 Mr '40.
9 CAHOW, ARTHUR C. "Relationships of Test Scores of Education College Freshmen to Grades in Selected Courses." *J Exp Ed* 8:284-9 Mr '40.

[1545]

Interpretation of Data: Test 2.71. Grades 7-9; 1940; 1 form; revision of Test 2.7; 5¢ per machine-scorable answer sheet; $1.50 per set of stencils for machine scoring; nontimed (60) minutes; Chicago, Ill.: Evaluation in the Eight Year Study, Progressive Education Association.

REFERENCES

1 HARTUNG, M. L. *Interpretation of Data.* Progressive Education Association, Evaluation in the Eight Year Study, Bulletin No. 3. Chicago, Ill.: the Study, October 1935. Pp. 11. Paper, mimeographed. Out of print.
2 *Evaluation Materials Developed for Various Aspects of Thinking.* Chicago, Ill.: Evaluation in the Eight Year Study, Progressive Education Association, March 1939. Pp. [22]. Paper, mimeographed. Out of print.
3 *The Evaluation of Abilities Involved in Dealing with Quantitative Relationships.* Chicago, Ill.: Evaluation in the Eight Year Study, Progressive Education Association, March 1939. Pp. [24]. Paper, mimeographed. Out of print.
4 *Social Sensitivity:* An Approach to Evaluation in Social Studies. Chicago, Ill.: Evaluation in the Eight Year Study, Progressive Education Association, March 1939. Pp. [34]. Paper, mimeographed. Out of print.

[1546]

Inventory of Reading Experiences. Grades 9-16; 1938-40; 1 form; $1.75 per 25; Frederick L. Pond; Stanford University, Calif.: Stanford University Press.

REFERENCES

1 POND, FREDERICK L. "A Qualitative and Quantitative Appraisal of Reading Experiences." *J Ed Res* 33:241-52 D '39.

[1547]

Iowa Silent Reading Tests, New Edition. Grades 4-9, 9-13; 1929-39; 2 forms, 2 levels; Yonkers, N. Y.: World Book Co.
a) ELEMENTARY TEST. Grades 4-9. $1.25 per 25; 25¢ per specimen set; 50(65) minutes. H. A. Greene and V. H. Kelley.
b) ADVANCED TEST. Grades 9-13. $1.60 per 25; 35¢ per specimen set; 5¢ per machine-scorable answer sheet; 47(60) minutes. H. A. Greene, A. N. Jorgensen, and V. H. Kelley.

REFERENCES

1 JORGENSEN, A. N. *Iowa Silent Reading Examinations.* University of Iowa. Studies, First Series No. 130; Studies in Education, Vol. 4, No. 3. Iowa City, Iowa: the University, May 1927. Pp. 76. $0.75. Paper.
2 STRANG, RUTH. "An Evaluation of Reading Tests for College Students (Abstract)," pp. 35-7. In *The Role of Research in Educational Progress*: Official Report, American Educational Research Association, A Department of the National Education Association, New Orleans, Louisiana, February 20-24, 1937. Washington, D. C.: the Association, May 1937. Pp. 255. $1.50. Paper.
3 DEARBORN, W. F., AND GORES, H. B. "Adult Reactions to a Silent Reading Test." *Harvard Ed R* 8:38-43 Ja '38.
4 LANDRY, HERBERT. "The Disparity of Test Norms," pp. 208-17. In *Yearbook of the New York Society for the Experimental Study of Education,* 1938. New York: the Society (c/o C. Frederick Pertach, Sec.-Treas., 500 Park Ave.). Pp. vii, 228. $1.00. Paper.
5 TRAXLER, ARTHUR E. "One Reading Test Serves the Purpose." *Clearing House* 14:419-21 Mr '40.
6 TRAXLER, ARTHUR E. "A Study of the New Edition of the Iowa Silent Reading Test for High Schools and Colleges," pp. 39-47. In *1939 Fall Testing Program in Independent Schools and Supplementary Studies.* Educational Records Bulletin, No. 29. New York: Educational Records Bureau, January 1940. Pp. x, 50. $1.00. Paper.

Ivan A. Booker, Assistant Director of the Research Division, National Education Association, Washington, D. C. An agreeable surprise but perhaps some measure of disappointment, too, is in store for test users who have long been familiar with the *Iowa Silent Reading Test* but have not yet made the acquaintance of the new, 1939 edition of it. Although in general scope and purpose the new edition closely resembles the earlier test battery, it differs from it both in appearance and in the technics of measurement employed.

The new edition of the *Iowa Silent Reading Test,* in common with its predecessor, is made up of several subtests. The types of subtests, however, are by no means the same. The new Elementary Test consists of: (*a*) a combined measure of rate and comprehension, (*b*) a test of "directed reading," (*c*) a vocabulary test, (*d*) a measure of paragraph comprehension, (*e*) a test of "sentence meaning," and (*f*) an exercise involving the "location of information." The Advanced Test contains all the foregoing subtests and an additional one on "poetry comprehension."

The directions for administering and scoring the new Iowa test are clear and easy to follow. Pupils should find it easy, too, to follow directions in doing the exercises. All the tests in the series are quite objective. The scoring is less time consuming and laborious than for most test batteries of comparable length. The test manual says nothing about the possibility of scoring the tests on the electrical test-scoring machines now available, but apparently the tests have been set up with that possibility in mind.

Strict and relatively brief time limits are enforced in administering the Iowa tests. Consequently, rate of work affects not only the pupils' rate scores but, to some extent, their scores on all parts of the test. Slow workers do not have time to finish the exercises, whereas rapid workers not only finish but have time to discover and correct their errors.

Each subtest yields a point score which is converted, by reference to a table of values in the test manual, into a standard score. The pupil's *median standard score* on the six (or seven) subtests is then computed and used as *the measure* of his silent reading ability. Tabled values are given for converting these median standard scores into age and grade equivalents or percentile ranks. The test manual points out, however, that the norms given are not valid as a basis for converting any given subtest score into an age-grade or percentile equivalent. For this reason the *Iowa Silent Reading Test* is, at present, primarily a survey test, affording a measure of the general level of silent reading achievement. In the absence of norms for each subtest, its potential diagnostic value can be realized only by test users who are willing and able to establish their own standards of achievement for the various parts of the test battery.

The information given in the new manual of directions is disappointingly scant with reference to procedures followed in constructing and standardizing the test—perhaps due to the newness of the revision. The only available data on the reliability of the Elementary Test were obtained by applying the Spearman-Brown formula to the scores of 120 seventh-grade pupils on Form A of the test. Similarly, the reliability of the Advanced Test is given in terms of the chance-half correlation of the scores of only 160 tenth-grade pupils. No data are presented on the equality of Forms A and B. Validity is established only by comparing the titles of the subtests included with a single outline of silent reading skills which was developed some fifteen years ago. Statements with reference to the basis for the age, grade, and percentile norms are too indefinite, vague, or general to admit of critical evaluation.

The suggestions given on interpreting the scores of individuals and groups of pupils on the new Iowa test also suffer by comparison with the corresponding helps given with the earlier form of the test. Much is left to the skill and ingenuity of the test giver in finding out what the test results mean in terms of pupil adjustment and corrective teaching.

Some of the least useful tests in the earlier edition have been abandoned, among them the exercise on "paragraph organization." Different technics have been introduced into other parts of the test which should result in definite improvement, particularly the technic of measuring reading rate and that of testing paragraph comprehension.

The new rate-comprehension subtest makes use of a technic which resembles, but is not quite identical with, the technic used in the *Traxler Silent Reading Test,* designed for junior high-school pupils. The student is required to read each of two selections ranging in length, in the different forms and at different grade levels, from 374 to 635 words. At the end of one minute he marks the word being read and continues to read for two more minutes. Then a check on comprehension is made by having him respond to 10 to 20 multiple-choice questions based on the selection. His rate score is based on the *sum of the number of sentences read in one minute for the two selections;* his comprehension score, on the total number of questions answered correctly. The scoring key makes it possible to obtain, also, a rate score in terms of number of words per minute. But the manual advises against this procedure, referring to it as an "unnecessary and probably an unjustified refinement." The type of comprehension measured by this particular exercise is perhaps best described as the *immediate recall of more or less significant details.*

The subtest, entitled "Directed Reading," makes use of the same identical selections used in the rate-comprehension part which precedes it. According to the manual, the purpose is "to measure the student's ability to comprehend general and specific situations expressed in the content without unduly stressing memory." Although no explanation is given as to why the same selections used in Subtest 1 are preferable to new material for use in Subtest 2, the purpose probably is to make it as easy as possible for students to *skim* the material, looking for the sentences pertinent to the questions asked. In this exercise the student is confronted with 20 questions to which he responds by giving the number of the sentence in the test selection in which the answer is found. In this exercise, the answer always is given in one of the five sentences occupying approximately the same horizontal plane as the question—a fact which automatically limits the students' search to those items. There is little difference in the type of question asked in Subtests 1 and 2. In Subtest 1, for example, the student may be asked to state from memory: "In what kind of climate does sugar cane grow best? 1 cool, 2 temperate, 3 very warm." Then in Subtest 2 he must find and give the number of the sentence which answers the question: "Does sugar cane grow better in a hot or a cold country?" The remainder of the subtests follow either the same technics employed in the original *Iowa Silent Reading Tests* or other technics commonly employed in reading scales. The subtest on "poetry comprehension" in the new Advanced Test represents an improvement over the earlier form but, in the judgment of this reviewer, is still one of the least valid and significant of the seven subtests.

The vocabulary section of the Advanced Test represents the "technical vocabulary" of four special fields: social science, science, mathematics, and English. Whether a test of technical vocabulary or one of general vocabulary is the more significant measure of reading achievement is a question on which authorities differ. It is pertinent here merely to point out that the Advanced Test includes only a test of technical vocabulary. In the Elementary Test, the first half is concerned with "general vocabulary"; the last, with "subject-matter vocabulary."

The tests of sentence meaning in both the elementary and advanced divisions measure reasoning power, and perhaps general information and intelligence, rather than ability to understand sentences of increasing complexity —as the title, "sentence meaning," might suggest. No sentence requires more than a single line of type. Each test exercise is a brief question, such as: "Should free people be expected to work for nothing?" This does not imply a criticism of the sentence meaning subtest, but is a fact which should be kept in mind in interpreting the test results.

In spite of certain obvious limitations, such as are more or less typical of new tests, the revised edition of the *Iowa Silent Reading Test* merits the attention and study of those who need both a comprehensive and diagnostic measure of silent reading achievement.

Holland D. Roberts, Associate Professor of Education, Stanford University. [Review of the Advanced Test.] This 1939 issue of a widely-used standard reading test for high schools and colleges follows the general form and approach of the earlier editions, using new material and improved methods. It is based essentially upon the traditional educational philosophy of the earlier test. The new work materially improves the effectiveness but does not substantially change its purposes or scope.

In constructing it the authors have made "an effort to go beyond the ordinary general survey of a single phase of silent reading ability." They state that it "measures three major aspects of silent reading ability; namely, (1) Rate of Reading at a Controlled Level of Comprehension, (2) Comprehension of Words, Poetry, Sentences, Paragraphs, and Longer Articles, and (3) Ability to Use Skills Required in Locating Information." To realize these purposes ten different types of tests are to be used in a 60- to 65-minute period.

This new Iowa test is one of the leading standardized instruments for diagnosis and evaluation of work type reading available at the time of publication. It is the work of thoroughly experienced test makers whose previous tests have given some years of satisfactory service. However, further study and insight would have resulted in significant improvements.

In this Iowa test, rate of reading and comprehension are checked for prose with short science and social studies selections. *Rate* consequently includes a measure of the total study-reading-response act and is not comparable to *rate* in words or lines per minute. The directions "Read this story about 'glass' very carefully so that you can answer questions about it" may produce word by word reading and increased regression.

Formal, religious verse of little significance to modern youth is used to test poetry comprehension. The archaic language of John Pryor's "knowledge" and the intensive analysis of the comprehension test are in disrepute among leading teachers of English as means of evaluating the "ability to read and interpret poetry." To realize that aim modern verse and an oral test are needed.

The vocabulary test is subject matter centered and designed to measure a pupil's understanding of significant words in social science, science, mathematics, and English. The large life areas of youth: sports, movies, radio, automobiles, aviation, adventure, friendship, and romance are not represented. The choice of material for the four subject-matter areas is traditional and does not recognize the important changes that have taken place within subject matter organization and viewpoint. Testing word meaning in the English section is chiefly through recognition of terms of formal grammar and literary form, such as "objective," "prologue," and "allegory." Clearly the authors have not realized their aim of cataloguing "the important concepts in that subject."

Tests of both word and sentence meaning are constructed of sentences presenting similar comprehension problems, and it seems probable that both measure the same interrelated abilities. Simple history, geography, and agriculture provide the content for testing paragraph comprehension. Item 3 perpetuates our current textbook mythology about the Eskimo exposed some years ago by Stefansson in *Adventures in Error*. Finding material in an index is used to test ability to locate information. It seems to be an excellent test of the mechanical skill of finding correct answers to questions in an index when neither the questions nor the answers are of interest or importance, and the student is motivated by the stop watch and the fear of a low score in the record. Such abilities as how to find the most interesting radio, theater, or movie programs, your friend's address or telephone number in a strange city, or how to find the best quality goods for the lowest price are not tested.

Scoring the test, except for rate, has been made simple and rapid by means of a perforated stencil scoring key. Percentile norms are based on some 10,000 cases and apply to the end of the school year. They are based upon "a random sampling of the entire school population of Iowa plus all the children in the requisite grades in two Eastern communities."

All standard reading tests now available have certain fundamental limitations which should be considered in evaluating this test.

1. The test experience is not one of the reading experiences which are frequently met in daily life situations. From the student viewpoint taking such a test does not meet his own needs and is nonfunctional. There is a serious question whether the reading power which we employ when we are striving to satisfy our own desires is operative when the motivation is external and compulsive as it necessarily is in standard tests. Standardized reading with teacher interruptions at the end of a minute, or a few minutes at most, obviously formalizes the reading process.

2. The content lacks significance in the life of the student. Neither the subject matter of the parts nor the form is unified, and there is a consequent handicap to those who have been prepared to look for related meanings in developmental reading and study.

3. The test makers do not guide the users to see the functional relationships of the test data in a complete diagnosis of the reading capacities of a student. Accordingly many teachers and schools base their entire reading programs on the necessarily incomplete data which the most satisfactory of tests give. For example, the test data provides no direct information on such crucial aspects of reading as attitudes and interests, habits, long-term concentration, and

scope and penetration in past reading experience.

4. The testing is upon specific forms of study reading, and excludes reading for enjoyment.

5. There is always the possibility that "test shock" may inhibit a student, and that the scores will not reflect actual power in daily life situations nor provide comparable measures.

It should be emphasized that these limitations do not invalidate a test when it is used for specific purposes as a part of a complete program of evaluation. They should qualify its use.

[1548]

Jenkins Oral Reading Test: Individualized Oral Diagnostic Test for Children with Serious Reading Difficulties. Children whose reading ability falls within the range of normal children in grades 1-3; 1939; 2 forms; 75¢ per 25; 10¢ per specimen set; Frances Jenkins and students; Cincinnati, Ohio: C. A. Gregory Co.

Guy L. Bond, Associate Professor of Education, The University of Minnesota. This test consists of eleven paragraphs of increasing difficulty. The pupil reads each paragraph orally until he reaches a paragraph where he has to be told ten words by the examiner. There are questions to measure comprehension. The test has some merit as an oral reading test but can hardly lay claim to giving a diagnosis of the difficulties. The examiner is supposed to estimate whether the reader is reading words or phrases. It is upon this estimate that the diagnosis rests. There is a rough scale given for locating the reader's approximate oral reading grade.

David Kopel, Department of Education, Chicago Teachers College. The Jenkins test is similar to and merits comparison with the better known *Standardized Oral Reading Paragraphs* by William S. Gray. Like the Gray, the Jenkins test consists of a series of increasingly difficult paragraphs, eleven in number. The material ranges in difficulty from primer to the fourth-grade level. The paragraphs are desirably longer and more episodic in character than those in the Gray test; they are followed by several "comprehension" questions which yield a percentage score. Unlike the Gray, this test is not timed. A record is kept, instead, of whether words are read singly or in groups. Number of errors is also recorded and the test continues until the child has to be told ten words in one paragraph. His test score is that of the selection preceding this.

This instrument possesses some of the obvious values and limitations mentioned in the writer's review of the Gray test. Thus it provides an opportunity for observing a child's reading and behavior in a "standardized" situation. The meaning of the test score must be validated in every instance, however, by observing the child's actual reading performance with several types of material.

The test suffers from a number of limitations. Not very serious is the poor typography: irregularities in inking, margination, and spacing between lines. More important is the omission of standardization data in the record sheet and manual which accompanies the test, although the chronological ages and grade scores on both the Jenkins and Gray tests are given for 36 pupils whose IQ's range from 51 to 99 (a non-representative group in terms of the intelligence distribution of poor readers generally). Comparative test scores are reported for several other retarded readers.

Perhaps the most serious criticism of the test is its oversimplification of the problem of diagnosis and remediation. The title page of the test bears several suggestions under the heading "Diagnosis and Remedial Measures." When one finds "sight words lacking"—presumably in the child's test performance—one should, it is to be inferred, provide "drill on small number of sight words from standard lists." As though children don't know "sight words" because they haven't had drills (usually countless drills) on words taken from "standard lists"! The approach in this test exemplifies that narrow point of view still held by some workers who (*a*) analyze reading problems into some of their superficial components (or symptoms) and (*b*) then proceed with "remedial" work by attempting to improve or strengthen these elementalistic skills through isolated and largely meaningless drill. Extensive studies and reviews of the literature by Jastak, Tinker, Gates, Gray, Bennett, Hildreth, Strang, Harrison, Witty and others have demonstrated the complexity of causation in reading disability—the lack of single "causes" —and the correlative need (*a*) in diagnosis, of a comprehensive study of the individual's development, and (*b*) in remedial work, for the use of techniques which are individually appropriate and which may contribute to the individual's progress in reading for meaning.

Clarence R. Stone, 2140 Los Angeles Avenue, Berkeley, California. This is a power test consisting of eleven short units ranging in difficulty from easy primer material to material on about college level. Consequently this test increases in difficulty more gradually than does Gray's test entitled *Standardized Oral Reading Paragraphs Test.* Apparently the material has been carefully selected and graded. The reader has no information as to the basis for gradation with respect to vocabulary or other factors. In this test no time record of the oral reading is taken as in the Gray test. Instead, the examiner indicates for each unit whether or not in his judgment the pupil reads word by word or in word groups. The examiner also records for each unit the number of words the examiner tells the child during the course of his oral reading of the unit. Immediately following the oral reading of the unit the child responds with pencil to one or more comprehension questions. The examiner records for each unit the percentage of correct answers. The child reads until he has to be told ten words in his oral reading of the unit. The score for the whole test is based on his record for the unit preceding this one.

While this test is somewhat easier to administer than the Gray test and is superior in construction in that it increases in difficulty more gradually and is apparently more carefully standardized as to the difficulty of the units, the reviewer's judgment is that this test will not yield sufficient information for an adequate diagnosis with respect to the oral reading of poor readers. A plan of recording on the test sheets different types of errors as is done in the Gray tests would greatly improve this test.

[1549]

Kansas Primary Reading Test. Grades 1-3; 1935; 2 forms; 40¢ per 25; 15¢ per specimen set; 12(20) minutes; Alma Hoag, Emma Humble, Bertha Robinson, Adeline Wipf, and H. E. Schrammel; Emporia, Kan.: Bureau of Educational Measurements, Kansas State Teachers College.

Alice K. Liveright, Principal of the Logan Demonstration School, Public Schools, Philadelphia, Pennsylvania. The *Kansas Primary Reading Test* is intended both as a survey and diagnostic measure of silent reading in grades 1-3. It comprises three distinct parts, so that ability in sentence reading, word knowledge, and paragraph reading may each be tested separately.

As a survey instrument the test appears to have many admirable features. It possesses adequate validity and a high degree of reliability. Norms available both for each part of the test and for the whole, as well as a table of percentile scores, assist the teacher in interpretation of results. Two forms render the repeated use of the test practicable. The brevity of the test, twelve minutes reading time, saves the time of the teacher and avoids fatigue of the young readers. As the method of registering response, underlining words, is simple and as the same response is used in all three parts, the reader's attention may be focused upon the reading problem solely and the scoring is simplified for the teacher. The test may be given to large numbers without great expenditure of money as it costs but $1.50 for one hundred copies.

The norms and the percentile scale records indicate that most first grade pupils receive quite low scores. This seems to indicate that the material is so difficult for pupils in the first grade as to prove very discouraging to them. As a survey measure, the test might well be delayed beyond the first year.

As an instrument for diagnosis it is probably as valuable as any short group test could be. In each part the material is well scaled from the simple to the more difficult so that the teacher can ascertain at a glance the level at which each pupil can attain success.

The multiple-choice method is used for indicating the response. The child must choose from among five words. This seems an unnecessarily long list. Many similar tests for older pupils use lists of four words only.

Part II is designed to test word knowledge. The words, however, are used in sentences. One who lacks ability to read the sentences, fails in this part of the test. There are ways of testing the word knowledge of young children without resorting to sentences. The ability required to succeed in Part II appears not to vary greatly from that required in Part I.

In Part III, two statements follow each paragraph. In each statement the child chooses the word from among three which makes the statement correct. The responses indicate both the understanding of the selection and grasp of details.

As a result of administering this test, the teacher knows the child's reading level. No causes of lack of ability are revealed. However, it should be said that it is difficult to find a short group test which diagnoses reading failures adequately.

In format the test is pleasing. It is likewise convenient to handle. The type is clear and bold. The spacing is good, with the exception of the first page of Part III, Form B. Here there is less space than in the similar portion of Form A, and the crowding might cause confusion to the reader. The format would be improved by the use of slightly thicker paper. The print from one side of a sheet shows somewhat on the other.

[1550]

Mathematics, Biology, Physical Science [Reading Test]: Booklet No. 2. Grades 10-16; 1938; 8¢ per test; 2¢ per machine-scorable answer sheet; 12¢ per sample test; 180(190) minutes; English Commission of the Association of Georgia Colleges; Athens, Ga.: the Association, c/o F. S. Beers, Memorial Hall.

[1551]

Metropolitan Achievement Tests in Reading. Grades 1, 2-3, 4-6, 7-8; 1931-35; 3 forms, 4 levels; edited by Jacob S. Orleans; Yonkers, N. Y.: World Book Co.
a) PRIMARY READING TEST. Grades 1-3; 1931-34; $1.25 per 25; 15¢ per specimen set; 40(60) minutes; Gertrude H. Hildreth.
b) INTERMEDIATE READING TEST. Grades 4-6; 1932-35; $1.00 per 25; 10¢ per specimen set; 37(45) minutes; Richard D. Allen, Harold H. Bixler, William L. Connor, and Frederick B. Graham.
c) ADVANCED READING TEST. Grades 7-8; 1932-35; $1.00 per 25; 10¢ per specimen set; 37(45) minutes; same authors as for *b*.

D. A. Worcester, Chairman of the Department of Educational Psychology and Measurements, The University of Nebraska. The primary test includes six subtests measuring respectively: word picture, word recognition, word meaning, reading completion, paragraph reading, and vocabulary. The intermediate and advanced tests measure reading and vocabulary, the reading subtest being divided into exercises requiring the supplying of missing words in paragraphs and the answering of questions on the content of paragraphs. No evidence of reliability or validity is presented in the directions for administering or other material contained in the specimen package.

Each of the subtests in the primary test is scored separately, and it is assumed that an accurate measure can be obtained from any one or any combination of the tests. The reader is told, moreover, that if a child's score exceeds a certain value, this test should not be used in obtaining his average reading grade equivalent. It is interesting to note that on this basis four of the six tests do not offer a sufficient range to measure the completion of the third grade, the highest grade equivalents which can be used for a general score being 3.1, 2.10, 3.7, 3.7, 4.7, and 5.4. If a child should make the highest score allowable on all six tests, his average reading equivalent would be 3.7, although on the two tests which allow a wider range, he would secure the equivalent of 4.7 and 5.4, respectively.

The instructions for the primary test present an interesting combination of the desire to appear very scientific and at the same time to be sensible. Paragraph five of the general directions, for example, says "Accurate administering requires implicit following of instructions. The precise wording of directions has been worked out with great care and any marked deviation may invalidate the results." Later in the same paragraph we read "Not all pupils respond in the same way to testing. Pupils totally unfamiliar with testing will need more preliminary help than others, and dull children may be expected to require more assistance. . . The examiner's own good sense must be relied upon to make necessary adaptions in the testing program"; then in paragraph six, "These tests are designed as measures of achievement of pupils—*not* tests of following directions. Consequently any method of making clear to the pupil what he is expected to do is allowable." Still later it is emphatically stated that the child may not ask questions during the examination, although it is pointed out that the examiner may walk about the room to see that the pupils are marking the answers instead of writing words, and so on. Why the child should not be allowed to ask if he is doing it rightly is, therefore, not made very clear.

The intermediate and advanced tests are not only very limited as to their diagnostic value, but are very similar in content. Twelve of the seventeen paragraphs in Part I of the reading test for grades 7-8, three of the four paragraphs in Part II, and forty of the sixty-five words in the vocabulary test are the same as those used in the test for grades 4-6. In addition to this similarity in test material, the table of grade equivalents for the intermediate test gives values from grade 4.0 to grade 9.0 (scores outside of these limits are extrapolated). There

scarcely seems to be, therefore, justification for the publication of the advanced form.

The scoring of the intermediate and advanced tests is quite largely subjective. The keys list several correct answers for some items but do not include all of the answers which may be correct, and do not suggest the possibility of several answers in some instances where the possibility exists. A single difference in the number of correct answers, however, may make as much as two months difference in a child's reading age equivalent.

The tests appear to this reviewer to be decidedly inferior to several other tests which are easily available; for example, the *Iowa Silent Reading Test* or the *Progressive Achievement Test in Reading.*

For reviews by Ivan A. Booker and Joseph C. Dewey, see 1105. For reviews by Jack W. Dunlap, Richard Ledgerwood, E. V. Pullias, and Hugh B. Wood of the total battery, see 874 and 1189.

[1552]

Metropolitan Readiness Tests. Kindergarteners and first-grade entrants; 1933-39; 1 form; $1.20 per 25; 15¢ per specimen set; (70) minutes; Gertrude H. Hildreth and Nellie L. Griffiths; Yonkers, N. Y.: World Book Co.

REFERENCES

1 HILDRETH, GERTRUDE. "Number Readiness and Progress in Arithmetic." *J Exp Ed* 4:1-6 S '35.
2 WRIGHT, WENDELL W. *Reading Readiness*: A Prognostic Study. Bulletin of the School of Education, Indiana University, Vol. 12, No. 3. Bloomington, Ind.: Indiana University Bookstore, June 1936. Pp. 46. $0.50. Paper.
3 CALVERT, EVERETT T. "Predicting Accomplishment in Beginning Reading." *Calif J El Ed* 6:34-44 Ag '37.
4 GRANT, ALBERT. "A Comparison of the Metropolitan Readiness Tests and the Pintner-Cunningham Primary Mental Test." *El Sch J* 38:118-26 O '37.
5 SENOUR, A. C. "A Comparison of Two Instruments for Measuring Reading Readiness," pp. 178-83. In *The Role of Research in Educational Progress*: Official Report, American Educational Research Association, A Department of the National Education Association, New Orleans, Louisiana, February 20-24, 1937. Washington, D. C.: the Association, May 1937. Pp. 255. $1.50. Paper.
6 FENDRICK, PAUL, AND McGLADE, CHARLES A. "A Validation of Two Prognostic Tests of Reading Aptitude." *El Sch J* 39:187-94 N '38.
7 GRANT, ALBERT. "The Comparative Validity of the Metropolitan Readiness Tests and the Pintner-Cunningham Primary Mental Tests." *El Sch J* 38:599-605 Ap '38.
8 HUGGETT, A. J. "An Experiment in Reading Readiness." *J Ed Res* 32:263-70 D '38.
9 KAWIN, ETHEL. "Implications of Individual Differences at the First Grade Level." Discussion by S. J. Beck. *Am J Orthopsychiatry* 8:654-72 O '38.
10 RANSOM, KATHARINE A. "A Study of Reading Readiness." *Peabody J Ed* 16:276-84 Ja '39.

W. J. Osburn, Professor of Education, The University of Washington. It is futile as well as dangerous to try to teach children who are not ready to learn what is taught. It is stupid to subject little children to impossible tasks upon their first contact with the school. Yet we have been doing just those things year after year with 25 per cent of our first grade children. It does no good to ascribe the high mortality in the first grade to such vague concepts as "lack of cooperation," "lack of interest," "naughtiness," "lack of attention," and the like when the real cause of the trouble is immaturity.

For these reasons all tests which purport to measure readiness are of major interest and importance. The *Metropolitan Readiness Tests* have been widely and successfully used as an objective means of identifying the children who are not yet mature enough to profit by ordinary first grade instruction.

In these tests maturity is defined in terms of perception vocabulary, the understanding and correct reaction to oral directions, number knowledge, information, and ability in drawing. While the total time required is 70 minutes at least four "sittings" are recommended. In addition the examiner is warned to stop at the end of any test when there is evidence of undue fatigue. The tests are to be used either at the close of the kindergarten or at the beginning of the first grade. Children who fail to score 60 points on the entire test are considered unready for ordinary reading instructions. The norms are based upon more than 7,000 cases.

The tests are entirely free from reading content. Test 1 is concerned with similarities in pictures. Test 2 requires the copying of forms. Tests 3 and 4 test vocabulary and the understanding of sentences by the use of pictures. Test 5 contains forty items involving ability in "number vocabulary, counting, ordinal numbers, recognition of written numbers, writing numbers, interpreting number symbols, the meaning of number terms, the meaning of fractional parts, recognition of forms, telling time, and the use of numbers in simple problems," all of which are markedly absent from most of our primary number tests. Test 6 is informational and Test 7 is concerned with freehand drawing.

It is obvious that the authors of the test would readily admit that their technique for the testing of readiness is far from perfect. With only one form they are unable to furnish measures of improvement in readiness. The validity problem is not solved adequately as yet. The ever difficult problem of reliability when testing very young children in groups is still with us. The authors warn clearly that some children who fail to achieve a total score of 60 are nevertheless ready to read. On the other hand some who achieve more than 60 are still unready.

Imperfections such as these are to be expected in all pioneer testing. In spite of them, however, the *Metropolitan Readiness Tests* are emphatically worth while.

[1553]
Michigan Speed of Reading Test, 1937 Revision. Grades 3-16; 1932-37; 2 forms; $1 per 25; 10¢ per specimen set; 7(15) minutes; Edward B. Greene; New York: Psychological Corporation.

REFERENCES

1 GREENE, EDWARD B. "Michigan Speed of Reading Tests." J Ed Res 28:283-8 D '34.
2 STRANG, RUTH. "An Evaluation of Reading Tests for College Students (Abstract)," pp. 35-7. In *The Role of Research in Educational Progress*: Official Report, American Educational Research Association, A Department of the National Education Association, New Orleans, Louisiana, February 20-24, 1937. Washington, D. C.: the Association, May, 1937. Pp. 255. $1.50. Paper.

[1554]
Minnesota Reading Examinations for College Students. Grades 9-16; 1930-35; 2 forms; $6 per 100; 35¢ per specimen set; 46(55) minutes; Melvin E. Haggerty and Alvin C. Eurich; Minneapolis, Minn.: University of Minnesota Press.

REFERENCES

1 EURICH, ALVIN C. *The Reading Abilities of College Students*: An Experimental Study, pp. 17-40. Minneapolis, Minn.: University of Minnesota Press, 1931. Pp. xv, 208. $2.50.
2 STRANG, RUTH. "An Evaluation of Reading Tests for College Students (Abstract)," pp. 35-7. In *The Role of Research in Educational Progress*: Official Report, American Educational Research Association, A Department of the National Education Association, New Orleans, Louisiana, February 20-24, 1937. Washington, D. C.: the Association, May 1937. Pp. 255. $1.50. Paper.
3 PATERSON, DONALD G.; SCHNEIDLER, GWENDOLEN G.; AND WILLIAMSON, EDMUND G. *Student Guidance Techniques*, pp. 91-4. New York: McGraw-Hill Book Co., Inc., 1938. Pp. xviii, 316. $3.00. (London: McGraw-Hill Publishing Co., Ltd. 18s.)

W. C. McCall, Director of the Personnel Bureau and Associate Professor of Education, University of South Carolina. This test contains two parts, the first is devoted to vocabulary measurement and the second to measuring silent reading comprehension through the medium of paragraph reading. The vocabulary part consists of a 100-word multiple-choice test, derived mostly from the *Haggerty Reading Examination, Sigma 3*, with additional items and arrangement of items in terms of difficulty. The time allowance is six minutes. The paragraph reading part consists of ten independent passages typical of textbook content at the college level. Three or four questions are attached to each passage, a total of 35 questions in all, devoted to testing grasp of factual information, comprehension of organization, and understanding of thought content. The time allowance for the ten paragraphs and 35 questions is 40 minutes.

The manual warns that timing must be adhered to precisely since "few pupils" are able to finish the vocabulary part within 6 minutes. The manual states, however, in reference to the paragraphs that "practically every pupil should finish in the time allowed." Thus, the test yields two part scores, the first of which, due to the short time limit, must be interpreted as a combined measure of vocabulary, rate of work, and "intelligence," and the second as essentially a power measure of silent reading comprehension.

That the vocabulary part measures "intelligence" to some extent, as is done by typical group intelligence tests, would naturally be assumed on the basis of the common characteristics of language content and speed emphasis. This assumption is supported by correlations cited in the manual which indicate that the "vocabulary" scores on Form A correlate with group intelligence tests to the extent of approximately .73. (Direct average of three correlations reported in the manual.) The authors report a reliability of .93 for the vocabulary part of Form A, based upon high school seniors' scores.

For the paragraph-reading part of Form A, the authors report a reliability coefficient of .78, based upon college juniors and seniors. The reliability for high school seniors is reported as only .69, an indication that the paragraph reading material is better suited to the upper-college level. The intercorrelation of the vocabulary and paragraph-reading parts is given in the manual as .54, based upon testing of high school seniors. It seems reasonable, therefore, to conclude that the paragraph-reading measure afforded by the *Minnesota Reading Examination* is a useful but not highly reliable index of a college student's ability to grasp facts and thought content in work-study reading material. From the intercorrelations it is evident that the two parts of the test measure partially separate abilities and it is therefore suggested that Part I scores may be used as rough indicators of whether or not respective pupils are as proficient in reading paragraphs as their "vocabulary-speed" scores would seem to warrant.

The extent to which total scores on Form A predict college marks is indicated by two correlations reported in the manual. Thesè correlations seem to justify an average correlation expectation of approximately .50 between total scores on the reading test and marks on college courses when marks are formulated indepen-dently by various instructors and reported in traditional five-letter symbolism. Thus, it is apparent that the test as a whole predicts college marks about as well as group intelligence tests usually predict.

All correlation studies reported in the manual are for Form A scores. Form B was constructed several years after Form A and both the item analysis and the standardization of Form B were based upon later generations of students. The manual contains tables of corresponding percentile ranks and standard scores for Forms A and B, based upon examining large numbers of separate generations of college sophomores, juniors, and seniors. Corresponding percentile ranks show only small differences in raw scores for the two forms and so the authors accordingly claim that "a high degree of comparability of total scores is apparent." The large numbers of cases on which the comparability tables are based obviously lend considerable support to their claim but the method of standardization was clearly faulty.

In several respects the format of the test and the scoring key suggest possibilities of improvement. The questions following the paragraphs are printed in type so small as to create eye strain for some students, especially if the lighting in the examination room is not entirely ideal. Also, the provisions for recording responses to the questions on paragraph reading invite scoring errors in that the alternatives are not numbered and the student is requested to check in some instances and to underscore in others. With answers thus falling in various positions on the paper, scoring is rendered laborious. The scoring key is of the old-fashioned strip-cut variety. A stencil-type key is needed to bring the answers conveniently adjacent to the recorded responses in the test booklet. Better still, the alternatives might be numbered and students directed to record their choices within parentheses in column, thereby making possible use of an easily manipulated fan-type key.

The examiner's manual is well written, conservative in claims for the test, instructive in discussion of reading and testing, and critical in analysis of what the Minnesota test accomplishes. The manual contains extensive norms data for Form A and reports a number of correlation studies, only a few of which have been referred to in this paper.

In conclusion, it may be said that the *Minne-*

sota Reading Examination for College Students is a useful instrument but that the test leaves much to be desired in that it is only roughly diagnostic to the extent of enabling description of a student's "reading" capability in terms of a "vocabulary" measure which is beclouded with emphasis upon speed and a measure of paragraph reading which is rather low in reliability and general in meaning. It is the writer's belief that much improvement could be made by increasing the time limit for Part I, increasing the content (and time allowance accordingly) of Part II, revising the format to facilitate scoring and reduce eye strain, and restandardizing Forms A and B as thus revised.

For a review by Ruth Strang, see 1106.

[1555]
Minnesota Speed of Reading Test for College Students. Grades 12-16; 1936; 2 forms; $2.75 per 100; 35¢ per specimen set; 6(15) minutes; Alvin C. Eurich; Minneapolis, Minn.: University of Minnesota Press.

REFERENCES
1 EURICH, ALVIN C. *The Reading Abilities of College Students*: An Experimental Study, pp. 54-61, Minneapolis, Minn.: University of Minnesota Press, 1931. Pp. xv, 208. $2.50.
2 PATERSON, DONALD G.; SCHNEIDLER, GWENDOLEN G.; AND WILLIAMSON, EDMUND G. *Student Guidance Techniques*, pp. 87-8. New York: McGraw-Hill Book Co., Inc., 1938. Pp. xviii, 316. $3.00. (London: McGraw-Hill Publishing Co., Ltd. 18s.)

J. R. Gerberich, Director of the Bureau of Educational Research and Statistical Service and Associate Professor of Education, University of Connecticut. Thirty-eight short paragraphs of material from such fields as history, geography, economics, government, psychology, education, and the sciences make up this test for measuring the reading speed of college students. The paragraphs, from 40 to 60 words in length, are sufficiently simple that the comprehension factor, which usually has variable and unpredictable influence on speed of reading test results, is largely controlled. Each paragraph contains an absurd phrase through which the student is to draw a line. The absurdities are on the whole rather cleverly worded and keyed to the context, so that a certain degree of comprehension is necessary on the part of the reader if the absurdity is to be detected. Students work as far through the thirty-eight paragraphs as they can during the six minutes for which the test is timed.

The manual for the test consists of eleven pages of mimeographed material in which are included directions for administration, directions for scoring, scoring keys for both Forms

A and B, and norms for both Forms A and B. No information of any kind is given concerning the validity or reliability of the instrument. Tables for converting raw scores to percentiles and to "scale values," which express deviations from the median in terms of the standard deviation, are based on college sophomores and juniors at the University of Minnesota, but the user of the test is left to conjecture concerning the number of such students upon which the norms are based. Obviously, the sampling is not likely to be highly representative of college students.

Although the manual makes no mention of any supplementary source of information, Eurich's, *The Reading Abilities of College Students*,[1] 1931 copyright, contains a chapter devoted to the development and standardization of the instrument. That the test is the same seems certain, despite the 1936 copyright of the test, because the manual contains tables of grade norms which are taken bodily from tables in the chapter of the book. The following data concerning reliability and validity are taken from the 1931 source. Reliability coefficients between the two forms of the test are reported as ranging from .81 for tenth grade pupils to .87 for graduate students in college. Correlation coefficients between scores on the two forms of the *Chapman-Cook Speed of Reading Test* and the two forms of the *Minnesota Speed of Reading Test for College Students* are reported as ranging from .63 to .76, while coefficients between scores on an informal reading exercise measuring words read per minute and on the two forms of the Minnesota test were .39 and .63. Eurich states that the validity coefficients listed above lead one "to the conclusion that the Minnesota Speed Test has marked validity as an instrument to measure the rate at which college students read."

Even though different speed of reading tests doubtless place varying emphases upon the speed and comprehension outcomes (by means of variations in difficulty of content, directions to the students, scoring methods, etc.), which justifies the acceptance of relatively low degrees of relationship between scores on such tests as evidence of satisfactory validity, it seems probable that a change in the placement of some of the absurdities in the paragraphs might well result in more valid scores. For example, in the 76 paragraphs from the combined

Forms A and B, 69 of the absurdities occur in whole or in part in the last two lines of the paragraphs. No paragraph has less than six lines, while the mode appears to be seven lines. It seems certain that at least occasional students would decide after brief experience with the test that reading the first parts of the selections is a waste of time, and would then go immediately to the last two or three lines of each paragraph through the remainder of the test. The comprehension level of the paragraphs is such that the absurdities can rather readily be detected without knowing the entirety of the context, so that such a technique might well effect a marked increase in rate scores for such students.

This test, despite the glaring inadequacy of the manual, the too-homogeneous sampling of college students used in establishing the norms, and validity which cannot be classed as high, appears to have considerable merit. The least improvement which would make the test acceptable as a scientific instrument would be the amplification of the manual to provide the information to which a test user is entitled or to indicate where such information is to be obtained.

For reviews by Frederick B. Davis and Ruth Strang, see 1107.

[1556]

Nature of Proof: Test 5.22. Grades 10-12; 1939-40; 1 form; revision of Tests 5.2a and 5.21; 5¢ per test; 1¢ per machine-scorable answer sheet; 5¢ per explanation sheet and interpretation guide; $1.50 per set of stencils for machine scoring; Chicago, Ill.: Evaluation in the Eight Year Study, Progressive Education Association.

REFERENCES

1 RATHS, LOUIS. "Evaluating the Program of Lakeshore School." *Ed Res B* 17:67-84 Mr 16 '38.
2 *Evaluation Materials Developed for Various Aspects of Thinking.* Chicago, Ill.: Evaluation in the Eight Year Study, Progressive Education Association, March 1939. Pp. [22]. Paper, mimeographed. Out of print.
3 *The Evaluation of Abilities Involved in Dealing with Quantitative Relationships.* Chicago, Ill.: Evaluation in the Eight Year Study, Progressive Education Association, March 1939. Pp. [24]. Paper, mimeographed. Out of print.

[1557]

Nelson-Denny Reading Test. Grades 9-16; 1929-30; 2 forms; $1.65 per 25 tests including 25 answer booklets; 75¢ per 25 answer booklets; single specimen set free; 30(35) minutes; M. J. Nelson and E. C. Denny; Boston, Mass.: Houghton Mifflin Co.

REFERENCES

1 THORNDIKE, E. L. *A Teacher's Word Book.* New York: Bureau of Publications, Teachers College, Columbia University, 1921. Pp. 134. $0.80.
2 HORN, ERNEST. *A Basic Writing Vocabulary:* 10,000 Words Most Commonly Used in Writing. State University of Iowa, Monographs in Education, Series 1, No. 4. Iowa City, Iowa: the University, 1926. Pp. 225. Cloth, $2.25; paper, $1.75.
3 STRANG, RUTH. "An Evaluation of Reading Tests for College Students (Abstract)," pp. 35-7. In *The Role of Research in Educational Progress:* Official Report, American Educational Research Association, A Department of the National Education Association, New Orleans, Louisiana, February 20-24, 1937. Washington, D. C.: the Association, May 1937. Pp. 255. $1.50. Paper.
4 HELD, OMAR C. "Nelson-Denny Reading Test as an English Placement Test." *Sch and Soc* 49:64 Ja 14 '39.
5 TRAXLER, ARTHUR E. "One Reading Test Serves the Purpose." *Clearing House* 14:419-21 Mr '40.
6 UPSHALL, C. C. "Reading Ability and Success in First Year College History." *Univ Wash Col Ed Rec* 6:33-6 Ja '40.

Hans C. Gordon, Division of Educational Research, Public Schools, Philadelphia, Pennsylvania. The vocabulary test contains 100 items which are short sentence completions with five answers from which to choose. The time for the vocabulary part is only ten minutes. Consequently, there is a large element of speed involved in answering 100 items. In addition, the student is obliged to find the proper place for the answer on a separate answer sheet. The fact that the time limits are quite short is evidenced in the norms reported. Thus, with 100 five-choice items an average score attained by marking answer spaces at random on the answer sheet would be 20 items right. There is no correction for wrong answers. The median for grade 9 is only 18 or two points less than a random or chance score. For grade 10 the vocabulary median is 21.

Most of the words in the vocabulary test were chosen from the Thorndike [1] and Horn [2] lists. The basis of choice is not described. The test follows good vocabulary test form in that the word given in the sentence occurs less frequently than the words given in the choices for the answers. It is evident, however, that in this vocabulary test other traits than breadth of vocabulary are measured, especially reading speed and clerical facility.

The paragraph test consists of nine selections of 200 words each followed by four multiple-choice questions (five choices). The time allowed for this section of the test is twenty minutes. Here again the comprehending reading rate is an important element in attaining high scores. In order to finish the test and to spend approximately half time on seeking and writing answers it is necessary for the student to read at the rate of 300 words a minute. Accordingly, high scores are attained by those who read rapidly and who after reading are able to answer relatively simple questions of fact. The paragraph selections are largely from college reading material. It is possible in some cases for a student with an adequate acquaintance with the general content of the selection to answer some questions without reading the selection carefully.

The first listed purpose of the test is "to predict probable success in college." Evidence of the value of the test for this purpose is cited in an *r* of .70 for the total scores correlated with an objective test in child psychology. In another reported study the test predicted "general scholastic success about as well or better than the better intelligence tests." Additional criteria for prediction of success in college are always welcome but, in view of the mass of evidence available in cumulative records and from scholastic aptitude tests, the addition of this test of reading is justified only when other evidence is quite meagre.

The second purpose of the test is listed: "to section incoming college or high-school classes." In view of the reported correlation between the test and at least one kind of college work, the value of this reading test for this purpose may be important. However, no suggestions are offered as to how the test may be used. The authors' satisfaction with the situation expressed in the high correlation coefficients might be interpreted to mean that the authors considered the test sufficiently accurate to be the sole criterion for sectioning. Where it is possible, it would seem to be a much more desirable procedure, however, to use a wider basis of fact in organizing classes in college or high-school subjects. Since these classes are usually organized separately in specific subjects, it is probably better to select those predictors which are of greatest value in the subject under consideration. It is hardly credible that any predictor will be equally valuable in all subjects.

The third purpose listed is diagnosis. The author makes no suggestion as to how the test might be used for this purpose. Since the vocabulary and reading tests involve a very considerable element of speed of reading which is not differentiated in score, it is obvious that the blend of reading ability indexed in the part score is not a satisfactory clue as to whether unusual pains should be taken to broaden the vocabulary or to deepen the power of paragraph comprehension. No reliability coefficients are reported for the part scores. The total test shows an *r* of .91 between Forms A and B for college freshmen. The *PE* of a score is about one-half year in grade norms.

Norms are reported for all grades from the third grade to the senior class in college. The value of some of these norms may be questioned in view of the fact that a random or

chance score on the total test is 34 which is the same as the norm for the eighth grade.

[1558]
Nelson Silent Reading Test. Grades 3-9; 1931-39; 3 forms; $1.65 per 25 tests including answer booklets; 75¢ per 25 answer booklets; single specimen set free; 30(35) minutes; M. J. Nelson; Boston, Mass.: Houghton Mifflin Co.

REFERENCES
1 GRANT, ALBERT. "Results of Nelson Silent Reading Test in Grade IX." *Sch R* 48:34-9 Ja '40.

Sch R 48:34-9 Ja '40. Albert Grant. "Results of Nelson Silent Reading Test in Grade IX." This report analyzes the results of the Nelson Silent Reading Test for more than three thousand ninth-grade pupils in Cincinnati. The Nelson test was originally issued as suitable for Grades III-VIII, inclusive. Recently, however, it has been described by the publishers as also suitable for Grade IX. The *Teacher's Manual* gives norms for Grade IX but gives no information on the size and the nature of the ninth-grade population used in the derivation of the norms. The author of the test, in a letter to the writer, states that he had been unable to secure the results of the test for the ninth-grade population of any large city. This dearth of information on the results of the test at the ninth-grade level suggested to the writer that an analysis of the results for the entire ninth grade of a large city might prove helpful to future users of the test. The test was given on a city-wide basis in Grade IX in Cincinnati during January, 1939. * The Nelson test consists of two parts, a vocabulary test and a paragraph test. The latter contains twenty-five paragraphs, each followed by three questions. Each question is intended to measure a distinct aspect of reading ability. Thus "A" questions are intended to measure ability to understand the general significance of the paragraph; "B" questions deal with ability to note details; and "C" questions have to do with ability to predict the probable outcome. The test is scored separately for each type of question—a fact which greatly increases the total scoring time required. The separate scores are intended to make possible a diagnosis of the pupil's status with respect to the three types of reading ability mentioned. The *Teacher's Manual* suggests ways in which these separate scores may be used as a basis for planning remedial work. * the coefficients of correlation between scores on Subtests A, B, and C were determined for a sampling of three hundred cases. The correlation between subtests A and B was found to be .91 ± .007; between Subtests A and C, .91 ± .007; and between Subtests B and C, .92 ± .006. Since all coefficients are above .90, close relationship is indicated. In fact, it is doubtful whether the coefficients of reliability for these subtests are any higher. In other words, the subtests correlate as closely with one another as they correlate with themselves. These findings definitely suggest that the various parts of the paragraph test measure functions which are either practically identical or closely related. It follows that the extra scoring time required to secure a score on the individual subtests is essentially wasted, since these scores yield no information which cannot be secured directly from the pupil's total score on the paragraph test. * This report gives a statistical analysis of results of the Nelson Silent Reading Test for more than three thousand ninth-grade pupils in Cincinnati. The essential findings are as follows: (1) The test is sufficiently difficult so that few ninth-grade pupils get maximum or nearly maximum scores. (2) In Grade IX the test yields scores the variability of which is as great as the variability of scores made by pupils in grades below the ninth. (3) The ninth-grade norms given in the *Teacher's Manual* agree closely with the median scores of the ninth-grade population of a large city (Cincinnati). (4) The three subtests of the paragraph test, which are intended to measure distinct aspects of reading ability, really measure functions which are closely related. Individual scores on these subtests yield little diagnostic information which cannot be secured from the total paragraph score.

[1559]

Ophthalm-O-Graph. 1936; a portable camera, using 35 mm. standard motion picture film, which photographs eye movements while the examinee is engaged in the act of reading; for A.C. or D.C., $275; Form R record card, 65¢ per 100; Southbridge, Mass.: American Optical Company.

REFERENCES

1 IMUS, HENRY A.; ROTHNEY, JOHN W. M.; AND BEAR, ROBERT M. *An Evaluation of Visual Factors in Reading.* The Dartmouth Eye Institute of the Dartmouth Medical School, Hanover, N. H.: Dartmouth College Publications, 1938. Pp. xiv, 144. $1.50. Paper.
2 DOLCH, EDWARD WILLIAM. *A Manual for Remedial Reading*, pp. 159-62. Champaign, Ill.: Garrard Press, 1939. Pp. x, 166. $2.00.

G. T. Buswell, Professor of Educational Psychology, The University of Chicago. The *Ophthalm-O-Graph* is a portable eye-movement camera patented by the American Optical Company. In common with most cameras built for this purpose, it has two lenses which may be used for photographing both eyes or one eye plus a head line. The instrument is suitable for ordinary clinical purposes but is not suitable for precise scientific work. The principal criticisms of the *Ophthalm-O-Graph* as a scientific instrument for the reading clinic are three in number.

First, the apparatus lacks a precise timing device, the only means of measuring the duration of a pause of the eye being to measure the length of the eye-line on the film and then translate this into units of time. Although a synchronous motor is used, the film runs slowly which allows a considerable margin of error in measuring brief pauses. Still more serious is the fact that precise measurement is impossible where there are vertical movements of the head, since these elongate or shorten the eye-line. The errors may compensate in computing averages, but the apparatus is not reliable for measuring duration of individual pauses.

A second criticism of the apparatus is that the material to be read is placed below the lenses in such a position that only a very short sample of reading material can be used. The reliability of such short records is open to serious question. There are various ways in which a camera might be constructed to obviate this difficulty. Longer samples of reading are necessary for either scientific study or accurate diagnosis.

A third criticism applies to the head rest device. In all of the models which the reviewer has seen, a chin rest has been used. This is the worst possible position to support the head, because any tendency to vocalize is immediately translated into vertical head movements which, in turn, cause errors in measuring the duration of fixations and in determining the exact position of a fixation.

Aside from the foregoing criticisms the apparatus is a convenient portable device for use in a reading clinic. It is compact, light in weight, and reasonably substantial in construction.

In order to use the *Ophthalm-O-Graph* for purposes of diagnosing reading ability, reliable standards are needed for studying growth from grade to grade. The writer has been unable to find the scientific data underlying the standards which appear in the advertising material distributed by the American Optical Company.

Furthermore, the reading materials on which the "norms" are based are not shown nor is there a description of precise conditions under which they were obtained. Without these qualifying facts the norms are scientifically useless. The nearest to a body of data of the type needed appeared in the Dartmouth College study.[1] However, the reliability of the samples in this study is open to serious criticism.

Since the research laboratory ordinarily develops and standardizes its own materials, the lack of adequate norms supplied by the distributor of the apparatus is not important. However, in view of the fact that by far the largest number of *Ophthalm-O-Graphs* used for educational purposes are found in schools where there are no adequately trained technicians, the absence of carefully standardized norms and reading materials is so serious that little educational value can result from the investment. An eye-movement camera is essentially a scientific rather than a clinical instrument.

The *Ophthalm-O-Graph* has certain values for the medical clinic quite apart from its value in the reading clinic. The criticisms expressed above apply to the employment of the *Ophthalm-O-Graph* as an instrument for use in the school.

Sch and Soc 52:205-8 S 14 '40. M. E. Broom. "The Reliability of the Reading Graph Yielded by the Ophthalmograph." * 1. The reliability coefficients of the tests of fixations, regressions and reading speed are too low in value to permit the use of these measures with individuals. 2. The reliability of the comprehension test is such that this test should never be used for the measurement of comprehension during silent reading. This is a minor defect, however, since this test functions primarily to motivate the subjects' actual reading performance. 3. The present information concerning the reliability of the tests is of doubtful value, and the truth as to the reliability of these measures probably will not be known until studies are made in which the same card is used for both the initial test and the re-test of the same individuals, and possibly not until adequately standardized duplicate and equivalent card materials are available for use with the ophthalmograph. While the present card test materials are not sufficiently reliable, they have served education through bringing be-

fore the public a better knowledge of the approximate recognition span that is found at various grade, and maturity, levels. The present card tests have rendered also a service in permitting the determination of gross progress made by groups of pupils. The writer still believes that the ophthalmograph has definite values as a prognostic and clinical instrument, but it is doubtful whether the full value of the instrument will be known until the card test materials have been scientifically standardized.

Dolch, Edward William. A Manual for Remedial Reading, pp. 159-62. (Champaign, Ill.: Garrard Press, 1939. Pp. x, 166. $2.00.) For many years, laboratories which studied reading problems have photographed eye movements. The machine used contained the usual 35-mm. motion-picture film which moved at a constant rate behind a pair of lenses. Each lens focused upon the film spots of light reflected from the reader's eyeballs and which were cast on the eye by a light shining through a small hole in a box which contained an electric bulb. Every movement of the pair of eyes was recorded upon the film by the movement of the spots of light reflected from the eyeballs. The standard procedure was to ask the subject to read five or six lines on a card placed at the proper reading distance and thus to secure on the film a record of the eye movements during this reading. The purpose of photographing the eye movements has been to study what were called "reading habits." It was assumed that the eyes of each individual moved in certain habitual ways during reading. If then a record of the eyes' habitual movements could be secured, it was assumed that remedial exercises could be given to change these habits. There has now been put on the market a very compact and effective machine for making eye movement photographs. Reading clinics everywhere have these machines and they are also found in the offices of school psychologists and others interested in the problems of poor readers. Many schools are wondering whether they should possess one of these machines or, if they have one, how they should use it. First of all, it must be said that no one should imagine, when he has secured an eye movement photograph for a child that he has fully adequate material for a diagnosis of that child's reading difficulties. The eye movement photograph tells what the child's eyes did in reading a certain short selection at a certain time. It does not tell what the child's eyes do in reading at all times. Two variables must be always kept in mind. (1) The child's reading changes as the material changes. The photograph shows the reading of a certain test card. Suppose an easier card had been used, or a harder one. It is easily shown in the photographing of the eye movement that we can change the record on the film in many ways by changing the material that the child is asked to read. This does not mean that the child does not have eye movement habits. Instead it shows either that he has various habits or that his habits change with changing conditions. (2) The other variable is the child's purpose, we find that we can change the record on the film by telling the child to read rapidly or to read very carefully or in some other special way. The standard directions for photographing eye movements are: You should read as rapidly as you can, remembering that you will answer a few questions about what you have read. It has been found that the direction "read rapidly" registers strongly with some children and causes them to hurry more than usual; while the warning about a "few questions" registers with others and causes them to slow down. These two limitations of the photograph secured by use of the machine are very important when we think of the kind of reading we are going to have the remedial case do. We are not going to have him read these standard cards with these standard directions. We are going to give him school books and other books of various degrees of difficulty and of interest for him. We are going to give him many purposes in reading and ask him all sorts of questions. Therefore, the eye movement photograph showing reading of a certain piece of text, following certain directions, is a *sample* of the child's eye movement. It is a *special* sample which must be taken as such. It is valuable if one remembers exactly the card the child was reading and the exact conditions which surrounded that reading. The photograph is valuable especially to a person who has personally taught many remedial cases how to read. Such a person understands how the child's mind works and what effects him and how. As a part of this total understanding of the remedial process, the sample given by the photograph is helpful. But a study of eye movement

photographs, apart from the child's total situation, is definitely misleading and may be clearly harmful. The concept that the child has a single reading habit, supposed to be very like a habit of handwriting, leads to mechanical exercises which may not at all fit the whole complicated situation. Such a partial and distorted view of the use of eye movement photographs is by all means to be avoided. Second, we wish to point out that eye movement photographs need to be interpreted in detail. Common practice is to count the forward movements, count the regressive movements, and give averages, including fixations per 100 words, regressions per 100 words, duration of fixations per 100 words, number of words per fixation, and num- of words per minute. These averages may or may not be very significant depending upon how uniform the child's performance was during the reading of the lines. But in a reading case the chances are against uniform performance. One line may consist of familiar words and may be read with ease. Another line may contain an unknown word which causes great confusion, with many regressions, long fixations, or a mere wavering of the eyes back and forth. And still another line may contain an unfamiliar idea which causes a mental confusion which shows itself in hesitating and confused eye movements. Therefore, to interpret a strip of film showing the reading of a number of lines of print, one must lay down beside the film the card which was read and compare the two line by line to try to discover the causes for the many kinds of movement which the film shows. While doing this one must remember the question raised above, whether the particular card was probably easy for the child to read, hard for him to read, contained certain unknown words or the like. It is in this interpretation of eye movement records that there has been the greatest failure to make proper use of them. Third, we must call attention to the check on comprehension which accompanies the usual photographing of eye movements. The standard procedure gives ten statements on the back of each card which is read. Immediately after the photographing, these statements are read to the child, and he answers "yes" or "no" depending on whether the statements agree with the paragraph just read. Thus the check on comprehension is planned to be immediate memory as determined by true or false statements. The percentage of statements which the pupil gets right is called his comprehension score. Several comments need to be made concerning this comprehension score. First, it is obvious that mere chance would give on the average a comprehension score of 50 per cent. This fact is keenly appreciated by all workers in education who use true and false or yes-no tests. It must not be forgotten here. Second, we must point out that many of the questions can be answered from previous knowledge. This has been found to be an especial difficulty with some of the cards which deal with facts in history. It is to some extent a difficulty with all the cards because about half of the statements are always false, and common sense or general experience will often detect falsity even without the reading of the cards. Third, it is found that the child, when first photographed, generally paid so much attention to the unusual experience that he was not trying hard enough to remember details. But after having tried to answer ten questions on one card he will be more cautious next time in his reading and therefore be able to answer more questions. We should know, therefore, whether an eye movement photograph is the first one made or whether it had been preceded by others. Finally, we must raise the question whether the kind of reading in which a child tries to remember ten details from six lines of text is the kind we are trying to teach in remedial reading. This is really part of the question which we raised in the last section, whether the type of reading done with the eye photographing machine is typical of the type of reading we are planning on teaching.

For reviews by Stella S. Center, David Kopel, Marion Monroe, Joseph Tiffin, and Miles A. Tinker, see 1108.

[1559.1]
Parr Skill-Ability Tests. Grades 9-16; 1938-40; 4 parts; Frank W. Parr; Corvallis, Ore.: O. S. C. Cooperative Association.
a) CONCENTRATION. 1940; 1 form; 4¢ per test, 50 or more.
b) OUTLINING. 1938; 1 form; 8¢ per test, 50 or more.
c) READING. 1938; 2 forms; 6¢ per test, 50 or more.
d) VOCABULARY. 1938; 2 forms; 10¢ per test, 50 or more; 28(35) minutes.

[1560]
Peabody Library Information Test, Revised Edition. Grades 13-16; 1938; 1 form; $1.25 per 25; 20¢ per specimen set; 32(40) minutes; Louis Shores and Joseph E. Moore; Minneapolis, Minn.: Educational Test Bureau, Inc.

[1561]
Poley Précis Test: A Test by Paragraph Summaries of Reading Comprehension. Grades 9-12; 1927; 2 forms; 75¢ per 25; 15¢ per specimen set; 40(45) minutes; Irvin C. Poley; Bloomington, Ill.: Public School Publishing Co.

Edward A. Tenney, Associate Professor of English, Cornell University. The *Poley Précis Test* is a sound device for determining a student's ability to read intelligently. In it, a student must judge the accuracy of forty précis (five each for eight selections), and he must label each précis as "right," "inadequate," or "wrong." The usefulness of the test is not confined to those who have studied précis-writing; it can readily be used to test anyone's ability to understand what he reads. A further advantage is that ample time is allowed. In consequence the ability to read rather than speed of reading is tested.

The publishers assert that "the test is also useful in diagnosing individual reading difficulties. . . . The eight selections in the test exemplify widely different fields of interest." The truth of this assertion is questionable, for six of the selections are literary; two are scientific. One of these two (Selection VI) by reason of its elaborate concluding simile is as "literary" as it is "scientific." Before a trustworthy diagnosis can be made, a series of précis tests including the same number of selections from poetry, from prose fiction, from expository prose, from argumentative prose, and from philosophical and scientific prose must be given.

This reviewer thinks that the attempt to carry the diagnosis to so fine a point is both futile and unnecessary. The ability to understand any passage of general writing, poetry or prose, literary or scientific, is based upon the accuracy and extent of the reader's vocabulary, upon his knowledge of the structure of sentences and paragraphs, and upon his ability to follow a logical argument or to imagine characters and scenes. If this is true, a diagnostic reading test should try to discover whether some one of these powers is weaker than another; for when they are well developed in a reader, he can encompass the meaning of all kinds of general writing. The *Poley Précis Test* does test these powers and is therefore useful; but it is not, in my opinion, a very accurate diagnosis of a student's capacity to interpret different kinds of literature.

363] *TESTS AND REVIEWS: READING* 1563

Those who are interested in testing not the speed at which a student reads nor his special powers but his general capacity to get the exact sense of what he reads will find these précis tests very useful.

[1562]
Primary Reading Test. Grade 1; 1939; 1 form; 85¢ per 25; single specimen set free; nontimed (40-55) minutes; Albert G. Reilley; Boston, Mass.: Houghton Mifflin Co.

[1563]
Progressive Reading Tests. Grades 1-3, 3-6, 7-9, 9-13; 1934-39; identical to the reading tests in the battery *Progressive Achievement Tests*; 4 levels; 75¢ per 25; 15¢ per specimen set of any one level; 2¢ per machine-scorable answer sheets; Ernest W. Tiegs and Willis W. Clark; Los Angeles, Calif.: California Test Bureau.
a) PRIMARY. Grades 1-3; 1934-37; 3 forms; 35(40) minutes.
b) ELEMENTARY. Grades 3-6; 1934-39; 3 forms; 35(40) minutes; *Machine Scoring Edition*: 2 forms; 5¢ per test.
c) INTERMEDIATE. Grades 7-9; 1934-39; 3 forms; 50(55) minutes; *Machine Scoring Edition*: 2 forms; 5¢ per test.
d) ADVANCED. Grades 9-13; 1934-39; 2 forms; 50(55) minutes; *Machine Scoring Edition*: 2 forms; 5¢ per test.

Frederick B. Davis, Reading and Professional Education Editor, Cooperative Test Service, New York, New York; and Educational Psychologist and Head of the Remedial Department, Avon Old Farms, Avon, Connecticut. The *Progressive Reading Tests* appear to be well-planned and carefully constructed measures of reading ability. In each manual particular emphasis is placed upon the fact that subtest scores, valuable for individual diagnosis, may be obtained in addition to the total score. On the cover of each test booklet is printed a diagnostic profile for graphic presentation of the subtest scores and a classification of the test items. These are unquestionably useful, but it is unfortunate that the manual contains no warning of the inevitable unreliability of subtest scores based on only a small number of items.

The writer consulted the manual for the Advanced Battery and, using data concerning the reliabilities of the tests and distributions of the scores at the eleventh grade level, estimated the standard errors of measurement for the vocabulary test and its four subtests and for the reading-comprehension test and its three subtests. The results of these calculations are somewhat discouraging because it appears that only the total reading score may be regarded as reasonably accurate in individual measurement. Subtest scores near the median may readily vary as much as thirty percentile-rank points on the diagnostic profile by pure chance.

It is clear that such great inaccuracy in the subtest scores means that the profile chart should be regarded as merely suggestive of possible variations in an individual pupil's reading skills. As such, it is of some value. Incidentally, the chart could be improved simply by relocating the percentile points in terms of the distances corresponding to standard deviation units.

The directions for all of the tests specify that pupils are to be stopped on each test when 90 per cent of the group has finished. Because the tests measure power rather than speed these directions are possible. However, the fact that the tests are often administered in schools where the practice of ability grouping is followed makes this kind of time limit undesirable. The better pupils in a low-ability group have an advantage over the poorer pupils in a high-ability group. For example, consider the case of two pupils of equal reading ability; one takes the test with a group of poor readers, the other takes the test with a group of good readers. The pupil in the group of poor readers is likely to obtain a higher score on the test simply because his companions take a longer time to finish.

Users of the Intermediate Battery should make sure that they have the proper norms. The most recent edition can be identified by the heading of the table on page 10, which should read: Norms (1937 Revision): Including revised extension of norms above 9.5 in 1939. One of the earlier editions, printed on pink paper, contained two misprints on page 10. At grade level 11.0 in the reading vocabulary norms, 99 should be read for 79; at grade level 15.0 in the age norms, 241 should be read for 214.

SUMMARY. The total reading test score derived from each of the four *Progressive Reading Tests* appears to be a valid and reliable index of reading ability. The Diagnostic Profile, however, is useful in individual measurement only to provide possible clues for remedial work or as the basis for further diagnostic testing.

For reviews by Ivan A. Booker and Joseph C. Dewey, see 1110. For reviews by D. Welty

Lefever, C. W. Odell, and Hugh B. Wood of the complete battery, see 876 and 1193.

[1564]

Reading Comprehension: Cooperative English Test, Tests C1 and C2. Grades 7-12, 11-16; 1940; 2 levels, Form Q; 5¢ per test, 10 to 99 copies; 1½¢ per machine-scorable answer sheet; 25¢ per specimen set; 40(45) minutes; Frederick B. Davis, F. S. Beers, Warner F. Gookin, D. G. Paterson, and Mary Willis with the cooperation of Walter F. Dearborn, Donald D. Durrell, Daniel D. Feder, William S. Gray, Arthur E. Traxler, and Louis C. Zahner; New York: Cooperative Test Service.

a) TEST C1, LOWER LEVEL. Grades 7-12.
b) TEST C2, UPPER LEVEL. Grades 11-16.

REFERENCES

1 Cooperative Test Service. *The Cooperative Reading Comprehension Tests*: Information Concerning their Construction, Interpretation, and Use. New York: Cooperative Test Service, 1940. Pp. 4. Gratis. Paper.
2 TRAXLER, ARTHUR. "The Cooperative English Test, Form Q: Correlations with School Marks and Intercorrelations," pp. 42-50. In *1940 Achievement Testing Program in Independent Schools and Supplementary Studies*. Educational Records Bureau Staff. Educational Records Bulletin, No. 30. New York: the Bureau, June 1940. Pp. xii, 76. $1.50. Paper, lithotyped.

[1565]

Sangren-Woody Reading Test. Grades 4-8; 1927-28; 2 forms; $1.25 per 25; 15¢ per specimen set; 27(35-40) minutes; Paul V. Sangren and Clifford Woody; Yonkers, N. Y.: World Book Co.

REFERENCES

1 SANGREN, PAUL V. "The Need for More Adequate Measures of Achievement in Silent Reading." *J Ed Res* 17:365-71 My '28.
2 DOUGLAS, JOSEPHINE, AND LAWSON, J. W. "Measurement of Reading Skills in Ability Groups." *J Appl Psychol* 13:494-8 O '29.
3 SANGREN, PAUL V. "The Sangren-Woody Silent Reading Test." *J Ed Res* 19:233-4 Mr '29.
4 FORAN, T. G., AND ROCK, ROBERT T., JR. *The Reliability of Some Silent Reading Tests.* Catholic University of America, Educational Research Bulletin, Vol. 5, No. 6. Washington, D. C.: Catholic Education Press, June 1930. Pp. 23. $0.35. Paper.
5 BROOM, M. EUSTACE; DOUGLAS, JOSEPHINE; AND RUDD, MARION. "On the Validity of Silent Reading Tests." *J Appl Psychol* 15:35-8 F '31.
6 "Report on Sangren-Woody Reading Test." *Pittsburgh Sch* 6:3-67 S '31.
7 SANGREN, PAUL V. Chapter 9, "Critical Study of a Silent Reading Test," pp. 165-76. *Improvement of Reading Through the Use of Tests.* Kalamazoo, Mich.: Extension Department, Western State Teachers College, 1932. Pp. 207. Paper. Out of print.

Alice K. Liveright, Principal of the Logan Demonstration School, Public Schools, Philadelphia, Pennsylvania. The *Sangren-Woody Reading Test* is admirably suited both for diagnostic purposes and to provide a comprehensive survey of silent reading ability. It consists of seven tests each of which deals with a distinct phase of the reading process. Silent reading vocabulary is tested through Part I, Word Meaning. The child indicates his knowledge of the meaning of a word by choosing from among four words that which best shows the use of the original word in a sentence.

In Part II, Rate, the child is asked to read a selection of about four hundred words as rapidly as is consistent with understanding. Rate is indicated by the number of words read during the first minute.

In Part III, Fact Material, the selection is the same as that used in Part II. Each paragraph, however, is followed by one or more factual questions. The answer, one or a few words, is written in the space provided.

Part IV, Total Meaning, likewise consists of a series of short paragraphs. Each is followed by a question which asks about the total meaning. Each question in turn is followed by four words. The pupil is asked to underline the word which best answers the question.

Part V, Central Thought, consists of paragraphs each followed by four statements. The pupil is expected to check the statement which expresses the central or important thought of the paragraph.

Part VI, Following Directions, contains ten paragraphs, each of which comprises one or more simple directions. The child's responses indicate whether he has understood the directions.

Part VII, Organization, consists of a number of sets of paragraphs with each set followed by a series of four statements in disarranged order. The pupil numbers them to indicate their correct order.

The authors have exercised great care to insure validity and reliability. A table of grade equivalents derived from the results of a huge number of pupils contains not only median scores for grades, but also for each month of the grade. Alternate forms are available.

Considering the comprehensive scope of the test, it is both short and simple to administer. The total time required is less than forty minutes. If necessary, the test may be given in two sittings. The scoring key may be fitted to each part of the test and the scoring is thus simplified as much as possible. Part VII alone is a bit complicated in arrangement and cumbersome to score. It requires the pupil to turn the paper both upside down and back and forward. This does prove confusing to some pupils and renders the scoring tedious.

Each test booklet includes a profile chart. The scores for each part of the test when indicated as directed on this chart form an individual reading profile. The pupil, parent, and teacher can at a glance note from the profile in which abilities the pupil is weak and in which he is strong. Pupils take a keen interest in the chart. They understand their reading strengths and weaknesses.

As the scores correlate well with those of shorter survey tests, the Sangren-Woody may be used for survey purposes. Its unique feature is its excellent diagnostic value. The most important skills required in study reading are all included. The organization test, however, covers one factor in organization only. To organize requires abilities other than arranging statements in proper sequence. The test is on the whole, nevertheless, quite comprehensive.

Both pupils and teachers receive the test enthusiastically. The child learns both his reading strengths and weaknesses. As few normal pupils fail in all parts, discouragement is avoided. After the test has been administered, each child may receive the special type of remedial exercise he needs and each may read with the specific purpose of making good his particular type of deficiency. When the teacher has administered the test, she is no longer satisfied with merely assigning more miscellaneous so-called remedial exercises. She helps each child to find the specific type of remedial exercise he requires.

[1566]

Schrammel-Gray High School and College Reading Test. Grades 7-13; 1940; 1 form; $1.50 per 25; 30¢ per specimen set; 25(30) minutes; H. E. Schrammel and W. H. Gray; Bloomington, Ill.: Public School Publishing Co.

[1567]

Shank Tests of Reading Comprehension. Grades 3-6, 7-9, 10-12; 1929; 3 forms, 3 levels; $3.20 per 25; 30¢ per manual;[1] 30¢ per specimen set, not including manual; quantity discounts; Spencer Shank; Cincinnati, Ohio: C. A. Gregory Co.
a) TEST I. Grades 3-6. 18(28) minutes.
b) TEST II. Grades 7-9. 20(30) minutes.
c) TEST III. Grades 10-12. 20(30) minutes.

REFERENCES

1 SHANK, SPENCER. *Student Responses in the Measurement of Reading Comprehension*: A Manual of Directions for the Shank Reading Tests. Cincinnati, Ohio: C. A. Gregory Co., 1929. Pp. 69. $0.30. Paper.
2 SHANK, SPENCER. "Student Responses in the Measurement of Reading Comprehension." *J Ed Res* 22:119-29 S '30.
3 TRAXLER, ARTHUR E. "One Reading Test Serves the Purpose." *Clearing House* 14:419-21 Mr '40.

James R. Hobson, Director of Child Placement, Brookline Public Schools, Brookline, Massachusetts. The author of this series of tests started with the assumption that reading comprehension is a composite of many separate but perhaps related abilities which cannot be measured by any single type of test response.

A complete analysis of forty-five reading tests then available for use in grades three through twelve showed that attempts had been made to measure at least seven general kinds of reading comprehension skills as indicated by the types of student response called for in the various tests.

The question of deciding which types of student response should be called for in the series under construction was solved partly by the logical consideration of the practical problems involved and partly by the construction and administration of two experimental forms of the test. Types of response which bore no relation to the content of the paragraph were eliminated as were also types of response requiring a particular kind of content and types requiring a special physical setup of the test. The response types remaining which are applicable to the reading of paragraph units as found in general literature are listed by the author as follows: (*a*) responses based upon giving details stated directly in the reading content, (*b*) responses based upon giving details implied in the content, (*c*) responses based upon giving thought implied in the content as a whole, (*d*) responses based upon determining whether or not the content stated a certain given idea, (*e*) responses based upon giving objects or thoughts to which given words refer, (*f*) responses based upon determining whether given statements are true or false, and (*g*) responses based upon selecting words of synonymous or similar meanings.

The next step in the development of this series of tests was an attempt to measure the effectiveness with which each of the above types of response measures reading comprehension when applied to the same paragraph. This was done by correlating the scores obtained from each response type with (*a*) the scores obtained from a test made up of all types, (*b*) teachers' marks, and (*c*) intelligence quotients. The results of these comparisons obtained through the administration of two experimental forms of the test series showed definite trends in the correlation of each of the types of comprehension skills included in the test with each of the three criteria chosen as a check on the validity of the test. These comparisons also revealed certain tendencies concerning the varying effectiveness from grade to grade with which each of the types of response included in the test measured reading comprehension. For example, it is of interest to note that Type *f* correlated highest on the whole with all three of the criteria while the correlation of Type *g* with each of the criteria increased with the increase in grade level. Apparently these results were used to justify the inclusion of four questions of Type *f* on each test paragraph as compared with one question requiring each of the other types of response. The trend just mentioned in regard to Type *g* as well as the fact that it was the only type to correlate more highly with IQ than with teachers' marks in reading resulted in the exclusion of questions of this type from Test I for grades 3-6.

The validity of the completed form of the test is indicated by mean *r*'s of .69, .62, and .63 between total test scores and average academic marks for Tests I, II, and III respectively, and by mean *r*'s of .66, .69, and .66 between total test scores and average IQ for the same tests. Multiple *R*'s from total scores, academic achievement marks, and IQ's averaged above .75. The number of cases in each grade averaged about 65.

The coefficient of reliability for each test obtained by the intercorrelation of the three forms of each test on more than 100 cases at each grade level is .90. The equivalence of the three forms of each test is indicated by the average score obtained from the administration of these three forms to an unmentioned number of pupils over the whole grade range of each test. No data are given regarding their equivalence from grade to grade. Age and grade norms based upon the administration of the three tests to approximately 5,000 pupils in grades 3-12 are given. These pupils represent both urban and rural districts in three states. The grade norms given are for the end of the semester in each case. The number of pupils in each grade or at each age upon which the norms are based is not given.

Criticisms of such well-constructed and altogether usable instruments as these tests must necessarily be minor ones. It does not appear to this reviewer that the evidence presented warrants four true-false questions about each paragraph as contrasted with one question of each of the other types. Incidentally, this would serve to make the correlation between Type *f* and the whole test spuriously high. The method of scoring the responses to this type of question is not in line with current practice and does not appear to be defended satisfactorily. The use of negative statements when false statements are to be marked introduces the idea of the double negative which is unnecessarily confusing to children in the elementary grades. The reasons for the elimination of certain response types which are included in other instruments of recognized value in this field seem in some instances at least to be trival and inconclusive.

There is no question, however, but that this series of tests will rate highly as judged by any objective check list of desirable test qualities which may be applied to them. Their diagnostic features should appeal to classroom teachers while such features as careful selection and editing of content and gradation of vocabulary and concept level make them interesting to the pupils to whom they are administered. The thoroughness and scientific nature of the procedures followed in the development of this series of tests may well serve as an example to test authors. The steps taken in the conception, development, and standardization of these tests are explained in detail in the manual which accompanies them. The completeness and objective quality of this report should commend this series of tests to the test consumer who objects to buying on faith alone.

[1568]

Silent Reading Comprehension: Iowa Every-Pupil Tests of Basic Skills, Test A. Grades 3-5, 6-8; 1940; Form L, 2 levels; 30¢ per manual; 12¢ per booklet of norms; 40¢ per 25 record cards; single specimen set free; H. F. Spitzer in collaboration with Ernest Horn, Maude McBroom, H. A. Greene, and E. F. Lindquist with the assistance of the faculty of the University Experimental Schools, State University of Iowa; Boston, Mass.: Houghton Mifflin Co.
a) ELEMENTARY BATTERY. Grades 3-5; $1.15 per 25; 44(50) minutes.
b) ADVANCED BATTERY. Grades 6-8; $1.25 per 25; 67(85) minutes.

[1569]

Southeastern Problems and Prospects, Social Studies and English [Reading Test]: Booklet No. 1. Grades 10-16; 1938; 8¢ per test; 2¢ per machine-scorable answer sheet; 12¢ per sample test; 180(190) minutes; English Commission of the Association of Georgia Colleges; Athens, Ga.: the Association, c/o F. S. Beers, Memorial Hall.

[1570]

Standardized Oral Reading Check Tests. Grades 1-2, 2-4, 4-7, 6-8; 1923; 5 forms, 4 levels; $1.50 per 20 tests, including all 5 forms; 50¢ per specimen set; 15¢ per specimen set of any one set; nontimed (1-3) minutes; William S. Gray; Bloomington, Ill.: Public School Publishing Co.
a) SET I. Grades 1-2.
b) SET II. Grades 2-4.
c) SET III. Grades 4-7.
d) SET IV. Grades 6-8.

REFERENCES
1 CAMP, CORDELIA, AND ALLEN, C. H. "How Oral Reading Was Improved through the Use of Gray's Check Tests." *El Sch J* 30:132-5 O '29.

David H. Russell, Assistant Professor of Education, The University of Saskatchewan. These tests consist of four sets, each containing five tests of approximately equal difficulty. Each test consists of a paragraph or paragraphs to be read orally in the presence of an examiner who records errors and the time required. One commendable feature of the tests, then, is the fact that the four sets allow testing at a reading level closer to the child's actual reading ability than is usually obtained in a reading test which is part of an achievement battery. Another advantage of the test is the availability of five forms of approximately equal difficulty, thus allowing for frequent retesting. These values are somewhat impaired for the test reviewer (if not the test user) by the fact that little information is given on how the material for the tests was selected or how the tests in any one set were equated. In the ten-line description of the construction of the tests it is stated that the tests "have been revised three times after each test of a set was given to no less than 120 pupils each time." There is no further statement on the sheet of directions regarding efforts to determine the validity or reliability of these tests at the four levels. The description states rather conservatively, then, that "the standard scores for rate and accuracy which follow are more or less tentative."

The uses to which a reading test may be put are probably at least as important as its material or grading. The *Standardized Oral Reading Check Tests* aim, first, to be a measure of oral reading. They probably accomplish this as well as other available oral reading tests but, like other tests, they make no attempt to measure such factors as rhythm, phrasing, interpretation, bodily position, etc., which, after all, are significant to the effectiveness of oral reading in the audience situation. Another weakness of the test is that there is no check on the comprehension of what is read. The accuracy records might include more than the actual errors made.

The second use that is suggested for these tests is to determine the specific nature of a pupil's difficulties. The diagnostic value of these, and certain other oral reading tests, would seem to be much greater than that of most silent reading tests. The Individual Record Sheet that accompanies the tests gives rather complete instructions for recording mis-

pronunciations, omissions, substitutions, repetitions, and insertions of words or parts of words. Space is provided for tabulating these errors on this sheet. Such a procedure should be valuable to the diagnostician. This value could be greatly enhanced, however, by additional information as to the seriousness of the number of these errors in relation to the number of errors usually made by children at a particular reading level. For example, the poor reader may make many more omissions and mispronunciations than insertions or repetitions on these tests, but this may not be atypical at his level, and so no hints as to causes of retardation can be obtained. The *Gates Oral-Context Test VI, 2* in the *Gates Reading Diagnosis Tests,* for example, allows for such comparisons and also analyzes types of mispronunciation more fully. The practised diagnostician, however, should find the analysis of errors on the Individual Record Sheet of considerable value.

The prospective purchaser of these tests should not confuse them with Gray's *Standardized Oral Reading Paragraphs* published by the same company.

Clarence R. Stone, 2140 Los Angeles Avenue, Berkeley, California. There are four sets or levels of these tests ranging from first-grade to seventh- or eighth-grade material. Each set or level has five forms of the test constructed to be of equal difficulty, thereby making possible repeated tests at intervals to measure progress. A very satisfactory plan of recording the child's errors on a copy of the test is provided. The reviewer has found these tests very valuable for measuring progress and for stimulating interest on the part of the individual in improving his oral reading. The progress can be easily graphed in terms of decreasing errors.

These tests were constructed before we had any graded vocabulary lists. Consequently, the series could now be improved by the use of graded vocabulary lists available and by providing one set or level for each school grade.

[1571]

Standardized Oral Reading Paragraphs. Grades 1-8; 1915; individual; 1 form; $1.00 per 100; 6¢ per specimen set; nontimed (5-15) minutes; William S. Gray; Bloomington, Ill.: Public School Publishing Co.

REFERENCES

1 GRAY, WILLIAM S. *A Tentative Scale for the Measurement of Oral-Reading Achievement.* Unpublished master's thesis, Columbia University, 1914.

2 GRAY, WILLIAM SCOTT. *Studies of Elementary-School Reading through Standardized Tests.* University of Chicago, Supplementary Educational Monographs, Vol. 1, No. 1. Chicago, Ill.: University of Chicago Press, 1917. Pp. viii, 157. Paper. Out of print.

3 MONROE, WALTER S. "A Simplified Method of Determining a Pupil's Score on Gray's Oral Reading Test." *Sch and Soc* 15:538 40 My 13 '22.

4 PAYNE, C. S. *The Derivation of Tentative Norms for Short Exposures in Reading.* Harvard Monographs in Education, No. 10. Cambridge, Mass.: Harvard University Press, 1930. Pp. 84. $1.00. Paper. (London: Oxford University Press. 4s. 6d.)

5 GATES, ARTHUR I. *The Improvement of Reading*: Revised edition, p. 533. New York: Macmillan Co., 1935. Pp. xvii, 668. $2.50. (London: Macmillan & Co., Ltd. 8s. 6d.)

6 BUCKINGHAM, B. R., AND DOLCH, E. W. *A Combined Word List.* Boston, Mass.: Ginn and Co., 1936. Pp. iii, 185. $1.50.

7 STONE, CLARENCE R. *Graded Vocabulary for Primary Reading.* St. Louis, Mo.: Webster Publishing Co., 1936. Pp. 61. $0.50. Paper.

David Kopel, Department of Education, Chicago Teachers College. This widely used individual test consists of twelve brief paragraphs arranged in order of difficulty of content. The first paragraph is primer material; each succeeding paragraph appears to represent an increment in difficulty of approximately one grade. The scoring of each paragraph is based upon the speed of reading and number of errors. The composite score is interpreted by reference to a table of norms or standards which are available for grades 1-8.

Several desirable qualities are to be found in the test. Its administration requires but a few minutes; directions are rather simple and easily learned; scoring is fairly objective (examiners will differ occasionally as to what represents an "error" and as to the meaning of "several seconds"—the amount of time one should wait before helping the child with a word he cannot pronounce). Use of the instrument yields a grade score which crudely classifies a child as to grade level of reading ability. An important by-product is the opportunity to observe many characteristics of the child's reading: type and frequency of errors, fluency and meaningfulness of reading, use of punctuation devices, skill in recognizing and analyzing words in context, emotional reactions to oral reading of increasingly difficult materials and to possible frustrating experiences that may be involved. Observations made during the test may have considerable diagnostic value as well as definite implications for therapy.

The following limitations in the test should be noted. Comparable forms of the test are not available; hence one must estimate practice effect when it is used more than once. Standardization data are not given in the manual provided by the publisher. However, Gates [5] states that grade scores on the test are usually

equivalent to mental grades and reading grades established on other tests. Comprehension of the material read must be checked informally. The validity of the test can and should be determined for the individual with whom it is being employed by having him read aloud *episodes* from various types of graded material chosen in accord with the test finding. An experienced teacher or clinician can readily and meaningfully determine in this manner the real status of the child's ability.

Clarence R. Stone, 2140 Los Angeles Avenue, Berkeley, California. This is a power test with one form consisting of twelve short units of reading matter increasing in difficulty from the primer level to the college level. The score on each unit depends upon the rate of reading and the number of errors made. An excellent plan of recording errors on a copy of the reading material is set forth in the directions. With this test it is possible to determine the level of material the child can read with reasonable accuracy and fluency. Since the test was constructed before we had available any standardized word lists, the material no doubt could be improved by a revision in which the vocabulary would be checked, level by level, against *Graded Vocabulary for Primary Reading* [7] and *A Combined Word List.* [6] The test would also be improved by a more gradual increase in the difficulty of the material.

[1572]

Stevens Reading Readiness Test. Grade 1; 1938; part individual; 1 form; $1 per 25; 10¢ per manual; 15¢ per specimen set; 10 daily sittings over a 2-week period; Avis Coultas Stevens; Columbus, Ohio: American Education Press, Inc.

[1573]

Student Skills Inventory. Experimental Edition. College; 1939; $1 per 25; 15¢ per specimen set; nontimed; Norman M. Locke; New York: Psychological Corporation.

REFERENCES

LOCKE, NORMAN M. "The Students Skills Inventory: A Study Habits Inventory." *J Appl Psychol* 24:493-504 Ag '40.

[1574]

Study-Habits Inventory. Grades 12-16; 1933-34; 1 form; $1.25 per 25; 25¢ per 25 sheets "What Your Score Means"; 10¢ per specimen set; nontimed (10-20) minutes; C. Gilbert Wrenn, assisted by R. B. McKeown; Stanford University, Calif.: Stanford University Press.

Edward S. Jones, Professor of Psychology and Director of Personnel Research, The University of Buffalo. This inventory is made up of a set of thirty items carefully selected from a much larger list of statements and attitudes previously submitted to 220 students at Stanford University. Half of them were in the upper 10 per cent of scholarship and the other half in the lower 20 per cent, the students being paired with each other on the basis of intelligence test scores, so that the difference would not be one of intelligence but a scholastic difference entirely. The 30 items are obviously related to attitudes or situations conducive to study. In fact, nearly half of them beg the question, such as: "I find myself too tired, sleepy, and listless to study efficiently," "I am conscious that I have been out of school too long, or took basic subjects too long ago," and "I read so slowly that I cannot get over all the assignments and outside readings." Naturally, some of the assignments have much greater weight than others. The item of greatest weight is, "My time is unwisely distributed; I spend too much time on some things and not enough on others." Obviously, the use of the adverb "too" presupposes that students knowing that they are good will be inclined to answer corresponding to their particular accomplishments. It is not amazing, therefore, that Wrenn comes out with scores in his tests such that the lowest quartile of the high-scholarship group is definitely above the highest quartile of the low-scholarship group.

It would seem to the reviewer much more satisfactory if a study-habits inventory could be worked up to include greater objectivity, one which could be applied to students before they know what kind of success they are going to achieve in college. Most of the attempts of this type, however, have not proved very diagnostic in differentiating between students because there are so many different standards of mental effort, and because intellectual background and motivation are more important than particular methods of work.

William A. McCall, Professor of Education, Columbia University. This inventory lists thirty habits of study, some good, some bad, and the student indicates whether each habit characterizes him rarely, sometimes, or often. Positive or negative scores of varying amounts are provided for each answer for each item.

The author evidently adopted the inventory instead of the test technique partly because some habits do not readily lend themselves to testing on paper. The inclusion of such habits is easily justified. Such, for example, is Item

27: "I study carefully the outlines in all courses where they are given."

Also the inventory method permits the author to cover much territory rapidly and inexpensively. Consider, for example, Item 5: "I read so slowly that I cannot get over all the assignments and outside readings." It would require much time to test this point, but there will be persons who believe that the more time-consuming procedure is preferable.

The entire inventory must depend upon the student for a truthful report, and, assuming his honesty, must further depend upon his being aware of what the truth is. In Item 8, the student is required to state whether his grades are lowered by faulty command of fundamental subjects. The student may not honestly know. The author commendably suggests uses for the inventory that encourage frank cooperation, thereby weakening somewhat the force of the former of these criticisms.

The items used are the thirty out of sixty-nine which discriminated best between high- and low-scholarship students whose intelligence test scores were approximately equal. Such correlation, even with intelligence partialed out, does not imply causation, yet the author makes several statements in his manual which fail to recognize this fact. If statements are properly guarded, the author is entitled to some leeway in this matter, pending an experimental proof of causal connection between these thirty habits and scholarship.

This reviewer is troubled about those discarded thirty-nine items. The technique of selection condemns these as being relatively unimportant. But are they? The possession of a brain may not distinguish a Nordic from a Mediterranean type but who would suggest therefore, that a brain is not important to a Nordic, and similarly for study-habit items. What better could the author have done? Without more reflection, and possibly with, the reviewer does not know.

Most serious of all, though we can scarcely blame the author for it, Item 23 and the atmosphere of many other items assume the indefensible *status quo* in college education. This is Item 23: "I study with others rather than by myself." When the long overdue revolution occurs in college education such an item, when answered with *often,* will not be heavily penalized. On the contrary, the student who answers *often* will be commended, and rewarded with a positive score, for in such education statistical considerations will be required to serve philosophical considerations.

[1575]

Study Outline Test. Grades 9-16; 1926; 1 form, 3 levels; 75¢ per package containing 25, 15, and 10 copies respectively of Tests I, II, and III; 10¢ per specimen set; nontimed; F. Dean McClusky and Edward William Dolch; Bloomington, Ill.: Public School Publishing Co.
a) TEST I.
b) TEST II. For examinees failing Test I.
c) TEST III. For examinees failing Test II.

REFERENCES

1 McCLUSKY, F. DEAN, AND DOLCH, EDWARD WILLIAM. "A Study Outline Test." *Sch R* 32:757-72 D '24.

Harriet Barthelmess Morrison, Research Assistant, Bureau of Reference, Research and Statistics, Public Schools, New York, New York. The test content consists of a three-paragraph selection. The testee is to designate for each sentence the appropriate number or letter to indicate its position in the outline presumably used by the author. A sample outline indicating the coordinate and subordinate letters and figures to be used is to be put on the blackboard.

The same content is used in all three tests, but with differing degrees of help on the part of the author in the way of "signs" of structure. Test I, the most difficult, is given first. Those pupils not getting a perfect score are given drill on outlining, and then are tested on Test II. Those unable to get a perfect score on this have more drill and then are given Test III, the easiest test. Diagnostic scores for coordination, subordination, and elaboration "give the clue as to the type of drill needed."

Neither the direction sheet nor the publisher's catalog gives any indication of validity or reliability. Nor do we know to what degree the results are conditioned by general reading ability.

The way in which the text is to be outlined is artificial and the pupil results may or may not be indicative of outlining ability in a more functional situation. Nor does the length of the test seem to offer high reliability. However, the development of the same content in three degrees of structural difficulty is ingenious and useful as a teaching aid.

Testing material in this field is limited and the type of test developed here deserves further experimentation.

[1576]

Test of Study Skills. Grades 4-9; 1940; 2 forms; $1.50 per 30, including 30 machine-scorable answer sheets; $1.50 per 100 machine-scorable answer sheets; 10¢ per specimen set; 60(70) minutes; J. W. Edgar and H. T. Manuel; Austin, Tex.: Steck Co.

[1577]

Test on the Use of Books and Libraries: Test 7.3. Grades 7-10; 1939; 2 forms; 10¢ per test; 1¢ per machine-scorable answer sheet; $1 per set of stencils for machine scoring; nontimed (60) minutes; Chicago, Ill.: Evaluation in the Eight Year Study, Progressive Education Association.

[1578]

Traxler High School Reading Test. Grades 10-12; 1938-39; 2 forms; $1.50 per 25; 10¢ per manual; 25¢ per specimen set; adapted to machine scoring; 50(55) minutes; Arthur E. Traxler; Bloomington, Ill.: Public School Publishing Co.

REFERENCES

1 TRAXLER, ARTHUR E. "Relationship between the Length and the Reliability of a Test of Rate of Reading." *J Ed Res* 32:1-2 S '38.

Alvin C. Eurich, Professor of Education, Stanford University. Like the authors of most of the available measures of reading ability, Traxler, in constructing this test, aimed to measure reading rate, understanding, and the ability to locate the central thought in reading a paragraph. The student is asked to read four and a half uninteresting looking pages of fairly easy social science material. The number of words read in five minutes translated into words read per ten seconds, gives the rate score. The understanding of the material read is tested by twenty items, each involving a choice of one of four possible answers. Part II, on finding the main ideas in paragraphs, consists of thirty short paragraphs, each followed by four statements, one of which the student designates as giving the central idea.

The validity of each comprehension question was determined by calculating the degree to which it distinguished the good readers or those in the top fourth of the distribution of total scores, from the poor readers, or those in the lowest fourth.

By discounting the coefficient of reliability derived through the use of the Spearman-Brown formula, the author estimates the reliability of the rate score to be .90. The reliability of the story comprehension score is only .72 for a group of tenth grade pupils. The author is to be commended for recognizing in the Manual that this part of the test is "reliable enough for group studies, but is of limited value for individual prediction." Few authors are so forthright in acknowledging the weaknesses of the instruments they produce. The reliability of Part II, on finding the main ideas in paragraphs is .80 for a group of twelfth grade students. Curiously, and with no explicit reason, the author combines the rate and comprehension scores into a total score for which he did not determine either the reliability or its meaning. The reviewer, therefore, is unable to interpret this total score. It appears much the same as adding up the distance run and the time taken to run it.

Norms for Part II were based on sixteen hundred high school pupils, and for Part I on twenty-one hundred. Percentiles for part scores are given for grades 10, 11, and 12. The directions for administering and scoring the test are clearly stated, and answer sheets are available for machine scoring.

Clearly the understanding and comprehension sections of this test are not as reliable as available reading tests for high school students, such as the *Iowa Silent Reading Test* and the *Nelson-Denny Reading Test*. The rate section, mainly because it is longer than other similar tests, is slightly more reliable. On the whole, the Traxler test does not provide a better instrument for measuring reading ability than those already available; in fact, it is not as good.

Constance M. McCullough, Assistant Professor of Education, Western Reserve University. This test is an upward extension of the *Traxler Silent Reading Test* for grades 7 through 10. Part I, Reading Rate and Story Comprehension, consists of rather easy story material of social studies content. The pupil is asked to read for understanding in order to answer questions at the end of his reading, and to mark his position when the examiner says, *mark* (after 150 and after 300 seconds). This part yields a score on the rate the pupil has chosen to read the passage with understanding. The twenty multiple-choice statements to which the pupil must respond without a second reading of the passage appear to refer to twelve of the twenty paragraphs and cover the "more important points" of the selection. A few concern main ideas; a few, simple inference; and the majority, important details. The score derived from these questions is labeled Story Comprehension. The time limit is generous and flexible so that all may finish responding to the statements.

Part II, Main Ideas in Paragraphs, comprises thirty paragraphs, each followed by four multiple-choice statements, one of which is to be selected as representative of the main idea. Groups of five paragraphs on history alternate with groups of five dealing with natural science. Various kinds of paragraph construction are represented, but none in which the main idea must be inferred. Of the multiple-choice statements, one is a main idea, three are details. The pupil is free to reread the paragraph if necessary. The time limit is generous.

The manual of directions is admirably frank, thorough, and practical. The validity of the test items was established on the performance of the 25 highest and 25 lowest scorers among 400 pupils in grades 10 and 11.

Tentative reliability indices based upon limited data are presented. From data secured by correlating the rates of reading during the first and second 2½-minutes of reading, the author estimates the reliability coefficient to be approximately .90 for pupils in grade 10. For the same group of pupils the reliability of the Story Comprehension score is .72. For the subtest, Main Ideas in Paragraphs, a reliability coefficient of .80 is reported for a group of twelfth grade pupils.

The tentative norms are based upon the scores of sixteen hundred public school pupils in the case of Part I and twenty-one hundred pupils in the case of Part II. Percentile norms for the subtest, Story Comprehension and Main Ideas, are given separately for each grade. The differences in rate among the three grades are so slight that percentile norms for Rate of Reading are given for the three grades combined.

The test may be scored by machine. However, a hand-scoring key is provided. The class record sheet is designed to show individual and class achievement on the parts of the test. Space is given in a column after the individual's name for recording the IQ. It would seem desirable in view of the part reading ability plays in tests of verbal intelligence to have two columns here, one for verbal intelligence scores and one for nonverbal.

Test users should hold certain facts in mind in considering this test. The rate score is more reliable than the rate scores of most speed of reading tests. The Story Comprehension section is practically the only standardized reading examination which tests pure rate of continuous reading for meaning. The reliabilities of the Story Comprehension and Main Ideas sections suggest that test users should not attempt interpretation of individual scores on these parts. However, if an individual conference can be held shortly after the administration of the examination, the pupil's reasons for various responses will give greater meaning to his score and fuller understanding of his particular difficulties.

Because the vocabulary of the test is not particularly difficult, the comprehension scores are chiefly measures of the pupil's ability to understand thought patterns in the social studies and natural science fields. Students of ancient history, however, may be familiar with the content of Part I and may profit by that familiarity in answering the comprehension items. The varied content of Part II would probably not give advantage to any particular pupil. As the entire test is concerned exclusively with materials in the social and natural science fields, it should be used to determine a student's reading abilities only in these types of subject matter.

Part I may be said to test a pupil's ability to identify from memory statements of the significant points of a story of social studies content, which he has just read at a rate freely chosen for the purpose of reading with understanding. Since no questions are given the pupil before the reading of the story, he must set his own standard of careful reading. Thus the score in Part I indicates his standard of careful reading modified by his ability to maintain it. It tests his reading judgment, which is of tremendous importance to efficient scholarship.

Part II is a test of the pupil's ability to recognize the main idea from among several details in a paragraph of social and natural science material. It could be wished that some multiple-choice statements in this section had included faulty statements of the main idea, such as overstatement, understatement, and the misinterpretation of the main idea, so that the test would involve more than the distinction between details and main ideas.

However, while Traxler has limited the scope of his test to a few rather specific reading abilities functioning in two special types of material, he has provided a diagnostic measure more thorough and explicit than most of the tests in this field can claim to be. His contribu-

tion is a reminder that reading abilities are many and varying, and that a 40-minute test which attempts to touch upon more than two or three abilities through a given type of material forfeits reliability in its parts and its utility in the schools. The test users need to recognize this fact and to select tests according to their appropriateness to specific situations. If they wish to survey a broad range of reading abilities with varied materials, they must be ready to devote more than an hour's time to testing.

C. Gilbert Wrenn, Professor of Educational Psychology, The University of Minnesota. The mechanical form of this test deserves first and favorable consideration. The inverted-page technique of questions on material read for rate is used but the reviewer found the familiar lack of relationship between comprehension and rate in computing rate of reading. Rate is determined *only* by the student's marking how far he has gone at the end of two and one-half and five minutes, but if he has skimmed or read absent-mindedly he still gets credit for what his eyes have covered mechanically since the questions on the material are figured in the "comprehension score" only. In other words, a "rate" score on a reading test would be much more significant if the comprehension has been perfect (in terms of the questions asked on the material) than if comprehension has been poor. Complete separation of "rate" and "comprehension" scores is artificial. The reviewer has had experience in trying to construct a test that would make a rate score more functionally meaningful in a test that was eventually built for use at Stanford University, and he knows full well the difficulty of the assignment. This is a task in test construction that still challenges and that the Traxler test has not solved. The rate section of this test is too short (62 lines) although the time limits are generous and the materials were taken from a selection that would not normally have been previously read by high school students. These are important factors.

Nine of the twenty questions on the rate section are so specific as to require the recall of one of a series of proper names, specific nouns, or figures. This is an unfortunately large proportion. The paragraph comprehension section follows the familiar form of multiple-choice questions on the main idea contained in short paragraphs. There are thirty of these paragraphs which is a much more satisfactory sample than the paragraph comprehension section of many other tests.

Simple reading rate, and comprehension of sixty-two lines of continuously read material and of thirty discrete paragraphs make up the test. We can be sure that these comprise the important elements of a reading test *only if* data are given as to the validity of the parts or totality of the test. This is lacking for the test under discussion. In fact validity data of any sort are lacking except for the selection of items in terms of internal consistency. Relationship of the test to intelligence test scores, scholarship groups or other external criteria leave one in doubt as to just what the test measures. Very tentative reliability coefficients are given but the number of cases involved is not stated. Reliability coefficients of .72 and .80 are quoted for the two comprehension sections. (The method of computing reliability is not given.) Percentile norms on sixteen hundred high school students are given but the number of cases for the norms of each of the three grades, 10, 11, and 12, is not stated. The medians and standard deviations for the three grades are provided and these show consistent rise in medians and fall in sigmas from grades 10 to 12, which may be considered an aspect of validity.

This test will be useful in senior high schools, particularly to those educators who have found the Traxler test for grades 7 to 10 helpful. Its value over other published tests will be more apparent when further standardization data are made available. It is a carefully made test of conventional form which adds but little to our knowledge of reading-test techniques.

Ed Res B 18:117-8 Ap '39. J. Wayne Wrightstone. * In measuring comprehension of the main ideas in paragraphs, the author has provided a sample of paragraphs based upon content found in typical social-science and natural-science textbooks. The method for presenting alternative responses is novel. * The author is to be commended because he has stated as precisely as he can the aspects of the reading process which various parts of his test measure. The test may be recommended for the measurement of the selected aspects of silent reading of high-school students that it purports to measure. It does not purport to measure

all phases of silent reading. The test is carefully constructed and easily administered, but the format of the story-comprehension part might be improved. *

Teach Col J 10:147 Jl '39. E. L. Abell. * The material and arrangement of this test seem to be very good, and the validity of each item in the comprehension test has been established by Ruch's commonly used method. Reliabilities of .92, .72, and .80 for the three tests would indicate, for this type of test very satisfactory consistency. * The test would seem to be a desirable addition to the list of high school reading tests.

[1579]

Traxler Silent Reading Test. Grades 7-10; 1934-39; 2 forms; $1.50 per 25; 15¢ per manual; 30¢ per specimen set; adapted to machine scoring; (50-55) minutes; Arthur E. Traxler; Bloomington, Ill.: Public School Publishing Company.

REFERENCES

1 RUCH, G. M., AND STODDARD, GEORGE D. *Tests and Measurements in High School Instruction*, p. 120. Yonkers, N. Y.: World Book Co., 1927. Pp. xxi, 381. $2.20.
2 TRAXLER, ARTHUR E. *The Measurement and Improvement of Silent Reading at the Junior High School Level.* Chicago, Ill.: University of Chicago Libraries, 1932. Pp. 218. Paper, lithotyped. Out of print.
3 TRAXLER, ARTHUR E. "One Reading Test Serves the Purpose." *Clearing House* 14:419-21 Mr '40.

Robert L. McCaul, Instructor of Remedial Reading in the Laboratory Schools and College of the University of Chicago. In *The 1938 Mental Measurements Yearbook* this test was thoroughly evaluated (*see* 1114). Last year's reviewers criticized: (*a*) The disproportionately heavy weighting of the rate score in determining total score; (*b*) The way in which the rate selection could be read superficially, no penalty being exacted; (*c*) The large standard errors of the part tests; (*d*) The coefficient of .80 obtained by correlating the comprehension parts of the test with their criterion of validity: a combination of scores from the *Monroe Standardized Silent Reading Test*, the *Thorndike-McCall Reading Scale*, and the paragraph-meaning part of the *New Stanford Achievement Test*; (*e*) The narrow range of the tentative norms contained in the teacher's handbook; (*f*) The limited value of the test for individual diagnosis, when used alone; and (*g*) The inconsistent sampling of the comprehension items.

His experience in administering and interpreting the Traxler test causes the present reviewer to agree with the criticism of the test's limitations for individual diagnosis and of the inadequacy of its norms. To these criticisms he would add that the vocabulary part test includes too large a percentage of words peculiar mainly to English literature and that this probably accounts for its high correlation with its validity criterion, the *Inglis Test of English Vocabulary*, which possesses almost solely literary words and indeed many poetic and some archaic terms. A better measure of whether a pupil has a vocabulary rich enough to enable him to read his school texts efficiently could be derived from a vocabulary test composed of more equal proportions of words from social studies, science, mathematics, and the other subject fields of the curriculum. Perhaps the Educational Records Bureau or some of Traxler's articles offer data bearing upon the matters criticized, but such data are not in the teacher's handbook and consequently are not available for the ordinary test purchaser.

Having set forth criticisms of the test, the reviewer must bring to the attention of schoolmen the following points in its favor. First, directions for administering the rate test emphasize comprehension and the necessity of answering questions about the rate story; these questions are placed where the pupils will see them before reading. Unless the pupils have become "test wise," it is most unlikely therefore that they will read the story superficially for the purpose of gaining a higher test score than their true reading speed merits. This is not intended to be a defense of the vulnerability of the rate test nor an argument against eliminating the excessive weight allotted to it in the calculation of total test scores. Second, the speed story is long and will appeal to pupils. Upon the essentials of the story, not details, the questions are focussed, and thus the pupils are not asked to read rapidly, then confronted with questions demanding information which can be secured only by slow, careful reading. Hence a contradiction inherent in many speed of reading tests is obviated. Third, the stimulus words of the vocabulary items are presented in sentence or phrase context and they are clearly synonymous with their proper response words. Fourth, because the time limit of the power of comprehension test is long, the speed factor is reduced to a degree that makes the test more nearly one of comprehension rather than of speed. All this is a relative matter, of course, for it is impossible to get an index of pure compre-

hension or of pure speed. The power of comprehension paragraphs, moreover, are representative of the materials which the pupil must read and study. Fifth, a "validity" coefficient of .80 between the comprehension parts of the Traxler test and the criterion tests by no means proves the former to be invalid. One of the criterion tests, the Monroe, is no model of perfection: of it Ruch and Stoddard remark that the test "cannot serve to cover even one phase of it [reading] adequately." [1] Likewise a coefficient of .80 does not compare so unfavorably with published correlations between other reading tests that the Traxler test deserves a peremptory condemnation. Sixth, the Traxler test has been employed successfully by the reviewer as a screen test to single out poor readers. It is not a dependable instrument for individual diagnosis when used alone; the reviewer is acquainted with no reading test which is. In the field of education what are called "diagnostic tests" are as common as the ubiquitous white rat of experimental psychology and have an equally high birth rate. Individual diagnosis, nevertheless, still remains a procedure based upon the results of specialized tests of oral reading, vocabulary, etc., and to an even greater extent upon personal observation of the reading method of the retarded child.

Miles A. Tinker, Associate Professor of Psychology, The University of Minnesota. There are many evidences that careful planning entered into the construction of this test. Three aspects of reading performance are measured: (a) rate of reading with a check on the story comprehension, (b) word meaning in which the word to be defined is presented within a sentence or phrase, and (c) power of comprehension for paragraphs varying in difficulty. The two published forms of the test are carefully equated to give practical equivalence. Directions for administration are clear and complete.

The test was standardized on several hundred pupils at each grade level. Unfortunately no measure of deviation is presented with the mean scores so that standard scores cannot be derived for those who might wish to use them. "Tentative" grade norms are given by months for the total score. Norms should be more than tentative. No reading test is entirely adequate unless the cited norms have been soundly established.

The validity of test scores appears adequate. For the rate test, with a composite score from several speed of reading measures as a criterion, the validity coefficient is .81. Similarly for word meaning, it ranges from .76 to .87 with one satisfactory criterion and .78 with another. Comprehension validity (story comprehension plus power of comprehension) with a composite criterion score was found to be .80. Total score validity with a composite score criterion is .88. When compared with school marks the total score has a validity of .56. Analysis of individual items revealed positive validity for all.

Correlation of scores on the two forms of the test yielded reliability coefficients ranging from .61 for story comprehension to .86 for word meaning. For total score, the coefficients ranged from .91 to .95.

In describing the nature of the test the author's statement "that the correlation between the rates of reading any two types of material is high" is misleading. There are ample data which show that such correlations are low.

In general this test may be designated as adequate. It is readily applicable to analysis of reading status and is suitable for research.

Ed Res B 19:59 Ja 17 '40. J. Wayne Wrightstone. * This test . . . has been criticized . . . because the special aspects of comprehension which it measures are not clearly defined or systematically examined by the test items. In this particular respect, however, the test is no better and no worse than many other silent-reading tests. The format of the story-comprehension part of the test could be improved. Despite these and other minor criticisms the test may be recommended as one of the better reading tests for junior-high-school pupils if a survey of the silent-reading skills is desired. The test is not recommended for diagnostic purposes.

For reviews by Frederick B. Davis and Spencer Shank, see 1114.

[1580]

Tyler-Kimber Study Skills Test. Grades 9-16;\ 1937; 1 form; $2.00 per 25; 15¢ per specimen set; nontimed (60-90) minutes; Stanford University, Calif.: Stanford University Press.

REFERENCES

1 UPSHALL, C. C. "The Study Skills of College Seniors." *Ed Adm and Sup* 26:139-44 F '40.

William A. McCall, Professor of Education, Columbia University. This test is arranged in the following eight parts: (*a*) finding what you want in a book; (*b*) using an index; (*c*) using general reference books; (*d*) recognizing common abbreviations; (*e*) using the library card catalog; (*f*) interpreting maps; (*g*) knowing current periodical literature; and (*h*) interpreting graphs.

Let me sum up its many merits in a sentence and detail what I deem to be its defects, not because I take a natural delight in dwelling on faults but because this is the way of progress.

MERITS. This is the best test of its kind for use in the secondary school and college—an important contribution to our list of useful tests.

DEFECTS. Some of the directions on the test proper appear to me to be unnecessarily difficult. This assumes the presence of the most important study skill, namely, reading ability.

In the case of certain tests, the students are asked not to guess at the answer. In other tests no directions as to guessing are given even though guessing could appreciably increase the score, albeit less so than where the caution is given. This tends to make the test measure degree of daring or willingness to gamble or lack of conscientiousness or something else alien to study skills.

In Test IV—a matching test for abbreviations—there is a startling neglect to disguise items to be matched. Thus the items determine whether a student *recognizes* that *pl.* is an abbreviation for *plural*, *par.* for *paragraph*, *obs.* for *obsolete*, *syn.* for *synonym*, *ant.* for *antonym*, *vol.* for *volume*, and *ch.* for *chapter*. Nothing more arduous mentally than simple perception such as that tested in the first grade is required to match these.

Not study skills but *study results* are tested too often. Items 101 to 110 illustrate this defect. For example, consider this item: "On the [outline] map of Europe which number corresponds to London? (1) 1 (2) 2 (3) 3 (4) 4 (5) 5." The difficulty in this item is to know the exact location of London—a knowledge which is the *result* of a study skill. Or consider again this item based on a dot map: "The second state in cattle production was (1) Texas (2) Kansas (3) Nebraska (4) Missouri (5) Iowa." Since the states are not labeled, probably the chief difficulty of this item is to remember which state is Kansas or Nebraska, etc.—a study result. Of course, even study skills are study results, and mere knowledge itself facilitates study, but the authors are obviously not trying to assay the amount of skill by the volume of knowledge produced by it.

As is to be expected of those who lovingly linger in California on their way to Heaven, the authors have given California's fruit industry a boost by basing all but one of their graphs upon it. Far be it from me to decry such loyalty, having been a fortunate guest in that far, fair land, but I do object to the upper half of the Thompson-Muscat-Sultana chart. It is misleading and mislabeled—an excellent example of improper charting technique. Such flaws probably subtract from the validity of the test.

Total scores are transmuted into percentiles, and subtest scores into quartiles. The authors state that they provide quartile scores for subtests because subtest scores are less reliable than total test scores. They seem to have adopted the fallacy, quite common in education, that coarsening the scale makes the scores more reliable. On the contrary it makes the transmuted scores less reliable. It would have been preferable to have kept the finer scale, and stated the probable error of the score (and not the prophecy formula reliability coefficient which is relatively unintelligible to the general consumer).

The authors have shown commendable zeal in determining the reliability of their test, and attempting to establish its validity. The time spent in applying a dubious check on validity should have gone toward freeing test items from faults which inherently impair validity. By and large, we test constructors have erred in giving relatively more attention to statistical considerations than to incisive criticism of the test itself.

Rachel Salisbury, Director of the Junior High School Department, State Teachers College, Platteville, Wisconsin. The *Tyler-Kimber Study Skills Test* is an 8-page booklet (8½ by 11 inches) providing scorable, objective answers to 175 items arranged in eight parts as follows: (*a*) finding what you want in a book (matching, from 10 printed response items); (*b*) using an index (same); (*c*) using general reference books (30 items with a response list of 10 reference books); (*d*) recognizing common abbreviations (2 groups of 10 items each);

(*e*) using the library card catalog (20 true-false questions); (*f*) interpreting maps (20 questions on 4 maps—Mercator, Mollweide, outline, and distribution types); (*g*) knowing current periodical literature (3 groups of 10 questions each); and (*h*) interpreting graphs (35 questions on 5 graphs).

The test is a power test which can ordinarily be taken in 60 to 90 minutes. A convenient cardboard scoring-key accompanies the test. A reliability coefficient of .90 was derived from a random sampling of 105 tests, scored from odd- and even-numbered items separately. Two validity procedures were used. Test scores on the *American Council on Education Psychological Examination for College Freshmen* and on the *Tyler-Kimber Study Skills Test* were correlated with each other and with the grade-point ratio of 343 unselected junior-college seniors, the coefficients ranging from .51 to .65. The study skills test appears to give as good an indication of academic success as either of the other two measures.

Then scores for 100 students with high grade-point ratios were compared with those for 225 students with low ratios. The difference in means between the two groups was found to be greatly in excess of that needed to prove a significant difference.

Both reliability and validity coefficients would be more convincing if a larger number of cases had been used; but the impracticability of isolating many of the factors involved in school success hampers any statistical procedure in this field, so that these values are probably as workable as any that could be obtained.

The diagnostic value of the test is limited. For each of the eight parts the raw scores may be translated only into quarters of a junior-college group. But these are not given by grades and they serve only to show outstanding gaps in training. Percentile norms, based on 2,163 cases, are presented for each of the first four semesters of the junior-college years only. Within this range the test should be definitely useful for placement. The number of cases and the range of norms are being extended by reports submitted by the present users of the test.

To this reviewer it appears unfortunate that the test is so heavily loaded with how-to-use-the-library items. Six of the eight skills measured seem to require more memory than study

power. Another, map study, contains too many
questions for which there must be factual recall before the study skill can operate (such as,
"Which letter applies to the Bay of Bengal?").
The last part is most truly a measure of interpretive skill, testing the pupil's power to find
facts from graphs which presumably have zero
familiarity; yet one wonders why one-fifth of
an eight-part test should be devoted to graphs.

On the whole, the test seems to be more
nearly a test of the ability to find materials
than of the power to study them. The reviewer
misses test items involving the more abstract
processes of study: such as (*a*) following directions in mathematical and scientific problems; (*b*) outlining, as evidence of the ability
to detect relations among ideas presented in
reading; (*c*) drawing inferences or conclusions
from data presented; (*d*) combining data from
several sources into effective speaking or writing experience; and (*e*) measuring directly or
indirectly the student's coefficient of concentration. Lack of attention to some, if not all, of
these more psychological aspects of study leaves
the teacher with only a partial picture of student ability to study, in which case the name of
the test is misleading. The present test, however, seems clearly to be an effective instrument for measuring the eight abilities presented in its pages.

*For reviews by Edward S. Jones and C. Gil-
bert Wrenn, see 1166.*

[1581]

Unit Scales of Attainment in Reading. Grades 1B,
1A, 2B, 2A, 3, 3-4, 5-6, 7-8, 9-12; 1932-34; 3 forms,
9 levels; identical to the reading tests in the battery
Unit Scales of Attainment; 75¢ per 25; 20¢ per specimen set; nontimed (45) minutes; M. J. Van Wagenen; Minneapolis, Minn.: Educational Test Bureau,
Inc.

*Ivan A. Booker, Assistant Director of the
Research Division, National Education Association, Washington, D. C.* The comprehensive
battery of tests which has been available for
several years under the title *Unit Scales of Attainment* was restandardized in 1937. It is a
general survey test of pupil achievement,
which, in grades beyond the third, is concerned
with eight fields: reading, arithmetic, spelling,
English usage, literature, history, geography,
and elementary science. The parts concerned
with reading achievement, *Unit Scales of Attainment in Reading*, are available not only in
the comprehensive test booklets designed for

various grade levels but also as separate reading tests. Whether used as part of the test battery or as separate tests, however, the reading
scales should be recognized as instruments designed primarily for general survey purposes
rather than for diagnosis.

Each of the *Unit Scales of Attainment in
Reading* has a narrow grade-level range. There
are nine separate booklets—or "Divisions" as
they are called. The reading tests employed in
grades 1, 2, and 3 measure knowledge of word
meaning (or vocabulary) and reading comprehension. In grades 4 to 12 the tests are concerned wholly with reading comprehension. No
time limits are set, the expectation being that
every pupil will complete the test within a 45-
minute period. In this way an attempt is made
to measure maximum "power of comprehension," relatively uninfluenced by speed of
reading.

Data with respect to the validity and reliability of the *Unit Scales of Attainment in Reading* are given in the manual which accompanies
the complete achievement test battery, but virtually no information on these points can be
found in the brief booklets which accompany
the scales in reading.

In validating the tests, reliance was placed
on expert opinion, texts, curricula, and "the
discriminatory capacity"—however that ambiguous phrase may have been interpreted by
the authors. The reliability of the tests—which
compares favorably with that of similar ones—
was determined by the usual statistical procedures. From the brief description given, it
would seem that these tests have been sufficiently well standardized and carefully scaled
so that they may be used with considerable assurance. Discriminating teachers, however,
would undoubtedly welcome more information
on standardization procedures than is now
given in the Directions for Administering and
Scoring. Also, many teachers would probably
like to have tables of age and grade medians,
and tables of quartile and percentile ranks for
the various groups, in addition to the table of
C-scores now provided.

The *Unit Scales of Attainment in Reading*
are highly satisfactory from the standpoint of
objectivity and ease of scoring. The multiple-
choice technic is employed throughout, with a
layout that is unusually favorable for rapid
scoring. The directions for administering and
scoring the tests are simple and clear, but the

explanations and directions for interpreting the tests leave much to be desired with respect to both accuracy in detail and clarity of statement.

The *Unit Scales of Attainment in Reading*, in common with most tests, have some few items that could be improved. For example, some paragraphs seem to call for unwarranted inferences; such as, that a boy was "angry" rather than "sorry" because he could not reach some berries, judging from the remark, "I don't want those berries. I know they are sour." There is at least some reasonable doubt whether this comment indicates either "sorrow" or "anger," or whether it registers only a bit of mild irritation and perhaps some measure of both disappointment and disgust. A few other instances of the same type might be cited, including one case where the reader must infer that a boy is "industrious," either from a casual reference to his return from doing an errand, or from the fact that he wanted very much to attend a new school which was opened in his village. One might readily attribute both to other forms of motivation!

Careful re-editing of the tests, particularly with reference to the spacing and arrangement of the comprehension exercises, would improve their usefulness. One evidence of superficial editing is an occasional "stray" line of bold type. Again, some of the comprehension exercises are needlessly crowded, the introductory questions or phrases running into the multiple-choice answers which follow.

Many of the test paragraphs are used in two or more "Divisions" of the *Unit Scales of Attainment in Reading*. One "Division" is made more difficult than the preceding one by dropping off some of the easier paragraphs and adding a few harder ones, rather than by using wholly new material. Hence, if different "Divisions" of the same form of the test are used with the same pupils within the year, or even from year to year, some degree of "practice effect" should be expected. The amount of overlap in the reading comprehension parts in the four upper "Divisions" of Form A is as follows: (*a*) Of the 10 paragraphs in the test for grades 3-4, 5 are also in the test for grades 5-6; 4, grades 7-8; and 2, grades 9-12. (*b*) Of the 9 paragraphs in the test for grades 5-6, 5 are also in the test for grades 3-4; 6, grades 7-8; and 4, grades 9-12. (*c*) Of the 8 paragraphs in the test for grades 7-8, 4 are also in the test for grades 3-4; 6, grades 5-6; and 6, grades 9-12. (*d*) Of the 8 paragraphs in the test for grades 9-12, 2 are also in the test for grades 3-4; 4, grades 5-6; and 6, grades 7-8.

In situations where a general survey of reading comprehension is desired, the *Unit Scales of Attainment in Reading* should prove quite satisfactory. Where information is wanted on other phases of reading achievement, however, or if one is interested in the specific nature of comprehension difficulties, some other test would probably be selected.

J. Wayne Wrightstone, Assistant Director, Bureau of Reference, Research, and Statistics, Public Schools, New York, New York. The exercises comprising the reading comprehension test of the *Unit Scales of Attainment in Reading* are scaled paragraphs with scaled items following each. These paragraphs overlap somewhat in the forms for succeeding grade levels. Some of the paragraphs used in the grade 5-6 form, for example, are used in the first part of the test grade 7-8 form.

Test items are arranged according to difficulty, and the number of correct responses is transmuted into a C-score, or so-called standard unit of measurement, comparable—according to the authors—to such standard units as inches or pounds in their respective fields. The reliability, or stability, of a C-score for any pupil is variable enough to limit the values claimed for this standard unit score versus a raw, or crude, score. The C-score for an individual pupil has a doubtful value and may influence many teachers to place more confidence in the pupil's score than it deserves. Its limitations as well as its values should be described more fully in the manual, lest the unwary teacher be misled in attempting to ascertain with too much certainty a pupil's progression or regression.

The test for grade three includes a section on vocabulary, or word meaning, and a section on comprehension. From grade four through the remaining series of grade forms, a comprehension section only is provided. Reading comprehension, however, is a general term that has been invested with various meanings in different reading tests. The author of this test has provided no clear designation of the particular aspects of reading comprehension which these scales purport to measure. From an analysis of the items which constitute these tests the reviewer has inferred that the following aspects of comprehension are measured in this series: (*a*) ability to identify the general sense of the paragraph; (*b*) ability to identify details in the paragraph; (*c*) ability to determine whether a definite idea is stated; and (*d*) ability to make simple inferences from the material presented in the paragraph.

Although the reviewer's analysis indicates that some items of the test will provide an index of the ability of pupils to make inferences, most of these items require only superficial inferences and sometimes the reproduction of facts stated directly or indirectly in the reading material rather than inferences drawn from a synthesis of data provided in the paragraph.

The test user who expects this series to provide a measure of such aspects of reading comprehension as reading to understand directions, to predict the outcome of events, to summarize ideas, or to apply these ideas to the solution of a problem will be disappointed. Certainly the author of this test should have stated more precisely the aspects of reading comprehension which his test purports to measure. Moreover, the validity of this test must be inferred from the structure of the items. The author presents no evidence of the validity or validation procedures for these tests, except general statements in the manual. Test authors should provide more adequate data regarding the validation of their tests.

The norms of this test are not clearly defined as to educational conditions of the pupil personnel. The population from which the norms were derived should be more clearly described in terms of educational, social, and economic factors, if the norms are to be used intelligently by teachers and administrators.

These reading comprehension tests are valuable for survey purposes, but do not seem to be especially valuable for diagnostic purposes. Al-

though the author apparently had a general scheme or pattern of items after each paragraph for selected aspects of reading comprehension, the pattern is too vaguely defined to be meaningful in interpreting the results of the test.

As compared with other reading comprehension tests, the *Unit Scales of Attainment in Reading* would seem, in general, to provide as valid measures of selected aspects of reading comprehension as any other test. Many, if not all, of the criticisms made against this test apply equally to most reading comprehension tests. The care that the author has exercised in selecting items and the fact that the norms are apparently revised frequently make this one of the more carefully constructed reading comprehension tests that are available.

For a review by Joseph C. Dewey, see 1115.

[1582]

Use of Library and Study Materials: A Test for High School and College Students. Grades 9-16; 1940; 2 forms; $6 per 100 tests including 100 machine-scorable answer sheets; $1.50 per 100 machine-scorable answer sheets; 10¢ per specimen set; 40(45) minutes; Mary Kirkpatrick, Lola Rivers Thompson, Helen Tomlinson in cooperation with the Texas Commission on Coordination in Education; Austin, Tex.: Steck Co.

[1583]

Work-Study Skills: Iowa Every-Pupil Tests of Basic Skills, Test B. Grades 3-5, 6-8; 1940; Form L, 2 levels; single specimen set free; 30¢ per manual; 12¢ per booklet of norms; 40¢ per 25 record cards; H. F. Spitzer in collaboration with Ernest Horn, Maude McBroom, H. A. Greene, and E. F. Lindquist with the assistance of the faculty of the University Experimental Schools, State University of Iowa; Boston, Mass.: Houghton Mifflin Co.
a) ELEMENTARY BATTERY. Grades 3-5. $1.15 per 25; 44(50) minutes.
b) ADVANCED BATTERY. Grades 6-8. $1.25 per 25; 78 (90) minutes.

[1583.1]

Ypsilanti Reading Test. Grades 6-8; 1940; 1 form; 8¢ per test, 1 to 10 copies; 5¢ per test, 25 or more copies; 35(40) minutes; B. H. Vanden Belt and Thelma McAndless; Hillsdale, Mich.: Hillsdale School Supply Co.

SCIENCE

Reviews by Charles L. Bickel, Francis D. Curtis, Max D. Engelhart, Hans C. Gordon, Louis M. Heil, Clark W. Horton, G. W. Hunter, Palmer O: Johnson, Andrew Longacre, Thomas F. Morrison, Victor H. Noll, Paul A. Northrop, Alvin W. Schindler, Ralph W. Tyler, Alan T. Waterman, Eugene A. Waters, Ralph K. Watkins, and Dael L. Wolfle.

BIOLOGY

[1584]

Application of Principles in Biological Science: Test 1.33A. Grades 10-12; 1940; revision of Test 1.33; 1 form, 2 parts (I and II); 10¢ per part; 1¢ per machine-scorable answer sheet for either part; 5¢ per explanation sheet and interpretation guide; $1.50 per set of stencils for machine scoring; 60(70) minutes for each part; Chicago, Ill.: Evaluation in the Eight Year Study, Progressive Education Association.

REFERENCES

1 RATHS, LOUIS E. *Application of Principles.* Progressive Education Association, Evaluation in the Eight Year Study, Bulletin No. 5. Chicago, Ill.: the Study, December 1936. Pp. 25. Paper, mimeographed. Out of print.
2 *Evaluation Materials Developed for Various Aspects of Thinking.* Chicago, Ill.: Evaluation in the Eight Year Study, Progressive Education Association, March 1939. Pp. [22]. Paper, mimeographed. Out of print.

[1585]

Cooperative Biology Test. High school; 1933-40; 40- and 90- minute editions; 25¢ per specimen set of either edition; Form P: F. L. Fitzpatrick and S. R. Powers; Form Q: F. L. Fitzpatrick with the editorial assistance of N. E. Bingham, Leslie Garlough, Donald H. Miller, Thomas F. Morrison, E. W. Sinnott, and Elmo Stevenson; New York: Cooperative Test Service.
a) FORMS 1934 AND 1937. Forms 1933, 1935, and 1936 are out of print; 6¢ per test, 10 to 99 copies; 90(95) minutes.
b) REVISED SERIES FORMS N, O, P, AND Q. 1937-40; 5¢ per test, 10 to 99 copies; 40(45) minutes.

Ralph W. Tyler, Chairman of the Department of Education; Professor of Education; and Chief Examiner, Board of Examinations, The University of Chicago. [Review of Form P.] The *Cooperative Biology Test* is a test of biological information which samples material most frequently included in courses in general biology. The test is to be commended for giving heavier weight to physiological material than to morphological material since this is in harmony with the trend in biology curricula. Another desirable characteristic of the test is the large proportion of functional information included in the items, that is information which young people have frequent opportunities to utilize.

The chief criticism of this biology test lies in the failure to emphasize either in the manual or in the title the fact that it is not a comprehensive biology test but is primarily an examination measuring the amount of biological information which the student has acquired. Although some problems are included which would require reasoning and the application of biological principles if the problems were new to the student, most biology students would have come in contact with the solution of these problems in their biology courses. In such cases the student's correct response may be due to his having remembered the answers given in the biology course rather than to his ability to think through biological problems and to apply appropriate principles.

It would not be difficult for the authors of this test to add sections which do measure some of the other important outcomes of biology teaching and to set up the test so as to distinguish answers arrived at solely from memorization and those arrived at through the correct processes of reasoning. The major change necessary would be to provide forms in which the student had opportunity to indicate the reasons which lead to the conclusions which he reaches. Enough experimental work has been done to demonstrate that tests of this type can be made highly objective. Such tests are more important for the teacher of biology than tests on information alone. If the *Cooperative Biology Tests* are to be tests of biology achievement, then they should be sufficiently comprehensive to cover most of the major kinds of achievement which are expected of biology students. The *Cooperative Biology Test* is not adequate for a comprehensive testing program in this field.

However, as a measure of information the *Cooperative Biology Test* is useful and is highly reliable. Furthermore, it can be quickly scored by machine or by manual methods.

For reviews by Francis D. Curtis and George W. Hunter, see 907.

[1586]

Hanes-Benz Biology Test. High school; 1939; 2 forms; $1 per 25; 10¢ per specimen set; 40(45) minutes; G. M. Hanes and H. E. Benz; Cincinnati, Ohio: C. A. Gregory Co.

REFERENCES

1 HANES, GLEN M. *An Information Test in Biology.* Unpublished master's thesis, Ohio University, 1938. Pp. 115.

Clark W. Horton, Department of Educational Research, Dartmouth College. The two equivalent forms of the test (Forms A and B) each contain the following parts: Part I, 30 true-false items. Part II, four diagrams of plant and animal structures, bearing a total of 30 numbered label lines, accompanied by 10 items in which the pupil is asked to write the name of a structure indicated by number (an alphabetically arranged list of 32 structure names is given for reference) and ten items in which the name of a structure is given and the pupil is asked to supply the proper number. An alphabetically arranged list of structures is given. Figures in Form A are: digestive system, woody twig, parts of flower, Paramecium. Figures in Form B are: grasshopper, fish, cross section of a leaf, Amoeba. Part III, 50 multiple-choice items each offering 5 possible answers.

The construction of the test involved ". . . the composition of a comprehensive outline of high school biology from two well-known outlines," and the checking of this outline against ". . . seven of the most widely used textbooks in the field." Only those items which occurred in at least five of the seven textbooks were retained. Five hundred test items were constructed, and "these were carefully studied by several persons, including some whose approach to the problem of testing does not coincide with that of the authors, and some who were subject matter experts in the field under consideration." The resulting four hundred items, in a multiple-choice form, were "divided into four forms of a hundred items each, and these forms were administered to three hundred pupils in nine schools of varying size and type." A statistical study of item validity was made "by determining the number of times each item was missed by pupils in the upper third, middle third, and lower third of the pupil population when arranged in terms of scores on the whole test." Too difficult, too easy, and ambiguous items were eliminated. Later 100 of these items were recast in the true-false form, and the material included in the drawings was prepared. The reliability of the test "as determined by a preliminary sampling of papers" is .88. The authors do not otherwise reveal how this coefficient of reliability was determined. Norms "based on scores made by 791 pupils from twenty different schools in seven different states" are available. The test is a time-limit test, allowing 10 minutes for Part I, 10 minutes for Part II, and 20 minutes for Part III.

The sterility of approaching test construction through an analysis of textbook and outline content is well illustrated by this test. The authors have produced only another test of pupil familiarity with items of information found in textbooks of biology. The test may be a very good device for finding out how many such facts a pupil knows. The danger inherent in tests of this type is that the score will be interpreted as a valid measure of *achievement*. The authors make two unfortunate statements. They write, "The purpose of this test is to provide an accurate and scientific instrument for the measurement of achievement in high school biology," and later, "An effort has been made to make this test conform to the best practice in the teaching of high school biology." Reasonable inferences from these statements are that *knowledge of isolated facts, such as those contained in the test, is the major objective of the best present practice in the teaching of high school biology*, and moreover, that *knowledge of these facts alone adequately represents achievement in high school biology*. This reviewer must deny the validity of both of these assumptions. When test makers learn to present information tests for what they are; when they stop assuming that knowledge of a smattering of facts found in biology textbooks adequately represents achievement; and when they begin to build tests in relation to other important objectives of instruction, we shall make real progress toward a more adequate evaluation of student achievement.

Reference to stated objectives of instruction in high school biology reveals that teachers *say* that their teaching is designed to bring about many changes in the student more significant than the learning of facts such as those included in this test. When will test makers stop wasting their time in statistical work on this kind of thing and really attack the problem of measuring other important aspects of achievement, for example, the development in students of thinking skills characteristic of scientific method?

The validity of this test as a test of the pupil's knowledge of a sampling of facts found in biology textbooks is not questioned. Its validity as a test of *achievement* in high school biology is denied. A valid measurement of achievement in high school biology implies measurement in relation to each of the important objectives of instruction in biology.

[1587]

Presson Biology Test. Grades 9-10; 1929-30; 2 forms, 2 parts; $1.20 per 25; 30¢ per specimen set; 38(45) minutes; John M. Presson under the direction of LeRoy A. King; Yonkers, N. Y.: World Book Co.
a) TEST I, PLANT BIOLOGY.
b) TEST II, ANIMAL BIOLOGY.

REFERENCES

1 PRESSON, J. M. *Achievement Tests in Biology for Secondary School Use as Based Upon an Analysis of the Content of the Subject.* Unpublished doctor's thesis, University of Pennsylvania, 1930. Pp. 149.
2 DIAMOND, L. N. "Testing the Test Makers." *Sch Sci and Math* 32:490-502 My '32.

Thomas F. Morrison, Head of the Science Department, Milton Academy, Milton, Massachusetts. It is too bad that some of the tests which appeared early in the history of testing have neither been revised with a view to the recent developments in the testing field nor have profited from direct criticisms which have appeared in reputable journals. Both of these faults can be found in the Presson series because no change has been made in them since they first appeared nine years ago. Diamond [2] has criticized these tests severely from the standpoint of their faulty subject-matter content, pointing out that of the 460 questions appearing in the tests 7.3 per cent of them demanded answers which were wrong. This reviewer feels that such a high percentage of informational errors is far from conducive to good educational practices, especially in a science field where exactness of detail is one of the desiderata.

Another general criticism which can be leveled at these tests is their close adherence to a knowledge of the details of subject matter. Some of these details are, in my opinion, of a difficulty beyond the scope of the average secondary student, although the tests were constructed after a careful study of texts and examinations in use in various parts of the country. If these tests were to be reconstructed in the light of the present-day methods of teaching biology, I believe that many of the de-

tails felt essential ten years ago would be omitted and some of the more general aspects of the subject stressed. It is unfortunate that what might have been a valuable measuring tool has become frozen into a form which perpetuates some of the least desirable features of testing.

Dael L. Wolfle, Assistant Professor of Psychology, The University of Chicago. The items for each test were selected from a study of standard texts, courses of study, teachers' final examinations, Regents' examinations, and College Entrance Board examinations. Each test consists of 15 matching items, 40 best-answer items with 5 choices, and 60 completion items. Completion items provide one of the most valid of objective test forms, but they present difficulties when scored by a large number of different teachers.

Since similar material is covered in different items, some questions are answered within the test. For example, in Test 1, Form B, one item asks: "That portion of the female reproductive organ in a flower which receives the pollen is called the ———"; another provides the answer: "The thread-like projection that develops when a pollen grain lodges on the stigma of the pistil is called a ———." In Test 2, Form B, two items which answer each other are: "The common name for the larval stage of the mosquito is ———," and "The wiggler stage of the mosquito is also known as the—pupa, tadpole, imago, polliwog, larva." How much such information can be utilized by a pupil hurrying to complete the test will depend upon a number of things, but in too many cases the information is there for him to use if he can.

Taken individually most of the items are satisfactory, but a few answers are surprising. Would biologists agree that the earthworm *moves* by means of setae, or that the majority of all *animals* move by means of legs? Some items which "in the estimation of the teachers giving the course, are most fundamental" seem trivial to the reviewer. Do the 115 most fundamental items in zoology include knowing that "The middle fin-like organ of the last segment of the abdomen of the crayfish is named the telson" or that the "Large scales found on the under surface of the snake are call scutes"? Well over half of the items deal with names of men, terminology, taxonomy, and structure, and less than half cover knowledge of physiological and embryological processes or plant and animal function.

The statistical criteria (reliability = .90, correlation with teachers' grades = .73 and with *Ruch-Cossmann Biology Test* scores = .81) are high enough to justify the test's use. But the emphasis on structure rather than function may give an unbalanced picture of what is important in biology.

[1588]

Ruch-Cossmann Biology Test. Grades 9-13; 1924; 2 forms; $1.30 per 25; 15¢ per specimen set; 38(45) minutes; Giles M. Ruch and Leo H. Cossmann; Yonkers, N. Y.: World Book Co.

REFERENCES

1 RUCH, G. M., AND COSSMANN, LEO H. "Standardized Content in High School Biology." *J Ed Psychol* 15:285-96 My '24.
2 RUCH, G. M., AND STODDARD, GEORGE D. *Tests and Measurements in High School Instruction,* pp. 142-4. Yonkers, N. Y.: World Book Co., 1927. Pp. xxi, 381. $2.20.
3 SYMONDS, PERCIVAL M. *Ability Standard for Standardized Achievement Tests in the High School.* New York: Bureau of Publications, Teachers College, Columbia University, 1927. Pp. x, 91. $1.05.

Thomas F. Morrison, Head of Science Department, Milton Academy, Milton, Massachusetts. Like the *Presson Biology Test*, this test relies on three types of questions: the multiple-choice, matching, and completion, and, like it, deals with the details of subject matter. There are, however, fewer questions in this series—224 in all—and in the keys which are supplied with the tests this reviewer has not been able to find any errors. On the whole the tests appear to be well constructed from the standpoint of the subject matter which they cover, but they do not attempt to test anything but factual knowledge.

The Ruch-Cossmann tests are among the oldest of the published biology tests having been on the market for fifteen years in exactly the same form.

Dael L. Wolfle, Assistant Professor of Psychology, The University of Chicago. The authors secured two thousand final examination questions from 126 high schools (in 23 states) doing high-grade work in biology, selected the 300 most frequently used items, and submitted these to 77 competent teachers and authorities on the teaching of biology. Those items getting the highest combined ratings were used in the test. It would be difficult to get a selection of items better designed to represent a "standardized content in high-school biology."

Each form of the test contains 40 information questions with seven choices each, 18 three-choice best-answer items, 15 items in which parts of a pictured plant, animal, or structure are to be matched against a list of names, two simple problems on Mendelian inheritance, and five short paragraphs in which the student is to supply missing words. Time limits are liberal enough so that for many students it will be a power test rather than a speed test. No data on validity are given. Correlations between the two forms for five small classes (*N* from 12 to 28) ranged from .76 to .87. Percentile norms are available.

Scoring the test is not as easy as it might be. In the first 40 items the correct answers are underlined instead of indicated by marks in a column. The score for part two is the number of right answers minus half the number of wrong answers. Scoring part five requires evaluating answers written in by the student, but the items are so chosen that few alternatives are correct. Scoring, on the whole, will take more time than it will for some of the newer tests.

The selection of items is good. Approximately two-thirds cover processes, ecological relationships, physiology, embryology, evolution, and heredity. Approximately one-third are on names of men, taxonomy, and (chiefly) names of structures. The individual items reflect the careful selective process; there are very few that are out of date or questionable.

In spite of its age and scoring difficulties, the *Ruch-Cossmann Biology Test* seems superior to the *Presson Biology Test* or the *Williams Biology Test*. It is subject to very much less technical criticism, and more than either of these other tests it emphasizes a vital functioning type of biology.

[1589]

Williams Biology Test. High school; 1934; 2 forms, 3 parts; 60¢ per 25; 20¢ per specimen set; 40(45) minutes; John R. Williams and H. E. Schrammel; Emporia, Kan.: Bureau of Educational Measurements, Kansas State Teachers College.
a) TEST I [STRUCTURAL ANIMAL BIOLOGY].
b) TEST II [HUMAN BIOLOGY].
c) TEST III [PLANT BIOLOGY].

REFERENCES

1 WILLIAMS, JOHN R. *The Construction of an Objective Achievement Test in Biology for High School.* Unpublished master's thesis, Kansas State Teachers College, Emporia, 1933. Pp. 73.

Clark W. Horton, Department of Educational Research, Dartmouth College. Much that was said about the *Hanes-Benz Biology Test* (*see* 1586) can also be said about this test. However, these authors have made use of important criteria other than occurrence of facts in outlines and textbooks, particularly the criterion of "social utility," and the sampling of facts seems to this reviewer to be much better. Moreover, they have made no claims that the test measures *achievement*, and undoubtedly recognize that it measures only one aspect of achievement, the acquisition of information. The danger still exists that users of the test will regard student scores on it alone as a valid measure of achievement. Or, is this reviewer wrong in assuming that high school biology teachers take seriously any objective of biology teaching other than the acquisition of information?

It is difficult to reconcile certain items in the test with the criterion of "social utility." For example, the items: "The chela is an organ of . . ."; "The green glands are structures found in . . ."; "The term 'altrical' refers to the young of . . ."; and certain others seem more like facts one would expect the biological specialist to know. However, items involving such detail are in the minority, and the authors have included a great majority of items of socially useful information.

Unfortunately this reviewer had a key to only Test I, Form A, hence could not critically review all items in relation to the expected answer. In Test I, Form A some errors are apparent. In Item 38 *respiration* is defined as "absorption of oxygen into the cell," an inadequate and erroneous concept. Surely concepts of oxidation and energy release are not too difficult for high school students! The same form contains an inaccurate usage of the term *osmosis*. In better usage the term *osmosis* is limited to the diffusion of the solvent, and is not used for diffusion of the solute. The proper answer to the item would have been *diffusion*. Item 7, Test III, Form B, is unanswerable. Digestion "usually" takes place in all of the plant parts listed, with the possible exception of flowers.

A table for converting raw scores into percentile scores is given. Percentile scores for Test I and Test II are based upon scores of over nine thousand students, those for Test III are based upon over seven hundred.

In addition to using true-false, multiple-choice, and matching items in each of the several tests, the authors use the device which requires the student to select the one word (in five) which is unrelated to the others. That is

a good device, for it appears to involve an understanding of relationships that is not measured by the other forms.

In general this test is a good test of biological information. We hope that students who make high scores on it are also learning to use biological facts and generalizations in the solution of common problems, are learning some skill in drawing sound inferences from biological data, are learning to plan experiments to test hypotheses, are gaining some understanding of the nature of proof, et cetera. This test, of course, does not give us that kind of information about the student. Why not devise some tests to get it?

Victor H. Noll, Head of the Department of Education and Professor of Education, Michigan State College. This test series appears to have several commendable features. The three tests are said to cover animal biology, human biology, and plant biology respectively. The first and third contain 100 items each; the second, 110 items. The items are entirely objective, each form containing multiple-choice, matching and true-false questions. Validity coefficients range from .46 to .68; reliability coefficients between Forms A and B of the three tests are .70, .65, and .69 respectively. Odd-even correlations range from .72 to .84 for the six forms. Norms for each of Tests I and II are based upon more than 9,000 cases; those for Test III are based on only 752 cases. The tests are practically self-administering and well-arranged for scoring.

The tests are cheaply printed, each form being found on one sheet of 8½ by 11 inch paper. The type is small but clear. The test items might be criticized as emphasizing too heavily, isolated and unrelated information of a factual nature. Many of the questions are purely vocabulary items. There is not a proportionate emphasis on understanding and application of principles. Some of the sets of matching questions may be criticized as being too long. Sets of matching questions should usually not contain more than about fifteen items so as not to make the burden of reading and eye movements excessive.

Although the validity coefficients of these tests are fairly high the reliability coefficients leave something to be desired. It would be helpful to know what the probable errors of the coefficients are. On the whole, these tests seem to be fairly accurate and rapid measures of factual knowledge in the field of biology.

Dael L. Wolfle, Assistant Professor of Psychology, The University of Chicago. The three tests are designed to measure knowledge of: structural animal biology; human biology and man's general relationships to animals and plants; and plant biology and the relations of plants to other organisms. Each test includes a group of multiple-choice items with four or five alternatives; a group of true-false questions; and a group of matching items. Some of the tests include a number of items in which the "odd" one of five terms is to be indicated.

There has been a definite attempt to include material on the economic aspects of biology (even including an item which asks when the open season for hunting wild ducks ends). The average reliability of the six forms is .75; the average correlation with teachers' marks is .58. The test is less reliable and perhaps less valid than the older *Ruch-Cossmann Biology Test.*

There are several technical criticisms, and one of content. A few words are misspelled. Essentially the same item is occasionally included on two different forms, or even included twice within the same form. Some of the matching lists are longer than they should be for greatest convenience, and some include the same number of items in both lists—making matching by elimination possible.

In order to get 100 or 110 items on both sides of a single sheet of 8½ by 11 inch paper, small type and considerable crowding has been necessary. In the worst case, the student is asked to write 11 two-place numbers in a column one-fourth by one and one-fourth inches. Attempts to score such crowded answers will add one more irritation to the teachers' lot.

The most important criticism of the test is that it depends too much upon memory and too little upon the ability to apply biological principles or to draw reasonable and meaningful conclusions from biological situations. I went over two of the forms trying to decide the types of information necessary to answer each item. In one I marked 83 and in the other 91 of the 100 items as answerable on no basis other than memory of specific facts, definitions, or names. The remaining items included such questions as "Animal life is entirely dependent upon plant life for food," which a student might answer on the basis of general biological

knowledge. Relationships are stressed in a number of instances, but they are highly specific—of the codling moth to the apple, of the anopheles mosquito to malaria, or of the head louse to man. These items represent useful knowledge, but they should not constitute the whole of biology.

Better tests than this one are available in biology.

CHEMISTRY

[1590]

Clinton-Osborn-Ware General Chemistry Test. High school and college; 1936; 2 forms; $1.40 per 25; 10¢ per specimen set; high school: 90(100) minutes; college: 60(65) minutes; R. A. Osborn, Glen C. Ware, and R. J. Clinton; Corvallis, Ore.: O. S. C. Cooperative Association.

[1591]

Columbia Research Bureau Chemistry Test. Grades 11-13; 1928-29; 2 forms; $1.50 per 25; 20¢ per specimen set; 110(120) minutes; Eric R. Jette, Samuel R. Powers, and Ben D. Wood; Yonkers, N. Y.: World Book Co.

Max D. Engelhart, Director of the Department of Examinations, The Chicago City Junior Colleges, Chicago, Illinois. Part I of each form contains 150 true-false items covering general informational material. Part II contains 22 exercises concerned with the completing and balancing of equations. Part III calls for the solving of 10 typical problems.

A reliability coefficient of .87, based on the use of the Spearman-Brown formula, is reported. The test also has a correlation of .56 with college marks in chemistry. In using this coefficient as evidence of the validity of the test, one should recognize the fallibility of the criterion.

The norms are based on data for Form A. The data were collected from 8,000 high-school students in one state. Although Form B is said to be equivalent, one could wish that its norms had been established independently and that the norms for both forms had been based on data obtained from a larger and more representative population.

The test seems to be valid with respect to the objectives of the typical high-school or college elementary chemistry course. It would be less valid for use in a course in which less emphasis is given to factual details and more emphasis is placed on general principles. There is almost nothing in either form on atomic structure. One can deprecate slightly the extensive list of true-false items of Part I and wish that a greater variety of objective exercises had been used. The scoring of Parts II and III is somewhat complex, but the directions for scoring are adequate.

[1592]
Cooperative Chemistry Test. High school; 1933-40; 40- and 90-minute editions; 25¢ per specimen set of either edition; Form P: Victor H. Noll, S. R. Powers, and Alexander Calandra; Form Q: Alexander Calandra with the editorial assistance of Theodore A. Ashford, M. D. Engelhart, R. N. Hilkert, G. E. Kimball, and V. H. Noll; New York: Cooperative Test Service.
a) FORMS 1936 AND 1937. Forms 1933, 1934, and 1935 are out of print; 6¢ per test, 10 to 99 copies; 90(95) minutes.
b) REVISED SERIES FORMS N, O, P, AND Q. 1937-40; 5¢ per test, 10 to 99 copies; 1½c per machine-scorable answer sheet; 40(45) minutes.

Charles L. Bickel, Science Department, The Phillips Exeter Academy, Exeter, New Hampshire. [Review of Form P.] The chemistry syllabus, which the *Cooperative Chemistry Test* is supposed to cover, is necessarily restricted to the barest fundamentals of the science. The limitations imposed by a one-year course make any departure from this minimum content quite impossible. However, a large number of good questions of the type used on the Cooperative test can be chosen from the material offered in this minimum syllabus.

There are too few questions in the 1939 examination which test the fundamentals of a beginning course and far too many questions which are concerned with material which is too specialized in its nature.

Factual questions are necessary and the results from them are indicative. However, questions which involve the use of factual material by a reasoning process are to be preferred and should be used if possible. The 1939 Cooperative test has few questions which require reasoning. Most of the items are factual and far too many of the factual questions are concerned with isolated material which is of no great importance in the one-year course. A forty-minute testing program can be carried out without including such foreign items.

The *Cooperative Chemistry Test* includes only four questions, Items 52-55 in Part I, of the problem type. In my opinion, achievement in chemistry can well be measured in this way. More of the problem types should have been tested.

An objective type question discriminates well only when the selection of the correct item is not too easy. Many questions are very poor in this respect. Many of the responses can be eliminated without any special ability or achievement in chemistry.

The interpretation of simple diagrams and charts appeals to me as a step in the right direction in testing. Items 28 and 29 in Part I and Item 9 in Part II are of this type. However, I object to Item 28 on the ground that the student should be tested on the solubility of salts in general rather than on the solubility of a particular salt. It is possible that a salt might have the solubility curve *EF*. Item 29, on the other hand, is very good because it deals with the general behavior of gases. It is my guess that the directions for Item 9 are too involved and that many students will misinterpret them.

I believe wholeheartedly in objective testing. It seems to me that a large mass of material can be tested more soundly by the objective method if the time of testing is limited. However, I feel very strongly that the *Cooperative Chemistry Test*, as a whole, is not a good test. The poor items outnumber the good. Such a condition can, however, be remedied by a more careful selection of questions. This problem is now being considered by a committee appointed last spring by the Educational Records Bureau.

Detailed Criticism of Questions.

GOOD QUESTIONS. Part I—Items 6, 10, 12, 14, 15, 21, 25, 29, 30, 32, 41, 45, 47, 50, 52, 53, 54, and 55. Part II—Items 2, 5, 8, 12, 13, 14, and 15.

GOOD QUESTIONS WITH QUALIFICATIONS. Part I—Item 2: may raise the question of silicon in the mind of a good student; Item 9: requires more than a casual acquaintance with organic chemistry; Item 11: good, if remembering a highly specialized word is a desirable achievement; Item 13: good, if "for preparing sulfuric acid" is inserted; Item 26: although the question depends on the word *Haber*, this process is used to illustrate so many elementary principles that use of question is justified; Item 44: good if student reasons. Part II—Item 1: good if the student does not consider the question carefully for although silver nitrate is used, other conditions must be fulfilled and, strictly speaking, no possible answer is a correct one. Item 4: could have had a better choice of responses than those numbered 2 and 5. Item 10: good, assuming that the equation is correct, which it is not. The good student will object that no answer is correct unless it is represented as an equilibrium reaction by double arrows, ⇌. Item 11: good although Mg Br Cl is a possible product. Items 31-35: good if directions are understood. It is suggested that an example be given for guidance.

POOR QUESTIONS. Part I—Item 1: too easy; Item 3: not chemistry, merely a vocabulary test; Item 4: requires no knowledge of Cd, As, or Ra; Item 5: responses 2, 3, and 4 are words about which students probably know nothing; Item 7: necessitates knowledge of the meaning of *flux*; Item 8: not elementary chemistry; Item 16: depends on remembering one uncommon word, *thermit*; Item 17: better responses than 2, 3, and 4 might be made; Item 18: not ordinarily studied; Item 19: depends too much on memory of colors, not fundamental; Item 20: too easy; Items 22 and 23: too specialized; Item 24: too easy; Item 27: too specialized; Item 28: a question whether or not the student should remember that the solubility of KNO_3 increases steadily with increase in temperature; Item 31: too easy; Item 33: in reviewer's opinion, specific organic knowledge should not be tested in an elementary test; Item 34: both responses 3 and 4 are good although 3 is much the better; Item 36: both responses 3 and 5 might be used, if oil means grease; Item 37: requires information outside the scope of an elementary course; Item 38: requires heats of combustion data which even a chemist of standing might not remember; Item 39: although textiles can be made from wood, glass, cotton, coal, and silk, coal is, however, presumably the correct answer; Item 40: too much organic chemistry required and, in any case, I do not believe that benzoic acid is indigenous to grape juice at any stage; Item 42: responses 1 or 2 might be correct, depending on the interpretation of the word *base*; Item 43: terms are not in common use in elementary chemistry; Item 46: requires specific information which is not fundamental to elementary chemistry; Item 48: too easy; Item 49: not chemistry, poorly worded, and, strictly speaking, there is no correct answer in a chemical sense; Item 51: too specialized. Part II—Item 3: requires too specific knowledge of physical and chemical properties of clay and wax; Item 6: too easy; Item 7: specific information about an element

which may not be studied extensively; Item 9: directions may be misinterpreted; Items 16-30: in my own experience with objective tests, this type of objective question gives very little useful data.

Louis M. Heil, Associate Professor of Education, The University of Chicago, and Research Associate in Science, Cooperative Study in General Education, American Council on Education. [Review of Form P.] The following review has been made on the basis of an examination of the revised Form P of the *Cooperative Chemistry Test* together with a statement of the purposes, construction, and possible uses of the tests found in the handbook of the Cooperative achievement tests and in the bulletin on directions for using the Cooperative tests.

The test consists of two parts, the first part of which contains 55 items and the second 35. The items in these two parts of the test seem to cover the field of classical or traditional chemistry quite adequately in terms of the knowledge of specific facts and terms. The field of modern chemistry, however, receives little emphasis. This omission is probably explained by the fact that the authors have attempted to base the test on the common content of four widely used chemistry textbooks; and frequently, a considerable time lag exists between the discoveries in chemistry and their appearance in textbooks.

According to the statement of the authors the test is expected to measure five main types of objectives in the field of chemistry. (*a*) "Knowledge and understanding of chemical laws, principles, and theories." (*b*) "Knowledge of, and ability to use, fundamental tools of chemistry." (*c*) "Understanding and appreciation of applications of chemistry in industrial processes and in daily life." (*d*) "Ability to perform correctly simple basic calculations in chemical problems involving the application of chemical principles." (*e*) "Knowledge and appreciation of great chemists and their contributions."

An analysis of the test shows that 62 of the 90 items may be classified under the heading of "a knowledge of, and ability to use, fundamental tools of chemistry," while 8 of the items ask for a knowledge of the "laws and principles" of chemistry. Twenty of the items of the test require an application of certain laws and principles in the field of chemistry. Nine of these 20, however, are devoted to an application of the principles of valence and the balancing of equations while 4 require that the student solve numerical problems which require knowledge of certain chemical principles. Seventeen of the items of the examination refer to chemistry in industrial processes and in everyday life.

Another reviewer might make a somewhat different assignment of the individual items of the test to the five objectives which the author has stated for the test; but it seems that an undue emphasis has been given in the test to the second objective, namely, "a knowledge of, and ability to use, the fundamental tools of chemistry."

The statistical reliability of the test is such that over a possible range of scores from 29 to 99 (scaled scores) the standard error of the average twelfth-grade student is two points. This means that the total score of any one student is determined with sufficient accuracy for the usual grading purposes.

In the booklet on directions for using the Cooperative tests the following uses, among others, are suggested for the test: "To give a preview of the status of an individual or of an entire class at the beginning of a course or curriculum so that appropriate placement may be made and later instruction intelligently modified." "Test results may be much better used as a basis for improved guidance and better adaptation of instructional materials to individual needs and capacities than as a stimulus to the teacher to put increased pressure on her pupils merely to learn more 'subject-matter'." If this test is to be used for these purposes it would be necessary to break the total score into partial scores indicating the extent to which an individual student or the class as a whole demonstrate achievement or lack of achievement in those purposes or aspects of the course which the teacher considers to be important. For example, in a chemistry test it might be possible to determine the extent to which students know the specific characteristics of certain elements and compounds, the extent to which they can apply such knowledge in arriving at conclusions in chemistry problems requiring the knowledge of the facts and principles, the extent to which students are able to work and solve numerical problems involving an application of chemical principles, etc. Un-

doubtedly, the degree to which any one student's score could be estimated in each of these specific or individual purposes would be low in comparison with the reliability of estimating the total score but the estimate should be high enough to make some fairly valid inferences concerning the kind of instruction which would be most appropriate for the student. Unless such a breakdown is made the teacher only knows that the student is good or poor in general. For purposes of improvement the instructor is forced to apply "heat" all through chemistry for those students who demonstrate or exhibit a low pretest score.

SUMMARY. The test seems to cover the field of classical or traditional chemistry quite well but contains omissions in modern chemistry. The relatively low standard error of measurement of the test indicates that it is quite discriminating of student achievement in those aspects of chemical knowledge which are included in it. Those teachers who wish to use the test for diagnostic purposes will have to study the test carefully, selecting those items which summarize the purposes of instruction in chemistry which are important to them.

For reviews by Edward E. Cureton and W. B. Meldrum, see 932.

[1593]

Cooperative Chemistry Test for College Students. 1938-40; Forms 1938, 1939, and 1940; 6¢ per test, 10 to 99 copies; 1½¢ per machine-scorable answer sheet; 25¢ per specimen set; 90(95) minutes; Form 1940: B. Clifford Hendricks, B. H. Handorf, O. M. Smith, Ralph W. Tyler, and Fred P. Frutchey with the collaboration of numerous others; New York: Cooperative Test Service.

REFERENCES

1 AMERICAN CHEMICAL SOCIETY, DIVISION OF CHEMICAL EDUCATION, COMMITTEE ON EXAMINATIONS AND TESTS, O. M. SMITH, CHAIRMAN. "The 1935-36 College Chemistry Testing Program." *J Chem Ed* 14:229-31 My '37.
2 PHELAN, EARL W. "The 1936-1937 College Chemistry Testing Program." *J Chem Ed* 14:586-90 D '37.
3 REED, RUFUS D. "The 1937-1938 College Chemistry Testing Program." *J Chem Ed* 16:184-90 Ap '39.
4 MARTIN, F. D. "The 1938-1939 College Chemistry Testing Program." *J Chem Ed* 17:70-6 F '40.
5 MARTIN, F. D., AND ALLEN, F. J. "The 'Clerical Facility' Factor for Students Taking Objectively Scored Tests by Direct Answer on the Test Sheet versus Separate Answer Sheets." *J Chem Ed* 17:76-7 F '40.

[1594]

Cooperative Chemistry Test in Qualitative Analysis. College; 1939-40; 1 form (Provisional Forms P and Q); 4¢ per test, 10 to 99 copies; 25¢ per specimen set; 60(65) minutes; prepared jointly by the Cooperative Test Service and the Division of Chemical Education of the American Chemical Society; Form P: Rufus D. Reed, Alexander Calandra, and W. B. Cortelyou; Form Q: Rufus D. Reed and Alexander Calandra with the assistance of J. Greenspan, D. Hart, G. Hinden, S. Leikind, L. S. Foster, J. R. Lacher, T. R. Hogness, L. P. Hammett, P. A.

Arthur, Allan Humphreys, O. M. Smith, L. A. Gold-blatt, D. W. Pearce, and W. B. Cortelyou; New York: Cooperative Test Service.

REFERENCES

1 REED, RUFUS D.; CORTELYOU, W. P.; AND CALANDRA, ALEXANDER. "Aims or Objectives of Qualitative Analysis." *J Chem Ed* 17:220-5 My '40.

[1595]
Cooperative Objective Tests in Organic Chemistry: 1939-1940 Series. First, second semesters: college; 1939; 9 subtests and a final test for the first semester; 17 subtests and a final test for the second semester; 20¢ per set, 5 or more sets; 25¢ per specimen set; (20-30) minutes per subject; Ed. F. Degering; Lafayette, Ind.: the Author, Chemistry Department, Purdue University.

[1596]
Glenn-Welton Chemistry Achievement Test. First, second semesters: high school; 1930-38; 2 forms, 2 levels; $1.30 per 25; 35¢ per specimen set; 71(80) minutes; Earl R. Glenn and Louis E. Welton; Yonkers, N. Y.: World Book Co.
a) TEST 1. First semester.
b) TEST 2. Second semester.

Max D. Engelhart, Director of the Department of Examinations, The Chicago City Junior Colleges, Chicago, Illinois. Each test is divided into the following parts: Part I, Range of Information; Part II, Practical Application of Chemical Principles; Part III, Vocabulary; Part IV, Laboratory Manipulation and Processes; and Part V, Formulas, Equations, and Problems.

The correlation between Forms A and B of Test 1 is .91. The reliability of both forms when administered together is estimated at .95. For Test 2, these coefficients are, respectively, .93 and .96.

The norms for both forms of Test 1 are based on 670 cases from nineteen schools in nine states. The norms for both forms of Test 2 are based on 595 cases from twelve schools in six states. These norms are labeled "tentative."

The exercises of the tests are based on analyses of six courses of study and ten textbooks. The content is claimed to be representative of what is taught in first-year high school chemistry. While this claim is no doubt justified, the tests should prove less valid in courses where less empsasis is placed on factual details and more emphasis is given to general principles. There is little mention of the newer concepts of atomic structure. The authors are to be commended for using a variety of types of objective exercises. Particularly pleasing is the number of exercises relating to diagrams.

Victor H. Noll, Head of the Department of Education and Professor of Education, Michi-gan State College. In content, Tests 1 and 2 are alike, covering range of information, practical applications of chemical principles, vocabulary, laboratory manipulation and processes, and formulas, equations, and problems.

Validity is inferential as based on courses of study and textbooks; also, on the dicriminating power of items. It is stated that "only those items were retained in which the number of students in the high group who passed the item was appreciably greater than the number in the medium group, and the same for the medium and poor groups." What the authors considered "appreciably greater" is not stated.

The reliability coefficients are high. The correlation between Form A and Form B of Test 1 is .91. For Form A and Form B of Test 2 it is .93. The types of items used are completion, multiple-choice, controlled association, matching or identification and problems. The scoring is said to be wholly objective but it is questionable whether this can be said of completion items.

In general, the arrangement of material in the test is good. Scoring is rapid and as easy as most standardized tests in chemistry. Some tests available now are somewhat more objective. One feature of the arrangement could be improved. In Part II and Part IV of each form, reference to drawing is necessary. If it were possible, it would be better to print all drawings and all questions pertaining thereto on facing pages to eliminate the necessity of turning the page back and forth. This test is well conceived and, except for minor criticisms mentioned, well executed. There is a genuine need for measuring instruments that pioneer beyond the safe zone of factual information and established chemical theory. Although this test is still weighted on the side of such knowledge, it goes beyond the kind of measurement which characterizes most of our work in this field. Among existing tests of chemistry for high school pupils it deserves a high rating.

Eugene A. Waters, Associate Professor of Education, The University of Tennessee. The Glenn-Welton test consists of two parts: Test 1, covering the parts of the subject usually taught in the first half year's work, to be used at the end of the first semester; and Test 2, covering the parts of the subject usually taught in the second half year, to be used at the close of the second semester. Each of the two tests is comprised of five parts: Part I, designed to yield a measure of the "students' range of information of chemical facts"; Part II, "contains drawings representing chemical principles and questions to determine whether the students understand the principles"; Part III, "measures associational vocabulary"; Part IV, "contains drawings of laboratory apparatus and questions concerning their use and operation"; and Part V, "measures the students' knowledge of and ability to solve equations and problems." The two forms are similar in content, organization, and difficulty.

According to the authors, validity of test items is based "on a study of six courses of study and ten textbooks." Also "the drawings for Parts II and IV, the vocabulary items, and the equations, formulas, and problems are based on tabulations of the occurrences of these types of items in the most widely used textbooks." From an analysis of data obtained from a preliminary edition those items which differentiated most completely between good and poor students were selected for inclusion in the present final edition. From this procedure the authors assume that "items were obtained each of which measured to some extent the students' total knowledge of chemistry." The coefficients of correlation between the two forms of Test 1 and between the two forms of Test 2 are reported as being .91 and .93 respectively.

One major limitation in the usefulness of this test, as is true of all similar tests, lies in its lack of appropriateness in those situations wherein significant changes in the content of chemistry courses has occurred. Another obvious, and perhaps intended, limitation of the test is its restriction to "right answers" and the type of educational outcomes associated with the theory of teaching which this point of view subsumes. Some few of the test items are seemingly not of sufficient specificity to actually permit a thoughtful student to arrive at *the* right answer within the strict limits of the factors obviously present or which *might* be present in the situation described by these items. This difficulty is not peculiar to this particular test but is a rather general restriction of many tests of its general type.

J Chem Ed 15:449 S '38. O. M. Smith. * A continuous period of seventy-one minutes is required to administer the test. This is a rather

long period of sustained attention for high-school students; to break the time would invalidate the reliability of the norms. * The questions are interesting and challenging and are arranged with increasing difficulty, thus encouraging the weaker students. In most cases the questions are clearly stated and should be easily understood. The ingenious use of many illustrations breaks the monotony of the usual test. In some instances the object or the diagram are not familiar to all students and in many cases the use of the illustration is of no aid, as, for example, a picture of a storage battery or a Pyrene fire extinguisher. The number of errors is small. The elimination of considerable duplication, the addition of the periodic chart and the E. M. F. series would improve the test. On the whole, the test is a good one, neither too difficult nor too easy for high-school students, for the authors have sampled the representative and interesting parts of the high-school course with discrimination.

[1597]

Intermediate Chemistry Test. "Students intending to sit for the Chemistry or Elementary Science examinations at the Junior Public or Intermediate stage; 1937; 2 forms, 2 booklets; 2 editions of Parts 3 and 4; 9d. per 12 booklets; 1s. 6d. per 12 complete tests; 7d. per manual; 85(90-95) minutes; Roy W. Stanhope; Melbourne, Australia: Australian Council for Educational Research.
a) PARTS 1 AND 2. 40(45) minutes.
b) PARTS 3 AND 4. 45(50) minutes. Issued in both the regular and the Victorian Edition.

GENERAL SCIENCE

[1598]

Analytical Scales of Attainment in Elementary Science. Grades 5-6, 7-8, 9; 1933; 1 form, 3 levels; 75¢ per 25; 15¢ per specimen set; (45) minutes; August Dvorak and M. J. Van Wagenen; Minneapolis, Minn.: Educational Test Bureau, Inc.
a) [DIVISION 2.] Grades 5-6.
b) [DIVISION 3.] Grades 7-8.
c) [DIVISION 4.] Grade 9.

Francis D. Curtis, Professor of Secondary Education and of the Teaching of Science, The University of Michigan. Each test consists of forty five-choice multiple-response items on each of three phases of material, namely, physiology and hygiene, biological sciences, and physical sciences. The test can be quickly and objectively scored by means of the keys provided, and the scores can be readily translated into "Elementary Science Ages." The opening statement under the "General Directions" states that "the Analytical Scales of Attainment are designed to measure the abilities and the ranges of information of the pupils. . . ." There is no explanation, however, of what the abilities in question are, nor is their nature evident from an inspection of the test items. One looks in vain in the materials accompanying the tests for any statements of the specific sources or materials used in selecting the items, and for any discussion of the validity and reliability of the tests. It is probable, however, that these important aspects are covered by the general statements in the materials distributed by the publishers. The tests are open to serious criticism on the grounds that they measure little or nothing other than retention of factual information. Test scores are expressed in C-scores. The only explanation of the method of determining these C-scores, however, consists in a reference in the sheet accompanying the tests to similar scores in another test. Moreover, the C-scores are translated into "Elementary Science Ages" which range from nine years (fourth grade) to seventeen years and six months. It is not clear why the scales are not designed to measure the achievement in elementary science of children in grades below the fourth and younger than nine years old. The directions for taking the test are somewhat perplexing owing to the fact that the second example has two correct responses, the second of which, but not the one given as the correct one in the paragraph of explanations, is, from the standpoint of the botanist, more rigorously correct than the accepted one. Among the various items of the tests are a few which have more than one correct response among the five given. There is some duplication of items in the tests provided for the various grade levels. Moreover, the items in the ninth-grade test which are not duplicated in the two tests for earlier grades embody no advance in difficulty over the items in tests for younger children. Some of the items in each of the tests may deserve criticism on the grounds that the purely factual information which they test is not especially significant or valuable information. These tests cover a wide range of factual information in a generally satisfactory way. Nevertheless such tests are open to the criticism that in testing mere factual information they test only the means to desirable ends and not any of the accepted goals of science teaching.

Victor H. Noll, Head of the Department of Education and Professor of Education, Michi- gan State College. These tests are in the series of achievement tests worked out under the direction of Van Wagenen. They are typical of a small number of carefully scaled tests now available in which the difficulty value of each item is carefully determined and expressed in probable error or similar units. The value of such techniques has been vigorously debated pro and con, and many studies have been made to determine whether tests so scaled provide demonstrably different results from those obtained by use of tests in which the elaborate scaling techniques have not been used. The outcomes of most such studies leave a serious doubt as to the value of the procedure.

Each division has three parts covering physiology and hygiene, biological sciences, and physical sciences. There are 120 items of the multiple-choice type in each scale, 40 in each part. Many items are found in all three divisions. The scale values for Division 2 run from 63 to 102; those for Division 3, from 70 to 109; and those for Division 4, from 75 to 114. The middle scale contains the same items as the lowest one except for a small number of the easiest items which are omitted and the addition of a few more difficult items. The same relationship holds as between the medium and the hardest scale. This would appear to be an undesirably large amount of duplication, especially in view of the fact that there is but one form of each scale. The tests purport to cover a body of subject matter often included in general science on the junior high school level. It is regrettable that no effort seems to have been made to establish their reliability or validity. No information is given on these matters nor on the source of materials on which the tests are based. They seem potentially useful but concrete evidence of their value, the basis for scaling and standardization, and their suitability for measuring attainment in general science at the junior high school level is almost wholly lacking.

[1599]

Application of Principles in Science: Test 1.3b. Grades 9-12; 1940; 1 form; a revision of Test 1.3; 5¢ per test; 1¢ per machine-scorable answer sheet for Test 1.3b; 5¢ per explanation sheet and interpretation guide; $1.50 per set of stencils for machine scoring; 60(70) minutes; Chicago, Ill.: Evaluation in the Eight Year Study, Progressive Education Association.

REFERENCES

1 RATHS, LOUIS E. *Application of Principles.* Progressive Education Association, Evaluation in the Eight Year Study, Bulletin No. 5. Chicago, Ill.: the Study, December 1936. Pp. 25. Paper, mimeographed. Out of print.

2 *Evaluation Materials Developed for Various Aspects of Thinking.* Chicago, Ill.: Evaluation in the Eight Year Study, Progressive Education Association, March 1939. Pp. [22]. Paper, mimeographed. Out of print.

[1600]

Cause and Effect Relationship Test in Science: Scientific Attitudes, Test 2. Grades 9-12; 1937-39; 1 form; $1.25 per 25; 40(45) minutes; State Science Committee of the Wisconsin Education Association; Milwaukee, Wis.: E. M. Hale and Co.

Louis M. Heil, Associate Professor of Education, The University of Chicago, and Research Associate in Science, Cooperative Study in General Education, American Council on Education. The *Cause and Effect Relationship Test in Science* represents an effort to measure one of the more elusive attitudes which the study of science purports to develop. The test consists of 66 pairs of "occurrences" taken mainly from the field of science. For example, "A flash of lightning illuminated the sky; the roll of thunder accompanied it." The first of each of the pairs of occurrences is to be judged by the student in one of four ways which represent a gradation from "total cause" of the second occurrence to "bears no causal relationship."

An inspection of the scoring key indicates that a considerable difference of opinion might exist concerning the judgment expected from the student. For example, in the pair "A flash of lightning illuminated the sky; the roll of thunder accompanied it," the first occurrence is keyed as "bearing no causal relationship" to the second. Depending upon the explanation which might be used to relate lightning and thunder it seems to the reviewer that the degree of causality would be greater than zero as the key indicates. The same criticism may be made of a number of the other items in the test.

The difficulty experienced in attempting to answer the items in the test probably results from the test directions which require that the judgment be made in terms of "degrees of causality." It would seem that a valid judgment of the degree to which students are able to assign "acceptable causality" to an event would not be revealed by the test until the directions are somewhat further clarified.

The analysis of the results of the use of the test reported by T. L. Torgerson indicate that the test has a reliability coefficient of .74 and a probable error of measurement of 2.4. The standard deviation of the scores obtained through the use of the test is 6.9. The data also seem to indicate that no significant growth

occurs for students who have had successively more science, that is, two or three years of science. This fact is explained by the authors to mean that "schools are not stressing learning of this nature." Although this inference may be true, it is also highly probable that students with more science training may make judgments on the test items which they could very easily justify but which do not agree with the key.

[1601]

Cooperative General Science Test. High school; 1933-40; 40- and 90-minute editions; 25¢ per specimen set of either edition; Form P: O. E. Underhill and S. R. Powers with the editorial assistance of Ralph D. Britton, Forrest W. Cobb, John C. Mayfield, Chester F. Protheroe, Myra Robinson, and Richard G. Sagebeer; Form Q: O. E. Underhill and S. R. Powers with the editorial assistance of John C. Mayfield, H. G. McMullen, Chester F. Protheroe, Myra Robinson, and P. Victor Peterson; New York: Cooperative Test Service.
a) FORMS 1933, 1934, 1935, AND 1936. Form 1937 is out of print; 6¢ per test, 10 to 99 copies; 90(95) minutes.
b) REVISED SERIES FORMS O, P, AND Q. 1937-40; Form N is out of print; 5¢ per test, 10 to 99 copies; 1½¢ per machine-scorable answer sheet; 40(45) minutes.

G. W. Hunter, Lecturer in Science Education, Claremont Colleges. [Review of Form P.] The Cooperative tests are so well known that it is not necessary to describe this one in detail. The test consists of 99 items in two groups. Most of the items show a four- or five-reponse multiple-choice arrangement, but there are two diagrams which have questions applying to them. The test shows considerable improvement over that of last year because several of the questions break away from the purely factual and conventional forms and are given as problems with a choice of several possible solutions. It is to be hoped that this type of question may increase in the future.

The test covers the field of general science admirably and presents a well-balanced group of questions. It seems to the writer that the test is rather difficult for the average student. This is perhaps to be expected when we realize that all the makers of the test are connected with private institutions or practice schools rather than secondary schools under state control. Especially is the emphasis on mathematical physics to be condemned. It is doubtful if students in the ninth grade of the average high school under state control would be able to answer some of these questions. Forty minutes seems too brief a period for the time given to the test.

It would seem to the writer that the best use for these tests would be as student self-help exercises since they are rather difficult and since they cover the ground of general science so completely.

For reviews by Alvin W. Schindler and W. B. Meldrum, see 1125.

[1602]

General Science Test: National Achievement Tests. Grades 7-9; 1936-39; 2 forms; $1.75 per 25; 5¢ per specimen set; nontimed (30-45) minutes; Robert K. Speer, Lester D. Crow, and Samuel Smith; Rockville Centre, N. Y.: Acorn Publishing Co.

Francis D. Curtis, Professor of Secondary Education and of the Teaching of Science, The University of Michigan. This test represents a commendable effort to provide a scientifically constructed test for general science. Scholarly attention has been given in its construction to such important aspects as standardization, validity, reliability, objectivity, and ease of administration and scoring.

In the descriptive leaflet accompanying the tests is the statement, "With rare exceptions each test measures not only the mastery of subject matter but *especially the pupil's ability to use knowledge.*" The statement is undoubtedly intended to apply generally to the large group of National Achievement Tests of which this test is one; it is seriously to be questioned, however, with respect to this test of general science. This test as a whole seems to reward unduly the mere memory of scientific facts and terminology. It would seem possible to make a high score on the test without demonstrating attainment in terms of accepted major goals of science teaching.

Part I, consisting of twenty four-choice multiple-response items on general concepts, is perhaps the best of the six parts. Most of the items test understanding of general concepts that are of undoubted value. A few items, however, are open to challenge on the grounds that they test specific rather than general information. Also, some of the vocabulary used in these items seems likely to be beyond the comprehension of most ninth-grade pupils.

Part II, consisting of twenty items on identification, seems to exemplify an undesirable extreme in testing memory of facts in some items, for example, those that require the identification of vitamins by their lettered designations. Moreover, there seems to be a good chance to guess at least one of the answers in the first group of items; also, the diagram of the lever seems likely to introduce undesired difficulty. This part of the test would seem capable, with practicable modifications, of being made into a test of understanding of scientific principles.

Part III, a matching test of ten items on association, seems to be an excellent test of its kind. It may be questioned, however, whether the association of noted scientists' names with their major achievements is important enough to be made one of six parts in a test on general science.

Part IV, a matching test of fifteen items on words and definitions, measures the ability to match scientific terms with their definitions. It does not, however, test understanding of these definitions.

Part V, consisting of twenty items on uses, tests the ability to match the name of a machine, a device, or an instrument with its use. It tests only knowledge of function. It makes no attempt to measure the more important aspect, namely, knowledge of *how* the machine, device, or instrument is used.

Part VI, a multiple-response test of thirty-five four-choice items on miscellaneous facts is just what the designation implies. One might question the importance of the facts measured by some of the items.

As a test of chiefly factual information, this *General Science Test* has many excellent features. It seems inevitable, however, that tests of this type must rapidly yield the field to tests measuring more important outcomes of science teaching.

G. W. Hunter, Lecturer in Science Education, Claremont Colleges. The test is one of the National Achievement series in their teach-study-test program. The objective, according to the statement of their editor, Robert K. Speer of New York University, is to help the instructor utilize the most efficient instruction methods in accordance with the requirements of his students. The purpose of the test is diagnostic, enabling the instructor to discover deficiencies of the student in any item of the test. The test was therefore constructed "to test the student's knowledge of general concepts; ability to match words and definitions; ability to match objects with their use; recognition of important men of science; ability to identify objects from illustrations and ability to recognize correct from incorrect; and miscellaneous facts in science."

The test is divided into six parts, having a total of 120 items. The areas are: I, General Concepts; II, Identifications; III, Important Men of Science; IV, Words and Definitions; V, Uses; and VI, Miscellaneous Facts. Several types of test construction are used, multiple choice with four alternate choices, matching, and identification of diagrams. A double check on the student's accuracy is found in the fact that the user is asked not only to place the proper letter in the parenthesis to the right of the word or sentence chosen as correct, but also to place a similar letter in the answer column at the right.

The question of the validity of the test is always a pertinent one. If we consider knowledge without practical application as a goal, then the test is excellent. Validity is, as Ralph W. Tyler sees it, a very *specific* concept and because of this teachers ought to consider carefully what is valid for their specific situation. If the objective here is a test for simple, factual knowledge without application of principles, then we have a well-balanced test so far as subject matter goes. If, however, as teachers we believe that science should result in more than pure memory work, then the test is little better than scores of other tests that are now on the market.

The test has a reliability coefficient of .93, which is quite high. We have, however, no guide to tell us how this reliability was obtained.

The makers of the test missed a good opportunity to get away from the mere factual point of view in the first group of questions in Part I, General Concepts. Here several questions deal with the scientific method and scientific attitude, but as the test is given, it is simply an opportunity for the pupil to reproduce textbook statements.

On the whole the test is relatively free from misstatements and ambiguity and gives an excellent sampling of general science subject matter as found in recent textbooks and courses of study. The test is not too difficult for the average "run of the mill" students and is easy to administer and score. It is a pity that the authors did not consider as an objective the solving of problems, for, as the test stands, it is purely factual.

[1603]

Science Information Test. Grades 4-6, 7-9; 1937; 2 forms, 2 levels; 75¢ per 25; 25¢ per specimen set; nontimed (60) minutes; Everett T. Calvert; Los Angeles, Calif.: California Test Bureau.
a) ELEMENTARY. Grades 4-6.
b) INTERMEDIATE. Grades 7-9.

Hans C. Gordon, Division of Educational Research, Public Schools, Philadelphia, Pennsylvania. These tests of science information modestly do not attempt to measure other objectives of science teaching. The content is entirely verbal; no pictorial material is presented. The author recognizes the subordinate importance to be attached to measures of information. However, the use of the test is recommended to determine whether more, or less, emphasis should be put on the science teaching in a local situation. The test results may also be used to guide the emphasis upon different phases of science instruction.

The content is derived from material used in widely different parts of the United States. Norms are those of children with an IQ of approximately 98 in cities and rural areas in central and southern California. This information is not given in the manual of directions although it is essential in using the test to determine whether more or less emphasis should be placed upon science teaching as a whole in a local situation. The test probably has one of its most important uses for teachers who wish to determine how well their children achieve in those formal phases of science study that are commonly offered in the larger communities of the United States. The nature of this analysis is shown by the subtest titles: Animal Life, Plant Life, Physical Changes, and Other Science in the Elementary Form; and Animal Life, Plant Life, Physical Information, Earth Study, Sky Study, and Elementary Chemistry in the Intermediate Form.

The analysis is probably reliable only for the averages of groups of children. The reliability coefficients for total scores are reported for spreads of three grades: .93 for grades 4-6 and .90 for grades 7-9. These have been attained, presumably, by the split-half method. Reliability coefficients for the individual grades (not given in the manual) are lower, ranging from .82 for grade 5 to .90 for grades 4 and 7. The reliability coefficients are not especially high for a test requiring about one hour. Reliability coefficients for various subtests are not available but it is to be assumed that they are correspondingly lower because of smaller numbers of items and the failure to establish time limits for the separate subtests. The test provides an individual profile chart upon the test paper, recording the grade scores in the subtests. The value of these scores, except in totals or averages, is somewhat questionable. It does not seem to be a worth-while activity to find that a given pupil is deficient in Earth Study, a 12-item subtest, if, upon repetition of another form of the test he shows a greater deficiency in Elementary Chemistry, also a 12-item subtest. This is almost certain to happen with subtests of low individual reliability.

The test is a valid test of science information as validity is ordinarily conceived. The items are a representative sampling of commonly taught items of information in science. Textbooks of the large publishing companies and courses of study in three large states and eleven large cities furnished the basic material for this test. Scientific accuracy of the items was checked by teachers of specialized science in the high school and junior college. The items used in the test were those found by acceptable statistical procedures to be those most valid in differentiating between pupils who had the highest and the lowest total scores in the preliminary test. In spite of this fact, the test contains the usual assortment of ambiguous items. This leads to questioning those methods of validation which depend largely upon the statistical procedure of comparing the results in one item with total scores obtained for many items, both valid and not valid. For example, in the Elementary Form A test, pupils are presented with the following item: A tiger and a lion are most like a ¹ dog ² kitten ³ puppy ⁴ bear. Pupils in grade 4 are credited with the correct science information only if they give the answer "kitten," recognizing that the kitten belongs to the family *Felidae* as does the tiger and the lion. However, at this stage of a child's development it would probably be quite as scientific to answer "bear" in that tigers, lions, and bears are *wild* animals while dogs, kittens, and puppies are not.

G. W. Hunter, Lecturer in Science Education, Claremont Colleges. This test is intended "to furnish a valid and reliable measure of the degree to which pupils in various grades have acquired information necessary to understand their natural environment." The maker of the tests evidently bases his informational material on California courses of study in science and on the pamphlets of science information put out for teachers by the California State Department of Education. Such tests of information may be valid for California, but not for other parts of the country. The material deals with a recognition of common flowers, trees, birds, and animals, a knowledge of weather conditions and the environmental forces that surround the child.

The tests are divided into several areas which deal respectively with animal life, plant life, physical information, earth study, sky study, and elementary chemistry. Some of us would take exception to the latter area if we recognize Hanor A. Webb's experimental work with children in this field.

The test items would certainly not always be a part of the information which urban children have. It seems to the writer that many of the items are obviously intended for rural children. Examples might be: "A rabbit thumps the ground when he is: ¹ drinking ² signaling ³ eating ⁴ sleeping; The ground is a poor bottom for a rabbit pen because rabbits ¹ catch cold ² burrow ³ eat grass ⁴ die"; and "The bird most apt to be found around the marshes is the ¹ eagle ² mud-hen ³ canary ⁴ woodpecker." There are several examples of inaccuracies or difficulties of interpretation. Examples might be: "When a frog's throat throbs, he is ¹ breathing ² swallowing ³ chewing ⁴ drinking"; and "A coral reef is composed of ¹ vegetable remains ² animal remains ³ iron ⁴ wood."

In both elementary and intermediate tests there is an overusage of difficult terms and in many of the items there is a very great chance for guessing. It seems to the writer that one great deficiency in the test is the entire absence of any items which deal with health or functional knowledge of the human body.

The makers of the tests claim validity based on actual teaching materials furnished by various leading publishers and the commonly accepted objectives of teachers. The writer would take exception to this statement. The coefficient of reliability for the elementary tests is .93 (grades 4-6) and for the intermediate tests, .91 (grades 7-9). Norms have been established based on the results of testing over 3,000 pupils in the elementary group and over

2,500 in the intermediate group, these pupils coming from about 80 different schools.

[1604]

Survey Test in the Natural Sciences: Cooperative General Achievement Test, Part II. High school and college placement; 1937-39; Forms N, O, and P; 6¢ per test, 10 to 99 copies; 1½¢ per machine-scorable answer sheet; 25¢ per specimen set; 40(45) minutes; Form P: Carl P. Swinnerton with the editorial assistance of F. N. Bennett, Alexander Calandra, Cuthbert Daniel, F. L. Fitzpatrick, G. Marshall Kay, T. F. Morrison, Duane Roller, and the Science Department, Loomis School; New York: Cooperative Test Service.

[1605]

Test of General Proficiency in the Field of Natural Sciences: Cooperative General Achievement Tests, Revised Series, Part II. High school and college; Form QR; 6¢ per test, 10 to 99 copies; 1½¢ per machine-scorable answer sheet; 25¢ per specimen set; 40(45) minutes; Richard E. Watson with the editorial assistance of Russell S. Bartlett, Thomas F. Morrison, Earle C. Sullivan, and Robert Widdop; New York: Cooperative Test Service.

REFERENCES

Cooperative Test Service. *The Cooperative General Achievement Tests (Revised Series):* Information Concerning Their Construction, Interpretation, and Use. New York: Cooperative Test Service, 1940. Pp. 4. Gratis. Paper.

PHYSICS

[1606]

Application of Principles in Physical Science: Test 1.34. Grades 10-12; 1940; 1 form, 2 parts (I and II) ; revision of Tests 1.31 and 1.32; 10¢ per part; 1¢ per machine-scorable answer sheet for either part; 5¢ per explanation sheet and interpretation guide; $1.50 per set of stencils for machine scoring; 60(70) minutes for each part; Chicago, Ill.: Evaluation in the Eight Year Study, Progressive Education Association.

REFERENCES

1 RATHS, LOUIS E. *Application of Principles.* Progressive Education Association, Evaluation in the Eight Year Study, Bulletin No. 5. Chicago, Ill.: the Study, December 1936. Pp. 25. Paper, mimeographed. Out of print.
2 *Evaluation Materials Developed for Various Aspects of Thinking.* Chicago, Ill.: Evaluation in the Eight Year Study, Progressive Education Association, March 1939. Pp. [22]. Paper, mimeographed. Out of print.

[1607]

Columbia Research Bureau Physics Test. Grades 11-14; 1926; 2 forms; $1.25 per 25; 30¢ per specimen set; 90(95) minutes; Hermon W. Farwell and Ben D. Wood; Yonkers, N. Y.: World Book Co.

REFERENCES

1 WOOD, BEN D. *New York Experiments with New-Type Modern Language Tests:* Including a Survey of Modern Language Achievement in the Junior High Schools of New York City, June, 1925; The Regents Experiment of June, 1925, with New-Type Tests in French, German, Spanish, and Physics; and A Second Survey of Modern Language Achievement in the Junior High Schools of New York City, June, 1926, pp. 105-319. Publications of the American and Canadian Committees on Modern Languages, Vol. 1. New York: Macmillan Co., 1927. Pp. xxii, 339. Paper. Out of print.

Eugene A. Waters, Associate Professor of Education, The University of Tennessee. This test, according to its authors, is designed to furnish a reliable, valid, and comparable measure of achievement in the conventional course in high school physics and is recommended by them for such varied purposes as a final examination following a course in high school physics, maintaining standards of achievement, selecting students for admission to college, and for correct placement and guidance of students already admitted to college who expect to continue the study of physics or allied sciences.

The test consists of 144 true-false statements, arranged in order of difficulty, involving informational materials common to the conventional content of high school and elementary college textbooks. According to the authors' statement "representation is given to the various topics in something like the following proportions: Mechanics, 16 per cent; Heat, 16 per cent; Sound, 8 per cent; Light, 16 per cent; Electricity, 32 per cent; and miscellaneous, 12 per cent." Two forms, Form A and Form B, practically equivalent in difficulty and variability (reported reliability between the two forms is .88) are available.

The test is largely self-administering and the "block" key supplied with the test assures speed and accuracy in its scoring. In 1925, Form A of the test was administered to 14,081 high-school students taking the regular Regents Examination in high-school physics and the distribution of these scores is supplied with the test.

The usefulness of this test is of course limited to situations wherein it is assumed that an objective measure of factual information acquired by students in physics classes represents a satisfactory measure of, or means to, the educational ends sought. Its usefulness in such situations may be limited by the fact that the items in the test relate to knowledge and principles in existence prior to the twentieth century. Measures of information in such areas as radio and television are not included in the test.

Teachers interested in educational outcomes other than the acquisition of factual information in physics and the ability to "work" problems based on such information will find this test of value only at such points as they may assume that measures of such information and ability are related to or involved in the realization of other outcomes.

[1608]

Cooperative Physics Test. High school; 1933-40; 40- and 90-minute editions; 25¢ per specimen set of

either edition; Form P: H. W. Farwell; Form Q: Carl P. Swinnerton with the editorial assistance of R. S. Bartlett, Duane Roller, S. M. Skinner, Frank Stewart, and G. W. Warner; New York: Cooperative Test Service.
a) FORMS 1934, 1935, AND 1936. Forms 1933 and 1937 are out of print; 6¢ per test, 10 to 99 copies; 90(95) minutes.
b) REVISED SERIES FORMS N, O, P, AND Q. 1937-40; 5¢ per test, 10 to 99 copies; 1½¢ per machine-scorable answer sheet; 40(45) minutes.

Andrew Longacre, Science Department, Phillips Exeter Academy, Exeter, New Hampshire. [Review of Form P.] This test is probably the best available in this field. All of the questions are of the selective-answer type and hence they are strictly objective. The questions relating to the various branches of the subject are thoroughly mixed and, more or less, in order of progressive difficulty. An analysis also shows that the number of questions concerned with each of the principal subdivisions is approximately proportional to the amount of time usually allotted for the treatment of that subdivision in a normal course. The correcting key and the sheet for machine scoring carry a table for the conversion of the raw scores to scaled scores based on 50 for the median of an unselected group.

My chief criticisms of this test are concerned with the number and general nature of the questions. Though the specific questions are all right for the course, the greater part of them are too easy and there are too many of them, 85, for the time allowed, 40 minutes. The published median raw score for a comparable test in 1937 for "Public Secondary Schools of the East, Middle West and West" is 35.5. This means that in the space of only 40 minutes the average examinee considered and came to some conclusion on at least 36 items and probably quite a few more, since the raw score is the number of correct items minus one-fourth of the wrong. These questions were in random order so that his mind was jumping all over the field during that time. Thus, the questions must be easy and depend almost entirely upon quick perception and memory of the obvious rather than upon reflection and judgment based upon the fundamentals. To be sure, facility and speed in handling the principles of physics are important but surely the evidence is against their being properly used in these answers. Further, the published standard deviations are what one would expect for a test pitched too low. Upon the lower side it

extends down from the median 18 units of raw score and on the upper side it only extends 13.5 units. Above a certain point the examinees fall off rapidly. It is a race against time rather than a test of ability or accomplishment in physics.

In the handbook of the Cooperative Test Service it is noted in regard to the physics test that "a few items on content not covered in the typical course are included to allow an opportunity for exceptional students who have gone beyond the usual course limits to demonstrate more nearly the true extent of their knowledge." There are a few questions of this nature which are all very simple. They are all extensions beyond the syllabus of the course and no test is made anywhere of the students who are superior because they are able to handle extensions in and refinements of the syllabus material itself.

There are also a few equivocal questions, a few trivial ones, and a few which require extremely careful reading to answer. Difficulty which is achieved by demanding careful reading belongs in a reading test and not in a physics tests at this level.

In closing let me note that the test is easy to administer and easy for the students to handle. Also the editing is vastly superior to that of the *Final Test in High School Physics.*

Alvin W. Schindler, Associate Professor of Education, University of Denver. [Review of Form P.] This test is composed of 85 five-reponse multiple-choice items. Each item is introduced with an incomplete statement. The test is accompanied by a handbook of directions for using the Cooperative tests, a booklet of norms, a handbook describing the purpose, content, and interpretation of the Cooperative achievement tests, and percentile norms for pupils in public secondary schools of the East, Middle West, and West, public schools of the South (11 grade systems), and independent secondary schools mostly in New England. Scale scores are provided. The tests are entirely objective, and the techniques for administering and scoring them are excellent. From the point of view of features and services referred to in this paragraph, the tests are not surpassed. The handbook on purpose, content, and interpretation, and the booklet of norms are both valuable contributions.

The items in the test are concerned with significant facts and principles, and in that respect they are valid for most high school pupils. At least one-half of the items require discrimination, application of principles, use of facts to solve problems, and interpretative reasoning. However, a number of items are concerned with definitions, quantitative facts, properties of substances, or one-step relationships without reference to real problematic situations. Since the functional approach should be stressed in high school classes, even with students who are preparing for advanced science in colleges and universities, the test may be criticized because of items of the latter type. Nevertheless, it gives more emphasis to the functional use of information than previous forms of the same test, and most certainly is superior in that respect to many of the physics tests now available.

The statements and responses in the items are free from ambiguity and reveal careful preparation. Irrelevant clues and specific determiners are relatively scarce. The organization reduces reading difficulties to a minimum. The content and form of the items indicate that the test deserves a high rating in validity, and there is no reason to doubt its reliability. It is definitely one of the better tests in high school physics, although it might be improved by introducing the items with challenging direct questions instead of incomplete statements and by replacing the purely factual items with some that demand reasoned understanding and use of information in relation to typical problems.

Ralph K. Watkins, Professor of Education, The University of Missouri. [Review of Form P.] This is the latest high school physics test of the Cooperative Test Service. The form is a multiple-choice of five items each; there are eighty-five exercises. The test will serve the same purposes any similar test sampling the whole field of physics can serve.

The reliability is high according to the data presented by the author. For many schools in the Middle West and Far West the validity may be questioned, since the basic selection of material was based upon syllabi of the College Entrance Examinations Committee and the New York Board of Regents. Norms are given for pupils in the eleventh grade. In many schools no distinction is made in the classification of pupils in physics as between grades eleven and twelve. It is apparently assumed that the norms are satisfactory for any pupils

classified in either grade eleven or twelve after having had one school year's work in physics.

The profile sheets given for the whole series of Cooperative tests for secondary schools indicate that comparisons are to be made as between the scores of individual pupils on other science tests, such as the Cooperative tests in general science, biology, and chemistry, with scores of the same pupils on the physics test. In spite of accurate scaling of these various tests, it is an extremely doubtful procedure to make comparisons of pupils on tests with differing content. The assumption that a pupil, having made a higher scale score on the physics test than he made at some previous time on the scaled general science test, has made a growth in science is a very doubtful assumption. In the same way, there may be some doubt concerning the practice of comparing scores of pupils on Form P of this test with scores of pupils having taken earlier forms of the Cooperative Physics Test, with content differing from the content of Form P.

It is recommended by the Cooperative Test Service that such tests can be used for diagnosis of the abilities of individual pupils in such fields as that of physics. Considerable caution should be used in drawing inferences from test scores of individual pupils on the administration of any one such test as that of the *Cooperative Physics Test.*

The chief value of this test will lie in the possibility of comparing scores of classes or of individuals with the scores of other classes or individuals on the same testing instrument.

For reviews by Ernest E. Bayles and A. W. Hurd, see 1088.

[1609]

Cooperative Physics Test for College Students. 1936-39; revision of Forms 1933, 1934, 1935, 1936, 1937, and 1938 of the earlier *Cooperative Physics Test for College Students* published in 6 parts (*see* 1089) ; 4 forms; 9¢ per test, 10 to 99 copies; 25¢ per specimen set; 1½¢ per machine-scorable answer sheet; 215(220-240) minutes; prepared by the Committee on Tests of the American Association of Physics Teachers; H. W. Farwell, C. J. Lapp, Harvey B. Lemon, Frederic Palmer, Jr., J. T. Tate, and A. G. Worthing; New York: Cooperative Test Service.

REFERENCES

1 AMERICAN ASSOCIATION OF PHYSICS TEACHERS, COMMITTEE ON TESTS, C. J. LAPP, CHAIRMAN. "The 1933-1934 College Physics Testing Program." *Am Physics Teach* 2:Sup:129-48 S '34.
2 AMERICAN ASSOCIATION OF PHYSICS TEACHERS, COMMITTEE ON TESTS, C. J. LAPP, CHAIRMAN. "The 1934-1935 College Physics Testing Program." *Am Physics Teach* 3:Sup:145-59 S '35.
3 AMERICAN ASSOCIATION OF PHYSICS TEACHERS, COMMITTEE ON TESTS, C. J. LAPP, CHAIRMAN. "The 1935-1936 College

Physics Testing Program." *Am Physics Teach* 4:Sup:153-66 S '36.
4 AMERICAN ASSOCIATION OF PHYSICS TEACHERS, COMMITTEE ON TESTS, C. J. LAPP, CHAIRMAN. "Where Are Superior Physics Students Found? Report of the 1936-37 College Physics Testing Program." *Am Physics Teach* 6:85-98 Ap '38.

Alan T. Waterman, Associate Professor of Physics, Yale University. [Review of Forms A and B.] These tests show a marked improvement in format over previous physics tests of the Cooperative Test Service. Printing is used in place of its less legible and less attractive substitutes and the options under each item are set in heavy type in column beneath, an arrangement that makes for clearness and speed in comprehension. There is greater variety of items both as to topic and difficulty; likewise there is an improved balance between easy and difficult, between numerical and descriptive material. The tests are quickly scored, either manually or by machine. The two tests, A and B, are comparable, thus being adapted directly for use in pretesting and post-testing.

These tests are without doubt the best in the field. The physics is sound, the tests show care and originality in construction, and they have a proved high degree of reliability and validity.

In spite of the present high standard of these tests it is felt that certain criticisms may be advanced.

1) It seems unfortunate that all items should be of the recognition type. Granted that this type is well adapted to wide coverage of a field in a short time, the use of one or two other types as well would broaden the test.

2) It is neither necessary nor desirable that all items have five options. This is an artificial procedure: some items lend themselves readily to many inviting options, others do not. As one important consequence too many questions appear padded, with perhaps a far-fetched or even farcical decoy. In such cases one might be justified in attempting to weight the various options differently and score on them all. In many items there are only one or two options in addition to the correct response which have real drawing power.

3) No item should raise a legitimate doubt in the mind of a specialist as to the uniqueness of the answer, otherwise able candidates with thorough preparation may be penalized.

4) Within a given item all options should apply to the point under consideration in the same sense. As outstanding, but not the only, instances where this principle is not complied

with, we have items with both numerical and descriptive options.

5) Items which are essentially double or triple questions in one should be used sparingly. This statement should not be interpreted as debarring items which cut across different divisions of the subject. Objectionable items clearly falling under this description are those which state a physical problem, difficult per se, containing awkward and unnecessary conversions of units.

6) It is believed that the majority of college teachers would favor the inclusion of more items aimed at testing laboratory experience and proficiency.

For a review by Paul A. Northrop, see 1089.

[1610]

Fulmer-Schrammel Physics Test. High school; 1934; 2 forms, 2 parts; 60¢ per 25; 15¢ per specimen set; 40(45) minutes; V. G. Fulmer and H. E. Schrammel; Emporia, Kan.: Bureau of Educational Measurements, Kansas State Teachers College.
a) TEST I [MECHANICS].
b) TEST II [HEAT, MAGNETISM, ELECTRICITY, AND SOUND].

Palmer O. Johnson, Professor of Education, The University of Minnesota. Each form of Test I consists of three parts: Part I is made up of 80 true-false statements; Part II of 10 multiple-choice items; and Part III of 20 matching items. Each form of Test II consists of two parts: Part I is comprised of 79 true-false statements; Part II of 47 matching items. The test is based upon textbooks and course of study content. The experience gained through a long testing program, the criticisms of teachers, and the analysis of the findings from preliminary forms, have been used in developing the present forms.

The scope of the tests is restricted largely to the measurement of vocabulary and of principles and other factual information. Some attention is given to application, but little to problem solving. The analysis, somewhat subjective, of one of the forms indicated that approximately 34 per cent of the items might be called vocabulary items and that 24 per cent of the items were based on principles, 24 per cent on other factual information, 12 per cent on application, and 5 per cent on problems. Because of the limited scope of the outcomes tested, the value of the tests would appear to be limited to such bases as they might provide for comparison of achievement of students in different schools for survey purposes. Those teachers of physics who emphasize outcomes of instruction in addition to the acquisition of vocabulary and of facts or principles would find restricted use for a test of this nature. This would hold especially for those teachers who are trying to vitalize the teaching of physics by stimulating the application of physical knowledge to problems and situations coming within the everyday experiences of their students. The content of this examination is very much devoted to the traditional outcomes of teaching physics and thus reflects little of the current developments that are taking place.

The reliability coefficient based on the correlation between Forms A and B of Test I is given as .77; between Forms A and B of Test II as .72. The reliability coefficients given for each test as determined by correlating odd- and even-numbered items are .84 and .86. Percentile norms based upon 4016 cases for Test I and 3666 cases for Test II are given. These norms are said to be based on the scores of students in physics classes of a large number of representative schools in many different states. No information is given as to the definition of a representative school, how the schools were chosen, nor of the characteristics of the students upon whom the norms were established.

Alvin W. Schindler, Associate Professor of Education, University of Denver. Each form of Test I includes 70 true-false items, ten four-response multiple-choice items, and one matching exercise consisting of 20 statements and 31 foils. Each form of Test II includes 79 true-false items and two matching exercises. One matching exercise is composed of 25 statements and 25 foils, and the second consists of 22 statements and 25 foils.

The authors report reliability of .77 between Forms A and B of Test I, and of .72 between Forms A and B of Test II. The reliability of each test and form independently by the method of correlating scores on even-numbered items with those on odd-numbered items is claimed to range "between .84 and .86, with an average of .85." The reliability is therefore relatively low. A survey of the items justifies some doubt in regard to the validity of the test, especially when the items are evaluated in the light of

sound objectives for high school physics classes.

The tests are accompanied by complete directions and by convenient scoring keys. They are entirely objective. A table of percentile norms is provided for each test. The percentiles in the table of norms are only the first, the ninety-ninth, and the multiples of five.

Most of the items emphasize fundamental facts and principles, and most of these are purely factual. About ten per cent of the items may be criticized because they demand information which is not fundamental or which should not be emphasized in high school classes. The validity of the test is certainly lowered by true-false items such as: "The shovel is an example of a second class lever"; "When burning, a pound of coal will combine with about twenty pounds of air"; "The coefficient of expansion of gases is nearly 0.00366"; "Charcoal absorbs about sixty times its volume of ammonia gas"; and "Loadstones are found in Asia Minor, Norway, and Sweden." Most of the true-false statements are very short. Likewise, the multiple-choice and matching exercises are concerned with unapplied facts which children and adults recall in life outside of school only in relation to a purpose.

When the objectives of high school physics are considered, it is evident that the tests fail to measure the ability of pupils to explain scientific phenomena or the applications of physics in everyday life. Classes in high school physics would be extremely dull and uninteresting if all of the attention was focused upon the types of situations which are used in the tests, and it follows that use of the tests would not encourage the more functional approach to learning.

[1611]
Hurd Test in High School Physics. End-of-Year; 1930; 3 forms; $2.10 per 100; 15¢ per specimen set; 40(45) minutes; A. W. Hurd; New York: Bureau of Publications, Teachers College, Columbia University.

Andrew Longacre, Science Department, The Phillips Exeter Academy, Exeter, New Hampshire. The three alternative forms of this test seem about equal as their published means and standard deviations indicate. However their serviceability as a final objective test in physics is a grave question. They are by no means "almost perfectly objective" as their author claims in the manual of directions. They include three types of questions. About fifty per cent of the questions are simple direct ones in which the examinee is required to formulate and write out his answer. Fifteen per cent of the questions are of the selective-answer type and the remainder are of the completion type. Obviously the questions of the first and last types are not wholly objective and the author really admits this in another part of the manual. "Some variations are allowable in certain answers. An answer which does not agree with the key may be scored correct if the meaning is synonymous. Variations of 1% in numerical answers are allowable." Even if far too many of the questions were not equivocal, upon such a basis of correction the published means and standard deviations can be of little or no value to the teacher correcting his own papers.

An analysis of the individual questions shows that, while there are several good questions on each form, as a rule the questions have been carelessly written. In some cases the units provided with the data are wrong not to mention the cases where the data are provided without units both in the questions and in the answers. Further it is left to the examinee whether or not he should include units with the numerical answers required in the questions (approximately fifty per cent of the total) in which he writes his own answer. From the general form of the paper it looks as though he would be better off to leave them out. Still, this is in contrast to the inclusion in the paper of from 10 to 12 per cent of the questions dealing entirely with subunits of the metric system and conversion between the metric and British systems.

There are far too many questions (82 to 83 per form) on the papers for the time allowed, 40 minutes, and they are, on the whole, far too easy. This is substantiated by the published means, about 46, and standard deviations, about 18. Presuming that these are for the raw scores, though this is not clear and should be made so, it means that the average student has considered and come to some conclusion regarding at least 46 items, and probably many more, in 40 minutes. The questions are all so easy that it becomes a race between memory and time and not a test of physics. In this regard it is worse than the *Cooperative Physics Test*. Thus it seems that the high scores in this test not only would not correlate well with the high scores in another test or teacher's

rating but would not provide a reliable prognostication of the examinee's success in further studies in engineering or science.

For a final test, its coverage of the various subdivisions of the field usually covered in course seems disproportionate. Far too much emphasis is given to details in mechanics and too little is given to electricity. Also it provides very little test of a grasp of the fundamentals of the subject, rather requiring simple definitions and trivial or unimportant, almost esoteric, facts. Whenever it goes beyond the syllabus it sets a technical application question rather than a question based upon an extension in reasoning.

In closing it must be said that each form contains a few questions which seemed to me to be of special merit. The arranging of possible numerical answers in computational form of the factors removes the chance for trivial arithmetical errors while testing physics, but units should have been included. Also the inclusion of a few questions having several correct alternatives and giving credit for all correctly selected, removes those from the answers based upon the lesser of the evils offered and puts them into the category of answers based upon a sound knowledge of physics. It is because of these few points that I wish the rest, and major part, of the papers had more merit.

Paul A. Northrop, Professor of Physics, Vassar College. These tests make use of three types of items, short-answer, completion, and multiple-choice. The short-answer and completion types permit few possible deviations from the logical answer and hence are sufficiently objective to be scored by a person with little training in physics. The multiple-choice type offer more than one correct answer in five cases of each form. This is a desirable feature but in some of the items it is not clearly indicated that more than one correct choice is offered. This type of question is of course entirely objective.

There are a few questions which are identical on two forms but the number is not great enough to effect the tests adversely. Only two errors were noted in a reasonably careful reading of the three forms. One was an error in an answer and the other was in the statement of a problem in which a difficult solution for "focal length" was required whereas a simple solution for object distance was desired. On the whole, however, the questions are clearly stated and of sufficient spread in difficulty to differentiate between students of varied ability and preparation. The apportionment of questions is not in agreement with the time spent on the divisions of physics in the usual course. Thus out of the 82 items in one form there are 39 hydrostatic and mechanic, 19 heat, 11 electricity, 8 light, and 5 sound items. As a consequence of this lack of balance which is similar in the three forms, they are not as revealing in electricity and light as they should be.

Percentile scores are offered for each form as are also "M" scores. By means of the latter the raw scores may be translated into marks of A, B, C, etc., according to a system which the author has found practical. Means and standard deviations which are useful for rough comparisons of large groups are also given based on 848, 528, and 444 cases, respectively, for the three forms. Reliability coefficients are given as found by the split-halves method for each form and also as between Forms A and B, and B and C. These coefficients indicate good reliability.

The test seems capable of yielding important information regarding the attainment of students at the end of their high school course in physics.

[1612]

Torgerson-Rich-Ranney Tests in High School Physics. First, second semesters; 1935; 2 forms, 2 levels; $1.25 per 25; 20¢ per specimen set; T. L. Torgerson, C. L. Rich, and Harriet Ranney; Cincinnati, Ohio: C. A. Gregory Co.

a) TEST 1, MECHANICS AND HEAT. First semester; 95(105) minutes.

b) TEST 2, ELECTRICITY AND MAGNETISM. Second semester; 100(110) minutes.

Palmer O. Johnson, Professor of Education, The University of Minnesota. These tests are designed primarily to measure informational outcomes and problem solving ability in the conventional course in high school physics consisting of the time-honoured divisions: mechanics, heat, magnetism and electricity, sound, and light. Each division is tested separately, and there are two forms for each division. Chief emphasis is placed upon the ability to recall information tested by means of completion tests including diagrams and by the problem tests which require knowledge of formulae involved in the solution. This form of examination is likely more exacting than those forms consisting chiefly of recognition

types of questions. An examination of the completion items indicates that the usual difficulty of securing exact responses without unexpected variations, or synonyms, has been largely overcome, although a small number of the completions are still open to this objection. Physics, in this sense, is likely more amenable to exact form of statement, than are other sciences. This is more especially true when the test compilers, as in the case of the present tests, have assigned themselves only the task of measuring the acquisition of standardized outcomes from standardized texts. The content of each test was based on common types treated by six "most widely used texts." With this restricted interpretation of the function of the tests, they are probably valid as claimed by the compilators, although the technique of sampling is not described and an examination of the content included would raise objections on the part of some teachers of physics as to why certain fundamental principles have been omitted. With its limited scope, the examination would be criticized by those teachers of physics who hold the view that content and instruction in physics should be more greatly vitalized than has been true of the past and is largely true of the present. Physics provides ample opportunity to introduce into its content and hence into the examination an abundance of materials that come within the range of experiences of students in his everyday living. This is especially true in the possible application that may be made of principles and other factual information acquired. Most of the applications of physical information whether of principles directly or the kinds of problems for solution in this examination are of the stereotyped kind. Would it detract from an examination if applications and problems could be made more interesting? Furthermore, the claim of testing functional knowledge would likely be more valid if opportunity were given to apply principles and solve problems which are more novel to the students than the usually stereotyped kinds found in textbooks and examinations.

While the statement is made that "all means, statistical and otherwise, were used to insure high validity, reliability and objectivity that the test and its divisions enjoy" the supporting evidence is not included in the test manuals. Percentile norms are given but the number and characteristics of the group of students upon whom these norms were based are not given. In the absence of this information, comparisons are not possible for the teacher of physics who might be interested in making them. .

In summary, it may be said that the examination within its limited scope may prove useful to teachers in measuring standardized outcomes, but they would require considerable supplementation when used by those teachers of physics who regard functional understanding of the nature of things and processes significant in every day life, the development of the ability to use the scientific method and to achieve through its application, and other such outcomes as of at least equal importance.

Paul A. Northrop, Professor of Physics, Vassar College. These tests cover the material taken up in the usual high-school course in physics and the questions are well proportioned among the different divisions of the subject. Four different types of questions have been used, completion, matching, true-false and problems. The matching test is limited to a few items in sound with a time allowance of three minutes, and the true-false type consists of 20 items in light with a time allowance of eight minutes. The remaining time of about 85 minutes is devoted to completion and problem types which are used in all the different divisions. Many diagrams have been used in mechanics and light to seek information which could not be asked by words alone. The authors of these tests are to be commended for their use of different types though it seems likely that either multiple-choice or short-answer questions would be more revealing than the true-false and matching types which are often disappointing in their results.

The type of question used is of secondary importance to the questions themselves, though it seems easier to devise good questions of certain types than of others. The questions in these tests are, on the whole, poor. The main reason for this is a lack of careful editing, although there is also evidence of poor proofreading. The questions were apparently carelessly constructed initially both from the standpoint of clear statement and also in some cases from that of the correct technical use of physical terms. For example in the completion question, "The principle involved in the manufacture of artificial ice is by a process of ———", the reader is confused by a principle

being called a process. Again, "The force which imparts to a gram of mass an acceleration of 1 cm. each second is called a ———" includes a wrong expression for the unit of acceleration which most teachers spend considerable time in attempting to displace from the minds and vocabularies of their students. And what answer is expected to the following? "A new dry cell of .05 ohms resistance causes an ammeter of negligible resistance to register 30 amperes. What is its terminal voltage?" The answer given is 1.5 volts indicating that the desired voltage is the open circuit voltage for a dry cell capable of the above performance. Unfortunately these are not isolated cases for a considerably greater number could be cited. The point, of course, is that these questions could have been greatly improved if they had been considered critically by a number of different persons. This reviewer also doubts if the questions contain a sufficient number of more difficult items to differentiate properly between students.

In the directions for scoring there are some omissions on the papers themselves which make it necessary to refer both to the directions and to corresponding parts of other papers before feeling certain of the correct procedure. There are no data to establish the reliability of the norms given. Incidentally the writer does not see why in a properly devised test, a working time of 15 minutes should be able to obtain a score of 28 in one division of the subject whereas a working time of 30 minutes could obtain a score of only 9.3 in another division of the subject as is true in these tests.

It would be wise for a teacher who contemplates using an objective test to consider also the *Final Test in High School Physics* and the *Cooperative Physics Test* before making a final selection.

[1613]

Wisconsin Achievement Test in Physics. High school; 1938-39; 2 forms; $1 per 25; 5¢ per sample test; 50(55) minutes; Bureau of Guidance and Records, School of Education, University of Wisconsin and the Wisconsin Physics Test Committee (W. P. Clarke, Ira C. Davis, A. H. Gould, Jerome Herreid, Charles Horwitz, M. J. W. Phillips, Severn Rinkob, F. W. Schuler, R. J. Suchy, J. H. Thorngate, and C. H. Walter); Milwaukee, Wis.: E. M. Hale and Co.

Louis M. Heil, Associate Professor of Education, The University of Chicago and Research Associate in Science, Cooperative Study in General Education, American Council on

Education. The *Wisconsin Achievement Test in Physics* is apparently designed to measure student achievement in the more conventional aspects of physics. The test items seem to fall under the following categories or objectives: (*a*) The knowledge of basic physical terms (density, diffusion, inertia, dispersion, conduction, etc.). (*b*) A knowledge of the effects produced by various physical devices (prism, condenser, lever, etc.). (*c*) An ability to solve numerical problems which require the application of physical principles (heat affusion, laws of motion, reflection, buoyancy, Ohm's Law, etc.). (*d*) A knowledge of the contribution of famous scientists. (*e*) A knowledge of physical constants (speed of sound, heat evaporation, absolute zero, mechanical equivalent of heat, etc.).

Of the 162 items in the test only 2 refer to developments in physics which date later than 1900. No reference is made to such topics as atomic structure, glow discharges, photoelectricity, polarized light (polaroids), etc. Alternating currents and the diffraction of light which represent two of the more important phases of classical or conventional physics likewise are not represented in the test.

The test is relatively free of ambiguities. Those identified by the reviewer occurred in Part 2 where the directions led to the possibility of several alternative responses equally valid. For example, they read "Write in the blank after each phrase the number of the term which the phrase suggests." In the list of alternatives for the phrase "rising of liquids in tubes of small diameter," the alternatives "capillarity," "service tension," and "cohesion" are offered. It seems to the reviewer that the students might very well use any one of these alternatives as the correct response to the phrase. Several other phrases in the same list might be answered by one or the other of the several suggested alternatives.

The data resulting from the use of the tests by 713 students reported by T. L. Torgerson indicate that the test has a reliability coefficient of .95 with a probable error of measurement equal to 3.8. The standard deviation of the scores of the 713 students is 25.4.

SUMMARY. The *Wisconsin Achievement Test in Physics* samples quite adequately the content of classical physics. Modern physics, on the other hand, is practically omitted from the test. Ambiguities are scarce. The probable error of measurement in the total score is sufficiently low so that one can safely infer that the test could be used as one basis of assigning the usual type of grades.

SOCIAL STUDIES

Reviews by Howard R. Anderson, Clinton C. Conrad, Warren G. Findley, Kenneth E. Gell, J. R. Gerberich, Grace Graham, Lavone A. Hanna, Robert E. Keohane, W. C. McCall, S. P. McCutcheon, Wilbur F. Murra, Pedro T. Orata, Jacob S. Orleans, Anna Parsek, Roy A. Price, G. M. Ruch, Hilda Taba, Wallace Taylor, Marie E. Trost, R. M. Tryon, Margaret Willis, Edgar B. Wesley, and Ernest C. Witham.

[1614]
Beard-Erbe Social Science Tests. Grade 12; 1937; 1 form; 5¢ per test; 20¢ per specimen set; nontimed (40-50) minutes; Marshall Rust Beard and Carl H. Erbe; Cedar Falls, Iowa: Holst Printing Co.

Kenneth E. Gell, Head of the Department of Social Studies, Washington High School, Rochester, New York; and Special Lecturer in Education, The University of Rochester. The reviewer does not feel that this test compares favorably with certain other tests produced by members of the faculty of the Iowa State Teachers College.

This test seeks to measure understanding in the whole field of social science including the several histories. It attempts to do this in 45 minutes with 148 questions. The sampling is too meager for such a wide field, and because the questions are arranged according to type of question construction rather than type of information tested there is almost no diagnostic value. It seems that the most a score on this test can tell is the number a student gets right out of this particular sampling, rather than his true knowledge of the field supposed to be covered. Not only are all fields of the social sciences included, but also the various elements of a total understanding of them—events, terms, dates, personages, causes and results, and so forth. All of these are in a confused order.

Too many of the items seem poorly chosen for their basic importance; for example, the date of George Washington's birth. Other items tested seem unimportant because of the maturity or involved understanding of the subjects studied; for example, such terms as "amnesty," "mandamus," and "extroversion." It is doubtful if such terms *in a short sampling* are valid in testing high school students. The ratio of the field to be tested to the length of the test makes it very sketchy, and a further disadvantage is that that sketchiness is "spotty," thereby making the remaining parts even thinner; for example, there is an emphasis upon legal terms, persons from American history, technical economic terms, etc. The testing of chronology is by 9 simple order-of-event groups of three each, and by 10 specific date items; some of these chronological items are not well chosen. There are a few other scattered time items. Ten questions are used to test the qualifications and responsibilities of senators as compared with United States representatives, which seems undue stress on these offices in an effort to test United States government as such.

Too many completion items and simple matching items are used.

The test is arranged to correct the raw score for chance, and there is a conversion table to turn these raw scores into percentiles; but the percentiles are based upon too few cases to have great meaning (only 1608 cases were used) except in the institution where the test was standardized.

The reviewer cannot recommend this test because it is too sketchy and too "spotty" to be of reasonable validity, because it is not based upon enough cases to have real measurement reliability (this despite the reliability table cited), and because the test is not arranged to provide for diagnostic analysis.

For a review by Edgar B. Wesley, see 1144.

[1615]

Cooperative Test of Social Studies Abilities. High school; 1936-39; Experimental Forms 1936 and Q; 6¢ per test, 10 to 99 copies; 25¢ per specimen set; Form 1936: 90(95) minutes; Form Q: 80(85) minutes; form 1936: J. Wayne Wrightstone; Form Q: J. Wayne Wrightstone with the assistance of Robert E. Keohane, William M. Shanner, Wilbur Murra, and Margaret Seder; New York: Cooperative Test Service.

Roy A. Price, Dual Professor of Social Science and Education, Syracuse University. This test consists of four parts. The first part measures students' ability to obtain facts from tables, graphs, and maps, and how to use indexes and card catalogs, and knowledge of the sources to utilize in seeking certain types of information. The second part measures students' ability to organize material and to distinguish between relevant and irrelevant material. Part III measures the ability to interpret facts. The final part of the test measures the ability to apply generalizations.

We have long recognized the need for measuring instruments in the social studies which would make possible an evaluation of students' achievement other than in terms of the amount of information required. Lip service has been paid to other types of objectives but we have not been able to measure in any objective manner the extent to which these objectives were being achieved. The *Cooperative Test of Social Studies Abilities* is one of a number of extremely promising attempts to devise instruments which will meet this need.

This test not only attempts to make possible measurement of a number of skills but does so in an ingenious manner. Evidence of the reliability and validity of the tests is not available.

The chief weakness of the test, in my opinion, is that certain items seem to lack objectivity, i.e., that experts could not agree with the published scoring key. Other technical difficulties appear also in that: (*a*) the directions to some parts of the test are complicated and confusing; (*b*) some graphic materials included are so small as to make exact reading difficult; and (*c*) in a few instances the meaning is not clear because of wording. Another difficulty is that the paragraphs of subject matter which are introduced are somewhat advanced. When a student is asked to read such a paragraph and then fails to apply a generalization to a specific event given, we are not able to ascertain whether his difficulty arose from inability to read and interpret the paragraph correctly, or whether he is unable to apply the generalization. Similarly, in the section on relevancy of statements, the particular statement in question may be relevant but not listed as a reason. Thus the validity of such items may be placed in some doubt.

The test is valuable not only as a measurement of achievement but perhaps even more important as a diagnostic device. Use of such a measuring scale as this would make the diagnosis of pupil weaknesses and subsequent remedial exercises a much simpler problem. There can be no question that this type of testing is greatly needed and this instrument illustrates the possibilities inherent in this relatively new field of evaluation.

For a review by Howard R. Anderson, see 1146.

[1615.1]

Illinois State Normal University Social Science Test, 1938 Edition. Grades 10-13; 1938; the instruction sheet refers to this test as the *Cooperative Social Science Test;* 1 form; $3.50 per 100; 5¢ per test; 50(55) minutes; John A. Kinneman and Clarence Orr; Bloomington, Ill.: McKnight & McKnight.

[1616]

Melbo Social Science Survey Test. Grades 10-16 and adults; 1937; 1 form; out of print; nontimed (40-45) minutes; Irving R. Melbo; Bloomington, Ill.: Public School Publishing Co.

REFERENCES

1 MELBO, IRVING R. *Information of High School Seniors on Contemporary Social, Political, and Economic Problems and Issues.* Unpublished doctor's thesis, University of California, 1935.
2 MELBO, IRVING R. "Information of High-School Seniors on Contemporary Problems." *Social Studies* 27:82-6 F '36.

Howard R. Anderson, Associate Professor of Education, Cornell University. According to the introductory statement in the teacher's handbook, the purpose of this test is "to measure the extent and nature of the information of high school students, college students, and adults on the major contemporary social, political, and economic problems and issues in American life." The handbook further suggests that the test has four uses: (*a*) to determine extent of information about major problems and issues; (*b*) to do this for specific issues; (*c*) to determine gains in information by making retesting possible; and (*d*) to serve as a basis for subsequent study of selected issues. There also is an account of the research underlying the test, i.e., criteria for the selection and validation of items, reliability coefficients (Form A—.885; Form B—.860), data indicating the equivalence of the two forms, a table of item difficulty, and norms expressed in terms of deciles. It perhaps should

be noted that the data pertaining to item difficulty as well as the norms are based on the administration of the test to 5,474 high school seniors in the spring of the years 1934 and 1935.

The test itself consists of 56 true-false items and 44 four-response best-answer items. In structure these conform to rules for the construction of good objective-type test questions except that the meaning of certain questions is not clear. For example, exactly what is the point of Item 38? "Even before the depression the United States maintained the shortest school term of any western nation." (True) Obviously the federal government does not dictate the length of the school term in the various states. And which are western nations: Brazil and Argentine, or Great Britain, Germany, and Sweden? Does "term" mean average total time spent in school? Item 88 reads: "Approximately one-half of the tax dollar is expended for . . ." Which unit of government is to be considered—federal, state, local, or all three?

Some of the items, as Item 80, "The first state-wide unemployment insurance law was passed by the state of . . . ," are rather narrowly factual; and others, as Item 87, "The per cent of the total national income regularly given to private religious, educational or charitable organizations is about (*a*) 2 per cent (*b*) 4 per cent (*c*) 8 per cent (*d*) 12 per cent," call for rather fine distinctions. The years that have passed since the test was developed cause other items to tend toward obsolescence. For example, Item 62, "The proposed federal pure food and drug laws . . ."; Item 78, "The total tax bill (federal, state, and local) is about (*a*) 4 billions (*b*) 6 billions (*c*) 8 billions (*d*) 10 billions"; Item 82, "By the terms of the present farm bill . . ."; etc.

A few of the items seem to be keyed incorrectly despite the claims made for the validation of concepts. For example, Item 11 states that "About one-half of the total population live in the metropolitan areas." (True) The 1930 census figures indicate that 56.2 per cent live in communities of more than 2,500. Surely all of these cannot be described as metropolitan areas. Then Item 23 reads, "With the exception of labor laws, the last century has witnessed but little change in the laws relating to marriage and children." (True) What about divorce and school attendance legislation?

The mechanical features of the test if considered from the viewpoint of the person who is to do the scoring are rather unsatisfactory. The teacher is provided with a key printed on both sides of a sheet of paper. The printing is not spaced so that this key can be cut into strips. Of course even a strip key requiring seven separate adjustments would be greatly inferior to the stencil keys supplied with many commercial tests.

R. M. Tryon, Professor of the Teaching of the Social Sciences, The University of Chicago. The subtitle of this test is "A Test of Information on Contemporary Problems and Issues in American Social, Political and Economic Life." The form under review is composed of 56 true-false items and 44 multiple-choice items. Its purpose is to measure both the extent and nature of the information on contemporary American life in the realms of politics, economics, and group activities possessed by groups of high school pupils, college students, and adults. Instead of testing information about affairs that are strictly contemporary, the test attempts to discover one's knowledge of established trends and broad movements. The author claims that it tests information relative to "currents of events" rather than "current events."

It would seem from the information in the handbook for the test that the author has given much attention to such technical aspects as validity, authenticity, reliability and norms. If a teacher desires a survey test, an inventory test, an achievement test or an instructional test, he could make use of this one in any or all of these capacities. Inasmuch, however, as the test is now three years old and the material used in determining its make-up is somewhat older, contemporariness is not its paramount attribute. In fact, the responses to many of the items today are not what they were three years ago. By confining the test chiefly to information about "currents of events" the author has limited the usefulness of his test and probably doomed it to a short and uneventful life.

For a review by Alvin C. Eurich, see 1150.

[1617]

Social Studies Test: National Achievement Tests. Grades 4-6, 7-9; 1937-39; 2 forms, 2 levels; $1.75 per 25; nontimed (35) minutes; Robert K. Speer and Samuel Smith; Rockville Centre, N. Y.: Acorn Publishing Co.

[1618]
Survey Test in the Social Studies: Cooperative General Achievement Test, Part I. High school and college placement; 1937-39; Forms N, O, and P; 6¢ per test, 10 to 99 copies; 1½¢ per machine-scorable answer sheet; 25¢ per specimen set; 40(45) minutes; Form O: H. R. Anderson, E. F. Lindquist, and J. E. Partington; Form P: Mary Willis and Charlotte Croon with the editorial assistance of Ronald Beasley, Robert E. Keohane, Robert L. Carey, Samuel McKee, Jr., Martin Y. Munson, J. Folwell Scull, Jr., and the Social Studies Department, Beaver Country Day School; New York: Cooperative Test Service.

Hilda Taba, Assistant Professor of Education and Research Associate, The University of Chicago. [Review of Form P.] As the title describes, this test surveys the achievement in social studies. The sampling of areas is quite broad and includes the following: Geography, Civics and American Government, the Contribution of Early Civilizations and the Middle Ages, the Rise of Modern European Nations, the Development of the United States, Economic Problems and Problems of Society. These sections are not scored separately, and only a total score is given on the whole test.

According to the accompanying handbook, this test is designed to measure "real or *reasoned* understanding of the information, ideas, relationships, and generalizations presented in the course of instruction" and "the ability to use these facts and ideas in the interpretation of movements, institutions, and practices," in contrast to "emphasis on memorization of unique or stereotyped textbook statements."

The test lives up fairly well to the first claim, namely, that of measuring reasoned understanding. Most questions deal with problems and generalizations significant either in their content or in their implications. With but few exceptions discrete and isolated facts, dates, and names are avoided. This is even true of the section on history. The phraseology is fresh and avoids successfully the textbook stereotype.

From the standpoint of construction, the statements are clear and precise. The "wrong" answers are plausible enough not to permit the guessing of the right responses by eliminating the obviously wrong ones. There are only a few items in which the alternative answers are too vague or too general to permit accurate judgment.

There is more doubt about the validity of the test in measuring the ability of students to apply information and ideas known to them in interpreting new problems. Even defining application rather loosely, namely, as including all questions which cannot be answered without a modicum of reorganization and synthesis of discrete facts and ideas learned, only about one-fifth of the 120 items can be said to call for this ability. Most of the items, while not purely descriptive and discrete, are nevertheless of the type which call more for memory than for interpretation and reorganization of ideas.

This test, along with others in the Cooperative test series, makes use of scaled scores. Raw scores can be converted into scaled scores of 1 to 100, in which the score of 50 represents the score of "average child in average school with the usual amount of instruction." This common scale facilitates the interpretation of scores considerably, both for groups and for individuals. Thus, the individual's scores from year to year on the same test, as well as his scores on different tests, can be easily compared. One wonders, however, to what degree of accuracy the "average child in an average school with an average amount of instruction" can be established, or by what criteria that average was established. Can, for instance, the "average amount" of instruction be determined by the number of years of study devoted to a given area, as was done in this case?

The test is supposed to help discover student needs, to facilitate advice concerning election of subjects, to diagnose causes of failure, to help in advising future scholastic activities of students, and to help appraise the quality of instruction. The authors of the test wisely advise caution in using the results from this test or other similar tests as a sole basis for educational guidance. They point out that a variety of other evidence is needed for adequate diagnosis for any of the purposes mentioned above. The users of this test should take this advice seriously. In spite of the fact that this test is called a survey test in social sciences, there are many other important outcomes of social science teaching not measured by this test which should be considered in making decisions about such matters as causes of failure, election of courses, or future academic career. And even when one assumes that achievement of intellectual understanding of content and mastery of information should be the main basis for educational guidance, the single score derived from the test is hardly diagnostic enough

to decide why a student has failed and whether he should take further work in history, economics, or other social science areas.

[1619]

Test of Critical Thinking in the Social Studies: Elementary School Series. Grades 4-6; 1938-39; 2 forms; $6.30 per 100; 20¢ per specimen set; 45(50) minutes; J. Wayne Wrightstone; New York: Bureau of Publications, Teachers College, Columbia University.

Warren G. Findley, Assistant Director, Division of Examinations and Testing, State Education Department, Albany, New York. The test consists of three 15-minute parts purporting to measure pupil growth in three aspects of critical thinking—namely, obtaining facts, drawing conclusions, and applying general facts. Part I, Obtaining Facts, is further subdivided into sets of questions involving reading tables, reading graphs, where to locate facts, and how to use an index.

It seems likely that this test will prove quite usable and helpful to classroom teachers. Its virtue resides in the fact that it provides a number of objective exercises related to significant skills in social studies in the elementary grades. In so doing, it gives concrete form to the newer goals of instruction in this area. Moreover, this virtue of the test proper is enhanced by inclusion in the test manual of practical, understandable suggestions to the teacher regarding instructional procedures to use with pupils who do poorly on the test. Without recourse to norms the teacher can pick out the weakest pupils for special assistance and otherwise apply information gained from test scores in the classroom situation.

All the above is said despite the large number of questions one must raise as to the test's reliability and validity as a measure of ability to do critical thinking and despite the presence of serious faults in the construction of several items. The test is far less useful than it might be and unless it is carefully revised, is certain to be superseded by other tests that will develop in this field.

The test items are poorly constructed. Several items contain specific determiners. The two false statements on the first page of Part II, Form A, both contain the word "only," while the true statements on the same page contain qualifiers like "some" and "many." Elsewhere in Part II, in which sets of four inferences follow each paragraph, two consecutive inferences will be mutually contradictory, so that the pupil gets credit for indicating as true that "bricks have many more lasting qualities than wood" and then indicating as false the statement that "bricks spoil rather quickly." In another set of four, two statements are identical except for vocabulary and both are contradicted by a third statement. In an item in Part I the examinee gains separate credit for responding first that in 1935 in Russia 12,500,000 goats were raised, and then responding that the country which raised 12,500,000 goats in 1935 is Russia. Such paired items are not merely inefficient; they render meaningless any reliability coefficients computed by the split-halves technique.

Statistical evidence of reliability is not given clearly enough to permit one to judge the reliability of scores on the parts of the test as indicators of pupil progress. One cannot find data from which to estimate the probable error of an individual score. Then, too, were reliability coefficients based on the 4,000 cases used for the norms or on the 64 cases used in estimating validity? Turning to the norms, how many pupils in each grade were used? Moreover, are the grade-scores above 7.0 based on seventh graders or derived by extrapolation from data accumulated on pupils in grades 4 to 6? The author states the limitations of norms and indicates that they should not be used for standards. This is well, but does not warrant omission of data necessary to determine the reliability of norms for interpretation of individual or group data.

Finally, one may raise questions concerning validity which for a test in this new area should be answered more fully than is done in the manual. The scores of the parts of the test, and even the responses to individual items, might well be correlated with independent criterions of the various skills covered by the test to show their validity and distinctness. Under the head of validity the author should also be asked to specify a clear working definition of "critical" thinking. Is the term well used if extended to cover all activity, such as reading tables and graphs, which is basic to the evaluative type of thinking, or is it better to restrict the term to evaluative thinking, inference, deduction, and the like? In either case should we not treat the reading of tables, charts, and graphs as similar in essential character to what is commonly called reading com-

prehension and hence either organize distinct tests of comprehension and critical thinking or else explain the presence of Part I in this test and the absence of ordinary reading comprehension material as due to the fact that reading comprehension tests are available to supplement the present test?

A basic defect of this test is that it is not built on a working definition of critical thinking which may be used to explain the inclusion in the "test of critical thinking" of whatever is used and the exclusion of other types of test exercise as either irrelevant or adequately represented by the material included in the test.

Pedro T. Orata, Special Consultant, Occupational Information and Guidance Service, United States Office of Education, Washington, D. C. Philosophers used to discuss at length the difference between appearance and reality. There is considerable need for the same kind of disputation in the field of "progressive" testing at the present time. *Test of Critical Thinking in the Social Studies* appears attractive as a title, but the validity of its content in measuring thinking, to say nothing of critical thinking, may well be questioned. What is thinking, and what does it mean to be critical? To what extent does this test measure either process?

In real life, thinking consists, as one writer puts it, of the finding and testing of meanings, with testing as the distinctive characteristic of being critical. *Test of Critical Thinking in the Social Studies* may have the first element, of *finding* meanings, in spots, but there is not a faint indication in any of the items in the test that would give evidence of the second element, the *testing* of meaning, which is really the test of critical thinking. Let us look at the tests to find out what processes are involved.

Part I, Obtaining Facts, is a verbal factual test, which requires the student to pick out certain specific facts from a group of facts according to precise directions. In each case the right answer to the question is given. All that is required is ability to match the answer with the fact given in the testing situation, viz., referring to the "Facts about some States" in Table III, Item 9, reading 91,058 in the column under *Population* after *Nevada* and matching it with the figure 91,058 in the test item that gives four possible answers.

Part II, Drawing Conclusions from Facts,

is a reading test, which requires one to compare one set of facts with another set of facts and to pick out those that correspond. The process consists of reading a paragraph and matching four statements with it in order to determine the extent to which each of them is, according to the facts, indicated in the paragraph—again a factual test requiring no interpretation or reinterpretation of meanings. The conclusions are *not* drawn; they are picked out from a given set of conclusions.

Part III, Applying General Facts, is more of the same, finding a fact that best explains another fact, both facts being given, along with other facts. The only differences between this part and Part II are that there are two columns instead of one and that the directions are more complicated. The principle is the same.

To sum the evidence: there is hardly any need for thinking in order for one to see that 91,058 is not 225,565; in like manner, the simple process of reading a sentence and determining whether or not it is given in a paragraph cannot be classified as a thinking process; and, again, the use of even the imagination is hardly necessary in order to know that "The invention of machines has caused the growth of factories" and not "In a new country the first settlers usually live near rivers or bays" "Explains big factories." In short, a 100 per cent factual test is not a test of critical thinking or of thinking of any other kind. While it is true that facts are needed in order for one to think at all, the mere possession of the facts is no evidence of ability to think.

Wrightstone is one of the few who have condemned paper-pencil tests severely on the ground that they merely test verbal information and book learning. His test is a paper-pencil test, which differs in no essential respect, except in name, from existing tests. In fact, we have better tests of the same kind rightly named.

Test of Critical Thinking in the Social Studies, like most other paper tests, suffers very much from unreality. Thinking is both creative and critical. In real life a thinking situation is of the nature of a puzzle. The thinker is confronted with a difficulty for which available data or information does not suffice. Hidden clues may exist, but they may not even suggest the answer. New material and new meanings must be introduced before

the solution will "dawn" upon one. One solution after another is tested before the right one is found. Not a single item in the test being reviewed qualifies for this kind of process. All the facts are there. All one has to do is to find the right pairs, and presto! one is said to have thought critically. Good reading ability is all that one needs to have a high score in the test. Why not call it a reading test?

In one of his Ford Sunday Evening Hour talks, Mr. W. J. Cameron said, in developing the topic, "Initiate—Don't Imitate," "Setting up another peanut stand on a corner where one peanut stand is already competently and completely serving the trade, that is not competition. It is not business expansion either." *Test of Critical Thinking in the Social Studies* is one more peanut stand on an overcrowded corner. Some years ago Wrightstone said that we needed new tests for new needs. We still do. The need will not be supplied until and unless we discard the old content and produce new material that really measures the power to think. There is no miracle in the change of names, and neither is there any gain by paying lip-service to progressive education and proceeding to make old-fashioned tests with a new set of names.

So much for the shortcomings. The following may be regarded as outstanding merits of the test: (*a*) focusing attention on a significant educational objective—the development of critical thinking; (*b*) breaking down the objective into areas for which evidence may be obtained; (*c*) suggesting a way of determining individual (if the test is in fact sufficiently reliable for such purpose) and group differences in three aspects of critical thinking; (*d*) presenting a new validation procedure; and (*e*) pointing the way toward using the test itself and the test results as a device for the improvement of teaching.

G. M. Ruch, Chief, Research and Statistical Service, United States Office of Education, Washington, D. C. Wrightstone has chosen for the purpose of this test, to divide thinking into three aspects: (*a*) obtaining facts, (*b*) drawing conclusions, and (*c*) applying general facts. The three parts of the test contain, respectively, 36, 32, and 27 exercises, or a total of 95. The working time is 15 minutes per section, or a total of 45 minutes, a seemingly adequate allowance.

The conception of the test includes as one element the logico-psychological analysis of the thinking process as formulated by Dewey and others. As another element may be mentioned the influence of progressive curriculum formulations in such states as New York, California, Colorado, and Virginia. The validation methods rightly distinguish between curricular and statistical analysis—despite the fact that the latter appears not to have been carried out. The curricular validation of this test has unique features. By means of a specially prepared interview, 64 pupils gave free-answer responses to the test elements. These were evaluated independently by an unstated number of (but apparently never less that three) judges or teachers. Space does not permit full descriptions of the validation of the three parts of the test; the methods differ from part to part, and the manual account is too compressed for the reader to feel sure of his comprehension of the exact methodology. The statistical validation is based largely (or entirely?) on the correlations of the test with the reading part of the *Modern School Achievement Test* and McCall's *Multi-Mental Scale,* and on the inter-part correlations. It is not stated whether the routine item-analysis techniques were applied; presumably not.

Reliabilities are reported for stepped-up split-halves and form vs. form methods. The population used is not adequately described, other than that it comprised pupils in grades 4-6. The reliabilities quoted are, therefore, considerably higher than may be expected when the test is applied to a single class despite the statement that "these scores may be reliably used for individual analysis."

Raw scores may be transmuted into both age and grade equivalents, part by part, and total scores. The norms are based upon 4,000 pupils in six states, tested in 1938. The age and grade equivalents are in close agreement with those of the *Modern School Achievement Test* and the *New Stanford Achievement Test;* agreement with the later is almost perfect.

The mechanical features of the test are better than average. Much waste space might have been utilized to advantage by larger type and extra leading in places. The use of 42-pica lines (about 7 inches) is objectionable in the intermediate grades according to many authorities. Scoring is objective, simple, and economical.

There is no question that this test has moved some distance in the right direction. Its title is overly ambitious; it might more aptly be called a "Test of Work Skills in the Social Studies." Part I calls for obtaining facts from tables, graphs, etc., and contains little that is not also taught in arithmetic or several other school subjects. Part II is fundamentally a reading comprehension test under a more pretentious caption. Part III lives up to the title of the test more nearly, and involves judgment, which is certainly one element in critical thinking.

The reader should be left with the feeling that Wrightstone has both complemented and supplemented our useful measures in the field of the social studies; if any critical statements in this review overshadow such a general impression, the net result has been unintentional.

Chicago Sch J 21:232 Mr-Ap '40. D(enton) L. G(eyer). This long-awaited measuring instrument comes to us after the expenditure of many thousands of dollars and several years of effort, and is by all odds the most successful attempt yet made to measure one of the major educational outcomes whose attainment we have so far been able only to hope for and guess at. Every teacher of the social studies in the elementary school ought to secure a copy of this test and make a study of it.

[1620]

Test of General Proficiency in the Field of Social Studies: Cooperative General Achievement Tests, Revised Series, Part I. High school and college; 1940; Form QR; 6¢ per test, 10 to 99 copies; 1½¢ per machine-scorable answer sheet; 25¢ per specimen set; 40(45) minutes; Mary Willis with the editorial assistance of Ronald Beasley, Wilson Colvin, John S. Custer, Edgar B. Wesley, and J. Wayne Wrightstone; New York: Cooperative Test Service.

REFERENCES

Cooperative Test Service. *The Cooperative General Achievement Tests (Revised Series):* Information Concerning their Construction, Interpretation, and Use. New York: Cooperative Test Service, 1940. Pp. 4. Gratis. Paper.

[1621]

Wesley Test in Political Terms. Grades 6-16; 1932; 4 forms; 40¢ per 25; 30¢ per specimen set, including the *Wesley Test in Social Terms;* nontimed (5) minutes; Edgar B. Wesley; New York: Charles Scribner's Sons.

REFERENCES

1 WESLEY, E. B. "Wesley Test in Social Terms," pp. 219-26; and "Terms in the Social Sciences," pp. 502-609. In *Tests and Measurements in the Social Sciences.* By Truman L. Kelley and A. C. Krey. New York: Charles Scribner's Sons, 1934. Pp. xiv, 633. $3.00.

Howard R. Anderson, Associate Professor of Education, Cornell University. These tests are "similar in nature" to the *Wesley Test in*

Social Terms, "but being brief and inexpensive are especially valuable for testing the achievement of an entire class." With this statement from the examiner's manual this reviewer agrees only in part.

The tests (there are four forms; each consisting of ten five-response best-answer statements) are brief and are made up of questions also found in the two forms of the *Wesley Test in Social Terms.* How a test so limited in its sampling can test "the achievement of an entire class" is not clear. For a test even of knowledge of political terms the sampling appears inadequate.

Norms are given for each of the four forms in terms of the average number of correct responses per grade from the eleventh through the sixteenth. These suggest that the forms are too short and too easy to be used to advantage in the last three grades.

[1622]

Wesley Test in Social Terms. Grades 6-16; 1932; 2 forms; $1.30 per 25; 30¢ per specimen set, including the *Wesley Test of Political Terms*; nontimed, (30) minutes. Edgar B. Wesley; New York: Charles Scribner's Sons.

REFERENCES

1 Wesley, E. B. "Wesley Test in Social Terms," pp. 219-26; and "Terms in the Social Sciences," pp. 502-609. In *Tests and Measurements in the Social Sciences.* By Truman L. Kelley and A. C. Krey. New York: Charles Scribner's Sons, 1934. Pp. xiv, 633. $3.00.
2 Bolton, F. B. "The Predictive Value of Three Kinds of Tests for a Course in United States History." *J Ed Res* 30:445-7 F '37.
3 Wilson, Howard E. *Education for Citizenship,* pp. 56, 96-7, 272. New York: McGraw-Hill Book Co., 1938. Pp. 272. $2.75. (London: McGraw-Hill Publishing Co., Ltd. 15s.)

Howard R. Anderson, Associate Professor of Education, Cornell University. The Wesley Test in Social Terms is described as a test to "measure the results of instruction as distinct from intelligence or *random information*" and "can be used (1) as a diagnostic test, (2) as a final examination in the social studies, (3) as a qualifying examination, and (4) in any situation in which accurate measurement in the social studies is desired." The parallel between the last claim and similar ones formerly advanced in behalf of certain patent medicines is palpable.

What is the formula? In this case 80 best-answer exercises which require that the student indicate which of five descriptions of a term is most apt, or which of five terms best fits a given description. (The research underlying the selection of these social terms is described in Kelley and Krey's *Tests and Measurements in the Social Sciences.*[1])

. The following items from Form A are more or less typical: "The county court house is located at the county (1) capital (2) capitol (3) court (4) metropolis (5) seat." "Utility is that quality of a good which makes it (1) beautiful (2) cheap (3) costly (4) desirable (5) unusual." Now to this reviewer it seems that even limited "intelligence" or "random information," or both, will suggest that "seat" complements "county" better than the other words, and that "desirable" brings to a happy ending the definition of utility commonly provided in economics textbooks.

Some of the other items also contain clues. For example, "A protective tariff is designed to . . . protect home industries"; "An injunction is a court order"; "Habeas Corpus is a . . . writ"; "A patroon is a . . . Dutch landlord in colonial New York"; etc.

Other questions call for information which scarcely seems related to instruction in the social studies. For example, "A sentinel is . . . a guard"; "An illegal act is contrary to . . . law"; "A notary is. . . an official"; "For purposes of consideration, ideas are classified into . . . categories"; "The condition of being related by blood to another constitutes an example of . . . consanguinity"; etc. That the keyed answer to "A gold certificate is issued by . . . the treasury" is correct seems doubtful.

Unquestionably instruction in the social studies will help a student answer these questions. But so will extensive reading and intelligence. The examiner's manual gives a correlation of only .391 between the *Otis Self-Administering Test of Mental Ability* and the *Wesley Test of Social Terms.* Later research seems to indicate a much higher correlation between intelligence and performance on this test. In the recent New York State Survey, Wilson[3] reports a coefficient of correlation of .70 between intelligence quotients and Wesley test scores.

The tentative norms provided in the examiner's manual are rather inadequate since they consist only of an average score for each of the grades 6 to 16. The scoring key also is unsatisfactory in that the answers to Form A are printed on one side and those for Form B on the reverse side.

[1623]

20th Century High School Civics Test. Grades 10-12; 1935; 1 form; 3¢ per test, 4 or more copies; 10¢ per sample test; 60(65) minutes; [Gale Smith]; Fowler, Ind.: Benton Review Shop.

ECONOMICS

[1624]

Cooperative Economics Test. High school and college; 1933-39; 40- and 90-minute editions; 25¢ per specimen set of either edition; Form P: Howard R. Anderson and J. E. Partington with the editorial assistance of Robert L. Carey, Howard C. Hill, and E. F. Lindquist; New York: Cooperative Test Service.
a) FORMS 1933 AND 1935. Out of print; 90(95) minutes.
b) REVISED SERIES FORM P. 1939; 5¢ per test, 10 to 99 copies; 1½¢ per machine-scorable answer sheet; 40(45) minutes.

Edgar B. Wesley, Professor of Education, The University of Minnesota. [Review of Form P.] This test has several merits. The matching and the best-answer forms are, next to clear recall, the best that have been devised, and they appear here in their most perfected style. The test includes names, terms, principles, facts, and problem situations. It thus embraces a wide sample of the field of economics. There are few available tests in economics, and this is certainly one of the best, if not the best, one available. A little more help from a skeptically disposed economist would make it even better.

In spite of its merits this test presents a series of confusions. One cannot see how many items there are. Part I opens with Item 10 and Part II opens with Item 20. A patient sort of teacher could figure out the number of items. The argument for convenience of the makers, printers, and scorers is unconvincing. The test reminds me of the accounting system in some stores where the customer is detained while the clerks and the office fill out their records.

Part I is made up of two kinds of items, and Part II continues with the same kind of items which appear in the second part of Part I. Those who have had courses in the mechanics of test construction can probably find clues and run down the significance, but prospective users may not be so kindly disposed nor so sleuth-like minded.

This test illustrates another easily defended, but nonetheless unfortunate, principle of test construction. It is probably suited to high school students of economics, but it causes the advanced student of economics considerable irritation and stirs many misgivings. Is it not possible to make items which are scholastically sound and at the same time fitted to high school students? For examples: Item 31—Is it a fact that people are buying more trademarked goods? Item 37—Who can say what form of organization is most temporary? Item 38—Which comes first, investment or control? Item 45—Does the word *public* mean *official* or the opposite of private? Item 48—What economist could answer the question at the time the item was written? Item 50—Is there a correct answer? Item 56—The facts contradict the "normal conditions" specified in the introductory phrase. Item 40—The correct answer is trivial and negates the significance of the whole item.

On the title page the student is told that "directions for each part are printed at the beginning of the part," but at the beginning of Part II, the student is merely told to continue. The mystery of why there are two parts thus deepens, and the confusion is increased by shifting the numbering scheme. Why does the publisher not explain the effect of the mechanical scoring machine?—if that is the answer. In spite of these defects the test seems to be entirely valid and useful.

GEOGRAPHY

[1625]

Analytical Scales of Attainment in Geography. Grades 6-7; 1933; 1 form; 75¢ per 25; 20¢ per specimen set; (45) minutes; M. E. Branom and M. J. Van Wagenen; Minneapolis, Minn.: Educational Test Bureau, Inc.

Ernest C. Witham, Associate Professor of Education, Rutgers University. This test is made up of geography information, in the form of multiple-choice statements, which ranges over the whole world. This does not conform well to many courses of study, as some parts of the world are not studied intensively before the eighth grade.

There are 160 statements divided equally into four groups as follows: (*a*) Geography Vocabulary, (*b*) Human Geography, (*c*) Industries, and (*d*) Products. While most of the statements are well selected, the division into such sections is rather meaningless, because many of the statements fall just as logically into one category as into another. Many of the statements could have been interchanged with equal geographical justification. For example, the statement "The country which imports the most lumber is (1) Great Britain (2) Germany (3) France (4) United States (5) Italy," seems to fit Industries or Products, but it is

Item 36 under Human Geography. The statement "Shoes are generally made from the hides or skins of (1) horses (2) cattle (3) sheep (4) goats (5) hogs," fits equally well Industries or Products. It is Item 11 under the latter. The statement "The fat of the hog is called (1) tallow (2) gristle (3) oil (4) margarine (5) lard," is listed in the Geography Vocabulary group. Just where is the geography vocabulary significance in such a question?

Specific directions for giving and scoring tests are indispensable, but all superfluous directions, in the interest of clarity and economy, should be dispensed with. For example, it is no longer necessary that every test shall give directions for clearing the desks and providing each child with two well-sharpened pencils.

The raw score results on this test are converted into C-scores and they in turn into geography ages. This seems unnecessarily complicated for the average geography teacher.

In the folder of directions for administering and scoring the test, there is no mention of validity and reliability.

In spite of the strictures mentioned the test has real value, and if I were a teacher of geography I would use it in my classes.

[1625.1]

Fourth Grade Geography Test. End of the fourth grade; 1940; 1 form; 8¢ per test; 4¢ per manual; 20¢ per scoring stencil; 3¢ per class record sheet; 30(35) minutes; Zoe A. Thralls, George Miller, and Marguerite Uttley; Bloomington, Ill.: McKnight and McKnight.

[1626]

Wiedefeld-Walther Geography Test. Grades 4-8; 1931; 2 forms; $1.15 per 25; 20¢ per specimen set; 60(65) minutes; N. Theresa Wiedefeld and E. Curt Walther; Yonkers, N. Y.: World Book Co.

Anna Parsek, Teacher in the Sixth Grade, Public School No. 6, West New York, New Jersey. This nine-year-old test was one of the first of the standardized tests in geography which purported to go beyond the measurement of geographical information alone to include the measurement of "skills in the finding, evaluation, and use of facts."

The authors state that Part 1, consisting of Subtests 1, 2, and 3, "measures the extent to which three necessary study abilities and skills have become part of a pupil's thinking and behavior in the effective study of geography."

Subtest 1, Reading, consists of sixteen 4-sentence paragraphs requiring the pupil to select the one sentence which "helps best to answer" the question following the paragraph.

In many cases the correct answer is too obvious and in other cases, such as Items 11 and 13, there are two answers equally correct. In light of the authors' claims that this subtest measures "the ability to read *various types* [reviewer's italics] of geographical material and comprehend their meaning for use in geographical interpretation," Subtest 1 does not appear to be valid.

Subtest 2, Organization, purports to measure "the ability to recognize the worth of geographical material with relation to geographical problems." Again many of the correct-according-to-the-key answers appear to be no better than other responses considered incorrect. Multiple-choice questions of this sort do not necessarily test reasoning ability. The examinee is given no freedom to suggest hypotheses or to marshal and organize data. This type of question does not test ability to think reflectively. Casting questions into objective-when-scored-according-to-the-key form must necessarily be at the expense of the validity of a test measuring "organizing ability."

Subtest 3, Map and Graph Reading, is excellent—it really tests ability to read and interpret maps and graphs. However, the maps are too small for the exacting reading required. Because of this, more than one answer ought to be considered acceptable for Items 10. 20, and 24. This subtest is too difficult for fourth and fifth grade pupils. Although most of the graphs are good, the circle graphs are too small. Item 44 may be answered correctly in two ways; the key accepts only one answer as correct.

Part 2, Geography Information, is similar to many other tests. The map exercise is needlessly confusing. With both political and physical divisions numbered in the same way, one frequently is at loss as to which the number represents.

The time allowed does not appear to be sufficient for a test which urges the students *"not to hurry."* It is unfortunate that the authors failed to name the "seven of the newest series of geography texts" which served as the basis for the choice and grade placement of the test items. Since omitted questions are penalized as much as wrong answers, a premium is placed upon guessing.

For measuring factual information and the reading of maps and graphs in grades 6, 7, and 8, the test should be of value. The test appears to be too difficult for grades 4 and 5. The authors state the test will enable the supervisor to "get objective information on the phases of the subject that need most improvement, the grades in which learning should be improved, and what assistance each teacher needs for the improvement of her instruction." Even though the test is hardly valid for these purposes, many supervisors will—unfortunately—use the test as the authors recommend.

Marie E. Trost, Teacher of Geography and Science in Grades 7 and 8, School No. 7, Belleville, New Jersey. Though intended for use in grades 4 through 8, this test is too difficult for children in grades 4 and 5. However, children in grades 6 through 9 should find the test stimulating. After taking the test, my own eighth graders wanted me to give them another test of the same kind.

Although most of the questions in Subtest 1 (10 minutes), Reading, are well-chosen, a few are not. For example, Item 9 asks, "Why is such a small part of Canada farmed?" The key gives as the correct answer, "The population is only about one-twelfth that of the United States."

Items 15-19 of Subtest 2 (10 minutes), Organization, are very involved and are arranged in a confusing manner. This subtest might better have been combined with Subtest 1 and a test on how to use the index put in its place.

Subtest 3 (15 minutes), Map and Graph Reading, is the most difficult subtest. The time allowed is much too short. At least ten minutes more is necessary if accuracy rather than speed is to be tested. For example, my own eighth graders earned on an average ten points more when given fifteen minutes extra for Subtest 3. The maps should be much larger and the relief map should have clearer markings. The questions on the silk graph should have been placed on the same page as the graph. As it is, the page must be turned eight times in order to answer the last four questions based upon the graph.

Subtest 4 (5 minutes), Geographical Vocabulary, appears to be a satisfactory test.

Subtest 5 (10 minutes), Geographical Relationships, consists of three exercises in which a total of twenty statements of effect are to be matched with twenty out of twenty-seven statements of causes.

Subtest 6 (10 minutes), Place Geography,

includes questions equally divided between the Eastern and Western Hemispheres. In the limited space used the maps are well arranged. The test requires the pupil to have an accurate knowledge of locations.

The *Wiedefeld-Walther Geography Test* is not just another test of factual information. The answers are not so obvious that a child needs to do no careful thinking. The test covers most of the major geographic skills. The questions indicate careful analysis of geographic subject matter and its relative importance. A great deal of research has gone into the preparation of this well-organized test. However, the mechanical setup of the test would have been much better had a larger size page been used.

The scoring mechanics could have been improved. Eleven adjustments of the answer strips must be made. To get total scores for three of the subtests, we must turn pages twice. On an average, I was able to score a test in four minutes.

If given at the beginning of a term, this test would be of considerable help to the teacher wishing to organize her geography instruction so as to be of most value to her pupils. The test should also serve as a guide in making test questions. Although the test is quite difficult, if used properly, it should make a definite improvement in geography teaching. Although published in 1931, it is still a very good tool for evaluating pupil growth in a rather progressive program of geography teaching.

[1627]
World Geography Test: The Dominion Tests. Grade 8; 1938; 2 forms; 2¢ per test, 10 or more; 5¢ per sample-copy; 15¢ per manual; 30(40) minutes; Toronto, Canada: Department of Educational Research, University of Toronto.

HISTORY

[1628]
American Council European History Test. Grades 10-15; 1929; 2 forms; $1.50 per 25; 20¢ per specimen set; 90(95) minutes; Harry J. Carman, Walter C. Langsam, and Ben D. Wood; Yonkers, N. Y.: World Book Co.

S. P. McCutchen, Assistant Professor of Education and Research Associate, Bureau of Educational Research, The Ohio State University. It seems reasonable to assume that one may carefully study the testing program and draw inferences as to the objectives of the course in which the tests are being used. On this basis one would have to say that the teacher who uses the *American Council European History Test* subscribes to a reservoir or cold storage theory of education. The chief justification for the things taught would be the assumption that the student would need this knowledge at some later date, presumably when he becomes an adult, in order to explain what is happening in his then contemporary world. Overlooking the factors of motivation and of retention, assuming that the teacher has persuaded, forced, or cajoled the student to learn the data selected, and that the student will retain it in useful form until the time of its later utility, there is still the question of accurate prediction to investigate. This test seems to operate on an assumption of eternal verities in history which all people need to know, and assumes, therefore, that every teacher will teach all of the facts to all students. In the main the items selected call for little association or constructive thought. Students are asked to indicate the truth or falsity of such items as "The *cahiers* were salt taxes" and "The *Zollverein* was a German customs union"; they are expected to identify Suleiman the Magnificent with Turkey, Henry Stanley with African exploration, and Dr. Quesnay with the Physiocratic movement; they should know what James Watt invented and the religion of George Fox; they must exercise selectiveness in indicating that General Foch was not a peaceful man, and that Blücher was not a scientist or writer.

Only occasionally does the necessity for thinking arise and the association is usually historical. This item in the true-false section is an illustration: "Being a leading aristocrat and believing in a policy of 'blood and iron,' Bismarck was always strenuously opposed to all forms of legislation tending to improve the condition of the working man." The item slyly identifies Bismarck with aristocracy and forthright methods, and challenges the student's naive assumption that such a person could not possibly have the interests of the working man at heart. Truly, a mental biography of Bismarck is required in order to attain the correct answer, false, for this item. The test illustrates the difficulty of standardized instruments in keeping pace with the tempo of modern events. These items are in the true-false section: "All the so-called Great Powers except the United States and Russia are at present members of the League of Nations." (The key

indicates that the statement is true.) "True to tradition, Austria still has a very undemocratic constitution." (To fit the key, this should be marked false.)

Very few people concerned with secondary education today advocate the complete elimination of testing, but the use of this test for measuring achievement seems a rather clear indication that the teacher has abdicated and is willing to let someone who does not know the uniquenesses of the community, uniquenesses of the teacher, uniquenesses of the student group prescribe the curriculum. There is probably no better way to contribute to a docile acceptance of authoritarianism.

[1629]
American History Test. First, second semester: high school; 1938; 1 form, 2 parts; 3¢ per test, 4 or more copies; 10¢ per sample test; 40(45) minutes; Gale Smith; Fowler, Ind.: Benton Review Shop.
a) FROM THE DISCOVERY OF AMERICA TO 1850.
b) FROM 1850 TO PRESENT TIME.

[1630]
American History Test: National Achievement Test. Grades 7-8; 1937-39; 2 forms; $1.50 per 25; 5¢ per specimen set; nontimed (45-60) minutes; Robert K. Speer, Lester D. Crow, and Samuel Smith; Rockville Centre, N. Y.: Acorn Publishing Co.

Jacob S. Orleans, Associate Professor of Education, The College of the City of New York. The purpose of this test, as indicated by the authors, is to measure the pupil's ability to interpret major lessons in American history, his mastery of the time sequence of events, his knowledge of historical associations, and recognition of important facts. There can be no question that the content of this test tends to go beyond the more typical factual tests in American history that have been published in the past. However, despite the names of the four parts of the test, it still is largely factual and may not be an improvement over some of the better elementary school history tests that have already appeared.

The only item available on content validity appeared in a circular which stated that: "The tests are in close agreement with numerous city and state courses of study, widely used textbooks, and the judgments of scores of school administrators and teachers. In most cases, each test includes not only the important subject matter, but especially questions to measure the pupil's power to use the knowledge he has acquired." Analysis of the content of the test shows a fairly good distribution for the various periods of American history with perhaps a little overemphasis on the Colonial Period and the period prior to the Civil War. It is interesting to note that of the 114 items in the test, 21 deal with the 5 specific items of. States' rights, taxation without representation, the Monroe Doctrine, the Emancipation Proclamation, and the cotton gin. No information is available as to whether the authors made an analysis of the questions in terms of types of content such as social, economic, political, chronological, and the like.

No information was at hand concerning the statistical validity of the test.

The data provided for reliability indicate a reliability coefficient of .88 for grades 7 and 8. Presumably this means for the two grades combined. The norms show a variation of 36 points representing 20 months of achievement, or slightly over one-half month per point. Since the probable error of a pupil's score is 2.6, the probable error of a pupil's score is less than one and one-half months of achievement. It is interesting to note that a shorter history test contained in the National Achievement Test Battery has a higher reliability coefficient for grade 6 alone.

The scoring is done without a key for three of the four parts of the test. The scorer is given a key word. Any answer is correct if preceded by a letter which is part of that word. There are only three choices for the multiple-choice questions in Parts 1 and 4, without any correction for guessing in the scoring. It is possible that the pupils may be somewhat confused in Part 2 by the continuous shifting in alternate questions from determining which of four items comes first to which of the four items comes last.

Despite the title of Part 1, Lessons of History, only 14 of the 29 questions deal with the lesson to be learned from a given situation. The other 15 items are almost entirely factual. In the case of several of the questions in Part 1, the authors may have difficulty justifying some of their answers. For example, our refusal to enter the League of Nations may be just as indicative of the fact that we do not understand European affairs as that we are opposed to political agreements with European countries. Although Part 4 is labeled "Miscellaneous Problems," the questions are purely items of historical fact.

Grade norms by months are given for grades 7 and 8 only. Therefore, it is not possible to give a specific equivalent measure for the poorest seventh grade pupils or the best eighth grade pupils.

Although the pupil's score on the entire test is undoubtedly reliable it is questionable that scores on the individual parts have meaning for analytical purposes. The diagnostic purpose which the test is meant to serve can then hardly be on the basis of reliable measurement in any one of the four parts of the test.

Wallace Taylor, Assistant Professor of Education and Supervisor in Social Studies, Milne High School, State College for Teachers, Albany, New York. The claims for the test seem extravagant. It is doubtful that it measures "power to interpret major lessons in American History; the ability to analyze principles; or ability in tracing cause and effect." It does fulfill its claim to test for a recognition of facts even though some of the facts seem scarcely important enough to deserve inclusion. Part VII, Historical Associations, tests for names of men, several of whom are not very important, and in addition employs the device of supplying the first name which certainly has the effect of encouraging verbal association.

The section dealing with time concepts would be more valuable if there was a definite relationship between each of the events that are to be placed in order.

Too many of the items deal with political history. Understanding of the aspects of the life of the common man which the better teachers of junior high school American history commonly stress, is not sufficiently stressed. Also, items in which the pupil is asked to use historical principles in the explanation of present-day problems are lacking.

The items are generally free from the more obvious defects of specific determiners, grammatical inconsistencies, and clues, but in many instances the incorrect responses are so obviously wrong as to require very little discrimination in arriving at the correct answer. It is probable that many of these items test for general intelligence rather than American history.

The element of guessing would have been reduced by the use of four rather than three responses. The opportunity for guessing probably results in spuriously high scores.

The use of code words in scoring seems

unnecessarily complicated. Any device of this type may possibly have the effect of causing the pupil to spend time trying to figure out the code that may be used in answering the questions. There is no apparent advantage resulting from its use.

[1631]

Analytical Scales of Attainment in American History. Grades 7-8; 1932-33; 1 form; 75¢ per 25; 20¢ per specimen set; (45) minutes; Mary G. Kelty and M. J. Van Wagenen; Minneapolis, Minn.: Educational Test Bureau, Inc.

Wilbur F. Murra, Executive Secretary, The National Council for the Social Studies, Washington, D. C. This test is intended for diagnosis only. It supplements the general achievement test by the same authors which is published as the American history section of the *Unit Scales of Attainment.* It claims to diagnose relative attainments in each of the following categories: historical vocabulary, historical background, persons, and places and conditions. Each section consists of 30 or 40 five-choice multiple-choice items.

The individual items are almost completely free from technical flaws. Directions are commendably clear and succinct. Format is excellent. It would seem unfortunate, however, that there is a 45-minute time limit on a test of this kind. Certainly many slower pupils will be unable to complete all 140 exercises in that time, and accordingly their scores on the fourth section will not be accurate measures.

Content is adequately representative of conventional courses in junior high school American history, but it will be found less well suited for those newer courses which put more emphasis on social and economic history and problems of the twentieth century. Out of a total of 140 items, only 11 deal exclusively with the twentieth century and 13 others—particularly places and terms—touch the twentieth century in part. Of the 11 which are exclusively concerned with events since 1900, three deal with the Panama Canal, six with military and diplomatic events of the World War, one with the Nineteenth Amendment, and one with the Kellogg Pact.

In a diagnostic test each trait separately measured should be identifiable and clearly distinguishable from every other trait. This important criterion is far from satisfactorily met by the instrument here under review. Such a short-

coming is due in part to the inherent nature of achievement in the field of history, where separate elements are scarcely distinguishable. It is, nevertheless, a specific fault of the *Analytical Scale of Attainment in American History* that its section titled Knowledge of Places and Conditions contains a miscellany of exercises touching such matters as legislation restricting immigration, motives for early exploration and settlement, and the founding of Harvard College. The teacher may well be in doubt as to the meaning of any pupil's score on this section. The section headed Historical Background is very similar, as its broad title more candidly indicates. The Historical Vocabulary subtest appears to demand "historical background" information almost as much as other sections, although a minority of its items treat exclusively of word meanings. The section headed Knowledge of Persons is least open to criticism on this ground.

With such indefinite limits for each section, it is quite to be expected that there is much overlapping. This fault is most indefensibly evident when one finds that Item 27 in the subtest Knowledge of Historical Background is repeated in its *identical* form as Item 37 in the subtest Knowledge of Places and Conditions. (The item deals with the effect of the Russian Revolution on the World War.)

Perhaps the most distinctive feature of this test is its scheme for expressing results in terms of "C-scores." This feature, of course, it shares with all its companion tests in the "Analytical Scales" and "Unit Scales" series by the same publishers. It admittedly affords a more valid basis for appraising the gains made by a pupil or class over a period of time, although it seems to have no advantage over other simpler systems of norms for *comparing* the attainment of a pupil or class in respect to the four traits measured in this test—or for comparing any one of them with other tests in the "Analytical" and "Unit" batteries. But the special claims which the publishers make for the C-score (the reference to a mythical "absolute zero point" and the "consistent unit of measurement") seem to this reviewer to afford no essential help to teacher-interpretation of test scores, however serviceable they may be for more sophisticated statistical analysis.

A table of norms for the "history age" equivalent of each C-score is provided. Such norms, however, are certainly not valid for interpreting achievement in American History. School curricula being what they are, attainment in this field cannot be thought of as continuous with advancing chronological age (as reading ability may be, for example). The pupil gains in knowledge of American history while he is studying that subject and rarely otherwise. Dependable surveys have demonstrated that the typical fifteen-year-old actually knows *less* American history than the typical fourteen-year-old, for the latter has normally just completed the study of the subject in grade 8, whereas the former has practically never had any study of it in grade 9.

Margaret Willis, Assistant Professor of Social Science Education, University School, The Ohio State University. This test includes four sections, Historical Vocabulary and Knowledge of Historical Background, each with thirty multiple-choice questions, and Knowledge of Persons and Knowledge of Places and Conditions, each with forty. The directions for scoring claim that "Since these Scales are like yard-sticks with a task of known value in place of the inch mark at each unit distance, the C-scores measure amounts of abilities just as numbers of inches measure amounts of height or numbers of pounds measure amounts of weight." The class analysis sheet is set up with norms for each section so that the "history age" of a pupil may be determined in each classification and the "Class Median Pc. Av. or IQ." calculated.

Since these are rather extensive claims it is interesting to examine the nature of test items which can be equated so accurately. The questions may also be examined for distribution of items as between periods of history and between the various aspects of living. Since the catalog of the Educational Test Bureau in which this test was listed points out that "no teacher believes a child learns only that which he is taught in the classroom," it is fair to watch for questions which an intelligent child might answer from his out-of-school experiences. Another point to consider is the opportunity which is offered for the exercise of the critical faculty.

It is not always easy to tell the historical period referred to by any particular question since time identifications are generally hazy, but the test seems to be heavily weighted toward the more distant past. Among the 40 persons included in the third section, 11 were connected with discovery and exploration, and 11 more with military affairs of the Civil War or earlier. Of the remaining 18, 6 were inventors and the other 12 scatter over all other fields during the whole period of our national life. In the section Knowledge of Places and Conditions, more than half of the items are pre-revolutionary. In the whole test not more than three or four living men are mentioned and they are wrong answers.

Throughout the test both facts and language are handled uncritically. For example, "The process of rebuilding the South after the Civil War was called: reconstruction." Was the South *rebuilt* during reconstruction? Also this: "Which one of these was the more important agricultural crop in America during the period from 1870 to 1900? (1) potatoes (2) cotton (3) wheat (4) rice (5) tobacco." The key says the answer is wheat, but how can anyone say which crop was more important unless there is some agreed standard for judging importance? Certainly throughout large sections of the country cotton seemed more important to the people whose whole living depended upon it.

Certain questions either repeat or contradict each other. The identical question appears as Item 27 under Historical Background and Item 37 under Places and Conditions. Under Historical Background the first question has *all* the English colonists raising Indian corn as their chief food, while the nineteenth question has the southern colonies raising rice as one of their most important occupations. The seventeenth question puts "most of the labor unions in the United States" in the American Federation of Labor, a contention which is certainly debatable in 1939. Throughout the test there are similar examples of carelessness in definition, in English usage, or in editing.

The test seems to this reviewer an instrument designed to measure and standardize the least desirable kind of history teaching now current. It bears little discernible relation to any part of a child's world except that of his textbook. As a measure of "ability" it is meaningless. The catalog of the Educational Test Bureau argues for standardized tests because where locally constructed tests are used instead "there is too apt to be the 'vicious circle' of tests modifying the curriculum and the curriculum modifying the tests." If such a situation were really a vicious circle, it would still be preferable to the standardization of an indefensible status quo.

[1632]

Bowman United States History Test. Grades 7-8 and 12; [1931]; 1 form, 2 parts (A and B); $1.00 per 25 of either part; 20¢ per specimen set; 45(50) minutes per part; Lela Gibson Bowman; Bloomington, Ill.: Public School Publishing Co.

Grace Graham, Department of History, Columbia High School, Columbia, South Carolina, and W. C. McCall, Director of the Personnel Bureau and Associate Professor of Education, The University of South Carolina. GENERAL CRITICISM. This test undertakes to measure both upper elementary grades and high school seniors. In view of the marked difference in the attainments of seventh or eighth graders and of twelfth graders, the difficulty, if not impossibility, of such a task should be immediately evident. As Samuel Adams said of the preamble to the Constitution, "I stumble at the threshold." Some items must certainly prove to be inoperative in both age groups. For instance, it seems inconceivable that any twelfth grader, or even any seventh grader, should fail to match "Discovered America in 1492" with Christopher Columbus. It seems equally unlikely that seventh graders should know Bryan as "a temperance advocate, an orator, and an unsuccessful candidate for president of the United States."

The Bowman test, it seems fair to say, is poorly balanced in content. Approximately 37 per cent of the items relate to the periods of Exploration, Colonization, and Revolution. Most of the textbooks of elementary classes devote only approximately 25 per cent of the space to these periods, although it is perhaps true that elementary teachers give nearly, if not as much as, 37 per cent of instructional time to these topics of American history. It is the writer's belief that in senior high school instruction the average time given to these topics is approximately 25 per cent.

Other fields of instruction generally regarded as essential parts of United States history courses are negligibly treated, if at all. Only four items of the total 282 relate to the period since the World War and only two items have to do with the Constitution. Scant reference is made to the development of American foreign policy, to causes and results of movements or happenings, to social and economic problems, such as labor, religion, tariffs, immigration, money and trusts.

One multiple-choice section is headed Causal Relationship but none of the items given except the sample exercise and one other express a causal relationship. The other questions require definite factual knowledge. Multiple-choice questions, when properly constructed, can stimulate more thought-provoking responses and make less appeal to memorization of factual information. To escape the stigma of being a test of memorized facts, the Bowman test might profitably have used the multiple-choice pattern to sound out concepts of various problems and to test for causes and results.

In the geographical sections, which include 48 per cent of the items of the entire test, the type of information called for is place geography exclusively, except for one section which requires knowledge of colonial possessions. Although this knowledge is necessary and desirable, certainly it does not represent 48 per cent of teachers' labors. The including of maps on which places are to be located is unusual and interesting. The items which ask for the states or countries in which cities are located tend to encourage drill teaching, reminiscent of the era when each child memorized states and their capitals. No items call for a knowledge of geographical influences on the lives of the people, or of products or natural resources. The chronological-relationships group of items rather than the identification of definite dates, as called for in another group, is more in line with current teaching.

The mechanical construction of this test invites scoring errors because the completion pattern makes scoring excessively laborious and also introduces the element of teacher opinion and generosity as to acceptance of misspelled answers. Scoring the section on geography is rendered doubly tiresome by the completion-fill-in arrangement together with the provision that pupils use letters instead of numbers to record identifications in one section. Due to the alignment of numbering of the sample exercises along with the test items, there is the added scoring danger of counting the sample-exercise answers in with the pupils' answers. The scoring "key" supplied by the publishers is nothing more than a condensed one-page list of correct answers. Scoring labors and errors could both be greatly reduced if the publishers would supply pasteboard stencil-type scoring keys throughout the test.

The author and publishers have failed to supply any information whatever about reliability of the test. Also, norms data ("standards," in the language of the test manual) are incomplete for the senior high school level and no information is given about the number of cases on which the table of seventh and eighth grade norms is based. In the language of the manual the norms are "tentative" and have apparently continued in that state since the test was published in 1931. In all fairness, it should be noted that the author reports an extensive and laborious investigation of curriculum content in American history and of examination questions used by teachers as a basis for item selection and validation in harmony with curriculum and teaching practices. The careful work done by the author suggests that the test content might well be used as a basis for a revised test designed for either junior high school or senior high school levels, reduced in content and modernized in mechanical respects.

CRITICISM OF SPECIFIC ITEMS. Four items in the identifications are poorly constructed in that they merely require memorized information concerning presidents, such as "was fourth president of the United States," and "was elected president in 1920." Identification of Calhoun as a "war-hawk from South Carolina" emphasizes a relatively unimportant part of his career. A few items are poorly worded, such as the multiple-choice question on the Monroe Doctrine and "The commander of the fleet at the battle of New Orleans was (*a*) McClellan (*b*) Farragut (*c*) Scott." Most students would identify the "battle of New Orleans" with 1812 rather than with the Civil War conflict. Two items test the discovery of America by Columbus for both identification of Columbus and for the date. Such items are a waste of testing space, especially since the information given in one item answers the other. Several of the items in the geographical section are ambiguous: the country owning Samoa, the state in which Chesapeake Bay is located. Others in the geographical section are unimportant, such as, the ownership of Staten Island and of the island of Yap.

[1633]

Cooperative American History Test. High school; 1933-40; 40- and 90-minute editions; 25¢ per specimen set of either edition; Form P: Howard R. Anderson, E. F. Lindquist, and Charlotte W. Croon; Form Q: Harry Berg, E. F. Lindquist, and Charlotte W. Croon with the editorial assistance of H. C. Hill, Tyler Kepner, Samuel McKee, Jr., Elmer J. Thompson,

and E. B. Wesley; New York: Cooperative Test Service.
a) FORMS 1934 AND 1937. Forms 1933, 1935, and 1936 are out of print; 6¢ per test, 10 to 99 copies; 90(95) minutes.
b) REVISED SERIES FORMS N, O, P, AND Q. 1937-40; 5¢ per test, 10 to 99 copies; 1½¢ per machine-scorable answer sheet; 40(45) minutes.

REFERENCES

1 LINDQUIST, E. F. "The Form of the American History Examinations of the Cooperative Test Service." *Ed Rec* 12:459-75 O '31.

Margaret Willis, Assistant Professor of Social Science Education, University School, The Ohio State University. [Review of Form P.] This test consists of 100 multiple-choice questions arranged in a rough chronological order which helps the reader to keep his bearings without elaborate time identifications. It is divided into two parts, apparently in order to insure that the slow worker will spend a fair part of his forty minutes on the last thirty-seven questions which deal with the period from the Spanish-American War to the present. Approximately half of the questions deal with the period of American history to the close of the Civil War, and only the first twelve with pre-revolutionary times. This proportion reflects newer emphases in teaching as does also the character of the questions themselves. The rote learner and the uncritical thinker will do very badly on this test, for the wrong choices are set up to make a particular appeal to him.

The booklet of directions, the booklet of norms and the handbook describing the purpose, content and interpretation of the coöperative tests all are cautious in their claims for the tests, and give some excellent advice as to the limits of their usefulness. The teacher who keeps in mind those limits and pays thoughtful attention to that advice may find the *Cooperative American History Test* a helpful instrument.

For a review by Edgar B. Wesley, see 1014.

[1634]

Cooperative Ancient History Test. High school; 1933-39; 40- and 90-minute editions; 25¢ per specimen set of either edition; Form P: Howard R. Anderson, E. F. Lindquist, Wallace Taylor, and Charlotte W. Croon with the editorial assistance of R. H. McFeely, J. H. Price, and F. S. Somerby; New York: Cooperative Test Service.
a) FORMS 1934, 1935, 1936, AND 1937. Form 1933 is out of print; 6¢ per test, 10 to 99 copies; 90(95) minutes.
b) FORMS O AND P. 1938-39; 5¢ per test, 10 to 99 copies; 1½¢ per machine-scorable answer sheet; 40(45) minutes.

S. P. McCutchen, Assistant Professor of Education and Research Associate, Bureau of Educational Research, The Ohio State University. [Review of Form P.] Since the American Council on Education is still printing a *Cooperative Ancient History Test* one must assume that there are still courses in ancient history being offered on the secondary level. The writer finds difficulty in figuring out why this is so. Of course, there are preparatory schools which have found that some of the Eastern colleges will accept, even prefer, to have students offer entrance examinations in ancient history, and perhaps there are teachers who still preserve high school ancient history courses because of the changeless nature of the course and its complete remoteness from practical modern concerns. Such people, however, having perfected the routine of their year's work so that they no longer have to take thought as to change, ought to have also their tests worked out and not require the aid of the Council. However, the *Cooperative Ancient History Test* exists, and it exists in two parts. Part I, labeled "Historical Facts," contains sixty-eight items using the multiple-choice technique. The thought process required of the student seems to be simple memorization in which the student is aided by the suggestions from which he makes his choice. Part II is called "Historical Judgment." The implication seems to be that the student exercises some independence of thinking in using the data furnished. The presence of an answer sheet, however, seems to question this inference for there is only one "right" judgment, and it seems likely that in this section also the student will fall back on his memory of what the textbook's comment was. (What textbook *does* one use for ancient history nowadays?)

Finally, it seems somehow anachronistic to see these "truths" of ancient history susceptible to machine scoring.

For a review by Wilbur F. Murra, see 1015.

[1635]

Cooperative Modern European History Test. High school; 1933-40; 40- and 90-minute editions; 25¢ per specimen set of either edition; Form O: Howard R. Anderson and E. F. Lindquist; Form P: Howard R. Anderson, E. F. Lindquist, and Charlotte W. Croon; Form Q: Wallace Taylor, E. F. Lindquist, Mary Willis, and Charlotte W. Croon with the editorial assistance of Howard R. Anderson, Margaret Hastings, Martin Y. Munson, Jean Stoner, and Elmer J. Thompson; New York: Cooperative Test Service.
a) FORMS 1934, 1935, 1936, AND 1937. Form 1933 is out of print; 6¢ per test, 10 to 99 copies; 90(95) minutes.
b) REVISED SERIES FORMS N, O, P, AND Q. 1937-40; 5¢ per test; 1½¢ per machine-scorable answer sheets; 40(45) minutes.

Lavone A. Hanna, Research Associate, School of Education, Stanford University. [Review of Form O.] In advertising this test, the publishers claim that it requires "the evaluation and understanding of fundamental movements and institutions as well as of personages, locations, and specific events" and that the recency of construction "permits the introduction of much contemporary material." These claims are not justified by the items covered in the test.

The test is divided into two parts. Part I deals with historical personages, historical terms, geographic terms, dates and events. Part II is called historical judgment. The items are all of the single-choice, best-answer type with each item containing four possible responses. Factual information is all that is required to select the correct answer in the first part, which contains such items as: Item 36, "At a time of crisis one member withdrew from the (1) Triple Entente (2) Triple Alliance (3) Entente Cordiale (4) Dual Alliance"; and Item 7, "The Reign of Terror came to an end after the execution of (1) Carnot (2) Danton (3) Mirabeau (4) Robespierre." Historical judgment seems a misnomer for the second section which uses the same technique used in Part I substituting a group of four phrases for names, places, terms, and events. Certainly little historical judgment is needed in selecting the right answer in such questions as: Item 87, "The country which produced the largest number of famous musical composers in the nineteenth century was (1) France (2) Italy (3) Germany (4) England"; and Item 77, "The office of prime minister in England developed (1) under the Restoration (2) during the arbitrary rule of the Stuarts (3) when the Bill of Rights was passed (4) during the reign of George the First." The second claim of the test, that it contains much contemporary material, is not very valid when only nine items out of the hundred deal with events of the last ten years.

If one is concerned with testing the factual information which students possess, the test has considerable value for the facts covered are well chosen and most of them are necessary to an understanding of contemporary Europe. The mere knowing of these facts does not, however, produce understanding and if one is concerned with appraising the understanding which students have of basal European problems as well as those fundamental to an understanding of international relations or with evaluating the grasp which students have of important concepts in world affairs, the test has little or no value. No attempt has been made either to evaluate the ability of students to see the relationship between the present situation and past events. Another defect in the test is that it follows the practice of most history tests in emphasizing political events and problems at the expense of economic and social ones.

The test is set up for machine scoring but can be easily and quickly hand scored. The reliability of the test (.908) is high but is based on a single grade or semester of group study.

For reviews by A. C. Krey and S. P. McCutchen, see 1016.

[1636]

Cooperative World History Test. High school; 1934-37; Forms 1934, 1935, 1936, and 1937; 6¢ per test, 10 to 99 copies; 25¢ per specimen set; 90(95) minutes; H. R. Anderson and E. F. Lindquist; New York: Cooperative Test Service.

Kenneth E. Gell, Head of the Department of Social Studies, Washington High School, Rochester, New York; and Special Lecturer in Education, The University of Rochester. [Review of Form 1937.] This test is a good one for both measurement and diagnosis. It is arranged in three parts by type of information to be tested, rather than by type of question as in many new type examinations. Part I tests recognition of names of 39 historical personages by 5-choice questions; 60 historical terms and 15 geographical terms are also tested in the same way. All items in Part I are well chosen for their basic importance and are well spread throughout history from ancient to modern times. The choices offered have high validity to world history and thereby add a further element to the value of the test. Part II tests eight sets of dates and events by the system of placing three significant events into one of five time intervals, marked off by five other important events, trends or periods. In this way 24 date elements are measured not by specific dates, which are so apt to be forgotten later, but by their relation to other events and

periods in the course of civilized history. All items in Parts I and II are well spaced throughout history, are well chosen for their importance, and place reasonable emphasis upon the social and cultural development of man rather than upon political events alone. The arrangement of Parts I and II should tell the instructor not only how much a student knows of the items tested but also indicates where the learning or teaching has been weak; they test whether or not the student knows by whom and when history was made, and whether or not he is acquainted with historical terminology. This is a very important point for prospective users of this test to keep in mind.

Part III, Historical Judgment, is tested by 47 5-choice questions. These items are more semifactual on matters of cause and result than on pure judgment, but they are none the less valuable by increasing the scope of measurement and the validity and the reliability of the test.

In criticism it may be said that the test is a little light on the more recent period of history, and makes no effort to test the place of United States history in the development of world history—which may or may not be a disadvantage depending upon how the students to be tested have been taught.

The test is a 90-minute test of 185 questions, which is a sufficient sampling to measure one field. The test is arranged so that the raw scores may be corrected for chance or guess answers, and a table for conversion to "scaled scores" is provided whereby relative marks on this test may be compared with relative scores in other subjects when measured by other tests in this series. The high diagnostic value of the test within the subject tested is thereby augmented by a diagnostic tool as between subjects.

The validity and reliability of the test has been worked out with a sufficient number of cases to make it worth while. Excellent tables of norms by both grades and geographic areas are provided. Thus a student's score can be compared with those of his fellow students, and the class as a whole can be matched against the achievement of other classes.

All told this is a good test, and compares very well with other Cooperative tests which the reviewer has used with good success (the reviewer has not used this test).

For a review by R. M. Tryon, see 1017.

[1637]
Ely-King Interpretation Tests in American History. Grades 7-8; 1929; 2 forms; $1.50 per 25; 15¢ per specimen set; nontimed; Lena A. Ely and Edith King; Los Angeles, Calif.; California Test Bureau.

Clinton C. Conrad, Lecturer in Education and Associate Director of Practice Teaching, The University of California; and Vice-Principal of the University High School, Oakland, California. This test is prepared in two forms. It is designed "to test pupils' ability to interpret meanings and evaluate historical situations." Its content includes "civic attitudes, appreciations, interpretations, and a minimum of merely factual response"; it is "not related to any given text, but contains materials suited to standard eighth grade courses in American History." These quotations are taken from the leaflet describing the tests.

Norms for the test in its two forms were obtained by giving over one thousand tests in different schools to 500 pupils at the end of the eighth grade. No evidence of the reliability of the test is adduced. No time limit is set for the test, save in the instruction, "Sufficient time should be allowed for most of the pupils to finish all of the exercises."

Each form of the test provides 75 opportunities for response to multiple-choice (including true-false), matching, and completion questions. In about half the exercises simple causal and temporal relationships are to be defined by the pupil. "Civic attitude" presumably is displayed in the pupil's choice of reasons for voting against a candidate for school office whose qualifications are set forth in a rather naive problem question.

To the reviewer's mind, this test places a premium upon the pupil's recall of a list of standardized facts and equally standardized relationships. Some of the latter seem unduly simplified; thus the sinking of the Lusitania is given as the cause of America's (sic) entering the World War. The political aspects of history are heavily weighted in nine of the eleven sections of the test.

The test may have limited usefulness in "standard eighth-grade courses in American History" to ascertain whether pupils have achieved standard results.

Edgar B. Wesley, Professor of Education, The University of Minnesota. This test was copyrighted in 1929. If one were to judge by its shortcomings, one would estimate its date as even earlier. The parts are not numbered; eight items constitute a true-false section; matching exercises involve only two possible answers; the cloudy device of cause-effect is tried; the true-false technique is applied to guessing as to which of two events occurred first; the word "always" appears in a true-false item; and a student problem situation is presented to call forth the proper attitudes. Altogether the prospective test user has a right to be discouraged; he may even be justified in resenting the continuation of tests which perpetuate the faults that could have been eliminated even ten years ago. Unless this test is revised it should be dropped from further consideration.

[1638]
Information Tests in American History. Grades 7-12 and teachers colleges; [1932]; 2 forms; 75¢ per 25; 20¢ per specimen set; nontimed (35) minutes; A. S. Barr and C. J. Daggett; Minneapolis, Minn.: Educational Test Bureau, Inc.

Roy A. Price, Dual Professor of Social Science and Education, Syracuse University. This test is available in two forms. Each form is composed of six subtests: 1, historical terms in contexts; 2, importance of events; 3, men-event relationship; 4, chronological facts; 5, causal relations; and 6, present-day problem relationships.

Although labeled *Information Tests in American History*, it is intended to measure not only information but also certain skills. For example, success in Test 1, Historical Terms in Contexts, depends more upon the ability to read and interpret verbal symbols than upon accumulated information about American history or the particular meaning of certain terms used.

No evidence of the validity or reliability of these tests is presented which is a serious hardship to those who would interpret the test scores. The percentile scores for junior high school, senior high school, and college levels are low. The relatively low achievement on the tests may be due to lack of objectivity in scoring. For example, in one item the student is expected to judge the "event which has been of the greatest importance in the political history of the United States," as among: the annexation of Texas, the Webster-Hayne debate, the Constitutional Convention, the Alien and Sedition Acts, and the first presidential election. The scoring key indicates that the annexation of Texas is the correct answer. It is understandable that some may have chosen the Constitutional Convention. In regard to Part I of the test, the same criticism holds true, i.e., that a board of experts would almost certainly disagree with several answers which are indicated as correct.

A number of the test items are based on insignificant events, and the wording of other items is confusing. The number of items included (55 on each form) is not sufficient to provide an adequate sampling of a student's knowledge of the field, and study of the items which are included leads one to question their validity in terms of measuring knowledge of significant phases of American development. However, the authors do point out that in addition to the use of a study on objectives of American history teaching by Miller, the "curricular validity is based on an analysis of over ten thousand examination questions in American History, gathered from all parts of the United States."

[1639]

Kansas American History Test. First, second semesters: high school and college; 2 forms, 2 levels; 50¢ per 25; 15¢ per specimen set; 40(45) minutes; Arthur Hartung, H. E. Schrammel, and C. Stewart; Emporia, Kan.: Bureau of Educational Measurements, Kansas State Teachers College.
a) TEST I. First semester.
b) TEST II. Second semester.

Wilbur F. Murra, Executive Secretary, National Council for the Social Studies, Washington, D. C. This is a test of slightly better than mediocre quality intended for measuring general achievement in the conventional senior high school American history course. It is published in two parts: Test I, covering the years before 1830, may be used at the end of the first semester; Test II covers the full range of American history with emphasis on the last century. Each test is available in alternate forms of supposedly equal difficulty. This latter feature commends itself as a distinctive advantage which does not pertain to many other tests in this field.

Each form of each test consists of 150 objective items, 75 true-false, 25 reverse multiple-choice, 35 matching, and 15 chronological order. The high proportion of true-false items is a serious shortcoming, this form being notoriously ill-adapted to testing understanding in any of the social studies. The complete absence of the best-answer form is equally to be deplored, as this form is certainly the most

generally useful of all test forms in the social studies and has several distinctive advantages. The reverse multiple-choice form (in which the testee selects the one of four choices which is wrong), on the other hand, has peculiar advantages and it is well utilized in the Kansas tests, whereas few other history tests have as yet made use of it. The chronology items are also good, avoiding as they do the pitfalls which so commonly beset items of this kind. The first matching exercise is very poor: it is too long (20 choices to be made from among 31 alternatives), and it lacks homogeneity of both content and grammatical form.

Perhaps the most critical weakness of the test as a whole is the generally poor phrasing of the individual items. Frequently found, especially in the true-false items, are: phrases with ambiguous or elastic meaning, pat phrases and rhetorical expressions, grammatical inconsistency, needless negative statements. To be sure, a majority of the items are free from these technical objections, freer than three-fourths of all teacher-made tests, but not so free as a test published in 1938 should be. Certainly, the defects that appear reduce the reliability of the tests—to what extent it is impossible to say. The test manual states that "preliminary studies . . . yielded reliability coefficients between .75 and .90." If the true reliability of the test is near the lower end of this range, it is *too low* for a test which is 150 items in length.

As compared with such admirable instruments as the American history tests published by the Cooperative Test Service and those published for use in or by the Iowa Every-Pupil High School Testing Programs, the Kansas test will reward pupils more for their memorized verbalisms, less for their reasoned understanding. As compared with published tests in this field other than those mentioned, however, the Kansas test is clearly well above the average in this regard. The sequence of items within each section is in accordance with chronological order of content rather than the preferable order of increasing difficulty of items. The format is annoyingly, but not critically, crowded. For many teachers, this defect may be compensated for in the resulting economy.

Percentile norms are provided for each part of the test. Based on 10,451 pupil scores from 364 schools, these norms should aid materially in the interpretation of results.

[1640]

Kansas Modern European History: Test II. High School; 1938; 1 form; 50¢ per 25; 15¢ per specimen set; 40(45) minutes; Alvin L. Hasenbank and H. E. Schrammel; Emporia, Kan.: Bureau of Educational Measurements, Kansas State Teachers College.

Clinton C. Conrad, Lecturer in Education and Associate Director of Practice Teaching, The University of California; and Vice-Principal of the University High School, Oakland, California. This test is designed to measure "the student's understanding of significant movements and events in relation to their social and economic consequences." It is intended for use in high schools and colleges which offer a one-year course in this subject. Form A, the only form now available, covers the period from the French Revolution to the present time. The items in the test were selected "from the basic content of several leading textbooks," and were validated by history teachers and supervisors and specialists in test construction. Percentile norms have been computed from 694 student scores. No evidence is given on the test's reliability.

The test is composed of three parts, made up respectively of 100 true-false, 30 multiple-choice, and 15 matching items. The inclusion of so many true-false questions is of course open to criticism. Some of the items are poorly worded (e.g., "Subjecting of races has been one of the chief troubles of the Balkan regions"); and in several (e.g., "Great Britain has always permitted workers to organize unions and to call strikes"), specific determiners aid the student in his choice of responses. The choice of items seems haphazard, rather than derived from the thoughtful study of the purposes and content of a well-planned course.

The validity of the test is open to serious question, for examination of the items shows a heavy stress upon the student's ability to respond correctly to items which measure only his knowledge of factual information, such as: (*a*) "Russia is the largest contiguous territory in the world under one flag"; (*b*) "Russia was defeated in the Crimean War"; (*c*) "Norway and Sweden separated peacefully in 1905"; and (*d*) "The Treaty of Versailles was drawn up in the year: (1) 1917 (2) 1919 (3) 1925 (4) 1922." Whatever the authors' avowed purpose, this is evidently a test of historical information which can hardly provide valid evidence of the student's "understanding of sig-

nificant movements and events in relation to their social and economic consequences."

[1641]

Taylor-Schrammel World History Test. First, second semesters: high school; 1936; 2 forms, 2 levels; 50¢ per 25; 15¢ per specimen set; 40(45) minutes; Wallace Taylor and H. E. Schrammel; Emporia, Kan.: Bureau of Educational Measurements, Kansas State Teachers College.
a) TEST I. First semester.
b) TEST II. Second semester.

J. R. Gerberich, Director of the Bureau of Educational Research and Statistical Service and Associate Professor of Education, University of Connecticut. This test, intended for use as a measure of achievement in one-year World History courses, provides Test I for the period from prehistoric man to the uprisings of 1820 and Test II for the period from 1820 to the present. These two tests, according to the authors, essentially cover the content of the first and second semesters of a typical course in the subject.

Users of this test are largely left to draw their own conclusions concerning test validity and reliability, the sole statement concerning these important criteria, contained in the one-sheet, mimeographed Manual of Directions, being that, "The test items were selected from the basic content of several leading textbooks in the field. All items were carefully checked by history teachers and supervisors and by test construction specialists."

The test format is not good, for the type is small and the print is crowded. The directions are consistently in error in using "parenthesis" where "parentheses" should be used. Punctuation is sufficiently in error in occasional items to change the literal meaning from what appears to be the intended meaning. The sample for Part II of all tests gives a three-response multiple-choice item in which one of the three alternatives is ruled out by the application of grammatical principles, for "education" does not correctly follow the indefinite article "a."

Pupils are allowed to draw their own conclusions concerning whether or not to guess on true-false sections, yet those parts are scored without correction for chance. Alternatives in multiple-choice sections vary in number from three to five for different items in at least one of the tests. The matching test sets are unbalanced and use items of such mixed categories that intelligence can well be applied to them in such manner that a tremendously better-than-chance result would be obtained without knowledge concerning content, and in some cases start at the bottom of one column and finish at the top of the other column on the page.

Percentile norms are based on 10,261 pupils from 412 schools which cooperated in four nation-wide programs, presumably those administered by the Bureau of Educational Measurements, Kansas State Teachers College of Emporia.

Despite the weaknesses of these tests, some of which are pointed out above, the test items themselves appear to be superior to the general impression obtained from an examination of the tests. In the main, the items do, as the authors point out, place emphasis upon the "cultural and social phases of history." Vocabulary, concepts, dates, persons, events, and movements of historical significance are covered. There seems to be a considerable over-weighting of items from contemporary history in Test II, and occasional items are no longer pertinent.

All tests are timed for 40 minutes, yet Test II consists of 136 items as compared with 77 items for Test I. Part IV of Test II consists of items of a type not found in Test I and probably requiring more time expenditure on the part of the pupil than most of the other item types in either test. It would seem that Test II should have a time allowance from 50 to 75 per cent greater than that for Test I.

It is unfortunate that the authors have not exerted more care in the mechanical and technical setup of the test, that they have not provided adequate evidence concerning its validity and reliability, and that they have not provided more comprehensive and meaningful norms, for the test items themselves appear to be so constructed that they could be made the foundation for a much more satisfactory test of achievement in world history than the authors have published.

[1642]

Test of Factual Relations in American History. Grades 10-12; 1936; 2 forms; 25¢ per specimen set; nontimed (100) minutes; Eugene S. Farley; Minneapolis, Minn.: Educational Test Bureau, Inc.
a) PERIOD I, 1000 TO 1763. 45¢ per 25; (15) minutes.
b) PERIOD II, 1763 TO 1783. 45¢ per 25; (10) minutes.
c) PERIOD III, 1783 TO 1840. 65¢ per 25; (25) minutes.
d) PERIOD IV, 1840 TO 1865. 45¢ per 25; (15) minutes.
e) PERIOD V, 1865 TO 1898. 45¢ per 25; (15) minutes.
f) PERIOD VI, 1898 TO 1930. 45¢ per 25; (20) minutes.

REFERENCES

1 FARLEY, EUGENE S. *A Test of Factual Relations in American History.* Unpublished doctor's thesis, University of Pennsylvania, 1934.

Robert E. Keohane, Instructor in Social Studies, The College, The University of Chicago. This test attempts "to measure relationships rather than isolated facts" for sixty topics in United States history to 1930. The topics used were selected by the so-called "objective" method of studying 7,000 examination questions used by teachers of United States history. Consequently, while the test may fairly represent the content of the more traditional courses, it is not well adapted to the needs of schools in which social and cultural history are strongly emphasized.

The pupil is expected to recognize the following items for each abstract topic: (a) a cause or purpose, (b) a fact or detail, (c) an effect or result, and (d) a related event. Historical personages are to be linked with (a) principles or significant facts, (b) position or occupation, (c) outstanding achievement, and (d) a related event. The topics are listed in groups of three. Five or six choices are offered in each of the four given categories. The pupil marks the number of the topic under the letter in front of the one correct answer in each category. In the reviewer's opinion, provision of a separate answer sheet for each pupil would combine economy with ease in scoring.

In a test such as this, oversimplification is perhaps to some extent unavoidable. The extremely complex character of historical causation is obscured, and the selection of *one* preceding condition as a cause is easily converted, in the pupil's mind, to its pre-eminence and *the* one true cause.

Failure to define rigidly "causes," "facts," and "related events," or at least to apply such definitions, results in a lack of consistency among the items placed in each category. Some of the topics are too general and others are poorly stated. A good verbal memory rather than real understanding is promoted by the use of slogans and conventional labels. There are several errors in spelling which careful proofreading would have corrected. In a very few cases two or more answers are equally correct, though usually the test secures rather fine discrimination between the one correct answer and the others which are good distractors. Some material of no real significance for understanding is included, and certain inaccuracies of fact and interpretation would call forth the criticism of subject specialists.

In spite of these serious drawbacks, this test may be useful in conventional courses in United States history, preferably in the senior high school (though the T-scores given are for twelve-year-old children). Often the correct answering of a question requires fine discrimination and a rather detailed fund of information, so much so, in fact, that the test often appears to test more for the latter than for the wider relationships involved. Use of this test will doubtless stimulate teachers to revise their own means of measuring such factual relationships as seem most important to them and may encourage the author to revise his work to meet legitimate criticisms.

For a review by Wilbur F. Murra, see 1024.

VOCATIONS

Reviews by Harold D. Carter, A. B. Crawford, W. D. Commins, John G. Darley, Stanley G. Dulsky, Jack W. Dunlap, Edward S. Jones, Forrest A. Kingsbury, G. Frederic Kuder, Herbert A. Landry, Irving Lorge, J. B. Miner, N. W. Morton, C. A. Oakley, Donald G. Paterson, John Gray Peatman, M. W. Richardson, Alec Rodger, Ruth Strang, Lorene Teegarden, Albert S. Thompson, M. R. Trabue, Arthur E. Traxler, Morris S. Viteles, E. G. Williamson, and C. Gilbert Wrenn.

[1643]

ABC Occupational Inventory. Grades 9 and over; 1935; 1 form; $1.44 per 30; 10¢ per specimen set; nontimed; N. A. Lufburrow; Baltimore, Md.: the Author, 3112 Milford Ave.

[1644]

Adjusted Graphic Analysis Chart. Applicants for professional and sub-professional positions; 2¢ per chart; 10¢ per specimen set; R. E. Dunford; Knoxville, Tenn.: the Author, University of Tennessee.

REFERENCES

1 DUNFORD, R. E. "The Adjusted Graphic Analysis Chart." *J Appl Psychol* 23:623-9 O '39.

[1645]

Aids to Self-Analysis and Vocational Planning Inventory. Grades 9-12; 1940; 8¢ per test; H. D. Richardson; Chicago, Ill.: Science Research Associates.

REFERENCES

1 RICHARDSON, H. D. *Analytical Devices in Guidance and Counseling.* Basic Occupational Plans, No. 3. Chicago, Ill.: Science Research Associates, 1940. Pp. 63. $1.00. Paper, lithotyped.

[1646]

Aptitude Index for Life Insurance Salesmen. Prospective life insurance agents; 1938; distribution restricted to life insurance companies which are members of the Life Insurance Sales Bureau; Hartford, Conn.: Life Insurance Sales Research Bureau.

REFERENCES

1 Life Insurance Sales Research Bureau. *Rating Prospective Agents.* Hartford, Conn.: the Bureau, 1937. Pp. 16. Privately distributed. Paper.
2 Life Insurance Sales Research Bureau. *Selection of Agents:* A Method of Relating Personal History Information to Probable Success in Life Insurance Selling. Hartford, Conn.: the Bureau, 1937. Pp. 24. Privately distributed. Paper.
3 Life Insurance Sales Research Bureau. *Measuring Aptitude for Life Insurance Selling.* Hartford, Conn.: the Bureau, 1938. Pp. 22. Privately distributed. Paper.
4 Life Insurance Sales Research Bureau. *The Prospective Agents Rating Plan in Use:* Report of Session on Selection of Agents, at Research Bureau Conference, Hartford, Connecticut, March 22, 1938. New Haven, Conn.: the Bureau, 1938. Pp. 44. Privately distributed. Paper.
5 KURTZ, ALBERT K. "Evaluating Selection Tests." *Managers Mag* 14:12-6 My-Je '39.

[1647]

Basic Interest Questionnaire: For Selecting Your Vocation or Avocation. Grades 9-16 and adults; 1938-39; 1 form; $2.50 per 25; key, $5; nontimed (75) minutes; Keith Van Allyn; Los Angeles, Calif.: National Institute of Vocational Research.

[1648]

Career Incentive and Progress Blank. For recording data concerning counselees in grades 9-16 and placement offices; 1939; $1.68 per 30; 10¢ per specimen set; N. A. Lufburrow; Baltimore, Md.: the Author, 3112 Milford Ave.

[1649]

Check List for Self-Guidance in Choosing an Occupation. Grades 9-16 and adults; 1940; $1.25 per 25; 15¢ per specimen set; Robert Hoppock; New York: Psychological Corporation.

[1650]

Check List of Occupations. High school and college; 1940; $1 per 25; 15¢ per specimen set; nontimed; Margaret E. Hoppock; New York: Psychological Corporation.

[1651]

Composite Inventory and Examination, Revised. Prospective salesman; 1940; 2 editions; $1 per specimen set; Verne Steward; Los Angeles, Calif.: Verne Steward & Associates, 5471 Chesley Ave.
a) FORM A. A 12-page booklet containing the following sections: (1) Mental Ability, (2) Personality Traits, (3) General Knowledge, (4) Vocational Interests, (5) Personality Trait Illustrations, (6) Personal History, and (7) Rating Form; $3 per 10; $7 per 25; (90-100) minutes.
b) FORM B. An 8-page booklet containing Sections 1, 5, 6, and 7 of Form A; $2.40 per 10; $5.50 per 25; (45-60) minutes.

REFERENCES

1 STEWARD, VERNE. *The Use and Value of Special Tests in the Selection of Life Underwriters.* Los Angeles, Calif.: Verne Steward and Associates, 5471 Chesley Ave., 1934. Pp. 93. $2.50.
2 STEWARD, VERNE. *Selection of Sales Personnel.* Los Angeles, Calif.: Verne Steward and Associates, 5471 Chesley Ave., 1936. Pp. 48. $2.75.

3 STEWARD, VERNE. "The Development of a Selection System for Salesmen." *Personnel* 16:124-36 F '40.

[1652-3]

[Cox Mechanical Aptitude and Manual Dexterity Tests.] Ages 11 and over; 1928-34; individual; according to the publisher, D. Draycon, Tests M1, D, and E constitute the battery usually employed in secondary and technical schools; J. W. Cox; Enfield, England: D. Draycon; London: National Institute of Industrial Psychology.

a) COX MECHANICAL MODELS TEST M1. Ages 14 and over. DRAYCON: £2 12s. per 10 wooden models; £6 13s. 4d. per 10 aluminum models; 6s. per 12 diagram booklets; 4s. per 50 answer sheets. N. I. I. P.: £6 13s. 4d. per set of metal models in box for transportation; 6d. per diagram booklet; 4s. per 50 answer sheets.

b) COX MECHANICAL MODELS TEST M2. DRAYCON: £3 5s. per 10 wooden models, more difficult than M1 (less 10s. if M1 and M2 are ordered together); 6s. per 12 diagram booklets; 4s. per 50 answer sheets.

c) COX MECHANICAL MODELS TEST M. Ages 11-14. DRAYCON: £2 per 5 wooden models constituting Part 1; £1 10s. per 5 wooden models constituting Part 2; 6s. per 12 diagram booklets for either part; 4s. per 50 answer sheets for either part; (20) minutes for Part 1.

d) COX MECHANICAL DIAGRAMS TEST D. DRAYCON: £2 2s. per 6 cardboard diagrams; £3 3s. per 6 linen diagrams; 6s. per 12 question booklets; 4s. per 50 answer sheets. N. I. I. P.: £3 3s. per 6 diagrams; 14s. per 50 question booklets.

e) COX MECHANICAL EXPLANATION TEST E. DRAYCON: 9s. 6d. per 12 test booklets; 4s. per 50 answer sheets.

f) COX EYEBOARD TEST. DRAYCON: 17s. 6d. N. I. I. P.: 17s. 6d.

g) COX NAILBOARD TEST. DRAYCON: 5s. 6d.

h) COX NAIL-STICK TEST. DRAYCON: 5s. 6d.

REFERENCES

1 Cox, J. W. *Mechanical Aptitude*: Its Existence, Nature and Measurement. London: Methuen & Co., Ltd., 1928. Pp. xiii, 209. 7s. 6d.
2 HARVEY, O. L. "Mechanical 'Aptitude' or Mechanical 'Ability'? A Study In Method." *J Ed Psychol* 22:517-22 O '31.
3 Cox, J. W. *Manual Skill*: Its Organizations and Development. London: Cambridge University Press, 1934. Pp. xx, 247. 16s. (New York: Macmillan Co. $5.00).
4 LAYCOCK, S. R., AND HUTCHEON, N. B. "A Preliminary Investigation into the Problem of Measuring Engineering Aptitude." *J Ed Psychol* 30:280-8 Ap '39.

C. A. Oakley, Scottish Area Officer of the British Air Ministry; in civil life, Scottish Divisional Director of the National Institute of Industrial Psychology, Glasgow, Scotland. In Scotland the best-known of the Cox tests is the Mechanical Models Test. Unfortunately until recently the test suffered from the unsatisfactory construction both of the wooden models and of the booklets. These matters have recently received the attention of the National Institute of Industrial Psychology.

The test (and other Cox mechanical tests, particularly the Diagrams Test) has the advantage of being a group test. Its disadvantage is that the instructions are complicated and difficult to follow. In practice this has led certain teachers to try to improve on the instructions—particularly by repeating difficult sections—without realising that they are invalidating the test.

Cox has standardised the tests with small groups but I have found his norms reasonably satisfactory. As few of the Scottish pupils to whom the tests have been given have done any other mechanical tests it is not possible to comment upon their validity.

Cox has, in my opinion, developed a useful technique but the tests themselves need revision to meet practical requirements in schools.

The Cox Eye-Board Test also has some defects in construction. It is inclined to warp and the eye-screws are easily broken or twisted out of position. For these reasons I have stopped using it, but again I should add that the general principles on which the test has been devised seem to me to be sound.

Alec Rodger, Head of the Vocational Guidance Department, National Institute of Industrial Psychology, London, England. Cox is a protagonist of Spearman's two-factor theory of ability. It is essential that this fact should be realized by those who make inquiries about his tests. He has aimed at producing measuring instruments for a "routine" manual dexterity which can be shown to be (*a*) relatively independent of such nonmanual abilities as general intelligence and mechanical aptitude and (*b*) useful for manual occupations.

No one is likely to dispute the fact that he has performed an important task with a most admirable degree of scientific ardour and detachment. In the reviewer's opinion, his work on manual dexterity and mechanical aptitude has been more searching than that of any other investigator or team of investigators. It would seem, however, that his research methods are probably of more importance than his research findings; the groups he used in his experiment were too small to warrant the formulation of anything more than broad conclusions.

Cox deals only briefly with a problem which arises in all testing work, but which is of almost paramount importance in manual dexterity testing; namely, the problem of incentives. He omits consideration of one aspect of this problem which seems to call for discussion. The reviewer has had a good deal of experience both in the use of Cox's eyeboard test and in the training of others in its use, and he is firmly of the opinion that the degree of "urgency" suggested by the tester's actions, voice inflections and so on, is nearly always very influential in the testing situation. A quiet, easygoing student who gives the test instructions in a deliberate way will tend to obtain a set of lower scores than a brisk, businesslike student (dealing with a comparable group) whose methods make the subjects feel "keyed up." Consequently, the reviewer holds the view that each tester should build up his own norms for this (and the other) Cox manual dexterity tests; the use of tables compiled by others is definitely unsatisfactory. Few testers are likely to be in a position to do this adequately.

For this reason—and, perhaps, for the additional reason that the variations shown by testers in their ability to time these tests play a substantial part in the determination of scores—the reviewer wonders whether other investigators, pursuing similar methods, using similar test material and testing similar subjects, might not reach rather different conclusions.

Briefly: the method by which Cox produced these tests was admirably scientific, but for the present it must be doubted whether their value can be taken as proven; in any case, they seem to be in some respects unsuitable for general or occasional use. It is to be hoped that research workers who are in a position to do so will include them in experimental "batteries" of tests.

[1654]

Detroit General Aptitudes Examination. Grades 6-12; 1938; 1 form; $2.00 per 25; 18¢ per *Ayres Handwriting Scale: Gettysburg Edition*; 25¢ per manual; 45¢ per specimen set; 60(85-90) minutes; Harry J. Baker, Paul H. Voelker, and Alex C. Crockett; Bloomington, Ill.: Public School Publishing Co.

G. Frederic Kuder, Examiner, Board of Examinations, The University of Chicago. The examination blank consists of sixteen tests—one to a page. Scores from different combinations of the various tests are added together to give scores for intelligence, mechanical aptitude, and clerical aptitude. The intelligence score is obtained from ten of the tests. The mechanical aptitude and clerical aptitude scores are each obtained from nine tests. More than half the tests in each battery are common with one of the other batteries. Four of the tests are included in all three batteries. Four others are common to two batteries. The intercorrelations of the three batteries are high, as might be

expected in view of the overlapping. These intercorrelations are .80, .78, and .73 for the intelligence-mechanical, intelligence-clerical, and mechanical-clerical pairs, respectively.

The high intercorrelations raise the question as to whether the overlapping is not so large as to make obtaining all three different scores superfluous. The best answer to this question would ordinarily be the size of the intercorrelations corrected for attenuation which would indicate the extent to which each pair of batteries measure the same thing. These coefficients, obtained by the usual formula, are .94, .93, and .82. However, the usual formula for attenuation is hardly applicable in this case since it rests on the assumption of uncorrelated errors—an assumption which is not met in the case of overlapping measures. If allowance is made for estimated identical errors, the correlation between true scores on the intelligence and mechanical batteries is about .87. The estimate of the extent to which the intelligence and clerical batteries measure the same thing is about .85, and for the mechanical and clerical batteries the correlation of true scores is .74. These figures were obtained on the assumption that for purposes of estimation, the standard deviations of the batteries are approximately equal and that the common error variance is about .07 of the total variance of each test. This latter estimate appears reasonable when it is considered that the total error variance is .200, .102, and .122 for the three tests, respectively, and that more than half of each test is common to each of the others.

From these figures it appears that the intelligence variance is so well accounted for by the other two scores that use of the test is superfluous if the others are used. Another consideration militating against use of the intelligence test is its reliability of .80 as compared with reliabilities of about .90 for most intelligence tests on the market. The effort of the authors to use relatively little verbal material in the intelligence test seems to have lowered the reliability usually obtained for tests of this type and to have driven the particular measure used close to the clerical and mechanical aptitude tests. It samples essentially the same things as the other two measures and does a poor job of it at that.

The case for the mechanical and clerical measures is much better. The two measures are unrelated enough to justify the use of both, and the reliabilities are satisfactory (.90 for mechanical aptitude, and .88 for clerical aptitude). It should be remembered that neither clerical nor mechanical ability has been demonstrated to be a unitary trait; the scores obtained are vectors in the respective fields which have been found to have some relation with other measures acknowledged to be of a mechanical or clerical nature.

Use of the page scores for individual diagnosis is urged in the directions for using the record form. This practice is hardly justified by the relatively low reliabilities of most of the single tests. The reliabilities range from .57 to .88 and have a median of .76. The reliabilities of the subsections (composed of two or more single tests) such as "motor," "visual imagery," "verbal," "educational," et cetera, are not given. However, judging from the reliabilities of the component tests, it is likely that some of these do have reliabilities high enough to justify use of their scores for individual measurement. The authors observe that the reliabilities of the single-page tests are very good considering the shortness of the tests. This statement is true, but it does not make the reliabilities high enough to justify use of the page scores in individual measurement.

The authors state that "among large groups of children representing a wide range of abilities, there tend to be rather high correlations between intelligence, mechanical, and clerical aptitudes. In individual cases there are many marked differences and this is particularly true within the individual pages or subparts of the entire test." It should be added that even when tests measure the same thing marked differences are inevitable if the tests are unreliable.

SUMMARY. The mechanical and clerical aptitude batteries are reliable measures which have been demonstrated to have some validity. They deserve consideration for measurement in their respective fields. Use of the intelligence test is hardly justified in view of the fact that there are much more reliable intelligence tests on the market. Even for purposes of predicting some criterion, use of the intelligence test can hardly be justified since its variance is almost entirely accounted for by the mechanical and clerical aptitude tests. It is unfortunate that the use of scores on individual tests is recommended for individual diagnosis in view of the inadequate reliabilities of most of the single tests.

Irving Lorge, Executive Officer of the Division of Psychology, Institute of Educational Research and Associate Professor of Education, Columbia University. The examination consists of sixteen subtests with time limits from 3 to 5 minutes each as follows: (1) handwriting; (2) general information; (3) arithmetic fundamentals; (4) motor speed (circles); (5) tool recognition; (6) disarranged pictures; (7) verbal opposites; (8) spelling errors; (9) size discrimination; (10) verbal analogies; (11) same-different for numbers, figures, etc.; (12) tool information; (13) classification; (14) belt and pulley; (15) disarranged sentences; (16) alphabetizing.

The scoring of the examination gives each subtest a maximum score ranging from 30 to 53 points. These scores are grouped into three subscores for intelligence, clerical aptitude, and mechanical aptitude. The intelligence score is the sum of Subtests 2, 3, 4, 6, 7, 8, 10, 13, 14, 15; the mechanical aptitude score is the sum of Subtests 1, 3, 4, 5, 6, 9, 12, 13, 14; and the clerical aptitude score is the sum of Subtests 1, 3, 4, 6, 8, 11, 13, 15, 16. It is regrettable so much overlap was allowed among these three group scores, five tests are common to intelligence and mechanical aptitude, six tests are common to intelligence and clerical aptitude, and five tests are common to clerical and mechanical aptitude. The commonality among scores is shown by reported correlations of .80, .70 and .73 between the group scores which if corrected for attenuation might indicate that the three group scores are probably measuring the same basic set of factors.

The intelligence group score was validated against the *Detroit Advanced Intelligence Test* (r = .90 for 188 twelfth grade pupils); estimated IQ's were correlated against 1916 Stanford Binet IQ's as criterion (r = .652 for 188 twelfth grade pupils) and the clerical group score was validated against *Detroit Advanced Intelligence Test* (r = .739 for 188 twelfth grade pupils). As far as the essential purpose of the examination is concerned, the authors have not demonstrated the validity of either the clerical or the mechanical aptitude scores. Basically, the authors demonstrate that the group scores are measures of intelligence.

Retest reliabilities for the group scores after six weeks are reported as .80 for intelligence, .90 for mechanical aptitude and .88 for clerical.

The subtest retest reliabilities range from .57 to .88 (259 eighth grade pupils).

Age norms are provided (based on 10,000 cases) for each of the group scores, and for each subtest score, as well as for another classification of subtest scores into verbal, educational, motor, mechanical information, visual imagery, etc., scores.

Since the authors have failed to demonstrate the differential validity of the clerical or mechanical aptitude scores, and, further, since they have failed to show the validity of other scores such as visual images, etc., the test must be used cautiously in guidance and in classification.

The test is not printed too well. Examination of several test copies shows differences in blackness, particularly in Subtests 4, 6, 9, 11, and 14. Subtest 5 is difficult for school children to take in its present format. Subtest 6 is badly drawn, and poorly reproduced. Subtest 9 is poor in format.

This test will not provide the ordinary guidance worker with those "aptitude facts essential to a direction of instruction-guidance of pupils in the first two years of high school" which are different from those measured by a good intelligence test.

John Gray Peatman, Assistant Professor of Psychology, The College of the City of New York. This aptitude examination has the useful feature of combining into one booklet of 16 pages, tests for three general areas of aptitude, viz., "intelligence, mechanical, and clerical." The superficial character of all of these areas is fairly clear, but it might have been more to the point to have named the first area "general scholastic aptitude," especially since the whole test is designed for school grades 6 to 12. Throughout the accompanying teacher's handbook, the authors employ the phrase "intelligence, mechanical, and clerical"—thus using the noun form for one aptitude area and the adjectival for the other two.

"Economy of testing has been achieved by using certain pages or tests in more than one type of aptitude. For example, if motor speed and skill are important in intelligence, in mechanical, and in clerical, two pages such as 4 and 13 accomplish this result for all three types of aptitudes. Other pages serve for two aptitudes while eight of the sixteen pages are used in only one of any of the three major aptitudes." This statement from the handbook further indicates something of the character of the authors' approach to the problem of standardizing the examination. Their selection and weighting of the various tests employed in each one of the three areas is evidently made chiefly on the basis of rational considerations. At least no satisfactory evidence of an empirical kind is cited to support the choices made. If it is argued that it is obvious that a symbol-checking test of paired items and a filing test (using word material) are especially relevant to clerical aptitudes but not to "intelligence and mechanical"; or that tests of general information, vocabulary and verbal analogies are obviously relevant to "intelligence" but not to "mechanical and clerical"; or that tests of tool and mechanical information and of form discrimination are especially relevant to "mechanical" but not to "intelligence and clerical," it should be clear that this is exactly the point. Argument and the appeal to reasonableness are indispensable to the empirical development of an aptitude test but they are not sufficient to warrant the public sale of such tests as presumably finished products. Of course this booklet of tests doesn't come first-born out of the blue; there is a precedent in the works of previous investigators for some of the choices of types of tests used. However it is not to the credit of the authors of the handbook that their booklet of 16 tests is made for sale to teachers *as if* it will measure all intended things in a functionally adequate manner. Presumably, all the teacher has to do is to follow the explicit directions for administration and scoring, consult the tables of norms at the end of the handbook and thereby be in a very good position to classify students or to execute the purposes of "individual counseling in cases of educational disability, in cases of uneven educational accomplishments, for educational guidance, and for possible causes of emotional or social maladjustment." It is to be hoped that the teacher or administrator who obtains this aptitude examination for any of these purposes is psychologically well-trained for the responsibility. This is probably but a pious hope, at least for the present. Sometime the day may dawn when the progenitors of this or that psychological test will not wish to put their premature offspring into the hands of our well-meaning but psychologically untrained school teachers.

More specifically, the handbook presents 13

tables of norms: letter ratings and mental age norms for each one of the 3 areas of aptitude, as well as mental age norms for each separate test and various test combinations. These norms are described as "based on 10,000 scores, chiefly the unselected groups of pupils at the eighth and ninth grade levels in Detroit." Whether this was a sample of 10,000 different pupils is not clearly stated nor do we learn anything further about the nature of the population used except that several hundred mentally subnormal children, some normal fifth- and sixth-grade pupils, and small groups in the senior high school were possibly used in the development of the norms. Separate norms for the sexes were not developed since, according to the authors, no appreciable differences could be detected between median values. Inasmuch as the examination is published for use considerably beyond the bounds of Detroit, and since all norms are evidently developed mainly in relation to the rankings of the individuals within the various age groups, and not at all with respect to really functional criteria, the nature of the sampling is obviously of fundamental importance.

Functional criteria in terms of later achievement in each one of the three areas of aptitude are nowhere in evidence. The possible validity of the scale is dealt with rather summarily. Later scholastic achievement records as relevant criteria for a validation analysis of the intelligence area (particularly as scholastic aptitude) are not even mentioned. The authors' case for the validation of the mechanical and clerical aptitude areas is just as inadequate and misleading. That something is being measured in a fairly reliable manner by these three aptitude groupings of the examination is suggested by retest reliability coefficients for a sample of 259 eighth grade pupils, evidently heterogeneous in age—the examination being repeated with them after an interval of six weeks. The coefficients range from .80 to .90. A good deal of attention has presumably been paid to item validation (using internal criteria). But this attention to important aspects of test construction and the possibly satisfactory reliability of the three test groupings obviously do not alter the fundamental fact that we have here a group of neatly arranged tests for which we discover practically no evidence that they are satisfactorily differentiating pupils' *aptitudes* for intellectual, mechanical, and clerical *achievement*. It is lamentable, to say the least, that an examination in this condition has been made generally available to school teachers and other test administrators. Nor is the fact that previous publishers of tests have sinned likewise a legitimate excuse.

[1655]
Detroit Clerical Aptitudes Examination. High school; 1937-38; 1 form; $4.50 per 100; 20¢ per specimen set; 30(40) minutes; Harry J. Baker and Paul H. Voelker; Bloomington, Ill.: Public School Publishing Co.

Irving Lorge, Executive Officer of the Division of Psychology, Institute of Educational Research and Associate Professor of Education, Columbia University. The test is offered as a means of measuring the special aptitudes required in commercial courses. It consists of eight subtests as follows: (1) rate and quantity of handwriting; (2) rate and accuracy in checking; (3) arithmetic fundamentals; (4) motor speed and accuracy; (5) commercial vocabulary; (6) disarranged pictures; (7) classification; and (8) alphabetizing. Seven of these subtests are common to the *Detroit General Aptitude Examination,* Form A as follows: $1 = 1$, $2 = 11$, $3 = 3$, $4 = 4$, $6 = 6$, $7 = 13$, and $8 = 16$ of the General Aptitudes Examination. Subtest 5 is not in the larger examination.

The scoring of the examination gives each subtest a maximum score ranging from 30 to 53 points. The examination should be easy to administer and to score.

The validity is given in terms of correlations of the examination with scholarship in commercial courses as .56 in bookkeeping, .37 in shorthand, and .32 for typewriting. The correlation between the examination and the *Detroit Advanced Intelligence Test* is reported as .44. The authors also report the inter-subtest correlations as well as the correlations of each subtest with the intelligence criterion as ranging from .26 to .53. The reviewer undertook a Hotelling component analysis of the intercorrelations which shows that about 41 per cent of the variance of the examinations scores may be attributed to a single factor which is common to intelligence tests. The factor loadings with the first factor for each subtest are: 1, .51; 2, .75; 3, .69; 4, .41; 5, .56; 6, .47; 7, .72; 8, .77; and the *Detroit Advanced Intelligence Test,* .77. A second factor accounts for about 11.5 per cent of the score variance. The factor loadings are: 1, .38; 2, .20; 3, −.14; 4, .45; 5,

−.41 ; 6, −.45 ; 7, .34 ; 8, .08 ; and *Detroit Advanced Intelligence Test,* −.39.

The second factor seems to be related to speed as opposed to information. There will be other factors in the test, but they will be unreliable. Basically, the test measures factors common to intelligence tests and to speed tests.

Retest reliability for a three weeks interval is reported as .85 which is satisfactory for group differentiation, but hardly high enough for individual prognosis or guidance.

Age norms are provided for the range 8-0 years to 21-11 years. The age norms are unusual in that almost uniformly through the range two points correspond to a month of chronological age.

The test is not printed well. Subtests 2, 4 and 6 particularly are badly reproduced. This test may contribute some basis for understanding and guiding pupils that will not be given by an intelligence test, but that contribution must wait upon a reweighting of the subtests. In its present form, it does not seem to be differentiating between a hypothetical clerical aptitude and general intellectual ability.

M. W. Richardson, United States Civil Service Commission, Washington, D. C. The eight subtests of which this examination is composed are (*a*) rate and quality of handwriting, (*b*) rate and accuracy in checking, (*c*) simple arithmetic, (*d*) motor speed and accuracy, (*e*) simple commercial terms, (*f*) visual imagery, (*g*) classification, and (*h*) alphabetical filing.

The total examination requires only thirty minutes; the separate subtests require two to five minutes each. Although perhaps eight different factors are not involved, nevertheless several different abilities basic to clerical proficiency are sampled. The test is designed to predict success in subsequent commercial courses in high school; it is not designed to select individuals for clerical positions.

The subtests seem to be well designed for their purpose. Moreover, the examination as a whole bears facial evidence of careful test construction.

Adequate norms are provided for each age group from 10 to 16 inclusive. The table of norms suggests that the correlation of the examination with chronological age is perhaps higher than its correlation with bookkeeping, shorthand, or typewriting. This circumstance adds a special difficulty to the interpretation of

the results. The user of the test may legitimately raise several questions on the matter of equivalence of scores as predicting success in clerical courses given in the table of letter ratings furnished by the authors. Not enough information is given by the authors on this point, and the obvious pitfalls in the interpretation of such tables are not sufficiently pointed out.

It is this reviewer's opinion that too many subtests are included for a thirty-minute test. The question is whether the amount of increase in validity gained by wide sampling of test materials is not lost by lowered reliability due to timing, bad starts, and other accidental factors. It is at least possible that two or three well-chosen subtests, lengthened to fill thirty minutes, would predict success in commercial courses quite as well. The examination is, perhaps necessarily, loaded with speed. No separate measures of speed and quality are provided, presumably because they are not necessary in the use of an empirical selection device.

The authors promise age norms for each part of the test, "so that special diagnosis of detailed abilities, as well as the general ability, may be made." It is questionable whether an interpretation of individual part-scores is worth while, since the reliability of each part-score is necessarily low, because of the short time limit.

[1656]

Detroit Mechanical Aptitudes Examination, Revised. Grades 7-16; 1928-39; 1 form; $3 per 100; 15¢ per specimen set; 31(40) minutes; Harry J. Baker, Paul H. Voelker, and Alex Crockett; Bloomington, Ill.: Public School Publishing Co.

REFERENCES

1 BAKER, HARRY J. "A Mechanical Aptitude Test." *Detroit Ed B* 12:5-6 Ja '29.

Irving Lorge, Executive Officer of the Division of Psychology, Institute of Educational Research and Associate Professor of Education, Columbia University. The examination is offered as a means of estimating mechanical aptitude. It consists of 8 subtests as follows: (1) tool recognition; (2) motor speed; (3) size discrimination; (4) arithmetic fundamentals; (5) disarranged pictures; (6) tool information; (7) belt and pulley; (8) classification. All of the subtests are common to the *Detroit General Aptitudes Examination* as follows: 1 = 5, 2 = 4, 3 = 9, 4 = 3, 5 = 6, 6 = 12, 7 = 14, and 8 = 13.

The scoring of the examination gives each subtest a maximum ranging from 31 to 53 points. The test should be fairly easy to administer and to score with possible exception of Subtest 7 (direction of pulleys). In this test, the pupil may be able to visualize whether the second wheel will be turning in the same or a different direction from the first, but may not be able to report correctly the direction of the second wheel if he changes orientation. For instance, if the arrow is considered to be applying to the movement at the bottom of the wheel, then the key would be wrong. The directions could be improved by telling the pupil that the directions refer to movement of the upper halves of the wheels.

The validity of the test is reported in terms of correlation with the *Detroit Advanced Intelligence Test* as .65. The items were presumably validated against the trial score as criterion.

The retest reliability is reported as .90 for an interval of six weeks, with the subtest reliabilities ranging from .57 to .88.

The age norms are given for the total score, for subtest scores, and for subtest groups for motor, visual, imagery and mechanical information.

The format of Subtest 1 could be improved. The reproduction of Subtest 3 and Subtest 5 is generally a poor printing job.

The authors have made a test of an undefined kind of aptitude called "mechanical aptitudes." By failing to show what the criterion is, the test consumer is at a loss in deciding whether he needs or can use the examination. It is hoped that sooner or later the authors will demonstrate what the test measures that is different from general intelligence.

Ed Res B 19:59 Ja 17 '40. J. Wayne Wrightstone. * The title of this test seems a misnomer because no evidence is provided to show that the examination does measure any vital or important mechanical aptitudes. As a sort of information test on tools and picture puzzles it may be interesting and informative, but as a basis for serious guidance in providing reliable indexes of mechanical aptitudes, the adequacy of this test must be questioned until the authors provide more convincing evidence that it measures mechanical aptitudes validly and reliably.

[1657]

Diagnostic Interviewer's Guide. For the selection of employees; 1937; 1 form; $1.50 per 50; 75¢ per specimen set; E. F. Wonderlic and S. N. Stevens; Chicago, Ill.: E. F. Wonderlic, 919 N. Michigan Ave.

REFERENCES

1 LAIRD, DONALD A. *The Psychology of Selecting Employees,* Third edition, pp. 114-8. New York: McGraw-Hill Book Co., Inc., 1937. Pp. xiv, 316. $4.00. (London: McGraw-Hill Publishing Co., Ltd. 24s.)
2 HOVLAND, CARL IVER, AND WONDERLIC, E. F. "Prediction of Industrial Success from a Standardized Interview." *J Appl Psychol* 23:537-46 O '39.

[1658]

Entrance Questionnaire and Experience Record. High school entrants; 1940; 8¢ per copy; H. D. Richardson; Chicago, Ill.: Science Research Associates.

REFERENCES

1 RICHARDSON, H. D. *Analytical Devices in Guidance and Counseling.* Basic Occupational Plans, No. 3. Chicago, Ill.: Science Research Associates, 1940. Pp. 63. $1.00. Paper, lithotyped.

[1659]

Finger Dexterity Test: Worksample No. 16. Ages 14 and over; 1926; 1 form; individual; worklimit (10-20) minutes; Johnson O'Connor; rents for $60 for the first year and $30 a year thereafter; the *Finger Dexterity Test* and the *Tweezer Dexterity Test* together rent for $90 the first year and $45 a year thereafter; Boston, Mass.: Human Engineering Laboratory. ($25 (No. 42069); Chicago, Ill.: C. H. Stoelting Co.) ($11; Minneapolis, Minn.: Mechanical Engineering Department, University of Minnesota.)

REFERENCES

1 HINES, MILDRED, AND O'CONNOR, JOHNSON. "A Measure of Finger Dexterity." *Personnel J* 4:379-82 Ja-F '26.
2 O'CONNOR, JOHNSON. *Born That Way,* pp. 21-3, 54-6, 141-2, 173-4 178-9, 181-2, 185-8, 191-9, 201-4, 213-5. Baltimore, Md.: Williams & Wilkins Co., 1928. Pp. 323. $2.00.
3 HAYES, ELINOR G. "Selecting Women for Shop Work." *Personnel J* 11:69-85 Ag '32.
4 BERGEN, GARRET L. *Use of Tests in the Adjustment Service,* p. 45. Adjustment Service Series Report [No.] 4. New York: American Association for Adult Education, 1935. Pp. 70. Paper. Out of print.
5 DVORAK, BEATRICE JEANNE. *Differential Occupational Ability Patterns.* Publications of the Employment Stabilization Research Institute, University of Minnesota, Vol. 3, No. 8. Minneapolis, Minn.: University of Minnesota Press, February 1935. Pp. 46. $1.00. Paper.
6 GREEN, HELEN J., AND BERMAN, ISABEL R.; under the direction of Donald G. Paterson and M. R. Trabue. *A Manual of Selected Occupational Tests for Use in Public Employment Offices,* pp. 5-7, 9-10, 23-31. University of Minnesota, Bulletins of the Employment Stabilization Research Institute, Vol. 2, No. 3. Minneapolis, Minn.: University of Minnesota Press, July 1936. Pp. 31. $0.50. Paper.
7 PATERSON, DONALD G., AND DARLEY, JOHN G., with the assistance of Richard M. Elliott. *Men, Women, and Jobs.* Minneapolis, Minn.: University of Minnesota Press, 1936. Pp. v, 145. $2.00. (London: Oxford University Press. 9s.)
8 BINGHAM, WALTER VAN DYKE. *Aptitudes and Aptitude Testing,* pp. 281-284. New York and London: Harper & Brothers, 1937. Pp. ix, 390. $3.00; 10s. 6d.
9 BROWN, FRED. "Selective Tests for Dental School Candidates." *Oral Hyg* 27:1172-7 S '37.
10 CANDEE, BEATRICE, AND BLUM, MILTON. "Report of a Study Done in a Watch Factory." *J Appl Psychol* 21:572-82 O '37.
11 DOUGLASS, HARL R. "Means of Predicting Scholastic Success in the College of Dentistry at the University of Minnesota," pp. 204-9. In *The Role of Research in Educational Progress:* Official Report, American Educational Research Association, A Department of the National Education Association, New Orleans, Louisiana, February 20-24, 1937. Washington, D. C.: the Association, May 1937. Pp. 255. $1.50. Paper.
12 O'CONNOR, JOHNSON. *Administration and Norms for the Finger Dexterity Test, Worksample 16, and the Tweezer Dexterity Test, Worksample 18.* Human Engineering Laboratory, Technical Report, No. 16. Boston, Mass.: the Laboratory, 1938. Pp. x, 136. $1.00. Paper, mimeographed.
13 PATERSON, DONALD G.; SCHNEIDLER, GWENDOLEN G.; AND WILLIAMSON, EDMUND G. *Student Guidance Techniques,* pp. 235-7. New York: McGraw-Hill Book Co., Inc., 1938. Pp. xviii, 316. $3.00. (London: McGraw-Hill Publishing Co., Ltd. 18s.)
14 TIFFIN, JOSEPH, AND GREENLY, R. J. "Employee Selection Tests for Electrical Fixture Assemblers and Radio Assemblers." *J Appl Psychol* 23:240-63 Ap '39.
15 BLUM, MILTON L. "A Contribution to Manual Aptitude Measurement in Industry: The Value of Certain Dexterity Measures for the Selection of Workers in a Watch Factory." *J Appl Psychol* 24:381-416 Ag '40.

Morris S. Viteles, Associate Professor of Psychology, and Albert S. Thompson, Instructor of Psychology, The University of Pennsylvania. The *Finger Dexterity Test*, one of the so-called worksamples developed by O'Connor, is so well known that it need not be described here. Since about 1925 it has had a prominent place in programs of industrial selection and vocational guidance.

Despite its wide use, relatively little was known about the reliability and validity of the test until recent years. Early references to the test by O'Connor [2] were divided between vague generalizations and categorical statements. Claims were made as to its value in forecasting industrial success in various occupations without adequate supporting data.

During recent years considerable data in the way of norms and of information on reliability and validity have been made available. These suggest that the test can be of service as an instrument in forecasting achievement in certain occupations. Bingham [8] reports differential norms for six manual occupations. The University of Minnesota Employment Stabilization Research Institute [5, 6, 7] has provided norms for an adult population and has used the test in developing occupational ability patterns. Independent studies [3, 10, 14] have shown the *Finger Dexterity Test* to be useful in the selecting of competent women shopworkers, watchmakers, and workers for various assembly jobs.

Although evidence is available to show that the test can be useful, the practitioner is handicapped by the absence of a satisfactory manual which brings into usable form the data which has accumulated over the past 10 years. Technical Report No. 16,[12] published in 1938 by the Human Engineering Laboratory of Stevens Institute of Technology, might have been expected to satisfy this need. Instead, in accordance with O'Connor's usual practice, this report is characterized by a complete disregard of the really significant work done outside the Laboratory. Its 138 mimeographed pages present a mass of improvement curves, age factors, and norms based on small age-group populations. No data on reliability are given and a few generalizations on validity are provided in a short paragraph, referring back to O'Connor's 1928 *Born That Way* and to a study of graduate nurses for further information. The chief value of the report is perhaps

in the presentation of tentative age norms— although the narrow range of differences between the ages of 14 and 19 make them of somewhat doubtful value in everyday practice.

Despite all these limitations, the test should receive the attention of the practicing psychologist. The Minnesota norms were carefully obtained; Bingham presents a few occupational norms; independent studies have shown that the test has an acceptable degree of validity for certain jobs involving rapid manipulation of small objects, etc. If information were assembled in convenient and standard form by a competent psychologist and critically presented, the usefulness of the *Finger Dexterity Test* as an experimental and practical instrument could be considerably increased.

[1659.1]

Guidance Questionnaire. High school; 1937; 1 form; 50¢ per 25; $1.25 per 100; 5¢ per specimen set; nontimed (25) minutes; Anthony J. Scholter; Milwaukee, Wis.: Department of Education, Archdiocese of Milwaukee.

[1660]

Individual Guidance Record. Grades 9-12; 1940; 8¢ per copy; H. D. Richardson; Chicago, Ill.: Science Research Associates.

REFERENCES

1 RICHARDSON, H. D. *Analytical Devices in Guidance and Counseling.* Basic Occupational Plans, No. 3. Chicago, Ill.: Science Research Associates, 1940. Pp. 63. $1.00. Paper, lithotyped.

[1661]

Kefauver-Hand Guidance Tests and Inventories. Grades 7-14; 1937; 8 parts; 50¢ per 25 student profile charts; 15¢ per manual; nontimed; Grayson N. Kefauver, Harold C. Hand, Virginia Lee Block, and William M. Proctor; Yonkers, N. Y.: World Book Co.
a) EDUCATIONAL GUIDANCE TEST. 1 form; $1.20 per 25 tests; 15¢ per specimen set; (30) minutes.
b) HEALTH GUIDANCE TEST. 1 form; $1 per 25 tests; 10¢ per specimen set; (25) minutes.
c) INVENTORY OF STUDENT PLANS. 1 form; $1.30 per 25 inventories; 5¢ per specimen set; (30) minutes.
d) INVENTORY OF STUDENT SELF-RATINGS. 1 form; $1.20 per 25 inventories; 5¢ per specimen set; (30) minutes.
e) RECREATIONAL GUIDANCE TEST. 1 form; $1 per 25 tests; 10¢ per specimen set; (25) minutes.
f) SOCIAL-CIVIC GUIDANCE TEST. 1 form; $1.20 per 25 tests; 15¢ per specimen set; (25) minutes.
g) STUDENT-JUDGMENT GUIDANCE TEST. 1 form; $1 per 25 tests; 10¢ per specimen set; (25) minutes.
h) VOCATIONAL GUIDANCE TEST. 1 form; $1 per 25 tests; 10¢ per specimen set; (25) minutes.

E. G. Williamson, Coordinator of Student Personnel Services and Associate Professor of Psychology, The University of Minnesota. This battery of six tests and two inventories may be used with students in grades 7 through 14. The Educational Guidance Test consists of selected questions concerning the purposes of secondary education and of specific courses;

the student's judgment of the relative difficulty of specific subjects; the student's knowledge of the specific courses offered in his own school. The latter two sections must be scored by means of a scoring key developed locally for each school; presumably the local teacher's judgment will determine the correct answers to questions about the relative difficulty of local courses, a characteristic of inventories and questionnaires rather than of standardized tests. The Health Guidance Test measures information of the importance of factors involved in physical and mental health. The Recreational Guidance Test includes questions on the importance and values of recreation and the facilities available in the local communities. The Social-Civic Guidance Test inventories the student's knowledge of general socio-economic conditions, the student's judgment of the importance of citizenship conditions in the local school and judgment of the number of "citizens" who "would have their well-being favorably affected (directly or indirectly) by each of the types of social action." The Vocational Guidance Test samples the student's knowledge of occupational trends, employment statistics and the duties of workers in a small number of occupations. The Student-Judgment Guidance Test contains questions on methods of character analysis and advertisements of proprietary training courses to be judged false or true. In each test, except the Educational Guidance Test, students are asked to indicate whom they should interview to secure assistance or information concerning a number of questions or problems.

The Inventory of Student Plans requires that the student name and give reasons for the selection of each school subject, the curriculum, extracurricular activities and his plans for future training beyond high school, his occupational choice and reasons for that choice, recreational and social-civic activities and plans for establishing a home. The Inventory of Student Self-Ratings requires that the student record his estimate of his capabilities in various subjects and activities and the extent to which he has learned to enjoy certain activities, his estimate of abilities to succeed in certain occupations and his physical disabilities.

Items and questions in both the tests and the inventories have been carefully selected by means of criticisms and judgments of guidance workers and by actual tryout in a number of survey-investigations. All items were selected in line with the definitive objectives of guidance activities. Questions in the six tests were subjected to item analysis to determine their differentiating values in terms of the total score. The test-retest (Form A vs. B) reliability coefficients for the six tests range from .77 to .89. The two forms have been equated. Although the manual states that a second form would be published in 1937, only one form is available at this time (fall, 1939).

The authors recommend that total raw scores be converted into percentages of the total possible scores. No norms are reported because the authors contend that local guidance workers might uncritically accept these norms as standards and because no one knows what score should be attained. As a matter of fact, all types of test norms could be misused in a similar manner. One wonders if the authors' investigations revealed such low standards of guidance activities as to make this danger of misuse of norms a special condition in this area of education.

These instruments make possible the collection of more or less objective data with which to identify the outcomes or effectiveness of the school's guidance activities. The authors advocate that the tests and inventories be given before and after the instituting of new types of guidance services. Such instruments are of self-evident importance in any serious attempt to evaluate objectively a guidance program and its many specific phases. It is to be hoped that these instruments will be used to determine whether widely used methods and techniques actually do produce the desirable effects claimed by many guidance workers. Specifically, experiments are needed to determine the outcomes of counseling, homerooms, extracurricular activities, and group guidance courses. Experiments are also needed to determine if these tests and inventories sample all of the important outcomes of guidance activities.

For reviews by Harold D. Carter, Gwendolen Schneidler, and M. R. Trabue, see 1170.

[1662]

Minnesota Rate of Manipulation Test. For selecting office and shop workers; 1933; a revision of the *Minnesota Manual Dexterity Test;* individual; $7.75 per testing outfit; worklimit (10-15) minutes; W. A. Ziegler; Minneapolis, Minn.: Educational Test Bureau, Inc. (*Minnesota Manual Dexterity Test*: $11;

Minneapolis, Minn.: Mechanical Engineering Department, University of Minnesota.)

REFERENCES

1 BERGEN, GARRET L. *Use of Tests in the Adjustment Service*, p. 47. Adjustment Service Series Report [No.] 4. New York: American Association for Adult Education, 1935. Pp. 70. Paper. Out of print.
2 GREEN, HELEN J., AND BERMAN, ISABEL R.; under the direction of Donald G. Paterson and M. R. Trabue. *A Manual of Selected Occupational Tests for Use in Public Employment Offices*, pp. 5-7, 10-11, 23-31. University of Minnesota, Bulletins of the Employment Stabilization Research Institute, Vol. 2, No. 3. Minneapolis, Minn.: University of Minnesota Press, July, 1936. Pp. 31. $0.50. Paper.
3 BINGHAM, WALTER VAN DYKE. *Aptitudes and Aptitude Testing*, pp. 278-81. New York and London: Harper & Brothers, 1937. Pp. ix, 390. $3.00; 10s. 6d.
4 PATERSON, DONALD G.; SCHNEIDLER, GWENDOLEN, G.; AND WILLIAMSON, EDMUND G. *Student Guidance Technique*, pp. 240-2. New York: McGraw-Hill Book Co., Inc., 1938. Pp. xviii, 316. $3.00. (London: McGraw-Hill Publishing Co., Ltd. 18s.)

Lorene Teegarden, Psychological Examiner, Public Schools, Cincinnati, Ohio. This test is intended to measure rapidity of movement in working with the hands and fingers. The long narrow board contains 60 holes in four rows of 15 each, into which fit 60 cylindrical blocks with one-sixteenth inch clearance. The test includes two parts, Placing and Turning, which are separate tests.

In Placing, the blocks are placed into the holes as rapidly as possible, following a definite procedure, and using one hand. The procedure is simple, and is readily learned in the first or practice trial. The score is a rating based upon the total time required for the second, third, fourth, and fifth trials. This is a measure of rapidity of movements involving the hand and arm, and not dependent upon co-ordination of the two hands working together, nor upon very delicate neuromuscular control.

Turning, the second test, measures rapidity and dexterity in manipulations requiring two-hand co-ordination. The board is presented with the blocks in place, and the subject picks up each block with one hand, turns the block over, and replaces with the other hand. With each change of rows the movement changes in direction, and the hands exchange functions. The first trial is used for practice, and the score is based upon time for the next four trials. Norms are given for adults, based upon the records of more than 5,000 employed workers. No appreciable sex difference is indicated. Time scores may be interpreted as a "percentile rank" (estimated from Z-scores) or as "per cent placement," (i.e., transmuted scores having a mean of 50 and a standard deviation of 10) in a ten quartile range.

Both parts of the test are useful for rating workers for routine manipulative operations.

Mean scores made by groups of packers, wrappers, and cartoners are reported to be distinctly above the median for the general population. For jobs requiring attention to numerous and varying details, it should be supplemented by some test, such as the *Minnesota Spatial Relations Test*, which involves reaction to observed details. For jobs requiring exact movements in the placing of small parts, it should be supplemented by some test of finger, tweezer, or plier dexterity. Few tests give so clear a picture of two-hand co-ordination as does the second part of the *Minnesota Rate of Manipulation Test*.

Morris S. Viteles, Associate Professor of Psychology, and Albert S. Thompson, Instructor in Psychology, The University of Pennsylvania. This test was devised by W. A. Ziegler to measure speed of rather gross movements of hand and fingers, of the kind frequently employed in occupational tasks calling for rapid manipulation of tools and materials. In its present form the *Minnesota Rate of Manipulation Test* is composed of a board containing 60 circular holes into which 60 slightly smaller circular blocks can be placed.

Two test situations are presented with the one board: (*a*) a "placing test," in which the blocks are transferred with one hand from a pre-positioned place on the table to their appropriate recesses in a set order; and (*b*) a "turning test," in which the blocks are lifted out of their holes, turned over by a two-handed operation, and replaced in the same holes. The "placing test," according to Ziegler, measures speed of hand manipulation; the "turning test" measures speed of finger manipulation, and a "speed index" is obtained by averaging the ratings on the two tests. Five trials of each test are given. The first trial is considered as a practice trial. The score is the sum of the times taken for the four test trials. About 20 minutes are required to administer the test.[2]

The test, in its present form, is a modification of the original *Minnesota Manual Dexterity Test* developed by Ziegler for the University of Minnesota Employment Stabilization Research Institute in order to determine "how much of the time required for the Minnesota Spatial Relations Test is consumed in the mere movement of the blocks." [2] In the original test 58 blocks and holes were provided. Only 4 trials were given and the score was the sum of all four trials. In addition to increasing the number of blocks to 60, Ziegler has made the instructions more specific, has increased the number of trials to 5, and has introduced an incentive by telling the subject the time for each trial. These modifications seem designed to increase the reliability of the test, which has been standardized on 2,000 adults engaged in a wide variety of occupations, tested by the University of Minnesota Employment Stabilization Institute during 1931 and 1932.

Just how reliable the revised test actually is, is not clear from the data supplied by the author in the manual accompanying the test. As a matter of fact, the entire treatment of "standards and interpretation" is confused by the assignment of unconventional and even novel meanings to everyday statistical concepts. So, for example, after wading through an involved discussion of "10 quartile ranges" and "per cent placements," the reader finally realizes that the latter represent "scores" obtained by transmuting raw scores to a scale with a mean of 50 and a probable error of 10 and a total range of $\pm$ 5PE's. The per cent placement score is obtained, however, by a counting process that makes no allowance for the skewness of the distribution which, in fact, appears, from inspection, to be a factor worthy of consideration in the case of the "turning test."

Data on the validity of the test are scarce. The Minnesota norms apply only to the original board and method of scoring.[2] Bingham presents occupational norms but these are also based on the original board, but with a different method of scoring.[3] Ziegler presents a table showing the range and median of speed indexes for 5 occupational groups including respectively 12 office workers; 60 package wrappers; 12 packet stuffers; 32 small parts factory assemblers, and 123 typing and stenographic students. In every case the mean is considerably higher than for the entire population and the range is within that of the better 50 per cent of adults. However, further analysis of the data is needed.

The test seems to have a fairly wide use in clinical practice. To the reviewers it appears to represent material for further experimental evaluation in specific selection and guidance situations.

[1663]

Minnesota Spatial Relations Test. Ages 11 and over; 1930; a revision of H. C. Link's *Spatial Relations Test*; 1 form; individual; $38 per testing outfit; worklimit (15-45) minutes; Donald G. Paterson,

Richard M. Elliott, L. Dewey Anderson, Herbert A. Toops, and Edna Heidbreder; Marietta, Ohio: Marietta Apparatus Co.

REFERENCES

1 ANDERSON, L. DEWEY. "The Minnesota Mechanical Ability Tests." *Personnel J* 6:473-8 Ap '28.
2 PATERSON, DONALD G.; ELLIOTT, RICHARD M.; ANDERSON, L. DEWEY; TOOPS, HERBERT A.; AND HEIDBREDER, EDNA. *Minnesota Mechanical Ability Tests*: The Report of a Research Investigation Subsidized by the Committee on Human Migrations of the National Research Council and Conducted in the Department of the University of Minnesota, pp. 59-61, 73-93, 109, 141, 204-19, 229-33, 235, 238-44, 250-4, 271-83, 291, 311-2, 339-45, 431-3, 461-6, 508-10, 531-2. Minneapolis, Minn.: University of Minnesota Press, 1930. Pp. xxii, 586. $5.00.
3 SCHIEFFELIN, BARBARA, AND SCHWESINGER, GLADYS C. *Mental Tests and Heredity*: Including a Survey of Non-Verbal Tests, pp. 216-7. New York: Galton Publishing Co., Inc. 1930. Pp. ix, 298. Out of print.
4 HARVEY, O. L. "Mechanical 'Aptitude' or Mechanical 'Ability'? A Study in Method." *J Ed Psychol* 22:517-22 O '31.
5 BERGEN, GARRET L. *Use of Tests in the Adjustment Service*, pp. 49-50. Adjustment Service Series Report [No.] 4. New York: American Association for Adult Education, 1935. Pp. 70. Paper. Out of print.
6 DVORAK, BEATRICE JEANNE. *Differential Occupational Ability Patterns*. Publications of the Employment Stabilization Research Institute, University of Minnesota, Vol. 3, No. 8. Minneapolis, Minn.: University of Minnesota Press, February 1935. Pp. 46. $1.00. Paper.
7 GREEN, HELEN J., AND BERMAN, ISABEL R.; under the direction of Donald G. Paterson and M. R. Trabue. *A Manual of Selected Occupational Tests for Use in Public Employment Offices*, pp. 5-7, 17-19, 23-31. University of Minnesota, Bulletins of the Employment Stabilization Research Institute, Vol. 2, No. 3. Minneapolis, Minn.: University of Minnesota Press, July, 1936. Pp. 31. $0.50. Paper.
8 BINGHAM, WALTER VAN DYKE. *Aptitudes and Aptitude Testing*, pp. 309-11. New York and London: Harper & Brothers, 1937. Pp. ix, 390. $3.00; 10s. 6d.
9 BROWN, FRED. "Selective Tests for Dental School Candidates." *Oral Hyg* 27:1172-7 S '37.
10 PATERSON, DONALD G.; SCHNEIDLER, GWENDOLEN G.; AND WILLIAMSON, EDMUND G. *Student Guidance Techniques*, pp. 225-7. New York: McGraw-Hill Book Co., Inc., 1938. Pp. xviii, 316. $3.00. (London: McGraw-Hill Publishing Co., Ltd. 18s.)

Lorene Teegarden, Psychological Examiner, Public Schools, Cincinnati, Ohio. This test was developed by the Employment Stabilization Research Institute of the University of Minnesota, from an earlier formboard devised by H. C. Link. It consists of a series of four boards, each with 58 holes of different shapes, into which 58 blocks are to be fitted. For the first two boards, A and B, the same blocks are used, the arrangement and spatial orientation being different in B from what it is in A, so that details of form and position must be observed anew in Board B. The last two boards, C and D, use a second set of blocks, slightly more difficult to discriminate and place than the first set. The time required is from 15 to 25 minutes.

The score is a percentile rank or standard score rating based upon the total time required for completion of B, C, and D, Board A being used as an introduction. This method is recommended as giving the highest reliability and being the most effective for individual diagnosis. There are separate norms for men and women based upon this method of scoring. Additional published norms include age norms for boys for each pair of boards and for the four boards combined; and grade norms for boys in grades 7 to 12, and for university groups. Reliability is quoted as .81 for boys, .91 for men, and .89 for women. Mean scores made by groups of workers in a number of different occupations are also given, including commercial, clerical, mechanical, and other occupations. The evidence given indicates a tendency to superior scores in mechanical occupations.

This test measures speed and accuracy in reacting to details of spatial relations. It gives a measure of the ability to work with a variety of details in handling things and materials. Since the score is influenced somewhat by rapidity of movement, it is important that the performance be so motivated as to secure the best possible interest, concentration, and effort, as indifference or distraction may appreciably increase the time and reduce the rating.

As a tryout for jobs requiring resourcefulness in solving problems of a mechanical nature it is probably surpassed by the Kent-Shakow or some other formboard which involves a series of graded problems. For jobs requiring the handling of small parts, or placement with great exactness, it should be supplemented by some test requiring fine neuromuscular control.

[1664]
Minnesota Vocational Test for Clerical Workers. Ages 17 and over for women and ages 19 and over for men; 1933-38; 1 form; $3 per 100; 25¢ per specimen set; 15(20) minutes; Dorothy M. Andrew under the direction of Donald G. Paterson and Howard P. Longstaff; New York: Psychological Corporation.

REFERENCES
1 POND, MILLICENT. "What Is New in Employment Testing." *Personnel J* 11:10-6 Je '32.
2 ANDREW, DOROTHY M., under the direction of Donald G. Paterson. *Measured Characteristics of Clerical Workers.* University of Minnesota Bulletins of the Employment Stabilization Research Institute, Vol. 3, No. 1. Minneapolis, Minn.: University of Minnesota Press, July 1934. Pp. 60. $1.00. Paper.
3 ANDREW, D. M. *"An Analysis of the Minnesota Vocational Test for Clerical Workers."* Unpublished doctor's thesis, University of Minnesota, 1935.
4 BERGEN, GARRET L. *Use of Tests in the Adjustment Service,* pp. 43-4. Adjustment Service Series Report [No.] 4. New York: American Association for Adult Education, 1935. Pp. 70. Paper. Out of print.
5 DODGE, ARTHUR F. *Occupational Ability Patterns.* Columbia University, Teachers College, Contributions to Education, No. 658. Harry Dexter Kitson, faculty sponsor. New York: Bureau of Publications, the College, 1935. Pp. v, 97. $1.60.
6 DVORAK, BEATRICE JEANNE. *Differential Occupational Ability Patterns.* Publications of the Employment Stabilization Research Institute, University of Minnesota, Vol. 3, No. 8. Minneapolis, Minn.: University of Minnesota Press, February 1935. Pp. 46. $1.00. Paper.
7 COPELAND, HERMAN A. "Some Characteristics of Three Tests Used to Predict Clerical Success." *J Appl Psychol* 20:461-70 Ag '36.
8 GREEN, HELEN J., AND BERMAN, ISABEL R.; under the direction of Donald G. Paterson and M. R. Trabue. *A Manual of Selected Occupational Tests for Use in Public Employment Offices,* pp. 5-9, 23-31. University of Minnesota, Bulletins of the Employment Stabilization Research Institute, Vol. 2, No. 3. Minneapolis, Minn.: University of Minnesota Press, July 1936. Pp. 31. $0.50. Paper.
9 ANDREW, DOROTHY M. "An Analysis of the Minnesota Vocational Test for Clerical Workers." *J Appl Psychol* 21:18-47, 139-72 F, Ap '37.
10 BINGHAM, WALTER VAN DYKE. *Aptitudes and Aptitude Testing,* pp. 322-7. New York and London: Harper & Brothers, 1937. Pp. ix, 390. $3.00; 10s. 6d.
11 CANDEE, BEATRICE, AND BLUM, MILTON. "A New Scoring System for the Minnesota Clerical Test." *Psychol B* 34:545 O '37.
12 COPELAND, HERMAN A. "Validating Two Tests for Census Enumeration." *J Appl Psychol* 21:230-2 Ap '37.
13 DAVIDSON, CHARLES M. "Analysis of Clerical Tests." *Personnel J* 16:95-8 S '37.
14 DAVIDSON, CHARLES M. "Evaluation of Clerical Tests." *Personnel J* 16:57-64 Je '37.
15 HALES, W. M. "Clerical Tests in State Reformatory." *Personnel J* 16:316-24 Ap '38.
16 PATERSON, DONALD G.; SCHNEIDLER, GWENDOLEN G.; AND WILLIAMSON, EDMUND G. *Student Guidance Techniques,* pp. 206-9. New York: McGraw-Hill Book Co., Inc., 1938. Pp. xviii, 316. $3.00. (London: McGraw-Hill Publishing Co., Ltd. 18s.)
17 DUDYCHA, GEORGE J. "Dependability and Clerical Aptitude." *J Appl Psychol* 23:332-6 Je '39.
18 BARNETTE, W. LESLIE. "Norms of Business College Students on Standardized Tests: Intelligence, Clerical Ability, English." *J Appl Psychol* 24:237-44 Ap '40.

W. D. Commins, Assistant Professor of Psychology, The Catholic University of America. The present test is accompanied by an illuminating manual containing many items relevant to the validity of the test, something that is sure to be appreciated by those interested in tests. There are data on the relation of test results to ratings, grades in accounting, speed of typing, employed vs. unemployed clerical workers, classes of clerical workers, future success, other clerical tests, age, sex, experience and training, formal education, intelligence, and speed of reading. Because of the generally favorable nature of this summary, as well as the convenience of having it at hand, one is impressed favorably by the test at the start. Correlations with intelligence, formal education, and experience and training are in general low, which offers considerable justification for the authors' claim that the test measures "an aptitude which is related positively to the abilities to discriminate small differences rapidly, to observe and compare, to adjust to a new situation, and to give attention to a problem." These, of course, are to be interpreted, for want of further evidence, in relation to the tasks imposed by the test, viz., number checking and name checking. Name checking correlates with speed of reading .45, and with spelling .65. Number checking correlates with verifying arithmetical computations .51. From an academic point of view, these results may be confusing if we think of the possible "uniqueness" of the test or the ability underlying it. It is just possible that we should not need a "clerical" test if we could identify the various mental "factors" in terms of certain fundamental operations. But until the day arrives when we can feel sure of our mental analysis, there will be a need of certain "on-the-job" specific tests which will have their justification in the practical selection of employees and promising workers. The present test ought to give considerable satisfaction in this respect, particularly because of its simple construction and relative ease of scoring. One might expect, however, that a more varied test, touching upon more aspects of clerical work, would ultimately be more satisfactory, although we do not now have adequate scientific data that such would be the case.

[1665]

N.I.I.P. Clerical Test: American Revision. Ages 16 and over; 1934; 1 form; $5 per 100; 25¢ per specimen set; (30) minutes; a revision of the *National Institute of Industrial Psychology Clerical Test, Series* 25; revision by Herbert Moore; New York: Psychological Corporation.

REFERENCES

1 MOORE, HERBERT. "The Institute's Clerical Test in America." *Human Factor* 7:407-9 N '33.
2 MOORE, HERBERT. "The Institute's Clerical Test in the Westinghouse Electric Company." *Human Factor* 10:221-4 Je '36.

Donald G. Paterson, Professor of Psychology, The University of Minnesota. This clerical test is printed in an 8-page booklet and consists of seven subtests as follows: Test I, Following oral instructions, seven statements with two questions each; Test II, Classification, each of 40 miscellaneous items is to be checked with reference to which of six categories of expense it is chargeable; Test III, Arithmetic, six simple addition problems and three problems each involving subtraction, multiplication, and division; Test IV, Copying 20 names and symbols; Test V, Checking names and numbers indicating in the case of each of 48 pairs of names and numbers whether the two members of a pair are the same or different; Test VI, Filing, two parts, one involving the arrangement of 17 numbers in increasing size, the other involving the arrangement of 17 names in alphabetical order; Test VII, Problems, 12 problems involving reasoning, number series completion, following printed directions, etc. Speed is emphasized in the general directions. The test can be administered in 30 minutes and corrected in 5. Only one form of the test is provided. It is designed for use with people whose academic training his reached the college level although norms are also provided for high school seniors.

Decile norms are provided for an unspecified number of high school seniors and college seniors and the median score for these two groups is given for each subtest. No norms for employed clerical workers are provided. Data regarding reliability are absent and little evidence bearing on validity is given. The correlation between intelligence and this test as a whole or the subtests is not given. The interrelation of the subtests is not given. There is a statement that secretarial workers would do well on all parts of the test whereas routine office workers would make a poor score on Tests I and VII and occasionally on Test V. Test V is mentioned as being of value in selecting persons for work involving close attention.

Neither the printed test nor the poorly mimeographed manual of directions mentions the publisher or distributor or cost. No references are given.

Judging solely on the basis of the test itself and the inadequate manual of directions, one is forced to suspend judgment as to the value of this test. Presumably, the present test is an experimental edition not intended for practical use in guidance and employment work, otherwise the author would supply sufficient information and data to permit a prospective consumer to judge its value for a given purpose.

[1665.1]

Occupational Analysis Form. For use with "Your Life Work Film" produced by Vocational Films, Inc., Des Moines, Iowa; 1940; 1 form; 50¢ per 25; Arthur P. Twogood; Bloomington, Ill.: McKnight & McKnight.

[1666]

Occupational Interest Blank. Boys of high school age; [1937]; 1 form; 75¢ per 25; 15¢ per specimen set; nontimed (10) minutes; Bruce V. Le Suer; New York: Psychological Corporation.

Stanley G. Dulsky, Chief Psychologist, Rochester Guidance Center, Rochester, New York. This is a one-page inventory consisting of 100 occupations to each of which the subject responds by circling *like, indifferent,* or *dislike.* The occupations are classified in ten groups: professional, technical, clerical, mercantile and sales, artistic or creative, skilled trades, semi-skilled occupations, adventuresome occupations, personal service, and agricultural occupations. There are ten occupations in each of the ten groups. A quick scoring method enables the user of the blank to determine the number of likes for each of the ten groups.

With respect to interpretation, the manual states: "No set rules can be given for the interpretation of scores. The information gained from the *Occupational Interest Blank* should be used to supplement information secured from other sources. The reactions to the individual items, and the summary of the responses should be examined critically and used as the basis for further discussion."

The question of paramount importance to a vocational counselor is: Can I do a more effective job of counseling by administering this blank to the counselee? The five-page manual accompanying the blank does not answer this question; in the reviewer's opinion the answer is a dubious "perhaps." The most serious objection to Le Suer's blank is a general one applying to all occupational interest blanks: Of what value is a response to the name of an occupation if the actual activities involved in pursuing that occupation are completely or partially unknown to the subject? The response is usually made on the basis of factors which the counselor can neither determine nor evaluate.

Comments specific to this occupational interest blank are:

(a) Three categories—like, indifferent, and dislike—are too few for anything but the crudest distinctions. A five-step scale might be better.

(b) Of what value is an occupation classification based mainly on census reports? Such a classification has no psychological basis. Why not a psychological classification of occupations for psychologists? Why consider a physician in the same category with a lawyer merely because both medicine and law are called professions? Aren't the psychological requirements and duties of a chauffeur (personal service occupation) more similar to those of a truck driver (semiskilled occupation) than to those of a barber (also personal service)?

(c) "The blank may be used without scoring, just as any similar form is used, but scoring increases its effectiveness by revealing the general trend of an individual's vocational interests as well as his specific job preferences." I disagree with the author. Because of the census classification employed, I believe one will learn more by merely inspecting the blank than by scoring it because scoring might easily mask important similarities. Circling "like" for occupations of chauffeur, machinist, auto mechanic, lathe hand, truck driver, and welder is important even though it represents three occupational groups. Certainly, those occupations have more in common than chauffeur, barber,

bellboy, and soda dispenser (all classified as personal service).

The author states that information from this blank should supplement information obtained from other sources. I would caution that information from this blank should never be used without a thorough discussion of it in a vocational interview. Finally, is the expenditure of money, time, and effort justified by the results secured from this blank? To this question I would reply: The author has given us no evidence that it is.

J. B. Miner, Professor of Psychology and Director of the Personnel Bureau, University of Kentucky. A boy of high school age checks L, I, or D through a list of 100 occupations and jobs. A comparison of the number of likes out of ten jobs in each of ten groups is assumed to indicate relative preferences for fields of work such as professional, clerical, skilled trades, etc. The blank might be of some use to introduce an interview, but the attempt to quantify the results is unfortunate and misleading. With so small a number as ten choices in a group, the difference between checking three or checking seven out of ten would not be statistically significant since the checks might differ this much if made and controlled by chance alone. The instructions for interpretation attempt to guard against misuse by a counselor who does not understand the fact that neither reliability nor validity of the scores is known. The author has used the blank to discover instances for interviews when a boy's choice of course in school seems to be out of line with a pronounced record as to his field of interest.

For reviews by W. V. Bingham and M. R. Trabue, see 1174.

[1667]
Occupational Orientation Inquiry. Grades 12-16; 1939; 1 form; $1.00 per 25; 15¢ per specimen set; nontimed (40-80) minutes; G. A. Wallar and S. L. Pressey; New York: Psychological Corporation.

REFERENCES

1 WALLAR, GENE A. "The Occupational Orientation Inquiry." *Sch and Soc* 46:507-10 O 16 '37.

John Gray Peatman, Assistant Professor of Psychology, The College of the City of New York. This inquiry is chiefly useful as a systematic aid in getting from a student a good deal of relevant information for vocational guidance purposes prior to the actual vocational counseling interview. On the first page, of the 4-page blank, the student is asked to review his vocational interests and experiences. Then on the two inside pages, two hundred and twenty-four occupations are listed in alphabetical order and self-estimates are asked for each—the student indicating his relative degree (on a 5-point scale) of knowledge, interest, ability, and opportunity for placement. Finally, on the back page, the student is asked to evaluate his vocational problems in the light of the preceding considerations. In the hands of a competent counselor, this inquiry should prove useful. Its chief improvement over most other occupational inventories is its use of the four categories of knowledge, interest, ability, and opportunity for each job self-estimate. The authors emphasize the value of the inquiry as a qualitative rather than a quantitative instrument. It is unfortunate that they do not confine themselves to this and forego the unhappy custom of citing as "first norms" data which have little or no normative value. The data they present will certainly be misleading to some and misused by others, and they are of practically no use to the competent counselor.

The table of so-called norms gives decile values for three groups of men and women students whom we are told are high school seniors, college freshmen, or college seniors. That is all we learn about their background except that the suggestion is made that the college groups resided in several sections of the country—"to insure against provinciality." The decile values are calculated for distributions of the *number* of jobs or occupations receiving a self-rating of "much" (4 points) or "above average" (3 points). At least the distributions for knowledge, interest, ability, and opportunity are presented separately which is more than can be said of a second table of data presented in the mimeographed manual of directions. In this second table, the authors present four lists of 20 occupations "ranking highest according to the sum of *total* ratings by (*a*) men and (*b*) women freshmen in (1) the science division of a technical college and (2) the college of education in a large university." These results are presented as a matter of "interest" in "showing the occupations rated highest by 400 freshmen in a college of education and by 200 freshmen in a science division of a technical college." Unfortunately, however, these results are *totally* ambiguous inasmuch as they are based on a summation of all four types of self-estimates, i.e., knowledge, inter-

est, ability, and opportunity are all thrown together. This hodgepodge of four very different kinds of self-estimates presents some results, especially among the men students, which at first glance are startling. Thus, for the men's technical college group, the occupations of gas station attendant, grocer, truck driver, and life guard rank 5th, 7th, 10th, and 17th respectively. And for the men's college of education group, grocer follows teacher and athletic director as the third highest ranking occupation in the group, with gas station attendant reduced to 10th position and truck driver to 16th. Since it is impossible to disentangle knowledge, interest, ability, and opportunity self-estimates from this ambiguous mass, the uselessness of this table of data should be apparent.

On the other hand, provided the inquiry will be found to have adequate reliability and functional value when used with groups of students, both tables of data indicate a possible usefulness of the inquiry in group surveys. Thus, it may be found to be helpful in ascertaining the occupational orientation of various kinds of groups, in terms of their own self-estimates of knowledge, ability, interest, and opportunities. But as for *norms*—why even try to simulate them for an instrument of this type?

The fact remains that this kind of instrument has its chief value in counseling as a systematic, timesaving device for getting information relevant to the particular student's vocational problems. As the authors themselves state—before giving way to a consideration of "norms"—"Interpretation of the scores on the *Occupational Orientation Inquiry* must ultimately be based on intensive study of the entire blank and is thus qualitative and largely an individual matter."

C. Gilbert Wrenn, Professor of Educational Psychology, The University of Minnesota. This 4-page blank is an aid to the interview and not a test or even a weighted inventory. This the authors wish to make very clear. The first page calls for a brief vocational history and the last page calls for the student's subjective analysis of what he considers to be his best occupational field. These two pages comprise something of an occupational autobiography. The two inside pages are taken up with columns of 224 occupations, opposite each of which the student is supposed to place his judgment as to his knowledge, interest, ability, and the opportunity for placement. The form of these inside pages looks somewhat complicated to the reviewer since each of these four ratings carry four possible steps, and it is necessary for the student to go back in his reading to the key at the top of the page until he has at least memorized the four steps under the four ratings. The blank makes a contribution in questioning the student on his opinion of his "knowledge" of each of these occupations and "the opportunity for placement" in addition to the ordinarily requested reactions on interest and ability.

If used by the counselor and not by the student, this blank can be helpful. Its real danger lies in the fact that the student may take his own judgment as prima facie evidence. The basic concept is that of self-analysis although the authors hope this will always be followed by counselor judgment and reaction. It is more specific in nature than Achilles' *Aids to the Vocational Interview* (*see* 493) although following the same general form of the provision of ideas suggested by the student that can be used in counseling with him. It may or may not be more helpful than the *Kefauver-Hand Guidance Tests and Inventories*, although subject to the same emphasis on self-analysis. The fault does not lie in the authors' concept of the use of such instruments, but in the student's unconscious or conscious assumption that what he thinks about himself is correct. It should be helpful to a counselor to know of what occupations the student thinks he has knowledge, opportunity for placement, ability, and interest, for this may provide the very point at which counseling begins, namely, the correction of false assumptions.

The total scores on such a blank as this are probably meaningless, for a summation of checks of unknown validity does not produce a score that has very much meaning. The reviewer does not see, therefore, much value in the percentile norms that are tentatively suggested. The blanks may, on the other hand, be of real value to a counselor as a basis for interviewing and as a technique for stimulating the student to think along certain specific vocational lines. It is built for and has been tried out with college students. The opportunity given for a statement and an evaluation of vocational history, when made in connection with a student's consideration of 224 specific occupations, may be the most valuable part of the blank.

[1668]

O'Rourke Mechanical Aptitude Test: Junior Grade. Grades 7-12; 1926-39; 3 forms; 5¢ per test; 10¢ per specimen set; 61(70) minutes; L. J. O'Rourke; Washington, D. C.: Psychological Institute.

REFERENCES

1 BINGHAM, WALTER VAN DYKE. *Aptitudes and Aptitude Testing*, pp. 318-20. New York and London: Harper & Brothers, 1937. Pp. ix, 390. $3.00; 10s. 6d.

Herbert A. Landry, Research Assistant, Bureau of Reference, Research and Statistics, Public Schools, New York, New York. This is essentially a test of mechanical information. The justification for its use as a measure of mechanical aptitude undoubtedly rests on the hypothesis that the amount of mechanical information possessed by an individual is an indirect measure of his interest in the realm of mechanical things. This interest is assumed to arise from the existence of mechanical aptitude. While it seems reasonable to believe that these assumptions are sound, conclusive proof has not been demonstrated.

It must be remembered that such inferential measurements rest upon the assumption that all individuals so measured have been subjected to uniformly operating environmental factors. It can be readily shown that this is not true. Variations of opportunity for contact with mechanical things are exceedingly marked. Any scores obtained, therefore, must be carefully interpreted in the light of the individual's opportunities and experience.

In presenting data concerning the validity of the tests, the author cites relationships obtained between test scores and shop ratings. While the exact nature of these ratings is not stated, it is assumed that they are either the periodic or end marks or ranks given by instructors since these are the most commonly used criteria. The coefficients of correlation obtained range from .64 to .84. From the limited data given, it would appear that the test can predict achievement in the types of courses mentioned with reasonable success.

Unlike the other pencil-and-paper tests of mechanical aptitude, this test limits itself to the measurement of a narrow sector of the total of these elements that constitute mechanical aptitude. For instance the *MacQuarrie Test for Mechanical Ability*, the *Detroit Mechanical Aptitudes Examinations*, and the tests devised by Cox, all seek to measure on a broader base. They include tests designed to measure power of visualization, ability to recognize spatial relationships, perception of mechanical relationships, hand-and-eye coordinations, etc. They attempt to measure a broader pattern of activities since inquiries into the nature of mechanical aptitude have shown that it is a complex of several elements among the important of which are those mentioned. The O'Rourke tests, however, restrict their area of measurement to that of information concerning tools and mechanical processes. Accordingly this must be held in mind and any results used within this limitation.

The reliability of the test is not known since it is not given on the single explanatory sheet which accompanies the test.

Percentile norms which are based upon scores made by 70,000 workmen who applied for mechanical jobs are provided. In addition average scores and standard deviations are given for thirty-three occupational groups (mechanical). The norms as such are limited in their use since they do not represent unselected cases. There is no way of knowing how much better these individuals scored on the test than unselected groups. It is reasonable to assume that the test performance of these 70,000 cases would be better than that of an unselected group because of their mechanical training and experience as well as their possible higher initial mechanical aptitude. While special occupational norms have some value, general norms based on unselected cases would be of greater value. For use in the secondary school grades, age norms would be especially useful, since most tests of mechanical aptitude have shown definite score increases with age up through the secondary school level.

About one-half the items of Part I are of the matching type. In all of the six groups there are the same number of stimuli and response items. Generally it is considered advisable to include more responses than stimuli items in order to avoid the selection of the last responses on an elimination basis. Aside from this, the structure of the items is satisfactory.

Physically the illustrations in Part I could be improved. To begin with they are all very small. Accordingly the details are frequently so fine as to make for difficulty of identification. In several instances the two related drawings differ considerably in proportion. This is apt to be confusing.

The test is simple to administer and should not present any difficulties to the individuals who are given the tests. The content has considerable interest value. The directions are clear and explicit.

It is to be regretted that there is so little information provided which is descriptive of the test. While the publishers may counter that few test users make use of the information this is no excuse for its omission. No doubt some less critical test users are willing to take a test on faith, many others, however, have a real desire to know "what it is all about," without implying any lack of confidence in the author or his test.

[1669]

Personal Data Blank. Counselees of high school age and over; 1934-38; $2 per 25; specimen set free; J. Gustav White; Stanford University, Calif.: Stanford University Press.

Edward S. Jones, Professor of Psychology and Director of Personnel Research, The University of Buffalo. This report is obviously designed for Y.M.C.A.'s and other institutions concerned with the guidance of youth. It would normally fit those in the upper high school level or in college. It includes the following sections: (*a*) Personal History which contains items about the family, health, and the finances of the person; (*b*) Your Problems; (*c*) Your Interests and Traits; (*d*) Your Education; (*e*) Your Occupation; and (*f*) Summary of Counseling Blanks and Discussion. It is not a test, but an inventory of items designed to help and guide the counselor to evaluate a student more completely. I see no objection to this sort of data blank, provided it is used with discretion. It is obviously an attempt to systematize a personal history or case study of the individual. No doubt White would agree that much of the material cannot be used at face value, since it is quite subjective, raising questions about attitudes, problems, and interests. In the section Your Problems, the student is asked to write on "what seems to be your particular problem, no matter in what area of life. Mention frankly any ambitions, difficulties, or doubts, though they may seem now relatively unimportant."

One can doubt the value of this sort of approach. Many students have been known to write nothing and others who would write extensively without any particular discrimination. There is not a clear enough directional instruction to the item. There is also the item, "What have you done to solve your problem?" This again may very easily lead to no response or to an indefinite amount of writing, which may be quite revealing.

The blank as a whole assumes at best a great deal of insight on the part of the student or inquirer and presumes a much more aggressive attitude than is present in a good many college freshmen and sophomores.

There is one check list, asking the individual to check once or twice his outstanding abilities, including such things as mechanical traits, dramatic ability, and management of finances. The reviewer is very skeptical of the value of a list of this sort. Most people do not have any basis of estimating abilities of this kind. In the reviewer's estimation a blank half as long with well-selected items, for the most part fairly objective ones, would probably be fully as useful. The last page of the blank contains a "Summary of Counseling Blanks and Discussions," which can be duplicated, a second copy to be used by other advisors. Most of this is quite objective data, and should be very useful to a person trained to evaluate the data properly.

Donald G. Paterson, Professor of Psychology, The University of Minnesota. The *Personal Data Blank* is designed to permit a counselee to record confidential case history information about himself and his problems prior to a counseling interview and thus to save the time of a counselor in securing pertinent data.

The blank is an eight-page booklet, 8½ by 11 inches. The first six pages are to be filled in by the counselee as a preliminary step in securing the help of a competent counselor. The data to be recorded are as follows: identifying information and family background; health data; data about finances; statement of problems prompting consultation; statement of present hobbies, interests, and characteristics together with an evaluation of accomplishments and failures; detailed record of educational history; and a detailed record of occupational history together with statements in regard to occupational information possessed and needed, vocational choice and self-estimates of vocational aptitudes, abilities, aims and ambitions. Page 7 is reserved for the counselor who is to use it to summarize his interpretation of the data, to record the highlights of the interview, and to list the specific and general recommenda-

tions made to the counselee. Page 8 is blank and can be used for recording additional case notes.

In addition to the eight-page booklet a duplicate of Page 7 accompanies the blank so that the counselor may make a carbon copy of his summary and give it to the counselee to serve as a memorandum of the interview.

The device for summarizing the interview is especially praiseworthy since it forces the counselor to record available test data in regard to abilities and interests, to interpret these in the light of the problem-areas in which the counselee is having difficulty and to formulate definite suggestions and recommendations to be followed by the counselee in attempting to solve his problems.

A one-page manual of suggestions for the counselor's use of the *Personal Data Blank* is also provided. These suggestions include a letter code for listing the areas in which the difficulty lies. Thirteen problem areas are specified including the need for: expert information, financial aid, employment placement, vocational guidance, educational guidance, health guidance, socialization, sex adjustment, moral and religious adjustment, and mental hygiene treatment.

The blank is comprehensive in its coverage without being loaded with a large number of items of doubtful value.

One may criticize the blank for not providing sufficient space for the recording of test data. It appears to be geared to a minimum battery of tests such as one mental test, two personality tests, and two vocational interest tests although provision is made for recording the scores from additional tests. This is in contrast to the counseling advantage to be found in a flexible profile form for recording a greater number and variety of test scores such as is found in the Psychological Corporation's *Aids to the Vocational Interview* (*see* 493). There is also the danger that an amateur counselor may become too dependent upon the blank as a basis for counseling. Such a counselor would tend to oversimplify his procedure and would tend to accept the recorded information *at face value* without adequate independent checks and attempts at verification. But this type of criticism is a bit unfair to the blank because the author of the blank rightly assumed that it would be used in conjunction with interview observations, psychological test results, and other sources of data by properly trained and competent counselors.

In the reviewer's opinion, this blank incorporates the good features of similar case history blanks and may be listed among the useful tools now available for systematizing the counseling interview and providing a permanent record of such interviews. Hence, this blank, when used properly, should lead to improved counseling work and should provide a partial basis for follow-up and evaluation studies which are so urgently needed in this type of service.

[1670]

Personal History. Prospective life insurance agents; 1937; this rating chart is also included as Part 1 of the *Aptitude Index for Life Insurance Salesmen*; distribution restricted to life insurance companies which are members of the Life Insurance Sales Bureau; Hartford, Conn.: Life Insurance Sales Research Bureau.

REFERENCES

1 Life Insurance Sales Research Bureau. *Rating Prospective Agents.* Hartford, Conn.: the Bureau, 1937. Pp. 16. Privately distributed. Paper.
2 Life Insurance Sales Research Bureau. *Selection of Agents:* A Method of Relating Personal History Information to Probable Success in Life Insurance Selling. Hartford, Conn.: the Bureau, 1937. Pp. 24. Privately distributed. Paper.
3 Life Insurance Sales Research Bureau. *Measuring Aptitude for Life Insurance Selling.* Hartford, Conn.: the Bureau, 1938. Pp. 22. Privately distributed. Paper.
4 Life Insurance Sales Research Bureau. *The Prospective Agents Rating Plan in Use*: Report of Session on Selection of Agents, at Research Bureau Conference, Hartford, Connecticut, March 22, 1938. New Haven, Conn.: the Bureau, 1938. Pp. 44. Privately distributed. Paper.
5 KURTZ, ALBERT K. "Evaluating Selection Tests." *Managers Mag* 14:12-6 My-Je '39.

[1671]

Preference Record. Grades 9-16; 1939; 1 form, 3 editions (differing only in the method of scoring); $1.25 per 25 forms for reporting scores and profiles to students; 50¢ per sample copy of any one edition; nontimed (40-60) minutes; G. Frederic Kuder; Chicago, Ill.: University of Chicago Bookstore.
a) FORM AM, EDITION FOR MACHINE-SCORING. $5.25 per 25; $2.50 per 100 answer sheets; $6.00 per set of scoring stencils.
b) FORM AH, EDITION FOR SCORING BY STENCILS. $5.00 per 25; $1.25 per 100 answer sheets; $2.00 per set of scoring stencils.
c) FORM AS, EDITION FOR SELF-SCORING. $6.00 per 25; $5.00 per 100 answer pads; $1.25 per 100 profile sheets.

REFERENCES

1 THURSTONE, L. L. "A Multiple Factor Study of Vocational Interests." *Personnel J* 10:198-205 O '31.
2 KUDER, G. F. "The Stability of Preference Items." *J Social Psychol* 10:41-50 F '39.

A. B. Crawford, Director of the Department of Personnel Study and Bureau of Appointments and Professor of Psychology, Yale University. Evaluation of this instrument is restricted, by lack of further evidence concerning its usefulness, to that offered in Kuder's own manual. The latter, however, presents such a clear picture of well-designed and carefully controlled experimentation, over a period of some six years, as to warrant distinct confidence in its possibilities and reported findings. Few of the many devices designed for guidance purposes have been as thoroughly tested and studied in advance of their release for general use, as this seems to have been.

The reviewer's opportunity actually to experiment with the *Preference Record* thus far has been limited to (*a*) a current study of 70 Yale freshmen, for which results are as yet incomplete and (*b*) an earlier administration to a few personal acquaintances. His opinions regarding its possible merits are, therefore, largely subjective. However, preliminary data on the freshman group indicate possibilities of differentiating arts, science, and engineering students rather clearly on some sections of the *Preference Record*. Moreover, test profiles of the other individuals well known to him did conform rather strikingly with his own estimates, and with those of several other qualified judges, as to the scores which these acquaintances might have been expected (in view of their known interests) to make. (Possibly the writer was unduly influenced in favor of the *Preference Record's* validity by the appropriately high "persuasive" rating of his wife.)

Although these various data, including such as have thus far been obtained concerning freshman students, are insufficient for statistically dependable conclusions, he can nevertheless endorse the primary aim of this device for "obtaining measures of motivation in various lines of study and of work." The premise that application or release of individual abilities and aptitudes is strongly affected by *motivation*—in plain words, that a person will "do his damndest" at what he most enjoys—seems wholly reasonable. Interest in any task, whether educational or vocational, supplies a natural drive for converting potentialities into effective achievement.

It is upon this premise that the work of Strong and others, in attempting to measure interest factors, has been founded. Kuder's objective is in the same direction, though his approach and methods are different. Strong developed and standardized the *Vocational Interest Blank* through its administration to successful representatives of various occupations. Thurstone [1] has shown that human interests are not actually classifiable into as many separate compartments as the Strong scales suggest; but instead fall into broader categories, each embracing certain *clusters* of the *Vocational*

Interest Blank groups. This is another way of saying that people cannot be specifically and individually labeled, respecting either their aptitudes or their interests, with the same manifold tags which distinguish vocations. The latter reflect far too much overlapping among the individual functions and abilities which they demand to parallel an occupational census. Hence, the Kuder approach, directed as it is toward identification of certain generalized activity patterns—each of which may find many career outlets—seems more fundamental in terms of observable human differences, than any preceding attempt to measure the motivating force of interests per se.

Kuder has proceeded, by the processes of experimental tryout and progressive analysis of many items, to develop a series of scores differentiating the following types of activity preferences: scientific, computational, musical, artistic, literary, social service, and "persuasive." His *Preference Record,* employing the technique of paired comparison, requires a preferential choice of one activity or interest versus another—e.g., "Go as a medical missionary to Africa" or "Establish a medical office in a fashionable suburb"; "Belong to an amateur astronomy club" or "Belong to a religious discussion group"; "Visit the Senate of the United States" or "Visit a museum of science"; "Own a good selection of tools" or "Own an encyclopedia"; "Browse in a library" or "Visit an art gallery." This method forces a selection even between "preferences" which, in fact, may be almost equally immaterial, attractive or repellent to the subject: he is offered no escape through such symbols as "I" (indifferent) or "?," as he is in most interest tests. No direct evidence is available as to relative validity of the two methods; but Kuder's recent article [2] discussing methods of selecting items for his *Preference Record* and their "stability" is well worth reading.

His immediate objective is educational guidance, although this is definitely associated with vocational choice. For each activity pattern suggestions are offered as to the occupations presumably offering it most scope. It is here that Kuder's work thus far is most vulnerable: the vocational groupings are admittedly speculative and include here and there some rather curious bedfellows. As yet, this instrument has not been validated in the occupational field at all, and its utility for the pur-

poses in view is, therefore, still open to question. Kuder's manual states: "These studies are being extended to people actually engaged in various occupations. In the course of time, it is expected to develop indexes which will reflect the degree to which a person's pattern of scores is characteristic of that of people in each of a number of occupations and of students in each of a number of curricula."

Reliability coefficients reported in the manual range from .85 to .90 for the several scales. The instrument is designed to permit repeated use of the test booklet itself, with independent answer sheets. The latter may be obtained in either machine, stencil, or self-scoring forms; with cost varying (according to the form of answer sheet and extent of re-use for the question booklet itself) from around 2 to 10 cents per student.

It is interesting, and indeed essential, to compare Kuder's subjectively chosen occupational clusters with those obtained from the Strong *Vocational Interest Blank* by Thurstone's objective factorial analysis. The latter yielded four interest groups, respectively associated with science, language, people, and business. Apart from Kuder's aesthetic categories (musical and artistic, which were insufficiently represented in the *Vocational Interest Blank* scores analyzed by Thurstone to yield recognizable factors), the two groupings—though bearing somewhat different sets of necessarily arbitrary labels—correspond rather closely. We can, indeed, pair them off as follows: science—scientific; language—literary; people—social service and persuasive; business—computational. Considering the fact that Strong has worked downwards toward the student body from already well-established representatives of their respective vocations; while Kuder is attempting to identify interest and activity patterns among youth directly, and feeling his way upwards toward their occupational significance, the degree of correspondence just noted between the two systems of classification is striking. As a result, at least a reasonable presumption of validity may be credited to both Kuder's system and Thurstone's factorial grouping of the Strong categories into analogous clusters. If the high promise thus far offered by Kuder's approach can in time be substantiated by further evidence and its discriminating power, his contribution toward guidance purposes should prove of undoubted significance.

This test appears to be more realistic and direct in procedure than its particular fore-runners, and is certainly much easier and more economical to score. Its use, at least experimentally, is recommended, although care should naturally be exercised in the interpretation of results. Kuder reports low intercorrelations between scores on Thurstone's *Tests for Primary Mental Abilities* and scores on the *Preference Record* and states: "It is apparent that *Preference Record* scores in general are not sufficient evidence of ability in the fields measured by the *Primary Abilities Tests*, nor is the converse true. The results suggest that, in guidance, use of the preference profile should always include a consideration of measures of ability." The latter measure may indeed effectively *supplement* (but not replace) aptitude or ability tests and, therefore, has a logical place in any comprehensive "evaluation" battery.

Arthur E. Traxler, Assistant Director, Educational Records Bureau, New York, New York. The measurement of interests has been hampered by various factors, two of the most important of which are the difficulty of obtaining scores that have high reliability and the instability of responses when the form of the items and the context in which they appear is changed. In view of this fact, it is surprising that in few of the many attempts that have been made to measure interests or motivation in recent years has any attention been given to the preference type of item, for this kind of item permits wide sampling per unit of time and is therefore conducive to increased reliability, and it is also promising from the standpoint of stability.

In a test that employs the preference type of item, either the rank-order or the paired-comparison technique may be used. If the rank-order procedure is followed, the kinds of activity are grouped and the subject is instructed to rank those in each group in order of preference. In the paired-comparison procedure, each activity included in the test is paired with every other activity and the subject indicates the one in each pair which he prefers. In the past, Miner, Plechaty, Furfey, Vernon and Allport, Sullivan, Hartson, and Weedon have used one or the other of these techniques. Recently, Kuder has experimented with both procedures and has constructed a

Preference Record which utilizes the paired-comparison type of item.

Kuder's purpose in the preparation of his *Preference Record* was "to develop a number of independent measures in the field of motivation." Briefly stated, the procedure followed in the preparation of the *Preference Record* was to start with a group of items that have psychological meaning and to develop and refine a series of scales, the items of which had high correlation with their own scale and low correlation with the other scales.

The Kuder *Preference Record* consists of 330 paired-comparison items arranged and scored in such a manner that a profile of preference scores is obtained with respect to scientific, computational, musical, artistic, literary, social service, and persuasive activities. Provision is made for showing the results of these seven scales both graphically and in the form of percentile ranks. It should be clearly understood that the scores are intended to show preference alone and are not expected to show anything concerning the ability of the individual in these fields.

The *Preference Record* is designed for use with both high school and college students. There is no time limit, but most persons can finish it within a class period of forty minutes.

The unique format of the *Preference Record* is worthy of comment. The test itself consists of a directions page and eleven pages of test items which are attached permanently by means of ten small rings within a heavy cardboard cover. A detachable answer sheet containing eleven columns corresponding to the eleven pages of the test rests inside the back cover. The pages of the test booklet are of unequal width so that when the subject turns from one page to the next the appropriate column of the answer sheet is exposed adjacent to the margin.

Used answer sheets may be removed and new ones inserted, and thus each test booklet may be used repeatedly. There are three types of answer sheets—one for hand-scoring, one for machine-scoring, and one for self-scoring. The self-scoring feature will appeal to schools with limited clerical resources. The reviewer has found by trial with several individuals that the self-scoring form works satisfactorily.

Kuder is to be commended in that he has provided more statistical data concerning his *Preference Record* than usually is available for a new test. He has shown that the preference type of item is fairly stable in that it measures about the same thing when set up in different form and context. He has also shown that when academic aptitude scores and average college grades were used as criteria of validity, the validity of items originally selected in rank-order form will, when tried out with a different group, hold up about as well in paired-comparison form as in the original form. In other words, "the preference item seems to be less sensitive to rather violent treatment than some other more common varieties of personality item." [2]

In the manual of directions, Kuder reports the following reliability coefficients for the different scales: scientific, .87; computational, .85; musical, .88; artistic, .90; literary, .90; social service, .84; persuasive, .90. On the surface, these reliability coefficients indicate that the *Preference Record* should be fairly satisfactory for individual diagnosis, although not highly so. However, it should be pointed out that these reliabilities were found by a method that is reputed to yield about the same results as the Spearman-Brown method. Since it is known that prediction of reliability with the Spearman-Brown formula sometimes gives spurious high results, it would be helpful if the author would check the reliabilities, as reported, by a test-retest procedure.

In the manual of directions, Kuder states further that the intercorrelations of the seven scores obtained by a form similar to the present one were all low (less than .30). This of course is highly desirable, for if the scores are to have real value in guidance they should be relatively independent. Kuder also presents data from preliminary studies which suggest that the *Preference Record* may have some validity for predicting marks in certain curricula. It also appears that there is considerable relation between patterns of scores and occupational choice.

The most crucial question that can be raised about the *Preference Record* is of course concerned with its validity. Are the scores obtained actually indicative of preference with respect to the seven fields it is designed to cover? Naturally there is no definite answer to the question, for there is no perfect criterion of validity. It is believed, however, that the considered judgment of mature persons concerning their preference for the seven gen-

eral kinds of activity should have some value as a criterion. With this thought in mind, the reviewer asked twenty-one adults to rate the seven fields in order of their preference and then obtained their scores on the *Preference Record*. He then computed Spearman correlations between the rank order of the expressed preferences of each individual and the rank order of his preferences as indicated by the record. The median of the twenty-one correlation coefficients was .75. All but one of the correlations were positive and all but six were above .60. The correlations for three individuals were .96. This procedure of evaluations was admittedly crude, but the results do offer three suggestions: (*a*) on the average there seems to be fairly high agreement between the expressed preferences and the tested preferences of adults for the seven groups of activities; (*b*) the agreement is very high for certain individuals; (*c*) for some individuals the results of the *Preference Record* either agree very poorly or are at variance with their expressed preferences.

The poor agreement in certain instances may have been due to misunderstanding on the part of these subjects concerning what their true interests were, although this is doubtful, for some of the most experienced persons had the lowest correlations. Another possible factor is that the items contributing to the scores may have been inadequate indices of interest in the different areas so far as certain individuals were concerned. For example, several of the subjects criticized the "persuasive" scale. They felt that it was more nearly indicative of interest in salesmanship than of interest in the broad field of persuasive activities, some of the most effective of which are exceedingly indirect and subtle. A study of the items contributing to the score for the persuasive field lends some support to this viewpoint, for 49 items, or 51 per cent of the 96 items contributing to the persuasive scale, deal with salesmanship or closely related persuasive activities, such as soliciting for charity, publicity, and so forth.

Notwithstanding a number of detailed criticisms of this kind that could be made concerning the different scales, the fact remains that Kuder has constructed one of the most interesting evaluative devices that has yet appeared in the broad field of interest and motivation and that he has made a laudatory attempt to build it on a sound basis of experimentation and to evaluate the finished product critically. At its present stage, no reviewer could more than guess at its probable value in guidance, but this one feels that the *Preference Record* is worthy of use in an experimental way by psychologists, counselors, and others who serve as advisers for students at the secondary school and college levels.

[1672]

Rating Forms for Use of Interviewers and Oral Examinations. Applicants for employment; 1938; 50¢ per 25; 5¢ per sample copy; W. V. Bingham; New York: Psychological Corporation.

REFERENCES

1 BINGHAM, W. V. *Oral Examinations in Civil Service Recruitment*: With Special Reference to Experiences in Pennsylvania. Civil Service Assembly of the United States and Canada, Pamphlet No. 13. Chicago, Ill.: the Assembly, February 1939. Pp. 30. $0.50. Paper.

Ruth Strang, Professor of Education, Columbia University. This rating form is an attempt to standardize the observational aspects of the interview. It calls the interviewer's attention to important, precisely described, nonverbal data obtainable in an employment interview. Moreover, it provides space for some descriptive support of the quantitative ratings given. In all these respects the form is commendable and would meet the approval of certain writers who believe that the kind of data in which interviewers are interested should be obtained through standardized methods.

Other writers in this field, on the contrary, believe that many of the impressions recorded in interviews are hardly susceptible of standardized measurements. Moreover, in directing the interviewer's attention to specific points, the blank may cause him to miss the most crucial evidence and its relation to the total situation. Even if the important impression was not lost, the task still remains of relating the specific items obtained on the form to the complex structure of the candidate's personality in relation to the job.

For the novitiate in the field, this form is a useful guide to observation. But it may hamper the expert interviewer in getting a total, properly high-lighted impression of the candidate's fitness for the position.

[1673]

Revised Minnesota Paper Formboard. Ages 9 and over; 1934; 2 forms, 2 editions; $3.50 per 100; 15¢ per specimen set; 14(30) minutes; Rensis Lickert and William H. Quasha; New York: Psychological Corporation.
a) SERIES AA AND BB. 1934; $3.50 per 100.
b) SERIES MA AND MB. 1940; $1.50 per 25; $5 per 100; $1.50 per 100 machine-scorable answer sheets.

REFERENCES

1 ANDERSON, L. DEWEY. "The Minnesota Mechanical Ability Tests." *Personnel J* 6:473-8 Ap '28.
2 PATERSON, DONALD G.; ELLIOTT, RICHARD M.; ANDERSON, L. DEWEY; TOOPS, HERBERT A.; AND HEIDBREDER, EDNA. *Minnesota Mechanical Ability Tests*: The Report of a Research Investigation Subsidized by the Committee on Human Migrations of the National Research Council and Conducted in the Department of the University of Minnesota, pp. 57-61, 73-6, 81-3, 93-101, 109-10, 141-3, 204-19, 227-44, 251-3, 271-83, 291, 299-305, 310-12, 335-9, 430-2, 467-76, 508-10, 531-2. Minneapolis, Minn.: University of Minnesota Press, 1930. Pp. xxii, 586. $5.00.
3 GARRETT, HENRY E., AND SCHNECK, MATTHEW R. *Psychological Tests, Methods, and Results*, pp. 84-6. New York and London: Harper and Bros., 1933. Pp. x, 137, 235. $2.75; 10s. 6d.
4 LICKERT, RENSIS. "A Multiple-Choice Revision of the Minnesota Paper Form Board." *Psychol B* 31:674 N '34.
5 QUASHA, W. R. *The Revised Minnesota Paper Form Board Test*: An Experiment in Test Construction. Unpublished master's thesis, New York University, 1935.
6 BINGHAM, WALTER VAN DYKE. *Aptitudes and Aptitude Testing*, pp. 312-3. New York and London: Harper & Brothers, 1937. Pp. ix, 390. $3.00; 10s. 6d.
7 QUASHA, WILLIAM H., AND LIKERT, RENSIS. "The Revised Minnesota Paper Form Board Test." *J Ed Psychol* 28:197-204 Mr '37.
8 PATERSON, DONALD G.; SCHNEIDLER, GWENDOLEN G.; AND WILLIAMSON, EDMUND G. *Student Guidance Techniques*, pp. 227-9. New York: McGraw-Hill Book Co., Inc., 1938. Pp. xviii, 316. $3.00. (London: McGraw-Hill Publishing Co., Ltd. 18s.)
9 SCHULTZ, RICHARD S. "Preliminary Study of an Industrial Revision of the Revised Minnesota Paper Form Board Test." *J Appl Psychol* 24:463-7 Ag '40.

Alec Rodger, Head of the Vocational Guidance Department, National Institute of Industrial Psychology, London, England. The second revision of this well-known test is characterised, it is claimed, by greater objectivity and by a reduction in scoring time. The claim is a just one. But there are matters, at least as important as these, which do not appear to have received marked attention from the authors.

In the first place, the occupational significance of the test is not discussed in the literature which accompanies the booklets. Norms, derived from the scores obtained by approximately 5,000 subjects, representative of various age and educational groups, are presented. No doubt the prospective user of the test is intended to draw his own broad conclusions about its occupational significance from the fact that groups of engineering students were found to produce higher average scores than groups of nonengineering students. The reviewer is well acquainted with the practical difficulties usually experienced by test constructors in establishing the value of their tests for vocational guidance or selection purposes, but he feels that such difficulties should, whenever possible, be faced more resolutely than they appear to have been faced by the Minnesota investigators.

Secondly, no indication is given by the authors of the extent to which success in this test is correlated with success in other tests for mechanical ability or with success in tests for general intelligence. Correlational data contained in the original report of their work is not directly relevant to this point, for the test now available is not the same as the original test. The reviewer is inclined to suspect that (on a two-factor theory of ability) the *g* saturation of the test may be quite as high as its saturation with any other factor, and his suspicions will not be removed until he is given reasonable evidence of the insecurity of their foundation. It has been found in other investigations that tests of this kind are often to a considerable extent merely nonverbal *g* tests.

A third, but relatively unimportant, flaw in the literature is to be found in its bare statement that the norms for the AA and BB series of the test are "identical." If the statement is perfectly true, it should, surely, be accompanied by a note drawing attention to this very remarkable phenomenon; if it is only approximately true, it should be modified. Doubtless the authors intended merely to suggest—perhaps very justifiably—that, for most practical purposes, the norms for the two series could be regarded as identical.

These criticisms are not intended to be purely destructive. It is clear from the data available that the test is an extremely interesting one from the vocational psychologist's point of view, and that it is worthy of very careful investigation. Could not the authors be persuaded to publish more information about it?

[1674]

Self-Administering Vocational Interest Locator, Revised Edition. Grades 9 and over; 1933-38; $1.68 per 30; 10¢ per specimen set; nontimed (30-40) minutes; N. A. Lufburrow; Baltimore, Md.: the Author, 3112 Milford Ave.

[1675]

Specific Interest Inventory: For Educational Diagnosis and Guidance. Ages 10 and over; 1932; 2 levels for each sex; $5.00 per 100; 50¢ per specimen set; nontimed (30-40) minutes; Paul P. Brainard and Frances G. Stewart; New York: Psychological Corporation.
a) FORM B. Boys: ages 10-16.
b) FORM G. Girls: ages 10-16.
c) FORM M. Men: ages 16 and over.
d) FORM W. Women: ages 16 and over.

REFERENCES

1 BRAINARD, P. P. "Interest Tests in Vocational Guidance." *Voc Guid Mag* 6:156-9 Ja '28.
2 ANDERSON, ROY N. "A Comparative Study of Three Vocational Interest Tests." *Psychol Clinic* 22:117-27 Je-Ag '33.
3 BILLINGS, ELIZABETH LOUISE. *The Use of Brainard's Specific Interest Inventories in a Secondary School.* Unpublished master's thesis, Columbia University, 1936.
4 FRYER, DOUGLAS. *The Measurement of Interests,* pp. 33-8, New York: Henry Holt and Co., Inc. 1931. Pp. xxxvi, 488. $4.50; student edition, $3.60. (London: George G. Harrap & Co., Ltd., 1937. 10s. 6d.)

Jack W. Dunlap, Associate Professor of Educational Psychology, The University of Rochester. Each of the four forms of the inventory consists of 20 groups of five items each, constructed to measure the individual's interest in a particular *mode* of expressing activity, such as physical work, mechanical work, vocal expression, experimenting, creative imagination, etc. The items in the adult forms differ from those in the adolescent forms only in that they are stated in more mature language. The forms for males are not identical in the groups of human modes of expression with those for females, and where the identical mode is used, the form of the statements is changed.

The subject is required to indicate his reaction to each item on a five point scale, where 1 means "dislike very much"; 2, "dislike it somewhat"; 3, "neutral or indifferent"; 4, "like it somewhat"; and 5, "like it very much." The average time for marking the blank is 30 minutes, and it may be filled out without supervision. In addition to the 100 items mentioned above, there are in each form 10 groups of statements with identical headings in which the subject is to underline those statements he is interested in and to double underline those of particular interest. The phrases are identical for the B and M blanks, and for the G and W blanks.

A score is determined for each mode of expression, and twenty modes are then ranked in descending order as to score. The examiner then looks at the first three or four modes, sees what general field is suggested, and notes this on a special blank. The next three modes are also examined and again the suggested field recorded. Finally, those modes are located that are least liked, i.e., have the smallest score. Special consideration is given those items marked 4 and 5 in the modes headed outdoor, scientific, experiment, observation, and creative imagination. Finally, the items underlined are examined and those that seem to fit in with the vocations suggested are recorded. The author states, "A definite vocational pattern now emerges, consisting of certain combinations of likes, limited by certain dislikes, and supported by items throughout the test marked 4 or 5, and by underlines. Select the occupation suggested most consistently by all factors, and apply other criteria such as intelligence, finances, personality, etc."

For the men's and boy's blanks a more mechanical method of scoring is proposed for various occupations. Certain items have been designated as indicative of interest in a given field, for example, 37 items supposedly indicate interest in agriculture. The number of items allocated to this group that the subject has marked with a 4 or 5 are determined and divided by 37 to give an indication of "fitness for the field." "Eighty per cent is considered to be standard. Anything less than that indicates same lack in the field."

No objective data are given as to the reliability or validity of the blank. However, some evidence as to reliability is given in terms of consistency of individuals as to order of groups on two testings. For sixty ninth-graders, foot-rule coefficients of consistency varied from .13 to .94 with an average of .68.

In view of the evidence given by the author, and a careful examination of the forms, the following conclusions are drawn: (*a*) The blank has merit and deserves consideration as a measure of interest. (*b*) More objective data as to the statistical validity, reliability, and the results of using the tests should be given. (*c*) The test is relatively simple to score, but will require care in recording underlined items and items marked 4 or 5. (*d*) It would appear that considerable instruction and practice is needed to interpret the results. A set of sample results to be interpreted by the prospective administrator, together with the authors' interpretation, would be valuable. (*e*) Data as to norms should be provided for the so-called "mathematical scores."

M. R. Trabue, Dean of the School of Education, The Pennsylvania State College. The publisher's catalogue describes the *Specific Interest Inventory* as follows: "An instrument to analyze tendencies which are significant in vocations. Each form includes 20 groups of 5 questions each, covering different phases of a particular mode of expression, and stated in terms of specific experiences."

The multigraphed four-page manual distributed with the test blanks suggests that the individual's record be listed under each head—"Outdoor, Scientific, Experiment, Observation, Creative Imagination," and the like. "A definite vocational pattern now emerges, consisting of certain combinations of likes, limited by certain dislikes, and supported by items

throughout the test marked 4 or 5, and by underlines. Select the occupation suggested most consistently by all factors, and apply other criteria such as intelligence, finances, personality, etc." One magazine article is cited, in which a study is reported of the persistence of 300 men in an engineering school—"43 engineers dropped out whose interest scores were above median and 62 dropped out whose scores were below median."

In the judgment of the reviewer, these inventories should not have been released for general use by untrained examiners. No group of five questions is likely to provide a highly reliable index of the amount of "Outdoor" interest or of "Scientific" interest. Even if these "basic interest groups" were each known to be reliably indicated by one's responses to five questions, not enough is known yet regarding the combinations of different "basic interest groups" that make success possible in various vocations. Relatively untrained and inexperienced persons will tend to take the scores of such instruments as these entirely too seriously or to give them no confidence at all. These and similar tools need extensive study, experimentation, and improvement at the hands of competent vocational psychologists before they are distributed for general use. It is unfortunate that those who make tests feel the financial necessity of selling them before adequate scientific evidence of their values and limitations has been collected and published.

For a review by Everett B. Sackett, see 1176.

[1676]

Stanford Scientific Aptitude Test. Entrants to schools of engineering and science; 1929-30; 1 form; $4 per 25; 50¢ per specimen set; nontimed (60-120) minutes; D. L. Zyve; Stanford University, Calif.: Stanford University Press.

REFERENCES

1 Zyve, D. L. *An Experimental Study of Scientific Aptitude.* Unpublished doctor's thesis, Stanford University, 1926.
2 Zyve, D. L. "A Test of Scientific Aptitude." *J Ed Psychol* 18:525-46 N '27.
3 Bingham, Walter Van Dyke. *Aptitudes and Aptitude Testing,* pp. 348-9. New York and London: Harper & Brothers, 1937. Pp. ix, 390. $3.00; 10*s*. 6*d*.

A. B. Crawford, Director of the Department of Personnel Study and Bureau of Appointments and Professor of Psychology, Yale University. The *Stanford Scientific Aptitude Test* (also called the Zyve test after its author) represents an ingenious attempt to measure directly certain mental factors or thought-processes presumably important for success in science. The test is composed of numerous exercises, each presenting problems designed to sample students' judgment, observation, reasoning power, etc., in ways which appraise not their *present* scientific achievement or knowledge; but rather their aptitude for acquiring such knowledge and consequently for contributing to *future* achievements in this division of learning. It is, therefore, essentially intended to serve as an index of educability in that particular area.

The various subtests employed in the hope of providing a composite measure of scientific aptitude (considered in the author's Explanatory Booklet to be a "complex conglomerate of mental and character traits") bear the following descriptive labels or titles: Experimental Bent; Clarity of Definition; Suspended versus Snap Judgment; Reasoning; Inconsistencies; Fallacies; Induction, Deduction, and Generalization; Caution and Thoroughness; Discrimination of Values in Selecting and Arranging Experimental Data; Accuracy of Interpretation; and Accuracy of Observation. The relative weights of subtest scores on these sections, as contributions to the total score, range from two to seven. There is no evidence that these weightings are other than arbitrary.

A mere glance at the titles just quoted shows what a wide and ambitious extent of mental traits—quite variant in specificity—this instrument purports to measure; and all within the space of 14 pages! Its reach far exceeds its grasp, as might be expected from the small number of individual items or problems allotted to each of the dozen subtests. There lies the undeniable weakness of this project. Even if its components had true separate significance, which is doubtful (compare the merger of "induction, deduction, and generalization" in Exercise S, with Thurstone's segregation of inductive and deductive reasoning), each of them would have to be extended, for satisfactory results, much beyond its present content of a few items only. One might surmise that adequate coverage of all the complex thinking abilities which this test sets out to evaluate in two hours could hardly be accomplished with success in less than six or eight. The consequence of its attempting so wide a range within such brief compass is to chop its contents up into subtests so short that their individual or total yield is quite unreliable.

The Explanatory Booklet concerning this test barely mentions reliability (in a footnote and with no indication of how the coefficients, there rather questionably employed to "correct" the validity coefficient for attenuation, were derived). Some evidence, based upon rather small numbers of subjects, is offered as to its validity; determined (*a*) through correlating test scores with the subjective ranking of 50 research students (21 in chemistry, 10 in physics, and 19 in electrical engineering) by 6 faculty representatives of those departments; and (*b*) through comparison of these "criterion group" scores on the test, with those made by "unselected" Stanford freshmen and by 79 other first-year students "intending to major either in science or engineering." While scores of the more advanced (criterion group) research scholars were distinctly higher than those of either freshman group, distributions of the "unselected" and the "science or engineering" freshmen, respectively, showed practically no difference. By an extraordinary *tour de force*, or sheer naïveté, Zyve deduces from these data "satisfactory proof of the validity of the SAT." But if the latter is intended to show *aptitude* for scientific studies, the performance of advanced "research" students or faculty members (21 in number who made the highest scores reported thereon) scarcely seems an appropriate index of its validity. Moreover, if Stanford freshmen expecting to enter science or engineering show no more educational aptitude (as thus measured) for these rather specialized fields than do "unselected" freshmen, something is curiously wrong either with matriculation guidance at Stanford or with this test. The reviewer, having both a high respect for Stanford and personal experience with the test in question, unhesitatingly attributes to the latter this anomaly.

Experimental administration of the Zyve test some years ago to a representative group of Yale freshmen (143 in number; considerably larger than the "criterion group" utilized originally for validation of this instrument) yielded the following results: (*a*) Validity—.30 (as indicated by correlation of test-scores in the fall with subsequent year-grades in science or pre-engineering courses). (*b*) Reliability—.60 (for *entire* test, by the method either of split-half, or of paired successive subtest, scores). Reliabilities for these separate subdivisions, where obtainable at all (i.e., when the number of individual items in an exercise permitted such an estimate) were still lower.

As stated earlier, the Zyve test is ingenious, and has interesting, provocative features. Unfortunately, it seems not to have been adequately "tried and proven" initially; nor has it ever been revised. No further data as to its validity (such as might, for example, have been sought through follow-up studies of the Stanford freshmen whose score distributions are depicted in the Explanatory Booklet; or its later administration to other groups) has been published since the test and Explanatory Booklet first appeared ten years ago. In fact, neither has been altered from its original form. Improvement of this instrument through further experimentation, item-analyses, and extension of its most promising sections is both desirable and necessary if it is to serve dependably the purpose for which it was designed. As the test stands, without either change in its content, or new evidence adduced in support of its value, it cannot be recommended. The chief beneficiary of its continued distribution would seem to be the Stanford University Press, whose announcements concerning it are as perennially optimistic as florid seed catalogues. Indeed, on the very day this review was written, there arrived from that press a "new test catalogue" advertising this same Stanford (Zyve) Scientific Aptitude Test as follows: "A test to detect those basic traits which comprise an aptitude for science or engineering." A measure which actually performed that function would be invaluable; but evidence as to the power of this particular instrument to do so is negative rather than positive. Consequently, neither students nor their educational advisors should place any reliance thereon. However, it will no doubt continue to be used (even if unimproved for still another decade) by vocational counselors and commercial "guidance" bureaus, since it is relatively inexpensive and easy to administer. Furthermore, it is ostensibly endorsed by Stanford University, which must give psychologists there—if they know about it—some troubled nights. That this initially promising experiment could not have been carried on to more valid and reliable forms is regrettable; that its sale in the original, unsatisfactory form is still being pushed (even by the Psychological Corporation), seems curious, to say the least.

[1677]

Stenographic Aptitude Test. Beginning secretarial students; 1939; 1 form; $4 per 100; 20¢ per specimen set; (22) minutes; George K. Bennett; New York: Psychological Corporation.

REFERENCES

1 BENNETT, GEORGE K. *Differential Aptitude Prognosis*, pp. 85-114. Unpublished doctor's thesis, Yale University, 1935.

[1678]

Tweezer Dexterity Test: Worksample No. 17. Ages 14 and over; [1928?]; 1 form; individual; worklimit (10-20) minutes; Johnson O'Connor; rents for $60 for the first year and $30 a year thereafter; the *Tweezer Dexterity Test* and the *Finger Dexterity Test* together rent for $90 the first year and $45 a year thereafter; Boston, Mass.: Human Engineering Laboratory. ($20(No. 42070); Chicago, Ill.: C. H. Stoelting Co.) ($11; Minneapolis, Minn.: Mechanical Engineering Department, University of Minnesota.)

REFERENCES

1 O'CONNOR, JOHNSON. *Born That Way*, pp. 56-9, 174-5, 179-180, 182-204, 216-7. Baltimore, Md.: Williams & Wilkins Co., 1928. Pp. 323. $2.00.
2 WELLS, F. L. "Comparative Reliability in Tests of Motor Aptitude." *J Genetic Psychol* 37:318-20 Je '30.
3 BERGEN, GARRET L. *Use of Tests in the Adjustment Service*, p. 46. Adjustment Service Series Report [No.] 4. New York: American Association for Adult Education, 1935. Pp. 70. Paper. Out of print.
4 DVORAK, BEATRICE JEANNE. *Differential Occupational Ability Patterns*. Publications of the Employment Stabilization Research Institute, University of Minnesota, Vol. 3, No. 8. Minneapolis, Minn.: University of Minnesota Press, February 1935. Pp. 46. $1.00. Paper.
5 GREEN, HELEN I., AND BERMAN, ISABEL R.; under the direction of Donald G. Paterson and M. R. Trabue. *A Manual of Selected Occupational Tests for Use in Public Employment Office*, pp. 5-7, 9, 23-31. University of Minnesota, Bulletins of the Employment Stabilization Research Institute, Vol. 2, No. 3. Minneapolis, Minn.: University of Minnesota Press, July 1936. Pp. 31. $0.50. Paper.
6 PATERSON, DONALD G., AND DARLEY, JOHN G., with the assistance of Richard M. Elliott. *Men, Women, and Jobs*. Minneapolis, Minn.: University of Minnesota Press, 1936. Pp. v, 145. $1.50. (London: Oxford University Press. 9s.)
7 BINGHAM, WALTER VAN DYKE. *Aptitudes and Aptitude Testing*, pp. 284-286. New York and London: Harper & Brothers, 1937. Pp. ix, 390. $3.00; 10s. 6d.
8 BROWN, FRED. "Selective Tests for Dental School Candidates." *Oral Hyg* 27:1172-7 S '37.
9 CANDEE, BEATRICE, AND BLUM, MILTON. "Report of a Study Done in a Watch Factory." *J Appl Psychol* 21:572-82 O '37.
10 HARRIS, ALBERT J. "The Relative Significance of Measures of Mechanical Aptitude, Intelligence, and Previous Scholarship for Predicting Achievement in Dental School." *J Appl Psychol* 21:513-21 O '37.
11 O'CONNOR, JOHNSON. *Administration and Norms for the Finger Dexterity Test, Worksample 16, and the Tweezer Dexterity Test, Worksample 18*. Human Engineering Laboratory, Technical Report, No. 16. Boston, Mass.: the Laboratory, 1938. Pp. x, 136. $1.00. Paper, mimeographed.
12 PATERSON, DONALD G.; SCHNEIDLER, GWENDOLEN G.; AND WILLIAMSON, EDMUND G. *Student Guidance Techniques*, pp. 237-40. New York: McGraw-Hill Book Co., Inc., 1938. Pp. xviii, 316. $3.00. (London: McGraw-Hill Publishing Co., Ltd. 18s.)
13 BLUM, MILTON L. "A Contribution to Manual Aptitude Measurement in Industry: The Value of Certain Dexterity Measures for the Selection of Workers in a Watch Factory." *J Appl Psychol* 24:381-416 Ag '40.

Morris S. Viteles, Associate Professor Psychology, and Albert S. Thompson, Instructor in Psychology, The University of Pennsylvania. This test, like O'Connor's *Finger Dexterity Test,* is well known and has had a somewhat similar history. Since the *Tweezer Dexterity Test* is considered a companion to the *Finger Dexterity Test,* the two have often been included in the same test battery.

Reports by the University of Minnesota Employment Stabilization Research Institute [4, 5, 6] and Bingham's text [7] represent the best sources of information on this test. Recent studies [9, 10] have shown the test to be of little value in predicting achievement in dental school but to be of considerable value in differentiating watchmakers from the general population.

The present equivocal position of the test as an instrument for forecasting vocational achievement is well reflected in Bingham's statement that "with the exception of workers engaged in fine instrument assembly jobs, the actual test achievements of large numbers of people succeeding or failing in ... occupations have not been published; and so the counselor has to rely largely on his good sense to guide him when considering what level of tweezer dexterity might be desirable in a specific occupation." [7]

One major handicap to the use of the test is uncertainty as to its reliability. In 1930 F. L. Wells suggested modifications of the board and of administrative procedures designed to reduce the variability of the scores. [2] Practically all the studies, nevertheless, have been made with the original board (known as O'Connor's *Worksample No. 17*) and instructions. A 1938 report [11] of the Human Engineering Laboratory of the Stevens Institute of Technology, reports the development of *Worksample No. 18*—a board constructed in line with Wells' suggestions, and including countersunk holes to reduce the possibility of jamming or catching of sleeves on the inserted pins— and in the future this will be the type of board leased or rented for use by the Human Engineering Laboratory. However, adequate data on the reliability of the new board, as on that of the old, is yet to be furnished. In general, much remains to be done with this test in the way of acceptable experimental analysis to make it a useful instrument in psychological practice.

[1679]

Vocational Aptitude Examination. Male high school graduates; 1935; 1 form; $4.00 per 25; $1.00 for manual, keys, and norms; 25¢ per sample test; part nontimed (85-100) minutes; Glen U. Cleeton and C. W. Mason; New York, N. Y.: Psychological Corporation.

REFERENCES

1 MASON, CHARLES W. *The Possibilities of an Objective Executive Aptitude Test.* Unpublished master's thesis, University of Buffalo, 1930. Pp. 65.
2 CLEETON, GLEN U., AND MASON, CHARLES W. *Executive Ability*: Its Discovery and Development. Yellow Springs, Ohio: Antioch Press, 1934. Pp. xvi, 210. $2.00.

3 MASON, CHARLES W., AND CLEETON, GLEN U. "Measuring Executive Ability." *Personnel J* 13:277-9 F '35.

Harold D. Carter, Research Associate, Institute of Child Welfare, The University of California. This examination was developed primarily for the measurement of executive ability. It appears to consist of a hard group test of intelligence, plus some information tests, an interest inventory, and a personality inventory. Those wishing to understand the method of approach will have to buy the authors' book entitled *Executive Ability*. In this book, analysis of the actual duties of modern executives furnishes an explanation of the choice of tests. Considerable thought has been given to the problem of measurement of executive ability, and the tests have a sound basis in job analysis and test work aimed at suitable quantification of the data needed for selection of executives. As the authors make clear, the tests are not quite adequate for the selection of men for executive positions, but they serve as a good basis for the elimination of those definitely without executive ability. This statement seems to be substantiated. However, such a claim could be made for any one of several tests.

Users of the test will be inconvenienced because the test is expensive and is not accompanied by a properly organized manual. The general explanations, scoring keys, instructions for administering, and interpretative material are not combined into a single booklet. Furthermore, the method of construction and validation is not made clear until one buys and studies a book and reads articles available only in scattered periodicals. Since the timed parts of the test take 61 minutes actual working time, the examination will be unsuitable for administration in most college classes. The scoring is objective, and can be made fairly rapid, but in the interests of convenience the user must make his own stencils and keys. The mimeographed set of keys is rather bulky, somewhat inconvenient, not perfectly accurate, and not arranged in a form which permits efficient scoring.

The materials offered for the interpretation of the test scores are not adequate. Apparently the reliability of this test is not known, and its validity is most inadequately expressed. There is, of course, no indication of the probable error of a score. The test has not been widely used, and the tentative norms are obviously inadequate. Medians are given for the separate tests and for the total score, for college students, for a group of accountants, and for a small group of business executives. These medians alone are not particularly useful, and the few sentences given in explanation are not convincing. Research has indicated to the authors some tendencies in scores of different groups, but data furnished with the tests are insufficient for fusing these indications into a definite judgment suitable for use by counselors. The norms are insufficiently quantified; larger groups should be tested, and percentile scores or standard scores should be furnished. High scores on the tests in general may be interpreted as indicating executive aptitude. High scores on Test 3 may indicate aptitude for sales work, especially if accompanied by lower scores on Tests 1, 2, 4, 5, and 6. High scores on Tests 1, 2, 4, 5, and 6 may indicate aptitude for technical work, especially if accompanied by lower scores on the parts of Test 8. But these tendencies which may be revealed by study of means for groups may lead to serious error in the classification of individuals. In the absence of definite correlational evidence of the reliability of the test, one is justified in questioning the reliability of such indications based upon the use of test score differences.

However, this test should not be lightly dismissed. Much care has gone into its construction, and enough work has been done to justify the belief that the test measures executive ability. Examination of the test suggests that it may turn out to be very practical, and widely useful. It may permit classification of individuals into executive groups, sales groups, technical groups, and clerical groups. Although the test looks promising, some spade work remains to be done before these values can be regarded as demonstrated.

M. R. Trabue, Dean of the School of Education, The Pennsylvania State College. This test includes eight different subtests, one of which is further subdivided into five distinct parts. Each of the twelve subtests is to be given a separate score and is to have its own local distribution of scores made, from which local norms are to be determined. A mimeographed report, supplied with the examination, gives the following "data on 450 miscellaneous cases, including executives, salesmen, accountants, engineers, and research workers":

median, third quartile, lower quartile, standard deviation, and reliability coefficient. The reliability coefficients given for the various tests range from .80 to .86; and for the total of Tests 1-6 inclusive, .94 is the reported reliability.

The mimeographed "Suggestions for interpretation of score patterns" attempts to give the user of the tests aid in their practical interpretation by such notes as the following: "Executives with general administrative and supervisory responsibilities tend to score above the median on Tests 1 to 6 inclusive." "Sales aptitude for fields requiring limited general ability is indicated when the median comparisons for Tests 1 and 3 are more favorable than the average for Tests 1, 2, 5, and 6." "Engineers, research, and technical groups tend to exceed the medians on Tests 2 and 4."

In the hands of a competent psychologist, such suggestions would be very useful, although less helpful than the actual distributions of scores made by general executives, salesmen of limited general ability, and other groups. In the hands of persons of less experience in psychological testing, suggestions of this type may lead to mechanical interpretations that cannot possibly be justified by the facts.

If one could be sure that no guidance or actual employment of men would be based on the results of these tests, except by persons who had read and fully understood the book entitled *Executive Ability: Its Discovery and Development,* [2] one could be more optimistic about the usefulness of the examination scores, for the authors have presented in the book most of the warnings needed in using such tests. The test forms now for sale are not, however, those directly reported upon in the text.

The authors have faced squarely an important task: the development of instruments for the selection of executives. They have approached the problem intelligently and have produced a trial form of an examination that offers considerable promise of being helpful in the selection of executives. The examination is only in tentative form, however, and cannot be turned over without many warnings to untrained examiners. The authors cannot be criticized for wanting to obtain test records from many different executives, but they have run a real risk in assuming that everyone who tries to use the examination will be familiar with their suggestions for caution in interpretation, which appear in the book only. Their plans for further validation and improvement of the examination are, in this reviewer's judgment, quite sound, but the administration and interpretation of the tests should not be turned over to inexperienced and untrained examiners.

[1679.1]

Vocational Guidance Questionnaire. High school; 1940; 1 form; 75¢ per 25; $2 per 100; 10¢ per specimen set; nontimed; Anthony J. Scholter; Milwaukee, Wis.: Department of Education, Archdiocese of Milwaukee.

[1680]

Vocational Interest Blank for Men, Revised. Ages 17 and over; 1927-38; revised scoring scales are available for measuring maturity of interest, masculinity-femininity, studiousness, thirty-five occupations, and six occupational groups (I, II, V, VIII, IX, X): Group I: artist, psychologist, architect, physician, and dentist; Group II: mathematician, engineer, chemist; Group III: production manager; Group IV: farmer, carpenter, printer, mathematics-physical science teacher, policeman, forest service man; Group V: Y.M.C.A. physical director, personnel manager, Y.M.C.A. secretary, city school superintendent, minister; Group VI: musician; Group VII: certified public accountant; Group VIII: accountant, office man, purchasing agent, banker; Group IX: sales manager, real estate salesman, life insurance salesman; Group X: advertising man, lawyer, author-journalist; Group XI: president of a manufacturing concern; 1 form; $2.00 per 25; 50¢ per 25 report blanks; $1 per scoring scale; 2 to 9 scales, 80¢ each; 10 or more scales, 70¢ each; $2.25 per 100 machine-scorable answer sheets; $5.00 per machine-scorable scale; nontimed (40) minutes; Edward K. Strong, Jr.; Stanford University, Calif.: Stanford University Press.

REFERENCES

1 COWDERY, KARL M. "Measurement of Professional Attitudes: Differences between Lawyers, Physicians and Engineers." *J Personnel Res* 5:131-41 Ag '26.
2 STRONG, EDWARD K., JR. "Interest Analysis of Personnel Managers." *J Personnel Res* 5:235-42 S '26.
3 STRONG, EDWARD K., JR. "An Interest Test for Personnel Managers." *J Personnel Res* 5:194-203 S '26.
4 STRONG, EDWARD K., JR. "Differentiation of Certified Public Accountants from Other Occupational Groups." *J Ed Psychol* 18:227-38 Ap '27.
5 STRONG, EDWARD K., JR. "Vocational Guidance of Engineers." *Ind Psychol* 2:291-8 Je '27.
6 STRONG, EDWARD K., JR. "Vocational Guidance of Executives." *J Appl Psychol* 11:331-47 O '27.
7 STRONG, EDWARD K., JR. "Vocational Interest Test." *Ed Rec* 8:107-21 Ap '27.
8 HOGG, MARY I. "Occupational Interests of Women." *Personnel J* 6:331-7 F '28.
9 STRONG, EDWARD K., JR. "Diagnostic Value of the Vocational Interest Test." *Ed Rec* 10:59-68 Ja '29.
11 STRONG, EDWARD K., JR. "Interests of Engineers: A Basis for Vocational Guidance." *Personnel J* 7:441-54 Ap '29.
12 RULON, PHILLIP JUSTIN, AND ARDEN, WESLEY. "A Scoring Technique for Tests Having Multiple Item-Weightings." *Personnel J* 9:235-41 O '30.
13 STRONG, EDWARD K., JR. "Procedure for Scoring an Interest Test." *Psychol Clinic* 19:63-72 Ap '30.
14 STRONG, EDWARD K., JR., AND MACKENZIE, HOPE. "Permanence of Interests of Adult Men." *J Social Psychol* 1:152-9 F '30.
15 GUNDLACH, RALPH H., AND GERUM, ELIZABETH. "Vocational Interests and Types of Ability." *J Ed Psychol* 22:505-11 O '31.
16 SHELLOW, SADIE MYERS. "Vocational Interest Blank as an Aid to Interviewing." *Personnel J* 9:379-84 F '31.
17 STRONG, EDWARD K., JR. *Change of Interests with Age*: Based on Examinations of More Than Two Thousand Men between the Ages of Twenty and Sixty Representing Eight Occupations. Foreword by Walter R. Miles. Stanford University, Calif.: Stanford University Press, 1931. Pp. xix, 235. $4.00. (London: Oxford University Press. 18s.)
18 THURSTONE, L. L. "A Multiple Factor Study of Vocational Interests." *Personnel J* 10:198-205 O '31.
19 GOODFELLOW, LOUIS D. "A Study of the Interests and Personality Traits of Prospective Teachers." *Ed Adm and Sup* 18:649-58 D '32.
20 HOLCOMB, G. W., AND LASLETT, H. R. "A Prognostic Study of Engineering Aptitude." *J Appl Psychol* 16:107-15 Ap '32.
21 STEINMETZ, HARRY CHARLES. "Measuring Ability to Fake Occupational Interest." *J Appl Psychol* 16:123-30 Ap '32.
22 STRONG, EDWARD K., JR., AND GREEN, HELEN J. "Short Cuts to Scoring an Interest Test." *J Appl Psychol* 16:1-8 F '32.
23 WOOD, BEN D. "New Method for Scoring the Strong Interest Test." *Sch and Soc* 36:718 D 3 '32.
24 ANDERSON, ROY N. "A Comparative Study of Three Vocational Interest Tests." *Psychol Clinic* 22:117-27 Je-Ag '33.
25 CARTER, HAROLD D., AND STRONG, E. K., JR. "Sex Differences in Occupational Interests of High School Students." *Personnel J* 12:166-75 O '33.
26 STRONG, EDWARD K., JR. "Interest Maturity." *Personnel J* 12:77-90 Ag '33.
27 ACHILLES, P. S., AND SCHULTZ, R. S. "Characteristics of Life Insurance Salesmen." *Personnel J* 12:260-3 F '34.
28 BERMAN, ISABEL R.; DARLEY, JOHN G.; AND PATERSON, DONALD G. *Vocational Interest Scales*: An Analysis of Three Questionnaires in Relation to Occupational Classification and Employment Status, pp. 5-23, 34-5. University of Minnesota, Bulletins of the Employment Stabilization Research Institute, Vol. 3, No. 5. Minneapolis, Minn.: University of Minnesota Press, August 1934. Pp. 35. $0.50. Paper.
29 Educational Records Bureau. *1934 Achievement Test Program in Independent Schools*: A Summary of the Results of Achievement Tests Given in Elementary and Secondary Independent Schools in April, 1934, pp. 8-13. Educational Records Bulletin No. 13. New York: the Bureau, 1934. Pp. iii, 64, 9. $1.50. Paper, lithotyped.
30 KELLEY, TRUMAN L. "The Scoring of Alternative Responses with Reference to Some Criterion." *J Ed Psychol* 25:504-10 O '34.
31 MANN, CLAIR V. *Experimentation to Discover Measurable Aptitudes for Engineering*, pp. 14-18 and charts 23-34. Journal of Educational Research, Vol. 1, No. 2. Rolla, Mo.: the Author, 210 East Eighth St., June 1934. Pp. 37. $0.50. Paper.
32 SEGAL, DAVID, AND BRINTLE, S. L. "The Relation of Occupational Interest Scores as Measured by the Strong Interest Blank to Achievement Test Results and College Marks in Certain College Subject Groups." *J Ed Res* 27:442-5 F '34.
33 STRONG, EDWARD K., JR. "Aptitudes versus Attitudes in Vocational Guidance." *J Appl Psychol* 18:501-15 Ag '34.
34 STRONG, EDWARD K., JR. "Classification of Occupations by Interests." *Personnel J* 12:301-13 Ap '34.
35 STRONG, EDWARD K., JR. "Interests and Sales Ability." *Personnel J* 13:204-16 D '34.
36 STRONG, EDWARD K., JR. "Permanence of Vocational Interests." *J Ed Psychol* 25:336-44 My '34.
37 STRONG, EDWARD K., JR. "Vocational Interest Test." *Occupations* 12:49-56 Ap '34.
38 BERGEN, GARRET L. *Use of Tests in the Adjustment Service*, pp. 52-4. Adjustment Service Series Report [No.] 4. New York: American Association for Adult Education, 1935. Pp. 70. Paper. Out of print.
39 BURNHAM, PAUL S., AND CRAWFORD, ALBERT B. "The Vocational Interests and Personality Test Scores of a Pair of Dice." *J Ed Psychol* 26:508-12 O '35.
40 CARTER, H. D.; PYLES, M. K.; AND BRETNALL, E. P. "A Comparative Study of Factors in Vocational Interest Scores of High School Boys." *J Ed Psychol* 26:81 98 F '35.
41 STRONG, EDWARD K., JR. "Predictive Value of the Vocational Interest Test." *J Ed Psychol* 26:331-49 My '35.
42 STRONG, E. K., JR., AND CARTER, H. D. "Efficiency Plus Economy in Scoring an Interest Test." *J Ed Psychol* 26:579-86 N '35.
43 BILLS, MARION A., AND WARD, L. W. "Testing Salesmen of Casualty Insurance." *Personnel J* 15:55-8 Je '36.
44 FLINNER, IRA A. "The Strong Vocational Interest Test and Its Use in Secondary Schools." *Ed Rec* 17:Sup 9:138-40 Ja '36.
45 STRONG, EDWARD K., JR. "Interests of Men and Women." *J Social Psychol* 7:49-67 F '36.
46 BINGHAM, WALTER VAN DYKE. *Aptitudes and Aptitude Testing*, pp. 72-5, 78-80, 354-7. New York and London: Harper and Brothers, 1937. Pp. ix, 390. $3.00; 10s. 6d.
47 MOSIER, CHARLES, I. "Factors Influencing the Validity of a Scholastic Interest Scale." *J Ed Psychol* 28:188-96 Mr '37.
48 WILLIAMSON, E. G. "An Analysis of the Young-Estabrooks Studiousness Scale." *J Appl Psychol* 21:260-4 Je '37.
49 YOUNG, C. W., AND ESTABROOKS, G. H. "Report on the Young-Estabrooks Studiousness Scale for Use with the Strong Vocational Interest Blank for Men." *J Ed Psychol* 28:176-87 Mr '37.
50 BILLS, MARION A. "Relation of Scores in Strong's Interest Analysis Blanks to Success in Selling Casualty Insurance." *J Appl Psychol* 22:97-104 F '38.
51 BILLS, MARION A., AND DAVIDSON, CHARLES M. "Study of Inter-relation of Items on Bernreuter Personality Inventory and Strong's Interest Analysis Test, Part VIII, and their Relation to Success and Failure in Selling Casualty Insurance." *Psychol B* 35:677 N '38.

52 CARTER, HAROLD D., AND JONES, MARY COVER. "Vocational Attitude Patterns in High-School Students." *J Ed Psychol* 29:321-34 My '38.

53 CROFT, LYSLE W. *An Empirical Comparison of the Thurstone Vocational Interest Schedule and the Strong Vocational Interest Blank Among Senior High School and Freshmen College Students.* Unpublished doctor's thesis, University of Kentucky, 1938.

54 DARLEY, JOHN G. "A Preliminary Study of Relations between Attitude, Adjustment, and Vocational Interest Tests." *J Ed Psychol* 29:467-73 S '38.

55 DWYER, PAUL S. "An Analysis of 19 Occupational Scores of the Strong Vocational Interest Test Given to 418 Students Entering the University of Michigan Medical School during the Years 1928, 1929, 1930." *J Appl Psychol* 22:8-16 F '38.

56 KOPAS, JOSEPH S. "The Point-Tally: A Modified Method of Scoring the Strong's Vocational Interest Blank." *J Appl Psychol* 22:426-36 Ag '38.

57 McQUITTY, LOUIS L. "An Approach to the Measurement of Individual Differences in Personality." *Char and Pers* 7:81-95 S '38.

58 PATERSON, DONALD G.; SCHNEIDLER, GWENDOLEN G.; AND WILLIAMSON, EDMUND G. *Student Guidance Techniques,* pp. 175-81. New York: McGraw-Hill Book Co., Inc., 1938. Pp. xviii, 316. $3.00. (London: McGraw-Hill Publishing Co., Ltd. 18s.)

59 SIMKEVICH, JOHN CHARLES. *An Item-Analysis of Strong's Interest Inventory:* With Recommendations for Lowering the Age Level to Which It May Be Applied. Unpublished master's thesis, Brown University, 1938. Pp. 36.

60 STARBUCK, EDMUND O. *Short-Cut Scoring of the Strong Vocational Interest Blank.* Unpublished master's thesis, Ohio State University, 1938. Pp. 57.

61 STUIT, DEWEY B. "A Study of the Vocational Interests of a Group of Teachers College Freshmen." *J Appl Psychol* 22:527-33 O '38.

62 TRAXLER, ARTHUR E. "Ratings of High School Boys on the Musician Scale of the Strong Vocational Interest Blank," pp. 57-8. In *1938 Achievement Testing Program in Independent Schools.* By Educational Records Bureau. Educational Records Bulletin No. 24, New York: the Bureau, June 1938. Pp. xi, 59, 14. $1.50. Paper, lithotyped.

63 WILLIAMSON, E. G. "A Further Analysis of the Young-Estabrooks Studiousness Scale." *J Appl Psychol* 22:105 F '38.

64 ESTES, S. G. AND HORN, D. "Interest Patterns as Related to Fields of Concentration among Engineering Students." *J Psychol* 7:29-36 Ja '39.

65 DYER, DOROTHY T. "The Relation between Vocational Interests of Men in College and Their Subsequent Occupational Histories for Ten Years." *J Appl Psychol* 23:280-8 Ap '39.

65.1 CARTER, HAROLD D. "The Development of Vocational Attitudes." *J Consulting Psychol* 4:185-91 S-O '40.

66 SARBIN, THEODORE R., AND BERDIE, RALPH F. "Relation of Measured Interests to the Allport-Vernon Study of Values." *J Appl Psychol* 24:287-96 Je '40.

67 SEDER, MARGARET. "Group Scales versus Occupational Scales for the Strong Vocational Interest Blank," pp. 51-6. In *1940 Achievement Testing Program in Independent Schools and Supplementary Studies.* Educational Records Bureau Staff. Educational Records Bulletin, No. 30. New York: the Bureau, June 1940. Pp. xii, 76. $1.50. Paper, lithotyped.

68 SEDER, MARGARET. "Some Data on the Revised Strong Vocational Interest Blank," pp. 48-50. In *1939 Fall Testing Program in Independent Schools and Supplementary Studies.* Educational Records Bulletin, No. 29. New York: Educational Records Bureau, January 1940. Pp. x, 50. $1.00. Paper.

69 SEDER, MARGARET. "Vocational Interests of Professional Women: Part I." *J Appl Psychol* 24:130-43 Ap '40.

70 SEDER, MARGARET. "The Vocational Interests of Professional Women: Part II." *J Appl Psychol* 24:265-72 Je '40.

71 SUPER, DONALD E. *Avocational Interest Patterns:* A Study in the Psychology of Avocations. Stanford University, Calif.: Stanford University Press, 1940. Pp. xiv, 148. $2.25. (London: Oxford University Press. 14s.)

Harold D. Carter, Research Associate, Institute of Child Welfare, The University of California. This test is based upon twenty years of research on the measurement of interests, and is at present the most outstanding of the several inventories of its type. Its advantages and limitations are primarily those inherent in the method of approach. It is undoubtedly of value in educational and vocational guidance, but the intelligent use of it demands some understanding of the technique, and some knowledge of the accumulated facts now available concerning interests, abilities, occupations, and the significance of vocational adjustment as a factor in the integration of personality.

The manual for the inventory contains a great store of information. It states clearly the purpose of the test, explains the technique, describes the standardization, contains instructions for administering and scoring, and furnishes devices for the interpretation of scores. The test may be scored by 35 different occupational scales, for which the intercorrelations are given in the manual along with a summary of the evidence on the reliability, validity, and general stability of the measures. The average reliability coefficient is .88 by the odd-even technique, .87 by the test-retest method with one week intervening, and .75 by the test-retest method with five years intervening. Norms are furnished with each published scale. In the manual is a bibliography of 35 references which furnish detailed information concerning particular aspects of the technique, and specific limitations, advantages, and applications of the test.

The test itself contains 400 items and takes about forty minutes to administer to the average person. It is not timed. The arrangement of the revised test is much more convenient than that of the earlier forms, both for persons taking the test and for those scoring it. The test is not too long; briefer inventories of this type are almost certain to be less reliable, less valid, and more liable to self-deception on the part of subjects. The type of item is not entirely self-explanatory; hence, mere inspection is no adequate basis for insight into the meaning of the scores. Persons wishing to use the test to full advantage are urged to read the manual most carefully and to read as many of the accompanying references as possible.

Psychologists who have made extensive use of this inventory in practical vocational guidance situations have reported that it has great value. This viewpoint is supported by results in the literature. The scoring is somewhat expensive, but unpublished studies by the writer indicate that about 80 per cent of those who take the test are benefited by it and feel that they get their money's worth. About 20 per cent are adversely critical. Comments by students who cooperate in such experiments indicate that in a majority of cases the test provides a correct appraisal of their attitudes. The inference is made that it provides a basis for insights which counselors could gain otherwise only through long acquaintance. I believe that the test reflects the cultural values assimilated by the individual during his life prior to the examination, and that the measures are useful in vocational guidance. Although primarily useful at the college level and with older persons, it is probably also of value when employed with selected high school students. The test results furnish some basis for insight into personality, but the method is technical and requires the good judgment and interpretative abilities of the trained psychologist. It is in a sense a projective method.

This test is a specific instrument to aid the vocational counselor, and not a panacea for all his ills. It is intended to indicate the vocation in which the individual is likely to be best satisfied in view of his interests. It is not intended to replace ability tests or aptitude tests, but rather to supplement them. It summarizes one's attitudes in terms of occupational significance, and for this purpose it is the best available test.

John G. Darley, Director of the University Testing Bureau and Assistant Professor of Psychology, The University of Minnesota. Since the last issue of the *Mental Measurements Yearbook* appeared, the revision of Strong's test has been made available. The revision includes: reduction of items from 420 to 400; increase in the number of specific occupational keys from 30 to 34; increases in the number of cases in each standardizing group; introduction of six so-called "group keys" and one new non-occupational key called "occupational level"; reduction in the range of score weights to plus 4 to minus 4. The specific occupational keys are located in functionally similar groupings by factor analysis techniques; there are more such functionally similar groupings than there were for the old form of the test. The six "group keys" now available are based on the item differentials between "men in general" and equal proportions of the representatives of specific occupations whose specific occupational keys fall together in the factor analysis. Thus, the responses of equal numbers of sales managers, life insurance salesmen, and real estate salesmen are compared with the responses of "men in general" to derive a "group key" that might

be given the general title of "business contact" or "sales" interests.

Our clinical experience with the revised test was checked in conferences with Mr. Strong. The following conclusions seem justified.

Two factors seem to operate to produce a higher proportion of A and B scores on the revised blank. These are: increases in the size (and presumably heterogeneity) of the standardizing groups; selection of a "men in general" sample more nearly proportional to United States census figures, where earlier "men in general" groups were loaded with representatives of upper-level jobs. These factors seem to offset the statistical effect of using one-half sigma rather than the semi-interquartile range as the starting point of the A grade range.

The "group keys" need further experimentation before being substituted for the specific occupational keys for this reason: even though certain keys show high intercorrelations in one group of subjects, the averages of a new group of subjects on a derived group key may be so divergent as to prevent certain of the new subjects from getting their expected proportion of A and B grades in the "group key" presumably as typical of their interests as of the interests of representatives of functionally similar occupations. The concept of the "group key" or "pillar key" is still promising, however, and if the present technical difficulty can be resolved, it may be possible to score the test first for "group keys" as a lead to dominant interests, following this with scoring for the specific keys indicated by the highest "group interests."

The "occupational level" key at present seems to this reviewer to give a clinically significant quantitative statement of "level of aspiration." Students with significantly low occupational level scores will probably find a satisfying adjustment in activities making relatively fewer demands on the worker than the more professionalized and exacting occupations in the upper ranges of socio-economic status.

Another clinical phase of interest measurement has evolved in our growing awareness of cases with no significant interest patterns, however often they may be tested. In such cases, guidance is extremely difficult and underachievement, transiency, or other symptoms may also appear. In this connection, it is to be hoped that the new interest-maturity scale will soon be available, since its use on the old form of the test made possible some diagnosis of lacking interests attributable primarily to maturity factors, rather than to more deep-seated conditions within the individual.

With this new scale—an improvement of an already invaluable measuring instrument—it seems even more imperative for users to stress pattern analyses rather than specific occupational keys, since the pattern analysis increases guidance usefulness by embracing a wider range of occupations that are functionally alike, even though specific keys are not now available for such a range. Furthermore, pattern analysis permits adjustments to be made for individual cases in terms of levels of the necessary abilities and aptitudes which will permit the realization of basic interests in actual job adjustments.

N. W. Morton, Assistant Professor of Psychology, McGill University. The immediate question for most persons concerned with the new Strong *Vocational Interest Blank* will be, "To what extent is it an improvement over the 1927 and 1930 forms?" The answer to this query, the reviewer believes, will depend largely upon whether one was convinced of the value of the Strong blank for one's own purposes in the first place. Some vocational psychologists have regarded it as undesirably rigid, laborious to score, costly in use and (because it deals only with *some* occupations of many) limited in significance. For them, there are grains of solace in the facts that the size of the scoring weights has been reduced whenever possible (and the time for scoring lessened a shade thereby), and one can now utilize the benefits of factor analysis by scoring for groups of psychologically related occupations rather than each occupation by itself. But in general the form and method are the same, and will doubtless be regarded by this group in much the same way. For other persons, more inclined to suffer its cumbrousness and other disadvantages for the sake of its positive values of thorough organization of material, extensive study of its validity, and knowledge about its relation to other psychological measurements, this new form will be attractive in several ways. First, it is more pleasingly and clearly printed. Second, odd points of inconvenience, such as the scoring of unchecked items in Part VI, have been dealt with. Third, a graphic

scheme of report is now provided which gives a more rapid picture of an individual's status, and which at the same time furnishes an idea of the better-than-chance value of his scores. Fourth, the old percentile values for each scale are replaced by the statistically more defensible standard scores, although for practical purposes letter-grades are emphasized as being easier to interpret, and as being safer anyway, since there is apparently no correlation with ability *within* the "A" group. Fifth, the size of the criterion samples has been increased to a minimum of 250 men, the number of occupations represented has been augmented, and other additions made, such as the aforementioned occupational groups and a scoring for occupational level. By this last is meant a measurement of distinction between laboring men's and business and professional men's interests (which is not individually diagnostic). The simplification of scoring by elimination of extreme weights has already been noted. This reviewer detects no deficiencies not already apparent in older forms.

There are given in the new manual no fresh data upon the validity of the *Vocational Interest Blank,* except as already published elsewhere. In this connection it is perhaps to be hoped that as time passes, data of a genetic kind are accumulating which will throw more direct light on the predictive value of the scales.

For a review by John G. Darley of an earlier edition, see 1178.

1681

Vocational Interest Blank for Women. Ages 17 and over; 1933-38; 1 form, 2 editions; scoring scales are available for measuring masculinity-femininity, and the following occupations: artist, author, dentist, housewife, lawyer, librarian, life insurance saleswoman, nurse, office worker, physician, social worker, stenographer-secretary, and high school teachers of each of the following subjects: English, mathematics-physical science, and social science; $2.00 per 25; 50¢ per 25 report blanks; $1.00 per scoring scale; $2.25 per 100 machine-scorable answer sheets; 2 to 9 scales, 80¢ each; 10 or more scales, 70¢ each; $5.00 per machine-scorable scale; Edward K. Strong, Jr.; Stanford University, Calif.: Stanford University Press.

REFERENCES

1 BERMAN, ISABEL R.; DARLEY, JOHN G.; AND PATERSON, DONALD G. *Vocational Interest Scales:* An Analysis of Three Questionnaires in Relation to Occupational Classification and Employment Status, pp. 5-6, 24-8, 35. University of Minnesota, Bulletins of the Employment Stabilization Research Institute, Vol 3, No. 5. Minneapolis, Minn.: University of Minnesota Press, August 1934. Pp. 35. $0.50. Paper.
2 BINGHAM, WALTER VAN DYKE. *Aptitudes and Aptitude Testing,* pp. 354-7. New York and London: Harper & Brothers, 1937. Pp. ix, 390. $3.00; 10s. 6d.
3 CARTER, HAROLD D., AND JONES, MARY COVER. "Vocational Attitude Patterns in High-School Students." *J Ed Psychol* 29:321-34 My '38.
4 PATERSON, DONALD G.; SCHNEIDLER, GWENDOLEN G.; AND WILLIAMSON, EDMUND G. *Student Guidance Techniques,* pp. 181-3. New York: McGraw-Hill Book Co., Inc., 1938. Pp. xviii, 316. $3.00. (London: McGraw-Hill Publishing Co., Ltd. 18s.)

5 STUIT, DEWEY B. "A Study of the Vocational Interests of a Group of Teachers College Freshmen." *J Appl Psychol* 22:527-33 O '38.

6 CRISSY, W. J. E., AND DANIEL, W. J. "Vocational Interest Factors in Women." *J Appl Psychol* 23:488-94 Ag '39.

6.1 CARTER, HAROLD D. "The Development of Vocational Attitudes." *J Consulting Psychol* 4:185-91 S-O '40.

7 DUFFY, ELIZABETH, AND CRISSY, W. J. E. "Evaluative Attitudes as Related to Vocational Interests and Academic Achievement." *J Abn and Social Psychol* 35:226-45 Ap '40.

8 SEDER, MARGARET. "Vocational Interests of Professional Women: Part I." *J Appl Psychol* 24:130-43 Ap '40.

9 SEDER, MARGARET. "The Vocational Interests of Professional Women: Part II." *J Appl Psychol* 24:265-72 Je '40.

Ruth Strang, Professor of Education, Columbia University. The *Vocational Interest Blank for Women* is not an aptitude test; it merely shows the degree of similarity between interests expressed by people taking the test and "successful" people in a limited number of occupations. A score of *A* in a particular occupation means similarity in interests and predicts a liking for the occupation, not success in it. This distinction between interests and success is quite understandable because many people succeed in occupations which they do not like.

The reported coefficients of reliability of the blank for five hundred married women, using the "odd versus even" technique stepped up by the Spearman-Brown formula, range from .74 to .94. As the reliability coefficients would undoubtedly vary with each group studied, they should be obtained for different age and occupational groups. No adequate information or validity of the blank has yet been obtained.

The following are difficulties involved in the development of the blank for women, many of which have been recognized by the author of the blank: (*a*) Women enter and continue in certain occupations for reasons other than interest in the occupation, and for that reason the criteria of success in the occupations is not entirely adequate. (*b*) The scale is standardized on adult women, whereas it is used for counseling purposes largely with young women whose interests are probably different from those of the older women. (*c*) A limited number of occupations are scaled—only seventeen, whereas the average person may be interested in as many as fifty and may possibly choose one of five hundred occupations. (*d*) The occupational groups on which the scales are validated are not homogeneous; they include a variety of positions having widely different interest values, as for example, the school nurse, the nurse in the hospital, and the visiting nurse—all of whom are included in the category, *nurse*.

In view of these limitations of the *Vocational Interest Blank for Women,* three courses of action are open to counselors of women. The first is to experiment with the more adequately developed blank for men. The second is to use the blank only in counseling women who do not know what kind of work they want to do and use the scores merely to suggest occupations for them to explore. The third course is to use the subject's responses on individual questions, rather than the scale scores, in order to obtain a general pattern of interests and leads for interviewing.

For a review by John G. Darley, see 1179.

[1682]

Vocational Interest Inventory. Grades 9-16 and adults; 1937-39; 1 form, separate inventories for men and women; $4.50 per 100; 25¢ per manual; 2¢ per machine-scorable answer sheet; nontimed (45-55) minutes; Glen U. Cleeton; Bloomington, Ill.: McKnight & McKnight.
a) MEN.
b) WOMEN.

Forrest A. Kingsbury, Associate Professor of Psychology, The University of Chicago. This inventory, designed for use in counseling high school students, but also usable with college students and adults, endeavors to rate the subject's interests in terms not of single occupations but of 9 types of related occupations. Two forms are provided, A for men, B for women, each in a 16-page pamphlet of which 3 pages are instructions; the remaining 13 pages contain 670 items, each to be marked + (yes or like) or 0 (no or dislike). A machine-scorable form is also available. The 670 items are grouped into 9 sections of 70 items each, based on occupational similarity, while a tenth "S-R" section lists 40 typical introversion-extraversion items. The inventory thus yields 10 scores, the introversion score for which a special key is provided, and 9 scores on occupational types, obtained by totaling the number of plus marks in any section.

A high score on any section indicates interests similar to those of persons of related occupations. For men these occupations are as follows: biological sciences (e.g., physician); selling (various fields); physical sciences (e.g., engineer, technologist, chemist, mathematician); social sciences (e.g., teacher, minister, social or YMCA worker); business administration (e.g., purchasing agent, business manager, clerk); legal and literary occupations (e.g., lawyer, journalist); mechanical occupations (e.g., various skilled trades); finance (e.g., accountant, statistician, banker, broker); creative or public performance occupations (e.g., actor, musician, artist). The women's inventory gives a somewhat different grouping. Letter-grade and percentile norms are provided for each form for grades 9, 10, 11, 12, college freshmen, and adults. Norms, it is implied, are identical for each of the 9 sections, although no information is given on this point. Reliability coefficients (odd vs. even) for 8 groups numbering from 150 to 1,000 range from .822 to .910, median .875. (Presumably, although not explicitly stated, these are corrected, and for the total form of 670 items, not for separately scored sections.) Repetition of administration after a month's interval showed a change of 6.1 per cent of the responses from 0 to +, or from + to 0.

Validity is inferred from the manner of selecting items. The inventory, we are told, was developed from items included in the original *Carnegie Interest Inventory*. New items were selected and classified on the basis of agreement with items of known significance. In addition, performance of 7,424 persons "successfully engaged in standard occupations" was analyzed to determine their relative standing on the 9 scales of the inventory. The highest inventory rating of each agreed with his actual occupation in 76 per cent of the cases; the first or second inventory rating, 82 per cent of the cases; and the first, second, or third inventory rating, 95 per cent.

The 24-page manual offers practical suggestions as to the use and interpretation of results in counseling and guidance. The author's position seems reasonable and moderate; he makes neither exaggerated claims for what it will do nor apologies for its inevitable limitations; but regards scores as bits of contributory evidence for the counselor.

A few errors in the edition examined will doubtless be corrected. The use of "page" when "section" is meant, both in manual and inventory, is confusing; so also is the 3-times misprint ECF for EFC on page 17. It would be interesting also to have more explicit information as to how the grouping of occupations into 9 types was effected, whether on the basis of occupational weightings of each item in other scales, or of inter-occupational correlations, or of factorial analyses of occupational interests, or otherwise.

This instrument appears to the reviewer to be a valuable and promising contribution to the techniques of counseling, yielding information which is sufficiently definite for most purposes, and at the same time obtained with sufficient ease and reliability to make it practicable and widely useful.

N. W. Morton, Assistant Professor of Psychology, McGill University. This inventory represents a successful attempt to provide in usable form a basis for judging vocational interests in terms of certain broad categories of occupations, such as biological science, selling, legal and literary occupations, etc. In accordance with much current research data and other vocational psychologists' views, the author has concluded that these broad categories offer a more valid means of estimating preferences than any attempt to specify at the outset particular callings. Like Strong's better-known *Vocational Interest Blank* the inventory utilizes, however, items referring to individual occupations as part of its material. The remaining items concern personal habits of feeling and acting, and likes and dislikes for people, things, and activities.

Each occupational group is dealt with in a subsection by itself. This has the effect of facilitating scoring, although how it may modify the attitudes of the person taking the test is a matter for conjecture. The basis of apportioning items to these subsections consists largely in the fruits of previously validated scales, such as Strong's and Manson's. New items, however, have been added by the device of considering their relation to older, well-tried ones. This occasionally results in a distribution of items difficult to rationalize, as when the item "watchmaker" is placed under the heading "biological sciences" rather than "physical science" or "mechanical occupations."

Among the more apparent assets which these inventories possess are the facts that they are put out in a handy, well-printed booklet form, are quickly scored by totaling positive responses for each section without weighting or use of minus values, and are readily interpreted. By some statistical magic or other device, raw point-scores on the nine main subsections of each form are directly comparable, as they have exactly equivalent letter grades or percentiles. No explanation is given of how this is accomplished. By way of deficiencies, either in the test itself or in the provision in the manual of information about it, there may be listed the lack of a middle category for "doubtful" responses (this is perhaps partially a consequence of the simplified method of scoring), the absence of any handy profile chart in the test booklet (which would readily fall in with the equivalent score device), and the failure of the author to give any data as to the intercorrelation between scores on each of the nine principal sections.

Determinations of the reliability of the individual scales by the split-half method indicate it to be in the neighborhood of .8 or .9, which is satisfactory, considering the nature of the functions measured. Although there is no indication as to the source of the agreement (whether a consequence of training, experience or temperament), there is demonstrated for employed adults a high degree of correlation between occupation followed and measured interest. Ninety-five per cent of the group have either their first, second, or third highest scores in the inventory scale corresponding to their occupation.

This reviewer feels that in Cleeton's *Vocational Interest Inventory*, taken altogether, we have a reasonably practical and useful addition to measuring instruments of this type. It would be desirable eventually to have information from genetic sources as to its prognostic value, but it is yet too early to expect this.

Occupations 18:347-52 F '40. Nora A. Congdon. "A Study of Cleeton's Vocational Interest Inventory." * The results of this study show that, although it is far from perfect, Cleeton's Vocational Interest Inventory is valuable as a guide in counseling students. The results of a reliable intelligence test should be used in connection with the results of the Inventory. The SR section, purporting to measure social adjustment, seems to have very little value. As an index of success in teaching, the intelligence test score appears to be the most valuable single factor for the men. For the women the Interest Inventory is quite valuable and should be used in connection with an intelligence test score. However, these results are not very reliable because they were based on small populations. In actual practice Cleeton's Inventory has proved especially valuable, when used

with intelligence and achievement tests, for counseling certain groups of students: (*a*) Those who cannot meet the requirements for the preparation of teachers. In attempting to persuade a student to change his vocational choice, objective scores and ratings such as these are often more convincing than subjective opinion. (*b*) Students who desire to teach in high school because of better salaries, but who are obviously better fitted to teach younger children. (*c*) Students who have no definite vocational goal or who have chosen a vocation for which they can not meet the preparation requirements. (*d*) Individual problem cases.

For reviews by Albert S. Thompson, M. R. Trabue, and E. G. Williamson, see 1181.

[1683]
Vocational Interest Schedule. College students; 1935-39; 1 form, 2 editions; nontimed (10-30) minutes; L. L. Thurstone; New York: Psychological Corporation.
a) 1935 EDITION. 1935; $2.00 per 25; 50¢ per specimen set.
b) MACHINE-SCORED FORM. 1939; $1.25 per 25 machine-scorable test-answer sheets; 25¢ per specimen set.

REFERENCES

1 THURSTONE, L. L. "A Multiple-Factor Study of Vocational Interests." *Personnel J* 10:198-205 O '31.
2 BINGHAM, WALTER VAN DYKE. *Aptitudes and Aptitude Testing*, pp. 75-80. New York and London: Harper & Brothers, 1937. Pp. ix, 390. $3.00; 10s. 6d.
3 CROFT, LYSLE W. *An Empirical Comparison of the Thurstone Vocational Interest Schedule and the Strong Vocational Interest Blank Among Senior High School and Freshman College Students.* Unpublished doctor's thesis, University of Kentucky, 1938.
4 LAYCOCK, S. R., AND HUTCHEON, N. B. "A Preliminary Investigation into the Problem of Measuring Engineering Aptitude." *J Ed Psychol* 30:280-8 Ap '39.

J. B. Miner, Professor of Psychology and Director of the Personnel Bureau, University of Kentucky. [Review of the 1935 Edition.] While it is useful for guidance to narrow choices to certain fields of related occupations, such value as Thurstone's blank might have in this respect is now superseded by provision for scoring the revised form of Strong's *Vocational Interest Blank* for eleven different groups. Strong's blank has the advantage that its reliability is known, and its data have been gathered from adults actually in the occupations.

The construction of Thurstone's blank and scoring method on the basis of factor analysis makes it a worth-while venture in research that has been decidedly valuable for later efforts in this direction. The self-consistency of the procedure for his group of college students leaves quite uncertain as yet its prediction value for interests in occupations they may later enter. How far interests are stabilized at the high school level is still so uncertain that the use of such blanks at that level is merely suggestive.

Unpublished results here on 350 high school seniors and college freshmen scored on both Thurstone's and Strong's blanks show that, when the occupations for Strong's blank are grouped as suggested by the Thurstone factors, the correlations between the median scores for the same individuals on the vocational groups ranged from −.03 to +.32. Without further evidence, it does not seem safe to assume that scores for a group of occupations named by Thurstone will correspond to a group of the same occupations scored on the Strong blank. It was also found that plus scores in Thurstone's groups are about as likely to agree with any one as another of seven out of twenty-one of Strong's occupations, for which both blanks were scored. The plan of the Strong blank is clearly more discriminative.

Thurstone's *Vocational Interest Schedule* is inexpensive, can be completed in fifteen minutes, and is easily scored. It might be used to introduce a vocational interview, but would be less useful for that purpose than the more comprehensive *Preference Record* of Kuder, or the *Basic Interest Questionnaire* of the National Institute of Vocational Research. Without further evidence the scores on it should not be assumed to predict scores on Strong's

blank or motivational interest in the actual vocations. Above all, a vocational counselor must be exceedingly cautious not to jump from vocational interest to the conclusion of vocational ability. It is even possible that a person's understanding of his own deep and persistent desire to enter a particular occupation would bring special success along some branch of the occupation not developed by those in the field whose interests were unlike his. He would be doing something different and distinctive in the field. For those who have had prolonged interests in one direction, their own choice of occupation may be quite as significant as their score on the interest blanks. This means that vocational interest blanks are mainly useful for those who are quite undecided. They should be used to direct attention to fields of work to be considered.

For reviews by Harold D. Carter and N. W. Morton, see 1180.

[1684*]

Vocational Inventory. Grades 8-16 and adults; 1940; 1 form; 10¢ per inventory; 5¢ per individual analysis reports; 25¢ per specimen set; nontimed (150) minutes; Curtis G. Gentry; Minneapolis, Minn.: Educational Test Bureau, Inc.

REFERENCES
1 GENTRY, CURTIS G. "Knoxville's Seven-Point Vocational Guidance Program." *Sch Executive* 59:10-2 Ap '40.

* In order to have the entry numbers continuous with the earlier publications in this series, the first entry number in the test section is 1182. The addition of 22 new entries—assigned fractional numbers—and the assignment of a double number to one test make the total number of tests listed in this volume 524.

Books and Reviews

* * * * *

The following roughly classified index has been prepared to assist readers to locate books on a particular subject. In addition to using this index, readers are urged to skim over titles and excerpts in search of works which otherwise may be overlooked.

467

BIBLIOGRAPHY AND REVIEW EXCERPTS

[B815*]

ALFANO, MARIE V. **English Vocabulary Distributions for Twenty-Nine Secondary Schools, Worksample 95, Form E.** Human Engineering Laboratory, Technical Report No. 33. Boston, Mass.: the Laboratory, 1939. Pp. vii, 58. $1.00. Paper, mimeographed.

[B816]

ALFANO, MARIE V. **Stimulus Words and Common Responses to the Free Association Test, Worksample 35, Form E.** Human Engineering Laboratory, Technical Report No. 28. Boston, Mass.: the Laboratory, 1939. Pp. vi, 98. $1.00. Paper, mimeographed.

[B817]

ALFANO, MARIE V. **Stimulus Words and Common Responses to the Free Association Test, Worksample 35, Form F.** Human Engineering Laboratory, Technical Report No. 29. Boston, Mass.: the Laboratory, 1939. Pp. vi, 98. $1.00. Paper, mimeographed.

[B818]

ALFANO, MARIE V. **Variation of Vocabulary Scores with Age and Schooling, Worksample 95.** Human Engineering Laboratory, Technical Report No. 35. Boston, Mass.: the Laboratory, 1939. Pp. viii, 72. $1.00. Paper, mimeographed.

[B819]

ALFANO, MARIE V. **Variation of Vocabulary Scores with Age, Sex, and Schooling, Worksample 176.** Human Engineering Laboratory, Technical Report No. 36. Boston, Mass.: the Laboratory, 1939. Pp. viii, 99. $1.00. Paper, mimeographed.

[B820]

ALLEN, E. PATRICIA, AND SMITH, PERCIVAL. **Selection of Skilled Apprentices for the Engineering Trades:** Third Report of Research. Birmingham, England: City of Birmingham Education Committee, January 1939. Pp. iii, 37. 1s. Paper.

Occupational Psychol 13:164 Ap '39. * This report deals mainly with the test results, academic entrance examination results, school ratings at the end of the course, and the industrial 'follow up' of 157 boys admitted to a junior technical school in 1932 and 1933. All the boys took an academic examination of the usual type, and were also given a battery of 'apprentice ability' tests on admission. Their results in the examination and in the test were compared with school ratings at the end of a two-year course. * The boys were then 'followed-up' in industry for a period of two to three years, and information as to their industrial success was obtained from them and from their employers. *

* Entries B1-B291 will be found in *Educational, Psychological, and Personality Tests of 1936.* By Oscar K. Buros. Rutgers University Bulletin, Vol. 14, No. 2A; Studies in Education, No. 11. New Brunswick, N. J.: School of Education, Rutgers University, August 1937. Pp. 141. $0.75. Paper.

Entries B292-B814 will be found in *The 1938 Mental Measurements Yearbook.* Edited by Oscar Krisen Buros. New Brunswick, N. J.: Rutgers University Press, 1938. Pp. xv, 415. $3.00.

[B821]

ALLPORT, GORDON W., AND VERNON, PHILIP E. **Studies in Expressive Movement.** Chapter 10, "Matching Sketches of Personality with Script," by Edwin Powers. New York: Macmillan Co., 1933. Pp. xiii, 269. $3.25.

Am J Psychol 46:667-8 O '34. Thos. H. Howells. This book presents an experimental study of consistency in bodily movements. It seeks to determine whether the typical movements of humans are marked by identifying characteristics, and whether there is correspondence in style between the various activities, indicative of some common permeating factor or factors. * Some 300 measurements were obtained of different aspects of various normal activities of twenty-five men. Typical measures were of normal speed in writing, drawing, talking and rhythmic activities; in area covered in writing and drawing; of the length of stride; of grip strength; of pressure in writing and tapping; of the estimation of distance between the hands and to various points outside the body; of weights and of the sizes of angles. There were also several ratings of action traits. More than 30 tests were given. * It is a matter of significance that this important study is truly inductive. It starts with no logical premise or hypothesis to be tested as does the traditional study of personality. Its categories are derived mechanically from the data. They are named and described, after discovery, through statistical analysis. To the reviewer this seems a very worthy achievement. The danger of the procedure seems to lie in the fact that the group measures are built up on the basis of some rather small differences in correlations. * A second question might arise in regard to the psychological "congruence" observed between the constituent items of the groups after they were constructed. There seems to be danger that one might "read in" or rationalize a meaningful relationship where it does not really exist. * As a trailblazing study, it is a worthy contribution. *

Am J Sociol 40:540 Ja '35. Herbert Blumer. The authors have devoted themselves to the interesting problem of the existence of consistency between different gestures, or forms of movement, in which personality is presumably expressed. *

Brit J Psychol 24:342 Ja '34. * a book which

stands out from among many as worthy of the most careful attention * [the authors use] throughout statistical measures with most admirable caution. The details of the conclusions must be studied in the book itself. As they are presented those conclusions appear to be both convincing and of far-reaching significance. * Especially interesting is their demonstration of the importance of what they call 'areal,' 'centrifugal' and 'emphasis' factors in movement, for this, as they show, indicates that "physical categories of movement are unsuitable models for the *psychological* study of expression." Theories of expressive movement are considered both critically and in a constructive manner, and there is a very attractive and sympathetic study of what may be called 'scientific graphology.' In sum, this is a good book of a fruitful kind which clears up many problems and points the way to a study of many more.

J Abn and Social Psychol 28:333-4 O-D '33. Dorothea Johannsen. * The emphasis in the whole volume is upon experimental technique, and it is certainly an interesting approach to a problem which is very largely slighted by American psychologists. * The approach is a behavioristic one which ought to appeal to many psychologists who have objected to the methods of impression and introspection which heretofore have been used in the study of personality. The book brings together historical material, much of which is not readily available, and discusses some theoretical concepts which are not often considered in connection with theories of personality, *e.g.*, transfer and the theory of identical elements.

J Ed Res 28:296-8 D '34. C. W. Brown. Most academic psychologists relegate to the realm of casuistry and "hocus-pocus" attempts of graphologists, character analysts and their kin to diagnose traits of personality. American psychologists, particularly, basing their opinion on one or two experimental investigations, have shown a vigorous skepticism toward research in a field which past associations have linked with astrology and the occult. Allport and Vernon have done a pioneering work in breaking through this peremptoriness and revealing a rich unexplored territory which challenges the analytical capacity of even the most exacting experimentalist. The book describes the methods, results and interpretations of a number of experiments designed to objectively unravel

the complex matrix of personality. * Part B, "Handwriting and Personality," presents the case for experimental graphology. An excellent critical review and evaluation of experimental studies is given. * Mention should be made of certain limitations of the study, some of which are acknowledged by the authors. Many of the conclusions of the first experiments were based upon constants obtained by the Spearman-Brown formula. In no instance do the authors show that the necessary conditions of the formula are met by their data. A cursory examination of the data indicates that these conditions were not fulfilled. The formula for the average intercorrelation between all related ratings or all related measures demands equality of means and sigmas among the separate variables. This condition was only remotely approached by the data of Allport and Vernon. Most of the raw coefficients were small, the authors depending upon correction formulas to boost up the constants to more acceptable sizes. A stronger case for expressive movement as a means of diagnosing personality would result if more reliable original measures were obtained. The reliabilities are not exceptionally high considering the amount of averaging and combining of the original scores and the fact that many of the coefficients were repeat-reliabilities. Many psychologists would attempt a case for specificity of function with data showing no greater consistency than manifested in these experiments. It must be admitted, however, that the corrected reliabilities in the studies of Allport and Vernon are considerably higher than those obtained by previous investigators studying similar functions.

Mental Hyg (New York) 20:320-1 Ap '36. Frank K. Shuttleworth. * As a pioneer study of an unexplored aspect of personality and as a stimulus to further research, this volume should prove to be an important landmark for both the theory and the measurement of personality. The volume is replete with arresting, disturbing, and thought-provoking contrasts. There are hundreds of correlations, 676 of them in a single table; yet there is constant depreciation of the hard mechanics of correlation and insistence on coherence, or congruence, or psychological consistency. All the devices dear to the statistician are on display; yet all of this elaboration applies at the most to twenty-five cases deliberately selected to provide a very heterogeneous group. The reader is introduced to a great array of newly devised tests of personality which rest on the solid foundation of quite objective observable behavior; yet a fourth of the volume labors mightily to provide evidence that graphologists can judge personality from handwriting. It is specifically stated that the objective tests were chosen without any particular hypotheses concerning what they might measure (sic); yet these tests seem to hang together both statistically and psychologically. Quite obviously there is nothing here for those who are busily engaged in the practical problems created by personality differences. This is a volume for those who are primarily interested in the theory and measurement of personality.

[B822]

AMERICAN COUNCIL ON EDUCATION. **The Construction and Use of Achievement Examinations:** A Manual for Secondary School Teachers. Edited by Herbert E. Hawkes, E. F. Lindquist, and C. R. Mann. Prepared under the auspices of a committee of the American Council on Education. Boston, Mass.: Houghton Mifflin Co., 1936. Pp. x, 497. $2.50. (London: George G. Harrap & Co., Ltd. 1937. 8s. 6d.)

Ed Res B 18:85-6 Mr '39. Norman Woelfel. * [This book] is unique . . . in that it analyzes the process of evaluation in terms of a progressive philosophy of education. The authors assume that good testing should penalize rote learning and should aim at getting away from non-interpretative material in favor of material which emphasizes functional values and interpretative ideas. The authors also assume that glorification of standards, which has been such a bugbear to the testing movement, should give way to an emphasis on individual differences, and that the wise use of tests will hasten the movement toward adaptation of instruction to individual needs. *

For additional reviews, see B6 and B295.

[B823]

AMERICAN COUNCIL ON EDUCATION. **Seventh Educational Conference, New York City, October 27 and 28, 1938:** Under the Auspices of the Educational Records Bureau, the Cooperative Test Service, the Committee on Measurement and Guidance of the American Council on Education, and the Commission on the Relation of School and College of the Progressive Education Association. Educational Record, Vol. 20, Supplement No. 12. Washington, D. C.: the Council, January 1939. Pp. 176. $0.25. Paper.

[B824]

AMERICAN COUNCIL ON EDUCATION. **Eighth Educational Conference, New York City, October 26 and 27, 1939:** Under the Auspices of the Educational Records Bureau, the Cooperative Test Service, the Committee on Measurement and Guidance of the American Council on Education, the Commission on the Relation of School and College of the Progres-

sive Education Association. Educational Record, Vol. 21, Supplement No. 13. Washington, D. C.: the Council, January 1940. Pp. 208. $0.50. Paper.

[B825]

ANDERSON, HOWARD R., and LINDQUIST, E. F. **Selected Test Items in American Government.** Foreword by Ruth West. National Council for the Social Studies, Bulletin No. 13. Washington, D. C.: the Council, National Education Association, September 1939. Pp. 68. $0.50. Paper.

[B826]

ANDERSON, HOWARD R., and LINDQUIST, E. F. **Selected Test Items in Economics.** Foreword by James A. Michener, Wilbur F. Murra, and Fremont P. Wirth. National Council for the Social Studies, Bulletin No. 11. Washington, D. C.: the Council, National Education Association, January 1939. Pp. 74. $0.50. Paper.

[B827]

ANDERSON, HOWARD R.; LINDQUIST, E. F.; and BERG, HARRY D. **Selected Test Items in American History,** Revised edition. National Council for the Social Studies, Bulletin No. 6, Revised edition. Washington, D. C.: the Council, National Education Association, April 1940. Pp. 90. $0.75. Paper.

[B828]

APPEL, KENNETH E., and STRECKER, EDWARD A. **Practical Examination of Personality and Behavior Disorders:** Adults and Children. New York: Macmillan Co., 1936. Pp. xiv, 219. $2.25. (London: Macmillan & Co., Ltd., 1937. 8s. 6d.)

Am J Med Sci 194:422 S '37. L. S. * Ideally the book should be used in conjunction with supervised teaching rather than independently by the individual student. As indicated by the subtitle it includes many examination methods useful for study of psychiatric disorders in children. If the book is used by workers with an eye to accurate investigation and observation, it will be found to be a valuable tool.

Ann Internal Med 10:1904 Je '37. J. C. S. There are many things in this book which serve to make it both an interesting and useful volume. Although the authors have presented the book ostensibly for medical students and neophytes in psychiatry, they have included material which may have a wider appeal. * The presentation is given largely in a very accessible outline form. It is noteworthy for its simple style and absence of flowery verbiage. The chapter on "The Art and Practice of the Psychiatric Examination" is especially practical and timely. * The greatest value of the work, in the opinion of the reviewer, lies in the portion devoted to the examination of children. The technic of obtaining information from the child by entering his phantasy life is especially interesting and practical. * In all it may be said that the book would be a valuable addition to the library of every practitioner of medicine.

Hygeia 15:564 Je '37. David Slight. * The first chapter, on the art of psychiatric examination, is excellent and should be "chewed and digested" by student and practitioner alike. * the book should prove of value for the guidance of students and especially for those intending to specialize in psychiatry.

For additional reviews, see B303.

[B829]

ARRINGTON, RUTH E. **Time-Sampling Studies of Child Behavior.** American Psychological Association, Psychological Monographs, Vol. 51, No. 2, Whole No. 228. Evanston, Ill.: the Association, 1939. Pp. xi, 193, 87. $4.00. Paper.

[B830]

ARTHUR, GRACE. **A Point Scale of Performance Tests:** Volume II, The Process of Standardization. New York: Commonwealth Fund, 1933. Pp. xi, 106. $1.50. (London: Oxford University Press. 6s. 6d.)

Personnel J 12:237 D '33. * Arthur in this volume completes her description of the construction and standardization of a non-verbal scale of intelligence tests. This scale, she feels, demonstrates that "intelligence as measured without recourse to the two types of abstract material known as words and numbers." * Standardization of two alternate forms greatly increases the scale's usefulness.

For additional reviews, see B19 and B304.

[B831]

BAILEY, EDNA W.; LATON, ANITA D.; AND BISHOP, ELIZABETH L. **Studying Children in School,** Second edition. [The first edition is entitled *Outline for Study of Children in Schools.*] New York: McGraw-Hill Book Co., Inc., 1939. Pp. vii, 182. $2.00.

Ed Abstracts 5:8 Ja '40. Charles M. Morris.
J Ed Psychol 31:238-9 Mr '40. C. M. Louttit. * The purpose of this book is to present an outline of child development and behavior which the teacher may follow in observing a child or children in his own room. * There is also an excellent annotated bibliography of books on all phases of child life. * The workbooks follow the same design as the text, and are arranged so that the record of observation in one area may be removed. The arrangement of materials is well executed, the topics are pertinent, and the text discussion well organized. This work should be of high value for courses in child psychology for teacher or parents, and it might well be used for independent study by anyone working with a child or several children.

J Home Econ 31:716 D '39. * Considerable change has been made in certain chapters, but the general plan and purpose remain the same. *

For reviews of the first edition, see B22 and B305.

[B832]

BAILEY, EDNA W.; LATON, ANITA D.; AND BISHOP, ELIZABETH L. **Workbook I, Study of Children in Preschool:** To Be Used with *Studying Children in School,* Second edition. New York. McGraw-Hill Book Co., Inc., 1939. Pp. iii, 40. $0.50. Paper.

[B833]

BAILEY, EDNA W.; LATON, ANITA D.; AND BISHOP, ELIZABETH L. **Workbook II, Study of Child in Elementary School:** To Be Used with *Studying Children in School,* Second edition. New York: McGraw-Hill Book Co., Inc., 1939. Pp. iii, 32. $0.50. Paper.

[B834]

BAILEY, EDNA W.; LATON, ANITA D.; AND BISHOP, ELIZABETH L. **Workbook III, Study of Youth in Secondary School:** To Be Used with *Studying Children in School,* Second edition. New York: McGraw-Hill Book Co., Inc., 1939. Pp. iii, 36. $0.50. Paper.

[B835]

BAKER, HARRY J., AND TRAPHAGEN, VIRGINIA. **The Diagnosis and Treatment of Behavior-Problem Children.** New York: Macmillan Co., 1935. Pp. xiv, 393. $3.00. (London: Macmillan & Co., Ltd., 1936. 12s. 6d.)

Hygeia 14:464 My '36. W. W. Bauer. This is an effort to reduce the subjective criteria of problem behavior in children to objective terms, through a scale known as the Detroit Behavior Scale, by which all the factors influencing behavior may be studied and scored numerically. It presents, of course, all the advantages and disadvantages of the application of mathematical scoring to personality variations. The authors acknowledge that, however objective may be the scoring of the several items the judgment on which the numerical score is based must still be subjective. That would seem to render it as fallible as ever. The fact that it is clothed with a semblance of objective exactness in the form of a score on the established scale may in itself be dangerous. As with any "yard stick" or appraisal the scale may be exceedingly useful in the hands of those who devised it or others equally capable of keeping in mind its limitations as well as its advantages. It will certainly be no help to the inexperienced person who might be tempted to pick it up and be deceived into thinking that here is a short-cut, nicely marked into definite milestones, by which the amateur may enter on the diagnosis and treatment of behavior-problem children. The high degree of statistical validity which the authors claim for their device may exist, but it depends on the validity of the underlying data, and this in turn springs out of the competence and the experience of the user. A serious defect in the book is the appearance of numerous inaccuracies and mis-statements which mar the section on health and physical factors. Surely the authors know better than to discuss rickets on a basis of insufficient food from mother's milk and without any reference to calcium-vitamin metabolism, or to state that the principal treatment of measles is eyebaths and catharsis with calomel. Surely they ought to be better informed about toxoid than to record the statement that diphtheria antitoxin is the main reliance in an immunizing program. There seems no good reason to include discussion of medical treatment in such a book, but if such references are to be made they should be accurate. A description of over-weight attributed to thyroid deficiency bears more resemblance to pituitary than to thyroid. Other points in this section badly need clarification and correction.

J Juvenile Res 22:209-10 Jl-O '38. Frederick L. Patry. Nowhere in the field of diagnosis and treatment of pupil maladjustments will one find a more effectively formulated book than that which the authors so happily and timely bring to the attention of all those working with the school child. The approach and method are on a highly scientific plane, taking root from many years of experience in dealing with the multifarious aspects of behavior maladjustments encountered in pupils in the Detroit public schools. * an outstanding example of a pioneer attempt in gaining an objective rating scale of behavior maladjustments * All workers in child guidance, and particularly the school psychologist and psychiatrist will feel deeply grateful to the authors for this much-needed publication.

J Nerv and Mental Dis 89:610 Ap '39. * The work affords material that cannot fail to stimulate the social worker toward a better grasp of the more obvious and tangible issues associated with child maladjustment. It is primarily a social survey, both in methods of diagnosis and suggested treatment. Little or no actual use is made of the inroads of psychoanalysis in this field. Matter relating to Freud is limited to part of a brief introductory section. Application of analytic concepts is general rather than specific.

Psychoanalytic Q 8:395-8 Jl '39. Marjorie R. Leonard. * presents a point of view that is fairly well rounded and certainly new to many teachers and social workers * one feels that the

authors have tried to make use of the knowledge psychoanalysis has made available. But one also senses confusion. In their introductory chapter, History of Treatment and Contribution to Theories, Freud, Adler, Jung and Healy are successively mentioned, briefly, and without any real understanding of their relation or lack of relation to each other. Throughout the book it does not become clear whether the authors really do not understand the concepts of Freud or whether they are making concessions and censoring their opinions with a view to the prejudices of their audience. Such a compromise is forgivable certainly, if by means of it they can reach a larger number of people and make them aware of the need to look behind the scenes, and provided the statements made are correct as far as they go. But one feels that the authors have tried to cover too much ground and have attempted to do justice to too many points of view with the result that the book lacks integration. Frequently we find a statement showing the retention of old-fashioned attitudes followed immediately by one which displays a great deal more insight. * Adequate explanation of the concepts of the unconscious and of repression are lacking. It is disturbing to find such behavior as stealing discussed as though the relation between it and the wish for love and affection were something of which the child were consciously aware. One also misses a recognition of the fact that the approach to the child and his problems must differ considerably according to the stage of the child's emotional development. The sex problems of childhood are touched upon, but not much more than that. Masturbation is mentioned with hesitancy, and circumcision is recommended as a cure or preventative. In the discussion of fears and anxieties, the authors mention that the cause for them may often be repressed and unknown to the child. However they proceed to recommend various methods of reassurance to enable the child to overcome them. Apparent lack of understanding also enters in the formulation and evaluation of certain questions. One shudders to think of the effect on a stuttering child when asked (factor 6): 'Do you speak plainly and easily? Have you ever had any trouble with speech, such as lisping or stuttering?' Dreams are considered under the heading of sleeping habits (factor 23) and the score is five points (very good) if there are no dreams or occasional meaningless (?!) ones. Factor 52, Number and Position in Siblings, is scored with no reference to whether or not the subject is the middle child although the authors, in their discussion of the relation between siblings in their chapter on Interpretation, apparently recognize that this position has special difficulties. One could easily find many other points where psychoanalysts would disagree with the authors or point out important omissions. But it is only fair to keep in mind the aim that Baker and Traphagen have in view. Realizing that the teachers and social workers, whose task is to try to enable the child to adjust, are often themselves individuals with prejudices and biased attitudes, they have attempted to develop a means of measurement of behavior problems which would not depend on the subjective opinion of any one person. Such a scale can never achieve what the 'free-association interview,' as Aichhorn calls it, can when conducted by a psychiatrically trained individual. However, for communities where such workers are not available, the Detroit Behavior scale is certainly a step in the right direction. It emphasizes the complexity of such problems, and teaches workers not to judge but to try to understand.

For additional reviews, see B24 and B306.

[B836]
BAKER, KENNETH H. **Item Validity by the Analysis of Variance:** An Outline of Method. *Psychological Record*, Vol. 3, No. 19. Bloomington, Ind.: Principia Press, Inc., November 1939. Pp. 242-8. $0.15. Paper.

[B837]
BALLARD, PHILIP BOSWOOD. **Teaching and Testing English.** London: University of London Press, Ltd., 1939. Pp. xi, 167. 5s.

Sch 28:914 Je '40. B. C. D. * contains much material that is entirely new * Like his earlier books, this one abounds in good sense and good humour. Not a page is without some point of interest to a teacher of English. Of the two parts into which the contents are divided, part I, *Teaching*, is, as may be expected, more suggestive and constructive than is part II, *Testing*. The most valuable chapters in part I are the following: The Making of Readers; The Making of Speakers; The Making of Writers; and The Hartog Method. In all of these chapters the reader will find more of common sense than of pedagogy. Dr. Ballard never appears either pompous or professional. He can chat with his reader without patronizing him; and

consequently he wins for his opinions a sympathetic reading. *

[B837.1]
BARNUM, ROBERT G. **Analysis of Time and Errors in Relation to Reliability of Two Clerical Tests, Worksample 1 and Worksample 223.** Human Engineering Laboratory, Technical Report No. 68. Boston, Mass.: the Laboratory, 1940. Pp. viii, 58. $1.00. Paper, mimeographed.

[B838]
BARSE, WILLIAM J. **Mental Tests for Civil Service Examinations.** New York: Grosset & Dunlap, Inc., 1939. Pp. xii, 225. $2.00.

[B839]
BAYLEY, NANCY. **The California First-Year Mental Scale.** University of California, Syllabus Series No. 243; Institute of Child Welfare. Berkeley, Calif.: University of California Press, May 1933. Pp. 24. $0.50. Paper.

[B840]
BECK, SAMUEL J. **Introduction to the Rorschach Method:** A Manual of Personality Study. Preface by F. L. Wells. Monograph No. 1 of the American Orthopsychiatric Association. New York: the Association, 1937. Pp. xv, 278. $4.00.

Arch Neurology and Psychiatry 42:187 Jl '39. * The manual represents careful work. The experimental records are models of skill and erudition. The Rorschach procedure itself is being widely used and compared with life histories and case records, with apparent advantage. The psychiatrist will find the manual useful in supplementing his diagnosis. The psychologist who accepts intuition as a valuable aid in the comprehension of the total personality will find a wealth of provocative relationships suggested for further investigation.

Char and Pers 6:159-60 D '37. S. H. MacColl. * a manual of Rorschach Test procedure which incorporates recent advances in technique and illustrates the particular practice of the writer. It is intended to be helpful to the neophyte and at the same time to offer a normative, objectively stable standard of procedure as a starting point for the accumulation of comparable material by different workers in the field. The bulk of the volume is given over to the recording and elaboration of fifty-nine cases * Among the many positive contributions of the book, however, one serious drawback must be noted. In connection with the compilation of normative tables, no serious attempt has been made to offer a clear statement of the criteria which may be used as a basis for the classification of responses which do not appear upon the tables. * The omission of theoretical discussion of interpretations is understandable (though regrettable) in consideration of the particular aims of the book, but lack of "theoretical" discussion of criteria in scoring cannot pass without comment.

Med J Australia 24:1043-4 D 11 '37. * The work is extremely technical and quite meaningless for the dilettante reader. It is apparent that much useful information is gleaned through the careful use of the ink-blot method, but it is questionable whether such tests will be of much use to the practicing psychiatrist. Dr. Beck himself has no illusions on this score. * Congratulations must be extended to Dr. Beck for his clear presentation of a difficult subject, and to the American Orthopsychiatric Association for such an excellently printed work. The type is clear and the arrangement of test scores excellent. It is to be hoped that other monographs will follow.

Psychoanalytic R 26:451-2 Jl '39. *G. C. Booth.* * The need for an English introduction to Rorschach's original conceptions . . . still exists, because considerable advance knowledge of the subject matter is taken for granted by Beck. He immediately concentrates on the presentation of 59 complete records, their interpretation and validation. Furthermore, in many respects his principles of scoring the records mean a departure from Rorschach's own conceptions. This is particularly in evidence in the treatment of the kinaesthetic element * On the other hand, Beck distinguishes with much greater statistical thoroughness between inferior and average quality of the form responses, gives closer attention to the contents of the responses, and introduces a new scoring element: the "Z response" as indicative of intellectual "organization energy." On the whole one may say that Beck's approach shifts the emphasis of the procedure and analysis from the introverted and instinctual towards the extraverted and intellectual elements in the personality structure. This brings the method into the danger of becoming a complicated intelligence test rather than an approach towards the dynamics which underlie external efficiency. * Although "theoretical discussion is conspicuous by absence," the book raises implicitly many important theoretical problems. * It is not an introduction in the usual sense of the word, but it represents an interesting, individual development of Rorschach's method. A great wealth of carefully presented, empirical material recommends Beck's contribution to the psychiatrist with one's own Rorschach experience for reference and critical study.

Psychol B 35:787-8 D '38. *Kurt Goldstein.* * The book is not only a review of the up-to-date experiences with the Rorschach test but reflects the author's own valuable results. * The book is written not so much for the beginner as for the experienced student, and the latter will find in it an abundance of material valuable for application of the Rorschach method to normal and sick people. * The expert will read with great interest the detailed interpretation of the individual responses. There is no doubt in the reviewer's mind that this is a publication which is highly recommendable, although the pertinent literature could have been considered somewhat more carefully.

For additional reviews, see B308.

[B841]

BECK, SAMUEL J. **Personality Structure in Schizophrenia:** A Rorschach Investigation in 81 Patients and 64 Controls. Preface by C. Macfie Campbell. Nervous and Mental Disease Monograph No. 63. New York: Nervous and Mental Disease Publishing Co., 1938. Pp. 88. $2.00.

Am J Orthopsychiatry 9:442-3 Ap '39. *Bruno Klopfer.* * Beck establishes the Rorschach method as a reliable instrument for differentiating schizophrenic subjects from normal ones. These quantitative findings, however, do not constitute the main theme of the study. * He amplifies the "psychological implications" by enumerating all the major questions about personality which the Rorschach method undertakes to answer, thus giving an excellent translation and condensation of the Rorschach terminology. * the most important new feature . . . [is] the ten pages (pp. 57-67) where he penetrates, further than in any of his previous publications, from the enumeration of important personality characteristics indicated in the Rorschach categories to an explicit personality description based on the structural relationships of the various characteristics. Included in this description is a very clever schematic representation of the interrelationship of four functions: "creativity," "affectivity," "organizing drive," and "form accuracy." *

Am J Psychiatry 95:1468-9 My '39. *W. Line.* * takes its place with the other well-known contributions of the author, who is in the first rank of those who sensed the possibilities of Rorschach's technique as a fruitful approach to personality analysis * a very clear account * The psychological implications are not so clear; but to the reviewer they point to the interesting generalization that the schizophrenics expressed themselves less personally than did the controls. * substantiates the view that Rorschach initiated a very subtle and significant psychological procedure. His findings should stimulate further researches of this kind. * The title of the monograph may be questioned, since the experimental findings are concerned mainly with ideational symptoms of schizophrenia—and are similar to those noted in current reports by such investigators as Kasanin. "Personality structure" is hardly an apt phrase for describing either the purpose of the study or its outcome.

Brit J Med Psychol 18:282 pt 2 '39. P. E. Vernon. Dr. Beck was one of the first English-speaking psychologists to take up the study of the Rorschach inkblot test, and is the author of the most thorough treatise on the use and interpretation of the test. * The investigation was carried out as carefully as we might expect, but its results do not appear to add very much to those previously obtained by Skalweit from a similar study in a Continental hospital. The outstanding differences between schizophrenics and normals were: greater numbers of *Dd, DG, Fb* and *FFb,* but fewer *FFb* responses; more irregular and confused *Sukzession;* much poorer *F* + % and fewer *V* responses. No reliable difference was found in the important *B* or chiaroscuro responses. Possibly Klopfer's and Piotrowski's more delicate method of handling such responses might have revealed more. * His discussion of the interrelations, and the significance, of his results will certainly be useful to those who employ the Rorschach test in mental hospitals.

Char and Pers 8:267 Mr '40. David Lester. * Beck uses the commendable method of presenting his investigation and his results in both the Rorschach technical and the English languages. Those not already familiar with the Rorschach Test will derive greater benefit from this publication if they will first read Dr. Beck's previously published *Introduction to the Rorschach Method, A Manual of Personality Study* and/or Dr. Rorschach's *Psychodiagnostik.* This applies particularly to the material contained in approximately the first half of this monograph which deals mostly with the technical aspects of the present examination. The latter half of this publication demands no previous familiarity with the Rorschach Test. The book will be valuable reading to all those interested in schizophrenia. Dr. Beck's conclusions herein regarding the schizophrenic supply of affect and the schizophrenic phantasy life should be given full consideration by those who still adhere to the older ideas concerning dementia praecox. It is worth serious study by those who intend to use the Rorschach method as a diagnostic and prognostic aid.

J Am Med Assn 112:1190 Mr 25 '39. This excellent monograph reports a study of the fantasies produced by persons when exposed to the observation of outlines created by the "ink blot method" and a critical analysis of the verbalizations regarding what they fantasied as a reaction to this observation. * Every psychiatrist and psychologist should familiarize himself with this test because it is certain to occupy a foremost position in any study of personality structure.

J Mental Sci 85:573-4 My '39. A. Guirdham. This book is a record of an investigation of cases of schizophrenia by the Rorschach test, and an outline of the personality traits revealed by it in that disease. In the former aim it is more happy. It is a valuable addition to the knowledge that schizophrenics show less concentration of movement responses than the control group. I feel, however, that two at any rate of the other findings occur, not specifically in schizophrenia, but in other conditions characterized by a diminution in co-ordinated affectivity and loss of interest. I refer to the interpretation of details usually overlooked, and the tendency to interpret the whole figure from consideration of a trifling detail. * The sections on the psychological implications of the test, and on the integration of personality, are very open to criticism in that they express characterological peculiarities which are very difficult to assess in ordinary psychological terms. * I cannot discover any very real addition to the knowledge of the schizophrenic personality, and much that might appear original is obfuscated by cloudy phrases. * The author describes the test as objective, but he seems to me not insistent enough on the criteria which accompany psychometry. * There is far too much loose phraseology . . . for the book to be impressive, and the description of a social and psychological personality does not help to eradicate this impression. * It seems a pity that the result of so much useful and obviously skilled work in the investigation of patients and controls should be mishandled in the vague generalizations of the last section of this book. It would, I think, be better to admit that orthopsychiatry is not an exact science, and I am beginning to believe that our best contributions to its study will be to avoid the inaccuracy occasioned by the psychometric utilization of psychological data. This book serves to confirm my opinion that the Rorschach test is being overworked as an aid to personality diagnosis. I still persist that the test fundamentals, e.g., the Erlebnistypus factors, are sound, but that other psychogramm elements are less important than enthusiasts would have us believe. I experience an intense relief on hearing that it is not yet possible to distinguish the different types of schizophrenia by the Rorschach test, but the fact that it will be attempted soon just makes me shudder.

J Nerv and Mental Dis 91:413 Mr '40. * a noteworthy book * We know of no better guide than the one under consideration, and can recommend it most heartily.

Med Times 67:299 Je '39. Joseph L. Abramson. * while technical, is well written, and stimulates a desire in the reader to investigate this method of psychological procedure further.

Psychiatric Q 13:370-1 Ap '39. * essentially an elaboration of the chapter on schizophrenics in Dr. Beck's Introduction to the Rorschach Method. * The contribution of this book lies mainly in its statistics, which are compatible with some of the statistical data compiled by Rorschach and others. It seems, however, that the value of Beck's statistical findings would have been enhanced if the author had taken a definite stand as to the justifiability of Rorschach's claim that several components of his method are specific in schizophrenia. * The Rorschach method has its own symbolic language. It is very difficult to master this language and it is not easy to translate the Rorschach findings into commonly used psychological terms. Beck attempted this difficult task and it is doubtful whether one could agree with him on all points. E.g., to interpret the C (or color response) as "emotional energy," "drive," "force," or "zestful experiences" does not seem to be quite accurate for in many patients we find a great emotional sensitivity without

strong drive and without any zest for emotional experiences. Then, too, the M (or human movement response) cannot always be considered an indicator of creative phantasy or of creativity; it would seem more prudent to define it as productivity omitting any implications as to whether or not the latter is desirable. It is open to question whether all schizophrenics have the same type of color and movement responses as normals. Thus, direct comparisons based on quantitative differences may be misleading. One of the problems of the book was to "tell us in what ways the Rorschach test . . . is valid in singling out members of this (schizophrenic) clinical group." This problem has not been solved clearly. In fact, most of the seven statistical differences which Beck enumerates as differentiating the schizophrenics from the controls are not specifically schizophrenic but are found in many other psychiatric groups. Apparently, Beck preferred not to repeat the rules which he laid down in the chapter on schizophrenics of his "Introduction"; this chapter is more helpful in recognizing schizophrenia in individual cases than is the present volume.

Psychoanalytic Q 9:134-6 Ja '40. John D. Benjamin. Dr. Beck has added another to his interesting series of publications on the Rorschach test. * Beck presents a short but unusually lucid introductory exposition of the fundamentals of the Rorschach technique itself. * As a study in technique this work contains much of value. The scoring and diagnostic interpretation of the one detailed schizophrenic record, for instance, can be warmly recommended as an example of sound Rorschach procedure, and there are many other pages and paragraphs in which the author's long experience with the test finds worthwhile expression. It has repeatedly been pointed out, however, that the Rorschach test is particularly unsuitable for statistical treatment because of the qualitative nature of many of the factors and because no single quantitative factor is of great importance except in relation to other aspects of the test. The best pages in this monograph, indeed, are devoted to a discussion of this very point: the significance of balance between various test factors. * To 'translate' these findings, however, as representative of the 'personality structure' of schizophrenics without reference to their total setting and without a deeper clinical and psychological understanding of schizophrenia appears to the reviewer to be unwarranted and above all unproductive. The same criticism applies to the author's general theory of personality, which will seem extraordinarily naïve to most students of the problem. It is for this reason primarily that the psychiatrist unfamiliar with the test will find little in the work to increase his knowledge of schizophrenia although much to sharpen his interest in the test itself and in its research potentialities.

Psychol B 36:296-8 Ap '39. Maria Rickers-Ovsiankina. * Everyone who has had some experience with schizophrenic "Rorschachs" is acquainted with the wide variety of reaction forms that one finds among these patients. It is therefore rather unfortunate that only one such record is reproduced in its entirety, especially in a monograph devoted to the subject. The presented case is well chosen, however. It brings out as many features characteristic of the disease group as can be expected in a single record * To beginners in the field, this case analysis may be warmly recommended. * By means of a diagram the interdependence, or inner balance, of the major categories is well illustrated. One regrets, however, that the analysis of the individual record has not been carried further into the finer, more qualitative aspects of the test * The statistical section is the best. * Unfortunately, original responses, which have proven a useful differentiating criterion, are not considered by the author. On the whole, however, this examination of the various test categories lends gratifying corroboration to Rorschach's own, Skalweit's, and the reviewer's findings in schizophrenic patients. Important, too, is the stress on the great variability within the schizophrenic group, well demonstrated by a histogram. Particularly illustrative is the diagram representing the relationship of color to movement. * should be a useful book. One wishes, however, that the author had used some of his broad experience in bringing out more fully the significance of the total individual record in all its quantitative and qualitative potentialities.

Q R Biol 14:266 Je '39. * This study is a valuable contribution to the problem of the schizophrenic personality, both as a demonstration of the possibilities of the Rorschach technique and in the specific conclusions emerging from its application in this particular sample of schizophrenic patients. *

[B842]

Bell, Hugh M. **The Theory and Practice of Personal Counseling:** With Special Reference to the Adjustment Inventory. A revision of *The Theory and Practice of Student Counseling.* Stanford University, Calif.: Stanford University Press, 1939. Pp. v, 167. $1.25. Paper, lithotyped. (London: Oxford University Press. 6s.)

Jun Col J 10: 55-6 S '39. * a revision of the author's earlier work *The Theory and Practice of Student Counseling,* published in 1935. It is written with special reference to the author's *Adjustment Inventory* which has proved helpful to so many junior college counselors in studying the adjustment difficulties of their students. The present volume reviews in detail the construction and use of the *Student Adjustment Inventory* and extends and revises the device in the form of a *School Inventory* and *Adult Adjustment Inventory.* The intelligent use of these instruments should aid materially the junior college counselor to secure reliable and valid information concerning certain aspects of personality in such a form as to be readily understood both by counselor and by student.

Loyola Ed Digest 14:11 My '39. Austin G. Schmidt. * a definite contribution to the theory and technic of measuring adjustment.

Occupations 17:835 Je '39. Ruth E. Salley. * essentially a handbook to accompany the Adjustment Inventory * The present edition includes, in addition to the earlier material, a statement of experimental work on the Adjustment Inventory since 1934, the development of the School Inventory and of the Adult Adjustment Inventory. * This book is an excellent introduction to the field of measurement in the personal areas sampled but one feels that the author is too optimistic about the possibility of obtaining "concrete and objective" descriptions of personality and reliable measuring instruments.

Scottish Ed J 23:546 Ag 2 '40. Counselling is the American term for what we call guidance. This work presents a method of diagnosing the difficulties that bring about failure of students during College life by means of adjustment inventories. Only when Universities and Colleges in this country come to assume responsibility for failure of their students will such a work as this be fully appreciated.

For reviews of the first edition, see B30 and B309.

[B843]
BENDER, LAURETTA. **A Visual Motor Gestalt Test and Its Clinical Use.** Preface by Paul Schilder. American Orthopsychiatric Association, Research Monographs, No. 3. New York: the Association, 1938. Pp. xi, 176. $3.50.

Am J Orthopsychiatry 9:441-2 *Ap '39 F. L. Wells.* * the chapters have . . . less of a *Gestalt* than might be looked for in a protagonist of these conceptions * The case material is readily followed * a wealth of fields for inquiry is opened * a most valuable clinical instrument * other avenues and levels of *Gestalt* functioning exist besides reproduction through drawing * Above it are the language functions, which have various limitations in large scale clinical work. Below are more manipulative procedures such as those developed by Goldstein; these would have been an interesting control of such observations as here reported. * there is the right to expect that considerable and competent attention be paid to rendering the procedure serviceable to other workers. The title itself implies such an endeavor. It is impossible to say that it has been effective. Actually no one could, by following the text, carry out the procedure with any assurance that essential conditions were being met. To this end, there should have been clear description of the manner of presenting the stimuli, time factors, and the like. There should have been far more detailed treatment along the lines of Ch. XI. * Viewed theoretically, the remark in the introduction that "the individual draws what he perceives," is a loose statement to come from one of Schilder's understanding. There is scant evidence for such one-to-one correspondence between perception and reproduction. The difference corresponds rather to what are called, in psychophysics, methods of "constant stimuli" and "average error." The present procedure does open up a critical way of studying this difference. One can, for example, have the standard figure drawn in the ordinary way, then call upon the subject to make visual comparisons of the standard with this and various other approximations to it. *

Brit J Psychol 29:434 *Ap '39.* * interesting * Bender has opened up a line of clinical research which may come to possess considerable importance, even though the assumptions underlying it have to be modified in the course of time.

Char and Pers 8:178-9 *D '39. Edward J. Stainbrook.* * This is a valuable, even a *must*, book for clinicians, and it should provoke extensive study and research since general clinical employment of the test reveals anomalies and contradictions not discussed in this monograph.

J Am Med Assn 113:1986-7 *N 25 '39.* * The author assumes a familiarity with the classic teachings of gestalt psychology, which are not reviewed in the book. * Of particular interest is Dr. Bender's standardization of the gestalt function in a performance test for children. * This book will be useful to physicians who are interested in problems of development and growth. The test devised by Dr. Bender will doubtless prove of clinical value as a performance test yielding specific information relative to preceptual functioning otherwise not ready available. It should prove to be particularly useful in diagnostic studies of retarded children and those suspected of being retarded. Where disturbances are primarily in the field of emotional development, the test will be of limited usefulness.

J Ed Psychol 31:78-9 *Ja '40. Miles A. Tinker.* * presents a very interesting approach to clinical abnormal psychology. Many will raise questions, however, concerning the usefulness of this visual motor gestalt test. It was standardized on normal subjects. The scoring is highly subjective. As yet we know nothing about its reliability. Obviously one must have a comprehensive knowledge of gestalt psychology and be sympathetic to the gestalt approach in order to obtain any value from use of the test.

J Nerv and Mental Dis 91:547 *Ap '40.* * Throughout, the applications to clinical problems are paramount. Case histories in greater or less detail are offered. The whole monograph is important and useful.

Med J Australia 26:762 *N 18 '39.* * The discussion opens up interesting lines of thought, and the test should provide an instrument to be considered in research projects, but it is likely to prove of limited use in its present form in routine work. However, it seems worth while to experiment with it in this country.

Psychiatric Q 13:382-4 *Ap '39.* In this small volume the author has taken gestalt psychology a considerable step forward. * The reviewer commends this book to the psychiatrist for its presentation not only of basic principles, but of clinical application. The study should be continued and expanded. Moderate defects of style, a number of typographical errors, an incomplete index, and monotonous reference to another writer mar the volume to some degree.

Psychoanalytic Q 9:441-2 Jl '40. J. F. Brown. * a very worthwhile publication * I think Dr. Bender is completely right in her belief that of all the academic psychologies gestalt psychology offers the greatest number of implications for clinical psychiatry and is equally right in thinking that gestalt psychology itself is enriched by her clinical data. The test she standardizes has already given us much and promises to give more semi-objective data to enlarge our knowledge of personality structure. The test gives us another valuable tool towards the investigation of the nature of the specific functional and organic neuroses. The presentation of standardized norms will do much to make the test available to other investigators in the fields of child and genetic psychology and experimental psychopathology. The visual motor gestalt test like the Rorschach test, the Luria technique and certain of the procedures of the topological psychologists is important as a pioneer attempt to create an experimental psychopathology. I have often expressed the belief that the future of psychopathology lies in this field. Consequently it is a pleasure to concur with the conclusion in Dr. Schilder's preface that this work 'opens up important vistas. It will help the psychologist and the psychiatrist. It will interest everyone who is interested in problems of development.'

Sociometry 2:101-2 O '39. Ernst Fantl. The author has made nine of Wertheimer's original patterns and one additional figure the basis of a performance test which she has given to normals, mental defectives, psychotic persons, children and adults at all age levels. The test consists of copying simple configurations, such as, a circle and a square touching at one point, or dots in a straight line, etc. It is interesting to observe how the insight into the whole and its parts gradually develops. * Bender again demonstrates clearly the evolution of the Gestalt function at different age levels. * This book is an interesting complement to Samuel J. Beck's book on the Rorschach method *

[B844]

BENNETT, WILHELMINA. **A Study of Several Well Known Personality Tests.** [New York: Psychological Corporation], October 1933. Pp. ii, 25. Paper, mimeographed. Out of print.

[B844.1]

BETTS, EMMETT ALBERT. **Data on Visual Sensation and Perception Tests:** Part I, Lateral Imbalance.

Meadville, Pa.: Keystone View Co., 1939. $0.25. Pp. 27.

Ed Abstracts 5:157 My '40. C. L. Nemzek. * An excellent bibliography of 101 references dealing with the visual sensation and perception tests of the Betts Ready to Read Battery is appended.

Ed Abstracts 5:191 Je '40. Howard E. Tempero. This report contains data about one technique for detecting cases with extreme lateral imbalance findings. It presents "previously unpublished data on the reliability and validity of the readings taken on the lateral imbalance slide (Slide DB-9) of the Visual Sensation and Perception Tests of the Betts Ready to Read Battery." The author discussed the purposes, limitations, and educational implications of the report. These topics are followed by the more technical discussions of the types of lateral imbalance, criteria for measuring lateral imbalance, and tests of imbalance. *

[B844.2]

BETTS, EMMETT ALBERT, WITH THE ASSISTANCE OF ARTHUR W. AYERS. **Data on Visual Sensation and Perception Tests:** Part II, Visual Efficiency. Meadville, Pa.: Keystone View Co., 1940. Pp. 66. $0.25. Paper, lithotyped.

[B845]

BINGHAM, W. V. **Administrative Ability:** Its Discovery and Development. Society for Personnel Administration, Pamphlet No. 1. Washington, D. C.: the Society, Box 266, April 1939. Pp. iii, 17. $0.25. Paper, lithotyped.

Pub Mgmt 21:188 Je '39. * thought-provoking *

[B846]

BINGHAM, WALTER VAN DYKE. **Aptitudes and Aptitude Testing.** Published for the National Occupational Conference. New York and London: Harper & Brothers, 1937. Pp. ix, 390. $3.00; 12s. 6d.

Civil Service Assembly News Letter 3:6 Mr '37. The author considers the problems of testing primarily from the point of view of vocational guidance * The public personnel administrator will be chiefly interested in Part III of the book. In this section Mr. Bingham discusses the selection, administration, and interpretation of tests. The appendix contains a careful resume of a number of tests with adequate instructions for their use.

Clearing House 13:377-8 F '39. * This illuminating book . . . consists of three parts: Aptitude and Guidance; Orientation within the World of Work; The Practice of Testing. The reviewer found Part II most constructive *

Ed Abstracts 3:179 Je '38. W. A. Stumpf.
* This volume seems to be virtually a handbook
in testing for the use of the vocational counselor, and of value to the general administrator
in determining what to expect from and in an
aptitude-testing program. The point of view
is that of common sense, and the style is readily
readable.

Eug News 22:42 My-Je '37. * well worth
study *

For additional reviews, see B313.

[B847]

BINGHAM, W. V. **Oral Examinations in Civil Service Recruitment:** With Special Reference to Experiences in Pennsylvania. Civil Service Assembly
of the United States and Canada, Pamphlet No. 13.
Chicago, Ill.: the Assembly, February 1939. Pp. 30.
$0.50. Paper.

*Civil Service Assembly News Letter 5:8 Mr
'39. James M. Mitchell.* * should prove of value
to personnel administrators and technicians as
a guide in improving oral examination methods
* As consultant to the Employment Board for
the Pennsylvania Department of Public Assistance, the author recently participated in a program requiring over eleven thousand such oral
interviews * Of especial interest to the personnel technician are two lengthly footnotes.
In one the author shows the disastrous results
caused by averaging the various parts of an
examination without taking into account the
range of marks in each such part. In the other,
a good defense of the graphic rating scale is
presented. However, some technicians will take
issue with Dr. Bingham on this point. * Bingham has done an excellent job of setting forth
improved interviewing practices and of describing their use on a large scale in Pennsylvania.
It is to be hoped that he will find it possible to
compare this wealth of examination data with
objective evidence as to the efficiency of these
candidates on the job.

Personnel Adm 1:12 Mr '39. D. T. Stanley.
* the most encouraging and instructive treatment of the use of oral examinations that has
been published in recent years * Bingham's
discussion is made concrete and enlivened considerably by anecdotes drawn from his experiences while he was working out his plan of
oral examinations for the Department of Public Assistance in Pennsylvania. An interesting
innovation was his use of the IBM electrical
test-scoring machine in computing the examiners' ratings of each candidate. Personnel administrators in the Federal service will find

the pamphlet helpful because of the part oral
examinations undoubtedly will play in departmental promotion plans.

Pub Mgmt 21:91 Mr '39.

[B847.1]

BLISS, ELISHA F., JR. **Standardized Tests and Educational Practice.** Brooklyn, N. Y.: the Author,
P. O. Box 267, 1940. Pp. 29. $0.75. Paper, lithotyped.

[B848]

BOVARD, JOHN F., AND COZENS, FREDERICK W. **Tests
and Measurements in Physical Education,** Second
edition. Philadelphia, Pa., and London: W. B. Saunders Co., 1938. Pp. 427. $3.00; 14*s*.

*Ed Abstracts 3:313-4 O '38. Evelyn B.
Spindler.* * Material in the original text of
1930 has been brought up to date and several
new and valuable chapters have been added.
This new edition is carefully footnoted and,
in addition, a selected bibliography is put conveniently at the end of each chapter. The appendix contains twenty pages of tables useful
in testing data and in scoring. Of the new
chapters, "Recent Advances in Measuring
Pupil Achievement" covers all recent research
plans *

Pub Health R 7:7 My '38 Virginia Peaseley.
* the most complete text available in the field
of testing dealing with physical activity * This
new edition of an already invaluable book
shows clearly the effort and progress that has
been made in recent years by research in physical education. It not only gives information
but serves also as a stimulation for others to
contribute to the work in testing which is constantly going on in this field.

For additional reviews, see B316.

[B849]

BRISTOL, MARGARET COCHRAN. **Handbook on Social
Case Recording,** Second edition. University of Chi-
cago, Social Service Monographs No. 36. Chicago,
Ill.: University of Chicago Press, 1937. Pp. xii, 219.
$1.50. (London: Cambridge University Press. 7*s*.)

*Sociol and Social Res 23:495-6 My-Je '39.
E(mory) S. B(ogardus).* The practical and
helpful nature of this book cannot be over-
emphasized. It has been developed out of extended and varied experiences in case recording. * It is clear, cautious, and constructive. *
The painstaking and thoughtful procedure of
the author is illustrated by many discriminating
statements. *

Survey 76:118 Mr '40. Maurice J. Karpf. *
is considerably more than a mere handbook for
recording, and a good deal less than an adequate guide for case work * The book is some-

what loosely organized and does not always seem to follow an inherently consistent and logical plan, at least one which this reviewer could easily recognize. However, the material itself is suggestive and stimulating, and should prove helpful and valuable to beginning students.

For reviews of the earlier edition, see B320.

[B850]

BROOM, M. E. **Educational Measurements in the Elementary School.** New York: McGraw-Hill Book Co., Inc., 1939. Pp. x, 345. $3.00. (London: McGraw-Hill Publishing Co., Ltd., 20s.)

Ed Abstracts 5:31 Ja '40. F. J. Adams.

El Paso Sch Standard 17:38-9 F '40. C. W. Webb. * The classroom teacher will find in the volume an excellent guide to existing standardized measuring instruments, as well as adequate information about procedures to be followed in constructing objective tests for classroom use. * simply written * The index is excellent. There are a few places in the volume where a student might be confused. * The typographical work and format of the book are excellent. * will be of great usefulness to educators working in the elementary school, and to students in training for elementary school teaching.

El Sch J 40:630-2 Ap '40. F. J. Adams. * some readers might wish that more consideration had been given to the interpretation and the utilization of mental-test findings * From the standpoint of the volume as a textbook, it includes many teacher helps, a great number of footnote references, short bibliographies at the ends of the chapter sections as well as at the close of the chapters themselves, and approximately forty pages of discussion topics and exercises. * While mental tests are considered in this book . . . one finds no mention of attempts to measure character and personality development, attitudes, or study habits. Rating scales are not discussed, interest inventories are not considered, and the discussion of the measurement of achievement in health and physical education is limited to less than a page. Only one test is described in the field of elementary science, as the author states that "science has had only a small place in the instruction program in elementary schools. . . ." and that "in all instances, it is a nonlaboratory course" (p. 244). The pupil-testing and evaluation procedures being developed by the progressive education movement fail to re-

ceive mention. In fact, since the median publication date for the writings of other authors mentioned in the footnote and bibliography citations is 1928, the reader may be encouraged to assume that little real advancement has been made in the elementary-school testing field during recent years.

Harvard Ed R 10:245-6 Mr '40. Eugene Shen. * the book as a whole is well balanced * The early treatment of statistical concepts and methods is particularly commendable, since these constitute the foundation of measurement, and are not merely useful, as so many other books seem to suggest, in summarizing test results. * Much of Chapter V is concerned with presenting evidence to show that teacher-made tests *can* be reliable and valid. Even if this may not be self-evident, it is certainly more important to know *how* to make a test reliable and valid. While the reviewer does not mean to suggest that the *how* is entirely neglected, it can certainly be more thoroughly discussed if much of the evidence on the other point is omitted. The chapters on standard tests for the various elementary-school subjects seem quite adequate. But some of the theoretical considerations on intelligence could perhaps well have given way to more discussion on the practical aspects. A number of inaccuracies, especially near the beginning of the book, are likely to make such unfavorable impressions on the reader that his judgment on the rest of the book may easily be prejudiced. The elementary nature of most of these errors, while rendering them more harmless than they otherwise might have been, certainly provides little excuse for their existence. *

J Ed (Boston) 123:68 F '40. * Administrators, teachers and those in training for the profession will find in "Educational Measurements in the Elementary School" a master key to guidance and the study of individual needs.

J Ed Res 33:714 My '40. J. Murray Lee. * prepared for the use of beginning classes. Its organization lends itself to class work very easily. * The volume can be commended from a teaching standpoint for its concise presentation, the short but carefully chosen references, and the many helpful exercises at the end of the chapters. * The reviewer would wish to include in a course on the elementary school level material dealing with attempts to study more carefully the personality of the child, the techniques which are developing of accumulating information on a pupil over a long period of time, and some of the newer attempts at evaluation. In some cases where obviously it was not practical to include a complete treatment of a topic it might have been better to omit it entirely. Examples of such points are the treatment of the constancy of the IQ and the scoring of the rearrangement test. * The beginning student will find the volume helpful, and teachers of measurement courses will find the volume usable.

Loyola Ed Digest 15:6 D '39. Austin G. Schmidt. * contains an abundance of material and deserves to be considered by instructors who wish their textbooks to be reasonably complete. The book in general is good but contains little that is strikingly new. *

Sch and Soc 51:352-3 Mr 16 '40. C. C. Crawford. * summarizes in sixty pages the main statistical concepts and processes that are used in treatment of measurement data. This statistical bird's-eye view is remarkably complete, concise and clear for a reader who has already studied a course in statistics, or as a preview to give a "gestalt" of what is to come. * six chapters on standardized tests . . . are specific descriptions of the principal tests, with samples to show the nature of testing devices employed. Also they include critical evaluations of the tests which would be of assistance to those who attempted to select or use tests for particular situations and purposes. *

Sch Executive 59:33 Ja '40. R. L. Bedwell. With definite purposes, practical organization, forceful presentation, and clear treatment, Dr. Broom has produced a valuable contribution to the field of educational measurement. * [The opening chapter on terminology is] an interesting discussion in which the nomenclature peculiar to this subject is used in such manner that the student reaches an understanding of technical terms "ere he is aware" of the difficulties involved. * The chapters end with good summaries, practical exercises, and frequently thorough objective examinations. * organized and presented from the viewpoint of a school administrator who has in mind the definite needs of public school teachers in regard to measurement. * Splendid treatment is given to the construction of teacher-made objective tests. This is a valuable book for teachers-in-service as well as teachers-in-training. There is a minimum of theory and a maximum of practice.

Univ Mich Sch Ed B 11:108 Mr '40. * gives concise and instructive descriptions of the better-known tests * There are two good chapters on teacher-made objective tests. The book represents an unusually sound approach to educational measurements * should find wide use in the education of teachers in the exercise of one of their important functions.

Univ Wash Col Ed Rec 6:79 Mr '40. Worth J. Osburn. * The history of the measurement of intelligence is particularly good. Good descriptions are given of the leading measurement instruments in the language arts, arithmetic, the social studies, and other elementary school subjects. The chapter on the uses of educational measurements is good but rather brief. Ample provisions are made in the way of bibliography. The sections dealing with questions and exercises show the effects of much thought and care. They should prove very useful for use in college classes. The book could have been improved in a number of details which cannot be named here because of limitations in space; none of them, however, is likely to be very objectionable. As a whole the book is as good as or even a bit better than any now on the market.

[B851]

BROWN, CLARA M. **Syllabus for Educational Measurement:** Home Economics Education 192, Part A. Minneapolis, Minn.: Division of Home Economics, University of Minnesota, 1938. Pp. iii, 147. $1.25. Paper, mimeographed.

[B852]

BROWN, MARION; MARTIN, VIBELLA; BOYD, EDNA M.; BROWNLEE, ROBERT E.; HILL, RUBY L.; INMAN-KANE, GRACE; JOSEPHSON, ALANN; KEENE, MANSEL; POWELL, ALVIN; AND SNYDER, DAVID P. **Techniques of Treating Data on Characteristics of High School Students:** The University High School Study of Adolescents: An Investigation Sponsored by the General Education Board and Directed in the Interest of Guidance Service and Curriculum Development. *University High School Journal,* Vol. 18, No. 1. Oakland, Calif.: the Journal, University of California, November 1939. Pp. 47. $0.25. Paper.

Ed Abstracts 5:125 Ap '40. Henry D. Rinsland. * The whole study gives an excellent description of the way data were gathered. *

[B852.1]

BROWN, W., AND THOMSON, G. H. **The Essentials of Mental Measurement,** Fourth edition. London: Cambridge University Press, 1940. Pp. x, 256. 21s. (New York: Macmillan Co. $5.00.)

[B853]

BROWNRIGG, WILLIAM, AND KROEGER, LOUIS J. **Toward Effective Recruiting:** A Method for Notifying Qualified Candidates of Scheduled Examinations. Civil Service Assembly of the United States and Canada, Pamphlet No. 7. Chicago, Ill.: the Assembly, January 1937. Pp. 22. $0.25. Paper, litho-typed.

[B854]

BRYAN, ROY C. **Pupil Rating of Secondary School Teachers.** Columbia University, Teachers College, Contributions to Education No. 708. Percival M. Symonds, faculty sponsor. New York: Bureau of Publications, the College, 1937. Pp. vi, 96. $1.60.

Calif J Sec Ed 14:117-8 F '39. William A. Smith. * Due to the very limited number of administrators participating in the rating, it is, in the opinion of the reviewer, hazardous to generalize upon the degree of agreement between pupil and administrative ratings. * this is a study of first rate importance in the field of secondary school practice. No one seriously concerned in the appraisal and improvement of teachers can afford not to give it thoughtful consideration.

Ed Adm and Sup 24:558-9 O '38. Silas Hertzler.

Ed Res B 18:138-9 My '39. Jesse J. Pugh.

High Points 21:74-5 My '39. A. H. Lass. * Bryan set out to discover what seems to us a rather odd tidbit: the validity of pupil ratings of teachers as compared with ratings given the same teachers by administrators and supervisors. We have heard of stranger ventures, 'tis true, but few seem to us basically so addled as this one. The not too startling conclusion that pupils and supervisors do not rate teachers alike would hardly seem to justify a study like this. The recommendation that pupils' ratings of teachers may even tentatively be employed to improve teaching is too fatuous to call for much comment here. This is the kind of learned impertinence that no self-respecting researcher ought ever to be guilty of. That pupils are shrewd and often accurate judges of teacher efficiency we have all discovered (without any elaborate research). That the little devils have an uncanny capacity for ferreting out teacher weaknesses and playing upon them is an equally common part of pedagogical lore. But that students can render an objective opinion on the teacher's sincerity and craftsmanship is in the realm of the purely conjectural. Certainly, no reputable study has yet indicated that pupil judgments are composed of anything but prejudices, hunches, resentments, "crushes," ennui, and sheer cussedness. * Maybe Dr. Bryan was just fooling. If so, then this is the first example we have encountered of a doctoral ukase delivered tongue in cheek. But we rather suspect that Dr. Bryan's suggestion was offered with

the usual sober albeit tentative objectivity. And we stand upon our homespun rights to discard what runs so brazenly counter to experience until it is proved to the hilt.

Sci Ed 22:336-7 N '38 C(larence) M. P(ruitt). * The data received sound statistical treatment and the study seems to be considerably above the average in worthwhileness.

For additional reviews, see B323.

[B855]

BRYAN, ROY C., AND YNTEMA, OTTO. **A Manual on the Evaluation of Student Reactions in Secondary Schools.** Kalamazoo, Mich.: Western State Teachers College, January 1939. Pp. ii, 56. $0.50. Paper, mimeographed.

Harvard Ed R 10:377-8 My '40. Clarence E. Howell. * Teachers who are sincerely interested in self-improvement through learning their pupils' opinions of them should find the proposals in this book most helpful. If the possibilities the authors offer for revealing the candid attitudes of pupils can be successfully put into effect, they should make a worthwhile contribution, regardless of how unjust those attitudes may be. * Perhaps the entire manual suffers from a lack of clearness and concise presentation, producing an unfavorable first impression. To one who has the time and patience to delve into it, however, the results depicted are most interesting, and the possibilities offered would appear to be well worth trying out.

Loyola Ed Digest 15:9 N '39. Austin G. Schmidt. If you have the courage to wish to know what your students truly think of you and of your methods, you will find here three rating scales (one for use in college) by means of which you should be able to obtain a picture of yourself as you exist in the minds of the members of your class. The authors discuss the larger problems connected with the use of rating scales, establish the reliability of their own scales, and explain how they are to be used.

Teach Col J 11:27 S '39. * an outgrowth of the doctorial dissertation of the first-named writer, although it is not acknowledged in the introduction or elsewhere. Some of the tables are exact copies from the dissertation, and the rating scales used or referred to are either identical or nearly identical in both books. * The *Manual* does not make much reference to the work of earlier investigators in the field, such as Bell, Bird, Book, Bowman, Davis, Engleman, Knight, Shannon, Tryon, and three dozen others. The dissertation, however, includes mention of all but the earlier ones of these. * The chief value of the *Manual* is the helpfulness to teachers who wish to employ a printed form in obtaining and using pupil estimates. Teachers who use some such formal device, or some less formal device, for obtaining pupil reactions will find them valuable means for self-improvement.

Univ Wash Col Ed Rec 5:111-2 Ap '39. Willis L. Uhl. The authors of this manual have published separately three teacher rating forms to be used by high school pupils and college students. These rating forms can be used by teachers without the manual. The manual itself, however, discusses reasons why teachers should obtain their pupils' reactions, procedures to be used in tabulating and interpreting pupils' reactions, and several important issues involved in teacher self-improvement after pupils' reactions have been obtained. * Teachers and administrators alike will find interesting reading in the pages devoted to the individual ratings of fifteen different teachers who range from excellent to very poor. * This material probably provides only the most stimulating supervisory means of improving teaching.

[B855.1]

BUEHLER [BÜHLER], CHARLOTTE, AND HETZER, HILDEGAARD. **Testing Children's Development from Birth to School Age.** Translated from the first German Edition (1932) by Henry Beaumont. New York: Farrar and Rinehart, Inc., 1935. Pp. xi, 191. Out of print. (London: George Allen & Unwin, Ltd. 12s. 6d.)

Brit Med J 3923:534 Mr 14 '36. * Great ingenuity is to be found in the methods evolved by the Viennese workers for the tests in the early months of life.

New R 4:504 N '36. T. J. Padshah. This book . . . satisfies a need long felt by those interested in the development of children. Written in a simple and interesting style, it should be of great use to parents, teachers and all those in charge of institutions for the guidance of the young. *

Times Lit Sup 1784:317 Ap 11 '36. * Those who are conversant with the subject will see that Dr. Buehler has advanced on the "behaviorists" in regarding as fundamental elements in a human personality such things as growth of bodily control, contact with other human beings, the ability of behavior to change on the basis of experience, and striving towards goals. *

For additional reviews, see B44 and B324.

[B856]

BUROS, OSCAR K. **Educational, Psychological, and Personality Tests of 1933, 1934, and 1935.** Rutgers University Bulletin, Vol. 13, No. 1; Studies in Education, No. 9. New Brunswick, N. J.: School of Education, Rutgers University, July 1936. Pp. 83. $0.50. Paper.

B Int Bur Ed 11:86 q 2 '37. * Detailed information is given about each test and there are useful indexes by authors, titles and publishers, and a comprehensive key to classification.

For additional reviews, see B46 and B325.

[B857]

BUROS, OSCAR K. **Educational, Psychological, and Personality Tests of 1936:** Including a Bibliography and Book Review Digest of Measurement Books and Monographs of 1933-36. Rutgers University Bulletin, Vol. 14, No. 2A; Studies in Education, No. 11. New Brunswick, N. J.: School of Education, Rutgers University, August 1937. Pp. 141. $0.75. Paper.

B Int Bur Ed 11:139 q 3 '37. * well arranged list of 364 tests in English speaking countries which have appeared during 1936 and a bibliography of publications in English concerning the measurement of psychology and education from 1933 to 1936 (291 titles). This bibliography is all the more useful because for the majority of the books extracts from reviews in various educational journals are given, amounting in some cases to 12 reviews for one book. *

J Nerv and Mental Dis 90:544 O '39. An extremely useful handy bibliography of the multitudinous tests used in educational work and in the study of personality chiefly from academic sources. A specially valuable feature for reference is the collection of reviews of the "Measurement Books." We find it a valuable extension of Gertrude Hildreth's *Bibliography of Mental Tests and Rating Scales* adapted to educational and psychological activities rather than psychiatric needs.

For additional reviews, see B326.

[B858]

BUROS, OSCAR KRISEN, EDITOR. **The 1938 Mental Measurements Yearbook of the School of Education, Rutgers University.** Foreword by Clarence Elmer Partch. New Brunswick, N. J.: Rutgers University Press, 1938. Pp. xv, 415. $3.00.

Am J Orthopsychiatry 9:659 Jl '39. (John Gray) Peatman. * represents a major accomplishment in the service it provides for anyone at all concerned with educational and psychological tests * For some reason, the Rorschach test, to mention an important omission, is not included. * Trade tests and vocational aptitude tests are not intended to be within the scope of the present Yearbook. There is a real need for an analogous service in the vocational field. If the American Association for Applied Psychology is planning to embark on such a project for this field, it is fortunate in having the present work as a fine example of what can be done in the way of bringing together in one volume a body of useful information with critical appraisals of various types of tests. Or perhaps Buros and his associates can expand the scope of their next yearbook so as to include the vocational field in the one volume. Such an extension would provide a service sorely needed at the present time.

Am J Psychiatry 96:508-9 S '39. W. Line. * a monumental piece of cooperative effort * The reviewer would like to see a section setting forth the main systematic trends from time to time, and a critical evaluation of the major signs of progress, both in test construction and in researches involving test usage. If possible, some of the more qualitative and highly significant psychological tests might also be included, with particular reference to their research application. The author and his collaborators are certainly to be congratulated on the excellence of their product, and on the service they are giving to all workers in this field.

Am J Psychol 53:165-6 Ja '40. John A. Long. * For educators faced with the problem of selecting appropriate tests from the vast reservoir of material on the market these reviews offer a very great service; they make unnecessary most of the guesswork which now characterizes much of the purchasing of standardized tests. Many of the reviews, of course, even though written by experts, will not be above criticism, but this can hardly be avoided, and it would be difficult to offer any important suggestions for the improvement of Buros's work. He is giving us a series of handbooks which should prove indispensable to those engaged in the work of educational measurement and research.

ASLIB Information 39:2 Mr '39. C(yril) B(urt). * the book will be of the utmost value to those who desire to use such tests: it will not only acquaint them with tests of whose existence they might have been unaware, but will also assist them to make a more discriminating selection from the large number on the market * The annotations consist of carefully selected extracts from the more important reviews of each volume * The project, the general plan,

and the mode of execution of the whole volume merit the highest praise. It is earnestly to be hoped that the School of Education of Rutgers University will continue the invaluable work that has thus been so successfully begun.

Austral J Psychol and Philos 17:171-3 Ag '39. C. A. Gibb. To say that this publication has brought up to date Buros's earlier series of "Educational, Psychological and Personality Tests" from 1933 to 1936 would in itself be a great compliment to its editor and co-operating reviewers. But it would still do a gross injustice to the "Yearbook." For the present work has been so greatly extended in scope as to be practically an entirely new publication. * The "Nineteen Thirty-Eight Mental Measurements Yearbook" has not only continued [the features of the earlier series] . . . but has surpassed all expectation in the execution of them and in the enormous extension of their scope. * [the book-review-excerpt section] alone is a contribution worthy of highest admiration. * [the] directories and indexes are very well executed as, indeed, is the whole work. * very nearly indispensable * We await the gift of some such service as this in the many other branches of Psychological and Research study. The School of Education of Rutgers University has pointed a way which none should be ashamed to tread; though many will quake at the mere contemplation of the organisation involved. * We trust it is with good reason that he [the editor] entertains the hope that, by the publication of critical test reviews, test authors and test publishers will be stimulated to produce fewer and better tests. There can be no doubt that in this way the "Yearbook" should make a constructive contribution. * It may be that the collation of book reviews . . . will awaken a professional pride among book reviewers. Should this be so the Mental Measurements Yearbook will have made yet another positive contribution to the science of mental measurement. Australian readers will probably experience some slight disappointment . . . [that the volume] does not include a single contribution from Australia. * In truth, Australia has contributed comparatively little * But still one can find contributions well worth consideration not only in this country, but beyond its shores. * Australian researchers, in particular, should be warned that though they will find a mine of invaluable information in Buros's "Yearbook of Mental Measurements," that information is not, for them at least, absolutely complete. Perhaps it is with insular conceit that one hopes to see future "Yearbooks" embrace the Australian and New Zealand contribution.

B. C. Teach 18:439-40 Ap '39. R. F. Sharp. * Although [the test review] . . . section . . . is a decided improvement over the earlier publications, Sandiford's criticism of the 1936 publication . . . is equally applicable here. He expresses the opinion that "since ninety out of every hundred tests published in the United States should be withdrawn because they have never been satisfactorily validated and standardized. Professor Buros's annual publication would be made much more useful if he would mark with a prominent star those which were valid, reliable, and had satisfactory norms. Then busy workers could neglect the rest, or if they wasted their money on 'gold bricks' the fault would be their own." * The book-review digest section proved very interesting. * The review excerpts have been chosen with discrimination; both appreciative and frankly critical statements have been included. The volume will undoubtedly be welcomed as a guide by those interested in educational and psychological tests. The book reviews should prove of genuine value to those teachers engaged in educational research. Buros goes beyond the confines of the United States and includes publications within the British Empire. Hence this book should prove of special interest to Canadian educationists.

B Int Bur Ed 13:84 q 2 '39.

Binet R 7:32-4 Ja '40. Gretchen P. Seiler. * serves as a beacon to befuddled test consumers and as a searchlight on cocksure test authors and publishers * The [excerpts from book] reviews are well selected being both appreciative and challenging. * The information in the Yearbook is unique, and has been presented scientifically and honestly. This comprehensive work has been done briefly and methodically so that any or all information is readily accessible. *

Brit J Ed Psychol 9:206-7 Je '39 Ll. W(ynn) J(ones). For several years Professor Buros has been regarded as one of the best friends of psychologists engaged in measurement. His *Educational, Psychological and Personality Tests of 1933, 1934 and 1935* is a bibliography of eighty-three pages. His corresponding volume for 1936, containing critical reviews of tests by experts, runs to 141 pages. Now, how-

ever, the tremendous activity of test technicians and writers of books on mental measurements has made it necessary to expand the scope of the service to the extent of 415 pages. * the task of keeping abreast of the times without its aid is almost hopeless * The venture deserves every encouragement and it is fervently to be hoped that the requisite finances will long be available to enable Professor Buros and his staff to continue these ambitious and helpful activities.

Brit J Med Psychol 18:281 pt 2 '39. Wm. Stephenson. * There can be no two minds about the important service afforded by this compilation, and once more Dr. Buros is to be congratulated. * extracts from reviews in current journals . . . make extremely interesting reading. We see the reviewers of every important psychological journal in harness. Most seem to be pulling in the same direction. An enormous number of publications are 'invaluable', 'real services', 'admirable for their clarity', 'excellent' and the like. But every now and then the horses run amok, greatly to our amusement. The arena is then full of contradictory opinions. These make the best reading—especially perhaps the long sections devoted to the Terman-Merrill Revision. * There are, I suppose, at least 200,000 words in this year-book. Everything looks accurate, expert, efficient, thorough, judicious; everything is in place; the format is pleasing; and the book is handy, easy for reference, and a veritable gold-mine of snippets. * Buros, and his large body of compilers, deserve every thanks for a successful venture. No mental tester can afford to miss the year-book. And seeing so much, he can feel a certain pride in being a cog in so extensive a machine.

Brit J Psychol 30:69 Jl '39. * very complete and comprehensive * All the articles and books dealt with are briefly described, and in general the descriptions are very clear and good. * It is to be hoped that the book will find a place in the libraries of all psychological departments and research centres, and that the editor will be encouraged to continue a task which, though it must be arduous, will be of undeniable service to all students who wish to engage in research in the general field covered.

Char and Pers 8:173-4 D '39. William A. Brownell. From the outset the user of standardized tests, whether of intelligence, educational achievement, or personality and aptitude, has been at the mercy of test authors and publishers. He has been at their mercy in the sense that, except for such facts about a test as he could glean from personal examination, he has had only the information that the authors and publishers have supplied him. And, as all critical users of such tests soon learned, this information has by no means always been accurate and complete. It is not unreasonable to hold that the prospective user of a test is entitled to all relevant facts relating to its validation and standardization. Nevertheless, obvious as this requirement seems to be, the essential facts have usually been withheld, with the consequence that tests have commonly been selected with little wisdom and the results obtained have been interpreted with equal lack of caution. Still, corrective measures have been almost wholly limited to the demand that "something ought to be done." Concrete steps for the improvement of the situation have been few in number, apparently in the pious, if unfounded, hope that criticism, alone would bring to test authors and publishers a sense of their moral responsibility. Fortunately, action of a vigorous character has at last been taken. * The reviews . . . represent honest, frank statements of the strengths and the weaknesses of the instruments considered. The editorial policy with regard to these reviews deserves comment. Once reviews had been received, they were retyped in Professor Buros's office (the reviewers' names being deleted) and submitted to the appropriate publishers. Errors of facts were then corrected, and the publishers' comments were sent to reviewers with the suggestion that any needed changes be made. Few reviewers found reason to alter their evaluations, and the editor then printed them exactly as finally received. * There are ample cross references, and the numbering system adopted permits easy keying with earlier books in the series. The whole book reveals a prodigious amount of painstaking work. One does not disparage the worth of the last three fourths of the book when one says that the first fourth, that devoted to evaluations of new tests, is the most valuable part—also the part which demanded the greatest courage to print. The test reviewers followed their instructions to the letter and said precisely what they thought about the tests assigned them. The anguish which must follow (and which has already been made vocal) on the part of test authors and publishers may well be imagined. In spite of objections and lack of co-operation from sources which have been offended, Professor Buros is going ahead with the series and has begun to collect reviews from an enlarged staff for the 1939 yearbook. Happily he is able to report marked change in the attitude of certain publishers, a change which should eventuate in fuller manuals and more comprehensive accounts of the procedures employed in validation. Had nothing else been accomplished by the 1938 yearbook, its appearance and the great labors which entered into its preparation would be justified. Appraisals of the 1938 yearbook have been uniformly favorable, whether made by psychologist or by educator. A few criticisms have appeared: some have decried the use of the term *mental* in the book title, on the ground that "mental tests" do not usually include tests of educational achievement; others have noted the relative absence of the names of prominent technicians in the list of reviewers (a circumstance, the reviewer hazards, which is not the result of oversight on the part of the editor); and still others have questioned the quality of certain reviews. Nevertheless, these criticisms are all minor. The yearbook marks an important milestone in the development of self-critical mental measurement. A job which badly needed to be done has been done—and has been well done.

Chicago Prin Club Rep 31:39 F '39. Turner C. Chandler. * a service to education for which all users of tests may well be grateful. In the past there has been very little information available, particularly concerning validity and reliability, about tests except that furnished by the authors and publishers of the tests. To make this book, more than 125 expert test technicians, subject matter specialists, and psychologists have cooperated to write descriptive, critical, and evaluative reviews of more than 300 commonly used tests of intelligence, achievements, and aptitudes. Each test is usually evaluated by two or more reviewers. * Every principal would do well to consult this book before purchasing tests: first, to get a frank evaluation of tests being considered; and, secondly, to keep informed about the large amount of material available. The publishers indicate that the continuation of this "time-consuming and expensive service" will depend upon whether or not there seems to be a demand for it. To this reviewer it seems to be a distinct contribution to all users of tests.

Civil Service Assembly News Letter 5:11 Je '39. Donald H. Nottage. * a most ambitiously executed compilation * the group intelligence tests and the small number of vocational tests included will be of most interest to personnel administrators. The large majority listed are, however, in the more academic fields and would not be of especial interest to persons in public personnel. * For public personnel administrators who are eager to use new standardized test material as it is put on the market, this book should be a most valuable source of reference for choosing specific tests in the general intelligence and vocational classifications on the basis of evaluations by test experts. For public personnel administrators who are beginning the use of standardized tests, this volume, together with previous yearbooks in the series, gives a most complete list of such material.

Ed 59:583 My '39. Guy M. Wilson. * the work of a conscientious editor and 133 test reviewers. Among the reviewers of the tests are the outstanding men in . . . testing throughout the country together with a great many others who, through the use of tests, have become competent judges as to their strengths and weaknesses. * [the] reviewers have not hesitated to offer adverse criticisms. The general impression . . . is that many of the tests have been constructed mechanically on the basis of textbooks and the traditional school load. It is evident that the day of complacent acceptance of anything labeled "standard tests" has passed, at least for the men who are in a position to view these tests critically. *

Ed Abstracts 4:148-9 Ap '39. Henry D. Rinsland. The importance of this compilation of all publications in the field of tests and measurements cannot be overestimated. To one who teaches or writes, such a complete bibliography and assembly of reviews of important tests, textbooks, and statistical and mechanical devices is of untold value. * These undertakings . . . should be commended by all editors. The many co-operating test reviewers and cooperation of publishers of books, magazines, and tests are to be complimented for their generous and useful contributions. * The classification of tests in the yearbook is well done. The information for each test is as complete as authors and publishers have published. The cross references for locating tests are very helpful,

and the reviews of tests are interesting, stimulating, and decidedly critical. The several indices which include a list of regional testing programs, a periodical dictionary, a publisher's dictionary, and index of titles, and an index of authors and reviewers, are most complete and apparently accurate to a degree seldom found with the publication of so many titles. The review of books in mental measurements is probably the most helpful compilation of information under one cover for any student in this field.

Ed Forum 3:518-9 My '39. * Feeling that those who use standardized tests have often no sound basis upon which to evaluate them, and believing that many tests have been published which are poorly prepared and inadequately validated, the present volume was projected and completed both as a guide to the users and as a deterrent to placing hastily-prepared and ill-advised tests on the market. * Altogether this furnishes a mine of reference materials which could be assembled only with great labor. The teaching profession, in particular those who are concerned with testing programs, are indebted to the School of Education of Rutgers University and to Dr. Buros, the editor, for making available this rich source of reference materials.

El Paso Sch Standard 17:33 S '39. M. E. Broom. * Many of the reviews are quite searching, evaluating in detail the parts of the tests, while others are merely perfunctory notices of the existence of the instruments. This inequality among the reviews is the greatest weakness in the volume. The book contains much valuable information, presented in well arranged form. The volume should have a salutory effect upon test makers and test users. The publication of frankly critical test reviews is likely to cause authors and publishers to publish fewer and better tests. The existence of accurate information about tests is likely to prevent test users from misusing them. This volume is worth while, and it should be continued as an annual publication.

El Sch J 40:154-5 O '39. Howard Easley. What is new in mental testing? What is a good test for a particular purpose? How can one find out about the tests available? This reviewer has been asked these questions frequently. Better answers than he, or any one person, is able to give are now to be found in Professor Buros' guide to the selection and the evaluation of tests and of works on tests and testing. * While it is true . . . that the reviewers do not always agree perfectly in their evaluations, nor with the opinions of others who might have contributed reviews, this disagreement is inevitable in any reviewing project. There is a minimum of contradiction on matters of major significance. The main source of variation is on points of emphasis. It is safe to say that it would be extremely difficult to secure so long a list of more competent reviewers. * The appearance of this volume makes it unnecessary for prospective users of tests to *guess* which tests to use or to ask others for equally bad guesses. Likewise, users of tests should be less at the mercy of the sales "ballyhoo" of test-publishers. These statements do not mean that all the relevant or necessary information concerning any test is available in this volume; but, if it is not, the reason usually is that the information is not available—and making the information available is, after all, the responsibility of the publishers and the authors of the test. If test-users will take this volume as a guide, they will make fewer mistakes than they would by using any other readily available source. It is even more important that such use should have a wholesome effect on the future publication of tests. * It is a small matter, but this reviewer believes that the title involves too broad use of the term "mental measurement." * The editor is to be commended for the idea of producing such a volume, for enlisting the co-operation of such a large number of competent reviewers, and especially for sticking to his guns in the face of objections from publishers and authors concerning certain evaluations of tests. Educators will look forward to the regular appearance of similar volumes in the future.

Family 20:309 Ja '40. Ruth M. Hubbard. * of value chiefly to psychologists in social agencies rather than to case workers, but its value to psychologists is great * a dependable basis for selection from among the multitude of new tests, and for the selection of books in this field for a personal or agency library.

H Sch J 22:211 My '39 A. M. Jordan. * Some reviews are extremely searching and evaluate in detail the various divisions of the test, while several reviews are rather perfunctory notices of the test contents. It is this inequality among the reviews which is the greatest weakness in the present volume. As a whole, users of tests will find in this *Yearbook* a storehouse of valuable information, well arranged, and easily accessible. Such a volume is abundantly worth while and needs to be published each year.

Harvard Ed R 9:370-2 My '39. J. W. M. Rothney. It seems that almost everyone who has worked extensively in the field of tests and measurements has at some time planned to provide a consumers' guide for the purchaser of tests, but the author of the volume under review is the first to make a serious attempt to do so. * The rendering of an opportunity to compare opinions of experts about measurement books is a service which ought to be continued, and the author should be heartily commended for this attempt. It is the test review section, however, about which the controversies will rage. * An examination of the list of co-operating test reviewers reveals many of the famous names of the mental-measurement movement, but one searches in vain for the names of Burt, Dearborn, Freeman, Hull, Kelley, Kuhlmann, Rulon, Spearman, Terman, Thomson, Thorndike, Thurstone, Tryon, and Wilson. It seems obvious that the inclusion of reviews by *more able* test technicians, subject-matter specialists, and psychologists would have strengthened the position taken by the author and it is hoped that their absence was not due to the fact that they did not consider the project worth their time and effort, for the task undertaken in this book requires the services of experts in the field. But even without the famous names, this reviewer believes that the person who turns to the *Mental Measurements Yearbook* for information concerning tests will rarely be misled by the reviewers selected. * an excellent attempt to satisfy a real need * educators . . . will receive much help in the selection of tests if they will read the critical reviews in the Yearbook, and then —remembering that reputation is only one of the many criteria to be used in the choice of test—follow up this first step with a very thorough quest for information about it.

High Points 21:80 O '39. A. H. Lass. The publication of this volume is an occasion to celebrate. For the first time it gives the users of educational tests access to an enormous number of critical appraisals of the tests now literally inundating the profession. Drawn from every conceivable source, these considered opinions enunciated without fear or equivocation supply what has long been needed: honest and detailed professional evaluation of the available measuring devices each of which, if we are to believe the publishers, is the open sesame to some phase or other of the human psyche. For those who would make intelligent use of the available tests, this volume is indispensable. It offers authoritative and unbiased guidance in place of the cloudy rhetoric and chimerical claims of special interests, addled testers, monomaniacal experts, and canny publishers riding high, wide, and not too handsome on the crest of a popular and professional hysteria. * The profession must be deeply indebted to Dr. Buros and his indefatigable colleagues, and to all the experts whose contributions make this volume so uniquely valuable.

Indian J Psychol 14:57-8 Ja '39. M. N. Banerji. None will dispute the claim of Prof. Clarence Elmer Partch . . . that this Yearbook "is likely to prove a landmark of considerable importance" in the literature and history of mental measurement. The volume is a record of very patient and laborious work. It places at the disposal of the readers not merely a mine of information but authoritative opinions regarding recent publications on mental tests. * The Year-book will prove extremely valuable to all users of tests by making available to them expert views on the principles and technique of various tests. The classification of material and indexing are all that can be desired in a volume like this. The critical reviews of the Year-book will have the effect of checking, as the editor says, authors from publishing inadequately validated tests and of encouraging preparation of "better tests." We commend the Editor's remark that "the tests not accompanied by detailed data on their construction, validation, uses and limitations should be suspect." We are convinced that further improvements as projected by the Editor will greatly enhance the value of the Year-books in future. We will only suggest the desirability of some of the old standard tests on the market being evaluated and incorporated as a special supplement in the next issue of the Year-book. All students of mental tests will be grateful to the publishers for bringing out this useful volume.

J Am Assn Col Reg 14:349-50 Ap '39. W. C. Smyser. * the book attempts to do for the users of standardized tests what *Consumers' Research* and similar organizations do for consumers of other goods; namely, make a careful analysis of offerings and present to the prospective buyer an impartial and accurate estimate of the validity of each test and the values to be expected from it. * Rutgers University and Professor Buros have made a notable contribution to educational literature with the publication of this book. It provides an indispensable tool for all who have occasion to administer, to interpret, or to evaluate tests and their results. The co-operating reviewers have been chosen from specialists both in subject-matter and in testing techniques, and they have in general presented their findings with scholarly thoroughness and impartiality. Careful editing and complete and accurate indexing have here placed within easy reach of the test worker an enormous amount of essential material.

J Am Med Assn 113:1058 S 9 '39. * Nothing but editing is contributed by the School of Education, for the comments on the included material are culled from the regular reviews of the tests in the current scientific literature. * a valuable source book for those who are doing mental testing.

J Consulting Psychol 4:77-8 Mr-Ap '40. (F. L. Wells.) This is a type of book that should continue very welcome in the psychometric field. * The usefulness of a book of this kind depends essentially on its editorial organization, and the practical considerations involved here seem to have been fairly met. The experience of the four previous cognate issues is behind it. Especial pains have been taken with indexing. A worthwhile and none too easy job has been well done. None but the most routine worker in the fields covered should try to do without it as a reference work. * an impression is gained that the critique of a test is commonly based on inspection of the record form and the manual for its use, rather than on personal experience with the procedure. This must not be laid heavily to the charge of the editor or writers, who had to obtain review material on relatively short notice, but it does limit the significance of criticisms. To this may also be ascribed some part of a relative stress laid on the observance of statistical canons. The Detroit Learning Aptitude test, for example, fares on this ground worse than it probably would do at the hands of workers experienced in its field use. As a means of evaluating mental powers this procedure compares favorably enough with its congeners, not without structural defects, but bearing a clear and none too usual impress of practical testing experience. * the method of such a volume facilitates comparisons, invidious or otherwise, between the productions of various authors in response to the same intellectual stimulus. It is not impossible for this to sustain, perhaps indeed improve, the critical standards to which offerings in this field are subjected. At all events the establishment of this Yearbook as an institution can hardly fail of favorable effects on the fields to which it is devoted.

J Ed (London) 71:180 Mr '39. * must prove an indispensable volume to educational psychologists and to all who interest themselves in mental tests * Test users, who may now simply turn the pages of the 1938 Yearbook to find reviews of any type of test they propose to use, owe a debt of gratitude to Prof. Buros for the time he has saved them in making their choice. The reviews are frankly critical and not merely descriptive. * Would that some benefactor would provide us with a similar volume dealing with school textbooks! * Unfortunately, the greater number of the tests here reviewed are American in origin, and so not directly applicable in this country. Several important tests published in England are listed but not reviewed.

J Ed Res 33:139-40 O '39. Carter V. Good. * Buros has performed an outstanding service to the field of measurement in his guide to mental measurements * The continuation of such an annual service should have a salutary effect on both authors and publishers of standard tests. * Even though in certain instances the criticisms of the tests may be of uneven value, and in some cases reviews of books are questionable guides for evaluation, it is hoped that this third yearbook of the series, in its expanded form, may be continued annually for the valuable service it renders to users and students of measurement and research instruments.

J Mental Sci 85:807 Jl '39. J. M. Blackburn. The clinical tester, faced with the multitude of tests that have been devised, is often at a loss to know which to choose. His task is made less formidable by the frank evaluative reviews of tests contained in this book. * The book is one that should be in every test clinic, and in view of its bulk it is to be hoped that the critical

reviews will, as the editor says in the preface, encourage "authors and publishers to publish fewer and better tests."

J Nerv and Mental Dis 91:405 Mr '40. * The general reference value of the work is enhanced by the extensive indices *

Jun Col J 9:283-4 F '39. * exceedingly valuable reference volume * Junior college educators interested in any phase of scientific tests and measurements (and this should mean all junior college educators) will find this volume a most valuable source of reference and critical appraisal. *

Labour Mgmt 21:93 My '39. * an extremely useful and careful piece of work * English psychologists who use American tests will find it a valuable book of reference.

Librarian 28:170 F '39. This is, strictly speaking, a bibliography. * American in tone * will certainly serve to make it easier for the teacher, or other tester, to select the most suitable tests for his purpose. The bibliographical information will be found valuable not only by practical psychologists but on occasion by librarians and others concerned with the selection of books and the formation of libraries. We cannot suggest any way in which the method of the book can be simplified, in fact there is every evidence that simplicity has been aimed at: but the fact remains that a certain amount of study is required for the successful use of the book: expressed another way, the more the book is used and understood so much the more will the user get used to it. *

Loyola Ed Digest 14:9 Ja '39. Austin G. Schmidt. * a real and a very substantial contribution. It will prove of help to serious-minded users of tests, to students of the theory of test construction, and to librarians who need to know whether or not a book is worth buying. It is put together in an intelligent and orderly fashion and well indexed. We are much in sympathy, too, with the editor's feeling to the effect that those who construct and publish tests should be forced to publish all available data on their validation, uses, and limitations. But while we are confident that this Yearbook will bring about an improvement, we believe that the editor is a little too sanguine concerning the ability of his reviewers to give dependable appraisals of test validity. Perhaps we are extreme on this point, but we do feel that the one criterion of validity is extended clinical trial under controlled conditions, the amount of trial that is necessary increasing with the delicacy of the function being measured. * Buros is quite right in being supremely interested in test validity. He will render a service by exposing a number of amateurish tests whose validity is palpably doubtful or certainly nil. He will be less successful in arriving at objective evidence as to how valid an apparently good test really is. But in his endeavor to arrive at this evidence he will carry us forward along that difficult path which must be trodden by everyone who works in the field of measurements.

*Math Gazette 23:222 My '39. C. E. Smith. * Competent specialists have been engaged to write critical reviews of each test, and extracts of these together with extracts from published reviews are included under each title. The list of tests covers a surprisingly wide field, the reviews are candidly critical and, as far as can be judged by those tests known to this reviewer, scrupulously fair. A few of them appear to be unnecessarily discursive. It would be an advantage if the reviews were presented in two sections; the first section giving briefly, under suitable uniform headings, such essential facts as purpose of the test, its reliability, validity, standardisation, etc., and the second section giving the reviewers' general criticism. Most of the tests have been prepared for Americans and would not be applicable without revision in this country. British tests are listed but in a number of instances without reviews. *

Mental Hyg (London) 5:38 F '39. Doris M. Odlum. This monumental volume provides an exhaustive survey of the vast body of tests employed in American colleges and schools. * Apparently the group test method is employed in the United States to an extent that has never been even contemplated in this country. * The book is of course purely referential, and only of interest to specialists; but it is undoubtedly valuable, and though it hardly applies to this country, it is interesting to us as an exposition of American testing methods.

Mgmt R 28:69-70 F '39. Richard S. Schultz. * a technical volume which may possess particular value for those interested in personnel research and statistical methods * More emphasis is placed on tests in educational institutions than on those of business organizations. The section on vocational tests, which will be of particular benefit to business organizations, is brief. * Too much emphasis is per-

haps placed on "consumer opinion concerning tests." Tests and measurement techniques are not established by mere opinion, as some of the reviews in this book appear to imply. The merit and practical value of tests in educational institutions and business organizations can be determined only by systematic and scientific criteria, and not by opinions of test users. Certain practical aspects of testing procedure may of course be clarified by obtaining opinions of supervisory and executive personnel, either in education or in industry. Nevertheless, statistical and factual evidence, rather than opinion, fall within the province of specialists in the field.

Nature 143:959 Je 10 '39. R(obert) H. T(houless). * invaluable. It is excellent to see at the end of the description of a test: "these tests serve to increase the number of mediocre tests that are now on the market, without making any scientific contribution to the development of group testing of intelligence." Whether or not this criticism is just in the particular case to which it is applied, it shows the right spirit. Let us hope that this Year-book marks the end of the period of merely listing psychological work without attempting to distinguish the bad from the good.

Occupational Psychol 14:114 Ap '40. * The editor's main aim has been to provide critical reviews of tests and of literature about tests. He has pursued it with a truly remarkable degree of persistence. The book's 400-odd pages are packed with information of value to vocational and educational psychologists. The work of psychologists outside the United States of America is not, perhaps, adequately represented, but it is not ignored.

Occupations 17:470 F '39. Harry D. Kitson. * Constructors of tests are prone to rush new tests on the market without testing them to see if they are reliable and valid, and without offering evidence concerning their practical significance. The editor of this yearbook conceived the idea that if all tests offered for public consumption could be publicly criticized and if their shortcomings could be pointed out and their approximate value appraised by experts, the entire plane of testing would be elevated. * While this volume will still not tell the superintendent or principal or teacher who wishes to "use some tests" exactly which tests he should use, it will at any rate indicate certain ones that may be avoided, and it will enlighten him regarding the considerations that make a test "good or bad." A feature of considerable value is a section (200 pages) of reviews of books on mental measurement, research, and statistics. * anyone who works with mental measurements is bound to need a copy at his elbow.

Personnel Adm 1:16 O '39.

Psychiatry 2:141-2 F '39. Ernest E. Hadley. * evokes admiration * a highly commendable work, foresightfully conceived, efficiently organized and brilliantly executed * Such collated material [excerpts from book reviews] will prove a guide and stimulus to the student. The critical treatment of the items presented will be a boon to the research worker who has specific problems of his own. Together with the *Educational, Psychological and Personality Tests of 1933 and 1934* and the *Educational, Psychological, and Personality Tests of 1936* an extremely fine reference library guide is available to all. *The Nineteen Thirty-Eight Mental Measurements Yearbook* is the continuation of these annual test bibliographies in a greatly expanded form. * Editor Buros has pointed to certain minor improvements. If in some details the present Yearbook does not quite approximate his ideal of perfection, it is none the less comprehensive in scope and unbiased in treatment.

Psychoanalytic Q 9:141-3 Ja '40. Michael B. Dunn. * an efficiently organized guide book * This yearbook and its predecessors . . . are attempts to guide the test user; as such, they are valuable additions to any tester's library. * The inadequacy of standardization of most tests makes it almost imperative for a tester to utilize an evaluating guide of this type before applying a test, or preferably, if he is properly equipped, carefully to evaluate the test himself. * It is this reviewer's opinion that the whole concept of psychological testing as it is used today misplaces the emphasis in the handling of personality problems. * man is at present conceived of as a conglomerate of I.Q.'s, E.Q.'s, P.Q.'s, percentiles, aptitudes, interests —everything but the whole man that he really is. Psychological, educational and technical journals are cluttered with these many new tests flooding an already deluged market, and there is of course an ever ready test user waiting for just such new gadgets. Testing which is based on an atomistic view of the personality inevitably leads to the segmentation that ulti-

mately produces an almost complete dissolution of the personality. It is not this reviewer's intent to imply that all tests are useless; rather that tests should receive only the emphasis which is their due. Testers tend to substitute for an organismic concept of personality a shopworn, outmoded point of view which is not far removed in its fundamental implications from that of the old multiple faculty psychologies. It is apparent from some of the tests that an occasional test developer tries to integrate a number of the segments. But here more than ever the ease with which a test lays claim to omnipotence is glaringly revealed. An 'expert' reviewing one of these tests says of it: 'The information which the test yields enables the teacher to become something of a sociologist, psychologist, mental hygienist, councilor, parent, friend and philosopher'; and it is further suggested that the test results can be a means of educating the community. This is certainly endowing a test with more significance than an entire educational institution dare assume. What is more, this reviewer has observed school guidance directors assuming this all powerful, all knowing rôle when using tests of this nature. The naïveté of this error is too obvious to discuss. The section of the book devoted to character and personality tests seems to have received less attention than some of the other sections. It is precisely in the field of personality tests where the greatest abuse of a test can take place. Consequently, it is in this particular field that the editor and reviewers should really be more thorough and exacting. That this is not the case, however, is especially evident when we come across definitions such as: 'Personality is measured by the ability to control oneself and to serve others' (p. 57); and, 'Emotional instability is a function of inadequate skills and habits' (p. 58). It is interesting to note that one of the few tests on the market today which attempts a qualitative, integrated understanding of personality is not once mentioned throughout the book. This is the Rorschach Personality Test. It would be well to use a test of this type to exemplify the differences between the two views of personality referred to here. Tests can give clues or they can be used as indicators, but their use should be merely a supplement to the psychologist's understanding of personality as a dynamic entity. In all fairness to the editor it must be stated that he appears unsympathetic to the attitude that produces superficial, inadequately standardized tests. It may have been this awareness that led him to the realization of the need for such a Yearbook.

Psychol B 36:698-9 O '39. A. R. Gilliland. * an excellent reference book for all those who are interested in the construction and use of any kind of psychological test. Here, the classroom teacher, the college teacher of tests and measurements, the clinical worker, the personnel director, and the research worker will find in concise, convenient form the pertinent facts about the recently constructed tests, as well as brief abstracts and references to practically all of the critical material about tests that has been written in the last few years. The 1938 Mental Measurements Yearbook is the most comprehensive compendium in the field, and it is to be hoped it will be followed up by later editions, if not annually, at least biennially. It constitutes a very complete psychological abstract in this one field.

Psychologists League J 3:47-8 Mr-Ap '39. M. M. Meyer. * The yearbook contains only a small sampling of tests in each field * Many of the reviews are simply uncritical descriptions of the tests; others include pertinent data but without any evaluation which leaves the reader in much the same quandary as before reference to the yearbook. More important is the problem of trying to take into account the competency and bias of the many reviewers. Whether a permanent Board of Reviewers or the presentation of the most pertinent data offers the best solution, seems to be a moot point. In view of the fact that present plans call for a yearly issue it would probably be more helpful to use a suitable looseleaf system rather than an additional book each year. More fundamental however is the author's plan of causing "test authors, publishers, and reviewers" to be more cautious in their work and to present the relevant data upon which their work is based. Certainly such an outlook is decidedly worthy of support, even though at the moment it may appear unduly optimistic. For the fulfilment of this goal it seems necessary that the process of reviewing be organized in a more precise fashion than the present which appears to be too dependent upon the fallible procedure of random sampling. It also requires that the individual reviews all be as objectively critical as a few contained in this volume. The editor indicates that as far as

possible each test was distributed among both conservative and progressive psychologists in order to obtain a fair sampling of criticisms. Such a procedure is either obviously absurd or a serious indictment against a profession which attempts to be scientific and yet cannot objectively evaluate one of its most objective instruments. It would seem far more desirable to distribute tests to psychologists in the various branches of the profession to determine the most suitable uses of each test and to submit the tests to the specialists for evaluation of the criteria on which they are based. Due consideration must be given to the fact that the monograph is a first venture in the present form and, despite its flaws, is definitely a beginning in the correct direction.

Psychometrika 4:73 Mr '39. Stanley G. Dulsky. * The reviews of the tests constitute the most important feature of the *1938 Yearbook*. A series of critical comments on tests is, of course, no stronger nor more valuable than the individual comments themselves. It is amazing to this reviewer to find in print so much fulsome praise heaped on tests, when in private conversations, these same tests are regarded as almost worthless. This is no reflection on Mr. Buros, who obviously attempted to secure as frank and evaluative comments as possible. What's the matter with the critics— are they afraid of hurting someone's feelings? As a result of sampling the reviews of some three dozen tests in a number of fields I find good critical comments in about sixty per cent, perfunctory remarks in thirty per cent, and definitely poor reviews in ten per cent. In general, the more reviews there were of a test the greater was the value of this service to the reader. The editor should continue to strive for at least two reviews of each test. The "Key to Classification of Tests" (pp. 9-13) should be revised because the physical features of these pages render the search for a section difficult; it would also be advisable to add the page number of the section. I agree with Sandiford and Traxler, two of the many reviewers of the 1936 Yearbook, that good tests should be starred, and that a brief descriptive statement concerning each test should be included whenever the purpose of the test is not clearly indicated by its title. No one can read the section "Cooperative Test Reviewing" (pp. 4-7) without realizing the tremendous effort Mr. Buros has put into this book.

Every psychologist will undoubtedly agree that the goal of the 1938 *Yearbook* is laudable; an auspicious start has already been made. Its value to us will depend on our efforts. Can we cooperate with Mr. Buros by contributing keen, fearless, criticism?

Q R Biol 14:383 S '39. * a comprehensive and systematic review and criticism of mental tests and books on mental tests. The book is frankly critical and starts with the assumption that ". . . ninety out of every hundred tests published in the United States should be withdrawn because they have never been satisfactorily validated and standardized." The value of the book is greatly enhanced by the cooperative reviewing of over a hundred specialists in the field of testing. This *Yearbook* is a "must have" for all those operating in the field of mental testing.

Sch 27:552 F '39. *J(ohn) A. L(ong).* If, as promised, this is but the forerunner of similar annual volumes, it can be accepted as marking a landmark in the literature of educational measurement. * No one who is actively engaged in the work of educational measurement can well do without so timely a reference. In his search for tests appropriate for his needs, he can save himself much time and expense by coming here for his information.

Sch R 47:468-9 Je '39. *Alvin C. Eurich.* Principals, teachers, test technicians, and educational research workers have long felt the need for a handbook on tests. * In the Introduction the editor indicates that the need for such a volume is more pressing than is ordinarily assumed. "There probably has never before been a two-year period," he says, "in which so many tests were published. Furthermore, there probably has never been a time when so little information was presented about published tests" (p. 3). The evidence for this statement is not given, but anyone working in the field of measurement is constantly impressed with the paucity of information about tests. * Practically all the 133 reviewers who co-operated with the editor of this book have contributed to the testing movement. * Obviously, with so many individual contributions, the reviews vary widely in providing critical appraisals of tests. * By and large, the editor was most scholarly in the preparation of the yearbook. The following generalization in the Introduction, however, needs to be challenged: "For most of its tests, the Cooperative Test Service

has given even less information than the commercial publishers" (p. 3). Having worked with information supplied by the Cooperative Test Service and by commercial publishers, the present reviewer is of the opinion that the information supplied by the former is far more adequate than that supplied by the average publisher of tests. Nevertheless, this criticism should not detract from the usefulness of the yearbook. It is indispensable to any person seriously interested in tests.

Social Ed 3:287-8 Ap '39. *Horace T. Morse.* * a work of major reference in the field of measurement * This is an excellent continuation of the previous similar volumes produced by Professor Buros. A new and highly desirable feature is the inclusion of original test reviews representing a wide range of reviewers, subject matter specialists as well as test technicians. The reviews are significant in revealing the common concern about improving the quality of tests published as well as for the variety of viewpoints presented. A particularly commendable feature is the relatively complete information given about each test. Thorough indexing and cross references aid the reader to get complete references concerning any field with an economy of time. It is unfortunate that many of the test reviewers use valuable space in describing the make-up, types of items of a test, etc., even when they are not criticizing these features. This information might have been incorporated with the other relevant data by the editor with little extra time or space. This volume is indispensable to any schools contemplating the use of standardized tests as well as to anyone who is interested in measurement. * Classroom teachers in any field would learn much from an examination of the section on tests, and would find particularly convenient the book review section representing a wider scope than that offered by the *Book Review Digest*. A book such as this should have a salutary effect in influencing authors and publishers to present better tests. A "Test Consumers' Research Bureau" has long been a desideratum, and the School of Education of Rutgers University should be commended for undertaking a service that will start clearing the way through the maze of tests and measurement material now available.

Social Service R 13:554 S '39. *S. J. Beck.* * The value of a work such as this hardly requires discussion. Any clinician who must choose from among the many new tests that issue yearly will be grateful for having so handy a reference volume. * With some of the proposals of the author this reviewer does not fully concur—as, for example, the suggested bureau of standards in the mental-test field * Buros' own volume will facilitate the assaying of psychological test material. In obtaining the capable co-operating test reviewers he is to be congratulated for what must have been a difficult task. The volume is recommended to psychologists, whether in clinics, schools, or personnel offices, who avail themselves of scientific test methods.

Sociol and Social Res 23:581-2 Jl-Ag '39. E(mory) S. B(ogardus). * A wide range of reviewers and of periodicals has been utilized. Many schools of thought are represented. * The School of Education of Rutgers University is deserving of high praise for sponsoring so valuable a Yearbook, and one that is certain to become increasingly useful. It is difficult to appreciate the vast amount of painstaking work which has been put into bringing together and preparing so well-executed a handbook.

Teaching 11:143 Mr '39. A most comprehensive and reliable guide to tests of all kinds and a book which no training college can afford to be without. * Thus test-users are given all possible help in selecting the tests which are most likely to meet their needs, and also receive valuable suggestions as to the right evaluation of a test. * The authoritative reviews included in the Yearbook will no doubt lead authors of tests to think over more carefully their own beliefs and values with respect to testing and to publish fewer but better tests. The first two sections of the book are likely to be of most interest to teachers in India * It is to be hoped that adequate financial support will be forthcoming to enable the Rutgers University to carry on its good work in the measurements field.

Training Sch B 36:77-8 Je '39. Alice W. Goodman. * The editor . . . essayed to have each test included critically evaluated by two or more persons, though space limitations, last minute refusals, and the like, caused many of the tests to have but single reviews. * well-arranged and completely indexed * If these yearbooks do no more than to make the test user more critical of the instrument he employs, and the test maker more concerned

with more careful test construction, they will have served a worthy and estimable purpose.

Univ Mich Sch Ed B 10:63 Ja '39. * co-operating reviewers of exceptional competence, from all parts of the country, provided detailed critical evaluations of the tests, most tests having several independent reviews * an unusually valuable source of information.

Univ Wash Col Ed Rec 5:128 My '39. Francis F. Powers. * serves the highly practical purpose of making a panoramic survey of the measurements available in a given field without exhaustive correspondence and examination of catalogues. The section . . . on "Research and Statistical Methodology Books" is particularly well done. The practical service value of this volume is increased by the accuracy and care with which the descriptive items are selected. * This book deserves a sale . . . among wide-awake personnel workers at all levels of the educational system.

Va Teach 20:37-8 F '39. W. J. Gifford. In this unusual volume the editor has utilized the help of the WPA and the American Council on Education. * a comprehensive guide to the whole matter of testing * Any one who uses tests at all or the results of tests will find genuine help and guidance in this volume. One cannot work with the volume, even for a brief period of time, without learning that here is the work of a fearless young educator who recognizes the fact that the testing movement, which purported to be *the* scientific development in education, has turned out to be quite otherwise. * While many of the reviews seem to be rather colorless, many on the other hand are very critical of the procedures in developing a given test and of the information available for those who use the test. If it proves possible for the editor to carry on this work for a period of years . . . there is no doubt that in a few years educational tests that are prepared will be much more carefully worked out and validated, and that the exorbitant claims, sometimes approaching those for patent medicines, will be greatly reduced. It is distinctly up to American educators and psychologists to stand definitely behind this genuinely fruitful and promising piece of scholarly investigation.

Voc Guid Digest 5:25 F '39. * Valuable reference book *

[B858.1]

CAPPS, HARRY MARCELLUS. **Vocabulary Changes in Mental Deterioration:** The Relationship of Vocabulary Functioning as Measured by a Variety of Word Meaning and Usage Tests to Clinically Estimated Degrees of Mental Deterioration in 'Idiopathic' Epilepsy. Columbia University, Archives of Psychology, No. 242. New York: the University, September 1939. Pp. 81. $1.25. Paper.

Am J Orthopsychiatry 10:638 Jl '40. * will be of interest to clinicians dealing with the problem of deterioration in general and its manifestation in epilepsy in particular. The writer studied 80 cases of "idiopathic" epilepsy in men and women at Craig Colony for Epileptics and controlled his work by similar investigations in 20 normal people resident there. The report is of value (*a*) for techniques used, pointing to methods of ingress into the difficult problem of the presence of real deterioration; (*b*) review of literature and previous work in the field; (*c*) findings, not entirely orthodox, e.g., "that vocabulary functioning is likewise closely related to the deterioration of mental functioning." The theoretical significance which Dr. Capps abstracts from his findings provokes some refreshing thinking on deterioration and methods of recognizing it.

[B859]

CATTELL, RAYMOND B. **The Fight for Our National Intelligence.** Introduction by Lord Horder, Major Leonard Darwin, and F. P. Armitage. London: P. S. King & Son, Ltd., 1937. Pp. xx, 166. 8*s.* 6*d.*

B Int Bur Ed 11:138 q 3 '37. * It may be that he exaggerates the danger and also that his view of England's stratified population is too static. * His book is a startling one and it should awaken the intelligent from their lazy indifference.

Brit Med J 3991:15-6 Jl 3 '37. * a painstaking psychological and statistical investigation of intelligence in a limited population in definite areas, alleged to be typical * Controls were lacking. Doubtless it was not possible to do much more, but these are very meagre materials on which to base the dogmatic and far-reaching conclusions to which the investigator invites us. * The very title of the book suggests a bias. * But if the book be read throughout in a cautious and alertly critical spirit much of it will be of value. Its facts are helpful, though by no means conclusive. Its arguments are well stated, though often specious. Its inference that our national intelligence has, since about 1875, been rapidly decreasing through a differential birth rate, whereas up to that time it had been increasing through a differential death rate, is not established. The

remedies suggested for such decline as there may be are perhaps more moderately stated than would seem to be justified by the course of the discussion. *

Lancet 5938:1475 Je 19 '37. * The facts adduced by Dr. Cattell are unquestionably interesting and suggestive; but the informed reader will feel that they hardly support the crushing superstructure of social and philosophical theorising which is built on them. The technical basis of the inquiry receives but the scantiest discussion. No details are given of the specially designed non-verbal intelligence tests which were employed; the reader is not told whether group tests were used; and the all-important question of sampling is dismissed in a footnote. *

For additional reviews, see B328.

[B860]

CATTELL, RAYMOND B. **A Guide to Mental Testing:** For Psychological Clinics, Schools, and Industrial Psychologists: Being a Handbook of Tests of Intelligence, Attainment, Special Aptitudes, Interest, Attitude, Temperament, and Character. Foreword by William Moodie. London: University of London Press, Ltd., 1936. Pp. xvi, 312. 10*s.* 6*d.*

Brit Med J 3969:221-2 Ja 30 '37. * Cattell has endeavoured "to provide sufficient instructions, test materials, and norms to aid the experimenter in assessing the principal aspects of personality so far made accessible to direct examination." In this he has undoubtedly succeeded. As a work of reference his book should prove invaluable. * As is usual in such a compilation some errors have crept into the list of tests. * These are but small drawbacks to a most valuable list. As a clinical manual the work is less satisfactory, and the psychiatrist or certifying officer seeking an introduction to the thorny subject of psychometrics from a clinical point of view will find the book's usefulness limited by its author's unswerving loyalty to the tenets of the factorial school of Spearman, both in his recommendation of tests and in his discussion of the psychological basis of testing. The statistical psychologist is interested primarily in the trait rather than in the patient, in mathematical validity rather than in clinical usefulness, an attitude which is justifiable in the laboratory but not in the consulting room. This is especially seen in the emotional field, where the clinician is particularly at home, the statistician particularly at sea. Dr. Cattell as a good statistician condemns, for example, the Rorschach test; it is inadequately standardized, it "measures" no "trait," and its interpretation is largely subjective. Yet the Rorschach is perhaps the most valuable weapon we have in the clinical approach to personality problems. Certainly it is of far greater use than the many question-and-answer methods which Dr. Cattell has listed so completely; the direct questionary approach to psychological patients is rarely useful and often dangerous; what physician would submit to a psychoneurotic a list of twenty leading questions dealing with his possible symptoms? Plainly the gulf between the statistician and the clinician is a wide one, and nowhere wider than in the field of dynamic psychology. Equally plainly there will come with increasing knowledge a narrowing of that gulf. Meanwhile the clinician may be grateful to Dr. Cattell for his statement of an opposing case, and may feel that in stating it he has added to the common store of knowledge, and in doing so has helped to bridge the gulf.

Civil Service Assembly News Letter 3:6 Ap '37. This book is an English counterpart of "Measurement in Psychology" by Thelma Hunt * well illustrated with examination material *

Lancet 231:379 Ag 15 '36. In a foreword to this book, Dr. William Moodie . . . aptly describes its place and function. "Here," he says, "for the first time is collected under one cover reliable information on all aspects of the subject." It is, in fact, a pioneer work and very efficiently achieves its purpose. * Inevitably at some places the book becomes a catalogue, for it is impossible to give all tests in detail, but each section contains a very full discussion of the rationale of the methods of testing and of the present position of research in the field concerned. The book ends with a chapter on the selection of tests for specific purposes and their interpretation, probably the most valuable chapter in the book to the examiner. * Cattell is extremely interesting on the question of proper interpretation of the meaning of the results of any test in themselves, and in their relation to other tests. *

For additional reviews, see B48 and B329.

[B861]

CEBOLLERO, PEDRO ANGEL. **Reactions of Puerto Rican Children in New York City to Psychological Tests.** San Juan, Puerto Rico: Puerto Rico School Review, 1936. Pp. 11. $0.25. Paper.

[B862]

CHAPPLE, ELIOT D., WITH THE COLLABORATION OF CONRAD M. ARENSBERG. **Measuring Human Relations:** An Introduction to the Study of the Interaction of Individuals. *Genetic Psychology Monographs,* Vol. 22, No. 1. Worcester, Mass.: Journal Press, February 1940. Pp. 147. $3.00. Paper.

[B863]

CLARKE, E. R. **Predictable Accuracy in Examinations.** British Journal of Psychology Monograph Supplements, Vol. 8, No. 24. London: Cambridge University Press, 1940. Pp. vi, 48. 5s. Paper.

[B864]

CLEETON, GLEN U., AND MASON, CHARLES W. **Executive Ability:** Its Discovery and Development. Yellow Springs, Ohio: Antioch Press, 1934. Pp. xvi, 210. $2.00.

Personnel J 14:32-3 My '35. Edward S. Cowdrick. In this latest attempt to isolate the germ of executive ability, the chief faults are due to the authors' ambition to talk to too large an audience. The thesis is directed sometimes to industrial managers, sometimes to personnel or educational specialists, sometimes to youthful aspirants to executive rank. Consequently it lacks cohesion of material and unity of purpose. It covers the fields of psychology, personnel administration and industrial engineering, with occasional sketchy incursions into the realm of general management. Mingled with up-to-the-minute reports of first class research in rating and tests, one finds some admonitions that are faintly reminiscent of the old courses in personal efficiency. But the reader who makes allowance for this defective method of approach will find in the book much that is of value. The analysis of executive functions, and of the traits of personality that conduce to their successful performance, is penetrating and honest. The authors are especially skillful in their discrimination between executive ability and leadership, pointing out that the latter is an essential ingredient of, but does not necessarily include, the former. They shrewdly indicate the difference between leadership qualities that are allied to executive capacity, and those that function most successfully in the field of politics. They emphasize the importance of the ability to reach decisions, which they consider a vital element in the executive's qualifications. * Much of the book is given up to descriptions of rating systems and tests designed to disclose executive possibilities. * The appendices present the details of a series of tests, mainly the work of Mason, which have been used in experimental work with moderate success. * Throughout the book, stress is laid upon the requirements of present-day industry and the essential difference between the old-fashioned domineering boss—however successful in his environment—and the many-sided expert in conference and coördination who has been brought to the top by the demands of depression and recovery. Here they are on solid ground and their conclusions are in line with those of the most advanced industrial thinkers.

[B865]
College Entrance Examination Board. **College Entrance Examination Board Questions Set at the Examinations of June, 1938.** Boston, Mass.: Ginn and Co., 1938. Pp. v, 139. $1.60.

[B866]
College Entrance Examination Board. **College Entrance Examination Board Questions Set at the Examination of June, 1939.** Boston, Mass.: Ginn and Co., 1939. Pp. v, 133. $1.60.

[B867]
College Entrance Examination Board. **Description of Examinations:** Edition of December 1938. New York: the Board, [1938]. Pp. 89. $0.30. Paper.

[B868]
College Entrance Examination Board. **Thirty-Eighth Annual Report of the Executive Secretary, 1938.** New York: the Board, [1938]. Pp. ix, 129. $0.25. Paper.

Loyola Ed Digest 14:12 Mr '39. Austin G. Schmidt. In addition to complete data on the number, distribution, and so forth, of boys and girls who took the College Entrance Examination Board examinations in 1938, this report contains painstaking and interesting studies of the Scholastic Aptitude Test and the Mathematics Attainment Test. There are also data on the accuracy with which tests are scored.

[B869]
College Entrance Examination Board. **Thirty-Ninth Annual Report of the Executive Secretary, 1939.** New York: the Board, [1939]. Pp. x, 114. $0.25. Paper.

Sch and Soc 51:679-81 My 25 '40. David Snedden. * discusses a year's operations devoted "chiefly to appraisal and review" *

[B870]
Collmann, R. D., and Jorgensen, C. **Three Studies in the Prediction of Scholastic Success.** Australian Council for Educational Research, Educational Research Series, No. 35. Melbourne, Australia: Melbourne University Press, 1935. Pp. 68. 3s. Paper. (London: Oxford University Press.) (New York: G. E. Stechert & Co. $0.75.)

[B871]
Congdon, Nora A. **The 1940 Report on the Cooperative Testing Program of the Teachers College Personnel Association.** Ninth Annual Report. Greeley, Colo.: Colorado State College of Education, February 1940. Pp. 32. $0.25. Paper.

[B872]
Conway, Clifford B. **The Hearing Abilities of Children in Toronto Public Schools.** University of Toronto, Ontario College of Education, Department of Educational Research, Bulletin No. 9. Toronto, Canada: the Department, 1937. Pp. 132. $0.75. Paper.

B Int Bur Ed 12:35-6 q 1 '38. * As an attempt to solve the problem of mass testing of hearing this report is valuable. *

Brit J Ed Psychol 9:210 Je '39. * The author quite rightly emphasises the great importance of accurate testing of the hearing of children as defects are more frequent than is generally realised.

For additional reviews, see B334.

[B872.1]
Cox, J. W. **Manual Skill:** Its Organization and Development. London: Cambridge University Press, 1934. Pp. xx, 247. 16s. (New York: Macmillan Co. $5.00.)

Brit Med J 3856:994 D 1 '34. * A number of conclusions were arrived at which should, if confirmed, be of very great advantage to industry. *

Times Lit Sup 1707:714 O 18 '34. * Cox . . . took about one hundred boys and girls, some backward, and forty grown-ups. Before each of them he set about twenty small parts, porcelain block, metal blocks, screws, nuts, springs, rings, covers, and asked the patient to fit them together. It is not clear whether any or all of them knew that the result would be an electric lampholder, but most of them succeeded within forty-five minutes. Then they spent an hour or so a day for eleven days in assembling and disassembling similar lampholders as fast as they could, Mr. Cox timing each operation in seconds. Some of them skipped most of the practice and received training instead, after which practisers and trainees were matched against each other. The purpose was to measure how far general intelligence, mechanical aptitude, routine skill and manipulative skill go together, and whether the improvement due to practice in one operation is transferable to other operations. * Sometimes Mr. Cox seems a little more optimistic than his own diagrams justify; for instance, Fig. 48 hardly justifies the claimed advantage of reasoned training over mere practice; trainees and practisers are equal at the end. The promise on page 76 to disentangle the two factors, mechanical skill and manipulative skill, is never fulfilled; indeed, page 181 acknowledges the failure to do so. Evidently more tests are needed yet.

For additional reviews, see B336.

[B873]

Cozens, Frederick Warren; Cubberley, Hazel J.; and Neilson, Neils P. **Achievement Scales in Physical Education Activities for Secondary School Girls and College Women.** New York: A. S. Barnes and Co., 1937. Pp. ix, 165. $2.00.

Ed Abstracts 3:234 Je '38. Wilda Logan. * These scales may be used advantageously in any part of the United States. Women and girl students will find real satisfaction when improvement in individual performance is found by a comparison of their first and subsequent achievement scores.

Ed Res B 18:82 Mr '39. Virginia Blunt. * contains carefully constructed tests in a wide variety of activities such as baseball, archery, hockey, basketball, and the like, with detailed instructions for their administration, as well as the achievement scales constructed from the tests. The techniques used in preparing the scales are also clearly propounded and their purposes and the uses to which they can be put elaborated. * it is well to keep in mind that measurement is but one phase of evaluation and the development of motor skill but one of many objectives. On the other hand, when such tests and scales are admittedly used as a part of a broader evaluation program, they are extremely valuable.

Pub Health R 7:6 Ap '38. Marie Hartwig. * should be in the possession of teachers wishing to use or develop achievement tests at these levels.

For additional reviews, see B337.

[B874]

Criswell, Joan Henning. **A Sociometric Study of Race Cleavage in the Classroom.** Columbia University, Archives of Psychology, No. 235. New York: the University, January 1939. Pp. 82. $1.25. Paper.

Sociometry 3:105-8 Ja '40. Barbara S. Burks. This is one of the most ingenious sociometric studies which the reviewer has had the pleasure of reading since "Who Shall Survive?" swam into her ken like a new planet in 1934. Taking her lead from Moreno's brief treatment of the absorption of minorities into class group structures, the author poses and answers questions which bear upon age and sex trends in attitudes toward minorities, attitudes of both white and Negro children when they constitute minorities and majorities, prestige status in white and Negro groups with respect to intra- and inter-racial choices, skin-color cleavages within majority-colored classes, and motivations for choices and rejections. * When a study is conceived with so much originality, insight, and sense of its social framework as this one, a reviewer would be making poor use of his space to carp about trivia. It seems highly relevant, however, to point out that a ratio—particularly when it is a ratio of two ratios (i.e., the "ratio of preference") is a statistic most sensitive to sampling fluctuations. While the chi-square treatment . . . indicates the improbability of a given result arising by chance, it gives us no information regarding the validity of *trends* which we find or believe we find in a series of ratios arranged according to some variable such as majority-minority composition of class groups. Many of the author's formulations appear so clearly from even a hasty digest of the tabular material that criteria of validity seem unnecessary, but in some comparisons the results are by no means consistent. When this happens, the author either draws an inference which she believes best to represent the data as a whole (e.g., "boys reject most strongly the small minorities," p. 33, based upon quite variable results in Tables 6 to 9), or she offers a formulation which can account for the disparities (e.g., "where whites outnumber Negroes, the colored membership either forms a very distinct group, thus greatly increasing cleavage, or they completely accept the whites," p. 24, based upon the "preference ratios" for only three classes of girls in Table 2). The reader will have to decide for himself which of the trends noted by Criswell seem established beyond cavil, excepting in the treatment by the *t-test* technique of differences in self-preference of large and small majority groups (pp. 68-69). The *t-test* or some other test of significance might appropriately be used much more extensively in Criswell's study. One other question deserves mention: this concerns the interpretation of the "ratio of preference." This ratio is the *pièce de résistance* of the investigation, and Criswell has assumed (by implication) that it provides a direct measure of the strength of a tendency to choose white or Negro children. It would appear, however, that the ratio of preference might be influenced by size of majority or minority in a purely mechanical fashion; that the strength of the tendency to select from one's own racial group might remain constant even while the ratio underwent considerable change. * It would doubtless be worth while to check some of the results by applying some other index of preference, e.g., an altogether simple and direct count of the actual proportions of white or Negro choices under varying conditions. The actual strength of tendency could then be assumed to lie somewhere between the margins delimited by the technique which was used and the one proposed.

[B875]

CROOK, MASON N. **Differential Responses to Personality Test Items.** *Psychological Record,* Vol. 1, No. 14. Bloomington, Ind.: Principia Press, Inc., August 1937. Pp. 187-94. $0.15. Paper.

[B876]

CURETON, THOMAS K., JR. **Beginning and Intermediate National Y.M.C.A. Progressive Aquatic Tests.** Y.M.C.A. Aquatic Literature, New Series, Vol. 2. New York: Association Press, 1938. Pp. 59. $0.50. Paper.

[B877]

DAVIS, EDITH A. **The Development of Linguistic Skill in Twins, Singletons with Siblings, and Only Children from Age Five to Ten Years.** Foreword by John E. Anderson. University of Minnesota, Institute of Child Welfare, Monograph Series, No. 14. Minneapolis, Minn.: University of Minnesota Press, 1937. Pp. x, 165. $2.00. (London: Oxford University Press. 9s.)

Am J Psychol 52:154-5 Ja '39. Martha G. Colby. Like Piaget, Mrs. Davis has emphasized the symbolic content, rather than the mechanical aspects of speech development. In addition, however, she has contributed a more objective technique, a more controlled selection of subjects, and a statistical analysis of her protocol data. *

Am J Sociol 44:463-9 N '38. Kimball Young.

J Juvenile Res 22:217-8 Jl-O '38. Juanita Pico.

For additional reviews, see B341.

[B878]

DAVIS, FREDERICK B. **Table of Equivalence Values for Intelligence Quotients Derived from the 1916 and 1937 Revisions of the Stanford-Binet Scales.** Avon, Conn.: Avon Old Farms, 1939. Pp. 4. Privately distributed. Paper.

[B879]

DEARBORN, WALTER F.; ROTHNEY, JOHN W. M.; AND SHUTTLEWORTH, FRANK K. **Data on the Growth of Public School Children:** From the Materials of the Harvard Growth Study. Monographs of the Society for Research in Child Development, Vol. 3, No. 1, Serial No. 14. Washington, D. C.: the Society, National Research Council, 1938. Pp. iii, 136. $1.00. Paper, lithotyped.

Am J Med Sci 196:739 N '38. J. S.

Childh Ed 16:187 D '39. John A. Hockett.

Endocrinology 23:245 Ag '38. Endocrinologists who are interested in research on growth and development will find this monograph a rich source of carefully obtained primary data. * As a source of normal control data, the collection is unique.

Sch R 47:309-11 Ap '39. Fowler D. Brooks. * should prove of value to persons interested in using the seriatim measurements for further investigation of growth and development during childhood and adolescence *

For an additional review, see B343.

[B880]

DEAVER, GEORGE G. **Fundamentals of Physical Examination.** Philadelphia, Pa., and London: W. B. Saunders Co., 1939. Pp. 299. $2.75; 12s. 6d.

Brit Med J 4086:874 Ap 29 '39. * It is difficult to believe that the bulk of this volume is really necessary for lay workers except as a book of reference, but Dr. Deaver's reputation stands high, and it can only be concluded that the world of American education differs greatly from its counterpart in this country. For any such audience, however, it is difficult to justify certain of the illustrations, such as that of a primary chancre on the penis.

Chicago Sch J 21:233 Mr-Ap '40. R. C. G. * In the few instances where the author's own opinions are expressed, they are conservative. Many of the illustrations found in the book are very instructive; a few are of extreme abnormalities rarely seen, except in textbooks, even by practicing physicians.

Ed Abstracts 4:272-3 O '39. N. P. Neilson. * As a handbook for administrators, teachers, nurses and others who aid the physician in the physical examination, this book is a significant contribution. An understanding of medical terms, tests, and measuring procedures in use today is necessary before the physical examination receives the consideration it merits.

Edinburgh Med J 47:144-5 F '40. * Several criticisms may be made of the information supplied. It seems doubtful whether it is desirable to describe in detail the delimitation of the heart by percussion and the value of the X-ray examination of the chest might well be emphasised. In summarizing the features of acute appendicitis the pain is described as occurring in the lower quadrant of the abdomen and no mention is made of the earlier central pain. Such an omission might easily give rise to a dangerous misconception in the mind of the non-medical reader. It is difficult to understand how the contents of this book could be usefully taught to any person who has not the average medical student's grounding in the basic sciences. In this country it will be of value only to the medical student and the physician. The illustrations tend to portray the extreme rather than the usual picture of abnormality.

Glasgow Med J 131:236 My '39. * The first part is concerned chiefly with procedure of examination, general bodily development and posture. It admirably fulfils the author's first purpose for his book, the early recognition of signs and symptoms of abnormal function. He avoids dogma, and shows a full grasp of his subject by presenting it in an interesting and concise manner. The "health records" recommended seem cumbersome but might work satisfactorily in the purpose for which they are intended. * The second part of the book deals with the special systems. It is questionable if the methods of examination are not too advanced for those for whom they are intended. * must be difficult reading for the non-medical student.

J Social Hyg 25:307-8 Je '39.

Lancet 138:225 F 3 '40. * Deaver argues that the physical instructor will cooperate more effectively with the doctor if he has a smattering of the doctor's language, and knows something of what the doctor is looking for when he examines a patient. So he has written this manual of physical examination, covering largely the same ground as the standard manuals for medical students, but simplified a little, and so written that the lay student can follow it easily and learn the meanings of medical terms as he goes along. There is special emphasis on methods of measurement and on posture and deformities, and enough simple explanation of disease processes to lend the story interest. The thing is done both well and thoroughly, and does not err on the side of being too elementary.

Loyola Ed Digest 14:8 Ap '39. Austin G. Schmidt. Written for school nurses, teachers of physical education, and workers in the field of public health * Numerous well-made illustrations add to the value of the work. The author combines the training of a physician with experience in school health work.

Q R Biol 14:372 S '39. * The information presented is, on the whole, highly superficial, with the inclusion of useless detailed medical

verbiage. The presentation is academic, each chapter being followed by Lessons to be Written, Laboratory Work and Self-Tests. The bulk of the subject matter seems to lie far outside the functions of the physical educator who can hardly be expected to acquire more than a dangerous mite of knowledge, or a false confidence in his diagnostic ability, from even complete mastery of this book. *

Va Teach 20:116 My '39. Rachel Weems. This book is of special value to physical educators and public health and school nurses; it offers a manual which aids them (1) in recognizing the early symptoms and signs of abnormal functioning of the body, and (2) in understanding the technics and medical nomenclature of the physician. * Excellent forms for the medical history and the physical examination are offered. Full explanation of each division of the physical examination is given in a clear-cut and definite manner. * From both the illustrations and the text the reader has a clear idea of the value of the physical examination, and an understanding of the tests made by the physical director and the examination made by the physician.

[B881]

DEUTSCHE, JEAN MARQUIS. **The Development of Children's Concepts of Causal Relations.** Foreword by John E. Anderson. University of Minnesota, Institute of Child Welfare, Monograph Series, No. 13. Minneapolis, Minn.: University of Minnesota Press, 1937. Pp. x, 104. $2.00. (London: Oxford University Press. 9s.)

Am J Psychol 52:318-20 Ap '39. John Irving Lacey. Employing a group-testing technique, Dr. Deutsche secured the written explanations of various phenomena by 732 children between the ages of 8 to 16 yr. * The quantitative method used in analyzing the data, however, is reported unclearly and, as we learned in correspondence with the author, incorrectly. As far as we have been able to understand it, the method was as follows. * The judges rated the answers on a 7-point scale each point of which was carefully defined. So much is clear, but from here on the exposition of the method is inadequate and erroneous. The raw median rating values thus obtained were then, apparently for purposes of weighting, expressed as percentages of the perfect score, *i.e.* of 7. These percentages were then converted into their corresponding sigma values and the sigma values were then *multiplied* by 2 (as we were informed by letter from the author—the monograph reports "divided by 2") ; 46 was subtracted from these results, and the remainders were divided by 10. The nearest whole numbers were taken as the "final quantified scores." Assuming a set of raw median rating values varying between 0 and 7, the reviewer carried through the calculations indicated. The resulting scores were all negative, and inversely related to the raw scores, and, if the nearest whole numbers were taken, the final scores obtained from such raw scores as 1, 3.5 and 5 were all −5. Dr. Deutsche's final results were all positive, ranging from 0 to 8, with the most adequate answers securing the highest scores. In every particular, then, our calculations ended with results different from those of the study. It is difficult to see how the author arrived at her values; and it is even more difficult to find a justification for her method. In the light of these inconsistencies and errors, it is difficult to discuss the quantitative results. * At the end of each chapter . . . there are convenient and good summaries. *

Am J Sociol 44:463-9 N '38. Kimball Young.

Brit J Ed Psychol 9:202-3 Je '39. C. W. V(alentine). * Questions were put to the children on such topics as follows: What makes the wind blow? What makes the snow? Why do boats float on water? What causes thunder? etc., and a number more decidedly of a type that might occur in early school work in general science. It is important to bear in mind the type of questions put because it no doubt explains several of the main findings, more particularly the surprising result that there was only a small connection between the scores and estimated intelligence, within any given age group; whereas the relation between score and school grade (age being held constant) was considerably higher. *

Ed Res B 18:48-9 F '39. Harold P. Fawcett. * a carefully controlled investigation * While this study makes no pretense of answering all the significant questions related to the thinking of children, it does give some insight into this important problem as well as direction to further desirable researches.

For additional reviews, see B344.

[B882]

DICKTER, MORRIS RICHARD. **The Relationship Between Scores on the Scholastic Aptitude Test and Marks in Mathematics and Science.** Philadelphia, Pa.: the Author, 2313 76th Avenue, 1937. Pp. 57. $1.00. Paper.

Sci Ed 23:177 Mr '39. A. W. H(urd). * aims to discover the relative validity of the prediction of scholastic success in college mathematics, chemistry, and physics courses from scores in the verbal and mathematical sections, respectively, of the college aptitude test taken before entrance to college *

[B883]

DIXON, ELIZABETH S., AND BROWNING, GRACE A., EDITORS. **Social Case Records:** Family Welfare. Chicago, Ill.: University of Chicago Press, 1938. Pp. x, 312. $2.00. (London: Cambridge University Press. 9s.)

Am Sociol R 5:656-7 Ag '40. Ray E. Baber. * The treatment of certain cases seems very brief (as few as 12 pages), but others are treated much more fully. There are no reports of staff conferences at the end of each case record in which ideas are exchanged. The case records are merely transplanted, without comment, from files to book to be used for analysis in training workers.

Cath Charities R 23:119-20 Ap '39. Alice Padgett. * The 16 selected case records . . . can be read with profit by practicing case workers anxious not to fall behind contemporary practice and by supervisors responsible for training others on the job. * Professional teaching will be not only easier but better coordinated as books like this one appear.

Jewish Social Service Q 16:302-3 Mr '40. Arnold Gurin.

Sociol and Social Res 24:483 My-Je '40. P(auline) V. Y(oung). * presents seventeen cases dealt with by public relief, by medical and family welfare agencies, by a child guidance clinic, juvenile court, and travelers' aid society. These cases present . . . the "general run" of problems * Most of the cases are well presented, though inadequately analyzed. As long as the book is used as a text (which is the intention of the editors), it will be of value only to those students who can have guidance and adequate case interpretation from competent instructors.

[B884]

DOLLARD, JOHN. **Criteria for the Life History:** With Analyses of Six Notable Documents. Yale University Institute of Human Relations Publications. New Haven, Conn.: Yale University Press, 1935. Pp. 288. $2.50. (Oxford University Press. 11s. 6d.)

Am J Psychol 49:331-2 Ap '37. Edwin A. Kirkpatrick. * The book is valuable as a stimulus to the growing appreciation of social psychology as chiefly concerned with the reactions of individuals to the culture traits of the society into which they are born. The method of arriving at the criteria and testing them by the study of typical life history documents is to be commended. To the reviewer, however, the criteria do not seem sufficiently clear, complete, or exact. They are not formulated in a way to impress one with their exact meaning and theoretical and practical value. One cannot readily carry them in mind as he reads a life history, and it is often difficult to tell which one is being applied in a given paragraph. * The omission of any criteria regarding sources and reliability of facts greatly restricts the value of this or any other criteria of life histories. Some persons, by reading a case study by Healy and one of Margaret Mead's anthropological studies, would get more help in writing life histories and in judging the value of a particular life history, than by studying and applying these criteria. The book will probably stimulate other work in this field, and ultimately prove useful to all persons dealing with life histories.

Brit J Psychol 26:454 Ap '36. * The author is inclined to be over-critical of the documents, and unless one has read the original, the abstracts, given only to show how they fulfil the criteria, are difficult to form into a coherent whole. This, along with the rather colloquial style, and the mannerism of paraphrasing, and then quoting the writer's words, are technicalities which detract from a very stimulating work. In the examples he gives, Dollard attributes small value to the *naïve* 'own story'; he fails to see that its very *naïveté* is a factor which reveals the basic culture patterns which interest him so much. Such material, he thinks, should be restated or augmented to a form which will satisfy his criteria. This book is one in which the reader will find points for dispute in each chapter, and in this it has its value. For the object of the work—namely, an attempt to systematize that elusive knowledge which is inherent in all life studies, whether biography, autobiography, or case history—is one in which even the 'lifeless' psychologists and sociologists are in fullest accord.

J Nerv and Mental Dis 83:753-4 Je '36. * extremely interesting work * a highly valuable work for the neuropsychiatrist.

Psychoanalytic Q 8:387-9 Jl '39. *Nathaniel Ross.* This lucidly conceived work is certainly an outstanding contribution to the methodology of the social sciences. The central theme, ingenious in its simplicity, is the measurement of the adequacy of life history techniques by means of highly specific criteria. * The criteria themselves are seven in number. Typical life histories representative of schools of psychiatry and sociology, and in addition, one literary venture (H. G. Wells' Experiment in Autobiography) are examined meticulously, and often brilliantly, to determine to what extent they adhere to these empirical standards. * In the specific application of the criteria the author brings out the defects and limitations of the techniques he is studying in so detailed a manner as to make his method of great practical value. * In presenting his critique, the author is careful to emphasize that he is not attacking interpretations as such, and while he is extremely fair, indeed leaning over backwards in his analysis of a life history done by a disciple of Rank, it is a tribute to his methodology that it brings out in bold relief the weaknesses and strengths of the techniques he discusses. * It is evidence of the author's fine psychological insight that he recognizes in the sociologists a strong tendency to be taken in by their subjects' rationalizations concerning the social situation. As one might expect, in their life histories the psychology is weak and unsystematic, if not amateurish. * Possessed for the most part of a crisp and incisive style, the author has a curious way of repeating quotations immediately after giving them, with practically no change. This constitutes an impediment to an otherwise smooth and logical account. * However difficult the task of establishing the relationships between culture and personality, it is a vital one. John Dollard has made a noteworthy attack upon it.

Psychoanalytic R 24:325-6 Jl '37. *N. D. C. Lewis.* * presents in an orderly and comprehensive fashion certain concepts from the field of social psychology and to demonstrate their application in the taking and evaluation of the life histories of individuals * The book as a whole is a worthy attempt to bring neglected factors into the foreground and should prove interesting to all workers dealing with clinical psychology and sociology.

Psychol B 33:838-41 D '36. *Percival Symonds.* * a significant and ingenious attempt to analyze and compare recent clinical studies and schools. The author is what might be called a psycho-sociologist or perhaps a socio-psychologist, although I believe that his original training was in the field of sociology and it is in that field that his most trenchant criticisms reside. * The book briefly described sets up seven criteria for judging a life history and then proceeds to apply these criteria to case studies or life histories by Adler, Taft . . . Freud . . . W. I. Thomas and Znaniecki, and Shaw . . . and H. G. Wells * an exceedingly illuminating analysis and comparison of the several psychoanalytical and sociological schools of thought. The whole study rests, however, on the seven criteria selected and Dollard is rather vague as to how they originated. Nothing is stated in the book to indicate whence these criteria came and we must assume that the author alone is responsible for them, gathering them up from the wealth of his own previous experience. * these criteria are, of necessity, relative to the particular culture and age in which we live, and another person writing at another time might give more or less emphasis to the present situation, family background, developmental factors, or cultural factors than Dollard has chosen to do. I should recommend Dollard's book to the psychology or sociology student as an easy way of becoming acquainted with the strengths and limitations of the various schools which have as their goal the clinical study of the individual.

Sat R Lit 13:17 F 29 '36. Horace M. Kallen. To judge by this book, the Institute of Human Relations down at New Haven is reliving the experience of one M. Jourdain set down in a play of Moliére's. M. Jourdain found great illumination in the discovery that he spoke prose. Mr. Dollard exhibits in a Ph.D. way a similar *éclairissement* at the idea that human relations are relations between individuals, and that consequently to know social causes as they actually operate is to know individuals. What Mr. Dollard calls "the life history" is a way of stating knowledge about an individual. Being "scientific," he believes that there is one best way of stating this knowledge. His "criteria" are the differentiae of this perfect way. * Much of his book is talk about papers by Alfred Adler, Jessie Taft, Freud, Thomas and Znaniecki, Clifford Shaw, and H. G. Wells in the light of these "criteria." He reproaches those who in his judgment have failed to employ them all. To which one can only say "as you like it" I myself don't. I find that Mr. Dollard does not deviate from the traditional

punditry of the field. He both labors the obvious and obscures it with professorial writing. It seems to me bad sense as well as bad logic to reproach any one for failing to do what he would have done if he had been somebody else doing something different. Criteria can be extrinsic or intrinsic. Extrinsically they are the consequences of an idea or a method. Intrinsically they are its logical structure—its clearness and distinctness, its consistency and economy. It is possible for a system or a method to be intrinsically perfect and extrinsically barren, or extrinsically rich and fertile and intrinsically defiant of all logics. So far as life-histories are concerned, there are fifty-seven ways of constructing sociological laws and every single one of them is right. The choice between them is esthetic and sectarian, not scientific and consequential. Adler and Freud, for example, whom Mr. Dollard finds less perfect, measured by his "criteria," than Thomas and Znaniecki, have thus far been far more fertile in consequences. Apart from consequences, the issue is *de gustibus*.

[B885]
DRAKE, RALEIGH M. **Work Book in Mental Tests.** Macon, Ga.: the Author, Wesleyan College, 1939. Pp. i, 37. $0.60. Paper, mimeographed. (Two "quizzes and final examination," $0.15 per set; key for work book and tests, $0.50; complete set, $1.00.)

[B886]
DRISCOLL, GERTRUDE PORTER. **The Developmental Status of the Preschool Child as a Prognosis of Future Development.** Columbia University, Teachers College, Child Development Monographs, No. 13. New York: Bureau of Publications, the College, 1933. Pp. xiv, 111. $1.50.

Am J Sociol 40:542-4 Ja '35. Ruth Pearson Koshuk. * The material in this volume on the reliability of the Kuhlmann-Binet and the Merrill-Palmer preschool intelligence tests should be read in connection with Miss Kawin's third study, *Tests for Children of Preschool Age.*

J Ed Res 28:629-30 Ap '35. Charles D. Flory. * This treatise concisely evaluates two mental tests and presents a combination of developmental indices which predicts future success of preschool children. The reliability of the Kuhlmann-Binet and the Merrill-Palmer tests is considered in the first part of the monograph. * Part II of the discussion is devoted to a follow-up study of 50 children who were retested after an interval of at least four years. * The first part of the monograph though brief is of more value than the proposed method for improving predictions by combining developmental indices. * The reader's attention was not called to the fact that reliability coefficients obtained with homogeneous subjects will be lower than the results obtained with a wide range of abilities. * This study should be of particular value to persons interested in mental testing. The attempt to develop a technique for making more accurate prognosis from preschool data is commendable. The results make it apparent that present methods of prognosis are in need of refinement.

For an additional review, see B88.

[B886.1]

EARLE, FRANK M. **Psychology and the Choice of a Career.** London: Methuen & Co., Ltd., 1933. Pp. vii, 103. *2s. 6d.*

Brit J Psychol 24:343 Ja '34. * a balanced and judicious account of its important topic * Earle has some particularly timely remarks to make on preparation for a career, in which he makes it clear that the mere diagnosis of occupational abilities must be supplemented by a well-arranged type of training. It is natural that in a book of this size and appeal the argument should for the most part run on a general plane. But sufficient illustrations are given to convince the most sceptical that psychology has an essential part to play in directing the choice of a career. Possibly something more might have been said about that provision and regulation of occupational opportunity which seems to be necessary if the psychological direction of careers is to be very efficient in actual life.

Occupations 12:84-5 Ja '34. *Donald G. Paterson.* * This little book aims to outline the principles which will remove vocational guidance from the realm of "art" and will permit the development of a science of vocational advising. A large order? To be sure! But progress is being made at an accelerated rate. For these reasons, the reviewer commends this book to those who would pause to survey the progress already made toward the realization of the goal. * The reader will be captured by Earle's ingenious attempt to portray in graphic form the development of the abilities and character qualities of the individual. * To the reviewer, the question of the adequacy of Earle's graphic chart is not crucial. Earle would probably be the first to admit that the multidimensional nature of personality precludes an accurate portrayal in two-dimensional space.

Furthermore, psychologists would disagree with respect not only to many details but also to some of the fundamental assumptions implied in the attempt to show the inter-relations between instincts, emotions, and sentiments on the one hand, and sensori-motor, perceptual, and symbolic modes of behavior on the other. Nevertheless, the reviewer believes that the attempt is worthwhile insofar as the complexities of personality analysis are clearly set forth, together with a much needed emphasis upon the genetic approach to personality study. * there is a wholesome attack on "general" education as adequate to meet the needs of all of the pupils. Unfortunately, Earle becomes somewhat vague at the point where one would expect him to describe the educational procedure best suited to the numerous company of pupils destined to enter the simpler occupational types of work. * The substance of Earle's book reflects the progress of vocational psychology in Great Britain and especially the contributions of the National Institute of Industrial Psychology. Since the findings fit in so nicely with recent developments in guidance here, the reviewer does not hesitate to urge working counselors to add this little gem to their professional libraries. Working counselors would further the guidance movement by commending it to school principals, superintendents, deans, and college presidents.

[B887]

EDUCATIONAL INSTITUTE OF SCOTLAND, CENTRAL MODERN LANGUAGES COMMITTEE. **Report of the Central Modern Languages Committee of the Educational Institute of Scotland on the Marking of Leaving Certificate Papers in French.** Reprinted from the *Scottish Educational Journal.* Edinburgh, Scotland: the Institute, 1938. Pp. 27. *6d.* Paper.

[B888]

EDUCATIONAL RECORDS BUREAU. **1938 Fall Testing Program in Independent Schools and Supplementary Studies.** Educational Records Bulletin No. 26. New York: the Bureau, January 1939. Pp. x, 69. $1.00. Paper, lithotyped.

[B888.1]

EDUCATIONAL RECORDS BUREAU. **1939 Fall Testing Program in Independent Schools and Supplementary Studies.** Educational Records Bulletin No. 29. New York: the Bureau, January 1940. Pp. x, 50. $1.00. Paper, lithotyped.

[B889]

EDUCATIONAL RECORDS BUREAU. **1939 Achievement Testing Program in Independent Schools and Supplementary Studies.** Educational Records Bulletin No. 27. New York: the Bureau, June 1939. Pp. xii, 76, 11. $1.50. Paper, lithotyped.

[B890]

EDUCATIONAL RECORDS BUREAU STAFF. **1940 Achievement Testing Program in Independent Schools and Supplementary Studies.** Educational Records Bulletin No. 30. New York: the Bureau, June 1940. Pp. xii, 76, 8. $1.50. Paper, lithotyped.

[B891]

EISNER, HARRY. **The Classroom Teacher's Estimation of Intelligence and Industry of High School Students.** Columbia University, Teachers College, Contributions to Education No. 726. Percival M. Symonds, faculty sponsor. New York: Bureau of Publications, the College, 1937. Pp. v, 108. $1.60.

High Points 20:71-2 D '38. A. H. Lass. * throws into a cocked hat many of the cherished illusions of the classroom teacher's intuition, observation, and judgment on such matters as pupil intelligence and industry. Dr. Eisner contends and proves that, at best, the teacher's guess (it's only a guess) is founded on haphazard impressions and the vaguest of data. * Only specially constructed and validated tests of these traits will yield the kind of information that is sound and usable. * This study . . . is an epicure's dish for the statistical gourmet. The general reader, however, will sit esurient at this Lucullan spread of mean and multiple correlations. * It is far from heartening to think that statistical formulae are going to prevent this really fine study from coming home as vitally as it might to the daily classroom practice of the average teacher. Dr. Eisner's patience, industry, ingenuity, careful study, and scrupulously controlled experimentation merit the serious consideration of all teachers. We hope this book finds its way into the hands of all concerned with making teaching a juster and hence profounder and more meaningful experience for the pupil. We feel it is worth reading and pondering this volume. It says something definite and important.

For additional reviews, see B353.

[B892]

ENGLEHART, MAX D. **Report of the January 1940 Comprehensive Examinations and the February 1940 Placement and Exemption Tests of the Chicago City Junior Colleges.** Chicago, Ill.: Department of Examinations, Chicago City Junior Colleges, 1940. Pp. 19. Gratis. Paper, mimeographed.

[B893]

ENGLISH, HORACE B. **A Student's Dictionary of Psychological Terms,** Fourth edition. New York and London: Harper & Brothers, 1934. Pp. x, 131. Cloth, $1.25; paper, $0.90; cloth, 7s. 6d.

Personnel J 13:61 Je '34. This clear and concise dictionary of psychological terms will be useful to the layman as well as to the student.

For an additional review, see B102.

[B894]

ESPENSCHADE, ANNA. **Motor Performance in Adolescence:** Including the Study of Relationships with Measures of Physical Growth and Maturity. Monographs of the Society for Research in Child Development, Vol. 5, No. 1, Serial No. 24. Washington, D. C.: the Society, National Research Council, 1940. Pp. viii, 126. $1.00. Paper, lithotyped.

J Pediatrics 16:677 My '40. * excellent graphs.

Loyola Ed Digest 15:10 My '40. Austin G. Schmidt. During a period of four years seriatim measures of gross motor performance were obtained for approximately 165 boys and girls * The mean performances of boys in all events were found to increase steadily with age, but those of girls in some events reached their maximum at fourteen years and declined thereafter. Sex differences were apparent at all ages, but were greater in older than in younger children. There were consistently wide variations within groups. The study was carefully controlled and the results add something of value to our knowledge of the motor ability and development of children.

Pub Health R 10:54-5 Je '40. Mabel E. Rugen. * Tests used by Espenschade to measure various elements of big muscle activity include: the distance throw, target throw, standing broad jump, jump and reach, Brace test, and 50-yard dash. Tests were repeated each six months for a period of 3½ years for the girls and 4 years for the boys. Results were analyzed thoroughly and compared with those of a control group. Interrelationships were made of: motor functions, performance and age and sex, performance and physical maturity. Comparative studies of inferior and superior motor performance and consistency of performance in selected cases was also made. It was found that mean performance for boys increased throughout the age range studies (12 to 17) while for girls a gradual decline was shown after 14 years of age. "Correlations between motor performances of girls and all measures of physical growth maturity are low and in most cases not statistically significant." (P. 118.) Just the opposite is true for boys. This fact has far-reaching implications for physical education as does the entire study. *

[B895]

Evans, Robert O. **Practices, Trends, and Issues in Reporting to Parents on the Welfare of the Child in School:** Principles Upon Which an Effective Program May Be Built. New York: Bureau of Publications, Teachers College, Columbia University, 1938. Pp. vi, 98. $1.05. Paper.

Ed Res B 19:237 Ap 10 '40. Charles C. Cowell. Mr. Evans has made a timely study of the evolution of the report card, an evaluation of past and present practices, and he concludes with some definite principles upon which an effective program of reporting to parents may be built. *

[B896]

Farmer, E., and Chambers, E. G. **A Study of Accident Proneness Among Motor Drivers.** Medical Research Council, Industrial Health Research Board, Report No. 84. London: H.M. Stationery Office, 1939. Pp. iii, 47. 9d.

J Royal Stat Soc 103:254-6 pt 2 '40. M. G. K(endall). * very interesting report * in only one out of four groups of London bus drivers (the group for which the largest experience was available) was there any significant relation between accidents and the aesthetokinetic tests, that relation being positive. The results of the perseveration and intelligence tests were not satisfactory, the subjects being obviously nervous * the general conclusion (which, one cannot help but feel, might have been foreseen) is that the tests were unsatisfactory * The authors' general conclusions are that the accident rate can be reduced by eliminating drivers with a strong degree of accident proneness. The question whether an individual has such a strong degree can be determined by examining his previous record and by psychological tests, preferably in conjunction. There is still room for doubt whether the psychological approach is really satisfactory—some further research with better tests and under more natural conditions seems indicated—but the general conclusion will probably be accepted. Its bearings on the training and selection of drivers need no emphasis. This report is admirably condensed, the authors being content to give their data and indicate their conclusions without any trimmings whatever. This is all the more commendable in view of the emotional atmosphere created around road accidents by the people who still believe that it is more dangerous to be outside a house than inside it. Obviously the report is not the last word on the subject, and it does not pretend

to be; but it is a valuable contribution which will be widely studied.

Lancet 238:418 Mr 2 '40.

[B897]

Farmer, E.; Chambers, E. G.; and Kirk, F. J. **Tests for Accident Proneness.** Medical Research Council, Industrial Health Research Board, Report No. 68. London: H.M. Stationery Office, 1933. Pp. iv, 37. 9d. Paper.

J Royal Stat Soc 96:685-6 pt 4 '33. A. B(radford) H(ill). * Intelligence and sensori-motor tests were applied to all the apprentices entering H.M. Dockyard at Portsmouth after 1923 and their test performances compared with their subsequent accident records over a period of five years. The results have been analysed critically and carefully by several alternative statistical methods, and, in general, confirm those of the authors' previous studies, namely that there is some association between success in the aestheto-kinetic tests and low accident rate. *

Personnel J 12:292 F '34. Charles S. Slocombe. * Five years ago Mr. Farmer gave a series of so-called sensori-motor tests to some apprentices entering mechanical trades. Now he compares the test records with the accident records of these boys. * [obtained no] correlation better than .3 between tests and accidents * [The results] are disappointing. * Farmer's tests, heavily weighted with reaction time, were good eight years ago, but would not be so regarded today. *

[B898]

Fenton, Norman, with the assistance of Ramona Wallace. **State Child Guidance Service in California Communities:** A Report on the Application of Mental Hygiene. A publication of the California Bureau of Juvenile Research. Sacramento, Calif.: Supervisor of Documents, 1938. Pp. xviii, 157. $1.50.

Am Sociol R 4:585-6 Ag '39. Katharine Whiteside Taylor. * most timely and welcome * includes . . . an excellent check list by which communities may rate themselves as to their present resources and greatest needs. This check list might well serve as the basis of pointed discussion for council or community meetings in areas wishing to develop such programs. *

Social Work Technique 4:68 Mr-Ap '39. * Because of limitations of space the book suffers from the inadequacy of the analysis of any of the above complex issues, each of which is of vital importance to students and workers in mental hygiene fields. The book is well written; has a good up-to-date bibliography.

[B899]

FERRY, MARGARET E. **Preliminary Study of Twenty Problem Students.** Human Engineering Laboratory, Technical Report No. 27. Boston, Mass.: the Laboratory, 1938. Pp. viii, 43. $1.00. Paper, mimeographed.

[B900]

FICK, M. LAURENCE. **The Educability of the South African Native.** Foreword by W. Eiselen. South African Council for Educational and Social Research, Research Series No. 8. Pretoria, South Africa: J. L. Van Schaik, Ltd., 1939. Pp. viii, 56. 2s. Paper.

[B901]

FICK, M. LAURENCE. **An Individual Scale of General Intelligence for South Africa:** The Standardization of Test Items for the Upper Levels of General Intelligence in an Existing Individual Scale. South African Council for Educational and Social Research, Research Series No. 7. Pretoria, South Africa: J. L. Van Schaik, Ltd., 1939. Pp. v, 51. 2s. Paper.

[B902]

FILLEY, MARY E. **The Construction of the English Vocabulary Test, Worksample 95, Form DB.** Human Engineering Laboratory, Technical Report No. 11. Boston, Mass.: the Laboratory, 1939. Pp. vii, 119. $1.00. Paper, mimeographed.

[B902.1]

FILLEY, MARY E. **Revision of Form A Leading to Form AA, Worksample 180.** Human Engineering Laboratory, Technical Report No. 57. Boston, Mass.: the Laboratory, 1940. Pp. v, 138. $1.00. Paper, mimeographed.

[B902.2]

FILLEY, MARY E. **Revision of Form A Leading to Form AA, Worksample 271.** Human Engineering Laboratory, Technical Report No. 62. Boston, Mass.: the Laboratory, 1940. Pp. vi, 16. $1.00. Paper, mimeographed.

[B903]

FILLEY, MARY E. **Revision of Form AB Leading to Forms AC and AD, Worksample 95.** Human Engineering Laboratory, Technical Report No. 41. Boston, Mass.: the Laboratory, 1939. Pp. vii, 157. $1.00. Paper, mimeographed.

[B903.1]

FILLEY, MARY E. **Revision of Form B Leading to Form BA, Worksample 176.** Human Engineering Laboratory, Technical Report No. 64. Boston, Mass.: the Laboratory, 1940. Pp. vi, 118. $1.00. Paper, mimeographed.

[B904]

FILLEY, MARY E. **Revision of Form BA Leading to Forms BB and BC, Worksample 95.** Human Engineering Laboratory, Technical Report No. 43. Boston, Mass.: the Laboratory, 1939. Pp. vi, 113. $1.00. Paper, mimeographed.

[B904.1]

FILLEY, MARY E. **Revision of Form EA Leading to Form EB, Worksample 95.** Human Engineering Laboratory, Technical Report No. 55. Boston, Mass.: the Laboratory, 1940. Pp. vi, 108. $1.00. Paper, mimeographed.

[B905]

FILLEY, MARY E. **Revision of Form F Leading to Forms FA and FB, Worksample 95.** Human Engineering Laboratory, Technical Report No. 42. Boston, Mass.: the Laboratory, 1939. Pp. v, 116. Paper, mimeographed.

[B905.1]

FILLEY, MARY E. **Revision of Form G Leading to Form GA, Worksample 95.** Human Engineering Laboratory, Technical Report No. 53. Boston, Mass.: the Laboratory, 1940. Pp. vi, 112. $1.00. Paper, mimeographed.

[B906]

FINDLEY, WARREN G. **A Program of Progress Testing for New York State Schools.** University of the State of New York Bulletin, No. 1158. Albany, N. Y.: University of the State of New York Press, February 1939. Pp. 11. $0.05. Paper.

[B907]

FLANAGAN, JOHN C. **The Cooperative Achievement Tests:** A Bulletin Reporting the Basic Principles and Procedures Used in the Development of Their System of Scaled Scores. New York: Cooperative Test Service, December 1939. Pp. v, 41. $0.25. Paper.

[B908]

FREEMAN, FRANK N. **Mental Tests:** Their History, Principles and Applications, Revised edition. Boston, Mass.: Houghton Mifflin Co., 1939. Pp. xi, 460. $2.50. (London: George C. Harrap & Co., Ltd. 10s. 6d.)

Am J Psychol 53:307-9 Ap '40. A. G. Bills. The reviewer, being no expert in psychometrics but . . . confronted with the problem of choosing a textbook suitable for a college class in measurement of intelligence and personality, proposes to evaluate the present book from that angle. * Knowing the author, one would expect a conservative, cautious and unbiased treatment. This expectation is, with some exceptions, borne out, especially so in Chapters I, XV, and XVI, which deal, respectively with the present status, meaning, and fields of application of mental tests; the interpretation of mental tests; and the nature of ability. No misguided layman, prejudiced either by an over- or under-confidence in psychological tests, could possibly read the sane appraisal contained in these chapters without profiting greatly by it. Both the limitations and advantages of the method are plainly presented. A good bibliography of texts in the field is appended to Chapter I. Students often puzzle over Spearman's tetrad difference method of proving his two-factory theory of ability. This and other uses of correlation are presented in such a simple, elementary way in Chapter III as to be clear to anyone. The same can be said of Chapters X, XI, and XII, which discuss "the technique and theory of mental tests," meaning such problems as the selection of materials and organization of items, and the setting up of norms and comparison of various types of scores. * The chapter on "Tests for the Analysis of Mental Capacity" deals with special abilities tests, like those for mechanical, musical, and art talent. The instructor would need to supplement the brief descriptions with a much fuller analysis to make this part of the book effective. Chapter VIII, dealing with tests of personality traits, is hardly adequate. Here, if anywhere, is needed a highly critical evaluation. The discussions of tests like the Vineland Social Maturity Test, and the Willoughby Emotional Maturity Test, are too sketchy, considering that these are prototypes along the lines of which further tests of these traits will in all likelihood develop. Granted the excuse that they are too new to be properly sized up, how about other earlier experimental attempts like the Downey Will Temperament Test? We find only casual mention of the fact that the consensus of opinion has relegated it to the discard; yet its validity is defended purely on the basis of the findings in the author's identical twin study in which four out of nineteen profiles came out nearly identical. What does this prove? One also looks in vain for a discussion of the logic of types and traits, which is practically indispensable to an understanding of the reason for the rejection by experts of the whole type theory and of the tests designed to isolate types. A good selected bibliography of tests of personality is appended. If supplemented by collateral readings, the book is quite usable.

Brit J Psychol 30:170 O '39. * thoroughly revised and brought up to date. It still remains in the main a factual book, concerned especially to describe and to illustrate a wide variety of tests, to give sufficient information about common methods of marking and scoring, and very briefly to characterize the main theories in the field. It is an extremely efficient piece of work, and should be of wide use in training college and university courses.

Ed Adm and Sup 25:474-5 S '39. A. S. *Edwards.* * Valuable historical facts are given, but are scattered through various chapters and will hardly give the student connected historical insight into the development of the testing movement. Historic orientation is not evenly provided for * the pioneer work of Pintner and Paterson is hardly given its due * In general, a very good selection of tests has been made, but one looks in vain for discussion of the very important and fundamental efforts that have been made in connection with vocabulary tests. The problem of social intel-

ligence also seems to be missing * Quantitative problems are discussed although such material belongs properly to a special text. * The three references to statistical texts, however, include none later than 1925; omit one of the best of the period, namely, Thurstone's * Excellent discussions of the IQ are scattered through the book. Recognition of the surprising increases in the IQ reported in recent years for children placed in greatly improved environment, is perhaps adequately dealt with; it is right to consider these reports with some question; but the great amount of increase afforded from some experiments is not made clear in the text. Generally excellent discussions of the various subjects are found. * The majority of the chapters are without references for further reading. * [The index] is, for the most part, well made. * the author's statement that no book has yet appeared with the scope of this one may at least be questioned, in view of . . . Hunt's book, *Measurements in Psychology* * Although excellent in conception, the organization will probably be found to be somewhat undesirable from the point of view of many students, because of the scattering found in the discussion of some of the subjects. On the whole it will be a very useful book.

El Paso Sch Standard 17:30-1 My '40. M. E. *Broom.* * presents quite complete analyses of problems and methods involved in the construction of mental tests, and excellent discussions on the interpretation of results of mental testing and of the uses of mental tests in education * Any attempt to cover the entire field of mental measurement in a single volume requires omitting much of the available information and data concerning this subject. For example, this reviewer was disappointed in the discussions of the constancy of the IQ and of the relationship between achievement and intelligence, because all of the available research findings were not presented and interpreted. However, this is not a serious criticism. In the opinion of this reviewer, the volume would have been more valuable if the materials dealing with aptitude tests and personality and character tests had been omitted, with the treatment of mental tests expanded in proportion to the omissions. The book should be very valuable to persons who have not studied mental testing extensively, despite the absence of extensive lists of references to the publications of other authorities in the field.

The treatment of controversial subjects in an impartial manner, with the presentation of evidence and opinion on both aspects, together with interpretation by the author, contributes to this value for students of mental measurement.

J Ed (Boston) 122:248-9 O '39.

J Ed Psychol 30:635-6 N '39. Stephen M. Corey. * The major additions in the second edition in comparison with the first are as follows: 1. An expansion of the treatment of "factor analysis" from one to six pages * 2. Some nine pages devoted to a description of new point scales which have appeared since 1925 * 3. About twelve pages of descriptions of new aptitude tests—music, art, clerical, academic, etc. * 4. A rather long section (seventeen pages) on personality and character tests * 5. Five pages calling attention to new methods of measuring increments of mental growth * 6. A revised and up-to-date discussion (seven pages) of the constancy of the IQ, and a new section (seven pages) on the relationship between conduct and intelligence * 7. Approximately twelve pages bringing the discussion on the inheritance of intelligence up-to-date * 8. A completely rewritten chapter on "The Nature of Ability." The reviewer studied Freeman's first edition shortly after it appeared in 1926 and was impressed by the author's ability to make judicious inferences from conflicting data. The relatively few changes in interpretation which appear in the revised edition are a tribute to a type of judgment which does not always characterize authors of texts in the field of psychological measurements. As is implied above, to those who were thoroughly familiar with the 1926 *Mental Tests* the revision will seem but slightly different. Certain sections have been added and one chapter completely rewritten but the reader gets no impression of a new text. Seventy five per cent of the pages have not been changed. * In his revision Freeman has paid no attention to achievement testing as such, and it would probably have been all to the good had he limited himself to intelligence without making any attempt to introduce his readers to mechanical aptitude, the measurement of character and other concepts and practices which are outside the area in which he has made many major contributions.

J Ed Res 33:536-8 Mr '40. F. Kuhlmann. * a comprehensive treatment . . . except that the discussion of application is limited to their use in education. It is particularly commendable for completeness of analysis of problems and methods involved in mental test construction, in interpretation of results and of their practical application in education. Its objective is to serve as a textbook for college and University classes studying mental testing, and, with the exception of the absence of well selected lists of references is well designed for this purpose. Attempt is made, and we believe reasonably successfully, to treat controversial subjects impartially by reviewing the evidence and opinions on both sides, while adding his own criticisms and conclusions. * Doubtless no reader will agree with all of the author's conclusions on the many controversial matters discussed, and some will feel that the evidence has not been fully or equally well presented on both sides. This reviewer would take special exception to the review that the chief problem in mental tests is the definition of the abilities being measured. * Knowing what particular ability each test in a Binet scale measured would not add one bit to its practical value, unless we knew also the correlation between each particular score and some particular activity of life in which there is some interest. We would also sharply disagree with the author's conclusions on the advantages and disadvantages of year scales and point scales, and that the former is on the way out. His discussion of the I.Q. especially with reference to its constancy is disappointing, both from the standpoint of presentation of the facts found empirically and from the standpoint of deductive reasoning. * As a textbook for students of mental tests, we believe it has at present no superior. Selected lists of references for supplementary reading should, however, be added, and "in Education" should be added to the subtitle.

Occupational Psychol 13:247 Jl '39. * Like most text books it is dull reading, and could not be recommended for the general reader. For the student of psychology and for others (for example, teachers) who intend to learn to administer tests for school purposes, the book should serve as a valuable indication of the uses and limitations of testing methods. * it is perhaps most valuable in its emphasis on the limitations of mental measurement * should have a particularly salutary effect on the unenlightened enthusiast who pins his faith upon a figure representing a test score without further inquiry into what the figure means * should be helpful in restraining the over-enthusiastic from rushing blindly into a testing programme without due preparation. The book gives, too, a healthy warning against regarding the score in a test of intelligence as the final and only measurement of 'educable capacity' *

Psychol B 36:694-7 O '39. Henry E. Garrett. * The revision represents no radical change in point of view. Rather, it consists in the expansion of certain chapters, in the addition of new material and of new references designed to bring the treatment up to date, and in the omission of certain special topics. The new book is forty-three pages shorter than the old. * Freeman can . . . be criticized (1) for inadequate treatment of several important subjects and (2) for frequent failure to bring his treatment up to date. Consider, first, the much discussed topic of factor analysis, to which several sections are devoted in Freeman's book. The discussion throughout is extremely general and not always accurate. * Of several other topics Freeman's new book gives a superficial and sketchy account. * the student is not told just what the most probable form of the mental growth curve is * On pages 295-296, Freeman makes a bow to the Heinis growth curve and the P.C., but no mention is made of Thurstone's and Thorndike's mental growth curves in which the attempt was made to measure changes with age in equal units and from an absolute zero. * there is no mention of item analysis and only the briefest treatment of test construction * The rather futile discussion of Burt's regression equation (pp. 401-403), repeated from the old book, is certainly not calculated to enlighten the student as to the factors which operate in determining Binet mental age. * Chapter VIII, on personality tests, devotes nine pages to the Downey Will-Temperament Test, although Freeman comments (all too correctly!) that ". . . the prevailing opinion among psychologists is that the test does not measure any real characteristics of the personality" (p. 214). Only one-half page is given to tests of introversion-extraversion; and the discussion of tests of neurotic tendencies, attitudes and opinions, and the like is so brief that the student will get from the book alone little more than a conversational acquaintance with these measures. It seems

rather remarkable that, after thirteen years, Chapter IV . . . "Age Scales: The Binet Scales," should need only one additional reference . . . in order to bring it up to date. * Careful perusal of Chapters XIV and XV, dealing with the application, interpretation, and uses of mental tests, may well leave the reader wondering whether anything important in mental measurement has happened since 1926. * F. S. Freeman's and Anastasi's comprehensive treatments of individual differences are omitted along with all recent research. In fact, the student must certainly gather that the last thirteen years have been marked by stagnation in the field of mental measurement. On the whole, Freeman's book strikes me as a hasty revision of his old book and as a not very thorough review of the field of mental measurement. * In a brief introductory course for undergraduates, Freeman's text will suffice. But for the serious student of psychometrics more and heartier fare should certainly be provided.

[B908.1]

GALLUP, GEORGE, AND RAE, SAUL FORBES. **The Pulse of Democracy:** The Public-Opinion Poll and How It Works. New York: Simon and Schuster, Inc., 1940. Pp. ix, 336. $2.50.

Sat R Lit 22:7+ Jl 27 '40. T. V. Smith. * The claims of the authors may be reduced to three: (1) public opinion can be measured; (2) public opinion is being measured by them; (3) public opinion should be measured, more and more and better and better. On the first two claims the book is fairly convincing * The third claim, is . . . the most important. *Should* public opinion be measured? Do the Gallup polls constitute *significant* contributions to the process and the progress of the democratic way of life? That is the question worthy of a philosopher and one being raised by not a few legislators. The authors devote a substantial segment of the book to that line of thought. But the answer to that question, while not negative, is yet not easy; for it goes beyond technology, and plows beneath science, in quest of a foundation for both. * I appreciate the Gallup polls for the minor contribution they make to a major enterprise. I am not greatly worried over the so-called dangers connected with them, primarily because I think most of our legislators and many of our citizens ignore them as cues to positive conviction and action. As maps for the journey ahead they are dangerous, as the authors of this book perhaps admit; as cautions for curves in the road they are valuable, as the authors claim. The less citizens rely upon them for their own opinions —I am tempted to say the less they know of them until their opinions are made up—the sounder the citizenship.

[B909]
GANSL, IRENE. **Vocabulary:** Its Measurement and Growth. Columbia University, Archives of Psychology, No. 236. New York: the University, March 1939. Pp. 52. $1.00. Paper.

Loyola Ed Digest 15:12 *Jl '40. Austin G. Schmidt.* * The vocabulary studied was passive, not active; that is, pupils were tested only for knowledge of the meaning of the words contained in the test. *

[B910]
GARRETT, HENRY E. **Differentiable Mental Traits.** *Psychological Record,* Vol. 2, No. 9. Bloomington, Ind.: Principia Press, Inc., June 1938. Pp. 259-98. $0.90. Paper.

[B911]
GATES, A. I.; BOND, G. L.; AND RUSSELL, D. H.; ASSISTED BY EVA BOND, ANDREW HALPIN, AND KATHRYN HORAN. **Methods of Determining Reading Readiness.** New York: Bureau of Publications, Teachers College, Columbia University, 1939. Pp. iv, 55. $0.60. Paper.

Ed Abstracts 5:51 *F '40. J. M. McCallister.*
Ed Adm and Sup 26:73-4 *Ja '40. A. S. Edwards.* * a quantitative study of pupils in four large New York city classes together with comparison of a similar study carried on in the Horace Mann school. Many tests, ratings, examinations, and appraisals were applied to each pupil. * The detailed information is of distinct value for those who deal directly with the problems of reading. *
Loyola Ed Digest 15:9 *N '39. Austin G. Schmidt.* Any piece of research on reading reported by Dr. Gates and his associates carries a great deal of weight. In the present study a number of pupils in four New York City classes were examined by means of practically every test that has ever been used for the purpose of determining reading readiness. The general conclusion is that the best predictive measures are tests that measure reading attainment * The only other tests found to possess any marked value were the Stanford-Binet and tests of auditory acuity. It is unsound to set up any given mental age as the proper one at which to begin reading. It is likewise unsound to assume that reading readiness is

a condition for the development of which the teacher can do no more than merely wait. *

[B912]
GESELL, ARNOLD. **Atlas of Infant Behavior:** A Systematic Delineation of the Forms and Early Growth of Human Behavior Patterns, Two volumes. Limited edition. Illustrated with 3,200 Action Photographs. New Haven, Conn.: Yale University Press, 1934. Pp. 921. $25.00. Loose-leaf. (London: Oxford University Press. Pp. 922. £5 10s.)

J Genetic Psychol 48:254-6 *Mr '36. G. E. Coghill.* This work presents two series of studies of the behavior of human infants through the first 56 weeks of post-natal life: a normative series, presented in Volume I; and a naturalistic series, in Volume II. The volumes are 12 × 2 × 12 inches, and elegantly bound in a special steel spring binder. This construction has the very important advantage of permitting the manipulation and assembling of the loose-leaf chromophotographs according to the particular interests and requirements of the student. * Gesell and his associates deserve the gratitude of neurologists for providing an exhaustive chronological panorama of behavior of the growing child with which structural studies of the nervous system of known ages can be compared. From this source and method information may be expected that cannot be acquired in any other way concerning behavior in its fundamental relations. This is a monumental work superbly presented. It is especially notable in accomplishment because it deals with a field of inquiry that is rigorously restricted in the application of the experimental method and beset with those difficulties which are allied with the traditional ideas and affects inherent in the subject matter with which it deals. It is a splendid realization of an unusual vision of research in human behavior.
J Pediatrics 6:424-5 *Mr '35. B(orden) S. V(eeder).* * an outstanding contribution * It is not only a unique but a most important contribution. * The mechanical make-up of the book is excellent. * The photographs . . . are clear and excellently produced. * The reviewer is overwhelmed with the obvious painstaking, time-consuming detail with which pictures have been studied, selected, and finally brought together in this Atlas. It can be stated without exaggeration that the Atlas is monumental in character and the possibilities of its use in teaching and research are tremendous. Everyone interested in the field of infancy can take

a just pride that such a work has come from an American clinic.

Sci 81:73 Ja 18 '35. John E. Anderson. In these well-planned and extraordinarily well printed volumes, Arnold Gesell, who for three decades has pioneered in research on the infant and young child, presents thirty-two hundred photographs, enlarged from motion picture frames, delineating the behavior of infants during the first year of life. Those in the first volume, taken in the photographic dome of the Yale Psycho-Clinic under laboratory conditions, show the development of 24 behavior sequences which cover posture, locomotion, perceptual, prehensive and adaptive behavior at 4, 6, 8, 12, 16, 20, 24, 28, 32, 36, 40, 44, 48 and 52 weeks, respectively. * The enlargements in the second volume show the behavior of infants in naturalistic situations—i.e., under a duplication of home conditions, in a special studio room to which both the infant and the mother, who was present, have been habituated. One purpose of the second volume is the portrayal of individual differences in development. * Each volume contains a description of the methods of securing and treating the films and of the apparatus, cameras and observation chambers used. * In the first volume the pictures are arranged by behavior patterns in age sequences; in the second volume by children. Both volumes are loose-leaf * Thus all the pictures dealing with the development of eating or bathing habits can be put together. The excellent quality of the enlargements in the first volume is exceeded by those of the second volume—indicating the superiority of 35 mm over 16 mm film. The approach to the study of infant behavior as presented in the atlas is so new that its evaluation is difficult. There is no doubt of its vivid and striking portrayal of infant behavior and its worth for teaching and demonstration and for directing the attention of scientists, students, parents, artists and other workers to various aspects of infant development. Only the future can determine its scientific value. The statistical data necessary for the interpretation of the normative and naturalistic pictures are not given. Nor is it clear how a particular picture or sequence was selected as normative. On the other hand, taken as a whole, rather than examined critically in detail, the sequences give a graphic and total picture of development that may for some purposes be of more value

than the fractionating of behavior into minute parts to which we have become so accustomed. *

[B913]

GESELL, ARNOLD; AMATRUDA, CATHERINE S.; CASTNER, BURTON M.; AND THOMPSON, HELEN. **Biographies of Child Development:** The Mental Growth Careers of Eighty-Four Infants and Children; A Ten-Year Study from the Clinic of Child Development at Yale University. New York: Paul B. Hoeber, Inc., 1939. Pp. xvii, 328. $3.75. (London: Hamish Hamilton, Ltd. 15s.)

Am J Dis Children 58:923 O '39. * interestingly and plainly written from the clinical point of view. It gives the best description of growth of intelligence which has been published.

Am J Psychol 53:476-7 Jl '40. Mary S. Ryan. * There is no indication anywhere in the book of the total number of cases which were predicted correctly or incorrectly, and the cases described were selected, as Gesell mentions in his introduction, not because they were typical but because they taught the members of the staff the most. Therefore these cases do not give a typical picture of development, and the study is of no value except as a comparison of the individual cases described. The book is of interest to those who have followed the earlier work at Yale and should be considered merely as a supplement to the earlier volumes, not as an independent work or general treatise on child development.

Ann Internal Med 13:373 Ag '39. H. W. N. * A great deal of valuable material is given to illustrate atypical growth complexes and the various factors that influence them. * The findings in this book are of particular interest to those professions dealing with children; pediatricians, educators, psychologists and social workers. The presentation is scientific in the strictest sense. There are no involved theories, nor does the reader have to wade through the strange jargons and terminologies characteristic of psychological schools of thought. The whole volume is readable, thought provoking and informative.

Brit J Ed Psychol 10:174 Je '40. C. W. V(alentine). * an account in detail of the mental development of eighty-four infants * In Part I we have records covering periods for the same child as long as from three or four months to ten or twelve years, or from one or two years to seventeen years. Dr. Gesell points out that the basis of selection has been the instructiveness of the record. There has been no attempt to illustrate the reliability of earlier tests. Indeed, the method of selection "tends to exaggerate the frequency of cases of irregular or a-typical development" (p. 5). * It should be clearly realized . . . that the present book is primarily a study of rather exceptional types of development, illustrating irregularities in development. * Furthermore, although these cases are, in a sense, a-typical, Dr. Gesell stresses the fact that they themselves follow a regular genetic pattern. * This section of the book is completed by a chapter of a more theoretical type on growth characteristics. This is short but very valuable, cautious yet highly suggestive. The most interesting idea is that of the "intrinsic insurance factors"; which enable the organism to compensate to some extent for certain defects and, into the places of missing elements, to push other elements as it were to fill up the gap * The volume is a further example of the valuable work which is being carried out under the guidance of Dr. Gesell in the collection of facts of infant development.

Brit J Psychol 30:264 Ja '40. * the reader is left with the impression of separate lines of development of isolated characteristics which never become synthesized into a completed personality. Useful as Dr. Gesell's technique undoubtedly is in predicting the future development of the more obviously apparent characteristics, it can as yet tell us little beyond the use of general terms such as "stable," "immature," "excitable," etc., about the kind of "person" the child will become. The type face employed is too "arty" and unsuitable for printing this kind of book, and, moreover, interferes distinctly with its legibility, at least for some readers.

Char and Pers 8:175-6 D '39. *Donald K. Adams.* * It is . . . gratifying to note that the cases, both typical and atypical, have been selected with such care and the observations reported are so relevant to the problems of development, despite the relative absence of theory, that the volume is one of unique value and convenience to the investigator and theorist. The fact that thirty of the biographies are of children whose development up to that date had already been described in Gesell's *Infancy and Human Growth,* published in 1928, not only adds scope to the lifespans covered but provides an opportunity for checking upon the prognostic utility of the developmental schedules. This exacting test, to which I believe no other developmental schedule has

been subjected, indicates that the Gesell schedule (at least as employed at the Yale Clinic) has done a highly creditable job of predicting the course of development. The unpretentious good sense of the book, and the clarity and relevance of its descriptions make it one which few students of human development will want to miss.

Ed Abstracts 4:247-8 O '39. *Raymond Fisher.*

J Abn and Social Psychol 35:468-71 Jl '40. *Mary Shirley.* * The authors courageously take from the files the clairvoyant remarks they made on the basis of infant examinations and assay them in the light of the actual achievement of the children several years later. In this respect the book is a unique and worthy contribution to literature on child development. The reader is doomed to disappointment, however, if he hopes that a "biography" implies not only a chronological account of the child's behavior over a period of several years, but also a description of the major experiences and environmental impacts that conceivably have influenced his life. For the sketches of individual children are brief, and in most instances they are singularly lacking in information concerning either the child's personality or the milieu in which his growth and development occur. The student or layman who seeks a simple and consistent statement of the practical prognostic value of developmental appraisals made in babyhood will be more confused than enlightened. * Another disappointing feature to one whose interest is primarily in "normal" children is that the cases selected for presentation represent such a distorted sample. * As nearly as one can estimate, only a fourth of the children treated in the volume could be considered healthy, non-problem youngsters growing up amidst their siblings under the guidance of their own parents. * A few of the cases reported by Amatruda show normal mental growth in spite of severe physical complications, and in discussing these the author takes occasion to bolster up Gesell's theory that "factors of insurance" safeguard growth and make for "developmental optimum." But in more than half the cases it is clear to her that the intervention of disease markedly and permanently altered the course of growth. None of the authors assembles for discussion the twenty-five cases in which Society did the experimenting—perhaps the most instructive of the lot. All these children were at one time or another victims of inferior circumstances. * more than two-thirds of the cases improved in a developmental rating after placement in a fairly desirable and permanent foster home. Gesell would explain the initial low scores and the subsequent rise of these children for whom environmental manipulation seemed to serve as a stimulant to development, as instances in which the examiner had failed to assess properly the "factors of insurance" at the early tests or in which these factors "came tardily to full force." But to the reviewer these cases seem to add their bit to the growing body of evidence that though potentiality for mental growth is basically dependent upon "deep-seated biochemical factors," as Gesell insists, the "trend and tempo" of mental development may be greatly altered by the impact of physical and cultural forces wholly outside the child himself.

J Am Med Assn 113:1156-7 S 16 '39. * While it might be difficult for one who is not fully acquainted with the literature and procedures of child study and child guidance to gain much from a case-study volume of this sort, the whole book presents an excellent argument in favor of careful child study from the standpoint of the pediatrician and psychiatrist and implies that predictions as to spontaneous cure or even the continuation of normal development must be made with some care. On the other hand, hope is given to those who have to deal with problem children in that many are shown not only to recover and reach the normal curve but to advance far beyond the average into the superior range. This book would be valuable for the child psychologist and the physician who has to do with developing children—the pediatrician or the orthopsychiatrist. It is scientifically done and carefully prepared, the cases are well selected and, while some perhaps are too short to show the mechanisms at work, at least they do show the principle involved in the success or failure of the child to develop.

J Ed (London) 71:638 S '39.

J Nerv and Mental Dis 91:549-50 Ap '40. * offers many correlative values which the psychiatric worker with children will find of great help. Together with its companion volumes the work is indispensable for those who would achieve a clearer insight to the vastly complicated psychobiological progressions comprised

in growth. It stresses throughout that it is only by keeping the dynamics of development in the foreground that any meaning can be found in the developmental diagnosis of behavior basing these studies. Such diagnosis does not aim, as does much of the abstract psychology of the textbooks, towards the useless accumulation of mental tests and measurements, but tries to perfect from a close study of living material means for appraising levels of maturation analytically, in point of specified behavior fields: postural, prehensory, perceptual, adaptive, language and social.

J Pediatrics 14:558 Ap '39. This is one of the most interesting books that has appeared from the Yale Clinic of Child Development. In contrast to some of the earlier publications, it has more to do with results than methods and for this reason appeals more to the average reader. * The value of Dr. Gesell's work and methods will undoubtedly find a permanent place in the study of child development.

Psychiatric Q 13:785 O '39. * a step forward in the scientific evaluation of mental growth processes, especially since we find in it repeated examinations of the same individual from infancy through childhood. * The graphs and charts reveal in a clear and impressive fashion the mental growth features in terms of relative maturity levels of the infant and child. * Part two of the book . . . commands our interest through . . . [its] studies of behavior growth, exemplified in individual biographies of children. * The book as a whole opens new vistas and possibilities of guidance and prognosis of behavior manifestations of children in discovering their individual progress possibilities. * The book is of decided value to all those scientifically and practically concerned with the development of infants and children. It is especially recommended to pediatricians and child guidance workers. The physical appearance of the book enhances its value by its beautiful binding, the clear graphs and good typography.

Psychol B 36:678-81 O '39. Nancy Bayley. * an instructive array of case histories showing a variety of trends of mental development in young children * The authors point out, repeatedly, that the cases presented in this volume are exceptional ones * Nowhere in the book do they give figures indicating the extent to which these cases are atypical in regard to either the entire population studied by them or the selected groups discussed (such as foster children, twins, or children with physical anomalies). The value of the material in this book would be increased if representative data were included, with statistical descriptions of the mental growth trends in a normal or unselected group of children. * That . . . clinical judgments actually give better prognosis than simple numerical test scores the reader is apparently expected to take on faith. * The semilogarithmic curves employed to represent development emphasize the continuity of growth and mask variations in relative scores. * Castner . . . presents six cases in which preschool prediction of reading disabilities was fulfilled. His criteria for prediction are interesting and appear to be well substantiated. * The case-history method should prove to be very fruitful in clarifying the qualitative aspects of growth and in bringing to light factors which influence trends of growth. As for the present series of cases, it makes interesting reading and illustrates well many of the generalizations made by the authors. However, the arguments will often prove unconvincing to those not already convinced. The reviewer would willingly accept many of the statements concerning the development of intelligence and would doubt, or take exception to, others; but they are little more than textbook statements which the pupil is expected to read and accept without verification. The principal conclusion that one can draw from these case histories is that early prediction of intelligence from even the Gesell type of clinical appraisal very often fails. In cases where it is important to know a child's mental level we must make frequent tests and rely primarily on recent tests of his ability. It appears in this book that Gesell, while protesting to the contrary, in effect admits that diagnosis in infancy of future mental status is relatively uncertain—except in cases of mongolism, untreated cretinism, or where there are other well-recognized stigmata of feeblemindedness.

Q R Biol 14:382 S '39. * In presenting these cases from their huge clinical records which run well into the thousands, the authors have mainly selected those cases which expose the difficulties and pitfalls of clinical diagnosis and prognosis and which are especially significant in clinical application and developmental psychology. *

[B914]

GESELL, ARNOLD; HALVERSON, HENRY M.; THOMPSON, HELEN; ILG, FRANCES L.; CASTNER, BURTON M.; AMES, LOUISE BATES; AND AMATRUDA, CATHERINE S. **The First Five Years of Life:** A Guide to the Study of the Preschool Child. From the Yale Clinic of Child Development. New York: Harper & Brothers, 1940. Pp. xiii, 393. $3.50.

Am J Orthopsychiatry 10:632 Jl '40. Ira S. Wile. * Gesell and his collaborators present in admirable manner the results of their careful studies of the mechanisms of growth. * Gesell's methods are exceedingly valuable because they constitute a developmental examination and facilitate the estimation of production at maturity, although there is no assumption that maturational genetics are continuous, universal and unchangeable * One error mars part of the helpful interpretive material: the statistical data, though in terms of percentages, are not convincing since the numbers are too limited, e.g., percentages based upon study of eighteen children. This minor criticism does not reflect on the potential value of the book, inherent in the running comment and definitive exposition, rather than upon mathematical statement of the facts. The study of larger groups under other conditions may alter figures but they probably will not affect the factual progressions noted during the preschool years.

Ed Abstracts 5:164-5 Je '40. D. G. Ryans. This is essentially a revision of Gesell's *The Mental Growth of the Pre-school Child,* published some fifteen years ago. The text has been entirely rewritten and extended. *

J Am Med Assn 115:408 Ag 3 '40. * will be of immense interest to all of those concerned in the study and training of children and is obviously invaluable particularly to the pediatrician, who must have far more than an ordinary knowledge of child psychology.

Loyola Ed Digest 15:8 Jl '40. Austin G. Schmidt. * Gesell's work represents a vast amount of careful observation, experimentation, and testing. Its contribution is threefold: it presents data on what normal child development is, it greatly broadens the concept of what should be included in a study of development, and it serves as a model of conservative and meticulously scientific methods of research.

Psychiatric Q 14:648-50 Jl '40. * Child guidance workers, nursery school and kindergarten teachers as well as other educators, parents, and all those interested in adequate guidance and sound mental growth of the child will do well to consult this book * They will be able to orient themselves toward the complex mental life and growth of the most important early years. They will find occasion to better prepare the road for optimal growth without the blinding emotional involvement and perplexity which so often create detrimental tension between children and their elders.

Survey Graphic 29:356 Je '40. Orvis C. Irwin. * Gesell long has been America's outstanding authority on the topography of infancy and childhood. * The uninitiated tourist will be charmed by the gentle dramatics of his descriptions of the vistas. The initiated perhaps will privately admire his skill in avoiding some of the roughest crags and the more resistant underbrush. Advanced students in the party, notebooks in hand, will be impressed by the competent summarizing remarks of the associate guides, who themselves have hewn out many interesting trails in difficult parts of the terrain. Occasionally the head guide slows his pace and indulges a pensive moment. Proper words seem to come falteringly. Perhaps it's the vistas, but neologisms do appear. Here are a few: The four-weeks child occasionally seems to be "staring at sound." He has a "picking up capacity of the eyes." At sixteen weeks "legs and feet have a very subsidiary status, but there are anticipations of their future responsibilities." "The twenty-eight-weeks-old infant crows and squeals. At sixteen weeks he cooed, at four weeks he mewed." "It takes the infant twelve weeks to rise from a twenty-four-weeks level of maturity to a thirty-six-weeks level." The one-year-old child "displays a dawning sense of aboveness and verticality." "He knows where things are, were, go, and belong." The two-year-old's "sense of self was not as totalitarian as it was at eighteen months." But after each of these lapses a new vista appears and it's all right, even with the old timer making his fourth trip. * At any rate, as Abe Lincoln is supposed to have said: This is an excellent book for anyone who likes this kind of book. Moreover, it is easily the best of this kind of book.

[B915]

GESELL, ARNOLD, AND THOMPSON, HELEN; ASSISTED BY CATHERINE STRUNK AMATRUDA. **Infant Behavior:** Its Genesis and Growth. New York: McGraw-Hill Book Co., Inc., 1934. Pp. viii, 343. $3.00. (London: McGraw-Hill Publishing Co., Ltd. 18s.)

Am J Sociol 42:285-6 S '36. Margaret Curti. * like the preceding books from Gesell's labora-

tory. There are more pictures of attractive babies behaving normally (different babies, I suppose, but looking about the same) ; many more details about the behavior of these babies in the situations familiar to those who follow Gesell's work; and the usual dignified generalizations about the profound significance which these facts must have. In the last chapters the writers use the words "maturational" and "organismic" as freely as the youngest of the writers in the periodicals. *

Brit J Ed Psychol 8:103 F '38. C. W. V(alentine). * important work * The volume is a welcome addition to the valuable contributions which Dr. Gesell has already made to the study of infant psychology.

Brit J Psychol 26:113-4 Jl '35. * presented and discussed with directness and clarity. Among the many studies of the early development of human behaviour which have appeared in recent years, this will take a very high place indeed. * a notable contribution to . . . [an] important topic.

J Ed Res 29:304-5 D '35. George D. Stoddard. * a refined account of what may be considered the expected sequence of responses for infants exposed to controlled environmental conditions. As such it is a useful reference book * A portion of the book is given over to a theoretical discussion of Gesell's well-known position which places great weight upon the inner lawfulness of child behavior. While the present observations lend support to his views, perhaps it should be pointed out that these children represent a great heterogeneity genetically, but a relatively even and comfortable environment. Were some strenuous person to coach and train infants in a way analogous to Myrtle McGraw's work with preschool children, we might well be faced with radical alternations in Gesell's normative patterns. But in delineating soundly a course of events which is likely to remain representative of infant behavior in a laissez faire (and probably desirably so) milieu, Gesell and Thompson, with the assistance of Amatruda and a staff of trained workers, have rendered an invaluable service to the young science of child development.

J Genetic Psychol 46:487-9 Je '35. Norman L. Munn. * The purpose in presenting this book is to "set forth normative data of development in such a way that the individual study and diagnosis of infant behavior status may be made more analytic and interpretive." Without the promised monograph on specific procedures and biometric conclusions and applications, however, this volume will probably be of restricted value to diagnosticians. The authors assume, of course, that diagnosticians will use it in connection with *An Atlas of Infant Behavior* and *Norms of Infant Development*. As it stands the book's chief value resides in its lucid and not too technical presentation of the methods and results of a significant approach to some problems of infant development. Genetic and child psychologists will find it a valuable supplement to their textbooks, since the student may trace for himself the developmental trends indicated in the tables and photographs. There is also much that will be of interest to the general reader.

J Nerv and Mental Dis 82:334-5 S '35. Dr. Gesell has contributed notably to further knowledge of the psychobiological foundations of human activity through his varied and detailed studies of the ontogenetic patternings of infant behavior. The present work . . . forms an important continuance of his studies in this field. * Gesell's use of morphographic methods in determining trends of "characteristicness" in the early behavior and psychical stages of child development is a major instance of his achievement in bringing some of the manifold inner dynamisms of psychobiological development further to light in terms of workable scientific formulation. These procedures are here applied to the investigation of mental development in infants during the first year of life ; recording results of the many-sided observation of the controlled conditions, and recounting through excellently oriented genetic interpretations the total reactions in the various behavior situations. * The authors, with the assistance of Catherine Strunk Amatruda as research pediatrist, have amply demonstrated through new and hard-won material the nature of mental growth as the dynamic progressions of inner behavior sequences; clearly substantiating their belief that "the action systems of embryo, fetus, and infant undergo orderly changes of pattern, which are so consistent that we may be certain that these changes are governed by mechanisms of form comparable with those which are being defined by the science of embryology." This is a work which no psychiatrist can afford to miss. On an invaluable and thoroughly mined level, it provides a stimulating approach, in terms of the first dynamic stages of life, to the problems of the nature of psychobiological function and mechanism manifest in the total development of the individual.

J Pediatrics 6:424-5 Mr '35. B(orden) S. V(eeder).

Lancet 230:668 Mr 21 '36. * There is scarcely a muscular movement of the human infant from birth to the second year which has not been carefully studied from day to day in order to investigate growth in coördination and the emergence of intelligent social behaviour. * No student of infancy can be without this important book. It should be of value to all those who are interested in the academic study of infant behaviour and also and particularly to those who find it so difficult to decide whether mental retardation has appeared in the early months of life. We must congratulate the authors in having produced in such an excellent form the results of their far-reaching researches.

Mental Hyg (New York) 19:477-8 Jl '35. Florence L. Goodenough. Those who have followed closely the long series of reports from the Yale Clinic of Child Development on the developmental sequences in infant behavior over the past decade can hardly help but be impressed, not only by the quality of the work itself, but also by the progress that the human eye makes in the art of seeing. * the book does not represent a new scientific construct, but a later stage of scientific morphology * As compared with the earlier reports, the present one is characterized by more precise description of the behavior situations used and by much greater minutiae in the presentation of results *

[B916]

GESELL, ARNOLD, AND THOMPSON, HELEN ; ASSISTED BY CATHERINE STRUNK AMATRUDA. **The Psychology of Early Growth:** Including Norms of Infant Behavior and a Method of Genetic Analysis. New York: Macmillan Co., 1938. Pp. ix, 290. $4.00. (London: Macmillan & Co., Ltd. 17s.)

Am J Dis Children 56:714 S '38.

Am J Nursing 38:1180 O '38. Gertrude Hildreth. * The precision with which the original behavior examinations have been elaborated would imply that anyone who expects to duplicate the tests should be equally precise. Since, however, the authors have not given the complete information that would be necessary to duplicate their apparatus, methods and technics, it is doubtful whether the book can serve one purpose the authors presumably intended it should have,—that of a testing manual in the hands of clinical workers outside the Yale laboratories. Incautious use of the materials under non-standardized conditions by child study enthusiasts might produce misleading results. Although the percentage norms for various age levels give some indication of individual variation in the group of infants studied, nevertheless more detailed information concerning the individual characteristics of these one hundred and seven children would have been a desirable addition to the book. All professional persons who work with children under a year of age will find it profitable to refer to this manual for behavior expectations at various age levels. *

Am J Orthopsychiatry 9:815-7 O '39. (John Gray) Peatman. * a companion volume to two other publications—the two-volume *Atlas of Infant Behavior* (a motion-picture record) and *Infant Behavior: Its Genesis and Growth.* The present work carries a normative survey of infant behavior at four-week intervals up through 56 weeks of age and is followed by a fourth volume on development from one to five years which will take the place of Gesell's earlier work, *The Mental Growth of the Pre-School Child.* * According to the preface of their 1934 volume *(Infant Behavior)* this book was to be called *Norms of Infant Development,* a phrase certainly more descriptive of the contents than *The Psychology of Early Growth.* * As suggested by the preceding, there is a great deal of overlapping in the 1934 and 1938 works. Just why Gesell and Thompson split their material between two volumes and two publishers is not clear. The result certainly detracts from the value of the whole. It is unfortunate that such an extended, painstaking, and methodologically refined investigation as this should suffer from this kind of publication. If the reader is acquainted with the 1934 work, the present volume is not difficult to use, but for the uninitiated the index at the end helps somewhat, but hardly makes the work a handbook until it has been explored as a whole. The normative data are based on a systematic, developmental investigation of a sample of 107 infants, studied extra-intensively. This is both the strength and the weakness of the work. Its strength of course derives from the great care with which the many behavioral observa-

tions have been carried out and minutely detailed for other research workers. Its weakness lies in the tendency to over-generalize results, based as they are on but a small sample of infants. * It is not to be wondered that the authors do not separate their groups with respect to sex and present behavioral data accordingly. * Aside from the fact that their sex samples are not large enough (they range in size from 13 to 26 cases) for generalized inferences about indifferences or lack of differences in behavior norms, the allusion to a possible sex difference in gross motor behavior is the reverse of results on walking presented by the data of several other investigators. Gesell and Thompson do not maintain that their sample is *fairly* representative of all infants, but they do infer it to be a representative of a delimited sector of our population. * it is highly improbable from the point of view of sampling theory that such a complex delimited "whole" could be randomly or fairly sampled so as to provide data for reliable norms * And the anthropometric data, with averages carried to two decimal places, can hardly be described as normative at all, based as they are on sex samples of from 13 to 26 cases. Fortunately, in presenting their behavior norms, the authors use a statistic which somewhat mitigates the hazards of generalizing from their small samples. Instead of presenting the *average* age at which a given behavior item is manifested, they tabulate the percentage frequencies of their subjects at each age level who manifest the item. * No doubt this work will be a valuable addition to the libraries of research workers interested in the atomization of behavior development in infants. * The work is apt to be confusing and misleading, however, to the lay mother who visits the library in search of knowledge about the psychology of early growth. Obviously the book was not published for the average mother, but the title belies this fact. For her, as well as for many professionals in child development, the 1934 volume will be sufficient. And, finally, it may not be amiss to point out that the Gesell-Thompson approach to child psychology will perhaps appear rather futile and fruitless to many, especially those with a *gestalt* or psychiatric orientation. * there are psychologists, psychiatrists and pediatricians who feel that the essence of child development is missed or but barely touched upon by this kind of normative survey. As Kurt Lewin might put it, the genotypical is neglected for the phenotypical. * Biometric central tendencies or critical ages . . . are certainly not indispensable to the detection and identification of this or that behavior character, since such norms are necessarily developed *after* the characters have been identified and measured.

Am J Psychol 51:604-5 Jl '38. Gilbert J. Rich. * The reviewer feels that the suggestions for the clinical use of the development schedules clearly imply that useful norms have now been set up. Is such an implication justified? The use of a homogeneous group of infants was ideal for the purpose of developmental study, when one age-level was to be compared to another. But one may question whether such a group is satisfactory as a norm to which infants not so chosen are to be compared. Until we know the effects of racial inheritance, socioeconomic status of parents, etc., upon development at this age, errors are likely to result if an infant is compared to a standard which is alien to him. This is, of course, only a minor criticism of a rather monumental work, one which is outstanding because of its scientific thoroughness and the completeness with which every detail is presented.

Am J Sociol 44:614-5 Ja '39. Ruth Pearson Koshuk. * To social psychologists, Part III presents something of a challenge. Here is described the diagnostic use of the norms established * no attempt is made to relate the level of the child's development to the type of care and social interaction to which he had been exposed *

Char and Pers 8:175-6 D '39. Donald K. Adams. * indispensable if for no other reason than that it presents the latest revision of the most comprehensive developmental schedule for the first year that we have.

Ed Abstracts 4:168-9 Je '39. Russell G. Leiter. * Throughout the volume an effort has been made to present the material in such a way that it may be serviceable for varying requirements of research and diagnosis.

Ed Adm and Sup 24:640 N '38. A. S. Edwards. * an indispensable volume for students of infants with a wealth of accurate and scholarly material. It is, of course, not an elementary textbook but the most thorough, detailed study of the early growth of human infants extant. The special value of the book lies in the details that are presented both of pro-

cedure and of results. The authors and the publishers are to be most highly congratulated in the production of this volume. Students of the subject are most fortunate in the fact that it is now available. Here is a magnificent piece of work in an exceedingly difficult field of measurement.

Ed Res B 18:27-8 Ja '39. Amalie K. Nelson. * Persons interested in child psychology will find this book an invaluable asset to their library.

El Sch J 39:311-3 D '38. Kai Jensen. * one of a series of brilliant books and researches which have come from the Yale Clinic of Child Development and which are outstanding in the field * both a research monograph and a handbook * *The Psychology of Early Growth* follows the highly commendable procedure of presenting all the data collected, so that others may check the conclusions reached and use any desired data for further research. The authors are also to be complimented on a very clear presentation of the methods and the procedures by which their data were collected. The need for better original data, rather than for more elaborate statistical treatment of inferior or incomplete data, is clearly seen. The section on the limitations of statistical treatment of data in this field is well worth the reading time of all interested in the scientific study of child development. Throughout, the volume stresses patterns of growth as well as developmental levels. Persons interested in child development at all ages would do well to study and to ponder the principles and the considerations laid down with respect to patterns of growth. A clear presentation of a new method of genetic analysis is an important contribution. The format of the book is particularly attractive and legible. * regrettably, the authors did not see fit to compare their work with similar research at Minnesota, Iowa, California, and other centers which have made important contributions in the field. Such a comparison would have been of great interest to many workers. There are also those who would like to have the Yale group tackle the problem of discovering the factors involved in the process called "maturation" and who would like more data on the possibilities and the consequences of speeding up developmental levels. These considerations in no way alter the fact that the book is clearly a notable contribution in the field of child development. It should prove of great value to intelligent parents and teachers generally, as well as to research workers in the field.

Int J Psycho-Analysis 21:107-8 Ja '40. Margarethe A. Ribble. * The book contains valuable studies of certain phases of motor and perceptual behaviour and of tendencies to explore *inanimate* reality. One cannot help feeling surprise that with so much carefully controlled material at hand such highly important behaviour manifestations as (1) the establishment and course of sucking, (2) crying behaviour, both in relation to the stabilization of breathing on the physiological side and as an emotional expression, (3) elimination behaviour, and (4) responses to presence or absence of the mother, are left out or only casually mentioned. For the diagnosis of latent brain disease or mechanical trauma the behaviour norms are of distinct value. For indications of instability which may be detrimental to good personality development they are not particularly helpful. This type of examination of infant behaviour is much like the performance tests given to older children to determine intelligence. The main criticism of it would be, particularly for the infant, that it gives so little consideration to the instinctual and emotional life whose full expression is always evidence of mental health.

J Consulting Psychol 3:70 Mr-Ap '39. Nancy Bayley. This volume is primarily a description of the Yale tests of behavior development during the first year of life. This description is detailed and careful. It includes the selection of the sample tested, the methods used in securing and recording the data, the exact manner of presenting the tests, norms based on these data, a method of scoring the tests, and summaries of behavior representative of each age level tested. The sample is rather small, there being from twenty-six to forty-nine cases tested at each four-week age level; but it was carefully selected to represent a strictly average socio-economic background. The age at testing has also been strictly regulated. * Although the authors argue that their method of appraising infant behavior is the best, they present no statistical or factual data to support their claims. * In spite of the fact that a fair proportion of the children were tested repeatedly there are no comparisons between test-retest scores, for either reliability or consistency. The authors content themselves

with the expression of a hope that the tests will make possible prognosis as well as diagnosis. They make no reference to any infant tests or test results of other investigators, and ignore the findings of others that predictions from infant tests cannot be made reliably. * As a treatise on the "psychology of early growth" which the title claims, this book is a great disappointment, for it concerns itself with only a small part of the subject. As an evaluation of a particular measure of infant development it also falls very short. It does have great value, however, as an acute clinical analysis of certain aspects of infant behavior, and as a detailed and complete description of the methods used in the Yale Clinic of Child Development for testing and scoring behavior development in infants from the ages four through fifty-six weeks. We have here for the first time an adequate description of the Gesell tests, making them generally available both for the purposes of testing, and for comparison with other infant scales. Whether these tests will justify their authors' claims is a matter which awaits the publication of their data on retests and the use of the tests by others.

J Nerv and Mental Dis 90:686-7 N '39. * No review can do justice to the enormous amount of factual material here presented. It is a fine bit of research and merits high praise and wide utilization.

Med Times 67:48 Ja '39. Stanley S. Lamm. * conclusions are carefully drawn *

Psychoanalytic Q 9:123-7 Ja '40. Lillian Malcove. * a volume quite complete in itself but more fully appreciated when supplemented by the two books of 1934, especially the Atlas * valuable for the student of clinical psychology as a textbook and for others as a handbook * particularly useful . . . [book] for the child psychiatrist, analyst, neurologist, endocrinologist and pediatrician * Certain of the test situations, as for instance the observations on the development of responses to external stimuli in the prehensory and perceptual examinations, afford an interesting opportunity to study, in addition to neuromuscular maturation, the growth of some aspects of ego function. To a limited extent the tests permit us to watch the infant's growing awareness of another person and the development of responses such as the comparison of that person with itself. * Another interesting observation is the time relationship between the diminution of oral activities (putting things in mouth) noted at forty-four weeks and the increase of poking activities noted at forty-eight weeks. * The limitation of the tests to five categories enhances the accuracy of the included data but emphasizes the need for extension of the observations to areas that have special interest for the analyst such as social adaptability, which soon involves ego defenses, and the development of responses to internal stimuli such as impulses. *

Psychol B 35:445-8 Jl '38. Nancy Bayley. * something which workers in the field of infant testing have long been waiting for—an accurate, detailed, and complete account of the methods of observation and measurement used in the Yale Clinic of Child Development, with norms for the first year of life * [the authors] argue that growth in behavior is not merely a matter of adding new responses, but also of dropping out old ones, as the organization of the infant changes. A test of development should, accordingly, include items which measure both types of developmental change in order to gain a complete picture of a child's level of ability. But the authors offer no proof of their thesis by presenting norms derived from different selections of test items. Hence they are not convincing in their arguments that for test scores the method they recommend is any better than the methods now generally used. As a matter of fact, other investigators who have worked with infant tests have noted this dropping out of immature behavior patterns, and have at times included such behavior changes in their test series. But the immature patterns are usually replaced by more advanced ones, so that a scale made up only of items whose frequency increases with age over a span of several months, actually does take into account most of these changing patterns. It seems unnecessary to include in a scale, for example, both the "decreasing" "head predominantly rotated" and the "increasing" "head predominantly midplane" (illustrated in figure 20) when the presence of the latter automatically excludes the former. * A single composite score they believe to be unjustified as an oversimplification of a complex array of behaviors. This may be true; but since they themselves say that many of the items might legitimately be placed in several of the categories, there being no way of dividing the behavior patterns into

independent functional units, one might hold equally well that the separation of scores is an unjustified complication serving to indicate only approximately the general fields in which a child (at the time of a particular test) may be retarded or advanced. The use of the scores *both* separately and in combination may very well be useful when their limitations and merits are taken into consideration. * This volume has great value as a careful and thorough presentation of the Yale material. But the authors tend to ignore related studies made elsewhere, from which it is not unthinkable they might occasionally have profited. If insularity is often a symptom of genius, it is scarcely the hallmark of science. The authors remark, in a concluding statement, that "the complex of growth is governed by inherent maturational mechanisms which carry every infant toward an optimal. These mechanisms are lawful. Herein lie the possibilities of prognosis as well as of diagnosis; for where there is lawfulness there is potential prediction." The reviewer is hopeful too, but is reminded of F. H. Bradley's comment: "It is *always* wet on half-holidays because of the Law of Raininess, but *sometimes* it is *not* wet, because of the Supplementary Law of Sunshine." At any rate, reliable predictions on the basis of infant tests appear unlikely for some time to come, not because of metaphysical guesses about the absence (or presence) of "lawfulness," but because of the accumulating empirical evidence that young children, who have been tested repeatedly over a span of years, are inconstant in their rates of growth, whatever the variable measured.

[B917]

GLASSOW, RUTH B., AND BROER, MARION R. **Measuring Achievement in Physical Education.** Philadelphia, Pa., and London: W. B. Saunders Co., 1938. Pp. 344. $2.75; 12s.

Ed Abstracts 3:273-4 O '38. Evelyn B. Spindler. * Intended for use in college courses, it is equally valuable for teachers and administrators who wish to learn more about testing methods. * A great need exists for standardization in tests and in test procedures which the book suggests. By collecting tests and summarizing recent literature it should be of great aid to workers in this field.

Ed Res B 19:237-8 Ap 10 '40. Charles C. Cowell. * At the very outset Miss Glassow and Miss Broer caution the users of this volume against testing and measuring as ends in themselves. Their prime purposes are to aid the student in evaluating tests, to know what tests are available, to know how to give tests, and to understand research techniques in order to interpret research studies. They have achieved these purposes to a high degree. * they fail to emphasize strongly the educational values affected by the testing process *

J Health and Phys Ed 9:528 O '38. * a novel approach * an excellent guide for courses in "tests and measurements."

Pub Health R 8:62 My 15 '39. Dorothy Beise. * an unusually fine piece of work * a real contribution to physical education and should be of value both to teachers and to strictly research workers.

Sch 27:548 F '39. H(elen) L. B(ryan). * a most comprehensive and readable book * Part I deals with the essential features of a good test, and the method of selecting one. Part II is an attempt "to compile all that literature has to offer in measuring skill in physical education." Much of this is presented in chart form, and the tests are then compared and evaluated. * will help much in the selection of suitable tests for team games, dual games and activities, dancing and rhythm, posture, motor ability, physical capacity and physical fitness. Part III is an excellent exposition of the interpretation of raw scores, the uses of standard deviation, and correlation. One of the most valuable features . . . is the bibliography which precedes each chapter.

Va Teach 19:208 D '38. H. M. * an intelligent and conservative estimate of the value of tests and measurements in physical education * statistical technique . . . is here made simple and clear * will be easily understood by any physical education major student.

For an additional review, see B364.

[B918]

GOLDBERG, WOOLF. **The Carnegie Examinations at Temple University:** A Study of the Examinations of the Carnegie Foundation in the Teachers College of Temple University. Philadelphia, Pa.: Temple University, 1938. Pp. vi, 105. $1.00. Paper.

Loyola Ed Digest 14:6 Ja '39. Austin G. Schmidt. * the Carnegie examinations were the ones used in the celebrated Pennsylvania Study. This doctoral dissertation, then, analyzes the results of the tests in Temple University. As usual, the academic group of students was definitely superior to the non-academic, and all made scores which were disappointingly low.

[B919]

GRAY, J. L. **The Nation's Intelligence.** London: C. A. Watts & Co., Ltd., 1936. Pp. v, 154. 2s. 6d. (Toronto, Canada: Ryerson Press. $0.85.)

B Int Bur Ed 12:33 q 1 '38. * written so as to be intelligible to the non-technical reader * [the author] describes what intelligence tests are and explains their use. He applies his findings to the English people, treating his subject from the angle of social psychology—which sets the book apart in a category of its own. He challenges the theory recently put forward of the decadence of the English intelligence, but he shows that, in England, opportunity is not sufficiently at the service of ability and he suggests necessary reforms. This book should be read by every one interested in the future of England.

Queen's Q 43:460 Winter '36-37.

For additional reviews, see B119 and B365.

[B920]

GRAYBEAL, ELIZABETH. **The Measurement of Outcomes of Physical Education for College Women.** Minneapolis, Minn.: University of Minnesota Press, 1937. Pp. viii, 80. $1.00. Paper. (London: Oxford University Press. 4s. 6d.)

Ed Abstracts 3:197-8 Je '38. Evelyn B. Spindler. * A definite stride forward in practical measurement which is becoming so necessary if physical education is to hold its place. Usable for justification of course, planning, classifying groups, ascertaining values. A challenge to the present haphazard system.

Pub Health R 7:7 F '38. Virginia Peaseley. * This small volume is not only interesting as research in physical education but is an encouragement to physical educators in successfully proving some of the claims made by the profession.

For additional reviews, see B366.

[B921]

GREAT BRITAIN, BOARD OF EDUCATION. **Supplementary Memorandum on Examinations for Scholarships and Special Places in Secondary Schools, July 1936.** Educational Pamphlets, No. 63 (Supplement, July 1936). London: H.M. Stationery Office, 1937. Pp. 9. 2d. Paper.

[B922]

GREULICH, WILLIAM WALTER; DAY, HARRY G.; LACHMAN, SANDER E.; WOLFE, JOHN B.; AND SHUTTLEWORTH, FRANK K. **A Handbook of Methods for the Study of Adolescent Children.** Introduction by Lawrence K. Frank. Monographs of the Society for Research in Child Development, Vol. 3, No. 2, Serial No. 15. Washington, D. C.: the Society, National Research Council, 1938. Pp. xix, 406. $2.25. Paper, lithotyped.

Am J Med Sci 196:739 N '38. J. S. * a very useful handbook. It contains a mine of new and revised information on many aspects of the physical structure and function of the adolescent. * will be a useful aid to physicians and educators dealing with the adolescent boy or girl.

Brit J Ed Psychol 10:83 F '40 O. W. This book is another interesting example of the value of the kind of corporate research which in many other fields has been more successfully employed in the United States of America than in this Country. * The authors have undoubtedly carried out with great thoroughness and competency a broad survey of the methods of study of adolescents now being successfully employed in their respective fields: and the Handbook will consequently prove a useful work of reference for all students of child development, though its value in this direction would have been increased by the inclusion of a good index. The most obvious limitation of the Handbook is the lack of balance between the treatment of the physical aspects of adolescence (to which 280 pages out of a total of 406 pages are devoted) and the psychological, and particularly the educational and social, aspects of development. *

Ed Res B 19:109 F 14 '40. F. P. Robinson. * a handbook compilation of specific techniques for measuring different aspects of growth during adolescence, and in most cases these means are also suitable for both before and after the adolescent period * Many may believe that the volume has underemphasized the importance of regular psychological testing * people who are interested in measurement techniques with adolescents will find much source material in this monograph that will be of value to them.

Endocrinology 23:245-6 Ag '38. * an indispensable addition to the libraries of students of human development * The bibliography is extensive and rigidly selected.

J Am Med Assn 111:2037-8 N 26 '38. * These two related works [reviewed jointly with *The Adolescent Period:* A Graphic and Pictorial Atlas (*see* B1071)] constitute a monumental achievement in selection and (in the handbook) of critical discussion of contributions from a vast and often confusing literature, which they now bring within relatively easy reach of the student or research worker. As a reference resource they amply justify the enormous labor they represent. As

the authors have set out to do, they indicate what structures, functions and activities of the growing child can and have been measured, and they aid the worker in making reliable measurements of his own. Despite its bigness, the handbook omits the neurologic, psychiatric and endocrinologic literature of adolescence, which omission, the authors explain, is due to limitations of time and personnel. From the standpoint of the medical research worker in adolescence this is a disappointing omission, and the authors' hope that others will be inspired to make up for this lack will be shared by medical workers. One cannot lightly dismiss, however, the almost cursory manner in which some relatively subjective methods of studying behavior are dismissed in chapter XXI. These include observation, personal report (interviews, psychoanalysis, case study) as discussed in the chapter on sexual behavior. These methods should be critically regarded as methods of study of behavior in general, sexual or otherwise. The possibilities of these methods are sufficiently great that serious students of behavior should not content themselves with the easy evasion "as the procedure (psychoanalysis) now stands, however, it appears to be too subjective to be classified as a scientific approach." The authors make tentative suggestions as to the possible "scientific" utilization of these methods. They persist in the curious attitude that methods which gain information about the mental life of the disturbed individual might not be useful in gaining information about the normal adolescent. According to this logic, study of an individual suffering with an infection might not be expected to throw light on the maintaining of immunity from disease by the normal individual who shows no sign of infection. Not infrequently it requires the observation of individuals presenting exaggerated reaction to undue stress (whether physical or psychologic) to suggest the reactive potentialities and the laws governing these for the normal individual. Observation, whether of individuals in health or in disease, may lead to the clues necessary to set up properly controlled conditions for scientific investigation. *

J Pediatrics 14:276 F '39. * of extreme value *

Loyola Ed Digest 14:7 Ja '39. Austin G. Schmidt. * a truly magnificent piece of work. Practically all known methods of observing, measuring, and testing are concisely and so far as we can see accurately described. The references are numerous and well selected.

Pub Health R 7:2 Je '38. Warren E. Forsythe. * a collection from the literature carefully and authoritatively selected and reviewed. It does not assume to be exhaustive in scope, but is scholarly and goes deeply into the areas included. * Workers in child hygiene, school health, human physiology, anthropometry, education, etc., should have this volume for reference.

Q R Biol 13:466 D '38. * A tremendous mass of material is made readily available through this handbook which should be invaluable to investigators in all fields of child development.

Sch R 47:309-11 Ap '39. Fowler D. Brooks. * The material is well organized and clearly presented. The general arrangement is to set forth important facts on a topic, the methods in use (with a critique of both facts and methods), and citation of the literature on the topic. Workers will find the bibliography on each topic more serviceable than a general or combined bibliography on all topics at the end of a chapter. * No index is given, but a good analytic table of contents makes the material in the volume readily accessible. This *Handbook of Methods* is distinctly valuable for workers interested in studying adolescence. *

[B923]

HAMILTON, GORDON. **Theory and Practice of Social Case Work.** Published for the New York School of Social Work. New York: Columbia University Press, 1940. Pp. viii, 388. $3.00. (London: Oxford University Press. 20s.)

Family 21:167-8 Jl '40. Leah Feder. * based upon a wide range of experience and knowledge; solidly grounded in practice, Miss Hamilton has a flair for extracting the essence of a situation as she sees it. Some portions of the book are brilliantly written and express with clarity and vividness remarkable insight into the meaning of practice, while in other parts the meaning is obscured by involved expression. The scope of the material is so broad that numerous subjects well worth further clarification by Miss Hamilton have had to be limited. For example, in describing the worker-client relationship, a single paragraph distinguishes between the point of view of relationship therapy as described by Virginia

Robinson and Dr. Taft and the point of view of others who interpret the "social situation and the client's feeling toward it." The values of both approaches are too significant to be treated so briefly, considering the quality of the contribution Miss Hamilton could make to the subject. * The use of group work in treatment is undoubtedly a significant new area in contrast to that of relief-giving, yet the omission of any lengthy discussion of the latter (which Miss Hamilton mentions as one of two areas in which the case worker may be said to be the "expert") cannot but be regretted, especially when the concept of relief-giving as outlined briefly seems potentially so valuable for case work practice in all fields. * The last chapter in the book, which states clearly and helpfully the ways in which case work may utilize the material and methods of psychiatry, will have special usefulness in helping case workers think through exactly where they may be going in their own particular use of their knowledge and the resources available for assistance. Miss Hamilton has related case work to the large field of social work and to certain special points of interest which are significant to her philosophy of social work. This interdependence of all movements for a better social order must not be overlooked. The extent of the subject matter has meant, however, a certain loss in the depth of the material. Unfortunately, also, the long case record excerpts have not been analyzed in sufficient detail to make clear always the relevance of their use. Miss Hamilton might have made a contribution in this area as well as in the articulation of the theory of social case work. From this angle, no doubt the book will offer ample opportunity for students to do their own case analysis, but it is too bad to lose so frequently Miss Hamilton's rare competence in the explanation of case work processes. Where she has done this the result is most gratifying.

[B924]

HAMLEY, H. R.; OLIVER, R. A. C.; FIELD, H. E.; AND ISAACS, SUSAN. **The Educational Guidance of the School Child:** Suggestions on Child Study and Guidance Embodying a Scheme of Pupils' Records. Foreword by Percy Nunn. Introduction by Keith Struckmeyer. London: Evans Brothers, Ltd., [1937]. Pp. 122. 3s. 6d.

B Int Bur Ed 11:190 q 4 '37. * shows the value of making pupils' records already in the infant school, and of using cumulative records right up through the school. Also how to interpret the records so as to give the measure of guidance that is within the power and capacity of teachers. Specimen records are given in an appendix.

For additional reviews, see B373.

[B925]

HARDY, MARTHA CRUMPTON, AND HOEFER, CAROLYN H. **Healthy Growth:** A Study of the Influence of Health Education on Growth and Development of School Children. Chicago, Ill.: University of Chicago Press, 1936. Pp. xii, 360. $3.50. (London: Cambridge University Press. 16s.)

El Sch J 38:151-2 O '37. Ruth Strang. The research . . . is unique in the literature of health education, representing, as it does, a thorough and scientific attempt to measure the effects of a health program. In contrast with its scope and elaborate statistical treatment of the data, the previously published descriptions of health programs appear obviously inadequate in their feeble evaluation based only on subjective opinion or quantitative study of one or two outcomes. * Even though conclusive evidence of the effectiveness of the health instruction was not secured, this research has made an invaluable contribution by developing more precise methods of measurement than have before been used, by analyzing the process of appraisal of children's health, and by frankly calling attention to sources of error in the experimental technique. It has emphasized the importance of setting up, in the beginning if possible, groups which are comparable with respect to the factors that are most likely to influence the physical development and educability of the pupils. The fullest possibilities of the original data are still unexhausted. If the wealth of data collected were reassembled as case studies, individual growth curves could be plotted and individual patterns of health behavior and status could be studied with reference to the associated environmental conditions.

J Ed Psychol 29:397-9 My '38. Roger T. Lennon. * Although the authors claim that the same children were followed over a twelve-year period, the data which they report cover only the four-year period from 1923 to 1927. * The equating . . . [of the experimental and control groups] was far from satisfactory, particularly in the case of socio-economic status and intelligence, and only by courtesy can the groups be said to be matched. For certain sub-analyses of the results, the authors have attempted to eliminate some of the errors which

might arise from this lack of equality by selecting more carefully matched groups; this procedure, however, reduces the number of cases on which their findings are based, and does not fully compensate for the initial lack of equality between the groups. * Unfortunately, the findings of the investigation are vitiated to a great extent by several factors. The poor equating of the groups has already been mentioned. Most of the measures employed in the study—physicians' ratings, estimates of socio-economic status, interest and attitude questionnaires, personality ratings, and the Performance Scale—are of unknown or disappointing reliability. The variable which was being studied, *viz.*, classroom instruction in health topics, varied from class to class, depending on the teacher and the individual needs of each class. The tables in which the data have been summarized are not always clear, and in some instances, *e.g.*, Tables 20 and 50, are marked by computational inaccuracy and erroneous headings. Critical ratios, which have been computed for almost all the group comparisons in the study, are sometimes given only for the difference between the initial and final status of each group, rather than for the differences in gains made by the two groups. The topical and author index is quite inadequate. It is regrettable that such a broadly conceived testing program, with such possibilities for a thorough developmental study of the whole child, did not yield more satisfactory results. In fairness to the authors, however, it should be pointed out that the investigation was planned more than fifteen years ago, and they were forced to employ less adequate measures, tests, and techniques than are available at present. Despite the above mentioned shortcomings, the authors present a wealth of information in this volume which is deserving of careful consideration by those interested in child health and development.

Med Times 65:322 Je '37. Stanley S. Lamm.

Q R Biol 12:378-9 S '37. * The figures as presented by the authors, however, do not warrant any very definite conclusions. The statistical technique, characterized by excessive faith in the correlation coefficient, is especially inadequate. Nevertheless, a great amount of data is given which will be found useful for other investigators.

Res Q 8:164 Mr '37. Ross L. Allen. * the report of a study which started in 1921 in the public schools of Joliet, Illinois, and was based on the investigation into the health, growth, development, accomplishment, habits, and social development of some four hundred children as they progressed from the third grade into the junior high school * The comprehensiveness of the work which preceded the publication of *Healthy Growth* may be demonstrated, for example, by the fact that a minimum of 132 pages of tests, measurements, and ratings, and 90 pages of questionnaire and observational data were collected for each child. The data included pediatric examinations, anthropometric, psychological, sociological, and academic tests, evaluations of health habits and knowledge, yearly accomplishment in physical achievement, behavior and personality schedules, personal activities, parent contact reports, etc. * There is little doubt that this publication will become a standard text in professional training courses for both health and physical education instructors and academic teachers.

[B926]

HARRISON, M. LUCILE. **Reading Readiness,** Revised edition. Boston, Mass.: Houghton Mifflin Co., 1939. Pp. xiii, 255. $1.40.

Childh Ed 16:133 N '39. Alice Temple. * This new edition of Miss Harrison's book deserves the study of all teachers.

El Engl R 16:168 Ap '39. Emmett Albert Betts. * a valuable contribution to primary education because it is a practical study of the major problems involved. The organization of the book is excellent * Statements made regarding "dominance" need further appraisal because no distinction is made between peripheral and central aspects of laterality. Furthermore, an unusual statement was made regarding the possibility "of changing eye dominance." This aspect of the problem can be overemphasized. * The book includes many features which should be appreciated by teachers and supervisors. First, there is a practical listing of means for detecting reading readiness deficiencies and of suggestions for guidance. In the writer's judgment, more emphasis should have been placed on first-teaching or prevention and less on "Remedial Measures." Second, the advantages and limitations of certain reading readiness tests are stated. Third, the professional bibliography (Appendix A) has been carefully selected. Fourth, a list of recommended books for the children's library is presented in Appendix B. These features, coupled with discus-

sions, make an excellent handbook for teachers and clinicians. One of the chief outcomes from reading this book should be an awareness of the wide range of individual differences presented to kindergarten and primary teachers. * The reviewer has found this book challenging for both graduate and undergraduate students.

El Paso Sch Standard 17:34 S '39. M. E. Broom. * should be of value to teachers in all subject fields in which reading is used for study purposes.

J Ed Res 33:466 F '40. Miles A. Tinker. The first edition of this book, which appeared in 1936, was concerned with problems of reading readiness in the primary grades. This material, with little change, appears in the revised text as Part I under the title of "readiness for the initial period of reading instruction." * Unfortunately, as in the first edition, Harrison tends to accept uncritically the claims made by authors of tests. Part II of the text concerns itself with reading readiness at educational levels beyond the preparatory level. Although in general all the higher levels are supposed to be covered, most of the discussion is confined to grades below the high school. The chapter on the nature of reading is exceptionally well done. Undue emphasis upon the mechanics of reading and other narrow viewpoints, such as the development of rhythm reading, are severely criticised. * This excellent book will help give due prominence to the problem of reading readiness at the higher levels as well as in the primary grades. Because a program of reading readiness at all educational levels is basically sound, this movement will without doubt become more widespread in the near future.

Sight-Saving R 10:167-8 Je '40. * The material is clearly presented and the very full bibliography should prove an excellent source of reference. The list of books for children on the preparatory level is very helpful. It might have been well to indicate pre-primer material that is available in the size and kind of type that is acceptable for the young child. *

For reviews of the first edition, see B127 and B375.

[B927]

HARTOG, PHILIP. **Secondary School Examinations and the Curricula of Secondary Schools:** With Suggestions for Reform. An address delivered to the Higher Education Meeting at the Portsmouth Conference of the N. U. T., 1937. London: National Union of Teachers, 1937. Pp. 34. Gratis. Paper.

B Int Bur Ed 11:144-5 q 3 '37. * The examination system is under review in many countries, therefore this pamphlet will be of general interest. *

For additional reviews, see B377.

[B928]
HARTOG, PHILIP, AND RHODES, E. C. **An Examination of Examinations:** Being a Summary of Investigations on the Comparison of Marks Alloted to Examination Scripts by Independent Examiners and Boards of Examiners, together with a Section on a Viva Voce Examination. International Institute Examinations Enquiry. London: Macmillan & Co., Ltd., 1935. Pp. 81. 1s. Paper.

Brit J Ed Psychol 6:81-6 F '36. *J. F. Duff.* * I am a member of the Board of one of the largest examining bodies; though not myself an examiner for the Board, I attend its meetings, and I know much more about the possibilities of achieving a high standard of consistency in marking by proper team-work, and of systematizing compensation for doubtful or hard cases, than is known, or at any rate recognized, by Sir Philip Hartog or Dr. Rhodes. This Board and others can, and I hope will, produce evidence that their procedure is more carefully thought out and their results more satisfactory than those recorded in this book. Unfortunately such evidence will get no headlines in the daily press. The birth of a two-headed calf is "news," of a one-headed calf is not. But for the two-headed calf to show only one head on a recount is worse than no news; it is bathos, it spoils sport, and every good publicist will hush it up. * securing scripts from one examining body, and a panel of examiners from another, and paying them on "the usual scale, or slightly higher," was not enough to ensure that the conditions of a real examination were reproduced * the book is misnamed; it is not an Examination of Examinations, but only of the marking of scripts. One of the three components of an examination, the paper set, is neglected. * I take for detailed comment that result which the Committee describe as "perhaps the most disturbing," namely the marking of School Certificate History scripts. Here the difference in one case between the marks allotted by two examiners to the same script was 30 marks out of the maximum of 96. And when the same panel of examiners re-marked the same set of scripts after an interval of not less than 12 months, out of a total of 210 verdicts it was found that in 92 cases the individual examiners gave on their second marking not merely a different mark, but a different category (Failure, Pass, Credit). This does undoubtedly sound bad; it shocks the layman, and (unlike many of the findings in the book) surprises even the more expert, who know that 100 per cent consistency can never be attained by a single examiner and that other means must be found to allow for and correct the vagaries of individual, unaided judgment. But note this, stated without comment by the investigators, and *not* noted by any review of the book which I have yet read. For this enquiry "15 scripts were selected which had been awarded exactly the same 'middling' mark by the School Certificate authority concerned." And these, with marks erased, were passed on to the 15 unfortunate examiners. What a sample! As a statistician, Dr. Rhodes might tell us what are the odds against it happening in a real examination that an examiner's whole batch of scripts deserve exactly the same "middling" mark. How does one set about finding a standard when marking? By looking for clear differences in merit, which in real life one always finds. Here there were none. No wonder if the examiners began to find imaginary differences or to magnify small ones. They had an unreal situation and an impossible task. "It may well be asked," says the book, "in view of the extreme differences of these results, what validity can be attached to the marking of School Certificate History papers." It may equally well be asked what validity can be attached to a report which does not point out how abnormal were the conditions confronting the examiners in this case, and treats the result as typical and "most disturbing." The really disturbing thing is not the result but the investigators' method of procedure. No doubt the purpose of the investigators was to see what scatter of marks a set of scripts already marked equal would produce. That is a reasonable enquiry in itself. But with the sending of none but equal scripts to the examiners the enquiry changed from a fair test to a trap; and the failure of the investigators to realize this is most surprising. * Heavy deductions must be made from the investigators' conclusions for the kind of reason just indicated, where a highly abnormal factor in the situation is passed over with no attempt to evaluate its influence on the result. In most of the enquiries we are told that there was a marking-scheme, though the thoroughness of such schemes seems to have differed widely. The general level of the precautions taken to standardize marking in these enquiries is without doubt lower than that of the only Board which I can use for purposes of comparison. * There is one piece of evidence in the book that distinctly suggests that examinees are more variable than examiners. That is the *viva voce* examination and its results, a part of the investigation which has not attracted much attention. * The examiners' tree is a mere bush compared to that in which the candidate lies hidden. If so, it is easy to see the direction in which we must move for improvement, though the road thither is not easy at all. We must apply the same treatment to the major variable, the candidate, as is applied by the statistician to the minor variable, the mark. * the best external evidence about school examinations is that of schoolmasters and schoolmistresses. Their evidence, as it has reached me, shows surprising unanimity; they say that they can forecast what *will* happen to their pupils—which is not the same thing as what *ought* to happen—in examinations with an accuracy which would be impossible if marking were anything like as variable as this book tries to show. If, as I have suggested, the investigators have strained at the gnat of variable marks and swallowed the camel of variable candidates, the schools' evidence indicates the gnat and camel together make no very great mouthful. That does not acquit the examination system. But let it be attacked on the wider field of educational principles, though the weapons there will be less sensational and the victory slow.

Brit J Ed Psychol 6:193-7 Je '36. Philip Hartog and E. C. Rhodes. "An Examination of Examinations—A Rejoinder." (*A rejoinder to the review by J. F. Duff.*)

Brit J Ed Psychol 6:198-9 Je '36. J. F. Duff. "An Examination of Examinations—A Reply." (*A reply to the rejoinder by Philip Hartog and E. C. Rhodes.*)

J Ed (London) 68:10-1 Ja '36. W. C. Burnet. (*A letter to the editor.*) May I be allowed to make some comments upon Sir Philip Hartog's report, and to ask certain questions? 1. Did he know that the procedure which he adopted was a mere travesty of the School Certificate Examination? If not, why not? 2. Did he inform his Committee of this fact, or did they accept responsibility for the Report in ignorance of it? 3. How does he account for the failure of panels of investigators, including heads and assistants in secondary schools and independent experts, assisted by statisticians, to recommend the abolition of examinations, if the discrepancies are of the order which he suggests? Does he suspect fraud, cowardice, or only incompetence? 4. How is it that the results of our examination are so closely in accordance with the estimates submitted by most of the schools? 5. Even the most bitter critic of examinations has never, so far as I know, alleged that they produce such chaotic results. Are the four Secondary Associations also partners in a great conspiracy of silence? * Sir Philip Hartog's investigation throws no light upon the validity of examinations conducted in our fashion, and that, so far as the School Certificate Examination is concerned, it has been a waste of time and money. *

J Ed (London) 68:11-2 Ja '36. P. J. Hartog. (*A reply to W. C. Burnet's letter.*) Mr. W. C. Burnet in his letter asks me a number of questions, some of which yield excellent examples of the old Aristotelian fallacy of "Many Questions" . . . a well-known instance is the question "have you left off kicking your mother?" Passing over these flaws, I will deal with his questions (for the sake of convenience) in the inverse order to that which he adopts. *

J Ed (London) 68:76 F '36. Invigilator. (*A letter to the editor.*) * will not astonish any one with any experience as an examiner or as a coach for examinations. There must be an element of chance, as there is in life itself. *

J Ed (London) 68:76-7 F '36. G. F. Bridge. (*A reply to the letter by P. J. Hartog.*) Decidedly the findings of the English Committee on Examinations demand further investigations. In the light of my several years' experience as one of the Senior Examiners in French in the Oxford School Certificate Examination, I find it quite impossible to understand how the results detailed in the paragraph "School Certificate French" could have been arrived at, if proper methods of marking and checking had been used. *

Lancet 229:1303-4 D 7 '35. * The methods of inquiry adopted appear eminently satisfactory. * To what conclusions does this important piece of work lead us? It is clear that the part played by chance in the verdicts given at different examinations on which careers depend must often at the present moment be a great one. * The present report must give everyone engaged in the conduct of examinations furiously to think, and in the interests both of the examined and the examining it is to be hoped that the further experimental work the committee plead for will be developed.

For additional reviews, see B130 and B378.

[B929]

HARTOG, PHILIP, AND RHODES, E. C. **The Marks of Examiners:** Being a Comparison of Marks Alloted to Examination Scripts by Independent Examiners and Boards of Examiners, together with a Section on a Viva Voce Examination. Memorandum by Cyril Burt. International Institute Examinations Enquiry. London: Macmillan & Co., Ltd., 1936. Pp. xix, 344. 8s. 6d.

Lancet 231:1470 D 19 '36. * It is perhaps legitimate to warn the non-mathematically minded student that in this search for truth there is little, from his point of view, to choose between the approach of the mathematical statistician and that of the psychologist. He will find them equally distressing. * The total is a book of real worth and interest.

Mind 46:256-7 Ap '37. F. C. S. Schiller.
For additional reviews, see B131 and B379.

[B930]

HARTOG, PHILIP, WITH THE ASSISTANCE OF GLADYS ROBERTS. **A Conspectus of Examinations in Great Britain and Northern Ireland.** International Examinations Enquiry. London: Macmillan & Co., Ltd., 1937. Pp. xiv, 182. 3s. 6d.

B Int Bur Ed 12:87 q 2 '38. * compiled to give the general public, as well as those specially interested in education, a bird's eye view of the width and variety of the field covered by the examination system in Great Britain and Northern Ireland *
Clearing House 14:318 Ja '40. Earl R. Gabler. * If the reader desires to discover the nature of the examinations used he should not read this book, for only in several instances (air pilot, motor driver) is there given any indication of the nature of the examinations. However, for its purpose it is a very worthwhile and valuable document.
New R 8:188 Ag '38. T. N. Siqueira. * Modest as its scope is, it stands for a great deal of patient inquiry and tabulation, and it is very useful to those who wish to read for English degrees. It contains in one cheap volume what is scattered in the several University Calendars.
Pub Adm 16:239-40 Ap '38. E. C. Rhodes. * A prodigious amount of labour must have gone to the making of this book, and the authors are

to be congratulated on the achievement of a task well done. Perhaps the most significant fact which emerges from a perusal of the book is the widespread interest which the University has in every-day affairs.
For additional reviews, see B380.

[B931]

HARTOG, PHILIP, AND OTHERS. **The Purposes of Examinations:** A Symposium. Reprinted from *The Yearbook of Education 1938.* London: Evans Brothers, Ltd., [1938]. Pp. 146. 3s. Paper.

Brit J Ed Psychol 9:110-1 F '39. * a symposium of contributions by many learned and distinguished authorities * It gathers together into one volume of modest size a statement of the relevant facts about a number of examinations which are taken by large groups of candidates at the present day. * Each chapter is written by an authority of special competence in his own field. * [the] expressions of opinion . . . give the book much of its interest and value; for, unlike the bare facts, they cannot be found in the ordinary works of reference. Two questions have been well to the fore in the minds of most of the writers. First, whether the examination under consideration is in itself a success or a failure, in relation to its avowed purpose. Second, whether the published results represent a fair verdict on the candidates. On the whole, the answers given to both questions are favourable, but there are some exceptions. * It is, perhaps, a little surprising that a book with this title did not include chapters on the principal secondary school examinations. But those whose main interest is university education will find in it a wealth of information and authoritative comment; and it is no mean achievement to have gathered so much into a volume of such moderate compass.
Electrician 121:788 D 30 '38. S. Parker Smith. This small book is worthy of wide attention. It sets out to tell us whether our school and university examinations fulfil their purpose and whether they are efficiently conducted. There are 22 contributions by acknowledged authorities, and every important course is intended to be scrutinised objectively and impartially. The book is to be thoroughly recommended to all interested in higher education. * In the first essay by Dr. P. B. Ballard on "The Free Place Examination," he sets .forth admirably the mode of selecting promising candidates for secondary and central schools. * Dr. R. Burrows describes "The Examinations for

the Bar" in a very able manner * The Final Honour School "Greats," Oxford, is described by Prof. H. Last. His statement on the aim and organisation of the course is a sound piece of philosophical pleading, but we may wonder how far the founders of the course had such ideals in mind. * From the account of the Final Honour School of Modern History, Oxford, by Prof. F. M. Powicke, the reader is left uncertain how far the purposes are fulfilled. The description of the Historical Tripos Parts I and II, Cambridge, by Prof. E. Barker, rather makes one wish to be a student again with his choice before him. * Two interesting essays on medical degrees * The Commerce Degree Course at Birmingham is described by Prof. J. G. Smith, who states that many students enter solely for the purpose of a *general* education, which, owing to the increasing specialisation in the Honour Schools of the Faculties, is becoming ever more difficult to obtain. One statement is both curious and encouraging: "It has more than once happened that business has preferred our examination failures to our branded Honours men, and quite properly, too." * In the last essay by Prof. L. B. Budden on the Architecture Degree at Liverpool, the reader will appreciate the blunt assertion that examinations should be vocational in character and aim; and he insists that a course of vocational study, if rightly conceived and directed, can afford in itself a liberal education. Would that all who train students for professional careers were as capable of such clear thinking! Most of the 22 essays are of a high order, and many are of absorbing interest.

New R 9:282 Ap '39. T. N. Siqueira. * a volume which every examiner in an Indian university would do well to ponder * It is interesting, in view of the disfavour into which classical studies seem to have now fallen, to find the Oxford Greats vindicated by Prof. Hugh Last. *

Scottish Ed J 22:941 Ag 11 '39.

[B932]

HAUCK, FLORENCE E. **First Approximation Norms and Fatigue Factors for the Grip Test, Work-sample 185.** Human Engineering Laboratory, Technical Report No. 30. Boston, Mass.: the Laboratory, 1937. Pp. vi, 34. $1.00. Paper, mimeographed.

[B932.1]

HAUCK, FLORENCE E. **Integrated Norms Forms BA, G, H for the Creative Imagination Test, Work-sample 161.** Human Engineering Laboratory, Technical Report No. 49. Boston, Mass.: the Laboratory, 1940. Pp. x, 150. $1.00. Paper, mimeographed.

[B933]

HAUCK, FLORENCE E. **The Relation of Assembly Practice Factors to Age and Sex.** Human Engineering Laboratory, Technical Report No. 26. Boston, Mass.: the Laboratory, 1938. Pp. vii, 40. $1.00. Paper, mimeographed.

[B934]

HERBST, R. L. **Report of the Spring Testing Program in Elementary Schools:** Unit Scales of Attainment, Form A, April 18-20, 1939. Dover, Del.: State Department of Public Instruction, 1939. Pp. 8. Gratis. Paper, mimeographed.

[B935]

HERBST, R. L. **Report of the Spring Testing Program in Secondary Schools, May 1939.** Dover, Del.: State Department of Public Instruction, 1939. Pp. 5. Gratis. Paper, mimeographed.

[B936]

HERTZ, MARGUERITE R. **Frequency Tables to be Used in Scoring the Rorschach Ink-Blot Test.** Cleveland, Ohio: Brush Foundation, Western Reserve University, 1936. Pp. vi, 283. $3.50. Paper, mimeographed.

[B937]

HILDRETH, GERTRUDE H. **A Bibliography of Mental Tests and Rating Scales,** Second edition. New York: Psychological Corporation, 1939. Pp. xxiv, 295. $4.00.

Civil Service Assembly News Letter 5:14 My '39. Thelma Hunt. All personnel administrators and personnel offices will want a copy of this bibliography. * There is a good index by subject and by author. *

Personnel Adm 1:15 Je '39. * 4,279 tests are listed, classified under a large number of subject headings, but very little information is given about each, and no evaluation is attempted. *

For reviews of the first edition, see B136 and B384.

[B938]

HOLLIS, FLORENCE. **Social Case Work in Practice: Six Case Studies.** New York: Family Welfare Association of America, 1939. Pp. x, 313. $2.50.

Am Sociol R 5:683-4 Ag '40. David K. Bruner. * There is meat for the sociologist in the discussion of the individual in relation to his social environment. The treatment of the concept of a norm (pp. 290 ff.) is stimulating, stressing as it does the factors of the individual's unique social environment and his conception of his role, and the idea of a relativity in behavior norms. There is more recognition of the importance of culture than in some case work and psychiatric writings. In short, the sociologist can study this volume with profit. Incidentally, these carefully edited records of a recognized agency remain tools for helping people out of trouble, and indicate that we have not realized the dream of a day when such records will lend themselves readily to statistical research.

Commonwealth R 22:129-30 My '40. Elon H. Moore. * One is impressed by the fact that these are ordinary cases such as any worker might encounter frequently in her work. The concluding chapter of the work, dealing with the principle underlying treatment, is most subject to criticism. The stressing of frustrations, anxiety, the unconscious, and various tensions follow a well-known emphasis which provides excuses and rationalizations for all sorts of failures which in a less extremely individualized culture would seldom appear. As with patent-medicine advertising, the number of ailments are increased through suggestion. Some day the social worker should frankly face this dilemma. The book is not a distinctive contribution in general analysis. The concepts of analysis and treatment are familiar to those who are acquainted with recent literature in this field. The distinctive contribution lies in the type of cases presented and the evaluative notes which accompany each case. The book should be of value to beginning students as a presentation of patterns of ideal case work, and to seasoned workers who wish to regain a sense of balance.

Fed Probation 4:41-2 My '40. Chas. H. Z. Meyer. * a book which gives the reader an x-ray view into an interesting profession at work. It reveals what case work is like in actual practice. * The felicitous organization of material makes it quite readable and stimulating. There is nothing high-sounding or deeply obscure in the book. It is logically sound and understandingly critical. The choice of case material is good and the bibliography is excellent. *

J Social Hyg 26:244 Je '40.

Survey 76:212-3 Je '40. Elizabeth McCord de Schweinitz. Detailed case analysis is combined here with general principles and basic philosophy in a way to be of inestimable value both to professional social workers and to interested lay people. The concise, clear-cut sentences which serve as chapter headings are only one indication of the workmanlike way in which Miss Hollis has approached the task of writing this book. The summaries which end each case give an excellent picture of what is involved in this kind of service to individuals. It is a real landmark in social case work writ-

ing. The more detailed comments on the case material restate and illuminate much that has become an accepted part of case work method and point of view over a period of years. The psychological theory underlying these cases is largely psychoanalytic, but there is little which would not be acceptable from any point of view, and there is much which should be reassuring to social workers who hope for unity in social work but whose own psychological theory stems from other sources. The whole discussion shows the extent to which social case work has moved away from psychological interpretation for its own sake and toward the understanding of people as the basis for helpful action. *

[B939]

HOLZINGER, KARL J., AND SWINEFORD, FRANCES. **A Study in Factor Analysis:** The Stability of a Bi-factor Solution. University of Chicago, Department of Education, Supplementary Educational Monographs, No. 48. Chicago, Ill.: the Department, March 1939. Pp. xi, 91. $1.00. Paper.

El Sch J 40:468-9 F '40. Douglas E. Scates.

Loyola Ed Digest 14:11 My '39. Austin G. Schmidt. The chief object of this highly technical study in factor analysis was to determine the stability of factor solutions for two groups of students in Illinois schools. Workers in the field of factor analysis will find some new material on technics.

Sch R. 47:709-11 N '39. A. H. Turney. The enthusiastic acceptance of factor analysis should not blind us to the fact that it is a relatively new and unproved technique. Since it is evident that basically the same methods may lead to astonishingly different conclusions, there seems still much to be done in studying the technique itself and in making practical applications of it. Holzinger and Swineford have added a work which contributes in both these directions. * The percentages of variance accounted for by each of the factors—general, spatial, verbal, speed, and memory—which were found for their two groups might be drastically altered over a truly developmental range. * Since Holzinger and Swineford's work brings factor analysis closer to practical application, the reviewer feels impelled to reiterate that a *rapprochement* between neurological and statistical data is sadly needed. If, in addition, the statisticians could put their house of disorder in greater harmony, the reciprocal contributions of psychological theory and of statistics would be enormously facilitated. *

presented in sober and unassuming language. If anything, it suffers from a paucity of discussion. It adds to Holzinger's well-deserved credit for long and patient work in his chosen field.

[B940]

HORCHOW, REUBEN. **Machines in Civil Service Recruitment:** With Special Reference to Experiences in Ohio. Introduction by Joseph W. Hawthorne. Civil Service Assembly of the United States and Canada, Pamphlet No. 14. Chicago, Ill.: the Assembly, October 1939. Pp. 43. $0.50. Paper.

Civil Service Assembly News Letter 5:10 D '39. Albert T. Helbing. * describes concisely, but at times in very technical jargon, the use of I.B.M. equipment by the State Civil Service Commission of Ohio in conducting examinations on a mass basis for the Unemployment Compensation Commission. * The Electrical Test Scoring Machine is the device that will be used increasingly by the larger examining jurisdictions, but more space is given in this pamphlet to the use of mechanical sorting, tabulating, and accounting equipment for handling test scores. * The most substantial portion of this article is devoted to a description of the machines, the forms and cards, and to the planning and scoring techniques. The benefits to be derived are adequately discussed, but only slight reference is made to the disadvantages. The chief difficulties will be found in the changed techniques of test construction and scoring and the need for having in the examining agencies, properly trained personnel —employees who can be adapted to the use of machine techniques. This booklet should be required reading for any agency with regular and heavy examination schedules.

Personnel Adm 2:16 D '39. Public personnel workers reading this pamphlet will be amazed at the complexity and variety of business machines which can be used in civil service recruitment. * clear and readable * numerous examples and illustrations.

[B941]

HORTON, CLARK W. **Achievement Tests in Relation to Teaching Objectives in General College Botany.** Botanical Society of America, Bulletin No. 120. Sponsored by the Committee on the Teaching of Botany in American Colleges and Universities. Charleston, Ill.: the Committee, c/o Ernest L. Stover, chairman, Eastern Illinois State Teachers College, 1939. Pp. 71. $0.50. Paper.

[B942]

HORTON, SAMUEL P. **An Analysis of the Pyramid, Worksample 68.** Human Engineering Laboratory, Technical Report No. 25. Boston, Mass.: the Laboratory, 1938. Pp. vii, 47. $1.00. Paper, mimeographed.

[B943]

HORTON, SAMUEL P. **The C Form of the Inductive Reasoning Test, Worksample 164.** Human Engineering Laboratory, Technical Report No. 24. Boston, Mass.: the Laboratory, 1939. Pp. ix, 69. $1.00. Paper, mimeographed.

[B943.1]

HORTON, SAMUEL P. **Experiments in the Scoring of a Measure of Creative Imagination, Worksample 161.** Human Engineering Laboratory, Technical Report No. 45. Boston, Mass.: the Laboratory, 1940. Pp. viii, 53. $1.00. Paper, mimeographed.

[B944]

HORTON, SAMUEL P. **Experiments with a New Form of Reasoning Test.** Human Engineering Laboratory, Technical Report No. 38. Boston, Mass.: the Laboratory, 1939. Pp. viii, 66. $1.00. Paper, mimeographed.

[B944.1]

HORTON, SAMUEL P. **First Experiments in Developing a Second Measure of Observation, Worksample 206.** Human Engineering Laboratory, Technical Report No. 51. Boston, Mass.: the Laboratory, 1940. Pp. viii, 52. $1.00. Paper, mimeographed.

[B944.2]

HORTON, SAMUEL P. **First Experiment with the Graded Series of Black Cube Tests.** Human Engineering Laboratory, Technical Report No. 47. Boston, Mass.: the Laboratory, 1940. Pp. viii, 54. $1.00. Paper, mimeographed.

[B944.3]

HORTON, SAMUEL P. **Further Experiments in the Development of a Reasoning Measure.** Human Engineering Laboratory, Technical Report No. 48. Boston, Mass.: the Laboratory, 1940. Pp. vii, 83. $1.00. Paper, mimeographed.

[B944.4]

HORTON, SAMUEL P. **Relationships among Nineteen Group Tests and Their Validity for Freshman Engineering Marks.** Human Engineering Laboratory, Technical Report, No. 46. Boston, Mass.: the Laboratory, 1939. Pp. viii, 141. $1.00. Paper, mimeographed.

[B945]

HORTON, SAMUEL P. **Reliability and Norms for the Tapping Test, Worksample 221.** Human Engineering Laboratory, Technical Report No. 39. Boston, Mass.: the Laboratory, 1939. Pp. vii, 37. $1.00. Paper, mimeographed.

[B946]

HORTON, SAMUEL P. **A Study of Factors in the Art Appreciation Test, Worksample 172.** Human Engineering Laboratory, Technical Report No. 23. Boston, Mass.: the Laboratory, 1939. Pp. vii, 42. $1.00. Paper, mimeographed.

[B947]

HORTON, SAMUEL P. **Two Experiments in the Measure of Memory for Design.** Human Engineering Laboratory, Technical Report No. 37. Boston, Mass.: the Laboratory, 1939. Pp. viii, 61. $1.00. Paper, mimeographed.

[B948]

HORTON, SAMUEL POMEROY. **An Objective Approach to Group-Influencing Fields,** Second edition. Boston, Mass.: Human Engineering Laboratory, 1939. Pp. 103. $1.00. Paper.

[B949]

HUMAN ENGINEERING LABORATORY. **Administration of Vocabulary Tests.** Boston, Mass.: the Laboratory, 1939. Pp. viii, 79. $1.00. Paper, mimeographed.

[B950]

HUMAN ENGINEERING LABORATORY. **An Analysis of the First Trial of the Black Cube, Worksample 167.** Human Engineering Laboratory, Technical Report No. 14. Boston, Mass.: the Laboratory, 1938. Pp. xi, 100. $1.00. Paper, mimeographed.

[B951]

HUMAN ENGINEERING LABORATORY. **An Analysis of the Second Trial of the Black Cube, Worksample 167.** Human Engineering Laboratory, Technical Report No. 18. Boston, Mass.: the Laboratory, 1938. Pp. ix, 100. $1.00. Paper, mimeographed.

[B951.1]

HUMAN ENGINEERING LABORATORY. **Characteristics of Graduate Nurses.** Human Engineering Laboratory, Technical Report No. 1. Boston, Mass.: the Laboratory, 1934. Pp. iv, 27. $1.00. Paper, mimeographed.

[B952]

HUMAN ENGINEERING LABORATORY. **The Common Responses to a New Form of the Free Association Test.** Human Engineering Laboratory, Technical Report No. 3. Boston, Mass.: the Laboratory, 1935. Pp. xiii, 18. $1.00. Paper, mimeographed.

[B952.1]

HUMAN ENGINEERING LABORATORY. **Comparative Scores of Two Groups of Graduate Nurses.** Human Engineering Laboratory, Technical Report No. 4. Boston, Mass.: the Laboratory, 1935. Pp. vi, 37. $1.00. Paper, mimeographed.

[B953]

HUMAN ENGINEERING LABORATORY. **First Analysis of the Traits of Fifty-Six Secondary School Boys.** Human Engineering Laboratory, Technical Report No. 17. Boston, Mass.: the Laboratory, 1937. Pp. x, 37. $1.00. Paper, mimeographed.

[B954]

HUMAN ENGINEERING LABORATORY. **First Purification of the Free Association Test, Worksample 35, Form DA.** Human Engineering Laboratory, Technical Report No. 12. Boston, Mass.: the Laboratory, 1937. Pp. v, 38. $1.00. Paper, mimeographed.

[B955]

HUMAN ENGINEERING LABORATORY. **First Revision of Form E of the English Vocabulary Test, Worksample 95.** Human Engineering Laboratory, Technical Report No. 5. Boston, Mass.: the Laboratory, 1935. Pp. viii, 92. Paper, mimeographed.

[B956]

HUMAN ENGINEERING LABORATORY. **The Formboard Worksample 173 as a Mental Measure.** Human Engineering Laboratory, Technical Report No. 13. Boston, Mass.: the Laboratory, 1937. Pp. v, 60. $1.00. Paper, mimeographed.

[B957]

HUMAN ENGINEERING LABORATORY. **An Individual Approach to Scientific Problems,** Second edition. Boston, Mass.: the Laboratory, 1939. Pp. 105. $1.00. Paper.

[B958]

HUMAN ENGINEERING LABORATORY. **The Measurement of Number Memory.** Human Engineering Laboratory, Technical Report No. 22. Boston, Mass.: the Laboratory, 1938. Pp. viii, 79. $1.00. Paper, mimeographed.

[B959]

HUMAN ENGINEERING LABORATORY. **Revision of Form A of Worksample 169, Judgment in Social Situations.** Human Engineering Laboratory, Technical Report No. 6. Boston, Mass.: the Laboratory, 1936. Pp. xii, 56. $1.00. Paper, mimeographed.

[B960]

HUMAN ENGINEERING LABORATORY. **Statistical and Graphic Analysis of Three Forms of Worksample 169, Judgment in Social Situations.** Human Engineering Laboratory, Technical Report No. 15. Boston, Mass.: the Laboratory, 1938. Pp. viii, 140. $1.00. Paper, mimeographed.

[B961]

HUMAN ENGINEERING LABORATORY. **Steps Toward the Isolation of Tonal Memory as a Mental Element.** Human Engineering Laboratory, Technical Report No. 21. Boston, Mass.: the Laboratory, 1938. Pp. vii, 49. $1.00. Paper, mimeographed.

[B962]

HUMAN ENGINEERING LABORATORY. **A Study of Methods of Computing Practice Factors.** Human Engineering Laboratory, Technical Report No. 19. Boston, Mass.: the Laboratory, 1938. Pp. viii, 50. $1.00. Paper, mimeographed.

[B963]

HUMAN ENGINEERING LABORATORY. **A Study of the Physics Technical Vocabulary Test, Worksample 181.** Human Engineering Laboratory, Technical Report No. 7. Boston, Mass.: the Laboratory, 1936. Pp. xxiv, 87. $1.00. Paper, mimeographed.

[B964]

HUNT, THELMA. **Measurement in Psychology.** New York: Prentice-Hall, Inc., 1936. Pp. xx, 471. $3.00.

Civil Service Assembly News Letter 2:6 D '36. * a clear and concise survey of the whole field of testing. It should prove helpful to personnel technicians who are interested in the various phases of psychological measurements. *

Training Sch B 37:18-9 Mr '40. H. Robert Otness. * Although the reader becomes aware of the sketchy nature of this work, he is at the same time impressed by the plan of this volume. It presents briefly a survey of the whole field of psychological testing, treating each field separately. The author suggests that this book be used as a college text in courses in tests and measurements. It seems well suited to this purpose provided it be supplemented with other more detailed materials. Such a text would undoubtedly bring to the student an awareness of the scope and importance of the whole field of psychological measurement since each field of application is presented. * The reviewer feels while reading the chapters dealing with measurement in the field of mental deficiency, of the mentally ill, of the superior, and others, that perhaps undue emphasis has been accorded the psychometric evaluation of these anomalies as a means to diagnosis. Since the social incompetence, or inadequacy, is a criterion foremost in detecting the mentally deficient and mentally ill, it seems that these chapters should be more closely related to Chapter XX—The Measurement of Social Attributes—or at least referred to in the discussion. * Although the book covers the broad field of measurement very well, one misses bibliographic references for the various chapters, presenting sources of current and historical interest that undoubtedly would be helpful in using it as a college textbook. A volume of this design has long been needed in unifying and at the same time broadening objectivity in the field of applied psychology and may well be found a profitable text in courses in tests and measurements and applied psychology at the college level with adequate supplementary reading.

For additional reviews, see B140 and B393.

[B965]

INDIANA UNIVERSITY, SCHOOL OF EDUCATION, BUREAU OF COOPERATIVE RESEARCH. **Twenty-Sixth Annual Conference on Educational Measurements:** Held at Indiana University, April 11, 1939. Bulletin of the School of Education, Indiana University, Vol. 15, No. 4. Bloomington, Ind.: Indiana University Bookstore, September 1939. Pp. 50. $0.50. Paper.

Ed Abstracts 5:61-2 F '40. Dewey B. Stuit.

[B965.1]

INDIANA UNIVERSITY, SCHOOL OF EDUCATION, BUREAU OF COOPERATIVE RESEARCH. **Twenty-Seventh Annual Conference on Educational Measurements:** Held at Indiana University, April 8, 1940. Bulletin of the School of Education, Indiana University, Vol. 16, No. 4. Bloomington, Ind.: Indiana University Bookstore, July 1940. Pp. 34. $0.50. Paper.

[B966]

INSTITUTE FOR JUVENILE RESEARCH, THE STAFF (PAUL L. SCHROEDER, DIRECTOR). **Child Guidance Procedures:** Methods and Techniques Employed at the Institute for Juvenile Research. New York: D. Appleton-Century Co., Inc., 1937. Pp. vii, 362. $2.50. (London: D. Appleton-Century Co., Inc., 1938. 10s. 6d.)

Am J Dis Children 56:714 S '38. * also of value to physicians *

Am J Psychiatry 95:1001-2 Ja '39. Esther L. Richards. * a clear presentation of the work of a good child guidance clinic * Part II presents the ingredients of "The Diagnostic Study" . . . made by five different specialists * the scope of each specialist is well covered in the respective outlines. In the chapter on "Medical Study" one misses however, reference to the biological set-up and habitus of the neuropathic constitution, for example, with its traits of undernutrition, tics, nervous insta-

bilities, etc. * Part III is devoted to "Therapy: Illustrative Cases." * The case histories . . . of children with superior or above average intelligence . . . are forceful and instructive. The case histories . . . of feebleminded children . . . also are excellent and to the point. The clinical worker in child behavior, however, finds himself wondering what treatment is recommended for the great mass of children between the precocious and feebleminded * The lay reader of these illustrative cases is very apt to get the impression that if he only could dig deeply enough and had the right techniques he could adjust every child behavior problem satisfactorily. Part IV, dealing with "The Relationship between the Clinic and the Community," is excellent.

Am J Psychol 51:790 O '38. Ethel B. Waring. * Apparently the different contributors had different readers in mind. * The book is interesting reading for general information and explains in understandable terms the functions and values of clinical service. It is excellent to put into the hands of community leaders who may be in a position to make such service readily available in their communities.

Am J Pub Health 28:1242 O '38. Henry C. Schumacher. * well written and well edited * There are chapters devoted to the Social History, the Medical Study, the Psychological Examination, The Psychiatric Interview—the so-called fourfold approach to the problem—and also a chapter entitled The Recreation Study. In the majority of clinics the latter is not assigned to special workers, and we see no particular reason for separating it as a special procedure. A good deal of the material investigated would quite naturally fall to the lot of social worker and, in particular, psychiatrist. In fact, one could well raise the question—and the authors hint at it—Whether this division into 4 or more parts at the hands of as many individuals of different and diverse training is either so valuable or so necessary. There has been a growing tendency in many clinics to ignore the so-called fourfold approach and to center the study and treatment in one or another of the staff, depending on the nature of the problem presented. * The illustrative cases, as is usual, do not clearly illustrate, though they do show what can be done, often under adverse conditions. * The book quite adequately presents what the title indicates—child guidance procedures. It undoubtedly will serve to give the reader not trained in a child guidance clinic an idea of the procedures, methods, and ideology of the average clinic. We recommend it to health officers, administrators and, in particular, those dealing with child Welfare.

Hygeia 16:1033 N '38. E. R. Eisler. * The book . . . is successful in presenting concisely an account of the functioning of the institute. It is especially well designed to meet the needs of parents, social workers, physicians or other persons who may wish to know what facilities are available for children who need these particular forms of service. A good bibliography is appended.

J Juvenile Res 22:219-20 Jl-O '38. Ella L. Bates. * well written and easy to read. It contains much valuable information and should serve as a good supplementary text. It presupposes, in its use of professional vocabulary, that the reader has had some acquaintance with technical terms. A glossary, giving definitions of terms and pronounciation, would have improved the book. *

J Nerv and Mental Dis 90:820-1 D '39. * The book we find to be very well written, condensed but not too much, and above all provocative and stimulating. It deals as well with the apparently trivial but really deep seated early problems, handles them with ease and good sense and gives an extensive panorama of the infinite variety of childhood reactions, and also enters into every nook and cranny of children's problems. We accord it the highest praise for its temperate and carefully considered presentation of the most significant aspect of the development of human beings. Could we all be as wise and understanding, a different world would not be so remote as it sometimes appears.

Pub Health R 9:15 N '39. L. E. Himler. * The opening chapter gives an excellent but regrettably brief introductory survey of the modern attitude toward the problems of childhood and guidance during these crucial years. * The broadly interpretative approach of this text should render it of value not only to the students for whom it was originally prepared, but also to physicians, educators, court and recreational workers whose field of interest necessarily carries over into the domain of child guidance.

For additional reviews, see B398.

[B967]

JACKSON, JOSEPH FRANCIS, AND STALNAKER, JOHN MARSHALL. **Report on the French Examination of June 1938:** A Description of the Procedures Used in Preparing and Reading the Examination in French and an Analysis of the Results of the Reading. New York: College Entrance Examination Board, April 1939. Pp. iii, 65. $0.25. Paper, lithotyped.

Loyola Ed Digest 14:10 Jl '39. Austin G. Schmidt. Describes the principles followed and the procedures used in constructing the College Entrance Examination Board examination in French of June 1938 and synopsizes the scores of items.

[B968]

JACOBSON, PAUL B. **The Place of Testing in the Supervisory Program:** Ways to Better High Schools. Prepared for the Committee on Supervision of the Illinois High School Principals' Association. University of Illinois Bulletin, Vol. 35, No. 89. Urbana, Ill.: High School Visitor, the University, July 1938. Pp. 34. Paper. Out of print.

[B969]

JACOBY, H. J. **Analysis of Handwriting:** An Introduction into Scientific Graphology. London: George Allen & Unwin, Ltd., 1939. Pp. 285. 12s. 6d.

Char and Pers 8:346-7 Je '40. Thea Steln Lewinson. * the first book in the English language on scientific graphology, in the past ten years, based on the psychology of expressive movement * In Part I . . . the author deals with three important points: he demonstrates the uniqueness of individual handwriting, proves its consistency, and explains the multifariousness of the graphological criteria. He treats the objections and limitations carefully and skillfully, in reference to the graphological method, and cites the statistically established reliability of .90 (for scientifically trained graphologists). In Part II, the author gives an insight into the practice of the graphologist, explaining the psychological meaning of the single characteristics of handwriting and their correlations. * In Part III, the author demonstrates the construction of a graphological analysis and the practical application of graphology to various fields * This part is very well illustrated. The author's dealing with the graphic expression of children is particularly skillful. Although not exhausting the methodological problems, the book represents a valuable contribution towards the progress of scientific graphology in English-speaking countries. The author is accurate in defining the purpose of graphology and that of his book, in the following manner: ". . . what one should expect is a deeper insight into the inner structure and dynamic nature of the human soul derived from the study and analysis of a person's handwriting. . . ." "The aim . . . will be fulfilled, if the author . . . has succeeded in creating confidence in a comparatively young science, which, if applied in a reasonable and critical way, is sure to produce valuable results."

Eug R 31:188-9 O '39. M. J. Mannheim. Graphology, the science of inferring character from handwriting, has not yet found the recognition it deserves. * The chief publications . . . have not been translated into English. It is the object of Mr. Jacoby's book to present the English public with an introduction into scientific graphology and to inform the reader about its development, foundations, limitations and applications. The approach is thorough and entirely based on a graphological analysis of expressive movements. It is a great merit of the book that it points out that graphology does not correlate each sign with a definite trait of character. * In spite of this subjective factor Mr. Jacoby is right in maintaining that graphology achieves a remarkably high degree of reliability reached by no other method. * The author has considerable psychological insight and succeeds well in creating confidence in a comparatively young science. The illustrations are well chosen and the reproduction is excellent. It is to be regretted that the brief account which appears on the wrapper of the book may lead the reader to believe that he might be able to analyse his own handwriting material after a careful perusal of the book. In fairness to Mr. Jacoby it must be said that he frequently warns against futile and amateurish attempts and that he makes it clear how many conditions (training, power of observation, psychological penetration, knowledge of psychiatry, etc.) have to be fulfilled, if graphological analysis is to be successful.

Nature 145:645 Ap 27 '40. R. A. S. Paget. * Many of the author's conclusions will be readily accepted, for example, that in handwriting, good spacing and regularity indicate orderliness and self-discipline: that exaggeratedly large writing denotes love of display, and that small and precise handwriting implies an unemotional or pedantic nature. Other dicta, such as that convex curves (arcades) indicate "shutting to the outside world," or that movements to the right manifest tendency towards the outside world (and *vice versa*) need further proof.

The book would be easier to read if the 161 illustrations—which are well reproduced—were more systematically related to the descriptive text. Fewer illustrations, more carefully chosen, would have been better. The index, too, could have been improved by additional headings. The author claims for 'graphology' a high percentage (87-95 per cent) of correct judgments as to character, psychological condition, ability, etc. To check this claim, the Institute of Industrial Psychology, for example, might provide Mr. Jacoby with specimens of the handwriting of a number of cases examined by them, so that the correlation between the findings of graphology and of psychological analysis might be measured. This book is certainly interesting, though somewhat discursively written.

New Era 20:237-8 S-O '39. E. I. Shanks. In this country, where much attention is given to individual education, it is surprising to find the subject of Graphology so largely neglected. The present volume sets out to supply this deficiency. The author's task has been arduous, since . . . he has had to reintroduce Graphology, and this has necessitated first removing all doubts of the genuineness of this science from the minds of sceptics, antagonized by their contacts with 'quack' graphologists. Mr. Jacoby has conducted his defence with broadmindedness and a strict regard for the limitations of his subject. * Part III deals with the application of Graphology, shows how a handwriting is analysed, deals briefly with children's scribblings and vocational guidance through Graphology—an extremely interesting subject and one well worth the study of educationists—shows how Graphology can usefully be applied to business, to matrimony, to criminology, to historical research and its essential usefulness in psychotherapy. The illustrations which conclude the book are both very plentiful and excellently reproduced. The chief usefulness of this book is that it constitutes an excellent introduction to Graphology as practised to-day, touching as it does on so many points and with its very good bibliography. Its chief defect lies in this very comprehensiveness; it is impossible, in so relatively few pages, to enlarge upon the most interesting points. * The question of the subconscious conception of zones is a most complicated and intriguing study and the book loses in ultimate conviction and interest through the lack of space to develop such points as this. The writer's style also suffers through this cramping necessity to condense and sometimes becomes unduly pedagogical. For those who wish for a wider understanding of their fellow-beings this book is, however, recommended, if only because it paves the way to such more constructive works as that of Minna Becker on Children's Handwriting or those of Anna Mendelsohn on the application of Graphology to Psychology.

Scottish Ed J 23:541 Ag 2 '40. * a clear and very complete account of the value of an analysis of handwriting for the diagnosing of character * Although the author gives many suggestive interpretations we have no method of checking them. The very full analysis of the characteristics of handwriting would, nevertheless, be very useful to any educationist preparing an analytic scale for measuring handwriting after the manner of Freeman.

[B970]
JAFFA, ADELE S. **The California Preschool Mental Scale:** Form A. Foreword by Herbert R. Stolz. University of California, Syllabus Series, No. 251; Institute of Child Welfare. Berkeley, Calif.: University of California Press, November 1934. Pp. v, 66. $0.75. Paper.

For reviews by B. M. Castner and Florence L. Goodenough, see 1383.

[B971]
JASTAK, JOSEPH. **Variability of Psychometric Performance in Mental Diagnosis.** Farnhurst, Del.: the Author, Delaware State Hospital, 1934. Pp. iv, 100. Out of print.

[B972]
JOHNSON, ALVIN D. **Sociometric Testing with Summer Camps.** New Haven, Conn.: the Author, 34 Shelton Ave., 1939. $0.50. Pp. 44. Paper, mimeographed.

[B973]
JOHNSTON, NORMAN J. **How to Pass Examinations.** London: Efficiency Magazine, [1934]. Pp. 32. 1s. Paper.

[B974]
JOINT COMMITTEE ON TESTS. **National Clerical Ability Tests:** Sponsored by National Office Management Association and National Council of Business Education As a Service to Trainers and Employers of Office Workers. Bulletin No. 1. Cambridge, Mass.: Joint Committee on Tests, Lawrence Hall, Kirkland St., November 1939. Pp. iv, 40. Gratis. Paper, mimeographed.

[B975]
JONES, LLOYD MEREDITH. **A Factorial Analysis of Ability in Fundamental Motor Skills.** Columbia University, Teachers College, Contributions to Education No. 665. Jesse Feiring Williams, faculty sponsor. New York: Bureau of Publications, the College, 1935. Pp. ix, 100. $1.60.

J Ed Res 31:218-9 N '37. A. R. Lauer. * a typical investigational monograph * The most

valuable part of the book for the busy reader will be the review of the literature and the general summary.

[B976]
JONES, MARY COVER, AND BURKS, B. S. **Personality Development in Childhood:** A Survey of Problems, Methods and Experimental Findings. Society for Research in Child Development, Monograph, Vol. 1, No. 4. Washington, D. C.: the Society, National Research Council, 1936. Pp. vi, 205. $1.00. Paper.

[B977]
KANDEL, I. L. **Examinations and their Substitutes in the United States.** Carnegie Foundation for the Advancement of Teaching, Bulletin No. 28. Preface by Walter A. Jessup. New York: the Foundation, 1936. Pp. xii, 183. Gratis. Paper.

B Int Bur Ed 11:85 q 2 '37. * it is of the greatest interest and importance the world over. The first chapter, on the problem of examinations and its social setting, with its summary of the differences between European and American education, and its study of the common problems of the U.S.A. and the countries of Europe, is illuminating. *

For additional reviews, see B152 and B405.

[B978]
KELLEY, GLENN ORVILLE. **The English Classification Tests Administered by the University of Nebraska:** An Analysis. Lincoln, Neb.: University of Nebraska Library, 1937. Pp. iii, 93. $0.75. Paper, mimeographed.

[B979]
KELLY, GEORGE A. **A Method of Diagnosing Personality in the Psychological Clinic.** *Psychological Record*, Vol. 2, No. 3. Bloomington, Ind.: Principia Press, Inc., March 1938. Pp. 95-111. $0.50. Paper.

[B980]
KENT, GRACE H. **Self-Derived Norms for Institutions.** Psychological Record, Vol. 3, No. 16. Bloomington, Ind.: Principia Press, Inc., October 1939. Pp. 195-208. $0.30. Paper.

[B981]
KENT, GRACE H. **Suggestions for the Next Revision of the Binet-Simon Scale.** *Psychological Record*, Vol. 1, No. 25. Bloomington, Ind.: Principia Press, Inc., November 1937. Pp. 409-33. $0.60. Paper.

For excerpts from this reference, see 1420.

[B982]
KENT, GRACE H. **Use and Abuse of Mental Tests in Clinical Diagnosis.** *Psychological Record*, Vol. 2, No. 17. Bloomington, Ind.: Principia Press, Inc., December 1938. Pp. 391-400. $0.25. Paper.

[B983]
KIRKPATRICK, FORREST H. **The Measurement of Personality.** *Psychological Record*, Vol. 3, No. 17. Bloomington, Ind.: Principia Press, Inc., October 1939. Pp. 211-24. $0.30. Paper.

[B983.1]
KNOWLES, ASA S. **Merit Rating in Industry.** Northeastern University, College of Business Administration, Bureau of Business Research, Bulletin No. 1. Boston, Mass.: the Bureau, February 1940. Pp. v, 36, v. Gratis. Paper.

[B983.2]
KROEGER, L. J., AND BYERS, K. Reports of Performance: A System of Service Ratings for the California State Civil Service. Sacramento, Calif.: State Personnel Board, 1939. $0.25. Paper.

Personnel Adm 2:15-6 Mr '40. Ward Steward. This substantial booklet represents one of the most thoroughgoing recent attempts to objectivize the most subjective phase of personnel administration—-the ratings of the services of employees by their supervisors. It is the culmination of several years of fundamental research and experimentation on the part of the California State Personnel Board and as such warrants careful scrutiny. Designed primarily as a manual of instructions for rating officers and only incidentally as an explanation of the system which it propounds, the booklet consists predominantly of forms and also contains a brief discussion which is well and carefully written and which describes the basic principles clearly and cogently. * The Board certainly deserves credit for a significant venture into troubled and troublesome waters. * In the past uncooperative supervisors have subverted every known rating instrument to their own purposes. If the new one from California makes this impossible, then indeed will the names of its designers be writ large on the sands of time.

[B984]
KUHLMANN, F. Tests of Mental Development: A Complete Scale for Individual Examination. Minneapolis, Minn.: Educational Test Bureau, Inc., 1939. Pp. xi, 314. $2.00.

For reviews by Grace H. Kent, Francis N. Maxfield, Myrtle Luneau Pignatelli, F. L. Wells and others, see 1426.

[B985]
LAIRD, DONALD A. The Psychology of Selecting Employees, Third edition. New York: McGraw-Hill Book Co., Inc., 1937. Pp. xiv, 316. $4.00. (London: McGraw-Hill Publishing Co., Ltd. 24s.)

[B986]
LAUER, ALVHH R. Methods of Measuring the Ability to Drive an Automobile: With Suggestions for Use as a Background for Research, Safety Training, and for Educational Purposes. Iowa State College of Agriculture and Mechanic Arts Official Publication, Vol. 35, No. 1; Engineering Extension Service, Bulletin [No.] 115. Ames, Iowa: the College, June 1936. Pp. 39. $0.10. Paper.

[B987]
LEARNED, WILLIAM S., AND HAWKES, ANNA L. ROSE. An Experiment in Responsible Learning: A Report to the Carnegie Foundation on Projects in Evaluation of Secondary School Progress, 1929-1938. Study of the Relations of Secondary and Higher Education in Pennsylvania, Carnegie Foundation for the Advancement of Teaching, Bulletin No. 31. New York: the Foundation, 1940. Pp. v, 61. Gratis. Paper.

[B988]
LEARNED, WILLIAM S., AND WOOD, BEN D. The Student and His Knowledge: A Report to the Carnegie Foundation on the Results of the High School and College Examinations of 1928, 1930, and 1932. Study of the Relations of Secondary and Higher Education in Pennsylvania. Foreword by Walter A. Jessup. Carnegie Foundation for the Advancement of Teaching, Bulletin No. 29. New York: the Foundation, 1938. Pp. xx, 406. Gratis. Paper.

Civil Service Assembly News Letter 4:13 Jl '38. M. W. Richardson. * deserves careful study in detail * It seems quite fair, from the evidence presented in the various tables and charts, to state that a reasonably good three hour objective examination given to an individual will yield more information about his knowledge and capacities than will a nicely engraved diploma, a transcript of "grades," and a letter of recommendation from a dean. The term "graduation from an accredited college" has little meaning. The civil service examiner may profitably ignore the academic record and proceed to test the applicant's knowledge. No other equivalent for college graduation has any meaning.

J Higher Ed 10:111-3 F '39. Lewis M. Terman. This is one of the most important contributions thus far made to the problems of higher education in the United States; in the reviewer's opinion, it is the most important since Abraham Flexner's memorable report more than a quarter-century ago on medical education. Flexner's report dealt chiefly with educational processes and teaching equipment; this deals with the raw material with which the college works and the measurable changes effected by the treatment to which it is subjected. It is a monumental investigation, by objective methods, of individual differences in achievement at the college level. To say that the data it summarizes are challenging is an understatement; in the better sense of the word, they are sensational. Unless the techniques used by the authors can be proved to be grossly fallacious and misleading, the material presented warrants a thorough overhauling of our collegiate educational procedures. * The bulk of the report . . . is devoted to the results of an eight-hour examination of the objective type given to fifty-seven hundred college students near the end of the sophomore year in forty-nine Pennsylvania colleges and repeated two years later near the end of the senior year. * The measures used are avowedly measures of knowledge. The authors admit that there are other values to be derived from a college education, although they are justifiably skeptical of some of the intangibles for which so much has been claimed. At any rate, knowledge is important. Whether a student can be "taught to think" is questionable, but there can be no question about his inability to think in a vacuum. * the achievement tests used in this study are probably not inferior to the best discursive examinations as measures of ability to think * The tests are admittedly not as good as can now be devised, but the scores they yield are in most cases highly reliable in the technical sense of this term. * the data show how enormously the forty-nine institutions differ among themselves * Even more significant than the comparison of institutional and departmental means are the enormous individual differences among students of a given class in the same college. * The authors show that in any given subject the correlation between knowledge possessed and units of credit in the subject is unbelievably low. * In the social sciences, especially, it is possible to accumulate credits without knowledge or knowledge without credits. In the face of such facts the prevailing course-credit system is not only indefensible, it is ridiculous. There is no escape from the author's conclusion that educational efforts in the college should be based upon broad and exact information regarding the abilities and achievement of the individual student. Without this, education proceeds in the dark. A week of testing at college entrance by the best available methods would make it possible to map the "intellectual geography" of every student. Repeated tests at the end of the sophomore and senior years would give an incomparably better measure of what has been achieved than the registrar's records of courses taken. Only thus can the total accomplishment of the student be taken into account or a basis be provided for intelligent counseling. * The authors have set the stage for a thoroughgoing reform of collegiate education. * The report is reasonably untechnical, but because of the tremendous mass of factual information presented it makes fairly slow reading. The authors have provided an excellent 69-page summary of the most important findings, and it is to be hoped that

this will be considerably expanded and published in book form.
Q R Biol 13:458-9 D '38.
*Sci Ed 22:330 N '38. E. R. D(owling). *There are valuable suggestions for the school administrator * The report should shatter any smug complacency that exists regarding the great superiority of our schools in these United States. Fortunately it will do more; it will point the way to needed reforms.
For additional reviews, see B412.

[B989]
LEITER, RUSSELL GRAYDON. **The Leiter International Performance Scale:** Vol. 1, Directions for the Application and Scoring of the Individual Tests. Santa Barbara, Calif.: Santa Barbara State College Press, 1940. Pp. ix, 95. $2.00.

*Ed Abstracts 5:157-8 My '40. Henry D. Rinsland. *A great deal of ingenuity and originality has been used in constructing this Scale although the principle is simple. Whether or not this simple technique is a valid sampling of the many kinds of intellectual performance which show the native intelligence of children from 2 to 12, cannot be judged from Volume I. No data of the relations between this test and other accepted criteria of intelligence are presented. Because of the obvious need of such a scale, the attractiveness of the problems to be solved by the subjects, and the backing of the National Research Council and the Rockefeller Fund in financing the production of the scale, one hopes that the validity is as high as the Revised Stanford-Binet Scales by Terman and Merrill.

[B989.1]
LIFE INSURANCE SALES RESEARCH BUREAU. **Measuring Aptitude for Life Insurance Selling.** Hartford, Conn.: the Bureau, 1938. Pp. 22. Privately distributed. Paper.

[B989.2]
LIFE INSURANCE SALES RESEARCH BUREAU. **The Prospective Agents Rating Plan in Use:** Report of Session on Selection of Agents, at Research Bureau Conference, Hartford, Connecticut, March 22, 1938. New Haven, Conn.: the Bureau, 1938. Pp. 44. Privately distributed. Paper.

[B990]
LIFE INSURANCE SALES RESEARCH BUREAU. **Rating Prospective Agents.** Hartford, Conn.: the Bureau, 1937. Pp. 16. Privately distributed. Paper.

[B991]
LIFE INSURANCE SALES RESEARCH BUREAU. **Selection of Agents:** A Method of Relating Personal History Information to Probable Success in Life Insurance Selling. Hartford, Conn.: the Bureau, 1937. Pp. 24. Privately distributed. Paper.

[B992]
LINDER, R. G. **The Use of Standard Tests as a Basis for a Remedial and Guidance Program.**

Western Illinois State Teachers College Quarterly, Vol. 18, No. 2. Macomb, Ill.: the College, September 1938. Pp. 36. Gratis. Paper.

[B993]

LINDQUIST, E. F. **The 1940 Iowa Every-Pupil Basic Skills Testing Program:** To be conducted January 17 to 31, 1940. Iowa City, Iowa: c/o E. F. Lindquist, State University of Iowa, 1939. Pp. 24. Gratis. Paper.

[B994]

LINDQUIST, E. F. **Summary Report of Results for The 1939 Iowa Every-Pupil High School Testing Program.** Iowa City, Iowa: c/o E. F. Lindquist, State University of Iowa, 1939. Pp. i, 18. $0.10. Paper, lithotyped.

[B995]

[LINDQUIST, E. F., AND OTHERS.] **Manual for Administration and Interpretation of 1939 Iowa Every-Pupil Tests of Basic Skills.** Iowa City, Iowa: Bureau of Educational Research and Service, State University of Iowa, 1939. Pp. 88. $0.25. Paper.

[B996]

LOBER, GERTRUDE. **Second Purification of the Free Association Test, Worksample 35, Form D.** Human Engineering Laboratory, Technical Report No. 34. Boston, Mass.: the Laboratory, 1939. Pp. vii, 42. $1.00. Paper, mimeographed.

[B997]

LOMBARDI, MARYELLAN MAHER. **The Inter-Trait Rating Technique.** Columbia University, Teachers College, Contributions to Education No. 760. William A. McCall, faculty sponsor. New York: Bureau of Publications, the College, 1938. Pp. vii, 99. $1.60.

Loyola Ed Digest 14:8 *My '39. Austin G. Schmidt.*

Pub Personnel R 1:61-2 *Jl '40. Margaret Marshall.* * The study represents primarily an exploration in the field of personality measurement and may suggest an approach for subsequent investigations. * clearly written and well organized * Many will disagree with the basic assumptions underlying the study, and the newness of the approach is questionable in view of the extensive use which is being made of "pattern" techniques in personality measurement. To the public personnel technician who is concerned with the problem of personality measurement, such experimental work as this should be of interest—not because it solves his problem, but because it may give some valuable clues to him in his quest for more valid techniques of measurement. * the chief value . . . lies in the personality pattern or profile which it yields. This would be useful for diagnostic purposes whenever individuals were being dealt with according to the case method. The fact that individuals cannot be safely compared on the basis of scores, because scores are not meaningful in relation to a universal scale, makes such an approach of doubtful value to the personnel examiner who must evaluate in-

dividuals relatively and rank them in order of their fitness to meet the requirements of a particular job.

[B998]

LOUTTIT, C. M. **Clinical Psychology:** A Handbook of Children's Behavior Problems. Foreword by L. T. Meiks. New York and London: Harper & Brothers, 1936. Pp. xx, 695. $3.50; 12s. 6d.

Brit Med J 399:16 *Jl 3 '37.*

Char and Pers 7:259-60 *Mr '39. Harry W. Crane.* In order to describe the text more definitely in terms of the author's own delimitations, the title should have been *A Clinical Psychology of Childhood and Adolescence.* His position that one person cannot "be equally skilled in dealing with both children and adults" is open to serious questioning. This is particularly true if one accepts the idea that the problems of adult adjustment are the result of unresolved childhood difficulties. Since the conception of what constitutes the field of clinical psychology definitely sets the limits of a text of this type, it is particularly important that an author's position on that point should be both clearly stated and sound. In the main, these criteria are met. * one must question the validity of the distinction made between mental hygiene and clinical psychology. The position is taken that the former is interested in prevention while the latter deals with "conditions already existing in the child." * There are some important points that seem to be treated too dogmatically. * A review is not the place for presenting arguments upon even important controversial questions. A comprehensive textbook, however, is not justified in presenting in relation to such questions only the position with which the author happens to be in agreement. While at times, particularly in the section on psychometrics, the treatment tends to be of survey or schematic type, one must bear in mind the breadth of the field covered. Sources for more detailed information are also supplied. There is an abundance of carefully selected illustrative case material. The organization is excellent. One is impressed with the author's recognition of the clinician's need to use all available sources of data and of the importance of the contributions of all environmental factors to the individual's behavior. As a whole, this book is a real contribution to the clinical psychology of childhood and adolescence. It is probably the best text now available in that field.

J Ed Res 31:217 *N '37. Francis N. Max-*

field. * a most satisfactory presentation of the theories, aims, and methods of clinical psychology. The author's treatment of his subject is inclusive, and his bibliography of forty-four pages covers a wide range. His illustrative case records, many of them of recent date from the files of the Indiana University Psychological Clinic, are well chosen. * Louttit's presentation of the facts and methods in regard to diagnosis and treatment of these problems will have important significance for [parents, employers, teachers, physicians, psychiatrists, social workers, visiting teachers, probation officers, et al.] . . . as well as for the student psychoclinician, for whom it is a fundamental textbook. *

J Pediatrics 10:844-6 Je '37. *S. I. S. and M. L.* * A vast amount of material is presented in systematic form. * the most useful book on clinical psychology that the present reviewer knows. It seems to contain all that is essential for the clinical psychologists as well as the psychiatrist or pediatrician with whom he works. The reviewer is impressed with the care and conscientiousness of the author in his task, the lack of prejudice, or any indication of a limited or narrow point of view. * clearly written, well arranged *

Lancet 232:88 Ja 9 '37. * As a text-book for students of clinical psychology this work is admirably adapted for its purpose. The treatment in each section is full, the arrangement systematic, the case-histories illustrative and helpful. It is written in an easy style and may be commended not only to workers in the child guidance movement but to the paediatrician, and especially to the practitioner who wishes to supplement his knowledge of the physical development of the child by some understanding of the concurrent psychological growth.

Med Times 65:272-3 My '37. *Stanley S. Lamm.* * The subject matter is presented with careful attention to detail. With each problem the author has offered, in an unbiased manner, various opposing theories with respect to cause and solution. This is particularly demonstrated in the chapter on speech defects. The chapters on the methods used for testing children and on educational abilities and disabilities are also well presented. Particularly of value is an extensive bibliography. One might question whether the subject material in its entirety should come under the realm of clinical psychology. To the reviewer it would seem that a

good portion of this work might better be left in the hands of the medical profession for diagnosis and treatment.
For additional reviews, see B418.

[B998.1]
LUQUEER, MARY O. **The Effect of Rearranging the Stimulus Words on Two Forms of the Free Association Test, Worksample 35, Forms A and D.** Human Engineering Laboratory, Technical Report No. 54. Boston, Mass.: the Laboratory, 1940. Pp. x, 138. $1.00. Paper, mimeographed.

[B999]
LUQUEER, MARY O. **Preliminary Norms for the Checking Series Test, Worksample 223.** Human Engineering Laboratory, Technical Report No. 31. Boston, Mass.: the Laboratory, 1939. Pp. viii, 80. $1.00. Paper, mimeographed.

[B999.1]
LUQUEER, MARY O. **Preliminary Study of the Fatigue and Practice Effects on the Tapping Test, Worksample 221, Form A.** Human Engineering Laboratory, Technical Report No. 40. Boston, Mass.: the Laboratory, 1939. Pp. viii, 67. $1.00. Paper, mimeographed.

[B999.2]
LUQUEER, MARY O. **Statistical Analysis of Five Discrimination Tests.** Human Engineering Laboratory, Technical Report No. 61. Boston, Mass.: the Laboratory, 1940. Pp. viii, 50. $1.00. Paper, mimeographed.

[B1000]
McCALL, WILLIAM A. **Measurement.** A revision of *How to Measure in Education.* New York: Macmillan Co., 1939. Pp. xv, 535. $4.00. (London: Macmillan & Co., Ltd. 18s.)

Brit J Ed Psychol 9:283-4 N '39. *Ll. W(ynn) J(ones).* * [McCall's] style of writing is occasionally racy and forceful. This is decidedly helpful, as, from the nature of his task, many of the pages are packed with dry-as-dust, yet necessary, rules of the technique of testing. * In spite of the prolific appearance of books on testing in recent years, the book can be strongly recommended even to those who possess the original edition, for, as already indicated, extensive additions have been made. * although the title "Measurement" has brevity to commend it, yet the book is very largely concerned with educational measurement in the United States * although the science of measurement is supposed to be international, yet there is no mention in the index of any British writer on measurement, if we except a solitary reference to Pearson's product moment formula, and another to the Spearman-Brown prophecy formula! * McCall's field is that of educational measurement. Every chapter has been carefully prepared and the author throughout is an enthusiastic champion of the possibilities of measurement. *

Very instructive and even amusing is the example on p. 313 when two of the author's close friends rated his personality traits. Very refreshing is the way in which he upholds subjective measurement. *

Bucknell J Ed 14:22-3 N '39. * McCall has done a good job * His seventeen theses set up in the first chapter covering the philosophy of measurement cover a field too often ignored in books on the subject. * One of the most usable reference lists of available standardized tests and their publishers consumes forty pages. * several good chapters dealing with tests and their use in measuring comprehension, diagnosing difficulties, and evaluating the work of faculty members * On the whole the volume is well done. It will undoubtedly serve as basic text in numerous measurement courses and will be a valuable reference in most others. It merits the scrutiny of those concerned with research or measurement problems in our schools.

Chicago Sch J 21:182 Ja-F '40. M(ax) D. E(ngelhart). * The classroom teacher will find this book . . . particularly useful, since it presents in an understandable fashion the important aspects of test theory in relation to their applications to educational practice.

Clearing House 14:181 N '39. Earl R. Gabler. * McCall is rather misleading when he states that this present book is a revision of *How to Measure in Education.* It is more than the term revision connotes. Prevision would be a better word to use, because it is truly a pioneering piece of work. Here we see an attempt to broaden the base of measurement to include the out-of-school as well as the in-school educationally significant experiences of children. The idea that teachers should become involved in the practice of measurement and that testing should be an integral part of the learning process and, above all, enjoyable to both pupil and teacher, is certainly worthwhile. Specifically, attention should be called to Chapter VII, covering some forty-two pages devoted to a comprehensive list of tests and test publishers, the best compilation of its kind to date. Also, Chapters XIV, XV, XVI, which deal with the program of measurement for progressive schools, represent a distinct contribution. Here we see a recognition of the neglected aspects of learning as exemplified by such areas as Living in the Community, Finding Information, Buying and Using Things, Keeping Your Temper, Man-

ners, etc. Read this book. It is not dry; it is not a statistical treatment of the factual outcomes of education; it has a soul.

Ed 59:518 Ap '39. Guy M. Wilson. This is more than a book; it is an accumulated growth. Dr. McCall wrote *How to Measure in Education* in 1932. Much has happened in the meantime, particularly to Dr. McCall. He has become more mature, more charitable. He has become riper and mellower. He sees that statistics in the hands of those who know only or chiefly statistics, may be devoid of the spirit that maketh alive. He sees that measurement is in real danger of becoming an ally of the *status quo.* * McCall has become concerned that measurement become available and helpful to teachers. * This new book is filled to the brim with McCall statistics, but they are accompanied by a philosophy. His T-scores are not forgotten, but more attention is given to grade scores and growth, to test construction, to interpretation of test results. Much of this is over the head of the average teacher, but the evident intention is to influence and improve the school room practices. * a favorable combination of handbook, teachers' manual and guide, and cyclopaedia of reference, in the field of measurement in education.

Ed Abstracts 4:307-8 O '39. Henry D. Rinsland. * McCall has, in his own language, infused in measurements a new spirit, sensitized it to the life that is outside as well as inside textbooks, placed it, as in former years, in the van of education (p. vii). It is true that he has "yanked measurements out of its statistical complacency" (p. vii), but not out of the absolute necessity or statistical interpretation. Measurements in the future will need more statistics. Educators must learn this tool of research before education will be a profession. But the logic and wholesome philosophy of Measurement will be a model for writing in this field for many years.

Ed Adm and Sup 26:320 Ap '40. Silas Hertzler. In *Measurement* McCall makes a noted contribution to American educational literature. * In this book he introduces a practical interpretation of statistics as related to the problems of the everyday life of children as they live and learn. His "philosophy of measurement" is the most comprehensive and the most challenging of anything the writer has seen in this field. * Although the suggestions of the book should be taken by the teacher into the classroom and used day after day, they seem quite technical to immature students. * There are pointed instructions on administering and interpreting tests, on pupil. classification, on the use of tests as a means of determining promotion ability. There is a long but able chapter on comprehensive intelligence and achievement tests, followed by a detailed set of directions for the use of such tests. * The writer heartily agrees with the underlying idea that tests are teaching instruments. *

Ed Forum 3:363-4 Mr '39. Although published as a revision . . . the present volume is practically a new work. It appears in a format expressive of modern book-art; it is written in a style that should win for it many readers * Chapter VII offers an exhaustive list of tests and publishers. Numerous tests are described in detail. In fact Dr. McCall does not seem to have omitted any material which can help teachers to measure. * There is more to this book than technics; it is a sound and sensible exposition of measurement as an indispensable aid to professional skill.

El Paso Sch Standard 17:35 S '39. M. E. Broom. * In his preface, the author writes: "This book has been written not only to preserve the good that is in the *status quo* but also to yank measurement out of its statistical complacency, infuse in it a new spirit, sensitize it to the life that is outside as well as inside textbooks, place it, as in former years, in the van of education." This is a large order, but it seems to be one that has been accomplished with more than average success. The volume will be of value to teachers interested in educational measurement.

El Sch J 40:310-3 D '39. H. T. Manuel. * To evaluate a book of such uneven merit is difficult. One is cheered to find an educator of the standing of Professor McCall not only militantly loyal to measurement in the face of the opposition which it has encountered but active also to keep it abreast of current educational thought. The very title, *Measurement,* is reassuring, for some who were once friends of measurement seem to have developed an emotional bias against the word itself. At various points the interpretative comments are distinctly forward looking. * The type of achievement test discussed and illustrated in some detail (pp. 246 ff.) should give a much needed impetus to experimentation with the measurement of objectives which are neglected in some

of the older tests. * the general trend of the discussion away from the marking systems in current use is commendable. On the other hand, the book has serious shortcomings. To start with a fault which the author himself recognizes (p. viii) relatively too much space is given to Professor McCall's own work. * It would be difficult to defend the scant attention given to the work of Tyler, Wrightstone, Wood, Thurstone, Lindquist, and the American Council on Education. The International test-scoring machine, hailed by many as a major development in testing, is given seven lines. Of the various methods of rendering test scores comparable, the author has given greatest prominence to the grade score—a score expressed in terms of school grade. The wisdom of this plan will undoubtedly be seriously questioned by technicians. The treatment of intelligence leaves much to be desired. * too little is said about the unreliability of test scores, and too much confidence is placed in the group intelligence test as a measure of the possibilities of school achievement. One of the most serious criticisms of the book is the tendency toward making the use of tests too mechanical. In classification, for example, one obtains a pupil's "grade score for placement" by the use of an algebraic formula. Table 7 is a "Table . . . Showing the Automatic [*sic*] Classification of Pupils into Grades on the Basis of Any G (Grade) Score." This mechanistic attitude toward test results, the reviewer believes, will hinder rather than help the attainment of the clinical point of view which an intelligent treatment of individual differences requires. This fault may be stated in another way by saying that there is a tendency through much of the book to deal with the results of tests in isolation from other pertinent data. The author has made a serious attempt to present measurement in its proper background, to show it as something to be used in carrying forward the processes of education. This point of view, of course, is sound (but now new). * It is a problem, however, which nobody seems to have solved to the satisfaction of his colleagues * In the reviewer's judgment, the problem of integrating measurement with the processes of education in a single textbook is still unsolved. In spite of these adverse comments, the reviewer believes that this book will find a useful place in the literature of measurement. Although the book does not fully meet the specifications set forth in the none too modest statement of the Preface (quoted above), it has substantial merit and it offers to the teacher of measurement a great deal of useful material. It will be of interest also from the standpoint of revealing the present thinking of a competent and productive leader.

Harvard Ed R 9:376-8 My '39. Eugene Shen. * Should one become too pessimistic about the place of measurement in education, one could find an effective antidote in McCall's new book. Here, educational measurement is justified on practical as well as on logical grounds. * The old title is appropriately abandoned for a broader one, since the author concerns himself with *why* and *what* and *when* as much as with *how* to measure. And there is often more need for wisdom to do the correct thing than technique to do it correctly! Nor is technique neglected. But many readers will probably find too many directions for specific procedures in place of more and fuller discussions of certain generally applicable concepts. The reviewer is particularly disappointed to find . . . no reference to the idea of regression of scores, which, be it noted, is no mere statistical technique, but wisdom incorporated into technique. But the outstanding weakness of the book is lack of integration. There seems to have been too much compilation and not enough organization. Excellent discussions of some questions are found, or rather lost, in the most unexpected places. Considerations of broad import are often subsumed under a topic of much narrower scope. * While the author has a liking for enumeration of steps, most parts of the book are far from dull or mechanical. They furnish interesting as well as instructive information which will be very useful to the classroom teacher and the student of educational measurement. The book will undoubtedly meet a warm reception which it deserves.

J Ed Psychol 31:157-8 F '40. Quinn McNemar. * We are told in the preface that one of the purposes of this book is to "yank measurement out of its statistical complacency." This has been easily accomplished by relegating statistical methods to the final twelve-page chapter, but unfortunately the author did not succeed in avoiding statistical concepts in the material presented between the preface and the last chapter. * As a sample of the materials included in this book, let us consider briefly

the discussion pertaining to measurement in progressive education. Professor McCall herein describes comprehensive tests of his own invention, but, if these tests are the best available, it can be said that measurement in progressive schools must be in a backward stage of development. For example, his "Comprehensive Achievement Test" of one hundred five questions "aims to measure, by sampling, everything important which a child ought to learn and which he can tell in a brief pencil-and-paper test" (p. 246). This sounds like a big order especially for so few items—indeed these one hundred five questions are so divided as to evaluate nineteen different aspects of achievement. Those who have been struggling with psychological and educational measurement will be surprised to know, for instance, that a subtest of four questions can be a reliable measure of "manners," that "modesty" can be evaluated by five questions, and that only three questions are required for the trait "keeping your temper." Not a few of the statistically complacent will wonder *how* reliably these different aspects are being measured. This bit of information is lacking, although the reliability coefficient for total score is reported as .92. However, the meaning of a total score, which is obtained by summing such diverse things as arithmetic, modesty, reading, manners, etc., would appear to be very nebulous. The uncritical presentation of such material as that just cited, plus a verbosity which would seem to be the antithesis of measurement, leads the reviewer to think that psychologists will not find this volume worth while.

J Ed Res 33:539-40 Mr '40. C. W. Odell. * contains much that is of high value from both theoretical and practical points of view, but unfortunately the method of organization and presentation is such as to make much of the content relatively difficult to locate and use * especially good features are the discussion of test validity, the section dealing with test instructions, the consideration of ability grouping, and the general style of writing, which is unusually interesting and in numerous instances seems to be evidence of dynamic thinking. The extensive list of tests is good but for many readers a shorter critically selected list might be more helpful. The procedures outlined appear in some cases to be too mechanical and in others the program contains so many features as probably to bewilder teachers who have had little or no training or experience in the use of tests. Too much emphasis is given the author's own instruments of measurement and also the grade score. The discussion of intelligence might well be strengthened. There are several statements in the book to which the reviewer objects as being either definitely erroneous or liable to lead to incorrect conclusions. * In a number of cases, points, usually minor, that seemed necessary to well-rounded treatments of the topics being dealt with, are omitted. * There are also several general points of view with which the reviewer disagrees. He believes that McCall is too unfavorable toward matching tests; that instead of encouraging guessing on alternative and perhaps other tests, the effort should be made to put a premium upon certainty of knowledge; and that the recommended marking system is subject to serious limitations because it is of little assistance in revealing inefficient teachers.

Jun Col J 10:55 S '39. * Most of the book concerns especially the elementary school field, from which the bulk of the illustrative material is drawn, but parts of it are sufficiently general to be of distinct value to junior college instructors. The first chapter, "A Philosophy of Measurement" is particularly stimulating. The 35-page list of available tests, classified by fields and subjects, will be helpful, but it would have been more useful if more information than only the name of the test and of the publisher had been given.

Loyola Ed Digest 14:9-10 Ap '39. Austin G. Schmidt. * A thesis fundamental to the book and one that is quite unique gives color to every page. McCall refuses to divorce the mechanics of measurement from the philosophy that directs us in what we should seek to measure. * The book is provocative throughout. The underlying philosophy is that of the progressive and the humanitarian. The author is frankly hedonistic, accepting happiness and broadly diffused satisfaction as the one supreme goal of life and brusquely brushing aside the theologian who would suggest a loftier aim. But the book, even though it may not change the current in American education or in the test movement, is so full of new points of view that it cannot be disregarded by anyone with even a mild interest in measurement.

Sch 28:276 N '39. J(ohn) A. L(ong). * McCall's earlier books . . . made him something of a pioneer in the field of educational experimentation and measurement * [This new book] is evidence that he is still in the forefront of the testing movement. Although it would be difficult to find anywhere a more comprehensive general discussion of the theory and practice of measurement in schools, particular attention is given in this book to those devices which have been nurtured mainly by the author, devices such as G-scores and the T-scale. Also, a large section of the book is devoted quite specifically to a discussion of the *Comprehensive Tests* * Many Canadian teachers will feel that Dr. McCall attaches an importance to educational measurement which is much greater than the matter deserves. * [To McCall] tests are genuine instruments of education, necessary tools in any intelligent programme of pupil guidance. He defends this position forcefully and convincingly.

Sci Ed 24:176 Mr '40. C(larence) M. P(ruitt). * in actuality a new book * a real compendium of knowledge in philosophy, psychology, tests and measurement, and evaluation. The author's philosophy of measurement is the finest treatise that the reviewer has ever read. It is indeed regrettable that so few classroom teachers will ever read it. * Altogether this monumental work well serves as a capstone to the writings of one of America's greatest teachers.

Scottish Ed J 22:1095 O 20 '39. The new edition is likely to maintain, if not to enhance, the reputation earned by its predecessor.

Univ Mich Sch Ed B 10:96 Mr '39. * this volume is for all practical purposes a new work. Book One is a doctrinaire "philosophy of measurement" consisting of a sequence of debatable theses presented as fundamental principles of measurement. The remainder of the volume relates to the construction and use of tests, and compares favorably with other current books on the subject. *

Univ Wash Col Ed Rec 6:95 Ap '40. August Dvorak. * [If McCall's] recent book, *Measurement,* were his last, it would be worthy an *opus magnum.* Into its 535 pages he has concentrated the best of his research, scholarship, and experience. The last twenty years have produced numerous excellent books on educational measurement. This reviewer concedes Professor McCall's book to be one of the best, if not the best, for teachers, administrators, and for students in colleges of education and in normal schools. This book should be in every professional, education, public school, and private library. * The reviewer has found Chapter VII, "A Comprehensive List of Tests and Test Publishers," well worth the cost of the book. *

[B1001]
McCLOY, C. H. **Appraising Physical Status:** Methods and Norms. University of Iowa Studies, New Series, No. 356; Studies in Child Welfare, Vol. 15, No. 2. Iowa City, Iowa: the University, 1938. Pp. 260. Cloth, $1.85; paper, $1.50.

B Menninger Clinic 3:126 My '39. W(eston) LaB(arre). Excellent and well-considered anthropometric [study] . . . of norms for child growth *

[B1002]
McCLOY, CHARLES H. **Appraising Physical Status:** The Selection of Measurements. University of Iowa Studies, New Series No. 319; Studies in Child Welfare, Vol. 12, No. 2. Iowa City, Iowa: the University, 1936. Pp. 126. Cloth, $1.35; paper, $1.00.

B Menninger Clinic 3:126 My '39. W(eston) LaB(arre). Excellent and well-considered anthropometric [study] . . . of norms for child growth *

For additional reviews, see B171.

[B1003]
McCLOY, CHARLES HAROLD. **Tests and Measurements in Health and Physical Education.** New York: F. S. Crofts & Co., 1939. Pp. xxi, 392. $3.00.

Cath Ed R 37:653-4 D '39. M. Immaculata. * presents briefly and clearly all recent developments * a wealth of detailed and specific information regarding tests of strength, power, endurance, motor educability, track and field athletics, special abilities, and health. The point of view is thoroughly practical. * No attempt has been made to treat the subject exhaustively. * a short chapter dealing with elementary statistical methods contributes much to the serviceableness of the volume as a text. A classified bibliography also enhances the pedagogical merit of the work. * the book is the best of its kind and meets a long felt need among administrators, teachers and students interested in the application or construction of tests in the field of health and physical education.

Chicago Sch J 21:132 D '39. N(ellie) B(ussell) C(ochran). While this book will have its most complete usefulness as a textbook for professional students, it contains valuable help for every teacher of physical education. * The text is scholarly, and yet informal and practical. *

Ed Abstracts 4:190-1 Je '39. Karl W. Bookwalter. * Certainly no physical education library is complete without this most practical volume. Much of the author's prolific contribution to the tests and measures in our field is brought together in this one text and the appendix is replete with valuable tables and norms for simplification of many desirable measures. The author's classification of tests leads to some repetition but this in no way detracts from the value of this book as a text for beginners or advanced students. *

J Health and Phys Ed 10:560 N '39. A complete resume of the whole tests and measurements field in both health and physical education has at last been written by one of the foremost research experts in the nation. Not only does the book cover most of the former tests, but it also adds many hitherto unpublished problems which have been worked out under the direction of the author. Another first in this splendid volume is the Iowa Classification Test with the Norms included. This should be on the must list of every health and physical education administrator.

J Home Econ 31:716 D '39. * a sound but not too theoretical discussion *

J Sch Health 9:218 S '39. Charles H. Keene. * Except for a short chapter devoted to measurement of size and maturity, the author purposely does not discuss anthropometric tests at length. With this exception, the field of physical tests is well covered. * The reviewer takes vigorous exception to the statement on page 27 regarding the Physical Fitness Index. "Where a low P. F. I. is found, the individual should be carefully examined by a competent physician before being assigned to strenuous physical activities." This exposes a dangerous fallacy in the author's point of view, since the P. F. I. is itself a strenuous physical activity, especially when used with adolescents. It should be given only *after* a careful physical examination given by a competent physician. With this reservation in mind, it is recommended that this text be made a part of the professional library of those engaged in or peculiarly interested in school health activities or programs.

Loyola Ed Digest 14:11-2 Je '39. Austin G. Schmidt. * a comprehensive presentation * there is manifest throughout a thorough familiarity with the literature. There are short but good discussions of the purposes of tests and of methods for utilizing them advantageously. The author has succeeded admirably in making the book comprehensible and useful to the average teacher.

Res Q 10:155-6 D '39. C. D. Giauque. * will be read by all alert physical educators * McCloy has been a pioneer in this comparatively new field and has probably developed, personally and through his students, more tests than any other person. Moreover, he is admirably fitted for the job through his knowledge of statistics, in which subject he is preeminent among physical educators. The author has described in detail a large number of tests and measurements in all the phases of health and physical education, many of them previously unpublished. Yet he has omitted the older, less specific tests and included just those which can be of practical value. * An excellent bibliography is included. The author also adds a ten-page chapter on statistical methods, which is the finest condensation of the necessary material in this field that I have ever seen. * The book is a valuable contribution to the field and should make an excellent text for courses in tests and measurements.

[B1004]
MACFARLANE, JEAN WALKER. **Methodology of Data Collection and Organization:** Studies in Child Guidance, I. Monographs of the Society for Research in Child Development, Vol. 3, No. 6, Serial No. 19. Washington, D. C.: the Society, National Research Council, 1938. Pp. vii, 254. $2.00. Paper.

[B1005]
McINTYRE, G. A. **The Standardization of Intelligence Tests in Australia.** Australian Council for Educational Research, Educational Research Series, No. 54. Melbourne, Australia: Melbourne University Press, 1938. Pp. 82. 4s. Paper. (London: Oxford University Press, 1939. 4s.) (New York: G. E. Stechert & Co. $1.00.)

Ed Abstracts 5:93-4 Mr '40. John W. Gittinger.

Times Ed Sup 1266:319 Ag 5 '39. * The Australian Council, having during the past five years constructed a number of objective tests of scholastic achievements and applied them throughout the Commonwealth, has recently applied intelligence tests over the same area. Two tests were used, one homemade test was non-verbal: it consisted of a multitude of little pictures. The American test was *The Otis Self-Administering Test,* which is very widely used in the United States and has been carefully standardized for that country. It is

called "self-administering" because the giver of the test has nothing to do except to distribute the booklets and collect them at the end of 30 minutes. There is no grouping and timing of the questions under different headings; the various types of subtests are mixed up and follow one another haphazard. This kind of group test—which, by the way, is becoming increasingly popular in England—has one disadvantage: it involves much more reading than the older kind where a score or so of little questions, all of exactly the same type, come under one and the same rubric. Hence the need felt by the Australian Council for balancing the Otis Test with a non-verbal test. The conclusions reached by the investigators are, in the main, the same as those that emerge wherever tests of this kind are set. *

[B1006]
MACMEEKEN, A. M. **The Intelligence of a Representative Group of Scottish Children.** Publications of the Scottish Council for Research in Education, [No.] 15. International Examinations Inquiry. London: University of London Press, Ltd., 1939. Pp. xvi, 144. 5s.

Brit J Psychol 30:263-4 Ja '40. * a lucid account of some of the results of . . . a most interesting and important experiment *

Occupational Psychol 14:67-8 Ja '40. Edith O. Mercer. * an account of the application of Binet and Performance tests to all Scottish children born on any of four specific dates in 1926. The 874 children thus tested constitute a sample that should be truly random in respect of intelligence. The simple clear-cut piece of research was evidently planned and carried out with praiseworthy thoroughness and the data it provides, both in the text and in a noteworthy accumulation of tables and diagrams, contribute valuably to our information about test norms and score distribution. It is a pity that it was necessary to use the 1916 Stanford Revision of the Binet tests rather than the recent Terman-Merrill revision * Altogether the report constitutes a satisfying account of a satisfactory piece of work.

Scottish Ed J 22:931 Ag 11 '39. * a truly representative sample [was] tested individually by one tester with both Binet and Performance scales * [the sample included] all children in Scotland born on 1st February, 1st May, 1st August and 1st November in the year 1926 * the group . . . numbered 874, of whom 444 were boys and 430 girls * it required two years and three months to overtake the testing, although the tester used all means of transport —land, water and air. The account of her journeys is one of the romantic chapters in Scottish education. * The better devised intelligence tests are, the less should they reveal sex or social class differences; if they disclose such differences they are not keeping constant all factors save intelligence, and are consequently self-condemned as intelligence tests. If this was more generally recognised a great deal of fruitless application of intelligence tests would be saved. * The present investigation included a Performance Battery, a new and valuable extension of previous national surveys, and should do much to enlighten us as to what reliance can be placed on this type of test. All who contributed to the success of the survey—Directors of Education, Teachers, the Research Council, and above all the tester —are to be congratulated on an enterprise which other countries may envy, but are not likely to be in a position to repeat.

Times Ed Sup 1270:351 S 2 '39. * The book on the whole serves as an excellent example of scientific procedure and of lucid exposition.

[B1007]

McQuitty, John Vredenburgh. **Statistical Analysis of the Comprehensive Examinations Used in the General College, University of Florida.** University of Florida, Education Series, Vol. 2, No. 1. Gainsville, Fla.: University of Florida Press, January 1940. Pp. v, 42. $0.75. Paper.

[B1007.1]

Macrae, Angus. **Talents and Temperaments:** The Psychology of Vocational Guidance. London: Cambridge University Press, 1933. Pp. xiii, 211. 5s. (London: James Nisbet & Co., Ltd. 5s.) (New York: D. Appleton-Century Co., Inc. $2.00.)

Occupations 12:74-6 N '33. Paul S. Achilles. The author of this book is well qualified to present the problems, methods, and achievements of psychology in the field of vocational guidance, as he has been actively engaged in the work of the National Institute of Industrial Psychology in London for the past seven years and is now head of its Vocational Guidance Department. The fact that London has been the locus of his experience in no way detracts from the value of the book for American readers, since some of the most extensive experiments in guidance have been conducted in England and are here summarized, and the author also comments freely on American methods with which he seems to be familiar. He has aimed to write a short and yet not superficial introduction to the subject for teach-

ers, parents, and social workers, and in the reviewer's opinion he has succeeded admirably. His chapter headings reveal both a logical development of this theme and a rather canny delineation of the degrees of certainty in the contributions of psychologists and others to guidance. * Although the book is avowedly introductory in character the reader feels at once that he is being brought face to face with the fundamental psychological problems involved. There is no dodging of controversial issues * Nor is there any hesitancy about disclosing the shortcomings of many of the tests and devices now utilized. And yet the author leads convincingly to the conclusion that the tests and procedures of the well-trained psychologist materially reduce the uncertainties in vocational guidance. On two points concerning which there is considerable misconception, this book seems to the reviewer to make particularly timely and valuable contributions. One is the view that tests are valueless unless they are perfect in validity. * Macrae shows that the value of the counsel which can be given an individual does not depend on the absolute validity of any one test but on the cumulative evidence of many tests, the scope and thoroughness of the examination, the training and experience of the examiner, and the amount and accuracy of the pertinent supplementary information systematically assembled and studied by the examiner. * The second point is the prevalent notion that vocational guidance is so simplified by the use of tests that it can be undertaken easily by untrained persons. Here Macrae cites Cyril Burt's statement that "there is no foot-rule for vocational guidance that can be put into the hands of teachers or welfare-workers and used with the ease of a thermometer or a pair of scales" * Macrae presents the case for psychology in this difficult field with due humility, as any scientist must, and in the reviewer's opinion he has added valuably to the literature by showing so clearly not only the shortcomings of psychologists, teachers, parents, doctors, and employers, but the need for a better understanding of the problem on the part of all of them and how they may better contribute to its solution. The chapter entitled, "The New Method on Trial," will be welcomed by American readers because it summarizes, for the first time in one place so far as known to the reviewer, the results of the so-called First and Second London Experiments and the Birmingham Experiment—three careful endeavors to measure through follow-up studies of large groups of children the effectiveness of vocational guidance given on the basis of tests and systematic procedures. While the findings are not so clear-cut and positive as might be wished, they nevertheless offer considerable encouragement and the experiments themselves contribute much toward refining the methods for determining the value of guidance. *

Survey 69:268 Jl '33. A simple, non-technical discussion of psychology as applied to vocational guidance, non-dogmatic in viewpoint, eclectic in outlook. Unfortunately a large measure of it is based upon facts derived from English rather than American experience.

Times Lit Sup 1621:116 F 23 '33. * The main impression left on one's mind by Mr. Macrae's useful summary of the present state of our knowledge is how very much we have yet to learn. In the 26 years that have elapsed since Binet originated the idea of mental testing the progress made has not been very striking. Certain fairly simple and easily recognizable abilities can be measured; but how closely they are related to each other and whether or not there is some general underlying capacity which can be separately determined are still matters of controversy. * we fear it is likely to be some time before man has conquered his environment so completely that he can devote himself to doing just exactly what he finds himself best qualified to do * The detection and classification of abilities and temperaments is one thing; that of determining for which of the available employments they were best fitted is quite another. Mr. Macrae's clear and well-arranged little handbook does not attempt to disguise the fact that what has so far been done in the way of vocational guidance is only a small beginning; but it is the beginning of a very important branch of research.

[B1008]
MANN, CECIL W. **Objective Tests in Fiji.** Suva, Fiji: Government Printer, 1939. Pp. i, 39. 1s. 6d. Paper.

[B1009]
MANN, CLAIR V. **Experimentation to Discover Measurable Aptitudes for Engineering.** *Journal of Educational Research,* Vol. 1, No. 2. Rolla, Mo.: the Author, 210 East Eighth St., June 1934. Pp. 37. $0.50. Paper.

[B1010]
MANUEL, HERSCHEL T. **The Guidance of Youth.** Texas Commission on Coordination in Education, Research Bulletin No. 11. Austin, Tex.: Administra-

tive Board, the Commission, April 1940. Pp. 71. Gratis. Paper, lithotyped.

[B1011]
MANUEL, HERSCHEL T. **Individual Guidance and Mental Health.** Texas Commission on Coordination in Education, Research Bulletin No. 10. Austin, Tex.: Administrative Board, the Commission, December 1939. Pp. 39. Gratis. Paper, lithotyped.

[B1012]
MANUEL, HERSCHEL THURMAN. **Spanish and English Editions of the Stanford-Binet in Relation to the Ability of Mexican Children.** University of Texas Bulletin, No. 3532. Austin, Texas: the University, 1935. Pp. 63. $0.25. Paper.

[B1013]
MANUEL, HERSCHEL THURMAN. **Test Results and Their Uses.** The Texas Commission on Coordination in Education, Research Bulletin No. 8. Austin, Texas: Administrative Board, the Commission, December 1938. Pp. 39. Gratis. Paper, lithotyped.

[B1014]
MARSTON, WILLIAM M. **The Lie Detector Test.** New York: Richard R. Smith, Inc., 1938. Pp. 179. $2.00.

Am Sociol R 4:607-8 Ag '39. Paul W. Tappan. Marston . . . performs a valuable service in clarifying for the lay public a technique usually viewed either as a mysterious and omnipotent *deus ex machina* or as a fraud. * one cannot but entertain considerable skepticism toward Marston's optimistic prognostications for the future accomplishments of "his test" * [Marston's] surprising naïveté displays more of feeling than scientific objectivity * though he . . . reiterates his discovery to be that of a "lie detection test," there is to be found nowhere in this work a clear statement of anything like a standardized "test" as that term is used in the sciences. Despite weaknesses, this book is of value as a clear and readable disquisition upon one among the several developing techniques in modern crime detection.

Fed Probation 4:41-2 F '40. Verne W. Lyon. If Dr. Marston's book could accomplish no other single purpose than to clarify and establish once and for all the existing confusion among lay groups as to "who invented the lie detector," it would represent a contribution of significant importance. * Marston emphasizes that the deception test should not be regarded as a "machine." "There never has existed, nor ever will exist a 'machine' which detects liars —it is a scientific test in the hands of an expert which does the lie detecting." The apparatus necessary for making these tests may be found in any moderately equipped psychological laboratory and is readily assembled. * Marston's book is replete with interesting case material which serves to illustrate more vividly the many practical applications of the deception test in criminal investigations. * *The Lie Detector Test* is well adapted for popular consumption. * It is commendable to note that while Marston is very enthusiastic and hopeful for the future, he nevertheless makes this cautionary observation. "Our chief concern is not to hasten the spread of deception test procedure but to make sure that its rapid growth does not outstrip its scientific control."

Survey 74:364 N '38. James Hargan. * Inaccurate feature articles have prejudiced many against the lie detector. This authoritative book, full of interesting cases, clarifies the subject. It is regrettable that Mr. Marston could not have obtained permission to examine Hauptmann.

For additional reviews, see B426.

[B1015]

MARTENS, ELISE H. **Clinical Organization for Child Guidance within the Schools.** United States Department of Interior, Office of Education, Bulletin 1939, No. 15. Washington, D. C.: Government Printing Office, 1939. Pp. vi, 78. $0.20. Paper.

[B1016]

MASE, WAYNE E. **A Self-Rating Scale for School Custodians.** Kansas State Teachers College of Emporia, Bulletin of Information, Vol. 19, No. 10; Studies in Education, No. 18. Emporia, Kan.: the College, 1938. Pp. 24. $0.20. Paper.

[B1017]

MENZEL, EMIL W. **Suggestions for the Use of New-Type Tests in India.** Teaching in India Series, No. 8. Bombay, London, and New York: Oxford University Press, 1939. Pp. xv, 261. Rs. 3.; 4s. 6d.; $1.50.

Teaching 12:94 D '39. This book provides as complete information as possible on the new-type tests, both psychological and educational, that have been standardized or used in India. Though much of the work done so far has been scrappy, some of it has been valuable, and it is a great convenience as well as a help to further research to have under one cover accounts of what has been achieved so far. * valuable suggestions for constructing tests, and recommendations regarding further reading are made * Specially helpful is the chapter on simple statistical devices * Besides tests of general intelligence the book contains fairly good descriptions of tests in the various school subjects * The book should find a place not only in the libraries of training colleges, but also in the teachers' libraries of all progressive

schools. * a most useful and helpful book * the author has done the cause he has at heart a real service.

Times Ed Sup 1296:81 Mr 2 '40. * gives so lucid and so helpful an account of the new style of examination that it may be read with profit by teachers and students in this country as well. It is excellent value for the price *

[B1018]

MERIAM, LEWIS. **Civil Service Testing for Social Work Positions.** Civil Service Assembly of the United States and Canada, Pamphlet No. 9. Chicago, Ill.: the Assembly, June 1937. Pp. 6. $0.25. Paper, lithotyped.

[B1019]

METROPOLITAN LIFE INSURANCE COMPANY, POLICYHOLDERS SERVICE BUREAU. **Testing Applicants for Employment.** New York: the Bureau, [1939]. Pp. iv, 32. Gratis. Paper.

Mgmt R 28:375 O '39. A brief review of the progress that has been made in testing employees for jobs. The study gives a general picture of the testing problem and indicates methods of planning and installing a testing program. It discusses the administration of tests, gives examples of testing programs, and contains other helpful information.

[B1020]

MILNE, F. T. **The Use of Scholastic Tests in South African Schools:** An Arithmetic Test Standardized on Witwatersrand Pupils. South African Council for Educational and Social Research, Research Series, No. 2. Pretoria, South Africa: J. L. Van Schaik, Ltd., 1937. Pp. 162. 1s. Paper.

B Int Bur Ed 12:33 q 1 '38. * The aim of the investigation recorded here was to construct scholastic tests suitable for children of ages from 8 to 16; to obtain norms of performance for the various age groups and standards, and to show how these tests may be used in conjunction with intelligence tests to study individual pupils and as the basis for re-organising the classroom.

[B1021]

MONROE, PAUL, EDITOR. **Conference on Examinations:** Under the Auspices of the Carnegie Corporation, the Carnegie Foundation, and the International Institute of Teachers College, Columbia University at the Hotel Royal, Dinard, France, September 16 to 19, 1938. New York: Bureau of Publications, Teachers College, Columbia University, 1939. Pp. xiii, 330. $3.15.

Clearing House 14:250 D '39. Earl R. Gabler.

Ed Abstracts 5:191 Je '40. Wm. Reitz. * Of particular interest in this volume are the French Committee's reports on the evaluation of general culture by means of essays and papers.

The French tenaciously cling to this form of examination, with the conviction that nothing is better suited to develop abilities, to present ideas clearly, to prepare good summaries, to adopt good examples, to treat subject matter at once lucid and, to choose an "elite." Also interesting is the English Committee's earnest endeavor to understand the chaotic examination practices in their country, and their attempt to break away from mere evaluation of mechanical aspects of essays and compositions and to adopt, instead, the principle: "Look after the *sense,* and the sentences will look after themselves." * Of significance in this volume is also Professor Thorndike's presentation—especially his plea for "purity" in measurement—and Professor Kandel's interesting summary of the conference and his prophetic view of the examination problem in relation to the issues of modern education as a whole. *Evaluation:* The conference on examinations presents without doubt the finest workshop on evaluation or tests and measurement that ever has been designed.

J Ed Psychol 31:316-7 Ap '40. Stephen M. Corey. These proceedings . . . suffer from the same weaknesses that limit the usefulness of so many convention reports. There is neither a table of contents nor an index, hence the only way in which a reader can locate what he wants is to turn the pages one by one. * the brief papers—surprisingly general and nontechnical to be read before a group of experts—and the discussion and chatter that followed make rather interesting reading. Good stories were reported faithfully and a few penetrating criticisms voiced. It would have been stimulating to have attended the conference. The report of it, however, this reviewer would not elect to read.

Loyola Ed Digest 14:7 Jl '39. Austin G. Schmidt. * One need only glance at the frontispiece showing thirty-seven of the most prominent educators of the world, to be assured that he cannot read this book without encountering new points of view well worth knowing. We hope that the proposal made at the final session to the effect that the conference should set up some sort of a permanent organization may be carried into effect.

Psychol B 37:116-7 F '40. Alvin C. Eurich. * The report as a whole recalls the early studies in the United States on the reliability of essay examinations and emphasizes similar conclu-

sions. * Like most reports of conferences, this volume includes much tedious and inconsequential material. Its weaknesses are those of the *Congressional Record.* The chief value of the book lies in its re-emphasis upon the common inadequacies of current examinations in all countries and its stress upon the need for intensive research to improve such measures.

Scottish Ed J 22:941 Ag 11 '39. * A new and interesting feature . . . is the frontispiece, a reproduction of a photograph of the delegates present at Dinard.

[B1022]

MORENO, J. L. **Who Shall Survive?** A New Approach to the Problem of Human Interrelations. Foreword by William A. White. Nervous and Mental Disease Monograph Series, No. 58. Washington, D. C.: Nervous and Mental Disease Publishing Co., 1934. Pp. xvi, 440. $4.00.

Am Social R 2:542-4 Ag '37. George A. Lundberg. The subtitle is an appropriate brief description of the contents of this volume, and herein lies its importance to sociologists. Why the main title was hung on remains a mystery after a careful study of the book. While it is unfortunate from the point of view of circulation that so misleading a title should have been attached, it does not detract from the solid merits of the volume, which are notable. For Dr. Moreno has definitely taken the lead in objectifying certain basic social processes which have always been recognized as fundamental to sociology. * Moreno's analysis, and the theoretical framework into which the data are fitted, are an ingenious and fascinating example of what a trained scientist can do when he turns his attention to sociological problems. To be sure, he draws on the other sciences for both terminology and theoretical suggestions. But as in the case of Comte, Ward, and others, this only adds strength and coherence to his system. * Space forbids a more detailed and critical account of the enormous detail and the theoretical system advanced in this volume. Perhaps it can best be summarized by saying that here are concrete data to illustrate Wiese's analysis of the smaller group-patterns. (See Wiese-Becker, *Systematic Sociology* Chs. 32, 39-41.) Not all of it is completely convincing as far as the present, perhaps inadequate, presentation of admittedly subtle data are concerned. For example, I should want a very much fuller account of the "spontaneity" testing and training, to which considerable space is devoted, before I could accept all of the author's claims for this technique. Also, I think the author assumes too readily the *priority* of the "emotional continuum of relations [which] lies below all the patterns of community life, families, clubs, labor, political or religious units" (p. 339). Actually these basic currents are themselves the results of interaction with the "upper structures" which are admittedly so often badly adapted to the underlying continuum. With this reservation, one must, however, welcome his illuminating analysis of and emphasis upon the importance of these underlying patterns. Less pardonable are the large number of minor infelicities which mar, although they do not greatly reduce, the value of this important work. There is, in the first place, a considerable number of errors and ambiguities, in addition to those listed in the Errata on the last page. The text and the diagrams do not agree in several cases (*e.g.*, p. 35). The percentages referred to in Fig. 4, p. 47, are not apparent from the charts. On p. 250 the author refers to the "accompanying triangle" but the triangle does not accompany or occur anywhere within 35 pages, if at all. There is a line or more omitted on p. 432. Failure to number numerous figures to correspond to text references is a great irritation to the reader (*e.g.*, pp. 104-106, 115, 116). On p. 241 there is reference to the "combination" of different criteria of choice, but I am unable to find any explanation of how this combination was effected. Also, it is not explained how individual attitudes were combined or averaged to get the relationship between cottages shown on p. 238. Added to these shortcomings are a number of atrocious examples of bad English (e.g., pp. 146, 185, 227) which mar an otherwise lucid style. The difficulty of proofreading so intricate a copy as this book presents must be recognized in partial extenuation of the defects noted, but they are none the less regrettable in a work otherwise so competent. The practical and theoretical implications of a more objective charting of the subtler social networks that underlie the more obvious and superficial community structures will be readily apparent. These networks stand in the same relation to readily observable overt social behavior as the atomic structure of matter stands in relation to the more obvious behavior of the physical universe. The formulation of the laws governing the "inner essence" of the latter has increased

enormously man's powers of adaptation to this universe. Sociologists, too, have always striven to formulate the "inner essence" of society. The volume under review makes powerful suggestions as to the direction in which a solution probably lies and the technique by which it may be approached. As such it must be regarded as one of the more important of contemporary contributions to sociological literature.

Ann Internal Med 8:104 Jl '34. J. L. McC. * There are many diagrams, percentage tables, and rather incomplete case histories. The book runs to 437 pages. The reviewer confesses it left him in a fog.

B Johns Hopkins Hosp 56:57 Ja '35. J. R. O. * one of the valuable monographs on Nervous and Mental Diseases * The book is not easy reading, but will be of interest to all teachers and psychiatrists.

J Hered 27:41-4 Ja '36. Gladys C. Schwesinger. The title of this book is altogether misleading. It affords no introduction to the text which, according to Dr. W. A. White's foreword, "is a study of the emotional relations between individuals who are functioning as a social group, or . . . the cross-currents of emotion as they play back and forth between individuals" (p. xi). The emotion studied is that of like-dislike. * The book might be dismissed from further consideration in a publication devoted to genetics and eugenics, were it not that it has received a rather favorable reception in certain quarters, and that some of its methods and conclusions may be evoked in future "social experimentation." For that reason it seems worth while to devote more space to this book than would otherwise be the case. The research, which is vaguely planned and poorly presented, covers data secured from children in a public school, a private school, and a state training school for girls. Some of these subjects were given a "sociometric test" which was, or was not, followed by a test for "spontaneability." The "sociometric test" is the basis on which the research rests; the test for spontaneity is offered to guide later social experimentation for a new order. To be more specific the procedure was as follows: "Our guiding principle in the research has been from the start, after we had decided working in an unexplored territory, to let the direction and the expansion of the research grow out of the situation" (p. 91). "The sociometric test requires an individual to choose his associates for any group of which he is or might become a member" (p. 11). This "test" is directed toward choice of housemother, of housemates and chums, of co-workers, and of cottage groups. These choices are elaborately pictorialized by colored lines, extending between chooser and chosen (or rejected). In the spontaneity tests, the subject improvises a standard life situation to his own satisfaction. He is told, for example, to "throw yourself into the state of anger" (p. 195). The test, it is claimed, "analyzed emotional, social, and vocational abilities" (p. 271). Proof that such is the case is conspicuously lacking. The training-school girls furnished the bulk of data for the report. At no time does the author describe clearly or in detail the precise make-up of any of the many groups analyzed, other than to assign a cottage number. He speaks casually of race and nationality differences, but rarely does he let the reader know whether the group he refers to is white or colored, or what its particular characteristics are. And in regard to socio-economic make-up, he sets down this surprising observation with respect to committed girls: "They are sent in from every part of N. Y. State by the courts; they are a cross-section of the nationality and social groups of New York" (p. 69). (Any elementary sociologist could tell Dr. Moreno that children committed through New York courts are *not* drawn from all social groups; much less do those in a state institution for children represent a "social cross-section" of any state.) The investigator makes repeated demands on the reader's scientific tolerances. He refers to his "sociometric test" as though it possessed an infallibility never yet accorded the most carefully standardized psychological test. Dr. Moreno's "test" is simply an offer of choice— of five choices—to the individual as to which individuals or group he wishes in the future to live with, work with, or play with. All five choices of mates are not always exhausted by the chooser. The persons chosen are later interviewed and their reaction to their choosers noted. The current which passes negatively or positively between any two people (or groups) is called a "tele." Needless to say the discovery is made that we are not always loved or sought by those whom we love or would seek! The investigator's talents are best revealed in his pictorial representation schemes of these affec-

tive currents, or "teles." A love that goes out earns a red line; a hate that returns becomes black. "Teles" between any two individuals or groups may be red, black, or half-black-half-red. Dr. Moreno also discovers with surprise the presence of "key" individuals, that is, persons who have a large, if inarticulate, following (which translated into "power" may be something to be reckoned with). He notes also the occurrence of "isolates," that is, those none-too rare individuals whom nobody loves. A "key" individual is strong; an "isolate" weak. There is also discovered the presence of "chains" (four to six or more people who form a closed circle, whose activities and line-up in the outside world might go by the name of "gang"). Acceptances and rejections of individuals from cottage to cottage are revealed by many red, green, and black lines, which crisscross in beautiful, lacy networks on paper. Some cottages, housemothers, jobs, and play activities are found to be more popular than are others. These discoveries have all been made by asking people to tell whom they like or dislike, and by transcribing their responses on a floor plan. The author's solution for the psychological salvation of group living is to have people live, play, and work with those individuals or groups whom they choose to live with, etc. Moreno cheerfully disregards the important implications of the fact that it is possible that at the time of having to choose the choosers' acquaintance with the alternative groups may have been new or definitely restricted. This social recommendation might be worth applying to society at large if only we could regulate, through personal choice, the particular companions with whom we must live, work and associate in all of our various interpersonal relationships. It might be made to work in some measure if we could be sure that our choice of today would hold for tomorrow. People then would never be dismissed from their jobs or divorced or forsaken or socially ostracised. It might even be made to work for a limited time if but to mention names were ever likely to be an open sesame to change in associates with change in experience and outlook. But even in a training school how can it work as this reporter in his enthusiasm would have us believe that it will? His technique assumes that children can make accurate and lasting choices of housemothers at sight, and from a distance, or known through hearsay only. How else can a child living in one cottage in an institution know whether she is going to be able to live permanently in "harmonious interrelationship" with a housemother in another cottage, or with one or more members of a group outside of her own? The author speaks of the likes and dislikes of these training-school girls for their housemothers and mates as though committed girls had equal opportunity with free citizens outside to form their friendships (p. 103). In all custodial institutions, social interaction is artificially controlled and restricted; necessarily so. He notes the waning of choices as later choices are given, but he does not sense the limitations imposed on the girls' opportunities to become intimately acquainted with 500 other inmates. He does not even consider the domination effect which different housemothers can have on the choices given by their charges, who are required to set down these choices in writing, over their signatures. Yet the author's recommendations for society must rest on the results obtained from these data, the validity of which is open to much serious question. Analogies are drawn between the "institution runaway" and the "problem of migration" (p. 31), on the naive assumption that girls in such a correctional school do not run away because they have no place to go or because the psychological forces attracting them to the institution are so strong that they do not want to run away to freedom (p. 204)! Perhaps in his creative preoccupation the author did not observe locked doors, night watchmen, or barbed-wire fences; nor did he hear of punishments and ostracism visited upon that greatest of all offenders in such a school—the (rather easily caught) returned runaway. The English of the text makes painful reading. Coined words, wrongly used words, mistakes in grammar and sentence structure may call for tolerance, even sympathy, for a foreigner's difficulties with English, but a report which is to attain the dignity of publication as a scientific monograph, surely ought to conform to elementary English usage. It is a great pity that one or more of the sixty-odd people to whom the author makes formal acknowledgment of help (pp. 434-435) could not have come to his rescue in the interests of verbal purity and of clarity. Infringements of the following kind occur on every page: "The ground . . . may lay in the first stage" (p.

62); "It apparently depends also upon whom are cut out" (p. 208); "radiated into all directions" (p. 19); "The opportunity to interject into the homestead project, besides agricultural and economic, also psychological planning was given" (p. 20); "pieces caught in the machine to an extent necessitating the forewoman to halt the steam roller to remove them" (p. 113); "There are millions of individuals among us, who, when they love a woman, at least five are ahead of him who are more attractive to her" (p. 250). "Who shall Survive?" This question, asked so intriguingly in the title is forgotten until it again appears as a chapter heading at the end of the book. Chapter 23 is not a summary of the 362 pages preceding it, but a rumination of ideas likely to occur to any thinking person of the 1930's. On page 366, one gathers that the author's "study of the integrating and disrupting forces in the development of society, by what means they operate and by what techniques they can be controlled" has disclosed characteristic "inner disturbances as a permanent feature of social organization," but the presentation of these disrupting forces or the revelation of their cause or control is confined to the likes-dislikes data revealed by the sociometric test. There is, of course, no question that our emotional attitudes toward and from our fellow men, separately and collectively, play a large part in our happiness and unhappiness, and it would invariably be helpful to understand in any given relationship the factors underlying the attitude. But to assume that one can offer a formula for determining the "emotional structure" so prettily depicted in Dr. Moreno's red and green diagrams is to assume an astounding simplicity of emotions as well as a static universe of attitudes which has no existence in fact. One knows *a priori* that there is an invisible structure of love and hate and various emotional hues in between, underlying social groups and individual relationships, but one cannot and never will be able to reveal this wealth of emotional coloring and complexity by straight red and green and black lines. In his ambition to pictorialize interpersonal relations, Dr. Moreno has overlooked too many things; the resistance, conscious and unconscious, of personality to reveal itself in its true form; the instability of emotion and attitude; their alteration and extension with experience; and above all, in a training-school situation, the "halo" effects injected into admissions made by the committed individuals accustomed to playing up to staff officers and official investigators. In his recommendations for an ideal social set-up in the world at large, the author constantly assumes a cohesion and a permanency for the likes and dislikes expressed by this choice test which he holds would be adequate for permanent group formations. He goes further; he draws eugenic implications! "Some groups classified today as unfit for propagation may be found unfit when in relation to certain groups, but fit in relation to other groups" (p. 369). And what are the contributions of this vast piece of work which has utilized the services of so many workers and subjects? At times one gets the feeling that the author is on the verge of an idea which, if one could thread his way through the mess of verbiage which enshrouds it, would be worthy of propagation. The main finding seems to be that some people like each other and that some do not, or what is even sadder, that we give our love to people who respond indifferently or negatively to our precious gift, and who in turn may meet with a similar fate at the hands of some one else. If we could live, play, and work with people whom we like and who like us in turn, life would be rosier. Perhaps the most valuable contribution of all, however, is the elaborately conceived system of codes and formulae for setting down "psychological cross currents" of love and hate. They are very pretty to look at on paper; and they do save words, which should appeal especially to the lovers of this world, if not to the haters.

J Nerv and Mental Dis 80:724-5 D '34. * a striking performance. It challenges attention both by its manner and matter, marking as it does a distinctly new mode of approach to an appraisal of human behavior and its values. Dr. Moreno has carried out a unique sociometric series of studies, chiefly at the Hudson School for Delinquent Girls. * While it is true, in the words of Dr. Wm. A. White to whom this work is indebted for an understanding and delightful Introduction, that "Dr. Moreno has discovered again many homely truths which have been recognized by others but he has rediscovered them by a different method and a method which permits of their development to a more highly differentiated degree and also their utilization for the benefit of the indi-

vidual." This is a truth that lies behind many great innovations and advances in thought. Many intuitively grasped truths, announced piecemeal through the centuries, become welded into a large generalization or theory by a stroke of genius which permits further and rapid advances in understanding of nature's phenomena. Dr. Moreno attempts an almost unsurmountable task when he would essay to determine the psychological processes which comprise a whole community. To arrive at valid formulations for such a procedure he utilizes his new sociometric method. As the biological unit develops in accordance with certain laws, so does the social unit. To essay to discern such fundamental processes is the purpose of this intriguing book. From the psychotherapeutic angle Dr. Moreno offers some interesting suggestions. * The diagrams are ingenious though at first baffling. Finally sociogenic "laws" appear. This very interesting and thought-provoking monograph is recommended particularly to those who have to house or care for large numbers of people. A consideration of the principles that Dr. Moreno has elaborated upon would be highly desirable, not only in communities, if they could be applied there, but if they held up under practical application they might be of inestimable value to the populations of large institutions such as State hospitals and prisons, etc. * These hints and suggestions are timely and valuable and it would seem that in the study of interhuman relations we are launched upon a study of the integration of the individuals with whom we have been working so long and that the principles of these integrations are of the highest significance to our various social organizations and institutions, and even to civilization itself. If Dr. Moreno's monograph does nothing else than to call attention to possibilities in this direction it will have served an exceedingly useful purpose.

J Social Psychol 6:388-93 Ag '35. Gardner Murphy. This extraordinary volume does genuinely contain "a new approach to the problem of human interrelations"; in fact, it contains two new approaches of the first magnitude, either of which would justify the very considerable enthusiasm with which the book has been greeted. * The book required nearly a week to read—one of the most valuable weeks of my year. Every simple drawing represents a complex social pattern, "frozen" for a moment for presentation on the printed page, and cut asunder from its context because of the necessity of starting with the simple "social atoms" in our social cosmos. The charts show the positive and negative affect of each individual towards many other individuals, considered with reference to participation in some social activity. * Sociometry is the study of positive and negative social responses between the members of groups, always considered in reference to some particular social situation. The technique of sociometric testing is rather complicated since a great deal depends upon the age, sex, IQ, and social characteristics of the persons tested, and the errors to be guarded against are complex and numerous. In essence, however, we have a living picture of the basis of social cohesion and social rejection. The result is a demonstration of "mutual pairs"; "triangles," where each one of a group of three is drawn to the other two; groups in which positive affect reaches on through a series A, B, C, D, E, until the end of the group is reached (these groups are called "chains"); "stars," individuals who receive positive affect from a whole cluster of associates; and "isolates," individuals who are accepted by no one. The social structure which appears in the diagrams reveals many things of theoretical and of practical significance. * of all the stimulating ideas offered by this book, I think the most novel and the most important is the conception of *"spontaneity training,"* which is organically related to sociometry but has further implications for personality study. * The book makes many contributions to social theory, yet meets the most acid test of practice, for example, in handling juvenile delinquency. It is primarily a book on method in social psychology, but the method is so well thought out and so shrewdly adapted to circumstances that we may fairly say a whole new field of research has been surveyed and thrown open to us. * one confronts, once in a blue moon, such a book as Moreno's. The book expresses a profound and deeply sensitive philosophy of social relations, based in some measure upon Nietzsche, Freud and Bergson, but given a three-dimensional quality by virtue of the dramatic imagination and expression of the author. * the concept of spontaneity training . . . puts the cap stone on a brilliant achievement. It might have been thought sufficient to

find here a new quantitative method which makes possible the study of many social groups in a truly experimental spirit, yet without the artificiality into which most such experiments have fallen. This book, however, has gone beyond the description of this new method and has offered a rich promise of psychiatric and educational usefulness in the unfolding of inarticulate and uncompleted personalities.

Lancet 228:213 Ja 26 '35. A foreword to this book, written by W. A. White, opens with the following sentence: "A crude concept of structure thinks of it as composed of parts after the fashion of a Mosaic." This is not an inspiring beginning, whether viewed as grammar or sense. Nor are the words with which Dr. Moreno opens his first chapter much more encouraging; "a true therapeutic procedure cannot have less an objective than the whole of mankind." Dr. Moreno's book resembles, in fact, a badly made sandwich. It consists of an interesting and original middle part wedged between unusually inept introductory and closing chapters. The following sentence from one of the last pages of the book is typical: "In consequence our emphasis upon any particular problem in Hudson, as racial tension, sex, or runaways, needs to be understood as arising from a penetration into the underlying factors which are uncovered when we examine beneath the surface of a community's psychological structure of organisation, whether this community be now Hudson or any other." * The method sounds simple, though perhaps somewhat unpracticable with shy or inhibited children; yet the amount of interesting information forthcoming from the total material which finally becomes available is surprising. Light is thrown on such general questions as the attitude to each other of children of different colour and racial groupings—Jews, Italians, Germans, etc., upon the psychology of sexual attraction, of leadership, and of group organisation. The method of investigation is time-consuming and it presupposes that the subjects do not lie in recording their attitudes and that they do not falsify their emotions in the spontaneity tests. The inquiries here described make no attempt to answer the question of who shall survive, which is posed in the title of the book, though a suggestion is made in the last chapter, a chef d'oeuvre of muddled thinking and writing, that those persons should survive who have "spontaneability."

Med Times 63:332 O '34. Irving M. Derby.
* The critical historical data supplied should be of interest to anyone interested in sociology.

Psychoanalytic R 22:231-4 Ap '35. Winifred Richmond. It is impossible to do justice to this extremely interesting and challenging piece of work within the limits of a review. To get its full meaning, to see the tremendous importance of what Dr. Moreno is driving at, one needs not only to read it carefully and give it thoughtful study, but to actually apply some of his tests, as the reviewer did, and to watch their working out within a group. Then it becomes apparent that here really is a method of observation of group reactions, or rather the reactions of individuals within the group, which not only throws light upon the personalities composing the group, but can aid in the arranging of people in communities so as to avoid a great part of the frictions and antagonisms which are the roots of much of our social disorder. * deserves careful reading by anyone interested in human nature from any angle, most of all by those interested in group psychology or group therapy.

Q R Biol 9:491-2 D '34. The student of human relations will find this an interesting book. *

[B1023]

MORTON, N. W. **Individual Diagnosis:** A Manual for the Employment Office. Foreword by Leonard C. Marsh. McGill University, McGill Social Research Series, No. 6. Montreal, Canada: McGill University, 1937. Pp. xvii, 123. $1.75. Paper. (London: Oxford University Press. 5s. 6d.)

Civil Service Assembly News Letter 4:12 Mr '38. As a handbook for persons engaged in vocational guidance and selection, Mr. Morton's manual for employment offices will find wide use. * A discussion of the statistical analysis of test data, the choice and administration of tests, the interpretation of test results and various other aspects of measurement of individuals should be helpful to test administrators.

For additional reviews, see B432.

[B1023.1]

MOWAT, ALEX S. **City and Rural Schools:** A Comparison of the "Qualifying" Candidates. Foreword by Godfrey H. Thomson. Publications of the Scottish Council for Research in Education, [No.] 11. London: University of London Press, Ltd., 1938. Pp. 79. 1s. Paper.

[B1024]

MURPHY, GARDNER, AND LIKERT, RENSIS. **Public Opinion and the Individual:** A Psychological Study of Student Attitudes on Public Questions, with a Retest Five Years Later. Prepared under the auspices of the Columbia University Council for Research in the Social Sciences. New York: Harper & Brothers, 1938. Pp. ix, 316. $3.00.

Am J Sociol 44:481 N '38. Elio D. Monachesi. * Murphy and Likert have made a significant contribution to the field of attitude study, and they have, in addition, indicated a number of new fields of research that should be cultivated in the near future.

J Abn and Social Psychol 34:283-5 Ap '39. Hadley Cantril. * especially concerned with the problem of combining qualitative data obtained from life histories with quantitative data obtained from questionnaires. The title of the book is, therefore, somewhat misleading. The term "public opinion" is meant to describe merely the public attitudes of the groups investigated. * The results obtained leave one with the feeling that we still know but little regarding the genesis of attitudes. * In respect to the question of generality-specificity, which is discussed in detail, one is somewhat puzzled to learn that the authors began with the "conviction" that they would find high specificity. This assumption, which goes so much against both common sense and laboratory findings, they discover to be wrong. * Since the authors presuppose specificity, they are also surprised to find that abbreviated attitude measures have reliabilities as high as the complete Thurstone scales. Here again, the authors seem to neglect the theoretical importance of recent demonstrations they and others have made that Thurstone's elaborate technique for measuring an attitude is comparable to cutting a tree with a razor rather than an axe. * A study of the personal involvement which different attitudes entail for different individuals might help to give more basic explanations for many of the contradictions found in the field of attitude measurement. *

Sociol and Social Res 23:189 N-D '38. E(mory) S. B(ogardus). * A unique inquiry consists of analyzing autobiographical materials and of quantifying the data. While the results are not wholly satisfactory, they are valuable enough to justify further research in this field. * All in all this study makes a very stimulating contribution to the measurement of the opinions and attitudes of individuals.

For an additional review, see B434.

[B1025]

MURPHY, LOIS BARCLAY. **Social Behavior and Child Personality:** An Exploratory Study of Some Roots of Sympathy. New York: Columbia University Press, 1937. Pp. ix, 344. $3.50. (London: Oxford University Press. Pp. viii, 344. 17s. 6d.)

Am J Orthopsychiatry 8:171-3 Ja '38. Ethel L. Ginsburg. * Murphy has made a real contribution to the understanding of the children's behavior and has raised many interesting questions for further study * our ultimate understanding of the total personality is hastened by the accumulation of just such minute, detailed data pertaining to each of the component parts of the personality. Psychiatrists, educators and social workers should find here much that is interesting and of value to them in their work with children; and, of equal importance, many suggestions for further explorations.

Am J Psychiatry 95:755-7 N '38. Eugenia S. Cameron. * an interesting and suggestive study of sympathetic behavior * In the discussion of detailed protocols there are many keen and helpful observations, and it is in these that the greatest value of the book lies for the child psychiatrists. *

Am J Psychol 51:440-1 Ap '38. Ellis Freeman. * This critical viewpoint which dominates the work reënforces one's confidence in the soundness of her tactfully presented and cautiously phrased conclusions. One of the great merits of this investigation lies in the heavy weighting of culture in the determination of personality. * especially serviceable in deepening and extending hypotheses, has defined a fruitful approach to the social aspects of personality.

Am J Sociol 44:463-9 N '38. Kimball Young. * There is throughout her description and her interpretation a keen recognition of the play of cultural factors in the induction of sympathetic and aggressive behavior. * Unfortunately, she was not in a position to indicate the detailed manner in which parental and school influences operated to produce some of the features of such behavior. Moreover, she ignores somewhat the possible effects of constitutional variability and especially neglects those influences of parents, siblings, playmates, and others which can scarcely be termed cultural in any sensible use of this term. * It seems to me that the social-psychological—that is, the interactional—basis of ambivalent reactions of co-operation and sympathy, on the one hand, and of antagonistic responses, on the other, is neglected. Regardless of cultural conditioning there seems to be evidence that everywhere rivalrous and oppositional attitudes and habits arise alongside of co-operative and sympathetic ones. * Unfortunately, the author in interpreting her data paid no attention to the theoretical contributions of George H. Mead and John Dewey. For example, much of her material would take on more significance if she had recognized the social nature of the rise of the self. * like most of the research workers with nursery-school children, Mrs. Murphy draws a false dichotomy between the egoistic and selfish references in behavior and those aspects of behavior directed to others * Until genetic psychologists reckon with the more fundamental social—that is, interactional—foundation of self in all its aspects, a completely deterministic and naturalistic interpretation of social behavior will be lacking. Yet, in spite of this limitation, Mrs. Murphy's study is worthy of serious attention from psychologists and sociologists alike. *

Am Sociol R 3:144-5 F '38. L. Guy Brown. * This high-grade study which could be used in every course in Methods, raised many questions in the thinking of the reviewer. Should we define situations as sympathetic situations or situations for politeness, etc., when the behavior of an individual concerns us? Situations that will elicit sympathy or politeness from one person will get quite different responses from others. Company in one's home is a situation for politeness, but the child often behaves badly. "Framed situations" are adult definitions and may not fit a child's definition at all. Would it not be better to study the daily reactions of an individual and see in what situations he expresses sympathy? In some of the verbal responses the reactions seemed to be group patterns rather than sympathy. Children do many things without the adult meaning, because they have seen them done. Even adults express sympathy merely because it is the conventional thing to do. Furthermore, a child may fail to express the sympathy he feels because he is shy or for other reasons. Professor Murphy views unsympathetic responses as egocentric, and sympathetic responses as social. All responses are both egocentric and social. On all occasions the person reacts to himself quite as much as he does to the object or situation. This statement does not mean that "everything one does is selfish." If a person admires a painting, he reacts to his own sense of beauty quite as much as he does to the picture. Sympathy is a reaction to one's own attitudes as much as it is a response to a distressing situation.

Ann Am Acad Pol and Social Sci 198:241-2 Jl '38. Ruth Arrington. * an investigation of sympathetic behavior in preschool children as revealed by an analysis of responses to distress in other children * the author undertook to coordinate "a variety of methods or techniques (observation, experiment, rating, interview) in *collecting data* on different aspects of behavior and personality," and to coördinate "different methods of *analysis* (description, statistics, systematic interpretation, cross-section and genetic relations)" in the evaluation of these data. The primary sources of data were objective diary records of distress situations occurring in two nursery-school play groups, social behavior ratings, experimental or framed situations, conferences with parents, and daily records kept by the parents of six children. *

Brit J Ed Psychol 8:315-6 N '38. * In her theory of the growth of sympathy Dr. Murphy is cautious and undogmatic. It is not clear how far she agrees with McDougall's theory of "sympathetically induced emotion" * The discussion tends at times to be carried on in unnecessarily abstract terminology, but undoubtedly the book makes a valuable contribution to the detailed study of this aspect of the development of a pre-school child.

Brit J Psychol 29:83 Jl '38. * this study marks an interesting transition from the 'cross-section' method of studying the distribution of a given trait in a group (so popular in the U. S. A.) to the 'longitudinal section' method of studying its relation to and development within a total personality. The author seems reluctant to abandon the former method, though secretly convinced of the superiority of the latter. Had she been surer of her convictions, and concentrated on tracing out the general response tendencies of the individual manifested in long period fluctuations of behaviour, she might have avoided the slight confusion from which the book suffers; and have demonstrated more clearly her interesting conclusions as to the importance of 'range of behaviour.' It is to be hoped that she will develop this technique more fully in future studies.

Commonwealth R 21:120-1 My '39. L. F. Beck. The reader who selects this book by its title is sure to be misled. Instead of a general discussion of social development in children, this volume is devoted to a naturalistic study of sympathetic, aggressive, and allied behavior in youngsters from two to four years of age. Specifically, an analysis is made of responses to distress in playmates. * [the] paucity of the psychological milieu brings into question the representativeness of the results of this study *

J Genetic Psychol 52:251-3 Mr '38. Florence L. Goodenough. * a very detailed account of the reactions of nursery school children to manifestations of distress in others * Some readers may feel that the amount of space devoted to these illustrative anecdotes is excessive, since a rough calculation indicates that they make up at least a third of the entire volume and in many instances the points in question are of such a simple direct character that the citation of concrete examples seems like elaborating the obvious. * The author wisely refrains from attempting to separate the closely interwoven strands of innate tendencies and environmental influences as determinants of sympathetic behavior. *

J Genetic Psychol 53:239-46 S '38. Barbara S. Burks. Unusual interest attaches to an experimental report by a critic and interpreter of developmental psychology who has contributed as much as this investigator to the clarification and consolidation of the field. * in so far as objective research tools are available Murphy uses them * much ingenuity is employed in working out techniques * We would want to make an analysis of Murphy's unpublished protocols, possibly supplement this by clinical interrogatory, and obtain observations upon older (school-age) Subjects before proposing such a schematization of "stages" with any urgency. But the formulation of true developmental stages in sympathetic feeling and behavior meanwhile remains a tantalizing possibility.

J Nerv and Mental Dis 90:288-9 Ag '39. * a serious, competent and well worth while work * Particular attention should be directed towards the elaboration of identification mechanisms, here following too closely, in our opinion, Scheler's excellent though not very profound work on *Sympathy*. In view of the definitely pragmatic issues which are well dealt with, it is perhaps of minor value to call attention to the inadequacies of the "sympathy" formulations here focussed upon. We find the work distinctly commendable. *

Mental Hyg (New York) 23:155-8 Ja '39. Helen L. Koch. * a discursive work rich in hypotheses * In only a few cases have the more formal of our techniques of analysis been used with sufficient refinement to establish a high degree of probability for the propositions suggested. * In fact, so plausible are most of the hypotheses that I should expect them to be established as highly probable were more adequate methods employed. * In its lack of conciseness—its essential content could have been set forth in one half the space—Murphy's volume can scarcely be offered as a model, but it has certainly helped to crystallize the problems, and it should stimulate an enthusiasm for illuminating some of the relatively dark areas of the psychological field.

Psychoanalytic Q 8:262-4 Ap '39. J. F. Brown. * an honest attempt to add to our knowledge of psychodynamics in childhood. It is concerned with the observation of emotional behaviors in natural social situations. * The subtitle of the book . . . more accurately describes the contents than does the title. The title is however not misleading. * Certainly a great deal of painstaking work went into this study. The study is a pioneer work that introduces a new type of attack and raises more questions than it answers. * a work which all psychoanalysts and particularly child analysts should read * This is a work in social psychology which complements rather than competes with the work of the child analyst. In the future there will probably be much active coöperation between workers like Murphy and the child analysts. My only major criticism is that Dr. Murphy is so wary of psychoanalytic concepts that her theoretical sections tend to lack conceptual and linguistic precision. Many of the actual behaviors described are, I believe, more easily translated into analytic concepts than those which are used. There are also minor criticisms to be made. Although Dr. Murphy writes very well, so many of the behavior protocols are included in detail that one loses the thread of the argument at times. Some examples were absolutely necessary, but very few busy readers will want so many. The various complicated dials and charts add I believe very little to the verbal text and are sometimes even confusing. (On the dials for instance in many cases two axes are marked

instead of one for reasons no place clearly indicated in the text.) Dr. Murphy is loose in her usage of those freudian conceptions she occasionally employs and rather inaccurate in some of the conceptions borrowed from Lewin. These are but minor points in a book in child psychology which sets a really important problem and investigates it in an intelligent fashion.

Psychol B 35:109-12 F '38. Helen Thompson. * The appendix gives in full the social behavior scale developed and used in the study. * The monograph is an excellent illustration of the importance of approaching a poorly understood phenomenon in an exploratory but scientific fashion. * The book abounds in explicit and implied suggestions for further research. * Although there are several instances of carelessness such as referring to a frontispiece which has been inserted elsewhere, omitting references, and other minor errors, and although there is some randomness of exposition, the general construction of the book and its important message definitely outweigh its faults. The book is heartily recommended not only to students of social behavior but to all investigators of child psychology as a refreshing antidote to the narrow delimited researches of recent years.

Psychologists League J 2:15-6 F '38. Helen Block. This monograph is a concrete example of the application of Lewin's concepts to a psychological problem. * Methodologically the study is of great importance since it illustrates the theoretical problems which a "field" analysis of behavior raises. * Mrs. Murphy's oversimplified description of the competitive-sentimental American culture-pattern presents us with a possible key to the conflicting behavior of individual children although her somewhat rambling discussion of this point leads to certain contradictions in her position. This is the only aspect of the book which the reviewer would criticize. *

Social Ed 2:64-5 Ja '38. Norman Frederiksen. The subtitle . . . expresses better than the title the actual content of the book. * The book deals with a type of research which is greatly needed in the psychology of personality. Genetic studies of behavior in natural rather than laboratory settings are more realistic and are likely to yield generalizations which more accurately describe the complex relationships involved in personality development. The book is a valuable contribution to the psychology of personality and might well serve as a model for additional studies dealing with other aspects of behavior.

Social Service R 12:151-3 Mr '38. Hyman S. Lippman. * One is impressed with her catholic approach to child behavior. She appears to be acquainted with the literature of various schools, but in attempting the difficult task of bringing together the philosophies of these schools she is less convincing than in the deductions from her experimental work. * The chapter on "Variations in Sympathetic Behavior in Relation to Motivation on the Playground" is most interesting. There is a lucid description of the variations of the child's behavior in different situations which reflects the instability of the young child. * Many valuable deductions may be drawn from the results obtained, which probably would apply to children of different ages. Those of us who deal with behavior problems in children realize the danger of accepting the opinion of a few people who are asked to describe the child's personality and behavior. As pointed out in this work, not only does behavior vary tremendously from day to day but also from one situation to another. Added to this, we must take into account the emotional relationship between the narrator and the child, for a child who is rejected is often described in a way that will emphasize his negative traits to such an extent that it is difficult to recognize him when he comes in for a study. The equally great danger of predicting how a child is going to behave on the basis of a few observations and tests is apparent from these studies. A great many problems for research are suggested by this book. The reviewer would like particularly to see a study that would explain why some children react with sympathy only when they are insecure, and others only when they are secure. It will probably be necessary to rely on psychoanalytic studies of children for this information. This book is highly recommended not only to those who are working with children in nursery schools but to every serious student of human behavior.

[B1026]

MURRAY, HENRY A., AND OTHER WORKERS AT THE HARVARD PSYCHOLOGICAL CLINIC. **Explorations in Personality:** A Clinical and Experimental Study of Fifty Men of College Age. New York and London: Oxford University Press, 1938. Pp. xiv, 761. $8.50; 42s.

Am J Psychiatry 96:1483-5 My '40. W. Line. This volume is both interesting and challenging. * The notes on psychological techniques employed are interesting, although the reader will not find much concrete reporting as to experimental results and conclusions. The most significant feature of this section . . . would seem to be the impressive degree of freedom in investigation that the enterprise encouraged. No one particular or stereotyped approach was emphasized. The studies obviously challenged the greatest versatility in attack and subtlety of qualitative insight in interpretation. How successful the outcomes were, however, we are unable to judge. From one point of view, the project may appear to be a mere elaboration of the usual clinical procedure, where a group of investigators examine a patient independently and discuss their findings in conference. Instead of being unduly concerned, however, with recommendations on therapeutic procedures in connection with the subject examined, as is usually the case in clinical work, the object of this project was apparently quite otherwise, although it is difficult to see how that object can be defined more clearly than in terms of general understanding of human personality. In a sense, this may be said to be a weakness of the project. One has the feeling that Dr. Murray's statement of a theory of personality is a common denominator to which all the workers would, in general, subscribe; but beyond that, each specialist would go to work from his own particular point of view. In another sense, however, it is possibly a strong point; for it creates a situation with great opportunities for following original insights and clarifying some challenging leads. Subsequent reports of the project or its continuation may indicate more clearly the degree to which it has justified its advantages as an investigatory setting. At present one feels that, for instance, the elaborate description of the "Case of Earnst" involved a very detailed enquiry into all sorts of experiences and events pertaining to the life of this individual, but that the case study as reported was decidedly lacking in purpose and bewildering in outcome.

Am J Sociol 45:130-1 Jl '39. Kingsley Davis. * The result is disappointing. Dr. Murray, who has his name on most of the chapters, is given to philosophizing, repetition, and neologisms (e.g., "scientification," "sentimentive," "harmavoidance"). The most useful chapter is the sixth (206 pages), in which each experimenter describes his procedure and results, giving such excellent sections as "Hypnotic Test," "Experimental Study of Repression," and "Violation of Prohibitions." An interesting chapter is the seventh, in which the group gives a full case study of one subject; significantly, however, this chapter fails to hang together, for the results of each experimenter are not too clearly related to the others. A basic defect in the volume is the misconception of scientific abstraction. It is fine to study the personality "as a whole." But the whole personality is the concrete personality, and science never reveals the concrete. The nearest one can come to concrete wholeness by the scientific route is the marshaling of all relevant sciences to describe the individual. The clinic did not do this. It stuck to "psychology," ignoring both biology and sociology. So naïve is Dr. Murray with respect to the social determinants of personality that he regards social institutions as the products of individual needs, thinks of them as something to which one can belong. He dismisses the sociological approach to personality by saying that the greater part of a person's life is private and subjective, hence could not be connected with his membership in organizations. By thus misconstruing the sociological approach, he fails utterly to understand the sociocultural determinants of personality. Under such auspices the "science of personology" gets off to a bad start. *

Am Sociol R 4:576-83 Ag '39. Kimball Young. * gives the results of several years of rather painstaking experimentation, testing, observation by experts, interviews, and collection of questionnaire and autobiographical materials from a group of 51 men of college age. Murray himself has written most of the theoretical and interpretative sections leaving only certain reports on particular items in the program to his co-workers. Yet the book is truly a joint enterprise, for the theory and interpretation were hammered out in the course of cooperative research and conferences. The basic standpoint . . . is drawn largely from psychoanalysis. * "The Genetical Investigation of Personality" dealing with "childhood events" is one of the best [chapters] * The fundamental aim of this project was the study of the person as a totality or unity rather than of segments of his make-up. This "organismal" standpoint,

according to Murray, implies a special subdivision of psychology which he calls "personology"—"the science of men, taken as gross units," with particular reference to "individual differences and types of personality." * excellent discussion of the fundamental developmental processes in the child * very ingenious and enlightening studies of fantasy, of dramatic and thematic interpretation of pictures and toys, and of tests of esthetic appreciation as means of discovering the subjects' latent motivations and interests * Although the intensive analysis of each individual counteracts, in part, the disadvantages of the small sample, it is evident that so far as the statistical treatment is concerned the results must be considered thoroughly tentative. * Moreover, all fifty-one subjects were not examined by the same methods or given equal attention. * Not the least of the contributions of this vast work is the narration of how constantly added findings forced the workers to new and usually more effective concepts and interpretations. Yet these alterations did not permit the complete comparability in the results of the various subjects. The data collected are of varying quality and completeness. From time to time the reader is struck by the great amount of theory and interpretation backed up by little concrete evidence * the new jargon imposed upon the reader . . . will tend to limit the future usefulness of this volume. Few will feel the need at this stage of personality studies for such elaborate subdivisions among our major concepts. * The . . . volume suffers . . . from a certain confusion of verbal minutiae.

B Johns Hopkins Hosp 64:447-8 Je '39. W. M. * A prodigious amount of work went into this book. * the wealth of detail is overwhelming * Of special interest is the series of questionnaires designed to elicit qualitative personality distinctions. * Not the least illuminating part of the whole case report is a retrospective account given by the subject some six months later, concerning the conference at which he was confronted by all the workers in the case. There is not enough of this sort of thing done in clinical practice. Usually too much is taken for granted concerning the patient's absorption of what is given him. This is a rather formidable book not to be dealt with lightly. The terminology is rather difficult * an unnecessarily large number of strange terms have been introduced * There is an enormous amount of interesting detail in the book. The reviewer misses in it what he would consider to be the proper emphasis of a dynamic psychology, namely, the importance of the biographical method in which various test situations serve only to give illustrations to the theme which is carried by the story. We do things in a much more economical way in clinical psychiatry, and I should think that the perfection of the method which has been so resolutely attempted by the Harvard group also would finally yield much more economical treatment of the problem.

B Menninger Clinic 3:94 My '39. K. A. M(enninger). * The theory contains brilliant elements, but is rather complicated and neologistic; the techniques, not all new, are well presented. The book is a great forward step in the construction of a science of personality study.

Brit J Psychol 29:432-3 Ap '39. It would be difficult to overrate the value of this study of personality * Though criticism may be levelled at the particular drives and themas selected, there is no doubt that they afford a very valuable and suggestive means for the combined analysis and synthesis of personality. The terminology used is sometimes to be deplored. It may also be objected that the psychoanalytic interests of four of the five members of the Diagnostic council have given an unduly Freudian bent to the themas; and indeed it would seem that the 'Case of Earnst', quoted in full, could be equally well interpreted without recourse to Freudian hypotheses. Prof. Murray, however, has in the Conclusions forestalled and to some extent met criticism on these grounds. But it is particularly with regard to method that the authors and experimenters, especially Prof. Murray, are to be congratulated; firstly, for the collaboration of experimentalists, psychometrists and clinicians, and their attempts to dovetail their results to produce a coherent whole, instead of merely contradicting one another (this collaboration extends to the writing of the book); secondly, for the study of each individual as far as possible as a whole, rather than the investigation of isolated functions in a variety of individuals. It is to be hoped that this study will be the forerunner of others; though it may be difficult to find a similar group of psychologists who can collaborate without losing their individual outlooks and methods of approach. *

Char and Pers 8:261-3 Mr '40. Henry C. Link. The nature of this book is accurately indicated by the title. * Although this book represents the work of a so-called psychological clinic in which a large group of psychoanalysts, psychiatrists, and psychologists participated, it remains essentially a thesis in psychoanalysis. In a sense, the effort is commendable. * However, in the present study the psychoanalytic leanings of the principal author are so dominant that the total result is further confusion rather than synthesis. The book starts with a tirade against scientific or "academic" psychology. This weaves itself in and out through the 742 pages of the book, slows it up, and detracts from the interest. While the analysis of personality is made by a strictly clinical approach, making use of interviews primarily and quantitative tests secondarily, Dr. Murray labors under the impression that the work is rigidly scientific. * Murray appears to hold the belief, common among psychoanalysts, that the scientific criterion "system" can be met by building a verbal system in which the definitions are interlocking. To this end, he makes up words, defines them with loose descriptions, attributes symbols to them, and then expresses himself in terms of equations constructed from functions of the symbols. His verbal system has been developed at the expense of great labor. However, it in no way makes the work more scientific. * In attempting to work out the philosophical fundamentals upon which his theory of personality is based, Murray mixes the philosophies of science indiscriminately, apparently unaware that they are mutually exclusive. For example, his theory rests at one place on the "organismal" view of nature (as expounded by Ritter). This is a Physical conception of nature and permits of no purpose or design. In another place, his theory rests on purpose in nature and is strictly teleological. Teleology is a property solely of the Functional conception of nature. In the Physical conception, the real is Being. In the Functional real is Becoming. The former requires mechanical causation; the latter excludes it. Dr. Murray is not at his best in writing on the philosophy of science. Following the speculative chapters by Murray, the organization of the work and the techniques used are described in detail by the other twenty-one authors listed above. This part of the book appears to the present reviewer to be the chief contribution, not to science, but to clinical psychology. * Murray expresses himself as being highly cautious in drawing conclusions. Every clinician must be, of course, because of the limitations of clinical logic. However, Murray frequently implies causal relations on what most clinical psychologists would regard as exceedingly flimsy grounds. For example, on page 734, he remarks: "In a number of cases it appeared that choice of a vocation had been guided by infantile or adolescent complexes. One subject who had fantasied the death of his parents in an automobile accident (a symbol of intercourse in his case) became a salesman of automobile insurance, which necessitated his hurrying to the scenes of accidents." The implications in this statement are interesting speculations and a priori conclusions of just the kind which the scientific method, and presumably this study, aim to do away with. The analyst or clinician can know there is a causal relationship between such a current form of behavior and such a remote experience, conscious or unconscious, only by going beyond the realm of scientific method into the method of mysticism, through which he can discover such causal efficacy by either intuition or divine revelations.

Isis 31:260 N '39. M. F. A(shley)-M(ontagu). * one of the most important works of its kind to appear within recent years. It is a very genuinely original work, originally conceived and executed, and its aim is to present a theory of personality and a series of techniques by means of which it may be investigated. These things are clearly achieved and Murray's book is bound to have profound repercussions not alone in the field of psychology but in all those disciplines in which the element of the social personality enters. *

J Abn and Social Psychol 35:283-5 Ap '40. *Kurt Lewin.* This is a most courageous book and an important step forward. Murray has set out to investigate personality problems on a level of depth, magnitude, and concreteness usually found only in the work of the psychiatrist or psychoanalyst. He tries to do this with procedures typical of scientific academic psychology. * this book tries to combine an unusual variety of procedures and methods * One gets the feeling that the relation between the experimental procedures and the conclusions in regard to individual differences is not as closely established as one might wish. * The authors

freely emphasize that their book is still a beginning. Probably many psychologists will find the whole procedure much too loose for a "scientific" approach. To my mind, however, it is a great step forward. *

J Appl Psychol 23:636-8 O '39. C. M. Louttit. * the most elaborate attempt to study personality in which many methods have been tried and either rejected or made an integral part of a total research program * In spite of the apparent open-mindedness shown in the preceding quotations, and by the author's consistent denials of finality, the most serious criticism of the whole work is a very real bias [in favor of Freudian psychoanalysis]. * While there are occasional criticisms of a minor nature of psychoanalysis they do not affect the essential influence that these doctrines have had on the investigation. * Lip service is paid to the importance of biological and environmental factors in behavior, but the failure to investigate these is explained on the ground that the Harvard Psychological Clinic had neither medical nor sociological services. Inasmuch as a physician and a sociologist might easily have been substituted for two members of the experimental group, one can only feel that the author's theoretical presuppositions did not require these contributors. * The locus assigned for the drives or needs . . . is naively traditional. * Limitation of space prohibits adequate reference to the many excellent ideas and hypotheses proposed in this volume—likewise to the unfinished and neglected possibilities. There can be no doubt that this is an important book. An original method of investigation is clearly outlined. While there is a definite psychoanalytic bias the authors have considered other methods (even statistical). That Dr. Murray does not consider his work final is indicated in the good advice of the book's last paragraph *

Psychiatry 2:296-7 My '39. *Edward N. Barnhart.* * The project involved three inter-related goals: the methodical construction of a theory of personality, the devising of techniques for analyzing and measuring some of its more important attributes as derived from the theory, and the discovery of basic facts about it. * [the] theoretical material is . . . the most provocative, and yet confusing, parts of the work * there is still the feeling that the possibilities of classification and conceptual development have run away with the theoreticians and it is difficult to see how, no matter how rigorous and well-intentioned they might have been, this structure was readily serviceable for conceptual use and for the interpretation of empirical data * Many of the procedures were highly ingenious and revealing, especially a series of projection tests which . . . seems destined to much greater use in this field. Some of these experiments, however, seem to have been undertaken without much knowledge of other work in the same fields and the statistical presentations are rather uneven in the completeness of their data. Despite these criticisms, what is most needed in the field of "personology" is given here in abundance: stimulating theories and insights which provoke experiments. Certainly an approach has been made here to tap the insights of the psychoanalysts and to make them accessible to the cold but not necessarily unfriendly light of quantitative research, and through such empirical testing to a reformulation of these concepts into usable and coherent form. The integration of theory and experiments carried out here mark the whole project as working in that pattern of thought which has brought understanding to other fields of scientific endeavor.

Psychoanalytic Q 8:389-92 Jl '39. Milton L. Miller. * There are some interesting chapters which deal with such tests as the measurement of types of reaction to frustration, as well as the thematic apperception tests. * From the point of view of emphasizing dynamic psychology in academic circles, the book is commendable. It does not however add much to our present knowledge of psychodynamics, since the approach, limited by the methods, gives us a relatively superficial picture. Many detailed facets of the personality are described in complicated terminology, and an attempt is made to place them in mathematical order. The value of these wide cross sections of personality structures would have been enhanced by the psychoanalysis of a few of the individuals studied. The procedures introduced by Murray and his co-workers, such as the tests for thematic apperception, reaction to frustration, etc., might be useful in psychoanalytic research—in investigating ego capacity, for instance. These tests, likewise, might eventually be of prognostic value: for example, in cases where schizophrenia is suspected.

Psychoanalytic R 27:127-8 Ja '40. * a very thought provoking book and a very worthwhile contribution in the field of the psychology of personality * The approach used by this group of investigators is original in that each is a specialist in investigating personality, but each uses his own technique. * should be of great value to all persons interested in investigating the problem of personality, and from the discussion of the many techniques used, it should be possible to make more thorough studies of individual personalities. Unfortunately, the cost of the book will limit its circulation *

Psychol B 36:288-91 Ap '39. Carney Landis. * The second chapter, "Proposals for a Theory of Personality," is a very long and involved argument advanced by Professor Murray * The theories and concepts are sometimes clearly expressed, but at other times the final product does not seem to justify the long arguments which have been used to maintain or elaborate the point. As a general psychological orientation it is at the same time illuminating and baffling. The third chapter, "Variables of Personality" . . . is extremely difficult reading and probably can be justified only in terms of the outcome. If . . . [it] will lead us . . . to a more complete and better understanding of personality, then the effort has been justified; otherwise, the conceptual framework is merely a logical play on words which seems intuitively correct but has no counterpart in reality. * Chapter IV, "Judgments of Personality," has been written by R. Wolf and H. A. Murray. Interesting material is presented here, bearing on the way in which opinions may be synthetically obtained from putting together both experimental findings and judgments by qualified experts. The authors point out that the data are insufficient and the sources of error many, but it seems that they have approached a problem which is central and important for all psychological work of this variety. Chapter V, "The Genetical Investigation of Personality: Childhood Events," is an excellent statement of the factors out of infancy and childhood which are of real importance in the adult personality. * a great deal of valuable thought and material is presented here which might well be incorporated into general academic textbooks * experiments [in Chapter VI] are given in detail . . . others are sketched in a brief and unsatisfactory fashion * First, the reviewer will present the . . . positive features of this study. The project in its entirety is psychology in the strict sense of that term. * A working terminology is developed, and a real attempt has been made to use the terminology consistently. * This is a frank, open, dynamic approach which draws much of its orientation from Freudian psychoanalysis. However, it is bigger, more inclusive, and more sophisticated * It lacks the mysticism and poetry so inherent in previous psychoanalytic presentations. Intuition is frankly acknowledged, accepted, and given its rightful place in a scientific procedure without recourse to unnecessary spirituality. The explorations are ingenious; most of the methods are shrewd and intelligent * Murray and his colleagues have actually attempted to do what others have spoken of for years. * The negative points which have impressed the reviewer are next in order. Personally, I dislike the terminology and the way in which the terminology all too frequently obscured the meaning which the authors were trying to present. * the vocabulary . . . is at present awkward, at times inexact, and in part meaningless * This volume contains an overload of philosophy and theory. The extended discourse of Chapter II seems unnecessary. Pragmatically speaking, the study should demonstrate its own worth without the long verbal defense. * It is exceedingly difficult and at times impossible for the reader to distinguish between experimentally determined fact and preconceived or derived theory. The two most glaring deficiencies in the work are in the selection of experimental methods and the statistical expression of the results. Many of the experiments are ingenious. They are new and carefully thought out. However, other experiments which are used are unbelievably naive. * several of the experiments reported give no reference to the body of previously determined experimental facts which should have added a great deal of meaning to the material. The presentation of statistical evidence is variable. Certain of the workers present tabular statements of correlation, probable error, etc.; other investigators report their results in such a fashion that only the most careful examination of the entire report gives the reader any notion concerning the true validity of the results. * a more adequate mathematical treatment of the results might have altered the conclusions and

probably would have brought about more positive suggestions for further work. A diagnostic council of experts was continually informed of the outcome of each experiment in order that they might prognosticate the outcome of future experiments as well as suggest new experiments. Their work constituted the keystone of the entire study. Unfortunately, the work of this committee is not adequately reported. * The case history which is given as the proof of the method leaves much to be desired. It is a nice anatomical dissection of a personality, but it certainly is weak in functional prediction, and functional prediction was the end-product desired. Furthermore, the various experimenters who report their findings do so in differing terms. Having read through the complete case, one is impressed by the "sour" or ultrasophisticated attitude of many of the experimenters. * the study . . . has been a gallant attempt; it is overloaded with philosophy, and suffers from poor experimental work in a fair number of experiments. Certain of the workers at the Clinic present brilliant and outstanding experimental findings and formulations which save the project as a whole. This study might be compared to an attempt to reach the top of Mount Everest. Other psychologists may learn by the failures of this expedition as well as other expeditions which have gone before. Those who took part in the expedition know better than anyone else who contributed and who failed. But over and above everything else the project again demonstrates the value of trained investigators who can make use, in an intelligent and ingenious fashion, of all previously accumulated psychological knowledge from whatever source.

Social Res 7:380-3 S '40. *Albert K. Cohen.* * a monument to the fruitfulness of cooperative enterprise in a field of science that has come to resemble a Hobbesian horde of rugged individuals, each brandishing a few deified concepts from behind a fence of polemical barbed wire. H. A. Murray and his coworkers have brought to bear a fine methodological sophistication on current conceptual schema. The experimenters seem to be a fair sample of all the principal "schools" of psychology, but they are endowed with a lively awareness that the scientific validity of a concept lies only in the degree to which, first, it is clear and unequivocal, second, it directs attention to a significant element of the personality, and third, it may be fitted into a generalized theoretical system that "works." * To reproach the authors of this volume for defects of emphasis and omission would be captious. The book does, however, fall short of realizing John Dollard's first criterion for life-history: "the subject must be viewed as a specimen in a cultural series." Murray talks of "the sociologist's assumption that a personality is the sum of its social relationships," but no respectable sociologist would insist on such an assumption. Murray protests rightly that before the personologist can make the fullest use of cultural materials the sociologist must perform his task of analyzing them into significant variables which can be handled by the personologist. But this is no reason why, pending such analysis, more adequate conceptual provision should not be made for group and cultural factors. * Personology must establish a more immediate nexus than even Murray and his associates have done between the individual and the cultural factors, with their varying incidence. The number, the variety, the relative congruity, intensity and imperiousness of the individual's affiliations are quantitative variables of significance. There are also qualitative factors, harder to handle. The frame of reference of this book will prove competent to deal with them but its potentialities have not been exploited. A related defect, attributable in large part to the disproportionate Freudian preoccupation with early childhood, is failure to deal adequately with adolescence. It is increasingly recognized that disturbances attendant on adolescence are not only due to racially uniform organic changes, but that they vary in individuals and cultures, and that an adequate, developmentally oriented psychology must make ample room for the pregnant processes, trauma and conflects engendered in a confused and mobile culture which prolongs adolescence inordinately, defines its limits and appropriate patterns ambiguously, and yet operates as a unique constellation on each individual subject to it. * The fact remains, however, that in this work one can begin to see the seething crucible of modern personology begin to cool and its most useful contents crystallize into an enduring substance.

[B1026.1]

National College of Education. **Curriculum Records of the Children's School.** Evanston, Ill.: Bureau of Publications, the College, 1940. Pp. xii, 606. $2.50.

[B1027]

National Education Association, American Educational Research Association. **Educational Tests and their Uses.** *Review of Educational Research,* Vol. 8, No. 5. Washington, D. C.: the Association, December 1938. Pp. 493-594. $1.00. Paper.

[B1028]

National Education Association, American Educational Research Association. **Pupil Personnel, Guidance, and Counseling.** *Review of Educational Research,* Vol. 3, No. 3. Washington, D. C.: the Association, June 1933. Pp. 183-278. $1.00. Paper.

[B1029]

National Education Association, American Educational Research Association. **Pupil Personnel, Guidance, and Counseling.** *Review of Educational Research,* Vol. 6, No. 2. Washington, D. C.: the Association, April 1936. Pp. 153-275. Out of print.

[B1030]

National Education Association, American Educational Research Association. **Pupil Personnel, Guidance, and Counseling.** *Review of Educational Research,* Vol. 9, No. 2. Washington, D. C.: the Association, April 1939. Pp. 143-252. $1.00. Paper.

[B1031]

National Industrial Conference Board, Inc. **Plans for Rating Employees.** Studies in Personnel Policy, No. 8. New York: the Board, 1938. Pp. 39. $2.00. Paper.

Civil Service Assembly News Letter 4:10 N '38. Donald J. Sublette. * primarily a fact-finding study . . . based on reports from ninety-four companies about equally distributed between manufacturing and non-manufacturing concerns, covering some 600,000 employees. This study is not a critical evaluation of service rating techniques, and for the most effective use by public personnel agencies should be studied in connection with [J. B. Probst's *Service Ratings* (St. Paul, Minn.: Probst Rating System, 1931)] * The various types of rating scales are described, although not critically evaluated. A better analysis will be found in Mr. Probst's bulletin. * Some attention is directed towards the problems involved in the development of rating scales, but in general the reader will be left in the dark as to the best approach to the problem. * In the appendix are illustrated thirteen different service rating forms. Again these are not critically evaluated, and are merely examples of a mine-run of forms, although some idea both as to what to do and what not to do may be gleaned by studying them. * a worthwhile contribution in a rather inadequately covered field and should encourage increased attention on a nation-wide scale to the problem of service ratings.

Personnel Adm 1:11-2 Ja '39. Ward Steward. To the large proportion of Federal officialdom prone to consider the annual rating of employees a part of governmental red tape, this survey may come as a distinct surprise. Not only is the evidence clear that many large and respectable private corporations are making ratings of their employees on a definite and periodic basis, but in roughly one-third of the companies that this particular study covers the practice has been going on for 15 years or more, ample evidence of its dollars-and-cents value. Is it possible that there is something in this rating business after all, something that has been obscured by the apologetic and backhanded manner in which it has been handled in too many Federal jurisdictions? As a study for the harassed public personnel man, this one is excellent. Compressed into a ridiculously small number of pages, the analysis of current rating practices is always cogent, and at times brilliant. Enough uses of ratings are outlined to satisfy even the most inquiring member of the Civil Service Commission's oral examining board, and the appendix is replete with specimen forms which leave the impression that perhaps our familiar forms 3200 and 3201 are not so complicated after all. * To any Federal personnel man interested in making our present rating standards mean something, this study is worth the two dollars, even if he has to pay it out of his own pocket.

[B1032]

NATIONAL INDUSTRIAL CONFERENCE BOARD, INC. **The Use of Tests in Employment and Promotion.** Studies in Personnel Policy, No. 14. New York: the Board, June 1939. Pp. 23. $1.00. Paper.

[B1033]

NATIONAL SOCIETY FOR THE STUDY OF EDUCATION, COMMITTEE ON GUIDANCE, GRAYSON N. KEFAUVER, CHAIRMAN. **Guidance in Educational Institutions.** Thirty-Seventh Yearbook, Part I. Edited by Guy Montrose Whipple. Bloomington, Ill.: Public School Publishing Co., 1938. Pp. viii, 313. Cloth, $2.50; paper, $1.75.

Occupations 17:84-5 O '38. George E. Meyers. * Briefly, one must conclude that even if the writers have had a clear conception of what guidance is, how it is related to the process of education, how it differs from methods of teaching, and how it is related to student personnel work, they have not succeeded in making these matters clear to their readers. However, [there is] much valuable material pertaining to the various services long recognized as essential to educational, voca-

tional and recreational guidance * the book as a whole leaves much to be desired as far as integration is concerned * The book deserves careful reading by all who are trying to do fundamental thinking on guidance. It certainly shows the need for much additional thinking in this challenging field. One wonders as he reads it whether the condition has not already developed against which Arthur J. Jones in his *Principles of Guidance* gave warning in 1930: "There is real danger that the (guidance) movement will become so broad as to be practically meaningless and dissipate itself into the thin air of general education or general instruction."

For an additional review, see B439.

[B1034]

NATIONAL SOCIETY FOR THE STUDY OF EDUCATION. **Intelligence:** Its Nature and Nurture, Two volumes. Thirty-Ninth Yearbook. Bloomington, Ill.: Public School Publishing Co., 1940. Pp. xviii, 471; xviii, 409, xlii. Cloth, $3.00 per volume; paper, $2.25 per volume.

Ed Meth 19:418-9 Ap '40. L(ois) C(offey) M(ossman). * There is apparently difference in definition as to what the members are studying and discussing. There seems to be confusion in the ways individuals interpret data and use statistical techniques. * A rather heavy weighting is given to the implication that tests now available are not to be trusted for measuring young children. * Yet all seem to be using the tests. * The question as to whether the tests measure native intelligence or effective intelligence is not fully dealt with. * It seems to the reviewer that there is then an area which the Yearbook has not considered fully. How is intelligent behavior to be developed; how shall learners build effective intelligence which will enable them to deal with their reality? This would seem to be as important a task as that of measuring the I.Q. Growth studies of individuals in their own group life, showing changes in the behavior of individuals along with detailed records of the processes of group living in which they engaged and of the environmental factors that were involved in what they did we would get some light on how teachers can contribute to the building of effective intelligence.

Sch Executive 59:29 Ap '40. Harold H. Bixler. * An elaborate discussion is given of means by which "cultural" or "environmental" influences on intelligence may be differentiated from those of a "physiological" nature. Indeed, throughout a large portion of the book, this distinction is the implied theme. As might be expected from the diverse beliefs of the group of authors, no accord is reached in the expositions. However, despite the non-conclusive nature of the reports and discussions, much light has been cast on this disputed question. Patterns are outlined for future research which may eventually result in more accord. * A great many of the questions frequently asked of the person working in the fields of testing and guidance are discussed, but in such a fashion as to render the likelihood very remote that any large number of teachers will ever refer to the yearbook for answers to these questions. *

[B1035]

NELSON, M. J. **Tests and Measurements in Elementary Education.** New York: Dryden Press, Inc., 1939. Pp. 351. $2.25.

Ed Abstracts 4:388-9 D '39. Henry D. Rinsland. * The presentation of the history and meaning of measurements is excellent. The presentation of the statistics involved in interpreting test scores is somewhat incomplete and not up to date. Many of the standard measures used for teacher-made tests and standardized tests, covered in previous publications, are not mentioned. * Percentile scores are mentioned but their calculation . . . is not given. Formulas for calculating the mean, standard deviation, correlation, median, and Q are not always given. The interpretation of the standard deviation, and the coefficient of correlation are very brief and incomplete. The meaning of standard deviation as a unit of measurement used for standard scores, R scores, and T scores is not explained, although the formula for calculation of T score is given. In the study of reliability the formula for the probable error of a score is not given, although this is easier understood and has more meaning than the coefficient of reliability. There is no suggestion as to how standardized test scores or teacher's grades may be numerically compared by the use of a standard deviation score, percentiles, or G scores. No mathematical definition for a grade in a marking system is given. No methods of improving teacher's subjective examinations or rating of quality are given. The third part of the book which treats of the use of standardized tests is much better written—fuller and more practical. * The use of tests in arithmetic is more

nearly complete than the use of tests in reading. Treatment of tests in other elementary subjects, such as, language, handwriting, and spelling, are very well done from the standpoint of the use of these tests for improving instructions. Very little of the newer measurements in the social science field are discussed. * The twenty pages devoted to measurement of intelligence are an excellent introduction to the problems for the elementary teacher. * The chapter on the use of educational tests, although brief, is one of the best presentations of the topic that this abstractor has seen in a number of books on educational measurements. One may disagree with Dr. Nelson about what to include in such a text, but this abstractor likes much of the presentation of what he has chosen.

Loyola Ed Digest 15:12 Ja '40. Austin G. Schmidt. * Any book intended for a first course must necessarily be limited to the essentials and follow certain clearly defined patterns. Hence we cannot say that Dr. Nelson's work is strikingly new, nor that it contains much not to be found elsewhere. But it is a clear book, an orderly book, and a book that should be easy to teach. We believe that it compares favorably with other works on its subject.

[B1036]

NETZER, ROYAL F. **The Evaluation of a Technique for Measuring Improvement in Oral Composition.** University of Iowa Studies, New Series, No. 367; Studies in Education, Vol. 10, No. 4; Research Studies in Elementary School Language, No. 2. Iowa City, Iowa: the University, February 1939. Pp. 48. $0.50. Paper.

Loyola Ed Digest 14:8 Ap '39. Austin G. Schmidt. This doctoral dissertation led to the conclusion that the Thurstone technic can be employed for the development of a valid scale for measuring improvement in oral composition. Since the effort was to measure content only, not delivery, what is said of oral composition can be applied to written composition.

Loyola Ed Digest 15:7 D '39. Austin G. Schmidt.

[B1037]

NOBLE, M. C. S., JR. **Practical Measurements for School Administration.** Scranton, Pa.: International Textbook Co., 1939. Pp. xix, 330. $2.50.

Ed Abstracts 5:32 Ja '40. Henry D. Rinsland. * Methods of drawing graphs, kind of graphs illustrated, and the illustrations themselves are very well done—all practical for school executives. * The distinctive contribution of the book lies in the measurement of strictly administrative problems: measuring state-school systems, by use of the Ayres and other indices; the N. E. A. self-survey plan; measuring local systems by surveys; measuring the school plant; measuring teacher efficiency. Each of these is presented with respect to the many subjective factors involved and the functional use of each measure. All show careful study of the literature and excellent choice of materials which are either best or representative of scales and measures in each field. * one does not understand why the work of the Co-operative Study of Secondary-School Standards was not presented. It is too bad that the writer never got beyond the use of the normal curve in suggesting improvements in grading when so much has been done.

H Sch J 23:142-3 Mr '40. Harl R. Douglass. Of books on statistical methods in education there have been more than enough—some mathematically sound, others obviously written by those with less than complete mastery of their field. Most of these have lacked in concrete application to the problems of the practical school man and, when not, have been pointed largely towards testing and experimental procedures. At last there is now in Dr. Noble's book a treatment of statistical methods which "carries the war into Africa": of statistical procedure into such applications as measuring school systems, the school plant, and teaching efficiency as well as intelligence and school efficiency. * The explanations are clear and well illustrated. Examples abound. Unnecessary technical terminology and verbiage have been avoided. Rarely used procedures are not discussed. To Dr. Noble go congratulations for a needed contribution to the wealth of books on statistical methods. *

Loyola Ed Digest 15:10-1 Mr '40. Austin G. Schmidt. * a concise, clear, and well-printed exposition of three things: the fundamentals of statistics, mental tests, and achievement tests. *

Sch and Soc 51:352-3 Mr 16 '40. C. C. Crawford.

Sch Executive 59:32 Mr '40. N. L. Engelhardt, Jr. * It is clear that a comprehensive handbook in measurements is needed which will clearly, simply, and frankly state the meanings and shortcomings of educational measuring devices and methods of interpretation. Mr. Noble's new book has done just this. It is de-

voted to problems which confront teachers and administrators in the operation of schools. Theories of statistics, pure methods of research, and elaborate treatments of statistics have been largely eliminated. * This book represents a forward step in the development of the use of educational measurements. Emphasis has been shifted from the programs for testing intelligence and achievement to a more comprehensive portrayal of types of measurements useful in other areas of school work.

[B1037.1]
OAKLEY, C. A., AND MACRAE, ANGUS. **Handbook of Vocational Guidance:** Secondary and Public Schools. With a section by Edith O. Mercer and a preface by C. S. Myers. London: University of London Press, Ltd., 1937. Pp. xvii, 337. 10s. 6d.

Brit Med J 3983:969 My 8 '37. * The modest, almost depreciatory tone of the claims made for this book disarm criticism. But we think that space might have been found for a fuller description of the methods and tests themselves, and for more guidance concerning the actual choice of tests. Perhaps, also, insufficient emphasis is placed upon the importance and the actual diagnosis of the "emotional background of success in work." It seems to us that wider use could be made of "vocational guidance" as a means of discovering those children who are in need of expert medical and psychological treatment. It is not enough to know that "John is unfit to be a doctor": it is more important to find out whether his unfitness is really "constitutional" or intellectual in origin, or whether it is due to faulty emotional habits or adjustments. It is more important still that these emotional faults should be properly treated. When further experience of vocational guidance has been obtained it will probably be found that occupations can be classified much more simply than Chapter VI of this book would suggest. Many of the intellectual, physical, manual, and other "dexterities" which are studied by persons engaged in vocational testing will take a subordinate place in career selection in comparison with the importance that will be accorded to emotional, social, and medical factors. * [contains a] short (and we feel inadequate) chapter on the technique of vocational guidance * [the survey] of "occupational requirements" . . . occupies nearly 200 pages, and contains valuable information, though with a good deal of repetition. This volume should be a useful reference book for teachers, doctors, and parents, and others who are concerned with the choice of a career for young people.

For additional reviews, see B443.

[B1038]
O'CONNOR, JOHNSON. **Two Knowledge Tests:** Architectural Technical Vocabulary, Worksample 250, and Knowledge of Painting, Worksample 183. Human Engineering Laboratory, Technical Report No. 32. Boston, Mass.: the Laboratory, 1939. Pp. vi, 60. $1.00. Paper, mimeographed.

[B1039]
ODENWELLER, ARTHUR LEONARD. **Predicting the Quality of Teaching:** The Predictive Value of Certain Traits for Effectiveness in Teaching. Columbia University, Teachers College, Contributions to Education No. 676. New York: Bureau of Publications, the College, 1936. Pp. xi, 158. $1.60.

B Int Bur Ed 11:33 q 1 '37.
Ed Res B 18:84-5 Mr '39. Robert W. Richey. * Administrators, teachers, and college personnel officers should find this book interesting and helpful.

For additional reviews, see B445.

[B1040]
ORDWAY, SAMUEL H., JR., AND O'BRIEN, JAMES C. **An Approach to More Objective Oral Tests.** Edited by M. Freyd. Society for Personnel Administration, Pamphlet No. 2. Washington, D. C.: the Society, June 1939. Pp. 31. $0.25. Paper.

Civil Service Assembly News Letter 5:7-8 S '39. W. V. Bingham. * reflects the experience of civil service administrators with a legal background, intimately familiar with the principles of evidence and the rules which courts have evolved governing admissibility, competence, and relevance. The writers modestly disclaim originality for either the theory or the practice here described. But the reviewer has not previously seen any statement of the problem so clearly formulated, nor any procedure suggested which offers greater promise of progress toward valid oral testing.
Occupations 18:156 N '39. A real contribution * features the application of evidence to the oral examination process, stresses forecasting future accomplishment from evidence of past accomplishment, and provides for ratings on quality as well as quantity of past accomplishment.

[B1040.1]
ORLEANS, JACOB S. **Measurement in Education.** New York: Thomas Nelson and Sons, 1937. Pp. xvi, 11-461. $2.75.

Ed Forum 3:230 Ja '39. * the theory underlying the use of tests is given emphasis, specific tests are mentioned only for the sake of illustration, and . . . stress is placed upon tests which have been constructed by the teacher * A clear notion of intelligence and intelligence tests is presented * There is a pertinent chapter on ability grouping and this is followed by an important chapter on the improvement of instruction. * The splendid appendix gives specific directions for constructing objective tests, which are illustrated by samples of the various types. The volume is designed to evaluate the place of testing in an instructional program rather than as a research device, and it serves well the function for which it is planned.

For additional reviews, see B446.

[B1041]
PATERSON, DONALD G., AND DARLEY, JOHN G., WITH THE ASSISTANCE OF RICHARD M. ELLIOTT. **Men, Women, and Jobs:** A Study in Human Engineering: A Review of the Studies of the Committee on Individual Diagnosis and Training. University of Minnesota, Employment Stabilization Research Institute. Minneapolis, Minn.: University of Minnesota Press, 1936. Pp. v, 145. $2.00; text edition, $1.50. (London: Oxford University Press. 9s.)

Am Econ R 27:372 Je '37. * will be of value to personnel officers, educators and civil service boards.
Civil Service Assembly News Letter 2:6 D '36.
Ed Res B 18:58 F '39. J. E. Bathurst. * quite readable, the facts presented have been well selected and organized * Those interested in methods and techniques of research in this field will find a wealth of useful information. The book is a signal contribution to basic scientific methods and procedures in solving the problem of human wastage in the vocational area. The ordinary layman may wonder if the results justify the enormous labor involved. The net results do seem rather scanty as far as conclusions are concerned, but the techniques evolved will no doubt be useful as a point of departure in developing more reliable and more useful techniques in this field. In the meantime, it is doubtful if society has yet reached the point where such refined techniques can be used *

For additional reviews, see B447.

[B1042]
PATERSON, DONALD G.; SCHNEIDLER, GWENDOLEN C.; AND WILLIAMSON, EDMOND G. **Student Guidance Techniques:** A Handbook for Counselors in High Schools and Colleges. New York: McGraw-Hill Book Co., Inc., 1938. Pp. xviii, 316. $3.00. (London: McGraw-Hill Publishing Co., Ltd. 18s.)

AVA J 13:253 N '38. F(ranklin) J. K(eller).
* develops in considerable detail an account of technical diagnostic instruments * Particularly interesting to members of A.V.A. will be the chapter on the treatment of vocational problems. *

J Ed Psychol 30:78-80 Ja '39. Mary Theresa Scudder. * Teachers who are giving courses in counseling will find this handbook valuable, and those who are engaged actively in guidance will discover some techniques which will help them in the diagnosis of the problems of students. * Only a few pages are devoted to a description of techniques other than tests, scant space being given to rating scales and observation. * a book which is planned to assist counselors in solving intricate problems of adjustment should not ignore to so great an extent the other techniques through the use of which one gains some insight into the difficulties besetting students. Tests are only one method of approach, and one which is still open to much controversial dispute. * If the problems presented by students are complex, involving so many facets, it is unfortunate that the discussion should be more or less limited to those concerned with educational guidance. * A stronger emphasis might well have been placed on the importance of trying to interpret one's findings correctly and, likewise, on the difficulty of interpreting them wisely, irrespective of the technique employed. * Greater stress might also have been made in regard to the counselor's need of a broad cultural background and a rich experience in life contacts * However, in spite of these criticisms, the book is recommended to those who are interested in personnel work, but with the final caution that tests do not tell all the story, especially those tests concerned with personality and aptitudes.

J Ed Res 32:140-1 O '38. Carter V. Good.

J Higher Ed 10:174 Mr '39. D. H. Gardiner. All educators who profess to advise students whether in secondary or higher education should read this book. To get the full value from it, however, Williamson and Darley's *Student Personnel Work* should be read first as this treatise is in the nature of a supplement. * Particularly significant is the chapter on "Personality Tests and Questionnaires" wherein constructive suggestions are made for the development of instruments in this debatable field of guidance. Especially valuable are the author's pungent criticisms of many widely held but poorly thought-out personnel principles. * The final chapter should be of great value to persons who contemplate entering the guidance field. It enumerates the qualifications for counselors and should excite considerable interest and discussion. The authors have contributed another vastly significant, and above all, useful volume to the field of student personnel service. The reviewer hopes that they will continue their contributions, giving special emphasis to adjustment techniques, as this volume stresses primarily diagnostic measures.

For additional reviews, see B448.

[B1043]
PERRY, RAYMOND CARVER. **A Group Factor Analysis of the Adjustment Questionnaire.** University of Southern California, Southern California Education Monographs, 1933-34 Series, No. 5. Los Angeles, Calif.: University of Southern California Press, 1934. Pp. xi, 93. $1.50.

Char and Pers 3:169-70 D '34. G. W. Allport. * a typical American doctoral dissertation in the field of the psychology of personality * The principal object of the study was to find how many independent (non-correlating) group factors are measured by the tests. According to the author there are four: one intellectual and three non-intellectual. For the latter the author finds the omnibus test of Bernreuter to be the most adequate measure— a finding not surprising in view of the fact that this test borrows heavily from some of the other scales employed, and itself figures most prominently in the battery. * The premises of this type of research are perhaps more significant than its results. Three of its premises are of special interest: the repudiation of linguistic analysis and full reliance upon statistical analysis, the preference for meager information concerning large numbers of subjects rather than for full information concerning a few, and the belief that it is desirable to discover independent (non-correlating) elements in personality. All three of these presuppositions are alien to the psychological point of view that favors a *direct* experimental or clinical approach to the problems of personality. * These criticisms apply to Dr. Perry's study no more than to every investigation employing the same presuppositions and methods. Dr. Perry's research is a competent representative of its type. The pity is that the type should be quite so common and influential as it is.

J Appl Psychol 18:725-6 O '34. M. E. Broom.
* This study is of significance because of its scope, and because of the care with which it was done. * The study should be of considerable interest to counsellors in secondary schools and colleges * the volume . . . is attractively bound. The printing is excellent. *

For additional reviews, see B451.

[B1044]

PETERS, MARY FRIDIANA. **A Comparative Study of Some Measures of Emotional Instability in School Children.** Lafayette, Ind.: St. Francis Community Press, 1939. Pp. xvii, 71. $2.00.

Loyola Ed Digest 15:8-9 Mr '40. Austin G. Schmidt. Using as her subjects 487 children in two elementary parochial schools, the author measured emotional stability by means of the Snoddy Stabilimeter Test and compared the resultant data with measures of emotional stability obtained from the Porteus Maze Test, the Mathews Personal Data Sheet, and teachers' estimates. * The author concludes that children in the elementary school are frequently overstimulated, that the emphasis on speed under competitive conditions can be productive of harm, and that the emotional health of teachers has a great influence upon the stability of children. While these conclusions are no doubt justified by the data, there is need for caution in applying them to present educational procedures. Dr. Snoddy has done notable work in the measurement of emotional stability, yet it must be recognized that the measurement of all such traits is only in its infancy. 'Over-stimulation' is an easy term to use, but it remains to be determined just what happens to a child who in the judgment of a psychologist is overstimulated. While we agree with Garry Meyers and the author that high-pressure classroom methods may easily disturb a child here and now, and may possibly produce injurious and lasting after-effects, the opposite extreme of slow motion, complacency, and phlegmatic satisfaction with present conditions is equally to be avoided.

[B1045]

PICKETT, HALE. **An Analysis of Proofs and Solutions of Exercises Used in Plane Geometry Tests.** Columbia University, Teachers College, Contributions to Education No. 747. William D. Reeve, faculty sponsor. New York: Bureau of Publications, the College, 1938. Pp. vii, 120. $1.60.

Ed Res B 19:115 F 14 '40. Harold Fawcett. Within recent years considerable attention has been given to the selection of what might be called the "essential" theorems of plane geometry. Mr. Pickett has studied this problem with great thoroughness and his "revised list of theorems" is derived from a most careful analysis of the geometry examinations given by certain public and state examining bodies during the period from 1923 to 1935 inclusive. *

H Sch J 22:255 O '39. H. F. Munch. * thorough and significant * should be widely read by mathematics teachers in order that they may keep informed of some of the trends in geometry teaching.

Loyola Ed Digest 14:6 D '38. Austin G. Schmidt. * The data and conclusions should prove of assistance to those who are interested in further improvements in the content of plane geometry.

Math Teach 32:42 Ja '39. I. S. Turner.

Nat Math Mag 14:292 F '40. Harold Fawcett. Within recent years considerable attention has been given to the selection of what might be called the "essential" theorems of plane geometry. Dr. Pickett has studied this problem with great thoroughness and his "revised list of theorems" is derived from a most careful analysis of the geometry examinations given by certain public and state examining bodies during the period from 1923 to 1935, inclusive. *

Sch Sci and Math 39:194 F '39. Joseph J. Urbancek. The book is the outcome of a study in which proofs and solutions of exercises used in plane geometry tests were analyzed. The writer collected geometry tests for the years 1923-1935 from five different sources. * the reader will find it profitable to read the book. The study shows a list of only 58 theorems needed to solve the problems in the 150 examinations.

Sci Ed 22:377 D '38. C(larence) M. P(ruitt).

Scripta Mathematica 6:47-8 Mr '39. Elizabeth M. Cooper. * This minimum list is interesting and may prove useful in simplifying and strengthening mathematics curricula, although to this reviewer the criteria of choice seems somewhat limited and artificial.

[B1046]

PORTEUS, S. D. **Primitive Intelligence and Environment.** New York: Macmillan Co., 1937. Pp. ix, 325. $3.00. (London: Macmillan & Co., Ltd. 15s.)

Am J Orthopsychiatry 9:658-9 Jl '39. (Samuel J.) Beck. As a work in psychology this book makes good anthropology; also most delightful travel reading. By these same tokens it is, for a change, a book in our field that makes pleasing reading. * As to the psychological findings in Porteus' expedition, one reads fourteen chapters of the book before finally coming to them. But really, you will not mind. Descriptions of land and people are too fascinating. An exciting and even a hero story now and then (pp. 166; 187) are thrilling. It is one of those books which you start reading the tired part of the evening and find yourself staying with it somewhere around the small hours of the morning. * The chief profit in the book to the psychologist as psychologist, would be in the orientation it provides relative to testing (a) for racial differences; (b) testing among those races which the white, in its conceit, likes to call "inferior" or primitive. The pitfalls appear to be many, hence the qualifications of the findings equally guarded. The author goes into detail regarding these difficulties. While he takes issue with Klineberg on a number of points, one can not help feeling but that in respect to underlying sympathies these two students are in essential agreement. To this reviewer the qualitative impressions which the book leaves are much more valuable than the quantitative. These latter justly take up only a small proportion of the 318 pages. Running through the work is a conviction whether intended by the author or not, of the invincible dynamism which the need for survival is, and the extraordinary ingenuity which man, among his fellow animals, can employ in shaping his adaptive mechanisms. * Returning to the psychologist as psychologist: the evidence which Porteus offers goes only skin deep. Nor does this reviewer believe that the author intended any profounder claims for his findings as evidence concerning racial differences. * He promises another volume on these aspects. The chief gain to the psychologist will, therefore, be information concerning tests, general methods, and pitfalls, in any program of psychometric investigation of race differences. Only one annoyance this reviewer confesses to, namely, the lack of some map, if only a sketch map, of the two areas traversed by the author. *

Geog R 28:517-8 Jl '38. Clark Wissler. * a study of adjustments to desert environments based on observations in the field and not a product of the library and the armchair. *

J Nerv and Mental Dis 90:667-9 N '39. * The first chapters form a fascinating account of the physical settings dealt with * There is much stimulating material here for the student of mental and psychical configurations in primitive groups; especially in those parts stressing the observable effects of physical environment. We would wish that the author's approach had had recourse to certain of the basic standpoints of psychoanalytic anthropological investigation as worked out by Roheim; the results of which give access to levels of genetic psychical and instinctual formations that cannot be comprised in the conscious orientations dealt with by mental tests.

J Social Philos 4:92-3 O '38. Kingsley Davis. * Professor Porteus, up to his old tricks, has written another book to prove the existence of racial differences in intelligence. Since he seems confused as to the nature of race, culture, and logic, this is a daring undertaking. His main resources in accomplishing the feat are a deep race prejudice (inadvertently but consistently manifest) and a few psychological tests. For him the Japanese and Chinese are "races," as are the Portuguese * His definition of race difference is ambiguous; generally he regards it as an inherent difference, and spends much time trying to eliminate cultural determinants of test performance. * The bulk of the volume is a travelogue * would make interesting reading for admirers of *Trader Horn*. The work was financed by the Carnegie Corporation of New York. *

Med J Australia 25:821-2 My 7 '38. * a very gracefully written book * Unfortunately, he was able to come in contact with only a very small group of Bushmen, numbering 25. They had had very little contact with whites, and were given the tests through interpreters. The principal test used was the Porteus maze, for though, as Professor Porteus says, it "is by itself far from being a satisfactory measure of intelligence," yet he regards its performance as an index of that complex of qualities which "seem to be valuable in making adjustments to our kind of society." This is important, because it is our kind of society which is being imposed on the native, and the author holds that "the question as to who is the most intelligent by native standards is beside the mark." * [this book] will be appreciated because of its candid examination of the tests used, for its summary of the work of this type previously done in Australia, for the comparison with research carried out amongst some Asiatic primitives, for the courteous attention paid to criticisms of earlier work, and as an indication of the value of psychological testing of peoples as a means of establishing race differences and cultural adaptability or its lack.

Sat R Lit 16:16 Jl 31 '37. Homer W. Smith.
* [Porteus] defines intelligence as "the capacity to enlarge the significance of environment," that is, he would go beyond mere adaptation, which is perfect in many lower animals, and include the potentialities for constructive interpretation. One wonders if this definition of intelligence has not outrun the methods by which it is being measured. But there is no argument that the author has a splendid talent for understanding and portraying primitive life, and for capturing those overtones which, so far as culture is concerned, distinguish man both black and white from his humanoid cousins.

Sociol and Social Res 22:294-5 Ja-F '38. E(mory) S. B(ogardus). * valuable treatise *
For additional reviews, see B454.

[B1047]

PREU, PAUL W. **Outline of Psychiatric Case-Study:** A Practical Handbook. Foreword by Eugen Kahn. New York: Paul B. Hoeber, Inc., 1939. Pp. xiv, 140. $1.85.

Am J Orthopsychiatry 10:408 Ap '40. T. H. Haines. * presents the outlines of psychiatric history-taking and of mental examination, developed at the New Haven Hospital, under the conviction that very full and careful studies of a few cases afford the student of psychiatry his best grounding in the subject. * In each division of the outline, topics are presented and questions are provided so skillfully that it is hard to imagine any important mental pathology escaping the attention of an examiner who uses this outline as his guide. It is well designed for the orderly and expeditious securing of all the information required in an adequate psychiatric study. For all who are interested in personality studies—psychiatrists, other physicians, psychologists, sociologists, anthropologists—Doctor Preu has performed a signal service in bringing this examinational guide to its present form and in making it available.

Am J Psychiatry 96:1258 Mr '40. K(arl) M. B(owman). * The material is covered systematically and, in general, along the lines accepted by American psychiatry. Certain individual attitudes appear from time to time, but no more than would be expected from any author of a book of this type. The reviewer finds himself in hearty accord with the statement: "Technical medical and psychological terms should not be used if it is possible to avoid them." The general directions given for taking a history and for making a mental examination are in keeping with the best psychiatric thought. The book is a very satisfactory one to place in the hands of all beginners in psychiatry.

Am J Psychol 53:475 Jl '40. Lowell S. Selling. This little manual is quite similar to one previously put out by Chaney several years ago. * The book is to be commended because it is so complete, but it is to be condemned because of the lack of sample questions given to enable the psychiatrist to make a study of patients, who does not carry with him standard, exemplary replies to questions. In other words, the student or beginning psychiatrist picks up this book with the idea of carrying on a psychiatric examination is provided with an extensive prospectus on how the history and examination are to be made but is not provided with any means of evaluating the responses and reactions that he gets. A number of words are used in improper text such as the term "visual field" with respect to hallucinations, the term being more properly used with sensory examination of the eye. There is no glossary to explain the technical terms to beginners for whom the book is supposedly designed.

Ann Internal Med 13:556 S '39. H. M. M. This outline seems essentially an expansion of the well-known, standard Kirby and Cheney Guide. Dr. Preu indicates most of the questions he considers necessary to obtain adequate information about an individual. He very wisely stresses the importance of putting things down in the terms actually used by the patient and the informant—not the historian's retrospective impression of what was said. The observations on history-taking technic (pp. 4-6) and method of mental examination (pp. 74-76) are good, although we do feel that the mental examination should contain only items directly observed at that time by the examiner (p. 81). Too much stress is laid on school record as a criterion of intelligence. We should like to have seen a section on the examination of uncoöperative patients included. We dislike the use of such obscure terms as "anancasm" (none of our dictionaries listed it). It is very easy to read. Like most guides, it should be most useful in making the historian think about things he wants to know about a well-studied case. Its skeleton outlines for practical use (no one could possibly sit down with it at a history-taking session) are a little lost in the mass of questions. It is a good guide for institutional beginners. But we wish someone, sometime, would devise a satisfactory outline of mental examination for non-psychotic, office and general hospital patients.

Arch Neurology and Psychiatry 41:1276 Je '39. * a valuable addendum to the library of a training institution, which may prove useful as a time-saving device for the senior resident or clinical director responsible for teaching elementary technics to the novice.

B Johns Hopkins Hosp 64:448 Je '39. W. M. * a good book, containing in its small, compact size a wealth of information, the usefulness of which, I am sure, psychiatric experience generally will corroborate * Long ago, we resorted to the practice of following the Complaint directly with the Present Illness, in order to get a rounded view of the current situation. This seems to us . . . definitely preferable to the older system which is perpetuated in Dr. Preu's book * However, this constitutes a minor matter in comparison with the general uniform excellence of the book.

J Am Med Assn 113:1157 S 16 '39. * an improvement on the older manuals * The paragraphs are brief, there is much abbreviation, and in a number of places words are inserted in lieu of extended explanations. In such a case it is obvious, of course, that the beginner or the nonpsychiatrically trained person would be obliged to have ancillary information if he wished to use the present volume as a guide. In some places the author shows a lack of knowledge of terminology used outside the field of psychiatry, for in examining mental changes in the visual sphere he uses the term "visual field," which of course applies to campimetry. Errors of this sort are not common in the book, however, and as a whole it can be considered a useful little handbook for the beginner provided he is given training and does not depend entirely on this volume. Most teachers, however, will find that it is more profitable to use their own methods of teaching how to make a psychiatric examination; but in lieu of the teacher's own guide the present volume is the best of its kind that has been produced so far to serve its purpose.

Med Times 67:345 Jl '39. Joseph Smith. * should be very helpful to psychiatric workers in getting anamneses and as an aid in the mental examination of psychiatric patients *

Mental Hyg (New York) 24:317 Ap '40. Nolan D. C. Lewis. * a worthy attempt to encourage careful, systematic recording of the pertinent events in the development of the individual, his difficulties in life, and the general and special factors that have contributed to the total situation * will certainly prove to be a valuable time-saver for the beginner, and at the same time it will be of value in orienting him in those procedures that are of outstanding importance in psychiatric medicine.

Psychiatric Q 14:650-1 Jl '40. * a practical outline of the psychiatric case-study. It has been modified repeatedly after adequate clinical use. * The book consists principally of sections dealing with the taking of the psychiatric history and the performance of the mental examination. Other examinations are described, the Snedden Vocabulary Test is outlined in some detail, charts and forms are reproduced, and an inclusive index is appended. Preu's treatment of the sexual history, the family emotional setting, the method of the mental examination, and the examination of the sensorium, mental grasp and capacity are excellent. * The book is surprisingly free from error of all types. One might quarrel with a usage on page 42; the order on page 44; the repetitions inherent in this system of recording medical and social histories; the insistence upon documentation by verbatim quotations at many points; and the inclusion of first attacks in the history of the present illness. These, however, are minor things. Preu's "Outline" is systematic, comprehensible, and practical. May its wide use endow with these virtues many of this reviewer's colleagues!

Psychoanalytic Q 9:420-2 Jl '40. J. Kasanin. * The present volume is an excellent reflection of that period in psychiatry when a good record was all that was necessary in a good psychiatric clinic. * It contains numerous questions which seem to be pertinent and intelligent and I have no doubt that if properly answered they would give us a good deal of knowledge about the patient's background, his physical and psychological reactions and his progress in the hospital. But there is the practical doubt that anyone would want to follow an outline containing one hundred and thirty-three pages of questions even if one had the leisure of a university psychiatric clinic. However, the outline is very satisfactory and one could undoubtedly learn a great deal by following it. The objection which the reviewer raises is not one of the value of this particular outline but the value of any complete formal outline used in the study of psychiatric cases. It seems to me that a perfectionistic pride in writing up a complete record with all questions properly and intelligently answered contains the danger of becoming an end in itself rather than the means of helping the patient. After all any psychiatrist has only a certain amount of time and energy at his disposal for each patient, and if the emphasis be on a formalist-ritualist compulsion to complete a good record which somebody some time might use for some research, one may easily lose track of the patient himself. There is too much danger in the purely historical point of view as contrasted to the therapeutic attitude which aims to mobilize as soon as possible the positive assets of the individual so that they can be worked with immediately in order to help the patient in his struggle for mental health. * The author of the outline carefully avoids any mention in the examination of the transference which probably is the most important basis for any plan for therapy. Somehow one has the feeling in looking over this particular outline that one is bagging around a skeleton rather than dealing with the flesh and blood of a human being. Perhaps this reflects too much the disillusionment of the reviewer in the formal, mechanistic approach to the problems of the psychotic patient, but this disillusionment must be shared by many who have more than a passing interest in problems of psychiatry and psychotherapy.

[B1048]

PULLIAS, EARL V. **Variability in Results from New-Achievement Tests.** Duke University Research Studies in Education, No. 2. Foreword by William A. Brownell. Durham, N. C.: Duke University Press, 1937. Pp. 100. $1.00. Paper. (London: Cambridge University Press. 4s. 6d.)

Ed Adm and Sup 25:77-8 Ja '39. Francis P. Robinson. * Pullias centers his study on the intercorrelations between the results of tests made by different teachers for the same assignment, between the results of final examinations made by different teachers for the same total course, and between the results of different standardized tests whose authors claim

that they measure common fields. * [The results indicate] excessive variability in objective test results. * Objectivity in scoring, according to the author, has tended to blind test users to other and very important causes of unreliability. The reviewer's main criticism of a rather straightforward, clean cut problem is the author's frequent averaging of correlation coefficients and the averaging of average correlations.

Personnel Adm 1:11 F '39.
For additional reviews, see B457.

[B1049]

PURNELL, RUSSELL T., AND DAVIS, ROBERT A. **Directed Learning by Teacher-Made Tests.** Boulder, Colo.: Bureau of Publications, Extension Division, University of Colorado, 1939. Pp. vii, 92. $1.00.

Ed Abstracts 4:389 D '39. Henry D. Rinsland. * a real contribution to the growing technique of evaluation. A distinctive contribution of the book is the clear discussion and illustration of the fact that tests must be built for particular purposes and that the nature of a test is contingent upon these purposes as well as the analysis of teaching objectives. A further contribution is the presentation of methods of formulating, analyzing and defining objectives of courses of study or programs, which have not been well covered by the usual objective test concerned more with measuring facts and information. * [This reviewer does not agree with the author's] effort to belittle skills, information and knowledge, for, as a matter of fact most of their items testing higher learnings—reasoning and thinking—are in themselves based upon facts. * This little book serves to organize and synchronize much valuable material scattered in many pages of many publications, and as such it should be a milestone in our progress towards achieving evaluations which will lead to more scientific and comprehensive measurement in the future.

Loyola Ed Digest 15:6 D '39. Austin G. Schmidt.

[B1049.1]

QUINN, P. JACK. **Experiments and Research on the Production of Tonal Memory Records.** Human Engineering Laboratory, Technical Report No. 60. Boston, Mass.: the Laboratory, 1940. Pp. vi, 22. $1.00. Paper, mimeographed.

[B1050]

REMMERS, H. H., EDITOR. **Further Studies in Attitudes, Series III.** Purdue University, Division of Educational Reference, Studies in Higher Education, [No.] 34. Lafayette, Ind.: the University, September 1938. Pp. 151. $1.50. Paper.

Ed Res B 19:56 Ja 17 '40. Lloyd L. Ramseyer. Only by the combined data secured from many studies can we hope eventually to learn to understand the factors involved in the formation of attitudes. This publication contains a series of excellent contributions toward this end. Eleven studies made by the editor and his associates are reported. In some of these studies an adaptation of the Thurstone technique, called the general-attitude scale, has been employed as the measuring instrument. Anyone deeply concerned with the study of attitudes should not miss reading this publication. Although too highly mathematical for the average reader, the specialist will find much in it of value.

Loyola Ed Digest 14:7 Ja '39. Austin G. Schmidt. Purdue University has done some conspicuously good work in the study of attitudes. The present volume contains eleven new studies, some of course more valuable and interesting than others. The reviewer takes sharp issue with Lee Hart Dixon, who on page 130 reports a study entitled "The Validation of a Three-Axial Scale to Measure Attitudes toward Any Existing or Proposed Social Activity." The first conclusion drawn by Mr. Dixon (p. 141) is that "while it is not statistically certain that the . . . scale . . . will always be valid . . . the chances of its being valid . . . are great." Nothing whatsoever in the study has the slightest bearing upon validity. All that Mr. Dixon established was the extent to which different portions of the measuring instrument measure the same thing. He knows no more now than he did before as to what that thing is. It may be an attitude and it may not be an attitude. An attitude is an inclination on the part of an individual to embrace a certain point of view or to follow a certain line of action. The greatest difficulty in applying any so-called attitude test is to distinguish between a mere knowledge of the socially acceptable response and an inclination to act in one way rather than in another. Delinquent boys can score high on a civic-attitude test; they know the right answer, but what their attitude may be is an entirely different question. Mr. Dixon used no external criterion. He established nothing as regards validity. Even Homer nods, and we feel that Dr. Remmers, usually a cautious worker, nodded when he gave his editorial approval to the title and conclusions of this study.

[B1051]
RICHARDSON, H. D. **Analytical Devices in Guidance and Counseling.** Basic Occupational Plans, No. 3. Chicago, Ill.: Science Research Associates, 1940. Pp. 63. $1.00. Paper, lithotyped.

[B1052]
RINSLAND, HENRY DANIEL. **Constructing Tests and Grading in Elementary and High School Subjects.** New York: Prentice-Hall, Inc., 1937. Pp. xvi, 323, $2.85. (London: George G. Harrap & Co., Ltd., 1938. 10s. 6d.)

Brit J Psychol 29:434-5 Ap '39. * a thorough and very detailed account of 'short answer' tests and examinations of every kind and in every subject * To those who use this kind of test it will be of value. The detailed discussion of methods of scoring . . . and of grading pupils . . . should be of interest to those in charge of large public examinations. But a teacher examining a single class should approach it with caution, since he cannot assume that the performances of a small sample of children will show a normal distribution. From the author's further dictum that "it is only through the experience and improvement of our measuring instruments of to-day, in the simpler phases of human learning, that we can push forward our scientific frontiers to a more accurate and comprehensive description of the personality of the whole child—the new centre of the educational world," we must, however, beg leave to dissent.

J Consulting Psychol 4:37-8 Ja-F '40. Gertrude Hildreth. * The book contains practical, commonsense suggestions which specialists in the field too often assume the beginner will think of himself. * No information is given as to how specific items are selected for experimental tests, how items are evaluated, or why they are retained in a final edition. * Applying the term "clinical grading system" as the author does to the grading scheme proposed, based on the "standard deviation" principle, is confusing to one who thinks of the term "clinical" as applying to the all-around study of individuals. There would seem to be little justification for calling a modification of the time-honored T-score scaling method a "clinical grading system." The author's modification of the T-score scale which he calls the R-score scaling method is, however, a practically useful contribution. * In this publication not much is contributed that is fundamentally new, but the illustrative material is original in character. A good list of references is appended to each chapter *

J Ed Res 32:620 Ap '39. C. W. Odell. By far the larger portion of this book is devoted to specimens and illustrations of single objective test elements and of short objective tests with relevant suggestions and comments. The many examples given make it one of the few largest single sources of such material and as such it will undoubtedly be frequently consulted by many teachers and others. The statements of principles and the discussions of various matters connected with testing and marking are, in general, quite direct and clearly stated, and should be understood with little difficulty. A rather unusual and distinctly helpful feature is that the author presents examples of both poor and good test elements with comments which point out why the latter are better. In some cases, however, only poor examples are given whereas it would seem better in all cases to include good ones also. * both the examples and the discussion are primarily concerned with the relatively mechanical aspects of measurement, and with the testing of memorized, factual material rather than with the objectives which should underlie measurement, and with the testing of those mental processes which, especially in the high school, are coming to be more and more accorded a place of prime importance * the author seems to condemn the essay or discussion examination to a position of little or no importance. Until objective tests are devised which will measure achievement of certain sorts far better than they do at present, it appears that the essay examination is needed. * Considerable attention is given to an R scale for use in marking, but this is so similar to the already well known T and Z scales and possesses so little, if any, advantage over them that its introduction seems unjustified. Moreover, it is expressed in terms of 100 points and because of the many misconceptions connected with the 100 point percent marking system, it seems to the reviewer desirable to avoid employing this same number. Despite the large number of examples, some of which present original forms, several types of fairly frequent use and some merit are omitted. * The discussion dealing with the criteria of a good examination is decidedly brief and weak. In portions of the book the absence of a sufficiently critical attitude is apparent. In conclusion, the reviewer believes that if used in class with the proper critical supplementation by the instructor this volume should be decidedly use-

ful to students preparing to teach. Likewise teachers in service who are sufficiently well grounded in the field of educational measurements to be familiar with many of the attitudes and principles not presented in this book will find it helpful as a source of new ideas of objective test construction. It does not, however, appear to merit strong recommendation as a sole guide or source for the individual who needs to construct tests.

Jun Col J 9:160-1 D '38. * has much that is of decided value to the junior college instructor * The numerous concrete rules and suggestions for construction of the different types of test items . . . should prove particularly helpful, even if one may have some doubt concerning the author's claim that by following them the teacher "will be able to build tests that are as reliable as, or, in many cases, more reliable than, many published standardized tests." The discussion of improving marks and grading systems is stimulating and helpful even though a careful reader may not necessarily accept every statement without qualification *

For additional reviews, see B466.

[B1053]

Rogers, Carl R. **The Clinical Treatment of the Problem Child.** Boston, Mass.: Houghton Mifflin Co., 1939. Pp. xiii, 393. $3.00. (London: George Allen & Unwin, Ltd. 15s.)

Am J Orthopsychiatry 10:401-2 Ap '40. Helen Speyer. * a very complete survey of the diagnostic and treatment methods actually in use in child guidance clinics in this country. The material is well-organized, is practical rather than theoretical and, fortunately, places emphasis on the child rather than on symptoms. * Rogers' own method of diagnosis, "the Component-Factor Method" . . . seems to be a valuable clinic tool, particularly as it brings out the multiple causation of behavior and concrete descriptive terms prevent reflecting the personal bias of the worker. Even though individual items may be wrongly evaluated one would grasp the dynamics involved. * This book is recommended as a valuable reference for all professional groups working with children. Dr. Rogers has not only collected material from many sources, including recent studies, presented it in a readable form, but he has given us the benefit of his personal clinical experience in evaluating it. The illustrative cases are well chosen and lend interest to the text, and there are excellent bibliographies at the end of chapters.

Am J Sociol 45:954 My '40. Ruth Shonle Cavan. * an excellent and detailed summary of procedures in use in child-guidance clinics in this country. Because it is a survey, it lacks definite focus and unity; its value will be in providing a background of information for the prospective clinician rather than in giving him the actual tools of a unified system of theory and practice. Part I on methods of diagnosis is rather weak. Too much emphasis is placed upon tests and upon methods of diagraming factors in the child's situation; too little emphasis is given to a needed theory of personality that should lie back of any diagnosis. Part II on treatment through the use of foster homes and institutions is especially thoughtful and thorough. Part III upon the use of family, school, camps, and clubs in treating a child is rather sketchy. Part IV on treatment through interviews of various 'sorts gives a comprehensive survey of methods that have been developed in different clinics; this section will inform on types of interviews but will not make the reader of the book into an interviewer. In spite of the shortcomings indicated, the book is exceedingly interesting and should be very useful to the group for which it is intended.

Am Sociol R 4:583-6 Ag '39. Katharine Whiteside Taylor. * among the most valuable recent contributions to clinical literature. Comprehensive, insightful, judicious, readably written and with ample illustrative case material, it gives an excellent over-view of significant findings, approaches, and techniques in the field, and suggests sound bases for further development. Although written primarily for clinical workers . . . it is equally valuable for students in the related fields of psychiatry, psychology, sociology, and education. Among its most distinctive contributions are the emphasis upon the continual *interaction* of all factors making for good and bad adjustment, and its presentation of the "Component-Factor Method of Diagnosis" developed in the Rochester Clinic. *

Brit J Ed Psychol 10:82 F '40. C. W. V(alentine). * a most useful volume * If one sought for one word to describe the chief characteristic of this book, it would, I think, be "comprehensive." * One of the most useful chapters of the book is that on the advisability of remov-ing a child from home. * A later chapter deals with the school's part in changing behaviour. A weak section here, it seems to me, is that which suggests that one way of giving "constructive help with the insecure attention-getting child" is by increasing the legitimate opportunities for gaining attention. * His defence of some of the play techniques, in which he does not refer to English workers, is, I think, one of the weaker parts of the book. Another weakness seems to me to be in the inadequate weight given to innate disabilities; but taken as a whole the volume deserves a welcome as one of the most useful contributions to this complex topic.

Brit J Psychol 30:373 Ap '40. * an excellent compendium of information about the methods of diagnosis and treatment of maladjusted children in the U.S.A. It consists of three main parts, the first on diagnosis, the second on treatment through modification of the environment, and the third on direct treatment of the child himself. The second section is far the best * The first and third parts of the book are somewhat superficial, suffering from a common tendency towards behaviourism and a lack of consideration of basic tendencies and mechanisms. The book thus contains little of great importance to the psychologist. But the sociologist and the social worker (especially in mental hygiene) should find the second section in particular most useful and suggestive.

Cath Charities R 23:55 F '39. Alice Padgett. * the title might just as accurately have read *The Individualized Treatment of the Handicapped Child*, whether handicapped from social, mental, physical, or emotional causes * Those preparing themselves for social work, psychiatric work, visiting teacher work, etc., as well as practitioners, will find that the book contains a world of well-arranged information on day-to-day problems. * another invaluable feature of this book is its detailed references to the most important pieces of research in the effectiveness of various treatment procedures * This book will be required reading for students of child welfare.

Char and Pers 8:258-9 Mr '40. C. M. Louttit. * Rogers has had much experience in dealing with behavior problems in children and he has worked with psychiatrists, social workers, and teachers. His personal grasp of the points-of-view of these various professions is abundantly evident in his whole discussion. * Perhaps the weakest chapters in this work are the second and third. The second considers methods of diagnosis, but it is so incomplete that it has little value. The third chapter and an appendix deal with the author's "component-factor method of diagnosis." There would appear to be nothing essentially new in this method, and since the author never mentions it in the real body of the book one wonders why it was included. However, the great weakness of these two chapters does not detract from the worth of the rest of the book. In this work Dr. Rogers has made a major contribution to clinical psychology. It is to be hoped that psychiatrists and social workers will read and profit as much as psychologists are certain to do.

J Abn and Social Psychol 34:544-5 O '39. Rose G. Anderson. This book represents a distinct departure from ordinary methods and a significant advance in devoting ten of its twelve chapters to the comprehensive and intensive consideration of methods of treatment and their results; that is, it takes up where a number of other useful books in clinical psychology stop. * One of the outstanding merits of this book is the author's ability to judge dispassionately both the positive value and the limitation of various methods and philosophies of treatment. * Throughout the book the author draws richly on his own clinical experience for illustrative cases and material. In addition, he has brought together many important descriptions of and evaluations of methods and results of treatment, a compilation of great value to any clinical worker. Bibliographies are particularly comprehensive. The book closes with an important chapter on considerations connected with the nature of the clinic set-up, inter-agency responsibility and cooperation in treatment, and the role of the different professional workers. * an indispensable book to every clinical or community worker, to every student of child and clinical psychology, and to his instructors in these subjects.

J Appl Psychol 23:423 Je '39. J. R. Gentry. * The material of the book is drawn from a wide experience and a sound point of view. It is well organized, and the style of writing is easy and pleasing.

J Consulting Psychol 4:37 Ja-F '40. Norman Fenton. * a stimulating book which should be an important and constructive contribution to the field * This reviewer . . . is doubtful of the adequacy of the author's interpretation and evaluation of the ego-libido method. * The author's own component-factor method is described. I wish he had given it more space. Part II includes a valuable discussion of change of environment as treatment which is not available elsewhere in so good and compact a form for students. The author draws upon his own extensive experiences in child placement to make this an interesting and authoritative section. Part III is concerned with treatment in the home, school and community. Again this reviewer is disappointed that the coordinating council is not included in the discussion * In the final section of the volume, the readers will find brought together all the newer techniques in clinical treatment. Naturally the discussions are brief, but there is ample documentation and the inquiring student has many sources suggested for his further enlightenment, if he will but seek them. The philosophy of child guidance is considered thoughtfully and interestingly throughout the book. * The format of the book is excellent. It is an example of superior textbook construction and printing. There is a good index * The book is really planned for the more advanced student who has already had the usual training experiences in general and child psychology, in the study of case histories, and perhaps in some introductory clinical work. * The book should also be of interest and value to professional workers. Over all there is a pleasant modesty and an experimental and tentative mood in the style and presentation. Dogma is nicely absent.

J Home Econ 32:254 Ap '40.

J Mental Sci 86:538-9 My '40. G. W. T. H. Fleming. The author . . . brings a wide practical experience to bear on the many difficulties which the problem child presents to the clinic. * the author very wisely is careful to point out how the whole subject, including its delinquency aspects, is as yet only in its infancy, and that we must have many therapeutic failures before the subject is on a really sound and successful foundation. The treatment of the difficult child is applied from so many angles that there is unlimited scope for extension, but a word of warning appears necessary, for much time and money may be spent on therapeutic measures which appeal very strongly to the lay mind but may have little scientific basis or therapeutic value.

Jewish Social Service Q 15:385-6 Je '39. Herbert H. Aptekar. * Rogers' book is not a dry study divorced from the treatment problems of the practitioner but, to my mind, it does lack some of the vitality and the stimulation which one finds in the less scholarly but more imaginative writings of some therapists and case workers in this field. Science alone is not enough. * Rogers makes a contribution to diagnostic thinking which he calls The Component Factor Method of Diagnosis. As its very name indicates, this is an eclectic approach to problems of diagnosis. * the diagnosis arrived at is meant to be a causal rather than a descriptive one. Here, too, Dr. Rogers' natural science method of approach to problems of diagnosis would be unsatisfying to many practitioners. * the medical conception of diagnosis has been found inadequate in the treatment of social difficulties. Dr. Rogers' eclectic method is essentially similar in character to the medical conception even though it is more elaborate. When social or psychological diagnosis is conceived of as something dynamic which develops along with treatment—indeed often follows, instead of preceding it—a formal diagnostic outline such as Dr. Rogers suggests hardly seems applicable. * In his consideration of the various therapies, Dr. Rogers gives prominent place to relationship therapy. Despite his own very scientific orientation, he sees in this type of therapy (which lays less claim to being strictly scientific than others) a significant and vital approach to the treatment of problem children and their parents. Dr. Rogers seems to recognize in his discussion of relationship therapy—if not elsewhere—that treatment involves living, experiencing, making mistakes and correcting them, and that living experience can be only partially scientific.

Med Officer 63:98 Mr 16 '40. This book sets out exactly what is implied by its title, and is therefore a welcome one. * simple, sober, well-written on the whole. While based mainly on the author's own practical experience, it is full of allusion to the methods and opinions of other workers. These are restricted almost entirely to Americans, which is a pity in one way, but makes for a more unified approach. * The whole book is, apart from its usefulness, a good illustration of that new attitude which has come to be adopted by all workers with children—all except the die-hard, Nazi-minded, or tough type who are always with us—that is,

the understanding, intelligent, sympathetic one, rather than suppression and moralizing. Of this child guidance is but one of the aspects, and this book an excellent example.

Med Times 68:48 Ja '40. Stanley S. Lamm. * The book shows evidence of thoughtful planning. It should be enjoyed by those interested in the subject.

Mental Hyg (New York) 23:656-8 O '39. James S. Plant. * clearly written * There is . . . a good discussion of the inadequacies—as well as the usefulness—of the various personality tests, and an appraisal of Dr. Kenworthy's ego-libido method. * the author puts forward his own component-factor method which involves plus and minus number ratings in each of seven areas * This he carefully guards against overenthusiasm and, in company with the originators of all other systems, he warns that his is meant to assist rather than to assimilate the worker. But he forgets that psychiatrists and psychologists revel in numbers, balances, and valencies, and that each counts himself successful when he has graduated to a sort of certified public accountancy. Three other chapters discuss foster-home care, institutional placement, and the broad question as to when it is advisable to remove a child from his own family. This section is fully documented and is the best thing the reviewer has seen in the way of a survey of the experiences that a large number of authorities have actually had with this question of change of environment as treatment. * The next three chapters cover treatment through modifying the environment. The first presents a good discussion of attitude therapy in the family. The second reviews possible resources in the school, and is helpfully suggestive to the worker if she will remember that over and above Dr. Rogers' suggestions there looms often just as much in the way of glorious help or baffling hazard in the teacher's personality and problems as in the case of the child's parents. The third chapter covers clubs, groups, and camps. It is an eye-opener for all that great group who "advise that Johnny go to camp" without the slightest notion of the advantages or disadvantages involved * Even the veteran will read this chapter with a little extra thrill of running onto new resources and new meanings for old resources. The final three chapters deal with the forms of treatment that have to do directly with the child himself. Most workers with children after a while evolve an approach of their own that is a little of this, a little of that, and—happily—something of themselves. For them these three chapters will be of little value. For the newcomer in the field, however, who becomes bewildered over interview therapy, deep therapy, and such-like, this is valuable reading. The discussion is straightforward, the criticisms fair; the reader never feels that Dr. Rogers is forcing his own point of view. It's a simple, unbiased analysis of a field that has tended toward much unwarranted mystery. * Rogers is to be congratulated on a readable, yet quite deft, untangling of threads in a field in which terms and discussions have tended to make everything seem very complicated. I am particularly struck with his ability to give all sorts of helpful suggestions as to diagnosis and treatment—never, however, going further than "for example, these things might be considered in this case." The reader will find little new ground. But for the confused furrows of the tilling of the last twenty years, here is an excellent guide.

Psychoanalytic R 27:395-6 Jl '40. * there is much good sense and sound understanding within the frame of reference utilized by the author. He discusses the Kenworthy Ego-Libido method, of which he apparently is not *au courant* with the more important backgrounds, thus thrusting somewhat diluted freudian conceptions into the foreground, instead of utilizing the more fundamental backgrounds of the unmodified freudian conceptions to say little of his apparent unawareness of the meanings of the terms Ego and Libido even after their rather copious dilutions from the Kenworthy sources. If "behavior" can be understood in any other terms than the "emotional reactions to experience"—the which is not accepted by the author—then the reviewer confesses he knows little of the whys and wherefores of behavior. The author utilizes what he calls a component factor method: Heredity, physical organization, mentality, family environment, family, economic and cultural factors, social factors, and the child's own insight. To us a very inadequate pot pourri of imperfectly thought out conceptions, made more or less ridiculous by tacking in figures + or − on arbitrary, blab-blab-scales.

Southw Social Sci Q 20:107-8 Je '39. Margaret Trippet Mitchell. * an intensely practical approach to the process of the readjustment of problem children * Part I, "Ways of Understanding the Child," has a very interesting chapter on the *component factor method* of diagnosis. This method, which was evolved at the Rochester Clinic where Dr. Rogers is director, was designed to help the clinician to analyze the difficulty and prescribe treatment and seems quite useful in clarifying concepts. * In a field which is as yet largely speculative, Dr. Rogers, with his nonacademic approach is peculiarly fitted to guide teachers, psychologists, counselors, and others in similar fields to an understanding and evaluation of the methods of treatment now being used. His bibliographies at the end of each chapter are particularly helpful, being restricted as they are to a few excellent selections of readings rather than consisting of comprehensive and confusing lists.

Survey 75:360 N '39. Ira S. Wile. * a simple textbook for the various professional groups trying to cope with the problems of children. Particularly useful is Dr. Rogers' exposition of the component-factor method of diagnosis *

[B1054]

ROSE, ANNA LORETTE. **Ability in Relation to School Progress:** An Analytical Study of the Relation between School Appraisal of Pupil Educational Development and Objective Measures of Pupil Achievement and Ability. Foreword by William S. Learned. Mansfield, Pa.: Mansfield Advertiser, 1933. Pp. xv, 131. $1.00.

[B1055]

RUCH, GILES M., AND SEGEL, DAVID. **Minimum Essentials of the Individual Inventory in Guidance.** United States Department of Interior, Office of Education, Vocational Division, Bulletin No. 202; Occupational Information and Guidance Series No. 2. Washington, D. C.: Government Printing Office, 1940. Pp. vi, 83. $0.15. Paper.

Occupations 18:630-1 My '40. Beatrice Candee. This book presents the problems of diagnosing individuals in a way that teachers and counselors will understand, not simply because the words are non-technical and the writing excellent, but because the problems appear as teachers and counselors know them and discuss them. I can recall scarcely any hard-fought issue in my experience in the public schools which is not mentioned and well defined. * The problem is stated and in most cases the prevailing opinion and the conviction of the authors, with reasons for these are given. There is one important exception to this: while the authors give a list of tests in common use, they do not offer any evaluation of these. I do not agree that evaluation of specific tests must wait for "comparative experimental studies of the worth of tests," nor have the authors in any other instance demanded such objectivity before summarizing existing experience and making suggestions. In contrast, the list of reference books and the comments on these are most valuable. * most of the procedures discussed require facilities beyond those of the majority of school systems at present * The administration of achievement tests and group intelligence tests sounds simple, but the giving of even one such test to all children in a school system of any size, with accurate scoring and recording of results, is a major administrative project. Even the dangers of the cumulative record cannot be dismissed in practice as easily as in this book * The authors of this book have done an excellent job of formulating problems in the diagnosis of individuals as counselors and teachers now perceive them; they have added to this the outline of a program as constructive as I have ever seen on the basis of these formulations; they have left us with the problem of how such a program can possibly be carried out in the usual school system, and the even more fundamental question of how accurate and how constructive are the present formulations of counselors and educators in the field of guidance.

[B1056]

SANDIFORD, PETER; CAMERON, M. A.; CONWAY, C. B.; AND LONG, J. A. **Forecasting Teaching Ability.** University of Toronto, Department of Educational Research, Bulletin No. 8. Toronto, Canada: the Department, 1937. Pp. 93. $0.50. Paper.

B Int Bur Ed 12:37-8 q 1 '38. * makes interesting reading *

Ed Res B 17:277 D '38. *Earl W. Anderson.* This thorough but discouraging report of two investigations undertaken in search of justifiable bases upon which to select student teachers in the Ontario College of Education is a definite contribution to the field of the education of teachers. * There is a thorough and concise review of previous research on the problem. *

For additional reviews, see B471.

[B1057]

SCHNEILER, FRANZ. **Students Examine Their Professors:** A Student-Reaction Plan at Work. Berkeley, Calif.: Pestalozzi Press, 1939. Pp. 32. $0.35. Paper.

Ed Abstracts 5:50 F '40. *F. J. Adams.*

Loyola Ed Digest 15:10 F '40. The author, a professor of German in the University of California, believes ardently in the obligation resting upon college professors of preparing students to meet the problems of the age in which they live. He believes, too, that students have a right to demand that professors be competent, and considers the task of keeping professors up to standard a joint responsibility of the faculty and the student body. For these reasons he was active in a movement to induce the administration to introduce a system of student rating of professors. The petition was rejected, whereupon groups of students circulated rating scales and delivered to the author for safe keeping 1,620 ratings turned in by students. The present brochure gives the history of the activity and reproduces a number of pen sketches of professors, good and bad.

[B1058]

SCHONELL, FRED J. **Diagnosis of Individual Difficulties in Arithmetic.** Edinburgh, Scotland: Oliver & Boyd, Ltd., 1937. Pp. xi, 115. 2s. 6d. (Toronto, Canada: Clarke, Irwin & Co., Ltd. $0.75.)

C. Ebblewhite Smith, Lecturer in the Department of Higher Degrees and Research, Institute of Education, University of London. It is symptomatic of the changing attitude towards teaching methods in the United Kingdom—where the systematic scientific approach to children's school problems has been too long delayed—that this book should appear at this time. Compiled as it is as a supplement to the *Schonell Diagnostic Arithmetic Tests* it serves both as an introduction for teachers in the elementary school to the technique of diagnosis and as a primary textbook on the whole subject of backwardness in arithmetic for students in training colleges. Though small, the book is comprehensive and is written with the authority of one who has an intimate, first hand, practical knowledge of this subject. It is perhaps in the nature of a book such as this, written for the non-specialist, that although the work is based on extensive research and statistical treatment it shall not back up all its statements with figures and experimental evidence. Dr. Schonell has the reputation for careful and reliable work and it may be assumed that his standardisations have been based on adequate samples.

The first part of the book concerns itself with the *Schonell Diagnostic Arithmetic Tests* —12 carefully constructed tests which are reviewed elsewhere. Very valuable is the section dealing by means of many examples, with interpretation of the test results in individual cases. The section on causes of backwardness in arithmetic agrees essentially with the generally accepted views on this subject. Is it too much to hope that in some future revision of this book the author will be able to give figures on the frequency of the different causes which he lists of backwardness in arithmetic found in the English elementary school?

The non-psychologist teacher will find all the information he needs to give him an insight into his classroom arithmetic teaching problems. The final chapter is concerned with such remedial work as may be carried on by the intelligent teacher under ordinary school conditions. As a supplement to this chapter there may be obtained sets of graded *Arithmetic Practice Cards* which may be used for controlled practice in the fundamental number facts.

This is a thoroughly sound little book and admirably fulfills its purpose as a handbook for teachers and students.

For additional reviews, see B474.

[B1059]
SCHRAMMEL, H. E., AND RASMUSSEN, OTHO M. **Report of the Thirtieth Nation-wide Every Pupil Scholarship Test for High Schools and Elementary Schools, April 12, 1939.** Kansas State Teachers College of Emporia, Bulletin of Information, Vol. 19, No. 4. Emporia, Kan.: Bureau of Educational Measurements, the College, April 1939. Pp. 24. Gratis. Paper.

[B1060]
SCHWESINGER, GLADYS C. **Heredity and Environment:** Studies in the Genesis of Psychological Characteristics. Studies in Social Eugenics, [No.] 1. Edited by Frederick Osborn. New York: Macmillan Co., 1933. Pp. xi, 484. (London: Macmillan & Co., Ltd., 1934.) Out of print.

Med Times 63:162 My '34. Stanley S. Lamm. * very objective in its method. It should be approached only with a studious attitude.

Personnel J 13:61 Je '34.

Sci 79:185 F 23 '34. Charles B. Davenport. * The history of mental measurement is traced from its beginning and the modern results skilfully classified and described. The measurement of personality is more difficult, but lines of approach are being followed; and these are fully set forth. * an excellent guide to a difficult field. The author has been industrious, selective, critical. Of much help will be the bibliographies and recommended readings. Nowhere else, we venture to say, can so comprehensive a survey be found. The book is recommended

to all who wish to understand the genetic basis for behavior and the way behavior may be studied.

For additional reviews, see B229 and B475.

[B1061]
SCOTTISH COUNCIL FOR RESEARCH IN EDUCATION, MENTAL SURVEY COMMITTEE. **The Intelligence of Scottish Children:** A National Survey of an Age-Group. Publications of the Scottish Council for Research in Education, [No.] 5. London: University of London Press, Ltd., 1933. Pp. x, 160. 5s.

Brit J Ed Psychol 3:295-7 N '33. Cyril Burt. The survey which this volume describes forms one of the most ambitious projects which educational psychologists have hitherto ever contemplated or carried out. The results are of great importance. They have an obvious bearing alike on educational and on social problems. * Bold as this undertaking may seem, it has been entirely successful. * The results are described in full; and incidentally valuable hints are given, not only on the construction of tests for this purpose, but also on the statistical devices to be used in analyzing such data. * It is difficult to praise too highly both the scheme and the results of the whole undertaking. Hitherto educationists in Scotland have had to depend on investigations in England or America for their assumptions regarding the distribution of general ability. Both the data and the conclusions will be not only of theoretical value to the psychologist and sociologist, but also of practical value to those in Scotland who have to interpret the results obtained by similar examinations carried out in schools or particular districts. The report, too, is of the first interest to every teacher and educationist, and, what is more, provides a solid contribution to the study of social problems.

For additional reviews, see B231 and B477.

[B1062]
SCOTTISH COUNCIL FOR RESEARCH IN EDUCATION, TERMAN REVISION COMMITTEE, D. KENNEDY-FRASER, CONVENER. **Modifications Proposed for British Use of the Revised Stanford-Binet Tests of Intelligence in Measuring Intelligence by Lewis M. Terman and Maud A. Merrill Published by George G. Harrap & Company, Ltd., 1937.** Edinburgh, Scotland: the Council, January 1939. Pp. iv, 16, i, 11. Apply. Paper, mimeographed.

Brit J Psychol 30:69 Jl '39. * Copies are available to accredited testers on application to the Research Council. These modifications have the approval of Prof. Terman and Dr. Merrill. They agree with some of the modifications suggested by the English Committee under Prof. Burt, but do not go as far as these. The original standardization is retained.

[B1063]
SEARLES, JOHN R., AND LEONARD, J. M. **Experiments in the Mental Testing of Detroit Policemen.** Schools of Public Affairs and Social Work of Wayne University, Report No. 5. Prepared under the direction of the Detroit Bureau of Governmental Research, Inc., Report No. 141. Detroit, Mich.: the Bureau, 1936. Pp. vi, 54. $0.75. Paper.

Civil Service Assembly News Letter 3:6 Ja '37. The Detroit Police Department has probably conducted more experiments on the selection of patrolman through the use of mental examinations than has any other American city. The authors of this pamphlet have made an excellent summarization of the findings of these studies. *

Nat Municipal R 26:160 Mr '37. * Having decided that the Army Alpha or . . . [a] similar general intelligence test was the most useful method of selecting applicants for police work, the Detroit police department set up a minimum requirement of an Army Alpha score of one hundred which it has been demonstrated is about the equivalent of completion of the second year of high school. The mental test is only one part of the process of selecting police personnel. *

[B1064]
SEDER, MARGARET, AND SHANNER, WILLIAM M. **Summary and Selected Bibliography of Studies Pertaining to Measurement in the Social Studies and the Natural Sciences.** Educational Records Supplementary Bulletin E. New York: Educational Records Bureau, March 1939. Pp. iii, 24. $0.25. Paper, lithotyped.

[B1065]
SEGEL, DAVID. **Differential Diagnosis of Ability in School Children.** Baltimore, Md.: Warwick & York, Inc., 1934. Pp. vii, 86. $1.40.

Brit J Psychol 25:502 Ap '35. Differential diagnosis in this book means a measure of the differing capacities of a child of school age in different school subjects. The methods and tests available for making this kind of measurement are clearly and concisely discussed, and their usefulness indicated.

For additional reviews, see B232 and B481.

[B1066]
SEGEL, DAVID. **Nature and Use of the Cumulative Record.** United States Department of the Interior, Office of Education, Bulletin 1938, No. 3. Washington, D. C.: Government Printing Office, 1938. Pp. v, 48. $0.10. Paper.

Sociol and Social Res 23:496 My-Je '39. E(dward) C. McD(onagh).

[B1067]
SEGEL, DAVID. **Tests for Preschool, Kindergarten, and Entering First-Grade Children.** United States Office of Education, Circular No. 180. Washington, D. C.: the Office, July 1939. Pp. 5. Gratis. Paper, mimeographed.

[B1068]
SEGEL, DAVID, AND HAAS, KENNETH B. **Tests in Business Education.** Washington, D. C.: United States Office of Education, August 1938. Pp. 16. Gratis. Paper, mimeographed.

[B1068.1]
SELLING, LOWELL SINN. **Diagnostic Criminology.** Ann Arbor, Mich.: Edwards Brothers, Inc., 1935. Pp. vii, 175. Out of print. Lithotyped.

Am J Sociol 42:291-2 S '36. Edwin H. Sutherland. * designed primarily for persons training in psychiatry who have had no experience in courts or reformatory institutions. The body of the book is composed of two chapters on the techniques which should be used in the examination of adult offenders and juvenile offenders, and one chapter on the syndromes which are found in such offenders. The fact that a psychiatrist with several years' experience in clinical work with offenders has found it necessary to write a book of this elementary nature justifies the inference that he believes the psychiatrist knows nothing about criminology when he finishes his medical work and has no general techniques which he can use in the study of patients of this nature.

J Nerv and Mental Dis 83:743 Je '36. * a remarkably clear, straightforward and readable outline of the function of the psychiatrist in the criminal courts. It goes further and also outlines modes of examination of juvenile and adult offenders, particularly the former, discusses important syndromes in both the adult and child, and closes with an appendix of actual case reports with samples of "Gutachten," as the Germans term their expert opinions on these types of situations. There is a short bibliography but no index in this excellent little manual. Incidentally it is a lithotype production, neat and novel.

Survey 72:95 Mr '36. William Healy. * pleasantly written and full of common sense. Methods of examination of the adult offender are considered in sixteen pages while seventy pages are devoted to instructions in examining juvenile offenders. * The author is not so concerned with the presenting symptoms of delinquency as he is with some of the underlying facts. The fundamental dynamic factors on the whole receive scant attention, although

Selling in some of his recommendations stands for more psychiatric investigation and even for psychoanalysis. His recommendations in general are essentially those a probation officer or a social agency would make. A sense of humor is shown in the pseudonyms given to his cases * The chapter, Historical Introduction, seems, at least in parts rather unnecessary in such a handbook. Professional psychiatrists will find the work too scanty to be of much service but the social worker may well be interested in its contents.

[B1069]
SHEEHY, LORETTA MARIA. **A Study of Preadolescents by Means of a Personality Inventory.** Washington, D. C.: Catholic University of America, 1938. Pp. x, 76. $1.50. Paper.

Loyola Ed Digest 14:11 Je '39. *Austin G. Schmidt.* The author of this doctoral dissertation constructed a personality test, administered it to 777 boys and girls, and made case studies of 36 children for the purpose of determining the validity of the test. She concludes that the test is a reasonably valid and useful index of a child's personality.

[B1070]
SHEVIAKOV, GEORGE V., AND FRIEDBERG, JEAN. **Evaluation of Personal and Social Adjustment: A Report** of Progress of the Study. Chicago, Ill.: Evaluation in the Eight Year Study, Progressive Education Association, University of Chicago, 1939. Pp. iii, 65. $0.75. Paper.

[B1071]
SHUTTLEWORTH, FRANK K. **The Adolescent Period:** A Graphic and Pictorial Atlas. Monographs of the Society for Research in Child Development, Vol. 3, No. 3, Serial No. 16. Washington, D. C.: the Society, National Research Council, 1938. Pp. v, 246. $2.00. Paper.

Am J Med Sci 196:739 N '38. *J. S.* * In graphic form, its information is easily and quickly referred to, and has a good index. It is also a very useful handbook for ready reference for the teacher or physician at a secondary school.

Brit J Ed Psychol 10:87 F '40. *O. W.* * contains an amazing amount of information * There is an excellent table of contents at the beginning which, with the useful index at the end, makes it easy to use the Atlas for reference. It might, however, have been an advantage, for the sake of clearness, to have had the section indicated in the Table of Contents carried through into the actual text; and to have had some of the graphs, where many details are included (such as in Figures 221, 244, 296, 309 and 310) drawn on a larger scale.

There is no discussion of the methods used to obtain the data nor of the significance of the facts collected, though in every case the sources of information are appended and the method of graphical or pictorial representation is clearly indicated. To the trained student, able to assess the probable degrees of validity of generalizations arrived at by very different means, this volume would be a most useful reference book concerning adolescence. It is a veritable mine of information, collected with care and efficiency, arranged with clearness and understanding, and expressed in graphical and pictorial form with surprising ingenuity.

Ed Res B 18:225-6 N '39. *F. P. Robinson.* * no attempt is made through narrative discussion to coordinate or evaluate the data . . . presented. In light of most students' lack of ability, and aversion, for reading graphs and because of the choppiness in style arising from such a form of presentation, this monograph may not be as useful for the average undergraduate as would the same material presented in prose style. However, for the teacher this monograph represents a very handy and excellent collection of data for presentation in class with suitable explanation. A wide area has been covered in selecting the material presented, although some readers may feel that pubescent changes and other aspects of physical growth receive a disproportionate emphasis. Such material, however, was probably found to be more available and more easily represented pictorially. The reviewer would not hesitate to recommend this monograph to any worker in the field of adolescence.

Endocrinology 23:246 Ag '38. * The material should prove of much use to endocrine investigators who have frequent need of reliable control data.

J Am Med Assn 111:2037-8 N 26 '38. * These two related works [reviewed jointly with *A Handbook of Methods for the Study of Adolescent Children* (see B922)] constitute a monumental achievement in selection and (in the handbook) of critical discussion of contributions from a vast and often confusing literature, which they now bring within relatively easy reach of the student or research worker. As a reference resource they amply justify the enormous labor they represent. As the authors have set out to do, they indicate what structures, functions and activities of the growing child can have been measured, and they aid the worker in making reliable measurements of his own. *

J Pediatrics 14:276 F '39. * a remarkable collection of graphs and pictures covering practically every phase of adolescence * a reference book that should be available to every student and teacher in the field of childhood.

J Pediatrics 16:677 My '40. * excellent graphs.

Pub Health R 10:54-5 Je '40. *Mabel E. Rugen.* * an excellent collection of factual data graphically presented that one would need to spend hours searching for in dozens of studies. This is a valuable source book on the adolescent. *

Q R Biol 14:84 Mr '39. * the author deserves much credit for a compilation which will be found very useful for purposes of reference.

Sch R 47:309-11 Ap '39. *Fowler D. Brooks.* * presents . . . 458 figures and photographs * nearly two hundred of . . . [the figures] are original drawings prepared especially for this volume * The material is well selected and well organized and is presented clearly and concisely. The volume should prove especially valuable to instructors offering courses in adolescent development, as well as to college and university students and teachers in secondary schools who are interested in problems of the adolescent period.

[B1072]
SICELOFF, MARGARET MCADORY, AND WOODYARD, ELLA, AND STAFF OF THE DIVISION OF PSYCHOLOGY, INSTITUTE OF EDUCATIONAL RESEARCH, TEACHERS COLLEGE. **Validity and Standardization of the McAdory Art Test.** New York: Bureau of Publications, Teachers College, Columbia University, 1933. Pp. v, 32. $0.75. Paper.

[B1072.1]
SIDSERF, EDWARD H. **English Vocabulary Distributions Converted to the General Vocabulary Scale for Forty-Two Secondary Schools:** Worksample 95, Forms A, B, C, D, and E. Human Engineering Laboratory, Technical Report No. 58. Boston, Mass.: the Laboratory, 1940. Pp. vii, 73. $1.00. Paper, mimeographed.

[B1073]
SIMMONS, ERNEST P., AND BIXLER, HAROLD HENCH. **The New Standard High School Spelling Scale:** Including Sixty-Four Lessons in Spelling for Junior and Senior High Schools. Atlanta, Ga.: Turner E. Smith & Co., 1940. Pp. ii, 64. $0.48.

[B1074]
SKEELS, HAROLD MANVILLE. **A Study of Some Factors in Form Board Accomplishments of Preschool Children.** University of Iowa Studies in Child Welfare, Vol. 7, No. 2. Iowa City, Iowa: the University, 1933. Pp. 148. Cloth, $1.35; paper, $1.00.

[B1075]
SLETTO, RAYMOND FRANKLIN. **Construction of Personality Scales by the Criterion of Internal Consistency.** Hanover, N. H.: Sociological Press, 1937. Pp. vii, 92. $1.75. Paper.

Am J Sociol 44:463-9 N '38. *Kimball Young.* * Sletto has made a useful criticism regarding the commonly accepted practice of determining test items in attitude scales by the method of "internal consistency." *

Civil Service Assembly News Letter 3:8 D '37.

Sociol and Social Res 22:189 N-D '37. *E(mory) S. B(ogardus).*

For additional reviews, see B486.

[B1076]
SMITH, B. OTHANEL. **Logical Aspects of Educational Measurement.** New York: Columbia University Press, 1938. Pp. x, 182. $2.50. (London: Oxford University Press. 12s. 6d.)

Am J Psychol 52:652-3 O '39. *Edward E. Cureton.* This book should be required reading for every student of psychophysics, psychometrics, and educational measurements. It is disturbing, and it is therefore important. The reviewer disagrees with practically every important conclusion which the author draws, but on trying to find specific flaws in the arguments advanced, and in trying to establish his own views on a rigorous logical basis, he finds extraordinary difficulty. Dr. Smith has raised important fundamental questions. His answers are unsatisfactory. So are the answers attempted by the present reviewer! The questions, therefore, remain, and they are important and fundamental. * it is doubtful if test builders have as strong a belief that they are measuring "real learning outcomes" as the author implies. They assume, more nearly, that they are measuring *one aspect* of these outcomes, which is correlated positively but imperfectly with the other important aspects. * In his treatment of the foundations of educational measurement in general, and of normal distribution in particular, the author exhibits unfamiliarity with certain fundamental statistical principles not found in the elementary texts. He seems, in particular, not to know the Taylor-series argument for the first-approximation validity of linear combinations of test items, nor the fact that the normal distribution has been derived without the assumption of equal, all-or-none, additively-combining elements. A great many of his criticisms lose some of their force in the light of these mathematical demonstrations. In spite of shortcomings in the analysis and solution of the problems raised, however, this book should be read, because it is the first, so far as the reviewer knows, which states these problems adequately, or even fully recognizes their existence.

Brit J Psychol 30:169 O '39. * The problem discussed in this book is one which is of importance to the increasing number of psychologists who rely on test scores and statistics for the basis of their theories. The exposition is reasonably clear but the reader is irritated by innumerable footnotes, most of which could be avoided by the usual system of reference to the comprehensive bibliography at the end of the book.

Curric J 10:187-8 Ap '39. Willis L. Uhl. * This volume has the distinctive value of going behind the measurements program and examining it critically step by step. This book will have a great value for any students of educational measurement, particularly for those in intermediate classes and in courses on test construction.

Ed Abstracts 4:232-3 Je '39. Henry D. Rinsland. * The author has confined his work to a critical examination of what might be called developmental tests and scales, and not to intelligence tests, aptitude tests, attitude tests or diagnostic tests. * The author makes a very sane criticism of our instruments of measure because they fail to give equal units and units that are additive. *

Ed Forum 3:362-3 Mr '39. * timely * a clear and definite analysis of the meaning of measurement and a well-drawn picture of the conditions under which it arose * This is in no sense a book on testing procedures and techniques; rather it is a critical statement of fundamental considerations which must enter into the construction of tests if they are to have validity.

H Sch J 23:143 Mr '40. A. M. Jordan. * scholarly and systematic *

Harvard Ed R 9:376-8 My '39. Eugene Shen. * devotes a good portion (80 pages) to a preliminary consideration of the theoretical requirements and historical antecedents * While these requirements and antecedents are clearly stated, they are not likely to appear to sophisticated readers as effective manoeuvering which adds to the ferocity of the final onslaught. The attack is most successful upon certain exaggerated claims of established quality between units of measurement. * Other attacks seem rather to aim at certain extrinsic

features of instruments and their uses. * If we do not seriously limit ourselves to logical aspects, the questions raised do furnish food for thought and are not without constructive suggestions. *

J Ed (London) 71:180 Mr '39. * traces historically the growth of educational testing and exposes a number of the errors commonly made in the interpretation of educational measurements. He discusses, on the usual lines, the theory of measurement, and concludes that it is unlikely that we shall secure much greater accuracy of educational measure; rather, future advance will be along the lines of factor analysis and of qualitative evaluation.

Loyola Ed Digest 14:9 Ap '39. Austin G. Schmidt. This is in certain respects a scholarly work, but we do not find in it much that is distinctly new. There is some good material on the theory of numbers and on the conditions necessary if measurement is to be made precise. These conditions are definitely not fulfilled in measurement as used today, the chief difficulty being the lack of a fixed zero point and of a unit of known and unchanging magnitude. The author is a materialist of an aggressive kind. * We cannot think of any churchman or any psychologist of standing who ever defended the thesis that mind and soul are supernatural. The author's lack of clear concepts on this subject and his illogical rejection of the spirituality of the soul weakens the foundations of his entire analysis.

Nature 143:960 Je 10 '39. * The logical treatment is nothing like so rigorous as that found, for example, in the paper by Mr. J. Guild on "Are sensation intensities measurable?", in the current Report of the British Association for the Advancement of Science, but it follows somewhat similar lines. *

Philos Sci 6:124-5 Ja '39. * points out very distinctly where criteria for measure are frequently not met. This it does by a careful account of the meaning of any kind of measurement, the logical foundations of measurement and the requirements of instruments. Specific instances are discussed rather destructively, and, one must add, deservedly so.

Psychol B 36:403-4 My '39. Quinn McNemar. * The reviewer finds himself in agreement with this verbal and logical knockout of those who claim to have established equal units in mental measurement. Those who have been skeptical of the equality of "equal" units will find herein some potent arguments to bolster their skepticism. * The first four chapters seem a bit oversimplified—hence tedious to read; Chapters V and VI, on the logical aspects of validity and the relationship between performance and validity, are somewhat lacking in conciseness and pointedness; the last three chapters are more succinct. The entire argument could be developed in one-third the space, but perhaps the intended audience will not be so concerned about verbal economy.

Social Ed 3:211-2 Mr '39. J. Wayne Wrightstone. * Serious questions may be raised about the adequacy of treatment and interpretation of such topics as factor analysis, newer trends in measurement, and the Gestalt psychology. The author rules out rating scales as instruments of measurement by his definition. At other places sweeping and unsupported generalizations are made, for example, about Quetelet's interpretation of the "average man" and about the manner in which concepts in physics were borrowed by psychology. The author's definition of validity ignores the operational definitions of validity called for by such test technicians as Tyler. The author fails to point out that conclusions on class size, methods of teaching, and homogeneous grouping are controversial, not only because of the faults inherent in measuring instruments, but also because of variable factors in methods, curricula, and pupil and teacher personnel of various studies. The merits of this book are: first, that it is a concise introduction to the logical bases of measurement; second, that it is a compilation and interpretation into one source of the postulates of measurement which are usually found, if at all, in many scattered sources; and, third, that it presents the psychological postulates upon which measurement is based, and gives clear cut statements of some of the most basic issues and controversies in this field. In spite of its faults of omission and commission, it provides a much needed and elementary handbook for students who may wish to study not only the manipulation and construction of tests and measurements but also the origins and development of the postulates and axioms upon which educational measurement is based.

Teach Col J 11:123-4 Mr '40. E. L. Abell. * In this book we find a very logical examination of the foundations of modern testing. Its helpfulness is admitted; its weaknesses laid bare.

It is a book which should be read and digested. It leaves the reader with the feeling that if measurement in education is to become scientific, more careful attention must be given to its foundations with perhaps new material and new techniques.

Va Teach 20:39-40 F '39. P(aul) H(ounchell). Although tests and scales are constantly used as instruments of research in education, the author is among the first to have examined the fundamental ideas that lie behind the construction of such instruments. *

[B1077]

SMITH, GEORGE MILTON, JR. **Group Factors in Mental Tests Similar in Material or in Structure.** Columbia University, Archives of Psychology, No. 156. New York: the University, 1933. Pp. 56. $1.00. Paper.

[B1078]

SOUTH, EARL BENNETT. **A Dictionary of Terms Used in Measurements and Guidance.** New York: Psychological Corporation, 1939. Pp. iv, 88. $1.00.

Civil Service Assembly News Letter 5:11 Je '39. Ross Pollock. * Personnel administrators may find this book useful in the training of junior technicians or in cramming immediately before lecturing a group of college psychology students. * Many of the terms are treated clearly, having definitions supplemented by examples or formulas. Unfortunately, the author does not handle the material uniformly so that some of the items are covered by discussions that do not include clear definitions. Cross referencing is only fair. * In a few cases as in the case of the *Factor Theory,* the definitions are so condensed as to be understandable only to the person already skilled in this field. An excellent feature of the book for readers who may wish to obtain further data is the inclusion, with page numbers, of specific references to sources. If the Civil Service Assembly were sponsoring a book of the month club, this glossary should be included as one of the choices for its readers.

Personnel Adm 1:16 O '39. This book is a boon to the many who are a little confused by the welter of technicalities encountered in modern testing literature. Well documented by references to leading texts in the field, definitions are further supplemented by relevant formulas and brief, clear explanations and examples.

[B1079]

SOUTH, EARL BENNETT. **An Index of Periodical Literature on Testing:** A Classified Selected Bibliography of Periodical Literature on Educational and Mental Testing, Statistical Method and Personality

Measurement, 1921-1936. New York: Psychological Corporation, 1937. Pp. xiii, 286. $4.50. Lithotyped.

Civil Service Assembly News Letter 3:6 N '37. * A most valuable part of the book is the appendix containing a comprehensive list of references on specific tests *

For additional reviews, see B489.

[B1080]

SOUTH, EARL BENNETT. **A Syllabus of Principles and Techniques of Educational Measurements.** Albany, N. Y.: State College Co-op Book Store, 1938. Pp. vii, 68. $1.00. Paper, mimeographed.

[B1081]

SPENCER, DOUGLAS. **Fulcra of Conflict:** A New Approach to Personality Measurement. Yonkers, N. Y.: World Book Co., 1938. Pp. xii, 306. $2.40.

Am J Orthopsychiatry 9:820-1 O '39. Luton Ackerson. * a novel effort to devise a measurement or "test" of personality traits other than intelligence * appears *a priori* to be a well-projected clinical instrument with the weakness, however, of considerable dependence upon arbitrary methods of scoring the responses * The monograph is unnecessarily difficult to read. If there is a revision of the present series a more concise "manual" should be prepared which will present the rationale and scoring methods in convenient form for the busy clinician, while the present volume may serve as a basic explanation for the student who wishes to study its methodology. Does the "Experience Appraisal" show promise of becoming a standard clinical instrument such as the well-known "intelligence test"? This reviewer as an incorrigible empiricist will not venture an answer until subsequent evidence of its actual use comes to hand, which we hope will soon be forthcoming.

Am J Orthopsychiatry 10:417-8 Ap '40. Eunice Acheson Pugh. [A note on the above review by Luton Ackerson.] In reading the recent review of Dr. Spencer's book in *The Journal,* it is evident that a number of unjustified criticisms were made and several important aspects of the study were entirely ignored. A thoughtful perusal of this book reveals a careful piece of scientific work. * one wonders if Dr. Ackerson is justified in saying that the chief weakness in [the] personality test is "its considerable dependence upon arbitrary methods of scoring." Since the Experience Appraisal is the only test of its kind which has yet been devised that does not rely entirely upon an arbitrary scoring key

for item evaluation, the above criticism seems unfounded. * Another weakness in Dr. Ackerson's review lies in the fact that he does not venture an opinion as to the value of the personality test. He states that he wishes rather to have this proved by its clinical performance and validation. When one reads that part of the text in which the author specifically indicates the methods by which the clinical validation is to be established, one feels that Dr. Spencer is unusually critical and conservative. This alone would lead to a considerable faith in the test's promise as a valuable clinical instrument. The present reviewer would also take issue with the statement that "the monograph is difficult to read, unnecessarily so." * Not only is the style good but the book is remarkable for its clarity and logical development. The intellectual level is high, judging by the fact that the second edition has already been sold out. The *Fulcra of Conflict* is proving its value to clinicians as well as to thoughtful students in related fields.

Am J Psychol 53:161-2 Ja '40. Henry A. Murray. The author starts off as if he were concerned with personality in general, but it dawns upon the reader sooner or later that he is interested in maladjustment, which is taken as synonymous with inner conflict. The book has nothing to say about the kinds, causes or treatment of conflict. It is a history, lucid and succinct, of the development of a new paper-and-pencil test for measuring the extent of conflict among normal adolescents. * The author's idea is a good one . . . but he has withheld from this volume the crucial information. There is only the promise of a later publication to appease the reader's reasonable curiosity on two points: Does this test measure inner conflict? Is inner conflict a good index of maladjustment? Maladjustment as measured by this test should prevail among children with high ideals and superior parents, and conflict (guilt feelings) should be common among those who are free and uninhibited in their behavior. Common experience tells us the opposite; high ideals tend to lift a person out of the slough of mediocrity (some tension between ambitions and attainments being normal and invigorating) ; and dilemmas of conscience are more frequent and disastrous among inhibited individuals whose conduct is exemplary. Nevertheless Dr. Spencer's test should be efficient in distinguishing most of the subjects with inferior complexes, even though some of the least normal cases will pass unnoticed. There should be a law against employing such a test to separate goats from sheep without adequate supplementary interviews by an experienced psychologist. *Fulcra of Conflict* is a neat report of work in progress rather than a finished book.

Clearing House 14:62 S '39. Charles E. Skinner.

J Ed Psychol 30:636-8 N '93. Carl R. Rogers. In spite of its esoteric title, this book represents a definite forward step in the complexities of personality measurement. * the book is a study of a new instrument for personality measurement * In essence his instrument provides more adequately than ever before for the comparison of the adolescent's self-rating with his rating of his own ideals, his parents' attitudes and behavior, and the behavior of his associates. * Not the least valuable part of the work is the thoroughgoing discussion of the philosophy as well as the techniques of personality measurement which constitute the first three chapters. This will be required reading for all those who plan new efforts in this field. The inadequacies of trait measurement, the over-use of statistical techniques, the lack of sound thinking and sound formulation of hypotheses for testing are forcefully presented. To this reviewer Spencer's discussion of personality conflict is definitely disappointing. Profound consideration of this problem, by those oriented to clinical work, is badly needed. Unfortunately the author contents himself with quoting others and then comfortably defines conflict for the purpose of his research as the discrepancy between the subject's views of his own behavior and his beliefs regarding the various "fulcra." This is too superficial a view. Another disappointment to clinicians is the meager practical outcome of the research. By additional questions Spencer finds that more than fifty per cent of the group would have answered questions untruthfully if the test had not been anonymous. Those with the most conflict show the greatest tendency toward distorting their responses, thus casting considerable doubt on the use of this type of procedure with clinical subjects of adolescent age. A relatively untapped field of discussion in the book is the wealth of revealing data as to adolescent attitudes in a fairly typical high-school group. *

In general the book places a needed emphasis on a soundly comparative approach for determining stress and strain within the individual. It is to be hoped that on the basis of Spencer's findings personality tests will be developed which can bring forth truthful responses, and yet concern themselves with these important conflict situations, rather than with hypothetical traits.

Mental Hyg (New York) 24:295-8 Ap '40. Henry C. Patey. Whether this is the book for which we have been looking is a question, but with either a psychoanalytic or a moralistic twist to our thinking, we are likely at least to agree that Dr. Spencer has written just what we wanted. He brings into harmony a variety of what have been conflicting views. * the reader will find this well-digested treatment of a wide variety of views most helpful—even if only as an orientation to the field of personality diagnosis in its measurement aspects * The author critically exposes the assumptions that underlie much of the research in personality measurement. * The discussion of conflict, complacency, and psycho-cultural processes is on a plane that wins the confidence of the reader in the author's mature grasp of clinical problems as well as in his facility in dealing with problems of philosophical and statistical research. * He expects to standardize the instrument later * With this further step in mind, it might be well to question what appears to be assumed to have been adequately considered. We shall not hesitate to borrow the author's criticisms of other work for this purpose. First, it does not appear that the author anticipates any further consideration of life circumstances than what is reflected in the experience appraisal. If this is true, he may become the object of his own criticism of Hadfield's view that the "psychoneurotic symptom is always the result of an endo-psychic conflict." The author has given such satisfactory recognition to environmental impacts that we may hope he will hold constant such facts as family disruption and types of home discipline when considering conflicts with parents' ideals and behaviors. * Possibly the conception of *complacency*, at least in its mathematical relationships, will need to be modified. On the continuum—probably not linear—complacency may lie not at the extreme pole from conflict, but at a point between *conflict* and a *static state*. Further, we sense an ambiguity in the use of the *conflict-complacency* idea as a continuum with the two terms defining the extremes, and on the other hand in the use of *complacency* to indicate a mental balance in which conflict is a valuable and necessary component. In the first instance, a *degree* on a scale is indicated. In the second instance, the *relationship* of two points on the scale is of interest. This second problem is one of *balance* or of *integration*. We then are left in doubt as to whether complacency is the opposite of conflict on a continuum or whether it is a ratio in which *facility to resolve conflict* is compared with *degree of conflict*. The author appears to think correctly in the clinical realm, but to have difficulty with the mathematical counterpart. Possibly he hopes to get a direct measure of integration and thereby to avoid the use of ratios. This view would be supported by his discussion of hazards. * In conclusion, we can agree that he has proved his argument that "a given attribute, behavior or experience . . . is significant . . . in conjunction with, and by reason of, the subjective relativities of the concrete experience"; and that he further has demonstrated the possibility of discovering the law and order in each individual life pattern and of measuring significant aspects of that individuality. The reading of the book will be a pleasanter experience than usually is anticipated. In fact, it has been difficult to refrain from quoting at least a few of the delightful paragraphs. Not only is the style good, but the organization is a model in logic. Altogether, a rare treat in psychological writing.

Muskingum Col Fac News B 9:35 Ap '39. J. J. Smith. * very interesting * I approve heartily the idea that personality is not a *sum* of factors—traits, attitudes, sets, acts, ideas, etc. The major problem in the understanding of personality is the pattern which makes the organism a unit. * This test shows reliability high enough for dealing with groups and perhaps for detecting individuals for clinical research. The most important validity factor mentioned—two hour interviews with examinees—is not yet reported. I question the generalization that students will not report their beliefs and attitudes honestly and that work of this kind must deceive the examinee. Does any one believe that deception as a policy will work more than once? I believe our only hope of aiding our students to build better

personalities is to work openly and honestly with them.

Psychiatry 2:290-1 My '39. Joseph Chassell. * In contrast to the usual personal inventory questionnaire, this test places little reliance upon the subject's description of his own symptoms or conflicts, but instead attempts to discover him in unwitting displays of actual conflict as shown in discrepancies between his report about his own attitude or behavior in personal, home, and social situations, and his report as to his own ideals in these regards as well as his conception of the attitudes and behavior of his parents and associates. * the author uses good sense throughout * This is probably a rather significant book, both for these attempting the personality-test approach and for those scoffing at it. * In the actual reading of the book one may easily become restive while wading through the preliminary discussion. In that case we suggest starting with the résumé on p. 56. Roughly speaking, the first chapters add up to the conclusion that, by and large, personality tests don't test, and that if a person answers YES to certain questions on a personal inventory, it does not necessarily follow that he is normal or introverted or neurotic. * When we enter the discussion of Dr. Spencer's own work we find a distinctly readable presentation, especially if we pick our way carefully around the twenty-four bristling tables. Being a Teachers College research, we may assume that Hollerith cards and calculating machines have been used, with no statistical stone left unturned. Nevertheless, all this is done with discrimination and without idolatory. *

Sociol and Social Res 23:580-1 Jl-Ag '39. M(elvin) J. V(incent). * valuable and arresting * a stimulating project in the whole field of personality measurement.

[B1082]
SPRAGUE, RUSSELL E. **Revision of Form C of the Physics Technical Vocabulary Test, Worksample 181 on the Basis of New Critical Ratios.** Human Engineering Laboratory, Technical Report No. 20. Boston, Mass.: the Laboratory, 1938. Pp. vi, 61. $1.00. Paper, mimeographed.

[B1083]
STEAD, WILLIAM H.; SHARTLE, CARROLL L.; OTIS, JAY L.; WARD, RAYMOND S.; OSBORNE, HERBERT F.; ENDLER, O. L.; DVORAK, BEATRICE J.; COOPER, JOHN H.; BELLOWS, ROGER M.; AND KOLBE, LAVERNE E. **Occupational Counseling Techniques:** Their Development and Application. Published for the Technical Board of the Occupational Research Program, United States Employment Service. New York: American Book Co., 1940. Pp. ix, 273. $2.50.

Bus Ed World 20:921 Je '40. *Marion M. Lamb.* * The book is solid and technical. It will no doubt be invaluable to those trained in vocational counseling; the lay reader will get from it little but a feeling of incompetency.

[B1084]

STEEL, JAMES H., AND TALMAN, JOHN. **The Marking of English Compositions.** London: James Nisbet and Co., Ltd., 1936. Pp. vii, 55. 2s.

[B1085]

STEVENSON, GEORGE S., AND SMITH, GEDDES. **Child Guidance Clinics:** A Quarter Century of Development. New York: Commonwealth Fund, 1934. Pp. vii, 186. $1.50. (London: Oxford University Press. 6s. 6d.)

Am J Psychol 48:549 Jl '36. *Wendell W. Cruze.*

Am J Sociol 41:417-8 N '35. *Ethel Kawin.* For anyone who wants to gain a thorough understanding of that significant phase of the mental hygiene movement which is represented by child-guidance clinics, this is a most valuable book. * The last two chapters include a frank, penetrating, and stimulating discussion of the many problems pressing for solution (notably the questions of evaluation and scientific research), and some consideration of the possible direction of future progress in child guidance, as suggested by present trends.

Ann Internal Med 8:104 Jl '34. *J. L. McC.* * an excellent review *

Arch Neurology and Psychiatry 32:1120-2 N '34. * a somewhat sketchy but interesting history of the child guidance clinic movement. Procedures are indicated rather than described. It will be of service to an agency contemplating the setting up of a new clinic and to all workers in the movement. As a manual of practice it is inadequate, however, and most of the concrete suggestions offered consist of warnings as to what to avoid rather than instructions as to what to do.

Brit J Psychol 25:258 O '34. * deals only with the development of the clinic in America, but is a very clear, unprejudiced, and fair piece of work. All child guidance workers in this country should study the report with care.

Brit Med J 3859:1150 D 22 '34.

J Ed Res 29:226-7 N '35. *Harry J. Baker.* The history of child guidance clinics has been well-presented and summarized. *

J Pediatrics 5:288 Ag '34. *B(orden) S. V(eeder).* * of considerable interest and should be read by pediatricians * the status of the

clinic, its weaknesses as well as its strength, is discussed in a broad, impartial manner * the authors have somewhat misunderstood the pediatric viewpoint. Pediatrics questions the place the so-called "clinical psychologist" has attempted to assume. * The reviewer feels that too much stress has been placed upon the relation of the child guidance clinic to social agencies rather than upon the family unit, although this may have been necessary in the early days of its development. * a fair and timely discussion * merits a widespread reading by pediatricians.

Med Times 63:298 S '34. *Stanley S. Lamm.* * should have an especial appeal to those physicians interested in the problem.

Mental Hyg (New York) 19:112-4 Ja '35. *Ralph P. Truitt.* * might be considered the *magnum opus* in the child-guidance-clinic field. In assembling their material, the authors have ignored no pertinent questions, and have discussed many delicate situations and controversial questions with great tact and skill. They have handled a difficult job well, and the book represents a distinct contribution to child guidance. * The chapters on approach to the case, the selection of cases, services, and procedures are exceptionally fine. * this book portrays a specialized effort to understand and help maladjusted children, for the most part in geographically unexplored and unprepared territories. It is an interesting account of rapidly changing affiliations, methods, and techniques, of failures and successes, and of the present status of a movement that has gained great momentum. The authors have no panaceas to offer, no axes to grind. Some questions are answered, but many remain to be solved. The outstanding feature of the book is its objectivity. No tendency is shown to lean toward this or that brand of therapy, and the possible value of all forms of approach is admitted. The insistence on open-mindedness is a healthy one. The book should attract the attention of a host of people besides those actively working in the child-guidance-clinic field. In make-up it has all of the usual excellent earmarks of the Division of Publications of the Commonwealth Fund.

For additional reviews, see B490.

[B1086]

STEWARD, VERNE. **Selection of Sales Personnel.** Los Angeles, Calif.: Verne Steward & Associates, 5471 Chesley Ave., 1936. Pp. 48. $2.75.

[B1087]

STRANG, RUTH. **Behavior and Background of Students in College and Secondary School.** New York: Harper & Brothers, 1937. Pp. xv, 515. $4.00.

Char and Pers 7:356-7 Je '39. *E. V. Pullias.* * a useful summary of the findings and conclusions of numerous researches touching . . . advisory work.

Ed Abstracts 4:350-1 D '39. *Roy N. Anderson.* * a monumental piece of work * a distinct service has been rendered to counsellors in secondary schools and colleges. No abstract can do justice to a volume that summarizes 1310 references covering such a wide variety of problems of adjustment of students. This volume should be in the professional library of all those who serve youth.

J Appl Psychol 22:667-8 D '38. *R. W. Husband.* * This volume must be considered a compendium more than anything else. Dr. Strang has worked in 1310 references, often as many as a dozen on a single page, yet has skillfully blended in quotations and citations to make the manuscript smooth and readable, as well as informative. * To the well trained psychologist or counselor, much of the material will seem superfluous * But to the individual who may be asked to do some counseling on the side, in addition to his regular teaching duties, the book should be remarkably handy in giving much valuable data, critical outlooks, and a well oriented point of view. *

J Consulting Psychol 3:39-40 Ja-F '39. *John G. Darley.* * Miss Strang has undertaken a much-needed task of synthesis and collation. Her efforts have yielded an indispensable and exhaustive bibliography, logically grouped and clearly annotated in relation to student personnel functions and problems. * Miss Strang has not written for easy or rapid reading, or for those whose basic grasp of certain aspects of theoretical psychology is weak. Her work presupposes a mastery of experimental methods in studying human behavior, skill in statistical interpretation, and a knowledge of psychological theory of human functioning. * The inclusion of so much material lends strength insofar as the [book is] . . . definitive and inclusive; the weakness springs from a relative lack of opportunity for sufficiently critical analysis of a small, but still representative, sampling of the literature. * of greatest value as source material for carefully delimited aspects of the field * specialists will find the . . .

[book] most valuable * should be compulsory reading for anyone who considers himself a personnel worker; without grasping Dr. Strang's ideas and without a minimum familiarity with the literature she has summarized, one lacks basic training in the field *

For additional reviews, see B492.

[B1088]

STRANG, RUTH. **Counseling Technics in College and Secondary School.** New York: Harper & Brothers, 1937. Pp. xi, 159. $2.00.

Char and Pers 7:356-7 Je '39. *E. V. Pullias.* * a very stimulating list of problems for further research . . . should be particularly suggestive to research students.

J Appl Psychol 22:667-8 D '38. *R. W. Husband.* * the outstanding feature . . . is the discussion of making the case study, handling the interview, making observations, and using rating scales. The various hidden angles, pitfalls, and traps into which the unwary counselor might fall are pointed out in very astute fashion. The necessity of keeping permanent records for cumulative purposes and to obviate probable loss of memory for details is well pointed out. * There is one limitation of this work, as well as of virtually every book on counseling, whether personal or vocational. This is the absence of a suggested constructive program. * Possibly a few case studies, reproduced more or less verbatim from actual interviews, with objective data which are to be considered interspersed, would give constructive advice of value.

J Consulting Psychol 3:39-40 Ja-F '39. *John G. Darley.* * Dr. Strang tends to emphasize equally each technic discussed, with too little discussion of relative merit or worth. Granting that all possible technics are of some value, it is still not inconsistent to expect a more critical evaluation of relative utility. To offset this impartiality, however, the reviewer finds her treatment of personality and of attitudes and interests to be infused with a caution that is at least theoretically defensible, in the present state of psychological knowledge; but this caution is somewhat extreme in clinical practice. In these chapters, also, the analysis of the literature emphasizes to a lesser extent the contribution of measurement or test methods to the study of the behavior in question. * it is disappointing to find so little discussion of the place of tests and psychometric procedures * should be compulsory reading for anyone who considers himself a personnel worker; without grasping Dr. Strang's ideas and without a minimum familiarity with the literature she has summarized, one lacks basic training in the field. *

J Ed Res 32:140-1 O '38. *Carter V. Good.* * Most of the chapters end with pointed suggestions for further research. *

J Higher Ed 9:408 O '38. *W. H. Cowley.* * a most valuable handbook for all personnel people. The reviewer has never seen a more thorough job and urges that it be within easy reach of every individual in schools and colleges who is seriously attempting to do counseling. The author's point of view is also significant. She not only summarizes the methods of counseling students, but she evaluates the underlying ideologies. Thus the reader has not only a compendium of valuable and otherwise inaccessible information but also a philosophy of counseling growing from long experience and built upon wise insight into the psychological and sociological problems involved.

Relig Ed 34:64 *Ja-Mr* '39. *Frank Meyerson.* * A reader-counselor will find much of value to aid him in his work.

For additional reviews, see B493.

[B1089]

SUPER, DONALD E. **Avocational Interest Patterns:** A Study in the Psychology of Avocations. Stanford, Calif.: Stanford University Press, 1940. Pp. xiv, 148. $2.25. (London: Oxford University Press. 14s.)

Loyola Ed Digest 15:6 *Jl* '40. *Austin G. Schmidt.* * The instrument used in the present study was the Strong Vocational Interest Blank. The study, painstakingly made, reveals certain patterns of avocational interest in men who have been successful in certain vocations. It is to be hoped that further research in the same field will lead to a solution of the problems which this pioneer investigation has opened up.

[B1090]

SYMONDS, PERCIVAL M. **Psychological Diagnosis in Social Adjustment:** Including an Annotated List of Tests, Questionnaires, and Rating Scales for the Study of Personality and Conduct. New York: American Book Co., 1934. Pp. ix, 362. $3.25.

Personnel J 13:299 *Ap* '35. * describes the uses of psychological measurement in the diagnosis of (1) criminal tendencies, (2) mental disorder, (3) citizenship and leadership, and (4) vocational fitness. The latter section would presumably be of chief interest to readers of this magazine, but unfortunately it is that one about which the author appears

to be least qualified to write. One gets the distinct impression that Dr. Symonds' knowledge about selecting employees has been gained through reading books and articles. An "annotated list of tests, questionnaires, and rating scales for the study of personality and conduct," comprising more than half the book, should prove useful for reference purposes.

For additional reviews, see B253 and B496.

[B1091]

TANSIL, REBECCA CATHERINE. **The Contributions of Cumulative Personnel Records to a Teacher-Education Program:** As Evidenced by their Use at the State Teachers College at Towson, Maryland. Columbia University, Teachers College, Contributions to Education No. 764. E. S. Evenden, faculty sponsor. New York: Bureau of Publications, the College, 1939. Pp. viii, 158. $1.60.

Ed Abstracts 5:19 *Ja* '40. *Roger M. Bellows.*
Ed Res B 19:241 *Ap* 10 '40. *F. C. Landsittel.* The utility of adequate records . . . becomes convincingly clear upon reading this report. * Any faculty member of a teachers' college will find profitable reading in Miss Tansil's study, for any faculty member has reason for being concerned about adequate personnel records and their use.

J Am Assn Col Reg 15:94 O '39. * a painstaking study * contains a good bibliography on personnel procedures, particularly as related to record-keeping * a significant contribution toward a better application and evaluation of personnel methods *

Loyola Ed Digest 14:7 *Jl* '39. *Austin G. Schmidt.* * The study was honestly and competently made, but the fact that the faculty numbered only thirty-five and the student body only about five hundred necessarily limits the value of both data and conclusions. Nevertheless, the work contains material that should prove helpful to institutions seeking to develop a personnel record system and is a good example of how the case-study method can be applied to the appraisal of a record system.

Mental Hyg (New York) 24:489-90 *Jl* '40. *Harry N. Rivlin.* * suggests many values that follow from the use of cumulative records * Dr. Tansil apparently agrees with Odenweller, whom she quotes, that the correlation between personality and success in teaching is greater than is the correlation between either college work or student teaching and teaching success. Her report becomes increasingly significant when it is viewed as one way of focusing attention on the personality development of prospective teachers. A program such as hers should foster the selection of future teachers with regard to their development as individuals as well as their attainments as students. This report should be helpful to those who are in a position to modify the records at teacher-training institutions. For such readers, the book presents a detailed analysis of the ways in which the records were used and evaluated. At times the reader will regret that the book appears as a doctoral dissertation, for it is essentially the report of a practical solution to a realistic problem. Appearing in the format of a research report, there is a tendency to employ statistical procedures with data that do not warrant elaborate treatment, and to include substantiating data even where the conclusions are obvious or the question trivial.

Occupations 18:233-4 D '39. M. E. Bennett. * a carefully planned appraisal * Administrators and guidance workers at all levels should gain valuable suggestions from this study for the development, evaluation, and improvement of a functional system of cumulative personnel records.

[B1092]
TERMAN, LEWIS M., AND MERRILL, MAUD A. **Directions for Administering Forms L and M, Revision of the Stanford-Binet Tests of Intelligence.** Boston, Mass.: Houghton Mifflin Co., 1937. Pp. v, 116. $1.35. Spiral binding.

[B1093]
TERMAN, LEWIS M., AND MERRILL, MAUD A. **Measuring Intelligence:** A Guide to the Administration of the New Revised Stanford-Binet Tests of Intelligence. Boston, Mass.: Houghton Mifflin Co., 1937. Pp., xiv, 461. $2.25. (London: George G. Harrap & Co., Ltd., 1939. 10s. 6d.)

Brit J Med Psychol 17:382-4 pts 3-4 '38. C. J. C. Earl. * the appearance of Terman's long-promised new revision is an event of major importance * contains no dogmatic statements of theory, but merely an account of the methods employed * the scales may be accepted as remarkably valid statistically * The mental-age method of scoring is adhered to, as is the I.Q. convention. The authors defend both points with spirit, but it seems a pity that this unique opportunity for the introduction of percentile scoring, at any rate as an alternative method, has been missed. * the new scale is infinitely better scored than was the old, its sensitivity ranging from 2 to 18 years * Scoring in terms of I.Q. is now more complicated than before * the term I.Q. is made even more artificial than formerly. With regard to the test items themselves, the principal novelty lies

in the pre-school years, now for the first time included in the scale. The material here . . . is admirable from the point of view of interest, but it would undoubtedly be better for its purpose if the toys were on a much larger scale. The test-matter of the remainder of the scale shows little change * It is a pity also that references to crime and punishment, and to violent death, all of which possess a strong emotional significance for many subjects tested in clinical work, are still included. The instructions for application and scoring should go far to make the new scale almost fool-proof; the scoring is admirably objective, and attention is directed, not only to the testing itself, but to the surroundings and circumstances in which it is carried out. One point for regret is that the serial method of administration is condemned; this is a pity, as the method is undoubtedly clinically useful, and places less strain on the examiner. * a very important book * there will be many clinical psychologists who would prefer a more flexible method consisting of single units either combined to form a battery or expressed configurationally as in the psychographs of Vermeylen or Rossolimo * the clinical value of such a figure as the intelligence quotient, however accurately measured, is definitely secondary to that of the interpretation of the test behaviour by a competent psychologist: it seems a pity then to use a test which gives so little scope for such interpretation as does the Binet. These, and many similar criticisms notwithstanding, there can be no doubt of the importance of the contribution made by Prof. Terman and his associates. * This may be the last of all the revisions of Binet's great scale. If so, it is not an unworthy finale.

Civil Service Assembly News Letter 3:9 O '37. * From the point of view of the public personnel technician, the most important change in the scales is the addition of two supplementary levels for superior adults. *

Lancet 5952:746 S 25 '37. * Binet, were he alive, might well have difficulty in recognizing these scales as revisions of his own. * This new scale may have to be modified for English children, but even in its original form the Terman revision was used with success in this country, and there is no reason to anticipate any more difficulty with the tests as revised.

For reviews by Francis M. Maxfield, J. W. M. Rothney, F. L. Wells, and others, see 1062, 1420, and B497.

[B1094]

TERMAN, LEWIS M., AND MILES, CATHERINE COX, ASSISTED BY JACK W. DUNLAP, HAROLD A. EDGERTON, E. LOWELL KELLY, ALBERT K. KURTZ, E. ALICE McANULTY, QUINN McNEMAR, MAUD A. MERRILL, FLOYD L. RUCH, AND HORACE G. WYATT. **Sex and Personality:** Studies in Masculinity and Femininity. New York: McGraw-Hill Book Co., Inc., 1936. Pp. xii, 600. $4.50. (London: McGraw-Hill Publishing Co., Ltd. 25s.)

Int J Psycho-Analysis 18:331-6 Ap-Jl '37. J. C. Flügel. * No attempt has been made, in selecting the items, to distinguish between constitutionally and environmentally determined differences * The unrestricted inclusion in the present test material of many items the responses to which must be largely determined by education and other social influences, may make it necessary to obtain fresh norms from each culture tested, even though the differences in culture are no greater than those that obtain between one western nation and another. * a very notable advance in the psychology of sex differences, as regards both methodology and the knowledge of new facts * There is no doubt that the book deserves careful study by all who are interested in sex differences, from whatever angle they approach the subject. * the authors never allow themselves to forget that they are primarily psychologists, for whom 'tests' and statistics may be useful tools but nothing more.

Int J Psycho-Analysis 18:336-40 Ap-Jl '37. William V. Silverberg. * *Sex and Personality* is unquestionably statistical in its approach, but it is informed with a humility, a breadth of viewpoint and a ripe wisdom not frequently encountered in the product of academic psychology. * Precisely what it is that is being tested remains somewhat doubtful, as the authors acknowledge * Psycho-analysts will be especially interested in the study of male homosexuality which forms several chapters of the work. * the authors are led to conclude that individuals admittedly competent in the field of psychology lack a basis for the observation of the 'behavioral correlates' of 'masculinity' and 'feminity'. * there is much in the data given which suggests that the quality tested under the title 'masculinity' is a certain defensiveness lest the individual be thought not to conform with the traditional expectations of his group * The study is dependent throughout upon psycho-analytical formulations which have been for the most part so well digested that the authors appear unaware of their source and make no acknowledgment, either expressed or implied, of their debt to Freud. The only reference to psycho-analysis in the course of this long and very valuable work is a remark to the effect that study of female inverts has been made by 'the psycho-analysts'. *

Occupations 17:563-4 Mr '39. Richard S. Uhrbrock. An important research tool has been provided for those who wish to investigate attitudes and interests. * It must be emphasized that the Attitude-Interest Analysis Test cannot be used in its present state of development, as an occupational classification device. Eventually it may have some bearing upon that important problem. Judgment regarding the ultimate value of this new research tool should be deferred. It is a data gathering device whose value could easily be destroyed if used by overzealous vocational counselors determined to discuss premature interpretation of the results.

For additional reviews, see B498.

[B1095]

Tests for Intermediate and Upper Grades. Dansville, N. Y.: F. A. Owen Publishing Co., 1935. Pp. 96. $0.50. Paper.

[B1096]

THOMAS, FRANK C. **Ability and Knowledge:** The Standpoint of the London School. Foreword by C. Spearman. Appendix by Elsa Walters. London: Macmillan & Co., Ltd., 1935. Pp. xx, 338. 15s. (New York: Macmillan Co. $4.50.)

New R 4:504 N '36. T. N. Siqueira. Professor Spearman's contribution to the psychology of cognition has made the London School justly famous; but his two classical volumes and numerous articles are inaccessible to the ordinary reader. Mr. Frank Thomas has therefore made this 'attempt to place before the novice in psychological studies a simple yet adequate and authoritative account of the theories associated with the name of Professor Spearman' (p. XIII). That this account is simple and clear has been acknowledged by Professor Spearman himself; that it is adequate and authoritative, every reader will feel who has already been in touch with the findings of the London School. * The effect of fatigue on ability is particularly well analysed. * The chapter on the part played by association in facilitation of retentivity is perhaps the most useful to the reader from the practical point of view; the well-known noëgenetic laws of cognition with their insistence on the eduction of relations are here better stated than in any other place I know, finally, some of the many rival theories which have in recent years been proposed both in Europe and in the United States are given a fair trial. *

For additional reviews, see B258 and B500.

[B1097]

THOMPSON, LORIN ANDREW, ASSISTED BY DANIEL C. LAURENCE AND ARCHIE ALLARDYCE. **Interview Aids and Trade Questions for Employment Offices.** Foreword by Henry M. Waite. New York and London: Harper & Brothers, 1936. Pp. xvii, 173. $2.50; 10s. 6d.

Civil Service Assembly News Letter 2:6 D '36. This publication grew out of the experiences of the Cincinnati Employment Service in interviewing and classifying applicants of the skilled trades. Examiners preparing tests on skilled trades will find it a useful source book as it contains specific questions for the most common trades with correct answers indicated, and rating tables for grading the answers.
Survey 72:159 My '36. * Based on the premise that trade knowledge correlates highly with trade skill, the authors make no extravagant claims for the tests. *

For additional reviews, see B501.

[B1097.1]

THOMSON, GODFREY H. **An Analysis of Performance Test Scores of a Representative Group of Scottish Children.** Publications of the Scottish Council for Research in Education, [No.] 16. International Examinations Inquiry. London: University of London Press, Ltd., 1940. Pp. vii, 58. 5s.

Scottish Ed J 23:482 Je 28 '40. * The tests selected comprised the Seguin Form Board, Manikin, Stutsman Picture, Red Riding Hood, Healy Picture Completion II., Knox Cube Imitation, Cube Construction and Kohs Block Design. All the children tested—444 boys and 430 girls between 8 years 11 months and 11 years 9 months of age—were given the performance tests on the same day as the Binet Tests * In assembling the performance tests the Committee did not consider the individual test results to be of primary importance. It was rather the result of the battery as a whole that was regarded as important, and it was recognised that if the tests were to be considered for any other purpose as separate tests of intelligence a less coarse scoring would be necessary. It is perhaps unfortunate that with this warning in mind Professor Thomson did not rescore the tests before subjecting the results obtained to a factorial analysis. The work is nevertheless an interesting example

of the new factorial technique in the evolution of which Professor Thomson has himself played so distinguished a part. * Thomson's examination of the data has disclosed that the correlation of the sum of the raw scores in three of the performance tests—Cube Construction, Kohs Block Design, Healy Picture Completion—with the Binet I.Q. is approximately .7, and this is not appreciably improved by taking the weighted sum of all the nine tests. * Thomson . . . arrived at the conclusion that two factors could be identified, a general factor and a rhythm or speed factor linking the first three tests. * Thomson regards the factor common to the Binet test and the performance tests as perhaps in some respects a more suitable measure of the ability of a child than the Binet I.Q. since it is presumably free from the verbal or linguistic bias of the Binet, and also from anything in the performance tests which is wholly unrepresented in the Binet Scale. He shows how from the raw score of a small battery composed of Kohs Block Design, Cube Construction and Red Riding Hood this factor can be computed. If the Binet I.Q. is also available a comparison of the two would indicate whether the pupil excelled in the linguistic type of ability or possessed some aesthetic flair or space factor causing him to excel in the common factor. Although the work is highly technical it has evidently interesting implications, and we are grateful to Professor Thomson for undertaking this analysis which to him was presumably a labour of love. He has also presented the data on which he worked in such a form as to invite other computers to exercise their ingenuity on them.

[B1098]

THOMSON, GODFREY H. **The Factorial Analysis of Human Ability.** London: University of London Press, Ltd., 1939. Pp. xv, 326. (Boston, Mass.: Houghton Mifflin Co. $3.75.)

Am J Psychol 53:303-4 Ap '40. J. P. Guilford. All who follow the development of factor theory or methods, or who apply the factorial techniques will surely wish to read this volume. * Thomson gives very clear accounts which can be grasped without the aid of greater mathematical sophistication than is afforded by elementary algebra, geometry, and trigonometry. * Early and frequently the author pays deep respects to Spearman, and like most of his countrymen, holds the conviction that a *g* factor will always be found among tests of ability, no matter whatever else may or may not be found. * As forecasted in his earlier writings, Thomson harmonizes his own theory with the *g* hypothesis. In early chapters the theoretical bases for the two-factor, sampling, and multiple-factor theories are laid. In every case, the assumption is made that any correlation between two tests is due to a great many small, identical elements, a conception of correlation which is at least as old as Poisson but which few writers accept explicitly. For Thomson, the psychological elements, or 'bonds' are the real constituents of mental ability and this conception dominates his theory. * His main support for the unreality of factors is given in his discussion of the effects of sampling. The factors and their loadings, he maintains, have no absolute meaning but are functions of the selected population of individuals and of tests. With this result few factorists would probably disagree. Different factors and different loadings do arise from different samplings of individuals, and in some methods, from different samplings of tests. But the conclusion is not inevitable that factors are therefore not 'real.' His elemental 'bonds' of the mind, however, he maintains are real, and are associated somehow with the "one hundred thousand million (sic) nerve cells" in each normal brain. On the basis of these atoms of ability one should expect Spearman's criterion for a single common factor to hold, particularly when a sufficiently large number of bonds are brought into play in tests. There is apparently no retreat from Thomson's early position that "the laws of probability alone will account for a tendency to zero tetrad differences among correlation coefficients" (p. 47). * Procedures for computing factor loadings by the methods of Spearman, Thurstone, Hotelling, and Burt are described. Holzinger's work receives but slight mention. * The book is full of information about factor analysis, and in spite of rapid developments in this field will serve as a standard reference book on the subject for some time.

Brit J Ed Psychol 9:188-95 Je '39. *Cyril Burt.* The theory of factors made its first appearance as an offshoot of the mental testing movement; but it has come to play much the same part in modern psychology as the theory of linear operators in modern physics. Indeed, as branches of mathematics both are closely akin. * The results of his work fully justify the eagerness with which they have been awaited. To the non-mathematical, factor-analysis wears a formidable aspect. But Prof. Thomson's book can be understood by students with little or no mathematical knowledge beyond what is ordinarily imparted in a secondary school. At the same time even professional statisticians will welcome, not merely the succinct compendium of formulae and proofs brought together in the mathematical appendix, but also the new light thrown on old problems and on familiar solutions at almost every turn of the page. Throughout the author reveals himself, not only as a brilliant mathematician, but also as a brilliant teacher. The structure of the book, the compact and lucid style, the ingenious devices used to illustrate geometrical conceptions and arithmetical proofs, make the whole work easy to follow and brimful of interest. * To the pioneer work of Prof. Spearman he pays a generous tribute. * Thomson makes a fruitful use of some of the neat expedients devised by his colleague, Dr. Aitken, for solving what are essentially problems in matrix algebra. Once again the technical explanations are most skillfully treated. * In Part IV we reach a topic of special interest to the educationist—the proposal to correlate persons instead of tests. As Prof. Thomson points out, the device of correlating persons, with or without the additional idea of extracting factors and determining types, has long been in use; but it is only during the last two or three years that it has come to the front as a topic of controversy. * To the educationist, however, the most interesting section of all will be the last. Part V brings the volume to a close with a full discussion of 'the interpretation of factors.' * a much-needed caution is registered against the common tendency to 'reify factors' * The sampling theory is the most far-reaching of Prof. Thomson's many original contributions to the subject. * Six postulates seem implied in Thomson's theory. * So far as they go, I believe every psychologist—including Spearman himself—would accept them. * the sampling theory, as developed by Thomson, is primarily opposed to the popular analysis of the mind into a few independent 'unitary abilities', 'factors', or 'traits', in much the same way as the associationist doctrine, as developed by Thorndike, was opposed to the traditional analysis of the mind into a composite of a dozen or so 'faculties'; and so far as it goes, it has much the same arguments in its favour. * Thomson does not propose to explain test-performances solely in terms of sampling; and he is by no means unaware of these further problems. Indeed, if, on a first perusal, the reader thinks he has discovered a grave objection to the theory, he may be warned to re-read the relevant pages with care: more often than not he will find Prof. Thomson has anticipated the difficulty and even tersely hinted how it can be met. In an introductory work, the primary object of which is to give a comprehensive and impartial survey of the whole subject, suitable for the elementary student, the author has rightly kept his own interpretations modestly in their place. We shall all, however, look forward with the greatest interest to the further elaboration of his views which he seems to promise. Meanwhile, the present volume not only gives a lucid and unbiassed account of the different theories and methods that have hitherto been advanced, but also, as I have tried to show, raises a number of interesting and important issues which factor-analysis has still to answer and on which the thoughtful student can reflect and perhaps research. Both to investigators in this special field and to every teacher or educationist who wishes to think with precision about such questions, the book is indispensable. It is a splendid culmination to twenty-five years' work, and at the same time supplies a solid foundation for work that is yet to come.

Brit J Psychol 30:167-8 O '39. E. G. C(hambers). * Thomson deals with this question in a manner calculated to satisfy the advanced mathematician and to instruct the person of average mathematical ability. * whilst the person of average mathematical ability might slavishly follow the arithmetical examples provided and even copy them using his own data, yet only one capable of clear and sustained mathematical thought would be able to understand what he was doing at all stages of the analysis. Such a one will, however, find in this book adequate and clear explanations of the analytic procedures adopted by Spearman, Thurstone, Hotelling, Burt and others, with actual worked examples and accounts of the various "short-cut" methods which have been devised. * There is a grave danger, as is pointed out in this book, of reifying mathematical factors—a danger which, though usu-

ally avoided by the leading exponents of factorial analysis, is frequently positively courted by their enthusiastic disciples. Of what use then is factorial analysis to the psychologist? the reader will ask. It is rather difficult to find an answer from this book except that the author is sceptical of the utility and pessimistic of the future of factor analysis. He concludes, however, that the factor theory will still continue in spite of all its dangers and imperfections, partly on account of its intrinsic interest and partly because it has undeniably been a guide and spur to many investigators. By examining and explaining *in extenso* the dangers and imperfections inherent in factorial analysis Professor Thomson has rendered a great service to the psychological investigator who has neither the time to study the vast body of original documents on the subject nor the mathematical ability to criticise and appraise the methods for himself. But the book is not easy reading for the non-mathematician.

J Am Assn Col Reg 14:344-5 Ap '39. G. E. Metz. * will be welcomed by non-mathematically-inclined personnel workers and others who are finding it as necessary today to become acquainted with factor analysis as it was a few decades ago to master the fundamentals of statistics and tests and measurements * The text is not only historical and comprehensive but also up-to-date. * The unique presentation of the various theories, concepts, and techniques of factor analysis renders the book casually understandable to the student with no mathematical background beyond the usual secondary school knowledge, more profitable to the student of statistics with a background in the algebra of determinants and matrices, and invaluable as a guide to the study of other works which are not so general or comprehensive but which deal more thoroughly and intensively with specific theories and techniques. *

Math Gazette 24:150-1 My '40. J. Wishart. * should . . . be of interest to all educationalists, and in particular mathematical teachers will be interested in a branch of psychology in which so much use is made of their own field of study. The book is interestingly and authoritatively written throughout, and is a pleasure to read. Also it is well documented with references, and dealing as it does with a branch of study which the author has made so much his own, it forms an invaluable source and reference book to all who would like to master this particular field of study. *

Nature 144:532-3 S 23 '39. C(yril) B(urt). * a single clear and systematic exposition [of] all the chief factorial methods that have hitherto been put forward. He explains their mathematical derivation in an elementary way for the student of psychology, and briefly compares their merits and their disadvantages. He also incorporates a summary of his own very valuable contributions, including more particularly a revised version of the sampling theory which he had put forward as an alternative to the two-factor theory of Prof. Spearman. From the first page to the last the treatment is remarkably lucid, suggestive, and impartial. * even the professional psychologist and statistician will welcome the compendium of formulae and proofs brought together in the mathematical appendix, and throughout the book will find new light continually shed on old problems * although these methods were originally developed for the analysis of the results of psychological testing, they would be almost equally applicable to the solution of analogous problems in many other fields—in physiology, biology, sociology, medicine, economics, agriculture and, indeed, in almost any science where causal factors are numerous and inextricably interlinked. The book must at once take its place as one of the most important publications of the year in the field of education and psychology; at the same time it should be of great interest to all who are engaged on statistical research, no matter what their special sphere.

Occupational Psychol 13:241-5 Jl '39. Patrick Slater. * From the beginning the reader will be delighted at the clearness of the style, the simplicity with which difficult mathematical problems are explained, the felicity of the diagrams, the convenience of the methods described for conducting complex statistical processes in simple steps. He will not have read far before he feels he has found his sea-legs in a multi-dimensional space with axes rotating gently to and fro. These feelings will remain, but their importance will fade as he reads on. He is likely to search in vain for a steady, consistent line of argument to lead him through the book. No such line is defined, its existence is only indicated by a series of

tangents to it. Although many methods of factor analysis are criticized mathematically, they themselves are not fully described. No complete description is given of Spearman's method or of its extension by Holzinger (Bi-factor analysis), or of Thurstone's, Kelley's or Burt's methods. The only method described in full is Hotelling's. And while the former are fully criticized, no detailed reference is given to the many serious criticisms, both mathematical and psychological, which have been brought against the latter (e.g., Thurstone, Vectors of Mind Chapter iv). Many limitations of the applicability of factor analysis to psychological problems are discussed, and deserve the careful consideration of those who use such methods for research work. Others given are more like exotic delicacies for the connoisseur of psychological statistics. It is characteristic of the book that both kinds of comment are given equal place and no attempt is made to segregate them. Two postulates run like themes through the book: the first, that the analysis of a table of correlations between test scores should account for the total variance of every test; the second, that factor analysis should provide a psychological parallelism to the physiology of the brain. Each of these postulates is open to criticism. * The [first] postulate . . . cannot ever be satisfied in practice, and Thomson's habitual insertion of communalities of 1 in the diagonals of his correlation tables seems to me therefore misleading in its implications and its consequences. Such a procedure has been criticized before, and Thomson notes the criticisms although he does not modify his practice. Surely it is better to estimate communalities at their most probable values than to equate them all to 1, a limiting value which is demonstrably unattainable. Thomson's second postulate . . . [is] his chief constructive contribution to factor analysis. * In my opinion psychological facts and findings are not compatible with Thomson's sampling theory. The theory seems to me still less adequate for explaining the known facts concerning other factors. * The Factorial Analysis of Human Ability is in my opinion not a reference book, not a guide to constructive research in mental testing, not a wholly unbiased or altogether reliable introduction to factor analysis; but it is, I consider, an excellent contribution to the controversial literature on the subject, and it deserves careful study as a conscientious warning against rash inferences from statistical data in psychology.

Scottish Ed J 22:372-3 Mr 31 '39. In this book Professor Thomson essays two of the most difficult tasks he could have chosen. . . . [First to inform] the non-mathematical reader of the different theories of factorial analysis * The second, and even more difficult task, is that of criticising the limitations in method and interpretation of the various theories in the field. * a very clear statement of the present position of factorial analysis and provides an excellent focal point for the discussion required to clear up the discrepancies and difficulties which abound in this field of research.

[B1098.1]

THORNTON, GEORGE R. **Factor Analysis of Tests Designed to Measure Persistence.** American Psychological Association, Psychological Monographs, Vol. 51, No. 3, Whole No. 229. Evanston, Ill.: the Association, 1939. Pp. 42. $0.65. Paper.

Loyola Ed Digest 15:10-1 Ja '40. Austin G. Schmidt. * The analysis revealed the presence of five approximately independent factors that are important in the tests studied. It is interesting to note that two of these factors—withstanding discomfort to achieve a goal and keeping on at a task—although they might have been expected to be closely associated, are not intercorrelated.

[B1099]

THURSTONE, L. L. **Primary Mental Abilities.** Psychometric Society, Psychometric Monograph No. 1. Chicago, Ill.: University of Chicago Press, 1938. Pp. ix, 121. $2.00. Paper. (London: Cambridge University Press. 9s.)

Brit J Ed Psychol 9:270-5 N '39. H. J. Eysenck. * reports the first large experimental inquiry, carried out by the methods of factor analysis described by Thurstone in *The Vectors of the Mind* * When the editor of this *Journal* first suggested a review of Professor Thurstone's new report, it appeared that the large collection of data contained in its tables would offer an admirable opportunity for testing recent statements about the mode of factor analysis, statements for the most part reached *a priori* and never yet verified by any concrete comparison. How, for example, do Thurstone's methods and results compare with earlier methods and results put forward by workers in this country? * Spearman, in a paper read at the recent Reading conference, has maintained that Thurstone's table could be fitted

by a two-factor analysis and that this procedure would reveal a single general factor. Thurstone, on the other hand, declares: "We cannot report any general common factor in Spearman's sense in the 56 tests that have been analyzed." This is rather surprising, since, in selecting the tests, "special emphasis was laid on those tests which are used as measures of intelligence." Now his Table III does, as a matter of fact, show a 'general common factor in Spearman's sense', i.e., a column of saturation coefficients, all positive, and larger than those in any other column; and its subsequent disappearance is plainly an inevitable result of his method of rotation: this aims, not only at abolishing negative saturations, but also at maximizing the zeros *in every column,* even where the saturations are large and positive throughout. No general factor could survive such a procedure. An analysis by Burt's procedure appears to reconcile the two conclusions: for, with Spearman, we discover a general factor, accountable for more of the total variance than any other, and with Thurstone we discover a number of group-factors having a clear psychological meaning. In their general nature the group-factors shown in Table I agree almost entirely with those of Professor Thurstone. They prove, indeed, to be much the same as those noted in the earlier researches of Burt and his co-workers on London school children * Perhaps, however, the most interesting result of our analysis is this. By the use of a very simple procedure we are able to demonstrate and calculate much the same factors as are demonstrated and calculated by Thurstone. Thurstone's own analysis depends first on making an elaborate formal analysis by the centroid method and then rotating the axes thus found by a somewhat prolonged and admittedly precarious graphical procedure. The submatrix method reaches the same results directly with one set of simple calculations. * To educationists one of the most interesting chapters in the monograph is the last. This deals with the uses of mental 'profiles'. * In conclusion we must express our admiration for the great care and thoroughness which has evidently been expended upon this research. It is, indeed, one of the most valuable educational experiments of its kind hitherto carried out. It provides a mass of figures for those who wish to test alternative methods of analysis; and anyone who wishes to be acquainted with the factorial technique in educational research will find this book a most lucid and instructive introduction.

Brit J Psychol 29:308-10 Ja '39. E. G. C(hambers). * The author of this monograph described, in *The Vectors of Mind* (1935), a method of factorial analysis which he has subsequently applied to a large body of experimental data, and has presented the results in this book. Without familiarity with the earlier work the reader would find difficulty in following certain sections in the present monograph, but if he is willing to accept without question the validity of the method of factorial analysis used, he will find the experiment and results obtained described in full, clear detail. * Doubts may arise in the reader's mind about the validity of this substitution [of tetrachoric coefficient for product-moment coefficients] * The monograph shows a sincere and painstaking attempt to exemplify the value of the author's method of analysing the factors involved in test performance, and the results are interesting and suggestive to psychologists. It must be borne in mind, however, that the isolation and naming of a factor by any method of factorial analysis does nothing further than prove the existence of this factor in the particular set of test scores under survey, and does not necessarily mean that there is an exact psychological counterpart in the subjects who originally performed the tests. The performance of the same tests by other groups of subjects might quite conceivably yield different results. In this case in particular, a highly selected group of subjects was tested, and it would be of great interest to see if the results were repeated, and the same factors isolated, if an unselected group of subjects (among whom the test intercorrelations would almost certainly be much larger) were given the same tests. Nor does the isolation and naming of a factor prove that a mental ability corresponding to it is possessed in fixed quantities by the subjects tested (and, arguing from them, by mankind in general), so that we can say of a certain person that he possesses abilities *A, B, C, D, . . .* to certain specified degrees. We are far yet from being able to do this and it may even be argued that envisaging such a procedure is undesirable, since it is suggestive of a retrogressive step in the history of psychology.

J Am Assn Col Reg 14:211 Ja '39. W. P. Shofstall. * will be valued highly by any who recognize that the nature of intelligence is still an open and vitally important question. Acceptance of the concept of mental abilities rather than mental ability would completely upset most of our present-day educational theories and practices. *

J Ed Psychol 30:74-7 Ja '39. Quinn McNemar. * An excellent nonstatistical introduction to the problem of factor analysis is provided in the opening chapter. * Unfortunately, despite the convincingness of Thurstone's monograph, the skeptic can still point to the subjective nature of the interpretations involved in assigning psychological meaning to the so-called primary abilities. * On page VII of the preface, Thurstone states that so far he has not found any evidence for a general common factor in Spearman's sense. It seems to the reviewer that no argument has been put forth which would deter Spearman and his followers from claiming that the first centroid factor corresponds to their common factor. * In this monograph a new criterion is proposed, and used, for determining how many centroid factors to extract. Had the discarded criterion (residual variance reduced to sampling variance of original mean intercorrelation) been used, only three factors would have been determined. The new criterion may be more valid, but certainly a part of the logic which led to its adoption is open to serious question. * The reviewer is unable to say to what extent the new criterion is invalidated because of the failure to allow for the proper operation of chance. Moreover, it seems extremely unlikely that an adequate criterion will be found which is independent of the number of cases in the sample. * In the application of the new criterion to the analysis of the fifty-seven tests, we note that the criterion value approaches its limiting value of .982 in the following manner: .556, .878, .941, .962, .959, .970, .974, .974, .978, .966, .960, .972, and .980, from which it is concluded that thirteen factors are needed. Perhaps the shade of difference between .970 and .980 means something, but until the criterion is more rigorously determined it seems a bit fortuitous to accept such a convergence as being of sufficient significance to indicate that more than six centroid factors are justified. What would happen if another sample were drawn? * Aside from the subjectivity involved in giving meaning to the factors, one also notes a disturbing arbitrariness in the selection of tests utilized in rationalizing some of the factors. * The points which the reviewer has raised are not to be regarded as major criticisms of a study which can very properly be considered as the outstanding experimental contribution in an important field of investigation. So far as the factorial methods are concerned it would seem that the weakest links in an otherwise strong chain are those which bridge the gap between mathematical factors and psychological meaning and the chasm between sample and universe values. In fact the latter link is practically missing, and from the reviewer's viewpoint this constitutes a serious limitation. * It cannot be said that Thurstone's basic data were faulty, or that he engineered his set-up so as to obtain seven factors, or that he generalizes too far beyond his findings, or that he is committed to any preconceived notion as to the organization of ability, or that he believes this study settles once and for all time the question as to the primary abilities of man.

Occupations 17:271-2 D '38. Henry E. Garrett. * Little criticism can be offered of the way in which this experiment was planned and carried out. The work was carefully done. It would be desirable, however, to administer the same test battery to a less highly selected group,—school children, perhaps. Also, it seems to the reviewer that the number, verbal comprehension, memory, and spatial factors were the most clearly identified. Verbal fluency as distinct from verbal comprehension, induction, and perceptual facility are still to be accepted tentatively.

Personnel Adm 1:11-2 D '38. Joseph N. Stonesifer. * Thurstone's first chapters are very readable and interesting but a grounding in statistical mathematics is helpful in following his treatment of the data. Anyone interested in this experimental report should first become familiar with his earlier *The Vectors of Mind*.

Psychoanalytic Q 8:534-5 O '39. Thomas M. French. * To many psychoanalysts who are accustomed to insist upon the importance of direct intuitive understanding of psychological connections, such a research as this one of Thurstone's may seem unpsychological and pedantic. The particular value of this work consists however in the very fact that it offers a strictly objective, non-psychological method for testing psychological preconceptions. Apparently paradoxical findings such as the discovery of a large S (spatial) factor in a test on sound grouping may even suggest questions that may lead to the discovery of unsuspected relations. In the opinion of the reviewer, a similar 'factor analysis' of dynamic tendencies might throw valuable light upon the psychoanalytic theory of the drives.

Psychol B 36:204-8 Mr '39. Joseph Zubin. * The author's purpose is to "describe the fundamental ideas of factor analysis in terms of only the simplest mathematical ideas . . ." * he succeeds quite well, with the single exception of Chapter IV, which is probably still beyond the average ability of those uninitiated in factorial mathematics * The general purpose of factorial analysis is to describe succinctly and adequately the individual differences in human abilities by finding the several primary abilities which underlie human behavor. * Ever since it became apparent that factorial analysis does not lead to a unique result, but that there were an infinite number of results possible, workers in this field have devoted their attention to finding some criteria for selecting one result rather than another. The criteria that have been proposed thus far are: invariance of results, psychological interpretation of results, and practical utility of results. In order that the results be invariant, the factorial structure of a given test must remain constant from one analysis to another. This is often not the case in the results obtained thus far. * In order that the results may be psychologically meaningful, some consistent hypothesis must be available for explaining the nature of the factors. Tests that correlate highly with a given factor must have something in common which is psychologically understandable. Unless some psychological explanation of this common bond is available, the results cannot be regarded as meaningful. Then, also, negative factor loadings crop up in many results. How a factor can affect a test by subtracting from it rather than contributing to it is difficult to comprehend. In order that the results have practical value the factor scores, *i.e.* the relative amount of each factor possessed by a single individual, must be utilizable in the description of the individual's ability or behavior. This, in the final analysis, is the purpose of all measurement. It is not sufficient for the results to be psychologically meaningful in the sense that they are explicable in terms of some hypothesis. The factor scores should also serve the same end as do test scores, but should serve it in a much better way. Unless the factor scores turn out to be superior to the original test scores, why spend all the time and effort in factor analysis? The first two conditions, invariance and meaningfulness of the results, are declared by Thurstone to be dependent upon our ability to find the simplest factorial structures for the test under analysis. * The purpose of maximizing the number of zero correlations needs more examination. * his conclusion that the number of zero loadings must be maximized does not seem to follow as a necessary result. Furthermore, the assumption that a simplified structure will remain more invariant than any other type of structure is an assumption that requires more empirical proof than is now available. But even granting that Thurstone's simplified structure will render the factor matrix independent of the removal or addition of any single test, the factorial structure may yet be altered by other means. One of these is the characteristics of the individuals in the sample. Thurstone pays little attention to this source of possible invariance, although there are studies pointing in that direction. One necessary result of the rotation of axes and the maximizing of the number of zero factor loadings is the elimination of the general factor running through all the tests which Spearman postulates. It is therefore somewhat difficult to follow Thurstone's conclusion: "So far we have not found the general factor of Spearman, but our methods do not preclude it." If conscious rotation to eliminate the general factor does not preclude it, what will? * Perhaps the most difficult problem of all is the problem of describing the factors after they are isolated. * it is doubtful whether unanimous agreement could ever be reached on the proper name or content of a given factor from a knowledge of the tests with which it correlates. Indeed, Thurstone himself finds difficulty in explaining the presence of high factor loadings for some tests and their absence in the case of others. In one or two instances some unusual *tour de force* is resorted to in order to explain the factor loading of a test. * The procedure of inferring the nature of the factor from the tests with which it correlates is a hazardous task and is in great need of supplementation by more objective de-

vices, if any can be found. The technique, disappointing as it is from the point of view of immediate returns, nevertheless seems to hold promise for the future. The succinctness of the approach must command the respect of all of those who become acquainted with it. The rapidity with which improvements are being made and difficulties removed is also striking. * The rotation of axes at the present time is conducted in a graphic, nonmathematical manner. It is hoped that within the next few years a more rigorous mathematical procedure for performing analytically the work which is now done graphically will become available. Despite the rapid advance that factor analysis has made in recent years, there is still much left to be done. * Perhaps one of the most outstanding difficulties is the question of the linearity of relationship between the original variables. Thurstone side-steps this issue completely by discarding the actual distribution surface and substituting for it a dichotomous distribution for each variable, the dichotomy being drawn at the line of the medians. This is done not only for the relationship between the variables but also for the reliability of each test. The tetrachoric correlations that are obtained in this manner are, of course, dependent upon the normality of the distribution surface as well as its continuity and on the linearity of the regression line. Whether these assumptions are at the basis of any of the difficulties that Thurstone finds in interpreting the results is well worth investigating. A second difficulty that Thurstone recognizes is the apparent nonsignificance of the individual profiles that emerge when the factor scores for each individual are determined. One wonders whether this result is not in part due to the above-mentioned artifact in the utilization of tetrachoric correlations. Perhaps a second reason for this result is the fact that the factors themselves are independent by definition. * Some of the difficulty which is being experienced in factor analysis today might be obviated if, instead of proceeding in the direction of factorial analysis of traits alone, we would supplement it by factorial analysis of individuals * The success that Thurstone's approach has won thus far seems to be limited to the field of mental abilities of the intelligence test type. He admittedly finds little success in the field of personality and vocational guidance, and is pessimistic enough about the personality tests of the paper-and-pencil variety to state that they are doomed to extinction. He expresses similar opinions about group tests in general and indicates that the future belongs to individual tests. * It makes very little difference at the present time, practically speaking, whether we regard a given test as made up of *g* or of *s* or of *v*. * A third difficulty that lies at the basis of the failure is perhaps fundamental to the entire factorial approach. Factorial analysis is primarily an attempt in the classification of human abilities and, in the last analysis, will stand or fall on the degree of usefulness which the classification system will provide. The assumption is made that a frame of reference exists in which human abilities can be described in terms of a comparatively small number of continuous, normally distributed, independent factors. Perhaps such a frame of reference exists, but if it does, it defies some of the concepts now current in psychological thought. It is difficult to make such a system compatible with Gestalt theory or with typology. * It is apparent that Thurstone has given us a very sharp tool which can cut keenly into our psychological problems, if used wisely. At present the tool is far sharper than it is useful. How to render it more useful is indeed one of the outstanding problems facing differential psychology. Perhaps by combining the contributions of differential psychology with those of typological psychology, both methods will be benefited and present-day psychology will be brought out of its chaotic condition.

Q R Biol 13:487 D '38. * This psychometric approach to the elusive data of psychology is too new to have yielded clear-cut results as yet. As an objective approach to the problems of psychology it is to be commended. * *For additional reviews, see B503 and 1427.*

[B1100]

THURSTONE, L. L. **Primary Mental Abilities:** This Supplement Contains the Experimental Psychological Tests that Were Used in the Factorial Analysis Described in the Monograph. Supplement to Psychometric Monograph No. 1. Published for the Psychometric Society. Chicago, Ill.: University of Chicago Press, 1938. Pp. 274. Paper, lithotyped. Out of print.

[B1101]

THURSTONE, L. L. **A Simplified Multiple Factor Method and an Outline of Computations.** Chicago: University of Chicago Bookstore, 1933. Pp. 25. $0.50. Paper, lithotyped.

J Gen Psychol 11:229-30 Jl '34. *Raymond Royce Willoughby.* A supplement to the recent monograph *The Theory of Multiple Factors;* in the former work the structure of the problem and the terminology were mapped out, and in the present one the principal modification is the elimination of sub-groups and the substitution of a "center of gravity method" (in hyperspace) for the former least square method. The saving is the difference between five hours and "several weeks" for the nine-variable problem used. * Spearman originally thought his findings pointed to a definite entity, which was great news; but with the gradual seeping in of one group-factor after another we seem to have come regretfully to the realization that the factor techniques are after all only methods of "as-if" description, whose ultimate usefulness is probably to enable a compact formulation of the interrelations of a set of coefficients. And so—with a perfected instrument, just where are we? To what realities of the mind do—or could—these wholly empirical factors to which the instrument will mechanically boil down any set of coefficients, and whose stability from set to set is entirely problematical, correspond? We await hopefully a thoroughgoing discussion of the matter, preferably by somebody with Thurstone's acumen (if there be any such) but without his "realist," or better impossibilist, philosophy.

[B1102]

TIEGS, ERNEST W. **Tests and Measurements in the Improvement of Learning.** Boston, Mass.: Houghton Mifflin Co., 1939. Pp. xxi, 490. $2.75.

Am J Psychol 53:480-1 Jl '40. *John G. Darley.* * an extension of the author's earlier *Tests and Measurements for Teachers* (1931)* The first four chapters give a straightforward and interesting discussion of measurement, use, and meaning of the IQ; and construction of the various types of "informal" diagnostic devices. 'Informal' seems in this usage to be synonymous with 'standardized' and one might take serious issue with the author for urging such judgment-making devices on the teacher if he had not stressed the frequent use of such casual objective tests primarily as means of diagnosing student difficulties interfering with mastery of clearly-stated objectives. The danger of having teachers come to rely on such *diagnostic* devices as *appraisal* devices must be pointed out. The next six chapters deal with diagnosis and appraisal in primary learning, elementary grades and secondary schools and colleges. This treatment, according to levels of education, leads to repetitious and cursory summaries of areas of diagnosis, even though it provides a convenient reference for teachers interested in a specific level. * The sections on personality and interest diagnosis are the least critically discussed throughout these chapters, with inadequate mention of the specialists who can and do contribute aid to the teachers in these areas. Furthermore, the tests used for illustration are not discussed critically in terms of their own reliability or validity. * As minor criticisms, the index is not well organized; the selected bibliographies carry occasional errors in authors' names; throughout the nineteen chapters ideas and concepts are too frequently repeated. On the whole, however, teachers in training and in service should find much of the book stimulating and helpful.

El Sch J 40:229-30 N '39. John B. White-law. * As a middle-of-the-road exposition of the place of evaluation in contemporary education . . . [this book] provides a sound, practical introductory textbook that will prove useful in beginning courses in educational measurement and helpful to supervisors working with young teachers. The educational writings of Tiegs have always been characterized by a concern for the practical problems of the average teacher. * There is a final chapter of twenty-two pages entitled "Questions and Answers about Tests and Measurements." The answers to many of these questions are much more conservative than one would expect from the general tone of the book as a whole. This book is definitely not a descriptive catalogue of tests . . . but many tests are discussed and there is adequate guidance to outstanding tests in each area of education. * Tiegs does not, in this book, make any unique contribution to the heavily documented field of measurement, but he has provided a comprehensive, substantial, and up-to-date guide for beginning students and for young teachers.

Harvard Ed R 10:388-9 My '40. Harold B. Gores. This book, a sequel to the author's previously published *Tests and Measurements for Teachers,* reflects the redirection which has characterized recent measurement. Accordingly, it subordinates the bibliographic approach to testing, and treats almost exclusively the basic problems of the nature and function of measurement, and the diagnosis and direction of learning. Of particular value is the

author's treatment of the natural concomitants of educational measurement: marking, promotion, ability grouping, curriculum building, and the diagnosis of teaching difficulties. Typical of books which attempt to cover a broad field by reducing its major areas to capsule form, the treatment of certain items is neither consistently thorough nor thoroughly consistent. * In nearly every instance the author has carefully presented the arguments for both sides of issues on which he takes a definite stand. For this he is to be commended. The pressure of brevity, however, occasionally makes it necessary for him to dismiss the opposition in an arbitrary fashion. * The author's treatment of diagnosis on the primary, elementary, and secondary levels is a distinct contribution to the sources available and understandable to the classroom teacher. These chapters alone are sufficient to justify the recommendation of this book. * The last thirty pages are given over to the quaint device of questions and answers. Perhaps this space could have been used more profitably to elaborate on techniques which classroom teachers could employ to meet the needs of pupils who have been found deficient in any of the factors isolated by these diagnostic tests of mental maturity which the author declares are fundamental to mental measurement.

J Ed Psychol 31:76-7 Ja '40. C. M. Louttit. * Throughout his discussion the author maintains a careful, common-sense point of view which should make the work invaluable for teachers and for teacher training. * In the last chapter there is an interesting and useful innovation of presenting questions frequently asked by school people and the author's answers to them. * As might be expected no subject is extensively treated. This must not be taken to mean that the book is shallow or scientifically unsound. As a general textbook for courses in educational measurements it should be eminently satisfactory. As a book for the individual teacher's guidance it is superior to most of the available works in the field.

J Ed Res 33:712-3 My '40. C. W. Odell. * In general the author's viewpoint is sound, his presentation direct and clear, and his selection of material appropriate for the purpose he had in mind. However, the breadth of his purpose is such as to render it impossible to cover adequately measurement at all school levels in a single volume of ordinary length. The reviewer believes that it is preferable to treat either one school level or one large phase of the movement more fully. In his effort to do the other, Tiegs has left a number of discussions, among which are those dealing with certain types of tests, the use of results from physical examinations, final conclusions as to a no-failing program and as to marking, decidedly incomplete. Among the commendable features of the book are the large number of figures and tables which help in clearness and forcefulness of presentation, the excellent statement of the need for better measurements, the brief history of the movement which might, however, well be longer, the discussion of the fallacy of the passing mark, and the concluding chapter with its questions frequently asked by students and the answers thereto. Some of the latter, however, are weak. * Many of the examples of elements and portions of tests are not in good form although the implication is that they may be taken as models. They include errors in English, unsatisfactory directions, and features that make them more difficult to take and to score than is necessary. The volume contains a number of statements that are either definitely in error or imply erroneous conclusions. * There are both misleading and definitely incorrect statements in the discussion of the accomplishment ratio. The index of reliability does not measure validity directly, as is implied on p. 386, but only indirectly through measuring reliability. * There are a few statistical errors. In two or three places the ranges of distributions are incorrectly given. In general the discussions of the significance of differences are based upon a conception of a sharply dividing critical point below which they are not significant and above which they are. This is a very misleading interpretation. * There are a number of minor omissions. * Any volume contains some typographical and similar errors and this is at least as good as most in this respect except for an unusual number of misspelled proper names. * There also are a few language errors * Points of view are of course largely subjective but several are expressed with which the reviewer feels he must disagree. Chief among these are that the value of the IQ for individual use seems seriously underestimated, as also is that of teacher-rating and a single index of teaching efficiency, whereas the low correlation of intelligence and scholastic suc-

cess, on the other hand, appears over-emphasized, and likewise the number of experimental data reported in connection with ability grouping, as compared with that bearing on other questions.

[B1103]

TOBIN, J. R. **What the Examiner Wants to Know.** London: A. Hammond & Co., 1937. Pp. 27. 2s. 6d. Paper.

[B1104]

TORGERSON, T. L., AND FROEHLICH, G. J. **Report of the 1939 Wisconsin Achievement Testing Program.** Madison, Wis.: Bureau of Guidance and Records, University of Wisconsin, August 1939. Pp. 27. $0.10. Paper, mimeographed.

[B1105]

TORGERSON, T. L.; FROEHLICH, GUSTAV J.; AND HELL-FRITZSCH, ALVIN G. **Report of the 1938 Wisconsin Achievement Testing Program.** Madison, Wis.: Bureau of Guidance and Records, University of Wisconsin, August 1938. Pp. ii, 37. $0.10. Paper, mimeographed.

[B1106]

TRAXLER, ARTHUR E., EDITOR. **Guidance in Public Secondary Schools:** A Report of the Public School Demonstration Project in Educational Guidance. Foreword by Ben D. Wood. Educational Records Bulletin No. 28. New York: Educational Records Bureau, October 1939. Pp. xxv, 329. Cloth, $2.50; paper, $2.00.

Ed Abstracts 5:77-8 Mr '40. Henry D. Rinsland. * The Editor's Preface is one of the most precise and convincing writings on guidance to be found, not on the whole program, but on parts of a program that can be worked out in public schools under practical situations. Of special note is the personal history of pupils developed in Plainfield; the description of the cumulative record and an illustration of its use by a most thrilling case study; the excellent results of the Colorado group to set up evaluations (not markings or grading) of many outcomes of learning and many abilities needed to succeed in normal life and the excellent detailed illustrations of how a testing program contributed to guidance.

Ed Meth 19:366-7 Mr '40. Philip W. L. Cox. * it is a great service to all educators that the Records Bureau has rendered, both in carrying through the demonstration and in making available a clear and convincing report of its progress and contributions. The volume will prove an indispensable reference book for college teachers of courses in guidance and for high school officers who recognize the great importance of adequate guidance procedures if their schools are truly to serve youth.

El Paso Sch Standard 17:31-2 My '40. J. M. Skiff. * The material in this volume is intensely practical since the entire program was carried out in public schools and under normal conditions. Anyone developing a guidance program will find the report very useful and it should be accessible to all guidance officers and administrators.

J Am Assn Col Reg 15:285-6 Ap '40. C. L. Murray. * The experiences in this project confirm a number of points of considerable value in developing guidance programs. The success of a guidance program depends much upon (1) the interest and perseverance of the administrators in charge of the school system; (2) the effectiveness of the re-education of teachers in the system; (3) the development, maintenance, and use of cumulative records; and (4) the ability of the school to adjust its program to the needs of the individual.

Loyola Ed Digest 15:7 F '40. Austin G. Schmidt. * The present volume . . . is not a complete and orderly treatise on guidance, but does contain a large amount of stimulating and useful material. There are numerous interesting case studies of pupils. The reproductions of record forms and the suggestions for the development of cumulative records suitable to the individual institution will be found particularly helpful.

N Central Assn Q 14:319 Ja '40. * another very helpful contribution to the literature on guidance.

Progressive Ed 17:284 Ap '40. Lois Meredith French. * In addition to its general appeal to all interested in guidance, the book has especial value for those who are directly involved in the development of a guidance program. Based on actual experience of seven school systems, it offers description and results of experiments, together with a careful analysis of problems and ways of meeting them. * Any administrator looking forward to developing a program, or already engaged in the endeavor will find the report full of helpful suggestions. He may even find short cuts in planning, and be forewarned by difficulties inherent in the task. He will appreciate the frankness with which problems are discussed and the unprejudiced appraisal of results. The book offers helpful material in answer to many questions. * One distinct contribution of the report lies in the detailed and practical discussion of the interpretation and uses of aptitude and achievement tests. * the survey offers not only stimulus and practical suggestion, but also a ready

reference for use in meeting problems as they arise.

Sch and Soc 51:679-81 My 25 '40. David Snedden. * a good example of such needed experimental ventures into complex fields * Dr. Wood, director of the Educational Records Bureau, infers in his foreword . . . that "The experience of this project confirms the already widely accepted view that the traditional academic curriculum is too narrow to care for the educational needs of all the pupils now in secondary schools." No serious student will dispute that. But have we yet produced anywhere in this country a realistic philosophy (body of beliefs) as to what such an adequate curriculum should or could be?

Sch R 48:467-8 Je '40. F. C. Rosecrance. * Among the more significant [chapters], in this reader's judgment, are "Six Years of an Experiment in Marking and Reporting in the Secondary School of the Colorado State College of Education"; "An Experiment with Anecdotal Records" at Plainfield, New Jersey; and the fifteen "Contributions to Guidance through Case Studies by Classroom Teachers." * While many readers will insist that the project has not conclusively demonstrated that it is feasible, desirable, and possible for public schools to utilize the type of instruments and services represented by the Cooperative Test Service and the Educational Records Bureau, all will be grateful for the record of experience given in this volume. Of particular value is the recurring emphasis on the role of the teacher in guidance and the practical methods which have been used to educate him and to enlist his interest. The reader is urged not to overlook the Foreword by Ben D. Wood and the Preface by the editor, Arthur E. Traxler.

Va J Ed 33:185 Ja '40.

[B1107]
TRAXLER, ARTHUR E. **The Nature and Use of Anecdotal Records.** Educational Records Supplementary Bulletin D. New York: Educational Records Bureau, January 1939. Pp. iii, 31. $0.25. Paper, lithotyped.

[B1108]
TRAXLER, ARTHUR E. **The Use of Tests and Rating Devices in the Appraisal of Personality.** Educational Records Bulletin, No. 23. New York: Educational Records Bureau, March 1938. Pp. vii, 80. $1.50. Paper, lithotyped.

Am J Psychol 52:320 Ap '39. Anthony J. Mitrano. * constructively critical *

Clearing House 14:378 F '40. * This bulletin presents an orderly statement of answers to questions that frequently arise in the minds of all concerned with the needs and achievements of pupils. *

Harvard Ed R 9:127-8 Ja '39. Phillip J. Rulon. * this bulletin was prepared to present a brief summary of the field of personality measurement, together with a description of some of the leading contemporary tests of personality and a summary of research dealing with them * the author [points out that] . . . the Bureau is . . . not recommending the use of personality tests, but only providing information about them * the author does in his summary make recommendations for types of tests to be used for certain purposes, and in the annotations for the tests themselves he presents obvious, even if implicit, recommendations and condemnations of particular tests * These recommendations and annotations are well done and are a valuable part of the work. When the author refuses to recommend "the use of personality tests," he must consider that the option in any given school situation may be to use no approach whatever to personality study, or use some approach even less commendable than the available tests. * I think he overrates Baker and Traphagen's work, although this is an act of omission (of criticism) rather than commission. He puts the Downey tests away nicely, but doesn't remark the weakness in Reavis's long-time dependence on them. He is properly skeptical of the Gilfords's statement of the validity of their scale, and properly skeptical of the Rorschach test. *

J Ed Psychol 30:77-8 Ja '39. Carl R. Rogers. This succinct digest of information about personality tests is the most practical, most useful, and most profound summary which has come to the attention of this reviewer. * There is a clear and remarkably thorough discussion—considering its brevity—of the different procedures for measuring and appraising behavior and personality traits and patterns. This is followed by a well-selected list of forty-five of the most useful tests, rating scales, and the like. * [this] bulletin is commended to all those who are using, or are interested in using, personality tests, whether in school, college, or behavior clinic.

Sch Life 23:332 My '38. David Segel. A good analysis of the possibilities of the use of various personality measures in schools * The Educational Records Bureau always has been conservative in the type of tests recommended

for use by its patrons, and it seemed surprising therefore that it should issue such a bulletin. However, the bulletin is throughout deliberately critical and retains the conservative approach of the bureau. *

For additional reviews, see B508.

[B1109]
Traxler, Arthur E. **The Use of Test Results in Secondary Schools.** Educational Records Bulletin No. 25. New York: Educational Records Bureau, October 1938. Pp. vi, 108. $1.00. Paper, lithotyped.

Ed Abstracts 4:73-4 F '39. Henry D. Rinsland. A questionnaire on the use of test results was sent to the schools cooperating with the Educational Records Bureau and replies from 140 schools were tabulated. * The author gives an excellent description of the value and use of cumulative records * The author describes some of the trends in marking although he omits the contribution by Rinsland in *Constructing Tests and Grading* (Prentice-Hall, 1937). He recommends very highly the analysis by the highly subjective marking system of the University of Chicago High School. One would question such an analytical report in all subjects to parents because parents are not actively engaged in teaching or following these details. (The report in language lists 22 items on a five-point scale.) The school treating the child's learning processes is interested in more accurate measurement of these details and many of the items listed in the sample report in language can be measured objectively with a much higher degree of reliability than by any opinion plan. * The author gives a descriptive list of a number of very excellent tests in all high school subjects. * An excellent bibliography of 124 titles is given. The copy of the complete questionnaire used in the study is very helpful in following the descriptions.

[B1110]
Tryon, Caroline McCann. **Evaluations of Adolescent Personality by Adolescents.** Monographs of the Society for Research in Child Development, Vol. 4, No. 4, Serial No. 23. Washington, D. C.: the Society, National Research Council, 1939. Pp. x, 83. $1.00. Paper, lithotyped.

Loyola Ed Digest 15:7 My '40. Austin G. Schmidt. Two groups of children, numbering approximately 350 and containing an almost equal number of boys and girls, were studied at the age of twelve and again at the age of fifteen for the purpose of discovering some of the qualities of personality which children consider desirable in one another. The data are subjected to careful statistical treatment. Sex differences and the effect of increased maturity are noted.

Pub Health R 10:54-5 Je '40. Mabel E. Rugen. * should be of particular value to those engaged in guidance and counselling of youth *

[B1111]

Tryon, Robert Choate. **Cluster Analysis:** Correlation Profile and Orthometric (Factor) Analysis for the Isolation of Unities in Mind and Personality. Berkeley, Calif.: Associated Students Store, University of California, 1939. Pp. ix, 122. $2.25. Paper, lithotyped.

Loyola Ed Digest 15:6 O '39. Austin G. Schmidt. * The author takes issue with both Spearman and Thurstone, which should be sufficient evidence that factor analysis, interesting and promising though it is, presents many unsolved and possibly unsolvable problems.

Psychol B 36:791-2 N '39. Dael L. Wolfle. Professor Tryon's aversion to the "mathematical magic" and the "ingenious but in many respects misleading activities of the 'factor analysts,'" together with his desire to obtain the fruits of factor analysis in some simple fashion, is responsible for his development of correlation profile analysis and orthometric analysis. * Tryon is neither always consistent nor always well acquainted with the methods which he criticizes. He condemns "factor" analysis because the mathematics is likely to be misunderstood, or worse, adopted uncritically by many psychologists, and recommends "orthometric" analysis because a knowledge of the derivations is quite unnecessary. In estimating the communality of a variable, Tryon averages the estimates made by two methods. He does not use Thurstone's method, Tryon explains, "because it is the hard way." Actually, both methods which Tryon uses are included in a list of eight suggested by Thurstone, and the *simpler* of his two methods is exactly the method commonly used and described by Thurstone and his students in a number of papers. The problems attacked by orthometric analysis are the same as those attacked by factor analysis. The method of naming an operational unity is the same as that of naming a factor; the resultant names are sometimes identical. When one strips orthometric analysis of its new vocabulary, what remains is a not very rigorous method of isolating factors—a method basically similar to some of Thurstone's earlier,

and discarded, attempts to solve the factor problem.

[B1111.1]

United States Office of Education. **List of Intelligence Tests.** Circular No. 179. Washington, D. C.: the Office, July 1939. Pp. 8. Gratis. Paper, mimeographed.

[B1112]

University of Minnesota, Committee on Educational Research. **The Effective General College Curriculum as Revealed by Examinations.** Minneapolis, Minn.: University of Minnesota Press, 1937. Pp. xvi, 427. $3.00. (London: Oxford University Press. 14s.)

Ed Res B 18:83-4 Mr '39. J. E. Bathurst. * As a contribution to more effective uses of examinations and to more effective teaching, the volume is valuable. To the curriculum technician it will be of interest and value, but whether a sound fundamental procedure for curriculum revision and construction has been presented is doubtful. That the philosophy on the basis of which the studies were made is sound no one who holds a democratic view of education can deny. In some places the volume is quite readable, in other places it is tedious.

J Higher Ed 10:169 Mr '39. H. E. Hawkes. This volume is useful in at least three different areas. It serves to inform the reader concerning the present state of the General College in the University of Minnesota; it provides an interesting analysis of collegiate curriculum building; and it includes a wealth of material on evaluation and analysis of the results of teaching by means of a carefully elaborated testing service. * The main portion of the volume is devoted to a careful scrutiny of the nature and results of the testing and evaluation system. Chapters are devoted to each of the main areas of the curriculum, and a wealth of illustrative material is given. The fine critical attitude taken with respect to the testing techniques is very interesting, and indicates an experimental state of mind on the part of all who are concerned with the College. These technical chapters cannot fail to be of interest and help to collegiate teachers who are interested in studying testing procedures.

For additional reviews, see B511.

[B1113]

Valentine, C. W. **Examinations and the Examinee:** Some Suggested Reforms. Birmingham, England: Birmingham Printers, Ltd., 1938. Pp. 39. 1s. 6d. Paper.

B Int Bur Ed 12:87 q 2 '38. * deals especially with the effects of the examination system on the individual. In the opinion of Prof. Valentine, the written test is a very unreliable vehicle for testing a child's suitability, or otherwise, for further education. *

New R 8:383 O '38. T. N. Siqueira. This booklet does in a restricted field the work already done on a large scale by the International Inquiry Committee: it examines the harm done by the School Certificate, the Scholarship, and the Matriculation examinations to the work of English schools. Too much is made in England (as in India) of these tests as tickets to employment, with the result that not only the candidates who appear for them but all the other pupils of high schools as well are terrorized by them. *

For additional reviews, see B513.

[B1114]

VERNON, P. E. **The Assessment of Psychological Qualities by Verbal Methods:** A Survey of Attitude Tests, Rating Scales, and Personality Questionnaires. Medical Research Council, Industrial Health Research Board, Report No. 83. London: H.M. Stationery Office, 1938. Pp. vi, 124. 2s. Paper.

Civil Service Assembly News Letter 5:7 Mr '39. Paul Horst. * a well-organized integration and stimulating critical evaluation of those psychological measuring devices for which "there are no right or wrong answers" * Doubtless many of those whose work is discussed in the report will take issue with the interpretations and criticisms of the writer, but this is inevitably true of any critical survey. The report should go far toward curbing much of the unimaginative empiricism which characterizes the particular field of research under discussion. * This report should prove of great value to all who are attempting to extend the borders of measurable human traits.

J Royal Stat Soc 102:89-92 pt 1 '39. B. B(abington) S(mith). * admirable report * presents very clearly an enormous amount of material in an extremely condensed form * It is noticeable that most of the techniques mentioned call for further development. * It is rather surprising that the short section on voting makes no reference to P. R. * where the average intercorrelation between raters is low, the author says that the resulting averages will not differ much, and recommends that the dispersion of the ratings be arbitrarily increased. This procedure seems unjustified if the intercorrelations are so low that the resulting averages do not differ significantly,

and in any case low dispersion is an important feature of the situation. Ranking is open to the objection that it assumes a "highly artificial distribution of items" (rectangular). It is, however, worth noting—what is not mentioned —that the greater difficulty experienced in ranking items in the middle of a group is not necessarily an indication, as suggested, that the differences are smaller there than at the ends. This can be demonstrated by ranking items known otherwise to differ by equal amounts. The greater difficulty in the middle of the group seems to be due, there, partly to the fact that the differences available for comparison are only half those between the extreme items. * The report describes methods available for assessing reliability, but validity is seldom a matter of measurement. Much remains to be done by psychologists in clarifying the principles underlying the tests used and in analysing the situations set up by the instructions to those who take them. * It would take too long to refer to all the techniques described in the report; surely the author is unduly modest when he says that "they are only a small, though we hope, representative sample." The same trait seems to have prevented him from giving a more than passing reference to the method of matching, to the development of which he has made considerable contributions. * Little has been said here about the types of tests used, but it would be a grave omission not to indicate the stress the author rightly lays on the great need for further analysis of the attendant psychological problems. For instance, it is too easy to accept the "measurements" at their face value and to suppose that because in any test the same instructions were given to all subjects, the situation produced in each subject was the same. One minor criticism is that the bibliography would have been more helpful if paragraph references had been added, as it is not always possible to trace an author to the text by way of the subject index. * The report as a whole is a most valuable and comprehensive survey of the field.

Personnel Adm 1:12 My '39. D. T. S(tanley). This rather ponderous title introduces a very complete but not-too-readable survey of the use of attitude tests, rating scales, and personality questionnaires. * Vernon's rather technical discussion offers interesting and valuable suggestions regarding the handling of factors which tend to alter the validity of interest scales and personality tests. * a convenient and very helpful handbook * It is not, however, recommended reading for convalescents.

For additional reviews, see B514.

[B1115]

Vernon, Philip E. **The Measurement of Abilities.** London: University of London Press, Ltd., 1940. Pp. xii, 308. 10*s*. 6*d*.

A.M.A. 35:112 My '40. * Teachers who examine the volume will appreciate its importance.

Librarian 29:207 My '40. * The author is critical of the ordinary examination, but mainly because the method of computing the results is not based on a scientific analysis of the marks awarded. He gives a sufficiency of basic psychology for his presentation of mental test procedure to be apprehended and put into practice. Many readers will find this a very useful book. *

Mental Health 1:91 Jl '40. J(ohn) C. R(aven). * The author's treatment of the principles of correlation and the statistical analysis of numerical data is neither as simple as he promises the reader it will be nor as clear as the student with more scientific interests would wish, and one is left to apply algebraic formulae by rule of thumb with no very adequate idea as to the real nature of the calculations carried out. The qualities of good mental tests are carefully considered and much sound, simple advice is given concerning the choice and use of appropriate tests. The last few chapters of the book are devoted, almost entirely, to the possible improvement of present day examination methods. The writer is keenly aware of the problems involved—almost too keenly. The book will appeal to teachers and examiners more than to students and psychologists interested in scientific or clinical work, but the author's contact with his particular problem, his experience and balanced judgment, make the book well worth reading by those who are interested in the uses of mental tests. As an introduction to the principles underlying mental measurement it undoubtedly covers the ground better than any one book yet published.

Nature 146:46 Jl 13 '40. J. I. Cohen. In the past five years or so, the work of the International Institute Examinations Enquiry in Great Britain and elsewhere has, to some extent, awakened the public to the need for some radical revision of the examination system.

Those who are alive to this social need will welcome Dr. Vernon's book, for it provides for teachers, school medical officers and students of education generally an up-to-date survey of simple methods which can readily be applied to this end. * About half of Dr. Vernon's book is devoted to elementary statistical techniques applicable in educational work. The author's aim is wholly practical, so considerations appropriate to statistical theory are omitted. A wealth of illustration is provided of almost every type of problem in evaluating ability or achievement that might arise in school or clinic. The remainder of the book is mainly a critical account of mental tests and examinations, especially of the new type. The sections on construction and improvements of new-type examinations are particularly useful. The author admits that contemporary psychological and educational research, unfortunately makes far too much use of correlational techniques, while neglecting such valuable methods as the analysis of variance. In spite of this, we find about fifty pages devoted to the former and a brief single page, conveying little, to the latter. The statement (p. 161) that most ways of factorizing tests "will lead to quite illogical results" must be questioned. If different results are obtained from different methods of factorial analysis, this is because these methods have different objectives and consequently vary in procedure as, for example, in estimating the diagonal cells in a correlation table. The final results of different methods may not be comparable, but they can scarcely be called "illogical."

Occupational Psychol 14:175-6 Jl '40. Alec Rodger. The debt which British psychology owes to Dr. Vernon is assuming considerable proportions. Not the least of the services he performs is the preparation of statements of the problems, methods and findings of other psychologists. These statements are almost invariably comprehensive and concise, and they are often accompanied by shrewd critical comments, the value of which derives mainly from Dr. Vernon's wide knowledge of experimental work in psychology, and from his wholly admirable impartiality. This book is typical of his writing. * It draws on the experience of many workers . . . in a fashion which indicates that Dr. Vernon's reading is indeed prodigious. Of particular interest to vocational psychologists are the chapters entitled "Analysis of Abilities," "Mental Tests" and "Hints to Testers." Some of the problems discussed in these—e.g. concerning the nature of factors —are important ones which have been sadly neglected by other authors * On two general points, especially, his treatment of these topics seems scarcely adequate. First, he does not deal in an entirely satisfactory way with the problem of defining the term 'ability.' In the reviewer's opinion, much of the present-day confusion about the use of psychological tests could be dispelled by a resolute attack on it by competent people. The line of thought sketched out some years ago by Dr. F. M. Earle, in his *Psychology and the Choice of a Career,* might profitably be pursued further. Secondly, it is doubtful whether Dr. Vernon's rather scattered references to the place of incentives in testing can be regarded as sufficient. It is apparent to the informed reader that he recognizes the importance of the matter, but it would not be impossible for a first-year student of psychology to gain the impression that on the whole Dr. Vernon subscribed to the common view that group testing is easy. His remark (on p. 187) that "group tests are easier (than ordinary tests) to procure, to apply and to score, and they demand much less training and experience on the part of the teacher" is, despite the cautionary comment which follows it, an unfortunate one. The reviewer has indicated briefly elsewhere his reasons for believing that, because it raises problems of incentive in an acute form, group testing is often fraught with even greater dangers than individual testing. A striking feature of Dr. Vernon's book is his discussion of 'new-type' examinations. He points out that the objectivity which is often held to put such examinations streets ahead of 'essay-type' examinations is limited. It is to be found only in the marking: the setting of the questions to be found in a 'new-type' examination is just as subjective as the setting of questions for 'essay-type' examinations. Equally notable is his discussion of Binet tests. There can be no doubt that this is a book which should be read, re-read and kept for reference. Its bibliography is good, but it should not have omitted mention of Bingham's *Aptitudes and Aptitude Testing,* which must be regarded with admiration equal to that due to Dr. Vernon's production. *

Times Ed Sup 1296:81 Mr 2 '40. * a book which may be recommended without reserve to all those who wish to know the principles on which the new tests are based and the uses to which they may profitably be put. It shows up the defects as well as the merits of the new tests, and it also points out the merits as well as the defects of the old examinations. It not only explains the most recent developments in the theory and practice of examining, but also takes into account the fusillade of criticism to which both types of examination have been subjected within recent years. * The statistical devices to which the new examiner is addicted are here justified and explained. Even the mysteries of "factor analysis" become, under the hands of the author, surprisingly clear. He is, however, no great stickler for statistics. He appears to prefer the mixed bag of mental faculties which make up what the plain man means by intelligence to that pure intelligence after which the psychologist hankers. Even Spearman's gives him no great joy. He accordingly believes that Binet's Scale, which is a hotch-potch of tests teeming with statistical defects, is a more useful instrument in the hands of a discerning examiner than many a battery of tests which satisfy the most rigid scientific criteria. Binet's Scale, which is the most used of all intelligence tests, is also the most abused, and Dr. Vernon's championship is a welcome change.

[B1116]

WALKER, WILMA, EDITOR. **Child Welfare Case Records.** University of Chicago Social Service Series. Chicago, Ill.: University of Chicago Press, 1937. Pp. xii, 584. $3.00. (London: Cambridge University Press. 13*s.* 6*d.*)

Family 21:96 My '40. Alan Keith-Lucas. * Social case workers have done much thinking since 1937. Nevertheless I cannot believe that this book represents the better thinking of its time. The factual problems presented by the clients are varied but the workers' handling of them essentially uniform. The workers are one and all efficient, conscientious, considerate, and humane. * Where then do we feel the work to have been inadequate? Most obviously because no worker has seen below the client's problems, recognized his deeper feelings about his difficulties, or seen him, indeed, as an individual subtly different from all others. * The records however show a fault nearer our own time. In no case have the workers considered what help the agency is set up to give, what help it is qualified to give, what help it were wise to give or for how long it could profitably be given. *

For additional reviews, see B518.

[B1117]
WANG, CHARLES K. A. **An Annotated Bibliography of Mental Tests and Scales,** Vol. 1. Publications of the College of Education, Catholic University of Peking, No. 1. Peiping, China: Catholic University Press, 1939. Pp. vi, 725. $5.00.

[B1118]
WATERMAN, ALAN TOWER, AND STALNAKER, JOHN MARSHALL. **Report on the Physics Examination of June 1938:** A Description of the Procedures Used in Preparing and Reading the Examination in Physics and an Analysis of the Results of the Reading. New York: College Entrance Examination Board, May 1939. Pp. iii, 43. $0.25. Paper, lithotyped.

Loyola Ed Digest 14:10 Jl '39. Austin G. Schmidt. * contains suggestive material on the principles underlying the construction and reading of examinations.

[B1119]
WEBB, L. W., AND SHOTWELL, ANNA MARKT. **Testing in the Elementary School.** A revised edition of *Standard Tests in the Elementary School.* New York: Farrar & Rinehart, Inc., 1939. Pp. xix, 407. $2.75.

J Ed Res 33:716 My '40. C. W. Odell. * the authors have wisely narrowed the field and have assumed a point of view that is not highly critical. The book appears to be best suited for elementary classroom teachers of little or no previous training along the line covered who are primarily interested in practical classroom testing and the use of the results obtained. For such individuals this volume should offer much that is helpful and not overly difficult to master. If they wish to enlarge upon the content of the book, the many references will greatly assist them, but in some cases those given are not so up-to-date as they might well be. * informal tests are accorded little attention and personality measurements none at all. School marks constitute another topic that is decidedly neglected. A number of terms common enough in educational literature that teachers who read anything at all in that line are almost certain to encounter are omitted. Moreover, opinions and statements are too often quoted with little or no comment as to whether they should be accepted or not. The general style is clear and understandable and the number of errors in English, spelling, and so forth small in comparison with some similar books. The effort to simplify material has occasionally resulted in statements that are not strictly accurate, perhaps through the omission of exceptions and

qualifications. In other instances errors appear without appearing to have this origin. * The selection of group intelligence tests discussed in the text is not so thoroughly in accord with general use and opinion as it might well be and in the instances of a few of the school subjects tests worth mentioning have been omitted. On the whole, this volume appears to deserve rank among the most helpful treatises on practical elementary school measurement, but may lead those for whom it is best suited to a degree of over-confidence in measurement techniques and an impression of over-simplification of the field covered.

Loyola Ed Digest 14:11 Je '39. Austin G. Schmidt. * a very substantial text * one of the better works in its field *

Sch Executive 59:31 S '39. J. Wayne Wrightstone. * an excellent background for testing in a traditional elementary school where the acquisition of facts and skills is the major concern of the teachers. Many of the specific tests described in the early volume have been supplanted by tests which have appeared more recently. * The material is presented in a non-technical manner which most teachers will welcome. The early chapters, however, present certain statistical methods and interpretations that may frighten those who are unaccustomed to the statistical approach. The reviewer feels that the revised handbook is still about five years behind the times and trends in testing. * References to the improved essay examination are also notable by their omission. * This volume may be recommended to the teacher, principal, or supervisor who wants a conventional book on traditional standard tests and measures . . . and who is willing to forego information relevant to newer tests of interests, basic study skills, and personal and social adjustment.

[B1120]
WEBSTER, E. C. **Guidance for the High School Pupil:** A Study of Quebec Secondary Schools. Foreword by W. D. Tait. McGill University, McGill Social Research Series, No. 8. Montreal, Canada: the University, 1939. Pp. xix, 153. Cloth, $1.50; paper, $1.25. Lithotyped.

Econ J 49:611 S '39. The purpose of this study is to consider how accurately the educational aptitudes of boys and girls can be forecast at certain crucial stages in the school system. *

Occupational Psychol 13:316 O '39. * extremely interesting and comprehensive study * describes a survey of a representative sample, consisting of some three thousand pupils, from the protestant secondary schools of Quebec. The cultural background of the children, their school marks, their scores in various tests of general and special aptitudes and in tests for the diagnosis and prognosis of achievement in several school subjects are detailed; these and other data are related to the success or failure of various sub-groups as they move through the secondary school system. * There are two major limitations to the work which the book describes. It relates only to the educational system of a minority in a single city. And, in the second place, the sub-groups with which Dr. Webster has had to deal are often extremely small. Nevertheless, these limitations by no means obscure the value of the volume. The detailed descriptions of the investigations and the suggestiveness of the results are alike commendable.

Occupations 18:150-1 N '39. Warren K. Layton. * presented clearly * An interesting foreword has been written by William D. Tait *

Sociol and Social Res 24:490 My-Je '40. E(dward) C. McD(onagh). This study reflects the growing belief in the value of mental testing as an aid to curriculum construction. * One of the important conclusions of this book is that the school needs a broadened curriculum for children which would provide opportunities for the development of their different abilities, skills, and interests. *

[B1121]

WECHSLER, DAVID. **The Measurement of Adult Intelligence.** Baltimore, Md.: Williams & Wilkins Co., 1939. Pp. ix, 229. $3.50. (London: Baillière, Tindall, and Cox. 16s.)

Am J Orthopsychiatry 9:808-10 O '39. George Lawton. In this book is described the first attempt to construct an intelligence scale specifically for adults and therefore it is required reading for those interested in mental measurement. Until now, most tests used with adults were not standardized for anyone over 18. This is as true of the new Terman-Merrill Scale as of the old Stanford-Binet. Those rare scales which did include adults in the standardization employed too few to be reliable. Moreover, many of the items in adult examinations had no appeal to mature persons. Too much emphasis is laid on speed as compared with power (accuracy). Credit for correctness of response very often depends upon the individual's manipulative ability, either of words or of objects, rather than on comprehension of meaning. The Stanford-Binet, for example, is a less successful measure of intelligence at the upper levels where it is overweighted with verbal items. However, to depend solely on performance items in the examination of adults would be equally unsatisfactory, for adults require tests of verbal and performance ability in equal degree. But where the so-called adult examinations are most invalid, as the author justifiably states, is in taking over from psychometric practice with children the concept of M. A. levels and M. A. scores. * Psychologists have not been really getting IQ's with adults at all, since an individual is compared not with others his own age, but with those 14 to 18 years old, the choice of divisor depending on where a given examiner locates the peak of the mental growth curve. * All this shows why the entire approach—both practical and theoretical—to appraising intelligence at maturity has been in urgent need of revision. * a long over-due attempt to deal with the problem as effectively as our psychological and statistical knowledge will permit today * Wechsler does not claim originality for individual test items * The discussion of mental deterioration is especially important and, incidentally, offers some valuable diagnostic leads to the psychiatrist dealing with seniles. He stresses the concept of "normal mental deterioration," that which occurs after maturity with the natural increase of age. Through the Tables it becomes possible, for the first time, to obtain a reliable estimate of the decrease in mental level of an older subject when compared with others his own age. * [The book] describes a fine job of test construction and offers the reader a very satisfying experience. A great deal of hard work has gone into it, but it is as honest as it is conscientious. Wechsler is not only critical of the shortcomings of other scales but of his own as well. In fact, he devotes an entire chapter entitled "Limitations and Special Merits" to analyzing the result of using the tests with more than 2000 subjects subsequent to standardization. All in all, the Bellevue Scales represent one of the most important pieces of psychometric pioneering to be brought forth in recent years. *

Am J Psychiatry 97:245-6 Jl '40. C. R. Atwell. * may be recommended to any physician who is interested in the measurement or the theories of intelligence * The [author's] definition [of intelligence] may be questioned, but it does have the pragmatic value of being a useful concept in developing a test for adult intelligence. The tests fill a long-recognized need by providing material suitable to and standardized for adults. The author's criticism of the concept of mental age as confusing . . . is justified but is probably not so seriously confusing as he indicates. * The author maintains that the average score on the test for the age group should be used in computing the I.Q. for any person of that group. He does, however, give efficiency quotients based on the I.Q.'s of the group from 20-24. For practical purposes, it is quite possible that the efficiency quotients would be more useful, since in considering the adjustment of a patient of 60, we are rather more interested in comparing his performance on a test with adults in general than with 60-year-old adults. * The reviewer has been fortunate to have had the privilege of using these tests for a little more than two years; shortly after they were tried out in this hospital, they were adopted as the basic testing material for our adult patients. The Bellevue Test may be whole-heartedly recommended for clinical use. The attention paid to the qualitative aspects of the tests both in the author's description of their uses and in his scoring criteria seems a particularly valuable contribution to the clinical worker. * If the statistical material is overlooked the book provides highly enjoyable reading.

B Menninger Clinic 4:28 Ja '40. W. A. V(arvel). * the Bellevue Adult Scale . . . has been devised with the requirements of the psychiatric clinic in mind and should prove to be a most useful instrument. The reliability is good, the validity has been checked with reference to clinical data, the test is easy to administer and it has been standardized on adult populations.

Ed Abstracts 4:390 D '39. Wm. Reitz. * an outstanding achievement in the field of intelligence testing. The Bellevue Scales not only furnish reliable and valid IQ's for age ranges 10 to 60 but their validation against clinical case study reports as well as the provision of both "verbal" and "performance" tests makes these scales especially adaptable to the diagnosis of psychopathic conditions and of cases of sensory or verbal defects and unusual conditions of environment. Wechsler's volume merits as important a position in the field of adult intelligence measurements as is held by Terman's "The Measurement of Intelligence" in regard to the lower age groups.

J Am Med Assn 114:683-4 F 24 '40. * All in all, the author presents a new technic which should be of some value to psychiatrists who have bemoaned the lack of the means of evaluating that trait which is so necessary of evaluation but so little understood—general adult intelligence. The present test certainly is a step forward, providing the psychologist working with the psychiatrist another tool in the diagnosis of mental patients.

J Nerv and Mental Dis 91:548-9 Ap '40.

Loyola Ed Digest 15:9 N '39. Austin G. Schmidt. The first part of this work consists of a discussion of the nature and measurement of intelligence. Though brief, the six chapters in this part contain observations and points of view that will be helpful even to the trained psychologist. The second part describes the development and standardization of the Bellevue Intelligence Scales, which are applicable to adults as well as to children. The third part contains the manual for use with the tests, appendices, and norms. The work as a whole is a substantial contribution to the practice and theory of mental testing.

Mental Hyg (New York) 24:312-3 Ap '40. Frank K. Shuttleworth. * an outstanding contribution to the measurement of adult intelligence. The tests represent that rare combination of competent execution, from a technical and statistical point of view, and of discriminating attention to a host of practical details, that is so important for effective clinical work. * But while the general procedures are familiar, all but one of the tests are either entirely new or represent considerable adaptations of existing tests. For the most part the individual questions or elements of each test were selected from a larger number which were tried on individuals of known intelligence and hence have been separately validated. While other test-makers have employed some mechanical or statistical rule-of-thumb in the selection of their test elements, Wechsler's selection is notable for the use of statistical procedures plus a high order of horse sense, insight, and discriminating judgment. Chapter 7, on test selection, must be read to be appreciated.

Ohio J Sci 40:51-2 Ja '40. Milton M. Parker. * There has finally been composed a good clinical test of adult intelligence * Without detracting one bit from Dr. Wechsler's accomplishment, it should be said that practically all of the principal concepts employed by him have been described before. His main contribution lies in his combination of these features into a practical and sound measure of adult intelligence. * One of the most interesting of the theoretical sections of the book deals with the problem of mental deterioration. * Wechsler gives adequate proof that the Bellevue scale is reliable as well as valid since it correlates highly with itself and with the Stanford-Binet. * The book is a clear account of that which the author has thought and done, and leaves few questions to be asked.

Personnel Adm 2:15 Mr '40. Walter V. Clarke. * [the] first 72 pages contain a general discussion of intelligence which is a real contribution to the literature on the subject * his discussion of mental deficiency and mental deterioration are [sic] of particular interest and value. Anyone interested in the problem of intelligence will find in Part One of this volume a real contribution to present day knowledge and an intense stimulant to thought. * To those interested in the subjects of intelligence or testing, this book is of fundamental value.

Psychiatry 2:430-3 Ag '39. Isabelle Kendig. It would be premature at this time to attempt an evaluation of the new Bellevue Scale; any judgment of its worth as a measure of adult intelligence must naturally await its thorough try-out by experienced workers throughout the country with groups of every type for whom it is designed. However it is not too early to extend the warmest and most hopeful welcome to such a well-considered and painstaking effort to supply the need for a suitable instrument for testing adults. * The text describing the new scale itself merits careful reading for, besides telling how the tests were selected and standardized, it discusses the nature of intelligence, criticizes our present concepts of mental age and I.Q., and offers new formulations of mental deficiency and mental deterioration. * [The] chapter on deterioration will make everyone over 30 squirm because of the insistence that mental decline sets in at least as early as that. To the present reviewer it is also disappointing because no careful distinction is made between such organic deterioration as Wechsler has

chiefly in mind and the purely functional impairment which frequently appears in dementia praecox and as quickly clears up with remission. * It should be noted that the I.Q. employed differs fundamentally from the concept as usually interpreted. * the book [is] worth thoughtful reading quite independently of the new scale for the presentation of which it was written. But the new scale itself may prove to be just that measure of adult intelligence for which psychologists everywhere have been devoutly praying. Certainly we trust that it will prove so and therefore recommend its immediate and widespread experimental use.

Q R Biol 15:117-8 Mr '40.

For reviews by F. L. Wells and others, see 1429.

[B1122]

WECHSLER, DAVID. **The Range of Human Capacities.** Baltimore, Md.: Williams & Wilkins Co., 1935. Pp. ix, 159. $2.50. (London: Baillière, Tindall, and Cox. 11s. 6d.)

Am J Med Sci 191:424 Mr '36. P. R. The modest dimensions of this book are by no means a measure of its inspiration or of the author's achievements. He attains brevity and clearness by a fine hand in the management of his materials and by the excellence of his writing. The first five chapters are a well-written exposition of the problem of measurement and range of human capacities. Even for those less conversant with the intricacies of statistical method, the author succeeds in making clear the method of approach and the pitfalls of statistical logic. His proposal to establish human values in terms of pure numbers is an advance in making intelligible the study of personality, and this method reveals a rather surprising fact, that human capacity as expressed as ratios between extremes of ability have "strikingly recurrent values which fall roughly with the range of 1.2:1 to 1.5:1; in brief, indicating that human variability is relatively limited. The author's discussion of the limitations of analysis, and particularly of the theory of probability as related to measurement of human abilities, should invite wide reading. The remaining four chapters will interest the less mathematically minded reader because of the novel treatment of exceptions, particularly of deficiency and genius and because of the author's developed contention that, contrary to the current doctrine, human capacity has a tendency to reach its zenith in youth and almost steadily to decline from that point on with the advance of age.

Am J Psychol 48:365-6 Ap '36. Edward Girden. * Without questioning the validity of the technique, one difficulty in evaluating these findings lies in the limited number of studies (7 in all) of perceptual and intellectual abilities presented in the analysis, Wechsler having omitted a considerable number as inadequate for his purposes. The paucity of adequate studies is, no doubt, in part due to the lack of satisfactory units of measurement for many mental abilities * The study of the maturation and decline of mental and physical abilities is today deservedly receiving more attention. Wechsler's work indicates a woeful lack of competent data in this field. This is further exemplified by present day conflicting opinion. Does "life begin at forty," or is the individual well on to decline by then as Wechsler contends? The unequivocal test of his conclusions cannot be made at present, but must await the judgment of more, competent, data than there are to be found in the journals at present. Well written and carefully developed, even for those whose knowledge of statistics is limited, this volume is indeed a contribution to the field. The tabular material is well coördinated in 3 appendices which do not conflict with the organization of the material in the text. The fundamentals of probability, "normal" curves, and other basic concepts are so well handled as to make the book admirably suited for collateral reading, particularly for courses in individual differences.

Brit J Psychol 26:456 Ap '36. There must be a great many people who have neither the time nor the inclination to study in detail the vast bulk of work which has been carried out on the measurement, the range and the significance of differences in human capacity, but to whom, nevertheless, the problems involved are of genuine practical and theoretical interest. To all such this monograph can be seriously commended. In the beginning some of the methods and some of the main difficulties of work in this field are critically reviewed, and thereafter a large mass of investigations are admirably summarized, their main conclusions indicated, and the significance of some of the principles they have laid bare is discussed in a lively, but unexaggerated manner. * The book is most excellently produced, though it seems rather a pity that it

could not have been offered to the public at less cost.

J Ed Res 31:225-7 N '37. Edward A. Lincoln. * interesting * Being a summary, the treatise contains much that is not new. However, the presentation is excellent. After the introductory chapter, there is a good discussion of the well-known difficulties which are involved in measuring human beings, especially when we try to measure those traits which are called mental. * He does not point out . . . the fairly obvious fact that the traits which do not appear to give normal distributions are just those traits which present the greatest difficulties when we attempt to measure them. * In Chapters IV and V we find some new ideas. * If we want the facts about range must we not consider the total range and not some selected part of it? * There is a good bibliography. The book is well-written and stimulating. What effect the proposal of the new method of studying variability will have cannot be foretold. Many investigators will still insist that units of variability are the best measures. Others will prefer isochrons, and still others will continue to search for "absolute" units and zero points. Some, like the reviewer, will incline to the belief that for practical purposes of school and clinic nothing is likely to surpass the natural time or age units. But what ever his present ideas and preference may be, no one who is interested in the problem of measuring human capacities can afford to miss reading this challenging book.

J Nerv and Mental Dis 83:744-5 Je '36. * a work of much interest. Suggestive of Pearson's *Grammar of Science,* the author discusses in a sound and satisfying manner such topics as the Measurement of Human Capacities, Distribution of Traits and Abilities, Limits of Human Variability, Exceptional Personalities, The Burden of Age, Genius and Deficiency, and the Meaning of Differences. We have been waiting for some such really vital and sound handling of these topics, which have been for many years confusedly dealt with by the "normal," "abnormal" misconceptions. Wechsler sidesteps these idealistic, nominalistic errors and deals with the facts of variation from top to bottom. In his own words he avoids the "nimble phrases of the essayist," as well as the "more heavy-footed ones of the philosophers." He sticks to the realistic and everyday working data of experience and avoids trying to ask or answer absurd questions by equally absurd irrelevancies, the which sprinkle, yes, even deluge, the pages of the avalanche of works on history, anthropology, psychology and the like. * Wechsler's discussion of the Meaning of Differences is for us both sensible and sound as well as being well put * Wechsler is sound and rational and a thorough advocate of the principle of relativity as were the better sophists of Greece. An excellent bibliography and index complete this highly commendable bit of work.

Mental Hyg (New York) 20:321-3 Ap '36. Frank K. Shuttleworth. The original and significant contribution of this volume appears in Chapter V and Appendix B. Available data from the field of individual differences have been treated in such a way as to yield a quantitative measure of the extreme range of human traits and capacities. * For the purpose of checking . . . similar ratios have been computed for seven linear measures on approximately a thousand New Haven six-year-old children. These average 1.36 with a range from 1.28 to 1.47, or in close conformity to Wechsler's data. * Even taking two to one as the typical ratio, this reviewer cannot agree that the range of human capacities is "exceedingly small." The smallness of the typical ratio is illusory. Another investigator might well have expressed a two-to-one ratio by saying that the largest measure is typically 200 per cent of the smallest. "Small" and "large" are, as the author insists elsewhere and forgets at this point, purely relative terms. Further, the numerical values of the ratios as computed are artifacts of the particular definition of the extremes. If the extremes had been defined as the next to the largest and next to the smallest measures out of a hundred thousand or a hundred million, then altogether different ratios would have resulted. * Chapters I to IV consist of a rather tedious statement of the problem and of the methods of analysis. * Chapters VII and VIII, which are concerned respectively with the downward trend of capacities during old age and with genius, contribute little or nothing to the major thesis of the volume. It is to be regretted that the social significance of the data is not more clearly suggested.

N Y Times Book R 40:12 S 1 '35.

Psychol B 33:108-12 F '36. Helen Peak. * the chief concern is with the presentation of

certain empirical data in an attempt to demonstrate that the difference between the limits of ability are "very small"; and that the ratios between extremes partake of the nature of natural constants, ranging in value from 1.2 to 2.5 or 3, "with a further probable maximum determined by the limit of organic rate of growth, namely the important mathematical constant, 2.718 (e)". * Since the book's main conclusions have to do with the characteristics of the range ratios considered as natural constants, the reviewer's task centers about the consideration of 2 questions: (1) To what extent can the ratios which the book presents be regarded as constant, and in what ways are they subject to possible variation? (2) What justification is there for the suggestion that the ratios of all human capacities will fall within the stated limits, with a maximum value of 2.718? The first necessity which confronts the user of a ratio is that of knowing the absolute zero of the scale in terms of which the measures are stated, and failure to take this into account makes certain ratios wholly meaningless. Although this problem does not arise for a majority of the values in the book, the author is evidently not aware of it, for he includes a range ratio of mental age without regard for the uncertain position of its zero, and even in the case of temperature measurement, for which an absolute scale is available, the results are given in Fahrenheit units. A second source of possible ambiguity in these constants is found in the necessarily arbitrary methods of setting the limits of true variability in any given distribution. The fact that in the present study 3 different methods are employed is itself difficult of evaluation, for there is no way of discovering from the data presented which methods were applied to which data. It is certain, however, that very different values might be obtained when setting the limits by means of the second individuals from each end than when using one of the other 2 methods. Furthermore, it is difficult to believe that any one arbitrarily determined portion of the popupulation (such as .1%) can ever be said to set the limits of significant variability in all human capacities * The author recognizes and discusses the fact that the nature of the group selected for measurement is a factor affecting the size of the range ratio. It is questionable, however, whether the difficulty has been handled satisfactorily, for it appears that any decision as to what factors are to be equated when choosing an experimental group is more or less arbitrary, since there are always other factors which might have been controlled with consequent changes in the range ratio. In general the author has selected studies where age, sex, and race of the group are the same. It has evidently proven impossible to adhere strictly to these arbitrary criteria in all the studies, however, for other limiting factors are clearly operating in certain sets of data. * This problem is really one aspect of the basic fact that no one is as yet able to define the boundaries of the traits and capacities whose limiting values are being sought, a fact which casts serious doubt on the values. * The limits of a trait are set by the wholly fortuitous circumstances under which an experiment happened to be carried out. * In view of the progressive and continuous increase in the size of the ratios as the capacities studied become more and more complex, a point which the book confirms, it is difficult to doubt that many ratios greater than the suggested maximum will be found. We offer but one suggestive example taken from Lemmon's investigation of the relation of reaction times to intelligence. This piece of research comprises the measures of reaction time under 6 different conditions, ranging from simple (which Wechsler includes in his tables) to complex. * We have calculated the range ratios for the 5 sets of reaction time results not included in the book and find them to have the following values: 1.88, 2.29, 3.32, 5.38, and 13.2. Though the psychological functions are simple when compared to other important functions not yet studied, 3 of these ratios far exceed the proposed maximum. In view of such empirical evidence on the subject, discussion of the *a priori* justifications for assuming such a maximum may be dispensed with at this time. * Our adverse comments have been intended chiefly to direct attention to certain serious limitations of the available methods of measuring variability and the conclusions derived therefrom. *

Q R Biol 11:115-6 Mr '36. The author proposes that human variability be measured by the ratio: maximum/minimum and discusses its statistical and biological significance. Though it seems strange that the proposed constant has not been used before, a superficial review of statistical literature confirms the author's assertion that his is the first publication in which it is mentioned. * The interval between the second and 999th is regarded by him as the range of normal variation. The author is of course free to use what limits seem more appropriate to him, but he goes further and attempts to give a rational justification of its use. This is unfortunate. Furthermore, he apparently does not foresee the case of J-shaped or other asymmetrical curves. * He is of the opinion that the value 2 is of special significance and discusses it at length. One can make a number of objections to such a statement. The principal objection is that this ratio, like all measures of variation, is affected by the scale of measurement. For example, the author finds this ratio = 1.03 for body temperature when measured in Fahrenheit degrees. If a centigrade scale had been used the ratio would have been different. * This book contains a number of interesting observations on the subject of variation and some valuable data. However, with regard to this ratio the author has apparently allowed himself to be carried away by his own enthusiasm.

Sat R Lit 12:14 Ag 17 '35. Upon the basis of a painstaking assemblage of measurements of bodily and mental capacities, Dr. Wechsler . . . concludes that the range of human differences is small * well put and documented. Yet the writer of the present note regards the thesis as misconceived, the interpretation unwarranted. There is slight reference to the naturalistic basis of the "capacities," which is the Hamlet of the play. There is a confusion between what is measurable (and the measure thereof) and what is important. The tables, though they have meaning, are conglomerates of incommensurables. Measurements in most mental "capacities" are not the correlates of such variations in pulse or breathing as nature permits. Much of the argument is too much like asking whether a salesman has to sell "twice as many" refrigerators to be "twice as good" a salesman; or make it stories for an author, or dates for a debutante. It is a treacherous thesis. Quantitativists and qualitativists are bound to disagree, which again shows that the present writer defends the *large* differences of man and man, and is as often amazed as depressed by them.

Survey 72:32 Ja '36. * Many interesting questions are raised in the discussion of the somewhat limited data which bear on the limits and range of human capacities.

[B1123]
WELLMAN, BETH L. **The Intelligence of Preschool Children as Measured by the Merrill-Palmer Scale of Performance Tests.** University of Iowa Studies, New Series, No. 361; Studies in Child Welfare, Vol. 15, No. 3. Iowa City, Iowa: the University, October 1938. Pp. 150. Cloth, $1.35; paper, $1.00.

Am J Orthopsychiatry 10:390-3 Ap '40. S. J. Beck. * specifically concerns the usefulness of the Merrill-Palmer schedule for very young children (281 children of 20 to 62 months life age). Skipping the mass of information given in the well-ordered tables and graphs which form a large part of the book, the net results demonstrate the effect of environmental stimulation in bringing out the child's potential intelligence. * Evaluation of the Merrill-Palmer scale, when many of us are at present concerned about adequate measurements for the very young child, is of course valuable. There is no doubt that this scale has certain advantages in administration, but the general feeling of comparative unreliability is confirmed. * Nevertheless the impact of these Iowa studies will make the psychologist more cautious and less fatalistic in utilizing true mothers' intelligence ratings as factors determining disposition of infant or young child. Equally, they will be more attentive to environment, both in patient's history and the prospective adoptive home. If these Iowa Studies result in giving adoptive children a better break, they will, of course, have been constructive. Meanwhile we should have more investigations from other centers, without the Iowa halo, relative to what a good home can do for the child of a low grade mother.

Am J Psychiatry 96:247-8 Jl '39. W. Line. * Certainly, the experimental data justify the conclusion that "pre-school attendance materially affected ability on the Merrill-Palmer test" * the reviewer would like to suggest caution in interpreting experimental data of the kind reported in the present monograph. It would be distinctly unwise if the stimulating, painstaking and discerning work of Dr. Wellman were to be regarded as representing a return to earlier conceptions of the IQ, with the simple revision that the constancy of the IQ is now being called into question. * The monograph is one of the most stimulating and significant productions of modern psychological

research. Adequate interpretation, however, must await a careful research programme initiated for that purpose.

J Abn and Social Psychol 35:457-62 Jl '40. Barbara S. Burks. * Much of the discussion is made highly cumbersome through the separate treatment of scores stated first in sigmas, then in IQ's, then in percentiles, with results so disparate that the direction of average change on retest is in some instances positive by one scoring technique and negative by another (Table 10). This fact indicates, of course, that the norms for the test are in need of thorough overhauling *

Loyola Ed Digest 14:9 F '39. Austin G. Schmidt. * One of the most important outcomes of the study is evidence that preschool experience brings about a growth in IQ which cannot be attributed to practice effects.

Volta R 41:44-5 Ja '39. * especially interesting *

[B1124]
WEST, JOE YOUNG. **A Technique for Appraising Certain Observable Behavior of Children in Science in Elementary Schools.** Columbia University, Teachers College, Contributions to Education No. 728. Gerald S. Craig, faculty sponsor. New York: Bureau of Publications, the College, 1937. Pp. vii, 118. $1.60.

Ed Res B 18:110-1 Ap '39. J. Wayne Wrightstone. A relatively new and interesting method of appraising observable behavior of children in science classes * All individuals who are interested in the newer trends in elementary-science objectives and especially in their measurement or evaluation should read this monograph.

Pub Health R 10:43-4 Ap '40. Mabel E. Rugen. * The technique described in this study should be helpful to educators in learning something of the health behavior of children. *

Sci Ed 22:209-10 Ap '38. C(larence) M. P(ruitt). * the technique developed in this study offers great possibilities for wide adaptation and as such should be listed among the better theses of recent years. We are in great need of more researches of this type. It is a direct method of controlled observation that provides teachers, supervisors, other administrators and curriculum workers with a direct method of making appraisals of classroom behavior of children in science.

For additional reviews, see B520.

[B1125]
WESTBURGH, EDWARD M. **Introduction to Clinical Psychology:** For Students of Medicine, Psychol-

ogy, and Nursing. Foreword by Edward A. Strecker. Philadelphia, Pa.: P. Blakiston's Son & Co., Inc., 1937. Pp. xiii, 336. $3.50.

J Ed Psychol 29:158-60 F '38. C. M. Louttit. In the first paragraph of his preface, Dr. Westburgh makes his first error when he says that, "students of psychology and medicine have no access to this accumulating knowledge of facts, principles, and methods" in clinical psychology. This was not true even at the time the book was written. Further on he says that this book is an attempt at a formulation of the "principles and philosophy of Clinical Psychology" and implies that it summarizes the facts and methods. It is impossible to demonstrate in a short review that neither methods, facts, nor principles are adequately dealt with. The book is largely devoted to methods. * In the chapter on "Test Results" there are praiseworthy cautions concerning the interpretation of IQ's, but at the same time the author says "IQ's are regarded as having approximately the same meaning for all tests." He devotes a page and a half to calculation of adult IQ's with sixteen as the divisor in spite of the changes in practice that started at least twenty years ago. Also in this chapter there is a disproportionate amount of space devoted to elementary statistics. In a clinical textbook one could reasonably expect to find a systematic discussion of the different kinds of problems encountered. Nowhere in this book is there any such discussion. There are two chapters on "Cognitive Factors" in which feeblemindedness is considered in the midst of an incoherent presentation of the theory of intelligence. * The last chapter . . . has a rather good summary of psychological types of therapy. * [The] bibliography does not include any of the published books on clinical psychology and does not mention a single book of cases, such as those published by the Commonwealth Fund. Surely these are serious lacks. Like so many books this one does not fulfill the promise of the preface. It can scarcely be considered even an *introduction* to clinical psychology.

J Nerv and Mental Dis 90:284-5 Ag '39. * We dissent . . . as biologists when he writes of "strong" and "weak" "instincts," much as we might should one speak of strong or weak T.N.T. He seems to have little awareness of the checks and counter-checks which guide, direct, block or symbolize the herculean ac-

tivities of the libido, beyond offering at times quaint and outmoded popular interpretations and phrasings. * we find the work of distinct pragmatic promise *

Mental Hyg (New York) 23:311-3 Ap '39. Wendell Muncie. The author defines clinical psychology "as a body of organized knowledge and as a systematic technique of adjusting individuals to themselves and their environment." Because only "a few men and women have learned through personal experience how to correct personality deviations and how to help keep children and adults in good mental and nervous health," and because "students of psychology and medicine have no access to this accumulating knowledge of facts, principles, and methods," this book has been written. The author adds: "If Clinical Psychology is to be established as a profession, a systematic presentation must be made of sound psychological techniques that shall be effective in correcting maladjustments, in changing specific emotional and behavior patterns, in improving the total personality picture." With this evidence of loose thinking and actual misstatement from the Preface, the reader is thoroughly warned as to the "scientific" monstrosity first gaining the light of day in the chapters to follow. With a fine disregard of the body of psychiatric experience as a practical working psychology based on the experiences of many workers, the author sees psychiatry being saved from the sterility of structuralism only through psychoanalysis and the data of clinical psychology. He appears to be unaware of the fact that those items he claims for his profession have been the common property of all psychiatrists for at least two generations * a further perusal of the book leads to two conclusions: 1. The Clinical Psychologist (author's capitals) has absorbed little of what is to be learned, to judge from the careless use of terms and concepts * These few illustrations will suffice to show the old shopworn stock-in-trade of those who never get beyond the jargon of "facing it," "escape," "compensation," "conversion," "sex drive," and so on, and the reliance on "techniques." * But the meagerness of the absorption of the considerable psychological knowledge already at hand, and the poor grasp of the real problems involved, are best exemplified by the author's introduction to a chapter headed, *Health History and Physical Factors* * What follows indicates how utterly dangerous such an arrangement would be if treatment is to be left to the clinical psychologist. The chapter is a tribute to the outmoded mind-body dualism, which, however, because of its vagueness and solemnity, would arouse only scorn from the past masters of dualism. 2. The strong need apparent throughout the book to establish a professional status for the clinical psychologist will meet with encouragement only in settings where loose thinking is allowed in regard to the fundamental concepts of human behavior. * The author's training qualifications for the competent clinical psychologist—from one to two years of internship under the guidance of a qualified clinical psychologist and in association with psychiatrists—will do nothing to lessen the alarm of serious workers for the welfare of patients whose "health or ill health, happiness or misery, success or failure depend on the wise or unwise guidance provided by the clinical psychologist." If the clinical psychologist really desires to achieve professional status, let him serve on apprenticeship in human biology in its broadest interpretation. The best part of the book is that which treats of the psychologist's most worth-while contribution—to the field of testing. The rest is a congeries of Freudism and borrowings from psychiatry put together in such a manner as to be wholly unacceptable to earnest workers. It will be a sad day for natural history when man is reduced finally to "mechanisms" and "techniques."

Psychoanalytic Q 8:398-400 Jl '39. Nina Ridenour. The table of contents of this book is an excellent summary of what students in medicine, nursing, and social work ought to know about clinical psychology. Unfortunately, the book itself does not sufficiently bear out the promise of the table of contents. The author is neither original enough to be stimulating, nor sufficiently orthodox to be dependable. He tries to cover far too much ground with the result that he fails to be definitive in any one aspect of his subject. His chief virtue lies in bringing together material not usually found within the compass of a single volume; but this advantage is rather offset by his poor presentation of the less controversial subjects, such as test results and cognitive factors, and by confusion worse confounded in the presentation of the more controversial material, especially affective factors. Throughout there is a lack of differential definitions and a failure to trace **cause** and effect relationships beyond the first

superficial level of explanation. The chapter on Test Results—Interpretation and Statistical Considerations is well conceived in that it selects important concepts for discussion, but the method of explanation would inevitably be confusing to a student. * By far the weakest part of the book is the section on Affective Factors. The presentation is based on McDougall's hormic psychology, but lacks the rigid definitions and admirable consistency of McDougall. * The terminology of the first part of this section is chiefly that of McDougall, with certain rather curious emphases of the author's own, such for instance as his frequent allusions to joyful rage. Psychoanalytic terms are interwoven with others . . . but without any real integration of ideas. The author appears satisfied with explaining motivation in superficial and ambiguous terms such as attention-getting, habits, ideals. The chapters on Family, Social, and Vocational History, History of Affective Experiences, and Health History and Physical Factors discuss the almost infinite variety of data that can go into a case history. These chapters would be better for the student if they were less exhaustive and more selective, with greater development of those types of data which are most important. The final chapter on Some Fundamental Concepts is perhaps better than most of the others. * There is bibliography of some 125 titles, and a very adequate index.

Psychol B 34:859-60 D '37. William A. Hunt. This is a curiously uneven book. Professedly written for "those who, at least, have had introductory courses in general, theoretical and experimental psychology," much of it is written at too elementary a level for its audience. One feels that the author has covered too much ground too superficially. The style is choppy and somewhat stilted, and the book does not make easy reading. The inclusion of numerous colloquialisms such as "house broken," "playing with fire," "dog's life," etc., all elaborately set off by quotation marks, creates an impression of deliberate condescension rather than the pleasant informality no doubt intended. * The chapter on "Test Results" is a simple, sane discussion of the significance of the statistical concepts found in testing. * The final chapter on "Some Fundamental Concepts" contains a defense of the clinical method as transcending the merely experimental, and a brief, but good, discussion of the rôle of the clinical psychologist and his relation to the patient. It is the best chapter in the book. The eighteen-page index is exceedingly thorough *

Psychologists League J 1:17, 19 S-O '37. Max L. Hutt. * eminently readable, free from encumbering footnotes and annotations, informal and non-scholastic in approach. According to the author it is intended primarily as an introduction to clinical psychology for students of medicine, psychology and nursing, altho it is hoped that it will also prove useful for "experienced psychologists and psychiatrists." It is difficult to see how one book whose main text comprises 269 chapters could possibly fulfill these dual functions and in the reviewer's opinion it fails in both. That is not to say that its viewpoint is fundamentally unsound or that it fails to introduce some basic concepts about which discussion has been sadly lacking. However by attempting to be at once profound and superficial, both intensive and extensive and both scientific and popular, it falls short of being satisfying. * If one reads this little volume diligently one is apt to find many thought-provoking statements but these are likely to be missed by a more casual perusal because they are hidden in a mass of verbiage. * To a certain extent the apparent haphazard sampling of problems or items for discussion becomes more meaningful when reference is made to the Appendix, An Outline for the Clinical Study of Personality. This appendix, perhaps the most useful feature of the book, is however not referred to in the text, although there is some attempt to follow it in the discussion nor is the basis for deriving the appendix explained. To the reviewer the shortcomings noted above are serious. They are especially so because Dr. Westburgh has a point of view which deserves serious consideration by all sincere clinicians and earnest students. A better organized volume treating the same areas, which may be inclusively described by the phrase, Clinical Techniques for psychological diagnosis, would be a fundamental and far-reaching contribution to clinical psychology. It is to be hoped that Dr. Westburgh will revise his book * There is literally a crying need for a clinical handbook, devoted not merely to psychometric diagnosis but to personality analysis in its broadest sense in which the psychological contributions of MacDougall, Meyer, Koffka, Lewin, Freud and others are

culled for the clinician and synthesized. Too long have psychologists been content with leaving entirely to psychiatrists the diagnosis of psychological problems and utilizing for themselves mainly routine psychometric techniques.

Pub Health R 7:6 F '38. L. E. Himler. * presents a scientifically sound formulation of the factual and practical, as well as the philosophic and theoretic, structures upon which modern clinical psychology is based * The three chapters devoted to the affective side of the personality will be especially valuable to those who desire a well-balanced orientation with respect to this most important aspect of the personality. There are excellent brief discussions of the influence of instincts, sentiments and interests on behavior, and on the development of compensation and defense mechanisms. * an admirably concise and well organized introduction to this field, presenting clearly and forcefully the basic principles and approach.

For additional reviews, see B521.

[B1126]

WILEY, LESTER E., AND WILEY, A. McBROOM, UNDER THE DIRECTION OF RAY G. WOOD. **Measurement of Educational Progress:** A Manual Describing a Procedure for the Measurement of the Development of a Class in Connection with the Ohio Every Pupil Tests. Bulletin of Research Activities, No. R-3. Columbus, Ohio: Ohio Scholarship Tests, State Department of Education, September 1939. Pp. 80, 19. $0.10. Paper.

[B1126.1]

WILKS, SAMUEL STANLEY. **Report on the Mathematics Attainment Test of June 1939:** A Description of the Procedures Used in Preparing and Reading the Mathematics Attainment Test and an Analysis of the Results of the Reading. New York: College Entrance Examination Board, May 1940. Pp. v, 61. $0.25. Paper.

[B1127]

WILLIAMSON, E. G. **How to Counsel Students:** A Manual of Techniques for Clinical Counselors. New York: McGraw-Hill Book Co., Inc., 1939. Pp. xx, 562. $3.75. (London: McGraw-Hill Publishing Co., Ltd. 21s.)

AVA J 15:72 F '40. F(ranklin) J. K(eller). * serves not only as "A Manual of Techniques for Clinical Counselors," but as a glorified check-list for the progressive principal who wishes to make his school a place for development of individuals as well as for mass training in skills * Williamson is justly skeptical of the quality of much of the current counseling, "At the present time most schools use a few personnel techniques in an isolated and sporadic manner, e.g., intelligence or entrance tests, faculty advising, etc. But nowhere is each student given adequate diagnostic and counseling service previous to, or parallel with, instruction." The word "adequate" saves the second sentence, for none of us can do all that we should for our students. But "nowhere" is a fighting word, and, while the reviewer has had the pleasure of seeing the excellent work of Dr. Williamson at Minnesota, he has not been around to see us. We are using this book to check on our guidance program, as should every other vocational educator, and as a result, we hope, may become almost "adequate."

Brit J Ed Psychol 10:171 Je '40. M. D. V(ernon). * Williamson is to be congratulated upon his enthusiasm in demonstrating the value of this work, and upon his method of approach to it * But Professor Williamson cannot be altogether commended upon the manner in which he describes the performance of this work. He groups the problems and difficulties with which he is faced according to their superficial and overt symptoms (personality, educational, occupational, financial and health problems), attempting little analysis of their fundamental causes. For instance, separate chapters are devoted to Uncertain Vocational Choice, Unwise Vocational Choice and No Vocational Choice. But he himself states that "the reader should conclude that the same causes operating in different students may produce an uncertain, an unwise or no choice at all." The reader is thus presented with a series of disconnected and repetitive descriptive statements, unrelated in any general scheme or classification based upon underlying psychological causes, and in consequence very hard to grasp or to remember. Moreover, the actual problems could be better understood and elucidated by anyone who took into consideration the much valuable work which has been devoted to these underlying psychological causes. Thus the author states that little is known about the lack of motivation as a cause of scholastic failure, while ignoring the work on unconscious motivation described, for instance, in several able American books on adolescent psychology. And no non-American work on these or any other problems is mentioned. Again the treatment of emotional difficulties is superficial to a degree; one cannot believe that problems resulting from sexual difficulties are so infrequent among American students as to be not worth mentioning. We hope that Professor Williamson will develop his interesting methods of counselling in the light of recent psycho-

logical and psychiatrical work, and will then describe them to us rather differently.

Ed 60:188 N '39. William P. Sears, Jr. * No teacher who is responsible for guidance (and that includes every teacher) and no counselor can afford to miss this volume. The contents are to be read, learned, marked, and inwardly digested.

Ed Abstracts 5:19 Ja '40. Roger M. Bellows. * one of the three or four most comprehensive and valuable works in this field *

Ed Trends 9:47-8 Ja-F '40. Frank S. Endicott. * a manual of techniques for those who function as counselors to individual students. It has not been written for classroom teachers since the author says frankly that he is "opposed to current efforts in the personnel movement to train teachers in the technicalities of guidance." These technical procedures he would reserve as the private domain of the clinical counselor or psychologist. * the most complete single source of suggestions for diagnostic and remedial work with individual students * Those who classify themselves as counselors, clinical workers, or school psychologists will welcome this manual. Its thoroughgoing and practical nature will appeal to all who use it. Since this reviewer is not among those who are fearful of attempts on the part of "ordinary" teachers to utilize these so-called "technicalities" of guidance, he suggests that the volume be made available to high school teachers through the principal's office or the school library.

El Paso Sch Standard 17:39-40 F '40. Josephine Skiff. * an outstanding contribution to the literature of the field of guidance and personnel work * The author has drawn extensively from the works of other writers in the field. He has quoted freely from them, commented upon many and cited numerous sources of additional material. This, coupled with the fact that the book is unusually replete with practical material makes the book valuable to the personnel worker. However, it would be helpful if the status of the clinical counselor in the school organization had been made clear. One feels a need for the clarification of such points as student load, number and type of assistants, and other duties, if any, which might be expected to devolve upon him. The book should fill a place in guidance literature. It should be valuable not only to clinical counselors, but to counselors in practical situations, even though less highly trained, to administrators building guidance programs, to teachers of guidance, and to all good classroom teachers, who fundamentally are personnel workers, for it points the way to the development of a better and more efficient guidance service.

H Sch J 23:190 Ap '40. A. J. Parkhurst. * The author has not been concerned in this book with quibbles over terminology carried on by the "philosophers" of the personnel movement. His more immediate concern has been *what to do* for the student who needs counseling. * This book should be on the "must have" list of every guidance worker.

J Higher Ed 11:167-8 Mr '40. J. E. Walters. * a timely book * gives to the counselor and personnel departments many valuable suggestions. It is a book which every counselor in educational work should read. * The book is an excellent exposition, and it is worthy of consideration because it is the work of one who has had experience in counseling. Though I recommend this book heartily, it seemed too long. * Williamson puts too much confidence in clinical psychologists. Some persons who have had clinical training in psychology cannot do good counseling, for even they have certain foibles. Though Mr. Williamson does not limit counseling to the clinical psychologists, he could have stressed more what the large number of non-clinical psychologists might do. Though used for emphasis, a too frequent use of the word *should* appeared. More definite facts to back up his opinion as to why counseling should be done in the suggested way might have been given. The author has a tendency to be an intellectualist about counseling. He might have emphasized that counselors should be more "personalized," so as to prevent them from making too many students "cases," and "problem students." There is some repetition in the book, particularly between the first and succeeding parts. This should be accepted, however, since the same techniques are often used to study personality problems as to study vocational problems. This book leans toward aggressiveness on the part of the counselor rather than passivity, whereas the informational approach, the middle road, is probably more often used in counseling. In general, the book is a good one and deserves a wide use.

Jun Col J 10:355 F '40. * [an] important new text * Selected readings are well chosen and a comprehensive index makes the wealth of material more convenient for ready reference.

Sch and Soc 52:76-7 Ag 3 '40. Hugh M. Bell. * without question, the most comprehensive and thorough treatment of student counseling that has yet appeared. It is consistently documented by reference to research studies. The treatment of problems of educational orientation and achievement is particularly effective and goes a long way toward placing this phase of student counseling on a scientific basis. The author is to be commended for his stress upon the "whole personality" of the counselee. * Some case histories of typical counseling problems might well have been included in this book. From such reports it is possible to show the interrelationships of adjustment problems and to indicate how quantitative data from tests and other sources are used to increase the effectiveness of the interview. Also, a discussion of sexual problems should have been included, since they constitute a considerable proportion of students' adjustment problems and fall naturally in the province of the clinical counselor. Dr. Williamson's book will be used widely as a text-book in courses in guidance and counseling, and will be read by many individuals outside the field of student personnel. It will do much to further the personnel point of view and to improve the quality of counseling in high schools and colleges.

Sch R 48:150-1 F '40. Julian C. Aldrich. * a real contribution to the guidance programs in secondary schools and colleges * It is this emphasis on the "clinical" counselor that bothered the reviewer. Williamson makes a real point in refusing to apply the term to the "untrained counselor who uses what has been called the single-interview method of counseling" (p. vii). The term is applied to those who "provide that technical diagnosis and counseling necessary to effective guidance and beyond the competency of teachers and untrained advisers" (p. 55). Too many "counseling" programs are valueless or actually harmful because of incompetent leadership. There is a real danger, however, that there will be created a new worker in the schools who knows the classroom only through his experience as a student. In Williamson's outline of the professional training needed by this worker, the only contact with teaching is a course in educational philosophy. In the reviewer's opinion, it is as important for the counselor to know the teaching problem as it is for the teacher to know the guidance problem. As a textbook to parallel a demonstration experience, this book is of great value in pre-service and in-service training programs. Teachers, principals, and superintendents will find in it a picture of an adequate counseling program and will see the need for training of persons assigned to the work. Every counselor should have this manual constantly at hand. Even superior counselors will profit from a study of Williamson's experience.

Univ Wash Col Ed Rec 6:14 N '39. Edwin B. Stevens. * Williamson uses direct statements, shows little patience for philosophers who quibble over words, and drives forward in an orderly procedure to the solution of some of the most baffling and complicated tasks in the educational program. * The emphasis is upon the types of problems most frequently met in a college counseling situation, but his discussions have almost as great value for the high school teacher-counselor. * Guidance officers will welcome a manual for consultation in terms of need, while the graduate students will find it a help in the laboratory or clinical work basic to seminar courses. To follow Williamson's treatment of a subject is a stimulating procedure. * the book is commended to the rapidly growing army of personnel workers in both the secondary schools and colleges. It is not light reading but will repay study.

[B1128]
WILLIAMSON, E. G., AND DARLEY, J. G. **Student Personnel Work:** An Outline of Clinical Procedures. Introduction by Donald G. Paterson. New York: McGraw-Hill Book Co., Inc., 1937. Pp. xxiv, 313. $3.00. (London: McGraw-Hill Publishing Co., Ltd. 18s.)

J Ed Psychol 29:553-4 O '38. Stephen M. Corey. The essential impracticability of any thoroughgoing treatment of guidance at the college level, such as is presented in this very good book, is that it assumes an educational philosophy quite at variance with current practice. The more realistic counsellors are aware of this, and attempt to make their position stronger by defining "personnel work" as an attempt "to deliver the student *to the classroom* in the optimum condition for profiting from instruction." This seems to the reviewer to be an empirical and unjustified delimitation. * Another characteristic type of optimism which

is illustrated in the writings of guidance specialists is the scope they give to formal education. Williamson and Darley, for example, imply that education should "provide . . . training not only in the realm of occupational activity but also in the total realm of life adjustments. . . ." (p. 19). This is rather broad to put it mildly. Schools, higher or lower, are not equipped to do everything, and this reviewer for one hopes the day may never come when formal educational institutions will attempt to provide training in the "total realm of life adjustments." There are, after all, other social institutions. * Williamson and Darley are at their best when they describe the excellent program at Minnesota, and this takes up the last two-thirds of the volume. * The treatment of "Analytic Techniques in Counseling" is superior and consists chiefly of a description and criticism of the many types of tests, inventories, and questionnaires which have developed primarily for use with college students. * The chapters dealing with "Student Problems and Treatment" and "Illustrative Case Histories" are valid, interesting, and informative. A frank evaluation of the work of the Minnesota Testing Bureau concludes the volume. *

For additional reviews, see B526.

[B1129]
WILLIAMSON, E. G., AND HAHN, M. E. **Introduction to High School Counseling.** New York: McGraw-Hill Book Co., Inc., 1940. Pp. ix, 314. $3.00. (London: McGraw-Hill Publishing Co., Ltd. 18s.)

Ed News B 10:112 Je '40. * considers in details the *how* as well as the *why* of student personnel work * will prove of great value in orienting the high school counselor, whether classroom teacher or counseling specialist, to the many ramifications of the student guidance program.

[B1130]
WITMER, HELEN LELAND. **Psychiatric Clinics for Children:** With Special Reference to State Programs. Foreword by George S. Stevenson. New York: Commonwealth Fund, 1940. Pp. xix, 437. $2.50. (London: Oxford University Press. 10s. 6d.)

Mental Hyg (New York) 24:470-5 Jl '40. James M. Cunningham. This book by Dr. Witmer is based on data on state-wide psychiatric services for children that were assembled by Miss Winifred Arrington and Miss Dorothy Brinker, of The National Committee for Mental Hygiene. To imply, however, that these data are the sole basis of the book would

do a serious injustice to the author, who brings to an analysis and evaluation of this material a wide knowledge of the theoretical basis for psychiatric clinics for children and a thorough understanding of the influence of cultural settings upon the effective operation of such clinics. This is not just another survey. The author has succeeded in taking extremely heterogeneous data regarding state-supported psychiatric clinics for children and giving them meaning by placing them in a perspective of psychiatric theory, social setting, and historical development. But this is by no means the full contribution of the book. On the basis of the material and the perspective developed, Dr. Witmer has arrived at certain principles for the development of future programs which should receive careful consideration by any one who is planning a clinical program for children, or, for that matter, any one who is now conducting such a program. * some may question the emphasis placed by Dr. Witmer on the contribution to psychiatric theory of Meyer as compared to that of Freud * while William A. White is mentioned, with others, as having influenced the development of psychiatric service to children, his major contribution is not indicated * In the third section of the book, the author develops certain principles for the development of future programs. With the majority of these one can agree, and their significance is such that no one planning a psychiatric program for children should fail to give them serious consideration. There are, however, one or two points on which there may be disagreement. In order to create a basis for the formulation of such principles, the author analyzes the objectives of psychiatric clinics. These are stated to be (1) the prevention of institutionalization, (2) the prevention of mental disorder, and (3) the treatment of children's problems for their own sake, without reference to any future outcome. The author believes that the first and the last are satisfactory and realizable objectives, but she would discard the second. Her reason is that there is no evidence to indicate that it is possible to identify the children who will later develop psychoses. While this is true in most cases, it would not seem a satisfactory reason for abandoning this objective. This reasoning is based on a descriptive rather than a dynamic psychiatry, and is unusual for this author, whose whole volume is a condemnation of a static, descriptive, diagnostic type of clinic. It may be said also that in public health in general many preventive procedures are undertaken—such as vaccination, for example—even though it is not possible to predict the future infection of any particular person. It is not necessary to identify the future psychotic in order to do a preventive piece of work. Many of the other objections that the author raises hinge on this matter of attaching labels. * Proceeding on the assumption that there are two valid objectives, the author then states that a clinic should choose one or the other. She does say that they are not mutually exclusive, but her major emphasis is on a staff organization and a training of personnel directed toward one or the other of these objectives. * It is questionable whether psychiatric clinics for children should become so specialized that a particular type of clinic will be available for each kind of psychiatric problem. * the author . . . uses the term "psychiatric treatment" in a very narrow sense. She would seem to limit it to psychotherapeutic interviews. Psychiatric treatment would seem to be much broader than this—broad enough to include any program of treatment that is based on adequate knowledge, whether it deals directly with the patient or with his family or social environment. * There is a question . . . as to the emphasis placed on what may be called "late Rankian" concepts. This is not the place to argue the merits of these concepts, but it is doubtful whether they have had the importance for clinic practice that is implied. * That the conclusions as to the feasibility of developing psychiatric clinics under public-health auspices are sound has been amply demonstrated by the program of the Connecticut State Department of Health. * Actual experience confirms the criteria that Dr. Witmer has set up as necessary for the formulation of state-financed clinical programs. * This volume of Dr. Witmer's meets a real need in this country. The orientation of the author, her presentation of the material of the survey, and the conclusions drawn show a high degree of objectivity. The significance both of the material and of the conclusions is such that no one planning a program of psychiatric clinics for children can afford to ignore it. Furthermore, as a basis for evaluating the present work of varied programs of this sort, it is invaluable. It should also be useful to those staff members who work both

in urban and in rural types of clinic in helping to orient them to their function in the total objective of bringing psychiatric service to children. Educators, probation officers, and others will also find in this volume much that will aid them to appreciate the function of psychiatric clinics in relation to their own programs.

Psychiatry 3:445-6 Ag '40. Paul J. Ewerhardt. * In the three main parts of the book the author deals with the theoretical and historical background of clinical child psychiatry, a survey of state financed clinics and, finally, principles for future programs. The first of these is an admirable discussion of the wide range of thinking out of which clinical efforts emerged. * The third part is especially interesting since it contains a wealth of material bearing upon the complexities implicit in a highly specialized technical service operating within a community culture having its own patterns of thought and action. The earlier and by no means extinct notion of the prevention of psychosis and crime as clinic objectives comes in for searching treatment. The words of the illustrious teacher, the late Dr. William A. White, when he discussed mental hygiene as "a positive program for life well lived, for mental health because of its values and not because of what it avoids" gain a much needed re-emphasis. This is followed by a full discussion of the essentials underlying effective clinical work in terms of clinic organization, personnel and function as such in relation to other community efforts. Here the author makes some cogent observations on inter-agency relationships. * Dr. Witmer is identified with Smith College School of Social Work, and also the National Committee for Mental Hygiene as Research Associate. Although accepting responsibility for points of view expressed it is probable that they also reflect the thinking of many others. There will be many who for one reason or another will not be in agreement with some of her more forward ideas and conclusions. Nevertheless free and frank discussion is a healthy procedure particularly in programs that may remain static. The volume should have wide reading among those already in the field, and others in the community who may have something to do with the introduction or extension of psychiatric services for children. There is an in-

troduction, a well documented index and also an index of authors and persons quoted.

[B1131]
WITTY, PAUL, EDITOR. **Intelligence in a Changing Universe.** *Educational Method,* Vol. 19, No. 2. Washington, D. C.: Department of Supervisors and Directors of Instruction, National Education Association, November 1939. Pp. 63-132. $0.50. Paper.

[B1132]
WOLF, RALPH ROBINSON, JR. **Differential Forecasts of Achievement and Their Use in Educational Counseling.** American Psychological Association, Psychological Monographs, Vol. 51, No. 1, Whole No. 227. Evanston, Ill.: the Association, 1939. Pp. v, 53. $0.75. Paper.

Loyola Ed Digest 15:7 N '39. Austin G. Schmidt. The author's purpose was to appraise the indices of ability in use at Yale University for the purpose of determining candidates' fitness for different curricula. The general conclusion is that measures of achievement now in use are relatively unreliable.

[B1133]
WOODSIDE, C. W., AND WANOUS, S. J. **Bibliography of Tests and Testing in Business Subjects.** Cincinnati, Ohio: South-Western Publishing Co., June 1939. Pp. 36. Gratis. Paper.

Balance Sheet 21:90 O '39. A bibliography of testing articles and tests that has been compiled from an extensive examination of government bulletins, books, commercial education periodicals, and printed tests obtained from various publishing companies. The articles on testing have been taken from periodicals dated since January, 1930, and from books with copyright dates later than 1920. The tests listed are those now in actual publication. At the end of the bibliography is given a list of the sources from which tests may be obtained yearly for contest purposes.

[B1134]
WOODY, CLIFFORD. **The Sophomore and Freshman Testing Program in the Accredited High Schools of Michigan.** University of Michigan, School of Education, Bureau of Educational Research and Service, Bulletin No. 149. Ann Arbor, Mich.: the School, 1937. Pp. viii, 129. $0.65. Paper.

[B1135]
WOODY, CLIFFORD. **Sophomore Testing Program in the Accredited High Schools of Michigan, 1936.** University of Michigan, School of Education, Bureau of Educational Reference and Research, Bulletin No. 148. Ann Arbor, Mich.: the School, April 1936. Pp. 95. $0.60. Paper.

Ed Res B 18:168 S '39. F. P. Frutchey. The American Council on Education Psychological Examination was given to 12,878

Sophomores in 176 high schools in Michigan during one week in January, 1936. At the same time an inquiry form was answered by the students to obtain sociological information, interests, activities, and future plans of the students. The pamphlet consists largely of the distributions of scores and medians of these students according to each item of information on the inquiry form. The tables include much interesting data. *

For additional reviews, see B290.

[B1136]

WOODY, CLIFFORD. **The Sophomore and Freshman Testing Program in the Accredited High Schools of Michigan, 1938.** University of Michigan, School of Education, Bureau of Educational Research and Service, Bulletin No. 150. Ann Arbor, Mich.: the School, September 1938. Pp. viii, 142. $0.65. Paper.

[B1137]

WRIGHTSTONE, J. WAYNE. **Appraisal of Experimental High School Practice.** New York: Bureau of Publications, Teachers College, Columbia University, 1936. Pp. xiv, 194. $2.25.

B Int Bur Ed 11:37 q 1 '37. * Graphs and charts add considerably to the value of the study.

Sci Ed 23:228-9 Ap '39. O(tis) W. C(aldwell). [Joint review of *Appraisal of Experimental High School Practices* and *Appraisal of Newer Elementary School Practices (See B1138).*] * In making statements drawn from these reports it needs to be clear that Dr. Wrightstone constantly says that the conclusions must be regarded as tentative awaiting further investigations, since his sampling in elementary schools aggregated a total of but 180 pupils. * The fact that the experimental schools used in this study regularly surpass the conventional schools used in this study is suggestive and encouraging, but not overwhelmingly convincing. So far as science is concerned, the results hardly justify a hasty rush to the methods of newer-type schools, unless self-initiated activities, and knowledge of unfounded beliefs are matters of deciding importance.

For additional reviews, see B529.

[B1138*]

WRIGHTSTONE, J. WAYNE. **Appraisal of Newer Elementary School Practices.** Graphs by Kathleen Corbett Wrightstone. New York: Bureau of Publications, Teachers College, Columbia University, 1938. Pp. xiii, 221. $2.25.

* In order to have the entry numbers continuous with earlier publications in this series, the first entry number in the book section is B815. The addition of 44 new entries—assigned fractional numbers—makes the total number of books listed in this volume 368.

Childh Ed 15:283 F '39. John A. Hockett. * the experimenter took great care in equating the two groups whose achievements were compared. * his findings are in general agreement with previous studies in which the outcomes of the older and newer types of schools have been compared.

Curric J 10:41-2 Ja '39. Hugh B. Wood. * a significant contribution * In achieving the stated purposes, the author has made an admirable contribution and met a real need in the first five chapters in summarizing concisely and yet pertinently the historical development of many experimental practices in schools today and in describing their general application. * The entire study, of course, is based on a philosophy which, if not accepted by the reader, invalidates the findings for him. Two minor criticisms include the definition of the conventional program in such a way that few of even the most conservative would accept it (p. 40), and the limited reference to outstanding curriculum bulletins * The book paves the way to better practices in measurement and provides an extremely useful handbook for developing a comprehensive program of evaluation.

El Sch J 39:629-30 Ap '39. C. L. Cushman. * The survey of trends in experimental and conventional elementary schools . . . should be helpful to persons who have had only limited contact with the development of elementary-school practices in recent years. The survey is, however, of necessity too brief to permit anything like a thorough review of these practices. To the writer it seems that the author has taken an unwarrantedly optimistic view toward recent progress at the elementary-school level. * The inclusive plan for appraising the outcomes of newer practices in elementary schools is ably set forth in chapter viii. * The statement of this appraisal technique and the report of its application represent the major contribution of the volume. * Unfortunately the author does not report how he gathered evidence to show that certain schools were experimental and others were conventional. Such distinctions are often made on a superficial basis. * In summary, this study provides (1) a valuable review of recent developments in the practices of elementary schools, (2) much information that can be used to refute the charges of the critics that these practices result in inferior work, and (3) an outline of new evaluation techniques that should be beneficial in the further development of new practices in elementary schools.

J Ed Sociol 12:256 D '38. Pioneer research of great significance and fine quality is reported in this book. * Along with his own studies, Wrightstone presents an excellent summary of the development and status of newer practices in the public schools of the United States. * This book is indispensable for teachers, supervisors, and administrators who want a clear interpretation of "activity programs" and the scientist's objective evaluation of the results from "progressive schools."

Loyola Ed Digest 14:6-7 D '38. Austin G. Schmidt. * Much of the material in the present volume has already appeared in periodical form. Schools of a progressive type were compared with schools of a conventional type in regard to six outcomes of instruction * The general result is a sweeping victory for the progressives. * In our judgment great caution should be observed in interpreting these results. The chief error to be avoided is that of an 'either-or' verdict. The choice is not necessarily between progressive education in its most extreme form and conventional education in its most rockbound form. Possibly the ideal school is one that combines the merits of both. Again, while so far as one can see the study was made as honestly and impartially as possible, it

is very probable that the teachers in the progressive schools were raised to a higher level of enthusiasm and given more help of various types than would be the case in the average and typical classroom. * Wrightstone has taken us a great step forward, but the last word has not yet been said. He himself interprets his findings temperately. We trust that the conclusion drawn from his book by smaller minds will not be that everything conventional must go out and everything progressive come in.

Sci Ed 23:228-9 Ap '39. O(tis) W. C(aldwell). [Same as review for B1137.]

Social Ed 2:661 D '38. Hazel Prehm. * The first part of this book makes no new contribution to the descriptive and illustrative literature already available on the newer type of schools. Chapter vi, however, which gives the author's interpretation of the six cardinal objectives of elementary education, should be a challenge to the thinking and practices of administrators and teachers. It seemed to the reviewer that the author devoted too little space to the outstanding feature of the study, the attempt to measure the so-called intangibles in education. A critical evaluation of the proposed techniques of measurement and their resulting educational implications should prove stimulating to graduate students and research workers in education, and should encourage further research toward more effective practices.

Periodical Directory and Index

* * *

References are to book and test entries. Numbers preceded by a B indicate book-review excerpts; other numbers refer to test-review excerpts. The name and address of the editor to whom books should be sent for review are given for each journal. Test references are not indexed.

A.M.A.—The A.M.A.: The Journal of the Incorporated Association of Assistant Masters in Secondary Schools. 10 issues (omitting Ap, Ag); vol. 35 started Ja '40; 6d. per issue; S. B. Lucas, editor, 29 Gordon Square, London, W.C.1, England: B1115

Am Econ R—The American Economic Review. Published by the American Economic Association. 4 issues; vol. 30 started Mr '40; $5; Davis R. Dewey, managing editor, 222 Charles River Road, Cambridge, Mass.: B1041

Am J Dis Children—American Journal of Diseases of Children. Published by the American Medical Association. 12 issues in 2 volumes; vol. 59 started Ja '40; vol. 60 started Jl '40; $8 per year; Clifford G. Grulee, editor, 636 Church St., Evanston, Ill.: B913, B916, B966

Am J Med Sci—The American Journal of Medical Sciences. 12 issues in 2 volumes; vol. 199 started Ja '40 (no. 814); vol. 200 started Jl '40 (no. 820); $6 per year; Edward B. Krumbhaar, editor, School of Medicine, University of Pennsylvania, Philadelphia, Pa.: B828, B879, B922, B1071, B1122

Am J Nursing—The American Journal of Nursing: Official Magazine of the American Nurses Association and the National League of Nursing Education. 12 issues; vol. 40 started Ja '40; $3; Mary M. Roberts, editor, 50 West 50th St., New York, N. Y.

Am J Orthopsychiatry—The American Journal of Orthopsychiatry: A Journal of Human Behavior. Published by the American Orthopsychiatric Association. 4 issues; vol. 10 started Ja '40; $6; Lawson G. Lowrey, editor, 25 West 54th St., New York, N. Y.: B841, B843, B858, B858.1, B914, B916, B1025, B1046-7, B1053, B1081, B1121, B1123

Am J Psychiatry—The American Journal of Psychiatry. Official organ of the American Psychiatric Association. 6 issues; vol. 97 started Jl '40; $6; Clarence B. Farrar, editor, 111th St. George St., Toronto, Ontario, Canada: B841, B858, B966, B1025-6, B1047, B1121, B1123

Am J Psychol—The American Journal of Psychology. 4 issues; vol. 53 started Ja '40; $6.50; Karl M. Dallenbach, editor, Cornell University, Ithaca, N. Y.; John G. Jenkins, review editor, University of Maryland, College Park, Md.: 1416, B821, B858, B877, B881, B884, B908, B913, B916, B966, B1025, B1047, B1076, B1081, B1085, B1098, B1102, B1108, B1122

Am J Pub Health—American Journal of Public Health and the Nation's Health: Official Publication of the American Public Health Association. 12 issues; vol. 30 started Ja '40; $5; Mazÿck P. Ravenel, editor, University of Missouri, Columbia, Mo.: B966

Am J Sociol—The American Journal of Sociology. 6 issues; vol. 46 started Jl '40; $5; Ernest W. Burgess, editor, 1126 East 59th St., Chicago, Ill.: B821, B877, B881, B886, B915-6, B1024-6, B1053, B1068.1, B1075, B1085

Am Sociol R—American Sociological Review: The Official Journal of the American Sociological Society. 6 issues; vol. 5 started F '40; $4; Read Bain, editor, Miami University, Oxford, Ohio; Howard Becker and T. C. McCormick, review editors, University of Wisconsin, Madison, Wis.: B883, B898, B938, B1014, B1022, B1025-6, B1053

Ann Am Acad Pol and Social Sci—The Annals of the American Academy of Political and Social Science. 6 issues; [no.] 210 is dated Jl '40; $5; Thorsten Sellin, editor, 3457 Walnut St., Philadelphia, Pa.: B1025

Ann Internal Med—Annals of Internal Medicine. Published by the American College of Physicians. 12 issues; vol. 14 (old series, vol. 19) started Jl

'40; $7; Maurice C. Pincoffs, editor, University Hospital, Baltimore, Md.: B828, B913, B1022, B1047, B1085

Arch Neurology and Psychiatry—Archives of Neurology and Psychiatry. Published by the American Medical Association. 12 issues in two volumes; vol. 43 started Ja '40; vol. 44 started Jl '40; $8 per year; H. Douglas Singer, chief editor, 1819 West Polk St., Chicago, Ill.: 1429, B840, B1047, B1085

ASLIB—ASLIB Information: The Bulletin of the Association of Special Libraries and Information Bureaux. 4 issues (Ja, Ap, Jl, S); no. 42 is dated Ja '40; distributed to members only; 31 Museum St., London, W.C.1, England: B858

Austral J Psychol and Philos—The Australasian Journal of Psychology and Philosophy. Published by the Australasian Association of Psychology and Philosophy. 3 issues; vol. 17 started My '39; 12s.; John Anderson, editor, The University, Sydney, New South Wales, Australia: B858

AVA J—AVA Journal and News Bulletin. Published by the American Vocational Association, Inc. 4 issues; vol. 15 started F '40; $1; L. H. Dennis, editor-in-chief, 1010 Vermont Ave. N.W., Washington, D. C.: B1042, B1127

B Int Bur Ed—Bulletin of the International Bureau of Education. 4 issues; year 13 started with 1st quarter '39 (no. 50); 5 Swiss francs; International Bureau of Education, Palais Wilson, Geneva, Switzerland: B856-9, B872, B919, B924, B927, B930, B977, B1020, B1039, B1056, B1113, B1137

B Johns Hopkins Hosp—Bulletin of the Johns Hopkins Hospital: The Publication of the Medical School and Hospital. 12 issues in two volumes; $6 per year; vol. 66 started Ja '40; vol. 67 started Jl '40; James Bordley III, managing editor, Johns Hopkins Hospital, Baltimore, Md.: B1022, B1026, B1047

B Menninger Clinic—The Bulletin of the Menninger Clinic. 6 issues; vol. 4 started Ja '40; $2; 3617 West Sixth Ave., Topeka, Kans.: B1001-2, B1026, B1121

B. C. Teach—The B. C. Teacher. Official organ of the British Columbia Teachers' Federation. 10 issues (omitting Jl, Ag); vol. 20 started S '40; $1.50; Norman F. Black, editor, 2565 West Seventh Ave., Edward T. Oliver, review editor, 3847 West 12th Ave., Vancouver, B. C., Canada: B858

Balance Sheet—The Balance Sheet. 9 issues (omitting Je, Jl, Ag); vol. 22 started S '40; gratis; 201-203 West Fourth St., Cincinnati, Ohio: 1478, B1133

Binet R—The Binet Review: A Publication Devoted to the Interests of Teachers in Binet Schools at Newark, New Jersey. 2 issues; vol. 7 started Ja '40; gratis; Elizabeth M. Kelly, editor-in-chief, Branch Brook School, Newark, N. J.: B858

Birmingham Med R—The Birmingham Medical Review: The Journal of the Birmingham Medical Institute. 4 issues; vol. 14 (new series) started Mr '39; 10s.; H. W. Featherstone, editor, 154 Great Charles St., Birmingham, England: 1526.1

Brit J Children's Dis—The British Journal of Children's Diseases. 4 issues; vol. 37 started Ja-Mr '40 (no. 433-5); 25s.; J. D. Rolleston, editor, 91 Bedford Gardens, Kensington, London, W.8, England: 1526.1

Brit J Ed Psychol—The British Journal of Educational Psychology. Issued on behalf of the British Psychological Society and the Training College Association. 3 issues (F, Je, N); vol. 10 started F '40; 20s.; C. W. Valentine, editor, The University, Edmund St., Birmingham, England: 1493, B858, B872, B881, B913, B915, B922, B928, B931,

B1000, B1025, B1053, B1061, B1071, B1098-9, B1127

Brit J Med Psychol—The British Journal of Medical Psychology: Being the Medical Section of the British Journal of Psychology. 4 issues; vol. 18 started with part 1 '39; 30s.; John Rickman, editor, 11 Kent Terrace, Regent's Park, London, N.W.1, England: 1220, B841, B858, B1093

Brit J Psychol—The British Journal of Psychology: General Section. Issued by the British Psychological Society. 4 issues; vol. 31 started Jl '40; 30s.; F. C. Bartlett, editor, Psychological Laboratory, University of Cambridge, Cambridge, England: B821, B843, B858, B884, B886.1, B908, B913, B915, B1006, B1025-6, B1052-3, B1062, B1065, B1076, B1085, B1098-9, B1122

Brit Med J—British Medical Journal: Journal of the British Medical Association. 52 issues in 2 volumes; no. 4122 is dated Ja 6 '40; no. 4148 is dated Jl 6 '40; 1s. 3d. per issue; Norman Gerald Horner, editor, Tavistock Square, London, W.C.1, England: B855.1, B859-60, B872.1, B880, B998, B1037.1, B1085

Bucknell J Ed—The Bucknell Journal of Education. Published by the Department of Education, Bucknell University. 4 issues; vol. 14 started N '39; gratis; Walter H. Sauvain and Frank G. Davis, editorial committee, Bucknell University, Lewisburg, Pa.: B1000

Bus Ed World—The Business Education World. 10 issues (omitting Jl, Ag); vol. 21 started S '40; $1; John Robert Gregg, editor-in-chief, Clyde I. Blanchard, managing editor, 270 Madison Ave., New York, N. Y.: 1213, 1477, 1480-1, 1486, 1489, B1083

Calif J Sec Ed—California Journal of Secondary Education. Published by the California Society of Secondary Education. 8 issues (omitting Je, Jl, Ag, S); vol. 15 started Ja '40; $3; Edward H. Redford. editor, Rooms 9-10, Haviland Hall, Berkeley, Calif.: B854

Cath Charities R—The Catholic Charities Review. The official organ of the National Conference of Catholic Charities and the Society of St. Vincent de Paul. 10 issues (omitting Jl, Ag); vol. 24 started Ja '40; John O'Grady, editor, 1317 F St., N.W., Washington, D. C.: B883, B1053

Cath Ed R—The Catholic Educational Review. Edited by the Department of Education, Catholic University of America. 10 issues (omitting Jl, Ag); vol. 38 started Ja '40; $3; 1326 Quincy St., N.E., Washington, D. C.: B1003

Char and Pers—Character and Personality: An International Psychological Quarterly. 4 issues; vol. 9 started S '40; $2; Charles Spearman, editor in Great Britain, 67 Portland Court, London, W.1, England; Karl Zener, editor in the United States, Drawer B, College Station, Durham, N. C.: B840-1, B843, B858, B913, B916, B969, B998, B1026, B1043, B1053, B1087-8

Chicago Prin Club Rep—Chicago Principals' Club Reporter. Published by the Chicago Principals' Club. 9 issues (omitting Jl, Ag, S); vol. 32 started O '39; publication temporarily suspended with issue for Je '40; George B. Masslich, editor, 185 North Wabash Ave., Chicago, Ill.: B858

Chicago Sch J—Chicago Schools Journal: An Educational Magazine for Chicago Teachers. 5 issues; vol. 22 started S-O '40; gratis to libraries; Sophia C. Camenisch, editor, John J. DeBoer, review editor, Chicago Teachers College, 6800 Stewart Ave., Chicago, Ill.: 1384, 1619, B880, B1000, B1003

Childh Ed—Childhood Education: The Magazine for Teachers of Young Children. Published by the Association for Childhood Education with the Cooperation of the National Association for Nur-

sery Education. 9 issues (omitting Je, Jl, Ag);
vol. 17 started S '40; $2.50; Frances Mayfarth,
editor, 1201 16th St., N.W., Washington, D. C.:
B879, B926, B1138

*Civil Service Assembly News Letter—Civil Service
Assembly of the United States and Canada News
Letter.* 12 issues; vol. 5 started Ja '39; distributed
to members only; 1313 East Sixtieth St., Chicago,
Ill.: B846-7, B858, B860, B937, B940, B964, B988,
B1023, B1031, B1040-1, B1063, B1075, B1078-9,
B1093, B1097, B1114

Clearing House—The Clearing House: A Journal for
Modern Junior and Senior High Schools. 9 issues
(omitting Je, Jl, Ag); vol. 15 started S '40; $3;
Forrest E. Long, editor, Philip W. L. Cox, review
editor, 207 Fourth Ave., New York, N. Y.: 1525,
B846, B930, B1000, B1021, B1081, B1108

Commonwealth R—The Commonwealth Review: A
Journal of Public Policy and Practice. Issued by
the University of Oregon, Oregon State System
of Higher Education. 4 issues; vol. 22 started Mr
'40; $2; Philip A. Parsons, editor, College of Social
Science, University of Oregon, Eugene, Ore.:
B938, B1025

Curric J—Curriculum Journal. Official publication of
the Society for Curriculum Study. 8 issues (omitting Je, Jl, Ag, S); vol. 11 started·Ja '40; $2.50;
Henry Harap, editor, George Peabody College for
Teachers, Nashville, Tenn.: B1076, B1138

Econ J—The Economic Journal: The Quarterly Jour-
nal of the Royal Economic Society. 4 issues; vol.
50 started Mr '40 (no. 197); 6s. per issue; J. M.
Keynes, editor, 4 Portugal St., Kingsway, London,
W.C.2; E. A. G. Robinson, review editor, Royal
Economic Society, Marshall Library, Downing St.,
Cambridge, England: B1120

Ed—Education: A Monthly Magazine Devoted to the
Science, Art, Philosophy and Literature of Edu-
cation. 10 issues (omitting Jl, Ag); vol. 61 started
S '40; $4; Raymond P. Palmer, managing editor,
370 Atlantic Ave., Boston, Mass.: B858, B1000,
B1127

Ed Abstracts—Education Abstracts. Published by the
Phi Delta Kappa. 11 issues (omitting Ag); vol. 5
started Ja '40; $4; Paul M. Cook, editor, 2034
Ridge Road, Homewood, Ill.: B831, B844.1, B846,
B848, B850, B852, B858, B873, B880, B911, B913-4,
B916-7, B920, B965, B989, B1000, B1003, B1005,
B1021, B1035, B1037, B1049, B1057, B1076, B1087,
B1091, B1106, B1109, B1121, B1127

*Ed Adm and Sup—Educational Administration and
Supervision:* Including Teacher Training. 9 issues
(omitting Je, Jl, Ag); vol. 26 started Ja '40; $4.50;
H. E. Buchholz, managing editor, 10 East Centre
St., Baltimore, Md.: B854, B908, B911, B916, B1000,
B1048

Ed Forum—The Educational Forum. Published by
the Kappa Delta Pi, 4 issues (N, Ja, Mr, My);
vol. 4 started N '39; $2; Alfred L. Hall-Quest,
editor, 311 East 72nd St., New York, N. Y.: B858,
B1000, B1040.1, B1076

Ed Meth—Educational Method. Published for the
Department of Supervisors and Directors of In-
struction of the National Education Association.
8 issues (omitting Je, Jl, Ag, S); vol. 20 started
O '40; $3; Lou L. LaBrant, managing editor, Ohio
State University, Columbus, Ohio: B1034, B1106

Ed News B—The Educational News Bulletin. Published by the Western State Teachers College.
5 issues (omitting Ag); vol. 10 started O '39;
gratis; Elmer H. Wilds, Western State Teachers
College, Kalamazoo, Mich.: B1129

Ed Res B—Educational Research Bulletin. Published

by the Bureau of Educational Research, Ohio
State University. 18 issues (fortnightly, omitting
Je, Jl, Ag); vol. 19 started Ja 3 '40; gratis; W. W.
Charters, editor, Ohio State University, Columbus,
Ohio: 1196, 1291, 1293, 1320, 1398, 1416, 1453, 1509,
1535, 1578-9, 1656, B822, B854, B873, B881, B895,
B916-7, B922, B1039, B1041, B1045, B1050, B1056,
B1071, B1091, B1112, B1124, B1135

Ed Trends—Educational Trends: A Journal of Interpretation. Published by the School of Education, Northwestern University. 6 issues; vol. 8
started Ja-F '40; $1.25; George T. Guernsey, editor,
Northwestern University, Evanston, Ill.: B1127

Edinburgh Med J—Edinburgh Medical Journal. 12
issues; vol. 47 started Ja '40; 40s.; D. Murray Lyon,
editor, 98 Great Russell St., London, W.C., England.: B880

El Engl R—The Elementary English Review. 8 issues (omitting Je, Jl, Ag, S); vol. 17 started Ja
'40; $2.50; C. C. Certain, editor, Box 67, North End
Station, Detroit, Mich.: B926

El Paso Sch Standard—El Paso Schools Standard.
Vol. 18 started S '40; M. E. Broom, editor, El
Paso Public Schools, El Paso, Tex.: B850, B858,
B908, B926, B1000, B1106, B1127

El Sch J—The Elementary School Journal: Emphasizing Instruction, Administration, Social Change.
Published by the Department of Education, University of Chicago. 10 issues (omitting Jl, Ag);
vol. 41 started S '40; $2.50; Newton Edwards,
editor, 5835 Kimbark Ave., Chicago, Ill.: B850,
B858, B916, B925, B939, B1000, B1102, B1138

Electrician—The Electrician. 52 issues in 2 volumes;
vol. 124 started Ja 5 '40; vol. 125 started Jl 5 '40
(no. 3240); 25s. per year; Bouverie House, 154
Fleet St., London, E.C.4, England: B931

Endocrinology—Endocrinology. Published by the Association for the Study of Internal Secretions. 12
issues in two volumes; vol. 26 started Ja '40, vol. 27
started Jl '40; $10.50 per year; Milton O. Lee,
managing editor, 25 Shattuck St., Boston, Mass.:
B879, B922, B1071

Eug News—Eugenical News. Official organ of the
American Eugenics Society. 4 issues; vol. 25
started Mr '40; $3; Rudolf C. Bertheau, secretary,
50 West 50th St., New York, N. Y.: B846

Eug R—The Eugenics Review. Published by the
English Eugenics Society. 4 issues; vol. 32 started
Ap '40; 12s.; Maurice Newfield, editor, 69 Eccles-
ton Square, London, S.W.1, England: 1420, B969

Family—The Family: Journal of Social Case Work.
Published by the Family Welfare Association of
America. 10 issues (omitting Ag, S); vol. 21 started
Mr '40; $1.50; Maurine Boie La Barre, editor, 122
East 22nd St., New York, N. Y.: B858, B923, B1116

Fed Probation—Federal Probation. Published by the
U. S. Probation System, Bureau of Prisons, De-
partment of Justice. 4 issues; vol. 4 started F '40;
gratis; Richard A. Chappell, editor, Room 4706,
Department of Justice, Washington, D. C.: B938,
B1014

Geog R—Geographical Review. Published by the
American Geographical Society. 4 issues; $5; vol.
29 started Ja '39; G. M. Wrigley, editor; Broadway at 156th St., New York, N. Y.: B1046

Glasgow Med J—Glasgow Medical Journal. Published for the Glasgow and West of Scotland
Medical Association. 12 issues in 2 volumes; vol.
133 [New (7th) Series, vol. 15] started Ja '40;
vol. 134 [New (7th) Series, vol. 16] started Jl
'40; 35s. per year; J. Leslie Orr and Alex H. Imrie,
editors, 104 West George St., Glasgow, C.2, Scotland: 1526.1, B880

H Sch J—The High School Journal. Published for the Department of Education of the University of North Carolina. 8 issues (omitting Je, Jl, Ag, S) ; vol. 23 started Ja '40; $1.50; W. Carson Ryan, editor, the University, Chapel Hill, N. C.: B858, B1037, B1045, B1076, B1127

Harvard Ed R—The Harvard Educational Review. Published for the Graduate School of Education, Harvard University. 4 issues (Ja, Mr, My, O) ; vol. 10 started Ja '40; $2.50; Howard E. Wilson, editor, 13 Lawrence Hall, Kirkland St., Cambridge, Mass.: B850, B855, B858, B1000, B1076, B1102, B1108

High Points—High Points: In the Work of the High Schools of New York City. Published by the Board of Education of the City of New York. 10 issues (omitting Jl, Ag) ; vol. 22 started Ja '40; $1; A. H. Lass, editor, Boys High School, New York, N. Y.: B854, B858, B891

Hygeia—Hygeia: The Health Magazine. Published by the American Medical Association. 12 issues; vol. 18 started Ja '40; $2.50; Morris Fishbein, editor, 535 North Dearborn St., Chicago, Ill.: 1501, B828, B835, B966

Indian J Psychol—Indian Journal of Psychology. The official organ of the Indian Psychological Association. 4 issues; vol. 15 started Ja '40; Rs 6; 9s.; H. P. Maiti, editor-in-charge, 92 Upper Circular Road, Calcutta, India: B858

Int J Psycho-Analysis—The International Journal of Psycho-Analysis. Official organ of the International Psycho-Analytical Association. 4 issues; vol. 21 started Ja '40; 30s.; James Strachey, editor, Lord's Wood, Marlow, Bucks, England: B916, B1094

Isis—Isis: International Review Devoted to the History of Science and Civilization. Organ of the History of Science Society and of the International Academy of the History of Science. 4 issues; vol. 31 started N '39 (no. 83) ; $6; George Sarton, editor, Harvard Library 185, Cambridge, Mass.: B1026

J Abn and Social Psychol—The Journal of Abnormal and Social Psychology. Published by the American Psychological Association. 4 issues; vol. 35 started Ja '40; $5; Gordon W. Allport, editor, Emerson Hall, Cambridge, Mass.; Stanley Estes, review editor, Northwestern University, Boston, Mass.: B821, B913, B1024, B1026, B1053, B1123

J Am Assn Col Reg—Journal of the American Association of Collegiate Registrars. 4 issues; vol. 15 started O '39; $3; M. E. Gladfelter, editor, Temple University, Philadelphia, Pa.; W. C. Smyser, reviews editor, Miami University, Oxford, Ohio: B858, B1091, B1098-9, B1106

J Am Med Assn—The Journal of the American Medical Association. 52 issues in two volumes; vol. 114 started Ja 6 '40; vol. 115 started Jl 6 '40; $8 per year; Morris Fishbein, editor, 535 North Dearborn St., Chicago, Ill.: B841, B843, B858, B913-4, B922, B1047, B1071, B1121

J Appl Psychol—The Journal of Applied Psychology. 6 issues; vol. 24 started F '40; $6; James P. Porter, editor, Ohio University, Athens, Ohio.: B1026, B1043, B1053, B1087-8

J Chem Ed—Journal of Chemical Education. Official monthly publication of the Division of Chemical Education of the American Chemical Society. 12 issues; vol. 17 started Ja '40; $3; Norris W. Rakestraw, editor, Metcalf Chemical Laboratory, Brown University, Providence, R. I.: 1596

J Consulting Psychol—Journal of Consulting Psy-

chology. Official journal of the American Association for Applied Psychology, Inc. 6 issues; vol. 4 started Ja '40; $3; J. P. Symonds, managing editor, 525 West 120th St., New York, N. Y.: 1426, B858, B916, B1052-3, B1087-8

J Ed (Boston)—The Journal of Education. 9 issues (omitting Je, Jl, Ag) ; vol. 123 started Ja '40; $2.25; Anson W. Belding, editor, 6 Park St., Boston, Mass.: B850, B908

J Ed (London)—The Journal of Education. 12 issues; vol. 72 started with Ja '40 (no. 846) ; 8s.; E. Salter Davies, editor, 40 Walton Crescent, Oxford, England: B858, B913, B928, B1076

J Ed Psychol—The Journal of Educational Psychology. 9 issues (omitting Je, Jl, Ag) ; vol. 31 started Ja '40; $6; Jack W. Dunlap, editor, Catherine Strong Hall, University of Rochester, Rochester, N. Y.; H. E. Buchholz, managing editor, 10 East Centre St., Baltimore, Md.: 1263, 1379, 1420, B831, B843, B908, B925, B1000, B1021, B1042, B1081, B1099, B1102, B1108, B1125, B1128

J Ed Res—Journal of Educational Research. 9 issues (omitting Je, Jl, Ag) ; vol. 34 started S '40; $3.50; A. S. Barr, editor, Kai Jensen, review editor, Department of Education, University of Wisconsin, Madison, Wis.: 1427, B821, B850, B858, B886, B908, B915, B926, B975, B998, B1000, B1037, B1042, B1085, B1088, B1102, B1119, B1122

J Ed Sociol—The Journal of Educational Sociology: A Magazine of Theory and Practice. 9 issues (omitting Je, Jl, Ag) ; vol. 14 started S '40; $3; E. George Payne, editor-in-chief, Harvey W. Zorbaugh, review editor, Room 41, New York University, 32 Washington Place, New York, N. Y.: B1138

J Gen Psychol—The Journal of General Psychology: Experimental, Theoretical, Clinical and Historical Psychology. 4 issues in 2 volumes; vol. 22 started Ja '40; vol. 23 started Jl '40; $14 per year; Carl Murchison, editor, 2 Commercial St., Provincetown, Mass.: B1101

J Genetic Psychol—The Pedagogical Seminary and Journal of Genetic Psychology: Child Behavior, Animal Behavior, and Comparative Psychology. 4 issues in 2 volumes; vol. 56 started Mr '40; vol. 57 started S '40; $14 per year; Carl Murchison, editor, 2 Commercial St., Provincetown, Mass.: B912, B915, B1025

J Health and Phys Ed—The Journal of Health and Physical Education. Official journal of the American Association for Health, Physical Education and Recreation. 10 issues (omitting Je, Ag) ; vol. 11 started Ja '40; $2; E. D. Mitchell, editor, 311 Maynard St., Ann Arbor, Mich.: 1503, B917, B1003

J Hered—The Journal of Heredity. Published by the American Genetic Association. 12 issues; vol. 31 started Ja '40; $3.50; Robert C. Cook, managing editor, Room 308, Victor Bldg., Washington, D. C.: B1022

J Higher Ed—The Journal of Higher Education. Published by the Bureau of Educational Research, Ohio State University. 9 issues (omitting Jl, Ag, S) ; vol. 11 started Ja '40; $3; W. W. Charters, editor, Ohio State University, Columbus, Ohio: B988, B1042, B1088, B1112, B1127

J Home Econ—Journal of Home Economics. Official organ of the American Home Economics Association. 10 issues (omitting Jl, Ag) ; vol. 32 started Ja '40; $2.50; Helen W. Atwater, editor, Mills Building, Washington, D. C.: B831, B1003, B1053

J Juvenile Res—The Journal of Juvenile Research. Published by the California Bureau of Juvenile Research. 4 issues; vol. 23 started Ja '39; discontinued publication with the issue for Ja 16 '40;

Norman Fenton, editor, School of Education, Stanford University, Stanford University, Calif.: B835, B877, B966

J Mental Sci—The Journal of Mental Science. Published by authority of the Royal Medico-Psychological Association. 6 issues; vol. 86 started Ja '40 (no. 360); 6s. per issue; Alexander Walk, editor, Horton Emergency Hospital, Epsom, Surrey, England; G. W. T. H. Fleming, managing editor, Barnwood House, Gloucester, England: B841, B858, B1053

J Nerv and Mental Dis—The Journal of Nervous and Mental Disease: An American Journal of Neuropsychiatry. 12 issues in 2 volumes; vol. 91 started Ja '40; vol. 92 started Jl '40; $10 per year; Smith Ely Jelliffe, managing editor, 64 West 56th St., New York, N. Y.: B835, B841, B843, B857-8, B884, B913, B915-6, B966, B1022, B1025, B1046, B1068.1, B1121-2, B1125

J Pediatrics—The Journal of Pediatrics: A Monthly Journal Devoted to the Problems and Diseases of Infancy and Childhood. Official organ of the American Academy of Pediatrics. 12 issues in 2 volumes; $8.50 per year; vol. 16 started Ja '40; vol. 17 started Jl '40; Borden S. Veeder, co-editor, 3720 Washington Ave., St. Louis, Mo., and Hugh McCulloch, co-editor, 325 North Euclid Ave., St. Louis, Mo.: B894, B912-3, B915, B922, B998, B1071, B1085

J Psychol—The Journal of Psychology: The General Field of Psychology. 4 issues in 2 volumes; vol. 9 started Ja '40; vol. 10 started with Jl '40; $14 per year; Carl Murchison, editor, 2 Commercial St., Provincetown, Mass.: 1200

J Royal Stat Soc—Journal of the Royal Statistical Society. 4 issues; vol. 103 started with pt 1 '40; 10s. per issue; 4 Portugal St., London, W.C.2, England: B896-7, B1114

J Sch Health—The Journal of School Health. Published by the American School Health Association. 10 issues (omitting Jl, Ag); $1.75; vol. 10 started Ja '40; Charles H. Keene, editor, 3335 Main St., Buffalo, N. Y.: B1003

J Social Hyg—Journal of Social Hygiene. Published by the American Social Hygiene Association. 9 issues (omitting Jl, Ag, S); vol. 26 started Ja '40; $3; Jean B. Pinney, managing editor, 60 West 50th St., New York, N. Y.: B880, B938

J Social Philos—Journal of Social Philosophy: A Quarterly Devoted to a Philosophic Synthesis of the Social Sciences. 4 issues; vol. 6 started O '40; $3; M. J. Aronson, managing editor, College of the City of New York, Convent Ave. and 139th St., New York, N. Y.: B1046

J Social Psychol—The Journal of Social Psychology: Political, Racial, and Differential Psychology. 4 issues in two volumes; vol. 11 started F '40; vol. 12 started Jl '40; $14 per year; John Dewey and Carl Murchison, editors, 2 Commercial St., Provincetown, Mass.: B1022

Jewish Social Service Q—The Jewish Social Service Quarterly: A Record of Communal Trends and Developments. Published by the National Conference of Jewish Social Welfare. 4 issues; vol. 16 started S '39; $2; Louis H. Sobel, chairman of the editorial board, David I. Cedarbaum, book review editor, 67 West 47th St., New York, N. Y.: B883, B1053

Jun Col J—The Junior College Journal. Official organ of the American Association of Junior Colleges. 9 issues (omitting Je, Jl, Ag); vol. 11 started S '40; $3; Walter C. Eells, editor, 730 Jackson Place, Washington, D. C.: B842, B858, B1000, B1052, B1127

Labour Mgmt—Labour Management: The Journal of the Institute of Labour Management. 11 issues (combined issue, Ag-S); vol. 22 started Ja '40; 1s. per issue; Thames House, Millbank, London, S.W.1, England: B858

Lancet—The Lancet: A Journal of British and Foreign Medicine, Surgery, Obstetrics, Physiology, Chemistry, Pharmacology, Public Health, and News. 52 issues in 2 volumes; vol. 238 started Ja 6 '40 (no. 6071); vol. 239 started Jl 6 '40 (no. 6097); £2 2s. per year; Egbert Morland, editor, 7 Adam St., Adelphi, London, W.C.2, England: B859-60, B880, B896, B915, B928-9, B998, B1022, B1093

Librarian—The Librarian and Book World and Curator: The Independent Professional Journal. 12 issues; vol. 30 started S '40; 12s.; Alex J. Philip, editor, Lodgewood, Windmill St., Gravesend, Kent, England: B858, B1115

Loyola Ed Digest—Loyola Educational Digest. 10 issues (omitting Ag, S); vol. 16 started O '40; $3; Austin G. Schmidt, editor, 3441 North Ashland Ave., Chicago, Ill.: 1228, 1264, 1426, 1535, 1537, B842, B850, B855, B858, B868, B880, B894, B909, B911, B914, B918, B922, B939, B967, B997, B1000, B1003, B1021, B1035-7, B1044-5, B1049-50, B1057, B1069, B1076, B1089, B1091, B1098.1, B1106, B1110-1, B1118-9, B1121, B1123, B1132, B1138

Math Gazette—The Mathematical Gazette. The organ of the Mathematical Association. Usually 5 issues (F, My, Jl, O, D); vol. 24 started F '40 (no. 258); 15s.; T. A. A. Broadbent, editor, 62 Coleraine Road, Blackheath, London, S.E.3, England: B858, B1098

Math Teach—The Mathematics Teacher: Official Journal of the National Council of Teachers of Mathematics. 8 issues (omitting Je, Jl, Ag, S); vol. 33 started Ja '40; $2; William David Reeve, editor-in-chief, 525 West 120th St., New York, N. Y.: B1045

Med J Austral—The Medical Journal of Australia. 52 issues in 2 volumes; 27th year, vol. 1 started Ja 6 '40; 27th year, vol. 2 started Jl 6 '40; £2; Mervyn Archdall, editor, The Printing House, Seamer St., Glebe, New South Wales, Australia: B840, B843, B1046

Med Officer—The Medical Officer: A Journal for Medical Men in the Government and Municipal Services. 52 issues in 2 volumes; vol. 63 started Ja 6 '40; vol. 64 started Jl 6 '40; 42s. per year; Whitefriars House, 68 Fleet St., London, E.C.4, England: B1053

Med Times—Medical Times: The Journal of the American Medical Association. 12 issues; $2; vol. 68 started Ja '40; Arthur C. Jacobsen, editor-in-chief, 95 Nassau St., New York, N. Y.; Alfred E. Shipley, review editor, 1313 Bedford Ave., Brooklyn, N. Y.: B841, B916, B925, B998, B1022, B1047, B1053, B1060, B1085

Mental Health—Mental Health. Published by the Central Association for Mental Welfare, the Child Guidance Council, and the National Council for Mental Hygiene. 4 issues; 3s. 6d.; vol. 1 started Ja '40; editorial board: Evelyn Fox, 24 Buckingham Palace Road, London, S.W.1, England; R. G. Gordon, 23 Queen Square, Bath, England; and Doris M. Odlum, 76-77 Chandlos House, Palmer St., London, S.W.1, England: B1115

Mental Hyg [London]—Mental Hygiene. Published by the National Council for Mental Hygiene. 4 issues (F, Ap, Jl, O); vol. 5 started F '39; amalgamated with *Mental Welfare* to form *Mental Health* which started Ja '40; 76-77 Chandos House, Palmer St., London, S.W.1, England: B858

Mental Hyg [New York]—Mental Hygiene. Quarterly magazine of the National Committee for Mental Hygiene, Inc. 4 issues; vol. 24 started Ja '40; $3; George S. Stevenson, editor, 50 West 50th St., New York, N. Y.: B821, B915, B1025, B1047, B1053, B1081, B1085, B1091, B1121-2, B1125, B1130

Mgmt R—The Management Review. Published by the American Management Association. 12 issues; vol. 29 started Ja '40; $5; James O. Rice, editor, 330 West 42nd St., New York, N. Y.: B858, B1019

Mind—Mind: A Quarterly Review of Psychology and Philosophy. Published for the Mind Association. 4 issues; vol. 49 started Ja '40 (no. 193); 16*s.*; G. E. Moore, editor, 86 Chesterton Road, Cambridge, England: B929

Muskingum Col Fac News B—Muskingum College Faculty News Bulletin. Irregularly issued; vol. 11 started O '40; gratis; Wm. Marshall French, editor, Muskingum College, New Concord, Ohio: B1081

N Central Assn Q—The North Central Association Quarterly. Official organ of the North Central Association of Colleges and Secondary Schools. 4 issues; vol. 15 started Jl '40; $5; Calvin O. Davis, managing editor, 1439 University Elementary School Building, Ann Arbor, Mich.: B1106

N Y Times Book R—The New York Times Book Review. 52 issues; $2; no volume or issue numbers; J. Donald Adams, editor; New York Times, Times Square, New York, N. Y.: B1122

Nat Math Mag—National Mathematics Magazine. 8 issues (omitting Je, Jl, Ag, S); vol. 14 started O '39; S. T. Sanders, editor, P. O. Box 1322, Baton Rouge, La.; H. A. Simmons, review editor, Northwestern University, Evanston, Ill.: B1045

Nat Munic R—National Municipal Review. Published by the National Municipal League. 12 issues; vol. 29 started Ja '40 (no. 283); $5; Howard P. Jones, editor, Elsie S. Parker, review editor, 299 Broadway, New York, N. Y.: B1063

Nature—Nature. 52 issues in two volumes; vol. 145 started Ja 6 '40 (no. 3662); vol. 146 started Jl 6 '40 (no. 3688); £3; Macmillan & Co., Ltd., St. Martin's St., London, W.C.2, England: B858, B969, B1076, B1098, B1115

New Era—The New Era in Home and School. 10 issues (double issues, Jl-Ag, S-O); vol. 21 started Ja '40; 8*s.*; Beatrice Ensor, editor, Latimer House, Church St., Chiswick, London, W.4, England: B969

New R—The New Review. 12 issues in 2 volumes; vol. 11 started Ja '40 (no. 61); vol. 12 started with Jl '40 (no. 67); Rs. 8 per year; A. Lallemand, editor, 3A Duff Lane, Calcutta, India: B855.1, B930-1, B1096, B1113

Occupational Psychol — Occupational Psychology. Published by the National Institute of Industrial Psychology. 4 issues; vol. 14 started Ja '40; £1; the Institute, Aldwych House, London, W.C.2, England: 1413, B820, B858, B908, B1006, B1098, B1115, B1120

Occupations—Occupations: The Vocational Guidance Magazine. Published by the National Vocational Guidance Association, Inc. 8 issues (omitting Je, Jl, Ag, S); vol. 19 started O '40; $3.50; Harry D. Kitson, editor, Teachers College, Columbia University, New York, N. Y.; Ralph B. Kenney, managing editor, 425 West 123rd St., New York, N. Y.: 1682, B842, B858, B886.1, B1007.1, B1033, B1040, B1055, B1091, B1094, B1099, B1120

Ohio J Sci—The Ohio Journal of Science. 6 issues; vol. 50 started Ja '40; $2; Laurence H. Snyder,

editor-in-chief, Ohio State University, Columbus, Ohio: B1121

Personnel Adm—Personnel Administration. Official Publication of the Society for Personnel Administration. 10 issues (omitting Jl, Ag); vol. 3 started S '40; $3; Richard W. Cooper, editor, P. O. Box 266, Washington, D. C.: B847, B858, B937, B940, B983.2, B1031, B1048, B1078, B1099, B1114, B1121

Personnel J—Personnel Journal: The Magazine of Labor Relations and Personnel Practices. Published by the Personnel Research Federation. 10 issues (omitting Jl, Ag); vol. 19 started My '40; $5; Charles S. Slocombe, managing editor, 60 East 42nd St., New York, N. Y.: B830, B864, B893, B897, B1060, B1090.

Philos Sci—Philosophy of Science. Organ of the Philosophy of Science Association. 4 issues; vol. 7 started Ja '40; $5; William Marias Malisoff, editor, 51 West 86th St., New York, N. Y.: B1076

Progressive Ed—Progressive Education. Published by the Progressive Education Association. 8 issues (omitting Je, Jl, Ag, S); vol. 17 started Ja '40; $3; W. Carson Ryan, editor, 221 West 57th St., New York, N. Y.: B1106

Psychiatric Q—The Psychiatric Quarterly. Official organ of the New York State Department of Mental Hygiene. 4 issues; vol. 14 started Ja '40; $2; Richard H. Hutchings, editor, Utica State Hospital, Utica, N. Y.: B843, B913-4, B1047

Psychiatry—Psychiatry: Journal of the Biology and the Pathology of Interpersonal Relations. Published by the William Alanson White Psychiatric Foundation, Inc. 4 issues; vol. 3 started F '40; $6. Harry Stack Sullivan, Ernest E. Hadley, and Thomas Harvey Gill, publication committee, 1835 Eye St., N.W., Washington, D. C.: B858, B922, B1028, B1081, B1121, B1130

Psychoanalytic Q—The Psychoanalytic Quarterly. 4 issues; vol. 9 started Ja '40; $6; Raymond Gosselin, managing editor, Room 1404, 57 West 57th St., New York, N. Y.: B835, B841, B843, B858, B884, B916, B1025, B1028, B1047, B1099, B1125

Psychoanalytic R—The Psychoanalytic Review: An American Journal of Psychoanalysis Devoted to an Understanding of Human Conduct. 4 issues; vol. 27 started Ja '40; $6; Smith Ely Jelliffe, managing editor, 64 West 56th St., New York, N. Y.: B840, B884, B1022, B1028, B1053

Psychol B—Psychological Bulletin. Published by the American Psychological Association, Inc. 10 issues (omitting Ag, S); vol. 37 started Ja '40; $7; John A McGeoch, editor, State University of Iowa, Iowa City, Iowa: 1429, B840-1, B858, B884, B908, B913, B916, B1021, B1025, B1028, B1076, B1099, B1111, B1122, B1125

Psychol Rec—The Psychological Record. Irregularly issued to make an annual volume of approximately 500 pages; vol. 4, no. 1 started with Ap '40; $4; J. R. Kantor, editor, Indiana University, Bloomington, Ind.: 1420

Psychologists League J—The Psychologists League Journal. Official organ of the Psychologists League. Issued irregularly; vol. 4 started Ja-Ap '40; $1 for 5 successive issues; Solomon Machover, managing editor, Kings County Psychiatric Hospital, Brooklyn, N. Y.: B858, B1025, B1125

Psychometrika—Psychometrika: A Journal Devoted to the Development of Psychology as a Quantitative Rational Science. Published by the Psychometric Society. 4 issues; vol. 5 started Mr '40; $5 to individuals, $10 to libraries and other institutions; Paul Horst, managing editor, Procter and Gamble Co., Cincinnati, Ohio: B 858

Pub Adm—Public Administration: The Journal of the Institute of Public Administration. 4 issues; vol. 18 started Ja '40; 4*s.* per issue; A. C. Stewart, editor, Palace Chambers, Bridge St., Westminster, London, S.W.1, England: B930

Pub Health R—Public Health Reviews. 9 issues (omitting Jl, Ag, S); vol. 9 started O '39; gratis; Charles H. Mann, editor, Division of Hygiene and Public Health, University of Michigan, Ann Arbor, Mich.: B848, B873, B894, B917, B920, B922, B966, B1071, B1110, B1124-5

Pub Mgmt—Public Management. Published by the International City Managers' Association. 12 issues; vol. 22 started Ja '40; $4; Clarence E. Ridley, editor, 1313 East 60th St., Chicago, Ill.: B845, B847

Pub Personnel R—Public Personnel Review: The Quarterly Journal of the Civil Service Assembly of the United States and Canada. 4 issues; vol. 1 started Ap '40; $5; G. Lyle Belsley, editor, 1313 East 60th St., Chicago, Ill.: B997

Q J Speech—The Quarterly Journal of Speech. Official publication of the National Association of Teachers of Speech. 4 issues (F, Ap, O, D); vol. 26 started F '40; $2.50; Giles Wilkeson Gray, editor, Louisiana State University, University, La.: 1535

Q R Biol—The Quarterly Review of Biology. 4 issues; vol. 15 started Mr '40; $5; Raymond Pearl, editor, Johns Hopkins University, Baltimore, Md.: B841, B858, B880, B913, B922, B925, B988, B1022, B1071, B1099, B1121-2

Queen's Q—Queen's Quarterly: A Canadian Review. Published by the Quarterly Committee of Queen's University. 4 issues; vol. 47 started with spring '40; $2; Alexander Macphail, chairman of the editorial board, Queen's University, Kingston, Ontario, Canada: B919

Relig Ed—Religious Education. Published by the Religious Education Association. 4 issues; vol. 35 started Ja-Ap '40; $3.50; Laird T. Hites, editor, 59 East Van Buren St., Chicago, Ill.: B1088

Res Q—The Research Quarterly: Of the American Association for Health, Physical Education, and Recreation. 4 issues (Mr, My, O, D); vol. 11 started Mr '40; $3; Elmer D. Mitchell, editor, 311 Maynard St., Ann Arbor, Mich.: B925, B1003

Safety Ed—Safety Education [Section One]. Published by the Education Division, National Safety Council. 12 issues; vol. 20 started S '40; $2; C. F. Scheer, editor, 20 North Wacker Drive, Chicago, Ill.: 1525

Sat R Lit—The Saturday Review of Literature. 52 issues in 2 volumes; vol. 22 started My 4 '40; vol. 23 started N 2 '40; $4 per year; Norman Cousins, executive editor, 420 Madison Ave., New York, N. Y.: B884, B908.1, B1046, B1122

Sch—The School (El Ed), or *The School (Sec Ed).* [The book review sections are identical in both editions.] Published by the Ontario College of Education, University of Toronto. 10 issues (omitting Jl, Ag); vol. 29 started S '40; one edition: $1.50; both editions: $2.25; Charles E. Phillips, managing editor, University of Toronto, Toronto, Canada: B837, B858, B917, B1000

Sch and Soc—School and Society. Published for the Society for the Advancement of Education, Inc. 52 issues in 2 volumes; vol. 51 started Ja 6 '40 (no. 1306), vol. 52 started Jl 6 '40 (no. 1332); $5 per year; William C. Bagley, editor, 525 West 120th Street, New York, N. Y.: 1427, 1559, B850, B869, B1037, B1106, B1127

Sch Executive—The School Executive: A National Magazine Dedicated to the Advancement of Education in General and to Administrative Problems in Particular as They Relate to the Board of Education and Its Administrative, Supervisory, and Teaching Staffs. 12 issues; vol. 60 started S '40; $2; Jesse H. Newlon and N. L. Engelhardt, editors, 470 Fourth Ave., New York, N. Y.: B850, B1034, B1037, B1119

Sch Life—School Life: Official Organ of the U. S. Office of Education. 10 issues (omitting Ag, S); vol. 26 started O '40; $1; Olga A. Jones, editor-in-chief, U. S. Office of Education, Washington, D. C.: B1108

Sch R—The School Review: A Journal of Secondary Education. Published by the Department of Education, University of Chicago. 10 issues (omitting Jl, Ag); vol. 48 started Ja '40; $2.50; Leonard V. Koos, editor, 5835 Kimbark Ave., Chicago, Ill.: 1558, B858, B879, B922, B939, B1071, B1106, B1127

Sch Sci and Math—School Science and Mathematics: A Journal for All Science and Mathematics Teachers. 9 issues; vol. 40 started Ja '40 (whole no. 350); $2.50; Glen W. Warner, editor, 7633 Calumet Ave., Chicago, Ill.: B1045

Sci—Science. Official organ of the American Association for the Advancement of Science. 52 issues in 2 volumes; vol. 91 started Ja 5 '40 (no. 2349); vol. 92 started Jl 5 '40 (no. 2375); $6 per year; J. McKeen Cattell, editor, Grand Central Terminal, New York, N. Y.: B912, B1060

Sci Ed—Science Education. Official organ of the National Association for Research in Science Teaching, The National Council on Elementary Science, and The Science Association of the Middle States. 7 issues (omitting My, Je, Jl, Ag, S); vol. 24 started Ja '40; $2.50; Charles J. Pieper, editor, 32 Washington Place, New York, N. Y.: 1500, 1503, B854, B882, B988, B1000, B1045, B1124, B1137-8

Scottish Ed J—The Scottish Educational Journal. The official organ of the Educational Institute of Scotland. 52 issues; vol. 23 started Ja 5 '40; 2*d.* per issue; the Editors, 47 Moray Place, Edinburgh, Scotland: 1403, 1423, B842, B931, B969, B1000, B1006, B1021, B1097.1, B1098

Scripta Mathematica—Scripta Mathematica: A Quarterly Journal Devoted to the Philosophy, History, and Expository Treatment of Mathematics. 4 issues (Mr, Je, O, D); vol. 7 started Mr '40; $3; Jekuthiel Ginsburg, editor, Lao G. Simons, review editor, Amsterdam Ave. and 186th St., New York, N. Y.: B1045

Sight-Saving R—The Sight-Saving Review. Published by the National Society for the Prevention of Blindness, Inc. 4 issues; vol. 10 started Mr '40; $2; Lewis H. Carris, editor, 50 West 50th St., New York, N. Y.: 1537, B926

Social Ed—Social Education: Official Journal of the National Council for the Social Studies. Published under the authority of the American Historical Association with the cooperation of the National Council for the Social Studies. 8 issues (omitting Je, Jl, Ag, S); vol. 4 started Ja '40; $2; Erling M. Hunt, editor, 204 Fayerweather Hall, Columbia University, New York, N. Y.: B858, B1025, B1076, B1138

Social Res—Social Research: An International Quarterly of Political and Social Science. Published by the New School for Social Research. 4 issues (F, My, S, N); vol. 7 started F '40; $3; Elizabeth Todd, managing editor, 66 West 12th St., New York, N. Y.: B1026

Social Service R—The Social Service Review: A Quarterly Devoted to the Scientific and Professional Interests of Social Work. 4 issues; vol. 14 started Mr '40; $4; Edith Abbott, editor, University of Chicago, Chicago, Ill.: B858, B1025

Social Work Technique—Social Work Technique: A Bimonthly Technical Journal for Social Workers. 6 issues; vol. 3 started Ja '38 (whole no. 13); discontinued with the issue Je '39; Erle F. Young, editor, 3474 University Ave., Los Angeles, Calif.: B898

Sociol and Social Res—Sociology and Social Research: An International Journal. 6 issues; vol. 25 started S-O '40; $3; Emory S. Bogardus, editor, 3551 University Ave., Los Angeles, Calif.: B849, B858, B883, B1024, B1046, B1066, B1075, B1081, B1120

Sociometry—Sociometry: A Journal of Inter-Personal Relations. 4 issues; vol. 3 started Ja '40; $4.50; Gardner Murphy, editor, City College of the City of New York, New York, N. Y.: B843, B874

Southw Social Sci Q—The Southwestern Social Science Quarterly. Published by the Southwestern Social Science Association. 4 issues; vol. 21 started Je '40; $3; Carl M. Rosenquist, editor-in-chief, O. Douglas Weeks, review editor, University of Texas, Austin, Texas: B1053

Survey—Survey Midmonthly. 12 issues; vol. 76 started Ja '40; $3; Paul Kellogg, editor, 112 East 19th St., New York, N. Y.: B849, B938, B1007.1, B1014, B1053, B1068.1, B1097, B1122

Survey Graphic—Survey Graphic: Magazine of Social Interpretation. 12 issues; vol. 29 started Ja '40; $3; Paul Kellogg, editor, 112 East 19th St., New York, N. Y.: B914

Teach Col J—The Teachers College Journal. Published by the Indiana State Teachers College. 6 issues; vol. 12 started S '40; gratis; J. E. Grinnell, editor, the College, Terre Haute, Ind.: 1196, 1291, 1578, B855, B1076

Teaching—Teaching: A Quarterly Technical Journal for Teachers. 4 issues; vol. 13 started S '40; Rs. 2-8; 4s.; M. S. H. Thompson, editor, c/o Oxford University Press, Post Box 31, Bombay, India: B858, B1017

Times Ed Sup—The Times Educational Supplement. 52 issues; 30th year started Ja 6 '40 (no. 1288); 15s. 2d.; Times Publishing Co., Ltd., Printing House Sq., London, E.C.4, England: B1005-6, B1017, B1115

Times Lit Sup—The Times Literary Supplement. 52 issues; 17s. 6d.; 39th year started Ja 6 '40 (no. 1980); Printing House Square, London, E.C.4, England: B855.1, B872.1, B1007.1

Training Sch B—The Training School Bulletin. 10 issues (omitting Jl, Ag); vol. 37 started Mr '40; $1; Helen Hill, editor, Training School, Vineland, N. J.: B858, B964

Univ Mich Sch Ed B—The University of Michigan School of Education Bulletin. 8 issues (omitting Je, Jl, Ag, S); vol. 12 started O '40; gratis; J. B. Edmonson, chairman of the editorial board, University of Michigan, Ann Arbor, Mich.: B850, B858, B1000

Univ Wash Col Ed Rec—The University of Washington College of Education Record. Published by the Bureau of Educational Research and School Service. 6 issues (N, D, Ja, F, Mr, Ap); vol 6 started N '39; gratis; Francis F. Powers, chairman, editorial board, the Bureau, College of Education, University of Washington, Seattle, Wash.: 1532, B850, B855, B858, B1000, B1127

Va J Ed—Virginia Journal of Education. Published by the Virginia Education Association, Inc. 9 issues (omitting Jl, Ag, S); vol. 33 started O '39; $1.50; Francis S. Chase, editor, 401 North Ninth St., Richmond, Va.: B1106

Va Teach—The Virginia Teacher. Published by Madison College. 9 issues (omitting Je, Jl, Ag); vol. 20 started Ja '39; discontinued with My '39; Conrad T. Logan, editor, Madison College, Harrisonburg, Va.: B858, B880, B917, B1076

Voc Guid Digest—Vocational Guidance Digest: A Digest of Material in Current Periodicals and in Unbound Form. 10 issues (omitting Jl, Ag); vol. 7 started S '40; $2.50; L. R. Martin, editor, 325 Sutter St., San Francisco, Calif.: B858

Volta R—The Volta Review. Official organ of the American Association to Promote the Teaching of Speech to the Deaf. 12 issues; vol. 42 started Ja '40; $2; Josephine B. Timberlake, editor, 1537 35th St., N.W., Washington, D. C.: B1123

Publishers Directory and Index

$*$ $*$ $*$ $*$ $*$

Bureau of Publications, National College of Education, Evanston, Ill.: B1026.1

Bureau of Publications, Teachers College, Columbia University, New York, N. Y.: 1190, 1214-5, 1228, 1238, 1244, 1257, 1259, 1263-4, 1325, 1336, 1340, 1343, 1500-1, 1535, 1537-9, 1611, 1619, B854, B886, B891, B895, B911, B975, B997, B1021, B1039, B1045, B1072, B1091, B1124, B1137-8

California. See State Personnel Board; and Supervisor of Documents

California Test Bureau, 3636 Beverly Boulevard, Los Angeles, Calif.: 1193, 1213, 1292, 1329, 1384, 1459, 1470, 1563, 1603, 1637

Cambridge University Press, Bentley House, 200 Euston Road, London, N.W.1, England: B849, B852.1, B863, B872.1, B883, B925, B1007.1, B1048, B1099, B1116

Carnegie Foundation for the Advancement of Teaching, 522 Fifth Ave., New York, N. Y.: B977, B987-8

Catholic University of America, Washington, D. C.: B1069

Catholic University Press, Peiping, China: B1117

Center for Psychological Service, George Washington University, Washington, D. C.: 1253, 1496.1

Center for Safety Education, New York University, 20 Washington Square North, New York, N. Y.: 1522-4, 1526

Character Research Institute, Washington University, St. Louis, Mo.: 1212

Chicago City Junior Colleges. *See* Department of Examinations

City of Birmingham Education Committee, Birmingham, England: B820

Civil Service Assembly of the United States and Canada, 1313 East 60th St., Chicago, Ill.: B847, B853, B940, B1018

Clarke, Irwin & Co., Ltd., 480-486 University Ave., Toronto, 2, Canada: B1058

College Entrance Examination Board, 431 West 117th St., New York, N. Y.: B867-9, B967, B1118, B1126.1

College Press, South Lancaster, Mass.: 1504

Colorado State College of Education, Greeley, Colo.: B871

Columbia University, Archives of Psychology, New York, N. Y.: B858.1, B874, B909, B1077. *See also* Bureau of Publications, Teachers College; and Columbia University Press

Columbia University Press, 2960 Broadway, New York, N. Y.: B923, B1025, B1076

Committee on Publications, Harvard Graduate School of Education, Harvard University, Cambridge, Mass.: 1265

Committee on the Teaching of Botany in American Colleges and Universities, Botanical Society of America, c/o Ernest L. Stover, Chairman, Eastern Illinois State Teachers College, Charleston, Ill.: B941

Commonwealth Fund, 41 East 57th St., New York, N. Y.: B830, B1085, B1130

Cooperative Test Service, 15 Amsterdam Ave., New York, N. Y.: 1182-4, 1271, 1276, 1286, 1298-9, 1318, 1346, 1349-50, 1358, 1360-2, 1364-5, 1373-4, 1431-4.1, 1438-40, 1467-8, 1474, 1564, 1585, 1592-4, 1601, 1604-5, 1608-9, 1615, 1618, 1620, 1624, 1633-6, B907

F. S. Crofts & Co., 41 Union Square, New York, N. Y.: B1003

Ed. F. Degering, Chemistry Department, Purdue University, Lafayette. Ind.: 1595

Delaware. See State Department of Public Instruction

Department of Education, Archdiocese of Milwaukee, 625 North Milwaukee St., Milwaukee, Wis.: 1659.1, 1679.1

Department of Education, University of Chicago, 5835 Kimbark Ave., Chicago, Ill.: B939

Department of Educational Research, Ontario College of Education, University of Toronto, 371 Bloor St. West, Toronto, 5, Canada: 1352-3, 1397, 1627, B872, B1056

Department of Examinations, Chicago City Junior Colleges, 6800 South Stewart Ave., Chicago, Ill.: B892

Department of Supervisors and Directors of Instruction, National Education Association, 1201 16th St., N. W., Washington, D. C.: B1131

Detroit Bureau of Governmental Research, Inc., 5135 Cass Ave., Detroit, Mich.: B1063

Morris Richard Dickter, 2313 76th Ave., Philadelphia, Pa.: B882

Division of Educational Reference, Purdue University, Lafayette, Ind.: 1202. *See also* Purdue University

Division of Home Economics, University of Minnesota, Minneapolis, Minn.: B851

Joseph Dominion, 2734 Milvia St., Berkeley, Calif.: 1383

Raleigh M. Drake, Wesleyan College, Macon, Ga.: B885

Dryden Press, Inc., 103 Park Ave., New York, N. Y.: B1035

Duke University Press, Durham, N. C.: B1048

R. E. Dunford, University of Tennessee, Knoxville, Tenn.: 1644

Thomas A. Edison, Inc., West Orange, N. J.: 1488

Educational Institute of Scotland, 46-47 Moray Place, Edinburgh, Scotland: B887

Educational Publishers, Inc. *See* Educational Test Bureau, Inc.

Educational Records Bureau, 437 West 59th St., New York, N. Y.: B888-90, B1064, B1106-9

Educational Test Bureau, Inc., 720 Washington Ave., S. E., Minneapolis, Minn.: 1197, 1237, 1281, 1295, 1315, 1332, 1404, 1407, 1426, 1428, 1445, 1447, 1463, 1472, 1511, 1532, 1560, 1581, 1598, 1625, 1631, 1638, 1642, 1662, 1684, B984

Edwards Brothers, Inc., 300 John St., Ann Arbor, Mich.: B1068.1

Efficiency Magazine, Kent House, 87 Regent St., London, W.1, England: B973

Evaluation in the Eight Year Study, Progressive Education Association, 6010 Dorchester Ave., Chicago, Ill.: 1211, 1225-7, 1245, 1250-1, 1254, 1283, 1288-9, 1294, 1297, 1302-3, 1305, 1328, 1527-8, 1530, 1544-5, 1556, 1577, 1584, 1599, 1606, B1070

Evans Brothers, Ltd., Montague House, Russell Square, London, W.C.1, England; WAR-TIME ADDRESS: 44-46 Clarence Road, St. Albans, Herts, England: 1403, 1519, B924, B931

Family Welfare Association of America, 130 East 22nd St., New York, N. Y.: B938

Farrar & Rinehart, Inc., 232 Madison Ave., New York, N. Y.: B855.1, B1119

Friends University. See Wichita Child Research Laboratory

Garrard Press, 119-123 West Park Ave., Champaign, Ill.: 1486

George Washington University. *See* Center for Psychological Service

Robert Gibson & Sons, Ltd., 45 Queen St., Glasgow, C.1, Scotland: 1421, 1493

Ginn and Co., 15 Ashburton Place, Boston, Mass.: B865-6

Government Printer, Colony of Fiji, Suva, Fiji: 1395, B1008
Government Printer, Kenya Colony, Nairobi, Kenya Colony, East Africa: 1396
Government Printing Office, Washington, D. C.: B1015, B1055, B1066
Gregg Publishing Co., 270 Madison Ave., New York, N. Y.: 1230
C. A. Gregory Co., 345 Calhoun St., Cincinnati, Ohio: 1186, 1282, 1536, 1548, 1567, 1586, 1612
Grosset & Dunlap, Inc., 1107 Broadway, New York, N. Y.: B838
William R. Grove, Behavior Clinic of the Criminal Court, County of Allegheny, Pittsburgh, Pa.: 1408
Gutenberg Press, 1619 West Seventh St., Los Angeles, Calif.: 1209

H. M. Stationery Office, York House, Kingsway, London, W.C.2, England: B896-7, B921, B1114
E. M. Hale and Co., 161 West Wisconsin Ave., Milwaukee, Wis.: 1452-3, 1531, 1600, 1613
Hamish Hamilton, Ltd., 90 Great Russell St., London, W.C.1, England: B913
A. Hammond & Co., 11 Lancashire Court, New Bond St., London, W.1, England: B1103
Mathilde Hardaway, Austin High School, El Paso, Texas, 1478
Harper & Brothers, 49 East 33rd St., New York, N. Y.; 90 Great Russell St., London, W.C.1, England: B846, B893, B914, B998, B1024, B1087-8, B1097. *See also* Paul B. Hoeber, Inc.
George G. Harrap & Co., Ltd., 182 High Holborn, London, W.C.1, England: 1267, 1386, 1389, 1399, 1410, 1413, 1416, 1420, 1423-4, 1462.1, B822, B908, B1052, B1093
Harvard Graduate School of Education. See Committee on Publications; and Psycho-Educational Clinic
Harvard University. See Committee on Publications; Joint Committee on Tests; and Psycho-Educational Clinic
High School Visitor, University of Illinois, Urbana, Ill.: B968
Hillsdale School Supply Co., 39 North St., Hillsdale, Mich.: 1583.1
His Majesty's Stationery Office. *See* H. M. Stationery Office
Paul B. Hoeber, Inc., 49 East 33rd St., New York, N. Y.: B913, B1047
Holst Printing Co., Cedar Falls, Iowa: 1614
Houghton Mifflin Co., 2 Park St., Boston, Mass.: 1188, 1198, 1268-9, 1290, 1398, 1420, 1451, 1543, 1557-8, 1562, 1568, 1583, B822, B908, B926, B1053, B1092-3, B1098, B1102
Human Engineering Laboratory, 381 Beacon St., Boston, Mass.: 1659, 1678, B815-9, B837.1, B899, B902-5.1, B932-3, B942-63, B996, B998.1-9.2, B1038, B1049.1, B1072.1, B1082

Indiana University Bookstore, Memorial Union Building, Bloomington, Ind.: B965, B965.1
Institute of the Pennsylvania Hospital. *See* Psychological Service
International Business Machines Corporation, 590 Madison Ave., New York, N. Y.: 1492
International Textbook Co., 1001 Wyoming Ave., Scranton, Pa.: 1327, B1037
Iowa. *See* Bureau of Educational Research and Service; and E. F. Lindquist
Iowa State College of Agriculture and Mechanic Arts, Ames, Iowa: B986

Joseph Jastak, Delaware State Hospital, Farnhurst, Del.: B971

Walther Joël, Los Angeles City College, Los Angeles, Calif.: 1210, 1235
Alvin D. Johnson, 34 Shelton Ave., New Haven, Conn.: B972
Joint Committee on Tests, National Office Association and the National Council of Business Education, 1 Kirkland St., Cambridge, Mass.: 1476, 1482-5, 1487, 1490-1, B974
Journal Press, 2 Commercial St., Provincetown, Mass.: B862

Kansas State Teachers College, Emporia, Kan.: B1016. *See also* Bureau of Educational Measurements
Kentucky Cooperative Testing Service, University of Kentucky, Lexington, Ky.: 1284, 1402
Keystone View Co., Meadville, Pa.: B844.1, B844.2
H. F. Kilander, Panzer College of Physical Education and Hygiene, East Orange, N. J.: 1503
P. S. King & Son, Ltd., Orchard House, 14 Great Smith St., Westminster, London, England: B859
Alma Jordan Knauber, 3331 Arrow Ave., Cincinnati, Ohio: 1323-4
Russell Graydon Leiter, 601 East Valerio St., Santa Barbara, Calif.: 1405
H. K. Lewis & Co., Ltd., 136 Gower St., London, W.C.1, England: 1417, 1526.1

Life Insurance Sales Research Bureau, Hartford, Conn.: 1646, 1670, B989.1-91
E. F. Lindquist, c/o, State University of Iowa, Iowa City, Iowa: B993-4
N. A. Lufburrow, 3112 Milford Ave., Baltimore, Md.: 1643, 1648, 1674

McGill University, Montreal, Canada: B1023, B1120
McGraw-Hill Book Co., Inc., 330 West 42nd St., New York, N. Y.: B831-4, B850, B915, B985, B1042, B1094, B1127-9. *See also* McGraw-Hill Publishing Co., Ltd.
McGraw-Hill Publishing Co., Ltd., Aldwych House, Aldwych, London, W.C.2, England: B850, B915, B985, B1042, B1094, B1127-9. *See also* McGraw-Hill Book Co., Inc.
McKnight & McKnight, 109-111 West Market St., Bloomington, Ill.: 1512.1, 1525, 1615.1, 1625.1, 1665.1, 1682
Macmillan Co., 60 Fifth Ave., New York, N. Y.: B821, B828, B835, B852.1, B872.1, B916, B1000, B1046, B1060, B1096. *See also* Macmillan & Co., Ltd.
Macmillan & Co., Ltd., 10 St. Martin's St., Leicester Square, London, W.C.2, England: B828, B835, B916, B928-30, B1000, B1046, B1060, B1096. *See also* Macmillan Co.
Management Service Co., 3136 North 24th St., Philadelphia, Pa.: 1425
Clair V. Mann, 210 East Eighth St., Rolla, Mo.: B1009
Mansfield Advertiser, Mansfield, Pa.: B1054
Marietta Apparatus Co., Marietta, Ohio: 1663
Mechanical Engineering Department, University of Minnesota, Minneapolis, Minn.: 1659, 1662, 1678
Melbourne University Press, Swanston St., Carlton, N3, Melbourne, Victoria, Australia: B870, B1005
Merrill-Palmer School, East 71 Ferry Ave., Detroit, Mich.: 1241-2
Methuen & Co., Ltd., 36 Essex St., London, W.C.2, England: B886.1
Metropolitan Life Insurance Co. *See* Policyholders Service Bureau
Milwaukee. *See* Department of Education, Archdiocese of Milwaukee

National Clerical Ability Tests. *See* Joint Committee on Tests

National College of Education. *See* Bureau of Publications, National College of Education

National Council for the Social Studies, National Education Association, 1201 16th St., N. W., Washington, D. C.: B825-7

National Council of Business Education. *See* Joint Committee on Tests

National Education Association. *See* American Educational Research Association; Department of Supervisors and Directors of Instruction; and National Council for the Social Studies

National Industrial Conference Board, Inc., 247 Park Ave., New York, N. Y.: B1031-2

National Institute of Industrial Psychology, Aldwych House, London, W.C.2, England: 1376, 1652-3

National Institute of Vocational Research, Suite 290, Outpost Building, 1707 North Las Palmas Ave., Los Angeles, Calif.: 1647

National Office Association. *See* Joint Committee on Tests

National Research Council. *See* Society for Research in Child Development

National Union of Teachers, Hamilton House, Mabledon Place, London, W.C.1, England: B927

Thomas Nelson and Sons, 385 Madison Ave., New York, N. Y.: B1040.1

Nervous and Mental Disease Publishing Co., 64 West 56th St., New York, N. Y.: B841, B1022

New York. *See* University of the State of New York Press

New York University. *See* Center for Safety Education.

Sven G. Nilsson, 16 Maverick Road, Worcester, Mass.: 1401

James Nisbet & Co., Ltd., 22 Berners St., London, W.1, England: B1007.1, B1084

Northeastern University. *See* Bureau of Business Research

O.S.C. Cooperative Association, P. O. Box 490, Corvallis, Ore.: 1316, 1321.1, 1475, 1479, 1495-6, 1559.1, 1590

Office of Education. *See* United States Office of Education

Ohio Scholarship Tests, State Department of Education, Columbus, Ohio: B1126

Oliver & Boyd, Ltd., Tweeddale Court, Edinburgh 1, Scotland: 1293.1, 1394.1, 1461, B1058

F. A. Owen Publishing Co., Dansville, N. Y.: B1095

Oxford University Press, Amen House, Warwick Square, London, E.C. 4, England; WAR-TIME ADDRESS: Press Road, Neasden Lane, London, N.W. 10, England; 114 Fifth Ave., New York, N. Y.: B830, B842, B870, B877, B881, B884, B912, B920, B923, B1005, B1017, B1023, B1025-6, B1041, B1076, B1085, B1089, B1112, B1130

Pestalozzi Press, 1114 Euclid Ave., Berkeley, Calif.: B1057

Policyholders Service Bureau, Metropolitan Life Insurance Co., 1 Madison Ave., New York, N. Y.: B1019

Prentice-Hall, Inc., 70 Fifth Ave., New York, N. Y.: B964, B1052

Principia Press, Inc., Bloomington, Ind.: 1518, B836, B875, B910, B979-83

Progressive Education Association. *See* Evaluation in the Eight Year Study

Psycho-Educational Clinic, Harvard University, Palfrey House, Rear 50 Oxford St., Cambridge, Mass.: 1390-1

Psychological Corporation, 522 Fifth Ave., New York, N. Y.: 1199, 1232-4, 1240, 1243.1, 1260, 1308, 1317, 1387, 1419, 1429, 1541, 1553, 1573, 1649-50, 1672-3, 1675, 1677, 1679, 1683, B844, B937, B1078-9

Psychological Institute, 3506 Patterson St., N.W., Washington, D. C.: 1668

Psychological Service, Institute of the Pennsylvania Hospital, 111 North 49th St., Philadelphia, Pa.: 1385

Public School Publishing Co., 509-513 North East St., Bloomington, Ill.: 1194-6, 1274, 1291, 1293, 1307, 1310, 1330, 1356, 1367, 1370, 1393, 1435, 1443, 1456, 1460, 1464, 1477, 1480, 1489, 1507-8, 1510, 1512, 1517, 1561, 1566, 1570-1, 1575, 1578-9, 1616, 1632, 1654-6, B1033-4

Puerto Rico School Review, San Juan, Puerto Rico: B861

Purdue University, Lafayette, Ind.: B1050. *See also* Division of Educational Reference

RCA Manufacturing Co., Inc., Camden, N. J.: 1338

Ralph R. Rice, 291 Lester Ave., Oakland, Calif.: 1481

Rorschach Institute, Inc., c/o Helen H. Davidson, Secretary of the Folder Committee, 601 West 115th St., New York, N. Y.: 1246

Rutgers University. *See* School of Education, Rutgers University; and Rutgers University Press

Rutgers University Press, New Brunswick, N. J.: B858

Ryerson Press, 299 Queen St., West, Toronto 2, Canada: 1411, B919

St. Francis Community Press, Lafayette, Ind.: B1044

Santa Barbara State College Press, Santa Barbara, Calif.: B989

W. B. Saunders Co., 218 West Washington Square, Philadelphia, Pa.: 7 Grape St., London, W.C.2, England: B848, B880, B917

School of Education, Rutgers University, New Brunswick, N. J.: B856-7

School of Education, University of Michigan, Ann Arbor, Mich.: B1134-6

Science Research Associates, 600 South Michigan Ave., Chicago, Ill.: 1645, 1658, 1660, B1051

Scott, Foresman and Co., 623 South Wabash Ave., Chicago, Ill.: 1322, 1454-5

Scottish Council for Research in Education, 46 Moray Place, Edinburgh 3, Scotland: B1062

Charles Scribner's Sons, 597-599 Fifth Ave., New York, N. Y.: 1621-2

Robert H. Seashore, Northwestern University, Evanston, Ill.: 1319

Sheppard and Enoch Pratt Hospital, Towson, Md.: 1219

Sheridan Supply Co., P. O. Box 837, Beverly Hills, Calif.: 1229

L. K. Shumaker, Friendly Hall, University of Oregon, Eugene, Ore.: 1278

Henrietta Silliman, Toulon, Ill.: 1301

Simon & Schuster, Inc., 1230 Sixth Ave., New York, N. Y.: B908.1

Richard R. Smith, 120 East 39th St., New York, N. Y.: 1014

Turner E. Smith & Co., 441 West Peachtree St., N.E., Atlanta, Ga.: 1287, 1296, 1312, 1313.1-4, B1073

Society for Personnel Administration, Box 266, Washington, D. C.: B845, B1040

Society for Research in Child Development, National Research Council, 2101 Constitution Ave., N.W., Washington, D. C.: B879, B894, B922, B976, B1004, B1071, B1110

Sociological Press, Hanover, N. H.: B1075

South-Western Publishing Co., 201-203 West Fourth St., Cincinnati, Ohio: B1133

Index of Titles

* * * * *

References are to book and test entries. Book titles are set in italic type and test titles in Roman type. Numbers preceded by B refer to book entries; other numbers refer to test entries. Test references are not indexed.

College English Test: National Achievement Test, 1269.1
College Entrance Examination Board Questions Set at the Examinations of June, 1938, B865
College Entrance Examination Board Questions Set at the Examination of June, 1939, B866
Columbia Research Bureau Algebra Test, 1436
Columbia Research Bureau Aural French Test, 1347
Columbia Research Bureau Chemistry Test, 1591
Columbia Research Bureau English Test, 1270
Columbia Research Bureau French Test, 1348
Columbia Research Bureau German Test, 1359
Columbia Research Bureau Physics Test, 1607
Columbia Research Bureau Plane Geometry Test, 1466
Columbia Research Bureau Spanish Test, 1372
Columbia Vocabulary Test, 1317
Colvin-Schrammel Algebra Test, 1437
Commercial Education Survey Tests, 1480
Common Responses to a New Form of the Free Association Test, B952
Comparative Scores of Two Groups of Graduate Nurses, B952.1
Comparative Study of Some Measures of Emotional Instability in School Children, B1044
Compass Diagnostic Tests in Arithmetic, 1454
Compass Survey Tests in Arithmetic, 1455
Composite Inventory and Examination, Revised, 1651
Comprehensive Examination in College Algebra, 1440
Concept Formation Test, 1216
Conference on Examinations: Under the Auspices of the Carnegie Corporation, the Carnegie Foundation, and the International Institute of Teachers College, Columbia University at the Hotel Royal, Dinard, France, September 16 to 19, 1938, B1021
Conspectus of Examinations in Great Britain and Northern Ireland, B930
Constructing Tests and Grading in Elementary and High School Subjects, B1052
Construction and Use of Achievement Examinations: A Manual for Secondary School Teachers, B822
Construction of Personality Scales by the Criterion of Internal Consistency, B1075
Construction of the English Vocabulary Test, Worksample 95, Form DB, B902
Construction Puzzle, 1391
Contributions of Cumulative Personnel Records to a Teacher-Education Program: As Evidenced by Their Use at the State Teachers College at Towson, Maryland, B1091
Cooperative Achievement Tests: A Bulletin Reporting the Basic Principles and Procedures Used in the Development of Their System of Scaled Scores, B907
Cooperative Algebra Test: Elementary Algebra Through Quadratics, 1438
Cooperative American History Test, 1633
Cooperative Ancient History Test, 1634
Cooperative Biology Test, 1585
Cooperative Chemistry Test, 1592
Cooperative Chemistry Test for College Students, 1593
Cooperative Chemistry Test in Qualitative Analysis, 1594
Cooperative Contemporary Affairs Test for College Students, 1182
Cooperative Contemporary Affairs Test for High School Classes, 1183
Cooperative Economics Test, 1624
Cooperative English Test, 1271, 1276, 1286, 1564
Cooperative English Test: Usage, Spelling, and Vocabulary, 1271
Cooperative French Test (Advanced Form), 1349
Cooperative French Test (Elementary Form), 1350

Cooperative General Achievement Test, 1434, 1604, 1618
Cooperative General Achievement Test, Revised Series, 1435.1, 1605, 1619
Cooperative General Culture Test, 1184
Cooperative General Mathematics Test for College Students, 1431
Cooperative General Mathematics Test for High School Classes, 1432
Cooperative General Science Test, 1601
Cooperative German Test (Advanced Form), 1360
Cooperative German Test (Elementary Form), 1361
Cooperative Intermediate Algebra Test: Quadratics and Beyond, 1439
Cooperative Italian Test, 1362
Cooperative Latin Test [Advanced Form], 1364
Cooperative Latin Test [Elementary Form], 1365
Cooperative Literary Acquaintance Test, 1298
Cooperative Literary Comprehension Test, 1299
Cooperative Mathematics Test for College Students: Comprehensive Examination in College Algebra, 1440
Cooperative Mathematics Test for Grades 7, 8, and 9, 1433
Cooperative Modern European History Test, 1635
Cooperative Objective Tests in Organic Chemistry: 1939-1940 Series, 1595
Cooperative Physics Test, 1608
Cooperative Physics Test for College Students, 1609
Cooperative Plane Geometry Test, 1467
Cooperative Solid Geometry Test, 1468
Cooperative Spanish Test [Advanced Form], 1373
Cooperative Spanish Test [Elementary Form], 1374
Cooperative Test of Social Studies Abilities, 1615
Cooperative Trigonometry Test, 1474
Cooperative Vocabulary Test, 1318
Cooperative World History Test, 1636
Cornell-Coxe Performance Ability Scale, 1388
Counseling Technics in College and Secondary School, B1088
Cowan Adolescent Personality Schedule: Revision No. 2, 1217
[Cox Mechanical Aptitude and Manual Dexterity Tests], 1652-3
Criteria for the Life History: With Analyses of Six Notable Documents, B884
Critical-Mindedness in the Reading of Fiction: Test 3.7, 1530
Cross English Test, 1272
Cube Construction Test, 1376
Curriculum Records of the Children's School, B1026.1

Data on the Growth of Public School Children: From the Materials of the Harvard Growth Study, B879
Data on Visual Sensation and Perception Tests: Part I, Lateral Imbalance, B844.1
Data on Visual Sensation and Perception Tests: Part II, Visual Efficiency, B844.2
Davis-Roahen-Schrammel American Literature Test, 1300
Davis-Schrammel Elementary English Test, 1273
Davis-Schrammel Spelling Test, 1311
Dawson Mental Test, 1389
Dearborn Formboards 2 and 2b, 1390
Dearborn Formboard 3, 1391
Dearborn-Anderson Formboards 2 and 2b, 1390
Description of Examinations: Edition of December 1938, B867
Detroit Advanced First-Grade Intelligence Test, 1392
Detroit Advanced Intelligence Test, 1393
Detroit Alpha Intelligence Test, 1393
Detroit Clerical Aptitudes Examination, 1655
Detroit General Aptitudes Examination, 1654

Index of Names

* * * * *

References are to book and test entries. Numbers preceded by a B refer to book entries; other numbers refer to test entries. Authors of books, references, reviews, and tests are indexed.

Aamodt, Geneva P., 1443-4
Abbott, Allan, 1270
Abell, E. L., 1196, 1578, B1076
Abramson, Joseph L., B841
Achilles, Paul S., 1199, 1325-6, 1329, 1680, B1007.1
Ackerson, Luton, 1420, B1081
Adams, Donald K., B913, B916
Adams, F. J., 1224, B850, B1057
Adams, Henry W., 1298
Adams, R. H., 1394.1
Adkins, Dorothy C., 1377, 1427
Albright, Norma A., 1508, 1511
Aldrich, Julian C., B1127
Alexander, W. P., 1279, 1376, 1400, 1414, 1422, 1450
Alfano, Marie V., B815-9
Allardyce, Archie, B1097
Allen, Bernard M., 1364
Allen, C. H., 1570
Allen, E. Patricia, B820
Allen, F. J., 1492, 1593
Allen, Frederick H., 1248
Allen, L. W., 1542
Allen, Richard D., 1189, 1337, 1458.1, 1551
Allen, Ross L., B925
Allport, Floyd H., 1198-9
Allport, Gordon W., 1198-9, 1243, B821, B1043
Almack, John C., 1310, 1315, 1499
Alster, Benjamin, 1201
Altman, Charlotte Hall, 1248, 1420
Amatruda, Catherine S., B913-6
Ames, Louise Bates, B914
Amidon, Edna P., 1509
Amoss, Harry, 1411
Amstutz, Wade S., 1182, 1225, 1250, 1544

Anastasi, Anne, 1377, 1398, 1424
Anderson, Earl W., B1056
Anderson, G. W., 1239, 1246
Anderson, Howard R., 1183-4, 1615-6, 1618, 1621-2, 1624, 1633-6, B825-7
Anderson, John E., 1390-1, B877, B881, B912
Anderson, L. Dewey, 1663, 1673
Anderson, Rose G., 1233, 1239, 1404, B1053
Anderson, Roy N., 1675, 1680, B1087
Anderson, W. A., 1197, 1315
Andrew, Dorothy M., 1664
Andrus, Lawrence, 1371, 1373
Appel, Kenneth E., B828
Appelt, E. P., 1358
Aptekar, Herbert H., B1053
Arden, Wesley, 1680
Arensberg, Conrad M., B862
Armitage, F. P., B859
Arndt, Christian O., 1371, 1374
Arnspiger, V. C., 1259
Arrington, Ruth E., B829, B1025
Arthur, Grace, 1379, 1420, B830
Arthur, P. A., 1594
Ashbaugh, Ernest J., 1271
Asher, Eston J., 1284, 1402
Ashford, Theodore A., 1592
Ashley-Montagu, M. F., B1026
Atkins, S. D., 1363, 1365, 1367
Atwell, C. R., 1420, B1121
Avery, George T., 1399, 1420, 1424
Axelrod, H. G., 1244
Ayers, Arthur W., B844.2

Babcock, Harriet, 1239, 1248
Babcock, James C., 1372, 1375

Babcock, Marjorie E., 1258
Baber, Ray E., B883
Badger, Alex J., 1517
Baer, Lenona Opal, 1239
Bagster-Collins, E. W., 1342, 1360
Bailey, Edna W., B831-4
Baird, Andrew H., 1376
Baker, Harry J., 1392-3, 1654-6, B835, B1085
Baker, Kenneth H., B836
Baldwin, Bird T., 1420
Balinsky, B., 1420, 1429
Ball, Rachel Stutsman, 1241-2, 1406-7, 1420
Ballard, Philip Boswood, B837
Banerji, M. N., B858
Barnes, Margaret R., 1248
Barnes, Walter, 1183
Barnette, W. Leslie, 1377, 1664
Barnhart, Edward N., B1026
Barnum, Robert G., B837.1
Barr, A. S., 1638
Barrera, S. E., 1246
Barrett, E. R., 1267
Barry, Herbert, Jr., 1246
Barse, William J., B838
Bartlett, Russell S., 1605, 1608
Bates, Ella L., B966
Bathurst, J. E., B1041, B1112
Bauer, W. W., 1501, B835
Baxter, Edna Dorothy, 1206-7
Baxter, Ernest W., 1514
Bayles, Ernest E., 1608
Bayley, Nancy, 1382, 1406-7, B839, B913 B916
Bear, Robert M., 1559
Beard, Marshall Rust, 1614
Beasley, Ronald, 1618, 1620
Beatley, Bancroft, 1342

Dvorak, Beatrice Jeanne, 1659, 1663-4, 1678, B1083
Dwyer, Paul S., 1680
Dyer, Dorothy T., 1680
Dyer, Henry S., 1271, 1485
Dysinger, Don W., 1223

Eads, Laura K., 1259
Earl, C. J. C., 1401, 1414, B1093
Earle, Frank M., B886.1
Easley, Howard, 1398, 1418, 1424, B858
Ebaugh, Franklin G., 1246
Eberhart, Wilfred, 1294
Eckerson, Lois D., 1319
Eckert, Ruth E., 1265
Edds, Jess H., 1272
Edgar, J. W., 1576
Edgerton, Harold A., B1094
Edwards, A. S., B908, B911, B916
Edwards, Bateman, 1344, 1351
Eiselen, W., B900
Eisler, E. R., B966
Eisner, Harry, B891
Elliott, Richard M., 1659, 1663, 1673, 1678, B1041
Ellis, D. B., 1222
Elwood, Mary Isabel, 1420
Ely, Lena A., 1637
Emery, M. A., 1350
Endicott, Frank S., B1127
Endler, O. L., B1083
Engelhardt, N. L., Jr., B1037
Engelhart, Max D., 1531, 1591-2, 1596, B892, B1000
Engle, Edna M., 1505
English, Horace B., B893
Erbe, Carl H., 1614
Ericson, Emanuel E., 1514-5
Espenshade, Anna, B894
Estabrooks, G. H., 1680
Estes, S. G., 1680
Eurich, Alvin C., 1182-4, 1259, 1325-6, 1554-5, 1578, 1616, B858, B1021
Evans, Marie Garrison, 1536
Evans, Robert O., B895
Evenden, E. S., B1091
Ewerhardt, Paul J., B1130
Eysenck, H. J., B1099

Fantl, Ernst, B843
Farley, Eugene S., 1642
Farmer, E., B896-7
Farnsworth, Paul R., 1239, 1326, 1330, 1338-9
Farram, Freda, 1198, 1243
Farwell, Hermon W., 1607-9
Faulkner, Ray, 1324, 1329
Fawcett, Harold P., 1438, 1465, B881, B1045
Fay, Jay W., 1332
Feder, Daniel D., 1200, 1243, 1564
Feder, Leah, B923
Fee, Mary, 1200, 1424
Feinberg, Henry, 1420
Fendrick, Paul, 1552
Fenton, Norman, B898, B1053
Ferguson, George Oscar, Jr., 1394
Ferguson, Leonard W., 1239
Ferry, Margaret E., B899
Fessenden, Seth A., 1535
Fetterman, Joseph L., 1248
Fick, M. Laurence, B900-1

Ficken, C. E., 1342, 1349
Field, H. E., 1519, B924
Filley, Mary E., B902-5.1
Finch, F. H., 1239, 1424
Findley, Warren G., 1259, 1619, B906
Fischer, Ferdinand A. P., 1515
Fisher, Raymond, B913
Fiske, Henry M., 1349-50
Fitzpatrick, F. L., 1184, 1585, 1604
Flanagan, John C., 1182, 1239, 1271, 1299, 1418, 1433, 1492, B907
Fleming, G. W. T. H., B1053
Flemming, Cecile White, 1537
Fletcher, Stevenson W., 1433
Flinner, Ira A., 1680
Flory, Charles D., 1377, B886
Floyd, J. A., 1430.1
Flügel, J. C., B1094
Foley, Louis, 1272
Foran, T. G., 1190, 1197, 1539, 1565
Ford, Gertrude C., 1476
Ford, H. E., 1342
Forlano, George, 1201, 1243-4
Forsythe, Warren E., B922
Fort, Tomlinson, 1431
Fosberg, Irving Arthur, 1246
Foster, Charlotte, 1458
Foster, Jeanette Howard, 1294
Foster, Josephine C., 1407
Foster, L. S., 1594
Foust, Judson W., 1433, 1465
Fowler, H. L., 1394, 1414
Fox, Charles, 1275, 1381
Fox, James Harold, 1496.1
Frank, Benjamin, 1239
Frank, Lawrence K., 1246, B922
Frantz, A. M., 1246
Franzen, Raymond, 1424, 1501
Frear, Florence D., 1507
Frederiksen, Norman, B1025
Freeman, Ellis, B1025
Freeman, Frank N., 1256, B908
Freeman, Frank S., 1377
French, Lois Meredith, B1106
French, Thomas M., B1099
Freyd, M., B1040
Frick, Norman K., 1322
Friedberg, Jean, 1225-6, B1070
Friend, Ruby S., 1338
Froehlich, Gustav J., B1104-5
Fromm, Erika Oppenheimer, 1246
Frutchey, Fred P., 1593, B1135
Fry, Dennis Butler, 1526.1
Fryer, Douglas, 1675
Fryklund, Verne C., 1512, 1517
Fulmer, V. G., 1610
Fusfeld, Irving S., 1239

G., R. C., B880
Gabler, Earl R., B930, B1000, B1021
Galbreath, Neva, 1420
Gallup, George, B908.1
Gambrill, Bessie Lee, 1215, 1256
Gansl, Irene, 1317, B909
Gardiner, D. H., B1042
Gardner, G. E., 1246
Garlough, Leslie, 1585
Garrett, Henry E., 1317, 1394, 1399, 1404, 1427, 1673, B908, B910, B1099
Garrison, Charlotte G., 1537
Garrison, Marie, 1536

Garrison, S. C., 1420
Gates, Arthur I., 1190, 1500, 1537-9, 1571, B911
Gaw, Frances, 1391
Gebhardt, Ann L., 1296, 1307
Gehrkens, Karl W., 1334
Gell, Kenneth E., 1614, 1636
Gentry, Curtis G., 1684
Gentry, J. R., B1053
Gerberich, J. R., 1377, 1555, 1641
Germany, Claude B., 1186
Gerum, Elizabeth, 1680
Gesell, Arnold, B912-6
Geyer, Denton L., 1619
Giauque, C. D., B1003
Gibb, C. A., B858
Gibbons, Charles C., 1233, 1250
Giduz, Hugo, 1344, 1349
Gifford, W. J., B858
Gilbert, Jeanne G., 1248
Gildersleeve, Glenn, 1336
Giles, H. H., 1183, 1296, 1304
Gilliland, A. R., 1239, 1338, B858
Ginsburg, Ethel L., B1025
Girden, Edward, B1122
Gittinger, John W., B1005
Gladfelter, M. E., 1271
Glaser, Edward M., 1228
Glassow, Ruth B., B917
Glenn, Earl R., 1596
Glick, Harry N., 1186
Goddard, Eunice R., 1342
Goddard, Henry H., 1204-5
Goldberg, Woolf, B918
Goldblatt, L. A., 1594
Goldman, Rosaline, 1420
Goldstein Kurt, 1246, B840
Goltry, Keith, 1273, 1282
Good, Carter V., B858, B1042, B1088
Goodenough, Florence L., 1382-3, 1406-7, B915, B970, B1025
Goodfellow, Louis D., 1680
Goodfellow, Raymond C., 1488
Goodman, Alice W., B858
Gookin, Warner F., 1360, 1564
Gordon, Hans C., 1557, 1603
Gordon, Kate, 1420
Gordon, R. G., 1406
Gores, Harold B., 1547, B1102
Gould, A. H., 1613
Graham, Frederick B., 1189, 1458.1, 1551
Graham, Grace, 1632
Graham, Jessie, 1477, 1480-1, 1489
Grant, Albert, 1552, 1558
Gray, Hob, 1187
Gray, J. L., B919
Gray, W. H., 1534, 1566
Gray, William S., 1564, 1570-1
Graybeal, Elizabeth, B920
Green, Helen J., 1420, 1659, 1662-4, 1678, 1680
Greenberg, Jacob, 1344, 1350, 1374
Greene, Edward B., 1320, 1420, 1553
Greene, Harry A., 1188, 1193, 1268, 1274, 1292, 1441, 1451, 1454-5, 1469, 1547, 1568, 1583
Greene, J. E., 1200, 1239
Greenly, R. J., 1659
Greenspan, J., 1594
Gregory, C. A., 1282
Gregory, Helen, 1282

Jewett, Stephen Perham, 1420
Joël, Janet, 1210, 1235
Joël, Walther, 1209-10, 1235
Johannsen, Dorothea, B821
John, Lenore, 1456
Johns, A. A., 1239
Johnson, Alvin D., B972
Johnson, Eleanor Hope, 1239
Johnson, Guy B., 1338
Johnson, John T., 1452-3
Johnson, Laura B., 1348, 1356
Johnson, Marie M., 1440
Johnson, Palmer O., 1434, 1610, 1612
Johnson, Winifred B., 1239
Johnston, Norman J., B973
Jones, Carleton C., 1271, 1295, 1298
Jones, Edward S., 1184, 1574, 1580, 1669
Jones, George A. A., 1377
Jones, Harold E., 1214, 1217, 1222, 1420
Jones, Harold J., 1230
Jones, Ll. Wynn. *See* Wynn Jones, Ll.
Jones, Lloyd Meredith, B975
Jones, Mary Cover, 1680-1, B976
Jordan, A. C., 1269.1
Jordan, A. M., 1191, 1197, 1295, 1392, 1424, B858, B1076
Jordan, John S., 1420
Jordon, R. C., 1430.1
Jorgensen, A. N., 1547
Jorgensen, C., 1377, B870
Josephson, Alann, B852
Joyal, Arnold E., 1237
Jurgensen, Clifford E., 1271

Kahn, Eugen, B1047
Kallen, Horace M., B884
Kandel, I. L., B977
Kaplan, A. H., 1246
Karpf, Maurice J., B849
Karve, B. D., 1220
Kasanin, Jacob, 1216, B1047
Katz, Siegfried E., 1239, 1243
Kaulfers, Walter V., 1340-1, 1350, 1355, 1374-5
Kawin, Ethel, 1256, 1406, 1552, B1085
Kay, G. Marshall, 1604
Keating, T. J., 1385, 1414, 1417
Keene, Charles H., B1003
Keene, Mansel, B852
Kefauver, Grayson N., 1424, 1661, B1033
Keith-Lucas, Alan, B1116
Keller, Franklin J., B1042, B1127
Keller, Victoria M., 1238
Kelley, Douglass M., 1246
Kelley, Glenn Orville, B978
Kelley, Truman L., 1427, 1621-2, 1680
Kelley, V. H., 1547
Kellogg, Chester E., 1377, 1419
Kellogg, Martha, 1447
Kelly, E. Lowell, B1094
Kelly, George A., B979
Kelly, T. B., 1202
Kelty, Mary G., 1631
Kemp, Gladys, 1458
Kendall, M. G., B896
Kendig, Isabelle, 1248, 1420, B1121

Keniston, Hayward, 1371-3
Kennedy, Stephanie, 1246
Kennedy-Fraser, D., 1420, B1062
Kent, Grace H., 1390-1, 1394, 1401, 1414, 1420, 1426, 1429, B980-2, B984
Kent, R. A., 1377
Keohane, Robert E., 1615, 1618, 1642
Kepner, Tyler, 1633
Kern, Grace, 1506
Kerr, Madeline, 1246
Kerridge, Phyllis M. T., 1526.1
Keys, Noel, 1200, 1237, 1239, 1424
Kilander, H. F., 1503
Kimball. G. E., 1592
King, Edith, 1637
King, LeRoy A., 1587
Kingsbury, Forrest A., 1223, 1682
Kinneman, John A., 1615.1
Kinney, L. B., 1432, 1436, 1489
Kintner, Madaline, 1325-6, 1329
Kirk, F. J., B897
Kirk, Samuel A., 1222
Kirkpatrick, Edwin A., B884
Kirkpatrick, Forrest H., 1239, 1243, 1416, B983
Kirkpatrick, Mary, 1582
Kirtland, John C., 1364-5
Kitson, Harry Dexter, 1239, 1664, B858
Klopfer, Bruno, 1246, B841
Knauber, Alma Jordan, 1323-4
Knight, F. B., 1454-5
Knight, James, 1430.1
Knight, Maxine Wisler, 1379, 1420
Knollin, Herbert E., 1420
Knowles, Asa S., B983.1
Knuth, William E., 1332
Koch, Helen L., B1025
Kogan, William, 1246
Kohn, Harold A., 1377
Kolbe, Laverne E., B1083
Kopas, Joseph S., 1680
Kopel, David, 1384, 1548, 1559, 1571
Koran, Sidney W., 1492
Korninger, Rupert C., 1544
Koshuk, Ruth Pearson, B886, B916
Krause, Carl A., 1356
Krey, A. C., 1621-2, 1635
Krieger, Laura B., 1190
Kroeger, Louis J., B853, B983.2
Kroll, Abraham, 1202
Krueger, Barbara L., 1223
Krug, Edward A., 1182-3
Krug, Othilda, 1246
Krugman, Morris, 1246, 1420
Kuder, G. Frederic, 1267, 1492, 1654, 1671
Kuhlmann, F., 1384, 1393, 1404, 1413, 1424, 1426, B908, B984
Kumin, Edythe, 1394
Kurtz, Albert K., 1646, 1670, B1094
Kuznets, George, 1239, 1243
Kwalwasser, Jacob, 1333-4

L., M., B998
LaBarre, Weston, B1001-2
LaBrant, Lou, 1298-9
Lacey, John Irving, B881
Lacher, J. R., 1594
Lachman, Sander E., B922

Laird, Donald A., 1657, B985
Lamb, Marion M., 1213, 1486, B1083
Lamm, Stanley S., B916, B925, B998, B1053, B1060, B1085
Lancaster, W. Elmer, 1466
Land, George A., 1364-5
Landis, Carney, 1239, 1243, B1026
Landry, Herbert A., 1196, 1320, 1539, 1547, 1668
Landsittel, F. C., B1091
Lane, Ruth, 1434, 1467
Langlie, T. A., 1492
Langsam, Walter C., 1628
Lanier, Lyle H., 1338
Lapp, C. J., 1609
Larson, Ruth Crewdson, 1338
Larson, William S., 1332, 1337-8
Laslett, H. R., 1198, 1239, 1377, 1680
Lass, A. H., B854, B858, B891
Laton, Anita D., B831-4
Lau, Louise Margaret, 1340
Lauer, Alvhh R., B975, B985
Laurence, Daniel C., B1097
Lauritsen, W. H., 1227
Lawson, J. W., 1565
Lawton, George, B1121
Laycock, S. R., 1239, 1652-3, 1683
Layton, Warren K., B1120
Learned, William S., 1184, B987-8, B1054
Ledgerwood, Richard, 1189, 1214, 1320, 1402, 1458.1, 1551
Lee, Dorris M., 1470
Lee, J. Murray, 1195, 1268, 1443, 1451, 1470, B850
Lefever, D. Welty, 1193, 1197, 1292, 1459, 1463, 1563
Leikind, S., 1594
Leiter, Russell Graydon, 1405, B916, B989
Lemon, Harvey D., 1609
Lemoster, J. Lloyd, 1479
Lennon, Roger T., B925
Lentz, Theodore F., 1212, 1239
Leonard, J. M., B1063
Leonard, J. Paul, 1193, 1282, 1285, 1292
Leonard, Marjorie R., B835
Leonard, Sterling A., 1269, 1271
Lester, David, B841
Le Suer, Bruce V., 1666
Levine, Michael, 1198
Levy, David M., 1246
Levy, Lydia, 1248
Lewerenz, Alfred S., 1329
Lewin, Kurt, B1026
Lewinson, Thea Steln, B969
Lewis, Don, 1338
Lewis, Nolan D. C., B884, B1047
Likert, Rensis, 1202, 1673, B1024
Limbert, Paul M., 1182
Lincoln, Edward A., 1390-1, 1420, B1122
Lincoln, Hazel, 1388
Lind, Christine, 1190
Linden, Arthur V., 1257
Linder, Maria G., 1406
Linder, R. G., B992
Lindquist, E. F., 1184, 1188, 1268, 1271, 1276, 1286, 1299, 1451, 1568, 1583, 1618, 1624, 1633-6, B822, B825-7, B993-5

Mosher, Raymond M., 1338
Mosier, Charles I., 1223, 1234, 1239, 1243, 1377, 1680
Moss, F. A., 1253
Mossman, Lois Coffey, B1034
Motz, Lloyd, 1184
Mowat, Alex S., B1023.1
Mowrer, Willie Mae C., 1406-7, 1420
Munch, H. F., B1045
Muncie, Wendell, B1125
Munn, Norman L., B915
Munroe, Ruth, 1246
Munson, Martin Y., 1184, 1618, 1635
Murphy, Gardner, B1022, B1024
Murphy, Lois Barclay, 1246, B1025
Murra, Wilbur F., 1615, 1631, 1634, 1639, 1642, B826
Murray, C. L., B1106
Murray, Elsie, 1326
Murray, Henry A., B1026, B1081
Mursell, James L., 1330, 1332-3, 1338
Myers, C. S., B1037.1
Myers, Charles Everett, 1192

N., H. W., B913
Neilson, Neils P., B873, B880
Nelson, Amalie K., B916
Nelson, Erland, 1492
Nelson, M. J., 1290, 1377, 1398, 1424, 1543, 1557-8, B1035
Nemzek, Claude L., 1239, 1399, 1404, 1420, B844.1
Neprash, J. A., 1243
Netzer, Royal F., B1036
Newcomb, Theodore, 1202, 1239
Newkirk, Louis Vest, 1516
Niles, Kathryn B., 1506
Noble, Isabel, 1506
Noble, M. C. S., Jr., B1037
Noll, Victor H., 1263, 1589, 1592, 1596, 1598
Norman, R. M., 1420
Northrop, Paul A., 1609, 1611-2
Nottage, Donald H., B858
Noyes, Arthur P., 1248
Noyes, Edward S., 1272, 1298
Nunn, Percy, 1519, B924
Nyberg, Joseph A., 1439

O., J. R., B1022
Oakley, C. A., 1652-3, B1037.1
Oberholzer, E., 1246
Oberlin, Diana S., 1406
O'Brien, James C., B1040
O'Connor, Johnson, 1659, 1678, B1038
Odell, Charles W., 1189, 1193, 1196, 1268, 1292, 1420, 1451, 1459, 1563, B1000, B1052, B1102, B1119
Oden, Melita H., 1420
Odenweller, Arthur Leonard, B1039
Odlum, Doris M., B858
Odoroff, M. E., 1424
Oeser, O. A., 1246
Oliver, R. A. C., 1396, 1519, B924
Olson, Willard C., 1222
Omwake, K. T., 1253
Orata, Pedro T., 1259, 1619
Ordahl, George, 1420
Ordahl, Louise Ellison, 1420

Ordway, Samuel H., Jr., B1040
Orleans, Jacob S., 1189, 1194, 1290, 1341, 1436, 1444, 1458.1, 1471, 1551, 1630, B1040.1
Orleans, Joseph B., 1436, 1444, 1471, 1473
O'Rourke, L. J., 1668
Orr, Clarence, 1615.1
Osborn, Frederick, B1060
Osborn, R. A., 1590
Osborne, Herbert F., B1083
Osburn, W. J., 1313, 1447, 1449, 1457-8, 1462, 1463-4, 1531-2, 1552, B850
O'Steen, Alton, 1331, 1335
Otis, Arthur S., 1413, 1415, 1436
Otis, Jay L., B1083
Otness, H. Robert, B964
Otterstrom, Ruth E., 1457
Owens, William A., 1377

Padgett, Alice, B883, B1053
Padshah, T. J., B855.1
Paget, R. A. S., B969
Pai, T., 1243
Pal, Satyajivan, 1420
Pallister, Helen, 1200
Palmer, Frederic, Jr., 1609
Parker, H. T., 1420
Parker, Milton M., B1121
Parkhurst, A. J., B1127
Parr, Frank W., 1321.1, 1559.1
Parsek, Anna, 1626
Parsons, A. Rebecca, 1194
Partch, Clarence Elmer, B858
Partington, J. E., 1618, 1624
Paterson, Donald G., 1182, 1184, 1189, 1193, 1197, 1200, 1202, 1223, 1239, 1271, 1318, 1325-6, 1360, 1401, 1424, 1554-5, 1564, 1659, 1662-5, 1669, 1673, 1678, 1680-1, B886.1, B1401-2, B1128
Patey, Henry C., B1081
Patry, Frederick L., B835
Patterson, Dale O., 1445
Patterson, M., 1246
Payne, C. S., 1571
Pazeian, Bessie, 1401
Peak, Helen, B1122
Peak, Mildred, 1457
Pearce, D. W., 1594
Pearse, Blythe, 1274
Pearson, John M., 1471
Peaseley, Virginia, B848, B920
Peatman, John Gray, 1420, 1654, 1667, B858, B916
Peatman, Lillie Burling, 1420
Pedersen, Ruth A., 1200
Peet, Telfair B., 1298
Penrose, L. S., 1417
Perkins, Ruth E., 1420
Perry, Fay V., 1508
Perry, Raymond Carver, 1198, 1239, B1043
Perry, Winona M., 1471
Pertach, C. Frederick, 1196, 1539, 1547
Pescor, M. J., 1246, 1394
Peters, Edwin F., 1252
Peters, Mary Fridiana, B1044
Peterson, P. Victor, 1601
Phelan, Earl W., 1593
Phillips, Arthur, 1420
Phillips, M. J. W., 1613

Pickett, Hale, B1045
Pico, Juanita, B877
Pierce, W. O'D., 1200
Pignatelli, Myrtle Luneau, 1387, 1426, B984
Pike, Ruth E., 1277
Pintner, Rudolf, 1201, 1239, 1243, 1244, 1253, 1379, 1384, 1413, 1416
Piotrowski, Zygmunt, 1246, 1420
Piper, Alva H., 1441
Pitcher, Stephen L., 1349-50
Plant, James S., B1053
Poley, Irvin C., 1294, 1560
Polleck, Ross, B1078
Pond, Frederick L., 1546
Pond, Millicent, 1664
Pooley, Robert C., 1267, 1276, 1286, 1304
Popper, Emma, 1361
Porter, E. H., Jr., 1426
Porteus, S. D., 1387, 1405, 1419, B1046
Potter, Mary A., 1438, 1462
Powell, Alvin, B852
Powell, Marjorie, 1246
Powers, Francis F., 1370, B858
Powers, S. R., 1585, 1591-2, 1601
Pratt, Bertha M., 1217
Pratt, Hiram E., 1434.1
Pratt, Norman T., Jr., 1364, 1366, 1370
Prehm, Hazel, B1138
Prescott, Daniel A., 1223, 1262
Pressey, L. C., 1196, 1243.1, 1274
Pressey, S. L., 1196, 1243.1, 1274, 1291, 1667
Presson, John M., 1587
Preu, Paul W., B1047
Price, H. Vernon, 1442
Price, J. H., 1634
Price, Roy A., 1615, 1638
Proctor, William M., 1661
Protheroe, Chester F., 1601
Pruitt, Clarence M., B854, B1000, B1045, B1124
Pugh, Eunice Acheson, B1081
Pugh, Jesse J., B854
Pullias, E. V., 1189, 1194, 1458.1, 1551, B1048, B1087-8
Purin, C. M., 1350, 1357, 1359-60
Purnell, Russell T., B1049
Puskin, Ruth, 1208
Pyles, M. K., 1680

Quance, F. M., 1309
Quasha, William H., 1673
Quinn, P. Jack, B1049.1

R., P., B1122
Rae, Saul Forbes, B908.1
Ramseyer, Lloyd L., B1050
Randall, Florence B., 1420
Randall, J. H., 1184
Ranney, Harriet, 1612
Ransom, Katharine A., 1552
Rasmussen, Otho M., B1059
Raths, Louis E., 1225-6, 1250, 1528, 1544, 1556, 1584, 1599, 1606
Raudenbush, Henry W., 1473
Raven, J. C., 1220, 1417, B1115
Redmond, Frank A., 1269
Reed, A. A., 1277
Reed, Clinton A., 1476
Reed, Rufus D., 1593-4

Reeve, Ethel B., 1511
Reeve, William D., 1433, 1438, B1045
Reidy, Ann., 1196, 1460
Reilley, Albert G., 1562
Reitz, Wm., B1021, B1121
Remmers, H. H., 1202, 1212, 1243, 1399, B1050
Rhinehart, Jesse Batley, 1253, 1377, 1420
Rhodes, E. C., B928-30
Ribble, Margarethe A., B916
Riccio, Peter, 1362
Rice, Leonard A., 1298
Rice, Ralph R., 1481
Rich, C. L., 1612
Rich, Gilbert J., B916
Richards, Esther L., B966
Richards, T. W., 1209
Richardson, C. A., 1420
Richardson, H. D., 1340, 1645, 1658, 1660, B1051
Richardson, M. W., 1431, 1434, 1440-1, 1655, B988
Richey, Robert W., B1039
Richmond, Winifred V., 1248, 1420, B1022
Rickers-Ovsiankina, Maria, 1246, B841
Ridenour, Nina, B1125
Rider, Paul R., 1434, 1440
Rieti, Ettore, 1246
Rietz, Henry L., 1440
Riggs, Winifred C., 1237
Riley, G., 1379, 1420
Rinkob, Severn, 1613
Rinsland, Henry D., 1195, 1271, 1284, 1293, 1310, 1535, B852, B858, B989, B1000, B1035, B1037, B1049, B1052, B1076, B1106, B1109
Rivlin, Harry N., B1091
Roach, Cornelia Bell, 1420
Roahen, R. L., 1300
Roback, A. A., 1249
Roberts, Arthur S., 1298
Roberts, Gladys, B930
Roberts, Holland D., 1547
Roberts, J. A. F., 1420
Roberts, Katharine Elliott, 1242
Robinson, Anna Belle, 1508
Robinson, Bertha, 1549
Robinson, Francis P., B922, B1048, B1071
Robinson, Myra, 1601
Rock, Robert T., Jr., 1539, 1565
Rodger, Alec, 1652-3, 1673, B1115
Rogers, Agnes L., 1343
Rogers, Carl R., 1237, 1240, 1258, B1053, B1081, B1108
Rogers, Frederick Rand, 1499, 1500
Rohrer, P. L., 1387
Roll, Rose, 1434
Roller, Duane, 1184, 1604, 1608
Rorschach, H., 1246
Rose, Anna Loretta, B1054
Rosecrance, F. C., B1106
Rosenzweig, Saul, 1246
Roslow, Sydney, 1199, 1233, 1240
Ross, C. C., 1187, 1195
Ross, Nathaniel, B884
Ross, W. D., 1246
Rossberg, Elizabeth, 1357
Rosskopf, M. F., 1434

Roth, Suzanne, 1348
Rothney, J. W. M., 1420, 1559, B858, B879, B1093
Rothwell, Easton, 1182-3
Roucek, Joseph S., 1525
Royer, O. O., 1182
Rubenstein, Boris B., 1246
Rubin, Beatrice, 1248
Ruch, Floyd L., B1094
Ruch, G. M., 1192, 1333, 1433, 1454-5, 1458, 1579, 1588, 1619, B1055
Ruckmick, Christian A., 1338
Rudd, Marion, 1565
Rugen, Mabel E., B894, B1071, B1110, B1124
Rugg, Harold, 1420
Ruggles, Richard, 1198
Ruhlen, Helen, 1274
Rulon, Phillip J., 1485, 1680, B1108
Rupp, Robert A., 1416
Russell, David H., 1309, 1537, 1570, B911
Russell, Harry J., 1372-3
Rust, Metta Maund, 1239
Ryan, Mary S., B913
Ryan, Teresa M., 1267
Ryans, B. G., B914
Ryans, David G., 1252

S., J., B879, B922, B1071
S., J. C., B828
S., L., B828
S., S. I., B998
Sackett, Everett B., 1675
Saetveit, Joseph G., 1338
Sagebeer, Richard G., 1601
St. Clair, Walter F., 1239
Salisbury, Frank S., 1338
Salisbury, Rachel, 1273, 1580
Salley, Ruth E., B842
Sammartino, Peter, 1356
Sánchez, George I., 1420
Sandiford, Peter, B1056
Sangren, Paul V., 1196, 1460, 1565
Sarbin, Theodore R., 1246, 1680
Saunders, Aulus Ward, 1326, 1329
Sayward, Ruth, 1433
Scates, Douglas E., 1259, 1259B
Schachtel, Ernst, 1246
Schieffelin, Barbara, 1390-1, 1394, 1401, 1663
Schilder, Paul, B843
Schiller, F. C. S., B929
Schindler, Alvin W., 1601, 1608, 1610
Schmidt, Austin G., 1228, 1264, 1426, 1535, 1537, B842, B850, B855, B858, B868, B880, B894, B909, B911, B914, B918, B922, B939, B967, B997, B1000, B1003, B1021, B1035-7, B1044-5, B1049, B1050, B1069, B1076, B1089, B1091, B1098.1, B1106, B1110-1, B1118-9, B1121, B1123, B1132, B1138
Schmitz, Sylvester B., 1377
Schneck, Matthew R., 1394, 1399, 1673
Schneidler, Gwendolen G., 1182, 1184, 1189, 1193, 1197, 1200, 1202, 1223, 1271, 1325-6, 1360, 1401, 1424, 1554-5, 1659, 1661-4, 1673, 1678, 1680-1, B1042

Schneiler, Franz, B1057
Schnell, Leroy H., 1449, 1467
Schnepp, Alfred, 1520
Schoen, M., 1338
Scholter, Anthony J., 1659.1, 1679.1
Schonell, F. Eleanor, 1293.1
Schonell, Fred J., 1293.1, 1394.1, 1448, 1450, 1461, B1058
Schoonover, Charles, 1513
Schorling, Raleigh, 1462
Schott, Emmett L., 1243, 1420
Schrader, W. A. B., 1250
Schrammel, H. E., 1196, 1267, 1273, 1300, 1311, 1321, 1339, 1363, 1366, 1368-9, 1437, 1457-8, 1465, 1499, 1513, 1534, 1549, 1566, 1589, 1610, 1639-41, B1059
Schreurs, Esther, 1377
Schroedel, E. C., 1492
Schroeder, Paul L., B966
Schuler, F. W., 1613
Schultz, Richard S., 1199, 1673, 1680, B858
Schumacher, Henry C., B966
Schwarz, Rudolph, 1248
Schweikhard, Dean M., 1513
Schwesinger, Gladys C., 1390-1, 1394, 1401, 1663, B1022, B1060
Scott, R. D., 1277
Scudder, Mary Theresa, B1042
Scull, J. Folwell, Jr., 1618
Seagoe, May V., 1341, 1393, 1424, 1444
Sealy, Glenn A., 1194
Searles, John R., B1063
Sears, William P., Jr., B1127
Seashore, Carl E., 1326, 1332, 1338-9
Seashore, Robert H., 1319
Seder, Margaret, 1377, 1433, 1615, 1680-1, B1064
Seegers, J. Conrad, 1239
Segel, David, 1377, 1680, B1055, B1065-8, B1108
Segner, Esther F., 1507
Seibert, Louise C., 1342, 1347
Seiler, Gretchen P., B858
Seitz, Clifford P., 1234
Seller, Mary Alice, 1363, 1368
Selling, Lowell S., B1047, B1068.1
Sells, Saul B., 1239
Semeonoff, Boris, 1334
Sender, Sadie, 1246
Senour, A. C., 1552
Shakow, David, 1246, 1248, 1401, 1420
Shank, Spencer, 1567, 1579
Shanks, E. I., B969
Shanner, William M., 1427, 1615, B1064
Sharp, R. F., B858
Shartle, Carroll L., B1083
Shaw, Amy I., 1190
Shaw, Edmond A., 1390-1
Sheehy, Loretta Maria, B1069
Shellow, Sadie Myers, 1680
Shen, Eugene, B850, B1000, B1076
Sheridan, Marion C., 1276, 1286
Sheviakov, George V., 1225-6, B1070
Shimberg, Myra E., 1390-1, 1394, 1401
Shirley, Mary, B913
Shlaudeman, Karl W., 1239

Shoemaker, Lois M., 1500, 1503
Shofstall, W. P., B1099
Shores, Louis, 1560
Shotwell, Anna Markt, B1119
Shuey, Herbert, 1246
Shumaker, L. K., 1270-1, 1278
Shuttleworth, Frank K., B821, B879, B922, B1071, B1121-2
Siceloff, L. P., 1184, 1431-2, 1434, 1438-9, 1467-8, 1473-4
Siceloff, Margaret McAdory, 1325, B1072
Sicha, Mary Hunter, 1246
Sidserf, Edward H., B1072.1
Silance, Ella Belle, 1202
Sill, Jane B., 1246
Silliman, Henrietta, 1301
Silverberg, William V., B1094
Simkevich, John Charles, 1680
Simmins, C. A., 1220
Simmons, C., 1248
Simmons, Ernest P., 1312, 1314, B1073
Simon, George B., 1485
Simon, Rosalind, 1506
Sinnott, E. W., 1184, 1585
Siqueira, T. N., B930-1, B1096, B1113
Sisson, E. Donald, 1326
Skaer, Mae, 1217
Skaggs, E. B., 1420
Skalet, Magda, 1420
Skeels, Harold M., 1379, 1404, 1420, B1074
Skiff, J. M., B1106
Skiff, Josephine, B1127
Skinner, Charles E., B1081
Skinner, S. M., 1608
Slater, Patrick, B1098
Sletto, Raymond Franklin, B1075
Slight, David, B828
Slocombe, Charles S., B897
Smith, Babington, B1114
Smith, B. Othanel, B1076
Smith, C. Ebblewhite, 1279, 1409, 1422, 1450, 1461, B858, B1058
Smith, Dorothy V., 1281
Smith, Elmer R., 1287, 1296
Smith, Gale, 1623, 1629
Smith, Geddes, B1085
Smith, George Milton, Jr., B1077
Smith, Hattie Nesbit, 1243
Smith, Harold B., 1338
Smith, Homer W., B1046
Smith, J. J., B1081
Smith, Joseph, B1047
Smith, Mary Katherine, 1319
Smith, O. M., 1593-4, 1596
Smith, Percival, 1381, 1389, B820
Smith, S. Parker, B931
Smith, Samuel, 1191, 1304, 1313, 1449, 1502, 1540, 1602, 1617, 1630
Smith, T. V., B908.1
Smith, William A., B854
Smyser, W. C., B858
Snedden, David, B869, B1106
Snedden, Donald, 1379
Snyder, David P., B852
Somerby, F. S., 1634
Soper, Wayne, 1336
South, Earl Bennett, B1078-80
Spache, George, 1404
Spaney, Emma, 1434, 1434.1, 1467

Spaulding, Geraldine, 1271, 1276, 1286, 1349-50, 1360, 1365, 1373-4
Spearman, C., 1417, 1427, B1096
Speer, G. S., 1239
Speer, Robert K., 1191, 1196, 1295, 1304, 1313, 1449, 1502, 1540, 1602, 1617, 1630
Speevack, Morris, 1420
Spence, Ralph B., 1190, 1258-9
Spencer, Douglas, 1233, 1243.1, B1081
Spencer, Peter L., 1189, 1458.1, 1463
Speyer, Helen, B1053
Spindler, Evelyn B., B848, B917, B920
Spitzer, H. F., 1188, 1268, 1451, 1568, 1583
Sprague, Russell E., B1082
Springer, N. Norton, 1240
Stackman, Harvey, 1420
Stagner, Ross, 1198, 1239, 1243, 1253
Stainbrook, Edward J., B843
Stalnaker, John M., 1183, 1192, 1271, 1293, 1320, 1377, 1427, B967, B1118
Stanhope, Roy W., 1597
Stanley, D. T., B847, B1114
Stanton, Hazel Martha, 1338
Starbuck, Edmund O., 1680
Starr, Natalie D., 1271, 1298
Staton, Thomas F., 1200, 1239
Stead, William H., B1083
Stecher, Lorle I., 1420
Steckel, Minnie L., 1404
Steel, James H., B1084
Steele, Isabel, 1198, 1243
Steeves, Harrison R., 1270
Steggerda, Morris, 1325, 1407
Stein-Lewinson, Thea, 1246
Stein, S. P., 1387
Stein, Saul, 1253
Steinmetz, Harry Charles, 1680
Stenquist, John L., 1420, 1505
Stephenson, William, 1423, B858
Stevens, Avis Coultas, 1572
Stevens, Edwin B., B1127
Stevens, Samuel N., 1198-9, 1657
Stevenson, Elmo, 1585
Stevenson, George S., B1085, B1130
Stevenson, L., 1510
Stevenson, Mary Lou, 1342
Steward, Verne, 1651, B1086
Steward, Ward, B983.2, B1031
Stewart, C., 1639
Stewart, Frances G., 1675
Stewart, Frank, 1608
Stewart, Howard Z., 1486
Stockard, Alfred H., 1420
Stoddard, George D., 1516, 1579, 1588, B915
Stogdill, Emily L., 1239
Stogdill, Ralph M., 1204-5, 1208
Stoke, Stuart M., 1420
Stokes, C. N., 1434
Stolper, B. J. R., 1294
Stolz, Herbert R., 1383, B970
Stone, Clarence R., 1548, 1570-1
Stoner, Jean, 1635
Stonesifer, Joseph N., B1099
Storck, John, 1184
Storment, Robert C., 1223
Stott, M. Boole, 1420

Stover, Ernest L., B941
Strang, Ruth, 1253, 1500, 1535, 1547, 1553-5, 1557, 1672, 1681, B925, B1087-8
Stratton, Clarence, 1269
Strecker, Edward A., B828, B1125
Strong, Edward K., Jr., 1680-1
Strouse, Catherine E., 1339
Struckmeyer, Keith, 1519, B924
Studebaker, J. W., 1454-5
Studman, L. G., 1220
Stuit, Dewey B., 1271, 1680-1, B965
Stull, DeForest, 1190
Stumpf, W. A., B846
Stutsman, Rachel, 1241-2, 1406-7, 1420
Suares, Nadine, 1246
Sublette, Donald J., B1031
Suchy, R. J., 1613
Sullivan, Earle C., 1605
Sullivan, Elizabeth T., 1384, 1420
Summey, George, Jr., 1276, 1286
Sumner, F. C., 1255
Sung, S. M., 1243
Sunne, Dagny, 1246
Super, Donald E., 1377, 1680, B1089
Sutherland, Edwin H., B1068.1
Sweeny, Mary E., 1241, 1406, 1420
Swineford, Frances, B939
Swinnerton, Carl P., 1184, 1604, 1608
Swope, Ammon, 1525
Symonds, Percival M., 1190, 1200, 1213, 1340, 1342, 1420, 1424, 1436, 1497-8, 1588, B854, B884, B891, B1090

Taba, Hilda, 1184, 1259, 1618
Tait, W. D., B1120
Talbert, Wilford, 1420
Tallman, Gladys, 1246
Talman, John, B1084
Tansil, Rebecca Catherine, B1091
Tappan, Paul W., B1014
Tate, J. T., 1609
Taylor, Katherine Whiteside, B898, B1053
Taylor, Marian W., 1406
Taylor, Wallace, 1630, 1634-5, 1641
Teagarden, Florence M., 1406-7
Teegarden, Lorene, 1401, 1662-3
Tempero, Howard E., B844.1
Temple, Alice, B926
Tenney, Edward A., 1299, 1561
Terman, Lewis M., 1420, 1424, B988, B1092-4
Tharp, James B., 1350, 1354-5
Thiele, C. L., 1193, 1433, 1459-60
Thomas, Charles Swain, 1267, 1271, 1293, 1299
Thomas, D. M., 1202
Thomas, Frank C., B1096
Thomas, Lenore, 1349-50
Thomas, Minnie E., 1239
Thompson, Albert S., 1659, 1662, 1678, 1682
Thompson, E. M., 1420
Thompson, Elmer J., 1633, 1635
Thompson, Helen, B913-6, B1025
Thompson, John H., 1271, 1298-9
Thompson, Lola Rivers, 1582
Thompson, Lorin A., Jr., 1236, B1097

Thomson, Godfrey H., 1386, 1427, B852.1, B1023.1, B1097.1, B1098
Thomson, William A., 1233, 1377
Thorndike, Edward L., 1271, 1315, 1557
Thorndike, Robert L., 1243.1, 1253, 1377
Thorngate, J. H., 1613
Thornton, George R., 1246, B1098.1
Thorpe, Louis P., 1213
Thouless, Robert H., B858
Thralls, Zoe A., 1625.1
Thurstone, L. L., 1243, 1377-8, 1420, 1427, 1671, 1680, 1683, B1099, B1100-1
Thurstone, Thelma Gwinn, 1243, 1377-8, 1531
Tiegs, Ernest W., 1192-3, 1213, 1292, 1384, 1459, 1563, B1102
Tiffin, Joseph, 1559, 1659
Tilson, Lowell Mason, 1338
Tinker, Miles A., 1533, 1559, 1579, B843, B926
Tobin, J. R., B1103
Tomlinson, Helen, 1582
Tomlinson, T. P., 1430
Toops, Herbert A., 1663, 1673
Torgerson, T. L., 1194, 1443-4, 1612, B1104-5
Townsend, M. Ernest, 1218
Townsend, Rebecca R., 1420
Trabue, M. R., 1320, 1342, 1659, 1661-4, 1666, 1675, 1678-9, 1682
Trafton, Helen, 1424
Traphagen, Virginia, B835
Traxler, Arthur E., 1195-6, 1239, 1276, 1286, 1299, 1320-1, 1377, 1384, 1547, 1557, 1564, 1567, 1578-9, 1671, 1680, B1106-9
Trebilcox, Russell D., 1298
Tressler, J. C., 1195
Trilling, Mabel, 1508, 1510
Trost, Helen, 1420
Trost, Marie E., 1626
Troup, Evelyn, 1246
Truitt, Ralph P., B1085
Tryon, Caroline McCann, B1110
Tryon, R. M., 1183, 1616, 1636
Tryon, Robert C., 1427, B1111
Tulchin, Simon H., 1233, 1244, 1246
Tully, Marguerite, 1337
Turner, Clarence E., 1347, 1351
Turner, Dodds M., 1457
Turner, I. S., B1045
Turney, Austin H., 1200, 1378, 1404, 1424, 1500-1, B939
Turse, Paul L., 1490.1
Twogood, Arthur P., 1665.1
Tyler, Henry T., 1200, 1252
Tyler, Ralph W., 1182, 1585, 1593

Uhl, Willis L., B855, B1076
Uhrbrock, Richard S., B1094
Umphrey, G. W., 1373
Underhill, O. E., 1601
Upjohn, Everard M., 1184
Upshall, C. C., 1253, 1377, 1557, 1580
Urbancek, Joseph J., B1045
Uttley, Marguerite, 1625.1

Vail, Curtis C. D., 1358, 1360-1
Vaillant, Paule, 1349

Valentine, C. W., 1247, B881, B913, B915, B1053, B1113
Van Allyn, Keith, 1647
Vanden Belt, B. H., 1583.1
Vander ,Beke, George E., 1342, 1346-7, 1349-50, 1355
Van Wagenen, M. J., 1197, 1295, 1407, 1428, 1447, 1463, 1532, 1581, 1598, 1625, 1631
Varnum, William H., 1327
Varvel, W. A., 1246, B1121
Vaughn, James, 1246
Veeder, Borden S., B912, B915, B1085
Vergil, Sister, 1340
Vernon, M. D., B1127
Vernon, Philip E., 1201, 1213, 1220, 1223, 1246, 1414, 1420, 1461, B841, B1114-5
Vincent, Melvin J., B1081
Viteles, Morris S., 1338, 1659, 1662, 1678
Voelker, Paul H., 1654-6
Vogel, B. K., 1202
Voorheis, Eloise B., 1467
Voss, Mildred Dow, 1325
Votaw, David F., Jr., 1446
Votaw, David F., Sr., 1187, 1446, 1492

W., O., B922, B1071
Waddle, Charles, 1420
Wadsworth, Guy W., Jr., 1223
Waite, A., 1417
Waite, Henry M., B1097
Waits, J. Virgil, 1377
Walcott, Fred G., 1269
Walker, Clyde, 1475
Walker, Helen M., 1438
Walker, M. J., 1346
Walker, Virgil R., 1472
Walker, Wilma, B1116
Wallace, Ramona, B898
Wallar, Gene A., 1667
Wallin, J. E. Wallace, 1420
Walston, Catherine L., 1298
Walston, Rosa Lee, 1184, 1298
Walter, C. H., 1613
Walters, Elsa, B1096
Walters, Fred C., 1420
Walters, J. E., B1127
Walther, E. Curt, 1261, 1626
Wang, Charles K. A., 1198, B1117
Wanous, S. J., B1133
Waples, Douglas, 1294
Ward, L. W., 1239, 1680
Ward, Raymond S., B1083
Ware, Glen C., 1590
Waring, Ethel B., B966
Warner, G. W., 1608
Washburne, John N., 1262
Wasson, Margaret M., 1198, 1223
Waterman, Alan T., 1609, B1118
Waters, Eugene A., 1596, 1607
Watkins, Ralph K., 1263, 1608
Watson, Goodwin, 1212, 1217
Watson, Richard E., 1184, 1605
Webb, C. W., B850
Webb, L. W., B1119
Webster, E. C., B1120
Wechsler, David, 1419-20, 1429, B1121-2
Weems, Rachel, B880

Weidemann, Charles C., 1433, 1467, 1469-71, 1499
Welles, Henry Hunter, 3rd., 1239
Wellman, Beth L., 1406, B1123
Wells, F. L., 1246, 1391, 1420, 1426, 1429, 1678, B840, B843, B858, B984, B1093, B1121
Welton, Louis E., 1596
Werner, Henry, 1394, 1420
Wertham, F., 1246
Wesley, Edgar B., 1614, 1620-2, 1624, 1633, 1637
West, Joe Young, B1124
West, M., 1420
West, Ruth, B825
Westbrook, H. T., 1184
Westburgh, Edward M., B1125
Wharton, LaVerna P., 1321
Wheat, Harry Grove, 1189, 1193, 1458.1, 1459
Wheeler, Dorothy S., 1433
Whipple, Guy Montrose, B1033
Whisler, Laurence, 1202, 1243
White, J. Gustav, 1669
White, Paul, 1224
White, William A., 1246, B1022
Whitelaw, John B., B1102
Whitley, Mary T., 1338
Whitmer, Carroll A., 1379, 1388
Wickman, E. K., 1222
Widdop, Robert, 1434.1, 1605
Wiedefeld, N. Theresa, 1626
Wile, Ira S., B914, B1053
Wiley, A. McBroom, B1126
Wiley, Lester E., B1126
Wilgus, George, 1492
Wilke, Walter H., 1308
Wilks, S. S., 1434, 1436, 1438-9, 1443-4, 1467, 1474, B1126.1
Will, Lucy, 1361
Williams, Allan J., 1196, 1310
Williams, C. O., 1338
Williams, G. Perrie, 1410
Williams, Griffith W., 1198, 1394
Williams, J. H., 1420
Williams, Jesse Feiring, B975
Williams, John R., 1589
Williams, Robert H., 1373-4
Williamson, Edmund G., 1182, 1184, 1189, 1193, 1197, 1200, 1202, 1214, 1218, 1223, 1233, 1271, 1325-6, 1360, 1401, 1424, 1554-5, 1659, 1661-4, 1673, 1678, 1680-2, B1042, B1127-9
Willing, M. H., 1271
Willis, Margaret, 1631, 1633
Willis, Mary, 1184, 1318, 1564, 1618, 1620, 1635
Willoughby, Raymond Royce, 1243, B1101
Wilner, Charles F., 1399, 1420
Wilson, Charles A., 1241, 1406, 1420
Wilson, Ellen, 1388
Wilson, Elmo C., 1182-3
Wilson, Frank T., 1537
Wilson, Guy M., 1189, 1194, 1315, 1447, 1458.1, B858, B1000
Wilson, Howard E., 1265, 1622
Wilson, J. H., 1424
Wilson, M. E., 1338
Wilson, Trudie, 1373
Wipf, Adeline, 1549
Wirth, Fremont P., B826